COLLECTOR'S GUIDE TO
Antique Radios

SIXTH EDITION

IDENTIFICATION AND VALUES

JOHN SLUSSER
& the staff of
RADIO DAZE

COLLECTOR BOOKS
A Division of Schroeder Publishing Co., Inc.

On the front cover:
Artwork by Norman Rockwell published on the cover of the
May 20, 1922, issue of Saturday Evening Post

Cover design by Beth Summers
Book design by Lisa Henderson

COLLECTOR BOOKS
P.O. Box 3009
Paducah, Kentucky 42002-3009

www.collectorbooks.com

Copyright © 2005 John Slusser

The current values in this book should be used only as a guide. They are not intended to set prices, which vary from one section of the country to another. Auction prices as well as dealer prices vary greatly and are affected by condition as well as demand. Neither the author nor the publisher assumes responsibility for any losses that might be incurred as a result of consulting this guide.

Searching For A Publisher?

We are always looking for people knowledgeable within their fields. If you feel that there is a real need for a book on your collectible subject and have a large comprehensive collection, contact Collector Books.

Contents

Dedication

This book is dedicated to all of those who help keep the charm of the golden age of radio alive yet today — antique radio clubs, collectors, enthusiasts, and restorers. We hope that in some small way the *Collector's Guide to Antique Radios* helps support that cause. And also to the many individuals who have warmly shared with us their personal memories of days sitting around the radio listening to their favorite dramas, comedies, or live breaking news of some of the major historical events of the twentieth century.

Acknowledgments

Ongoing love and appreciation to my children, Adam, Michael, and Callie for their continuing support and understanding as Dad pursues his "hobby." A very special thank you to my lady, Kim, for her encouragement, editing help, and infinite patience. And of course, to Phil Hazen and Bill Rindfuss of our Radio Daze team for their help once again in putting together this new sixth edition. Warmest regards and sincere appreciation to the many individuals who have contacted us with comments and suggestions for this new edition as well as to all of those who supported the efforts that went into the five past editions of this book.

About the Author

John Slusser has been fascinated by the world of antique radios ever since he was given his grandfather's Atwater Kent cathedral radios in his early teens. In fact, it was his interest in restoring and listening to that radio that motivated him to pursue an education in electrical engineering. He has been involved in the computer and telecommunications arena for over 30 years.

long before the hobby became an obsession and then a new business — Radio Daze, LLC! Today, Radio Daze maintains an inventory of over 500,000 vacuum tubes and additionally offers a broad range of components and supplies for radio repair and restoration to antique radio enthusiasts all over the world.

In the early 1990s, John decided to renew his interest in antique radios as a "casual" hobby and a relaxing diversion from the high-tech world. However, it wasn't

Many vintage radio collectors have literally hundreds of radios from various manufacturers in their personal collections. In addition, they also often focus on those made by a specific radio manufacturer. In John's case, his passion is for radios made by E.H. Scott Radio Laboratories. In 2003, John published (under Radio Daze Press) another radio book, *E.H. Scott — The Dean of DX*. It was an opportunity of a lifetime for John to work closely with the book's author, the late Marvin Hobbs, who was a chief engineer at E.H. Scott from 1939 to 1947 — during the glory days of American radio design and manufacturing.

Welcome to the World of Antique Radios

Thousands of individuals all over the world are enchanted with the hobby of antique radios. During the golden age of radio (1920s – 1950s) millions of radios were produced in the United States by hundreds of companies. Radio manufacturers such as RCA, Philco, Zenith, GE, Stromberg-Carlson, and many others were once among the largest firms in the country. The radios that they built had a quality of materials and construction techniques that simply don't exist in today's consumer electronics. Although the vast majority of these radios and their manufacturers have long since vanished, many of the sets produced during the golden age of radio do still exist. To the antique radio enthusiast, nothing quite compares to finding a classic radio at a flea market, garage sale, antique shop, or even Grandpa's attic. Often, with just the right dose of tender loving care, these radios can be restored to their original warm sound and visual elegance.

Newcomers to antique radios will be pleased to find that many excellent books and reference sources are available to help them learn more about the history, technology, and restoration of vintage radio sets. Antique radio organizations and clubs, such as the Antique Wireless Association (AWA) based in Bloomfield, New York, can be a great source of help and guidance.

Components and supplies required for antique radio restoration remain generally available. Radios of the golden age used vacuum tubes — the predecessor of today's solid state electronics. Vacuum tube have filaments similar to light bulbs and they do degrade in the normal course of operation. The life of a tube is generally in inverse proportion to the amount of time the radio is in operation. However, some tubes will last for 10+ years in average use, while others may need replacement within a year or two. Although vacuum tubes are no longer in production on a broad scale, there are a few active manufacturers of specific types of tubes. More importantly for the radio enthusiast, billions of tubes were manufactured during the tube era and most types are still available from various sources that currently serve the antique radio community. Most other electronic components necessary for radio restoration, such as capacitors and resistors, are still

being manufactured. Although replacement parts originally supplied by the manufacturer are usually not available, functionally equivalent parts that can substitute for the original parts can generally be found.

Part of an antique radio's charm can be its original, albeit sometimes used, look. As with other antiques, complete refinishing of a radio should only be done when absolutely necessary. Often what appears to be a marginal finish can be brought back to a great appearance with a rub down and spot touch up. Many products are readily available for working on the appearance of wood, Bakelite, and plastic radios. In addition, several sources offer reproduction grille cloth, knobs, etc. to help appearance restoration.

For those not interested in doing radio restoration themselves, there are several dozen quality repair shops and individuals across the country specializing in antique radio restoration.

And now an important note of caution. The excitement of a novice antique radio enthusiast finding his first classic set can often yield unfortunate results. Many of the parts in a tube radio do not deteriorate with age and should last for decades yet to come. However, some parts do deteriorate and offer a much higher possibility of failure. If you have or find a vacuum tube radio that hasn't been used for several years or more, please note that there are several good reasons not to plug it in and "check it out." Most classic radios are not fused and therefore do not protect the radio from abnormal operating conditions. The parts in the radio that may have deteriorated can heavily stress or ruin other good parts. If this happens, the radio may become unrepairable. The insulation on your radio power cord may also be questionable and offer both a shock and a fire hazard. Many newcomers understand that vacuum tubes need to "warm up" and often will plug-in sets for many minutes, expecting a long warm up period. Often, what they don't realize is that some of the other radio components themselves are actually "warming up" and heading toward "burning up"! Best bet is not to give in to temptation and only plug in your radio under controlled circumstances or after basic checkout and/or restoration.

About This Edition

There were several goals for this sixth edition of *The Collector's Guide to Antique Radios.* Certainly first and foremost was the updating of any pricing to reflect changes that have occurred over the past three years since the last edition. The valuation of some of the radios listed has changed very little — perhaps a reflection of the relatively low inflation rate in the overall economy during that time. However, other radios, especially the rarer or unique pieces have seen some meaningful changes in value.

The actual number of distinct antique radio models designed in the United States will never be precisely known. Based upon manufacturers' documentation and advertising, our guess would be at least 30,000 and perhaps many more. Additional models, flavors, and brands continue to be uncovered by radio enthusiasts. We are also contacted from time to time by individuals who have come across a radio that is not in our guide and we highly welcome that input. We could readily add many more listings just based on documented models. However, our second goal was to add additional listings based upon ongoing exposure to models and brands that appear to have been produced in a quantity that they may well confront the collector community. To that end, this guide now has grown to over 10,000 listings.

A third goal was to add more color photo illustrations. This edition has nearly twice the number of photos as the last edition.

Please note that in order to provide more radio images, radios with photos are not included in the listings themselves but are illustrated in sequential order under a given company. If a model number is not found in the listings, look for it as a potential illustration.

Explanation of Pricing

Pricing for vintage radios, like many other antiques and collectibles, is extremely variable and dependent on many factors. The pricing information in this book is drawn from many different sources: regional and national radio meets, flea markets, auctions, private collectors, antique radio classified ads, and the authors' real world experience. The price ranges listed represent an average of these various pricing information sources. Many prices remain reasonably consistent over time — especially for those radios of average design and/or those originally produced in reasonable volumes resulting in higher numbers remaining still today. Rarer or more functionally sophisticated sets, and aesthetically unique sets such as Deco designs, novelties, or Catalins, tend to enjoy a trend of ever-increasing prices. Some radio prices have decreased somewhat over time as well.

The primary factor when considering whether an old radio is worth the price is its *condition*. We have tried to provide pricing that reflects sets in good condition, using the following guidelines.

1. Physical condition. All knobs and pushbuttons are intact and original. Tuning dials/scales are fully readable and complete. Dial covers, escutcheons, bezels, and other trim items are intact and undamaged. Radio does not appear to have had exposure to weather or moisture and chassis shows very little or no rust or corrosion. Wooden cabinets should have intact veneer, no meaningful chips, be structurally sound, and have a finish in reasonable condition (should not require complete refinishing). Plastic cabinets should have no cracks, chips, heavy scratches, or gouges. Cloth covered, leatherette, etc. cabinets should have no rips, tears, stains, or heavily worn areas.

2. Electronic condition. This is often difficult to fully determine from a visual inspection. Pricing does not assume the radio is working (see earlier caution on the turning on radios of unknown operational condition). However, the radio should have all the components intact, including tubes and other sub-assemblies such as record players, etc. where applicable. Speaker(s) should be in place and have no damage. The radio should also not appear to have had obvious functional problems that might be indicated by visible signs of overheating, burn marks, component melting, etc.

Several specific factors may well support prices above those listed. Radios that have been professionally restored by skilled technicians certainly may be substantially higher in price. Proper restoration can involve a great deal of labor and investment, especially in higher tube count radios. Professional cabinet refinishing can also involve substantial expense. Occasionally a radio will be found in as-is "mint" condition. Such a "mint" radio, due to its rarity, would obviously be worth more than the price listed herein. Original user manuals or other original documentation accompanying a given radio may also dictate higher pricing.

If you have a radio that you would like to sell, it is important to be realistic about its true condition. Although it is obviously quite old and may even be a family heirloom, the radio's condition will primarily dictate its value to a potential buyer.

Geographic location is also a factor in determining a fair price for an antique radio. Prices generally tend to be higher on the West Coast than the East Coast, due in part to the greater supply of sets in the east due to population distribution during the golden age of radio. Sale/purchase venue is also a factor. Antique shop and auction prices tend to be more expensive than flea markets and yard sales, etc.

Setting price guidelines for rare and/or highly collectible radios is somewhat challenging. Pricing can vary quite dramatically depending upon what might be at first perceived to be slight differences in condition. For example, Catalin radios are still some of the most highly sought radios. Yet, because there are so many factors that significantly affect the price of Catalin radios, i.e. specific color, the smallest stress cracks, heat discoloration, etc., it is impossible to establish a reasonably firm price range. Similarly, slight imperfections in the appearance of novelty radios can result in wide price swings. High end radios, such as those of E.H. Scott, often were produced with a wide variety of cabinet types. Pricing for radios with the same basic model electronics varies dramatically depending upon the specific cabinet model. Because of these dynamics, we have indicated some prices followed by a "+," which means you should expect to pay at least this much for a set in good condition, with specific price depending on the above mentioned variables.

Terms and Key to Descriptive Information

COMPANY ADDRESSES

We have included addresses for as many of the companies in our listings as possible. For some of the larger or more well-known companies, we have also included a brief history. The address and history information is not necessarily complete. Many radio companies, especially during the 1920s and the during the Great Depression, went in and out of business so fast, or merged with one another so often, or moved so frequently that it is sometimes impossible to pinpoint exact addresses and complete historical background.

MODEL NUMBERS

Some model number formats for a given company can be very inconsistent and confusing. We have often found company literature and advertising to show the same model number in several different ways! For example: A model #36WG-715 might be written 36-WG-715 or 36WG715 or even 36-WG715. We have attempted to list radios in a logical sequence to help locate models quickly. However, you may need to consider some of the format variations above when looking for a specific model and try different combinations until you find the one you are looking for. Also note that in order to provide more radio images, radios with photos are not included in the listings themselves but are illustrated in sequential order under a given company. If a model number is not found in the listings, look for it as a potential illustration.

STYLE

There are many different types or styles of radios available. We have used various common descriptive terms in this guide. The following is a basic description of each.

Breadboard: An early radio with the tubes and other component parts attached to a rectangular board that usually has "breadboard" ends. Breadboard radios have no cases or covers, all parts and tubes are exposed.

Cathedral: Sometimes referred to as "beehives," cathedrals are taller than wide with a top that is usually rounded or with a rounded peak, generally thought to resemble a cathedral window in shape. The cathedral is the classic radio shape.

Chairside: A console radio with a low shape made to sit beside an armchair, usually with the controls on the top within easy reach.

Console: The console is also called a floor model. It can consist of a cabinet on legs or just a rectangular (higher than wide) case that sits directly on the floor.

Portable: A radio made to be used in the home as well as outdoors or in a location with no electricity. Most portables run on battery power, although a great many are three-way sets, using electricity or batteries.

Table: A general term used to describe many shapes and sizes of radios that are tabletop sets.

Tombstone: These are sets that are rectangular in shape, higher than they are wide and flat on top; generally they resemble the shape of a tombstone. They are sometimes called upright table models.

C: Clock — radio includes a clock as one of its design features.

N: Novelty. This is a very broad term and covers all radios that are highly collectible due to their unusual cases, whether they sport a Mickey Mouse, a Charlie McCarthy, a built-in camera, look like a baseball, a bar, a bottle, or any other design where one would not expect to find a radio.

R/P: Radio/phono combination.

R/P/Rec: Radio/phono/recorder combination.

R/P/Rec/PA: Radio/phono/recorder/public address system combination.

YEAR

We have tried to provide the correct first year of availability for most of the sets listed. However, the actual date of manufacture for a specific radio set that you may own, or are looking to purchase, may vary somewhat. Keep in mind that many radio companies overlapped models from one year to the next. In addition, popular models were often made for several years or more. Therefore the year data should be used primarily to give a general idea of the age of the radio. In some cases we have placed a "c" before the date, e.g. "c1937," to indicate that to our best knowledge the radio was introduced around or "circa" the year given.

CASE MATERIAL

Radio cases/cabinets are made from a variety of materials. We have classified most radio sets into one of the following categories.

Cloth-Covered: Many radio cabinets were designed with an underlying wood or composition material structure covered by a decorative cloth of various kinds. Specific kinds of cloth designs included simulated alligator, leather, called "leatherette," and snakeskin.

Metal: Used to designate radio cabinets that are primarily or totally constructed of painted metal.

Luggage-style: A radio cabinet that looks very similar to a piece of luggage and utilized for portable radio designs. Often cloth-covered in some fashion, with hinged cover/lid and handle.

Plastic: We have used the word "plastic" as a generic term to cover most, but not all, plastics. In the case of Catalin plastics, we have used the word "Catalin" specifically rather than the generic word plastic because of the much higher pricing structure of Catalin sets.

Repwood: A type of pressed wood popular in the 1930s and used to make various decorative items, including ornate radio cases that have a beautiful carved appearance.

Wood: We have used the word "wood" to cover a wide range of radio cases comprised of either solid wood or a combination of outer wood/paper veneers and inner wooden framework and typically finished in clear or toned lacquers. In some cases we have indicated the type or color of the wood/finish, i.e. walnut, mahogany, etc.

DESCRIPTION

In addition to the other listing items, we have attempted to include, wherever possible, a description of the radio's shape, placement of the dial and grille, etc. to help in identifying a specific model. Some of the following terms are frequently used in the descriptions.

"Airplane" Dial: A round dial with a pointer covering a full 360 degrees. Named for an appearance similar to aircraft gauges and instrumentation.

Bakelite: A thermosetting phenolic resin developed in the early 1900s — essentially the first "plastic." Utilized for many front panels of battery sets and the complete cabinet for many table radios until the advent of more modern plastics in the 1950s. Bakelite

is molded under very high temperature and is naturally black or brown in color. Some Bakelite cases were painted in order to offer more color variety, e.g. ivory.

Dial: Battery sets (see power sources below), prior to around 1927 – 1928, had one or more round, typically large, knobs for station selection. The knobs would either have a pointer to front panel scale markings or the knobs would be marked with a scale (typically 0 – 100) and have an associated front panel pointer. Later sets would usually have a single tuning knob and some form of associated station/frequency indicator — also called a "dial" - such as the "airplane" or "slide rule" dials.

Escutcheon: An ornamental and/or protective plate typically around a radio dial or knobs.

Feet: Attached or molded standoffs on radios used to maintain some space between the bottom of the radio and the table/floor itself.

Grille: The face area of a radio cabinet, often of a decorative design, behind which the radio speaker is typically mounted. Most radios also have an associated color coordinated cloth, the "grillecloth," mounted between the grille and the speaker.

Highboy: A floor model radio whose legs (usually 4 – 6) typically are half or more of the total height of the case.

Lowboy: A floor model radio whose legs (usually 4 – 6) are considerably lower than a highboy's, generally, less than half the height of the case.

Midget: A small table set, usually less than seven inches in its longest measurement.

"Movie" Dial: A dial, which features a projected image from a circular film, rotating around a bulb.

Pushbuttons: Control "buttons," typically ganged together in groups, that are operated by being "pushed" in rather than turned like knobs. Pushbuttons are most often utilized to easily select specific preset radio stations. Also sometimes used to control other functions such as tone, phono, on/off, etc.

"Robot" Dial: A feature of some Zenith radios, the robot dial is really three dials in one — standard broadcast, shortwave, and police/amateur. Only one dial is visible at any time and can be changed by the turn of a lever.

"Slide Rule" Dial: A rectangular dial, usually horizontal, which features a thin sliding indicator.

Stretcher Base: A radio cabinet style, most typically a "highboy," with a framework of braces interconnecting and strengthening the cabinet's legs.

Tuning Eye: A special purpose vacuum tube mounted to be visible from the front of the radio cabinet and used to aid tuning in a station by indicating the station's signal strength. The name is derived from its typical appearance as an "eye" which opens and closes. Also sometimes called a "magic eye" or "cats-eye."

KNOBS

As an aid in identification, we have included, whenever the information was available, the number of "knobs" for a given radio. For this purpose, we consider sets with multiple functions on one common control shaft, e.g. a tuning control and a band selector, as one knob from a visual perspective. Sets with dials that are themselves knobs are included in the knob counts.

TYPES OF RECEPTION

The vast majority of radios listed were primarily designed for consumer use. We have not generally included sets that were designed for amateur radio, commercial, or special purpose reception. Some of the radios listed were designed to receive multiple "bands" or frequency ranges and in some descriptions we indicate the number of such bands for a given radio set. In general we have categorized the reception capability of a radio into one or more of the following categories.

BC: Broadcast — typically synonymous with the AM (amplitude modulation) band still in existence today. Almost all the radios listed were designed to provide BC reception. The BC frequency range varied as radio evolved, but typically covered from around 550 kilocycles or KC (now "kilohertz") to 1600 kilocycles. Radio sets in the 1930s would often extend this range to above 1700 KC to include the then existing "police" band.

FM: Frequency Modulation — both a new type of reception and frequency range that evolved just before World War II. Pre-war FM reception consumer radios were fairly rare and typically covered the range of 42 – 50 megacycles or MC. When known, these sets are designated as "FM1" in the listings. The FM band was moved in 1945 to its present day allocation at 88 – 108 MC and the vast majority of sets listed with frequency modulation receiving capabilities cover this frequency range.

LW: Long Wave — reception in a frequency range below the BC band. Typically some segment within 100 KC to 500 KC.

SW: Short Wave — a general term used to indicate reception in some segment of the range from 1600 KC, just above the BC band, to 30 megacycles or MC. Often this capability would be referred to as "Foreign Broadcast" reception and many sets, primarily in the 1930s, would actually show foreign cities on the radio dial. Some radios had a separate "Police" band, covering 1700 KC and above, to allow reception of police calls. In such cases, we have designated them as "SW" as well.

NUMBER OF TUBES

The number of vacuum tubes utilized in the radio. For listing purposes we have included "tuning eyes" and ballast tubes in the totals.

POWER

Antique radios typically utilize one or more of the following sources of operating power.

AC: Alternating Current — typically the standard household 110 volt, 60 cycle (hertz) power in use today. AC powered radio sets first started to appear in the latter half of the 1920s in conjunction with the development of compatible vacuum tube technology and the increasing electrification of major population centers in the United States. Early AC powered sets were actually battery sets (see below) with separate power supplies commonly referred to as "battery eliminators."

DC: Direct Current — many rural/farm areas in the United States did not become "electrified" with today's standard AC power until as late as the early 1950s. Instead, electric power tended to be derived from generators, etc. that supplied DC power. A fair number of radio sets were designed to operate on DC power for use in such rural areas and they were often referred to as "farm" sets. Many radios were ultimately designed to readily operate on either AC or DC power, including the vast majority of the table radios produced in the late 1940s through mid 1960s.

Battery: All early radio sets, until the latter half of the 1920s, required several batteries for operation — an "A" battery to power tube filaments, such as a rechargeable automobile battery, and "B" and sometimes "C" batteries for other operating power. These sets are collectively called "battery sets." Later on, radios designed to be portable also utilized different forms of batteries as one source of operating power.

PICTURES

We have tried, to the best of our ability, to photograph only sets that are as close to original as possible. There may be a few pictures included herein that show radios with new finishes or replacement parts such as knobs or grillecloth. In general, we believe such modifications do not detract from the value of the given radio set.

Keep in mind that this book is a guide — intended to guide the reader with identification and current pricing information. Because there are so many dynamic variables to consider, we recommend that you also rely upon your own judgment when making an antique radio purchase or sale decision.

We welcome your comments and constructive criticisms about this edition. We also would be interested in any suggestions or informative contributions that you might have for future editions.

John Slusser & Radio Daze
7620 Omnitech Place
Victor, New York 14564
Phone (585) 742-2020   Fax (800) 456-6494
web: www.radiodaze.com
e-mail: info@radiodaze.com

A-C DAYTON
The A-C Electrical Mfg. Co., Dayton, Ohio
The A-C Dayton Company, Dayton, Ohio

The A-C Electrical Manufacturing Company began business in Dayton, Ohio, in 1901, as a manufacturer of electric motors. By 1922 they were manufacturing and selling radios and radio parts. The company was out of business by 1930.

AC-9990 "Navigator," console, 1929, wood, highboy, inner window dial with large metal escutcheon, upper cloth grille with cut-outs, double doors, 3 knobs, BC, 9 tubes, AC, $150.00-180.00.

AC-63, table, 1928, wood, low rectangular case, center front dial with large escutcheon, lift top, 3 knobs, BC, 7 tubes, AC..**$110.00-130.00**
AC-65, table, 1928, wood, low rectangular case, center front dial with large escutcheon, lift top, 3 knobs, BC, 7 tubes, AC..**$110.00-130.00**
AC-98 "Navigator," table, 1929, wood, low rectangular case, center front window dial with escutcheon, lift top, 3 knobs, BC, 8 tubes, AC **$110.00-130.00**
AC-9960 "Navigator," console, 1929, wood, lowboy, upper front window dial, metal escutcheon, lower round grille, 3 knobs, BC, 8 tubes, AC **$120.00-140.00**
AC-9970 "Navigator," console, 1929, wood, lowboy, inner window dial, metal escutcheon, lower round grille with cut-outs, double sliding doors, 3 knobs, BC, 8 tubes, AC **$120.00-150.00**
AC-9980 "Navigator," console, 1929, wood, lowboy, upper front window dial, metal escutcheon, lower grille with vertical bars, 3 knobs, BC, 9 tubes, AC **$120.00-140.00**
R-12, table, 1924, mahogany finish, low rectangular case, 3 dial front panel, 8 knobs, BC, 4 tubes, battery **$140.00-150.00**
XL-10, table-glass, 1925, plate glass, low see-through rectangular case, 3 dial front panel, 7 knobs, BC, 5 tubes, battery **$530.00-580.00**
XL-10, table, 1924, wood, low rectangular case, 3 dial front panel, lift top, 5 knobs, BC, 5 tubes, battery **$130.00-160.00**
XL-15, console, 1923, wood, highboy, 3 dial front panel, storage, 5 knobs, BC, 5 tubes, battery **$190.00-210.00**

XL-5, table, 1925, wood, low rectangular case, 3 dial front panel, lift top, 7 knobs, BC, 5 tubes, battery, $120.00-140.00.

XL-20, table, 1926, wood, high rectangular case, slanted 3 dial front panel, lift top, 5 knobs, BC, 5 tubes, battery...........................**$130.00-160.00**
XL-25, table, 1926, wood, low rectangular case, 2 dial front panel, lift top, 2 versions, 6 knobs, BC, 5 tubes, battery **$180.00-200.00**
XL-30, table, 1925, wood, low rectangular case, 2 dial front panel with escutcheons, meter, fluted columns, 6 knobs, BC, 6 tubes, battery **$130.00-150.00**
XL-50, table, 1927, walnut, low rectangular case, 1 front dial with metal escutcheon, 2 knobs, BC, 6 tubes, battery **$85.00-95.00**
XL-60, console, 1927, wood, lowboy, inner dial & knobs, fold-down front, battery storage, BC, 6 tubes, battery **$270.00-320.00**
XL-61, table, 1928, wood, low rectangular case, center front dial with large escutcheon, BC, 6 tubes, battery **$85.00-105.00**
XL-71 "Navigator," table, 1929, wood, low rectangular case, center front window dial with metal escutcheon, 3 knobs, BC, battery ..**$85.00-95.00**

ABBOTWARES
Los Angeles, California

Z477, table-N, 1949, metal, various horse or horse & rider designs standing on radio base, horizontal grille bars, 2 knobs, BC, 5 tubes, AC/DC, $300.00-350.00.

ACE
The Precision Equipment Co., Inc.
Peebles Corner, Cincinnati, Ohio

In 1922, Crosley bought Precision Equipment but continued to use the old Precision "Ace" trademark on this line until 1924.

Type V, table, 1923, wood, low rectangular case, 1 dial black front panel, lift top, 3 knobs, BC, 1 tube, battery, $200.00-230.00.

Type 3B, table, 1923, wood, low rectangular case, 1 dial black front panel, lift top, 5 knobs, BC, battery **$190.00-210.00**

ACRATONE
Federated Purchasers, Inc.
25 Park Place, New York, New York

87, console-R/P, 1934, wood, upper front dial, lower cloth grille with cut-outs, lift top, inner phono, feet, BC, SW, 8 tubes, AC ..**$150.00-180.00**
1938, cathedral, wood, center front half-round dial, upper cloth grille with cut-outs, 3 knobs, BC **$300.00-350.00**

ADDISON
Addison Industries, Ltd.
Toronto, Ontario, Canada

5F, table, 1940, Catalin, shouldered, upper front slide rule dial, lower cloth grille with 5 vertical bars, 3 "pinwheel" knobs, various colors, 3 knobs, BC, SW, AC, $1100.00+.

2A, table, Catalin, Deco, right front dial, left vertical wrap-over grille bars, 2 "pinwheel" knobs, various colors, 2 knobs, BC, AC.........**$850.00+**
A2A, table, 1940, plastic, Deco, right front dial, left vertical wrap-over grille bars, 2 "pinwheel" knobs, BC, AC **$300.00-350.00**
B2B, table, Catalin, Deco, right front dial, left vertical wrap-over grille bars, 2 "pinwheel" knobs, BC, AC ....**$850.00+**
B2E, table, plastic, Deco, right front dial, left vertical wrap-over grille bars, 2 "pinwheel" knobs, BC, AC..............................**$300.00-350.00**

A2A, table, 1940, Catalin, Deco, right front dial, left vertical wrap-over grille bars, 2 "pinwheel" knobs, BC, AC, $850.00+.

ADLER
Adler Manufacturing Co.
881 Broadway, New York, New York

199 "Royal," table, 1924, wood, low rectangular case, 3 dial front panel, 2 knobs, BC, 5 tubes, battery **$150.00-180.00**
201-A "Royal," table, 1924, walnut or mahogany, low rectangular case, 3 dial front panel, 2 knobs, BC, 5 tubes, battery **$140.00-160.00**
324, console, 1930, wood, highboy, inner dial, cloth grille with cut-outs, double front doors, stretcher base, BC, AC ..**$150.00-180.00**
325, console, 1930, wood, highboy, inner dial, cloth grille with cut-outs, double front doors, stretcher base, BC, AC ..**$150.00-180.00**

ADMIRAL
Continental Radio & Television Corporation
3800 W. Cortland Street, Chicago, Illinois
Admiral Corporation, 3800 W. Cortland St., Chicago, Illinois

Admiral was founded as the Continental Radio & Television Corporation in 1934 by a group of four investors, some of whom literally sold their belongings to raise the initial capital. Growing rapidly due to the production of good products at affordable prices, the company ranked #5 in sales volume by 1939. Because of quality control problems and competition from Japanese TV manufacturers, the company was forced to close its last plant in 1979.

4A4, table, plastic, lower right front dial knob & lower left front on/off/volume knob over large textured grille area, feet, 2 knobs, BC, AC/DC **$15.00-20.00**
4D11, portable, 1948, plastic, right side dial knob, front vertical wrap-over grille bars, stand-up handle, 2 knobs, BC, 4 tubes, battery ..**$40.00-55.00**
4E21, portable, 1956, charcoal gray plastic, right side dial knob, front V-shaped perforated grille area, top pop-up Rotoscope antenna, 2 knobs, BC, 4 tubes, AC/DC/battery **$30.00-40.00**
4F22, portable, 1956, holiday red/polar white plastic, right side dial knob, front V-shaped perforated grille area, top pop-up Rotoscope antenna, 2 knobs, BC, 4 tubes, AC/DC/battery **$30.00-40.00**
4F24, portable, 1956, Arizona tan/polar white plastic, right side dial knob, front V-shaped perforated grille area, top pop-up Rotoscope antenna, 2 knobs, BC, 4 tubes, AC/DC/battery **$30.00-40.00**
4F26, portable, 1956, tropic yellow/polar white plastic, right side dial knob, front V-shaped perforated grille area, top pop-up Rotoscope antenna, 2 knobs, BC, 4 tubes, AC/DC/battery **$30.00-40.00**
4F28, portable, 1956, turquoise/polar white plastic, right side dial knob, front V-shaped perforated grille area, top pop-up Rotoscope antenna, 2 knobs, BC, 4 tubes, AC/DC/battery **$30.00-40.00**
4F28N, portable, 1956, turquoise/polar white plastic, right side dial knob, front V-shaped perforated grille area, top pop-up Rotoscope antenna, 2 knobs, BC, 4 tubes, AC/DC/battery **$30.00-40.00**
4H22, portable, 1956, holiday red/polar white plastic, right side dial knob, front V-shaped perforated grille area, top pop-up Rotoscope antenna, 2 knobs, BC, 4 tubes, AC/DC/battery **$30.00-40.00**
4H24, portable, 1956, Arizona tan/polar white plastic, right side dial knob, front V-shaped perforated grille area, top pop-up Rotoscope antenna, 2 knobs, BC, 4 tubes, AC/DC/battery **$30.00-40.00**
4H26, portable, 1956, tropic yellow/polar white plastic, right side dial knob, front V-shaped perforated grille area, top pop-up Rotoscope antenna, 2 knobs, BC, 4 tubes, AC/DC/battery **$30.00-40.00**
4H28, portable, 1956, turquoise/polar white plastic, right side dial knob, front V-shaped perforated grille area, top pop-up Rotoscope antenna, 2 knobs, BC, 4 tubes, AC/DC/battery **$30.00-40.00**
4L21, table, 1958, ebony plastic, upper right front dial overlaps vertical grille bars, 2 knobs, BC, 4 tubes, AC/DC **$20.00-25.00**
4L24, table, 1958, shell pink plastic, upper right front dial overlaps vertical grille bars, 2 knobs, BC, 4 tubes, AC/DC ..**$20.00-25.00**
4L25, table, 1958, carnival red plastic, upper right front dial overlaps vertical grille bars, 2 knobs, BC, 4 tubes, AC/DC ..**$20.00-25.00**
4L26, table, 1958, harvest yellow plastic, upper right front dial overlaps vertical grille bars, 2 knobs, BC, 4 tubes, AC/DC **$20.00-25.00**
4L27B, table, 1958, plastic, upper right front dial overlaps vertical grille bars, 2 knobs, BC, 4 tubes, AC/DC..............................**$20.00-25.00**
4M22, table-C, 1959, mahogany plastic, upper right front dial, left square alarm clock, center checkered grille area, feet, 3 knobs, BC, 3 tubes, AC **$20.00-25.00**
4M23, table-C, 1959, ivory plastic, upper right front dial, left square alarm clock, center checkered grille area, feet, 3 knobs, BC, 3 tubes, AC **$20.00-25.00**
4M25, table-C, 1959, tan coral plastic, upper right front dial, left square alarm clock, center checkered grille area, feet, 3 knobs, BC, 3 tubes, AC **$20.00-25.00**

4L28, table, 1958, turquoise plastic, upper right front dial overlaps vertical grille bars, 2 knobs, BC, 4 tubes, AC/DC, $20.00-25.00.

5G32N, table, 1954, plastic, raised top, upper front slide rule dial, lower horizontal bars, 2 knobs, BC, 6 tubes, AC/DC, $35.00-45.00.

4M28, table-C, 1959, turquoise plastic, upper right front dial, left square alarm clock, center checkered grille area, feet, 3 knobs, BC, 3 tubes, AC **$20.00-25.00**

4R12, portable, 1950, plastic, front half-round pop-up dial, center front metal perforated grille panel, flex handle, top right button, 2 knobs, BC, 4 tubes, AC/DC/battery **$30.00-40.00**

4T12, portable, plastic, upper front half-round dial, lower high-low grille area, top thumbwheel on/off knob, flex handle, 2 knobs, BC, AC/DC/battery **$25.00-35.00**

4V18, portable, 1952, plastic, upper front half-round dial, lower lattice grille area, top thumbwheel on/off knob, flex handle, 2 knobs, BC, 4 tubes, AC/DC/battery **$25.00-35.00**

4W19, portable, 1951, plastic, front half-round pop-up dial, center front lattice grille, flex handle, top right button, 3 knobs, BC, 4 tubes, AC/DC/battery **$30.00-40.00**

4Z12, portable, 1954, maroon plastic, top dial, front metal perforated grille with center emblem, handle, 2 knobs, BC, 4 tubes, AC/DC/battery **$40.00-50.00**

4Z14, portable, 1954, beige plastic, top dial, front metal perforated grille with center emblem, handle, 2 knobs, BC, 4 tubes, AC/DC/battery **$40.00-50.00**

4Z18, portable, 1954, green plastic, top dial, front metal perforated grille with center emblem, handle, 2 knobs, BC, 4 tubes, AC/DC/battery **$40.00-50.00**

4Z19, portable, 1954, light gray plastic, top dial, front metal perforated grille with center emblem, handle, 2 knobs, BC, 4 tubes, AC/DC/battery **$40.00-50.00**

5A32/16, table-C, 1953, mahogany plastic, metal front panel, right round dial, left round alarm clock, 4 knobs, BC, 5 tubes, AC ..**$30.00-40.00**

5A33, table-C, 1952, ivory plastic, round clock & round dial faces, gold front, 4 knobs, BC, 5 tubes, AC **$30.00-40.00**

5A42, table-C, 1956, mahogany plastic, right front square dial, left front square clock, center perforated grille, 4 knobs, BC, 5 tubes, AC..**$25.00-35.00**

5A43, table-C, 1956, ivory plastic, right front square dial, left front square clock, center perforated grille, 4 knobs, BC, 5 tubes, AC ..**$25.00-35.00**

5A44, table-C, 1956, sand beige plastic, right front square dial, left front square clock, center perforated grille, 4 knobs, BC, 5 tubes, AC, ...**$25.00-35.00**

5A48, table-C, 1956, olive green plastic, right front square dial, left front square clock, center perforated grille, 4 knobs, BC, 5 tubes, AC...**$25.00-35.00**

5C41, table, 1956, ebony plastic, upper right front dial, left grille area with center 5 star logo, feet, 2 knobs, BC, 4 tubes, AC/DC ..**$20.00-25.00**

5C45, table, 1956, rose coral/white plastic, upper right front dial, left grille area with center 5 star logo, feet, 2 knobs, BC, 4 tubes, AC/DC **$20.00-25.00**

5C48, table, 1956, turquoise/white plastic, upper right front dial, left grille area with center 5 star logo, feet, 2 knobs, BC, 4 tubes, AC/DC **$20.00-25.00**

5C49, table, 1956, London grey/white plastic, upper right front dial, left grille area with center 5 star logo, feet, 2 knobs, BC, 4 tubes, AC/DC **$20.00-25.00**

5D31A, table-R/P, 1954, mahogany finish, low square case, center front dial, 3/4 lift top, inner phono, 2 knobs, BC, 5 tubes, AC..**$45.00-55.00**

5E22, table, 1951, plastic, center front round dial with inner perforated grille, handle, 2 knobs, BC, 5 tubes, AC/DC **$30.00-40.00**

5F11, portable, 1949, plastic, inner right dial, center lattice grille, flip-up front, handle, 2 knobs, BC, 4 tubes, AC/DC/battery....**$35.00-45.00**

5G22, table-C, 1951, plastic, right front square dial & left square alarm clock over vertical bars, 4 knobs, BC, 5 tubes, AC **$30.00-40.00**

5G23X, table-C, 1951, plastic, right front square dial and left front square alarm clock overlays vertical bars, 4 knobs, BC, 5 tubes, AC..........**$30.00-40.00**

5G44, table-C, 1956, desert rose/white plastic, upper right front dial, left square clock, center checkered grille, feet, 3 knobs, BC, 4 tubes, AC **$15.00-20.00**

5G45, table-C, 1956, fiesta red/white plastic, upper right front dial, left square clock, center checkered grille, feet, 3 knobs, BC, 4 tubes, AC **$15.00-20.00**

5G46, table-C, 1956, golden tan/white plastic, upper right front dial, left square clock, center checkered grille, feet, 3 knobs, BC, 4 tubes, AC **$15.00-20.00**

5G49, table-C, 1956, London grey/white plastic, upper right front dial, left square clock, center checkered grille, feet, 3 knobs, BC, 4 tubes, AC **$15.00-20.00**

5H44, table-C, 1956, laurel pink plastic, right front dial & left square clock over horizontal bars, 5 knobs, BC, 4 tubes, AC ..**$20.00-25.00**

5H47, table-C, 1956, cameo tan plastic, right front dial & left square clock over horizontal bars, 5 knobs, BC, 4 tubes, AC ..**$20.00-25.00**

5H49, table-C, 1956, London grey plastic, right front dial & left square clock over horizontal bars, 5 knobs, BC, 4 tubes, AC ..**$20.00-25.00**

5J21, table, 1951, plastic, right trapezoid dial, left horizontal grille openings, 2 knobs, BC, 5 tubes, AC/DC **$30.00-40.00**

5J21N, table, 1951, plastic, right trapezoid dial, left horizontal grille openings, 2 knobs, BC, 5 tubes, AC/DC **$30.00-40.00**

5J38, table-C, 1953, plastic, right side dial knob, large front clock face, brass trim, 3 knobs, BC, AC **$50.00-65.00**

5J44, table-C, 1956, laurel pink/white plastic, right front dial & left front clock over horizontal bars, 5 knobs, BC, 4 tubes, AC ..**$20.00-25.00**

5J45, table-C, 1956, fiesta red/white plastic, right front dial & left front clock over horizontal bars, 5 knobs, BC, 4 tubes, AC....**$20.00-25.00**

5J48, table-C, 1956, turquoise/white plastic, right front dial & left front clock over horizontal bars, 5 knobs, BC, 4 tubes, AC ..**$20.00-25.00**

5J49, table-C, 1956, London grey/white plastic, right front dial & left front clock over horizontal bars, 5 knobs, BC, 4 tubes, AC ..**$20.00-25.00**

5K32, portable, 1954, maroon plastic, top dial, front metal perforated grille with emblem, handle, 2 knobs, BC, 5 tubes, AC/DC/battery **$40.00-50.00**

5K34, portable, 1954, beige plastic, top dial, front metal perforated grille with emblem, handle, 2 knobs, BC, 5 tubes, AC/DC/battery **$40.00-50.00**

5K38, portable, 1954, green plastic, top dial, front metal perforated grille with emblem, handle, 2 knobs, BC, 5 tubes, AC/DC/battery **$40.00-50.00**

5K39, portable, 1954, light gray plastic, top dial, front metal perforated grille with emblem, handle, 2 knobs, BC, 5 tubes, AC/DC/battery **$40.00-50.00**

5L21, table-C, 1952, plastic, right front square dial with inner perforations & left square alarm clock over vertical bars, 4 knobs, BC, 5 tubes, AC **$30.00-40.00**

5M21, table-R/P, 1952, plastic, front round dial with inner concentric circular louvers, 3/4 lift top, inner phono, 2 knobs, BC, 5 tubes, AC...**$45.00-55.00**

5R11, table, 1949, plastic, right front square dial, left square checkerboard grille, 2 knobs, BC, 5 tubes, AC/DC **$30.00-40.00**

5R11UL, table, 1949, plastic, right front square dial, left square checkerboard grille, 2 knobs, BC, 5 tubes, AC/DC **$30.00-40.00**

5J23, table, 1951, painted plastic, right trapezoid dial, left horizontal grille openings, 2 knobs, BC, 5 tubes, AC/DC, $30.00-40.00.

5R12-N, table, 1949, plastic, right front square dial, left square checkerboard grille, 2 knobs, BC, 5 tubes, AC/DC $30.00-40.00

5RP42C, table-R/P, 1958, plastic, low square case, right front dial, horizontal bars overlay center front cloth grille, 3/4 lift top, 4 knobs, BC, 5 tubes, AC $45.00-55.00

5R35N, table, 1955, plastic, upper right front dial knob over horizontal bars, left lattice grille area, feet, 2 knobs, BC $20.00-25.00

5S21AN, table, 1953, ebony plastic, right front curved dial, off-center concentric circular louvers, 2 knobs, BC, 5 tubes, AC/DC .. $40.00-50.00

5S22AN, table, 1953, mahogany plastic, right front curved dial, off-center concentric circular louvers, 2 knobs, BC, 5 tubes, AC/DC ..$40.00-50.00

5S232AN, table, 1953, ivory plastic, right front curved dial, off-center concentric circular louvers, 2 knobs, BC, 5 tubes, AC/DC $40.00-50.00

5T12, table-R/P, 1949, plastic, upper front slide rule dial, lower criss-cross grille, lift top, inner phono, 3 knobs, BC, 5 tubes, AC......$45.00-55.00

5T32, table, 1956, mahogany plastic, large right front dial overlaps left perforated grille, 2 knobs, BC, 4 tubes, AC/DC $30.00-35.00

5T35, table, 1956, rose coral/white plastic, large right front dial overlaps left perforated grille, 2 knobs, BC, 4 tubes, AC/DC $30.00-35.00

5T36, table, 1956, turquoise/white plastic, large right front dial overlaps left perforated grille, 2 knobs, BC, 4 tubes, AC/DC $30.00-35.00

5T37, table, 1956, ebony/white plastic, large right front dial overlaps left perforated grille, 2 knobs, BC, 4 tubes, AC/DC....$30.00-35.00

5W12, table-R/P, 1949, plastic, center front round dial with inner concentric circular louvers, 3/4 lift top, inner phono, 2 knobs, BC, 5 tubes, AC...$50.00-65.00

5X12, table, 1949, plastic, right front round dial over horizontal grille bars, 2 knobs, BC, 5 tubes, AC/DC $30.00-40.00

5X12N, table, 1949, plastic, right front round dial over horizontal grille bars, 2 knobs, BC, 5 tubes, AC/DC..............................$30.00-40.00

5X13, table, 1949, plastic, right front round dial over horizontal grille bars, 2 knobs, BC, 5 tubes, AC/DC $30.00-40.00

5X22, table-C, 1953, plastic, lower front slide rule dial, large upper alarm clock, side grille, 4 knobs, BC, 5 tubes, AC..$40.00-50.00

5X23, table-C, 1953, plastic, lower front slide rule dial, large upper alarm clock, side grille, 4 knobs, BC, 5 tubes, AC..$40.00-50.00

5Y22, table-R/P, 1952, plastic, center front round dial with inner concentric circular louvers, 3/4 lift top, inner phono, 2 knobs, BC, 5 tubes, AC $50.00-65.00

5Z, table, 1937, plastic & chrome, can be used horizontally or vertically, 2 grille bars, BC, 5 tubes, AC $95.00-105.00

5Z22, table, 1952, mahogany plastic, large center front metal dial with inner perforated grille area, 2 knobs, BC, 5 tubes, AC/DC $35.00-45.00

5Z23, table, 1952, ivory plastic, large center front metal dial with inner perforated grille area, 2 knobs, BC, 5 tubes, AC/DC ..$35.00-45.00

6C11, portable, 1949, plastic, inner right dial, center lattice grille, flip-up front, molded handle, 2 knobs, BC, 5 tubes, AC/DC/battery $35.00-45.00

6C22, table, 1954, mahogany plastic, large center front gold metal dial over cloth grille, feet, center knob, 1 knob, BC, 6 tubes, AC/DC $45.00-55.00

6C22AN, table, 1954, mahogany plastic, large center front gold metal dial over cloth grille, feet, center knob, 1 knob, BC, 6 tubes, AC/DC $45.00-55.00

6C23, table, 1954, ivory plastic, large center front gold metal dial over cloth grille, feet, center knob, 1 knob, BC, 6 tubes, AC/DC...... $45.00-55.00

6C23AN, table, 1954, ivory plastic, large center front gold metal dial over cloth grille, feet, center knob, 1 knob, BC, 6 tubes, AC/DC $45.00-55.00

6P32, portable, 1946, simulated alligator, inner right dial, left palm tree grille, fold-down front, double handle, 2 knobs, BC, AC/DC/battery, $75.00-85.00.

6C71, console-R/P, 1946, wood, upper front slide rule dial, 6 pushbuttons, center pull-out phono with doors, lower grille, 4 knobs, BC, SW, 10 tubes, AC $85.00-105.00

6J21, table-R/P, 1949, plastic, front round dial with inner concentric circular louvers, 3/4 lift top, inner phono, 2 knobs, BC, 6 tubes, AC...$50.00-65.00

6J21N, table-R/P, 1950, plastic, front round dial with inner concentric circular louvers, 3/4 lift top, inner phono, 2 knobs, BC, 6 tubes, AC...$50.00-65.00

6N26, console-R/P, 1952, wood, inner pull-out radio/phono, slide rule dial, double doors, lower grille, 3 knobs, BC, 6 tubes, AC $50.00-65.00

6Q12, table, 1949, plastic, right front round dial over horizontal louvers, 2 knobs, BC, FM, 6 tubes, AC/DC...................................$35.00-45.00

6Q13-N, table, 1949, plastic, right front round dial over horizontal louvers, 2 knobs, BC, FM, AC/DC $35.00-45.00

6R11, table-R/P, 1949, plastic, upper front slide rule dial, lower criss-cross grille, lift top, inner phono, 3 knobs, BC, FM, 6 tubes, AC...$45.00-55.00

6RT42A, table-R/P, 1947, wood, lower front slide rule dial, upper grille with 3 horizontal bars, lift top, inner phono, 2 knobs, BC, AC $35.00-45.00

6RT43-5BL, table-R/P, 1946, wood, lower front slide rule dial, upper horizontal louvers, 3/4 lift top, inner phono, 2 knobs, BC, 5 tubes, AC $30.00-40.00

6RT44, table-R/P, 1947, wood, lower front dial, upper horizontal grille bars, 3/4 lift top, inner phono, 4 knobs, BC, SW, 7 tubes, AC $35.00-45.00

6RT44A-7B1, table-R/P, 1947, wood, lower front slide rule dial, upper horizontal louvers, lift top, inner phono, 4 knobs, BC, SW, 7 tubes, AC $35.00-45.00

6S12, table-R/P, 1950, plastic, front round dial with inner concentric circular louvers, 3/4 lift top, inner phono, 2 knobs, BC, 6 tubes, AC...$50.00-65.00

6T01, table, 1946, plastic, lower front slide rule dial, upper horizontal louvers, 2 knobs, BC, 6 tubes, AC/DC $35.00-45.00

6T04, table, 1946, wood, lower front slide rule dial, upper grille with horizontal louvers, 2 knobs, BC, 5 tubes, AC/DC............... $35.00-45.00

6T05, table, 1946, wood, lower front slide rule dial, upper grille with horizontal louvers, 2 knobs, BC, 6 tubes, AC/DC............... $40.00-50.00

6T06, table, 1946, two-tone wood, lower front slide rule dial, upper cloth grille with circular cut-outs, 2 knobs, BC, 4 tubes, battery $45.00-55.00

6T11, table, 1946, wood, rounded sides, lower front slide rule dial, upper rectangular grille, 2 knobs, BC, 5 tubes, AC/DC $35.00-45.00

6V12, table-R/P, 1949, plastic, upper front slide rule dial, lower criss-cross grille, lift top, inner phono, 3 knobs, BC, 6 tubes, AC......$45.00-55.00

6W12, table-R/P, 1949, plastic, upper front slide rule dial, lower criss-cross grille, lift top, inner phono, 3 knobs, BC, FM, 6 tubes, AC..$45.00-55.00

6Y18, portable, 1949, leatherette, inner right dial, center lattice grille, fold-down front, handle, 2 knobs, BC, 5 tubes, AC/DC/battery.$30.00-40.00

7C60M, console-R/P, 1948, wood, inner slide rule dial, phono, lift top, lower record storage, 4 knobs, BC, 6 tubes, AC............$65.00-75.00

7C62, console-R/P, 1947, wood, upper front dial with large escutcheon, center fold-down phono door, lower grille, 4 knobs, BC, 6 tubes, AC $65.00-75.00

6A22, table, 1950, plastic, right front round dial with center crest over horizontal grille bars, 2 knobs, BC, 6 tubes, AC/DC, $35.00-45.00.

6T02, table, 1946, plastic, lower front slide rule dial, upper horizontal louvers, 2 knobs, BC, 5 tubes, AC/DC, $35.00-45.00.

7C63-UL, console-R/P, 1947, wood, upper front dial with large escutcheon, center fold-down phono door, lower grille, 4 knobs, BC, SW, 7 tubes, AC...**$65.00-75.00**

7C65W, console-R/P, 1948, wood, inner right dial, door, left pull-down phono door, lower 2 section grille, 4 knobs, BC, 7 tubes, AC **$65.00-75.00**

7C73, console-R/P, 1947, wood, inner right dial, door, left fold-down phono door, lower grille & storage, 3 knobs, BC, FM, 9 tubes, AC **$65.00-75.00**

7G14, console-R/P, 1949, wood, inner right dial, door, left fold-down phono door, lower grille & storage, 3 knobs, BC, 7 tubes, AC **$65.00-75.00**

7P33, portable, 1947, briefcase-style, inner slide rule dial, checkered grille, fold-down front, handle, 2 knobs, BC, 5 tubes, AC/DC/battery **$30.00-40.00**

7RT42, table-R/P, 1947, wood, upper front slide rule dial, lower cloth grille with metal cut-outs, lift top, inner phono, 4 knobs, BC, 6 tubes, AC **$30.00-40.00**

7RT42N, table-R/P, 1947, wood, upper front slide rule dial, lower cloth grille with metal cut-outs, lift top, inner phono, 4 knobs, BC, 6 tubes, AC **$30.00-40.00**

7T01C-N, table, 1948, plastic, lower front slide rule dial, upper horizontal louvers, 2 "A" knobs, BC, 5 tubes, AC/DC **$35.00-45.00**

7T01M-N, table, 1948, plastic, lower front slide rule dial, upper horizontal louvers, 2 "A" knobs, BC, 5 tubes, AC/DC **$35.00-45.00**

7T01M-UL, table, 1948, plastic, lower front slide rule dial, upper horizontal louvers, 2 knobs, BC, 5 tubes, AC/DC.....................**$35.00-45.00**

7T04-UL, table, 1948, two-tone, lower front slide rule dial, upper cloth grille, 2 knobs, BC, 5 tubes, AC/DC **$35.00-45.00**

7T10, table, 1947, plastic, right front square dial, left horizontal louvers, 2 "A" knobs, BC, 5 tubes, AC/DC **$40.00-50.00**

7T10M-N, table, 1947, plastic, right front square dial, left horizontal louvers, 2 "A" knobs, BC, 5 tubes, AC/DC **$40.00-50.00**

7T12, table, 1947, plastic, upper front slanted slide rule dial, large lower grille area, 2 knobs, BC, 4 tubes, battery **$30.00-40.00**

8D15, console-R/P, 1949, wood, right front tilt-out black dial, left fold-down phono door, 3 knobs, BC, FM, 8 tubes, AC **$65.00-75.00**

9B14, console-R/P, 1948, wood, right front tilt-out black dial, left fold-down phono door, 4 knobs, BC, FM, 9 tubes, AC **$65.00-75.00**

9E15, console-R/P, 1949, wood, right front tilt-out black dial, left fold-down phono door, 4 knobs, BC, FM, 9 tubes, AC **$65.00-75.00**

12-B5, table, 1940, ebony plastic, right front dial, left horizontal louvers, 2 bands, 2 knobs, BC, SW, 5 tubes, AC/DC **$45.00-55.00**

13-C5, table, 1940, mahogany plastic, right front dial, left horizontal louvers, handle, 2 knobs, BC, 5 tubes, AC/DC **$45.00-55.00**

14-B5, table, 1940, ivory plastic, right front dial, left horizontal louvers, handle, 2 bands, 2 knobs, BC, SW, 5 tubes, AC/DC **$45.00-55.00**

14-C5, table, 1940, ivory plastic, right front dial, left horizontal louvers, handle, 2 knobs, BC, 5 tubes, AC/DC **$45.00-55.00**

15-B5, table, 1940, walnut plastic, streamline, right front dial, left horizontal wrap-around louvers, 2 bands, 2 knobs, BC, SW, 5 tubes, AC/DC **$95.00-115.00**

15-D5, table, 1940, mahogany plastic, streamline, right front dial, left horizontal wrap-around louvers, 2 knobs, BC, 5 tubes, AC/DC ..**$95.00-115.00**

16-B5, table, 1940, chartreuse/ivory plastic, streamline, right front dial, left horizontal wrap-around louvers, 2 bands, 2 knobs, BC, SW, 5 tubes, AC/DC **$150.00-180.00**

16-D5, table, 1940, ivory plastic, streamline, right front dial, left horizontal wrap-around louvers, 2 knobs, BC, 5 tubes, AC/DC .. **$110.00-130.00**

17-B5, table, 1940, walnut wood, right front dial, left horizontal louvers, handle, 2 bands, 2 knobs, BC, SW, 5 tubes, AC/DC **$50.00-65.00**

18-B5, table, 1940, walnut wood, right front dial, left horizontal louvers, 2 bands, 2 knobs, BC, SW, 5 tubes, AC/DC **$50.00-65.00**

20-A6, table, 1940, walnut plastic, streamline, right front dial, rounded left with horizontal wrap-around louvers, 2 bands, 2 knobs, BC, 6 tubes, AC/DC **$95.00-115.00**

21-A6, table, 1940, ivory plastic, streamline, right front dial, rounded left with horizontal wrap-around louvers, 2 bands, 2 knobs, BC, 6 tubes, AC/DC **$110.00-130.00**

22-A6, table, 1940, walnut wood, right front dial, left vertical grille bars, 2 bands, 2 knobs, BC, 6 tubes, AC/DC **$50.00-65.00**

23-A6, table, 1940, walnut wood, right front dial, left vertical grille bars, 2 bands, 2 knobs, BC, 6 tubes, AC/DC **$50.00-65.00**

25-Q5, table, 1940, walnut wood, right front dial, left horizontal louvers, 4 pushbuttons, BC, 5 tubes, AC/DC **$50.00-65.00**

28-G5, portable, 1942, inner dial, horizontal louvers, fold-open front door, handle, 2 knobs, BC, AC/DC/battery............................**$50.00-65.00**

29-G5 "Bantam," portable, 1941, plastic/leatherette, inner dial/grill/2 knobs, AC/DC/battery switch, fold-open front door, handle, 2 knobs, BC, AC/DC/battery **$65.00-75.00**

33-F5, portable, 1940, upper front slide rule dial, lower square grille area, handle, 2 knobs, BC, 5 tubes, AC/DC/battery **$25.00-30.00**

34-F5, portable, 1940, leatherette, upper front slide rule dial, lower horizontal louvers, handle, 2 knobs, BC, 5 tubes, AC/DC/battery.......**$25.00-30.00**

35-G6, portable, 1940, brown leatherette, inner slide rule dial, horizontal louvers, detachable cover, handle, 2 knobs, BC, 6 tubes, AC/DC/battery **$30.00-40.00**

37-G6, portable, 1940, upper front slide rule dial, lower horizontal louvers, handle, 2 knobs, BC, 6 tubes, AC/DC/ battery **$30.00-35.00**

43-B4, table, 1940, wood, upper right front dial, left grille with 2 vertical bars, 2 knobs, BC, 4 tubes, battery **$35.00-45.00**

44-J5, table, 1940, ebony plastic, right front dial, left horizontal louvers, 3 bullet knobs, BC, SW, 5 tubes, AC/DC **$45.00-55.00**

45-J5, table, 1940, ivory plastic, right front dial, left horizontal louvers, 3 bullet knobs, BC, SW, 5 tubes, AC/DC.........................**$45.00-55.00**

47-J55, table, 1940, walnut wood, right front dial, left horizontal louvers, 2 bands, 3 knobs, BC, SW, 5 tubes, AC/DC **$45.00-55.00**

48-J6, table, 1940, mahogany plastic, right front dial, left horizontal louvers, pushbuttons, 2 bands, 3 knobs, BC, SW, 5 tubes, AC/DC ..**$50.00-65.00**

49-J6, table, 1940, ivory plastic, right front dial, left horizontal louvers, pushbuttons, 2 bands, 3 knobs, BC, SW, 5 tubes, AC/DC **$50.00-65.00**

50-J6, table, 1940, walnut wood, right front dial, left horizontal wrap-around grille bars, 4 pushbuttons, 3 knobs, BC, SW, 6 tubes, AC/DC **$50.00-65.00**

51-J55, table, 1940, mahogany plastic, right front dial, left horizontal louvers, 2 bands, 3 knobs, BC, SW, 5 tubes, AC/DC **$45.00-55.00**

51-K6, table, 1940, mahogany plastic, right front dial, left horizontal wrap-around louvers, 2 bands, 3 knobs, BC, SW, 6 tubes, AC .. **$45.00-55.00**

52-J55, table, 1940, ivory plastic, right front dial, left horizontal louvers, 2 bands, 3 knobs, BC, SW, 5 tubes, AC/DC **$45.00-55.00**

52-K6, table, 1940, ivory plastic, right front dial, left horizontal wrap-around louvers, 2 bands, 3 knobs, BC, SW, 6 tubes, AC **$45.00-55.00**

53-K6, table, 1940, walnut wood, right front dial, left horizontal wrap-around grille bars, 2 bands, 3 knobs, BC, SW, 6 tubes, AC **$40.00-50.00**

54-XJ55, table-R/P, 1940, wood, right front dial, left horizontal louvers, lift top, inner phono, 2 band, BC, SW, 5 tubes, AC **$35.00-45.00**

55-A7, table, 1940, walnut wood, right front dial, left grille with bars, pushbuttons, 2 bands, 3 knobs, BC, SW, 7 tubes, AC **$50.00-65.00**

56-A77, console, 1940, walnut, upper slanted front dial, lower vertical grille bars, pushbuttons, 2 bands, 3 knobs, BC, SW, 7 tubes, AC ..**$200.00-120.00**

57-B7, console-R/P, 1940, wood, inner dial & push buttons, phono, front vertical bars, BC, SW, 7 tubes, AC................................**$85.00-115.00**

58-A11, console-R/P, 1940, wood, lift top, front grille with 3 vertical bars, tuning eye, pushbuttons, 5 bands, BC, SW, 12 tubes, AC .. **$110.00-130.00**

59-A11, console-R/P, 1940, wood, inner dial, pushbuttons, tuning eye, phono, lift top, front grille, 5 bands, 5 knobs, BC, SW, 12 tubes, AC **$150.00-180.00**

61-K7, table-R/P/Rec, 1940, walnut, inner dial/phono/recorder, lift top, right & left front wrap-around louvers, BC, 6 tubes, AC .. **$50.00-65.00**

62-B7, console-R/P, 1940, walnut, upper front dial, lower horizontal grille bars, doors, inner phono, pushbuttons, 3 knobs, BC, SW, 7 tubes, AC **$85.00-115.00**

63-A11, console, 1940, walnut, upper front slanted dial, tuning eye, lower vertical grille bars, 5 bands, BC, SW, 12 tubes, AC **$85.00-115.00**

64-K5, table-R/P, 1940, walnut, inner dial/phono, lift top, right & left front wrap-around louvers, 4 knobs, BC, 5 tubes, AC **$40.00-50.00**

69-M5, table-R/P, 1941, walnut, right front dial, left grille with horizontal bars, lift top, inner phono, 2 knobs, BC, 5 tubes, AC/DC **$35.00-45.00**

70-K5, table-R/P, 1941, wood, inner right dial, left phono, lift top, right & left horizontal wrap-around bars, 4 knobs, BC, 5 tubes, AC **$35.00-45.00**

70-N6, table-R/P, 1941, walnut, inner right dial, left phono, lift top, right & left front horizontal wrap-around bars, 4 knobs, BC, 6 tubes, AC **$40.00-50.00**

71-M6, console-R/P, 1941, walnut, upper front dial, center pull-out phono behind double doors, lower grille with horizontal bars, 2 bands, 3 knobs, BC, SW, 6 tubes, AC **$85.00-115.00**

74-M5, console-R/P, 1942, walnut, double front doors, horizontal grille bars, lower storage, BC, 5 tubes, AC **$85.00-115.00**

76-P5, portable, 1941, mahogany plastic, right front dial, left horizontal grille bars, handle, 2 knobs, BC, 5 tubes, AC/DC/battery **$30.00-40.00**

77-P5, portable, 1941, cloth-covered, right front dial, left patterned grille, handle, 2 knobs, BC, 5 tubes, AC/DC/battery **$25.00-35.00**

78-P6, portable, 1941, leatherette, inner right dial, left patterned grille, fold-down front, handle, 2 knobs, BC, 6 tubes, AC/DC/battery **$25.00-35.00**

79-P6, portable, 1941, leatherette, inner right dial, left patterned grille, fold-down front, handle, 2 knobs, BC, 6 tubes, AC/DC/battery .. **$25.00-35.00**

81-F4, table, 1942, walnut, right front slide rule dial, left grille with horizontal bars, 2 knobs, BC, 4 tubes, battery **$30.00-40.00**

102-6B, table, 1938, walnut, right front slide rule dial, left cloth grille with cut-outs, 6 pushbuttons, 4 knobs, BC, SW, 6 tubes, AC .. **$65.00-75.00**

103-6B, table, 1938, wood, right front slide rule dial, left cloth grille with cut-outs, 6 pushbuttons, 4 knobs, BC, SW, 6 tubes, AC **$65.00-75.00**

104-4A, table, 1940, wood, right front slide rule dial, left square grille, 2 knobs, BC, 4 tubes, battery **$30.00-40.00**

113-5A, table, 1938, black plastic, right front magnifying lens dial, left vertical grille bars, pushbuttons, 2 knobs, BC, 5 tubes, AC **$120.00-150.00**

114-5A, table, 1938, walnut plastic, right front magnifying lens dial, left vertical grille bars, pushbuttons, 2 knobs, BC, 5 tubes, AC .. **$120.00-150.00**

115-5A, table, 1938, ivory plastic, right front magnifying lens dial, left vertical grille bars, pushbuttons, 2 knobs, BC, 5 tubes, AC **$120.00-150.00**

123-5E, table, 1938, black plastic, midget, right front round dial knob, vertical wrap-over grille bars, 2 knobs, BC, 5 tubes, AC **$85.00-95.00**

124-5E, table, 1938, walnut plastic, midget, right front round dial knob, vertical wrap-over grille bars, 2 knobs, BC, 5 tubes, AC **$85.00-95.00**

125-5E, table, 1938, ivory plastic, midget, right front round dial knob, left vertical wrap-over grille bars, 2 knobs, BC, 5 tubes, AC...... **$100.00-110.00**

126-5E, table, 1938, red plastic, midget, right front round dial knob, left vertical wrap-over grille bars, 2 knobs, BC, 5 tubes, AC **$140.00-160.00**

129-5F, table, 1938, two-tone walnut, right front dial, left cloth grille with vertical bars, 2 knobs, BC, 5 tubes, AC **$50.00-65.00**

139-11A, console, 1939, wood, upper front slide rule dial, pushbuttons, lower cloth grille with vertical bars, 3 bands, BC, SW, 11 tubes, AC **$85.00-115.00**

141-4A, table, 1939, two-tone wood, right front slide rule dial, left cloth grille with 2 horizontal bars, 2 knobs, BC, 4 tubes, battery **$35.00-45.00**

142-8A, console-R/P, 1938, wood, inner slide rule dial, pushbuttons, Deco front grille with horizontal bars & discs, 3 bands, BC, SW, 8 tubes, AC **$150.00-180.00**

144-16S, console-R/P, 1938, wood, upper right front dial, left phono, lower grille with center vertical divider, 13 pushbuttons, 3 bands, BC, SW, 16 tubes, AC.. **$300.00-350.00**

148-6K, table, 1939, walnut, right front slide rule dial, left horizontal grille bars, 4 pushbuttons, thumbwheel knobs, 2 knobs, BC, 6 tubes, AC... **$65.00-85.00**

153-5L "The Gypsy," portable-R/P, 1939, fold-down front, inner right dial, left grille, lift top, inner phono, handle, luggage case style, 2 knobs, BC, AC **$30.00-40.00**

156-5J, table, 1939, walnut plastic, right front dial, left vertical wrap-over grille bars, 2 knobs, BC, 5 tubes, AC/DC **$50.00-60.00**

157-5J, table, 1939, ivory plastic, right front dial, left vertical wrap-over grille bars, 2 knobs, BC, 5 tubes, AC/DC **$100.00-120.00**

158-5J, table, 1939, onyx "beetle" plastic, right front dial, left vertical wrap-over grille bars, 2 knobs, BC, 5 tubes, AC/DC .. **$170.00-190.00**

159-5L, table-R/P, 1939, wood, right front dial, left horizontal wrap-around louvers, lift top, inner phono, 2 knobs, BC, AC **$40.00-50.00**

7P33-4, portable, 1947, brief-case-style, inner slide rule dial, checkered grille, fold-down front, handle, 2 knobs, BC, 5 tubes, AC/DC/battery, $30.00-40.00

162-5L, table, 1939, plastic, right front dial, left horizontal wrap-around louvers, 2 knobs, BC, 6 tubes, AC/DC **$50.00-65.00**

164-4D, portable, 1939, striped fabric, right front dial, left grille area, handle, airplane luggage style, 2 knobs, BC, 4 tubes, battery **$25.00-30.00**

166-5D, table, 1939, walnut plastic, streamline, right front dial, rounded left with horizontal wrap-around louvers, 4 pushbuttons, 2 knobs, BC, 6 tubes, AC/DC **$110.00-140.00**

167-5D, table, 1939, ivory plastic, streamline, right front dial, rounded left with horizontal wrap-around louvers, 4 pushbuttons, 2 knobs, BC, 6 tubes, AC/DC **$150.00-180.00**

168-5D, table, 1939, onyx "beetle" plastic, streamline, right front dial, rounded left with horizontal wrap-around louvers, 4 pushbuttons, 2 knobs, BC, 6 tubes, AC/DC **$260.00-290.00**

169-5D, table, 1939, wood, right front dial, left horizontal wrap-around louvers, pushbuttons, 2 knobs, BC, 6 tubes, AC/DC **$50.00-65.00**

202, portable, 1958, leatherette, right front half-round dial, perforated grille, handle, 2 knobs, BC, 4 tubes, AC/DC/battery **$35.00-45.00**

217, portable, 1958, two tone tan fabric, right front dial, left front grille, flex handle, 2 knobs, BC, 4 tubes, AC/DC/battery **$35.00-45.00**

242, table, 1958, maroon plastic, right round dial over horizontal front bars, "Admiral" logo, 2 knobs, BC, 5 tubes, AC/DC...... **$20.00-25.00**

244, table, 1958, pink/white plastic, right round dial over horizontal front bars, "Admiral" logo, 2 knobs, BC, 5 tubes, AC/DC...... **$20.00-25.00**

245, table, 1958, red/white plastic, right round dial over horizontal front bars, "Admiral" logo, 2 knobs, BC, 5 tubes, AC/DC...... **$20.00-25.00**

248, table, 1958, turquoise/white plastic, right round dial over horizontal front bars, "Admiral" logo, 2 knobs, BC, 5 tubes, AC/DC.. **$20.00-25.00**

284, table-C, 1958, plastic, lower right front dial over horizontal louvers, left alarm clock, feet, 4 knobs, BC, 5 tubes, AC......... **$25.00-30.00**

292, table-C, 1958, plastic, lower left front dial, upper alarm clock, right horizontal louvers, 4 knobs, BC, 5 tubes, AC............... **$25.00-30.00**

303, table, 1959, wood, lower front slide rule dial, large upper grille, 2 knobs, BC, FM, 6 tubes, AC/DC................................... **$25.00-30.00**

331-4F, portable, 1939, striped fabric, upper front dial, lower square grille, handle, 2 knobs, BC, battery................................ **$25.00-30.00**

335-4Z, portable, 1940, gray tweed fabric, fold down front cover, inner right dial, left square grille, handle, 2 knobs, BC, 4 tubes, battery **$25.00-30.00**

336-5N, portable, 1940, striped fabric, fold down front cover, inner right dial, left square grille, handle, 2 knobs, BC, 5 tubes, AC/DC/battery **$30.00-35.00**

351-4A, console, 1940, wood, step-down top, upper center sloping panel with center slide rule dial, lower grille with two vertical bars, 2 knobs, BC, 4 tubes, battery **$50.00-60.00**

352-5R, table, 1940, walnut wood, right front dial, curved left, left grille with horizontal louvers, step-down top right with 4 pushbuttons, 2 knobs, BC, 5 tubes, AC/DC **$80.00-100.00**

361-5Q, table, 1940, walnut plastic, step-down top on right side with pushbuttons, right front dial, left horizontal wrap-around louvers, 2 knobs, BC, 5 tubes, AC **$50.00-65.00**

362-5Q, table, 1940, ivory plastic, step-down top on right side with pushbuttons, right front dial, left horizontal wrap-around louvers, 2 knobs, BC, 5 tubes, AC **$50.00-65.00**

366-6J, table, 1940, walnut plastic, streamline, right front dial, rounded left with horizontal wrap-around louvers, 4 pushbuttons, 2 front knobs, 1 right side knob, BC, 6 tubes, AC/DC **$110.00-140.00**

7RT41-N, table-R/P, 1947, plastic, upper front slide rule dial, lower cloth grille with metal cut-outs, lift top, inner phono, 4 knobs, BC, 6 tubes, AC, $45.00-55.00.

367-6J, table, 1940, ivory plastic, streamline, right front dial, rounded left with horizontal wrap-around louvers, 4 pushbuttons, 2 front knobs, 1 right side knob, BC, 6 tubes, AC/DC **$150.00-180.00**

368-6J, table, 1940, onyx "beetle" plastic, streamline, right front dial, rounded left with horizontal wrap-around louvers, 4 pushbuttons, 2 front knobs, 1 right side knob, BC, 6 tubes, AC/DC.... **$260.00-290.00**

369-6J, table, 1940, walnut wood, right slide rule dial with lower 4 pushbuttons, left front extended grille with horizontal louvers, 2 front knobs, 1 right side knob, BC, 6 tubes, AC/DC **$80.00-100.00**

371-5R, table, 1940, walnut plastic, right front dial, curved left with horizontal wrap-around bars, step-down top right with 4 pushbuttons, 2 knobs, BC, 5 tubes, AC/DC **$110.00-140.00**

372-5R, table, 1940, ivory plastic, right front dial, curved left with horizontal wrap-around bars, step-down top right with 4 pushbuttons, 2 knobs, BC, 5 tubes, AC/DC **$150.00-180.00**

373-5R, table, 1940, onyx "beetle" plastic, right front dial, curved left with horizontal wrap-around bars, step-down top right with 4 pushbuttons, 2 knobs, BC, 5 tubes, AC/DC **$260.00-290.00**

380-7H, console, 1940, wood, step-down top, upper center slide rule dial, pushbuttons, lower grille with vertical bars, 4 knobs, BC, SW, 7 tubes, AC **$110.00-140.00**

381-7H, console, 1940, wood, step-down top, upper center slide rule dial, pushbuttons, large lower grille, 4 knobs, BC, SW, 7 tubes, AC **$110.00-140.00**

382-7H, console-R/P, 1940, wood, inner slide rule dial and pushbuttons, larger lower grille, inner phono, 4 knobs, BC, SW, 7 tubes, AC.... **$110.00-140.00**

383-7H, console-R/P, 1940, wood, inner slide rule dial and pushbuttons, larger lower grille, inner phono, 4 knobs, BC, SW, 7 tubes, AC **$110.00-140.00**

384-5S, table, 1939, walnut, right front dial, left horizontal grille bars, handle, 2 knobs, BC, 5 tubes, AC/DC **$50.00-65.00**

394-11B, console, 1940, wood, step-down top, upper center slide rule dial, pushbuttons, lower grille with center vertical bar, 4 knobs, BC, SW, 11 tubes, AC **$120.00-150.00**

395-11B, console-R/P, 1940, wood, inner slide rule dial and pushbuttons, larger lower grille, inner phono, 4 knobs, BC, SW, 11 tubes, AC **$120.00-150.00**

396-6M, table, 1940, walnut plastic, streamline, right front dial, rounded left with horizontal wrap-around louvers, 4 pushbuttons, 3 knobs, BC, SW, 6 tubes, AC/DC **$110.00-140.00**

397-6M, table, 1940, ivory plastic, streamline, right front dial, rounded left with horizontal wrap-around louvers, 4 pushbuttons, 3 knobs, BC, SW, 6 tubes, AC/DC **$150.00-180.00**

398-6M, table, 1940, onyx "beetle" plastic, streamline, right front dial, rounded left with horizontal wrap-around louvers, 4 pushbuttons, 3 knobs, BC, SW, 6 tubes, AC/DC **$260.00-290.00**

399-6M, table, 1940, walnut wood, right front dial, left horizontal louvers, 4 pushbuttons, 2 bands, 3 knobs, BC, SW, 6 tubes, AC/DC .. **$80.00-100.00**

512-6D, table, 1938, two-tone wood, right front slide rule dial, left cloth grille with Deco cut-outs, 4 knobs, 2 bands, 4 knobs, BC, SW, 6 tubes, DC **$50.00-65.00**

516-5C, table, 1938, plastic, right front dial, raised left with vertical grille bars, 2 knobs, 2 bands, 2 knobs, BC, LW, 5 tubes, AC/DC **$45.00-55.00**

521-5C, table-R/P, 1938, two-tone wood, right front dial, left cloth grille with 3 horizontal bars, lift top, inner phono, 2 knobs, BC, 5 tubes, AC **$35.00-45.00**

521-5F, table-R/P, 1938, two-tone wood, right front dial, left cloth grille with horizontal bars, lift top, inner phono, BC, 5 tubes, AC **$35.00-45.00**

549-6G, console-R/P, 1939, walnut, inner slide rule dial, 8 pushbuttons, phono, large front grille, 2 band, BC, 6 tubes, AC **$85.00-95.00**

920-6Q, tombstone, 1937, wood, center front dial, upper horizontal grille bars, 4 knobs, BC, SW, battery **$65.00-75.00**

930-16R, console, 1937, wood, upper front slanted slide rule dial, lower cloth grille with vertical divider, 7 knobs, BC, SW, 16 tubes, AC... **$180.00-200.00**

935-11S, console, 1937, walnut, upper front slide rule dial, lower cloth grille with 3 vertical bars, 5 knobs, BC, SW, 11 tube, AC **$120.00-150.00**

940-11S, console, 1937, walnut, rounded sides, upper front slide rule dial, lower cloth grille with 3 vertical bars, 5 knobs, BC, SW, 11 tube, AC **$120.00-150.00**

945-8K, console, 1937, walnut, upper front round dial, lower cloth grille with center vertical bar, 4 knobs, BC, SW, 8 tubes, AC........ **$120.00-150.00**

945-8T, console, 1937, walnut, upper front round dial, lower cloth grille with center vertical bar, BC, SW, 8 tubes, AC **$120.00-150.00**

950-6P, console, 1937, wood, upper front dial, lower cloth grille with center vertical bar, 4 knobs, BC, SW, 6 tubes, battery **$75.00-95.00**

955-8K, chairside, 1937, walnut, Deco, top dial, streamline semi-circular front with ashtray, BC, SW, 8 tubes, AC.................... **$240.00-270.00**

955-8T, chairside, 1937, walnut, Deco, top dial, streamline semi-circular front with ashtray, BC, SW, 8 tubes, AC/DC **$240.00-270.00**

960-8K, table, 1937, wood, right front round dial, left horizontal louvers, pushbuttons, feet, 4 knobs, BC, SW, 8 tubes, AC **$75.00-85.00**

960-8T, table, 1937, wood, right front round dial, left horizontal louvers, pushbuttons, feet, 4 knobs, BC, SW, 8 tubes, AC/DC .. **$75.00-85.00**

965-6P, table, 1937, wood, right front dial, left grille with 3 horizontal bars, 4 knobs, BC, SW, 6 tubes, battery **$45.00-55.00**

965-7M, table, 1937, wood, right front dial, left grille with 3 horizontal bars, 4 knobs, BC, SW, 7 tubes, AC........................... **$55.00-65.00**

975-6W, table, 1937, wood, right front dial, left cloth grille with 3 horizontal bars, 3 knobs, BC, SW, 6 tubes, AC **$55.00-65.00**

980-5X, table, 1937, wood, right front dial, left cloth grille with Deco cut-outs, 3 knobs, BC, SW, 5 tubes, AC............................. **$55.00-65.00**

985-5Z, table, 1937, ivory & gold plastic, can be used horizontally or vertically, 2 grille bars, BC, 5 tubes, AC **$65.00-85.00**

985-6Y, table, 1937, ivory & gold plastic, can be used horizontally or vertically, 2 grille bars, BC, SW, 6 tubes, AC...................... **$65.00-85.00**

990-5Z, table, 1937, ebony plastic & chrome, can be used horizontally or vertically, 2 grille bars, BC, 5 tubes, AC **$95.00-115.00**

990-6Y, table, 1937, ebony plastic & chrome, can be used horizontally or vertically, 2 grille bars, BC, SW, 6 tubes, AC **$95.00-115.00**

4202-B6, table, 1941, plastic, upper front slide rule dial, lower horizontal grille bars, 2 knobs, BC, 6 tubes, AC/DC **$40.00-50.00**

4204-B6, table, 1941, two-tone wood, upper front slide rule dial, cloth grille with lyre cut-out, 2 knobs, BC, SW **$65.00-75.00**

4207-A10, console-R/P, 1941, walnut, upper front dial, pushbuttons, inner pull-out phono, doors, 4 knobs, BC, SW, 10 tubes, AC **$120.00-150.00**

4207-B10, console-R/P, 1941, walnut, upper front dial, push buttons, inner pull-out phono, doors, 3 bands, 4 knobs, BC, SW, FM1, 10 tubes, AC **$120.00-150.00**

4214-L5, table-R/P, 1942, two-tone wood, upper front slide rule dial, lower horizontal grille bars, lift top, inner phono, 2 knobs, BC, AC **$30.00-40.00**

A126, table, 1936, wood, large center front round airplane dial, top grille cut-outs, 3 bands, 4 knobs, BC, SW, 5 tubes, AC **$95.00-105.00**

AM6, console, 1936, wood, rounded upper front with oval 4 band dial area, lower cloth grille with vertical bars, 4 knobs, BC, SW, LW, 10 tubes, AC **$140.00-160.00**

AM488, console, 1936, rounded upper front with oval 4 band dial area, lower cloth grille with vertical bars, 4 knobs, BC, SW, LW, 12 tubes, AC **$140.00-160.00**

AM786, console, 1936, wood, upper front dial area with oval escutcheon, lower cloth grille with 3 vertical bars, 4 knobs, BC, SW, LW, 11 tube, AC **$140.00-160.00**

AM787, console, 1936, wood, rounded upper front with oval dial area, lower cloth grille with 4 vertical bars, 4 knobs, BC, SW, LW, 11 tube, AC **$140.00-160.00**

AM889, console, 1936, walnut, rounded upper front with oval dial area, lower cloth grille with vertical bars, 4 bands, 4 knobs, BC, SW, LW, 17 tubes, AC **$200.00-230.00**

AZ593, console, 1936, wood, upper front round dial, lower cloth grille with center vertical divider, 4 knobs, BC, 6 tubes, battery **$75.00-85.00**

B125, table, 1936, walnut, right front round airplane dial, left round grille with cut-outs, 3 bands, 3 knobs, BC, SW, 5 tubes, AC .. **$55.00-65.00**

B225, table, 1936, walnut, right front round airplane dial, left round grille with cut-outs, 3 bands, 3 knobs, BC, SW, 6 tubes, AC/DC **$55.00-65.00**

CL-684, console, 1936, wood, upper front round airplane dial, lower cloth grille with cut-outs, 3 bands, 4 knobs, BC, SW, 8 tubes ..**$110.00-130.00**

L767, tombstone, 1936, wood, lower front round airplane dial, upper cloth grille with cut-outs, 4 knobs, BC, SW, 7 tubes, battery .. **$65.00-75.00**

L783, console, 1936, wood, upper front round airplane dial, lower cloth grille with 3 vertical bars, 4 knobs, BC, SW, 7 tubes, battery **$65.00-85.00**

M169, table, 1936, wood, left front round airplane dial, right round cloth grille with cut-outs, 3 bands, 4 knobs, BC, SW, 6 tubes .. **$75.00-85.00**

R58-B11, console-R/P/Rec, 1940, wood, front grille with 3 vertical bars, tuning eye, pushbuttons, recorder, BC, SW, 11 tube, AC .. **$120.00-150.00**

R59-B11, console-R/P/Rec, 1940, wood, inner dial & push buttons, phono, wire recorder, front grille, BC, SW, 11 tube, AC **$120.00-150.00**

Y2993 "Avalon," table, 1961, dove white plastic, upper right front dial knob, left horizontal grille bars, feet, 2 knobs, BC, 4 tubes, AC/DC **$15.00-20.00**

Y2996 "Avalon," table, 1961, harvest yellow plastic, upper right front dial knob, left horizontal grille bars, feet, 2 knobs, BC, 4 tubes, AC/DC **$15.00-20.00**

Y2998 "Avalon," table, 1961, turquoise plastic, upper right front dial knob, left horizontal grille bars, feet, 2 knobs, BC, 4 tubes, AC/DC **$15.00-20.00**

Y2999 "Avalon," table, 1961, charcoal gray plastic, upper right front dial knob, left horizontal grille bars, feet, 2 knobs, BC, 4 tubes, AC/DC **$15.00-20.00**

Y3004 "Ashley," table, 1961, shell pink plastic, right front half-round dial, vertical grille bars with lower left Admiral logo, 2 knobs, BC, 5 tubes, AC/DC **$15.00-20.00**

Y3006 "Ashley," table, 1961, harvest yellow plastic, right front half-round dial, vertical grille bars with lower left Admiral logo, 2 knobs, BC, 5 tubes, AC/DC **$15.00-20.00**

Y3008 "Ashley," table, 1961, turquoise plastic, right front half-round dial, vertical grille bars with lower left Admiral logo, 2 knobs, BC, 5 tubes, AC/DC **$15.00-20.00**

Y3012 "Argyle," table, 1962, reef coral/white plastic, right front dial over vertical grille bars, feet, 2 knobs, BC, 5 tubes, AC/DC ..**$15.00-20.00**

Y3016 "Argyle," table, 1962, harvest yellow/white plastic, right front dial over vertical grille bars, feet, 2 knobs, BC, 5 tubes, AC/DC.........**$15.00-20.00**

Y3019 "Argyle," table, 1962, charcoal gray/white plastic, right front dial over vertical grille bars, feet, 2 knobs, BC, 5 tubes, AC/DC **$15.00-20.00**

Y3021 "Winston," table, 1961, starlight black/white plastic, right front dial knob/left volume knob overlap center oval grille area, feet, 2 knobs, BC, 5 tubes, AC/DC **$20.00-25.00**

Y3027 "Winston," table, 1961, walnut grained finish/white plastic, right front dial knob/left volume knob overlap center oval grille area, feet, 2 knobs, BC, 5 tubes, AC/DC **$20.00-25.00**

Y3037 "Sinclair," table-C, 1962, desert beige/white plastic, upper right front dial knob, left alarm clock, center vertical grille bars, 3 knobs, BC, 4 tubes, AC **$20.00-25.00**

Y3046 "Welborne," table-C, 1962, harvest yellow/white plastic, left front half-round dial and clock face, right horizontal grille bars, feet, 4 knobs, BC, 5 tubes, AC **$20.00-25.00**

Y3048 "Welborne," table-C, 1962, turquoise/white plastic, left front half-round dial and clock face, right horizontal grille bars, feet, 4 knobs, BC, 5 tubes, AC **$20.00-25.00**

Y3049 "Welborne," table-C, 1962, charcoal gray/white plastic, left front half-round dial and clock face, right horizontal grille bars, feet, 4 knobs, BC, 5 tubes, AC **$20.00-25.00**

Y3051 "Duncan," table-C, 1962, starlight black plastic, left front panel with quarter round dial/volume windows and alarm clock, right vertical grille bars, top pushbuttons, feet, 3 knobs, BC, 5 tubes, AC **$20.00-25.00**

Y3053 "Duncan," table-C, 1962, dove white plastic, left front panel with quarter round dial/volume windows and alarm clock, right vertical grille bars, top pushbuttons, feet, 3 knobs, BC, 5 tubes, AC **$20.00-25.00**

Y3058 "Duncan," table-C, 1962, Nassau green plastic, left front panel with quarter round dial/volume windows and alarm clock, right vertical grille bars, top pushbuttons, feet, 3 knobs, BC, 5 tubes, AC **$20.00-25.00**

7T10E-N, table, 1947, plastic, right front square dial, left horizontal louvers, 2 "A" knobs, BC, 5 tubes, AC/DC, $40.00-50.00.

Y3061 "Walton," table, 1962, starlight black/white plastic, right front dial knob/left volume knob overlap center oval grille area, feet, 2 knobs, FM, 5 tubes, AC/DC..**$20.00-25.00**

Y3067 "Walton," table, 1962, walnut grained finish/white plastic, right front dial knob/left volume knob overlap center oval grille area, feet, 2 knobs, FM, 5 tubes, AC/DC **$20.00-25.00**

Y3071 "Dexter," table, 1961, starlight black/white plastic, right vertical slide rule dial, left oval grille with horizontal bars, 2 knobs, BC, FM, 6 tubes, AC/DC **$20.00-25.00**

Y3077 "Dexter," table, 1961, walnut grained finish/white plastic, right vertical slide rule dial, left oval grille with horizontal bars, 2 knobs, BC, FM, 6 tubes, AC/DC **$20.00-25.00**

Y3079 "Dexter," table, 1961, cherry grained finish/white plastic, right vertical slide rule dial, left oval grille with horizontal bars, 2 knobs, BC, FM, 6 tubes, AC/DC **$20.00-25.00**

Y3083 "Stanton," table, 1962, desert beige/white plastic, right front window dial over horizontal grille bars, feet, 2 knobs, FM, 5 tubes, AC/DC **$15.00-20.00**

Y3083A "Stanton," table, 1962, desert beige/white plastic, right front window dial over horizontal grille bars, feet, 2 knobs, FM, 5 tubes, AC/DC **$15.00-20.00**

Y3100 "Sonnet," table, 1963, granite gray plastic, lower right front dial knob/lower left volume knob over vertical grille bars, feet, 2 knobs, BC, 5 tubes, AC/DC **$15.00-20.00**

Y3100A "Sonnet," table, 1963, magna gray plastic, lower right front dial knob/lower left volume knob over vertical grille bars, feet, 2 knobs, BC, 5 tubes, AC/DC **$15.00-20.00**

Y3104 "Sonnet," table, 1963, fiesta pink plastic, lower right front dial knob/lower left volume knob over vertical grille bars, feet, 2 knobs, BC, 5 tubes, AC/DC **$15.00-20.00**

Y3104A "Sonnet," table, 1963, cameo pink plastic, lower right front dial knob/lower left volume knob over vertical grille bars, feet, 2 knobs, BC, 5 tubes, AC/DC **$15.00-20.00**

Y3107 "Sonnet," table, 1963, boulder beige plastic, lower right front dial knob/lower left volume knob over vertical grille bars, feet, 2 knobs, BC, 5 tubes, AC/DC..**$15.00-20.00**

Y3107A "Sonnet," table, 1963, Brighton beige plastic, lower right front dial knob/lower left volume knob over vertical grille bars, feet, 2 knobs, BC, 5 tubes, AC/DC..**$15.00-20.00**

Y3109 "Sonnet," table, 1963, strata blue plastic, lower right front dial knob/lower left volume knob over vertical grille bars, feet, 2 knobs, BC, 5 tubes, AC/DC..**$15.00-20.00**

Y3109A "Sonnet," table, 1963, beryl blue plastic, lower right front dial knob/lower left volume knob over vertical grille bars, feet, 2 knobs, BC, 5 tubes, AC/DC..**$15.00-20.00**

Y3137 "Chaperone," table-C, 1962, boulder beige plastic, left front oval alarm clock face and dial knob over vertical grille bars, feet, 3 knobs, BC, 4 tubes, AC **$20.00-25.00**

Y3146 "Celebrity," table-C, 1962, sun gold plastic, left front clock face and dial knob over vertical grille bars, feet, 4 knobs, BC, 5 tubes, AC **$20.00-25.00**

Y3147 "Celebrity," table-C, 1962, boulder beige plastic, left front clock face and dial knob over vertical grille bars, feet, 4 knobs, BC, 5 tubes, AC **$20.00-25.00**

218, portable, 1958, leatherette, right front half-round dial, metal perforated grille with logo, handle, 2 knobs, BC, 4 tubes, AC/DC/battery, $35.00-45.00.

Y3149 "Celebrity," table-C, 1962, strata blue plastic, left front clock face and dial knob over vertical grille bars, feet, 4 knobs, BC, 5 tubes, AC **$20.00-25.00**

Y3153 "Capri," table-C, 1963, slate white plastic, left front clock face and dial knob over vertical grille bars, feet, 4 knobs, BC, 5 tubes, AC **$20.00-25.00**

Y3154 "Capri," table-C, 1963, fiesta pink plastic, left front clock face and dial knob over vertical grille bars, feet, 4 knobs, BC, 5 tubes, AC **$20.00-25.00**

Y3158 "Capri," table-C, 1963, reseda green plastic, left front clock face and dial knob over vertical grille bars, feet, 4 knobs, BC, 5 tubes, AC **$20.00-25.00**

Y3203 "Waverly," table, 1962, mist green/white plastic, right front window dial over horizontal grille bars, feet, 2 knobs, BC, FM, 6 tubes, AC/DC **$15.00-20.00**

Y3221 "Citadel," table, 1962, starlight black/white plastic, right vertical slide rule dial, left oval grille with horizontal bars, 3 knobs, BC, FM, 6 tubes, AC/DC..............................**$20.00-25.00**

Y3227 "Citadel," table, 1962, walnut grained finish/white plastic, right vertical slide rule dial, left oval grille with horizontal bars, 3 knobs, BC, FM, 6 tubes, AC/DC **$20.00-25.00**

Y3229 "Citadel," table, 1962, fruitwood finish/white plastic, right vertical slide rule dial, left oval grille with horizontal bars, 3 knobs, BC, FM, 6 tubes, AC/DC.....................................**$20.00-25.00**

Y3303 "Minuet," table, 1963, ermine white plastic, lower front dial knob overlaps left vertical grille bars, feet, 2 knobs, BC, 4 tubes, AC/DC.............................**$15.00-20.00**

Y3308 "Minuet," table, 1963, tempra turquoise plastic, lower front dial knob overlaps left vertical grille bars, feet, 2 knobs, BC, 4 tubes, AC/DC.............................**$15.00-20.00**

Y3309 "Minuet," table, 1963, magna gray plastic, lower front dial knob overlaps left vertical grille bars, feet, 2 knobs, BC, 4 tubes, AC/DC.............................**$15.00-20.00**

Y3313 "Melody," table, 1963, ermine white plastic, right front oval dial over vertical grille bars, feet, 2 knobs, BC, 5 tubes, AC/DC **$15.00-20.00**

Y3318 "Melody," table, 1963, tempra turquoise plastic, right front oval dial over vertical grille bars, feet, 2 knobs, BC, 5 tubes, AC/DC **$15.00-20.00**

Y3321 "Overture," table, 1963, Baltic black plastic, center round dial, right and left grille bars, dual speakers, feet, 2 knobs, BC, 5 tubes, AC/DC.............................**$15.00-20.00**

Y3323 "Overture," table, 1963, ermine white plastic, center round dial, right and left grille bars, dual speakers, feet, 2 knobs, BC, 5 tubes, AC/DC.............................**$15.00-20.00**

Y3337 "Serenade," table-C, 1963, Brighton beige plastic, right clock face with lower dial knob over lattice patterned front panel, feet, 3 knobs, BC, 4 tubes, AC **$20.00-25.00**

Y3343 "Lyric," table-C, 1963, ermine white plastic, left oval clock face and dial knob over patterned front panel, feet, 3 knobs, BC, 5 tubes, AC **$20.00-25.00**

Y3346 "Lyric," table-C, 1963, Ming yellow plastic, left oval clock face and dial knob over patterned front panel, feet, 3 knobs, BC, 5 tubes, AC **$20.00-25.00**

Y3353 "Duet," table-C, 1963, ermine white plastic, left oval clock face and dial knob over patterned front panel, feet, 3 knobs, BC, 5 tubes, AC **$20.00-25.00**

Y3354 "Duet," table-C, 1963, cameo pink plastic, left oval clock face and dial knob over patterned front panel, feet, 3 knobs, BC, 5 tubes, AC **$20.00-25.00**

Y3359 "Duet," table-C, 1963, beryl blue plastic, left oval clock face and dial knob over patterned front panel, feet, 3 knobs, BC, 5 tubes, AC **$20.00-25.00**

Y3363 "Tempo," table-C, 1963, ermine white plastic, left front clock face and dial knob over vertical grille bars, feet, 4 knobs, BC, 5 tubes, AC **$20.00-25.00**

Y3364 "Tempo," table-C, 1963, cameo pink plastic, left front clock face and dial knob over vertical grille bars, feet, 4 knobs, BC, 5 tubes, AC **$20.00-25.00**

Y3368 "Tempo," table-C, 1963, grotto green plastic, left front clock face and dial knob over vertical grille bars, feet, 4 knobs, BC, 5 tubes, AC **$20.00-25.00**

Y3376 "Fiesta," table-C, 1963, Ming yellow plastic, left front clock face and dial knob over vertical grille bars, top pushbuttons, feet, 2 knobs, BC, 5 tubes, AC **$20.00-25.00**

Y3377 "Fiesta," table-C, 1963, Brighton beige plastic, left front clock face and dial knob over vertical grille bars, top pushbuttons, feet, 2 knobs, BC, 5 tubes, AC **$20.00-25.00**

Y3379 "Fiesta," table-C, 1963, beryl blue plastic, left front clock face and dial knob over vertical grille bars, top pushbuttons, feet, 2 knobs, BC, 5 tubes, AC **$20.00-25.00**

Y3381 "Marquis," table-C, 1963, Baltic black plastic, lower front dial, upper round clock face, top push buttons, feet, dual speakers, 2 knobs, BC, 5 tubes, AC **$20.00-25.00**

Y3383 "Marquis," table-C, 1963, ermine white plastic, lower front dial, upper round clock face, top pushbuttons, feet, dual speakers, 2 knobs, BC, 5 tubes, AC **$20.00-25.00**

Y3399 "Fanfare," table, 1962, beryl blue/white plastic, right round dial over patterned front panel, feet, FM, 6 tubes, AC/DC....**$15.00-20.00**

Y3408 "Lark," table, 1962, grotto green/white plastic, right round dial over patterned front panel, feet, BC, FM, 6 tubes, AC/ DC **$15.00-20.00**

Y3411 "Balladier," table-C, 1963, Baltic black/white plastic, right round dial and round clock face, left patterned panel, feet, BC, FM, 6 tubes, AC/DC **$20.00-25.00**

Y3412 "Balladier," table-C, 1963, sea coral/white plastic, right round dial and round clock face, left patterned panel, feet, BC, FM, 6 tubes, AC/DC **$20.00-25.00**

Y3421 "Minstrel," table, 1963, Baltic black/white plastic, right vertical slide rule dial, left vertical grille bars, feet, 3 knobs, BC, FM, 6 tubes, AC/DC **$15.00-20.00**

Y3426 "Minstrel," table, 1963, Ming yellow/white plastic, right vertical slide rule dial, left vertical grille bars, feet, 3 knobs, BC, FM, 6 tubes, AC/DC **$15.00-20.00**

Y3431 "Maestro," table-C, 1963, Baltic black/white, right vertical slide rule dial, left clock face, center vertical bars, 5 knobs, BC, FM, 6 tubes, AC/DC....................................**$20.00-25.00**

Y3436 "Maestro," table-C, 1963, Ming yellow/white, right vertical slide rule dial, left clock face, center vertical bars, 5 knobs, BC, FM, 6 tubes, AC/DC....................................**$20.00-25.00**

Y3443 "Skylark," table-C, 1963, ivory white plastic, right clock face and dial knob over pattern front panel, feet, 3 knobs, BC, 4 tubes, AC **$15.00-20.00**

YG763, table-C, 1963, plastic, lower front dial knob, large upper left oval clock face overlaps patterned grille area, feet, 3 knobs, BC, AC **$25.00-30.00**

YR503, table, 1964, plastic, lower right front dial knob & lower left front on/off/volume knob over vertical grille bars, feet, 2 knobs, BC, $15.00-20.00.

ADVANCE ELECTRIC
Advance Electric Company
1260 West Second Street, Los Angeles, California

Advance Electric was founded in 1924 by Fritz Falck. He had previously manufactured battery chargers and transformers and did repair work and rewinding of electric motors. By 1924, the company was producing radios and continued to do so until 1933, when it dropped the radio line and continued in business with the production of electrical relays and electronic parts.

4, table, 1924, wood, high rectangular case, 2 dial slant front panel, lift top, BC, 3 exposed tubes, battery.............................**$160.00-180.00**
4 Junior, table, C1924, wood, high rectangular case, 2 dial slant front panel, lift top, BC, 2 exposed tubes, battery **$160.00-180.00**
69, cathedral, 1930, two-tone wood, center front window dial, upper scalloped cloth grille with cut-outs, 3 knobs, BC, AC...... **$200.00-230.00**
88, cathedral, 1930, wood, center front window dial, upper scalloped cloth grille with cut-outs, 3 knobs, BC, 6 tubes, AC.. **$240.00-270.00**
89, cathedral, 1930, two-tone wood, center window dial, scalloped grille with cut-outs, 3 knobs, BC, 6 tubes, AC **$200.00-230.00**
F, cathedral, 1932, wood, lower front half-round dial with escutcheon, upper round cloth grille with cut-outs, 3 knobs, BC, 5 tubes **$180.00-200.00**

AERMOTIVE
Aermotive Equipment Corp.
1632-8 Central Street, Kansas City, Missouri

181-AD, table, 1947, wood, right front black dial with airplane, left round grille area with horizontal bars, 2 knobs, BC, 8 tubes, AC/DC **$35.00-45.00**

AERODYN
Aerodyn Co.
1780 Broadway, New York, New York

Special, table, 1925, wood, rectangular case, slanted three dial black front panel, 5 knobs, BC, 5 tubes, battery.................**$120.00-150.00**

AETNA
Walgreen Co.
744 Bowen Avenue
Chicago, Illinois

19-A66W, tombstone, wood, center front dial, upper grille with cut-outs, 4 knobs, BC, SW, AC **$110.00-120.00**
255, table, 1937, upper front dial, large lower grille area with horizontal bars & Aetna logo, 4 knobs, BC, 5 tubes, AC/DC **$65.00-75.00**
M-253, table, wood, large front oval three-colored dial with Aetna logo, top speaker & grille area with cut-outs, 3 knobs **$75.00-85.00**

500, tombstone, c1935, wood, large center round dial, metal escutcheon, upper grille cloth with cut-outs, 4 knobs, BC, SW, 5 tubes, AC, $90.00-110.00.

AIR CASTLE
Spiegel, Inc.
1061- 1101 West 35th Street
Chicago, Illinois

7B, console-R/P, 1948, wood, inner right slide rule dial, left pull-out phono drawer, 4 knobs, BC, FM, AC **$65.00-75.00**
9, table, 1948, plastic, upper slanted slide rule dial, lower horizontal louvers, 3 knobs, BC, FM, 6 tubes, AC/DC **$35.00-45.00**
102B, portable, 1950, plastic, lower slide rule dial, upper curved horizontal louvers, handle, 2 knobs, BC, 5 tubes, AC/DC/battery ..**$35.00-40.00**

106B, table, 1947, plastic, streamline, right square dial, left horizontal louvers, 2 knobs, BC, 5 tubes, AC/DC, $120.00-150.00.

121, console, wood, upper front dial, pushbuttons, tuning eye, lower grille with vertical bars, BC, SW, AC **$85.00-115.00**
153, console-R/P, 1951, wood, inner slide rule dial, center pull-out phono, double doors, 4 knobs, BC, 7 tubes, AC **$50.00-65.00**
171, table, 1950, plastic, lower front slide rule dial, upper horizontal grille bars, 2 knobs, BC, 5 tubes, AC/DC............................**$40.00-50.00**
179, portable, 1948, upper front slide rule dial, lattice grille, handle, 2 knobs, BC, 4 tubes, battery.....................................**$35.00-45.00**
180, portable, 1948, upper front slide rule dial, lattice grille, handle, 2 knobs, BC, 5 tubes, AC/DC/battery...............................**$35.00-45.00**
198, table, 1950, wood, lower slide rule dial, upper recessed grille, feet, 2 knobs, BC, FM, 8 tubes, AC **$30.00-40.00**
201, table, 1950, plastic, lower slide rule dial, recessed checkerboard grille, 2 knobs, BC, 6 tubes, AC/DC **$45.00-55.00**
211, table, 1949, plastic, right round dial over front lattice grille, 2 knobs, BC, 4 tubes, AC/DC...**$35.00-40.00**
212, table, 1949, plastic, lower slide rule dial, upper vertical grille bars, 2 knobs, BC, FM, 8 tubes, AC **$35.00-45.00**
213, portable, 1949, plastic, lower slide rule dial, upper lattice grille, handle, 2 knobs, BC, 5 tubes, AC/DC/battery.....................**$30.00-35.00**
227I, table, 1950, plastic, right square dial, left horizontal wrap-around louvers, 2 knobs, BC **$65.00-75.00**
350, console-R/P, 1951, wood, inner slide rule dial, pull-out phono, double doors, 4 knobs, BC, FM, 8 tubes, AC **$50.00-65.00**
472-053VM, console-R/P, 1952, wood, pull-out front drawer contains right dial, left phono, 3 knobs, BC, 5 tubes, AC **$45.00-55.00**
472.254, console-R/P, 1953, wood, inner right slide rule dial, pull-out phono, double doors, 4 knobs, BC, 7 tubes, AC **$50.00-65.00**
568, table, 1947, upper right front slide rule dial, left round grille, 3 recessed knobs, BC, SW, 5 tubes, AC/DC **$35.00-45.00**
572, console-R/P, 1949, wood, inner right dial, left phono, lift top, front grille, 4 knobs, BC, 7 tubes, AC **$50.00-65.00**
603.880, table-R/Rec, 1954, leatherette, inner left dial, disc recorder, lift top, outer grille, handle, 4 knobs, BC, 6 tubes, AC **$20.00-25.00**
603-PR-8.1, table-R/P/Rec, 1951, leatherette, inner left dial, phono, recorder, mike, lift top, handle, 4 knobs, BC, 6 tubes, AC **$20.00-25.00**
606-400WB, table, 1951, wood, right rectangular dial, left cloth grille with cut-outs, 2 knobs, BC, 4 tubes, battery.........................**$35.00-45.00**
607.299, table, 1952, plastic, right half-round dial, left horizontal grille bars, 2 knobs, BC, 4 tubes, AC/DC...............................**$40.00-50.00**
607-314, table, 1951, plastic, large front dial with horizontal decorative lines, 2 knobs, BC, 6 tubes, AC/DC.............................**$35.00-45.00**
607-316-1, table, 1951, plastic, right front round dial, diagonally divided grille area, 2 knobs, BC, 5 tubes, AC/DC **$30.00-40.00**
611-1, tombstone, C1940, wood, lower front cylindrical dial, upper cloth grille, 6 pushbuttons, 4 knobs, BC, SW, 6 tubes, battery ..**$85.00-95.00**
651, table, 1947, plastic, upper slide rule dial, lower horizontal louvers, 2 knobs, BC, 5 tubes, AC/DC...**$40.00-50.00**

629, table, 1937, wood, right slide rule dial, 6 pushbuttons, tuning eye, left grille with cut-outs, 4 knobs, BC, SW, 7 tubes, AC, $85.00-105.00.

652.505, table-R/P, 1952, leatherette, inner right round dial, left phono, lift top, handle, 3 knobs, BC, 5 tubes, AC **$20.00-25.00**

652.5X5, table-R/P, 1955, wood, right side dial knob, large front grille, 3/4 lift top, inner phono, 3 knobs, BC, 6 tubes, AC **$30.00-35.00**

659.511, table-C, 1952, plastic, center front round dial, right checkered grille, left alarm clock, 5 knobs, BC, 4 tubes, AC **$30.00-40.00**

659.520E, table-C/N, 1952, plastic, clock/radio/lamp, center round dial knob, left alarm clock, 5 knobs, BC, 4 tubes, AC **$75.00-85.00**

751, table, 1937, wood, right front black slide rule dial, left grille with diagonal bars, black top, 3 knobs, BC, 7 tubes, AC...... **$40.00-50.00**

782.FM-99-AC, table, 1955, plastic, lower front slide rule dial, large upper grille, 2 knobs, BC, FM, 9 tubes, AC **$45.00-55.00**

935, table-C, 1951, plastic, right round dial, horizontal center bars, left clock, 4 knobs, BC, 5 tubes, AC................................... **$35.00-40.00**

5000, table, 1947, plastic, right front dial, left grille with 3 horizontal bars, step-down top, 2 knobs, BC, 5 tubes, AC/DC **$50.00-65.00**

5001, table, 1947, plastic, right front square dial, left cloth grille, 2 knobs, BC, 5 tubes, AC/DC...**$35.00-45.00**

5002, table, 1947, plastic, right front square dial, left vertical wrap-over louvers, 2 knobs, BC, 6 tubes, AC/DC **$65.00-75.00**

5003, table, 1947, plastic, upper front slide rule dial, lower wrap-around louvers, 2 knobs, BC, 5 tubes, AC/DC **$50.00-65.00**

5008, table, 1948, two-tone wood, upper slanted slide rule dial, lower grille area, 3 knobs, BC, 6 tubes, AC/DC **$40.00-50.00**

5011, table, 1947, two-tone wood, upper slanted slide rule dial, lower cloth grille, 4 knobs, BC, SW, 6 tubes, AC/DC **$50.00-65.00**

5015.1, table, 1950, plastic, raised top, upper slide rule dial, lower horizontal louvers, 2 knobs, BC, 5 tubes, AC/ DC **$65.00-75.00**

5020, portable, 1947, luggage-style, right square dial, left cloth grille, handle, 3 knobs, BC, 4 tubes, AC/DC/battery...............**$20.00-25.00**

5022, portable, 1951, "snakeskin" with plastic front panel, right dial, handle, 3 knobs, BC, 4 tubes, AC/DC/battery......................**$55.00-65.00**

5024, table, 1948, wood, upper slanted slide rule dial, lower cloth grille, top burl veneer, 3 knobs, BC, 4 tubes, AC/DC/battery ..**$35.00-40.00**

5025, portable, 1947, "snakeskin" with plastic front panel, top dial, front horizontal louvers, handle, 3 knobs, BC, 4 tubes, AC/DC/battery **$35.00-40.00**

5027, portable, 1948, leatherette, top slide rule dial, front horizontal louvers, handle, 3 knobs, BC, 4 tubes, AC/DC/battery **$30.00-35.00**

5028, portable, 1948, "alligator," right front dial, left horizontal louvers, handle, 3 knobs, BC, 5 tubes, AC/DC/battery...............**$35.00-45.00**

5029, portable, 1948, "alligator," right front square dial, left horizontal louvers, handle, 2 knobs, BC, 4 tubes, battery **$30.00-40.00**

5035, table-R/P, 1948, leatherette, outer "horseshoe" dial, horizontal louvers, lift top, inner phono, 3 knobs, BC, 5 tubes, AC **$20.00-25.00**

5036, table-R/P, 1949, wood, outer front slide rule dial, lift top, inner phono, 3 knobs, BC, 4 tubes, AC................................. **$25.00-30.00**

5044, table-R/P, 1951, wood, outer front slide rule dial, lift top, inner phono, 3 knobs, BC, 4 tubes, AC................................. **$25.00-30.00**

5050, table, 1948, leatherette, right front dial, left large square cloth grille, 2 knobs, BC, 5 tubes, AC/DC **$35.00-40.00**

5052, table, 1948, plastic, right front dial, left horizontal grille bars, step-down top, 2 knobs, BC, 5 tubes, AC/DC........................**$45.00-55.00**

5056-A, table, 1951, plastic, small case, right front dial, left checkered grille, 2 knobs, BC, 5 tubes, AC/DC **$50.00-65.00**

6042, table-R/P, 1949, wood, outer front slanted slide rule dial, lift top, inner phono, 4 knobs, BC, 5 tubes, AC **$30.00-35.00**

6050, table-R/P, 1949, wood, outer front slanted slide rule dial, lift top, inner phono, 4 knobs, BC, 5 tubes, AC **$30.00-35.00**

6053, table-R/P, 1950, wood, outer front slanted slide rule dial, lift top, inner phono, 4 knobs, BC, 5 tubes, AC **$30.00-35.00**

6514, table, 1947, wood, upper slanted slide rule dial, lower cloth grille with 5 horizontal bars, 2 knobs, BC, 5 tubes, AC/DC **$40.00-50.00**

6541, table-R/P, 1947, wood, outer slide rule dial, horizontal louvers, lift top, inner phono, 4 knobs, BC, 5 tubes, AC................. **$30.00-40.00**

6547, table-R/P, 1947, wood, outer slide rule dial, horizontal louvers, lift top, inner phono, 4 knobs, BC, 5 tubes, AC................. **$30.00-40.00**

6634, table-R/P, 1947, leatherette, slide rule dial with small cover, lift top, inner phono, handle, 4 knobs, BC, SW, 6 tubes, AC .. **$30.00-40.00**

7553, table, 1948, plastic, upper front slide rule dial, lower wrap-around louvers with "x," 2 knobs, BC, 5 tubes, AC/DC **$50.00-65.00**

9008W, table, 1950, plastic, right front dial, left vertical wrap-over grille bars, 2 knobs, BC, 4 tubes, AC/DC...............................**$45.00-55.00**

9009W, table, 1950, plastic, streamline, right front dial, horizontal wrap-around louvers, 2 knobs, BC, 5 tubes, AC/DC **$65.00-75.00**

9012W, table, 1950, plastic, Deco, right front dial, left wrap-around horizontal louvers, 2 knobs, BC, 4 tubes, AC/DC **$75.00-85.00**

9151-W, table-C, 1951, plastic, right half-round dial, left alarm clock, perforated center grille, 4 knobs, BC, 4 tubes, AC **$30.00-40.00**

9904, tombstone, 1934, wood, lower round dial, upper grille with cut-outs, 4 knobs, BC, SW, 7 tubes, AC, $150.00-160.00.

1200, table, two-tone wood, right dial, 4 pushbuttons, left grille with cut-outs, 5 knobs, BC, $50.00-65.00.

10002, table, 1949, plastic, upper slide rule dial, lower horizontal wrap-around louvers, 3 knobs, BC, 6 tubes, AC/DC **$40.00-50.00**

10003-I, table, 1949, plastic, streamline, right front square dial, left horizontal wrap-around louvers, 2 knobs, BC, 5 tubes, AC/DC ..**$75.00-85.00**

10005, table, 1949, plastic, upper front slide rule dial, lower horizontal wrap-around louvers, 4 knobs, BC, FM, 8 tubes, AC/DC............**$40.00-50.00**

10023, table-R/P, 1949, leatherette, outer right front round dial, handle, lift top, inner phono, 3 knobs, BC, 5 tubes, AC **$25.00-30.00**

108014, table, 1949, plastic, upper slanted slide rule dial, lower horizontal grille bars, 4 knobs, BC, 6 tubes, AC **$40.00-45.00**

121104, console-R/P, 1949, wood, right tilt-out dial, left pull-out phono drawer, 4 knobs, BC, FM, 10 tubes, AC **$65.00-75.00**

121124, console-R/P, 1949, wood, outer right slide rule dial, left lift top, inner phono, 4 knobs, BC, FM, 10 tubes, AC................ **$65.00-75.00**

127084, console-R/P, 1949, wood, outer front dial, lower grille, lift top, inner phono, 4 knobs, BC, SW, 4 tubes, AC **$50.00-65.00**

131504, table, 1949, plastic, upper slanted slide rule dial, lower horizontal grille bars, 4 knobs, BC, FM, 10 tubes, AC/DC **$40.00-45.00**

132564, table, 1949, wood, right square dial, left cloth grille with crossed bars, 2 knobs, BC, 4 tubes, battery **$35.00-40.00**

138104, console-R/P, 1949, wood, outer right front slide rule dial, left lift top, inner phono, 5 knobs, BC, 6 tubes, AC **$65.00-75.00**

138124, console-R/P, 1949, wood, right tilt-out slide rule dial, left pull-out phono drawer, 5 knobs, BC, 6 tubes, AC **$65.00-75.00**

147114, portable, 1949, metal, inner right dial, lattice grille, flip-up front, handle, 2 knobs, BC, 4 tubes, AC/DC/battery **$40.00-50.00**

149654, table, 1949, plastic, upper slanted slide rule dial, lower horizontal grille bars, 4 knobs, BC, FM, 8 tubes, AC **$40.00-45.00**

150084, console-R/P, 1949, wood, slide rule dial, lift top, inner phono, criss-cross grille, 4 knobs, BC, FM, 8 tubes, AC **$50.00-65.00**

A-2000, table, c1940, wood, center cylindrical dial, pushbuttons, tuning eye, upper cloth grille, 4 knobs, BC, SW, 8 tubes, AC, $85.00-105.00.

G-516, table-R/P, 1948, wood, outer slanted slide rule dial, lower grille, lift top, inner phono, 4 knobs, BC, 5 tubes, AC **$30.00-40.00**

G-521, portable, 1949, leatherette, slide rule dial, tambour top, checkered grille area, telescope antenna, 3 knobs, BC, SW, 5 tubes, AC/DC/battery **$40.00-50.00**

G-722, console-R/P, 1948, wood, inner right dial, pushbuttons, door, left pull-out phono drawer, BC, 7 tubes, AC **$65.00-75.00**

G-724, table, 1948, wood, upper slanted slide rule dial, large criss-cross grille, 4 knobs, BC, FM, 7 tubes, AC/DC **$40.00-45.00**

G-725, console-R/P, 1948, wood, inner right dial, door, left pull-out phono drawer, 4 knobs, BC, FM, 7 tubes, AC **$65.00-75.00**

L-6, tombstone, 1936, wood, large lower front round airplane dial, upper cloth grille with cut-outs, 4 knobs, BC, SW, 8 tubes, AC, $160.00-180.00.

PX, table, 1947, wood, upper slanted slide rule dial, lower cloth grille with side cut-outs, 2 knobs, BC, 4 tubes, battery **$30.00-40.00**

REV248, table, 1951, plastic, upper curved slide rule dial, lower horizontal louvers with center divider, 3 knobs, BC, 6 tubes, AC/DC **$55.00-65.00**

WEU-262, table, 1950, plastic, right front dial, left cloth grille, decorative case lines, 4 knobs, BC, FM, 8 tubes, AC/DC...............**$55.00-65.00**

AIR KING
Air King Products Co., Inc.
1523 63rd Street
Brooklyn, New York

66, tombstone, 1935, plastic, Deco, center front round dial, upper insert with globes, 2 band, various colors, 3 knobs, BC, SW, 6 tubes, AC/DC, $3,000.00+.

5H110, table, 1946, plastic, right front round dial with gold pointer, left lattice grille, 2 knobs, BC, AC **$45.00-55.00**

47, table, 1937, wood, rounded sides, lower front round dial, upper cloth grille with 3 vertical bars, 2 knobs, BC, SW, 5 tubes, AC.. **$85.00-95.00**

52, tombstone, 1933, plastic, Deco, center window dial, upper insert with Egyptian figures, various colors, 3 knobs, BC, 5 tubes, AC .. **$4,000.00+**

222, table, 1938, plastic, midget, right front dial, left grille, 2 knobs, BC, 5 tubes, AC **$80.00-100.00**

770, tombstone, 1935, plastic, Deco, center front square dial, upper cloth grille with vertical bars, 4 knobs, BC, SW, 6 tubes, AC/DC ..**$1000.00+**

800, console-R/P, 1949, wood, right tilt-out slide rule dial, pull-out phono drawer, 4 knobs, BC, FM, 8 tubes, AC **$65.00-75.00**

911, table, 1938, wood, right front dial, left horizontal louvers, 6 pushbuttons, 3 knobs, BC, 6 tubes, AC/DC **$45.00-55.00**

4129, table-R/P, 1941, wood, lower front slide rule dial, upper grille, lift top, inner phono, 2 knobs, BC, AC............................... **$30.00-40.00**

4603, table, 1946, wood, upper slanted slide rule dial, lower horizontal grille bars, 2 knobs, BC, 6 tubes, AC/DC **$35.00-45.00**

4604, table, 1946, wood, upper slanted slide rule dial, lower criss-cross grille, 4 knobs, BC, SW, 6 tubes, AC **$35.00-45.00**

4604-D, table, 1946, wood, upper slanted slide rule dial, lower grille area, 4 knobs, BC, SW, 6 tubes, AC **$35.00-45.00**

815 "Comet," table, 1938, wood, right front dial, left cloth grille with 3 vertical wrap-over bars, 3 knobs, BC, SW, 6 tubes, AC/DC, $55.00-65.00.

4706, table, 1946, painted plastic, right round dial with gold pointer, left lattice grille, 2 knobs, BC, 6 tubes, AC/DC, $45.00-55.00.

4608, table, 1946, plastic, right vertical slide rule dial, left perforated grille, 2 knobs, BC, 5 tubes, AC/DC **$50.00-65.00**

4609, table, 1947, wood, right vertical slide rule dial, left horizontal louvers, 2 knobs, BC, 5 tubes, AC/DC **$45.00-55.00**

4610, table, 1947, plastic, right vertical slide rule dial, left horizontal louvers, 2 knobs, BC, 5 tubes, AC/DC **$40.00-45.00**

4700, console-R/P/Rec, 1948, wood, inner right slide rule dial, left phono, lift top, criss-cross grille, 5 knobs, BC, 7 tubes, AC......**$50.00-65.00**

4704, table-R/P, 1947, wood, outer top slide rule dial, louvers, lift top, inner phono, 4 knobs, BC, 6 tubes, AC **$40.00-50.00**

4705, table, 1946, plastic, right round dial with gold pointer, left lattice grille, 2 knobs, BC, 6 tubes, AC/DC **$45.00-55.00**

9209, table, plastic, right front vertical slide rule dial, left metal perforated grille with center crown logo, 2 knobs, BC **$55.00-65.00**

A-400, table, 1947, plastic, right half-moon dial, left checkered grille, 2 knobs, BC, 4 tubes, AC/DC **$55.00-65.00**

A-403 "Court Jester," table-R/P, 1947, wood, outer right front dial, left cloth grille with 3 horizontal bars, open top phono, 3 knobs, BC, 4 tubes, AC **$35.00-40.00**

A-410, portable/Camera, 1948, "alligator," lower front dial, perforated grille, inner camera, strap, 2 knobs, BC, 4 tubes, battery **$120.00-150.00**

A-426, portable, 1948, plastic, inner metal grille, louvers, flip-open door, handle, 2 thumbwheel knobs, BC, 4 tubes, battery **$50.00-55.00**

A-502, table, 1948, plastic, right front dial, left lattice grille, 3 knobs, BC, SW, 5 tubes, AC/DC **$50.00-65.00**

A-510, portable, 1947, leatherette, right front dial, horizontal grille bars, handle, 2 knobs, BC, 4 tubes, AC/DC/battery................**$25.00-30.00**

A-511, table, 1947, plastic, right front dial, left lattice grille, 2 knobs, BC, 5 tubes, AC/DC **$45.00-55.00**

A-520, portable, 1948, plastic, recessed lower right dial, vertical grille bars, handle, 2 knobs, BC, 4 tubes, AC/DC/battery **$40.00-45.00**

A-600 "Duchess," table, 1947, two-tone Catalin, lower slide rule dial, recessed lattice grille, various colors, 2 knobs, BC, 6 tubes, AC/DC ....**$750.00+**

A-604, table, 1950, wood, upper slanted slide rule dial, lower horizontal louvers, 4 knobs, BC, SW, 6 tubes, AC **$35.00-40.00**

A-625, table, 1948, two-tone plastic, lower slanted slide rule dial, upper horizontal louvers, 2 knobs, BC, 6 tubes, AC/DC **$65.00-75.00**

A-450, table, plastic, midget, raised top, right front half-round dial, left grille area, 2 knobs, BC, AC, $65.00-75.00.

A-650, table, 1948, two-tone plastic, lower slide rule dial, upper horizontal louvers, 2 knobs, BC, FM, 6 tubes, AC/DC **$65.00-75.00**

AIR KNIGHT
Butler Brothers
Randolph & Canal Streets
Chicago, Illinois

CA-500, table, 1947, wood, right square dial, left cloth wrap-around grille, 2 knobs, BC, AC/DC **$35.00-40.00**

N5-RD291, table-R/P, 1947, wood, outer front square dial, right/left cloth grills, lift top, inner phono, 2 knobs, BC, 5 tubes, AC.... **$30.00-40.00**

AIR-WAY
Air-Way Electric Appliance Corp
Toledo, Ohio

The Air-Way Company began business in 1920 as a manufacturer of vacuum cleaners and electrical parts. They made radios and radio parts briefly during the mid-twenties but by 1926 they had ceased radio production.

41, table, 1924, wood, low rectangular case, 2 dial front panel, lift top, 5 knobs, BC, 4 tubes, battery **$150.00-160.00**

51, table, 1924, wood, low rectangular case, 3 dial front panel, lift top, 7 knobs, BC, 5 tubes, battery **$180.00-200.00**

61, table, 1925, walnut, low rectangular case, 2 front window dials, fluted columns, BC, 6 tubes, battery **$150.00-180.00**

62, table, 1925, walnut, high rectangular case, 2 front window dials, built-in loud speaker, BC, 6 tubes, battery **$170.00-190.00**

B, table, 1922, wood, high rectangular case, detector & 1 stage amp, 2 dial front panel, 6 knobs, BC, 2 tubes, battery **$650.00-760.00**

C, table, 1922, wood, high rectangular case, detector & 2 stage amp, 3 dial front panel, 8 knobs, BC, battery **$1,400.00-1,600.00**

F, table, 1923, wood, high rectangular case, 2 dial front panel, 6 knobs, BC, 4 tubes, battery..**$530.00-650.00**

G, table, 1923, wood, high rectangular case, 3 dial front panel, 9 knobs, BC, 5 tubes, battery..**$1,200.00-1,400.00**

AIRADIO
Airadio, Inc., Stamford, Connecticut

3049, table-R/P, wood, outer slide rule dial, horizontal grille bars, lift top, inner phono, 4 knobs, BC, 5 tubes, AC **$30.00-40.00**

3100, table, 1948, wood, upper front slide rule dial, lower cloth grille area, 4 knobs, FM, 8 tubes, AC/DC **$30.00-35.00**

AIRITE

3000, table-N, 1936, desk set radio, center radio with top grille bars, right pen/inkwell, left clock face, 2 knobs, BC...................**$410.00-460.00**

AIRLINE
Montgomery Ward & Co.
619 Chicago Avenue, Chicago, Illinois

Airline was the brand name used for Montgomery Ward's radio line. Airlines were second only to Sears' Silvertones in mail order radio sales. In the 1930s, Airline sets were made for Montgomery Ward by several companies: Wells-Gardner & Co., Davidson-Hayes Mfg. Co., and US Radio & Television Corp.

04BR-397A, table, 1940, wood, large center front multi-band dial with escutcheon, side grille bars, 4 knobs, BC, SW, 5 tubes, AC/DC..**$55.00-65.00**

04BR-508A, table, 1940, plastic, rounded right side, right front tubular dial and four lower pushbuttons, left grille with 4 vertical bars, brown/ivory, 1 front and 1 right side knob, BC, 5 tubes, AC/DC **$160.00-180.00**

04BR-511A, table, 1940, plastic, lower slide rule dial, upper horizontal louvers, rounded top, 2 knobs, BC, 5 tubes, AC/DC, $55.00-65.00.

04BR-513A, table, 1940, plastic, Deco, right slide rule dial, 5 pushbuttons, left horizontal louvers, 2 knobs, BC, 5 tubes, AC/DC **$85.00-105.00**
04BR-514B, table, 1940, plastic, Deco, right slide rule dial, 5 pushbuttons, left horizontal louvers, 2 knobs, BC, 5 tubes, AC/DC **$85.00-105.00**
04BR-609A, table, 1940, wood with inlay, right slide rule dial, 6 pushbuttons, left grille with horizontal bars, 4 knobs, BC, SW, 6 tubes, AC/DC **$65.00-75.00**
04WG-754C, table, 1940, wood, center front cylindrical dial, 6 pushbuttons, upper grille with cut-outs, 4 knobs, battery **$50.00-65.00**
05GAA-992A, table-R/P, 1950, cloth covered, outer front round dial, 3/4 lift top, inner phono, 4 knobs, BC, 5 tubes, AC **$30.00-35.00**
05GCB-1540A "Rudolph," table-N, 1951, plastic, right round dial knob, Rudolph on rounded left, side louvers, 2 knobs, BC, 4 tubes, AC/DC ....**$800.00+**
05GCB-1541 "Lone Ranger," table-N, 1950, plastic, Lone Ranger & Silver on rounded left front, right round dial knob, 2 knobs, BC, 4 tubes, AC/DC ....**$800.00+**
05GCB-1541A "Lone Ranger," table-N, 1950, plastic, Lone Ranger & Silver on rounded left front, right dial knob, 2 knobs, BC, 4 tubes, AC/DC ....**$800.00+**
05GHM-1061A, portable, 1950, leather case, right front round dial knob over grille, handle, 3 knobs, BC, 4 tubes, AC/DC/battery ..**$30.00-35.00**
05WG-1813A, table, 1950, wood, right front rectangular dial over large cloth grille, 4 knobs, BC, FM, 9 tubes, AC **$30.00-35.00**
05WG-2748F, console-R/P, 1950, wood, inner right slide rule dial, pull-out phono, double doors, 4 knobs, BC, FM, 9 tubes, AC **$65.00-75.00**
05WG-2749D, console-R/P, 1950, wood, inner right slide rule dial, left pull-out phono drawer, 4 knobs, BC, FM, 9 tubes, AC ..**$65.00-75.00**
05WG-2752, console-R/P, 1950, wood, inner right slide rule dial, left pull-out phono drawer, 4 knobs, BC, FM, 7 tubes, AC **$65.00-75.00**
5D8-1, table, plastic, right front dial, left horizontal louvers, handle, 2 knobs, 5 tubes, AC/DC **$45.00-55.00**
14BR-521A, table, 1941, plastic, small case, lower front dial, upper horizontal grille bars, 2 knobs, BC, 5 tubes, AC/DC **$65.00-75.00**

04BR-566A, portable, 1940, cloth covered, inner right slide rule dial, left cloth grille, fold-in front, handle, 2 knobs, BC, 6 tubes, AC/DC/battery, $25.00-30.00.

14BR-514B, table, 1941, painted plastic, Deco, right slide rule dial, pushbuttons, left horizontal louvers, 2 knobs, BC, 5 tubes, AC/DC, $85.00-105.00.

14BR-522A, table, 1941, plastic, lower front slide rule dial, upper horizontal louvers, rounded top, 2 knobs, BC, 5 tubes, AC/DC ..**$65.00-75.00**
14BR-525A, table, 1941, plastic, large center front dial, right & left side horizontal wrap-around grille bars, 5 pushbuttons, 2 knobs, BC, 5 tubes, AC/DC **$55.00-65.00**
14BR-526A, table, 1941, plastic, large center front dial, right & left side horizontal wrap-around grille bars, 5 pushbuttons, 2 knobs, BC, 5 tubes, AC/DC **$55.00-65.00**
14BR-734A, table, 1941, plastic, large center front dial, right & left side horizontal wrap-around grille bars, 6 pushbuttons, 4 knobs, BC, SW, 7 tubes, AC/DC **$65.00-75.00**
14BR-735A, table, 1941, plastic, large center front dial, right & left side horizontal wrap-around grille bars, 6 push buttons, 4 knobs, BC, SW, 7 tubes, AC/DC **$65.00-75.00**
14BR-736A, table, 1941, wood, center front dial, right & left horizontal wrap-around grille bars, pushbuttons, 4 knobs, BC, SW, 7 tubes, AC/DC **$75.00-85.00**
14WG-625A, table, 1941, plastic, right front dial, left vertical grille bars, 2 knobs, BC, 6 tubes, AC/DC **$65.00-75.00**
14WG-680A, portable, 1941, inner right slide rule dial, left grille, fold-down cover, handle, 3 knobs, BC, 6 tubes, AC/DC/battery **$30.00-35.00**

14WG-806A, table, 1941, wood, right slide rule dial, curved left with vertical grille bars, pushbuttons, 4 knobs, BC, SW, 8 tubes, AC, $65.00-75.00.

15BR-1535B, table, 1951, plastic, lower front slide rule dial, upper quarter-round louvers, 4 knobs, BC, FM, 5 tubes **$50.00-65.00**
15BR-1536B, table, 1951, plastic, right slide rule dial, left lattice grille, 6 pushbuttons, 2 knobs, BC, 5 tubes, AC/DC **$55.00-65.00**
15BR-1544A, table, 1951, plastic, lower front slide rule dial, upper lattice grille, 2 knobs, BC, 5 tubes, AC/DC **$40.00-45.00**
15BR-1547A, table, 1951, plastic, lower front curved slide rule dial, upper lattice grille, 4 knobs, BC, 4 tubes, AC/DC **$45.00-55.00**
15GAA-995A, table-R/P, 1951, leatherette, outer front dial, switch, 3/4 lift top, inner phono, 3 knobs, BC, 5 tubes, AC..................**$25.00-30.00**
15GHM-934A, table-R/P, 1951, suitcase-style, inner right dial, left phono, lift top, handle, 4 knobs, BC, 5 tubes, AC **$20.00-25.00**
15GHM-1070A, portable, 1951, suitcase-style, right front round dial over grille, handle, 3 knobs, BC, 4 tubes, AC/DC/battery **$30.00-35.00**
15GSE-2764A, console-R/P, 1951, wood, right front dial, left pull-out phono drawer, storage, 4 knobs, BC, 6 tubes, AC........ **$55.00-65.00**
15WG-1545A, table, 1951, plastic, top curved slide rule dial, lower horizontal wrap-around louvers, 4 knobs, BC, FM, 8 tubes, AC ..**$55.00-65.00**

25BR-1542A, table, 1952, plastic, lower front slide rule dial, upper lattice grille, 4 knobs, BC, 4 tubes, AC/DC, $50.00-55.00.

15WG-2745C, console-R/P, 1951, wood, inner right slide rule dial, pull-out phono, storage, double doors, 4 knobs, BC, FM, 10 tubes, AC **$50.00-65.00**

15WG-2758A, console-R/P, 1951, wood, inner right slide rule dial, pull-out phono, double doors, 4 knobs, BC, FM, 8 tubes, AC **$50.00-65.00**

20, cathedral, 1931, wood, small case, left front half- round dial, cloth grille with cut-outs, scalloped top, 2 knobs, BC, 4 tubes, AC.. **$200.00-230.00**

25BR-1549B, table-C, 1952, plastic, perforated front panel, right dial, left clock, center horizontal lines, 4 knobs, BC, 4 tubes, AC .. **$30.00-35.00**

25GAA-996A, table-R/P, 1952, cloth covered, outer center front round dial & knobs, 3/4 lift top, inner phono, handle, 3 knobs, BC, 5 tubes, AC **$30.00-35.00**

25GSE-1555A, table, 1952, plastic, right front round dial over large woven grille area, lower left "Airline" logo, 2 knobs, BC, 5 tubes, AC/DC **$30.00-35.00**

25GSG-2016A, table-R/P, 1952, wood, right front dial over large grille, 3/4 lift top, inner phono, 4 knobs, BC, 5 tubes, AC **$30.00-35.00**

25GSL-1560A, table-C, 1952, plastic, right side dial, large front rectangular alarm clock, 4 knobs, BC, 4 tubes, AC **$35.00-40.00**

25GSL-1814A, table, 1952, wood, front half-round dial over criss-cross grille, 2 knobs, BC, 6 tubes, AC/DC **$30.00-35.00**

25GSL-2000A, table-R/P, 1952, plastic, outer right front round dial, left vertical grille bars, open top phono, 3 knobs, BC, 4 tubes, AC.. **$35.00-45.00**

25WG-1573A "Global," table, 1952, plastic, right front vertical slide rule dial, left perforated grille, 4 knobs, BC, SW, 6 tubes, AC.. **$45.00-55.00**

35GAA-3969A, table-R/Rec, 1953, leatherette, inner left dial, disc recorder, lift top, outer grille, handle, 4 knobs, BC, 6 tubes, AC.. **$20.00-25.00**

35GSE-1555D, table, 1953, plastic, right front round dial over large woven grille area, lower left "Airline" logo, 2 knobs, BC **$30.00-35.00**

62-84, console, 1933, wood, lowboy, upper half-round dial, lower cloth grille with cut-outs, 6 legs, 3 knobs, BC, 10 tubes, AC, $120.00-150.00.

35GSL-2770A, end table-R/P, 1953, wood, step-down top, slide rule dial, front pull-out phono drawer, 4 knobs, BC, 6 tubes, AC .. **$85.00-115.00**

35WG-1573B "Global," table, 1953, plastic, right front vertical slide rule dial, left perforated grille, 4 knobs, BC, SW, 6 tubes, AC.. **$45.00-55.00**

54BR-1501A, table, 1945, plastic, lower slide rule dial, upper horizontal louvers, 2 knobs, BC, 5 tubes, AC/DC **$65.00-75.00**

54BR-1503A, table, 1945, plastic, upper slide rule dial, lower horizontal wrap-around louvers, 2 bullet knobs, BC, 5 tubes, AC/DC............**$50.00-65.00**

54BR-1505B, table, 1945, plastic, large center dial, horizontal side louvers, 5 pushbuttons, 2 knobs, BC, 5 tubes, AC/DC **$55.00-65.00**

54BR-1506A, table, 1945, plastic, large center front dial, horizontal side louvers, 5 pushbuttons, 2 knobs, BC, 5 tubes, AC/DC ..**$55.00-65.00**

54KP-1209B, table, 1945, two-tone wood, upper slide rule dial, lower cloth grille, 2 knobs, BC, 5 tubes, battery **$30.00-35.00**

54WG-2500A, console-R/P, 1945, wood, upper front slanted slide rule dial, lower cloth grille with vertical bars, 4 knobs, BC, SW, 7 tubes, AC **$65.00-75.00**

54WG-2700A, console-R/P, 1945, wood, upper front slanted slide rule dial, lower tilt out phono unit, 4 knobs, BC, SW, 7 tubes, AC .. **$65.00-75.00**

62-77, cathedral, 1933, wood, center front window dial, upper cloth grille with cut-outs, 3 knobs, BC, battery............................**$120.00-150.00**

62-114, tombstone, 1934, wood, shouldered, lower front round dial, upper grille with 3 vertical bars, 3 knobs, BC, 7 tubes, battery **$85.00-95.00**

62-123, console, 1935, two-tone wood, upper round dial, lower cloth grille with cut-outs, fluted front & side panels, 4 knobs, BC, SW, 7 tubes, AC **$150.00-180.00**

62-131, tombstone, 1935, wood, shouldered, lower airplane dial, upper grille with 3 vertical bars, 4 knobs, BC, SW, 7 tubes, AC, $95.00-115.00.

62-140, tombstone, 1937, wood, two-toned right and left front sides, center front round dial, upper cloth grille with cut-outs, 2 knobs, BC, 5 tubes, AC **$95.00-115.00**

62-148, tombstone, 1934, wood, rounded shoulders, lower round dial, upper cloth grille with cut-outs, 2 knobs, BC, 5 tubes, AC **$95.00-115.00**

62-169, tombstone, 1936, wood, lower front center airplane dial, upper grille, wide cabinet with room for batteries, 3 knobs, BC, 4 tubes, battery **$90.00-100.00**

62-177, tombstone, 1936, wood, lower round dial, upper cloth grille with black cut-outs, horizontal fluting on base, 4 knobs, BC, SW, 7 tubes, AC **$85.00-105.00**

62-211, tombstone, 1936, wood, lower round dial, stripes around dial, stars in each upper front corner, upper cloth grille, 2 knobs, BC, 5 tubes, battery **$85.00-95.00**

62-217, table, 1935, wood, wide case, center recessed area with lower airplane dial, upper decorative grille with center rectangle, step-down top, 4 knobs, BC, SW, 7 tubes, battery **$110.00-130.00**

62-245, table, 1936, wood, right airplane dial, left decorative cut-out grille, rounded shoulders, 2 knobs, BC, SW, 7 tubes, 6VDC **$80.00-90.00**

62-304, table, 1937, wood, Deco, rounded left top and rounded right side, right center airplane dial, left decorative round grille with cut-outs, 2 knobs, BC, 4 tubes, battery **$160.00-180.00**

62-306, table, 1937, wood, right front round "telephone" dial, tuning eye, left horizontal wrap-around louvers, 4 knobs, BC, SW, 6 tubes, AC **$75.00-85.00**

62-316, table, 1935, wood, off-center oval dial, tuning eye, left cloth grille with Deco cut-outs, 3 knobs, BC, SW, 6 tubes, AC **$95.00-105.00**

62-318, table, 1935, wood, off-center "movie dial," tuning eye, left grille with cut-outs, 4 knobs, BC, SW, 8 tubes, AC............. **$95.00-105.00**

62-320, table, 1939, ivory plastic, right front dial, left graduated horizontal wrap-around louvers, 2 knobs, BC, 5 tubes, AC/DC....**$85.00-105.00**

62-325, table, 1939, brown plastic, right front dial, left graduated horizontal wrap-around louvers, 2 knobs, BC, 5 tubes, AC/DC **$85.00-105.00**

62-336, table, 1938, wood, center front oval dial, left grille with horizontal bars, right horizontal lines, 3 knobs, BC, SW, 5 tubes, battery **$50.00-65.00**

62-351, table, 1939, brown plastic, Deco, rounded right side with slot, right side window dial and pushbuttons, left vertical wrap-over top grille bars, 1 front and 1 right side knob, BC, 5 tubes, AC **$160.00-180.00**

62-352, table, 1939, ivory plastic, Deco, rounded right side with slot, right side window dial and pushbuttons, left vertical wrap-over top grille bars, 1 front and 1 right side knob, BC, 5 tubes, AC .. **$160.00-180.00**

62-370, console, 1938, wood, upper front slide rule dial, tuning eye, lower grille with vertical divider, pushbuttons, 4 knobs, BC, SW, 7 tubes, AC **$110.00-120.00**

62-370, table, 1938, wood, right front slide rule dial, left round cloth grille with horizontal bars, 6 pushbuttons, 4 knobs, BC, SW, 7 tubes, AC **$75.00-85.00**

62-376, table, 1939, wood, right oval dial, tuning eye, left wrap-around grille bars, 4 knobs, BC, SW, 6 tubes, battery...............**$50.00-65.00**

62-386, table, 1939, plastic, right front "telephone" with tuning eye above, left grille with vertical bars, decorative top, case also encloses back, 2 knobs, BC, 6 tubes, AC...........................**$160.00-180.00**

62-416, table, 1935, wood, right front multi-colored oval dial, left cloth grille with vertical bars, tuning eye, 3 knobs, BC, SW, 6 tubes, AC.. **$55.00-65.00**

62-425, table, 1936, wood, right front round dial, left cloth grille with free-form cut-outs, 2 knobs, BC, 5 tubes, AC **$65.00-75.00**

62-437, table, 1936, wood, off-center "movie dial," left cloth grille with Deco cut-outs, 4 knobs, BC, SW, 7 tubes, battery **$85.00-95.00**

62-455, table, plastic, rounded right with "telephone" dial, left grille with vertical wrap-over bars, 2 knobs, BC, 5 tubes, AC .. **$110.00-130.00**

62-288 "Miracle," table, 1939, plastic, right front dial, 6 push buttons, finished all sides, tuning eye, 1 front and 1 right side knob, BC, 6 tubes, AC, $120.00-150.00.

62-476, table, 1941, plastic, right front "telephone" dial, tuning eye, left vertical grille bars, 2 knobs, BC, 6 tubes, AC **$95.00-115.00**

62-600, table, 1939, wood, right front slide rule dial with tuning eye above, left round grille with cut-outs, rounded shoulders, 3 knobs, BC, SW, 6 tubes, AC.. **$120.00-150.00**

62-606, table, 1938, plastic, right front "telephone" dial, tuning eye, left vertical wrap-over grille bars, 2 knobs, BC, 6 tubes, AC **$95.00-115.00**

62-2714, console-R/P, wood, upper front slide rule dial, large lower cloth grille area, tilt-out phono, 4 knobs, BC, FM, AC.......... **$95.00-115.00**

64BR-1051A, portable, 1946, luggage style, small upper slide rule dial, lower grille area, handle, 2 knobs, BC, 5 tubes, AC/DC/battery **$25.00-30.00**

64BR-1205A, table, 1946, plastic, center front dial, right & left side horizontal wrap-around louvers, 2 knobs, BC, 4 tubes, battery ..**$35.00-40.00**

64BR-1208A, table, 1946, wood, right slide rule dial, left wrap-around grille, 6 pushbuttons, 4 knobs, BC, SW, 5 tubes, battery **$40.00-45.00**

64BR-1501A, table, 1946, plastic, lower slide rule dial, upper horizontal grille bars, rounded top, 2 knobs, BC, 5 tubes, AC/DC..**$55.00-65.00**

64BR-1808, table, 1946, wood, left front slide rule dial, right criss-cross grille, pushbuttons, 3 knobs, BC, SW, 8 tubes, AC **$50.00-55.00**

64BR-1808A, table, 1946, wood, left front slide rule dial, criss-cross grille, 8 pushbuttons, 5 bands, 3 knobs, BC, SW, 8 tubes, AC **$50.00-55.00**

62-403, console, 1939, wood, upper front "movie dial," pushbuttons, lower grille with vertical divider, BC, SW, 13 tubes, AC, $160.00-180.00.

64WG-1050A, portable, 1946, inner right half-round dial, center square grille, left volume knob, flip-up lid, BC, 4 tubes, AC/DC/battery **$40.00-50.00**

64WG-1052A, portable, 1946, inner right slide rule dial, left grille, fold-down front, handle, 3 knobs, BC, 6 tubes, AC/DC/battery **$35.00-40.00**

64WG-1207B, table, 1946, wood, upper front slide rule dial, large center cloth grille, 2 knobs, BC, 5 tubes, battery **$30.00-35.00**

64WG-1511A, table, 1946, plastic, lower recessed slide rule dial, recessed cloth grille, 2 knobs, BC, 6 tubes, AC/DC **$40.00-45.00**

64WG-1801C, table, 1946, wood, right square dial over criss-cross grille area, round sides, 2 knobs, BC, 5 tubes, AC/DC **$40.00-45.00**

64WG-1804B, table, 1946, wood, lower recessed slide rule dial, recessed cloth grille, 2 knobs, BC, 6 tubes, AC/DC **$45.00-50.00**

64WG-1807A, table, 1946, wood, lower recessed slide rule dial, recessed cloth grille, 4 knobs, BC, SW, 6 tubes, AC **$35.00-40.00**

64WG-1809A, table, 1946, wood, lower recessed slide rule dial, upper recessed cloth grille, base, 2 knobs, BC, 6 tubes, AC/DC...**$35.00-40.00**

64WG-2007B, table-R/P, 1946, wood, outer right dial, criss-cross grille, lift top, inner phono, 2 knobs, BC, 5 tubes, AC **$30.00-35.00**

64WG-2009A, table-R/P, 1946, wood, outer slide rule dial, cloth grille, lift top, inner phono, 3 knobs, BC, 6 tubes, AC..................**$30.00-35.00**

74BR-1053A, portable, 1947, upper slide rule dial, lower horizontal louvers, handle, 2 knobs, BC, 4 tubes, AC/DC/battery **$30.00-35.00**

74BR-1055A, portable, 1947, upper slide rule dial, lower lattice grille, handle, 2 knobs, BC, 4 tubes, AC/DC/battery...............**$30.00-35.00**

74BR-1502B, table, 1947, ivory plastic, lower slide rule dial, upper horizontal louvers, metal back, 2 knobs, BC, 5 tubes, AC/DC **$75.00-85.00**

74BR-1514B, table, 1947, plastic, lower slide rule dial, large upper grille, 6 pushbuttons, 4 knobs, BC, SW, 6 tubes, AC/DC **$50.00-55.00**

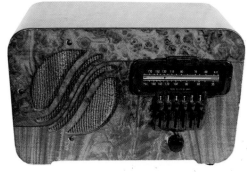

62-553, table, 1939, wood, right front slide rule dial, 6 pushbuttons, left round grille with Deco cut-outs, 2 knobs, BC, 5 tubes, AC/battery, $120.00-150.00.

64BR-1514A, table, 1946, painted plastic, lower slide rule dial, 6 pushbuttons, upper metal grille, 4 knobs, BC, SW, 6 tubes, AC/DC, $50.00-55.00.

74BR-1812B, table, 1947, wood, lower slanted slide rule dial, upper recessed cloth grille, 4 knobs, BC, FM, 9 tubes, AC **$50.00-55.00**

74BR-2001A, table-R/P, 1947, right front slanted slide rule dial, left wrap-around grille, open top phono, 3 knobs, BC, 5 tubes, AC.. **$50.00-65.00**

74BR-2001B, table-R/P, 1947, right front slanted slide rule dial, left wrap-around grille, open top phono, 3 knobs, BC, 5 tubes, AC.. **$50.00-65.00**

74BR-2701A, console-R/P, 1947, wood, inner right slide rule dial, pushbuttons, left pull-out phono drawer, 5 knobs, BC, SW, 8 tubes, AC **$65.00-75.00**

74BR-2702B, console-R/P, 1947, wood, inner right slide rule dial, phono, lift top, vertical grille bars, 4 knobs, BC, FM, 9 tubes, AC...... **$65.00-75.00**

74KR-1210A, table, 1947, wood, lower slide rule dial, upper cloth grille, rounded sides, 2 knobs, BC, 4 tubes, AC/DC/battery....**$40.00-45.00**

74KR-2706B, console-R/P, 1947, wood, see-through slide rule dial in front of grille, pull-out phono drawer, 3 knobs, BC, 6 tubes, AC... **$50.00-65.00**

74KR-2713A, console-R/P, 1947, wood, inner right slide rule dial, left pull-out phono drawer, 3 knobs, BC, 6 tubes, AC **$65.00-75.00**

74WG-1054A, portable, 1947, leatherette, right front half-round dial, center perforated grille, handle, 2 knobs, BC, 5 tubes, AC/DC/battery **$30.00-35.00**

74WG-1056A, portable, 1947, cloth covered, inner right dial, left grille, fold-down front, handle, 3 knobs, BC, 5 tubes, AC/DC/battery **$25.00-30.00**

74WG-1057A, portable, 1947, leatherette & plastic, inner right dial, center perforated grille, flip-up front, 2 knobs, BC, 4 tubes, AC/DC/battery **$40.00-45.00**

74WG-1510A, table, 1947, plastic, lower slide rule dial, upper recessed cloth grille, 2 knobs, BC, 6 tubes, AC/DC **$40.00-45.00**

74WG-1802A, table, 1947, wood, right round dial over large woven grille area, rounded corners, 2 knobs, BC, 5 tubes, AC/DC ..**$25.00-30.00**

74WG-2002A, table-R/P, 1947, wood, outer front slide rule dial, cloth grille, lift top, inner phono, 3 knobs, BC, 6 tubes, AC .. **$30.00-35.00**

74BR-1501B, table, 1947, walnut plastic, lower slide rule dial, upper horizontal louvers, metal back, 2 knobs, BC, 5 tubes, AC/DC, $75.00-85.00.

74WG-2004A, table-R/P, 1947, wood, outer front round dial, lift top, inner phono, 2 knobs, BC, 5 tubes, AC **$30.00-35.00**

74WG-2010B, table-R/P, 1947, wood, inner right slide rule dial, left phono, lift top, criss-cross grille, 4 knobs, BC, SW, 6 tubes, AC **$30.00-35.00**

74WG-2504A, console, 1947, wood, upper front slide rule dial, lower cloth grille with 3 horizontal bars, 4 knobs, BC, SW, 6 tubes, AC **$65.00-75.00**

74WG-2505A, console, 1947, wood, upper slanted slide rule dial, 6 push-buttons, tuning eye, lower grille with 2 horizontal bars, 4 knobs, BC, SW, FM, 10 tubes, AC **$65.00-75.00**

74WG-2704A, console-R/P, 1947, wood, upper slide rule dial, tilt-out phono, cloth grille with vertical bars, 4 knobs, BC, SW, 6 tubes, AC **$65.00-75.00**

74WG-2709A, console-R/P, 1947, wood, upper slide rule dial, tilt-out phono, vertical grille bars, 4 knobs, BC, SW, 7 tubes, AC............. **$65.00-75.00**

83BR-351A, table, 1938, plastic, Deco, rounded right side, pushbuttons, left vertical wrap-over grille bars, 1 front and 1 right side knob, BC, 5 tubes, AC **$110.00-130.00**

84BR-1065A, portable, 1948, inner slide rule dial, horizontal louvers, plays when front is opened, handle, 2 knobs, BC, 5 tubes, AC/DC/battery **$35.00-45.00**

84BR-1065B, portable, 1948, inner slide rule dial, horizontal louvers, plays when front is opened, handle, 2 knobs, BC, 5 tubes, AC/DC/battery **$35.00-45.00**

84BR-1065C, portable, 1948, plastic, inner slide rule dial, horizontal louvers, plays when front is opened, handle, 2 knobs, BC, 5 tubes, AC/DC/battery **$35.00-45.00**

84BR-1502B, table, 1948, plastic, lower front slide rule dial, upper horizontal louvers, rounded top, 2 knobs, BC **$55.00-65.00**

84BR-1517A, table, 1948, walnut plastic, upper right front slide rule dial, left lattice grille area, 6 push buttons, 1 front and 1 side knob, BC, 6 tubes, AC/DC...**$65.00-75.00**

84BR-1518A, table, 1948, ivory plastic, upper right front slide rule dial, left lattice grille area, 6 pushbuttons, 1 front and 1 side knob, BC, 6 tubes, AC/DC...**$65.00-75.00**

84BR-1815B, table, 1948, wood, large plastic recessed half-round dial/circular louvers, 2 knobs, BC, 5 tubes, AC/DC........**$50.00-65.00**

84GCB-1062A, portable, 1948, leatherette & plastic, inner round dial, flip-up front, side handle, 2 knobs, BC, 4 tubes, battery......**$45.00-55.00**

84GSE-2731A, console-R/P, 1948, wood, top dial, lift cover, inner phono, lower storage, BC, 4 knobs, BC, 5 tubes, AC **$40.00-50.00**

84HA-1529A, table, 1948, plastic, slanted slide rule dial, upper recessed grille, 4 knobs, BC, FM, 7 tubes, AC/DC **$35.00-45.00**

84HA-1810, table, 1948, wood, slanted slide rule dial, large metal perforated grill/front, 4 knobs, BC, FM, 7 tubes, AC/DC, $30.00-35.00.

84HA-1810A, table, 1948, wood, slanted slide rule dial, large perforated grill/front, 4 knobs, BC, FM, 7 tubes, AC/DC **$30.00-35.00**

84HA-1810C, table, 1948, wood, slanted slide rule dial, large perforated grill/front, 4 knobs, BC, FM, 7 tubes, AC/DC **$30.00-35.00**

84KR-1520A, table, 1948, metal, right vertical slide rule dial, left horizontal louvers, various colors, 2 knobs, BC, 4 tubes, AC/DC **$65.00-75.00**

84KR-2511A, end table, 1948, wood, "2 drawer" end-table, tilt-out front with slide rule dial, 2 knobs, BC, 5 tubes, AC................ **$85.00-95.00**

84WG-1056B, portable, 1948, cloth covered, inner right slide rule dial, fold-down front, handle, 3 knobs, BC, 5 tubes, AC/DC/battery **$30.00-35.00**

5A, table, 1931, wood, right window dial, center round grille with cut-outs, gold pinstriping, 2 knobs, BC, 5 tubes, AC, $85.00-95.00.

5C, console, 1931, wood, upper front dial, lower criss-cross grille, bowed front legs, BC, AC **$120.00-150.00**

10, tombstone, C1935, two-tone wood, small case, lower round dial, cloth grille with cut-outs, 3 knobs, BC, AC **$85.00-95.00**

18, console, 1929, wood, decorative case, inner dial, grille with urn cut-out, sliding doors, 3 knobs, BC **$240.00-270.00**

20-L, console, 1931, wood, ornate case, upper window dial, lower grille with cut-outs, stretcher base, 3 knobs, BC, 8 tubes, AC...... **$200.00-230.00**

27 "Amborada," console, 1926, wood, plain cabinet looks like dresser, feet, inner 2 dials & knobs, BC, 7 tubes, battery ...**$180.00-200.00**

28, table, 1928, wood, low rectangular case, center front window dial with escutcheon, 3 knobs, BC, 8 tubes, AC............. **$130.00-160.00**

35 "Cruiser," table, 1926, wood, upper front window dial, lift top, feet, 3 knobs, BC, 5 tubes, battery **$120.00-150.00**

35 "Imperial Cruiser," console, 1926, walnut, low cabinet, inner front dial, double front doors, feet, 3 knobs, BC, 5 tubes, battery ..**$150.00-180.00**

35 "Royal Cruiser," table, 1926, walnut, upper front window dial, lift top, feet, 3 knobs, BC, 5 tubes, battery **$120.00-150.00**

36, console, 1929, wood, lowboy, upper center dial, lower decorative grille with cut-outs, stretcher base, 2 knobs, BC, 6 tubes, AC..**$120.00-150.00**

48A, console, 1929, wood, highboy, stretcher base, sliding doors, metal dial panel, lower cloth grille with cut-outs, 3 knobs, BC, 7 tubes, AC **$150.00-170.00**

57, console, 1927, wood, lowboy, inner dial, fold-down front, lower double doors, inner grille, BC, 7 tubes, battery **$150.00-170.00**

58A, console, 1930, wood, upper front dial, lower cloth grille with cut-outs, BC, 8 tubes, AC **$150.00-160.00**

60, console, wood, inner window dial, cloth grille with cut-outs, sliding doors, decorative case moldings, 5 knobs, BC, 9 tubes, AC...... **$150.00-180.00**

66 "Cruiser," table, 1927, wood, front window dial with escutcheon, lift top, horizontal moldings, 3 knobs, BC, 6 tubes, battery **$140.00-160.00**

66AC, table, 1927, wood, front window dial with escutcheon, lift top, horizontal moldings, separate A & B power unit, 3 knobs, BC, 6 tubes, AC **$140.00-160.00**

76 "Cruiser," console, 1927, wood, lowboy, inner window dial with escutcheon, fold-down front door, lower grille, BC, 6 tubes, battery **$130.00-160.00**

87 "Cruiser," table, 1927, wood, low rectangular case, center front window dial with escutcheon, BC, 7 tubes, battery **$120.00-150.00**

96, console, 1927, wood, lowboy, inner front window dial with escutcheon, fold-down front, lower grille, BC, 6 tubes, AC..............**$120.00-140.00**

107, console, 1927, wood, lowboy, inner dial, fold-down front, lower fancy grille with double doors, 3 knobs, BC, 7 tubes, AC **$180.00-200.00**

116, table, 1927, wood, front window dial with escutcheon, right & left front panels, feet, 3 knobs, BC, 6 tubes, AC **$85.00-115.00**

126, table, 1927, wood, right front thumbwheel window dial, lift top, 2 lower knobs, BC, 6 tubes, AC................................... **$110.00-130.00**

205-A, table, 1932, mahogany finish, right front window dial, center round grille with cut-outs, 2 knobs, BC, 5 tubes, AC **$75.00-85.00**

210, table, wood, right front window dial, center round cloth grille with cut-outs, gold pinstriping, 2 knobs, BC, AC **$75.00-85.00**

226-F "Fireside," console, 1932, wood, upper front window dial, lower grille with cut-outs, 3 knobs, BC, 8 tubes, battery **$85.00-115.00**

236-A, table, 1932, mahogany with inlay, upper front dial, lower grille with cut-outs, 2 knobs, BC, 6 tubes, AC **$75.00-85.00**

242 "Empire," console, 1932, wood, lowboy, upper front dial, lower square grille with cut-outs, 3 knobs, BC, 8 tubes, AC **$150.00-180.00**

250-M "Mansion," console, 1932, wood, upper front dial, lower square grille with cut-outs, stretcher base, 3 knobs, BC, 10 tubes, AC... **$150.00-180.00**

16 "Amborola," table, 1925, wood, 2 dial Bakelite panel with escutcheon, lift top, feet, burl front, 4 knobs, BC, 6 tubes, battery, $270.00-300.00.

260-C "World Cruiser," console, 1932, wood, upper front dial, lower grille with cut-outs, feet, 4 knobs, BC, SW, 10 tubes, AC .. **$160.00-190.00**

260-R "World Rover," console, 1932, wood, upper front dial, lower 2-section grille, stretcher base, 4 knobs, BC, SW, 10 tubes, AC **$160.00-190.00**

312-C "Grand Concert," console, 1932, wood, upper front dial, lower grille with cut-outs, feet, 3 knobs, BC, SW, 12 tubes, AC **$180.00-200.00**

312-G, console, 1932, wood, lowboy, double front doors, inner upper dial and lower grille, 6 legs with stretcher base, 3 knobs, BC, SW, 12 tubes, AC **$190.00-210.00**

350, table, 1933, mahogany with inlay, right front window dial, center grille with scrolled cut-outs, 4 knobs, BC, SW, 5 tubes, AC .. **$75.00-85.00**

355, table, 1933, mahogany with inlay, right front window dial, center grille with scrolled cut-outs, 4 knobs, BC, SW, 5 tubes, AC/DC **$75.00-85.00**

360-M, console, 1933, wood, upper front dial, lower cloth grille area, 4 knobs, BC, SW, 7 tubes, AC...................................... **$95.00-115.00**

360T, tombstone, 1933, wood, center front dial, upper cloth grille with cut-outs, 4 knobs, BC, SW, 7 tubes, AC **$120.00-150.00**

370S, console, 1933, wood, lowboy, upper front dial, lower grille with cut-outs, stretcher base, 4 knobs, BC, 7 tubes, AC.. **$160.00-180.00**

370T, tombstone, 1933, wood, center front dial, upper cloth grille with cut-outs, 4 knobs, BC, SW, 7 tubes, AC **$120.00-150.00**

402, table, 1934, wood, right front window dial, center round cloth grille with star cut-out, 2 knobs, BC, 5 tubes, AC/DC **$65.00-75.00**

420, table, 1934, wood, right front window dial, center 3-section cloth grille, 4 knobs, BC, 5 tubes, AC **$85.00-95.00**

440-C, console, 1934, wood, upper front round compass dial, lower grille with cut-outs, 4 knobs, BC, SW, 6 tubes, AC........... **$160.00-180.00**

440-T, tombstone, 1934, wood, center front round compass dial, upper cloth grille with cut-outs, rounded top, 4 knobs, BC, SW, 6 tubes, AC **$320.00-350.00**

460-A, tombstone, 1934, wood, center front rectangular dial, upper grille with circular cut-outs, 4 knobs, BC, SW, 7 tubes, AC .. **$110.00-130.00**

460-B, tombstone, 1934, wood, center front rectangular dial, upper square grille with cut-outs, 4 knobs, BC, SW, 7 tubes, AC **$110.00-130.00**

46 "Little Six," table, 1927, walnut, high rectangular case, right thumbwheel window dial, 2 lower knobs, BC, 6 tubes, $150.00-160.00.

200-A "Treasure Chest," table, 1932, wood, chest-style, inner dial & grille, lift top, fancy "carved" front, 2 knobs, BC, 5 tubes, AC, $300.00-320.00.

605, table, 1936, wood, right front round airplane dial, left cloth grille with horizontal bars, 3 knobs, BC, SW, 5 tubes, AC, $50.00-65.00.

470-G, console, 1935, wood, upper front slanted dial with escutcheon, lower grille with scroll cut-outs, BC, SW, 7 tubes, AC .. **$120.00-140.00**

470-U, tombstone, 1935, wood, lower front dial, upper grille with cut-outs, right & left fluted columns, BC, SW, 7 tubes, AC........ **$120.00-140.00**

480-D, console, 1934, wood, inner slanted dial, fold-back top, lower cloth grille with cut-outs, BC, SW, 10 tubes, AC............... **$180.00-200.00**

500, table, 1933, wood with inlay, right front window dial, center grille with cut-outs, 2 knobs, BC, 5 tubes, AC/DC................. **$75.00-85.00**

501, table, 1933, wood with inlay, right front window dial, center grille with cut-outs, 2 knobs, BC, 5 tubes, AC/DC................. **$75.00-85.00**

505, table, 1935, wood, right front square black dial, left square cloth grille, center star, 3 knobs, BC, SW, 5 tubes, AC.......... **$65.00-75.00**

510, tombstone, 1935, wood, small case, lower round airplane dial, cloth grille with cut-outs, 3 knobs, BC, SW, 5 tubes, AC **$75.00-85.00**

510-E, console, 1935, wood, upper front round dial, lower grille with scroll cut-outs, 3 knobs, BC, SW, 5 tubes, AC............ **$95.00-115.00**

565-W, tombstone, 1935, wood, center front round dial, upper cloth grille with intersecting cut-outs, 3 knobs, BC, SW, 6 tubes, AC **$85.00-95.00**

575-F, tombstone, 1935, wood, lower front round airplane dial, upper grille with vertical bars, 4 knobs, BC, SW, 7 tubes, AC **$85.00-95.00**

575-Q, console, 1935, wood, upper round airplane dial, lower cloth grille with vertical bars, 4 knobs, BC, SW, 7 tubes, AC **$110.00-130.00**

585-Y, tombstone, 1935, wood, lower front round airplane dial, upper grille with scroll cut-outs, 4 knobs, BC, SW, 8 tubes, AC **$110.00-130.00**

585-Z, console, 1935, wood, upper front round airplane dial, lower cloth grille with cut-outs, 4 knobs, BC, SW, 8 tubes, AC .. **$110.00-130.00**

595-P, console, 1935, wood, upper front round dial, lower cloth grille with cut-outs, 4 knobs, BC, SW, 10 tubes, AC **$120.00-140.00**

604, table, 1935, wood, right front dial, left cloth grille with horizontal bars, 3 knobs, BC, SW, 5 tubes, AC/DC **$40.00-50.00**

604A2, table, 1935, wood, right front dial, left grille area, 3 knobs, BC, 5 tubes **$40.00-50.00**

610A2, table, 1936, wood, right front square airplane dial, left grille with horizontal bars, 3 knobs, BC, SW, 6 tubes, AC/DC........**$45.00-55.00**

625, console, 1936, wood, upper front round dial, lower cloth grille with center vertical bar, 4 knobs, BC, SW, 7 tubes, AC.... **$110.00-130.00**

650, console, 1936, wood, upper front round dial, lower grille with center vertical bars, 4 knobs, BC, SW, 6 tubes, AC **$110.00-130.00**

660T, table, 1936, wood, right round dial, left & right grills with horizontal bars, 4 knobs, BC, SW, 7 tubes, AC............................. **$65.00-75.00**

670C, console, 1936, wood, front recessed black dial, lower grille with vertical bars, 4 knobs, BC, SW, 9 tubes, AC **$140.00-150.00**

805, table, 1936, wood, right front window dial, center grille with cut-outs, two shield-shaped escutcheons, gold pin-striping, 2 knobs, BC **$75.00-85.00**

809, table, 1937, wood, right front dial, left cloth grille, 3 knobs, BC, SW, 6 tubes, AC/DC **$45.00-55.00**

680, console, 1934, two-tone wood, upper front black dial, lower cloth grille with vertical bars, 5 knobs, BC, SW, 13 tubes, AC, $180.00-200.00.

460-R, console, 1934, wood, inner slanted dial, fold-back top, "horseshoe" grille with splayed bars, 4 knobs, BC, SW, 7 tubes, AC, $180.00-200.00.

AMERICAN RADIO
American Radio Corp.
6116 Euclid Ave., Cleveland, Ohio

3-A "Arc-Lininger," table, 1925, wood, low rectangular case, 2 dial front panel, BC, 3 tubes, battery **$120.00-150.00**

4 "Arc-Lininger," table, 1925, wood, low rectangular case, 2 dial front panel, BC, 4 tubes, battery **$140.00-160.00**

Super 5 "Arc-Lininger," table, 1925, wood, low rectangular case, 2 dial front panel, BC, 5 tubes, battery **$150.00-180.00**

AMERICAN SPECIALTY
American Specialty Co.
Bridgeport, Connecticut

Standard "Electrola," table, 1925, wood, high rectangular case with arched top, 3 dial front panel, upper built-in speaker with cut-outs, BC, 5 tubes, battery.....................................**$200.00-230.00**

AMNECOGRAND
American Chest Co.
Waukesha, Wisconsin

Corner Console (no #), console, wood, unique triangular case design made to fit into a corner, front window dial, lift top, 3 legs, 3 knobs, BC, AC **$530.00-580.00**

AMPLEX

De Exer, table, c1925, wood, low rectangular case, brown Bakelite 3 dial front panel with gold trim, 5 knobs, BC, battery, $150.00-180.00.

C "Lectrosonic," table, metal, low rectangular case, center window dial, lift-off top, switch, 2 knobs, BC **$85.00-105.00**
Touradio, portable, leatherette, inner right dial, center cloth grille with cut-outs, fold-down front, handle, 2 knobs, BC **$85.00-105.00**

AMRAD
The Amrad Corporation
Medford Hillside, Massachusetts
American Radio & Research Corporation
Medford Hillside, Massachusetts

The name Amrad is short for American Radio & Research Corporation. The company began business manufacturing transmitters and receivers for the government during WW I and produced its first crystal set in 1921. By 1925 Amrad was in serious financial trouble and was bought out by Crosley although their radios still retained the Amrad label. A victim of the Depression, Amrad closed in 1930.

70 "Concerto," console, 1928, walnut, highboy, inner dial & escutcheon, double doors with brass hardware, stretcher base, BC, 8 tubes, AC **$150.00-180.00**

2575/2776, table, 1922, wood, 2 units, crystal receiver and 2 stage amp, black front panels, 3 knobs, battery, $1,300.00-1,400.00.

3500-1 (3475/2634), table, 1923, two unit "double-decker," receiver & tuner, front Bakelite panels, top screens, 4 tubes, battery, $1,300.00-1,500.00.

70 "Nocturne," console, 1928, walnut, highboy, inner dial & escutcheon, double doors, stretcher base, BC, 8 tubes, AC **$150.00-180.00**
70 "Sonata," console, 1928, walnut, highboy, inner dial with escutcheon, double doors, stretcher base, BC, 8 tubes, AC **$160.00-190.00**
81 "Aria," console, 1929, walnut, inner front window dial, lower grille, double doors, stretcher base, 3 knobs, BC, 8 tubes, AC .. **$180.00-200.00**
81 "Duet," console-R/P, 1929, wood with inlay, lowboy, inner dial & escutcheon, large double doors, stretcher base, BC, 8 tubes, AC **$120.00-140.00**
81 "Serenata," console, 1929, wood, highboy, inner front dial, double doors, stretcher base, BC, 8 tubes, AC **$150.00-180.00**
81 "Symphony," console, 1929, wood, Art Moderne, highboy, inner front dial, double doors, stretcher base, BC, 8 tubes, AC .. **$140.00-160.00**
2575, table, 1922, wood, square case, crystal receiver, black Bakelite front panel with 1 center dial, 1 knob **$760.00-880.00**
2596/2634, table, 1921, "double-decker," detector/two-stage amp & short-wave tuner, Bakelite panels, 8 knobs, battery **$1,200.00-1,400.00**
3366, table, 1923, wood, low rectangular case, crystal set, 2 dial Bakelite panel, top screen, 1 tube, battery **$1,300.00-1,400.00**
3500-3 "Inductrole," table, 1925, wood, high rectangular case, upper 2 dial panel, lower storage, doors, 4 tubes, battery **$530.00-650.00**
3500-4 "Cabinette," table, 1925, wood, high rectangular case, 2 dial black front panel, 4 tubes, battery............................**$410.00-430.00**
3500-6 "Jewel," table, 1925, wood, chest-type case, inner 2 dial panel, double front doors with carvings, 4 tubes, battery **$430.00-470.00**
AC-5, table, 1926, wood, low rectangular case, 3 front window dials, front columns, 4 knobs, BC, 5 tubes, AC **$270.00-300.00**
AC-5-C, console, 1926, mahogany, lowboy, 3 inner window dials, fold-down front door, 4 knobs, BC, 5 tubes, AC **$270.00-300.00**
AC-6 "The Warwick," table, 1927, walnut, low rectangular case, center front dial with escutcheon, 3 knobs, BC, 6 tubes, AC.. **$130.00-150.00**
AC-6-C "The Berwick," console, 1927, walnut, lowboy, inner dial with escutcheon, fold-down front, 3 knobs, BC, 6 tubes, AC.. **$150.00-190.00**
AC-7 "The Windsor," table, 1927, wood, low rectangular case, center dial with escutcheon, 3 knobs, BC, 7 tubes, AC **$140.00-150.00**
AC-7-C "The Hastings," console, 1927, wood, lowboy, inner dial, large double doors, stretcher base, 3 knobs, BC, 7 tubes, AC **$150.00-190.00**
AC-9, table, 1926, mahogany, low rectangular case, 2 window dials, front columns, 5 knobs, BC, 7 tubes, AC **$140.00-160.00**
AC-9-C, console, 1926, wood, lowboy, 2 inner front dials, 5 knobs, BC, 7 tubes, AC **$180.00-200.00**
S-522, table, 1926, wood, low rectangular case, 3 window dials, lift top, front columns, 4 knobs, BC, 5 tubes, battery **$170.00-190.00**

Neutrodyne, table, 1923, wood, low rectangular case, 2 dial front panel, lift top, 3 knobs, BC, $160.00-190.00.

S-522-C, console, 1926, two-tone mahogany, lowboy, inner front panel with 3 window dials, fold-down front door, 4 knobs, BC, 5 tubes, battery $180.00-200.00

S-733, table, 1926, two-tone mahogany, low rectangular case, 2 front window dials, lift top, 4 knobs, BC, 7 tubes, battery ..$150.00-160.00

S-733-C, console, 1927, wood, lowboy, 2 inner front window dials, fold-down front door, 4 knobs, BC, 7 tubes, battery $150.00-180.00

ANDREA
Andrea Radio Corporation
27-01 Bridge Plaza North
Long Island, New York

The Andrea Radio Corporation was begun by Frank D'Andrea in 1934 after the sale of his previous radio company — F. A. D. Andrea, Inc.

2-D-5, table, 1937, walnut, right front lighted dial, left grille with diagonal bars, 3 knobs, BC, SW, 5 tubes, AC............................$55.00-65.00

2-D-8, table, 1937, wood, slanted front, right dial, left cloth grille with wrap-over bars, BC, SW, 8 tubes $50.00-65.00

2-E-6, table, 1938, wood, upper front slanted slide rule dial, lower horizontal grille bars with center vertical divider of 6 pushbuttons, 3 bands, 4 knobs, BC, SW, 6 tubes, AC $110.00-130.00

2-E-8, table, 1938, wood, right front slide rule dial, rounded left with vertical grille bars, 8 pushbuttons, 4 knobs, BC, SW, LW, 8 tubes, AC $120.00-140.00

5-E-11, console, 1939, wood, upper front dial, pushbuttons, lower grille with horizontal bars, 4 knobs, BC, SW, LW, 11 tubes, AC $85.00-105.00

6-E-6, console-R/P, 1938, wood, upper front slanted slide rule dial, lower horizontal grille bars, pushbuttons, lift top, inner phono, 4 knobs, BC, SW, 6 tubes, AC...................................$110.00-130.00

6G63, portable, 1940, brown striped cloth, inner right dial, left grille, fold-up front, handle, 3 bands, BC, SW, 6 tubes, AC/DC/battery..$25.00-30.00

6G63A, portable, 1940, "alligator" leatherette, inner right dial, left grille, fold-up front, handle, 3 bands, BC, SW, 6 tubes, AC/DC/battery $30.00-35.00

6H44, table, 1941, two-tone walnut with black trim, right front dial, left grille, 3 bands, 4 knobs, BC, SW, 6 tubes, AC $55.00-65.00

8-E-11, console-R/P, 1938, wood, upper front slide rule dial, center pull-out phono drawer, lower horizontal grille bars, pushbuttons, 4 knobs, BC, SW, 11 tubes, AC...................................$120.00-140.00

14-E-6, table, 1938, walnut/rosewood, right front vertical slide rule dial, left horizontal wrap-around louvers, pushbuttons, 4 knobs, BC, SW, 6 tubes, AC $50.00-65.00

826, upright table, 1940, wood, lower front rectangular dial, upper grille with horizontal bars, 5 tubes, battery $65.00-75.00

CO-UI5, table-R/P, 1947, wood, outer slanted slide rule dial, lift top, inner phono, 5 knobs, BC, SW, 5 tubes, AC $30.00-35.00

P-I63, portable, 1947, luggage-type, inner right black dial, fold-up door, handle, 3 knobs, BC, SW, AC/DC/battery $30.00-35.00

T-16, table, 1947, two-tone wood, upper slanted slide rule dial, lower U-shaped cloth grille with 2 vertical bars, 4 knobs, BC, SW, 6 tubes, AC $55.00-65.00

T-U15, table, 1947, plastic, upper slanted slide rule dial, lower lattice grille, 4 knobs, BC, SW, 5 tubes, AC/DC.......................$45.00-55.00

T-U16, table, 1947, two-tone wood, upper slanted slide rule dial, lower U-shaped grille with 2 vertical bars, 4 knobs, BC, SW, 7 tubes, AC/DC $55.00-65.00

W69P "Spacemaster Deluxe," portable, 1957, leatherette, flip-up front with map, telescope antenna, handle, 9 bands, 2 knobs and 13 pushbuttons, BC, SW, 6 tubes, AC/DC/battery...........$85.00-105.00

ANDREWS
Andrews Radio Co.
327 S. LaSalle St.
Chicago, Illinois

De Luxe "Deresnadyne," table, 1925, wood, low rectangular case, 3 dial front panel, 6 knobs, BC, 5 tubes, battery..................$120.00-140.00

ANSLEY
Ansley Radio Corp.
41 St. Joes Avenue
Trenton, New Jersey

53, console-R/P, 1947, wood, modern, inner right dial, 8 pushbuttons, left phono, lift top, storage, 5 knobs, BC, SW, FM, 13 tubes, AC $120.00-150.00

105, piano console-R/P, 1948, upright piano-style, unusual piano/radio/record player combination, 5 radio knobs, BC, SW, FM, 24 tubes, AC.. $1,500.00+

D-4, table-R/P, 1933, wood, outer front grille with vertical bars, lift top inner phono, BC, 5 tubes, AC $30.00-35.00

D-10 "Dynaphone," table-R/P, 1935, wood, outer front dial & grille, lift top, inner phono, 4 knobs, BC, SW, 7 tubes, AC $30.00-35.00

D-17 "Dynaphone," console-R/P, 1936, wood, front tilt-out radio unit, lower grille, lift top, inner phono, BC, SW, 7 tubes, AC.. $95.00-105.00

D-23 "Dynaphone," chairside-R/P, 1937, wood, inner dial & phono, "glider top" slides sideways, front grille, BC, SW, 7 tubes, AC $85.00-95.00

D-10-A "Dynaphone," table-R/P, 1941, wood, right front slide rule dial, front/right/left grills, lift top, inner phono, 5 knobs, BC, SW, 7 tubes, AC, $30.00-35.00.

APEX
Apex Electric Manufacturing Company
1410 West 59th Street, Chicago, Illinois
Apex Radio & Television Corp.
United States Radio & Television Corporation
Chicago, Illinois

The Apex Electric Manufacturing Company began business selling parts for automobiles. By 1925 they were producing radios. Financial difficulties forced a merger with Case to form the United States Radio & Television Corporation in 1928.

5, table, 1926, wood, low rectangular case, single front window dial, feet, 3 knobs, BC, battery $95.00-115.00

6, table, 1926, wood, low rectangular case, inner window dial, fold-down front, 3 knobs, BC, battery..............................$120.00-140.00

8A, cathedral, 1931, wood, center front dial, upper scalloped grille with cut-outs, fluted columns, 2 right side toggle switches, 3 knobs, 8 tubes, AC $240.00-270.00

10B, console, 1931, wood, lowboy, inner quarter-round dial, lower grille with cut-outs, doors, stretcher base, BC, 10 tubes, AC $120.00-150.00

11, console, 1930, wood, lowboy, upper front dial, lower scalloped grille with cut-outs, BC, AC $120.00-150.00

12B, console, 1932, wood, upper front curved dial, lower grille with Gothic cut-outs, 6 legs, stretcher base, BC, 12 tubes, AC $150.00-180.00

60, console, 1928, walnut, upper front dial, lower grille with cut-outs, stretcher base, 2 knobs, BC, 7 tubes, AC $120.00-150.00

70, console, 1928, walnut, highboy, lower cloth grille with cut-outs, stretcher base, 2 knobs, BC, 9 tubes, AC .. $160.00-190.00

89, table, 1929, metal, low rectangular case, center front window dial with escutcheon, 2 knobs, BC, 9 tubes, AC.................$65.00-75.00

106, console, 1926, wood, highboy, inner window dial, fold-down front, lower storage, 3 knobs, BC, battery $150.00-170.00

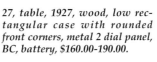

ARBORPHONE

27, table, 1927, wood, low rectangular case with rounded front corners, metal 2 dial panel, BC, battery, $160.00-190.00.

47A, console, 1929, wood, lowboy, upper front window dial, metal escutcheon with emblem, lower cloth grille with cut-outs, 2 knobs, BC, 7 tubes, AC, $120.00-150.00.

ARC
ARC Radio Corp.
523 Myrtle Avenue, Brooklyn, New York

601, portable, 1947, shoulder bag-style, "alligator," front grille, strap, 2 top thumbwheel knobs, BC, 4 tubes, battery **$40.00-50.00**

ARCADIA
Whitney & Co.

116, console, 1926, wood, highboy, inner window dial, upper speaker grille, double doors, storage, 3 knobs, BC, battery **$160.00-190.00**

120B, console, 1932, wood, lowboy, ornate cabinet, double front doors, 6 legs, stretcher base, BC, 12 tubes, AC **$180.00-200.00**

37D14-600, table, 1946, wood, upper slanted slide rule dial, lower criss-cross grille, 3 knobs, BC, SW, 7 tubes, AC/DC.............**$45.00-55.00**

160, console, 1930, wood, highboy, lower window dial, upper grille with cut-outs, stretcher base, BC, 9 tubes, AC **$140.00-160.00**

Baby Grand, console, 1925, wood, spinet piano-style, inner 3 dial panel, fold-down front door, 5 knobs, BC, battery...............**$240.00-270.00**

ARGUS

Corsair, table, 1927, wood, low rectangular case, center front dial with escutcheon, fluted columns, 2 knobs, BC....................**$95.00-105.00**

Deluxe, table, 1925, wood, high rectangular case, lower 3 dial front panel, upper built-in speaker, 5 knobs, BC, battery ..**$150.00-170.00**

Lyric, table, 1927, wood, low rectangular case, inner window dial, fold-down front, 3 knobs, BC **$120.00-140.00**

Milan Electric, console, 1927, wood, lowboy, inner front dial, lower Gothic grille, double doors, 2 knobs, BC, 6 tubes, AC **$120.00-140.00**

Minstrel, console, 1927, wood, inner dial, lower Gothic grille, double doors, stretcher base, 2 knobs, BC, AC **$120.00-150.00**

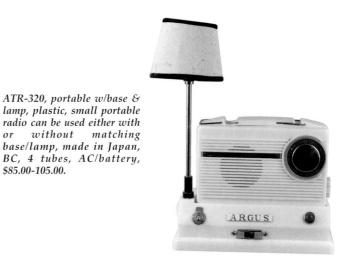

ATR-320, portable w/base & lamp, plastic, small portable radio can be used either with or without matching base/lamp, made in Japan, BC, 4 tubes, AC/battery, $85.00-105.00.

Music Chest, table, 1928, wood, low rectangular case, center front dial & escutcheon, 2 knobs, BC, 6 tubes, battery **$85.00-95.00**

Neutrodyne, table, 1930, walnut finish metal rectangular case, front illuminated dial, 2 knobs, BC, 7 tubes, AC **$65.00-75.00**

Super Five, table, 1925, wood, low rectangular case, 3 dial front panel, lift top, feet, 5 knobs, BC, 5 tubes, battery **$140.00-160.00**

Troubadour, console, 1927, wood, inner front dial, grille with Gothic cut-outs, double doors, stretcher base, storage, 2 knobs, BC, AC **$240.00-270.00**

APEX INDUSTRIES
Apex Industries
192 Lexington Avenue, New York, New York

4B5, table, 1948, plastic, right square dial, left horizontal louvers, 2 knobs, BC, 5 tubes, AC/DC...**$45.00-55.00**

ARIA
International Detrola Co.
Detroit, Michigan

APPLEBY
Appleby Mfg. Co.
250 N. Juniper St., Philadelphia, Pennsylvania

571, table, plastic, right front slide rule dial, left horizontal louvers, 2 knobs, BC, AC, $55.00-65.00.

60, table, wood, low rectangular case, 2 dial metal front panel, meter, lift top, 4 knobs, BC **$140.00-170.00**

593, table, wood, right front dial, left curved grille with vertical bars, 3 (1 on grill) knobs, BC, AC/DC, $85.00-105.00.

554-1-61A, table-R/P, 1946, wood, outer top right dial, inner phono, lift top, 3 knobs, BC, 6 tubes, AC **$35.00-40.00**
572-10, table, wood, right front slide rule dial, left & right metal perforated grills, feet, 3 knobs, BC, AC **$45.00-55.00**
572-21, table, wood, right front slide rule dial, cloth grille with chrome molding, 3 knobs, BC **$45.00-55.00**

ARKAY
R-K Radio Laboratories, Inc.
Chicago, Illinois

421, table, 1934, wood, right front dial, center grille with cut-outs, 2 knobs, BC, 4 tubes, AC/DC **$85.00-105.00**
633, console, 1934, wood, upper front round dial, lower cloth grille with vertical bars, fluting, BC, SW, 6 tubes, AC **$120.00-150.00**

ARLINGTON

AH, table, plastic, right front dial, left horizontal wrap-around grille bars, 2 knobs, BC, AC/DC **$65.00-75.00**

ARTHUR ANSLEY
Arthur Ansley Mfg. Co.
Doylestown, Pennsylvania

R-1, table, 1953, wood, inner right vertical slide rule dial, left grille, fold-up front, 4 knobs, BC, FM, 10 tubes, AC **$45.00-55.00**

ARTONE
Affiliated Retailers, Inc.
Empire State Building, New York, New York

524, table-C, 1949, wood, upper front slide rule dial, center alarm clock, grille bars on case top, 5 knobs, BC, 5 tubes, AC **$40.00-45.00**

ARVIN
Noblitt-Sparks Industries, Inc.
13th Street & Big Four R. R., Columbus, Indiana
Arvin Industries, Inc., Columbus, Indiana

10R16, table, 1961, ice green plastic, lower front dial and volume knobs over vertical bars, feet, 2 knobs, BC, 5 tubes, AC/DC .. **$15.00-20.00**
10R17, table, 1961, white plastic, lower front dial and volume knobs over vertical bars, feet, 2 knobs, BC, 5 tubes, AC/DC **$15.00-20.00**
10R18, table, 1961, beige plastic, lower front dial and volume knobs over vertical bars, feet, 2 knobs, BC, 5 tubes, AC/DC **$15.00-20.00**
10R22, table, 1961, plastic, lower right front dial, square grille with vertical and horizontal bars, 2 knobs, BC, 5 tubes, AC/DC ..**$20.00-25.00**

10R32, table, 1961, persimmon plastic, upper center front dial window, right and left vertical bars, feet, dual speakers, 2 knobs, BC, 5 tubes, AC/DC **$20.00-25.00**
10R38, table, 1961, sandstone plastic, upper center front dial window, right and left vertical bars, feet, dual speakers, 2 knobs, BC, 5 tubes, AC/DC **$20.00-25.00**
10R39, table, 1961, gray plastic, upper center front dial window, right and left vertical bars, feet, dual speakers, 2 knobs, BC, 5 tubes, AC/DC **$20.00-25.00**
12R23, table, 1963, sunset plastic, large right front dial overlaps horizontal grille bars, feet, 2 knobs, BC, 5 tubes, AC/DC **$15.00-20.00**
12R25, table, 1963, blue plastic, large right front dial overlaps horizontal grille bars, feet, 2 knobs, BC, 5 tubes, AC/DC **$15.00-20.00**
12R27, table, 1963, white plastic, large right front dial overlaps horizontal grille bars, feet, 2 knobs, BC, 5 tubes, AC/DC **$15.00-20.00**
12R29, table, 1963, charcoal plastic, large right front dial overlaps horizontal grille bars, feet, 2 knobs, BC, 5 tubes, AC/DC **$15.00-20.00**
30R12, table, 1961, persimmon plastic, right front slide rule dial, left checkered grille area, 2 knobs, FM, 5 tubes, AC......**$20.00-25.00**
30R18, table, 1961, sandstone plastic, right front slide rule dial, left checkered grille area, 2 knobs, FM, 5 tubes, AC...........**$20.00-25.00**
30R58, table, 1961, plastic, lower left front slanted slide rule dial, grille above, 4 knobs, BC, FM, 6 tubes, AC **$20.00-25.00**
31R25, table, 1962, moonstone plastic, large right front dial, left vertical grille bars, feet, 3 knobs, BC, FM, 7 tubes, AC/DC **$20.00-25.00**
31R26, table, 1962, mint green plastic, large right front dial, left vertical grille bars, feet, 3 knobs, BC, FM, 7 tubes, AC/DC **$20.00-25.00**
32R43, table, 1963, wood, bottom right front corner half round dial panel overlays cloth grille, 4 knobs, BC, FM, 7 tubes, AC/DC ..**$20.00-25.00**
32R89 "Stereophonic," table, 1962, plastic, front slide rule dial, step-back raised top with speaker grille, pushbuttons, 2 speakers, 4 knobs, BC, FM, 10 tubes, AC **$55.00-65.00**
33R28, table, 1963, beige plastic, large right front dial, left vertical grille bars, feet, 3 knobs, BC, FM, 6 tubes, AC/DC **$20.00-25.00**
33R29, table, 1963, charcoal plastic, large right front dial, left vertical grille bars, feet, 3 knobs, BC, FM, 6 tubes, AC/DC **$20.00-25.00**
35R28, table, 1965, plastic, right front dial, left front lattice grille, 6 knobs, BC, FM, 5 tubes, AC **$20.00-25.00**
52R35, table-C, 1962, moonstone plastic, center front dial, right alarm clock face, left lattice grille area, 4 knobs, BC, 5 tubes, AC **$20.00-25.00**
52R37, table-C, 1962, white plastic, center front dial, right alarm clock face, left lattice grille area, 4 knobs, BC, 5 tubes, AC **$20.00-25.00**
58, table, 1939, black plastic, right front dial, left round grille with horizontal bars, 2 knobs, BC, 5 tubes, AC/DC **$85.00-95.00**
58A, table, 1939, ivory plastic, right front dial, left round grille with horizontal bars, 2 knobs, BC, 5 tubes, AC/DC **$85.00-95.00**
68, table, 1938, brown plastic, right pushbutton tuning, left round grille with horizontal bars, 3 knobs, BC, 5 tubes, AC...........**$85.00-105.00**
78, table, 1938, wood, right front dial, left grille with horizontal bars, 4 pushbuttons, 3 knobs, BC, SW, 5 tubes, AC **$65.00-75.00**
88, table-R/P, 1938, wood, outer right dial, left grille with vertical bars, lift top, inner phono, 2 knobs, BC, SW, 6 tubes, AC **$35.00-40.00**
89, table, 1939, wood, right front dial, left grille with vertical bars, pushbuttons, tuning eye, 4 knobs, BC, SW, 6 tubes, AC **$65.00-75.00**
91, console, 1939, walnut, slanted front rectangular dial, pushbuttons, tuning eye, 4 knobs, BC, SW, 6 tubes, AC **$120.00-140.00**
140-P, portable, 1947, two-tone, upper slide rule dial, lattice grille, handle, 2 (on top) knobs, BC, 5 tubes, AC/DC/battery **$35.00-45.00**

40 "Mighty Mite," table, 1938, metal, midget, right front dial, left horizontal louvers, rounded top, 2 knobs, BC, 2 tubes, AC/DC, $85.00-95.00.

150TC, table-R/P, 1948, mahogany veneer, outer slide rule dial, horizontal grille bars, 3/4 lift top, 4 knobs, BC, 6 tubes, AC **$30.00-35.00**

151TC, table-R/P, 1948, walnut veneer, outer slide rule dial, horizontal grille bars, 3/4 lift top, 4 knobs, BC, 6 tubes, AC **$30.00-35.00**

152T, table, 1948, plastic, left half-round dial, horizontal wrap-around bars, 2 knobs, BC, 5 tubes, AC/DC......**$35.00-45.00**

160T, table, 1948, plastic, upper slide rule dial, lower metal perforated grille, case top is ribbed, 3 knobs, BC, 6 tubes, AC/DC..**$35.00-45.00**

182TFM, table, 1948, wood, upper slide rule dial with clear escutcheon, lower perforated grille, 4 knobs, BC, FM, 8 tubes, AC/DC..**$40.00-50.00**

240-P, portable, 1948, plastic, center vertical slide rule dial, checkered grille, handle, 2 knobs, BC, 4 tubes, battery, $40.00-50.00.

241P, portable, 1949, plastic, center vertical slide rule dial, checkered grille, handle, 2 knobs, BC, 4 tubes, AC/DC/battery **$40.00-50.00**

242T, table, 1948, metal, small case, right front dial, vertical grille bars with oblong cut-outs, 2 knobs, BC, 4 tubes, AC/DC...**$85.00-95.00**

243T, table, 1948, metal, small case, right front dial, vertical grille bars with oblong cut-outs, 2 knobs, BC, 4 tubes, AC/DC......**$85.00-95.00**

250-P, portable, 1948, metal, upper slide rule dial, vertical lattice louvers, handle, 2 knobs, BC, 5 tubes, AC/DC/battery **$35.00-45.00**

253T, table, 1949, black plastic, right front round dial over vertical grille bars, 2 knobs, BC, 5 tubes, AC/DC...........................**$40.00-50.00**

254T, table, 1949, walnut plastic, right front round dial over vertical grille bars, 2 knobs, BC, 5 tubes, AC/DC.........................**$40.00-50.00**

255T, table, 1949, ivory plastic, right front round dial over vertical grille bars, 2 knobs, BC, 5 tubes, AC/DC.............................**$40.00-50.00**

256T, table, 1949, green plastic, right front round dial over vertical grille bars, 2 knobs, BC, 5 tubes, AC/DC.............................**$40.00-50.00**

264T, table, 1949, wood, lucite covered slide rule dial on top of case, large lower grille, 4 knobs, BC, 6 tubes, AC/DC............**$40.00-50.00**

280TFM, table, 1948, wood, lucite covered slide rule dial on top of case, large lower grille, 4 knobs, BC, FM, 8 tubes, AC/DC......**$40.00-50.00**

302A, table-R/P, 1939, metal, rounded front with left dial and center vertical grille bars, open top phono, 3 knobs, BC, 4 tubes, AC......**$75.00-85.00**

350P, portable, 1949, plastic, right dial part of centered circular grille bars, handle, 2 knobs, BC, 5 tubes, AC/DC/battery **$40.00-50.00**

350PL, portable, 1950, plastic, right dial part of centered circular grille bars, handle, 2 knobs, BC, 5 tubes, AC/DC/battery......**$40.00-50.00**

351-P, portable, plastic, right dial part of centered circular grille bars, handle, 2 knobs, BC, 5 tubes, AC/DC/battery...............**$40.00-50.00**

356T, table, 1949, sandalwood plastic, right round dial knob over vertical grille bars, 2 knobs, BC, 5 tubes, AC/DC **$35.00-45.00**

357T, table, 1949, willow green plastic, right round dial knob over vertical grille bars, 2 knobs, BC, 5 tubes, AC/DC **$35.00-45.00**

358T, table, 1948, plastic, left raised half-round dial over horizontal wrap-around louvers, 2 knobs, BC, 5 tubes, AC/DC **$45.00-55.00**

360TFM, table, 1949, plastic, raised top with curved slide rule dial, large lower grille, 3 knobs, BC, FM, 6 tubes, AC/DC **$40.00-50.00**

402, table, 1939, walnut metal, midget, right front dial, left horizontal louvers, 2 knobs, BC, 3 tubes, AC/DC **$85.00-95.00**

402-A, table, 1939, ivory metal, midget, right front dial, left wrap-around louvers, 2 knobs, BC, 3 tubes, AC/DC **$85.00-95.00**

422, table, 1941, brown, midget, right front dial, left wrap-around louvers, 2 knobs, BC, 4 tubes, AC/DC **$75.00-85.00**

422-A, table, 1941, ivory, midget, right front dial, left wrap-around louvers, 2 knobs, BC, 4 tubes, AC/DC **$75.00-85.00**

440T, table, 1950, metal, midget, right front round dial knob, left round checkered grille, 2 knobs, BC, 4 tubes, AC/DC.............**$65.00-75.00**

341T, table, 1950, metal, midget, right round dial knob, left horizontal louvers, rounded top, 2 knobs, BC, 4 tubes, AC/DC, $75.00-85.00.

441-T "Hopalong Cassidy," table-N, 1950, metal-Black version, aluminum front Hopalong Cassidy, right dial, rear "lariatenna," 2 knobs, BC, 4 tubes, AC/DC...**$410.00-460.00**

442, table, 1948, metal, midget, right front dial, left horizontal louvers, rounded top, 2 knobs, BC, 4 tubes, AC/DC...............**$85.00-95.00**

444, table, 1946, metal, midget, right front dial, rounded corners, horizontal louvers, 2 knobs, BC, 4 tubes, AC/DC **$85.00-95.00**

444A, table, 1946, metal, midget, right front dial, horizontal louvers, raised top, 2 knobs, BC, 4 tubes, AC/DC **$85.00-95.00**

444AM, table, 1947, metal, midget, right front dial, horizontal louvers, raised top, 2 knobs, BC, 4 tubes, AC/DC **$85.00-95.00**

446P, portable, 1950, plastic, center front vertical louvers, handle, right side dial and left side volume knobs, BC, 4 tubes, battery........**$35.00-45.00**

450T, table, 1950, plastic, center round dial with inner metal perforated grille, 2 knobs, BC, 5 tubes, AC/DC **$55.00-65.00**

451T, table, 1950, plastic, center round dial with inner metal perforated grille, 2 knobs, BC, 5 tubes, AC/DC **$55.00-65.00**

451-TL, table, 1950, plastic, center round dial with inner metal perforated grille, 2 knobs, BC, 5 tubes, AC/DC **$55.00-65.00**

460T, table, 1950, plastic, right see-through dial, left horizontal grille bars, 3 knobs, BC, 6 tubes, AC/DC **$35.00-40.00**

462-CM, console-R/P, 1950, wood, upper front dial, center front pull-out phono drawer, lower grille, 3 knobs, BC, 6 tubes, AC....**$40.00-50.00**

467 "Rhythm Belle," table, 1936, wood, left front round dial, right round grille, 3 knobs, BC, SW, 4 tubes, AC **$75.00-85.00**

502, table, 1939, metal, midget, right front square dial, left wrap-around louvers, 2 knobs, BC, 5 tubes, AC/DC **$85.00-95.00**

502A, table, 1939, metal, midget, right front square dial, left wrap-around louvers, 2 knobs, BC, 5 tubes, AC/DC **$85.00-95.00**

517 "Rhythm Junior," tombstone, 1936, wood, center front round dial, upper oval grille with 3 splayed bars, 4 knobs, BC, SW, 5 tubes, AC **$190.00-210.00**

417 "Rhythm Baby," tombstone, 1936, wood, lower round dial, upper oval grille with 3 splayed bars, 2 knobs, BC, SW, 4 tubes, AC, $190.00-210.00.

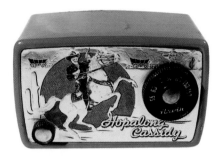

441-T "Hopalong Cassidy," table-N, 1950, metal-Red version, aluminum front Hopalong Cassidy, right dial, rear "lariatenna," 2 knobs, BC, 4 tubes, AC/DC, $550.00-610.00.

518 "Phantom Baby," table, 1937, wood, lower front round dial, upper cloth grille with horizontal bars, 4 knobs, BC, SW, 5 tubes, AC ..$85.00-95.00

518DW "Phantom Pal," table, 1937, ivory/mahogany wood, lower front round dial, upper cloth grille with horizontal bars, 4 knobs, BC, SW, 5 tubes, AC $130.00-150.00

522, table, 1941, brown metal, midget, right front square dial, left horizontal louvers, raised top, 2 knobs, BC, 5 tubes, AC $85.00-95.00

522A, table, 1940, ivory metal, midget, right front square dial, left horizontal louvers, raised top, 2 knobs, BC, 5 tubes, AC $85.00-95.00

524, table, 1940, walnut, right front square dial, left horizontal louvers, raised top, 2 knobs, BC, 5 tubes, AC/DC $85.00-95.00

524A, table, 1940, ivory, right front square dial, left horizontal louvers, raised top, 2 knobs, BC, 5 tubes, AC/DC $85.00-95.00

527 "Rhythm Senior," console, 1936, wood, upper front round dial, lower oval grille with 3 splayed bars, 4 knobs, BC, SW, 5 tubes, AC $160.00-190.00

528CS "Phantom Mate," chairside, 1938, wood, top round dial and knobs, side grille with horizontal bars, storage, BC, SW, 5 tubes, AC $150.00-160.00

532, table, 1941, burgundy & onyx Catalin, left front dial, raised right with vertical wrap-over grille bars, 2 knobs, BC, 5 tubes, AC/DC..$1,250.00+

532A, table, 1941, onyx & amber Catalin, left front dial, raised right with vertical wrap-over grille bars, 2 knobs, BC, 5 tubes, AC/DC ......$1,250.00+

540T, table, 1951, painted metal, large right round dial knob over lattice grille, 2 knobs, BC, 4 tubes, AC/DC $85.00-95.00

541TL, table, 1950, plastic, large center front round dial with stars & inner perforated grille, 2 knobs, BC $50.00-65.00

542J, table, 1947, metal, right front round dial knob, horizontal grille bars, lower left knob, 2 knobs, BC $65.00-75.00

544, table, 1946, plastic, left front dial, right wrap-over vertical grille bars, rounded corners, 2 knobs, BC, 6 tubes, AC/DC $55.00-65.00

544A, table, 1946, plastic, left front dial, right wrap-over vertical grille bars, rounded corners, 2 knobs, BC, 6 tubes, AC/DC ..$55.00-65.00

547, table, 1948, plastic, left front dial, right vertical wrap-over grille bars, 2 knobs, BC, 5 tubes, AC/DC $55.00-65.00

552N, table, 1947, plastic, upper slide rule dial, lower vertical grille bars, 2 knobs, BC, 5 tubes, AC/DC $45.00-55.00

555, table, 1947, walnut plastic, upper slide rule dial, lower vertical grille bars, 2 knobs, BC, 5 tubes, AC/DC.............................$45.00-55.00

555A, table, 1947, ivory plastic, upper slide rule dial, vertical grille bars, 2 knobs, BC, 5 tubes, AC/DC...$45.00-55.00

558, table-R/P, 1946, wood, lower front slide rule dial, upper cloth grille, lift top, inner phono, 4 knobs, BC, 5 tubes, AC/DC........$30.00-35.00

568A "Phantom Blonde," table, 1938, lower round dial, upper wrap-over vertical grille bars, 4 knobs, BC, 5 tubes, AC $85.00-95.00

568DW "Phantom Ace," table, 1937, ivory/mahogany, lower round dial, upper wrap-over vertical grille bars, 4 knobs, BC, SW, 5 tubes, AC...$85.00-95.00

580TFM, table, 1951, plastic, right front see-through dial, left horizontal bars, 3 knobs, BC, FM, 8 tubes, AC $35.00-45.00

581TFM, table, 1953, plastic, right front see-through dial, left cloth grille, feet, 3 knobs, BC, FM, 8 tubes, AC $35.00-45.00

602, table, 1939, walnut plastic, right front dial, left round grille with horizontal bars, handle, 3 knobs, BC, 6 tubes, AC/DC $85.00-95.00

602A, table, 1939, ivory plastic, right front dial, left round grille with horizontal bars, handle, 3 knobs, BC, 6 tubes, AC/DC $85.00-95.00

616, table, 1941, walnut plastic, left front dial, right vertical wrap-over grille bars, 2 knobs, BC, 6 tubes, AC/DC $75.00-85.00

616-A, table, 1941, ivory plastic, left front dial, right vertical wrap-over grille bars, 2 knobs, BC, 6 tubes, AC/DC $75.00-85.00

617 "Rhythm Maid," tombstone, 1936, wood, center front round dial, upper oval grille with 3 splayed bars, BC, SW, 6 tubes, AC $280.00-310.00

618 "Phantom Maid," table, 1937, two-tone wood, off-center round dial, left side grille with horizontal bars, tuning eye, 4 knobs, BC, SW, 6 tubes, AC $75.00-85.00

622, table, 1941, walnut plastic, right front dial, horizontal wrap-around grille bars, rounded top, 2 knobs, BC, 5 tubes, AC/DC..$75.00-95.00

622-A, table, 1941, ivory plastic, right front dial, horizontal wrap-around grille bars, rounded top, 2 knobs, BC, 5 tubes, AC/DC..$75.00-95.00

627 "Rhythm Master," console, 1936, wood, upper front round dial, lower oval grille with 3 splayed bars, 5 knobs, BC, SW, 6 tubes, AC $300.00-350.00

628CS "Phantom Bachelor," chairside, 1937, two-tone wood, Deco, top dial, rounded front with vertical bars, BC, SW, 6 tubes, AC $240.00-270.00

632, table, 1941, walnut, right front rectangular dial, left cloth grille with vertical bars, 2 knobs, BC, 5 tubes, AC/DC $50.00-65.00

638 "Phantom Fawn," console, 1938, wood, upper front dial, lower grille with vertical bars, 4 knobs, BC, SW, 6 tubes, AC $140.00-160.00

638CS "Phantom Grad," chairside, 1938, wood, top round dial, step-down front with horizontal louvers, lower storage, 4 knobs, BC, SW, 6 tubes, AC $150.00-180.00

650-P, portable, 1952, large center front round dial, flex handle, right side dial and left side volume knobs, BC, 5 tubes, AC/DC/battery $40.00-50.00

655SWT, table, 1952, plastic, right see-through dial, left horizontal grille bars, 3 knobs, BC, SW, 5 tubes, AC/DC $35.00-45.00

657-T, table-C, 1952, plastic, lower right front slide rule dial, left square alarm clock, 2 side and 3 front knobs, BC, 5 tubes, AC..$30.00-35.00

664, table, 1947, plastic, right front square dial, left vertical grille bars, handle, BC, 6 tubes, AC/DC $50.00-65.00

665, console-R/P, 1947, wood, inner right slide rule dial, left phono, lift top, legs, 4 knobs, BC, 6 tubes, AC $50.00-65.00

669, table-R/P, walnut, lower front dial, pushbuttons, horizontal grille bars, lift top, inner phono, 4 knobs, BC, 6 tubes, AC $40.00-45.00

702, table, 1940, walnut, right front dial, left louvers, step-down top with pushbuttons, 3 knobs, BC, 6 tubes, AC/DC $85.00-95.00

722, table, 1941, walnut plastic, right front square dial, left vertical grille bars, handle, 3 knobs, BC, 6 tubes, AC $50.00-65.00

722-A, table, 1941, ivory plastic, right front square dial, left vertical grille bars, handle, 3 knobs, BC, 6 tubes, AC $50.00-65.00

732, table, 1941, walnut, right front dial, left horizontal louvers, 3 knobs, BC, 6 tubes, AC $45.00-55.00

741T, table, 1953, plastic, right front round dial, left criss-cross grille, 2 knobs, BC, 4 tubes, AC/DC $35.00-40.00

746P, portable, 1953, plastic, large front metal lattice grille with logo, handle, top dial and volume knobs, BC, 4 tubes, battery......$75.00-85.00

751-TB, table, C1951, blonde wood, large front see-though dial over cloth grille area, large center pointer, 2 knobs, BC, 5 tubes, AC $35.00-45.00

751-TM, table, C1951, mahogany wood, large front see-though dial over cloth grille area, large center pointer, 2 knobs, BC, 5 tubes, AC $35.00-45.00

753T, table, 1953, plastic, right front see-through round dial over oblong cloth grille, 2 knobs, BC, 5 tubes, AC/DC $35.00-45.00

758T, table-C, 1953, plastic, right vertical slide rule dial, left clock face, woven grille, 5 knobs, BC, 5 tubes, AC $30.00-35.00

760T, table, 1953, plastic, right front dial, left cloth grille, feet, 3 knobs, BC, 6 tubes, AC/DC $30.00-35.00

802, portable, 1939, cloth with lower stripe, right front dial, left grille, handle, 2 knobs, BC, 5 tubes, AC/DC/battery.....................$25.00-30.00

480TFM, table, 1950, plastic, right see-through dial, left horizontal grille bars, 3 knobs, BC, FM, 8 tubes, AC, $45.00-55.00.

840T, table, 1954, metal, right round plastic dial knob over vertical bars, lower left plastic knob, 2 knobs, BC, 4 tubes, AC/DC, $65.00-75.00.

822, portable, 1940, inner right dial, left grille, fold-down front, handle, 3 knobs, BC, 5 tubes, AC/DC/battery..............................$25.00-30.00

828AT "Phantom President," console, 1937, two-tone wood, upper front dial, lower cloth grille with 2 vertical bars, 5 knobs, BC, SW, 8 tubes, AC $180.00-200.00

838AT "Phantom Princess," console, 1938, wood, upper front dial, lower cloth grille with 2 vertical bars, 5 knobs, BC, SW, 8 tubes, AC $180.00-200.00

838CS "Phantom Deb," chairside, 1938, wood, inner dial and controls, fold-over top, side grille area, storage, BC, 8 tubes, AC $150.00-180.00

842J, table, 1954, metal, right front round dial knob over lattice grille bars, lower left volume knob, 2 knobs, BC, 4 tubes, AC/DC....**$65.00-75.00**

842T, table, 1954, metal, right front round dial knob over lattice grille bars, lower left volume knob, 2 knobs, BC, 4 tubes, AC/DC....**$65.00-75.00**

848CS "Phantom Vogue," chairside-R/P, 1938, wood, top round dial and knobs, lift top, inner phono, side grille with horizontal bars, storage, BC, SW, 8 tubes, AC $180.00-200.00

850T, table, 1955, plastic, large right round dial over oval metal perforated grille, 2 knobs, BC, 5 tubes, AC/DC $35.00-45.00

857T, table-C, 1955, plastic, modern, lower slide rule dial, center front alarm clock, 5 knobs, BC, 5 tubes, AC $30.00-35.00

927 "Rhythm Queen," console, 1936, wood, large upper front round dial, lower oval grille with 3 splayed bars, 5 knobs, BC, SW, 9 tubes, AC $600.00-700.00

950T, table, 1955, plastic, upper right front round dial over horizontal grille bars, 2 knobs, BC, 5 tubes, AC/DC $25.00-30.00

950T2, table, 1958, plastic, upper right front round dial over checkered grille, 2 knobs, BC, 5 tubes, AC/DC $25.00-30.00

951T, table, 1955, plastic, upper right front round dial over horizontal grille bars, 2 knobs, BC, 5 tubes, AC/DC $25.00-30.00

952P, portable, 1955, plastic, large right front round dial over checkered grille area, top right thumbwheel knob, handle, BC, 4 tubes, AC/battery $30.00-35.00

954P, portable, 1955, plastic, large right front round dial over checkered grille area, top right thumbwheel knob, handle, BC, 4 tubes, AC/battery $30.00-35.00

956T, table, 1955, plastic, lower front dial, large upper grille area with center vertical treble/bass indicator, twin speakers, 2 knobs, BC, 5 tubes, AC/DC..$25.00-30.00

956T1, table, 1955, plastic, lower front dial, large upper grille area with center vertical treble/bass indicator, twin speakers, 2 knobs, BC, 5 tubes, AC/DC..$25.00-30.00

957T, table-C, 1956, plastic, lower right front slide rule dial, large left alarm clock face, feet, side knobs, BC, 5 tubes, AC $25.00-30.00

958T, table-C, 1956, plastic, lower slide rule dial, center alarm clock with day-date, 5 knobs, BC, 5 tubes, AC $25.00-30.00

1127 "Rhythm King," console, 1936, wood, large upper front round dial, lower oval grille with 3 vertical bars, 5 knobs, BC, SW, 11 tube, AC $750.00-850.00

1237 "Phantom Prince," console, 1937, wood, upper front round telephone dial, lower horseshoe-shaped grille with 3 vertical bars, BC, 12 tubes, AC $400.00-450.00

1247 "Phantom Queen," bookcase, 1937, wood, upper front round dial, right & left bookcases, BC, SW, 12 tubes, AC............$450.00-500.00

1247D, bookcase, 1938, wood, center front round dial, pushbuttons, right & left 3 shelf bookcases, BC, 12 tubes $350.00-380.00

1427 "Phantom King," console, 1937, walnut, upper front round front dial, pushbuttons, tuning eye, 2 speakers, BC, SW, 14 tubes, AC $500.00-550.00

1581, table, 1958, plastic, front lattice grille, right side dial and left side volume knobs, BC, 4 tubes, AC/DC $25.00-30.00

2410P, portable, 1948, plastic, center front vertical slide rule dial, checkerboard grille, handle, 2 knobs, BC, 4 tubes, AC/DC/battery **$35.00-45.00**

2563, table, 1957, plastic, right front vertical slide rule dial, left lattice grille, 2 knobs, BC, 5 tubes, AC/DC $25.00-30.00

2572, table, 1958, ivory or willow green plastic, lower right front dial knob, upper vertical grille bars, feet, 2 knobs, BC, 5 tubes, AC/DC $20.00-25.00

2573, table, 1958, flame or turquoise plastic, lower right front dial knob, random patterned perforated grille area, feet, 2 knobs, BC, 5 tubes, AC/DC $35.00-45.00

2581, table, 1959, plastic, front lattice grille, right side dial and left side volume knobs, BC, 5 tubes, AC/DC $25.00-30.00

2584, table, 1959, plastic, large center round dial with "steering wheel" pointer, horizontal front bars, twin speakers, feet, 2 knobs, BC, 5 tubes, AC/DC $30.00-35.00

2585, table, 1959, plastic, lower left front slide rule dial, large upper cloth grille area with center logo, twin speakers, 3 knobs, BC, 5 tubes, AC/DC $25.00-30.00

3561, table, 1957, plastic, center vertical slide rule dial & tone control, right/left lattice grills, twin speakers, 2 knobs, BC, 6 tubes, AC/DC $30.00-35.00

3582, table, 1959, plastic, lower front slide rule dial, raised upper grille area with hi/fi logo, 4 knobs, BC, 7 tubes, AC/ DC $50.00-65.00

3586, table, 1959, plastic, lower front slide rule dial, raised upper grille area, pushbuttons, 4 knobs, BC, FM, 9 tubes, AC $50.00-65.00

5561, table-C, 1957, pink plastic, lower left dial with alarm clock face, right front checkered grille, 4 knobs, BC, 5 tubes, AC ..$25.00-30.00

5571, table-C, 1958, plastic, right round dial knob over horizontal bars, left alarm clock face, feet, BC, 5 tubes, AC....................$20.00-25.00

5572, table-C, 1958, plastic, right round dial knob, left alarm clock face, feet, BC, 5 tubes, AC $20.00-25.00

5581, table-C, 1957, green plastic, lower left dial with alarm clock face, right front checkered grille, 4 knobs, BC, 5 tubes, AC ..$25.00-30.00

5591, table-C, 1960, plastic, lower right thumbwheel dial, lower left thumbwheel on/off/volume, center front alarm clock face, BC, 5 tubes, AC $35.00-45.00

6640, table, 1948, walnut, right front square dial, left cloth grille with Deco cut-outs, 3 knobs, BC, 6 tubes, AC/DC........................$50.00-65.00

8565, portable, 1957, British tan leatherette, right front round dial, left grille area with lattice cut-outs, top right thumbwheel knob, handle, BC, 4 tubes, battery..$25.00-30.00

8571 "Voyager," portable, 1958, lower front lattice grille area, pull-up handle, right side dial and left side volume knobs, BC, 4 tubes, AC/DC/battery $30.00-35.00

8571-1, portable, 1958, cloth-covered, lower front lattice grille area, pull-up handle, right side dial and left side volume knobs, BC, 4 tubes, AC/DC/battery $30.00-35.00

8572, portable, 1958, leather, front perforated grille with random lines, handle, right side dial and left side volume knobs, BC, 4 tubes, AC/DC/battery $35.00-45.00

8583 "Velvet Voice," portable, 1959, leatherette/aluminum, front horizontal bars, rotatable handle, upper right front thumbwheel dial knob, upper left thumbwheel on/off/volume knob, BC, 4 tubes, AC/DC/battery $40.00-50.00

952P1, portable, 1956, plastic, large right front round dial over checkered grille area, top right thumbwheel knob, handle, BC, 4 tubes, AC/battery, $30.00-35.00.

ATKINS
Atkins Concert Hall
Frederick Wholesale Corp.
New York, New York

12N27-11, table, 1963, plastic, large right front dial knob overlaps grille area, left on/off/volume knob, BC, 5 tubes, AC/DC........**$15.00-20.00**

13N49-11, table, 1964, plastic, lower left front slide rule dial, large upper grille area, feet, 3 knobs, BC, 6 tubes, AC/DC **$15.00-20.00**

31N28-11, table, 1963, plastic, lower right panel with dial & knobs over large patterned grille area, feet, 3 knobs, BC, FM, 6 tubes, AC/DC **$15.00-20.00**

32N43-11, table, 1963, wood, lower right panel with half-round dial and knobs over large grille area, 4 knobs, BC, FM, 6 tubes, AC/DC **$15.00-20.00**

42N25-11, table-C, 1963, plastic, lower right front dial, center round alarm clock face, left vertical grille bars, 5 knobs, BC, FM, 6 tubes, AC **$15.00-20.00**

51N28-11, table-C, 1963, plastic, right round dial over horizontal grille bars, left alarm clock face, feet, BC, 5 tubes, AC **$15.00-20.00**

ATLANTIC
Atlantic Radio Corp., Brooklyn, New York

31AC, grandfather clock, 1931, wood, Colonial-style grandfather clock, front dial, knobs and grille, BC, AC **$410.00-460.00**

AC, cathedral, wood, center front quarter-round dial with brass escutcheon, upper cloth grille with cut-outs, 3 knobs, BC, AC **$410.00-460.00**

ATLAS
Atomic Heater & Radio Co.
102-104 Park Row, New York, New York

AB-45, table, 1947, wood, right front square dial, left cloth grille with vertical bars, 3 knobs, BC, SW, AC/DC **$40.00-50.00**

ATWATER KENT
Atwater Kent Manufacturing Company
4703 Wissahickon Avenue
Philadelphia, Pennsylvania

Atwater Kent began business manufacturing electrical items and parts for automobiles. In 1922 the Atwater Kent Manufacturing Company began to market component parts for radios and the first of their large line of breadboards. By 1924 the company produced the first of their cabinet sets. Both the Pooley Company and the Red Lion Cabinet Company were among several furniture manufacturers who made radio cabinets for Atwater Kent. From 1925 to 1927, the company sponsored the Atwater Kent Radio Hour, a popular Sunday night show of radio music. A victim of the Depression, Atwater Kent was out of business by 1936.

2, breadboard, 1922, small rectangular wooden board, 1 left & one center dial, BC, 3 right side tubes, battery, $950.00-1,150.00.

9C, breadboard, 1923, rectangular wooden board, 1 left & 1 center dial, BC, 4 tubes, battery, $1,200.00-1,400.00.

1, breadboard, 1922, small rectangular wooden board, 1 left & 1 center dial, BC, 2 right side tubes, battery **$1,000.00-1,200.00**

5, breadboard, 1923, small rectangular wooden board, 1 left side dial, BC, 5 right side tubes, battery **$3,500.00-4,500.00**

9, breadboard, 1923, rectangular wooden board, 1 left & 1 center dial, BC, 4 tubes, battery **$1,200.00-1,400.00**

9A, breadboard, 1923, rectangular wooden board, 1 left and 1 center dial, BC, 4 tubes, battery **$1,200.00-1,400.00**

10, breadboard, 1923, rectangular wooden board, 1 left & 2 centered dials, BC, 5 tubes, battery **$1,050.00-1,150.00**

10, console, 1923, wood, model 10 breadboard unit built into large ornate "Valley Tone" cabinet, BC, 5 tubes, battery.....................**$1,400.00+**

10A, breadboard, 1923, rectangular wooden board, 1 left & 2 centered dials, BC, 5 tubes, battery **$950.00-1,050.00**

10B, breadboard, 1924, rectangular wooden board, 1 left & 2 centered dials, BC, 5 tubes, battery **$950.00-1,050.00**

10C, breadboard, 1924, rectangular wooden board, 1 left and 2 centered dials, BC, 5 tubes, battery, $950.00-1,050.00.

12, breadboard, 1924, rectangular wooden board, 1 left & 2 centered dials, BC, 6 tubes, battery **$1,200.00-1,400.00**

20 "Big Box," table, 1924, wood, low rectangular case, 3 dial black front panel with AK logo, lift top, 6 knobs, BC, 5 tubes, battery...........**$85.00-115.00**

20 "Deluxe," table, 1924, wood, low rectangular case with molding, 3 dial black front panel with AK logo, lift top, 6 knobs, BC, 5 tubes, battery...**$85.00-115.00**

20C, table, 1925, wood, low rectangular case, 3 dial front panel with center AK logo, lift top, 6 knobs, BC, 5 tubes, battery......**$85.00-115.00**

21, table, 1925, wood, low rectangular case, 3 dial black front panel with AK logo, lift top, 6 knobs, BC, 5 tubes, battery **$240.00-270.00**

24, table, 1925, wood, low rectangular case with overhanging lid, 3 dial front panel, button feet, 6 knobs, BC, 5 tubes, battery..........**$200.00-230.00**

30, table, 1926, wood, low rectangular case, 1 dial front panel with center AK logo, lift top, 3 knobs, BC, 6 tubes, battery **$120.00-150.00**

32, table, 1926, wood, low rectangular case, 1 dial front panel with center AK logo, lift top, 3 knobs, BC, 7 tubes, battery **$120.00-140.00**

33, console, 1927, wood, 1 dial front panel with center AK logo, built into various console cabinets, 4 knobs, BC, 6 tubes, battery **$245.00-295.00**

33, table, 1927, wood, low rectangular case, 1 dial metal panel with center AK logo, lift top, 4 knobs, BC, 6 tubes, battery......**$95.00-115.00**

36, console, 1927, wood, model 36 built into various console cabinets, left front dial, center AK logo, 3 knobs, BC, 7 tubes, AC ..**$150.00-180.00**

36, table, 1927, wood, low rectangular case, left front dial, center AK logo, 3 knobs, BC, 7 tubes, AC **$120.00-150.00**

37, table, 1927, metal, low rectangular case, left front dial, top gold ship logo, lift-off top, 2 knobs, BC, 7 tubes, AC **$75.00-95.00**

19, table, 1924, wood, low rectangular case, black 2 dial front panel with AK logo, lift top, 5 knobs, BC, 4 tubes, battery, $410.00-460.00.

38, table, 1927, metal, low rectangular case, left front dial, lift-off top with AK ship logo, 2 knobs, BC, 8 tubes, AC **$65.00-75.00**
40, console, 1928, wood, model 40 built into various console cabinets, left front dial, 2 knobs, BC, 7 tubes, AC **$150.00-180.00**
40, console, 1928, wood, model 40 built into a Pooley cabinet with double front doors, Spanish style with card and pipe racks, small interior doors for storage & pipes, 2 knobs, BC, 7 tubes, AC..**$410.00-460.00**
41, table, 1928, metal, low rectangular case, left front dial, lift-off top, feet, 2 knobs, BC, 7 tubes, DC **$75.00-85.00**
42, table, 1928, metal, low rectangular case, left front dial, lift-off top with gold AK logo, 2 knobs, BC, 7 tubes, AC **$55.00-65.00**
42F, table, 1928, metal, low rectangular case, left front dial, lift-off top, feet, 2 knobs, BC, 7 tubes **$55.00-65.00**
43, table, 1928, metal, low rectangular case, left front dial, lift-off top, feet, 2 knobs, BC, 8 tubes, AC **$85.00-95.00**
44, console/bar, 1928, wood, model 44 built into Pooley bar cabinet, lift top, inner bar supplies, 2 knobs, BC, 8 tubes, AC...............**$900.00+**
44, table, 1928, metal, low rectangular case, left front dial, lift-off top with AK logo, feet, 2 knobs, BC, 8 tubes, AC **$75.00-85.00**
44F, table, 1928, metal, low rectangular case, left front dial, lift-off top with gold AK logo, feet, 2 knobs, BC, 8 tubes **$75.00-85.00**
45, table, 1929, metal, low rectangular case, left front dial, lift-off top with AK logo, 2 knobs, BC, 8 tubes, AC **$75.00-85.00**
46, console, 1929, wood, model 46 built into various console cabinets, left front dial, 2 knobs, BC, 8 tubes, AC **$160.00-190.00**
46, table, 1929, metal, low rectangular case, left front dial, lift-off top with AK logo, 2 knobs, BC, 8 tubes, AC **$85.00-95.00**

20C, console, 1925, wood, model 20C in Pooley cabinet, built in speaker, fold down front door, battery storage, 6 knobs, BC, 5 tubes, battery, $245.00-295.00.

30, console, 1926, wood, 1 dial front panel with center AK logo, built into various console cabinets, 3 knobs, BC, 6 tubes, battery, $185.00-235.00.

47, console, 1929, wood, model 47 built into various console cabinets, left front dial, 2 knobs, BC, 9 tubes, AC **$180.00-200.00**
47, table, 1929, metal, low rectangular case, left front dial, center gold AK logo, lift-off top, 2 knobs, BC, 9 tubes, AC **$75.00-85.00**
48, table, 1928, wood, low rectangular case, front panel with left dial & center AK logo, lift top, 3 knobs, BC, 6 tubes, battery .. **$75.00-85.00**
49, table, 1928, wood, low rectangular case, metal front panel with left dial, lift top, 4 knobs, BC, 6 tubes, battery **$65.00-75.00**
50, table, 1928, wood, low rectangular case, front panel with left dial, shielded interior, 4 knobs, BC, 7 tubes, battery .. **$1,000.00-1,200.00**
52, console, 1928, metal, upper left front dial, lower large center round "caned" grille, legs, 2 knobs, BC, 7 tubes, AC **$120.00-140.00**
55, console, 1929, wood, center front window dial with escutcheon, various console cabinets, 3 knobs, BC, 7 tubes, AC **$120.00-150.00**
55, Kiel table, 1929, wooden 6 legged table, inner front window dial with escutcheon, fold-down door, lift-top, 3 knobs, BC, 7 tubes, AC **$245.00-295.00**
55, table, 1929, metal, low rectangular case, center front window dial with escutcheon, 3 knobs, BC, 7 tubes, AC **$75.00-85.00**
55-C, Kiel table, 1929, wooden 6 legged table, inner front window dial with escutcheon, fold-down door, lift-top, 3 knobs, BC, 7 tubes, AC **$245.00-295.00**
55-C, console, 1929, wood, model 55-C built into various console cabinets, window dial with escutcheon, 3 knobs, BC, 7 tubes, AC ..**$120.00-150.00**
56, console, 1929, metal, upper left front dial, lower round grille with 7 circular cut-outs, legs, 2 knobs, BC, 7 tubes, AC **$85.00-115.00**
57, console, 1929, metal, upper left front dial, lower round grille with 7 circular cut-outs, legs, 2 knobs, BC, 7 tubes, AC **$85.00-115.00**

35, table, 1926, metal, low rectangular case, right front dial, top gold AK logo, 2 knobs, BC, 6 tubes, battery, $65.00-75.00.

37, console, 1927, wood, model 37 built into various console cabinets, speaker, left front dial, 2 knobs, BC, 7 tubes, AC, $245.00-295.00.

53, console, 1929, metal, upper left front dial, lower round "caned" grille, center AK logo, legs, 2 knobs, BC, 8 tubes, AC, $120.00-140.00.

60, Kiel table, 1929, wooden 6 legged table, inner front window dial with escutcheon, fold-down door, lift-top, 3 knobs, BC, 8 tubes, AC **$260.00-310.00**

60, table, 1929, metal, low rectangular case, center front window dial with escutcheon, 3 knobs, BC, 8 tubes, AC **$75.00-85.00**

60C, console, 1929, wood, model 60C built into various console cabinets, window dial with escutcheon, 3 knobs, BC, 8 tubes, AC **$200.00-230.00**

60C, Kiel table, 1929, wooden 6 legged table, inner front window dial with escutcheon, fold-down door, lift-top, 3 knobs, BC, 8 tubes, AC **$260.00-310.00**

61, table, 1929, metal, low rectangular case, center front window dial with escutcheon, lift-off top, 3 knobs, BC, 7 tubes, DC **$65.00-75.00**

66, console, 1929, wood, inner window dial, upper cloth grille with cut-outs, sliding doors, 3 knobs, BC, 7 tubes, AC............**$180.00-200.00**

67, table, 1930, metal painted to look like wood, center front window dial, lift-off top, 3 knobs, BC, 7 tubes, battery **$75.00-85.00**

70, console, 1930, wood, lowboy, upper front quarter-round dial, lower cloth grille, 3 knobs, BC, 7 tubes DC, 8 tubes AC, available in AC or DC or battery versions **$120.00-140.00**

72, console, 1930, wood, highboy, upper front quarter-round dial, lower cloth grille, stretcher base, 3 knobs, BC, 8 tubes, AC ..**$160.00-190.00**

74, console, 1930, wood, lowboy, upper front quarter-round dial, lower cloth grille, 3 knobs, BC, 7 tubes DC, 8 tubes AC, available in AC or DC versions **$160.00-190.00**

75, console-R/P, 1930, wood, lowboy, front quarter-round dial, lower cloth grille, lift top, inner phono, 3 knobs, BC, 8 tubes, AC..**$180.00-220.00**

76, console, 1930, wood, highboy, inner dial and knobs, lower grille, double front doors, 3 knobs, BC, 7 tubes DC, 8 tubes AC, available in AC or DC or battery versions....................................**$150.00-180.00**

80, cathedral, 1931, wood, front half-round dial, upper cloth grille with cut-outs, twisted columns, 3 knobs, BC, 6 tubes, AC **$380.00-430.00**

81, console, 1932, wood, lowboy, inner quarter-round dial, double doors, stretcher base, 6 legs, BC, 12 tubes, AC....................**$160.00-190.00**

82D, cathedral, 1931, wood, front half-round dial, upper grille with Gothic cut-outs, twisted columns, 3 knobs, BC, 6 tubes, DC..**$470.00-530.00**

82Q, cathedral, 1931, wood, front half-round dial, upper grille with Gothic cut-outs, twisted columns, 3 knobs, BC, 7 tubes, battery **$410.00-460.00**

83, console, 1931, walnut, lowboy, upper front half-round dial, lower grille with cut-outs, BC, 6 tubes, AC **$140.00-160.00**

84, cathedral, 1931, wood, center front half-round dial, upper cloth grille with Gothic cut-outs, 3 knobs, BC, 6 tubes, AC **$470.00-530.00**

84, grandfather clock, 1931, wood, center front half-round dial, lower grille, upper clock face, 3 knobs, BC, 6 tubes, AC **$700.00-760.00**

84D, cathedral, 1931, wood, center front half-round dial, upper cloth grille with Gothic cut-outs, 3 knobs, BC, 6 tubes, DC **$430.00-500.00**

60, console, 1929, wood, model 60 built into various console cabinets, window dial with escutcheon, 3 knobs, BC, 8 tubes, AC, $200.00-230.00.

40, table, 1928, metal, low rectangular case, left front dial, lift-off top with gold AK logo, 2 knobs, BC, 7 tubes, AC, $75.00-85.00.

82, cathedral, 1931, wood, front half-round dial, upper grille with Gothic cut-outs, twisted columns, 3 knobs, BC, 7 tubes, AC, $470.00-530.00.

90, cathedral, 1931, wood, front half-round dial, upper cloth grille with cut-outs, twisted columns, 3 knobs, BC, 7 tubes, AC, $470.00-530.00.

85, console, 1931, wood, lowboy, upper front quarter-round dial, lower cloth grille with cut-outs, 3 knobs, BC, 7 tubes, AC ..**$140.00-160.00**

85Q, console, 1931, wood, lowboy, upper front quarter-round dial, lower cloth grille with cut-outs, 3 knobs, BC, 7 tubes, battery .. **$140.00-160.00**

87D, console, 1931, wood, available as highboy or lowboy, quarter-round dial, grille cut-outs, BC, 8 tubes, DC **$140.00-160.00**

89, console, 1931, wood, highboy, inner quarter round dial, double sliding front doors, 3 knobs, BC,10 tubes, AC **$180.00-200.00**

92, cathedral, 1931, wood, center front half-round dial, upper cloth grille with cut-outs, twisted columns, 3 knobs, BC, 8 tubes, AC **$470.00-530.00**

94, console, 1931, wood, available as highboy or lowboy, upper front quarter-round dial, lower grille cut-outs, BC, 7 tubes, AC ..**$140.00-160.00**

96, console, 1931, wood, available as highboy or lowboy, upper front quarter-round dial, lower grille cut-outs, BC, 8 tubes, AC ..**$180.00-190.00**

99, console, 1932, wood, available as highboy or lowboy, upper front quarter-round dial, lower grille cut-outs, BC, 10 tubes, AC ..**$180.00-190.00**

112N, console, 1934, wood, upper front quarter-round dial, lower cloth grille with scrolled cut-outs, 5 knobs, BC, SW, 12 tubes, AC...**$275.00-325.00**

112S, console, 1934, wood, upper front quarter round dial, lower cloth grille with scrolled cut-outs, 5 knobs, BC, SW, 12 tubes, AC...**$325.00-375.00**

145, tombstone, 1934, wood, lower front round dial, upper cloth grille with cut-outs, fluting, 4 knobs, BC, SW, 5 tubes, AC.........**$160.00-190.00**

155, table, 1933, wood, right front window dial, large center cloth grille with cut-outs, 2 knobs, BC, 5 tubes, AC/DC................**$85.00-105.00**

165Q, cathedral, 1933, wood, right front window dial, cloth grille with scrolled cut-outs, 3 knobs, BC, 5 tubes, battery **$240.00-270.00**

184, tombstone, 1935, two-tone wood, lower right front window dial, upper cloth grille with cut-outs, 3 knobs, BC, 4 tubes, AC **$180.00-200.00**

185, tombstone, 1934, wood, Deco, lower right front window dial, center cloth grille with right & left cut-outs, 3 knobs, BC, SW, 5 tubes, AC **$180.00-210.00**

185A, tombstone, 1934, wood, Deco, lower right front window dial, center cloth grille with right & left cut-outs, 3 knobs, BC, SW, 5 tubes, AC **$180.00-210.00**

188, console, 1932, wood, lowboy, upper front quarter-round dial, lower cloth grille with cut-outs, BC, 8 tubes, AC.................**$140.00-170.00**

217, table, 1933, wood, right front window dial, center grille with cut-outs, round top, 4 knobs, BC, SW, 7 tubes, AC **$380.00-430.00**

225, tombstone, 1932, wood, lower front round airplane dial, upper cloth grille with cut-outs, 3 knobs, BC, SW, 5 tubes, AC....**$160.00-190.00**

228, cathedral, 1932, wood, center front half-round dial, upper cloth grille with Gothic cut-outs, 3 knobs, BC, 8 tubes, AC **$410.00-430.00**

237Q, tombstone, 1935, wood, lower front round airplane dial, upper cloth grille with cut-outs, 4 knobs, BC, SW, 6 receiver tubes, 1 power unit, 6VDC...**$200.00-230.00**

246, table, 1933, two-tone wood, right front window dial, center grille with cut-outs, rounded top, 3 knobs, BC, 6 tubes, AC **$320.00-350.00**

260, console, 1932, wood, lowboy, upper quarter-round dial, lower cloth grille with cut-outs, 6 legs, 4 knobs, BC, 10 tubes, AC..**$150.00-180.00**

266, console, 1933, wood, small upper right window dial, lower cloth grille with cut-outs, 6 legs, 3 knobs, BC, 6 tubes, AC **$140.00-160.00**

286, console, 1935, wood, upper center airplane dial, lower grille with cut-outs, 4 knobs, BC, SW, 6 tubes, AC **$200.00-230.00**

84B, cathedral, 1931, wood, center front half-round dial with escutcheon, upper grille with cut-outs, 3 knobs, BC, 6 tubes, AC, $470.00-530.00.

165, cathedral, 1933, wood, right front window dial, cloth grille with scrolled cut-outs, 3 knobs, BC, 5 tubes, AC, $300.00-350.00.

206, cathedral, 1934, wood, lower front round dial, upper grille with cut-outs, fluted columns, 4 knobs, BC, SW, 6 tubes, AC, $380.00-430.00.

356, tombstone, 1935, wood, lower front round airplane dial, upper grille with cut-outs, fluting, 4 knobs, BC, SW, 6 tubes, AC, $270.00-300.00.

305, tombstone, 1935, wood, lower front round airplane dial, upper cloth grille with cut-outs, 4 knobs, BC, SW, 4 tubes, DC....**$130.00-160.00**

310, console, 1933, wood, upper front quarter-round dial, lower grille with scrolled cut-outs, 6 legs, 5 knobs, BC, SW, 10 tubes, AC **$240.00-270.00**

317, console, 1935, wood, upper front round dial, lower cloth grille with vertical bars, 4 knobs, BC, SW, 7 tubes, AC **$160.00-190.00**

318, console, 1934, wood, upper front quarter-round dial, lower grille with cut-outs, 5 knobs, BC, SW, 8 tubes, AC.........**$200.00-230.00**

318K, console, 1934, wood, upper front quarter-round dial, lower grille with cut-outs, 6 legs, 5 knobs, BC, SW, 8 tubes, AC ..**$200.00-230.00**

325E, console, 1934, wood, lowboy, upper front round dial, lower grille with cut-outs, 6 legs, 4 knobs, BC, SW, 5 tubes, AC ..**$180.00-200.00**

328, console, 1935, wood, upper front quarter-round dial, lower cloth grille with cut-outs, 5 knobs, BC, SW, 8 tubes, AC **$200.00-230.00**

337, tombstone, 1935, wood, lower front round airplane dial, upper grille with cut-outs, fluted columns, 4 knobs, BC, SW, 7 tubes, AC...**$240.00-300.00**

376, console, 1934, wood, lowboy, stretcher base, 6-legs, upper front round dial, lower cloth grille with cut-outs, 4 knobs, BC, SW, 6 tubes, AC **$130.00-160.00**

387, cathedral, 1934, wood, center front half-round dial, upper cloth grille with cut-outs, 3 knobs, BC, SW, 7 tubes, battery **$300.00-320.00**

427, console, 1933, wood, lowboy, small right front window dial, lower cloth grille with cut-outs, 6 legs, 4 knobs, BC, SW, 7 tubes, AC **$130.00-160.00**

427D, console, 1933, wood, lowboy, small right front window dial, lower cloth grille with cut-outs, 6 legs, 4 knobs, BC, SW, 7 tubes, DC **$130.00-160.00**

435, console, 1935, wood, upper front round airplane dial, lower cloth grille with cut-outs, 3 knobs, BC, SW, 5 tubes, AC **$160.00-190.00**

447, tombstone, 1934, wood, rounded shoulders, lower quarter-round dial, upper grille cut-outs, 5 knobs, BC, SW, 7 tubes, AC....**$270.00-300.00**

448, console, 1933, wood, lowboy, upper front quarter- round dial, lower cloth grille with cut-outs, 6 legs, 4 knobs, BC, 8 tubes, AC........**$240.00-280.00**

456, tombstone, 1936, wood, lower front round dial, upper cloth grille with cut-outs, 4 knobs, BC, SW, 6 tubes, AC **$270.00-300.00**

465Q, tombstone, 1934, wood, rounded top, lower round airplane dial, upper grille cut-outs, 4 knobs, BC, SW, 5 tubes, battery **$240.00-280.00**

469, console, 1932, walnut, lowboy, upper front quarter- round dial, lower grille cut-outs, 4 knobs, BC, 9 tubes, available in AC or DC or battery versions..**$170.00-200.00**

475, console, 1935, wood, upper front round airplane dial, lower cloth grille with cut-outs, 4 knobs, BC, SW, 5 tubes, AC....**$180.00-200.00**

485Q, console, 1936, wood, upper front round airplane dial, lower cloth grille with cut-outs, 3 knobs, BC, SW, 5 tubes, battery **$150.00-180.00**

487, console, 1935, wood, upper front quarter-round dial, lower grille with cut-outs, 5 knobs, BC, SW, 7 tubes, AC **$200.00-230.00**

509, console, 1935, wood, center front quarter-round dial, upper "tune-o-matic" clock, 5 knobs, BC, SW, 9 tubes, AC...............**$270.00-300.00**

509-W, console, 1935, wood, center front quarter-round dial, upper "tune-o-matic" clock, 5 knobs, BC, SW, 9 tubes, AC...........**$270.00-300.00**

510, console, 1933, wood, modern, upper front quarter-round dial, lower grille with cut-outs, 5 knobs, BC, SW, 10 tubes, AC..**$240.00-300.00**

511W, console, 1934, wood, center front quarter-round dial, upper "tune-o-matic" clock, 5 knobs, BC, SW, 11 tube, AC **$270.00-300.00**

521N, console, 1930, metal, upper left front dial, large lower center "caned" grille, legs, 2 knobs, BC, 7 tubes **$120.00-150.00**

535, console, 1936, wood, upper front round dial, lower cloth grille with center vertical bars, 3 knobs, BC, 5 tubes, AC **$150.00-180.00**

275, table, 1933, wood, right front window dial, center cloth grille with Deco cut-outs, 4 knobs, BC, SW, 5 tubes, AC/DC, $180.00-200.00.

480, console, 1932, wood, lowboy, stretcher base, top center dial, ornate top front border, lower cloth grille with cut-outs, 4 knobs, BC, SW, 10 tubes, AC, $260.00-290.00.

555, table, 1933, inlaid walnut, chest-style, lift top, inner metal panel, front grille with cut-outs, 2 knobs, BC, 5 tubes, AC, $410.00-430.00.

725, tombstone, 1936, wood, lower front round dial with globes, upper grille with cut-outs, 3 knobs, BC, SW, 5 tubes, AC, $160.00-190.00.

545, tombstone, 1935, wood, lower round airplane dial, upper grille with cut-outs, 3 knobs, BC, SW, 5 tubes, AC **$150.00-180.00**
558, cathedral, 1932, wood, center front half-round dial, upper cloth grille with cut-outs, 4 knobs, BC, 8 tubes, available in AC or DC or battery versions... **$410.00-460.00**
559N, console, 1934, wood, upper front quarter-round dial, lower cloth grille with cut-outs, 5 knobs, BC, SW, 9 tubes, AC....**$150.00-180.00**
567, cathedral, 1932, wood, center front half-round dial, upper grille with Gothic cut-outs, front carved columns, 3 knobs, BC, 7 tubes, AC **$410.00-460.00**
612, console, 1932, wood, lowboy, upper front quarter-round dial, lower cloth grille with cut-outs, 2 speakers, 4 knobs, BC, 12 tubes, AC...**$200.00-230.00**
637, tombstone, 1932, wood, lower front round multicolored dial, upper cloth grille with cut-outs, 4 knobs, BC, 7 tubes.........**$150.00-180.00**
649, console, 1935, wood, upper quarter-round dial, lower cloth grille with cut-outs, 5 knobs, BC, SW, 9 tubes, AC **$160.00-190.00**
667, console, 1933, wood, modern, upper front window dial, lower grille with cut-outs, 4 knobs, BC, SW, 7 tubes, AC **$240.00-270.00**
676, console, 1936, wood, upper round "rainbow" dial, lower cloth grille with vertical bars, 4 knobs, BC, 6 tubes, AC **$120.00-150.00**
708, table, 1933, wood, right front dial, cloth grille with cut-outs, rounded top, 4 knobs, BC, SW, 8 tubes, AC **$300.00-320.00**
711, console, 1933, wood, lowboy, inner quarter-round dial, double doors, 6 legs, 5 knobs, BC, SW, 11 tube, AC **$240.00-270.00**
735, cathedral, 1935, wood, lower front round airplane dial, upper cloth grille with cut-outs, fluted columns, 4 knobs, BC, SW, 5 tubes, AC **$300.00-350.00**
808, console, 1933, wood, upper front dial, lower cloth grille with cut-outs, 6 legs, 4 knobs, BC, SW, 8 tubes, AC **$240.00-270.00**
810, console, 1935, wood, upper front quarter-round dial, lower cloth grille with cut-outs, 5 knobs, BC, SW, 10 tubes, AC..**$200.00-230.00**

812, console, 1932, wood, lowboy, inner quarter-round dial, cloth grille with cut-outs, double sliding doors, 6 legs, BC, 12 tubes, AC ..**$200.00-230.00**
825, table, 1934, wood, right front window dial, center cloth grille with Deco cut-outs, 4 knobs, BC, SW, 5 tubes, AC/DC **$160.00-180.00**
854, tombstone, 1935, wood, small right front window dial, upper cloth grille with cut-outs, 3 knobs, BC, AC.........................**$180.00-200.00**
856, tombstone, 1935, wood, lower round airplane dial, upper grille with cut-outs, 4 knobs, BC, SW, 6 tubes, AC **$130.00-150.00**
976, console, 1935, wood, upper front round airplane dial, lower grille with cut-outs, 4 knobs, BC, SW, 6 tubes, AC **$140.00-160.00**

944, cathedral, 1934, two-tone wood, right front window dial, upper cloth grille with cut-outs, 2 knobs, BC, 4 tubes, AC, $300.00-350.00.

627, cathedral, 1932, wood, center front half-round dial, upper grille with cut-outs, front columns, 3 knobs, BC, 7 tubes, AC, $410.00-430.00.

AUDAR
Audar, Inc., Argos, Indiana

AV-7T, table-R/P, 1952, wood, inner dial, fold-down front door, lift top, inner phono, 5 knobs, BC, 7 tubes, AC **$30.00-35.00**
PR-6, table-R/P, 1947, inner dial, phono & knobs, lift top, outer grille, handle, 3 knobs, BC, 4 tubes, AC **$20.00-25.00**
PR-6A, table-R/P, 1947, inner dial, phono & knobs, lift top, outer grille, handle, BC, AC **$20.00-25.00**
RER-9 "Telvar," console-R/P/Rec, 1949, wood, vertical dial, left inner phono, sliding door, storage, 4 knobs, BC, 8 tubes, AC ..**$50.00-65.00**

AUDIOLA
Audiola Radio Co.
Chicago, Illinois

5W, table, 1933, wood, front dial, center grille with cut-outs, 2 knobs, BC, 5 tubes, AC/DC **$75.00-85.00**
22, table/stand, 1932, wood, highboy, short-wave converter table, half-round dial, 4 legs with criss-cross stretcher, 3 knobs, SW, 2 tubes, AC..**$120.00-150.00**

Jr, cathedral, 1931, wood, center front window dial, metal escutcheon, upper cloth grille with cut-outs, 3 knobs, BC, 5 tubes, AC, $220.00-260.00.

67-10AW, console, 1932, wood, lowboy, receiver with separate short-wave converter, one half round dial and one quarter round dial, six ornate legs, 6 knobs, BC, SW, 10 tubes, AC.............**$180.00-220.00**

517, cathedral, 1932, wood, ornate scrolled front, lower half-round dial, upper grille with cut-outs, BC, SW, 5 tubes, AC **$350.00-410.00**

610, cathedral, 1931, wood, center front quarter-round dial, upper grille with scrolled cut-outs, 3 knobs, BC, AC **$240.00-270.00**

612, console, 1931, wood, lowboy, upper front quarter-round dial, lower grille with scrolled cut-outs, BC, 6 tubes, AC **$150.00-180.00**

811, cathedral, 1932, wood, center front quarter-round dial, upper cloth grille, fluted columns, 3 knobs, BC, 8 tubes, AC **$220.00-260.00**

814, console, 1931, wood, lowboy, upper front quarter- round dial, lower cloth grille with scrolled cut-outs, stretcher base, 3 knobs, BC, 8 tubes, AC **$140.00-160.00**

1168, console, 1932, wood, lowboy, upper front half- round dial, lower cloth grille with cut-outs, 6 legs, BC, 11 tubes, AC.....**$160.00-190.00**

10300D, console, 1933, wood, lowboy, upper front half-round dial, lower cloth grille with cut-outs, 6 legs, BC, 10 tubes, AC....**$150.00-180.00**

Skyraider, tombstone, 1933, Deco, peaked top, cloth covered, lower front half-round dial, upper cloth grille with cut-outs, BC, 4 tubes **$350.00-410.00**

AUTOCRAT
Autocrat Radio Co.
3855 N. Hamilton Ave.
Chicago, Illinois

101, table, 1938, plastic, right front dial panel over horizontal grille bars, decorative case lines, 2 knobs, BC, 4 tubes, AC/DC **$65.00-75.00**

AUTOMATIC
Automatic Radio Mfg. Co., Inc.
122 Brookline Avenue
Boston, Massachusetts

The Automatic Radio Manufacturing Company began in 1920. The company is well known for its line of car radios and farm tractor sets as well as for their "Tom Thumb" line of home radios. The company is still in business as manufacturers of solid state products and test equipment.

8-15, table, 1937, plastic, Deco, right front square dial, left cloth grille with Deco cut-outs, step-down top, 2 knobs, BC, 5 tubes, AC/DC **$150.00-170.00**

141, table-R/P, 1941, wood, outer right front dial, left grille with diagonal bars, lift top, inner phono, 3 knobs, BC, AC **$30.00-40.00**

145, table-R/P, 1941, walnut, outer right front dial, left grille, lift top, inner phono, 3 knobs, BC, 6 tubes, AC **$30.00-40.00**

602, table, 1947, plastic, right front square dial, left vertical louvers, curved sides, 2 knobs, BC, 5 tubes, AC/DC, $65.00-75.00.

152, table-R/P, 1941, wood, right front dial, left grille with Deco bands, open top phono, 2 knobs, BC, 4 tubes, AC....................**$30.00-35.00**

219, table, plastic, Deco, right front square dial, left cloth grille with Deco cut-outs, 2 knobs, BC **$85.00-115.00**

434-A, table-R/P, 1940, walnut, center front square dial, right & left vertical grille bars, lift top, inner phono, BC, 5 tubes, AC......**$35.00-45.00**

458, table, 1939, wood, upper front rectangular dial, lower horizontal louvers, tapered cylindrical sides, 3 knobs, BC **$85.00-115.00**

601, table, 1947, plastic, right front square dial, left vertical louvers, curved sides, 2 knobs, BC, 5 tubes, AC/DC **$65.00-75.00**

612X, table, 1946, wood, right front round convex dial, "S" curve on top of case, 2 knobs, BC, 6 tubes, AC/DC **$85.00-105.00**

1975, table, 1935, wood, right front slide rule dial, left horizontal wrap-around louvers, 3 knobs, BC, SW, AC, $40.00-50.00.

613X, table, 1946, wood, right front round convex dial, "S" curve on top of case, 2 knobs, BC, 6 tubes, AC/DC **$85.00-105.00**

614X, table, 1946, plastic, right round starburst dial, left grille with concentric squares, 2 knobs, BC, 6 tubes, AC/DC **$65.00-75.00**

620, table, 1947, two-tone wood, upper front slanted slide rule dial, lower criss-cross grille, 2 knobs, BC, 6 tubes, AC/DC **$40.00-50.00**

640, table-R/P, 1946, wood, outer right square dial, criss-cross grille, lift top, inner phono, 3 knobs, BC, 5 tubes, AC **$30.00-35.00**

662, table, 1947, wood, upper front slanted slide rule dial, lower horizontal grille bars, 3 knobs, BC, SW, 6 tubes, AC/DC **$45.00-55.00**

CL-100, table-C, 1959, plastic, right front square dial, left alarm clock, center vertical wrap-over bars, 4 knobs, BC, 5 tubes, AC, $35.00-45.00.

P-64, portable, leatherette, front plastic panel, center round dial with inner perforations, handle, 2 knobs, BC, $40.00-50.00.

Tom Thumb Camera, portable-camera, 1948, leatherette, top reflex camera, lower horizontal grille bars, top rear slide rule dial, strap, 2 knobs, BC, 4 tubes, battery, $180.00-200.00.

677, table-R/P, 1947, wood, inner right dial, phono, lift top, wooden grille, 4 knobs, BC, 6 tubes, AC **$35.00-40.00**

720, table, 1947, wood, right front black dial, left criss-cross grille, rounded sides, 2 knobs, BC, 6 tubes, AC/DC **$45.00-55.00**

933 "Tom Thumb," table, 1939, Catalin, small case, right front dial, left grille with Deco cut-outs, various colors, 2 knobs, BC, 4 tubes, AC/DC ....**$2,000.00+**

955 "Tom Thumb," table, 1938, Catalin, small case, right front oval dial, left wrap-around cloth grille with center horizontal bars, feet, 2 knobs, BC, 4 tubes, AC/DC ....**$2,000.00+**

986, table, 1939, wood, right front dial, left cloth grille with vertical bars, 6 pushbuttons, 3 knobs, BC, SW, AC **$85.00-105.00**

ATTP "Tom Thumb," portable, 1947, leatherette & plastic, inner half-moon dial & grille, door, handle, 2 knobs, BC, 4 tubes, AC/DC/battery **$85.00-105.00**

B-44 "Tom Thumb," portable-bike, 1949, bike radio, left front vertical slide rule dial, right horizontal louvers, bottom mounting brackets, telescope antenna, handle, 2 knobs, BC, 4 tubes, battery ..**$85.00-115.00**

Bluebird, table, 1926, leatherette, low rectangular case, 2 dial black Bakelite front panel with bluebird decal, 3 knobs, BC, 1 tube, battery **$580.00-650.00**

C-51, portable, 1952, leatherette, center front round dial with inner perforations, handle, 2 knobs, BC, 5 tubes, AC/DC/battery .. **$35.00-45.00**

C-60, portable, 1946, luggage style, right front dial, left horizontal louvers, handle, 3 knobs, BC, 5 tubes, AC/DC/battery **$35.00-45.00**

C-60X, portable, 1947, two-tone leatherette, right front dial, left horizontal louvers, handle, 3 knobs, BC, 4 tubes, AC/DC/battery .. **$40.00-50.00**

C-65, portable, 1942, leatherette, right front dial, left horizontal louvers, handle, 3 knobs, BC, AC/DC/battery **$35.00-45.00**

CL-61, table-C, plastic, raised top, lower slide rule dial, large center front clock face, right/left horizontal wrap-around bars, feet, 5 knobs, BC, AC **$50.00-65.00**

CL-152B, table-C, 1953, plastic, right front square dial, center horizontal grille bars, left alarm clock, 5 knobs, BC, 5 tubes, AC ..**$30.00-40.00**

CL-175, table-C, wood, right front dial, left alarm clock, center lattice grille panel, 4 knobs, BC, AC.......................................**$30.00-40.00**

Companion Bed Lamp Radio, headboard, 1940, wood, right bottom vertical dial, built in lamp, attaches to head of bed, 3 knobs, BC, 5 tubes, AC **$190.00-230.00**

F-790, console-R/P, 1947, wood, modern, inner right half- round dial, left pull-out phono drawer, 4 knobs, BC, 9 tubes, AC.........**$65.00-85.00**

Tom Thumb Jr., table, 1933, Bakelite, Deco-black with chrome trim, left front dial, center grille, chrome ball feet, 2 knobs, BC, AC, $220.00-245.00.

P-72, portable, 1939, cloth covered, upper front dial, lower grille, handle, 2 knobs, BC, 5 tubes, AC/DC/battery...........................**$30.00-40.00**

Tom Boy, portable, 1947, two-tone leatherette, right front dial, left criss-cross grille, handle, 2 knobs, BC, 4 tubes, battery........**$35.00-45.00**

Tom Thumb Buddy, portable, 1949, leatherette & plastic, inner slide rule dial, vertical grille bars, flip-open front, handle, 2 knobs, BC, 4 tubes, AC/DC/battery **$65.00-75.00**

Tom Thumb Cathedral, cathedral-C, wood, center front quarter-round dial, upper cloth grille with cut-outs and center clock face, 3 knobs, BC, AC **$530.00-580.00**

Tom Thumb Jr., portable, 1947, "snakeskin," right front square dial, left horizontal grille bars, handle, 2 knobs, BC, 5 tubes, battery .. **$35.00-45.00**

Tom Thumb Portable, portable, 1929, leather case, inner engraved metal one dial panel, hinged front cover, handle, 3 knobs, BC, 4 tubes, battery **$350.00-410.00**

TT528, portable, 1957, plastic, right front dial, left lattice grille, handle, top right thumbwheel volume and right tuning knobs, BC, 4 tubes, battery **$180.00-200.00**

TT600, portable, 1957, plastic, right front dial, left checkered grille, handle, 2 transistors, 2 knobs, BC, 3 tubes, battery, $180.00-200.00.

AVIOLA
Aviola Radio Corp.
Phoenix, Arizona

509, table-R/P, 1946, wood, right front dial, left octagonal grille, feet, lift top, 3 knobs, BC, 5 tubes, AC.......................................**$25.00-30.00**

601, table, 1947, plastic, upper slanted slide rule dial, lower checkerboard grille, 2 knobs, BC, 6 tubes, AC/DC **$50.00-65.00**

608, table-R/P, 1947, wood, inner right slide rule dial, phono, lift top, criss-cross grille, 3 knobs, BC, 6 tubes, AC **$35.00-40.00**

612, table, 1947, wood, upper slanted slide rule dial, lower horizontal louvers, 2 knobs, BC, AC/DC **$40.00-50.00**

AZTEC
The Fred W. Stein Radio Company
Atchison, Kansas

Model unknown, cathedral, 1931, wood, right front window dial, metal escutcheon, upper cloth grille with lyre cut-out, thumb-wheel dial knob plus on/off volume knob, BC, 8 tubes, AC, $320.00-360.00.

Model unknown, cathedral, 1931, wood, "gambrel roof" top, front corner "bedposts," scalloped bottom, center window dial, upper grille with "fleur-di-lis" cut-out, 3 knobs, BC, 9 tubes, AC **$400.00-450.00**

B. F. GOODRICH
B. F. Goodrich Co., Akron, Ohio

92-523, table, 1951, plastic, right front round dial over rectangular grille bars, 2 knobs, BC, 5 tubes, AC/DC **$35.00-45.00**

BALDWIN
Nathaniel Baldwin, Inc.

50 "Baldwinette," tombstone, 1930, wood, arched top, left front window dial, upper scalloped grille with cut-outs, BC, AC......**$180.00-200.00**

BALKEIT
Balkeit Radio Corporation
Clinton & Randolph Streets, Chicago, Illinois

The Balkeit Radio Company was formed as subsidiary of the Pfanstiehl Radio Company in 1929.

C, console, 1929, wood, inner front window dial, upper cloth grille with scalloped cut-outs, double doors, 2 knobs, BC, 9 tubes, AC, $200.00-230.00.

44, table, 1933, two-tone case, center front grille with vertical cut-outs, BC, 4 tubes, battery $75.00-85.00
A-3, table, 1928, metal, low rectangular case, center front slanted thumb-wheel dial, BC, 8 tubes, AC...........................**$140.00-160.00**
A-5, table, 1928, wood, low rectangular case, center front slanted thumb-wheel dial, BC, 8 tubes, AC...........................**$150.00-180.00**
A-7, console, 1928, wood, highboy, inner slanted thumb wheel dial, lower grille, double front doors, BC, 7 tubes, AC **$180.00-200.00**
B-7, console, 1928, wood, inner slanted thumbwheel dial, upper speaker grille with cut-outs, double front doors, BC, 9 tubes, AC **$270.00-300.00**
B-9, console-R/P, 1928, wood, inner front thumbwheel dial, speaker grille with cut-outs, double doors, lift top, inner phono, BC, 9 tubes, AC **$200.00-230.00**

BARBAROSSA

Beer Bottle, table-N, 1934, Bakelite, looks like large Barbarossa beer bottle, base with switch, BC, AC, $350.00-410.00.

BELLETONE

125-P, table, plastic, upper front slide rule dial, lower horizontal wrap-around grille bars, 2 knobs, BC, AC **$55.00-65.00**

BELLTONE
Jewel Radio Corp.
583 Sixth Avenue, New York, New York

500, table, 1946, wood, upper slanted slide rule dial, lower horizontal grille bars, 2 knobs, BC, AC/DC **$40.00-50.00**

BELMONT
Belmont Radio Corp.
5921 West Dickens Avenue
Chicago, Illinois

4B17, table, 1946, wood, lower front slide rule dial, upper vertical grille openings, 2 knobs, BC, 4 tubes, battery $30.00-35.00
4B112, table, 1946, plastic, right front dial, left horizontal wrap-around louvers, 2 knobs, BC, 4 tubes, battery $40.00-50.00
4B115, table, 1948, plastic, rounded top, front half- round dial curves over checkered grille, 2 knobs, BC, 4 tubes, battery .. $85.00-115.00
5D110, table-R/P, 1947, wood, lower front slide rule dial, upper cloth grille, 3/4 lift top, inner phono, 2 knobs, BC, 5 tubes, AC $30.00-35.00
5D118, table, 1948, plastic, center front airplane dial inside concentric circular grille, 2 knobs, 5 tubes, AC/DC.....................**$110.00-130.00**
5D128, table, 1946, plastic, streamline, right front slide rule dial, left horizontal bars, 5 pushbuttons, 1 front and 1 right side knob, BC, 5 tubes, AC/DC..**$180.00-200.00**

5D137, table, 1947, plastic, Deco, right front dial, left round grille with lower horizontal bars, 4 pushbuttons, 1 front and 1 right side knob, BC, 5 tubes **$180.00-200.00**

5P19, portable, 1946, luggage-style, upper front slide rule dial, lower grille area, handle, 2 knobs, BC, 5 tubes, AC/DC/battery **$30.00-35.00**

5P113 "Boulevard," portable, 1947, very small case, dial on top of case, earphone only, 2 knobs, BC, 5 tubes, battery **$240.00-270.00**

6D120, table, 1947, plastic, streamline, right front half-round dial, left horizontal wrap-around louvers, 6 pushbuttons, 1 front and 1 right side knob, BC, 6 tubes, AC/DC..**$150.00-180.00**

8A59, console-R/P, 1946, wood, inner right slide rule dial, pushbuttons, left pull-out phono drawer, 4 knobs, BC, SW, 8 tubes, AC **$65.00-75.00**

407, portable, 1939, striped cloth, luggage-style, top dial & knobs, front grille, handle, BC, 4 tubes, battery **$30.00-35.00**

425, table, 1933, metal, front center grille with diagonal bars, dial "knob," decorative lines, 2 knobs, BC, 4 tubes, AC/DC.............**$60.00-70.00**

507, portable, C1938, cloth covered, right front dial, left grille area, handle, 2 knobs, BC, 6 tubes, AC/DC/battery **$30.00-35.00**

509, table, 1940, wood, lower front slide rule dial, upper grille with vertical bars, pushbuttons, BC, SW, 5 tubes, battery................**$75.00-85.00**

510, table, 1938, plastic, streamline, right front dial, left horizontal wrap-around louvers, 2 knobs, BC, 5 tubes, AC/DC **$85.00-95.00**

519, table, 1939, plastic, streamline, right front dial, left circular grille with horizontal bars, 6 pushbuttons, 1 front and 1 right side knob, BC, 5 tubes, AC/DC...**$180.00-200.00**

522, table, 1936, wood, right front round dial, left cloth grille with Deco cut-outs, 2 knobs, BC, 5 tubes, battery **$45.00-55.00**

525, table, 1933, wood, Deco case lines, right front dial, center cloth grille with cut-outs, 2 knobs, BC, 5 tubes, AC/DC.................**$85.00-95.00**

526, table, 1938, plastic, Deco, right front "Bel- Monitor" tuning system, left vertical grille bars, BC, 5 tubes, AC **$95.00-115.00**

533-D, table-R/P, 1941, wood, right front square dial, left grille, lift top, inner phono, 2 knobs, BC, 5 tubes, AC **$30.00-35.00**

534, table, 1940, plastic, streamline, right front slide rule dial, left horizontal louvers, pushbuttons, 1 front and 1 right side knob, BC, 5 tubes, AC/DC **$150.00-180.00**

571, table-C, 1940, walnut, lower front slide rule dial, upper electric clock face, ribbed sides, 2 knobs, BC, 5 tubes, AC **$55.00-65.00**

575, tombstone, 1934, wood, shouldered, center front round dial, upper cloth grille with cut-outs, BC, 5 tubes, AC.................**$110.00-130.00**

602 "Scotty," table, 1937, plastic, raised right top, right front dial, left vertical wrap-over grille bars, 2 knobs, BC, 6 tubes, AC/DC ..**$85.00-95.00**

636, table, 1939, plastic, right front dial, left wrap-around louvers, 5 pushbuttons, 1 front and 1 right side knob, BC, 6 tubes, AC/DC ..**$95.00-115.00**

675, tombstone, 1934, wood, center front round dial, upper cloth grille with cut-outs, BC, SW, 6 tubes, AC **$120.00-140.00**

675E, console, 1934, two-tone wood, upper front round dial, lower cloth grille with cut-outs, BC, SW, 6 tubes, AC **$120.00-140.00**

686, table, 1936, wood, right front oval dial, left/right cloth grille areas, 3 knobs, BC, SW, 6 tubes, AC **$55.00-65.00**

770, console, 1936, wood, upper front oval dial, lower cloth grille with vertical bars, 4 knobs, BC, 7 tubes **$120.00-150.00**

777, tombstone, 1935, wood, lower front round airplane dial, upper cloth grille with cut-outs, 4 knobs, BC, 7 tubes, AC............**$120.00-140.00**

778A, table, 1936, wood, right front oval dial, left cloth grille with cut-outs, 4 knobs, BC, SW, 7 tubes, AC **$75.00-85.00**

401, cathedral, 1935, two-tone wood, lower front round airplane dial, upper grille with cut-outs, 3 knobs, BC, 4 tubes, AC, $240.00-270.00.

787, console, 1936, wood, upper front oval dial, lower recessed "speaker tone chamber," tuning eye, 4 knobs, BC, SW, 7 tubes, AC **$140.00-160.00**

792, console, 1939, wood, upper front rectangular dial, lower grille area, pushbuttons, 4 knobs, BC, SW, 6 tubes, AC **$85.00-115.00**

797, console-R/P/Rec, 1940, wood, inner right rectangular dial, pushbuttons, left phono, lift top, BC, SW, 7 tubes, AC **$85.00-115.00**

840, console, 1937, wood, upper front oval dial, tuning eye, lower grille with vertical bars, 4 knobs, BC, SW, 8 tubes, AC **$160.00-180.00**

878, console, 1936, wood, upper front oval dial, lower recessed "speaker tone chamber," rounded top front, tuning eye, 4 knobs, BC, SW, 8 tubes, AC **$140.00-160.00**

1070, console, 1935, wood, upper front oval dial, lower cloth grille with vertical bars, 4 knobs, BC, SW, 10 tubes, AC...........**$150.00-180.00**

1170, console, 1936, wood, upper front oval dial, tuning eye, lower cloth grille with vertical bars, 4 knobs, BC, SW, 11 tubes, AC **$150.00-180.00**

A-6D110, table, 1947, plastic, right front slide rule dial, left vertical grille bars, 6 pushbuttons, 1 front and 1 right side knob, BC, 6 tubes, AC/DC **$85.00-115.00**

C640, table, 1946, plastic, streamlined, right front half- round dial, left horizontal grille bars, 6 pushbuttons, 1 front and 1 right side knob, BC, AC **$150.00-180.00**

BENDIX
Bendix Radio/Bendix Aviation
Baltimore, Maryland

The company began in 1937 as a division of Bendix Aviation. During World War II, Bendix was a major supplier of radio-related aircraft equipment for the British and American governments.

6D111, table, 1946, plastic, streamlined, right front half-round dial, left horizontal grille bars, 6 pushbuttons, 1 front and 1 right side knob, BC, 6 tubes, AC/DC, $150.00-180.00.

55L3U, table, plastic, upper front slide rule dial, lower metal perforated grille, rear hand-hold, 2 knobs, BC, 5 tubes, AC/DC, $45.00-55.00.

75P6U, table, 1949, walnut plastic, upper front slide rule dial, lower wood-grained grille, rear hand-hold, 3 knobs, BC, FM, 6 tubes, AC/DC, $45.00-55.00.

55L2, table, 1949, ivory plastic, upper front slide rule dial, lower vertical grille bars, rear hand-hold, 2 knobs, BC, 5 tubes, AC/DC **$45.00-55.00**

55L3, table, 1949, ivory plastic, upper front slide rule dial, lower wood-grained grille, rear hand-hold, 2 knobs, BC, 5 tubes, AC/DC **$45.00-55.00**

55P2, table, 1949, walnut plastic, upper front slide rule dial, lower vertical grille bars, rear hand-hold, 2 knobs, BC, 5 tubes, AC/DC ..**$40.00-50.00**

55P3, table, 1949, walnut plastic, upper front slide rule dial, lower wood-grained grille, rear hand-hold, 2 knobs, BC, 5 tubes, AC/DC **$45.00-55.00**

55P3U, table, 1949, walnut plastic, upper front slide rule dial, lower wood-grained grille, rear hand-hold, 2 knobs, BC, 5 tubes, AC/DC **$45.00-55.00**

55X4, portable, 1949, plastic, inner slide rule dial, horizontal louvers, flip-up front, 2 knobs, BC, 5 tubes, AC/DC/battery **$40.00-50.00**

65P4, table, 1949, plastic, upper front slide rule dial, lower metal grille, rear hand-hold, 3 knobs, BC, 6 tubes, AC/DC **$40.00-50.00**

65P4U, table, 1949, plastic, upper front slide rule dial, lower metal grille, rear hand-hold, 3 knobs, BC, 6 tubes, AC/DC..............**$40.00-50.00**

69B8, console-R/P, 1949, blonde wood, inner right radio/phono, left storage, double front doors, 3 knobs, BC, FM, 6 tubes, AC..**$65.00-75.00**

69M8, console-R/P, 1949, mahogany, inner right radio/phono, left storage, double front doors, 3 knobs, BC, FM, 6 tubes, AC..**$65.00-75.00**

69M9, console-R/P, 1949, wood, inner right slide rule dial, pull-out phono, door, 3 knobs, BC, FM, 6 tubes, AC **$65.00-75.00**

75B5 "Fairfax," console-R/P, 1949, blonde wood, top left dial & knobs, right front pull-out phono drawer, storage, 3 knobs, BC, FM, 6 tubes, AC **$65.00-75.00**

75M8 "Heritage," console-R/P, 1949, mahogany, upper front dial and knobs, inner pull-out phono drawer & storage, door, 3 knobs, BC, FM, 6 tubes, AC **$75.00-85.00**

75P6, table, 1949, walnut plastic, upper front slide rule dial, lower wood-grained grille, rear hand-hold, 3 knobs, BC, FM, 6 tubes, AC/DC **$45.00-55.00**

75W5 "York," console-R/P, 1949, walnut wood, top left dial, right front pull-out phono drawer, 3 top knobs, BC, FM, 6 tubes, AC **$65.00-75.00**

110, table, 1948, walnut plastic, upper front slide rule dial, lower vertical grille bars, rear hand-hold, 2 knobs, BC, 5 tubes, AC/DC, $50.00-65.00.

79M7, console-R/P, 1949, wood, inner right slide rule dial, lower pull-out phono, door, 3 knobs, BC, FM, 7 tubes, AC **$65.00-75.00**

95B3 "Boulevard," console-R/P, 1949, blonde wood, right tilt-out radio, left pull-out phono drawer, 3 knobs, BC, FM, 9 tubes, AC **$75.00-85.00**

95M3 "Wiltondale," console-R/P, 1949, mahogany, right tilt-out radio, left pull-out phono drawer, 3 knobs, BC, FM, 9 tubes, AC **$75.00-85.00**

95M9 "Wayne," console-R/P, 1949, mahogany, right tilt-out radio, left pull-out phono drawer, 3 knobs, BC, FM, 9 tubes, AC ..**$75.00-85.00**

110W, table, 1948, ivory plastic, upper front slide rule dial, lower vertical grille bars, rear hand-hold, 2 knobs, BC, 5 tubes, AC/DC ..**$50.00-65.00**

111, table, 1949, walnut plastic, upper front slide rule dial, lower vertical grille bars, rear hand-hold, 2 knobs, BC, 5 tubes, AC/DC **$50.00-65.00**

111W, table, 1949, ivory plastic, upper front slide rule dial, lower vertical grille bars, rear hand-hold, 2 knobs, BC, 5 tubes, AC/DC ..**$50.00-65.00**

112, table, 1948, walnut, upper front slide rule dial, large lower perforated grille area, 2 knobs, BC, 5 tubes, AC/DC **$40.00-50.00**

114, table, 1948, tan & brown plastic, upper front slide rule dial, lower horizontal wrap-around grille bars, 2 knobs, BC, 5 tubes, AC/DC **$300.00-320.00**

115, table, 1948, ivory & burgundy plastic, upper front slide rule dial, lower horizontal wrap-around grille bars, 2 knobs, BC, 5 tubes, AC/DC, $300.00-320.00.

300, table, 1948, brown plastic, upper front slanted slide rule dial, lower vertical grille bars, 3 knobs, BC, 6 tubes, AC/DC **$40.00-50.00**

300W, table, 1948, ivory plastic, upper front slanted slide rule dial, lower vertical grille bars, 3 knobs, BC, 6 tubes, AC/DC **$40.00-50.00**

301, table, 1948, wood, upper front slanted slide rule dial, lower horizontal grille bars, 3 knobs, BC, 6 tubes, AC/DC **$35.00-45.00**

302, table, 1948, wood, upper front slanted slide rule dial, lower horizontal grille bars, 3 knobs, BC, 6 tubes, AC/DC **$35.00-45.00**

416A, table, 1948, wood, upper front slide rule dial, lower horizontal louvers, small base, 2 knobs, BC, 4 tubes, battery **$35.00-45.00**

516A, table, 1946, plastic, Deco case, upper front slide rule dial, lower vertical louvers, 2 knobs, BC, AC/DC **$65.00-75.00**

526A, table, 1946, plastic, Deco case, upper front slide rule dial, lower vertical louvers, 2 knobs, BC, 5 tubes, AC/DC **$65.00-75.00**

526B, table, 1946, plastic, Deco case, upper front slide rule dial, lower vertical louvers, 2 knobs, BC, 5 tubes, AC/DC **$65.00-75.00**

526D, table, 1946, plastic, Deco case, upper front slide rule dial, lower vertical louvers, 2 knobs, BC, 5 tubes, AC/DC **$65.00-75.00**

526MB, table, 1947, plastic, Deco case, upper front slide rule dial, lower vertical grille bars, 2 knobs, BC, 5 tubes, AC/DC **$50.00-65.00**

613, table-R/P, 1948, wood, outer slide rule dial over large grille area, lift top, inner phono, 4 knobs, BC, 5 tubes, AC **$30.00-35.00**

626-A, table, 1947, plastic, upper front slanted slide rule dial, lower vertical louvers, rear hand-hold, 3 knobs, BC, SW, 6 tubes, AC/DC..**$50.00-65.00**

626-C, table, 1947, plastic, upper front slanted slide rule dial, lower vertical louvers, rear hand-hold, 3 knobs, BC, SW, 6 tubes, AC/DC **$50.00-65.00**

636A, table, 1947, plastic, upper front slanted slide rule dial, lower vertical louvers, 3 knobs, BC, 6 tubes, AC/DC......................**$40.00-50.00**

636B, table, 1947, wood, upper front slanted slide rule dial, lower woven grille, 3 knobs, BC, 6 tubes, AC/DC **$65.00-75.00**

636C, table, 1947, wood, upper front slanted slide rule dial, lower woven grille, 3 knobs, BC, 6 tubes, AC/DC **$65.00-75.00**

526C, table, 1946, Catalin, green & black, upper front slide rule dial, lower horizontal louvers, 2 knobs, BC, 5 tubes, AC/DC, $650.00+.

656A, table-R/P, 1946, wood, inner right dial, left phono, lift top, outer louvers, 3 knobs, BC, 6 tubes, AC, $30.00-35.00.

636D, table, 1947, wood, upper front slanted slide rule dial, lower woven metal grille, 3 knobs, BC, 6 tubes, AC $65.00-75.00
646A, end table, 1946, wood, drop leaf end table, dial lights up across lower panel, 4 knobs, BC, 6 tubes, AC/DC $120.00-150.00
676D, console-R/P, 1946, wood, inner right vertical slide rule dial, left phono, lift top, front grille, 4 knobs, BC, SW, 6 tubes, AC $65.00-75.00
687A, portable, 1949, leatherette, inner slide rule dial, vertical grille bars, fold-down front, handle, 4 knobs, BC, 6 tubes, AC/DC/battery $35.00-45.00
697A, end table-R/P, 1947, wood, step-down end table, radio in top, phono in base with sliding door, 4 knobs, BC, 6 tubes, AC $120.00-150.00
736-B, console-R/P, 1946, wood, inner right vertical dial, left phono, lift top, 4 knobs, BC, SW, 7 tubes, AC $75.00-85.00
753F, table-C, 1953, cherry wood, lower slide rule dial, large front alarm clock, side louvers, handle, feet, 5 knobs, BC, 5 tubes, AC $65.00-75.00
753W, table-C, 1953, blonde wood, lower slide rule dial, large front alarm clock face, handle, feet, 5 knobs, BC, 5 tubes, AC $65.00-75.00
847-B, console-R/P, 1947, wood, inner right dial, pushbuttons, left phono, lift top, 4 knobs, BC, FM, 8 tubes, AC................$75.00-85.00
1217B, console-R/P, 1947, wood, inner right dial, push buttons, lift top, front pull-out phono drawer, BC, SW, FM, 12 tubes, AC..$65.00-75.00
1217D, console-R/P, 1948, wood, inner right slide rule dial, lift top, left front pull-out phono, oval grille, BC, SW, FM, 14 tubes, AC $65.00-75.00
1518, console-R/P, 1948, mahogany, inner dial, pushbuttons, lift-up lid, left pull-out phono, BC, FM, 8 tubes, AC $65.00-75.00
1519, console-R/P, 1948, walnut, inner dial, pushbuttons, lift-up lid, left pull-out phono, BC, FM, 8 tubes, AC $65.00-75.00
1521, console-R/P, 1948, wood, inner right slide rule dial, door, lift top, inner phono, 4 knobs, BC, FM, 8 tubes, AC $75.00-85.00
1524, console-R/P, 1948, mahogany, inner right dial, pushbuttons, lift-up lid, left pull-out phono, BC, FM, 10 tubes, AC...............$65.00-75.00
1525, console-R/P, 1948, walnut, inner dial, pushbuttons, lift-up lid, left pull-out phono, BC, FM, 10 tubes, AC $65.00-75.00
PAR-80, portable, 1948, luggage style, inner slide rule dial, vertical grille bars, fold-down front, handle, 4 knobs, BC, SW, LW, 6 tubes, AC/DC/battery $35.00-45.00

PAR-80A, portable, 1948, luggage style, inner slide rule dial, vertical grille bars, fold-down front, handle, LW, 4 knobs, BC, SW, LW, 6 tubes, AC/DC/battery $35.00-45.00

753M, table-C, 1953, mahogany wood, lower slide rule dial, large front alarm clock face, handle, feet, 5 knobs, BC, 5 tubes, AC, $65.00-75.00.

BENRUS
Benrus Watch Co., Inc.
50 West 44th Street, New York, New York

526E, table, 1946, wood, upper front slanted slide rule dial, lower vertical grille bars, rounded sides, 2 knobs, BC, 5 tubes, AC/DC, $50.00-65.00.

10B01B15B, table-C, 1955, metal, large front clock face, right side dial knob, left side on/off/volume knob, BC, 5 tubes, AC, $50.00-65.00.

BEST

221, table, 1936, wood, rounded right side, right front oval dial, left grille with chrome wrap-around bars, 3 knobs, BC, $110.00-130.00.

BETTS & BETTS
**Betts & Betts Corp.
643 W. 43rd St., New York, New York**

T8 "Trans-Continental," table, 1925, wood, high rectangular case, 2 dial front panel, BC, 8 tubes, battery................................ **$240.00-270.00**

BOSWORTH
The Bosworth Mfg. Co., Cincinnati, Ohio

B-2, table, 1926, wood, rectangular case, 2 dial fancy slanted metal panel, lift top, 4 knobs, BC, 5 tubes, battery **$180.00-200.00**

BOWMAN
**A. W. Bowman & Co.
Cambridge, Massachusetts**

Airophone, table, 1923, wood, low rectangular case, 2 dial black Bakelite front panel, 4 knobs, BC, battery, $240.00-270.00.

BRADFORD
**The W.T. Grant Company
1441 Broadway, New York, New York**

96628, table-C, 1963, plastic, front off-center alarm clock face, left random-patterned grille area, 1 top and one front knob, BC, 5 tubes, AC **$25.00-30.00**
96636, table-C, 1962, plastic, right front dial over horizontal bars, left alarm clock face, 2 knobs, BC, 5 tubes, AC **$20.00-25.00**
96651, table, 1962, plastic, lower right front dial panel over large patterned grille area, feet, 3 knobs, BC, FM, 6 tubes, AC/DC.........**$20.00-25.00**

BRANDES
**J. F. Brandes Corp.
35½ Oxford St., Newark, New Jersey**

B10, table, 1929, wood, low rectangular case, center front window dial with escutcheon, 3 knobs, BC, 7 tubes, AC **$140.00-160.00**

B15, console, 1929, wood, upper front window dial with escutcheon, lower cloth grille with cut-outs, 3 knobs, BC, 8 tubes, AC **$150.00-180.00**
Brandola, table, 1925, wood, low rectangular case, one center front dial, storage, BC, 6 tubes, battery **$180.00-210.00**

BREMER-TULLY
**Bremer-Tully Manufacturing Company
520 South Canal Street, Chicago, Illinois**

Bremer-Tully was begun in 1922 by John Tully and Harry Bremer. The company started in business manufacturing radio parts and kits and by 1925 they were selling fully assembled radios. The company was sold to Brunswick in 1928.

81, console, 1929, wood, highboy, center front dial, upper grille with oval cut-out, stretcher base, 3 knobs, BC, 8 tubes, AC, $150.00-180.00.

6-22 "Counterphase," table, 1927, two-tone wood, rectangular case, center front dial with escutcheon, BC, battery **$120.00-150.00**
6-35 "Counterphase," table, 1927, wood, rectangular case with slant front, 2 center front dials with escutcheon, BC, 6 tubes, battery...**$140.00-160.00**
6-37 "Counterphase," console, 1927, wood, lowboy, 2 inner front dials with escutcheon, fold-down front, 4 knobs, BC, 6 tubes, battery **$160.00-190.00**
6-40C, console, 1928, wood, lowboy, upper front dial with escutcheon, lower cloth grille with cut-outs, 2 knobs, BC, 7 tubes, AC **$160.00-190.00**
6-40R, table, 1928, wood, low rectangular case, center front dial with escutcheon, right & left decorative emblems, BC, 7 tubes, AC **$130.00-150.00**
6-40S, table, 1928, wood, low rectangular case, center front dial with escutcheon, right & left decorative emblems, BC, 7 tubes, AC **$130.00-150.00**
7-70, table, 1928, wood, low rectangular case, recessed center front dial with escutcheon, BC, 8 tubes, AC............................**$140.00-160.00**
7-71, console, 1928, wood, highboy, center front dial with escutcheon, upper grille with cut-outs, BC, 8 tubes, AC **$180.00-200.00**
8 "Counterphase," table, 1926, wood, rectangular case with slant front, center dial with escutcheon, lift top, BC, 7 tubes, battery **$140.00-160.00**
8-12 "Counterphase," table, 1927, wood, rectangular case with slant front, center dial with escutcheon, lift top, BC, 7 tubes, battery.. **$140.00-160.00**
8-20, table, 1928, wood, low rectangular case, recessed center front dial with escutcheon, lift top, BC, 9 tubes, AC.................**$140.00-160.00**
8-21, console, 1928, wood, upper front dial, lower cloth grille with cut-outs, BC, 9 tubes, AC **$120.00-160.00**
80, console, 1929, wood, upper front window dial, lower grille with cut-outs, 3 knobs, BC, 6 tubes, AC **$120.00-150.00**
82, console, 1929, walnut, highboy, center front dial, upper grille with cut-outs, double doors, 3 knobs, BC, 8 tubes, AC **$180.00-200.00**

BREWSTER
Meissner Mfg. Div.
Maguire Industries, Inc., Mt. Carmel, Illinois

9-1084, table, 1946, plastic, recessed right, slide rule dial, left horizontal bars, step-down top, 3 knobs, BC, SW, 6 tubes, AC/DC, $55.00-65.00.

9-1086, table, 1946, plastic, recessed right, slide rule dial, left horizontal bars, step-down top, 3 knobs, BC, SW, 6 tubes, AC/DC ..**$55.00-65.00**

BROWNING-DRAKE
Browning-Drake Corporation
353 Washington Street
Brighton, Massachusetts

Frederick Drake and Glenn Browning created the Browning-Drake circuit in 1924. In 1925 their Browning-Drake Company was selling fully assembled radios. Their business slowly decreased until the partners went their separate ways in 1937.

5-R, table, 1926, wood, low rectangular case, 2 dial black front panel, lift top, BC, 5 tubes, battery.. **$150.00-180.00**
6-A, table, 1927, wood, low rectangular case, inner front dial, double front doors, lift top, 5 knobs, BC, 6 tubes, battery **$110.00-130.00**
7-A, table, 1927, walnut, low rectangular case, inner dial & knobs, double front doors, lift top, BC, 7 tubes, battery **$120.00-140.00**
30, table, 1928, wood, low rectangular case, center front dial, 3 knobs, BC, AC **$140.00-160.00**
32, console, 1928, wood, lowboy, upper front dial, lower cloth grille with Gothic cut-outs, 3 knobs, BC, AC **$200.00-230.00**
34, table, 1928, wood, low rectangular case, center front window dial with escutcheon, 3 knobs, BC, 8 tubes, AC **$120.00-150.00**
53, table, 1929, wood, low rectangular case, center window dial with escutcheon, 3 knobs, BC, 9 tubes, AC **$120.00-140.00**
54, console, 1929, wood, lowboy, upper front window dial with escutcheon, lower round grille with cut-outs, 3 knobs, BC, 9 tubes, AC **$150.00-180.00**
56, console, 1929, wood, lowboy, upper front window dial with escutcheon, lower decorative grille with cut-outs, stretcher base, 3 knobs, BC, 9 tubes, AC **$150.00-180.00**

4-R, table, wood, low rectangular case, 2 dial black front panel, lift top, BC, 4 tubes, battery, $140.00-160.00.

57, console, 1929, wood, upper front window dial with escutcheon, lower scalloped grille with cut-outs, 3 knobs, BC, 9 tubes, AC..**$150.00-180.00**
84, console, 1929, wood, lowboy, upper front window dial, lower round grille with cut-outs, 3 knobs, BC, 7 tubes, battery **$85.00-115.00**
B-D "Junior," table, 1925, wood, low rectangular case, 2 dial front panel, lift top, 6 knobs, BC, 5 tubes, battery **$120.00-140.00**
B-D "Senior," table, 1925, wood, lower radio with 2 dial front panel, upper speaker with scroll grille, BC, 6 tubes, battery........... **$200.00-230.00**
B-D "Standard," table, 1925, mahogany, low rectangular case, 2 dial front panel, lift top, 6 knobs, BC, 5 tubes, battery **$150.00-180.00**
Regenaformer, table, wood, low rectangular case, 2 dial front panel, lift top, battery **$150.00-180.00**

28, table, 1928, wood, low rectangular case, center front window dial, large metal escutcheon with emblem and model, 5 knobs, BC, 5 tubes, battery, $120.00-140.00.

BRUNSWICK

The "Brunswick" name was utilized by a succession of companies including the Brunswick-Balke-Collender Co., the Brunswick Radio Corporation, Mershman Brothers Corp., and Radio & Television, Inc.

5KR, table, 1928, wood, low rectangular case, center front dial with escutcheon, lift top, 2 knobs, BC, 7 tubes, AC, $120.00-140.00.

5-WO, table, 1928, wood, low rectangular case, center window dial with escutcheon, lift top, 2 knobs, BC, 9 tubes, AC **$120.00-150.00**
11, tombstone, 1931, wood, shouldered case, center front window dial, upper grille with cut-outs, BC, 7 tubes, AC **$200.00-230.00**
14, console, 1929, wood, upper front dial, lower grille with cut-outs, stretcher base, 3 knobs, BC, 9 tubes, AC or DC models **$140.00-170.00**
15, console, 1930, wood, upper front window dial, lower scalloped grille, stretcher base, 2 knobs, BC, 7 tubes, AC **$140.00-170.00**
16, console, 1931, wood, lowboy, upper front window dial, lower cloth grille with cut-outs, BC, 7 tubes, AC **$120.00-150.00**
21, console, 1929, wood, highboy, inner front dial & knobs, double doors, stretcher base, BC, 9 tubes, AC or DC models **$150.00-180.00**
22, console, 1930, wood, inner front dial & knobs, double doors, stretcher base, BC, 7 tubes, AC **$160.00-190.00**
31, console-R/P, 1929, wood, inner front dial & knobs, double doors, phono, arched stretcher base, BC, 9 tubes, AC or DC models **$160.00-190.00**
33, console-R/P, 1931, wood, upper front dial, lower grille with cut-outs, lift top, inner phono, BC, 7 tubes, AC **$130.00-160.00**
50, console, wood, upper front window dial, lower tapestry grille with cut-outs, right & left medallions, 2 knobs........................**$150.00-180.00**

1580, table, wood, rectangular case, inner right dial, left grille with cut-outs, double doors, 2 knobs, $65.00-85.00.

1559, side table, 1939, wood, French Provincial styling, inner right dial/left grille, double front doors, 3 knobs, BC, 5 tubes, AC/DC **$130.00-160.00**

1669, side table, 1939, wood, Hepplewhite styling, inner right dial/left grill/pushbuttons, double front doors, 4 knobs, BC, SW, 6 tubes, AC **$150.00-180.00**

2559, side table, 1939, wood, Early American styling, inner right dial/ left grille, double front doors, 3 knobs, BC, 5 tubes, AC/DC...........**$110.00-130.00**

2689, side table, 1939, wood, Duncan Phyfe styling, inner dial/tuning eye/pushbuttons, double doors, 4 knobs, BC, SW, 6 tubes, AC **$180.00-200.00**

3689, side table, 1938, wood, French styling, half-round table, front dial, pushbuttons, BC, SW, 6 tubes, AC **$150.00-180.00**

4689, console, 1939, wood, Queen Anne styling, inner dial/tuning eye/pushbuttons, double doors, 4 knobs, BC, SW, 6 tubes, AC **$200.00-230.00**

5000, console-R/P, 1948, wood, inner right front slide rule dial, fold-back door, 4 knobs, BC, FM, 11 tubes, AC **$85.00-115.00**

8109, console-R/P, 1939, wood, Queen Anne styling, inner dial/grill/tuning eye/pushbuttons, lift top, inner phono, 4 knobs, BC, SW, 8 tubes, AC **$200.00-230.00**

BJ-6836 "Tuscany," end table-R/P, 1947, wood, step-down end table, dial in top, doors, phono in base, 5 knobs, BC, 9 tubes, AC **$120.00-150.00**

D-1000, console-R/P, 1949, wood, inner right slide rule dial, left pull-out phono drawer, double doors, 4 knobs, BC, FM, 14 tubes, AC **$65.00-75.00**

T-2580, table, 1939, wood, inner right dial, left cloth grille with cut-outs, double doors, 2 knobs, BC, 5 tubes, AC/DC.................**$75.00-85.00**

A-2700, console-R/P, 1939, wood, inner right front slide rule dial, pushbuttons, "tambour" doors, lift top, inner phono, 3 knobs, BC, SW, 7 tubes, AC, $150.00-180.00.

80, table, 1929, metal, low rectangular case, large front escutcheon with window dial, lift top, 3 knobs, BC, 8 tubes, AC, $150.00-180.00.

BULOVA
Electronics Guild, Inc.
Sunrise Highway, Valley Stream
Long Island, New York

100, table-C, 1957, plastic, left front dial & clock, right metal grille, step-down top, 3 front and 2 side knobs, BC, 5 tubes, AC, $40.00-50.00.

110, table-C, 1957, plastic, left front dial & clock, right grille, step-down top, side knobs, feet, 3 front and 2 side knobs, BC, 5 tubes, AC **$40.00-50.00**

170, table-C, 1961, plastic, lower right front half-round dial, center clock face, feet, 4 knobs, BC, 5 tubes, AC **$30.00-35.00**

180 Series, table-C, 1961, plastic, lower right front dial, large left clock face, 5 top pushbuttons, feet, 2 knobs, BC, 5 tubes, AC...........**$30.00-40.00**

201 "The Companion," portable, 1955, walnut plastic, large center front dial over horizontal bars, top right thumb wheel on/off/volume knob, fold-down handle, BC, 4 tubes, AC/DC/battery **$30.00-40.00**

202 "The Companion," portable, 1955, ebony plastic, large center front dial over horizontal bars, top right thumb wheel on/off/volume knob, fold-down handle, BC, 4 tubes, AC/DC/battery **$30.00-40.00**

203 "The Companion," portable, 1955, ivory plastic, large center front dial over horizontal bars, top right thumb wheel on/off/volume knob, fold-down handle, BC, 4 tubes, AC/DC/battery **$30.00-40.00**

204 "The Companion," portable, 1955, forest green plastic, large center front dial over horizontal bars, top right thumb wheel on/off/volume knob, fold-down handle, BC, 4 tubes, AC/DC/battery .. **$30.00-40.00**

205 "The Companion," portable, 1955, maroon plastic, large center front dial over horizontal bars, top right thumb wheel on/off/volume knob, fold-down handle, BC, 4 tubes, AC/DC/battery **$30.00-40.00**

206 "The Companion," portable, 1955, teal blue plastic, large center front dial over horizontal bars, top right thumb wheel on/off/volume knob, fold-down handle, BC, 4 tubes, AC/DC/battery .. **$30.00-40.00**

208 "The Companion," portable, 1955, pearl gray plastic, large center front dial over horizontal bars, top right thumb wheel on/off/volume knob, fold-down handle, BC, 4 tubes, AC/DC/battery .. **$30.00-40.00**

120, table-C, plastic, left front dial & clock, right grille with center logo, step-down top, side knobs, feet, 3 front and 2 side knobs, BC, 5 tubes, AC, $40.00-50.00.

360, table, 1961, plastic, upper right window dial, center front dial knob overlaps upper metal perforated grille area, 2 knobs, BC, FM, 7 tubes, AC/DC.....................................**$25.00-30.00**
400 Series, table-C, plastic, lower right front dial knob, large left clock face, lattice grille area, feet, 3 front and 2 side knobs, BC, AC **$25.00-30.00**
A, table-C, plastic, left front dial & clock, right grille, step-down top, feet, BC, AC **$45.00-55.00**
M-701, cathedral-C, 1932, wood, center front half-round dial, upper grille with round clock face & cut-outs (at least two grille variations), 3 knobs, BC, 7 tubes, AC **$430.00-500.00**

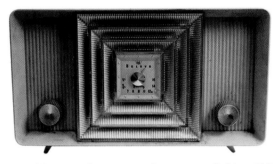

300, table, 1957, plastic, center front square dial in middle of concentric square louvers, feet, 2 knobs, BC, 5 tubes, AC/DC, $40.00-50.00.

BUSH & LANE
Bush and Lane Piano Company
Holland, Michigan

11K, console, 1930, wood, lowboy, Deco, shouldered, upper front dial, lower square grille with cut-outs, variegated veneers, BC, AC...**$200.00-230.00**
34, console, 1929, wood, upper front dial, lower scalloped grille with cut-outs, stretcher base, BC, 7 tubes, AC **$150.00-180.00**
40, console, 1929, wood, inner front dial & knobs, double doors, stretcher base, BC, AC **$180.00-200.00**

CAMEO
Columbus, Ohio

14N18-03, table, 1964, beige/wood grain, center front panel with dial, right and left twin speakers, 3 knobs, BC, 5 tubes, AC/DC **$15.00-20.00**
52N17-03, table-C, 1960, plastic, upper lattice grille area, left alarm clock face, 3 knobs, BC, 5 tubes, AC **$20.00-25.00**

52N18-03, table-C, 1960, plastic, upper lattice grille area, left alarm clock face, 3 knobs, BC, 5 tubes, AC **$20.00-25.00**

CAPEHART
Farnsworth Television & Radio Corp.
Fort Wayne, Indiana

C14, table-C, 1954, plastic, lower slide rule dial, large upper alarm clock face, step-down top, feet, 4 knobs, BC, AC, $35.00-45.00.

1P55, portable, 1955, plastic, center front round dial over horizontal grille bars, top thumbwheel knob, handle, BC, 4 tubes, AC/DC/battery ..**$35.00-45.00**
2P56, portable, 1956, center front round dial over grille, top thumbwheel knob, handle, BC, 4 tubes, AC/DC/battery.....................**$30.00-40.00**
3T55E, table, 1954, plastic, right front round dial over large woven grille area, feet, BC, 5 tubes, AC/DC **$30.00-35.00**
10, portable, 1952, plastic, upper front half-round dial over lattice grille, top left thumbwheel knob, fold-down handle, BC, battery **$30.00-40.00**
17RPQ155F, console-R/P/Rec, 1955, wood, inner center slide rule dial, right phono, left recorder, lift top, BC, FM, 11 tubes, AC ..**$50.00-65.00**
29P4, console-R/P, 1949, wood, inner right black dial, left pull-out phono, double doors, 5 knobs, BC, FM, 11 tubes, AC **$65.00-75.00**
33P9, console-R/P, 1949, wood, inner dial, phono, lift top, lower front grille with cut-outs, storage, 4 knobs, BC, FM, AC **$75.00-85.00**
75C56, table-C, 1956, wood, right side dial, center front square alarm clock face over recessed grille, 4 knobs, BC, 5 tubes, AC **$30.00-35.00**
88P66BNL, portable, 1956, leatherette, flip-up front with map, inner multi-band slide rule dial, telescope antenna, handle, 8 band, BC, 5 tubes, AC/DC/battery **$75.00-85.00**
1002F, console-R/P, 1951, wood, inner right slide rule dial, inner left pull-out phono, doors, 4 knobs, BC, FM, 11 tubes, AC **$65.00-75.00**
1006-M, console-R/P, 1951, wood, inner right slide rule dial, left pull-out phono drawer, 4 knobs, BC, 8 tubes, AC **$65.00-75.00**
1007AM, console-R/P, 1951, wood, inner right slide rule dial, left pull-out phono drawer, 4 knobs, BC, FM, 11 tubes, AC.............**$75.00-85.00**
P-213, portable, 1954, plastic & metal, front V-shaped plaid grille, handle, 2 knobs, BC, 4 tubes, AC/DC/battery **$45.00-55.00**
RP-152, console-R/P, 1953, wood, inner front slide rule dial, lower phono, large double doors, 4 knobs, BC, 7 tubes, AC ..**$50.00-65.00**
T-30, table, 1951, plastic, right front half-round dial, center raised patterned grille, feet, 2 knobs, BC, 5 tubes, AC/DC **$30.00-40.00**
T-522, table, 1953, plastic, large front dial with inner perforations, slanted feet, 2 knobs, BC, 5 tubes, AC/DC **$40.00-50.00**
TC-20, table-C, 1951, plastic, right side dial, left front alarm clock, step-down top, 5 knobs, BC, 5 tubes, AC **$30.00-40.00**
TC-62, table-C, 1953, plastic, right side dial, left front alarm clock, step-down top, 2 knobs, BC, 6 tubes, AC **$30.00-40.00**

CAPITOL
Capitol Radio Corp.

UN-61 "Music Master," table, 1948, upper slanted slide rule dial, lower horizontal louvers, 2 knobs, BC, 6 tubes, AC/DC **$40.00-50.00**

UN-72, table, 1949, two-tone wood, upper slanted slide rule dial, lower horizontal louvers, 4 knobs $45.00-55.00
UN-72P "High Fidelity Symphonic," table-R/P, 1948, wood, outer slanted slide rule dial, horizontal louvers, lift top, inner phono, 4 knobs, BC, SW, 7 tubes, AC $30.00-35.00

CARDINAL
Cardinal Radio Manufacturing Co.
2812 South Main St., Los Angeles, California

60, cathedral, 1931, wood, center front quarter-round dial, upper 4-section grille, 3 knobs, BC, AC $300.00-320.00
60, tombstone, 1931, wood, arched top, center quarter-round dial, upper grille with cut-outs, 3 knobs, BC, AC.........................$150.00-180.00

CARLOYD
Carloyd Electric & Radio Co.
342 Madison Ave., New York, New York

Mark II "Malone-Lemmon," table, 1925, wood, high rectangular case, 3 dial slanted front panel, lift top, 6 knobs, BC, 5 tubes, battery, $300.00-320.00.

CASE
Indiana Mfg. & Elec. Co.
570 Case Avenue, Marion, Indiana

61C, console, 1926, two-tone walnut, center front dial, upper speaker grille with cut-outs, BC, 6 tubes, battery $150.00-180.00
62C, console, 1927, wood, center front dial with escutcheon, upper speaker grille with cut-outs, BC, 6 tubes, AC $160.00-190.00
66A, table, 1928, wood, low rectangular case, center illuminated window dial with escutcheon, BC, 6 tubes, AC $120.00-140.00
73B, console, 1928, wood, highboy, upper window dial with escutcheon, lower grille with cut-outs, 3 knobs, BC, 8 tubes, AC..$120.00-150.00
73C, console, 1928, wood, lowboy, inner dial & knobs, double front doors, stretcher base, BC, 8 tubes, AC.................$160.00-190.00
90A, table, 1927, walnut, low rectangular case, center front dial, left side loop antenna, feet, BC, battery.................................$200.00-230.00
90C, console, 1927, wood, lowboy, large case, inner dial & knobs, front doors, BC, battery $200.00-230.00
500, table, 1925, mahogany, low rectangular case, slanted 3 dial front panel, lift top, BC, tubes $85.00-105.00
503, table, 1926, wood, low rectangular case, front panel with 3 pointer dials, 5 knobs, BC, 6 tubes, battery $120.00-150.00
510, tombstone, 1935, wood, center front "Tell- Time Jumbo Dial," upper cloth grille with cut-outs, BC, 5 tubes $150.00-160.00

60A, table, 1926, wood, low rectangular case, 2 dial front panel, lift top, feet, 3 knobs, BC, 6 tubes, battery, $85.00-115.00.

701, console, 1926, walnut, inner left 3 dial panel, right grille, fold-down front, fold-up top, BC...$240.00-300.00
710, tombstone, 1935, wood, center front "Tell-Time Jumbo Dial," upper cloth grille with cut-outs, BC, SW, 7 tubes, AC.........$150.00-160.00
1015, console, 1935, wood, upper front round dial, lower cloth grille with cut-outs, BC, 10 tubes...$180.00-200.00
1017, console, 1935, wood, upper front round "Tell-Time Jumbo Dial," lower cloth grille with cut-outs, BC $180.00-200.00

CAVALCADE
Cavalcade Radio Company
2341 Wolfram St., Chicago, Illinois

361, table, 1935, walnut, center front round airplane dial over cloth grille with cut-outs, 2 knobs, BC, 5 tubes, AC $85.00-115.00
3651, console, 1935, two-tone wood, upper front airplane dial, lower cloth grille with cut-outs, 3 bands, 4 knobs, BC, 6 tubes, AC $120.00-150.00

CAVALIER
Hinners-Galanek Radio Corp.
2514 Broadway, Long Island, New York

4CL4, table-C, 1955, plastic, right side dial, center front clock over checkered grille, 5 knobs, BC, 4 tubes, AC...................$35.00-45.00
5C1, table-C, 1954, plastic, right side dial, center front clock over checkered grille, 5 knobs, BC, 5 tubes, AC....................$35.00-45.00
603, table, 1957, plastic, right side dial, large front perforated grille with crown logo & "V," BC, 6 tubes, AC/DC $40.00-50.00
LK-447, cathedral, 1933, two-tone wood, center front half-round dial, upper cloth grille with cut-outs, 2 knobs, BC $160.00-190.00
SF-547, cathedral, 1933, two-tone wood, center front half-round dial, upper cloth grille with cut-outs, 2 knobs, BC $160.00-190.00

CBS-COLUMBIA
CBS-Columbia Inc.
3400 47th Avenue, Long Island, New York

515A, table, 1953, plastic, large right front round dial, diagonally divided lattice grille, 2 knobs, BC, 5 tubes, AC/DC, $35.00-45.00.

525, portable, 1953, plastic, lower right front dial, left patterned grille area, handle, 2 knobs, BC, 4 tubes, AC/DC/battery $35.00-45.00
541, table-C, 1953, plastic, right round dial, left alarm clock face, center checkered panel, 5 knobs, BC, 5 tubes, AC $35.00-40.00
5165, table, plastic, large half-round metal dial with inner horizontal lines, large dial pointer, feet, 2 knobs, BC, 5 tubes $45.00-55.00
5220, portable, 1954, plastic, right side dial, upper front horizontal bars, fold-down handle, 2 knobs, BC, 4 tubes, AC/DC/battery ..$25.00-30.00
5440, table-C, 1956, plastic, right round dial, left round alarm clock face, center panel, 5 knobs, BC, 5 tubes, AC $30.00-35.00
T200, table, 1956, plastic, recessed front panel with right "steering wheel" dial over horizontal bars, 2 knobs, BC, 5 tubes, AC $45.00-55.00
T202, table, 1956, plastic, recessed front panel with right "steering wheel" dial over horizontal bars, 2 knobs, BC, 5 tubes, AC $45.00-55.00

CHANCELLOR
Radionic Equipment Co.
170 Nassau Street, New York, New York

35P, portable, 1947, leatherette, plastic front panel with right dial over horizontal bars, handle, 2 knobs, BC, 4 tubes, AC/DC/battery **$30.00-35.00**

CHANNEL MASTER
Channel Master Corp.
Ellenville, New York

6532, table, 1960, two-tone plastic, center front dial, right & left twin speakers, 2 knobs, BC, AC **$25.00-30.00**
6533, table-C, 1960, two-tone plastic, center alarm clock & dial, right & left twin speakers, snooze bar, 4 knobs, BC, 5 tubes, AC **$25.00-30.00**
6535, table, 1960, walnut, two right front slide rule dials, left lattice grille, 4 knobs, BC, FM, 6 tubes, AC **$25.00-30.00**
6536, table-C, 1960, walnut, right front clock & slide rule dial, left lattice grille, 4 knobs, BC, FM, 6 tubes, AC **$25.00-30.00**

CHELSEA
Chelsea Radio Co.
150 Fifth Street, Chelsea, Massachusetts

102, table, 1923, wood, high rectangular case, 2 dial black front panel, 6 knobs, BC, 3 tubes, battery, $150.00-180.00.

107 "Regenodyne," table, 1925, wood, low rectangular case, 2 dial front panel, 5 knobs, BC, 4 tubes, battery **$120.00-150.00**
Super Five, table, 1925, wood, slant front, 3 oval window dials, curved sides, 5 bakelite knobs, BC, 5 tubes, battery **$130.00-150.00**
Super Five, table, 1925, wood, three dial slant front wooden panel, lift top, 5 knobs, BC, 5 tubes, battery.............................**$130.00-150.00**
Super Six, table, 1925, wood, high rectangular case, slant front, three window dials, curved sides, 5 knobs, BC, 6 tubes, battery **$140.00-150.00**

122, table, 1925, wood, high rectangular case, slant front 2 dial black Bakelite panel, lift top, 4 knobs, BC, battery, $140.00-160.00.

Super Five, table, 1925, wood, metal front panel, three window dials with brass escutcheons, 5 knobs, BC, 5 tubes, battery, $130.00-150.00.

CHEROKEE

571-X50-2A, table, wood, upper right front rectangular dial over large plastic horizontal louvers, 2 knobs, BC **$40.00-50.00**

CHUN-KING

ATR-210, portable, plastic, right front dial over horizontal grille bars, fold-down handle, made in Japan, 2 knobs, BC, battery **$45.00-55.00**

CISCO
Cities Service Oil Co.
New York, New York

1A5, table, 1948, wood, right front square dial, left horizontal louvers, 2 knobs, BC, 5 tubes, AC/DC **$40.00-50.00**
9A5, table, 1947, plastic, right front square dial, left horizontal louvers, handle, 2 knobs, BC, 5 tubes, AC/DC **$75.00-85.00**

CLAPP-EASTHAM
Clapp-Eastham Company
136 Main Street, Cambridge, Massachusetts

The Clapp-Eastham Company was formed in 1908 to manufacture X-rays and wireless parts and eventually produced complete radio sets. The company declined during the early 1920s and was out of business by 1929.

Baby Emerson, table, 1927, small case, 1 dial front panel, Emerson Multivalve, 3 knobs, BC, 1 tube, battery **$1,050.00-1,150.00**
DD Radak, table, 1925, leatherette or wood, low rectangular case, 2 dial black front panel, 5 knobs, BC, 3 tubes, battery **$300.00-350.00**

Gold Star, table, 1925, wood, low rectangular case, black front panel with 3 pointer dials and gold trim, BC, 5 tubes, battery, $300.00-350.00.

HR, table, 1922, wood, high rectangular case, 2 dial black Bakelite front panel, 4 knobs, BC, 1 tube, battery, $350.00-410.00.

320 "Clarion Jr.," tombstone, 1937, wood, center front window dial with escutcheon, upper cloth grille with cut-outs, 3 knobs, BC, 5 tubes, AC, $85.00-105.00.

HR/HZ, table, 1922, wood, 2 units with black Bakelite front panels, BC, battery **$720.00-820.00**

R-4 Radak, table, 1924, wood, high rectangular case, black Bakelite front panel, 3 knobs, BC, 1 tube, battery...................**$350.00-410.00**

RZ Radak, table, 1922, wood, rectangular case, black Bakelite front panel, 7 knobs, BC, 3 tubes, battery **$820.00-920.00**

R-3 Radak, table, 1923, wood, high rectangular case, black Bakelite front panel, 4 knobs, BC, 1 tube, battery, $350.00-410.00.

340, tombstone, wood, center front window dial, upper cloth grille with cut-outs, 3 knobs, BC, 8 tubes, AC **$85.00-105.00**

400, table, 1937, wood, step-down top, right front dial, center grille with cut-outs, 2 knobs, BC, 5 tubes, AC/DC **$110.00-130.00**

422, table, 1933, wood, rounded top, right front dial, center grille with cut-outs, 2 knobs, BC, 5 tubes, AC/DC **$85.00-105.00**

450, table, 1933, wood, right front dial, center grille with cut-outs, ribbed sides, 2 knobs, BC, 6 tubes, AC/DC........................... **$85.00-105.00**

470, tombstone, 1933, wood, center front window dial with escutcheon, upper cloth grille, 4 knobs, BC, 6 tubes, AC **$95.00-115.00**

691, table, 1937, two-tone wood, right front round telephone dial, left horizontal louvers, 4 knobs, BC..................................**$85.00-105.00**

770, table, 1937, wood, large right front dial, left cloth grille with 2 horizontal bars, 3 knobs, BC, SW **$45.00-55.00**

11011, portable, 1947, leatherette, slide rule dial, horizontal louvers, handle, 2 knobs, BC, 4 tubes, AC/DC/battery **$30.00-35.00**

11305, table-R/P, 1947, wood, outer front dial, criss-cross grille, lift top, inner phono, 2 knobs, BC, AC **$30.00-35.00**

11411-N, portable, 1947, plastic, inner right dial, lattice grille, switch, flip-up cover, 2 knobs, BC, 4 tubes, AC/DC/battery **$35.00-45.00**

11801, table, 1947, plastic, lower slanted slide rule dial, upper horizontal louvers, 2 knobs, BC, 5 tubes, AC/DC **$50.00-65.00**

12110M, console-R/P, 1949, wood, right tilt-out dial, left pull-out phono drawer, 4 knobs, BC, FM, AC **$65.00-75.00**

12310W, console-R/P, 1948, wood, upper slanted slide rule dial, center pull-out phono drawer, 5 knobs, BC, SW, 6 tubes, AC ..**$75.00-85.00**

12708, console-R/P, 1948, wood, upper front slide rule dial, lower criss-cross grille, lift top, inner phono, 4 knobs, BC, 4 tubes, AC **$50.00-65.00**

12801, table, 1949, plastic, right front square dial, left lattice grille, ridged base, 2 knobs, BC, 4 tubes, AC/DC **$45.00-55.00**

13101, table, 1948, plastic, upper slanted slide rule dial, horizontal grille bars, 4 knobs, BC, FM, 10 tubes, AC/DC..................... **$40.00-50.00**

CLARION
Warwick Mfg. Corp.
4640 West Harrison Street, Chicago, Illinois

80, tombstone, 1931, wood, shouldered top, front half-round dial, upper grille with cut-outs, 3 knobs, BC, 8 tubes, AC...........**$200.00-230.00**

81, console, 1931, wood, lowboy, upper front half-round dial, lower cloth grille with cut-outs, BC, 8 tubes, AC **$120.00-160.00**

85, cathedral, 1931, wood, center front half-round dial, upper cloth grille with cut-outs, 3 knobs, BC **$320.00-350.00**

90, tombstone, 1931, wood, shouldered top, front half-round dial, upper grille with cut-outs, 3 knobs, BC, 8 tubes, AC...........**$160.00-190.00**

91, console, 1931, wood, lowboy, upper front half-round dial, lower cloth grille with cut-outs, BC, 8 tubes, AC **$150.00-180.00**

280, console, 1932, wood, lowboy, upper front half-round dial, lower cloth grille with cut-outs, 6 legs, BC, 12 tubes, AC **$150.00-180.00**

300, console, wood, inner half-round dial, double doors, lower criss-cross grille area, decorative columns, 2 speakers, 2 knobs, BC, 14 tubes, AC **$200.00-230.00**

321, tombstone, wood, center front window dial with escutcheon, upper cloth grille with cut-outs, 3 knobs, BC, 5 tubes...........**$85.00-105.00**

322, console, wood, lowboy, upper front window dial, lower cloth grille with cut-outs, 3 knobs, BC **$120.00-150.00**

470, cathedral, 1933, wood, small case, center front window dial, upper grille with cut-outs, 4 knobs, BC, 6 tubes, AC, $180.00-200.00.

AC-40 "Junior," cathedral, 1931, wood, center front window dial with escutcheon, upper cloth grille with decorative cut-outs, 2 knobs, BC, 5 tubes, AC, $270.00-295.00.

13201, table, 1949, plastic, right square dial, left horizontal wrap-around louvers, 2 knobs, BC, 4 tubes, battery $35.00-40.00
14601, table, 1949, plastic, right square dial, left checkerboard grille, ridged base, 2 knobs, BC, 5 tubes, AC/DC $45.00-55.00
14965, table, 1949, plastic, upper slanted slide rule dial, lower horizontal grille bars, 4 knobs, BC, FM, 8 tubes, AC $40.00-50.00
AC-51, console, 1929, wood, lowboy, upper front window dial, lower scalloped grille, stretcher base, 3 knobs, BC, 8 tubes, AC ..$120.00-150.00
AC-53, console, 1929, wood, lowboy, upper front window dial, lower scalloped grille, stretcher base, 3 knobs, BC, 8 tubes, AC ..$120.00-150.00
AC-61, cathedral, 1931, wood, off-center front window dial, upper scalloped grille with cut-outs, 3 knobs, BC, 6 tubes, AC..$200.00-230.00
AC-70, cathedral, 1931, wood, off-center front window dial, upper round grille with ornate cut-outs, unique convex-concave top, 3 knobs, BC, 7 tubes, AC $320.00-350.00
AC-85, cathedral, 1931, wood, center front half-round dial, upper cloth grille with cut-outs, 3 knobs, BC, 7 tubes, AC...........$320.00-350.00
C100, table, 1946, plastic, right front square dial, left horizontal wrap-around louvers, 2 knobs, BC, 5 tubes, AC/DC $55.00-65.00
C101, table-R/P, 1946, wood, right front square dial, left horizontal louvers, lift top, inner phono, 3 knobs, BC, AC $30.00-35.00
C102, table, 1946, plastic, upper front slide rule dial, lower horizontal wrap-around grille bars, 2 knobs, BC, 5 tubes, AC/DC..$40.00-50.00
C103, table, 1946, plastic, upper front slide rule dial, lower cloth grille with horizontal bars, 4 knobs, BC, AC...........................$35.00-45.00
C104, table, 1946, wood, upper front curved dial, lower cloth grille with horizontal louvers, 4 knobs, BC, 6 tubes, AC/DC.........$45.00-55.00
C105-A, console-R/P, 1946, wood, upper front slide rule dial, lower horizontal louvers, doors, lift top, inner phono, 4 knobs, BC, 6 tubes, AC $50.00-65.00
C108, table, 1946, wood, upper slanted slide rule dial, lower cloth grille with harp cut-out, 2 knobs, BC $40.00-50.00
TC-2, console, 1934, wood, Deco, upper front quarter-round dial, lower grille with geometric cut-outs, 3 knobs, BC, SW, 7 tubes, AC $150.00-180.00

AC-60 "Junior," cathedral, 1932, walnut, off-center window dial, upper scalloped cloth grille with cut-outs, 3 knobs, BC, 6 tubes, AC, $200.00-230.00.

CLARK'S
30 Boylston St.
Boston, Massachusetts

Acme Reflex, table, wood, low rectangular case, 2 dial black front panel, lift top, BC, battery..$130.00-150.00

CLEARFIELD

D, table, 1925, wood & glass, low rectangular case with clear plate glass top and sides, 3 dial front panel, wooden base, BC, 6 tubes, battery $800.00-900.00

CLEARSONIC
U. S. Television Mfg. Co.
3 West 61st Street, New York, New York

5C66, table, 1947, wood, right front square dial, left cloth grille with horizontal bars, 2 knobs, BC, 5 tubes, AC/DC $35.00-45.00
5D66, table-R/P, 1947, wood, right front dial, criss-cross grille, lift top, inner phono, 2 knobs, BC, 5 tubes, AC/DC $30.00-35.00

CLEARTONE
Cleartone Radio Company
2427 Gilbert Avenue, Cincinnati, Ohio

60 "Goldcrest," table, 1925, wood, low rectangular case, front panel with 3 pointer dials, 7 knobs, BC, 4 tubes, battery $110.00-130.00
70 "Clear-O-Dyne," table, 1925, wood, low rectangular case, front panel with 2 pointer dials, 5 knobs, BC, 4 tubes, battery $110.00-130.00
72 "Clear-O-Dyne," console, 1925, wood, inner panel with 2 pointer dials, drop front, built-in speaker, 5 knobs, BC, 4 tubes, battery...........$240.00-270.00
80 "Super Clear-O-Dyne," table, 1925, wood, low rectangular case, front panel with 3 pointer dials, 5 knobs, BC, 5 tubes, battery ..$140.00-160.00
82, console, 1925, wood, inner panel with 3 pointer dials, drop front, built-in speaker, 5 knobs, BC, 5 tubes, battery $240.00-270.00
100, table, 1926, wood, high rectangular case, slant front panel, lift top, 5 knobs, BC, 5 tubes, battery $140.00-160.00
Mayflower, console, 1926, wood, upper front dial with escutcheon, lower built-in speaker with scrolled grille, BC, 5 tubes, AC....$200.00-230.00

CLEVELAND
Cleveland Products Co.
714 Huron Rd., Cleveland, Ohio

A-5, table, 1925, wood, low rectangular case, 3 dial front panel, 5 knobs, BC, 5 tubes, battery...$120.00-150.00

CLIMAX
Climax Radio & Tel. Co., Inc.
513 South Sangamon Street, Chicago, Illinois

Emerald, table, 1937, walnut veneer, streamlined, right oval convex dial, left wrap-around grille bars, BC, AC/DC $140.00-160.00

35 "Ruby," table, 1937, walnut veneer, ultra streamlined, teardrop shaped, right oval dial, left horizontal grille bars, tuning eye, 3 knobs, BC, SW, 7 tubes, AC/DC, $420.00-470.00.

CLINTON
Clinton Mfg. Co.
1217 West Washington Boulevard, Chicago, Illinois

216, table, 1935, wood, rounded sides, right front dial, left grille with Deco cut-outs, 3 knobs, BC, SW, 5 tubes, AC/DC **$85.00-115.00**

254, portable, 1937, leatherette, inner right front dial, left round grille, fold-open front door, handle, BC, battery **$65.00-85.00**

1102, console, 1937, wood, large upper front round dial, tuning eye, lower cloth grille with vertical bars, BC, SW, AC **$150.00-180.00**

620XP, table, wood, right front airplane dial, left cloth grille with 2 horizontal bars, 6 pushbuttons, feet, 3 knobs, BC, SW, AC, $65.00-85.00.

CO-OP
National Cooperatives Inc.
343 South Dearborn, Chicago, Illinois

6A47WT, table, 1949, wood, lower front slide rule dial, large upper recessed grille, 4 knobs, BC, SW, 6 tubes, AC **$35.00-45.00**

COCA-COLA
Point of Purchase
Displays, Inc.

Coke cooler, table-N, 1949, red plastic, looks like Coca-Cola cooler, upper front slide rule dial, 2 knobs, BC, 5 tubes, $650.00-700.00.

Coke bottle, table-N, Bakelite, large bottle-shaped set complete with "Drink Coca-Cola" slogan, small front window dial, 2 knobs, BC, $2,500.00+.

COLBLISS
The Colbliss Radio Company
827 South Hoover St., Los Angeles, California

500 "Petite," cathedral, 1931, wood, lower front window dial, upper scalloped grille with cut-outs, 3 knobs, BC **$240.00-270.00**

COLONIAL
Colonial Radio Corporation
Buffalo, New York
Colonial Radio Corporation
Long Island, New York

36, cathedral, 1931, wood, lower front window dial with escutcheon, upper grille with cut-outs, 4 knobs, BC, 6 tubes, AC, $245.00-270.00.

3, grandfather clock, wood, bookcase-style with center front radio unit, window dial, round cloth grille with cut-outs, upper round clock face, BC, AC **$410.00-460.00**

16, table, 1925, wood, low rectangular case, 3 dial front panel, 3 knobs, BC, 5 tubes, battery **$120.00-150.00**

17, table, 1925, wood, low rectangular case, 2 dial front panel, BC, 4 tubes, battery **$130.00-160.00**

20-6, table, 1925, wood, low rectangular case, 3 dial front panel, 4 knobs, BC, 6 tubes, battery **$150.00-180.00**

31AC, console, 1929, wood, lowboy, double doors, inner upper radio with pinter dial, lower ornate grille, 3 knobs, BC, 7 tubes, AC **$130.00-160.00**

31DC, console, 1929, wood, lowboy, double doors, inner upper radio with pinter dial, lower ornate grille, 3 knobs, BC, 7 tubes, DC **$110.00-120.00**

39, cathedral, 1931, wood, lower front window dial, upper scalloped grille with cut-outs, 2 knobs, BC, 5 tubes, AC **$200.00-230.00**

41C, grandfather clock, 1931, wood, front window dial, lower grille with cut-outs, rectangular clock face, BC, 5 tubes, AC **$410.00-460.00**

250, table, 1933, walnut with inlay, right front dial, center cloth grille with cut-outs, 2 knobs, BC, SW, 5 tubes, AC **$95.00-115.00**

279, table, 1933, walnut with inlay, arched top, right front dial, center 3-section cloth grille with cut-outs, 2 knobs, BC, 5 tubes, AC.. **$95.00-115.00**

300, table, 1933, plastic, Deco, right front dial, center circular chrome cut-outs, ribbed sides, feet, 2 knobs, BC, SW, 5 tubes, AC/DC... **$320.00-350.00**

301, table, 1933, wood, Deco, right front dial, center cloth grille with chrome cut-outs, 2 knobs, BC, 5 tubes, AC **$270.00-300.00**

315EV, tombstone, 1935, wood, lower front dial, upper cloth grille with cut-outs, 5 knobs, BC, SW, 8 tubes, AC **$110.00-130.00**

600A, console, 1934, wood, upper front window dial, lower cloth grille with 2 vertical bars, 3 knobs, BC, SW, 6 tubes, AC ..**$120.00-140.00**

601, console, 1934, wood with metal inlay, upper front window dial, lower cloth grille with 4 vertical columns, 5 knobs, BC, SW, 10 tubes, AC **$150.00-180.00**

603, console, 1934, wood, upper front round airplane dial, lower cloth grille with cut-outs, feet, 5 knobs, BC, SW, 6 tubes, AC **$120.00-150.00**

New World, table-N, 1933, plastic, world globe on stand, front window dial, side knobs, top vents, BC, SW, 5 tubes, AC/DC, $880.00-930.00.

604, console, 1934, wood, upper front round airplane dial, lower cloth grille with 3 vertical bars, 5 knobs, BC, SW, 8 tubes, AC.....**$120.00-150.00**

605, console, 1934, wood, inner front airplane dial, door, lower front cloth grille with cut-outs, BC, SW, 7 tubes, AC **$140.00-170.00**

651, table, 1934, wood, raised top, center cloth grille with cut-outs, 2 knobs, BC, SW, 5 tubes, AC **$75.00-85.00**

652, tombstone, 1934, wood, lower front round airplane dial, upper cloth grille with cut-outs, 3 knobs, BC, SW, 5 tubes, AC......**$85.00-115.00**

653, tombstone, 1934, wood with metal inlay, arched top, lower front dial, upper cloth grille with cut-outs, 3 knobs, BC, 5 tubes, AC **$180.00-200.00**

654, table, 1934, wood with inlay, center cloth grille with cut-outs, 2 knobs, BC, 5 tubes, AC/DC..**$75.00-85.00**

655, table, 1934, wood, raised top, center cloth grille with oblong cut-outs, 2 knobs, BC, SW, 6 tubes, AC **$75.00-85.00**

656, tombstone, 1934, wood, lower front round airplane dial, upper cloth grille with cut-outs, 3 knobs, BC, SW, 6 tubes, AC....**$150.00-180.00**

658, table, 1934, wood, center cloth grille with cut-outs, 2 knobs, BC, SW, 6 tubes, AC **$95.00-115.00**

T345, cathedral, wood, lower front quarter-round dial, upper cloth grille with cut-outs, 3 knobs, BC **$180.00-200.00**

COLUMBIA PHONOGRAPH
Columbia Phonograph Company, Inc.
55 Fifth Avenue, New York, New York

C-1, table, 1928, wood, center front window dial with escutcheon, lift top, switch, 3 knobs, BC, 7 tubes, AC **$120.00-150.00**

C-81, upright table, 1932, two-tone walnut, center front window dial, upper grille with cut-outs & "notes," 3 knobs, BC, 8 tubes, AC **$240.00-270.00**

C-83, console, 1932, walnut, lowboy, upper front window dial, lower grille with cut-outs & "notes," 6 legs, 3 knobs, BC, 8 tubes, AC........**$150.00-190.00**

C-84, console, 1932, walnut, highboy, upper front window dial, lower twin grilles with cut-outs, 6 legs, BC, 8 tubes, AC **$180.00-200.00**

C-150, table, wood, right front dial, center cloth grille with cut-outs, left volume, 2 knobs, BC, $75.00-85.00.

C-85, console-R/P, 1932, walnut, center front dial, lower grille with cut-outs & "notes," lift top, inner phono, 3 knobs, BC, 8 tubes, AC ..**$180.00-200.00**

C-93, console, 1932, walnut, lowboy, upper front dial, lower grille with cut-outs & "notes," 6 legs, 3 knobs, BC, 11 tubes, AC......**$180.00-200.00**

C-95, console, 1932, walnut, upper front window dial, lower twin grilles with cut-outs, 6 legs, 3 knobs, BC, AC **$150.00-180.00**

C-103, console, 1932, walnut, upper front dial, lower grille with scalloped cut-outs & "notes," 3 knobs, BC, AC..........................**$120.00-150.00**

COLUMBIA RECORDS
799 Seventh Avenue
New York, New York

530, console-R/P, 1957, wood, inner right dial & knobs, left phono, lift top, front grille, legs, BC, FM, 11 tubes, AC **$40.00-50.00**

COMMONWEALTH
Commonwealth Radio Mfg. Co.

170, cathedral, 1933, wood, center front quarter-round dial, upper cloth grille with cut-outs, BC, SW, 7 tubes, AC **$240.00-270.00**

CONCERT
Concert Radiophone Co.
626 Huron Rd., Cleveland, Ohio

Concert Grand, table, 1925, wood, low rectangular case, 3 dial front panel, 5 knobs, BC, 4 tubes, battery **$130.00-150.00**

Concert Sr., portable, 1925, leatherette, inner 2 dial panel, built-in loop antenna, handle, 3 knobs, BC, 2 tubes, battery **$240.00-270.00**

CONCORD
Concord Radio Company
901 West Jackson Boulevard, Chicago, Illinois

1-400, portable, 1948, leatherette, lower front center slide rule dial, upper center recatngular grille, plastic strap top handle, 2 knobs, BC, 4 tubes, battery...**$25.00-35.00**

1-402, table, 1948, brown plastic, streamline, right front dial, left horizontal wrap-around louvers, 2 knobs, BC, 4 tubes, AC/DC......**$75.00-85.00**

1-403, table, 1948, ivory plastic, streamline, right front dial, left horizontal wrap-around louvers, 2 knobs, BC, 4 tubes, AC/DC **$75.00-85.00**

1-404, table, 1948, ivory plastic, right front rectangular airplane dial, left grille with wrap over top vertical louvers, 2 knobs, BC, 4 tubes, battery **$35.00-45.00**

1-405, table, 1948, brown plastic, right front rectangular airplane dial, left grille with wrap over top vertical louvers, 2 knobs, BC, 4 tubes, battery **$35.00-45.00**

1-407, console-R/P, 1948, wood, upper front slide rule with horizontal bar grille below, lower double doors for record storage, top lift lid for phono, 4 knobs, BC, 4 tubes, AC.....................................**$75.00-85.00**

1-408, portable, 1948, plastic, front hinged door, inside knob dial, inside center grille with louvers, leather strap handle, 2 knobs, BC, 4 tubes, AC/DC/battery **$65.00-75.00**

1-411, table, 1948, plastic, streamline, right front half-round dial, left horizontal wrap-around louvers, 2 knobs, BC, 4 tubes, AC/DC **$50.00-65.00**

1-500, table, 1948, ivory plastic, upper right front slide rule dial, dial outline and left grille with horizonal lovers in brown plastic, rounded edges, 2 knobs, BC, 5 tubes, AC/DC **$40.00-50.00**

1-501, table, 1948, walnut plastic, upper front sloping slide rule dial, lower grille with horizontal louvers, handle, 2 knobs, BC, 6 tubes, AC/DC **$40.00-50.00**

1-502, table, 1948, wood, upper front sloping slide rule dial, lower grille with horizontal louvers, recessed base, 2 knobs, BC, 5 tubes, AC/DC **$35.00-45.00**

1-504, table, 1949, plastic, upper slanted slide rule dial, lower horizontal grille bars, 3 knobs, BC, SW, 5 tubes, AC....................**$40.00-50.00**

1-505, table-R/P, 1948, wood, front lattice gille and rounded corners, left top slide rule dial, right top lid with inside phono, 3 knobs, BC, 5 tubes, AC **$40.00-50.00**

1-506, portable-R/P, 1948, leatherette, front door with inside slide rule dial and grille with horizontal cut-outs, top rear lid with inner phono, leather handle, 4 knobs, BC, 5 tubes, AC **$30.00-40.00**

1-507, table, 1948, brown plastic, sloping front, right airplane dial, left grille with vertical bars, 3 knobs, BC, SW, 5 tubes, AC/DC **$30.00-40.00**

1-508, table, 1948, ivory plastic, sloping front, right airplane dial, left grille with vertical bars, 3 knobs, BC, SW, 5 tubes, AC/DC **$30.00-40.00**

1-513, portable, 1949, plastic, right front rectangular dial, patterned grille area, handle, 3 knobs, BC, 5 tubes, AC/DC/battery **$35.00-45.00**

1-514, table, 1949, plastic, right front airplane dial, left horizontal louvers, 2 knobs, BC, AC/DC **$35.00-45.00**

1-516, table-R/P, 1948, leatherette, slanted front slide rule dial, lower grille, open top phono, 2 knobs, BC, 5 tubes, AC **$25.00-30.00**

1-518, portable, 1948, two-tone case, right front oval recessed dial area, handle, BC, AC/DC/battery..**$30.00-40.00**

1-602, chairside-R/P, 1948, mahogany wood, upper double doors with inside slide rule dial and controls, lower sliding top with inner phono, 4 legs, 4 knobs, BC, SW, 6 tubes, AC **$45.00-55.00**

1-603, chairside-R/P, 1948, blond mahogany wood, upper double doors with inside slide rule dial and controls, lower sliding top with inner phono, 4 legs, 4 knobs, BC, SW, 6 tubes, AC............**$45.00-55.00**

1-604, table, 1948, walnut plastic, upper slanted slide rule dial, lower grille with horizontal louvers, rounded shoulders, 2 knobs, BC, SW, 6 tubes, AC/DC **$40.00-50.00**

1-605, table, 1948, ivory plastic, upper slanted slide rule dial, lower grille with horizontal louvers, rounded shoulders, 2 knobs, BC, SW, 6 tubes, AC/DC **$40.00-50.00**

1-606, table, 1948, plastic, upper slanted slide rule dial, lower horizontal grille bars, 3 knobs, BC, FM, 6 tubes, AC/DC **$40.00-50.00**

1-607, portable, 1946, alligator, upper slanted slide rule dial, lower recessed grille and knobs, top leather handle, 3 knobs, BC, 6 tubes, AC/DC/battery **$30.00-40.00**

1-611, portable, 1948, leatherette, upper front slide rule dial, horizontal grille bars, handle, 2 knobs, BC, 6 tubes, AC/DC/battery..........**$35.00-45.00**

1-700, table, 1948, wood, upper front center sloping slide rule dial, lower cloth grille, recessed base, 4 knobs, BC, 7 tubes, AC/DC ..**$30.00-40.00**

1-702, chairside-R/P, 1948, wood, front top recessed slide rule dial, front grille with vertical bars, left side pull-out phono, 4 knobs, BC, 7 tubes, AC **$80.00-100.00**

1-1101, console-R/P, 1948, wood, upper right door with inside slide rule dial, upper left phono drawer, lower center lattice grille, 6 knobs, BC, FM, 11 tubes, AC **$60.00-70.00**

1-1501, console-R/P, 1948, wood, chippendale cabinet with upper and lower double doors, upper right slide rule dial and 10 pushbuttons, upper left phono, lower right grille, 6 knobs, BC, SW, FM, 15 tubes, AC **$80.00-100.00**

6C51B, table, 1947, plastic, streamline, right front dial, left horizontal wrap-around louvers, 2 knobs, BC, 5 tubes, AC/DC **$75.00-85.00**

6D61P, table-R/P, 1947, wood, outer right slide rule dial, lift top, inner phono, 3 knobs, BC, 6 tubes, AC **$30.00-40.00**

6E51B, table, 1947, plastic, upper slanted slide rule dial, lower horizontal louvers, handle, 2 knobs, BC, 5 tubes, AC/DC..............**$40.00-50.00**

6F26W, table, 1947, wood, upper slanted slide rule dial, lower cloth grille, 4 knobs, BC, SW, 6 tubes, AC/DC **$40.00-50.00**

6T61W, table, 1947, wood, right front square dial, left horizontal louvers, 3 knobs, BC, 6 tubes, AC/DC **$35.00-45.00**

7E51W, table, 1947, wood, upper front center sloping slide rule dial, lower grille with horizontal louvers, recessed base, 2 knobs, BC, 5 tubes, AC/DC **$35.00-45.00**

7E71PR, portable, 1947, alligator, right front airplane dial, left grille, handle, 2 knobs, BC, 7 tubes, AC/DC/battery......................**$30.00-40.00**

7E71W, table, 1947, wood, upper front center sloping slide rule dial, lower cloth grille, rounded front top, 4 knobs, BC, 7 tubes, AC/DC **$30.00-40.00**

CONTINENTAL
Spiegel, Inc.
1061 West 35th Street, Chicago, Illinois

44, table, plastic, streamline bullet shape, large right front dial, left horizontal wrap-around bars, feet, 2 knobs, BC, AC............**$60.00-70.00**

K6, table, 1940, plastic, right front dial, left horizontal wrap-around louvers, 3 knobs, BC, SW, 6 tubes, AC, $40.00-50.00.

1000, table, plastic, streamline, right front dial, left horizontal wrap-around bars, 2 knobs, BC **$120.00-150.00**

1600, table-C, plastic, streamline, upper front thumbwheel dial, left horizontal wrap-around bars, right round clock face, 5 knobs, BC, AC **$75.00-95.00**

C-45, table-C, 1957, plastic, center round dial, right circular louvers, left alarm clock face, 5 knobs, BC, 4 tubes, AC **$30.00-40.00**

M-500, portable, plastic, large center front round dial, lower metal perforated grille area, fold-down handle, 2 knobs, BC **$35.00-45.00**

R-20 "Star Raider," console, 1929, walnut finish, highboy, inner dial & knobs, double front doors, stretcher base, BC, 11 tubes, AC **$160.00-180.00**

R-30 "Star Raider," console, 1929, wood, lowboy, inner front dial & knobs, double doors, stretcher base, BC, 11 tubes, AC **$160.00-180.00**

Piano, table-N, 1940, radio shaped like grand piano, lift-up lid covers dial & G clef grille, BC, $300.00-350.00.

CONTINENTAL ELECTRONICS
Continental Electronics, Ltd.

82 "Sky Weight," table-R/P, 1947, luggage-style, alligator, lift top, inner phono, handle, 3 knobs, BC, AC **$25.00-30.00**

CORONADO
Gamble-Skogmo, Inc.
The Gamble Stores
Minneapolis, Minnesota

05RA1-43-7755A, console-R/P, 1950, wood, upper front slide rule dial, center pull-out phono drawer, 4 knobs, BC, FM, AC **$50.00-65.00**

05RA1-43-7901A, console-R/P, 1950, wood, inner right slide rule dial, door, left pull-out phono drawer, 4 knobs, BC, FM, 10 tubes, AC **$50.00-65.00**

05RA2-43-8230A, table, 1952, plastic, upper front slide rule dial, lower metallic grille, 2 knobs, BC, 5 tubes, AC/DC **$30.00-35.00**

05RA2-43-8515A, table, 1950, plastic, lower center raised round dial overlaps large recessed grille area, 2 knobs, BC, FM, 8 tubes, AC **$35.00-45.00**

05RA4-43-9876A, portable, 1950, leatherette, upper front slide rule dial, lower metal grille, handle, 2 knobs, BC, 5 tubes, AC/DC/battery **$30.00-40.00**

05RA33-43-8120A, table, 1950, plastic, oblong case, right front round dial, left round grille with horizontal bars, 2 knobs, BC, 4 tubes, AC/DC **$65.00-85.00**

05RA37-43-8360A, table, 1950, two-tone plastic, right raised round dial over lattice louvers, 2 knobs, BC, 6 tubes, AC/DC....... **$40.00-50.00**

15RA1-43-7654A, console-R/P, 1951, wood, upper front slide rule dial, center pull-out phono drawer, 4 knobs, BC, FM, 8 tubes, AC...**$45.00-55.00**

15RA1-43-7902A, console-R/P, 1951, wood, inner right slide rule dial, door, left pull-out phono drawer, 4 knobs, BC, FM, 10 tubes, AC **$75.00-85.00**

15RA2-43-8230A, table, 1952, plastic, upper front slide rule dial, lower metallic grille, 2 knobs, BC, 5 tubes, AC/DC **$40.00-50.00**

15RA33-43-8246A, table, 1952, plastic, center front round dial over checkered grille, 2 knobs, BC, 5 tubes, AC/DC.............**$35.00-40.00**

15RA33-43-8365, table, 1952, plastic, lower front round raised dial overlaps large upper grille area, 2 knobs, BC, 6 tubes, AC ..**$40.00-50.00**

15RA37-43-9230A, table-R/P, 1952, wood, right front square dial, left grille, left 2/3 lift top, inner phono, 2 knobs, BC, 5 tubes, AC **$35.00-40.00**

35RA4-43-9856A, portable, 1953, leatherette, center front round dial over criss-cross grille, handle, 2 knobs, BC, 5 tubes, AC/DC/battery **$35.00-40.00**

35RA33-43-8125, table, 1953, plastic, right front square dial, left horizontal grille bars, 2 knobs, BC, 4 tubes, AC/DC **$35.00-40.00**

35RA33-43-8145 "Ranger," table, 1953, plastic, right front round dial, left lattice grille, 2 knobs, BC, 5 tubes, AC/DC............. **$35.00-40.00**

35RA33-43-8225, table, 1953, plastic, right front dial, left vertical grille bars, center horizontal wrap-around strip, 2 knobs, BC, 5 tubes, AC/DC **$30.00-35.00**

35RA37-43-8355, table, 1953, plastic, recessed slide rule dial, upper recessed lattice grille, 3 knobs, BC, 6 tubes, AC/DC.... **$35.00-45.00**

35RA40-43-8247A, table-C, 1954, plastic, square case, right side dial, large front alarm clock, 6 knobs, BC, 5 tubes, AC **$35.00-40.00**

43-6301, table, 1946, wood, upper slanted slide rule dial, lower cloth grille, 2 knobs, BC, 4 tubes, battery **$35.00-40.00**

43-6321, table, 1948, wood, lower front slide rule dial, large upper cloth grille, 2 knobs, BC, 4 tubes, battery **$35.00-40.00**

43-6451, table, 1946, two-tone wood, upper slanted slide rule dial, large lower cloth grille, 2 knobs, BC, 5 tubes, battery **$35.00-40.00**

43-6485, table, 1948, wood, upper slanted slide rule dial, large lower cloth grille, 2 knobs, BC, 5 tubes, battery **$35.00-40.00**

43-6927, console, 1948, wood, upper slanted slide rule dial, large lower cloth grille area, 4 knobs, BC, AC **$75.00-85.00**

43-6951, console, 1948, wood, upper slanted slide rule dial, large lower cloth grille, 4 knobs, BC, FM, AC...............................**$75.00-85.00**

43-7601, console-R/P, 1946, wood, upper slide rule dial, lower pull-out phono drawer, 4 knobs, BC, SW, 6 tubes, AC **$75.00-85.00**

43-7651, console-R/P, 1946, wood, inner right slide rule dial, pushbuttons, left pull-out phono drawer, 4 knobs, BC, SW, 8 tubes, AC...**$75.00-85.00**

43-7652, console-R/P, 1948, wood, inner right slide rule dial & pushbuttons, left pull-out phono, BC, SW, AC **$75.00-85.00**

43-7851, console-R/P, 1948, wood, inner right slide rule dial, door, left pull-out phono drawer, 4 knobs, BC, FM, 7 tubes, AC ..**$75.00-85.00**

43-8160, table, 1947, plastic, center round dial inside concentric circular louvers, base, 2 knobs, BC, 5 tubes, AC/DC **$110.00-130.00**

43-8178, table, 1947, plastic, right half-round dial, wrap-around horizontal bands, 2 knobs, BC, 5 tubes, AC/DC **$65.00-85.00**

43-8180, table, 1946, plastic, right front dial, left horizontal wrap-around louvers, 4 knobs, BC, 5 tubes, AC/DC **$45.00-55.00**

43-8190, table, 1947, plastic, contrasting plastic oblong front panel encircles grille, handle, 2 knobs, BC, 5 tubes, AC/DC **$200.00-230.00**

43-8213, table, 1946, wood, upper slanted slide rule dial, lower criss-cross grille, 2 knobs, BC, 5 tubes, AC/DC **$40.00-50.00**

43-8240, table, 1947, plastic, upper slanted slide rule dial, lower horizontal louvers, 2 knobs, BC, 5 tubes, AC/DC..................... **$40.00-50.00**

43-8305, table, 1946, plastic, lower front slide rule dial, upper cloth grille, curved base, 2 knobs, BC, 6 tubes, AC/DC **$55.00-65.00**

43-8312, table, 1946, plastic, lower front slide rule dial, large upper cloth grille, curved base, 2 knobs, BC, 6 tubes, AC/DC **$55.00-65.00**

43-8312A, table, 1946, plastic, lower front slide rule dial, large upper cloth grille, curved base, 2 knobs, BC, 6 tubes, AC/DC **$55.00-65.00**

43-8330, table, 1947, wood, lower front slide rule dial, upper recessed horizontal louvers, 2 knobs, BC, 5 tubes, AC/DC **$40.00-50.00**

1070A, table, 1940, wood, front slide rule dial, upper cloth grille with cut-outs, 6 pushbuttons, 4 knobs, BC, SW, AC, $65.00-75.00.

43-8351, table, 1947, plastic, upper front slide rule dial, lower horizontal louvers, 6 pushbuttons, 2 knobs, BC, 6 tubes, AC/DC .. **$50.00-65.00**

43-8354, table, 1947, plastic, upper front slide rule dial, lower cloth grille with 2 horizontal bars, 5 pushbuttons, 2 knobs, BC, 6 tubes, AC/DC **$45.00-55.00**

43-8420, table, 1947, wood, lower front slide rule dial, upper cloth grille with 2 horizontal bars, 2 knobs, BC, 5 tubes, AC/DC. **$35.00-45.00**

43-8470, table, 1946, wood, lower front slide rule dial, upper cloth grille with 2 horizontal bars, 2 knobs, BC, 6 tubes, AC/DC.... **$35.00-45.00**

43-8471, table, 1946, wood, lower front slide rule dial, upper cloth grille with 2 horizontal bars, 2 knobs, BC, 6 tubes, AC/DC.... **$35.00-45.00**

43-8576, table, 1946, wood, lower front slide rule dial, large upper cloth grille, 4 knobs, BC, SW, 6 tubes, AC **$35.00-45.00**

43-8685, table, 1947, wood, lower front slide rule dial over large cloth grille area, 3 knobs, BC, 6 tubes, AC.............................**$35.00-45.00**

43-9196, table-R/P, 1947, wood, front slide rule dial, horizontal louvers, 3/4 lift top, inner phono, 4 knobs, BC, AC.................**$35.00-40.00**

43-9201, table-R/P, 1947, wood, front slide rule dial, large grille, 3/4 lift top, inner phono, 2 knobs, BC, 5 tubes, AC **$30.00-35.00**

43-9865, portable, 1948, inner lower right dial, lattice grille, flip-up front, handle, 2 knobs, BC, AC/DC/battery.............................**$30.00-40.00**

94RA1-43-6945A, console, 1949, wood, upper front slide rule dial, large lower cloth grille, 4 knobs, BC, FM, 7 tubes, AC...........**$65.00-75.00**

94RA1-43-7605A, console-R/P, 1949, wood, upper front slide rule dial, lower tilt-out phono, 4 knobs, BC, SW, 6 tubes, AC **$65.00-75.00**

94RA1-43-7656A, console-R/P, 1949, wood, inner right slide rule dial, door, left pull-out phono drawer, 4 knobs, BC, FM, 10 tubes, AC...**$65.00-75.00**

94RA1-43-7751A, console-R/P, 1950, wood, upper front dial, center pull-out phono drawer, lower grille, 4 knobs, BC, FM, 7 tubes, AC...**$65.00-75.00**

94RA1-43-8510A, table, 1949, plastic, upper slanted slide rule dial, lower off-center lattice grille, 4 knobs, BC, FM, 7 tubes, AC ..**$45.00-55.00**

94RA1-43-8510B, table, 1949, plastic, upper slanted slide rule dial, lower off center lattice grille, 4 knobs, BC, FM, 7 tubes, AC....**$45.00-55.00**

94RA1-43-8511B, table, 1949, plastic, upper slanted slide rule dial, lower off center lattice grille, 4 knobs, BC, FM, 7 tubes, AC....**$45.00-55.00**

94RA4-43-8130A, table, 1949, plastic, lower front slide rule dial, upper horizontal louvers, 2 knobs, BC, 5 tubes, AC/DC......... **$30.00-35.00**

94RA31-43-8115A "Cub," table, 1950, plastic, right front round dial overlaps lattice wrap-around grille, 2 knobs, BC, 4 tubes, AC/DC .. **$50.00-65.00**

94RA31-43-9841A, portable, 1949, inner slide rule dial, lattice grille area, fold-down front panel, handle, 2 knobs, BC, 5 tubes, AC/DC/battery **$30.00-40.00**

94RA33-43-8130C, table, 1949, plastic, lower front dial, large upper grille with horizontal bars, 2 knobs, BC, 5 tubes, AC/DC........**$30.00-40.00**

686, table, 1935, wood, right front oval dial, left cloth grille with horizontal bars, 4 knobs, BC, SW, 7 tubes, AC **$65.00-85.00**

C5D14, table, 1942, plastic, center round dial inside concentric circular louvers, base, 2 knobs, BC, 5 tubes, AC/DC **$95.00-115.00**

RA12-8121-A, table, 1957, plastic, right front round dial, left horizontal bars, 2 knobs, BC, 4 tubes, AC/DC **$20.00-25.00**

RA37-43-9240A, table-R/P, 1955, wood, right side dial, large front grille, lift top, inner phono, 4 knobs, BC, 6 tubes, AC $25.00-30.00

RA37-43-9855, portable, 1954, plastic, top right dial, front vertical grille bars, handle, 2 knobs, BC, 4 tubes, AC/DC/battery $30.00-35.00

RA42-9850A, portable, 1955, plastic, large center front round dial over horizontal grille bars, handle, 2 knobs, BC, 4 tubes, battery..$30.00-35.00

RA48-8157A, table, 1958, plastic, right front half-round dial, horizontal grille bars, feet, 2 knobs, BC, 4 tubes, AC/DC $20.00-25.00

RA48-8158A, table, 1958, plastic, lower front slide rule dial, large upper grille, feet, 2 knobs, BC, 5 tubes, AC/DC $30.00-35.00

RA48-8159A, table, 1958, plastic, lower front slide rule dial, large upper grille, feet, 2 knobs, BC, 6 tubes, AC/DC $30.00-35.00

RA48-8342A, table, 1957, plastic, recessed front, right dial over lattice grille area, feet, 2 knobs, BC, 5 tubes, AC/DC $25.00-30.00

RA48-8351A, table, 1957, plastic, right side dial, large front perforated grille with crest & "V," 2 knobs, BC, 6 tubes, AC/DC $35.00-45.00

RA48-8352A, table, 1957, plastic, lower front slide rule dial, upper grille with center vertical divider, 2 knobs, BC, 6 tubes, AC/DC.......$30.00-35.00

CORONET
Crystal Products, Co.
1519 McGee Trafficway, Kansas City, Missouri

IouC-2, table, 1946, two-tone, slide rule dial on top of case, front cloth grille with horizontal bars, 2 knobs, BC, AC/DC............$40.00-50.00

COTO-COIL
Coto-Coil Co.
87 Willard Ave., Providence, Rhode Island

Coto Symphonic, table, 1925, wood, rectangular case, 3 dial black front panel, 6 knobs, BC, 4 tubes, battery, $180.00-200.00.

CRESTLINE

ATR 210, portable, plastic, right front dial, horizontal grille bars, handle, 2 knobs, BC, $45.00-55.00.

CROSLEY
The Precision Equipment Company, Inc.
Peebles Corner, Cincinnati, Ohio
Crosley Manufacturing Company, Cincinnati, Ohio
The Crosley Radio Corporation, Cincinnati, Ohio
Crosley Corporation, 1329 Arlington Street, Cincinnati, Ohio

The Crosley company was begun in 1921 by Powel Crosley, who believed his radio company should offer the consumer a good quality product at the lowest possible price and he called his sets the "Model T's" of radio. In 1923, Crosley bought out The Precision Equipment Company. The Crosley Radio Corporation enjoyed success until the late 1920s. One of the most sought-after of Crosley sets today is the "Pup," a small one tube set made to sell for only $9.75 in 1925 and known as the "Sky Terrier."

5-38, table, 1926, wood, 2 styles, high rectangular case, slanted front panel with 3 dials, 5 knobs, BC, 5 tubes, battery, $85.00-115.00.

02CA, console, 1941, wood, large upper front slanted round dial, lower cloth grille with vertical bars, pushbuttons, 2 knobs, BC, SW, 10 tubes, AC $150.00-180.00

02CP, console-R/P, 1941, wood, large upper front slanted round dial, center pull-out phono, lower cloth grille with vertical bars, pushbuttons, 2 knobs, BC, SW, 10 tubes, AC $150.00-180.00

03CB, console, 1941, wood, large upper front slanted round dial, lower cloth grille with vertical bars, pushbuttons, 2 knobs, BC, SW, 10 tubes, AC $150.00-180.00

1-K "Merry Maker," console, wood, lowboy, upper front window dial, lower cloth grille with cut-outs, 3 knobs, BC $85.00-115.00

1-N "Litlfella," cathedral, 1932, wood, small case, center front window dial, upper 3-section grille, scalloped base, 3 knobs, BC, AC...$200.00-230.00

4-29, portable, 1926, leatherette, inner 2 dial front panel, fold-back top, fold-down front, handle, BC, 4 tubes, battery $180.00-210.00

4-29, table, 1926, two-tone wood, high rectangular case, slanted 2 dial panel, wood lid, BC, 4 tubes, battery $150.00-180.00

5-50, table, 1926, wood, high rectangular case, right front thumbwheel dial, BC, 5 tubes, battery $85.00-95.00

5-75, console, 1926, mahogany, highboy, upper right front dial, built-in speaker, BC, 5 tubes, battery $150.00-180.00

6-60, table, 1927, wood, high rectangular case, slanted front panel, right thumbwheel dial, BC, 6 tubes, battery $85.00-95.00

6H2, tombstone, 1933, wood, center front round dial, upper cloth grille with cut-outs, 3 knobs, BC, SW, 6 tubes, AC $110.00-130.00

8H1, console, 1934, wood, upper front round dial, lower cloth grille with cut-outs, BC, SW, 8 tubes, AC $120.00-150.00

9-101, table, 1949, plastic, upper front curved slide rule dial, lower "boomerang" louvers, 3 knobs, BC, 5 tubes, battery $35.00-45.00

5M3, tombstone, 1934, wood, center front window dial with metal escutcheon, upper grille with cut-outs, 2 knobs, BC, 5 tubes, AC, $85.00-115.00.

9-102, table, 1948, plastic, upper front curved slide rule dial, lower "boomerang" louvers, 3 knobs, BC, 6 tubes, AC **$55.00-65.00**

9-103, table, 1949, plastic, lower front slide rule dial, large upper perforated grille area with center crest, 3 knobs, BC, 6 tubes, AC/DC.................**$50.00-65.00**

9-104W, table, 1949, plastic, lower front slide rule dial, large upper grille area with center crest, 3 knobs, BC, 6 tubes, AC/DC **$50.00-65.00**

9-105, table, 1949, plastic, lower front slide rule dial, large upper grille area with center crest, 3 knobs, BC, SW, 6 tubes, AC/DC **$50.00-65.00**

9-106W, table, 1949, plastic, lower front slide rule dial, large upper grille area with center crest, 3 knobs, BC, SW, 6 tubes, AC/DC..**$50.00-65.00**

9-113, table, 1949, plastic, lower slanted slide rule dial, upper metal perforated grille, 2 knobs, BC, 5 tubes, AC/DC **$40.00-50.00**

9-114W, table, 1949, plastic, lower slanted slide rule dial, upper metal perforated grille, 2 knobs, BC, 5 tubes, AC/DC..............**$40.00-50.00**

9-117, table, 1948, plastic, large right front square dial, left vertical wrap-over grille bars, 3 knobs, BC, 4 tubes, battery **$35.00-45.00**

9-118W, table, 1948, plastic, upper front curved slide rule dial, lower "boomerang" louvers, 3 knobs, BC, 6 tubes, AC **$55.00-65.00**

9-119, table, 1948, plastic, right front round dial, left cloth grille with horizontal bars, 2 knobs, BC, 5 tubes, AC/DC **$45.00-55.00**

9-121, table, 1949, plastic, raised top with slide rule dial, lower horizontal wrap-around louvers, 2 knobs, BC, 5 tubes, AC/DC......**$40.00-50.00**

9-122W, table, 1949, plastic, raised top with slide rule dial, lower horizontal wrap-around louvers, 2 knobs, BC, 5 tubes, AC/DC .**$40.00-50.00**

9-201, console-R/P, 1948, wood, 2 upper front slide rule dials, center pull-out phono, lower grille, 4 knobs, BC, FM, 8 tubes, AC....**$65.00-75.00**

9-202M, console-R/P, 1948, wood, inner right slide rule dial, door, left pull-out phono drawer, 4 knobs, BC, FM, 8 tubes, AC ..**$65.00-75.00**

9-120W, table, 1948, plastic, right front round dial, left cloth grille with horizontal bars, 2 knobs, BC, 5 tubes, AC/DC, $45.00-55.00.

7H2, tombstone, 1934, wood, shouldered, center front round dial, upper cloth grille with cut-outs, 4 knobs, BC, SW, 7 tubes, AC, $150.00-180.00.

9-203B, console-R/P, 1948, wood, inner right dial, left pull-out phono, lower storage & grille, 4 knobs, BC, FM, 8 tubes, AC **$65.00-75.00**

9-204, console-R/P, 1949, wood, inner right dial, left pull-out phono, lower storage & grille, BC, FM, 9 tubes, AC **$75.00-85.00**

9-205M, console-R/P, 1949, wood, right tilt-out slide rule dial, left pull-out phono drawer, 4 knobs, BC, FM, 9 tubes, AC..........**$65.00-75.00**

9-207M, console-R/P, 1949, wood, right tilt-out slide rule dial, left pull-out phono drawer, 5 knobs, BC, SW, FM, 11 tubes, AC **$65.00-75.00**

9-209, console-R/P, 1949, walnut, inner slide rule dial, pull-out phono drawer, criss-cross grille, 3 knobs, BC, 6 tubes, AC......**$75.00-85.00**

9-209L, console-R/P, 1949, walnut, inner slide rule dial, pull-out phono drawer, criss-cross grille, BC, 6 tubes, AC....................**$65.00-75.00**

9-212M, console-R/P, 1949, mahogany, inner right slide rule dial, door, left pull-out phono drawer, criss-cross grille, 3 knobs, BC, 6 tubes, AC **$65.00-75.00**

9-212ML, console-R/P, 1949, mahogany, inner slide rule dial, pull-out phono drawer, criss-cross grille, BC, 6 tubes, AC **$65.00-75.00**

9-213B, console-R/P, 1949, blonde, inner slide rule dial, pull-out phono drawer, criss-cross grille, BC, 6 tubes, AC **$65.00-75.00**

9-214M, console-R/P, 1949, wood, right tilt-out slide rule dial, pull-out phono drawer, 4 knobs, BC, FM, 11 tubes, AC.............**$65.00-75.00**

9-214ML, console-R/P, 1949, wood, right tilt-out slide rule dial, left pull-out phono drawer, 4 knobs, BC, FM, 11 tubes, AC **$65.00-75.00**

9-302, portable, 1948, alligator, metal front panel with upper slide rule dial, handle, 2 top knobs, BC, 5 tubes, AC/DC/battery..**$35.00-45.00**

10-135, table, 1950, white plastic, center front circular chrome dial with inner metal perforated grille, 2 knobs, BC, 5 tubes, AC/DC **$110.00-130.00**

10-137, table, 1950, chartreuse plastic, center front circular dial with inner perforated grille, 2 knobs, BC, 5 tubes, AC/DC **$110.00-130.00**

10-138, table, 1950, maroon plastic, center front circular dial with inner perforated grille, 2 knobs, BC, 5 tubes, AC/DC **$110.00-130.00**

10-139, table, 1950, aqua plastic, center front circular chrome dial with inner metal perforated grille, 2 knobs, BC, 5 tubes, AC/DC **$110.00-130.00**

10-140, table, 1950, green plastic, center front circular chrome dial with inner metal perforated grille, 2 knobs, BC, 5 tubes, AC/DC **$110.00-130.00**

10-145M, table-R/P, 1949, wood, center front round dial, right & left grilles, lift top, inner phono, 3 knobs, BC, AC **$30.00-35.00**

10-307M, portable, 1949, mahogany plastic, upper front slide rule dial, lower horizontal grille bars, handle, 2 knobs, BC, 5 tubes, AC/DC/battery **$30.00-35.00**

10-308, portable, 1949, gray plastic, upper front slide rule dial, lower horizontal grille bars, handle, 2 knobs, BC, 5 tubes, AC/DC/battery **$30.00-35.00**

10-309, portable, 1949, green plastic, upper front slide rule dial, lower horizontal grille bars, handle, 2 knobs, BC, 5 tubes, AC/DC/battery **$30.00-35.00**

11, table, C1940, plastic, right front dial, left horizontal wrap-around louvers, 2 knobs, BC, 5 tubes, AC/DC **$45.00-55.00**

11-100U, table, 1951, white plastic, large center round dial with inner circular louvers, side "fins," 2 knobs, BC, 5 tubes, AC/DC ..**$150.00-180.00**

111-102U, table, 1951, green plastic, large center round dial with inner circular louvers, side "fins," 2 knobs, BC, 5 tubes, AC/DC **$150.00-180.00**

11-103U, table, 1951, red plastic, large center round dial with inner circular louvers, side "fins," 2 knobs, BC, 5 tubes, AC/DC **$150.00-180.00**

11-104U, table, 1951, ebony plastic, large center round dial with inner circular louvers, side "fins," 2 knobs, BC, 5 tubes, AC/DC....**$150.00-180.00**

11-105U, table, 1951, chartreuse plastic, large center round dial with inner circular louvers, side "fins," 2 knobs, BC, 5 tubes, AC/DC **$150.00-180.00**

11-106U, table, 1952, black plastic, center front square dial with inner checkered grille & crest, 2 knobs, BC, 5 tubes, AC/DC ..**$65.00-75.00**

11-108U, table, 1952, burgundy plastic, center front square dial with inner checkered grille & crest, 2 knobs, BC, 5 tubes, AC/DC ..**$65.00-75.00**

11-109U, table, 1952, green plastic, center front square dial with inner checkered grille & crest, 2 knobs, BC, 5 tubes, AC/DC ..**$65.00-75.00**

10-136E, table, 1950, ebony plastic, center front circular dial with inner perforated grille, 2 knobs, BC, 5 tubes, AC/DC, $110.00-130.00.

11-AB, table, 1940, plastic, right front dial, left horizontal wrap-around louvers, base, 2 knobs, BC, SW, 5 tubes, AC/DC, $50.00-65.00.

11-114U "Serenader," table, 1951, ivory plastic, right front round dial, left concentric circular louvers with horizontal center ridge, 2 knobs, BC, 5 tubes, AC/DC..$110.00-130.00

11-115U "Serenader," table, 1951, red plastic, right front round dial, left concentric circular louvers with horizontal center ridge, 2 knobs, BC, 5 tubes, AC/DC $110.00-130.00

11-116U "Serenader," table, 1951, gray plastic, right front round dial, left concentric circular louvers with horizontal center ridge, 2 knobs, BC, 5 tubes, AC/DC $110.00-130.00

11-117U "Serenader," table, 1951, green plastic, right front round dial, left concentric circular louvers with horizontal center ridge, 2 knobs, BC, 5 tubes, AC/DC.....................................$110.00-130.00

11-118U "Serenader," table, 1951, beige plastic, right front round dial, left concentric circular louvers with horizontal center ridge, 2 knobs, BC, 5 tubes, AC/DC.....................................$110.00-130.00

11-119U "Serenader," table, 1951, blue plastic, right front round dial, left concentric circular louvers with horizontal center ridge, 2 knobs, BC, 5 tubes, AC/DC $110.00-130.00

11-120U, table-C, 1951, white plastic, right front round dial with inner perforations, left alarm clock, center crest, 5 knobs, BC, 5 tubes, AC $120.00-150.00

11-121U, table-C, 1951, ebony plastic, right front round dial with inner perforations, left alarm clock, center crest, 5 knobs, BC, 5 tubes, AC $120.00-150.00

11-122U, table-C, 1951, chartreuse plastic, right front round dial with inner perforations, left alarm clock, center crest, 5 knobs, BC, 5 tubes, AC $120.00-150.00

11-123U, table-C, 1951, maroon plastic, right front round dial with inner perforations, left alarm clock, center crest, 5 knobs, BC, 5 tubes, AC $120.00-150.00

11-124U, table-C, 1951, blue plastic, right front round dial with inner perforations, left alarm clock, center crest, 5 knobs, BC, 5 tubes, AC $120.00-150.00

11-125U, table-C, 1951, green plastic, right front round dial with inner perforations, left alarm clock, center crest, 5 knobs, BC, 5 tubes, AC $120.00-150.00

11-126U, table, 1951, brown plastic, upper right front dial, left round grille with center crest, 3 knobs, BC, FM, 7 tubes, AC/DC **$40.00-50.00**

11-101U, table, 1951, blue plastic, large round dial with inner circular louvers, side "fins," 2 knobs, BC, 5 tubes, AC/DC, $150.00-180.00.

11-127U, table, 1951, green plastic, upper right front dial, left round grille with center crest, 3 knobs, BC, FM, 7 tubes, AC/DC **$40.00-50.00**

11-128U, table, 1951, ebony plastic, upper right front dial, left round grille with center crest, 3 knobs, BC, FM, 7 tubes, AC/DC **$40.00-50.00**

11-129U, table, 1951, maroon plastic, upper right front dial, left round grille with center crest, 3 knobs, BC, FM, 7 tubes, AC/DC **$40.00-50.00**

11-132U, table, 1951, plastic, center front round see-through filigree dial with inner grille area, rear label states "made exclusively for the leading jewelers of America by Crosley," 2 knobs, BC, 5 tubes, AC/DC **$120.00-150.00**

11-207MU, console-R/P, 1951, wood, inner right slide rule dial, door, left pull-out phono drawer, 3 knobs, BC, 8 tubes, AC..........**$50.00-65.00**

11-301U, portable, 1951, blue plastic, flip up semi-circular front with crest, inner dial, handle, 2 knobs, BC, 4 tubes, AC/DC/battery **$45.00-55.00**

11-302U, portable, 1951, green plastic, flip up semi-circular front with crest, inner dial, handle, 2 knobs, BC, 4 tubes, AC/DC/battery **$45.00-55.00**

11-303U, portable, 1951, red plastic, flip up semi-circular front with crest, inner dial, handle, 2 knobs, BC, 4 tubes, AC/DC/battery..**$45.00-55.00**

11-304U, portable, 1951, brown plastic, flip up semi-circular front with crest, inner dial, handle, 2 knobs, BC, 4 tubes, AC/DC/battery **$45.00-55.00**

11-305U, portable, 1951, ebony plastic, flip up semi-circular front with crest, inner dial, handle, 2 knobs, BC, 4 tubes, AC/DC/battery **$45.00-55.00**

11-107U, table, 1952, beige plastic, center front square dial with inner checkered grille & crest, 2 knobs, BC, 5 tubes, AC/DC, $65.00-75.00.

11-550MU, console-R/P, 1951, wood, inner front round metal dial, lower pull-out phono, double doors, 3 knobs, BC, 5 tubes, AC ..**$65.00-75.00**

13-BK, table, 1940, plastic, right front square dial, left horizontal wrap-around grille bars, handle, 3 knobs, BC, SW, 5 tubes, AC/DC **$40.00-50.00**

15-16, console, 1937, wood, large upper front round dial, lower cloth grille with 3 vertical bars, 5 knobs, BC, 15 tubes **$180.00-200.00**

16AL, table, 1940, walnut, right front dial, left vertical grille bars, pushbuttons, 3 knobs, BC, 5 tubes, AC/DC........................**$65.00-75.00**

20AP "Fiver," table, 1941, wood, right front square dial, left cloth grille with diagonal bars, 3 knobs, BC, SW, 5 tubes, AC **$45.00-55.00**

21, table, 1929, metal, rectangular case, center window dial, Deco corner details, 3 knobs, BC, 6 tubes, battery **$85.00-115.00**

22, console, 1929, walnut veneer, highboy, upper front window dial, lower round grille with cut-outs, 3 knobs, BC, 6 tubes, AC **$140.00-160.00**

22-AS, table-R/P, 1940, wood, right front dial, left grille with horizontal bars, lift top, inner phono, 3 knobs, BC, SW, AC **$30.00-35.00**

22CA, console, 1941, walnut, large upper front slanted round dial, lower cloth grille with vertical bars, pushbuttons, 2 knobs, BC, SW, 12 tubes, AC **$200.00-230.00**

22CB, console, 1941, wood, large upper front slanted round dial, lower vertical grille bars, BC, FM1, 12 tubes, AC **$200.00-230.00**

28AZ "Recordola," console-R/P/Rec/PA, 1940, wood, inner dial, phono, recorder, PA system, front grille with 3 vertical bars, BC, 8 tubes, AC **$110.00-130.00**

31, table, 1929, metal, rectangular case, center window dial, Deco corner details, 3 knobs, BC, 7 tubes, AC **$85.00-115.00**

33-BG, table-R/P/Rec, 1940, wood, outer right front square dial, left horizontal louvers, lift top, inner phono, 3 knobs, BC, 5 tubes, AC...**$35.00-45.00**

11-112U, table, C1952, plastic, center front round see-through filigree dial with inner grille area, rear label states "made exclusively for the leading jewelers of America by Crosley," 2 knobs, BC, 5 tubes, AC/DC, $120.00-150.00.

33-S, console, 1929, wood, lowboy, upper front window dial, lower grille with cut-outs, 3 knobs, BC, 7 tubes, AC ....**$110.00-130.00.**

34-S, console, 1929, wood, lowboy, inner dial & controls, double front doors, BC, 7 tubes, AC ....**$120.00-150.00.**

35AK, table-R/P, 1941, wood, right front square dial, left grille, lift top, inner phono, 3 knobs, BC, 6 tubes, AC ....**$30.00-35.00.**

36AM, table, 1940, wood, right front dial, left cloth grille with cut-outs, 2 knobs, BC, 4 tubes, battery.....................................**$30.00-35.00.**

41, table, 1929, metal, rectangular case, center window dial, Deco corner details, 3 knobs, BC, 8 tubes, AC ....**$85.00-115.00.**

43BT, table, 1940, wood, right front square dial, left horizontal louvers, 3 knobs, BC, 5 tubes, AC/DC/battery.............................**$45.00-55.00.**

46FB, table, 1947, wood, large center front square dial, right & left cloth wrap-around grilles, 3 knobs, BC, SW, 4 tubes, battery..**$40.00-50.00.**

48 "Johnny Smoker," small console, 1931, repwood, ornate "carved" front panel, lower round cloth grille with cut-outs, 3 knobs, BC ....**$410.00-460.00.**

48 "Widgit," cathedral, 1931, repwood, ornate "carved" front panel, upper grille with cut-outs, 2 knobs, BC, 5 tubes, AC ....**$470.00-530.00.**

50A, table-amp, 1925, wood, amplifier, black Bakelite front panel, lift top, 2 tubes, battery ....**$180.00-200.00.**

50/50A, table, 1925, wood, low rectangular case, receiver/amplifier in one unit, lift top, BC, 3 tubes, battery ....**$350.00-380.00.**

50 Portable, portable, 1924, wood, inner 1 dial black front panel, fold-back top, fold-down front, storage, BC, 1 tube, battery.......**$320.00-350.00.**

51, table, 1924, wood, low rectangular case, 1 dial black front panel, lift top, 4 knobs, BC, 2 tubes, battery.............................**$140.00-170.00.**

51A, table-amp, 1924, wood, box, 2-stage amplifier, 2 tubes, battery ....**$160.00-190.00.**

51 Portable, portable, 1924, leatherette, inner 1 dial front panel, fold-back top, fold-down front, handle, 4 knobs, BC, 2 tubes, battery ....**$180.00-200.00.**

51SD "Special Deluxe," table, 1924, wood, high rectangular case, left front half-round pointer dial, lift top, 4 knobs, BC, 2 tubes, battery...**$150.00-180.00.**

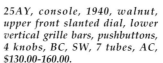

25AY, console, 1940, walnut, upper front slanted dial, lower vertical grille bars, pushbuttons, 4 knobs, BC, SW, 7 tubes, AC, $130.00-160.00.

52-FC, table, 1942, wood, right front airplane dial, left cloth grille with horizontal bars, 3 knobs, BC, 5 tubes, AC/DC/battery ..**$45.00-55.00.**

52P, portable, 1924, leatherette, inner 1 dial front panel, fold-down front, handle, BC, 3 tubes, battery ....**$180.00-200.00.**

52PA, portable, 1941, right front dial over large grille area, handle, 2 knobs, BC, 5 tubes, AC/DC/battery.................................**$30.00-35.00.**

52-S "Special," table, 1924, wood, high rectangular case, slant front panel with left dial, lift top, 5 knobs, BC, 3 tubes, battery ......**$130.00-150.00.**

52SD "Special Deluxe," table, 1924, wood, high rectangular case, slanted panel, left half-round pointer dial, 4 knobs, BC, 3 tubes, battery ....**$130.00-150.00.**

52TA, table, 1941, walnut, right front square dial, left cloth grille with 2 horizontal bars, 2 knobs, BC, 5 tubes, AC/DC ....**$40.00-50.00.**

52TD, table, 1941, plastic, right front airplane dial, right and left horizontal wrap-around bars, 3 knobs, BC, SW, 5 tubes, AC/DC ..**$45.00-55.00.**

52TL, table, 1942, wood, large center front dial, side grille, 3 knobs, BC, SW, 5 tubes, AC..**$55.00-65.00.**

52TP, table-R/P, 1942, wood, outer right front airplane dial, left grille area, lift top, inner phono, 3 knobs, BC, SW, 5 tubes, AC ......**$35.00-40.00.**

52TQ, table-R/P, 1941, wood, outer right front airplane dial, left grille area, lift top, inner phono, 3 knobs, BC, 5 tubes, AC ....**$35.00-40.00.**

56FA, table, 1948, plastic, large center front dial, right & left horizontal wrap-around louvers, 4 knobs, BC, SW, 5 tubes, battery ....**$55.00-65.00.**

56PA, portable, 1946, plastic, upper front slide rule dial, lower horizontal louvers, handle, 2 top knobs, BC, 5 tubes, AC/DC/battery......**$55.00-65.00.**

56PB, portable, 1946, plastic, upper front slide rule dial, lower horizontal louvers, handle, 2 top knobs, BC, 5 tubes, AC/DC/battery ..**$55.00-65.00.**

56TA-L, table, 1946, plastic, right front dial over horizontal wrap-around grille bars, 3 knobs, BC, SW, 5 tubes, AC/DC...............**$45.00-55.00.**

56TC, table, 1946, wood, right front square dial, left grille with horizontal bars, 3 knobs, BC, SW, 5 tubes, AC/DC ....**$40.00-50.00.**

14-AG, table, 1940, wood, right front square dial, left grille with horizontal bars, handle, 3 knobs, BC, SW, 5 tubes, AC/DC, $50.00-65.00.

46FA, table, 1947, plastic, large center front square dial, right and left horizontal wrap-around louvers, 3 knobs, BC, SW, 4 tubes, battery, $50.00-65.00.

50, table, 1924, wood, 1 dial black Bakelite front panel, lift top, 4 knobs, BC, 1 tube, battery, $120.00-150.00.

52, table, 1924, wood, low rectangular case, 1 dial black front panel, lift top, 4 knobs, BC, 3 tubes, battery, $140.00-160.00.

56TC-L, table, 1946, wood, right front square dial, left grille with horizontal wrap-around bars, 3 knobs, BC, SW, 5 tubes, AC/DC....$40.00-50.00

56TD "Duette," table, 1947, plastic, modern, top slide rule dial, lower vertical grille bars, 3 knobs, BC, 5 tubes, AC/DC $120.00-150.00

56TD-R "Duette," table, 1947, plastic, modern, top slide rule dial, lower vertical grille bars, 3 knobs, BC, 5 tubes, AC/DC $120.00-150.00

56TG, table, 1946, plastic, upper front slide rule dial, lower horizontal wrap-around louvers, 2 knobs, BC, 5 tubes, AC/DC.....$45.00-55.00

56TJ, table, 1946, wood, upper slanted slide rule dial, center cloth grille, 2 knobs, BC, AC/DC $35.00-45.00

56TN, table, 1948, wood, right front dial, left wrap-around grille with horizontal bars, 3 knobs, BC, SW, 5 tubes, AC/DC..............$50.00-65.00

56TN-L, table, 1946, wood, right front dial, left wrap-around grille with horizontal bars, 3 knobs, BC, SW, 5 tubes, AC/DC........$50.00-65.00

56TP, table-R/P, 1946, wood, right front black dial, left cloth wrap-around grille, lift top, inner phono, 3 knobs, BC, SW, 5 tubes, AC.................................. $35.00-45.00

56TP-L, table-R/P, 1948, wood, right front black dial, left cloth wrap-around grille, lift top, inner phono, 3 knobs, BC, SW, 5 tubes, AC.................................$35.00-45.00

56TR, table-R/P, 1948, wood, center front slide rule dial, right/left wrap-around grilles, lift top, inner phono, 3 knobs, BC, 5 tubes, AC $30.00-35.00

56TS, table-R/P, 1947, wood, center front slide rule dial, right/left wrap-around cloth grilles, lift top, inner phono, 3 knobs, BC, 5 tubes, AC $30.00-35.00

56TU, table, 1946, plastic, upper slide rule dial, lower wrap-around louvers, handle, 2 knobs, BC, 5 tubes, AC/DC $55.00-65.00

56TU-O, table, 1949, plastic, upper slide rule dial, lower wrap-around louvers, handle, 2 knobs, BC, 5 tubes, AC/DC $55.00-65.00

56TV-O, table, 1949, wood, upper slide rule dial, large center front grille, BC, 5 tubes, AC/DC.......................................$30.00-40.00

56TW, table, 1946, plastic, right front square dial, right/left horizontal wrap-around grille bars, base, 3 knobs, BC, SW, 5 tubes, AC/DC $50.00-65.00

56TX-L, table, 1946, plastic, right front square dial, right/left horizontal wrap-around grille bars, base, 3 knobs, BC, SW, 5 tubes, AC/DC $50.00-65.00

56TY, table, 1948, wood, upper slide rule dial, lower horizontal grille bars, 2 knobs, BC, AC/DC $50.00-65.00

56TZ, table-R/P, 1948, two-tone wood, inner right slide rule dial, phono, 3/4 lift top, 3 knobs, BC, 5 tubes, AC $30.00-35.00

57TK, table, 1948, plastic, upper front slide rule dial, lower vertical grille bars, 2 knobs, BC, 5 tubes, AC/DC...............................$45.00-55.00

57TL, table, 1948, plastic, upper front slide rule dial, lower vertical grille bars, 2 knobs, BC, 5 tubes, AC/DC.............................$45.00-55.00

58 "Buddy Boy," cathedral, 1931, ornate repwood case, thumbwheel tuning, cloth grille with cut-outs, 2 knobs, BC, AC.... $470.00-530.00

58TK, table, 1948, plastic, right front round dial, left cloth grille with horizontal bars, 2 knobs, BC, 5 tubes, AC/DC $45.00-55.00

58TL, table, 1948, plastic, upper slanted slide rule dial, lower vertical grille bars, 2 knobs, BC, 5 tubes, AC/DC $50.00-65.00

58TW, table, 1948, plastic, upper slanted slide rule dial, lower wrap-around louvers, lucite handle, 2 knobs, BC, 5 tubes, AC/DC $65.00-75.00

59 "Oracle," grandfather clock, 1931, wood, window dial, ornate grille, raised top, Deco clock face, 3 knobs, BC, 5 tubes, AC ..$470.00-530.00

59 "Show Boy," cathedral, 1931, ornate repwood case, center front window dial, upper grille area, 3 knobs, BC, 5 tubes, AC .. $380.00-430.00

61, tombstone, 1934, wood, shouldered, center front round airplane dial, upper grille with cut-outs, 3 knobs, BC, SW, 6 tubes, AC $140.00-160.00

62PB, portable, 1942, leatherette, inner right front dial, left grille, fold-down front, handle, 2 knobs, BC, 6 tubes, AC/DC/battery $30.00-35.00

64 MD, console, 1934, wood, upper front round dial, lower cloth grille with cut-outs, BC, SW, AC $110.00-130.00

66CS, console-R/P, 1947, wood, large inner right dial, phono, lift top, front grille with 2 vertical bars, 4 knobs, BC, SW, 6 tubes, AC..$65.00-75.00

66-T, table, 1946, wood, large center front square dial, right & left wrap-around grilles, 4 knobs, BC, SW, 6 tubes $55.00-65.00

66-TC, table, 1946, wood, large center front square dial, right & left wrap-around grilles, 4 knobs, BC, SW, 6 tubes, AC $55.00-65.00

66TW, table, 1946, plastic, large center front square black dial, right & left wrap-around louvers, 4 knobs, BC, SW, 6 tubes, AC .. $55.00-65.00

68CP, console-R/P, 1948, wood, inner right slide rule dial, phono, lift top, front criss-cross grille, 4 knobs, BC, SW, 6 tubes, AC..$65.00-75.00

68CR, console-R/P, 1948, wood, upper front slide rule dial, center pull-out phono, lower grille, 4 knobs, BC, SW, 6 tubes, AC $65.00-75.00

51-S "Special," table, 1924, wood, slanted 1 dial black Bakelite front panel, lift top, 3 knobs, BC, 2 tubes, battery, $110.00-140.00.

54G "New Buddy Boy," table, 1930, repwood, ornate "carved" front panel, lower right dial, upper cloth grille, 2 knobs, BC, AC, $300.00-350.00.

56TD-W "Duette," table, 1947, plastic, modern, top slide rule dial, lower front vertical grille bars, 3 knobs, BC, 5 tubes, AC/DC, $120.00-150.00.

63TA "Victory," table, 1946, wood, large red, white & blue center front dial with stars & stripes, right & left wrap-around grilles, 4 knobs, BC, SW, 6 tubes, AC, $65.00-85.00.

68TA, table, 1948, plastic, upper front curved slide rule dial, lower "boomerang" louvers, 3 knobs, BC, 6 tubes, AC **$55.00-65.00**

68TW, table, 1948, plastic, upper front curved slide rule dial, lower "boomerang" louvers, 3 knobs, BC, 6 tubes, AC **$55.00-65.00**

72AF, tombstone, 1934, wood, shouldered, lower front round airplane dial, upper cloth grille with cut-outs, 3 knobs, BC, SW, 7 tubes, AC.. **$120.00-140.00**

72CP, console-R/P, 1942, wood, upper front slanted airplane dial, center pull-out phono, lower grille with vertical bars, 4 knobs, BC, SW, 7 tubes, AC **$110.00-130.00**

75, table, wood, low rectangular case, 3 upper front window dials, lift top, 5 knobs, BC **$120.00-140.00**

80, cathedral, 1934, wood, center front window dial, upper 3-section cloth grille, 4 knobs, BC, AC **$180.00-200.00**

82-S, console, 1929, wood, highboy, inner dial & controls, double front doors, stretcher base, BC, 8 tubes, AC......................**$130.00-150.00**

86CR, console-R/P, 1947, walnut, top slanted dial, center pull-out phono, lower grille, storage, 4 knobs, BC, SW, FM, 8 tubes, AC ..**$110.00-130.00**

86CS, console-R/P, 1947, mahogany, top slanted dial, center pull-out phono, lower grille, storage, 4 knobs, BC, SW, FM, 8 tubes, AC **$110.00-130.00**

87CQ, console-R/P, 1948, wood, upper slanted slide rule dial, center pull-out phono drawer, lower grille, 4 knobs, BC, SW, FM, 8 tubes, AC **$110.00-130.00**

88CR, console-R/P, 1948, wood, inner right dial & knobs, left pull-out phono, criss-cross grille, BC, SW, FM, AC **$65.00-75.00**

88TC, table, 1948, wood, upper curved slide rule dial, lower cloth grille, 3 knobs, BC, FM, 8 tubes, AC/DC **$50.00-65.00**

117, console, 1936, wood, upper front round dial, lower cloth grille with center vertical bar, 5 knobs, BC, SW, 9 tubes, AC **$110.00-130.00**

124, cathedral, 1931, wood, low case, center front window dial, upper 3 section grille, fluted columns, 3 knobs, BC, 8 tubes, AC **$240.00-300.00**

124 "Playtime," grandfather clock, 1931, wood, front window dial, lower grille with cut-outs, 3 knobs, BC, 8 tubes, AC...........**$430.00-500.00**

124-M "Playtime," grandfather clock, 1931, wood, front window dial, lower grille with cut-outs, 3 knobs, BC, 8 tubes, AC..**$430.00-500.00**

125, cathedral, 1932, wood, center front window dial, upper 3 section grille, fluted columns, 3 knobs, BC, 5 tubes, AC **$150.00-180.00**

125, console, 1931, wood, upper front window dial with escutcheon, lower cloth grille with cut-outs, 3 knobs, BC, 5 tubes, AC **$120.00-150.00**

127, tombstone, 1931, wood, center front window dial, upper grille with cut-outs, scalloped base, curved top, 3 knobs, BC, 10 tubes, AC **$270.00-300.00**

129, cathedral, 1932, wood, center front window dial with escutcheon, upper grille with cut-outs, 3 knobs, BC, 6 tubes, AC ..**$270.00-300.00**

137, console, 1936, wood, upper front large round dial, lower cloth grille with 3 vertical bars, 5 knobs, BC, SW, 10 tubes, AC ..**$110.00-130.00**

140, table-N, 1931, looks like set of books, inner left window dial, right grille, double doors, 2 knobs, BC, 5 tubes, AC **$350.00-410.00**

141 "Library Universal," table-N, 1931, looks like set of books, inner right window dial, center round grille, double doors, BC, 5 tubes, AC..**$350.00-410.00**

146, cathedral, 1932, wood, center front window dial, upper 3 section cloth grille, fluted columns, 4 knobs, BC, 9 tubes, AC **$240.00-270.00**

146CS, console-R/P, 1947, wood, inner right half-round dial, pushbuttons, left pull-out phono drawer, 2 knobs, BC, SW, FM, 14 tubes, AC **$65.00-75.00**

148 "Fiver," cathedral, 1931, wood, center front window dial with escutcheon, upper cloth grille with cut-outs, 2 knobs, BC, 5 tubes, AC **$240.00-270.00**

148CP, console-R/P, 1948, wood, inner right half-round dial, pushbuttons, left pull-out phono drawer, 2 knobs, BC, SW, FM, 14 tubes, AC **$65.00-75.00**

157, cathedral, 1933, two-tone wood, center front window dial, upper cloth grille with cut-outs, 3 knobs, BC, 10 tubes, AC ..**$240.00-270.00**

166 "Travo," table, C1936, metal, right front dial, center 3-section cloth grille, top vertical slots, 2 knobs, BC, 4 tubes, AC/DC ..**$85.00-115.00**

167, console, 1936, wood, upper front round dial, lower cloth grille with vertical bars, 4 knobs, BC, SW, 13 tubes, AC **$120.00-150.00**

168, cathedral, 1933, wood, center front window dial, upper cloth grille with cut-outs, 4 knobs, BC, SW, 7 tubes, AC **$200.00-220.00**

169, cathedral, 1934, wood, center front window dial, upper sectioned cloth grille, 2 knobs, BC, SW, 4 tubes, AC **$200.00-230.00**

56TX, table, 1946, plastic, right front square dial, right/ left horizontal wrap-around grille bars, base, 3 knobs, BC, SW, 5 tubes, AC/DC, $50.00-65.00.

66TA, table, 1946, plastic, large center front dial, right & left horizontal wrap-around grille bars, 4 knobs, BC, SW, 6 tubes, AC, $55.00-65.00.

88TA, table, 1948, plastic, upper front curved slide rule dial, lower "boomerang" louvers, 3 knobs, BC, FM, 8 tubes, AC/DC, $55.00-65.00.

154, cathedral, 1933, wood, center front window dial with escutcheon, upper cloth grille with cut-outs, 2 knobs, BC, 4 tubes, AC, $200.00-230.00.

176 "Travette," table, 1934, metal, Deco case design, right front dial, center 4-section grille, 2 octagonal knobs, BC, SW, 5 tubes, AC/DC $85.00-115.00

179, tombstone, 1934, wood, Deco, shouldered, center front window dial, upper sectioned grille, silver flutings, BC, SW, 7 tubes, AC $240.00-300.00

182 "Travette Moderne," table, 1934, wood, Deco, right front dial, center grille with chrome cut-outs, 2 knobs, BC, 5 tubes, AC/DC $160.00-190.00

250, tombstone, 1936, wood, large front round dial, upper cloth grille with cut-outs, 4 knobs, BC, SW, 5 tubes $85.00-115.00

251, table, 1936, wood, lower front dial, upper sectioned cloth grille area, 2 knobs, BC, SW, 5 tubes, AC/DC $65.00-75.00

295, table, 1936, wood, right front round dial, left cloth grille with cut-outs, fluted side, 4 knobs, BC, SW, AC........................$85.00-115.00

349, tombstone, 1936, wood, lower front round dial, upper sectioned cloth grille, 4 knobs, BC, SW, 5 tubes $110.00-130.00

395, table, 1936, wood, right front round dial, left cloth grille with cut-outs, 4 knobs, BC, SW, 5 tubes....................................$85.00-115.00

401 "Bandbox Jr.," table, 1928, metal, low rectangular case, center window dial with escutcheon, 3 knobs, BC, 4 tubes, battery ..$75.00-95.00

418 "Vanity," table, 1938, plastic, sloping front with grille and two horizontal bars, lower four pushbuttons, 1 right side dial knob, 1 left side knob, BC, 4 tubes, AC/DC..$80.00-90.00

428 "Vanity Deluxe," table, 1938, plastic, sloping front with grille and two horizontal bars, lower four pushbuttons, 1 right side dial knob, 1 left side knob, BC, 4 tubes, AC/DC $80.00-90.00

449, tombstone, 1936, wood, center front round dial, upper cloth grille with 2 vertical bars, 4 knobs, BC, SW, 6 tubes $110.00-130.00

458 "Vanity," table, 1939, plastic, sloping front with grille and two horizontal bars, lower four pushbuttons, 1 right side dial knob, 1 left side knob, BC, 4 tubes, battery..$50.00-60.00

495, table, 1936, wood, Deco, off-center round dial, left oblong grille with Deco cut-outs, 4 knobs, BC, SW, 6 tubes, AC $85.00-115.00

515, tombstone, 1934, two-tone wood, lower round airplane dial, upper grille with cut-outs, 4 knobs, BC, SW, 5 tubes, AC......$85.00-105.00

517 "Fiver," tombstone, 1934, wood, lower front round airplane dial, upper cloth grille with cut-outs, 3 knobs, BC, SW, 5 tubes, AC $75.00-85.00

527, tombstone, 1937, wood, lower front round dial, upper cloth grille with horizontal bars, 2 knobs, BC, 5 tubes, battery........$40.00-50.00

527A, table, C1938, two-tone wood, right front square dial, left cloth grille with horizontal bars, 2 knobs, BC, 5 tubes, battery........$45.00-55.00

555, tombstone, 1935, wood, lower front round dial, upper sectioned grille, side fluting, BC, SW, 5 tubes, AC $85.00-105.00

556, tombstone, 1936, wood, lower front round dial, upper sectioned cloth grille, 4 knobs, BC, SW, 5 tubes, battery $85.00-105.00

568 "Trouper," table, 1939, plastic, round front round airplane dial, left grille with horizontal bars, rounded shoulders and inward sloping sides, 2 knobs, BC, 5 tubes, AC/DC $70.00-80.00

588 "Super Vanity Fiver," table, 1939, plastic, sloping front with grille and two horizontal bars, lower four pushbuttons, 1 right side dial knob, 1 left side knob, BC, 5 tubes, AC/DC $80.00-90.00

598 "Vanity," table, 1938, plastic, sloping front with grille and two horizontal bars, lower four pushbuttons, 1 right side dial knob, 1 left side knob, BC, 5 tubes, AC/DC..$80.00-90.00

601 "Bandbox," table, 1927, metal, low rectangular case, front dial with escutcheon, 3 knobs, BC, 6 tubes, battery $65.00-75.00

608 "Gembox," table, 1928, metal, low rectangular case, center front window dial with escutcheon, 3 knobs, BC, 6 tubes, AC...$75.00-95.00

609 "Gemchest," console, 1928, metal, upper front window dial, fancy Chinese grille & corner "straps," legs, 2 knobs, BC, AC......$350.00-410.00

610 "Gembox," table, 1928, metal, low rectangular case, front window dial with escutcheon, 3 knobs, BC, 7 tubes, AC $75.00-95.00

614EH, tombstone, 1934, wood, shouldered, center front round dial, upper sectioned grille, BC, SW, AC...........................$120.00-150.00

614PG, console, 1934, wood, upper front round dial, lower cloth grille with cut-outs, BC, SW, AC $120.00-140.00

122 "Super Buddy Boy," cathedral, 1931, repwood case, lower window dial, upper 3 section grille, 3 knobs, BC, 7 tubes, AC, $470.00-530.00.

160, cathedral, 1933, wood, center front window dial, upper cloth grille with cut-outs, 4 knobs, BC, 12 tubes, AC, $270.00-300.00.

167, cathedral, 1936, wood, center front window dial, upper grille with cut-outs, 3 knobs, BC, SW, 5 tubes, AC ..$180.00-200.00.

587, tombstone, 1939, wood, small case, lower front round dial, upper cloth grille with 2 vertical bars, 2 knobs, BC, AC, $75.00-95.00.

617, chairside, 1937, wood, top round dial and knobs, front grille area with horizontal bars, storage, BC, SW, 6 tubes, AC ..**$120.00-150.00**

628B, table, 1937, plastic, raised top, lower front slide rule dial, upper horizontal grille bars, 5 pushbuttons, 2 knobs, BC, SW........**$65.00-75.00**

637-A, table, 1937, wood, large right round dial, left cloth grille with horizontal bars, 3 knobs, BC, SW, 6 tubes, AC/DC............**$50.00-65.00**

648 "Super Sextette," table, 1939, plastic, center vertical slide rule dial, right and left side horizontal wrap around louvers, 4 top pushbuttons, 2 knobs, BC, 6 tubes, AC/DC............**$65.00-75.00**

649, console, 1937, wood, upper front round dial, lower cloth grille with 2 vertical bars, 4 knobs, BC, SW, 6 tubes **$120.00-150.00**

649A, table, 1940, plastic, center front vertical dial, right & left wrap-around side louvers, top pushbuttons, 2 knobs, BC, 5 tubes, AC/DC **$85.00-115.00**

656, tombstone, 1936, wood, lower front large round dial, upper cloth grille with cut-outs, 4 knobs, BC, 6 tubes, AC...........**$130.00-150.00**

699, console, 1936, wood, upper front round dial, lower cloth grille with vertical bars, BC, SW, 6 tubes.................................**$120.00-150.00**

704 "Jewelbox," table, 1928, metal, low rectangular case, center front dial with escutcheon, 3 knobs, BC, 7 tubes, AC **$75.00-95.00**

704 "Perfecto," side table, 1928, model 704 built into a 6 legged lift top wood table with drop front panel, 3 knobs, BC, 8 tubes, AC **$300.00-320.00**

705 "Showbox," table, 1928, metal, low rectangular case, front window dial with escutcheon, 3 knobs, BC, 8 tubes, DC **$75.00-95.00**

714GA, tombstone, 1934, wood, shouldered, lower round dial, upper grille with cut-outs, 3 knobs, BC, SW, 7 tubes, AC **$120.00-150.00**

714NA, console, 1934, wood, upper front round dial, lower cloth grille with cut-outs, BC, SW, 7 tubes, AC **$120.00-140.00**

725, tombstone, 1935, wood, center front round dial, upper cloth grille with cut-outs, 4 knobs, BC, SW, 7 tubes, AC **$130.00-150.00**

744, table, 1937, wood, center front round airplane dial, grille on top with speaker facing upward, 4 knobs, BC, SW, 7 tubes, AC ..**$100.00-120.00**

745, tombstone, 1937, wood, center front round airplane dial, upper grille with two vertical bars, right and left front corner columns, 4 knobs, BC, SW, 7 tubes, AC **$110.00-130.00**

769, console, 1937, wood, upper front large round dial, lower cloth grille with vertical bar, BC, 7 tubes, AC **$120.00-150.00**

804 "Jewelbox," table, 1929, metal, low rectangular case, center window dial with escutcheon, 3 knobs, BC, 8 tubes, AC **$75.00-95.00**

814FA, tombstone, 1934, wood, center front round dial, upper sectioned grille, 3 knobs, BC, SW, 8 tubes, AC **$110.00-130.00**

814QB, console, 1934, wood, upper front round dial, lower cloth grille with cut-outs, BC, SW, 8 tubes, AC **$120.00-140.00**

817, table, 1937, wood, right front round dial, left cloth grille with horizontal bars, 4 knobs, BC, SW, 8 tubes, AC....................**$65.00-75.00**

819M, console, 1939, wood, upper front slanted dial, lower grille with 3 vertical bars, pushbuttons, 4 knobs, BC, SW, AC......**$150.00-180.00**

865, console, 1935, wood, upper front round dial, lower cloth grille with center vertical divider, 6 feet, 4 knobs, BC, SW, 8 tubes, AC **$150.00-180.00**

899, console, 1936, wood, upper front round dial, lower cloth grille with vertical divider, 5 knobs, BC, SW, 8 tubes, AC **$120.00-150.00**

989, console, 1937, wood, upper front large round dial, lower cloth grille with vertical bar, 5 knobs, BC, 9 tubes, AC...............**$130.00-160.00**

1117, console, 1937, wood, upper front round dial, lower cloth grille with vertical bars, 4 knobs, BC, SW, 11 tubes, AC...........**$150.00-180.00**

1127, console, 1937, wood, upper front round dial, lower cloth grille with vertical bars, 4 knobs, BC, SW, 11 tubes, AC...........**$140.00-170.00**

516, tombstone, 1936, wood, small case, lower front red, white & blue dial, upper cloth grille, 4 knobs, BC, SW, 5 tubes, AC, $75.00-85.00.

612, tombstone, wood, shouldered, center front round dial, upper cloth grille with cut-outs, 4 knobs, BC, $110.00-130.00.

637 "Super 6," table, 1937, wood, large right round dial, left cloth grille with horizontal bars, 3 knobs, BC, SW, 6 tubes, AC, $50.00-65.00.

1199, console, 1937, wood, upper front round dial, lower cloth grille with vertical bar, 5 knobs, BC, SW, 11 tubes, AC..............**$150.00-180.00**

1211, console, 1937, wood, upper front round dial, lower cloth grille with vertical bar, 5 knobs, BC, SW, 12 tubes, AC.............**$150.00-180.00**

1313, console, 1937, wood, upper front round dial, lower cloth grille with vertical bars, 5 knobs, BC, SW, 13 tubes, AC...........**$150.00-180.00**

3716 "WLW," console/PA, 1936, wood, massive console, upper front round dial, 4 chassis, 6 speakers, 4' 10" high, 5 knobs, BC, SW, 37 tubes, AC..**$12,000.00+**

5519, table, 1939, plastic, center front vertical slide rule dial, right & left vertical grille bars, handle, 2 knobs, BC, 5 tubes, AC/DC **$50.00-75.00**

5628-A, table, plastic, lower front slide rule dial, upper horizontal louvers, raised top, 5 pushbuttons, 2 knobs, BC **$75.00-95.00**

AC-7, table, 1927, wood, high rectangular case, slanted front panel with right thumbwheel dial, BC, 7 tubes, AC.....................**$110.00-130.00**

AC-7C, console, 1927, wood, upper right front thumbwheel dial, thumbwheel knobs, lower speaker, BC, 7 tubes, AC **$140.00-160.00**

Ace 3B, table, 1923, wood, low rectangular case, 1 dial front panel, BC, 3 tubes, battery **$180.00-200.00**

Ace 3C, console, 1923, wood, upper Ace 3C table model with feet removed, lower storage area, BC, 3 tubes, battery....**$240.00-270.00**

Ace 3C, table, 1923, wood, high rectangular case, inner 1 dial panel & speaker, double doors, BC, 3 tubes, battery..............**$200.00-230.00**

Arbiter, console-R/P, 1930, walnut veneer with ornate repwood front panel, center dial, lift top, inner phono, BC, AC **$180.00-200.00**

B-429A, portable, 1939, cloth covered, high case, right front square dial, left grille, handle, 2 knobs, BC, 4 tubes, battery **$30.00-35.00**

706 "Showbox," table, 1928, metal, low rectangular case, front window dial with escutcheon, 3 knobs, BC, 8 tubes, AC, $75.00-95.00. (Speaker shown is not included in value.)

B-439A, portable, 1939, striped case, right front dial, left grille, handle, 2 knobs, BC, 4 tubes, battery...**$35.00-40.00**

B-549A, portable, 1939, brown striped cloth, right front dial, left grille, handle, 2 knobs, BC, 5 tubes, AC/DC/battery...............**$30.00-35.00**

B-667A, tombstone, 1937, walnut, center front round dial, upper grille with cut-outs, 4 knobs, BC, 6 tubes, AC/battery...........**$65.00-85.00**

B-5549-A, portable-R/P, 1939, cloth covered, right front dial, left grille, lift top, inner crank phono, handle, 2 knobs, BC, 5 tubes, AC/DC/battery **$30.00-35.00**

CA-12, console, 1941, wood, upper front slide rule dial, lower cloth grille with vertical bars, 4 knobs, BC, SW, 11 tubes, AC **$120.00-140.00**

Centurion, console, 1935, wood, upper front round airplane dial, lower cloth grille with cut-outs, BC, SW, 10 tubes, AC........**$120.00-150.00**

Chum, side table, 1930, walnut veneer with inlay, 28" high, front window dial with escutcheon, 3 knobs, BC, 6 tubes, AC.......**$160.00-190.00**

Comrade, side table, 1930, walnut veneer, 29" high, inner front window dial, double front doors, BC, AC **$140.00-160.00**

D10BE, table, 1951, blue plastic, large center round dial with inner circular louvers, side "fins," 2 knobs, BC, 5 tubes, AC/DC **$150.00-180.00**

D10CE, table, 1951, chartreuse plastic, large center round dial with inner circular louvers, side "fins," 2 knobs, BC, 5 tubes, AC/DC ..**$150.00-180.00**

D10GN, table, 1951, green plastic, large center round dial with inner circular louvers, side "fins," 2 knobs, BC, 5 tubes, AC/DC ..**$150.00-180.00**

D10RD, table, 1951, red plastic, large center round dial with inner circular louvers, side "fins," 2 knobs, BC, 5 tubes, AC/DC **$150.00-180.00**

D10TN, table, 1951, tan plastic, large center round dial with inner circular louvers, side "fins," 2 knobs, BC, 5 tubes, AC/DC **$150.00-180.00**

D10WE, table, 1951, white plastic, large center round dial with inner circular louvers, side "fins," 2 knobs, BC, 5 tubes, AC/DC ..**$150.00-180.00**

655, tombstone, 1935, wood, center front round dial, upper cloth grille with cut-outs, fluting, 4 knobs, BC, SW, 6 tubes, AC, $130.00-150.00.

818-A "Super 8," table, 1938, wood, right front round dial, left 3-section grille, 5 pushbuttons, 4 knobs, BC, SW, 8 tubes, AC, $75.00-85.00.

1014, tombstone, 1935, wood, shouldered, lower front round dial, upper cloth grille with cut-outs, 4 knobs, BC, SW, 10 tubes, AC, $85.00-105.00.

E10BE, table, 1953, blue plastic, large front dial with center pointer & inner criss-cross grille, 2 knobs, BC, 5 tubes, AC/DC, $75.00-95.00.

D25BE, table-C, 1953, blue plastic, right round metal dial with inner perforations, left alarm clock, center crest, 5 knobs, BC, 5 tubes, AC **$120.00-150.00**

D25CE, table-C, 1953, chartreuse plastic, right front round dial with inner perforations, left alarm clock, center crest, 5 knobs, BC, 5 tubes, AC **$120.00-150.00**

D25GN, table-C, 1953, green plastic, right front round dial with inner perforations, left alarm clock, center crest, 5 knobs, BC, 5 tubes, AC **$120.00-150.00**

D25TN, table-C, 1953, tan plastic, right front round dial with inner perforations, left alarm clock, center crest, 5 knobs, BC, 5 tubes, AC **$120.00-150.00**

D25WE, table-C, 1953, white plastic, right round metal dial with inner perforations, left alarm clock, center crest, 5 knobs, BC, 5 tubes, AC **$120.00-150.00**

Director, console, 1930, walnut veneer with ornate repwood front panel, lowboy, center window dial, BC, AC **$180.00-200.00**

E10CE, table, 1953, chartreuse plastic, large front dial with center pointer & inner criss-cross grille, 2 knobs, BC, 5 tubes, AC/DC..**$75.00-95.00**

E10RD, table, 1953, red plastic, large front dial with center pointer & inner criss-cross grille, 2 knobs, BC, 5 tubes, AC/DC....**$75.00-95.00**

E10WE, table, 1953, white plastic, large front dial with center pointer & inner criss-cross grille, 2 knobs, BC, 5 tubes, AC/DC....**$75.00-95.00**

E15BE, table, 1953, blue plastic, upper front dial, perforated grille area with center horizontal bar, crest, 2 "steering wheel" knobs, BC, 5 tubes, AC/DC **$85.00-115.00**

E15CE, table, 1953, chartreuse plastic, upper front dial, perforated grille area with center horizontal bar, crest, 2 knobs, BC, 5 tubes, AC/DC **$85.00-115.00**

E15TN, table, 1953, tan plastic, upper front dial, perforated grille area with center horizontal bar, crest, 2 "steering wheel" knobs, BC, 5 tubes, AC/DC..........................**$85.00-115.00**

E15WE, table, 1953, white plastic, upper front dial, perforated grille area with center horizontal bar, crest, 2 "steering wheel" knobs, BC, 5 tubes, AC/DC..........................**$85.00-115.00**

E20GN, table, 1953, green plastic, large center front dial with inner cloth grille & gold pointer, 2 knobs, BC, 5 tubes, AC/DC........**$65.00-85.00**

E20GY, table, 1953, grey plastic, large center front dial with inner cloth grille & gold pointer, 2 knobs, BC, 5 tubes, AC/DC........**$65.00-85.00**

E20MN, table, 1953, maroon plastic, large center front dial with inner cloth grille & gold pointer, 2 knobs, BC, 5 tubes, AC/DC **$65.00-85.00**

E20TN, table, 1953, tan plastic, large center front dial with inner cloth grille & gold pointer, 2 knobs, BC, 5 tubes, AC/DC........**$65.00-85.00**

E30BE, table, 1953, blue plastic, right front dial, left round grille with center crest overlaps lower checkered panel, 3 knobs, BC, 7 tubes, AC **$40.00-50.00**

E30GN, table, 1953, green plastic, right front dial, left round grille with center crest overlaps lower checkered panel, 4 knobs, BC, FM, 7 tubes, AC **$40.00-50.00**

E30MN, table, 1953, maroon plastic, right front dial, left round grille with center crest overlaps lower checkered panel, 3 knobs, BC, FM, 7 tubes, AC **$40.00-50.00**

E30TN, table, 1953, tan plastic, right front dial, left round grille with center crest overlaps lower checkered panel, 3 knobs, BC, FM, 7 tubes, AC **$40.00-50.00**

E75CE, table-C, 1953, chartreuse plastic, perforated front panel with lower right "Crosley," left front clock, right side dial knob, 6 knobs, BC, 5 tubes, AC **$30.00-35.00**

E75GN, table-C, 1953, green plastic, perforated front panel with lower right "Crosley," left front clock, right side dial knob, 6 knobs, BC, 5 tubes, AC **$30.00-35.00**

E75RD, table-C, 1953, red plastic, perforated front panel with lower right "Crosley," left front clock, right side dial knob, 6 knobs, BC, 5 tubes, AC **$30.00-35.00**

E75TN, table-C, 1953, tan plastic, perforated front panel with lower right "Crosley," left front clock, right side dial knob, 6 knobs, BC, 5 tubes, AC **$30.00-35.00**

E85CE, table-C, 1953, chartreuse plastic, perforated front panel with lower right "Crosley," left front clock, right side dial knob, 6 knobs, BC, 5 tubes, AC **$30.00-35.00**

E85GN, table-C, 1953, green plastic, perforated front panel with lower right "Crosley," left front clock, right side dial knob, 6 knobs, BC, 5 tubes, AC **$30.00-35.00**

D25MN, table-C, 1953, maroon plastic, right front round dial with inner perforations, left alarm clock, center crest, 5 knobs, BC, 5 tubes, AC, $120.00-150.00.

Elf, cathedral, 1931, pressed wood case, ornate "carved" front, upper cloth grille with cut-outs, 2 knobs, BC, AC, $470.00-530.00.

Pup "Sky Terrier," table, 1924, metal, square case, side knobs, BC, 1 top exposed tube, battery, $470.00-530.00.

T60CL, table, 1955, charcoal plastic, lower right front oblong slide rule dial over large checkered grille, upper left front "Crosley," feet, 2 knobs, BC, 5 tubes, AC/DC, $30.00-35.00.

E85RD, table-C, 1953, red plastic, perforated front panel with lower right "Crosley," left front clock, right side dial knob, 6 knobs, BC, 5 tubes, AC **$30.00-35.00**

E85TN, table-C, 1953, tan plastic, perforated front panel with lower right "Crosley," left front clock, right side dial knob, 6 knobs, BC, 5 tubes, AC

E90BK, table-C, 1953, black plastic, large front grille with left square alarm clock, right side dial knob, 5 knobs, BC, 5 tubes, AC **$30.00-35.00**

E90CE, table-C, 1953, chartreuse plastic, large front grille with left square alarm clock, right side dial knob, 5 knobs, BC, 5 tubes, AC ..**$30.00-35.00**

E90GY, table-C, 1953, grey plastic, large front grille with left square alarm clock, right side dial knob, 5 knobs, BC, 5 tubes, AC **$30.00-35.00**

E90RD, table-C, 1953, red plastic, large front grille with left square alarm clock, right side dial knob, 5 knobs, BC, 5 tubes, AC **$30.00-35.00**

E90WE, table-C, 1953, white plastic, large front grille with left square alarm clock, right side dial knob, 5 knobs, BC, 5 tubes, AC **$30.00-35.00**

F5CE, table, 1954, chartreuse plastic, left front lattice grille, right front insignia, right side dial knob, 2 knobs, BC, 5 tubes, AC/DC **$35.00-45.00**

F5IY, table, 1954, ivory plastic, left front lattice grille, right front insignia, right side dial knob, 2 knobs, BC, 5 tubes, AC/DC **$35.00-45.00**

F5MY, table, 1954, mahogany plastic, left front lattice grille, right front insignia, right side dial knob, 2 knobs, BC, 5 tubes, AC/DC **$35.00-45.00**

F5RD, table, 1954, red plastic, left front lattice grille, right front insignia, right side dial knob, 2 knobs, BC, 5 tubes, AC/DC **$35.00-45.00**

F5TWE "Musical Chef," table-timer, 1954, plastic, left side kitchen radio/timer knob, left front lattice grille, right front insignia, right side dial knob, 3 knobs, BC, 5 tubes, AC/DC **$50.00-65.00**

F110BE "Skyrocket," portable, 1953, blue plastic, right front round dial over lattice grille with crest, handle, 2 knobs, BC, 4 tubes, battery **$30.00-35.00**

F110BK "Skyrocket," portable, 1953, black plastic, right front round dial over lattice grille with crest, handle, 2 knobs, BC, 4 tubes, battery **$30.00-35.00**

F110CE "Skyrocket," portable, 1953, chartreuse plastic, right front round dial over lattice grille with crest, handle, 2 knobs, BC, 4 tubes, battery **$30.00-35.00**

F110GE "Skyrocket," portable, 1953, green plastic, right front round dial over lattice grille with crest, handle, 2 knobs, BC, 4 tubes, battery **$30.00-35.00**

F110RD "Skyrocket," portable, 1953, red plastic, right front round dial over lattice grille with crest, handle, 2 knobs, BC, 4 tubes, battery **$30.00-35.00**

G1465, table, 1938, Catalin, right front dial, left horizontal wrap-around louvers, flared base, 2 knobs, BC, AC ....**$1,300.00+**

Harko Senior, table, 1922, mahogany finish, low rectangular case, 1 dial front panel, BC, 1 tubes, battery **$530.00-650.00**

JC-6BK, table-C, 1956, black leatherette, right/left side metal perforated grilles, center front round alarm clock face, wire stand, 4 knobs, BC, 5 tubes, AC **$35.00-45.00**

JC-6BN, table-C, 1956, brown leatherette, right/left side metal perforated grilles, center front round alarm clock face, wire stand, 4 knobs, BC, 5 tubes, AC **$35.00-45.00**

JC-6TN, table-C, 1956, tan leatherette, right/left side metal perforated grilles, center front round alarm clock face, wire stand, 4 knobs, BC, 5 tubes, AC **$35.00-45.00**

JC-6WE, table-C, 1956, white leatherette, right/left side metal perforated grilles, center front round alarm clock face, wire stand, 4 knobs, BC, 5 tubes, AC **$35.00-45.00**

JM-8BG "Musical Memories," portable-N, 1956, leather, looks like small book, inner thumbwheel dial, metal grille, tubes & 2 transistors, 2 knobs, BC, 3 tubes, battery **$150.00-180.00**

Mate, console, 1930, walnut veneer with ornate repwood front panel, upper dial, stretcher base, BC, AC **$180.00-200.00**

Minstrel, console, 1931, wood, inner front window dial, lower cloth grille with cut-outs, double front doors, BC **$120.00-150.00**

Pal, consolette, 1931, wood with ornate repwood front & sides, lowboy, window dial, 3 knobs, BC, 5 tubes, AC **$180.00-200.00**

Playmate, console, 1930, walnut veneer, low case, 29 ½" high, inner front window dial, double doors, BC, AC **$140.00-160.00**

RFL-60, table, 1926, mahogany, low rectangular case, 3 dial panel engraved with woodland scene, 5 knobs, BC, 5 tubes, battery...**$140.00-160.00**

RFL-75, table, 1926, mahogany, low rectangular case, slanted ornately engraved 3 dial front panel, 5 knobs, BC, 5 tubes, battery ..**$190.00-210.00**

Sheraton, cathedral, 1933, wood, Sheraton-style, center front window dial, pedimented top with finial, 3 knobs, BC, 5 tubes, AC, $350.00-410.00.

Trirdyn 3R3, table, 1924, wood, low rectangular case, 2 dial front panel, lift top, 5 knobs, BC, 3 tubes, battery, $95.00-115.00.

Trirdyn Super Regular, table, 1925, wood, low rectangular case, front panel with 2 pointer dials, lift top, 5 knobs, BC, 3 tubes, battery, $140.00-160.00.

RFL-90, console, 1926, mahogany, upper front double dial with escutcheon, lower built-in speaker, BC, 6 tubes, battery **$180.00-200.00**

T60GN, table, 1955, green plastic, lower right front oblong slide rule dial over large checkered grille, upper left front "Crosley," feet, 2 knobs, BC, 5 tubes, AC/DC..**$30.00-35.00**

T60GY, table, 1955, light gray plastic, lower right front oblong slide rule dial over large checkered grille, upper left front "Crosley," feet, 2 knobs, BC, 5 tubes, AC/DC..**$30.00-35.00**

T60IY, table, 1955, ivory plastic, lower right front oblong slide rule dial over large checkered grille, upper left front "Crosley," feet, 2 knobs, BC, 5 tubes, AC/DC..**$30.00-35.00**

T60RD, table, 1955, red plastic, lower right front oblong slide rule dial over large checkered grille, upper left front "Crosley," feet, 2 knobs, BC, 5 tubes, AC/DC..**$30.00-35.00**

TA-62, table, 1941, wood, right front dial, left grille with vertical bars, 5 pushbuttons, 3 knobs, BC, SW, 5 tubes, AC/DC **$65.00-75.00**

TH-52, table, 1941, plastic, right front dial, left horizontal wrap-around grille bars, handle, 3 knobs, BC, SW, 8 tubes, AC/DC ..**$45.00-55.00**

TK-52, table, 1941, wood, right front dial, left vertical grille bars, pushbuttons, 3 knobs, BC, SW, 8 tubes, AC/DC **$65.00-75.00**

Travo Deluxe, table, 1932, Deco case, center cloth grille with cut-outs, top fluting, 2 knobs, BC, AC **$85.00-115.00**

Trirdyn, table, 1925, wood, low rectangular case, 2 dial front panel, lift top, 5 knobs, BC, 3 tubes, battery...............................**$85.00-115.00**

Trirdyn 3R3 Special, table, 1924, walnut, low rectangular case, 2 dial front panel, lift top, feet, 5 knobs, BC, 3 tubes, battery **$120.00-150.00**

Trirdyn Newport, table, 1925, wood, slanted 2 dial black front panel, feet, 5 knobs, BC, 3 tubes, battery **$120.00-150.00**

Trirdyn Regular, table, 1925, wood, low rectangular case, 2 dial front panel, lift top, BC, battery **$95.00-105.00**

Trirdyn Special, table, 1925, wood, low rectangular case, 2 dial front panel, lift top, 5 knobs, BC, 3 tubes, battery **$120.00-150.00**

Trirdyn Super Special, table, 1925, wood, low rectangular case, slanted black panel with 2 pointer dials, lift top, 5 knobs, BC, 3 tubes, battery **$150.00-190.00**

IV, table-amp, 1922, wood, low rectangular case, amplifier, black Bakelite front panel, lift top, battery.........................**$240.00-300.00**

V, table, 1922, wood, low rectangular case, 1 dial black Bakelite front panel, lift top, BC, 1 tube, battery, $240.00-300.00.

VI, table, 1923, wood, low rectangular case, 2 dial black Bakelite front panel, lift top, BC, 2 tubes, battery, $240.00-270.00.

VI Special, table, 1923, wood, low rectangular case, 2 dial front panel, lift top, rear storage, BC, 2 tubes, battery **$270.00-320.00**

VIII, table, 1923, wood, low rectangular case, 2 dial black Bakelite front panel, lift top, BC, 3 tubes, battery **$580.00-700.00**

VIII Portable, portable, 1923, wood, inner 2 dial panel, storage, fold-down front, handle, loop antenna, BC, 3 tubes, battery ..**$1,050.00-1,150.00**

XJ, table, 1923, wood, low rectangular case, 2 dial black Bakelite front panel, lift top, 7 knobs, BC, 4 tubes, battery **$220.00-250.00**

XL, table, 1923, wood, low rectangular case, inner left 2 dial panel, double doors, BC, 4 tubes, battery **$580.00-700.00**

XV, table, 1922, wood, high rectangular case, upper 2 dial panel, lower built-in speaker, 7 knobs, BC, 4 tubes, battery **$580.00-700.00**

X, table, 1922, wood, low rectangular case, 2 dial black Bakelite front panel, lift top, BC, 4 tubes, battery, $240.00-300.00.

CROWN

PR-535, portable, plastic, right front round dial, left perforated grille area, fold-down handle, BC, battery.......................................**$35.00-45.00**

CROYDON

530, tombstone, two-tone wood, lower front airplane dial, upper cloth grille with cut-outs, 3 knobs, BC, SW, AC **$140.00-170.00**

CUTTING & WASHINGTON
Cutting & Washington Radio Corporation
Minneapolis, Minnesota

Cutting & Washington was formed in 1917 by Fulton Cutting and Bowden Washington in the business of making radio transmitters. In 1922 the company marketed its first radio but was out of business by 1924 due to legal difficulties and marketing problems.

11, table, 1922, wood, low rectangular case, 2 dial front panel, lift top, 8 knobs, BC, 3 tubes, battery **$1,000.00-1,200.00**

12A, table, 1923, wood, high rectangular case, 2 dial front panel, removable front, 7 knobs, BC, 3 tubes, battery **$850.00-950.00**

11A, table, 1922, wood, low rectangular case, 3 dial black front panel, lift top, 7 knobs, BC, 3 tubes, battery, $690.00-740.00.

CYARTS

B "Deluxe," table, 1946, Lucite, streamline bullet shape, slide rule dial, rounded left with round cloth grille, 3 knobs, BC, AC........**$1,100.00+**

DAHLBERG
The Dahlberg Company
Minneapolis, Minnesota

4130-D1 "Pillow Speaker," coin op-N, 1955, plastic, mounts on motel bed headboard, slide rule dial, moveable pillow speaker, 2 thumbwheel knobs, BC, AC...**$200.00-230.00**
4130-D11 "Pillow Speaker," coin op-N, 1955, plastic, mounts on motel bed headboard, slide rule dial, moveable pillow speaker, 2 thumbwheel knobs, BC, AC...**$200.00-230.00**

DALBAR
Dalbar Mfg. Co.
1314 Forest Avenue, Dallas, Texas

100-1000 Series, table, 1946, wood, right front dial, left horizontal grille bars, 4 knobs, BC, 5 tubes, AC/DC...............................**$35.00-45.00**
400, table, 1946, wood, right front dial, left diamond-shaped grille, 2 knobs, BC, 6 tubes, AC/DC...**$35.00-45.00**
Barcombo Jr., table-R/P, 1946, wood, right front dial, diamond-shaped grille, lift top, inner phono, 4 knobs, BC, 6 tubes, AC **$30.00-35.00**

DAVID GRIMES
David Grimes, Inc.
1571 Broadway, New York, New York

5B "Baby Grand Duplex," table, 1925, wood, low rectangular case, metal front panel with 2 pointer dials, 5 knobs, BC, 5 tubes, battery, $240.00-300.00.

3XP "Inverse Duplex," table, 1925, wood, rectangular case, slanted 3 dial front panel, BC, 3 tubes, battery **$180.00-200.00**
4DL, table, 1924, wood, 3 inner pointer dials, fold-down front, columns, BC, 4 tubes, battery...**$270.00-300.00**

6D, table, 1925, wood, low rectangular case, inner panel with 3 pointer dials, fold-down front, BC, battery.............................**$300.00-320.00**

DAY-FAN
The Dayton Fan & Motor Company
Dayton, Ohio
Day-Fan Electric Company, Dayton, Ohio

Day-Fan began business as the Dayton Fan & Motor Company in 1889 producing fans. The company marketed a line of radio component parts in 1922 and by 1924 was producing complete radio sets. Day-Fan was bought out by General Motors in 1929.

25 (5069), table, 1928, wood, ornate cabinet with center window dial and large metal escutcheon, lift top, 3 knobs, BC, 9 tubes, AC, $135.00-160.00.

5 (5049), table, 1925, wood, low rectangular case, 1 dial slant front panel, lift top, 5 knobs, BC, 5 tubes, battery **$85.00-105.00**
Daycraft, table, 1925, mahogany, low rectangular case, 1 dial slant front panel, right built-in speaker, BC, 5 tubes, battery **$120.00-150.00**
Daygrand, console, 1926, wood, inner 1 dial slanted panel, left built-in speaker, fold-down front, storage, BC, 5 tubes, battery **$150.00-180.00**
Dayola (5112), table, 1925, mahogany, inner 3 dial slanted panel, fold-down front, feet, BC, 4 tubes, battery **$120.00-140.00**
Dayradia (5107), table, 1924, wood, high rectangular case, lower slant front panel, upper built-in speaker, BC, battery **$200.00-230.00**
Dayroyal, console, 1926, mahogany, desk-style, inner 1 dial panel, upper built-in speaker & storage, doors, BC, 5 tubes, battery ..**$160.00-190.00**
Daytonia, console, 1926, wood, inner 1 dial slanted panel, fold-down front, right built-in speaker, storage, BC, 5 tubes, battery **$160.00-190.00**
OEM-5, table, wood, low rectangular case, 3 dial black front panel, 5 knobs, BC, 5 tubes, battery **$150.00-180.00**
OEM-11 (5106) "Duo-Plex," table, 1924, wood, low rectangular case, 3 dial front panel, lift top, 6 knobs, BC, 3 tubes, battery..........**$110.00-130.00**
OEM-12, table, 1925, mahogany finish, low rectangular case, 3 dial front panel, lift top, 5 knobs, BC, 4 tubes, battery **$85.00-105.00**

OEM-7 (5106), table, 1925, wood, low rectangular case, 3 dial front panel, lift top, 5 knobs, BC, 4 tubes, battery, $130.00-150.00.

DEARBORN
Dearborn Industries, Chicago, Illinois

100, table-R/P, 1947, wood, right front square dial, left cloth grille with oblong cut-outs, open top phono, 4 knobs, BC, 5 tubes, AC **$20.00-25.00**

DEFOREST
The Radio Telephone Company
49 Exchange Place, New York, New York
Deforest Radio Telephone & Telegraph Company
1415 Sedgwick Avenue, New York, New York
Deforest Radio Company
Jersey City, New Jersey

Between 1900 and the end of WW I, Lee Deforest and his various companies produced much electrical equipment for the government. By 1922, the company was fully involved in the production of radio sets for the public. After many legal entanglements, the company was sold to RCA in 1933.

D-4 "Radiophone," table, 1923, wood, square case with fold-back top, inner 2 dial panel, 3 knobs, BC, 1 exposed tube, battery, $480.00-580.00.

D-6, table, 1922, wood, low rectangular case, 2 dial front panel, BC, 3 tubes, battery...**$1,250.00-1,350.00**
D-7 "Radiophone," table, 1922, wood, square case, 2 dial front panel, top loop antenna, BC, 3 tubes, battery...................**$900.00-1,000.00**
D-7A, table, 1923, wood, square case, 2 dial black front panel, top loop antenna, 4 knobs, BC, 3 tubes, battery **$900.00-1,000.00**
D-10, table, 1923, leatherette or mahogany, inner 2 dial panel, doors, top loop antenna, 5 knobs, BC, 4 tubes, battery **$850.00-950.00**
D-14 "Radiophone," table, 1925, wood, tall case, inner slanted 2 dial panel, loop antenna, 3 knobs, BC, 5 exposed tubes, battery ..**$740.00-850.00**
D-17A, table, 1925, wood, upper 2 dial front panel, lower built-in speaker, top loop antenna, BC, 5 tubes, battery **$740.00-850.00**
D-17L, table, 1925, leatherette, upper 2 dial front panel, lower built-in speaker, top loop antenna, BC, 5 tubes, battery........**$640.00-740.00**
D-17M, table, 1925, mahogany, upper 2 dial front panel, lower built-in speaker, top loop antenna, BC, 5 tubes, battery........**$740.00-850.00**
DT-600 "Everyman," table, 1922, wood, square case, crystal set, inner panel and storage, lift lid, BC **$610.00-690.00**

D-12 "Radiophone," table, 1924, leatherette or mahogany cabinet, 2 dial front panel, top loop antenna, BC, 4 tubes, battery, $740.00-850.00.

D-556A, table, plastic, upper slanted slide rule dial, large cloth grille with 4 vertical bars, 2 knobs, BC, $45.00-55.00.

DT-800, table-amp, 1922, wood, two-step amplifier, inner panel, BC, 2 exposed tubes, battery **$900.00-1,000.00**
F-5 "Radiophone," table, 1925, wood, low rectangular case, 3 dial front panel, lift top, feet, 5 knobs, BC, 5 tubes, battery......**$320.00-380.00**
F-5-AL, table, 1925, embossed leatherette, low rectangular case, 3 dial front panel, 5 knobs, BC, 5 tubes, battery..................**$300.00-350.00**
F-5-AW, table, 1925, walnut, low rectangular case, 3 dial front panel, 5 knobs, BC, 5 tubes, battery **$300.00-350.00**
F-5L, table, 1925, leatherette, upper 3 dial front panel, lower built-in speaker, BC, 5 tubes, battery **$300.00-350.00**
F-5M, table, 1925, mahogany, upper 3 dial front panel, lower built-in speaker, 5 knobs, BC, 5 tubes, battery **$300.00-350.00**
"Interpanel," table, 1922, 4 units - tuner, audion control, 1-step amp, transmitter, battery ....**$2,000.00+**

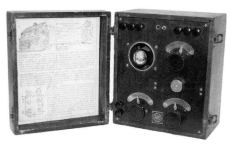

DT-700 "Radiohome," table, 1922, wood, square case, removable lift lid, 3 dials, 3 knobs, BC, 1 exposed tube, battery, $580.00-690.00.

DELCO
Delco Radio, Division of G. M. Corp.
Kokomo, Indiana

608, table, 1949, wood, large multi-band slide rule dial over front grille, 4 knobs, BC, SW, AC **$45.00-55.00**

1102, tombstone, 1935, wood with inlay, center front dial with escutcheon, upper grille with vertical bars, 4 knobs, BC, SW, 6 tubes, AC, $120.00-140.00.

1107, tombstone, 1935, wood, round airplane dial, upper cloth grille with 3 vertical bars, 4 knobs, BC, SW, AC, $120.00-150.00.

R-1116, table, 1938, wood, right front round black dial, left cloth grille with 3 horizontal bars, 4 knobs, BC, AC, $55.00-65.00.

1106, tombstone, 1935, wood, lower front round airplane dial, upper cloth grille with 3 vertical bars, 4 knobs, BC, SW, AC **$120.00-150.00**

R-1125, table, 1937, wood, right front airplane dial, left cloth grille with cut-outs, 2 knobs, BC, AC...........................**$50.00-65.00**

R-1127, table, 1937, wood, right front airplane dial, left cloth grille with cut-outs, tuning eye, 4 knobs, BC, SW **$75.00-95.00**

R-1134, table, plastic, top right wrap-over slide rule dial, right & left wraparound horizontal bars, 5 pushbuttons, 2 knobs, BC, AC..**$120.00-150.00**

R-1135, table, plastic, top right wrap-over slide rule dial, right & left wraparound horizontal bars, 5 pushbuttons, 2 knobs, BC, AC..**$120.00-150.00**

R-1141, table, 1937, wood, lower front slide rule dial, upper cloth grille with horizontal bars, pushbuttons, 4 knobs, BC, SW, AC **$65.00-85.00**

R-1227, table, 1947, plastic, upper slanted slide rule dial, lower horizontal grille bars, decorative case lines, 3 knobs, BC, 6 tubes, AC/DC **$55.00-65.00**

R-1229, table, 1947, two-tone wood, upper slanted slide rule dial, lower horizontal louvers, 3 knobs, BC, 6 tubes, AC/DC **$40.00-50.00**

R-1230, table, 1948, ivory plastic, right front dial, left vertical bars with center "ribbon candy" cut-out, 2 knobs, BC, 5 tubes, AC/DC **$75.00-85.00**

R-1231, table, 1948, brown plastic, right front dial, left vertical bars with center "ribbon candy" cut-out, 2 knobs, BC, 5 tubes, AC/DC..**$75.00-85.00**

R-1231A, table, 1948, brown plastic, right front dial, left vertical bars with center "ribbon candy" cut-out, 2 knobs, BC, 5 tubes, AC/DC **$75.00-85.00**

R-1232, table, 1948, walnut, right front square dial, left vertical grille bars, 2 knobs, BC, 5 tubes, AC/DC **$50.00-65.00**

R-1233, table, 1948, plastic, right front dial, left vertical bars with center "ribbon candy" cut-out, 2 knobs, BC, 5 tubes, AC/DC ..**$75.00-85.00**

R-1235, table, 1946, plastic, upper slanted slide rule dial, lower horizontal louvers, 3 knobs, BC, 6 tubes, AC/DC **$40.00-50.00**

R-1236, table, 1947, plastic, upper slanted slide rule dial, lower horizontal louvers, 3 knobs, BC, 6 tubes, AC/DC **$40.00-50.00**

R-1241, table-R/P, 1949, wood, lower front slide rule dial, large grille, 3/4 lift top, inner phono, 4 knobs, BC, 5 tubes, AC **$30.00-35.00**

R-1242, table-R/P, 1948, wood, right front square dial, lift top, inner phono, 2 knobs, BC, 5 tubes, AC/DC **$30.00-35.00**

R-1243, table, 1948, wood, upper slanted slide rule dial, large lower grille area, 3 knobs, BC, 6 tubes, AC **$35.00-45.00**

R-1244, table-R/P, 1948, walnut, lower front slide rule dial, 3/4 lift top, inner phono, 4 knobs, BC, 6 tubes, AC **$30.00-35.00**

R-1245, console-R/P, 1948, walnut, upper front slide rule dial & grille area, center phono, lower storage, 4 knobs, BC, 6 tubes, AC ..**$50.00-65.00**

R-1246, console-R/P, 1948, mahogany, upper front slide rule dial & grille area, center phono, storage, 4 knobs, BC, 6 tubes, AC ..**$50.00-75.00**

R-1249, console-R/P, 1949, wood, inner right dial, door, left pull-out phono drawer, 4 knobs, BC, FM, 10 tubes, AC.............**$65.00-75.00**

R-1251, console-R/P, 1947, wood, inner right dial, left pull-out phono drawer, lower grille with cut-outs, 6 knobs, BC, SW, FM, 15 tubes, AC **$65.00-75.00**

R-1254, console-R/P, 1948, wood, inner right slide rule dial, pushbuttons, left pull-out phono drawer, 6 knobs, BC, SW, FM, 12 tubes, AC **$65.00-75.00**

R-1407, portable, 1941, inner right front dial, left grille bars, removable front cover, handle, 3 knobs, BC, 6 tubes, AC/DC/battery **$25.00-30.00**

3201, tombstone, C1935, wood, center front dial with escutcheon, upper grille with vertical bars, 3 knobs, BC, 6 tubes, AC, $95.00-115.00.

R-1228, table, 1947, plastic, upper slanted slide rule dial, lower horizontal grille bars, decorative case lines, 3 knobs, BC, 6 tubes, AC/DC, $55.00-65.00.

R-1230A, table, 1947, ivory plastic, right front dial, left vertical bars with center "ribbon candy" cut-out, 2 knobs, BC, 5 tubes, AC/DC, $75.00-85.00.

R-1408, portable, 1947, cloth covered, right square dial, left grille with circular cut-outs, recessed handle, 3 knobs, BC, 6 tubes, AC/DC/battery **$30.00-35.00**

R-1409, portable, 1947, cloth covered, right square dial, left grille with circular cut-outs, recessed handle, 3 knobs, BC, 6 tubes, AC/DC/battery **$30.00-35.00**

R-1410, portable, 1948, luggage-type, front slide rule dial, handle, 2 knobs, BC, 6 tubes, AC/DC/battery..............................**$30.00-35.00**

R-1238, table, 1948, wood & plastic, right front dial, left grille with circular cut-outs, Lucite handle, 2 knobs, BC, 5 tubes, AC/DC, $65.00-75.00.

DELUXE

Junior, table, two-tone wood, right front dial, center chrome grille with cut-outs, 2 knobs, BC **$240.00-270.00**

DETROLA
International Detrola Corp.
1501 Beard Street, Detroit, Michigan

4D, cathedral, 1934, wood, small case, center front round dial, cloth grille with cut-outs, 3 knobs, BC, 4 tubes, AC, $200.00-230.00.

219 "Super Pee Wee," table, 1938, plastic, Deco, right front dial, left wrap-around louvers, 2 knobs, BC, SW, 5 tubes, AC/DC, $400.00+.

7A3, tombstone, 1934, wood, center front round dial, upper cloth grille with vertical bars, BC, SW, AC **$120.00-140.00**

159, table, wood, right front oval dial with red & yellow bands, left cloth grille with horizontal bars, 3 knobs, BC, SW, 5 tubes, AC/DC....**$50.00-65.00**

172A "Glen," table, 1937, wood, right front round dial, left grille with horizontal bars, 3 knobs, BC, SW, 5 tubes, AC/DC.............**$75.00-85.00**

173EC "Lark," console, 1937, wood, upper front dial, lower grille with vertical bars, corner louvers, BC, SW, 8 tubes, AC **$140.00-160.00**

174EC "Martin," console, 1937, wood, upper front dial, cloth grille with vertical bars, corner louvers, BC, SW, 8 tubes, AC/DC **$140.00-160.00**

197 "Pee Wee," table, 1938, plastic, midget, right front dial, left wrap-around louvers, 2 knobs, BC, 4 tubes, AC/DC ....**$350.00+**

218 "Pee Wee," table, 1939, midget, plastic, right front dial, left wrap-around louvers, 2 knobs, BC, SW, 4 tubes, AC/DC.............**$350.00+**

258EPC, console-R/P, 1938, wood, upper front dial, lower grille with horizontal bars & drawer, lift top, inner phono, BC, SW, 8 tubes, AC **$120.00-150.00**

310, table, 1940, wood with inlay, right front dial, left cloth grille, 6 top pushbuttons, handle, 2 knobs, BC, SW, 7 tubes, AC **$75.00-85.00**

378, portable, 1941, leatherette & plastic, inner dial & knobs, fold-open door, handle, BC, 5 tubes, AC/DC/battery **$50.00-65.00**

383, portable, 1941, cloth covered, right front square dial, left grille, handle, 2 knobs, BC, 5 tubes, AC/DC/battery.....................**$35.00-40.00**

417, table-R/P, 1941, wood, center front dial, right & left grille areas, lift top, inner phono, BC, 5 tubes, AC................................**$30.00-35.00**

419, table-R/P, 1941, wood, front slide rule dial, grille with cut-outs, lift top, inner phono, BC, 6 tubes, AC................................**$30.00-35.00**

558-1-49A, table-R/P, 1946, wood, front dial, horizontal louvers, lift top, inner phono, 3 knobs, BC, 5 tubes, AC **$30.00-35.00**

568-13-221D, table, 1946, metal, upper right front slide rule dial, left round perforated grille, 3 knobs, BC, SW, 5 tubes, AC/DC **$35.00-40.00**

571L, table, 1946, wood, upper right front slide rule dial, left cloth grille with horizontal bars, 2 knobs, BC, 5 tubes, AC/DC........**$40.00-50.00**

281 "Split Grill," table, 1939, Catalin, right front dial, left 2-section wrap-around horizontal louvers, 2 pin-wheel knobs, BC, SW, 5 tubes, AC/DC, $2,000.00+.

302, cathedral-C, 1938, wood, triangular shaped case, lower right front dial, left cloth grille, upper round clock face, feet, 2 knobs, BC, 5 tubes, AC, $350.00-410.00.

571X-21-94D, table, 1946, plastic, right front slide rule dial, left horizontal louvers, 2 knobs, BC, 5 tubes, AC/DC **$45.00-55.00**

572-220-226A, table, 1946, wood, right front slide rule dial, right & left cloth grille areas with horizontal bars, feet, 3 knobs, BC, SW, 6 tubes, AC **$40.00-50.00**

576-1-6A, table, 1946, wood, upper slanted slide rule dial, lower cloth grille with vertical bars, 3 knobs, BC, 6 tubes, AC/DC ..**$75.00-85.00**

579-2-58A, table, 1946, wood, upper slanted slide rule dial, lower cloth grille with 2 horizontal bars, 2 knobs, BC, 6 tubes, AC/DC.........**$40.00-50.00**

582, chairside, 1947, wood, top dial, lift top, inner phono, lower record storage, feet, 3 knobs, BC, SW, AC **$75.00-95.00**

610-A, table, 1949, wood, right front round dial, horizontal grille bars, rounded corners, feet, 2 knobs, BC, 4 tubes, battery **$35.00-45.00**

611-A, table, 1948, wood, right front round dial, horizontal grille bars, rounded corners, feet, 4 knobs, BC, SW, 5 tubes, battery **$35.00-45.00**

2811, table, 1939, wood, right front dial, left horizontal wrap-around louvers, 2 knobs, BC, SW, 5 tubes, AC/DC **$45.00-55.00**

3281, table-C, 1941, wood, mantle clock style with arched top, lower right front airplane dial, left cloth grille, upper round clock face, 2 knobs, BC, SW, 6 tubes, AC **$350.00-410.00**

3861, table-R/P, 1941, walnut veneer, right front dial, left grille, lift top, inner phono, 3 knobs, BC, 5 tubes, AC **$30.00-35.00**

7156, table-R/P, 1948, wood, lower front slide rule dial, horizontal louvers, 3/4 lift top, inner phono, 4 knobs, BC, 5 tubes, AC **$30.00-35.00**

7270, table-R/P, 1947, wood, top slide rule dial, front grille with cut-outs, lift top, inner phono, 3 knobs, BC, 7 tubes, AC **$35.00-40.00**

571, table, 1946, wood, right front slide rule dial, left horizontal louvers, 2 knobs, BC, 5 tubes, AC/DC, $45.00-55.00.

DEWALD
Dewald Radio Mfg. Corp.
440 Lafayette Street, New York, New York
Pierce-Aero, Inc.
New York

406, table, 1938, plastic, small case, right front round dial, left vertical wrap-over grille bars, feet, 2 knobs, BC, 4 tubes, AC/DC, $85.00-115.00.

54 "Dynette," portable, leatherette, inner wood panel with right dial, center grille, removable front, handle, BC, 5 tubes, AC/DC/battery **$85.00-115.00**

54A, table, 1933, wood, rounded top, center grille with cut-outs, raised side panels, 2 knobs, BC, 5 tubes, AC/DC/battery **$95.00-115.00**

60-3, tombstone, 1933, wood, center front window dial with escutcheon, upper grille with Gothic cut-outs, 3 knobs, BC, 6 tubes, AC/DC **$120.00-150.00**

60-42, console, 1933, wood, upper front window dial with escutcheon, lower grille with cut-outs, 6 legs, 3 knobs, BC, AC **$150.00-170.00**

410, portable, leatherette, left side dial, front rectangular metal grille, handle, 2 knobs, BC, 4 tubes, battery **$35.00-40.00**

511, table-R/P, 1949, alligator, slide rule dial, lift top, inner phono, handle, 4 knobs, BC, SW, 5 tubes, AC.......................................**$30.00-35.00**

522, table, 1936, wood, Deco, right front dial, left grille with wrap-over vertical bars, tuning eye, BC, 5 tubes, battery................**$65.00-75.00**

530, table, 1939, walnut or ivory plastic, right front dial, left grille with checker board center, 2 knobs, BC, 5 tubes, AC/DC **$75.00-85.00**

531, table-R/P, 1939, two-tone wood, right front dial, left grille, lift top, inner phono, 2 knobs, BC, 5 tubes, AC **$40.00-45.00**

532, table-R/P, 1939, two-tone wood, right front dial, left grille, lift top, inner phono, 2 knobs, BC, 8 tubes, AC/DC...................**$40.00-45.00**

533, table, 1939, wood, right front recessed dial, left wrap-around horizontal louvers, 2 knobs, BC, 5 tubes, AC/DC **$50.00-65.00**

555, tombstone, C1933, wood, center front window dial with escutcheon, upper grille with Gothic cut-outs, rounded top, 3 knobs, BC, 5 tubes, AC, $120.00-140.00.

615, table, 1935, wood, lower front round airplane dial, upper cloth grille, rounded sides, 2 knobs, BC, SW, 6 tubes, AC/DC, $75.00-85.00.

534, table, 1939, wood, right front recessed dial, curved left grille with vertical bars, 2 knobs, BC, 5 tubes, AC/DC **$65.00-75.00**

548 "Organ-Tone," table, 1940, plastic, raised top & flared base, lower front slide rule dial, upper vertical wrap-over grille bars, 4 pushbuttons, 2 knobs, BC, SW, 5 tubes, AC/DC **$110.00-130.00**

550 "Dynette," table, 1933, walnut with inlay, right front dial, center grille with cut-outs, arched top, 2 knobs, BC, 5 tubes, AC/DC **$95.00-115.00**

551 "Deluxe," table, 1933, walnut, right front dial, center grille with cut-outs, vertical front lines, 2 knobs, BC, AC/DC.............**$85.00-115.00**

561 "Jewel," table, 1941, Catalin, upper front slide rule dial, lower horizontal grille bars, handle, 2 knobs, BC, 5 tubes, AC/DC .....**$650.00+**

562 "Jewel," table, 1941, Catalin, upper front slide rule dial, lower horizontal grille bars, handle, 2 knobs, BC, 5 tubes, AC/DC .....**$650.00+**

564 "Companionette," portable, 1941, leatherette, inner dial, vertical grille bars, fold-open front, handle, 2 knobs, BC, AC/DC/battery...**$40.00-50.00**

565, portable, 1941, leatherette, inner slide rule dial, cloth grille, front cover, handle, 2 knobs, BC, AC/DC/battery **$35.00-45.00**

580, table, 1933, wood, lower front window dial, upper cloth grille with vertical bars, 3 knobs, BC, 5 tubes, AC.........................**$75.00-95.00**

643, table, 1939, wood, right front dial, left grille with horizontal bars, tuning eye, 4 knobs, BC, SW, 6 tubes, AC **$65.00-75.00**

645, table, 1939, wood, right front slide rule dial, left horizontal wrap-around grille bars, 3 knobs, BC, 6 tubes, AC/DC **$50.00-65.00**

648, table, 1939, wood, right front dial, curved left with vertical bars, 6 pushbuttons, 4 knobs, BC, SW, 7 tubes, AC/DC **$75.00-85.00**

649, table, 1939, wood, right front dial, left wrap-around horizontal grille bars, 6 pushbuttons, 4 knobs, BC, SW, 6 tubes, AC **$75.00-85.00**

901, tombstone, wood, large case, lower front round airplane dial, upper cloth grille with vertical bars, 4 knobs, BC, $120.00-140.00.

666, table, plastic, right front dial, left grille area, horizontal wrap-around decorative lines, 2 knobs, BC, 6 tubes, AC/DC.............**$40.00-50.00**

669 "Super Six," table-R/P, 1941, wood, right front dial, left horizontal louvers, lift top, inner phono, 2 knobs, BC, 6 tubes, AC..**$35.00-40.00**

670, table, 1941, wood, upper front slanted slide rule dial, lower grille, 4 knobs, BC, SW, 6 tubes, AC/DC **$45.00-55.00**

701, table, 1939, wood, right front dial, left grille with 3 horizontal bars, 6 center pushbuttons, 3 knobs, BC, 7 tubes, AC/DC........**$55.00-65.00**

708, table, 1941, two-tone wood, upper front slanted slide rule dial, lower grille, 4 knobs, BC, SW, 7 tubes, AC **$45.00-55.00**

802, tombstone, 1934, wood, Deco, center front round airplane dial, upper cloth grille with triangular cut-out, 4 knobs, BC, SW, 8 tubes, AC **$120.00-150.00**

907, console-R/P, 1940, wood, inner right dial & knobs, left phono, lift top, front grille with vertical bars, BC, SW, 9 tubes, AC..........**$65.00-75.00**

1200, table, 1937, wood, right front dial, left 3-section cloth grille, BC, SW, 12 tubes, AC...**$50.00-65.00**

A-500, table, 1946, plastic, upper front slide rule dial, lower horizontal louvers, 2 knobs, BC, 5 tubes, AC/DC **$40.00-50.00**

A-501 "Harp," table, 1946, Catalin, harp-shaped case, upper front slide rule dial, lower cloth grille with 5 vertical bars, 2 knobs, BC, 5 tubes, AC/DC ....**$700.00+**

A-502, table, 1946, Catalin, upper front slide rule dial, lower horizontal louvers, 2 knobs, BC, 5 tubes, AC/DC, $700.00+.

A-503, table, 1946, wood, upper front slide rule dial, lower horizontal louvers, 2 knobs, BC, SW, 5 tubes, AC/DC **$45.00-55.00**

A-505, table, 1947, plastic, upper front slide rule dial, lower horizontal louvers, 4 knobs, BC, SW, 5 tubes, AC/DC....................**$40.00-50.00**

A-507, portable, 1947, leatherette, inner slide rule dial, fold-down front, handle, 2 knobs, BC, 5 tubes, AC/DC/battery...............**$35.00-40.00**

A-509, table, 1948, plastic, upper front slide rule dial, lower horizontal louvers, 3 knobs, BC, SW, 5 tubes, AC/DC....................**$45.00-55.00**

A-514, table, 1947, plastic, right front dial, left horizontal wrap-around louvers, 2 knobs, BC, 5 tubes, AC/DC **$50.00-65.00**

A-602, table-R/P, 1947, wood, inner slide rule dial, fold-down front, lift top, handle, 4 knobs, BC, 6 tubes, AC **$30.00-35.00**

A-605, table-R/P, 1947, wood, front slide rule dial over horizontal louvers, lift top, inner phono, 4 knobs, BC, 6 tubes, AC **$35.00-40.00**

B-400, portable, 1948, two-tone leatherette, right front square dial, left cloth grille, handle, 2 knobs, BC, 4 tubes, battery.........**$35.00-40.00**

B-402, portable, 1948, plastic, lower front slide rule dial, upper horizontal grille bars, handle, 2 knobs, BC, 4 tubes, battery **$35.00-45.00**

B-403, table-C, 1948, Catalin, harp-shaped case, upper front slide rule dial, center clock face, right & left cloth grilles, 2 knobs, BC, 4 tubes, AC..**$700.00+**

B-504, portable, 1948, plastic, lower front slide rule dial, upper horizontal louvers, handle, 2 knobs, BC, 4 tubes, AC/DC/battery..**$35.00-45.00**

B-506, table, 1948, plastic, lower front slide rule dial, upper checkered grille area, 2 knobs, BC, 5 tubes, AC/DC **$30.00-35.00**

B-510, table, 1948, plastic, upper front slide rule dial, lower horizontal louvers, 3 knobs, BC, SW, 5 tubes, AC/DC....................**$35.00-40.00**

B-512, table-C, 1948, Catalin, upper front slide rule dial, center clock face, grille bars on top of case, 5 knobs, BC, 5 tubes, AC ..**$600.00+**

B-515, portable, 1949, plastic, lower front slide rule dial, upper horizontal grille bars, handle, 2 knobs, BC, SW, 4 tubes, AC/DC/battery **$35.00-40.00**

B-614, table-R/P, 1949, alligator, slide rule dial, lift top, inner phono, handle, 4 knobs, BC, 6 tubes, AC **$35.00-40.00**

B-401, table, 1948, plastic, right front round dial, left vertical wrap-over grille bars, 2 knobs, BC, 4 tubes, AC/DC, $75.00-85.00.

C-516, table, 1949, plastic, lower front slide rule dial, upper checkered grille, 3 knobs, BC, SW, AC/DC.....................................$40.00-45.00

C-800, table, 1949, plastic, upper slanted slide rule dial, lower horizontal louvers, 4 knobs, BC, FM, 8 tubes, AC/DC $40.00-45.00

D-508, portable, 1950, alligator, upper front slide rule dial, lower grille, handle, telescope antenna, 3 knobs, BC, SW, 4 tubes, AC/DC/battery $40.00-45.00

D-517, portable, 1951, plastic, lower front slide rule dial, upper perforated grille, handle, 2 knobs, BC, 4 tubes, AC/DC/battery $30.00-35.00

D-518, table, 1950, plastic, lower front slide rule dial, upper perforated grille, 2 knobs, BC, 5 tubes, AC/DC $40.00-45.00

D-519, table, plastic, lower front slide rule dial, upper checkered grille area, 2 knobs, BC $40.00-45.00

D-616, table, 1950, plastic, upper front slide rule dial, lower perforated grille, top vents, 2 knobs, BC, 6 tubes, AC/DC $40.00-45.00

E-520, table, 1955, plastic, upper front slide rule dial, lower horizontal louvers, 4 knobs, BC, SW, 5 tubes, AC/DC...................$40.00-45.00

E-522, table-R/P, 1951, wood, upper front slide rule dial, horizontal grille bars, 3/4 lift top, inner phono, 4 knobs, BC, 5 tubes, AC ..$30.00-35.00

F-404, table, 1952, plastic, right front round dial, left horizontal wrap-around louvers, 2 knobs, BC, 4 tubes, AC/DC $45.00-55.00

F-405, table, 1953, plastic, upper front slanted slide rule dial, lower horizontal louvers, 4 knobs, BC, SW, 4 tubes, battery $35.00-40.00

G-408, portable, 1953, plastic, lower front round dial, upper vertical grille bars, handle, 2 knobs, BC, 4 tubes, battery $35.00-40.00

H-528, table-C, 1954, plastic, right front round dial, left clock, center checkered panel, 3 knobs, BC, 5 tubes, AC $30.00-35.00

H-533, table-C, 1954, plastic, right side dial, front clock, vertical wrap-over grille bars, 5 knobs, BC, 5 tubes, AC.....................$45.00-55.00

H-537, table, 1955, plastic, right front dial, left volume, center checkered grille, 3 knobs, BC, SW, 5 tubes, AC/DC........................$40.00-45.00

D-E517A, portable, 1952, plastic, lower front slide rule dial, upper checkered grille, handle, 2 knobs, BC, AC/DC/battery, $40.00-45.00.

J-802, table, plastic with contrasting trim, upper front slide rule dial, lower horizontal louvers, 2 knobs, BC, FM $40.00-45.00

JD-519, table, plastic, lower front slide rule dial, upper checkered grille area, 2 knobs, BC $35.00-40.00

K-412 "The Moderne," table, 1957, plastic, right front dial, recessed left side with checkered grille, 2 knobs, BC, 4 tubes, AC/DC ..$30.00-35.00

K-545, table-C, 1957, plastic, right front clock, recessed left side with checkered grille, 3 knobs, BC, 5 tubes, AC $30.00-35.00

M-550, table, 1959, plastic, right front dial, recessed left side with checkered grille, 2 knobs, BC, 5 tubes, AC/DC $25.00-30.00

DISTANTONE
Distantone Radio, Inc.
Lynbrook, New York

C "Single Control," table, 1926, wood, slant front polished Bakelite panel, one center dial, BC, 5 tubes, battery $120.00-140.00

DORON
Doron Bros. Electric Co.
Hamilton, Ohio

R-5 "Super-Equidyne," table, 1925, wood, low rectangular case, 3 dial front panel, BC, 5 tubes, battery $120.00-140.00

DUMONT
Allen B. Dumont Labs, Inc.
2 Main Street, Passaic, New Jersey

R-1110, table, plastic, right side dial, diagonally divided front with horizontal lines, feet, $30.00-35.00.

RA-354 "Beachcomber," portable, 1957, leather case with front criss-cross grill, right round dial, strap, 2 knobs, BC, 4 tubes, AC/DC/battery $35.00-40.00

RA-346, table, 1956, plastic, several variations, including a clock radio version, lower right front dial over lattice grille area with "tree" design, 2 knobs, BC, AC/DC, $120.00-150.00.

DYNAVOX
Dynavox Corp.
40-35 21st Street, Long Island, New York

3-P-801, portable, 1948, two-tone leatherette, inner dial, flip-open door, handle, 3 knobs, BC, 4 tubes, AC/DC/battery...............**$35.00-45.00**

EAGLE
Eagle Radio Company
16 Boyden Place, Newark, New Jersey

The Eagle Radio Company began business in 1922. After an initial surge of business, the company began to decline and in 1927 was sold to Wurlitzer.

A, table, 1923, wood, low rectangular case, 3 dial front panel, lift top, 5 knobs, BC, 5 tubes, battery.........................**$120.00-150.00**
B "Neutrodyne," table, 1924, wood, low rectangular case, 3 dial front panel, 5 knobs, BC, 5 tubes, battery..........................**$150.00-180.00**
C-1, console, 1925, wood, contains table model F receiver, fold-down front door, lower storage, 5 knobs, BC, 5 tubes, battery......**$160.00-190.00**
C-2, console, 1925, wood, contains table model F receiver, fold-down front door, lower storage, 5 knobs, BC, 5 tubes, battery......**$160.00-190.00**
C-3, console, 1925, wood, contains table model F receiver, fold-down front door, lower storage, 5 knobs, BC, 5 tubes, battery......**$160.00-190.00**
D, table, 1925, wood, low rectangular case, 3 dial black Bakelite front panel, 5 knobs, BC, 5 tubes, battery..........................**$120.00-140.00**
F "Neutrodyne," table, 1925, wood, low rectangular case, black Bakelite front panel, 3 window dials, 5 knobs, BC, 5 tubes, battery........**$120.00-140.00**
H, table, 1926, wood, low rectangular case, 3 dial front panel, 5 knobs, BC, 5 tubes, battery.....................................**$110.00-130.00**
K, console, 1926, wood, inner 3 dial panel with Eagle emblem, fold-down front door, storage, BC, 5 tubes, battery...................**$200.00-230.00**
K-2, table, 1926, wood, low rectangular case, inner 3 dial panel, fold-down front door, BC, 5 tubes, battery.......................**$150.00-170.00**

EARLE

4, tombstone, wood, shouldered, center front window dial, upper round grille with cut-outs, 2 knobs, BC, AC..........................**$120.00-150.00**

ECA
Electrical Corp. of America
45 West 18th Street, New York, New York

101, table, 1946, wood, upper front curved slide rule dial, lower horizontal louvers, 2 knobs, BC, 5 tubes, AC/DC **$35.00-40.00**
102, table, 1947, plastic, upper front curved slide rule dial, lower vertical grille openings, 2 knobs, BC, 5 tubes, AC/DC...............**$45.00-50.00**
104, table-R/P, 1947, wood, front slide rule dial, lower horizontal louvers, lift top, inner phono, 4 knobs, BC, 5 tubes, AC **$30.00-35.00**
105, table-R/P, 1947, leatherette, inner slide rule dial, phono, lift top, 4 knobs, BC, 5 tubes, AC **$30.00-35.00**
106, table-R/P, 1946, wood, front slide rule dial, horizontal louvers, lift top, inner phono, 4 knobs, BC, 5 tubes, AC **$30.00-35.00**
108, table, 1946, plastic, shouldered top, upper front curved slide rule dial, lower textured grille, 4 knobs, BC, 7 tubes, AC/DC.........**$45.00-55.00**
121, console-R/P, 1947, wood, top left dial, right front pull-out phono drawer, 4 knobs, BC, 7 tubes, AC **$85.00-105.00**
131, table-R/P, 1947, alligator, inner slide rule dial, fold-down side door, lift top, handle, 4 knobs, BC, 5 tubes, AC **$30.00-35.00**
132, table, 1948, wood, upper front slanted slide rule dial, lower criss-cross grille, 4 knobs, BC, 7 tubes, AC/DC....................**$30.00-35.00**
201, table, 1947, two-tone wood, upper front slanted slide rule dial, lower horizontal grille openings, 2 knobs, BC, 5 tubes, AC/DC **$40.00-45.00**
204, portable, 1948, alligator, inner right dial, left grille, fold-down front, handle, 2 knobs, BC, 7 tubes, AC/DC/battery...............**$30.00-35.00**

ECHOPHONE
Echophone Radio, Inc.
1120 North Ashland Avenue, Chicago, Illinois
The Hallicrafter Co.
2611 South Indiana Avenue, Chicago, Illinois
Radio Shop
Sunnyvale, California
Echophone Radio Mfg. Co.
968 Formosa, Los Angeles, California

The trade name "Echophone" was used on many sets made by different manufacturers.

3, table, 1925, wood, high case, slanted two dial black panel, lift top, 3 knobs, BC, 3 exposed tubes, battery, $320.00-380.00.

4, table, 1925, wood, high case, slanted front panel with 2 pointer dials, 4 knobs, BC, 4 exposed tubes, battery **$380.00-410.00**
6, cathedral, wood, right front thumbwheel dial, upper round grille with lyre cut-out, 2 knobs, BC...................................**$240.00-270.00**
17, upright table, 1932, wood, unusually shaped case with upper front quarter-round window dial, lower cloth grille area with cut-outs, finials, 2 speakers, 3 knobs, BC, 8 tubes, AC **$350.00-410.00**
40 "Echoette," cathedral, 1931, wood, lower half-round dial with escutcheon, upper "cathedral arch" grille, 2 knobs, BC, 4 tubes, AC **$200.00-240.00**
46, console, 1928, wood, rectangular cabinet on 4 legged stand, center front dial with escutcheon **$240.00-270.00**
60, cathedral, 1931, walnut, lower front quarter-round dial, upper ornate pressed wood grille, 3 knobs, BC, 7 tubes, AC.........**$350.00-410.00**

4, cathedral, 1932, wood, front window dial with escutcheon, upper cloth grille with cut-outs, 2 knobs, BC, 4 tubes, AC, $240.00-300.00.

80, cathedral, 1931, walnut, lower front quarter-round dial with escutcheon, upper ornate pressed wood grille, 3 knobs, BC, 8 tubes, AC, $350.00-410.00.

81, cathedral, 1932, wood, lower front quarter-round dial with escutcheon, upper ornate pressed wood grille, 3 knobs, BC, 8 tubes, AC **$350.00-410.00**
90, console, 1931, wood, lowboy, upper front quarter-round dial, lower ornate Gothic grille, 3 knobs, BC, 8 tubes, AC **$180.00-200.00**

EC-112, table, 1946, plastic, center front square dial over large cloth grille with vertical bars, 4 knobs, BC, SW, 6 tubes, AC/DC, $45.00-55.00.

173, tombstone, 1935, two-tone wood, lower front dial, upper cloth grille with cut-outs, 4 knobs, BC, 7 tubes, battery................**$85.00-105.00**
185, tombstone, 1935, two-tone wood, lower front dial, upper cloth grille with cut-outs, 4 knobs, BC, 6 tubes **$85.00-105.00**
A, table, 1923, wood, high rectangular case, 2 dial front panel, 5 knobs, BC, 3 tubes, battery...**$200.00-230.00**
EC-113, table, 1946, wood, center front square dial, right & left grille areas, 4 knobs, BC, SW, 6 tubes, AC/DC **$35.00-45.00**

S-4, cathedral, 1931, wood, right front window dial, upper round grille with lyre cut-out & vertical bars, BC, 6 tubes, AC, $240.00-270.00.

EC-306, table-R/P, 1947, wood, center front dial, right & left grille areas, lift top, inner phono, 4 knobs, BC, SW, AC **$30.00-35.00**
EC-403, console-R/P, 1947, wood, inner top right dial & knobs, center front pull-out phono drawer, BC, SW, FM, 15 tubes, AC **$85.00-105.00**
EC-600, table, 1946, wood, upper front slanted slide rule dial, lower cloth grille, round corners, 4 knobs, BC, 4 tubes, battery **$35.00-40.00**
EX-102, table, 1949, plastic, center front square dial, large vertical grille bars, 4 knobs, BC, SW, AC/DC **$50.00-65.00**
S-3, cathedral, 1930, wood, right front window dial, upper round grille with lyre cut-out & vertical bars, BC, 5 tubes, AC **$240.00-270.00**
S-10, cathedral, wood, center front quarter-round dial, upper cloth grille with cut-outs, 4 knobs, BC **$350.00-410.00**
V-3, table, 1925, wood, high rectangular case, slanted two dial front panel, 3 knobs, BC, 3 exposed tubes, battery **$380.00-410.00**

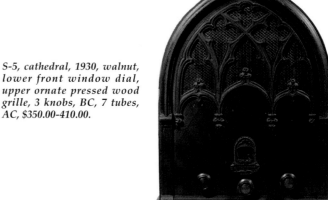

S-5, cathedral, 1930, walnut, lower front window dial, upper ornate pressed wood grille, 3 knobs, BC, 7 tubes, AC, $350.00-410.00.

ECODYNE
Ecodyne Radio Co.
Irwin, Pennsylvania

R-5, table, 1925, wood, low rectangular case, 4 dial front panel, BC, 5 tubes, battery **$120.00-140.00**
RT-13, table, 1925, wood, low rectangular case, 4 dial front panel, BC, 5 tubes, battery **$110.00-130.00**

EDISON
Thomas A. Edison, Inc.

C-4, console-R/P, 1929, wood, lowboy, inner front dial/knobs/grille, double doors, lift top, inner phono, BC, 8 tubes, AC........**$350.00-410.00**
R-5, console, 1929, wood, inner front dial/grille, sliding doors, 3 knobs, BC, 8 tubes, AC **$180.00-200.00**

EISEMANN
Eisemann Magneto Corporation
165 Broadway, New York, New York

The Eisemann Magneto Corporation was formed in 1903 for the manufacture of automobile magnetos. The company began to produce component parts for radios in 1923 and in 1924 briefly manufactured only a few complete radios.

6-D, table, 1924, mahogany, low rectangular case, 3 dial front panel, feet, BC, 5 tubes, battery...**$85.00-105.00**
RF-2, table, 1924, wood, low rectangular case, 2 dial front panel, BC, 5 tubes, battery **$85.00-105.00**

ELCAR
Union Electronics Corp.
38-01 Queens Blvd., Long Island, New York

602, table, 1946, wood, upper front slide rule dial, lower cloth grille with 2 horizontal bars, 2 knobs, BC, SW, AC/DC......................**$40.00-45.00**

ELECTONE
Northeastern Engineering Inc.
Manchester, New Hampshire

T5TS3, table, 1947, plastic, right front half-round dial, left horizontal wrap-around grille bars, 2 knobs, BC, 4 tubes, AC/DC..**$50.00-65.00**

ELECTRO
Electro Appliances Mfg. Co.
102-104 Park Row, New York, New York

B20, table, 1947, wood, right front square black dial, left cloth grille with vertical bars, 2 knobs, BC, AC/DC **$40.00-50.00**

ELECTRO-TONE
Electro-Tone Corp.
221 Hudson Street, Hoboken, New Jersey

555, table-R/P, 1947, wood, inner left vertical dial, lift top, outer horizontal louvers, 4 knobs, BC, AC **$30.00-35.00**

ELECTROMATIC
Electromatic Mfg. Corp.
88 University Place, New York, New York

26, table, 1941, ivory plastic, right front dial, left grille, horizontal & vertical decorative lines, 3 knobs, BC, 6 tubes, AC/DC **$45.00-55.00**
607A, table-R/P, 1946, wood, streamline, front slide rule dial, louvers, lift top, inner phono, 2 knobs, BC, AC **$75.00-85.00**

ELECTRONIC LABS
Electronic Laboratories, Inc.
122 West New York Street, Indianapolis, Indiana

710-PC, console-R/P, 1947, wood, inner right vertical dial, left phono, lift top, lower doors, 4 knobs, BC, 10 tubes, AC/DC **$50.00-65.00**
710-W, table, 1947, wood, lower front slide rule dial, right & left wrap-around grilles, 4 knobs, BC, 10 tubes, AC/DC **$40.00-50.00**
2701, table, 1946, wood, lower front slide rule dial, large upper grille, 2 knobs, BC, 6 tubes, AC/DC **$30.00-35.00**
3000 "Orthosonic," table, 1948, right front dial, 3 center horizontal louvers, 2 knobs, BC, 4 tubes, AC/DC **$30.00-35.00**

ELGIN
Elgin Radio Supply

4X "Compact Air Roamer," table, 1939, wood, right front dial, left grille with horizontal bars, 2 knobs, BC, 4 tubes, AC/DC........**$40.00-45.00**
35 "Economy Air Roamer," table, 1939, wood, right front dial, left cloth grille with curved cut-outs, 2 knobs, BC, 5 tubes, AC/DC ..**$40.00-45.00**
77 "Tiny-Tot Air Roamer," table, 1939, wood, midget, slant front case, left front dial, right wrap-around grille with horizontal bars, 2 knobs, BC, AC/DC...**$65.00-75.00**
80B "De Luxe Air Roamer," table, 1939, wood, right front dial, curved left with horizontal bars, 3 knobs, BC, SW, 5 tubes, AC/DC ..**$65.00-75.00**

210A "Universal Air Roamer," table, 1939, wood, right front dial, left cloth grille with horizontal bars, 2 knobs, BC, SW, 6 tubes, AC/DC **$40.00-50.00**
A115 "Super Air Roamer," table, 1939, wood, right front dial, left cloth grille with horizontal bars, tuning eye, 3 knobs, BC, SW, 7 tubes, AC/DC **$65.00-75.00**

ELKAY
The Langbein-Kaufman Radio Co.
511 Chapel Street, New Haven, Connecticut

Senior, table, 1926, wood, low rectangular case, slanted front panel with center thumbwheel dial, BC, 6 tubes, AC **$120.00-150.00**

EMERSON
Emerson Radio & Phonograph Company
111 8th Avenue, New York, New York

The Emerson Radio & Phonograph Company was founded in 1923. To keep costs down during the Depression, the company began to produce "midget" radios and consistently geared their pricing to lower income customers. With this marketing strategy, Emerson became one of the leaders in radio sales.

25A, table, 1933, wood, curved top, right front dial, center cloth grille with cut-outs, 2 knobs, BC, 4 tubes, AC/DC, $85.00-105.00.

17 "Miracle Six," table, 1935, plastic, Deco, right front dial, center cloth grille with vertical chrome bars, 2 knobs, BC, 4 tubes, AC/DC **$140.00-160.00**
19 "Miracle Six," table, 1935, plastic, Deco, right front dial, center cloth grille with vertical bars, 2 knobs, BC, 4 tubes, AC/DC..**$110.00-130.00**
20A, table, 1933, plastic, small case, right front dial, center ornate molded grille, 2 knobs, BC, 4 tubes, AC/DC **$85.00-115.00**
23, table, 1935, wood, rectangular box with base trim, center grille with cut-outs and Emerson logo below, 2 knobs, BC, 4 tubes, AC ..**$75.00-90.00**
26, tombstone, 1934, two-tone wood, center front window dial, upper cloth grille with cut-outs, 3 knobs, BC, SW, 5 tubes, AC **$85.00-105.00**

32, table, 1934, walnut, right front dial, center cloth grille with cut-outs, rounded top, 2 knobs, BC, SW, 5 tubes, AC/DC, $110.00-130.00.

38, table, 1934, wood, arched top, lower front round dial, upper cloth grille with cut-outs, 4 knobs, BC, SW, 6 tubes, AC/DC, $120.00-150.00.

28, tombstone, 1934, walnut, front window dial, upper grille with circular cut-outs, 3 knobs, BC, SW, 5 tubes, AC **$110.00-130.00**

30, portable, 1933, burl walnut with inlay, inner dial, grille with cut-outs, fold-down front, handle, 2 knobs, BC, SW, 5 tubes, AC/DC **$110.00-130.00**

30-AW, portable, 1933, burl walnut with inlay, inner dial, grille with cut-outs, fold-down front, handle, 2 knobs, BC, SW, 5 tubes, AC/DC **$110.00-130.00**

31-AW, table, 1934, pressed wood, right front dial, center vertical grille bars, 2 knobs, BC, SW, 5 tubes, AC/DC **$85.00-115.00**

33-AW, table, 1933, walnut with black lacquer and chrome, right front dial, center octagonal grille, handle, 2 knobs, BC, SW, 5 tubes, AC/DC **$150.00-180.00**

34-C, tombstone, 1935, walnut, center front round airplane dial, upper grille with vertical bars, 4 knobs, BC, SW, 6 tubes, AC **$110.00-130.00**

34-F7, tombstone, 1935, walnut, center front round airplane dial, upper grille with vertical bars, 4 knobs, BC, SW, 6 tubes, battery **$75.00-95.00**

35, table, 1933, walnut, Sheraton design, center front window dial, upper grille with cut-outs, pediment top, 2 knobs, BC, SW, 6 tubes, AC/DC **$270.00-300.00**

36, tombstone, 1934, two-tone wood, center front dial, upper cloth grille with 3 vertical bars, 3 knobs, BC, SW, 5 tubes, AC **$85.00-105.00**

39, tombstone, 1934, wood, lower front round airplane dial, upper cloth grille with vertical bars, 3 knobs, BC, SW, 5 tubes, AC..**$110.00-130.00**

40, side table, 1933, walnut, French Provincial design, inner front window dial and knobs, drop front, BC, 6 tubes, AC/DC **$120.00-150.00**

49, upright table, 1934, walnut, lower front round dial, upper cloth grille with cut-outs, curved top, BC, SW, 6 tubes, AC/DC..**$180.00-200.00**

50B-1, table, plastic, lower front slide rule dial, upper perforated grille area with center round logo, 2 knobs, BC, AC/DC **$35.00-45.00**

45, tombstone, 1934, walnut, center front round airplane dial, upper grille with cut-outs, 3 knobs, BC, SW, 6 tubes, AC, $120.00-150.00.

107, table, 1935, walnut, arched top, lower front dial, upper cloth grille with cut-outs, finished front & back, 4 knobs, BC, SW, 6 tubes, AC/DC, $160.00-180.00.

50-M, side table, 1933, walnut, Louis XVI design with gold carvings, inner front window dial and, tambour doors, 3 knobs, BC, SW, AC **$180.00-200.00**

69, console, 1934, walnut, upper front round dial, lower cloth grille with 3 vertical bars, step-down top, BC, SW, 6 tubes, AC ..**$120.00-140.00**

71, tombstone, 1934, walnut, center front round airplane dial, upper grille with geometric cut-outs, 4 knobs, BC, SW, 7 tubes, AC.........**$120.00-150.00**

77, console, 1934, walnut, upper front window dial, lower grille with Deco cut-outs, chrome trim, 3 knobs, BC, 7 tubes, AC **$200.00-230.00**

100, console, 1934, walnut, upper front round dial, lower cloth grille with vertical bars, step-down top, BC, AC **$120.00-150.00**

101, console, 1935, walnut, upper front round airplane dial, lower cloth grille with vertical bars, 4 knobs, BC, SW, 6 tubes, AC **$120.00-140.00**

101-F7, console, 1935, walnut, upper front round airplane dial, lower cloth grille with vertical bars, 4 knobs, BC, SW, 6 tubes, battery **$75.00-85.00**

101-U, console, 1935, walnut, upper front round airplane dial, lower grille with vertical bars, 4 knobs, BC, SW, 6 tubes, AC/DC ..**$120.00-140.00**

102, console, 1935, walnut, upper front round airplane dial, lower cloth grille with vertical bars, 5 knobs, BC, SW, 8 tubes, AC **$120.00-140.00**

102-LW, console, 1935, walnut, upper front round airplane dial, lower cloth grille with vertical bars, 5 knobs, BC, SW,LW, 8 tubes, AC ..**$120.00-140.00**

103, tombstone, 1935, walnut, upper front round airplane dial, lower cloth grille with vertical bars, BC, SW, 5 tubes, battery **$75.00-85.00**

104, tombstone, 1935, walnut, arched top, center front round airplane dial, upper grille cut-outs, 5 knobs, BC, SW, 8 tubes, AC ..**$140.00-160.00**

104-LW, tombstone, 1935, walnut, arched top, center front round airplane dial, upper grille cut-outs, 5 knobs, BC, SW, LW, 8 tubes, AC **$140.00-160.00**

105, console, 1935, walnut, upper front round airplane dial, lower grille with cut-outs, step-down top, 5 knobs, BC, SW, 11 tubes, AC..**$160.00-190.00**

149, table, plastic, right front dial, left cloth grille with 3 horizontal bars, decorative case lines, 2 knobs, BC, $85.00-115.00.

250-AW, table, 1933, burl walnut, right front dial, center cloth grille with cut-outs, arched top, 2 knobs, BC, SW, 5 tubes, AC/DC, $85.00-115.00.

400 "Aristocrat," table, 1940, Catalin, right front round dial, left horizontal wrap-around grille bars, handle, 2 knobs, BC, 5 tubes, AC/DC, $525.00+.

105-LW, console, 1935, walnut, upper front round airplane dial, lower grille with cut-outs, step-down top, 5 knobs, BC, SW, LW, 11 tubes, AC **$160.00-190.00**

106, table, 1935, wood, lower front dial, upper cloth grille with cut-outs, finished front & back, 2 knobs, BC, SW, 6 tubes, AC/DC..**$140.00-160.00**

107-AC "Duo-Tone," table, 1935, walnut, arched top, lower front dial, upper cloth grille with cut-outs, finished front & back, 4 knobs, BC, SW, 5 tubes, AC..........................**$160.00-180.00**

107-LW, table, 1935, walnut, arched top, lower front dial, upper cloth grille with cut-outs, finished front & back, 4 knobs, BC, SW, LW, 6 tubes, AC/DC **$160.00-180.00**

108, tombstone, 1935, plastic, black or ivory, lower front round airplane dial, cloth grille with vertical bars, 2 knobs, BC, SW, 5 tubes, AC/DC **$240.00-270.00**

108-LW, tombstone, 1935, plastic, black or ivory, lower front round airplane dial, cloth grille with vertical bars, 2 knobs, BC, SW, LW, 5 tubes, AC/DC...**$240.00-270.00**

109, table, 1934, plastic, center front round airplane dial over cloth grille with vertical bars, 2 knobs, BC, SW, 4 tubes, AC/DC **$120.00-150.00**

110, tombstone, 1935, wood, lower front round airplane dial, upper cloth grille with vertical bars, 2 knobs, BC, SW, 5 tubes, AC/DC **$85.00-105.00**

110-LW, tombstone, 1935, wood, lower front round airplane dial, upper cloth grille with vertical bars, 2 knobs, BC, SW, LW, 5 tubes, AC/DC **$85.00-105.00**

111, table, 1935, walnut, lower front dial, upper cloth grille with cut-outs, arched top, 4 knobs, BC, SW, 6 tubes, AC/DC.........**$110.00-130.00**

111-LW, table, 1935, walnut, lower front dial, upper cloth grille with cut-outs, arched top, 4 knobs, BC, SW, LW, 6 tubes, AC/DC **$110.00-130.00**

116, tombstone, 1936, walnut, lower front round airplane dial, upper cloth grille with vertical bars, 4 knobs, BC, SW, 5 tubes, AC..**$85.00-95.00**

117, tombstone, 1936, wood, lower front round airplane dial, upper cloth grille with vertical bars, 4 knobs, BC, SW, 5 tubes, AC..**$85.00-95.00**

118, table, 1936, wood with repwood front, round airplane dial over cloth grille area, 2 knobs, BC, 5 tubes, AC/DC **$85.00-115.00**

119, tombstone, 1936, walnut, arched top, lower front dial, upper cloth grille with cut-outs, 4 knobs, BC, SW, 6 tubes, AC/DC ..**$85.00-115.00**

126, table, 1936, plastic, front round airplane dial, cloth grille with vertical bars, decorative case lines, 2 knobs, BC, 5 tubes, AC/DC **$85.00-105.00**

157, table, plastic, small case, upper front dial with center pointer, decorative case lines, 2 knobs, BC **$75.00-85.00**

199, table, 1938, plastic, front round dial, cloth grille with vertical bars, decorative case lines, 2 knobs, BC, AC.......................**$85.00-105.00**

238, table, 1939, wood, chest-type, inner right square dial, left grille with horizontal bars, lift top, 2 knobs, BC, 5 tubes, AC/DC..**$270.00-300.00**

239, consolette, 1939, wood, upper front square dial, right & left horizontal louvers, lower shelves, 2 knobs, BC, 5 tubes, AC/DC ..**$110.00-130.00**

240, consolette, 1939, wood, upper front square dial, right & left horizontal louvers, lower shelves, 2 knobs, BC, 5 tubes, AC/DC ..**$120.00-150.00**

241, table-R/P, 1939, wood, right front square dial, left vertical grille bars, lift top, inner phono, 2 knobs, BC, 5 tubes, AC **$45.00-55.00**

250, table, 1933, burl walnut, right front dial, center cloth grille with cut-outs, arched top, 2 knobs, BC, 5 tubes, AC/DC **$85.00-115.00**

257, kitchen radio, 1939, white finish, right front square dial, left horizontal louvers, top shelf, 2 knobs, BC, 5 tubes, AC/DC **$75.00-95.00**

300, table, 1933, wood, chest-type, inner right dial, right/left vertical grille bars, center cloth grille area, lift top, cylindrical side handles, 2 knobs, BC, 5 tubes, AC **$180.00-200.00**

321-AW, table, 1933,wood, Oriental case design in ebony and gold Chinese lacquer, inner dial/grille with cut-outs, double front doors, handle, 2 knobs, BC, SW, 5 tubes, AC/DC **$240.00-270.00**

330-AW, table, 1934, walnut with chrome trim, right front dial, center grille with cut-outs, base, handle, 2 knobs, BC, SW, 5 tubes, AC/DC **$180.00-200.00**

341, table, wood, front rectangular slide rule dial with center tuning eye, top grille, 4 knobs, BC, AC **$50.00-65.00**

343, table, 1940, plastic, right front dial, left horizontal grille bars with center overlapping vertical bars, 2 knobs, BC, SW, 5 tubes, AC/DC **$50.00-65.00**

336, table, 1940, plastic, right front dial, left grille with geometric cut-outs, 2 knobs, BC, 5 tubes, AC/DC, $40.00-50.00.

410 "Mickey Mouse," table-N, 1933, wood, black & silver with metal trim, center octagonal grille with Mickey & cello, 2 knobs, BC, 4 tubes, AC/DC, $1,600.00+.

414, table, 1933, pressed wood, ornate case with fleur-de-lis designs, lower right front dial, 2 knobs, BC, AC, $180.00-200.00.

504, table, 1946, wood, right front round dial, clear lucite grille panel with circular cut-outs, 2 knobs, BC, 5 tubes, AC/DC, $50.00-65.00.

349, table, 1941, wood, right front dial, left curved grille with vertical bars, 2 knobs, BC, SW, AC/DC **$65.00-75.00**

350-AW, table, 1933, wood, ornately carved case, inner right dial, center cloth grille with cut-outs, double front doors, 2 knobs, BC, SW, 5 tubes, AC/DC **$180.00-200.00**

357, portable, 1940, tan & maroon leatherette, right front dial, left horizontal louvers, handle, 2 knobs, BC, AC/DC/battery **$30.00-35.00**

357A, portable, 1940, right front dial, left grille with horizontal louvers, handle, 2 knobs, BC, AC/DC/battery.......................**$30.00-35.00**

359, table, 1940, two-tone wood, right front dial, left grille with horizontal louvers, 2 knobs, BC, AC/DC/battery **$35.00-40.00**

363, portable, 1940, blue leatherette, right front dial, left horizontal louvers, handle, 2 knobs, BC, SW, AC/DC/battery **$35.00-40.00**

364, table-R/P, 1940, wood, center front dial, right & left horizontal louvers, lift top, inner phono, BC, AC **$30.00-35.00**

365, table, 1940, walnut, center front slide rule dial, rounded sides, tuning eye, hi-fi, 4 knobs, BC, 8 tubes, AC.........................**$65.00-75.00**

368, console, 1940, walnut, upper front dial, 6 push buttons, lower grille with vertical bars, 4 knobs, BC, SW, AC **$110.00-130.00**

370, console-R/P, 1940, walnut, center front dial, 6 pushbuttons, lower horizontal grille bars, tuning eye, lift top, inner phono, 4 knobs, BC, SW, 8 tubes, AC..**$110.00-130.00**

375, table, 1933, walnut, inner window dial/grille cut-outs, double tambour doors, 2 knobs, BC, 6 tubes, AC/DC **$150.00-180.00**

380, portable, 1940, pocket-size, top slide rule dial, front vertical grille bars, handle, 2 knobs, BC, 4 tubes, battery **$45.00-55.00**

382, portable-R/P, 1940, leatherette, inner dial, knobs & phono, outer horizontal louvers, lift top, handle, BC, 5 tubes, AC **$30.00-35.00**

383, table-R/P, 1940, walnut, right front square dial, left grille with vertical bars, lift top, inner phono, 2 knobs, BC, AC **$30.00-35.00**

384, table-R/P/Rec, 1940, inner right square dial, left horizontal louvers, fold-down front, lift top, inner phono, handle, BC, AC ..**$30.00-35.00**

385, portable, 1940, cloth, inner right dial, left horizontal louvers, fold-down front, handle, 2 knobs, BC, 6 tubes, AC/DC/battery **$30.00-35.00**

400 **"Patriot,"** table, 1940, red, white & blue plastic, right front round dial, left wrap-around grille bars, handle, 2 knobs, BC, 5 tubes, AC/DC ....**$675.00+**

403, table-R/P, 1942, wood, right front dial, left horizontal louvers, lift top, inner phono, 4 knobs, BC, 5 tubes, AC **$35.00-40.00**

409 **"Mickey Mouse,"** table-N, 1933, wood, ivory & light green with metal trim, center octagonal grille with Mickey & cello, 2 knobs, BC, 4 tubes, AC/DC ....**$1,600.00+**

411 **"Mickey Mouse,"** table-N, 1933, pressed wood, side/top/front Mickey musical "carvings," 2 knobs, BC, 4 tubes, AC/DC........**$2,500.00+**

413, table, 1942, two-tone plastic, upper front slide rule dial, lower horizontal grille bars, 4 knobs, BC, SW, 6 tubes, AC/DC **$50.00-65.00**

414 **"Big Six,"** table, 1941, plastic, right front dial, left horizontal grille bars, 2 knobs, BC, 6 tubes **$45.00-55.00**

415, table, 1933, walnut plastic, right front dial, center grille area with cut-outs, 2 knobs, BC, 4 tubes, AC/DC **$85.00-105.00**

416 **"Intimate,"** table, 1934, walnut, center front octagonal grille with cut-outs, horizontal fluting, 2 knobs, BC, 4 tubes, AC/DC ..**$75.00-95.00**

420, table, 1933, plastic, right front dial, center grille area with cut-outs, 2 knobs, BC, 4 tubes, AC/DC/battery............................**$85.00-105.00**

421, table, 1941, walnut plastic, upper slanted slide rule dial, lower horizontal louvers, 4 knobs, BC, 5 tubes, AC **$35.00-45.00**

423, table-R/P, 1941, wood, front slide rule dial over horizontal louvers, lift top, inner phono, 3 knobs, BC, 6 tubes, AC.............**$30.00-35.00**

424, portable, 1941, leatherette, right front round dial, left horizontal wrap-around louvers, handle, 2 knobs, BC, 6 tubes, AC/DC/battery **$35.00-40.00**

426, portable, 1941, plastic, top dial, horizontal wrap-around grille bars, handle, 2 knobs, BC, AC/DC/battery.............................**$35.00-45.00**

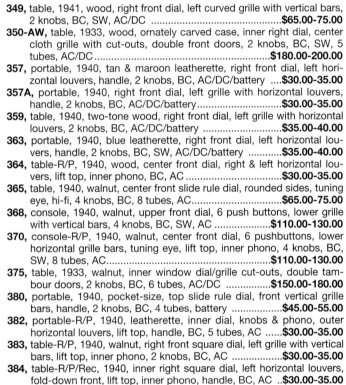

455, table, jewelry box style ornate case, opening hinged lid turns radio on, feet, 2 thumbwheel knobs, BC, 4 tubes, battery, $85.00-105.00.

510, table, 1946, wood, right front round dial, plastic grille panel with circular cut-outs, 2 knobs, BC, 5 tubes, AC/DC, $50.00-65.00.

511 "Moderne," table, 1946, plastic, raised see-through plastic dial over large grille, top hand-hold, 2 knobs, BC, 5 tubes, AC/DC, $55.00-65.00.

541, table, 1947, wood, right raised see-through plastic dial over large perforated grille, 2 knobs, BC, 5 tubes, AC/DC, $40.00-45.00.

427, portable, 1941, leatherette, right front round dial, left horizontal louvers, handle, 2 knobs, BC, 6 tubes, AC/DC/battery **$35.00-40.00**

428, portable, 1941, leatherette, inner right front round dial, left horizontal louvers, fold-down front, handle, 2 knobs, BC, 6 tubes, AC/DC/battery **$35.00-40.00**

432 "Power Mite," portable, 1941, plastic, horizontal grille bars, flip-open lid, inner dial & knobs, handle, 2 knobs, BC, 4 tubes, battery **$65.00-75.00**

437, table-R/P, 1942, walnut, lower right front dial, left horizontal grille bars, lift top, inner phono, 3 knobs, BC, 7 tubes, AC **$35.00-40.00**

447, table-R/P, 1941, walnut, front slide rule dial over horizontal louvers, lift top, inner phono, 3 knobs, BC, 7 tubes, AC **$30.00-35.00**

450, portable-R/P, 1942, leatherette, inner dial/knobs/phono, front horizontal louvers, lift top, handle, 3 knobs, BC **$30.00-35.00**

456, table, 1941, walnut, upper slanted slide rule dial, lower horizontal grille bars, 4 knobs, BC, SW, 7 tubes, AC/DC...............**$45.00-50.00**

459, table, 1941, walnut, upper slanted slide rule dial, lower horizontal grille bars, 4 knobs, BC, SW, 6 tubes, AC **$45.00-50.00**

461, table, 1942, simulated leather, right front dial, left horizontal louvers, 2 knobs, BC, 5 tubes, AC/DC **$35.00-40.00**

462, console-R/P, 1942, wood, front dial, upper slide-away tambour door, inner phono, 4 knobs, BC, 6 tubes, AC **$150.00-180.00**

503, table, 1946, wood, right round dial over perforated front panel, 2 knobs, BC, 5 tubes, AC/DC **$30.00-35.00**

505, portable, 1946, leatherette, right front dial over perforated grille, handle, 2 knobs, BC, 6 or 7 tube versions, AC/DC/battery ..**$35.00-40.00**

506, table-R/P, 1946, wood, inner left vertical dial, right automatic phono, lift top, 3 knobs, BC, 6 tubes, AC **$30.00-35.00**

507, table, 1946, plastic, right front dial, left grille with Deco cut-outs & Emerson logo, feet, 2 knobs, BC, 5 tubes, AC/DC **$40.00-45.00**

508, portable, 1946, plastic, flip open lid, inner dial, handle, 2 knobs, BC, 4 tubes, battery **$65.00-75.00**

509, table, 1946, plastic, right front dial, left grille with circular cut-outs, handle, 2 knobs, BC, 5 tubes, AC/DC **$40.00-45.00**

512, table, 1946, wood, upper front slanted slide rule dial, lower perforated grille, 4 knobs, BC, 6 tubes, AC/DC **$35.00-40.00**

514, table, 1947, plastic, upper front slanted slide rule dial, lower horizontal louvers, 4 knobs, BC, SW, 6 tubes, AC/DC **$45.00-55.00**

515, table, 1947, plastic, upper front slanted slide rule dial, lower horizontal louvers, 4 knobs, BC, 6 tubes, AC/DC **$45.00-55.00**

516, table, 1947, plastic, upper front slanted slide rule dial, lower horizontal louvers, 4 knobs, BC, 6 tubes, AC/DC **$45.00-55.00**

517 "Moderne," table, 1947, plastic, raised see-through plastic dial over large grille, top hand-hold, 2 knobs, BC, 5 tubes, AC/DC..**$55.00-65.00**

519, table, 1947, wood, right front round dial over perforated grille, 2 knobs, BC, 5 tubes, AC/DC...**$35.00-40.00**

520, table, 1946, two-tone Catalin, right front round dial, white panel with checkered grille, 2 knobs, BC, 5 tubes, AC/DC.........**$180.00-200.00**

523, portable, 1946, luggage style, cloth covered, right front round dial over perforated grille area, handle, 2 knobs, BC, 6 or 7 tube versions, AC/DC/battery..**$25.00-30.00**

524, table, 1947, wood, upper front slanted slide rule dial, lower perforated grille, 4 knobs, BC, SW, 10 tubes, AC **$50.00-65.00**

525, table-R/P, 1947, wood, center front round dial, lift top, inner phono, 4 knobs, BC, 5 tubes, AC **$25.00-30.00**

528, table, 1947, wood, upper front slanted slide rule dial, lower perforated grille, 4 knobs, BC, FM, 8 tubes, AC **$50.00-65.00**

530, table, 1948, wood, upper front slanted slide rule dial, lower horizontal grille bars, 4 knobs, BC, 6 tubes, AC/DC **$45.00-55.00**

531, table, 1947, two-tone wood, upper front slanted slide rule dial, lower perforated grille, 4 knobs, BC, 5 tubes, battery..............**$35.00-40.00**

532, table, 1947, plastic, upper front slanted slide rule dial, lower horizontal louvers, 4 knobs, BC, 5 tubes, battery **$35.00-40.00**

535, table, 1947, wood, right front square dial over large perforated grille, 2 knobs, BC, 5 tubes, AC/DC **$40.00-45.00**

536, portable, 1947, leatherette, upper front slide rule dial, lower perforated grille, handle, 2 top knobs, BC, 7 tubes, AC/DC/battery ..**$30.00-35.00**

536A, portable, 1947, leatherette, upper front slide rule dial, lower grille area, handle, 2 top knobs, BC, 6 tubes, AC/DC/battery **$30.00-35.00**

537, console-R/P, 1947, wood, inner right slide rule dial, left phono, 2 lift tops, scalloped base, 4 knobs, BC, FM, 6 tubes, AC **$75.00-85.00**

539, table, 1946, wood, right front round dial over perforated grille, 2 knobs, BC, 5 tubes, AC/DC...**$35.00-40.00**

540 "Emersonette," table, 1947, plastic, midget, right front vertical slide rule dial, checkered grille, 2 knobs, BC, 5 tubes, AC/DC ....**$175.00+**

522, table, 1946, plastic, right front dial, left grille with cut-outs, handle, feet, 2 knobs, BC, 5 tubes, AC/DC, $40.00-50.00.

544, table, 1947, two-tone wood, right round dial, left horizontal grille bars, 2 knobs, BC, 5 tubes, AC/DC, $50.00-65.00.

558, portable, 1948, plastic, inner slide rule dial, horizontal louvers, lift-up lid, handle, 2 knobs, BC, 4 tubes, battery, $50.00-65.00.

570 "Memento," table, 1949, jewelry box-style, inner vertical slide rule dial, photo frame in lid, 2 knobs, BC, 4 tubes, battery, $85.00-105.00.

540A, table, 1947, plastic, midget, right front vertical slide rule dial, checkered grille, 2 knobs, BC, 5 tubes, AC/DC ....**$175.00+**

543, table, 1947, plastic, right round dial over metal wrap-around grille, handle, 2 knobs, BC, 5 tubes, AC/DC **$50.00-65.00**

546, table-R/P, 1947, wood, front slanted slide rule dial, lower horizontal grille bars, lift top, inner phono, 4 knobs, BC, 5 tubes, AC............**$35.00-40.00**

547, table, 1947, plastic, lower front slide rule dial, upper louvered grille, 2 knobs, BC, 5 tubes, AC/DC **$40.00-50.00**

547A, table, 1947, plastic, lower front slide rule dial, upper louvered grille, 2 knobs, BC, 5 tubes, AC/DC **$40.00-50.00**

550, table, 1947, wood, upper slanted slide rule dial, lower horizontal louvers, 4 knobs, BC, 6 tubes, AC/DC **$40.00-50.00**

551, portable, 1947, leatherette, inner slide rule dial, horizontal louvers, drop-front, handle, 2 knobs, BC, AC/DC/battery **$30.00-35.00**

551A, portable, 1947, leatherette, inner slide rule dial, horizontal louvers, drop-front, handle, 2 knobs, BC, 6 tubes, AC/DC/battery ..**$30.00-35.00**

552, table-R/P, 1947, wood, center front round dial, 3/4 lift top, inner phono, 4 knobs, BC, 5 tubes, AC **$35.00-40.00**

553, portable, 1947, leatherette, upper front slide rule dial, lower horizontal grille bars, handle, 2 knobs, BC, AC/DC/battery **$40.00-45.00**

553A, portable, 1947, leatherette, upper front slide rule dial, lower horizontal grille bars, handle, 2 knobs, BC, 6 tubes, AC/DC/battery **$40.00-45.00**

556 Series A, table, 1949, plastic, lower front slide rule dial, upper recessed woven grille, 4 knobs, BC, FM, 7 tubes, AC/DC **$40.00-50.00**

557, table, 1948, plastic, lower front slide rule dial, upper recessed lattice grille, 4 knobs, BC, FM, 7 tubes, AC/DC **$45.00-55.00**

557 Series B, table, 1948, plastic, lower front slide rule dial, upper recessed lattice grille, 4 knobs, BC, FM, 7 tubes, AC/DC.................**$45.00-55.00**

559, portable, 1948, alligator, lower front slide rule dial, upper vertical grille bars, handle, 2 knobs, BC, 5 tubes, AC/DC/battery **$40.00-50.00**

559A, portable, 1948, alligator, lower front slide rule dial, upper vertical grille bars, handle, 2 knobs, BC, 5 tubes, AC/DC/battery **$40.00-50.00**

560, portable, 1947, plastic, lower front slide rule dial, upper vertical grille bars, handle, 2 knobs, BC, 4 tubes, battery **$40.00-45.00**

561 Series B, plastic, lower front curved slide rule dial, upper right & left vertical grille bars, 2 knobs, BC, AC/DC **$55.00-65.00**

564, table, 1940, Catalin, midget, right vertical slide rule dial, lattice grille area, 2 knobs, BC, 5 tubes, AC/DC ....**$500.00+**

565, table, 1949, wood, lower front slide rule dial, upper cloth grille, 4 knobs, BC, FM, 7 tubes, AC **$45.00-55.00**

568, portable, 1949, plastic, upper front curved slide rule dial, checkered half-round grille, handle, 2 thumbwheel knobs, BC, 5 tubes, AC/DC/battery **$40.00-45.00**

568A, portable, 1949, plastic, upper front curved slide rule dial, checkered half-round grille, handle, 2 thumbwheel knobs, BC, 5 tubes, AC/DC/battery **$40.00-45.00**

569, portable, 1948, plastic, inner slide rule dial, horizontal grille bars, flip-up front, 2 knobs, BC, 4 tubes, AC/DC/battery.............**$50.00-65.00**

569A, portable, 1948, plastic, inner slide rule dial, horizontal grille bars, flip-up front, 2 knobs, BC, 4 tubes, AC/DC/battery.......**$50.00-65.00**

572, table, 1949, plastic, center front square dial with inner perforated metal grille & large pointer, 2 knobs, BC, 5 tubes, AC/DC ..**$125.00+**

572 Series A, table, 1949, plastic, center front square dial with inner perforated metal grille & large pointer, 2 knobs, BC, 5 tubes, AC/DC ....**$125.00+**

573B, console-R/P, 1948, wood, inner right front dial, left pull-out phono drawer, lower cloth grille with cut-outs, scalloped base, 4 knobs, BC, 9 tubes, AC **$65.00-75.00**

574 "Memento," table, 1949, wood, jewelry box-style, inner vertical slide rule dial, photo frame in lid, 2 knobs, BC, 4 tubes, battery........**$85.00-105.00**

575, portable, 1950, plastic, upper front curved slide rule dial, lower checkered half-round grille, handle, 2 thumbwheel knobs, BC, 6 tubes, AC/DC/battery **$40.00-45.00**

561, table, 1949, plastic, lower front curved slide rule dial, upper right & left vertical grille bars, 2 knobs, BC, 6 tubes, AC/DC, $55.00-65.00.

587 Series B, table, 1949, plastic, lower front slide rule dial, upper perforated metal grille with center Emerson logo, 2 knobs, BC, 5 tubes, AC/DC, $50.00-65.00.

616A, table, 1949, wood, lower front cylindrical slide rule dial, upper "woven" grille, 2 side knobs, BC, 5 tubes, AC/DC, $55.00-65.00.

576, console-R/P, 1948, wood, inner left vertical slide rule dial, pull-out phono drawer, lower criss-cross grille, 4 knobs, BC, 5 tubes, AC **$50.00-65.00**

576A, console-R/P, 1948, wood, inner left vertical slide rule dial, pull-out phono drawer, criss-cross grille, 4 knobs, BC, 5 tubes, AC ..**$50.00-65.00**

577, table, 1948, wood, center front slide rule dial, upper criss-cross grille, 4 knobs, BC, 8 tubes, AC..................................**$55.00-65.00**

577B, table, 1948, wood, center front slide rule dial, upper criss-cross grille, 4 knobs, BC, 8 tubes, AC....................................**$55.00-65.00**

578A, table, 1946, walnut, large gold plastic front grille with lower slide rule dial, horizontal louvers, 2 knobs, BC, AC **$55.00-65.00**

579, table-R/P, 1949, plastic, lower front slide rule dial, vertical grille bars, open top phono, 4 knobs, BC, 5 tubes, AC....................**$35.00-40.00**

579A, table-R/P, 1949, plastic, lower front slide rule dial, vertical grille bars, open top phono, 4 knobs, BC, 5 tubes, AC **$35.00-40.00**

580 "Memento," table, 1949, jewelry box-style, inner vertical slide rule dial, photo frame in lid, 2 knobs, BC, 4 tubes, battery ..**$85.00-105.00**

581, table, 1949, plastic, right front round dial over horizontal wrap-around grille bars, handle, 2 knobs, BC, 5 tubes, AC/DC...........**$45.00-55.00**

581A, table, 1949, plastic, right front round dial over horizontal wrap-around grille bars, handle, 2 knobs, BC, 5 tubes, AC/DC **$45.00-55.00**

586, console-R/P, 1949, wood, inner right slide rule dial, left pull-out phono drawer, large lower grille area, 4 knobs, BC, FM, AC **$75.00-85.00**

587A, table, 1949, plastic, lower front slide rule dial, upper grille with center Emerson logo, 2 knobs, BC, 5 tubes, AC/DC **$50.00-65.00**

591, table, 1949, plastic, upper slanted slide rule dial, lower horizontal grille bars, 2 knobs, BC, 6 tubes, AC/DC **$40.00-50.00**

596, table-R/P, 1949, wood, lower front slide rule dial, horizontal louvers, lift top, inner phono, 2 knobs, BC, 5 tubes, AC **$35.00-40.00**

599, table, 1949, plastic, lower front slanted slide rule dial, upper recessed lattice grille, 4 knobs, BC, 8 tubes, AC/DC **$50.00-65.00**

602, table, 1949, plastic, lower front cylindrical slide rule dial, upper lattice grille, 2 side knobs, FM, 6 tubes, AC/DC **$40.00-50.00**

603, console-R/P, 1949, wood, inner right slide rule dial, left pull-out phono drawer, lower criss-cross grille, 4 knobs, BC, FM, 11 tubes, AC **$50.00-65.00**

640, portable, 1950, plastic, inner vertical slide rule dial, horizontal louvers, flip-up front, handle, 2 knobs, BC, 4 tubes, battery, $55.00-65.00.

605, console-R/P, 1949, wood, center front dial, fold-up front panel, pull-out phono, lower criss-cross grille, 4 knobs, BC, FM, 7 tubes, AC **$50.00-65.00**

610, table, 1949, plastic, lower front cylindrical slide rule dial, upper "woven" grille, 2 side knobs, BC, 5 tubes, AC/DC **$55.00-65.00**

610A, table, 1949, plastic, lower front cylindrical slide rule dial, upper "woven" grille, 2 side knobs, BC, 5 tubes, AC/DC **$55.00-65.00**

613A, portable, 1949, plastic, large round front dial with inner concentric circular grille louvers, flex handle, 2 side knobs, BC, 4 tubes, AC/DC/battery **$40.00-45.00**

615, table, 1949, wood/plastic, flared front with center slide rule dial, upper right & left vertical grille bars, 2 knobs, BC, 6 tubes, AC/DC...**$55.00-65.00**

634B, table-R/P, 1950, wood, inner slide rule dial, outer horizontal louvers, lift top, inner phono, 2 knobs, BC, AC **$35.00-40.00**

636A, table, 1950, plastic, lower front cylindrical slide rule dial, upper lattice grille, 2 knobs, BC, 5 tubes, AC/DC **$55.00-65.00**

641B, table, 1951, plastic, right front slide rule dial, left geometric grille design, 3 knobs, BC, 7 tubes, AC/DC **$40.00-45.00**

642, table, 1950, plastic, right front round dial over horizontal grille bars, handle, 2 knobs, BC, 5 tubes, AC/DC.........................**$45.00-55.00**

643A, portable, 1950, leatherette, upper front curved slide rule dial, lower checkered half-round grille, handle, telescoping antenna, 2 knobs, BC, SW, 5 tubes, AC/DC/battery...................................**$35.00-40.00**

645, portable, 1950, plastic, round front dial with inner concentric circular grille louvers, flex handle, pull-up "fan-tenna," 2 knobs, BC, 4 tubes, battery **$50.00-65.00**

646, portable, 1950, plastic, front slide rule dial overlaps left circular "woven" grille, handle, 2 knobs, BC, 5 tubes, AC/DC/battery **$40.00-45.00**

646A, portable, 1950, plastic, front slide rule dial overlaps left circular "woven" grille, handle, 2 knobs, BC, 5 tubes, AC/DC/battery **$40.00-45.00**

646B, portable, 1950, plastic, front slide rule dial overlaps left circular "woven" grille, handle, 2 knobs, BC, 5 tubes, AC/DC/battery **$40.00-45.00**

652-B, table, 1950, plastic, right front slide rule dial overlaps left round grille with checkered cut-outs, 2 knobs, BC, 5 tubes, AC/DC....**$40.00-45.00**

635, table-R/P, 1950, plastic, top slide rule dial, vertical wrap-over grille bars, 3/4 lift top, inner phono, 2 knobs, BC, 5 tubes, AC, $65.00-75.00.

652, table, 1950, plastic, right front slide rule dial overlaps left round grille with checkered cut-outs, 2 knobs, BC, 5 tubes, AC/DC, $40.00-45.00.

657, portable, 1950, leatherette, upper front curved slide rule dial, lower checkered half-round grille, handle, 2 thumbwheel knobs, BC, AC/DC/battery, $40.00-45.00.

705, portable, 1953, plastic, center front round dial overlaps checkered grille, handle, 2 knobs, BC, battery, $40.00-50.00.

653, table, 1950, plastic, lower front slide rule dial, large upper lattice grille area, 2 knobs, BC, 5 tubes, AC/DC **$35.00-40.00**

653B, table, 1950, plastic, lower front slide rule dial, large upper lattice grille area, 2 knobs, BC, 5 tubes, AC/DC **$35.00-40.00**

656, portable, 1950, plastic, upper front curved slide rule dial, lower checkered half-round grille, handle, 2 thumbwheel knobs, BC, AC/DC/battery **$40.00-45.00**

659, table, 1949, plastic, right front slide rule dial, left grille with concentric squares, 3 knobs, BC, FM **$45.00-55.00**

672B, table-R/P, 1951, wood, inner slide rule dial, phono, lift top, criss-cross grille, 2 knobs, BC, 5 tubes, AC..............................**$30.00-35.00**

679B, console-R/P, 1951, wood, inner right slide rule dial, left phono, double doors, 3 knobs, BC, FM, 8 tubes, AC **$50.00-65.00**

691B, table, 1952, plastic, lower front slide rule dial, large upper lattice grille, 2 knobs, BC, SW, 5 tubes, AC/DC......................**$35.00-40.00**

695B, table-C, 1952, plastic, center vertical slide rule dial, right clock, left checkered grille, 4 knobs, BC, 5 tubes, AC...................**$35.00-40.00**

702B, table, 1952, wood, lower front slide rule dial, upper right & left horizontal grille bars, 2 knobs, BC, 5 tubes, AC/DC **$35.00-40.00**

703B, table-R/P, 1952, wood, inner dial, knobs & phono, lift top, front horizontal grille bars, 2 knobs, BC, 5 tubes, AC **$40.00-45.00**

704, portable, 1952, plastic, center front round dial overlaps checkered grille, handle, 2 knobs, BC, 4 tubes, battery **$40.00-50.00**

706, table, 1952, plastic, small case, lower half-round dial over large checkered grille, Emerson logo, 2 knobs, BC, 5 tubes, AC/DC **$55.00-65.00**

707-B, table, 1952, plastic, "sun-burst" front, lower half-round dial, upper "rayed" grille, 2 knobs, BC, 5 tubes, AC/DC **$75.00-85.00**

718B, table-C, 1953, plastic, left front square dial, right square alarm clock, feet, 5 knobs, BC, AC **$25.00-30.00**

724, table-C, 1953, plastic, large front half-round dial with inner round clock, side grille bars, 5 knobs, BC, AC **$40.00-50.00**

724B, table-C, 1953, plastic, large front half-round dial with inner round clock, side grille bars, 5 knobs, BC, AC **$40.00-50.00**

729 Series B, table, 1954, plastic, diagonally divided front with right half-round dial, left checkered grille area, feet, 2 knobs, BC, 5 tubes, AC/DC **$40.00-50.00**

744B, table, 1954, plastic, raised dome-shaped top, large front half-round dial, 2 thumbwheel knobs, BC, 5 tubes, AC/DC..........**$320.00-350.00**

745B, portable, 1954, leatherette, left front dial, right plaid grille, handle, 2 knobs, BC, 5 tubes, AC/DC/battery...............................**$35.00-45.00**

746B, portable, 1954, left front dial, right plaid grille, handle, telescope antenna, 2 knobs, BC, SW, 5 tubes, AC/DC/battery **$35.00-45.00**

747, portable, 1954, plastic, right front dial, left horizontal grille bars, handle, 2 knobs, BC, 4 tubes, battery **$180.00-200.00**

755-M, cathedral, 1933, walnut, center front window dial, upper cloth grille with cut-outs, 4 knobs, BC, AC.........................**$270.00-300.00**

778 Series B, table, 1954, plastic, center front round dial surrounded by curved grille bars, feet, 2 knobs, BC, 5 tubes, AC/DC ..**$50.00-65.00**

788-B, table-C, 1954, plastic, modern, raised center dial, right perforated grille, left recessed clock, 3 knobs, BC, 5 tubes, AC......**$50.00-65.00**

790, portable, 1954, plastic, right front round dial, left wrap-around horizontal grille bars, handle, 2 knobs, BC, AC/DC/battery ..**$35.00-40.00**

790 Series B, portable, 1954, plastic, right front round dial, left wrap-around horizontal grille bars, handle, 2 knobs, BC, AC/DC/battery **$35.00-40.00**

671B, table-C, 1950, plastic, left front slide rule dial, horizontal wrap-around grille bars, right clock, 5 knobs, BC, 5 tubes, AC, $40.00-50.00.

706-B, table, 1952, plastic, small case, lower half-round dial over large checkered grille, Emerson logo, 2 knobs, BC, 5 tubes, AC/DC, $55.00-65.00.

713 Series A, table, 1952, wood, "sun-burst" front, lower half-round dial, upper "rayed" grille, 2 knobs, BC, 5 tubes, AC/DC, $65.00-75.00.

810B, table, 1955, plastic, lower front dial scale, upper pointer under semi-circular plastic panel, 2 side knobs, BC, 5 tubes, AC/DC, $40.00-50.00.

801, portable, two-tone plastic, upper front round dial overlaps center checkered grille area, fold-down handle, 2 knobs, BC, battery...**$45.00-55.00**

805-B, table, 1954, plastic, left dial area over large front grille with circular perforations, 2 knobs, BC, AC/DC **$25.00-30.00**

808B, table, 1955, plastic, center concentric grille with outer 5/8 circle dial, inward sloping sides with horizontal lines, upper right front Emerson logo, 2 knobs, BC, 5 tubes, AC/DC **$40.00-50.00**

810, table, 1955, plastic, lower front dial scale, upper pointer under semi-circular plastic panel, 2 side knobs, BC, 5 tubes, AC/DC ..**$40.00-50.00**

811, table, 1955, plastic, small case, front half-round dial over horizontal grille bars, feet, 2 knobs, BC, 5 tubes, AC/DC **$40.00-50.00**

811B, table, 1955, plastic, small case, front half-round dial over horizontal grille bars, feet, 2 knobs, BC, 5 tubes, AC/DC **$40.00-50.00**

812B, table, 1955, plastic, large front center dial knob, "bow-tie" louvered grille, inward sloping sides, 1 front knob, 1 right side knob, BC, 5 tubes, AC/DC...**$35.00-45.00**

814B, table-R/P, 1955, wood, outer front round dial over large grille, ¾ lift top, inner phono, 4 knobs, BC, 5 tubes, AC **$25.00-30.00**

816B, table-C, 1955, plastic, modern, raised center dial, right perforated grille, left recessed clock, 3 knobs, BC, 5 tubes, AC.....**$50.00-65.00**

823, table, plastic, center front slide rule dial, upper & lower horizontal bars & vertical dots, 3 knobs, BC, 7 tubes, AC/DC **$30.00-35.00**

825B, table-C, 1955, plastic, center rectangular clock, left grille with horizontal louvers, right fake grille, pedestal base, 2 front, 2 right side knobs, BC, 5 tubes, AC **$25.00-30.00**

826B, table-C, 1955, plastic, large front center lucite clock face, horizontal grille, pedestal base, 3 front, 2 right side knobs, BC, 5 tubes, AC **$50.00-60.00**

832B, table, 1956, plastic, right side dial, front horizontal bars with center "Emerson" band, BC, 5 tubes, AC/DC **$25.00-30.00**

838, portable, 1956, plastic, right front round dial, left checkered grille, handle, 2 transistors, BC, 3 tubes, battery **$150.00-180.00**

851 Series B, table, 1957, plastic, lower right front dial, upper lattice grille area, feet, 2 knobs, BC, 5 tubes, AC/DC **$20.00-25.00**

852 Series B, table, 1957, plastic, lower right front dial window, lower left on/off/volume window, large recessed checkered grille area, 2 knobs, BC, AC/DC **$25.00-30.00**

867B, console-R/P, 1958, wood, inner right dial, phono, lift top, lower front grille, feet, BC, 5 tubes, AC **$35.00-40.00**

876B, table, 1958, plastic, large right airplane dial, left grille with horizontal louvers, feet, 2 knobs, BC, 5 tubes, AC/DC **$25.00-30.00**

881B, table-C, 1958, plastic, right clock, left grille with horizontal louvers and vertical bars, dial knob, feet, 6 knobs, BC, 5 tubes, AC **$25.00-30.00**

883B, table-C, 1958, plastic, center front window dial, right alarm clock, left horizontal louvers, top right "snooze" bar, 4 knobs, BC, 5 tubes, AC **$25.00-30.00**

915B, table, 1960, plastic, lower right front dial over large textured grille area, 2 knobs, BC, 5 tubes, AC/DC **$30.00-35.00**

918B, table-C, 1960, plastic, lower front center dial, right clock, left grille with horizontal louvers, top right "snooze" bar, 4 knobs, BC, 5 tubes, AC **$25.00-30.00**

1002, table, 1947, plastic, upper front slanted slide rule dial, lower horizontal louvers, 4 knobs, BC, 7 tubes, AC/DC **$45.00-55.00**

1003, table, 1947, wood, upper front slanted slide rule dial, large lower perforated grille area, 4 knobs, BC, 7 tubes, AC/DC.....**$30.00-35.00**

A-130, table, 1936, walnut, right front gold dial, left cloth grille with horizontal bars, 2 knobs, BC, 6 tubes, AC/DC **$45.00-55.00**

A-148, table, 1936, wood, slanting front panel, right front gold dial, left grille with three vertical bars, 2 knobs, BC, 6 tubes, AC/DC ..**$180.00-220.00**

AA-204, table, 1938, wood, right front dial, left wrap-around horizontal louvers, 3 knobs, BC, SW, 6 tubes, AC/DC...................**$55.00-65.00**

AA-207, table, 1938, plastic, right front dial, left horizontal louvers, decorative case lines, 3 knobs, BC, SW, 6 tubes, AC/DC......**$45.00-55.00**

AB-182, console, 1937, walnut, upper front dial, lower cloth grille with vertical bars, BC, SW, 14 tubes, AC **$120.00-150.00**

756 Series B, table, 1953, plastic, right front slide rule dial, left grille with concentric squares, 3 knobs, BC, AC, $40.00-45.00.

813B, table, 1955, plastic, large round center dial over gold grille, upper left Emerson logo, feet, 1 front knob, 1 right side knob, BC, 5 tubes, AC/DC, $30.00-35.00.

848, portable, 1957, plastic, top dial, front checkered grille, handle, 2 knobs, BC, AC/DC/battery, $35.00-40.00.

AH, table, two-tone wood, right front gold airplane dial, left cloth grille with horizontal bars, 4 knobs, BC, SW, 6 tubes, AC/DC **$45.00-55.00**

AM-169, table, 1937, walnut, right front airplane dial, rounded left side with vertical bars, 3 knobs, BC, SW, 6 tubes, AC/DC **$65.00-75.00**

AP-176, table, 1937, wood, large center front airplane dial, upper wrap-over grille with vertical bars, 4 knobs, BC, SW, LW, 6 tubes, AC/DC **$85.00-115.00**

AR-165, chairside-R/P, 1937, wood, Deco, step-down top, rounded front with horizontal louvers, inner phono, BC, SW, 6 tubes, AC **$200.00-230.00**

AU-213, table, 1938, walnut, tombstone shape, lower front half-round dial, upper vertical bars, 3 knobs, BC, 5 tubes, AC/DC ..**$120.00-150.00**

AX-212, table, 1938, walnut or maple, Deco, right front square dial, left round grille with concentric circle louvers, 2 knobs, BC, 5 tubes, AC/DC **$200.00-230.00**

AX-217, table, 1938, walnut or maple, right front square dial, left horizontal louvers, 2 knobs, BC, 5 tubes, AC/DC **$40.00-50.00**

AX-219, table-R/P, 1938, wood, right front square dial, left horizontal louvers, open top phono, 2 knobs, BC, 5 tubes, AC **$35.00-40.00**

AX-221, table-R/P, 1938, wood, right front dial, curved left with vertical bars, lift top, inner phono, 2 knobs, BC, 5 tubes, AC **$30.00-35.00**

AX-221-AC-DC, table-R/P, 1938, wood, right front dial, curved left with vertical bars, lift top, inner phono, 2 knobs, 5 tubes, AC/DC ..**$30.00-35.00**

AX-222, portable-R/P, 1938, cloth-covered, inner dial & grille, fold-down front, lift top, inner phono, handle, 2 knobs, BC, 5 tubes, AC/DC **$35.00-40.00**

850, portable, plastic, upper front round dial, center lattice grille panel, handle, 2 knobs, BC, AC/DC/battery, $45.00-55.00.

A-132, table, 1936, wood with Repwood front panel, right front gold dial, left cloth grille with cut-outs, 2 knobs, BC, 6 tubes, AC/DC, $45.00-55.00.

AX-232, portable-R/P, 1938, alligator, inner dial & grille, fold-down front, lift top, inner phono, handle, 2 knobs, BC, 5 tubes, AC ..**$35.00-40.00**

AX-232 AC-DC, portable-R/P, 1938, alligator, inner dial & grille, fold-down front, lift top, inner phono, handle, 2 knobs, BC, 5 tubes, AC/DC **$35.00-40.00**

AX-235 "Little Miracle," table, 1938, Catalin, right front square airplane dial, left horizontal louvers, flared base, 2 knobs, BC, 5 tubes, AC/DC ....**$1,000.00+**

B-131, table, 1936, wood, right front gold dial, left cloth grille with horizontal bars, 3 knobs, BC, SW, 6 tubes, AC **$40.00-50.00**

BA-199, table, 1938, plastic, center front round dial, cloth grille with vertical bars, 2 knobs, BC, 4 tubes, AC/DC **$95.00-115.00**

BB-208, table, 1938, plastic, right front airplane dial, left horizontal louvers, decorative case lines, pushbuttons, 2 knobs, BC, 5 tubes, AC/DC **$65.00-75.00**

BB-209, table, 1938, wood, right front airplane dial, left horizontal louvers, pushbuttons, 2 knobs, BC, 5 tubes, AC/DC **$65.00-75.00**

BD-197 "Mae West," table, 1938, wood, curved case, right front conical dial, left conical grille, 4 knobs, BC, SW, 6 tubes, AC ......**$1,000.00+**

BF-169, table, 1938, wood, right front dial, curved left with vertical bars, 3 knobs, BC, SW, 6 tubes, AC/DC **$65.00-75.00**

BF-204, table, 1938, wood, right front airplane dial, left wrap-around horizontal louvers, 3 knobs, BC, SW, 6 tubes, AC/DC **$55.00-65.00**

BF-207, table, 1938, walnut or ivory plastic, right front dial, left horizontal louvers, decorative case lines, 3 knobs, BC, SW, 6 tubes, AC/DC **$45.00-55.00**

AE-163, table, 1937, wood, raised top, lower front airplane dial, upper cloth grille with cut-outs, 2 knobs, BC, 6 tubes, AC/DC, $85.00-115.00.

AL-132, table, 1936, wood with Repwood front panel, right front gold dial, left cloth grille with cut-outs, 2 knobs, BC, AC, $45.00-55.00.

AX-211 "Little Miracle," table, 1938, plastic, midget, right front dial over horizontal grille bars & front lines, 2 knobs, BC, 5 tubes, AC/DC, $85.00-115.00.

BF-316, table, 1938, wood, right front gold airplane dial, rounded left side with wrap-around horizontal grille bars, 3 knobs, BC **$75.00-85.00**

BJ-200, table, 1938, walnut or ivory plastic, right front dial, left horizontal louvers, decorative case lines, 2 knobs, BC, 6 tubes, AC/DC ..**$55.00-65.00**

BJ-214, table, 1938, wood, right front airplane dial, curved left with horizontal wrap-around louvers, 2 knobs, BC, 6 tubes, AC/DC **$75.00-85.00**

BJ-218, table-R/P, 1938, wood, right front dial, curved left with horizontal bars, lift top, inner phono, 2 knobs, BC, 6 tubes, AC/DC ..**$45.00-55.00**

BJ-220, table-R/P, 1938, wood, right front dial, left horizontal grille bars, lift top, inner phono, 2 knobs, BC, 6 tubes, AC/DC........**$40.00-45.00**

BL-200, table, 1938, walnut or ivory plastic, right front gold dial, left horizontal louvers, decorative case lines, 2 knobs, BC, SW, 5 tubes, AC **$65.00-75.00**

BL-210, table, 1938, wood, right front airplane dial, curved left with vertical bars, 2 knobs, BC, 5 tubes, AC **$65.00-75.00**

BL-214, table, 1938, wood, right front airplane dial, curved left with horizontal wrap-around louvers, 2 knobs, BC, 5 tubes, AC ..**$75.00-85.00**

BL-218, table-R/P, 1938, wood, right front dial, curved left with horizontal bars, lift top, inner phono, 2 knobs, BC, 5 tubes, AC **$40.00-45.00**

BL-220, table-R/P, 1938, wood, right front dial, left horizontal bars, lift top, inner phono, 2 knobs, BC, 5 tubes, AC **$35.00-40.00**

BM-204, table, 1938, plastic, right front airplane dial, left horizontal louvers, 2 knobs, BC, AC/DC **$35.00-40.00**

BM-206, table, 1938, walnut or ivory plastic, right front airplane dial, left horizontal louvers, 2 knobs, BC, 5 tubes, AC/DC **$40.00-50.00**

BM-216, table-R/P, 1938, wood, right front airplane dial, left horizontal louvers, open top phono, 2 knobs, BC, 5 tubes, AC **$30.00-35.00**

BM-242, table-R/P, 1939, wood, right front airplane dial, left horizontal louvers, lift top, inner phono, 2 knobs, BC, 5 tubes, AC..**$30.00-35.00**

BM-247 "Snow White," table-N, 1938, Snow White and Dwarfs in pressed wood, right front airplane dial, left cloth grille, 2 knobs, BC, 5 tubes, AC/DC ....**$1,500.00+**

BN-216, table-R/P, 1938, wood, right front airplane dial, left horizontal louvers, open top phono, 2 knobs, BC, 5 tubes, AC.....**$25.00-30.00**

BQ-223, console-R/P, 1938, wood, upper front conical dial, pushbuttons, lower horizontal grille bars, left lift top, inner phono, 4 knobs, BC, SW, 6 tubes, AC...**$180.00-200.00**

BQ-225 "Symphony Grand," console, 1938, wood, upper front conical dial, pushbuttons, lower horizontal grille bars, 4 knobs, BC, SW, 6 tubes, AC **$150.00-180.00**

BQ-228, table, 1938, wood, right front conical dial, left horizontal louvers, pushbuttons, 4 knobs, BC, SW, 6 tubes, AC **$85.00-115.00**

BR-224, console-R/P, 1938, wood, right front conical dial, pushbuttons, lower horizontal louvers, left lift top, inner phono, 4 knobs, BC, SW, 13 tubes, AC **$400.00-450.00**

BR-224-A, console-R/P, 1938, wood, right front conical dial, pushbuttons, lower horizontal louvers, left lift top, inner phono, 4 knobs, BC, SW, 13 tubes, AC..**$400.00-450.00**

BR-226 "Symphony Grand," console, 1938, wood, upper front conical dial, pushbuttons, lower horizontal louvers, 4 knobs, BC, SW, 13 tubes, AC **$500.00-550.00**

BS-227 "Queen Anne," console, 1938, wood, lowboy, Queen Anne style, upper front conical dial, pushbuttons, tuning eye, lower shell cut-out and horizontal grille bars, 4 knobs, BC, SW, 15 tubes, AC...**$900.00-1,100.00**

BT-245, tombstone, 1939, Catalin, lower front scalloped dial, upper 3-section grille with inset horizontal louvers, 3 knobs, BC, 6 tubes, AC/DC ....**$1,200.00+**

BU-229, table, 1938, wood, right front conical dial, left horizontal grille bars, pushbuttons, tuning eye, 4 knobs, BC, SW, 7 tubes, AC...**$120.00-150.00**

BU-230 "Chippendale," console, 1938, wood, upper front conical dial, lower oval grille with horizontal louvers, pushbuttons, tuning eye, BC, SW, 7 tubes, AC **$120.00-150.00**

AU-190, tombstone, 1938, Catalin, lower front scalloped gold dial, upper cloth grille with vertical bars, 3 knobs, BC, SW, 5 tubes, AC, $1,200.00+.

AX-238, table, 1939, wood, chest-type, inner right dial, left grille with horizontal bars, lift top, 2 knobs, BC, AC/DC, $270.00-300.00.

BJ-210, table, 1938, wood, right front airplane dial, curved left with vertical bars, 2 knobs, BC, 6 tubes, AC/DC, $65.00-75.00.

BW-231, table, 1938, wood, right front conical dial, left horizontal louvers, 4 knobs, BC, SW, 6 tubes, AC......................**$85.00-95.00**

BX-208, table, 1939, plastic, right front airplane dial, left horizontal louvers, decorative case lines, pushbuttons, 2 knobs, BC, 5 tubes, AC/DC **$55.00-65.00**

BY-233, tombstone, 1939, plastic, lower front round dial, upper cloth grille with vertical bars, 2 knobs, BC, 6 tubes, AC/DC **$180.00-200.00**

C-134, tombstone, 1936, walnut, lower front dial, upper cloth grille with cut-outs and center tuning eye, 5 knobs, BC, SW, 8 tubes, AC **$110.00-130.00**

C-138, console, 1936, walnut, upper front dial, tuning eye, lower cloth grille with vertical bars, 5 knobs, BC, SW, 8 tubes, AC **$120.00-150.00**

C-142, console, 1936, walnut, upper front dial, tuning eye, lower cloth grille with vertical bars, 5 knobs, BC, SW, 8 tubes, AC **$120.00-150.00**

C-145, console-R/P, 1936, walnut, upper front dial, tuning eye, lower cloth grille with vertical bars, lift top, inner phono, 5 knobs, BC, SW, 8 tubes, AC **$120.00-150.00**

CE-259, portable, 1939, luggage-style, center front square dial, side grille, handle, 2 knobs, BC, 5 tubes, battery **$30.00-35.00**

CE-260, table, 1939, wood, center front square airplane dial, right & left horizontal louvers, 2 knobs, BC, 5 tubes, battery **$40.00-45.00**

CG-268, table, 1939, walnut or onyx plastic, right front airplane dial, left horizontal wrap-around louvers, 3 knobs, BC, SW, 6 tubes, AC/DC **$40.00-50.00**

CG-276, table, 1939, wood, right front square dial, left grille with vertical bars, 3 knobs, BC, SW, 6 tubes, AC/DC **$55.00-65.00**

CG-293, console-R/P, 1939, wood, inner right dial & knobs, center phono, lift top, front horizontal bars, BC, SW, 6 tubes, AC..........**$75.00-85.00**

CG-294, console-R/P, 1939, wood, inner right dial & knobs, left phono, lift top, vertical front bars, BC, SW, 6 tubes, AC **$75.00-85.00**

CG-318, table, 1939, walnut with inlay, right front square dial, left vertical grille bars, 3 knobs, BC, SW, 5 tubes, AC/DC................**$65.00-75.00**

CH-246, table, 1939, plastic, right front dial, raised left with horizontal wrap-around louvers, 2 knobs, BC, 5 tubes, AC/DC......**$65.00-75.00**

CH-253, table, 1939, ivory, red or brown embossed leatherette, right front half-round dial, left horizontal louvers, 2 knobs, BC, 5 tubes, AC/DC **$55.00-65.00**

CH-256 "Strad," table, 1939, wood, violin shape, front off-center dial, left horizontal louvers, top cut-out, 2 knobs, BC, 5 tubes, AC/DC..**$470.00-530.00**

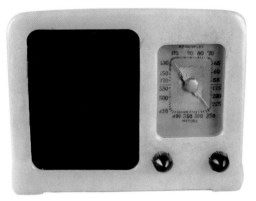

BM-258, table, 1937, Catalin, small case, right front airplane dial, left inset horizontal louvers, 2 knobs, BC, 5 tubes, AC/DC, $1,000.00+.

CJ-238, table, 1939, wood, chest-type, inner right dial, left horizontal louvers, lift top starts and stops radio, 2 knobs, BC, 5 tubes, AC/DC **$270.00-300.00**

CJ-257, kitchen radio, 1939, white finish with black stripes, right front square airplane dial, left horizontal louvers, top shelf, 2 knobs, BC, 5 tubes, AC/DC..**$75.00-95.00**

CQ-269, table, 1939, plastic, right front dial, left horizontal wrap-around louvers, 4 pushbuttons, 3 knobs, BC, SW, 5 tubes, AC/DC ..**$40.00-50.00**

CQ-271, table, 1939, wood, rounded top, right front dial, left vertical bars, 4 pushbuttons, 3 knobs, BC, SW, 7 tubes, AC/DC **$65.00-75.00**

CR-1-303, portable-R/P, 1939, leatherette, inner dial & louvers, fold-down front, handle, lift top, inner phono, BC, 5 tubes, AC/DC..**$30.00-35.00**

CR-261, table, 1939, walnut or maple, right front square dial, curved left with vertical grille bars, 2 knobs, BC, 5 tubes, AC/DC....**$65.00-75.00**

CR-262, table, 1939, wood, curved front with recessed right dial/left vertical grille bars, 2 knobs, BC, 5 tubes, AC/DC................**$75.00-85.00**

CR-274, table, 1939, walnut or onyx plastic, right front dial, raised left with horizontal wrap-around louvers, 2 knobs, BC, 5 tubes, AC/DC **$50.00-65.00**

CR-297, console-R/P, 1939, wood, inner right dial & knobs, left phono, lift top, front vertical grille bars, BC, 5 tubes, AC **$50.00-65.00**

CR-303, portable-R/P, 1939, leatherette, inner dial & louvers, fold down front, handle, lift top, inner phono, 2 knobs, BC, 5 tubes, AC........**$30.00-35.00**

CS-268, table, 1939, walnut or onyx plastic, right front dial, left wrap-around horizontal louvers, 3 knobs, BC, SW, 7 tubes, AC/DC **$40.00-50.00**

CS-270, table, 1939, wood, rounded top, right front square dial, left vertical grille bars, 3 knobs, BC, SW, 7 tubes, AC/DC **$65.00-75.00**

CS-272, table, 1939, wood, right front square dial, curved left with vertical bars, 3 knobs, BC, SW, 7 tubes, AC/DC **$65.00-75.00**

CS-317, table, 1939, walnut, right front square dial, left vertical grille bars, "waterfall" top & base, 3 knobs, BC, SW, 6 tubes, AC/DC ..**$65.00-75.00**

BM-215, table, 1938, two-tone wood, right front gold airplane dial, left horizontal louvers, 2 knobs, BC, 5 tubes, AC/DC, $45.00-55.00.

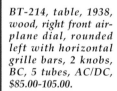

BT-214, table, 1938, wood, right front airplane dial, rounded left with horizontal grille bars, 2 knobs, BC, 5 tubes, AC/DC, $85.00-105.00.

*CF-255 "Emersonette,"
table, 1939, plastic, midget,
right front vertical slide rule
dial, horizontal grille bars,
2 knobs, BC, 2 tubes,
AC/DC, $150.00+.*

*CQ-273, table, 1939, wood,
right front square dial, curved
left with vertical bars, 4 pushbuttons, 3 knobs, BC, SW, 7
tubes, AC/DC, $75.00-85.00.*

CS-320, table, 1939, two-tone walnut, right front square dial, left vertical grille bars, 3 knobs, BC, SW, 7 tubes, AC/DC...............**$55.00-65.00**

CT-275, portable, 1939, cloth covered with stripes, right front dial, left grille, handle, 2 knobs, BC, 5 tubes, battery **$30.00-35.00**

CU-265, table, 1939, plastic, right square dial over horizontal front bars, 2 knobs, BC, 5 tubes, AC/DC **$50.00-65.00**

CV-1-290, portable-R/P, 1939, cloth covered, inner dial & louvers, fold-down front, lift top, inner phono, BC, 5 tubes, AC/DC ..**$30.00-35.00**

CV-1-291, table-R/P, 1939, wood, right front square dial, curved left with horizontal bars, lift top, inner phono, BC, 5 tubes, AC/DC..**$30.00-35.00**

CV-264, table, 1939, ivory, brown or red embossed design, right front square dial, left horizontal louvers, 2 knobs, BC, 5 tubes, AC/DC **$50.00-65.00**

CV-280, portable, 1939, cloth covered, inner right dial, left horizontal louvers, fold-down front, handle, 2 knobs, BC, 5 tubes, AC/DC **$35.00-40.00**

CV-289, table-R/P, 1939, wood, right front square dial, left vertical grille bars, lift top, inner phono, 2 knobs, BC, 5 tubes, AC **$40.00-45.00**

CV-290, portable-R/P, 1939, cloth covered, inner dial & louvers, fold-down front, lift top, inner phono, 3 knobs, BC, 5 tubes, AC **$30.00-35.00**

CV-291, table-R/P, 1939, wood, right front square dial, curved left with horizontal bars, lift top, inner phono, 2 knobs, BC, 5 tubes, AC ..**$40.00-50.00**

CV-295, table, 1939, wood, right front square dial, curved left with vertical grille bars, 2 knobs, BC, 5 tubes, AC/DC..................**$65.00-75.00**

CV-298 "Strad," table, 1939, wood, violin shape, right front square dial, left horizontal louvers, top cut-outs, 2 knobs, BC, 5 tubes, AC/DC **$480.00-560.00**

CV-313, table, 1939, walnut, right front square dial, left vertical grille bars, rounded sides, 2 knobs, BC, 5 tubes, AC/DC **$85.00-95.00**

CV-316, table, 1939, walnut, right front square dial, left horizontal louvers, rounded sides, 2 knobs, BC, 5 tubes, AC/DC **$95.00-115.00**

CW-279, table, 1939, plastic, right front dial, right & left wrap-around horizontal bars, 4 pushbuttons, 2 knobs, BC, 5 tubes, AC/DC **$65.00-75.00**

CX-263, portable, 1939, cloth covered, right front dial, left horizontal louvers, handle, 2 knobs, BC, 5 tubes, battery **$30.00-35.00**

CX-283, portable, 1939, cloth covered, right front dial, left horizontal louvers, handle, 2 knobs, BC, 5 tubes, battery **$30.00-35.00**

CX-284, portable, 1939, cloth covered, inner right dial, left louvers, slide-in door, handle, 2 knobs, BC, 5 tubes, battery **$30.00-35.00**

CX-285, table, 1940, wood, center front dial, right & left horizontal louvers, 2 knobs, BC, 5 tubes, battery **$30.00-35.00**

CX-292, portable-R/P, 1939, cloth covered, right front dial, left louvers, lift top, inner phono, handle, 2 knobs, BC, 5 tubes, battery ..**$25.00-30.00**

CX-305, portable, 1939, walnut, right front recessed dial, left horizontal grille bars, handle, 2 knobs, BC, 5 tubes, battery **$40.00-50.00**

CY-269, table, 1939, walnut or onyx plastic, right front dial, left wrap-around horizontal louvers, 4 pushbuttons, 3 knobs, BC, SW, 5 tubes, AC/DC...**$45.00-55.00**

CY-286, table, 1939, wood, right front dial, left horizontal grille bars, 4 pushbuttons, 3 knobs, BC, SW, 5 tubes, AC/DC **$45.00-55.00**

CY-288, table, 1939, wood, right front square dial, curved left with horizontal bars, 4 pushbuttons, 3 knobs, BC, SW, 5 tubes, AC/DC....**$75.00-85.00**

CZ-282, table, 1939, wood, curved right with top recessed pushbuttons, left vertical bars, 2 knobs, BC, 5 tubes, AC/DC **$85.00-95.00**

D-139, console, 1936, walnut, upper front dial, tuning eye, lower cloth grille with 3 vertical bars, 5 knobs, BC, SW, 10 tubes, AC....**$120.00-150.00**

D-140, tombstone, 1936, walnut, center front dial, upper cloth grille with cut-outs and center tuning eye, 5 knobs, BC, SW, 10 tubes, AC **$110.00-130.00**

D-146, console, 1936, walnut, upper front dial, tuning eye, lower cloth grille with vertical bars, 5 knobs, BC, SW, 10 tubes, AC **$120.00-150.00**

DB-247 "Snow White," table-N, 1939, Snow White & Dwarfs in pressed wood, right front dial, left cloth grille, 2 knobs, BC, 5 tubes, AC/DC ....**$1,500.00+**

DB-296, table, 1939, wood, right front dial, left horizontal louvers, pull-up handle, 2 knobs, BC, 5 tubes, AC/DC **$45.00-55.00**

DB-301, table, 1939, plastic, right front dial, left horizontal louvers, pull-up handle, 2 knobs, BC, 5 tubes, AC/DC **$40.00-50.00**

DB-315, table, 1939, walnut, right front dial, left conical grille, handle, 2 knobs, BC, 5 tubes, AC/DC **$85.00-95.00**

DB-350, table, wood, right front dial, left raised curved grille with horizontal bars, 2 knobs, BC, AC/DC **$65.00-75.00**

DC-308, portable, 1939, leatherette, right front dial, large left grille, handle, 2 knobs, BC, 5 tubes, battery **$30.00-35.00**

DF-302, portable, 1939, walnut with inlay, right front dial, left horizontal louvers, handle, 2 knobs, BC, 6 tubes, AC/DC/battery ..**$50.00-65.00**

DF-306, portable, 1939, cloth covered, inner dial & louvers, fold-down front, handle, 2 knobs, BC, 6 tubes, AC/DC/battery **$30.00-35.00**

DH-264, table, 1939, brown embossed design, right front square dial, left horizontal louvers, 2 knobs, BC, 5 tubes, battery **$50.00-65.00**

*CL-256 "Strad," table, 1939, wood, violin shape,
front off- center dial, left horizontal louvers, top
cut-out, 2 knobs, BC, AC/DC, $470.00-530.00.*

*CV-296 "Strad," table, 1939,
wood, violin shape, right front
square dial, left horizontal
louvers, top cut-outs, 2 knobs,
BC, 5 tubes, AC/DC, $480.00-
560.00.*

95

Emerson

DA-287, table, 1939, walnut, right front dial, left horizontal bars, 3 knobs, BC, SW, 6 tubes, AC, $50.00-65.00.

LA, table, plastic, decorative case design, right dial, center cloth grille with cut-outs, 2 knobs, BC, $85.00-115.00.

DJ-200, table, 1939, plastic, right front airplane dial, left horizontal louvers, decorative case lines, 2 knobs, BC........................**$85.00-95.00**
DJ-310, portable, 1939, leatherette, right front dial, left horizontal louvers, handle, 2 knobs, BC, 6 tubes, AC/DC/battery...............**$30.00-35.00**
DM-331, table, 1939, two-tone wood, right front dial, left two-section grille with vertical bars, 3 knobs, BC, SW, 6 tubes, AC/DC **$40.00-50.00**

DQ-334, table, 1940, two-tone wood, right front square dial, left horizontal grille bars, 2 knobs, BC, 5 tubes, AC/DC, $45.00-55.00.

DW-358, table, plastic, right front airplane dial, left horizontal wrap-around grille bars, decorative case lines, 2 knobs, BC ..**$85.00-95.00**
EC-301, table, 1940, plastic, right front dial, left horizontal louvers, handle, 2 knobs, BC, 5 tubes **$50.00-65.00**
EP-375 "5+1," table, 1941, Catalin, right front square dial, 5 left grille bars and 1 right bar, handle, 2 knobs, BC, AC ....**$900.00+**
EP-405, table, wood/chest-type, inner off-center dial, right and left vertical bars, lift top, rope handles, scalloped base, 2 knobs, BC **$120.00-150.00**
EQ-368, console, wood, upper front slide rule dial, lower vertical grille bars, 6 pushbuttons, 4 knobs, BC, SW, 6 tubes, AC ..**$120.00-150.00**
FL-715, table, plastic, right front dial, left horizontal grille bars, 2 knobs, BC, AC/DC...**$40.00-50.00**
FU-427, portable, 1941, cloth covered, right front round dial, left horizontal louvers, handle, 2 knobs, BC **$30.00-35.00**
FU-428, portable, 1942, inner right round dial, left horizontal louvers, fold-down front, handle, 2 knobs, BC, AC/DC/battery ..**$30.00-35.00**
G-127, portable-R/P, 1936, cloth covered, inner front dial and grille, fold-down front, fold-back top, inner phono, 3 knobs, BC, SW, 6 tubes, AC/DC **$35.00-40.00**

H-130, table, 1936, walnut, right front airplane dial, left cloth grille with horizontal bars, 2 knobs, BC, 6 tubes, battery **$30.00-35.00**
H-137, portable, 1936, walnut with metal design, upper right front dial, left cloth grille with cut-outs, handle, 2 knobs, BC, 6 tubes, battery **$45.00-55.00**
J-106, table, 1935, walnut with ebony base, lower front oval dial, upper cloth grille with cut-outs, rounded sides, 2 knobs, BC, 6 tubes, AC/DC **$110.00-130.00**
K-121, table, 1936, walnut, right front airplane dial, left cloth grille with 2 horizontal bars, 4 knobs, BC, 5 tubes, AC.....................**$40.00-50.00**
K-123, table, 1936, walnut, right front airplane dial, left cloth grille with vertical bars, 4 knobs, BC, 5 tubes, AC.........................**$45.00-55.00**
L-117, tombstone, 1936, wood, lower front dial, upper cloth grille with vertical bars, 4 knobs, BC, SW, 5 tubes, AC **$85.00-105.00**
L-141, tombstone, 1936, wood, two-tone cabinet, lower center gold airplane dial, rounded front corners, speaker grille on top, 4 knobs, BC, SW, 5 tubes, AC...**$150.00-170.00**
L-143, table-R/P, 1936, wood, high case, lower right gold dial, left grille, lift top, inner phono, 4 knobs, BC, SW, 5 tubes, AC **$45.00-55.00**
L-150, chairside, 1935, walnut, oval, step-down top with upper level drawer & lower dial & knobs, BC, 5 tubes, AC **$150.00-170.00**
L-456, cathedral, 1932, two-tone wood, front window dial, upper cloth grille with cut-outs, 2 knobs, BC, 4 tubes, DC **$180.00-210.00**
L-458, table, 1932, two-tone walnut, right front window dial, center round grille with cut-outs, 2 knobs, BC, 4 tubes **$75.00-85.00**
L-459, table, 1932, wood, chest-type, inner top dial & knobs, lift-up lid, fancy front grille, 2 knobs, BC, 4 tubes, DC **$200.00-230.00**
L-556, cathedral, 1932, two-tone wood, front window dial, upper cloth grille with cut-outs, 2 knobs, BC, 5 tubes, AC...........**$200.00-230.00**
L-559, table, 1932, wood, chest-type, inner top dial & knobs, lift-up lid, fancy front grille, 2 knobs, BC, 5 tubes, AC...............**$240.00-270.00**
M-755, cathedral, 1932, two-tone burl walnut, center front window dial, upper cloth grille with cut-outs, 3 knobs, BC, 7 tubes, AC **$320.00-350.00**

Q-236 "Snow White," table-N, 1939, Snow White & Dwarfs in pressed wood, center front dial & cloth grille, 2 knobs, BC, AC, $1,800.00+.

F-133, table, 1936, two-tone wood, right front gold dial, left wrap-around grille with horizontal bars, horizontal decorative metal bands, 4 knobs, BC, SW, 6 tubes, AC/DC, $95.00-115.00.

96

U-6D, table, 1934, wood, lower front round dial, upper cloth grille with cut-outs, 2 knobs, BC, 6 tubes $140.00-160.00

U-6F, table, 1936, wood, lower front dial, upper cloth grille with cut-outs, rounded top, rounded sides, 4 knobs, BC, 6 tubes, AC/DC $120.00-150.00

X-175, console-R/P, 1937, wood, Deco, right upper gold dial with tuning eye above, raised and rounded left side with horizontal bars, 5 knobs, BC, SW, 15 tubes, AC $1,000.00-1,200.00

Z-159, upright table, 1937, wood, slanted front panel, center dial, upper grille with vertical bars, BC, 6 tubes, AC $75.00-95.00

Z-160, table, 1937, wood, right front airplane dial, left wrap-around cloth grille with cut-outs, 4 knobs, BC, SW, 6 tubes, AC $65.00-75.00

U-5A, tombstone, 1935, plastic, Deco, round dial, cloth grille with vertical bars, plastic back, 2 knobs, BC, 5 tubes, AC, $200.00-230.00.

EMOR
Emor Radio, Ltd.
400 East 118th St., New York, New York

100, floor-N, 1947, chrome, Deco, round globe-shaped radio on adjustable floor stand, top grille bars, 3 knobs, BC, SW, 5 tubes $410.00-430.00

EMPIRE
Empire Electrical Products, Co.
102 Wooster Street, New York, New York

30, table, 1933, wood, front dial, center cloth grille with cut-outs, arched top, 2 knobs, BC, 5 tubes, AC/DC $85.00-95.00

EMPRESS
Empire Designing Corp.
1560 Broadway, New York, New York

55 "Chalet," table-N, 1946, wood, cottage-shaped case, dial in door, knobs in windows, upper lattice grille, 2 knobs, BC, 5 tubes, AC/DC, $240.00-270.00.

ERLA
Electrical Research Laboratories
2500 Cottage Grove Avenue, Chicago, Illinois

The name Erla is short for Electrical Research Laboratories. The company began in 1921 selling component parts and radio kits and by 1923 they were marketing complete sets. After much financial difficulty, Erla was reorganized as Sentinel Radio Corporation in 1934.

22P, cathedral-C, 1930, wood, scalloped top, lower front horizontal dial, upper cloth grille with cut-outs and center clock face, 2 knobs, BC, AC $350.00-410.00

30, console, 1929, wood, highboy, lower front window dial with escutcheon, upper grille with cut-outs, BC, 8 tubes, AC $160.00-190.00

271, cathedral, 1931, wood, squared top, lower front window dial, upper round grille with cut-outs, 2 knobs, BC, 7 tubes, AC .. $160.00-190.00

De Luxe Super-Five, table, 1925, wood, low rectangular case, 3 dial front panel, scalloped molding, feet, BC, 5 tubes, battery .. $140.00-170.00

Duo-Reflex, table, wood, high rectangular case, 2 dial front panel, 6 knobs, BC, 3 tubes, battery $170.00-190.00

S-11, table, 1925, wood, low rectangular case, slanted front panel with 3 pointer dials, button feet, 5 knobs, BC, battery, $160.00-190.00.

ESPEY
Espey Mfg. Co., Inc.
33 West 46th Street, New York, New York

7-861, end table, 1938, mahogany or walnut, Duncan Phyfe style, drop-leaf, inner dial & controls, BC, SW, 6 tubes, AC $150.00-180.00

18B, table, 1950, wood, upper front slide rule dial, large center cloth grille, 2 knobs, BC, 5 tubes, AC/DC $40.00-50.00

31 "Roundabout," table, 1950, two-tone plastic, cylindrical fluted case, right front dial, 2 knobs, BC, 5 tubes, AC/DC $180.00-230.00

651, table, 1946, plastic, upper front slanted slide rule dial, lower horizontal wrap-around louvers, 2 knobs, BC, 5 tubes, AC/DC $45.00-55.00

861B, portable, 1938, inner right front dial, left grille, removable cover, handle, 3 knobs, BC, SW, 6 tubes, AC $30.00-35.00

6545, table-R/P, 1946, wood, top slide rule dial, front criss-cross grille, open top phono, 3 knobs, BC, 5 tubes, AC $20.00-25.00

6547, table-R/P, 1946, wood, front slide rule dial, lower horizontal louvers, lift top, inner phono, 4 knobs, BC, 5 tubes, AC $30.00-35.00

6613, table, 1947, wood, upper front slanted slide rule dial, lower horizontal louvers, 4 knobs, BC, SW, 6 tubes, AC/DC $40.00-50.00

RR13, table, 1947, wood, upper front slanted slide rule dial, lower cloth grille with "X" cut-out, 2 knobs, BC, SW, 6 tubes, AC/DC $55.00-65.00

ESQUIRE
Esquire Radio Corp.
51 Warren Street, New York, New York

60-10, table, 1947, plastic, right front half-round dial over large grille area, horizontal decorative lines, 2 knobs, BC, AC/DC $65.00-75.00

65-4, table, 1947, plastic, right half-round dial, left horizontal wrap-around louvers, 2 knobs, BC, AC/DC $55.00-65.00

511, table-C, 1952, plastic, center front round dial, right checkered grille, left alarm clock, 5 knobs, BC, 4 tubes, AC $35.00-40.00

520, table-N-C, 1952, plastic, clock/radio/lamp, center front round dial, left alarm clock, 5 knobs, BC, 4 tubes, AC **$65.00-75.00**
550, table-C, 1952, plastic, center front round dial, right checkered grille, left alarm clock, 5 knobs, BC, 5 tubes, AC **$30.00-35.00**
550U, table-C, 1952, plastic, center front round dial, right checkered grille, left alarm clock, feet, 5 knobs, BC, 5 tubes, AC ..**$30.00-35.00**

ETHERPHONE
Radio Apparatus Co.
40 West Montcalm Street, Detroit, Michigan

RX-1, table, 1923, wood, square case, lift top, inner black panel, BC, 1 exposed tube, battery, $470.00-530.00.

EVEREADY
National Carbon Co.
New York - San Francisco

1, table, 1927, gumwood with maple finish, low rectangular case, center front window dial, 3 knobs, BC, 8 tubes, AC, $120.00-150.00.

1, console, 1928, gumwood with maple finish, table model #1 on four legs, center front window dial, 3 knobs, BC, 8 tubes, AC **$150.00-180.00**
2, console, 1928, metal, table model #2 on aluminum legs, center front window dial, 3 knobs, BC, 8 tubes, AC **$120.00-150.00**
2, table, 1928, metal, low rectangular case with decorative lines, center front window dial, 3 knobs, BC, 8 tubes, AC...............**$85.00-105.00**
3, console, 1928, wood, table model #3 on four legs, center front window dial, 3 knobs, BC, 8 tubes, AC.....................**$120.00-150.00**
3, table, 1928, wood, low rectangular case, center front window dial with escutcheon, 3 knobs, BC, 8 tubes, AC **$85.00-105.00**
20, table, 1928, wood, high rectangular case, upper front window dial, lift top, 3 knobs, BC, 6 tubes, battery................................**$95.00-115.00**
31, table, 1929, wood, low rectangular case, center front dial in carved panel, 3 knobs, BC, 8 tubes, AC **$110.00-130.00**
32, console, 1929, wood, inner ornate panel with upper window dial, sliding doors, 3 knobs, BC, 8 tubes, AC **$180.00-200.00**

33, console, 1929, wood, inner ornate panel with upper window dial, sliding doors, 3 knobs, BC, 8 tubes, AC **$180.00-200.00**
54, console, 1929, wood, inner ornate front panel with upper window dial, sliding doors, 3 knobs, BC, 8 tubes, AC **$200.00-230.00**
100X, table, wood, right front square black dial, left cloth grille with vertical bars, 3 knobs, BC, SW, AC/DC **$40.00-45.00**
101, table, 1947, wood, right front square black dial, left criss-cross grille, 3 knobs, BC, SW, AC/DC **$40.00-50.00**

EXCEL
Excel Corp. of America
9 Rockefeller Plaza, New York, New York

KR-451, portable, right front dial, upper right thumbwheel on/off/volume knob, left grille area with circular cut-outs, handle, BC, battery **$35.00-45.00**
Super T-211, portable, 1959, plastic, right front half-round dial, lower right thumbwheel on/off/volume knob, metal perforated grille area, pull-up handle, BC, battery **$45.00-65.00**
XL-45, portable, 1959, plastic, upper front round dial overlaps horizontal grille bars, pull-up handle, made in Japan, 2 knobs, BC, 4 tubes, battery **$35.00-45.00**

EXCELLO
Excello Products Corporation
4822 West 16th St., Cicero, Illinois

154, console-R/P, 1931, wood, lower front window dial, upper grille with cut-outs, lift top, inner phono, BC **$180.00-200.00**
172, console, 1931, wood, highboy, ornately carved, inner front window dial, scrolled grille, doors, Queen Anne legs, BC **$300.00-350.00**
D, cathedral, 1931, wood, scalloped top, center front window dial, upper cloth grille with cut-outs, 3 knobs, BC **$350.00-410.00**
D-6, console-R/P, 1931, wood, upper front window dial, lower circular grille with cut-outs, lift top, inner phono, 3 knobs, BC..**$120.00-150.00**

FADA
Fada Radio & Electric Company
30-20 Thomson Avenue, Long Island, New York
F.A.D. Andrea, Inc.
1581 Jerome Avenue, New York, New York

Fada was named for its founder — Frank Angelo D'Andrea. The company began business in 1920 with the production of crystal sets. Business expanded until the mid-twenties, but over-production and internal problems took their toll and by 1932 the company had been sold and the name changed to Fada Radio & Electric Corporation. Fada continued to produce radios through the mid-1940s and is probably best known for the Fada Bullet, their ultra-streamlined Catalin radio made in the 1940s.

7 "FADA Seven," table, 1926, wood, low rectangular case, center front dials, loop antenna folds out of left side, lift top, 3 knobs, BC, 7 tubes, battery, $190.00-220.00.

5F60, table, 1939, Catalin, small case, right front square airplane dial, left horizontal louvers, 2 fluted knobs, BC, 5 tubes, AC/DC ...... **$800.00+**

6A39, table, 1948, plastic, right front dial, left horizontal wrap-around louvers, 2 knobs, BC, SW, 6 tubes, AC/DC...................... **$65.00-75.00**

7, console, 1926, wood, highboy, inner dial, fold down front, optional side loop antenna, 3 knobs, BC, 7 tubes, battery **$270.00-300.00**

8 "FADA Eight," table, 1926, wood, center front metal escutcheon with two dial scales, loop antenna stores inside when not in use, lift top, 5 knobs, BC, 8 tubes, battery **$240.00-300.00**

10, table, 1928, wood, low rectangular case, center front dial with escutcheon, switch, 3 knobs, BC, 7 tubes, AC **$110.00-130.00**

11, table, 1928, wood, low rectangular case, center front window dial with escutcheon, 3 knobs, BC, 7 tubes, AC **$120.00-150.00**

12, table, 1928, wood, low rectangular case, center front dial with escutcheon, switch, 3 knobs, BC, 6 tubes, DC **$95.00-115.00**

16, table, 1928, wood, low rectangular case, center front window dial, 3 knobs, BC, 8 tubes, AC **$110.00-130.00**

17, table, 1928, wood, low rectangular case, center front window dial with escutcheon, 3 knobs, BC, 8 tubes, AC **$120.00-150.00**

20, table, 1929, two-tone metal, low rectangular case, center front window dial, 3 knobs, BC, 8 tubes, AC...........................**$110.00-130.00**

20-T, table, 1938, walnut, right front illuminated dial, left grille with Deco cut-outs, BC, 6 tubes, AC/DC **$45.00-55.00**

20-W, table, 1938, plastic, small right front dial, left cloth grille with Deco bars, decorative case lines, 2 knobs, BC, 5 tubes, AC, $85.00-115.00.

20-Z, table, 1929, two-tone metal, low rectangular case, center front window dial, 3 knobs, BC, 8 tubes, AC..............................**$95.00-115.00**

22, table, 1929, wood, large front bronze escutcheon with window dial, 3 knobs, BC, 6 tubes, battery..**$95.00-115.00**

25, console, 1929, walnut, upper front recessed window dial with escutcheon, lower grille with cut-outs, 3 knobs, BC, 8 tubes, AC **$120.00-150.00**

33 Series, portable, 1940, cloth covered, inner metal panel with lower dial and upper vertical grille bars, fold-open front, handle, 2 knobs, BC, battery, $50.00-65.00.

43, cathedral, 1931, wood, scalloped top, ornate pressed wood front, center window dial, upper grille, 3 knobs, BC, 7 tubes, AC, $300.00-350.00.

25-Z, console, 1929, walnut, upper front recessed window dial with escutcheon, lower grille with cut-outs, 3 knobs, BC, 8 tubes, AC **$120.00-150.00**

30, console, 1928, wood, highboy, inner window dial, fold-down front, lower oval grille with cut-outs, 3 knobs, BC, 7 tubes, AC.......**$140.00-160.00**

30J, table, wood, right front airplane dial, left cloth grille with cut-outs, 4 knobs, BC, AC **$55.00-65.00**

31, console, 1928, wood, highboy, inner front window dial, fold-down front, upper speaker with doors, 3 knobs, BC, 7 tubes, AC ..**$200.00-230.00**

32, console, 1929, walnut, highboy, inner front window dial, upper "scallop shell" grille, double front doors, 3 knobs, BC, 8 tubes, AC..**$150.00-180.00**

35, console, 1929, walnut, highboy, inner front window dial, upper "scallop shell" grille, double front doors, 3 knobs, BC, 7 tubes, AC..**$180.00-200.00**

35-B, console, 1929, walnut, highboy, inner front window dial, upper "scallop shell" grille, double front doors, 3 knobs, BC, 8 tubes, AC..**$160.00-190.00**

35-C, console, 1929, walnut, highboy, inner front window dial, upper "scallop shell" grille, double front doors, 3 knobs, BC, 8 tubes, AC..**$160.00-190.00**

35-Z, console, 1929, walnut, highboy, inner front window dial, upper "scallop shell" grille, double front doors, 3 knobs, BC, 7 tubes, AC..**$160.00-190.00**

41, console, 1930, wood, highboy, inner dial & knobs, double front doors, stretcher base, BC, 9 tubes **$160.00-190.00**

42, console, 1930, wood, lowboy, ornate center front panel with upper window dial, lower grille with cut-outs, BC, 9 tubes, AC....**$180.00-210.00**

44, console, 1930, wood, lowboy, inner dial & knobs, double front sliding doors, stretcher base, BC, 9 tubes, AC.....................**$190.00-210.00**

51, cathedral, 1931, wood, center front window dial, upper cloth grille with cut-outs, front pillars, 3 knobs, BC, 6 tubes, AC, $320.00-350.00.

Fada

53, table, 1938, Catalin, right front square airplane dial, left horizontal louvers, 2 fluted knobs, BC, AC, $900.00+.

44, table, 1939, plastic, right front dial, left and right horizontal wrap-around louvers, 2 knobs, BC **$50.00-65.00**

45, console, 1931, wood, lowboy, upper front window dial, lower cloth grille with cut-outs, 3 knobs, BC, 8 tubes, AC...........**$150.00-180.00**

46, console, 1930, wood, highboy, ornate, inner dial & knobs, double doors, 6 legs, stretcher base, BC, 9 tubes, AC **$190.00-210.00**

47, console-R/P, 1930, wood, lowboy, ornate, inner dial & knobs, double front doors, BC, 9 tubes, AC **$200.00-230.00**

49, console, 1931, wood, highboy, inner window dial, grille with cut-outs, double doors, 6 legs, 3 knobs, BC, 10 tubes, AC **$180.00-200.00**

52, table, 1938, Catalin, right front square airplane dial, left horizontal wrap-around louvers, 2 fluted knobs, BC, SW ....**$1,100.00+**

55, table, 1932, wood, upper right front window dial, center cloth grille with vertical bars, 2 knobs, BC, 5 tubes, AC **$85.00-115.00**

60W, table, plastic, right front airplane dial, left grille with Deco cut-outs, decorative case lines, 3 knobs, BC, $75.00-85.00.

66, console, 1932, wood, lowboy, two upper window dials, lower cloth grille with cut-outs, stretcher base, 5 knobs, BC, SW, 10 tubes, AC ..**$150.00-180.00**

70, console, 1928, wood, lowboy, inner dial, fold-down front, lower speaker, doors, side loop antenna, 3 knobs, BC, 9 tubes, AC..**$240.00-300.00**

72, console-R/P, 1928, wood, lowboy, ornate, inner window dial, lower grille with cut-outs, double front doors, BC, 9 tubes, AC **$240.00-300.00**

73, tombstone, 1932, two-tone walnut, center front quarter-round dial, upper cloth grille with diamond-shaped cut-out, 3 knobs, BC, 7 tubes, AC **$85.00-115.00**

74, console, 1932, wood, lowboy, upper front quarter-round dial, lower cloth grille with cut-outs, stretcher base, 3 knobs, BC, 9 tubes, AC **$200.00-230.00**

75, console, 1929, two-tone walnut, lowboy, inner window dial, fold-down front, lower speaker with double doors, 3 knobs, BC, 8 tubes, AC **$150.00-180.00**

136, table, 1941, Catalin, right front airplane dial, left horizontal wrap-around louvers, flared base, handle, 2 knobs, BC, 5 tubes, AC/DC, $1,200.00+.

76, console, 1932, wood, lowboy, inner quarter-round dial, cloth grille with vertical bars, double sliding front doors, stretcher base, 3 knobs, BC, 9 tubes, AC **$120.00-150.00**

77, console-R/P, 1929, walnut, lowboy, inner front window dial, lower grille with cut-outs, double front doors, lift top, inner phono, 3 knobs, BC, 8 tubes, AC **$240.00-300.00**

78, console, 1932, walnut, inner quarter-round dial, cloth grille with cut-outs, double sliding front doors, stretcher base, 3 knobs, BC, 11 tubes, AC **$120.00-150.00**

79, console, 1932, wood, highboy, inner dial, double front doors, 6 legs, stretcher base, 3 knobs, BC, 11 tubes, AC **$150.00-180.00**

97, console, 1932, wood, lowboy, upper front quarter-round dial, lower cloth grille with cut-outs, 6 legs, stretcher base, 3 knobs, BC, 9 tubes, AC **$120.00-150.00**

98, console, 1933, wood, upper front quarter-round dial, lower cloth grille with cut-outs, 6 legs, stretcher base, 3 knobs, BC, 7 tubes, AC **$120.00-150.00**

100, portable, alligator, inner right slide rule dial, left grille area, fold-down front, handle, 3 knobs, BC, 5 tubes, AC/DC/battery **$35.00-40.00**

110AM, table, 1935, wood, rectangular with black accent trim, center grille with cut-outs, right front dial knob, 2 knobs, BC, 4 tubes, AC/DC **$110.00-140.00**

115 "Bullet," table, 1941, Catalin, streamlined, right front round airplane dial, left horizontal grille bars, handle, 2 knobs, BC, 5 tubes, AC/DC .... **$550.00+**

119, table, 1940, plastic, right front airplane dial, left cloth grille with "T" design, decorative case lines, 3 knobs, BC, 6 tubes, AC/DC **$55.00-65.00**

130, table, 1935, wood, right front window dial, center cloth grille with cut-outs, rounded top, BC, 5 tubes, AC/DC.................. **$75.00-95.00**

160 "One-Sixty," table, 1923, mahogany, low rectangular case, 3 dial black Bakelite front panel, lift top, 4 knobs, BC, 4 tubes, battery, $140.00-160.00.

169, table, 1939, wood, right front square airplane dial, left grille with vertical bars, 4 knobs, BC, SW, 7 tubes, AC/DC, $55.00-65.00.

263W, table, 1936, plastic, small right front dial, left cloth grille with Deco bars, plastic back, 3 knobs, BC, AC, $85.00-115.00.

135, table, 1935, wood, right front window dial, center grille with lighter wood and vertical cut-outs, step-down top, 2 knobs, BC, 5 tubes, AC/DC **$80.00-100.00**

140, table, 1935, wood, upper right front window dial, recessed center grille with decorative cut-outs, rounded shoulders, feet, 3 knobs, BC, 5 tubes, AC/DC **$120.00-140.00**

144MT, table, 1940, wood, right front square dial, left cloth grille with vertical cut-outs, 3 knobs, BC, 4 tubes, battery **$65.00-75.00**

150-CA, console, 1935, wood, upper front round dial, lower cloth grille with cut-outs, 4 knobs, BC, SW, 5 tubes, AC **$120.00-150.00**

155, table, 1935, two-tone wood, right front dial, center cloth grille with cut-outs, 2 knobs, BC, 4 tubes, AC/DC **$75.00-95.00**

160-A "One-Sixty," table, 1925, wood, low rectangular case, 3 dial black front panel, lift top, 4 knobs, BC, 4 tubes, battery......**$140.00-160.00**

160-CA, console, 1935, wood, upper front round dial, lower cloth grille with cut-outs, 4 knobs, BC, SW, 6 tubes, AC **$120.00-150.00**

160T, tombstone, 1935, wood, center front round airplane dial, upper cloth grille with cut-outs, 4 knobs, BC, SW, 6 tubes, AC **$110.00-130.00**

167, table, 1936, wood, lower front dial, upper cloth grille with cut-outs, BC, SW, 6 tubes, AC/DC **$85.00-115.00**

168, table, 1936, wood, lower front dial, upper cloth grille with cut-outs, BC, SW, 6 tubes, AC/DC **$85.00-115.00**

175-A "Neutroceiver," table, 1924, mahogany, low rectangular case, 3 dial slanted front panel, 6 knobs, BC, 5 tubes, battery **$110.00-130.00**

175/90-A "Neutroceiver Grand," console, 1925, wood, model 175-A on a lowboy cabinet, 3 dial front panel, double doors, 6 knobs, BC, 5 tubes, battery...**$150.00-180.00**

182G, table-N, 1940, metal, looks like baby grand piano, dial & G-clef speaker grille under keyboard, 2 knobs, BC, SW, 5 tubes, AC/DC **$530.00-580.00**

185-A "Neutrola," table, 1925, wood, inner 3 dial panel, fold-down front, upper speaker, 6 knobs, BC, 5 tubes, battery............**$190.00-210.00**

185/90-A "Neutrola Grand," console, 1925, wood, model 185-A on a lowboy cabinet, inner 3 dial panel, speaker, 6 knobs, BC, 5 tubes, battery **$240.00-270.00**

192-A "Neutrolette," table, 1925, wood, rectangular case, 3 dial black slanted front panel, 6 knobs, BC, 5 tubes, battery **$150.00-180.00**

195-A "Neutro-Junior," table, 1924, wood, low rectangular case, 2 dial black front panel, lift top, 3 knobs, BC, 3 tubes, battery **$150.00-180.00**

203, table, plastic, Deco, right front dial, left cloth grille with Deco cut-outs, handle, 3 knobs, BC, AC/DC **$55.00-65.00**

209 Series, table, 1942, wood, right front airplane dial, left grille with vertical bars, 2 knobs, BC, 5 tubes, AC/DC **$55.00-65.00**

209V, table, 1941, ivory plastic, right front dial, left vertical grille bars, 2 knobs, BC, 5 tubes, AC/DC **$50.00-65.00**

209W, table, 1941, walnut bakelite, right front dial, left vertical grille bars, 2 knobs, BC, 5 tubes, AC/DC...................................... **$50.00-65.00**

252 "Temple," table, 1941, Catalin, upper front dial, lower horizontal grille bars, rounded corners, 2 knobs, BC, 6 tubes, AC/DC .... **$550.00+**

260, table, 1936, plastic, right front dial, left cloth grille with Deco bars, 2 knobs, BC, SW, 6 tubes, AC/DC **$85.00-115.00**

260B, table, 1936, black plastic, right front dial, left cloth grille with Deco bars, 2 knobs, BC, 6 tubes, AC/DC **$85.00-115.00**

260D, table, 1936, black plastic with chrome trim, right front dial, left cloth grille with Deco bars, 2 knobs, BC, 6 tubes, AC/DC .. **$270.00-300.00**

260G, table, 1936, ivory plastic with gold trim, right front dial, left cloth grille with Deco bars, 2 knobs, BC, 6 tubes, AC/DC .. **$270.00-300.00**

260V, table, 1936, ivory plastic, right front dial, left cloth grille with Deco bars, 2 knobs, BC, 6 tubes, AC/DC **$85.00-115.00**

265-A "Special," table, 1927, mahogany, low rectangular case, 2 front window dials, 3 knobs, BC, 6 tubes, battery **$120.00-150.00**

177, table, 1940, wood, right front slide rule dial, left vertical grille bars, base, 3 bands, 4 knobs, BC, SW, 9 tubes, AC/DC, $65.00-75.00.

358, table, 1937, wood, right front dial, left cloth grille with horizontal wrap-around bars, feet, 5 knobs, BC, SW, AC/DC, $75.00-95.00.

605, table, 1946, plastic, upper front slanted slide rule dial, lower horizontal louvers, 2 knobs, BC, 5 tubes, AC/DC, $45.00-55.00.

790, table, 1948, plastic, right front square airplane dial, left criss-cross grille with "T" design, 4 knobs, BC, FM, 9 tubes, AC/DC, $85.00-95.00.

280CA, console, 1936, wood, upper front center airplane dial, tuning eye, lower grille with center vertical bars, rounded shoulders, 4 knobs, BC, SW, 8 tubes, AC/DC **$90.00-110.00**

290-C, console, 1936, wood, upper front round dial, lower cloth grille with vertical bars, tuning eye, 6 knobs, BC, SW, 9 tubes, AC **$150.00-180.00**

290-T, tombstone, 1936, walnut, lower front round dial, upper cloth grille with cut-outs, tuning eye, 6 knobs, BC, SW, 9 tubes, AC **$150.00-180.00**

351, table, 1937, wood, right front gold dial, left cloth grille with Deco cut-outs, 4 knobs, BC, SW, 5 tubes, AC **$55.00-65.00**

366T, table, 1937, wood, right front dial, left wrap-around grille with center horizontal bar, 6 station indicator lights, 5 knobs, BC, SW, 5 tubes, AC **$85.00-115.00**

454V, table, 1938, ivory plastic, right front square dial, left cloth grille with Deco cut-outs, 3 knobs, BC, 5 tubes, AC **$85.00-115.00**

461K, table, 1939, wood, right front airplane dial, left grille with vertical bars, 4 knobs, BC, SW, 5 tubes, AC/DC **$50.00-65.00**

480-B, table, 1927, walnut, large front escutcheon with 2 window dials, fold-out loop antenna, BC, 8 tubes, battery **$200.00-230.00**

602, table-R/P, 1947, wood, upper front slide rule dial, lower dial, lift top, inner phono, 4 knobs, BC, 6 tubes, AC **$30.00-35.00**

609W, table, 1946, plastic, right front square dial, left vertical grille bars, 2 knobs, BC, 5 tubes, AC/DC **$50.00-65.00**

637, portable-R/P, 1947, leatherette, inner slide rule dial, phono, 2 fold-back covers, 4 knobs, BC, 6 tubes, AC..........................**$20.00-25.00**

700, table, 1948, Catalin, right front round dial, left horizontal grille bars, handle, curved sides, 2 knobs, BC, 6 tubes, AC/DC ....**$600.00+**

711, table, 1947, Catalin, right front dial, left cloth grille, handle, rounded corners, 2 knobs, BC, 5 tubes, AC/DC ....**$500.00+**

740, table, 1947, plastic, stepped top, right front dial, left horizontal wrap-around louvers, 2 knobs, BC, 5 tubes, AC/DC **$65.00-75.00**

795, table, 1948, plastic, FM tuner, upper front slide rule dial, lower horizontal louvers, 2 knobs, FM, 5 tubes, AC **$45.00-55.00**

830, table, 1950, plastic, upper curved slide rule dial, lower horizontal louvers, 2 knobs, BC, 5 tubes, AC/DC **$45.00-55.00**

845, table, 1947, plastic, Deco, right front round dial, left horizontal grille bars, handle, 2 knobs, BC, 6 tubes, AC/DC ....**$275.00+**

1000 "Bullet," table, 1946, Catalin, streamline bullet shape, right front round dial, left horizontal grille bars, handle, 2 knobs, BC, 6 tubes, AC/DC ....**$550.00+**

1452A, tombstone, 1934, walnut, front round airplane dial, upper cloth grille with Deco cut-outs, 4 knobs, BC, SW, 5 tubes, AC **$110.00-130.00**

1452F, console, 1934, walnut, upper front round airplane dial, lower cloth grille with cut-outs, 4 knobs, BC, AC........................**$110.00-130.00**

1462D, table, 1935, wood, lower front round airplane dial, upper cloth grille with cut-outs, 4 knobs, BC, SW, 6 tubes, AC/DC..........**$95.00-115.00**

1470C, tombstone, 1934, wood, center front round dial, upper cloth grille with cut-outs, 4 knobs, BC, SW, 7 tubes, AC **$110.00-130.00**

1470E, console, 1934, wood, upper front round dial, lower cloth grille with cut-outs, 4 knobs, BC, SW, AC **$120.00-150.00**

A66PC, console-R/P, 1939, wood, lift top with inner right dial and pushbuttons, lower recessed cloth grille with vertical bars, rounded front corners, 4 knobs, BC, SW, 6 tubes, AC.....................**$120.00-150.00**

A66SC, console, 1939, wood, pushbuttons, lower cloth grille with vertical bars, 4 knobs, BC, SW, 6 tubes, AC..**$120.00-150.00**

C-34, portable, 1941, leatherette, inner dial, vertical grille bars, flip-open front, handle, BC, 5 tubes, AC/DC/battery **$55.00-65.00**

F55, table, 1939, plastic, right front dial, right and left horizontal wrap-around louvers, 2 knobs, BC, 5 tubes, AC/DC **$55.00-65.00**

652 "Temple," table, 1946, Catalin, upper front dial, lower horizontal grille bars, rounded corners, 2 knobs, BC, 6 tubes, AC/DC, $650.00+.

855, table, 1950, plastic, lower front slide rule dial, upper recessed horizontal grille bars, 2 knobs, BC, 5 tubes, AC/DC, $45.00-55.00.

1001, table, 1947, burl veneer, upper front slanted slide rule dial, lower horizontal louvers, 2 knobs, BC, 6 tubes, AC/DC, $50.00-65.00.

F55T, table, 1939, walnut, Deco, right front square dial, left horizontal grille bars, 2 knobs, BC, 5 tubes, AC/DC **$65.00-75.00**

KG, console, 1931, wood, lowboy, ornate front, upper window dial, lower cloth grille with cut-outs, 3 knobs, BC, 7 tubes, AC ..**$240.00-270.00**

L56 "Bell," table, 1939, Catalin, right front dial, left horizontal wrap-around louvers, flared base, handle, 2 knobs, BC, SW, 5 tubes, AC/DC .... **$1,250.00+**

P-40, portable, 1939, cloth covered, right front recessed dial, left 2-section grille, handle, 2 knobs, BC, 4 tubes, battery...........**$20.00-25.00**

P-41, portable, 1940, leatherette, inner slide rule dial, square grille, slide-out front, handle, 2 knobs, BC, 5 tubes, AC/DC/battery ..**$20.00-25.00**

P-82, portable, 1947, leatherette, inner right slide rule dial, slide-in door, handle, 3 knobs, BC, 6 tubes, AC/DC/battery...............**$30.00-35.00**

P-100, portable, 1947, snakeskin, inner right slide rule dial, fold-down front, handle, 3 knobs, BC, 6 tubes, AC/DC/battery **$40.00-45.00**

P-111, portable, 1952, plastic, inner right round dial, lattice grille, flip-up front, handle, 2 knobs, BC, 4 tubes, AC/DC/battery **$50.00-65.00**

P-130, portable, 1951, leatherette, inner slide rule dial, lift front, telescope antenna, handle, 4 knobs, BC, SW, 5 tubes, AC/DC/battery...**$45.00-55.00**

PL24, portable, 1940, leatherette, inner right dial, left horizontal louvers, slide-up door, handle, 3 knobs, BC, SW, 7 tubes, AC/DC/battery **$35.00-40.00**

PL41, portable, 1941, leatherette, inner slide rule dial, lower grille area with Fada logo, removable front, handle, 2 knobs, BC, 5 tubes, AC/DC/battery **$35.00-40.00**

PL50, table-R/P, 1939, wood, right front square dial, left horizontal louvers, lift top, inner phono, BC, 5 tubes, AC **$30.00-35.00**

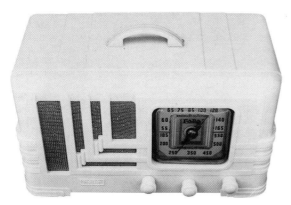

L-96W, table, 1939, plastic, right front square airplane dial, left cloth grille with Deco cut-outs, handle, 3 knobs, BC, 5 tubes, AC/DC, $85.00-105.00.

P-80, portable, 1947, plastic, inner right dial, Deco grille cut-outs, flip-up lid, 3 knobs, BC, 4 tubes, AC/DC/battery, $75.00-95.00.

PL58, portable, 1939, leatherette, fold down front with inner right airplane dial, left grille, top handle, 3 knobs, BC, 5 tubes, AC/DC/battery **$35.00-40.00**

PT-208, table-R/P, 1941, walnut, center front dial, right & left grilles, lift top, inner phono, 4 knobs, BC, 5 tubes, AC **$30.00-35.00**

RE1843, tombstone, wood, center front quarter-round dial, upper cloth grille with diamond-shaped cut-out, 3 knobs, $110.00-130.00.

FAIRBANKS-MORSE
Fairbanks-Morse Home Appliances
430 South Green Street, Chicago, Illinois

6AC-7, chairside, 1937, two-tone wood, top "Great Circle" dial, tuning eye, front grille with vertical bars, 4 knobs, BC, SW, 6 tubes, AC **$120.00-140.00**

9AC-4, console, 1937, wood, upper front round dial with automatic tuning, lower cloth grille with vertical bars, 5 knobs, BC, SW, 9 tubes, AC **$170.00-190.00**

9AC-5, console, 1937, wood, upper front round dial with automatic tuning, lower cloth grille with vertical bars, 5 knobs, BC, SW, 9 tubes, AC **$170.00-190.00**

12-C-6, console, 1936, wood, upper front "semaphore dial," lower grille with bowed vertical bars, 4 knobs, BC, SW, LW, 12 tubes, AC **$240.00-280.00**

57-TO, table, 1936, wood, right front round dial, left cloth grille with cut-outs, cabinet finished on back, 3 knobs, BC, SW, 5 tubes, AC..**$85.00-95.00**

58-T-1, table, 1936, wood, right front round dial, left grille with Deco cut-outs, rounded left side, BC, SW, 5 tubes, AC **$85.00-105.00**

72-C-2, console, 1936, wood, upper front round airplane dial, lower cloth grille with splayed vertical bars, tuning eye, 4 knobs, BC, SW, 7 tubes, AC **$120.00-150.00**

91-C-4, console, 1936, wood, upper front "semaphore dial," lower grille with center vertical bars, 4 knobs, BC, SW, 9 tubes, AC........**$200.00-240.00**

91-T-4, tombstone, 1937, wood, lower front "semaphore dial," upper grille with horizontal louvers, step-down top, 4 knobs, BC, SW, 9 tubes, AC **$120.00-140.00**

746, console, 1935, wood, upper front round airplane dial, lower cloth grille with cut-outs, 4 knobs, BC, SW, 7 tubes, battery..**$65.00-75.00**

814, tombstone, 1934, wood, Deco, lower front half-round dial, upper wrap-over vertical grille bars, 4 knobs, BC, SW, 8 tubes, AC **$300.00-350.00**

5106, cathedral, 1934, wood, center front window dial, upper scalloped-top grille with cut-outs, 3 knobs, BC, 5 tubes, AC **$300.00-320.00**

5312, tombstone, 1934, walnut, Deco, lower front round airplane dial, upper wrap-over vertical grille bars, 3 knobs, BC, SW, 5 tubes, AC..**$110.00-130.00**

5341, console, 1934, wood, upper front round airplane dial, lower cloth grille with cut-outs, 6 legs, BC, SW, 5 tubes, AC **$120.00-140.00**

7014, tombstone, 1934, wood, Deco, lower front round dial, upper wrap-over vertical grille bars, 4 knobs, BC, SW, 7 tubes .. **$140.00-160.00**

7040, console, 1934, wood, Deco, upper front round dial, lower cloth grille with vertical bars, 6 legs, 4 knobs, BC, SW, 7 tubes, AC **$130.00-150.00**

7117, tombstone, 1935, wood, lower front round dial, upper cloth grille with cut-outs, 4 knobs, BC **$120.00-150.00**

7146, console, 1935, wood, upper front round dial, lower cloth grille with cut-outs, 3 band, 4 knobs, BC, SW, 7 tubes, AC **$120.00-140.00**

FAIRVIEW
Fairview Electric Shop
35 Fairview Avenue, Binghamton, New York

J-400 "Lasher Capacidyne," table, 1925, wood, high rectangular case, 3 dial front panel, storage, 5 tubes **$140.00-160.00**

FARNSWORTH
Farnsworth Television & Radio Corp.
Fort Wayne, Indiana

AC-55, console, 1939, wood, upper front slide rule dial, pushbuttons, lower grille with 2 vertical bars, 4 knobs, BC, SW, 7 tubes, AC **$120.00-140.00**

AC-70, console, 1940, wood, upper front 3 section dial, push buttons, lower grille with vertical bars, 4 knobs, BC, SW, 8 tubes, AC..**$110.00-130.00**

BT-54, table, 1942, wood, right front dial, left cloth grille with cut-outs, 2 knobs, BC, 5 tubes, AC/DC, $40.00-50.00.

DT-55, table, 1942, wood, upper front slide rule dial, lower 3-section wrap-around grille, 2 knobs, BC, $40.00-50.00.

AC-90, console, 1939, wood, upper front slanted dial, push buttons, lower grille with vertical bars, 4 knobs, BC, SW, 10 tubes, AC...**$130.00-150.00**

AC-91, console, 1939, wood, wide cabinet, upper front dial, pushbuttons, lower grille with 2 vertical bars, 4 knobs, BC, SW, 10 tubes, AC **$150.00-180.00**

AK-17, table-R/P, 1939, walnut, right front half-round dial, left wrap-around grille, lift top, inner phono, 2 knobs, BC, 5 tubes, AC **$30.00-35.00**

AK-59, console-R/P, 1939, wood, inner dial & phono, push buttons, lower grille with center vertical bar, BC, SW, 7 tubes, AC **$130.00-160.00**

AK-76, console-R/P, 1939, wood, inner dial & phono, push buttons, lower front grille with vertical bars, BC, SW, 8 tubes, AC......**$130.00-160.00**

AK-86, console-R/P, 1940, wood, inner dial & phono, push buttons, lower front grille with vertical bars, BC, SW, 8 tubes, AC......**$140.00-170.00**

AK-95, console-R/P, 1939, wood, inner dial & phono, pushbuttons, lower front grille with vertical bars, BC, SW, 10 tubes, AC ..**$140.00-160.00**

AK-96, console-R/P, 1940, wood, Chippendale design, inner dial & phono, pushbuttons, front grille cut-outs, BC, SW, 10 tubes, AC **$120.00-150.00**

AT-11, table, 1939, plastic, right front half-round dial, left horizontal wrap-around louvers, handle, 2 knobs, BC, 5 tubes, AC/DC.. **$120.00-150.00**

AT-12, table, 1939, plastic, right front half-round dial, left horizontal wrap-around louvers, handle, 2 knobs, BC, 5 tubes, AC/DC.. **$120.00-150.00**

AT-14, table, 1939, plastic, right front half-round dial, top pushbuttons, left horizontal wrap-around louvers, handle, 2 knobs, BC, 5 tubes, AC/DC.. **$120.00-150.00**

AT-15, table, 1939, plastic, right front half-round dial, top pushbuttons, left horizontal wrap-around louvers, handle, 2 knobs, BC, 5 tubes, AC/DC.. **$120.00-150.00**

AT-16, table, 1939, wood, Deco, step-down top, right front half-round dial, top pushbuttons, left grille with horizontal bars, 2 knobs, BC, 5 tubes, AC/DC **$85.00-105.00**

AT-31, portable, 1939, cloth covered, inner right slide rule dial, left grille, fold-down front, handle, 3 knobs, BC, 5 tubes, AC/DC/battery...**$30.00-35.00**

AT-50, table, 1939, wood, lower front slide rule dial, push buttons, upper grille with horizontal bars, 4 knobs, BC, SW, 7 tubes, AC..**$75.00-85.00**

BC-80, console, 1940, wood, upper front dial, lower cloth grille with vertical bars and cut-outs, pushbuttons, 4 knobs, BC, SW, 8 tubes, AC **$120.00-150.00**

BC-81, console, 1940, wood, upper front slide rule dial, pushbuttons, lower grille with vertical bars, 4 knobs, BC, SW, 8 tubes, AC **$120.00-150.00**

BC-82, console, 1940, wood, upper front slide rule dial, lower cloth grille with center vertical divider, pushbuttons, 4 knobs, BC, SW, 8 tubes, AC **$130.00-150.00**

BC-102, console, 1940, wood, upper front slide rule dial, pushbuttons, lower grille with vertical bars, 4 knobs, BC, SW, 10 tubes, AC...**$130.00-150.00**

BC-103, console, 1940, wood, upper front dial, lower cloth grille with center vertical bars, pushbuttons, 4 knobs, BC, SW, 10 tubes, AC...**$120.00-140.00**

BK-69, table-R/P, 1941, wood, right front slide rule dial, pushbuttons, left grille, lift top, inner phono, 3 knobs, BC, AC **$30.00-35.00**

BK-73, chairside-R/P, 1940, walnut, top dial & knobs, front horizontal louvers, lift top, inner phono, side storage, 4 knobs, BC, 7 tubes, AC **$120.00-150.00**

BK-88, console-R/P, 1940, wood, front tilt-out dial panel, lower horizontal grille bars, lift top, inner phono, 4 knobs, BC, 8 tubes, AC ..**$85.00-115.00**

BKR-84, table-R/P/Rec, 1940, wood, right front slide rule dial, pushbuttons, left grille, lift top, inner phono & recorder, 4 knobs, BC, SW, 8 tubes, AC **$40.00-45.00**

BT-20, table, 1940, plastic, right front airplane dial, raised left horizontal wrap-around louvers, rounded top, 3 knobs, BC, SW, 6 tubes, AC/DC **$50.00-65.00**

BT-22, table, 1940, wood, right front slide rule dial, push buttons, left grille with vertical bars, 3 knobs, BC, SW, 6 tubes, AC/DC **$75.00-85.00**

BT-40, table, 1940, two-tone wood, right front dial, left horizontal louvers, BC, battery **$35.00-40.00**

BT-55, table, 1940, wood, right front slide rule dial, left grille with cutouts, pushbuttons, 2 knobs, BC, 5 tubes, AC/DC **$65.00-75.00**

BT-57, table, 1940, wood, right front slide rule dial, left horizontal grille bars, 3 knobs, BC **$45.00-55.00**

BT-61, table, 1940, wood, right front slide rule dial, left grille with cutouts, pushbuttons, 3 knobs, BC, 6 tubes, AC/DC **$55.00-65.00**

BT-68, portable, 1946, leatherette, inner dial & grille with cut-outs, fold-down front, handle, 2 knobs, BC, 6 tubes, AC/DC/battery **$35.00-45.00**

BT-70, table, 1940, wood, lower front slide rule dial, upper cloth grille, pushbuttons, 4 knobs, BC, AC **$55.00-65.00**

BT-71, table, 1940, wood, lower front slide rule dial, upper cloth grille with cut-outs, pushbuttons, 4 knobs, BC, AC **$55.00-65.00**

BT-1010, table, 1938, wood, right front slide rule dial with plastic escutcheon, left horizontal louvers, 4 knobs, BC, SW, 10 tubes, AC **$50.00-65.00**

CC-70, console, 1941, wood, upper front dial, lower grille with vertical bars, pushbuttons, 4 knobs, BC, 7 tubes, AC **$110.00-120.00**

CC-90, console, 1941, wood, upper front dial, lower grille with cut-outs, pushbuttons, 4 knobs, BC, 9 tubes, AC **$110.00-120.00**

CK-58, table-R/P, 1941, wood, upper front slide rule dial, lower grille, lift top, inner phono, 2 knobs, BC, 5 tubes, AC **$30.00-35.00**

CK-66, table-R/P, 1941, wood, front slide rule dial, lower grille area, lift top, inner phono, 4 knobs, BC, 6 tubes, AC **$40.00-45.00**

CK-73, chairside-R/P, 1941, wood, top dial & knobs, front horizontal wrap-around grille bars, lift top, inner phono, side storage, BC, SW, 7 tubes, AC **$120.00-150.00**

CT-41, table, 1941, mahogany plastic, right front dial, left horizontal wrap-around louvers, 2 knobs, BC, 4 tubes, battery......**$35.00-40.00**

CT-42, table, 1941, walnut, right front slide rule dial, left grille with Deco cut-outs, 2 knobs, BC, 4 tubes, battery.........................**$40.00-45.00**

CT-43, table, 1941, two-tone mahogany plastic, right front dial, left horizontal wrap-around louvers, 2 knobs, BC, 4 tubes, battery **$40.00-45.00**

CT-50, table, 1941, mahogany plastic, upper front slide rule dial, lower horizontal louvers, handle, 2 knobs, BC, 5 tubes, AC **$50.00-65.00**

ET-065, table, 1946, plastic, upper slanted pointer dial, lower grille with metal insert, handle, 2 knobs, BC, 6 tubes, AC/DC, $75.00-95.00.

GT-050, table, 1948, brown plastic, Deco design, right front round dial, horizontal wrap-around louvers, 2 knobs, BC, 5 tubes, AC/DC, $120.00-150.00.

CT-51, table, 1941, ivory plastic, upper front slide rule dial, lower horizontal louvers, handle, 2 knobs, BC, 5 tubes, AC **$50.00-65.00**

CT-52, table, 1941, mahogany plastic with gold trim, upper front slide rule dial, lower horizontal louvers, handle, 2 knobs, BC, SW, 5 tubes, AC **$55.00-65.00**

CT-53, table, 1941, ivory plastic with brown trim, upper front slide rule dial, lower horizontal louvers, handle, 2 knobs, BC, SW, 5 tubes, AC **$55.00-65.00**

CT-54, table, 1941, walnut, upper front slide rule dial, lower 3-section wrap-around grille, 2 knobs, BC, SW, 5 tubes, AC **$65.00-75.00**

CT-59, portable, 1941, leatherette & plastic, inner dial & horizontal grille bars, flip-open front, handle, 3 knobs, BC, 5 tubes, AC/DC/battery **$45.00-55.00**

CT-60, portable, 1941, leatherette, luggage-type, inner right front dial, left grille, fold-down front, handle, 2 knobs, BC, 6 tubes, AC/DC/battery **$35.00-40.00**

CT-61, table, 1941, mahogany plastic, upper front slide rule dial, lower grille, handle, 2 knobs, BC, 6 tubes, AC/DC................**$45.00-55.00**

CT-62, table, 1941, ivory plastic, upper front slide rule dial, lower grille, handle, 2 knobs, BC, 6 tubes, AC/DC **$45.00-55.00**

CT-63, table, 1941, mahogany plastic, upper front slide rule dial, lower grille, 2 knobs, BC, SW, 6 tubes, AC/DC **$45.00-55.00**

CT-64, table, 1941, wood, upper front slide rule dial, lower cloth grille with horizontal bars, 2 knobs, BC, SW, 6 tubes, AC/DC **$40.00-50.00**

EC-260, console, 1946, wood, dial on top of case, front cloth grille, 3 knobs, BC, 6 tubes, AC **$75.00-85.00**

EK-264, console-R/P, 1946, wood, dial on top of case, front criss-cross grille, lift top, inner phono, 3 knobs, BC, 6 tubes, AC..**$120.00-150.00**

EK-264WL, console-R/P, 1946, wood, dial & knobs on top of case, front criss-cross grille, lift top, inner phono, 3 knobs, BC, 6 tubes, AC **$120.00-150.00**

ET-060, table, 1946, plastic, upper front slide rule dial, lower wrap-around checkered grille, 2 knobs, BC, SW, 6 tubes, AC/DC **$45.00-55.00**

ET-061, table, 1946, plastic, upper front slide rule dial, lower wrap-around checkered grille, 2 knobs, BC, SW, 6 tubes, AC/DC **$45.00-55.00**

ET-063, table, 1946, wood, upper front slide rule dial, lower cloth grille with cutouts, curved sides, 2 knobs, BC, SW, 6 tubes, AC/DC **$50.00-65.00**

ET-064, table, 1946, plastic, upper slanted pointer dial, lower cloth grille with metal insert, 2 knobs, BC, 6 tubes, AC/DC...........**$75.00-95.00**

ET-066, table, 1946, wood, upper front pointer dial, lower cloth grille with "X" cut-outs, scalloped base, 2 knobs, BC, 6 tubes, AC/DC ..**$50.00-65.00**

ET-067, table, 1946, wood, upper front slide rule dial, lower grille, vertical fluting on case top, 2 knobs, BC, AC **$40.00-50.00**

GK-102, console-R/P, 1947, wood, inner right slide rule dial, pushbuttons, left phono, lift top, 4 knobs, BC, FM, 10 tubes, AC **$75.00-85.00**

GK-111, console-R/P, 1949, wood, inner right dial, pushbuttons, left pull-out phono drawer, 4 knobs, BC, FM, 10 tubes, AC........**$75.00-85.00**

GK-141, console-R/P, 1947, wood, inner right slide rule dial, 8 pushbuttons, left phono, lift top, 5 knobs, BC, SW, FM, 14 tubes, AC....**$65.00-75.00**

GP-350, portable, 1947, metal & leatherette, inner right round dial, left metal grille, flip-open front, 2 knobs, BC, 4 tubes, AC/DC/battery **$35.00-45.00**

GT-051, table, 1948, ivory plastic, Deco design, right front round dial, horizontal wrap-around louvers, 2 knobs, BC, 5 tubes, AC/DC... **$120.00-150.00**

GT-064, table, 1948, plastic, upper front slanted dial, lower cloth grille, vertical fluting, 2 knobs, BC, 6 tubes, AC/DC................**$40.00-50.00**

GT-065, table, 1948, plastic, upper front slanted dial, lower cloth grille, vertical fluting, handle, 2 knobs, BC, 6 tubes, AC/DC ..**$40.00-55.00**

FEDERAL
Federal Telephone & Radio Corporation
591 Broad Street, Newark, New Jersey
Federal Telephone & Telegraph Company
Buffalo, New York
Federal Radio Corporation
(Division of the Federal Telephone Manufacturing Corp.)
Buffalo, New York

Federal Telephone & Telegraph began in 1908 with the manufacture of telephones and soon began to produce radio parts as well. The company produced its first complete radio in 1921 and began to manufacture a high quality, relatively expensive line of sets. As time went on and less complicated radios began to appear on the market, Federal's business declined and by 1929 the company had been sold.

110, table, 1924, metal or wood, polished black Bakelite front panel, lift top, 7 knobs, BC, 3 tubes, battery, $800.00-850.00.

57, table, 1922, metal, 1 dial polished black Bakelite front panel, top right door, 7 knobs, BC, 4 tubes, battery, $690.00-740.00.

59, table, 1923, metal or wood, polished black Bakelite front panel, lift top, 12 knobs, BC, 4 tubes, battery.....................**$1,000.00-1,050.00**
61, table, 1924, metal or wood, polished black Bakelite front panel, lift top, 16 knobs, BC, 6 tubes, battery.....................**$1,250.00-1,450.00**
102, portable, 1924, wood, rectangular case, inner Bakelite panel, removable front, handle, 4 knobs, BC, 4 tubes, battery **$640.00-690.00**
141, table, 1925, mahogany, inner 2 dial Bakelite front panel, double front doors, 4 knobs, BC, 5 tubes, battery.........................**$530.00-580.00**
142, table, 1925, wood, rectangular case, right two dial panel, left built-in speaker, 4 knobs, BC, 5 tubes, battery **$450.00-500.00**

143, console, 1925, wood, lowboy, inner right two dial panel, left built-in speaker, 4 knobs, BC, 5 tubes, battery **$450.00-500.00**
144, console, 1925, wood, lowboy, inner right two dial panel, left built-in speaker, 4 knobs, BC, 5 tubes, battery **$450.00-500.00**
301, console-R/P/Rec, 1940, wood, inner right dial, left phono & recorder, lift top, front grille, BC, AC..**$65.00-75.00**
306, console-R/P/Rec, 1940, wood, inner right dial, left phono & recorder, lift top, BC, AC **$65.00-75.00**
1024TB, table, 1948, black Catalin, upper front slanted slide rule dial, large lower wire mesh grille, 3 knobs, BC, 5 tubes, AC/DC **$350.00-410.00**
1030T, table, 1946, wood, upper slanted slide rule dial, lower grille, 3 knobs, BC, SW, 6 tubes, AC/DC **$40.00-50.00**
1040T, table, 1947, plastic, right front dial, horizontal wrap-around grille bars, 2 knobs, BC, 5 tubes, AC/DC **$35.00-45.00**
1040-TB, table, 1947, plastic, right front dial, horizontal wrap-around grille bars, 2 knobs, BC, 5 tubes, AC/DC **$35.00-45.00**
6001-PO, portable, C1948, alligator, inner right slide rule dial, left grille, fold-down front, handle, 3 knobs, BC, 6 tubes, AC/DC/battery **$30.00-40.00**
A-10 "Orthosonic," table, 1925, wood, low rectangular case, slanted 3 dial front panel, 5 knobs, BC, 5 tubes, battery **$120.00-150.00**
B-20 "Orthosonic," table, 1925, mahogany, low rectangular case, slanted panel with 3 window dials, 4 knobs, BC, 5 tubes, battery **$120.00-150.00**
B-30 "Orthosonic," table, 1925, mahogany, slanted front panel with 3 window dials, rounded top speaker, 4 knobs, BC, 5 tubes, battery **$270.00-300.00**
B-35 "Orthosonic," console, 1925, mahogany, inner right 3 dial panel, left built-in speaker, fold-down front, storage, 4 knobs, BC, 5 tubes, battery **$180.00-200.00**
B-36 "Orthosonic," console, 1925, mahogany, inner right 3 dial panel, left built-in speaker, fold-down front, storage, 4 knobs, BC, 5 tubes, battery **$180.00-200.00**

58 DX, table, 1922, metal or wood, polished black Bakelite front panel, top right door, 8 knobs, BC, 4 tubes, battery, $850.00-900.00.

1028T, table, wood, right front dial with red pointer, left criss-cross grille, 3 knobs, BC, $45.00-55.00.

C-20 "Orthosonic," table, 1925, mahogany, low rectangular case, slanted front panel with 2 dials, 3 knobs, BC, 7 tubes, battery **$120.00-150.00**

C-30 "Orthosonic," table, 1925, mahogany, slanted front panel with 2 dials, rounded top speaker, 3 knobs, BC, 7 tubes, battery **$270.00-300.00**

D-10, table, 1926, mahogany, low rectangular case, center pointer dial, lift top, 2 knobs, BC, 5 tubes, battery **$100.00-120.00**

E-10 "Orthosonic," table, 1926, mahogany, low rectangular case, center window dial with escutcheon, 3 knobs, BC, 6 tubes, battery **$120.00-150.00**

Milan, console, 1927, wood, large ornate cabinet, double front doors, inner fold-down door over dial panel, upper grille with ornate cut-outs, 3 knobs, BC, 7 tubes, battery ....**$800.00+**

H-10-60 "Orthosonic," table, 1928, wood, low rectangular case, center front window dial with escutcheon, 3 knobs, BC, 7 tubes, AC, $120.00-150.00.

FENTONE
L. T. Labs
Beach & Sheridan Rd., Waukegan, IL

M-1851, portable, plastic, right front thumbwheel dial, left thumbwheel volume, center horizontal grille bars, handle, telescoping antenna, 2 knobs, BC, AC/battery, $35.00-45.00.

FERGUSON
J. B. Ferguson
80 Beaver St., New York, New York
Ferguson Radio & Television Co., Inc.
745 Broadway, New York, New York

3, table, 1925, wood, low rectangular case, 3 dial front panel, 3 knobs, BC, 4 tubes, battery.....................................**$120.00-150.00**

4, table, 1925, wood, low rectangular case, slanted 2 dial front panel, 5 knobs, BC, 4 tubes, battery **$120.00-150.00**

6, table, 1925, wood, low rectangular case, 2 dial front panel, battery storage, 4 knobs, BC, 6 tubes, battery **$120.00-150.00**

8, table, 1925, wood, rectangular case, slanted front panel with window dial, 2 knobs, BC, 6 tubes, battery **$160.00-180.00**

214, table, 1937, walnut, slanted front, right airplane dial, left grille with cut-outs, tuning eye, 3 knobs, BC, SW, 14 tubes, AC/DC .. **$85.00-115.00**

12, table, 1926, wood, low rectangular case, right & left front window dials, 3 knobs, BC, battery, $120.00-140.00.

FERRAR
Ferrar Radio & Television Corp.
55 West 26th Street, New York, New York

C-81-B, console, 1947, two-tone wood, upper front slide rule dial, lower grille, 4 knobs, BC, SW, 8 tubes, AC/DC **$85.00-95.00**

T-61-B, table, 1948, wood, right front slide rule dial, left horizontal grille bars, 3 knobs, BC, SW, 6 tubes, AC/DC **$30.00-35.00**

TA61B, table, 1948, wood, upper front slanted slide rule dial, lower diamond shaped grille, 4 knobs, BC, SW, 6 tubes, AC **$35.00-45.00**

FIDELITY

N31, table, plastic, right front round dial over large lattice grille area, feet, 2 knobs, BC, AC, $25.00-30.00.

FIRESTONE
The Firestone Tire & Rubber Company
1200 Firestone Parkway, Akron, Ohio

4-A-1 "Mercury," table, 1948, plastic, lower front slanted slide rule dial, upper horizontal louvers, 2 knobs, BC, 5 tubes, AC/DC .. **$40.00-50.00**

4-A-2 "Commentator," table, 1947, plastic, upper front slide rule dial, lower horizontal louvers, 2 knobs, BC, 5 tubes, AC/DC .. **$40.00-50.00**

4-A-3 "Diplomat," table, 1948, plastic, right front dial, left vertical wrap-over grille bars with lower loops, 2 knobs, BC, 6 tubes, AC/DC **$50.00-65.00**

4-A-10 "Reporter," table, 1947, plastic, upper front slide rule dial, lower horizontal wrap-around louvers, 2 knobs, BC, 5 tubes, AC/DC **$45.00-55.00**

4-A-11, table, 1948, plastic, lower front slide rule dial, upper horizontal wrap-around louvers, 2 knobs, BC, 5 tubes, AC/DC **$40.00-50.00**

4-A-15, console-R/P, 1948, wood, inner right slide rule dial, pushbuttons, lift top, left pull-out phono drawer, BC, SW, FM, 15 tubes, AC **$65.00-75.00**

4-A-12 "Narrator," table, 1948, plastic, elongated base, lower slide rule dial, upper horizontal wraparound louvers, 2 thumbwheel knobs, BC, FM, 6 tubes, AC/DC, $45.00-55.00.

4-A-17, table-R/P, 1948, wood, outer top right dial, front grille with cutouts, lift top, inner phono, 3 knobs, BC, 7 tubes, AC **$35.00-40.00**

4-A-21 "Adam," table, 1947, wood, right front slide rule dial, left cloth grille with cut-outs, 6 pushbuttons, 4 knobs, BC, SW, 6 tubes, AC **$50.00-65.00**

4-A-23 "Interceptor," table, 1946, wood, upper front slanted slide rule dial, lower cloth grille, 6 pushbuttons, 4 knobs, BC, SW, 7 tubes, AC **$45.00-55.00**

4-A-24, table, 1947, wood, upper front slanted slide rule dial, lower cloth grille with "X" cut-out, 2 knobs, BC, 4 tubes, battery **$35.00-40.00**

4-A-25, table, 1947, plastic, upper front slide rule dial, lower horizontal louvers, 2 knobs, BC, 5 tubes, AC/DC **$40.00-50.00**

4-A-27 "Cameo," table, 1947, plastic, lower front slanted slide rule dial, upper horizontal louvers, 2 knobs, BC, 5 tubes, AC/DC..**$40.00-50.00**

4-A-30, console, 1949, wood, upper front slide rule dial, lower cloth grille with vertical bars, pushbuttons, 4 knobs, BC, SW, 10 tubes, AC **$85.00-95.00**

4-A-31 "Rhapsody," console-R/P, 1947, wood, upper front slanted slide rule dial, lower tilt-out phono drawer, 3 knobs, BC, 8 tubes, AC **$85.00-95.00**

4-A-37, console-R/P, 1947, wood, upper front slide rule dial, 6 pushbuttons, lower tilt-out phono, 4 knobs, BC, SW, 8 tubes, AC **$75.00-85.00**

4-A-41, table, 1948, plastic, upper front slanted slide rule dial, lower horizontal louvers, 2 knobs, BC, 5 tubes, AC/DC................**$35.00-45.00**

4-A-20, table, 1947, wood, upper front slanted slide rule dial, lower cloth grille with "X" cut-out, 3 knobs, BC, SW, 6 tubes, AC/DC, $50.00-65.00.

4-A-42 "Georgian," console-R/P, 1947, wood, upper front slide rule dial, 6 pushbuttons, lower tilt-out phono, 4 knobs, BC, FM, 10 tubes, AC **$75.00-85.00**

4-A-60, console-R/P, 1948, wood, inner right slide rule dial, left pull-out phono drawer, 4 knobs, BC, FM, 9 tubes, AC..............**$65.00-75.00**

4-A-61 "Cameo," table, 1948, plastic, lower front slanted slide rule dial, upper horizontal louvers, 2 knobs, BC, 5 tubes, AC/DC..**$45.00-55.00**

4-A-62 "Marlborough," console-R/P, 1949, wood, inner right black dial, left lift top, inner phono, 3 knobs, BC, FM, 8 tubes, AC ..**$50.00-65.00**

4-A-64 "Contemporary," console-R/P, 1949, wood, upper right front dial, left lift top, inner phono, 3 knobs, BC, FM, 9 tubes, AC ..**$50.00-65.00**

4-A-66, console-R/P, 1949, wood, inner top right slide rule dial, front pull-out phono, 4 knobs, BC, FM, 12 tubes, AC **$50.00-65.00**

4-A-67, table, 1949, plastic, upper front slanted slide rule dial, lower horizontal louvers, 2 knobs, BC, 4 tubes, battery **$30.00-35.00**

4-A-68, table, 1949, plastic, right front round dial, left checkerboard grille, ridged base, 2 knobs, BC, 5 tubes, AC/DC **$35.00-45.00**

4-A-69 "Sunrise," table-C, 1949, plastic, upper front slide rule dial, center electric clock, grille on case top, 5 knobs, BC, 5 tubes, AC...**$35.00-40.00**

4-A-70, table, 1951, plastic, right front half-round dial with large tuning knob, left horizontal grille bars, 2 knobs, BC, 4 tubes, AC/DC..**$35.00-40.00**

4-A-71, table-R/P, 1949, wood, center front dial, right & left horizontal louvers, lift top, inner phono, 4 knobs, BC, 5 tubes, AC **$30.00-35.00**

4-A-78, table, 1950, walnut plastic, oblong front panel, right half-round dial, left grille, 2 knobs, BC, 5 tubes, AC/DC **$35.00-45.00**

4-A-26 "Newscaster," table, 1948, plastic, upper front slanted slide rule dial, lower horizontal louvers, 2 knobs, BC, 5 tubes, AC/DC, $40.00-50.00.

4-A-79, table, 1950, ivory plastic, oblong front panel, right half-round dial, left grille, 2 knobs, BC, 5 tubes, AC/DC **$35.00-45.00**

4-A-85, table, 1950, walnut plastic, large front half-round dial, lower panel with vertical lines, 2 knobs, BC, 6 tubes, AC/DC............**$30.00-35.00**

4-A-86 "Westmoreland," console-R/P, 1951, wood, inner right front slide rule dial, lower pull-out phono drawer, left storage, 4 knobs, BC, FM, 8 tubes, AC **$65.00-75.00**

4-A-87 "Waverly," console-R/P, 1951, wood, upper front slide rule dial, center pull-out phono drawer, lower grille, 4 knobs, BC, 6 tubes, AC **$50.00-65.00**

4-A-89, table, 1950, white plastic, large front half-round dial, lower panel with vertical lines, 2 knobs, BC, 6 tubes, AC/DC **$30.00-35.00**

4-A-92, table-C, 1951, plastic, right front dial, left clock, center vertical wrap-over grille bars, 4 knobs, BC, 5 tubes, AC **$30.00-35.00**

4-A-108, table, 1953, plastic, center front half-round dial surrounded by perforated grille area, feet, 2 knobs, BC, 5 tubes, AC/DC **$30.00-35.00**

4-A-110, table-C, 1953, wood, right front square dial, left alarm clock, center lattice grille, 5 knobs, BC, 5 tubes, AC...............**$30.00-35.00**

4-A-115, table, 1953, wood, center front round dial over large woven grille, 2 knobs, BC, 6 tubes, AC **$35.00-40.00**

4-A-134, table-C, 1956, plastic, right side round dial, left front clock, right lattice grille, 5 knobs, BC, 5 tubes, AC **$25.00-30.00**

4-A-143, table, 1956, plastic, lower front dial, large upper grille with center strip, twin speakers, 2 knobs, BC, 5 tubes, AC/DC.......**$40.00-50.00**

4-A-149, table, 1957, plastic, right front round dial, left horizontal bars, BC, 4 tubes, AC/DC **$20.00-25.00**

4-A-152, table-R/P, 1957, right side dial, large front grille, 3/4 lift top, inner phono, handle, 3 knobs, BC, 5 tubes, AC **$20.00-25.00**

4-A-124, table, metal, right front round dial overlaps vertical grille bars with center wedge-shaped divider, 2 knobs, BC, $65.00-75.00.

4-C-5, portable, 1948, plastic, top right dial, rounded center top, rounded sides, strap, 2 knobs, BC, 4 tubes, AC/DC/battery, $40.00-50.00.

4-A-153, table, 1957, plastic, center front vertical slide rule dial & tone control, right & left lattice grilles, 2 knobs, BC, 6 tubes, AC/DC **$20.00-25.00**

4-A-154, table-C, 1957, plastic, front off-center vertical dial, right square clock, 3 knobs, BC, 5 tubes, AC **$20.00-25.00**

4-A-159, table, 1957, plastic, right front vertical slide rule dial, large left lattice grille, 2 knobs, BC, 5 tubes, AC/DC....................**$20.00-25.00**

4-A-160, table-C, 1957, plastic, right side round dial, front alarm clock, left step-down top, 3 knobs, BC, 4 tubes, AC..............**$20.00-25.00**

4-A-162, table-C, 1957, plastic, lower front dial, center square clock face with day-date, 5 knobs, BC, 5 tubes, AC **$25.00-30.00**

4-A-164, table-C, 1957, plastic, right side dial, off-center clock over checkered panel, 4 knobs, BC, 5 tubes, AC **$25.00-30.00**

4-A-167, table-C, 1958, plastic, right front round dial, left square clock, side half-round cut-outs, feet, BC, 5 tubes, AC **$25.00-30.00**

4-A-175, table-R/P, 1958, right side dial, large front grille, 3/4 lift top, inner phono, handle, 3 knobs, BC, 5 tubes, AC **$20.00-25.00**

4-A-176, table, 1958, plastic, right front dial with wedge-shaped pointer, left lattice grille, 2 knobs, BC, 4 tubes, AC **$20.00-25.00**

4-A-179, table-C, 1958, plastic, right side dial, left front clock, right horizontal louvers, 4 knobs, BC, 5 tubes, AC **$20.00-25.00**

4-C-3, portable, 1947, leatherette, inner front slide rule dial, fold-back top, lower grille, 2 knobs, BC, 6 tubes, AC/DC/battery ..**$30.00-35.00**

4-C-13, portable, 1949, lower right front dial, upper horizontal wrap-around grille bars, handle, 2 knobs, BC, 4 tubes, AC/DC/battery **$30.00-35.00**

4-C-16, portable, 1951, plastic, lower front slide rule dial, upper vertical grille bars, flex handle, 2 knobs, BC, 4 tubes, AC/DC/battery **$35.00-40.00**

4-C-18 "Vacationer," portable, 1950, leatherette, center front slide rule dial over large grille area, handle, 2 knobs, BC, 5 tubes, AC/DC/battery **$25.00-30.00**

4-C-19 "The Caravan," portable, 1952, maroon plastic, "alligator" front panel with center circular louvers, flex handle, 2 side knobs, BC, 4 tubes, AC/DC/battery **$35.00-40.00**

4-C-20 "The Caravan," portable, 1952, green plastic, "alligator" front panel with center circular louvers, flex handle, 2 side knobs, BC, 4 tubes, AC/DC/battery **$35.00-40.00**

4-C-21, portable, 1952, two-tone leatherette, center front round dial with inner perforated grille, handle, 2 knobs, BC, 5 tubes, AC/DC/battery...**$35.00-40.00**

4-A-163, table, 1957, plastic, right front dial over random patterned panel, left checkered grille, feet, 2 knobs, BC, 5 tubes, AC/DC, $25.00-30.00.

4-C-22, portable, 1954, plastic, lower front round dial, upper vertical grille bars, handle, 2 knobs, BC, 4 tubes, battery **$30.00-35.00**

4-C-29, portable, 1956, plastic, hybrid/tubes and transistors, right front dial, left checkered grille, handle, 2 knobs, BC, 3 tubes, battery **$200.00-230.00**

4-C-30, portable, 1957, leather, right front slide rule dial, left grille, lower map, telescope antenna, handle, 4 knobs, BC, SW, 5 tubes, AC/DC/battery **$40.00-50.00**

4-C-31, portable, 1957, leather case, front grille cut-outs, upper right round dial, handle, helmet logo, right side thumbwheel knob, BC, 4 tubes, battery...**$30.00-35.00**

4-C-32, portable, 1957, leather case, front grille cut-outs, upper right round dial, handle, helmet logo, 2 knobs, BC, 4 tubes, AC/DC/battery **$30.00-35.00**

4-C-35, portable, 1958, leatherette, upper front slide rule dial, lower map/grille area, telescope antenna, handle, 4 knobs, BC, SW, 5 tubes, AC/DC/battery **$40.00-50.00**

S-7398-1, table, 1940, wood, right front square dial, left cloth grille with cut-outs, 2 knobs, BC, 6 tubes, AC/DC **$40.00-50.00**

S-7398-5, table, 1940, wood, right front slide rule dial, left horizontal grille bars, decorative columns, 6 pushbuttons, 4 knobs, BC, 6 tubes, AC/DC...**$50.00-65.00**

S-7403-2, table, 1940, plastic, right front dial, left vertical wrap-over grille bars with lower loops, 2 knobs, BC, 6 tubes.................**$45.00-55.00**

S-7403-3, table, 1940, wood, right front slide rule dial, left horizontal grille bars, handle, 2 knobs, BC, 5 tubes, AC **$45.00-55.00**

S-7426-6, table, 1939, plastic, right front dial with statue & globe, horizontal grille bars, 2 knobs, BC, 6 tubes, AC, $40.00-50.00.

FIVE STARS

M-1832, portable, plastic, right front dial, left lattice grille area, handle, upper right thumbwheel on/off/volume knob, BC, 4 tubes, battery **$45.00-55.00**

FLUSH WALL
Flush Wall Radio Co.
58 East Park Street, Newark, New Jersey

5P, wall radio, 1947, Catalin front panel, right dial, left horizontal grille openings, 2 knobs, BC, 5 tubes, AC/DC **$180.00-230.00**

FRANKLIN
Franklin Radio Corporation
Dayton, Ohio

105, cathedral, 1933, wood, center front dial, upper cloth grille with cut-outs, BC, 4 tubes, AC **$200.00-230.00**

FREED-EISEMANN
Freed Radio Corporation
200 Hudson Street, New York, New York
Freed-Eisemann Radio Corporation
255 Fourth Avenue, New York, New York

The Freed-Eisemann Radio Corporation began in 1922. Business was good for the company until 1924 when, with the onslaught of less expensive radios from the competition, the company began to decline. Most of the Freed-Eisemann stock was sold to the Freshman Company in 1928 and the final blow was the stock market crash in 1929. Two later companies also formed by the Freed Brothers were the Freed Television and Radio Corporation begun in 1931 and the Freed Radio Corporation begun in 1940.

40, table, 1926, wood, high rectangular case, slanted front, center window dial with escutcheon, 4 knobs, BC, 6 tubes, battery, $120.00-140.00.

10, table, 1926, wood, low rectangular case, 3 dial black front panel, 5 knobs, BC, 5 tubes, battery.......................................**$95.00-115.00**
11 "Electric 11," console, 1927, wood, fold-down front, inner window dial, lower double doors, inner grille, 3 knobs, BC, 6 tubes, AC...**$200.00-230.00**
11 "Electric 11," table, 1927, wood, low rectangular case, inner window dial, fold-down front, 3 knobs, BC, 6 tubes, AC **$140.00-160.00**
26, portable, 1937, leatherette or cloth, inner right dial, left grille, fold-down front, handle, 3 knobs, BC, AC/DC......................**$30.00-35.00**
27D, table, 1937, wood, right front airplane dial, left grille with cut-outs, tuning eye, BC, SW, 7 tubes, AC/DC **$75.00-85.00**
28, table, 1937, two-tone wood, right front square airplane dial, left grille with horizontal bar, BC, SW, AC **$45.00-55.00**
29-D, table, 1937, walnut, right front airplane dial, left grille with horizontal bars, tuning eye, 4 knobs, BC, SW, 11 tubes, AC/DC....**$65.00-75.00**

FE-15, table, 1924, wood, low rectangular case, 3 dial black front panel, lift top, 5 knobs, BC, 5 tubes, battery, $140.00-160.00.

30, table, 1926, mahogany, slanted front panel, 2 window dials with escutcheons, 5 knobs, BC, 6 tubes, battery **$130.00-150.00**
30-D, table, 1937, wood, right front airplane dial, left grille with horizontal bars, tuning eye, 3 knobs, BC, SW, 10 tubes, AC/DC .. **$65.00-75.00**
46, console-R/P, 1947, wood, inner right slide rule dial, left phono, lift top, doors, 6 knobs, BC, SW, FM, 20 tubes, AC...........**$50.00-65.00**
48, table, 1926, wood, inner center dial with escutcheon, fold-down front, side columns, BC, 6 tubes, battery **$120.00-150.00**
50, table, 1926, mahogany, inner center dial with escutcheon, fold-down front, side columns, 4 knobs, BC, 7 tubes, battery **$120.00-140.00**
51, table, 1941, walnut, right & left front vertical slide rule dials, large center grille area, tuning eye, 5 knobs, BC, SW, FM, 14 tubes, AC..**$75.00-85.00**
350, table, 1933, walnut with black & silver trim, right front window dial, center grille with cut-outs, 3 knobs, BC, 5 tubes, AC **$85.00-95.00**
800, table, 1926, wood, low rectangular case, slanted front with center dial, loop antenna, BC, 8 tubes, battery **$200.00-230.00**
800-C-8, console, 1927, wood, console on roller wheels, center front dial, lower speaker grille with cut-outs, top loop antenna, BC, 8 tubes, battery **$300.00-350.00**
850, console, 1926, wood, tall Italian Renaissance cabinet, inner dial, fold-down front, upper speaker with doors, BC, 8 tubes, battery **$320.00-350.00**
BG-357-P, table, 1936, silver, pink, green or blue mirror glass, center front round dial surrounded by vertical grille bars, 2 knobs, BC, 5 tubes, AC/DC .... **$1,200.00+**
FE-18, table, 1925, wood, high rectangular case, 3 dial slanted front panel, storage, 5 knobs, BC, 5 tubes, battery **$120.00-150.00**
FE-24, table, 1937, wood, right front dial, left grille with cut-outs, BC, 5 tubes, AC/DC **$50.00-65.00**
FE-28, table, 1937, wood, right front square airplane dial, left cloth grille with horizontal bars, 3 knobs, BC, SW **$50.00-65.00**
FE-30, table, 1925, wood, low rectangular case, inner three dial panel, fold-down front, 5 knobs, BC, 6 tubes, battery **$140.00-160.00**

NR-5, table, 1923, mahogany, low rectangular case, 3 dial black front panel, lift top, 5 knobs, BC, 5 tubes, battery, $110.00-130.00.

FE-60, table, 1936, two-tone wood, right front dial, left grille with bars, BC, 6 tubes, AC/DC $45.00-55.00

FM-40, table, 1940, walnut, right & left front vertical slide rule dials, large center grille area, 5 knobs, BC, FM1, 16 tubes, AC/DC .. $65.00-75.00

FM-42, console-R/P, 1941, wood, Hepplewhite cabinet, inner slide rule dials and record player, inner large grille, tuning eye, 5 knobs, BC, FM1, 16 tubes, AC $200.00-240.00

NR-6, table, 1924, wood, low rectangular case, 3 dial front panel, lift top, 6 knobs, BC, 5 tubes, battery $110.00-130.00

NR-7, table, 1925, wood, low rectangular case, 3 dial black front panel, lift top, 5 knobs, BC, 6 tubes, battery $110.00-150.00

NR-8, console, 1927, wood, inner panel with 2 window dials, upper speaker, double doors, 5 knobs, BC, 6 tubes, battery $180.00-200.00

NR-8, table, 1927, mahogany, slanted front panel with 2 window dials, 5 knobs, BC, 6 tubes, battery $110.00-140.00

NR-9, console, 1927, wood, inner panel with window dial, fold-down front, upper speaker, 3 knobs, BC, 6 tubes, battery ..$150.00-180.00

NR-9, table, 1927, wood, slant front panel with window dial & brass escutcheon, 3 knobs, BC, 6 tubes, battery $95.00-115.00

NR-12, table, 1924, wood, low rectangular case, 2 dial black front panel, lift top, 4 knobs, BC, 4 tubes, battery $200.00-230.00

NR-20, table, 1924, wood, low rectangular case, inner 3 dial panel, fold-down front, columns, 5 knobs, BC, 5 tubes, battery ..$200.00-230.00

NR-55, console, 1929, walnut veneer, upper front window dial, lower grille with cut-outs, 3 knobs, BC, 8 tubes, AC $150.00-180.00

NR-60, console, 1927, wood, inner dial with large escutcheon, drop front, lower cloth grille with cut-outs, double doors, 3 knobs, BC, 7 tubes, AC $150.00-180.00

NR-60, table, 1927, wood, low rectangular case, front window dial, 3 knobs, BC, 7 tubes, AC $95.00-115.00

NR-66, table, 1927, wood, low rectangular case, front window dial, 3 knobs, BC, 6 tubes, battery $95.00-115.00

NR-67, table, 1927, wood, low rectangular case, inner front window dial with large escutcheon, fold-down front, lift top, 3 knobs, BC, 7 tubes, AC $120.00-150.00

NR-77, table, 1927, wood, low rectangular case, front window dial, right side fold-out loop antenna, 3 knobs, BC, 7 tubes, battery $120.00-150.00

NR-78, console, 1929, walnut, highboy, upper front window dial, lower grille with cut-outs, 3 knobs, BC, 8 tubes, AC............$120.00-150.00

NR-79, console, 1929, walnut, highboy, center front window dial, upper grille with cut-outs, 3 knobs, BC, 8 tubes, AC...........$120.00-150.00

NR-85, table, 1928, metal, rectangular case with decorative decals, center front thumbwheel dial, 2 knobs, BC, 8 tubes, AC........$120.00-150.00

NR-90, console, 1929, walnut, upper front dial, lower cloth grille with cut-outs, stretcher base, BC, 8 tubes, AC $140.00-160.00

NR-95, console, 1929, walnut, highboy, inner window dial, upper grille with cut-outs, doors, 3 knobs, BC, 9 tubes, AC $140.00-160.00

NR-45, table, 1925, wood, low rectangular case (2 versions), 3 dial black front panel, 5 knobs, BC, 6 tubes, battery, $190.00-220.00.

FRENCH
Jesse French & Sons Piano Co.
New Castle, Indiana

"Junior," cathedral, 1931, wood, lower front window dial, upper "bell-shape" grille with cut-outs, ornate edge trim, 2 knobs, BC, 5 tubes, AC $400.00-450.00

"Tudor," console, 1931, wood, lowboy, upper front center window dial, lower round grille with decorative cut-outs, 4 legs, 3 knobs, BC, 7 tubes, AC $130.00-150.00

FRESHMAN
Chas. Freshman Co., Inc.
Freshman Building
240-248 West 40th Street, New York, New York

In 1922 the Charles Freshman Company was formed for the manufacture of radio parts. The popular, low-cost Freshman Masterpiece was introduced in 1924 in both kit as well as completed radio form. The company was plagued by quality control problems and by 1928, in spite of a merger with Freed-Eisemann, the stock market crash dealt the final blow.

G-10 "Equaphase," console, 1927, wood, inner dial, fold-down front, lift top, lower inner speaker, 3 knobs, BC, 7 tubes, AC, $180.00-200.00.

5-F-2, table, 1925, wood, low rectangular case, slanted 3 dial front panel, 5 knobs, BC, 5 tubes, battery $95.00-115.00

5-F-4, table, 1925, mahogany, low rectangular case, slanted 3 dial front panel, 5 knobs, BC, 5 tubes, battery $110.00-130.00

5-F-5, table, 1925, mahogany, low rectangular case, 3 dial front panel, left built-in speaker, 5 knobs, BC, 5 tubes, battery $160.00-180.00

6-F-1 "Masterpiece," console, 1926, mahogany, inner 3 dial panel, fold-down front, upper speaker grille with cut-outs, lower storage, 5 knobs, BC, 5 tubes, battery $200.00-230.00

6-F-2 "Masterpiece," console, 1926, burled walnut, inner 3 dial panel, fold-down front, upper speaker grille with cut-outs, lower storage, 5 knobs, BC, 5 tubes, battery $200.00-230.00

6-F-3 "Masterpiece," console, 1926, mahogany, right 3 dial front panel, left built-in speaker, lower storage, 5 knobs, BC, 5 tubes, battery $160.00-190.00

6-F-4 "Masterpiece," console, 1926, mahogany, right 3 dial front panel, left built-in speaker, lower storage, 5 knobs, BC, 5 tubes, battery $160.00-190.00

6-F-5 "Masterpiece," table, 1926, mahogany, low rectangular case, right 3 dial front panel, left built-in speaker, 5 knobs, BC, 5 tubes, battery $140.00-160.00

6-F-6 "Masterpiece," table, 1926, wood, low rectangular case, 3 dial slanted front panel, 5 knobs, BC, 5 tubes, battery $95.00-115.00

6-F-9 "Masterpiece," console, 1926, mahogany, inner right 3 dial panel, left built-in speaker, fold-down front, lower storage, 5 knobs, BC, 5 tubes, battery $200.00-220.00

6-F-10 "Masterpiece," console, 1926, walnut, inner right 3 dial panel, left built-in speaker, fold-down front, lower storage, 5 knobs, BC, 5 tubes, battery $200.00-220.00

6-F-11 "Masterpiece," console, 1926, mahogany, inner 3 dial panel, fold-down front, lower double doors, inner speaker, 5 knobs, BC, 5 tubes, battery $200.00-230.00

6-F-12 "Masterpiece," console, 1926, walnut, inner 3 dial panel, fold-down front, lower double doors, inner speaker, 5 knobs, BC, 5 tubes, battery $200.00-230.00

Masterpiece, table, 1925, wood, 2 styles, low rectangular case, 3 dial front panel, lift top, 5 knobs, BC, 5 tubes, battery, $85.00-105.00.

7-F-2, table, 1927, wood, low rectangular case, center front window dial with escutcheon, 2 knobs, BC, 6 tubes, battery **$75.00-95.00**
7-F-3, console, 1927, mahogany, upper front window dial, lower built-in speaker with round grille, 2 knobs, BC, 6 tubes, battery ..**$120.00-150.00**
7-F-5, console, 1927, mahogany, inner window dial, fold-down front, lower double doors, inner speaker, 2 knobs, BC, 6 tubes, battery...................**$180.00-200.00**
21 "Earl," table, 1929, metal, low rectangular case, front window dial with escutcheon, 3 knobs, BC, 8 tubes, AC **$75.00-95.00**
22 "Earl," console, 1929, walnut finish, highboy, upper front window dial, lower grille with circular cut-outs, 3 knobs, BC, 8 tubes, AC **$180.00-200.00**
31 "Earl," console, 1929, walnut finish, upper front window dial, lower grille with cut-outs, stretcher base, 3 knobs, BC, 8 tubes, AC..**$180.00-200.00**
32 "Earl," console, 1929, highboy, walnut finish, inner front window dial, double doors, stretcher base, 3 knobs, BC, 8 tubes, AC........**$200.00-230.00**
41 "Earl," console, 1929, wood, highboy, inner window dial and speaker grille with cut-outs, double doors, BC, 9 tubes, AC ..**$180.00-200.00**
Concert, table, 1925, mahogany, tall case, inner 3 dial panel, fold-down front, upper built-in speaker, 5 knobs, BC, 5 tubes, battery **$180.00-200.00**
F-1 "Equaphase," table, 1927, wood, low rectangular case, center front dial, 3 knobs, BC, 6 tubes, battery **$85.00-105.00**
Franklin "Masterpiece," console, 1927, mahogany, inner right 3 dial panel, left built-in speaker, fold-down front, lower storage, 5 knobs, BC, 5 tubes, battery...**$180.00-200.00**
Franklin "Masterpiece," table, 1927, mahogany, right 3 dial panel, left built-in speaker, fold-down front, 5 knobs, BC, 5 tubes, battery **$140.00-160.00**
G-4 "Equaphase," console, 1927, wood, inner front dial & round speaker grille, double doors, lower storage, 3 knobs, BC, 7 tubes, AC **$190.00-210.00**
G-7 "Equaphase," console, 1927, wood, inner dial, fold-down front, lower double doors, inner speaker, 3 knobs, BC, 7 tubes, AC...**$180.00-200.00**

Masterpiece with speaker, table, 1925, wood, low rectangular case with built-in speaker, 3 dial panel, lift top, 5 knobs, BC, 5 tubes, battery, $120.00-150.00.

M, table, 1927, metal, center front window dial with escutcheon, lift-off top, switch, 2 knobs, BC, 7 tubes, AC...........................**$75.00-95.00**
N-12, console, 1928, walnut, lowboy, upper front window dial, lower grille with cut-outs, stretcher base, 3 knobs, BC, 7 tubes, AC..**$140.00-160.00**
Q-15 "Little Giant of the Air," table, 1928, metal, center front dial, lift-off top, 3 knobs, BC, 5 tubes, AC **$75.00-95.00**

FROST MINTON
Frost-Minton Corporation
New York, New York

Bookshelf Model, table, 1931, composition, looks like 9 books on a shelf, BC, 4 tubes, AC **$320.00-360.00**

GAROD
Garod Radio Corporation
70 Washington Street, Brooklyn, New York
Garod Corporation
8 West Park Street, Newark, New Jersey

The name Garod is short for the original Gardner-Rodman Corporation which manufactured crystal sets in 1921. The name was changed to the Garod Corporation in 1923 when the company began to produce radios. Due to legal and quality control problems, the original company was out of business by 1927 but the Garod name had appeared once again in radio manufacturing by 1933.

4A-1B, portable, 1947, inner right dial, upper grille with horizontal slots, flip-up front w/loop antenna, handle, 2 knobs, BC, 4 tubes, battery, $45.00-55.00.

1B55L, table, 1940, Catalin, right square airplane dial over horizontal wrap-around grille bars, recessed handle, 2 knobs, BC, 5 tubes, AC/DC .... **$1,000.00+**
3B123, table, wood, large right front slide rule dial, left cloth grille with cut-outs, 4 knobs, BC, SW **$50.00-65.00**
3P85, table-R/P, 1941, wood, right front dial, left vertical grille bars, lift top, inner phono, 3 knobs, BC, SW, 8 tubes, AC **$30.00-35.00**
4A-2B, portable, 1947, inner right dial, upper grille with horizontal slots, flip-up front w/loop antenna, handle, 2 knobs, BC, 4 tubes, battery **$45.00-55.00**
4B-1, portable, 1948, plastic, inner left dial, geometric grille design, flip-up front, handle, 2 knobs, BC, 4 tubes, battery.............**$40.00-50.00**
5A1 "Ensign," table, 1947, plastic, upper front slide rule dial, lower grille area with vertical bars, rounded corners, 2 knobs, BC, 5 tubes, AC/DC **$55.00-65.00**
5A2, table, 1946, plastic, upper front slide rule dial, lower inset vertical grille design, 2 knobs, BC, 5 tubes, AC/DC **$55.00-65.00**
5A2-Y, table, 1946, plastic, upper front slide rule dial, lower inset vertical grille design, 2 knobs, BC, 5 tubes, AC/DC **$55.00-65.00**
5A3, table, 1948, plastic, right front dial, horizontal louvers, rounded corners, 2 knobs, BC, 5 tubes, AC/DC **$35.00-45.00**

5A4 "Thriftee," table, 1948, plastic, upper front slanted slide rule dial, lower horizontal wrap-around grille bars, 2 knobs, BC, 5 tubes, AC/DC, $45.00-55.00.

5AP1-Y "Companion," table-R/P, 1947, plastic, upper front slide rule dial, lower vertical grille bars, open top phono, 2 knobs, BC, 5 tubes, AC $50.00-65.00

5D-2, portable, 1947, alligator, inner right vertical dial, left horizontal louvers, flip-up front, 2 knobs, BC, 5 tubes, AC/DC/battery............$40.00-45.00

5D-5, portable, 1948, metal, inner right triangular slide rule dial, left grille, flip-up lid, 2 knobs, BC, 4 tubes, AC/DC/battery $40.00-45.00

5RC-1 "Radalarm," table-C, 1948, plastic, right front dial, left alarm clock, center horizontal louvers, 5 knobs, BC, 5 tubes, AC $30.00-35.00

6A-2, table, 1947, wood, upper front slide rule dial, lower horizontal louvers, 2 knobs, BC, 6 tubes, AC/DC $45.00-55.00

6AU-1 "Commander," table, 1946, Catalin, upper front slide rule dial, lower horizontal wrap-around louvers, handle, 2 knobs, BC, 6 tubes, AC/DC .... $800.00+

6BU-1A, table, 1947, plastic, lower front slide rule dial, upper horizontal louvers, flared base, 2 knobs, BC, 6 tubes, AC/DC $55.00-65.00

6DPS-A, console-R/P, 1947, wood, inner right front slide rule dial, left pull-out phono drawer, legs, 4 knobs, BC, SW, 6 tubes, AC ..$65.00-75.00

8A4, table, 1938, wood, step-down top, right front airplane dial, left cloth grille with horizontal wrap-around bars, 4 knobs, BC, SW, AC/DC $85.00-105.00

11FMP, console-R/P, 1948, wood, inner right slide rule dial, door, left pull-out phono drawer, legs, 4 knobs, BC, SW, FM, 11 tubes, AC $65.00-75.00

62B, table, 1947, plastic, lower front slide rule dial, upper horizontal louvers, flared base, 4 knobs, BC, SW, 6 tubes, AC/DC.... $50.00-65.00

126, table, 1940, Catalin, upper front dial, lower cloth grille with overlapping circle cut-outs, handle, 2 knobs, BC $50.00-65.00

306, table-R/P, 1948, wood, center front dial, 3/4 lift top, inner phono, 4 knobs, BC, 5 tubes, AC $30.00-35.00

5D-3A, portable, 1947, metal, inner right triangular slide rule dial, left grille, flip-up lid, 2 knobs, BC, 5 tubes, AC/DC/battery, $40.00-45.00.

309-P8, console-R/P, 1938, wood, large front dial area, lower grille with center vertical bar, lift top, inner phono, BC, SW, 9 tubes, AC **$85.00-115.00**

711-P, table-R/P, 1941, walnut veneer, right front dial, left vertical grille bars, lift top, inner phono, 3 knobs, BC, 7 tubes, AC **$40.00-45.00**

769, table, 1935, wood, Deco, right front dial, pushbuttons, step-down left grille with vertical bars, 4 knobs, BC, SW **$120.00-140.00**

1450, table, 1940, Catalin, arched top, right front square airplane dial, left cloth grille with horizontal bars, handle, 2 knobs, BC, 5 tubes, AC/DC .... **$900.00+**

4159, table, 1938, wood, right front slide rule dial, push buttons, left rounded grille with horizontal bars, BC, SW, LW, 15 tubes, AC **$75.00-85.00**

BP20, portable, 1941, leatherette, inner dial and horizontal grille bars, flip-open front, handle, BC, 5 tubes, AC/DC/battery......**$35.00-45.00**

EA, console, 1926, wood, highboy, slanted front panel with 3 dials, 4 legs, 5 knobs, BC, 6 tubes, AC **$200.00-230.00**

EB, console-R/P, 1926, wood, inner 3 dial panel, fold-down front, lower storage & phono, doors, 5 knobs, BC, 6 tubes, AC ..**$200.00-230.00**

EC, console, 1926, wood, highboy, fold down upper door with inner window dial, 4 legs with stretcher base, BC, 7 tubes, AC..**$200.00-230.00**

EM, table, 1926, wood, slanted front panel with two dials, separate AC power supply, 5 knobs, BC, 6 tubes, AC....................**$120.00-150.00**

Georgian, console, 1924, wood, drop down upper door with inner radio, lower right side door with built-in loudspeaker, inner storage for batteries, 4 legs, 5 knobs, BC, 5 tubes, battery **$350.00-400.00**

M, table, 1925, wood, low rectangular case, 3 dial slanted front panel, 5 knobs, BC, 5 tubes, battery **$85.00-115.00**

V, table, 1924, mahogany, low rectangular case, 3 dial slanted front panel, feet, 5 knobs, BC, 5 tubes, battery **$120.00-150.00**

RAF, table, 1923, mahogany, low rectangular case, 3 dial front panel, lift top, 5 knobs, BC, 4 tubes, battery, $200.00-230.00.

GENERAL ELECTRIC
General Electric Co. - Electronics Department
Bridgeport, Connecticut

GE began manufacturing radios in 1919 and marketed them through RCA until 1930, when they began to use their own General Electric trademark on their products.

41 "Musaphonic," console-R/P, 1948, wood, inner right slide rule dial, 9 pushbuttons, left pull-out phono drawer, double doors, 5 knobs, BC, SW, FM, FM1, 16 tubes, AC **$75.00-85.00**

42 "Musaphonic," console-R/P, 1948, wood, inner slide rule dial, 9 pushbuttons, pull-out phono, 5 knobs, BC, SW, FM, FM1, 16 tubes, AC **$75.00-85.00**

43 "Musaphonic," console-R/P, 1948, wood, inner slide rule dial, 9 pushbuttons, pull-out phono, 5 knobs, BC, SW, FM, FM1, 16 tubes, AC **$75.00-85.00**

44 "Musaphonic," console-R/P, 1948, wood, inner slide rule dial, 9 pushbuttons, pull-out phono, 5 knobs, BC, SW, FM, FM1, 16 tubes, AC **$75.00-85.00**

45 "Musaphonic," console-R/P, 1948, wood, inner slide rule dial, 9 pushbuttons, pull-out phono, 5 knobs, BC, SW, FM, FM1, 16 tubes, AC **$75.00-85.00**

50, table-C, 1946, plastic, lower right front dial, upper lattice grille, left square clock, 4 knobs, BC, 4 tubes, AC **$40.00-50.00**

50W, table-C, 1948, ivory plastic, lower right front dial, upper lattice grille, left square clock, 4 knobs, BC, 4 tubes, AC **$40.00-50.00**

54, table, 1940, plastic, Deco, right front vertical slide rule dial, left round grille with horizontal bars, 4 knobs, BC, $85.00-105.00.

140, portable, 1947, metal & plastic, inner metal panel with dial & grille, flip-open door, pull-up handle, 2 knobs, BC, 4 tubes, AC/DC/battery, $30.00-40.00.

60, table-C, 1948, mahogany plastic, upper front thumbwheel dial, left clock, right horizontal grille bars, 4 knobs, BC, 5 tubes, AC **$45.00-55.00**

62, table-C, 1948, ivory plastic, upper front thumbwheel dial, left clock, right horizontal grille bars, 4 knobs, BC, 5 tubes, AC **$45.00-55.00**

64, table-C, 1949, mahogany plastic, upper front thumbwheel dial, left round alarm clock, right vertical grille bars, 5 knobs, BC, 5 tubes, AC **$45.00-55.00**

65, table-C, 1949, ivory plastic, upper front thumbwheel dial, left round alarm clock, right vertical grille bars, 5 knobs, BC, 5 tubes, AC **$45.00-55.00**

66, table-C, 1949, mahogany plastic, upper front thumbwheel dial, left round alarm clock, right horizontal louvers, 4 knobs, BC, 5 tubes, AC **$45.00-55.00**

67, table-C, 1949, ivory plastic, upper front thumbwheel dial, left round alarm clock, right horizontal louvers, 4 knobs, BC, 5 tubes, AC **$45.00-55.00**

102, table, 1948, brown plastic, lower front slide rule dial, upper horizontal grille bars, 2 knobs, BC, 5 tubes, AC/DC **$35.00-45.00**

102W, table, 1948, ivory plastic, lower front slide rule dial, upper horizontal grille bars, 2 knobs, BC, 5 tubes, AC/DC **$35.00-45.00**

103, table, 1946, wood, lower front black dial, upper "woven" grille, 2 knobs, BC, 5 tubes, AC/DC **$50.00-65.00**

106, table-R/P, 1946, wood, right front round black dial, lift top, inner phono, 3 knobs, BC, 5 tubes, AC **$30.00-35.00**

107, table, 1948, brown plastic, lower front slide rule dial, upper horizontal wrap-around louvers, 2 knobs, BC, 5 tubes, AC/DC **$35.00-45.00**

107W, table, 1948, ivory plastic, lower front slide rule dial, upper horizontal wrap-around louvers, 2 knobs, BC, 5 tubes, AC/DC **$35.00-45.00**

113, table, 1948, plastic, right front half-round dial, left horizontal grille bars, 2 knobs, BC, 5 tubes, AC/DC **$35.00-45.00**

114, table, 1946, brown plastic, lower front slide rule dial, upper horizontal louvers, 2 knobs, BC, 5 tubes, AC/DC...................... **$35.00-45.00**

114W, table, 1946, ivory plastic, lower front slide rule dial, upper horizontal louvers, 2 knobs, BC, 5 tubes, AC/DC...................... **$35.00-45.00**

115, table, 1948, brown plastic, lower front slide rule dial, upper plastic perforated grille, 2 knobs, BC, 5 tubes, AC/DC **$40.00-50.00**

115W, table, 1948, ivory plastic, lower front slide rule dial, upper plastic perforated grille, 2 knobs, BC, 5 tubes, AC/DC **$40.00-50.00**

119W, console-R/P, 1948, wood, inner right dial, phono, lift top, front criss-cross grille, 3 knobs, BC, 6 tubes, AC **$50.00-65.00**

123, table, 1949, brown plastic, large right front dial, left vertical wrap-over grille bars, 2 knobs, BC, 5 tubes, AC/DC **$35.00-45.00**

124, table, 1949, ivory plastic, large right front dial, left vertical wrap-over grille bars, 2 knobs, BC, 5 tubes, AC/DC **$35.00-45.00**

135, table, 1950, brown plastic, lower front slide rule dial, upper recessed vertical grille bars, 2 knobs, BC, 5 tubes, AC/DC.......... **$35.00-45.00**

136, table, 1950, ivory plastic, lower front slide rule dial, upper recessed vertical grille bars, 2 knobs, BC, 5 tubes, AC/DC.......... **$35.00-45.00**

141, portable, 1949, plastic, lower front slide rule dial, upper horizontal louvers, 2 thumbwheel knobs, BC, 4 tubes, battery **$35.00-45.00**

143, portable, 1949, plastic, lower front slide rule dial, upper horizontal louvers, 2 thumbwheel knobs, BC, 4 tubes, AC/DC/battery **$35.00-45.00**

145, portable, 1949, inner slide rule dial, lattice grille, lift-up top, handle, 2 knobs, BC, 4 tubes, AC/DC/battery...............................**$35.00-45.00**

150, portable, 1949, leatherette, upper front slide rule dial, lower horizontal grille bars, handle, 2 knobs, BC, 5 tubes, AC/DC/battery ..**$35.00-45.00**

160, portable, 1949, plastic, upper front slide rule dial, lower lattice grille, handle, battery charger, 2 thumbwheel knobs, BC, 5 tubes, AC/battery **$30.00-40.00**

165, portable, 1950, maroon plastic, upper front slide rule dial, lower horizontal grille bars, handle, 2 knobs, BC, 5 tubes, AC/DC/battery **$35.00-45.00**

100, table, 1946, plastic, lower front half-round dial, upper horizontal wrap-around grille bars, 2 knobs, BC, 5 tubes, AC/DC, $45.00-55.00.

200, table, 1946, plastic, lower front black dial, upper horizontal wrap-around grille bars, 2 knobs, BC, 6 tubes, AC/DC, $35.00-45.00.

180, table, 1947, wood, right front dial over cloth grille with horizontal bars, rounded corners, feet, 2 knobs, BC, 4 tubes, battery **$30.00-35.00**

201, table, 1946, plastic, lower front black rectangular dial, upper metal criss-cross grille, 2 knobs, BC, 6 tubes, AC/DC........... **$35.00-45.00**

202, table, 1947, plastic, lower front rectangular dial, upper metal criss-cross grille, 2 knobs, BC, AC/DC **$35.00-45.00**

203, table, 1946, wood, lower front black rectangular dial, upper metal woven grille, 2 knobs, BC, 6 tubes, AC/DC **$45.00-55.00**

210, table, 1948, mahogany plastic, right front round dial, recessed cloth grille, 2 knobs, BC, FM, 7 tubes, AC/DC **$35.00-40.00**

211, table, 1948, ivory plastic, right front round dial, recessed cloth grille, 2 knobs, BC, FM, 7 tubes, AC/DC **$35.00-40.00**

212, table, 1948, wood, right front dial over plastic wrap-around panel, cloth grille, 2 knobs, BC, FM, 7 tubes, AC/DC **$35.00-40.00**

218, table, 1951, mahogany plastic, right front dial, lattice grille, lower diagonal panel with, 3 knobs, BC, FM, 6 tubes, AC/DC, $35.00-40.00.

220, table, 1946, plastic, lower front slide rule dial, checkered grille area, top vertical fluting, 2 knobs, BC, SW, 6 tubes, AC/DC.. **$40.00-45.00**

221, table, 1946, wood, large lower slide rule dial, upper criss-cross grille, 2 knobs, BC, SW, 6 tubes, AC/DC **$40.00-50.00**

226, table, 1950, brown plastic, lower front slide rule dial, upper recessed checkered grille, 2 knobs, BC, 6 tubes, AC/DC **$35.00-45.00**

250, portable, 1946, metal, inner top slide rule dial, flip back lid, lower horizontal louvers, 4 knobs, BC, 5 tubes, AC/battery **$40.00-50.00**

254, portable, 1948, cloth covered, inner right dial, left grille, fold-down front, handle, 2 knobs, BC, 6 tubes, AC/DC/battery **$30.00-35.00**

260, portable, 1947, metal, inner top slide rule dial, 1 knob, 12 pushbuttons, flip-up lid, lower horizontal louvers, 2 knobs, BC, SW, 6 tubes, AC/battery **$40.00-50.00**

280, table, 1947, wood, right front dial over large grille with 2 horizontal bars, rounded corners, 4 knobs, BC, SW, 5 tubes, battery ..**$25.00-30.00**

303, table-R/P, 1947, wood, upper front slide rule dial, lower horizontal louvers, lift top, inner phono, 4 knobs, BC, 6 tubes, AC..**$30.00-35.00**

304, table-R/P, 1948, wood, upper front slide rule dial, lower horizontal grille bars, lift top, inner phono, 4 knobs, BC, 6 tubes, AC **$30.00-35.00**

324, console-R/P, 1949, mahogany, right front tilt-out slide rule dial, left pull-out phono drawer, lower grille & storage, 4 knobs, BC, FM, 8 tubes, AC **$65.00-75.00**

328, console-R/P, 1949, blonde wood, right front tilt-out slide rule dial, left pull-out phono drawer, lower grille & storage, 4 knobs, BC, FM, 8 tubes, AC **$65.00-75.00**

356, table, 1948, plastic, step-down top, upper front slide rule dial, lower horizontal louvers, 2 knobs, BC, FM, 8 tubes, AC/DC .. **$40.00-50.00**

376, console-R/P, 1948, wood, left tilt-out slide rule dial, right pull-out phono drawer, lower grille, 4 knobs, BC, FM, 9 tubes, AC **$65.00-75.00**

401, table, 1950, ivory plastic, slanted right front dial, left vertical grille bars, 2 knobs, BC, 5 tubes, AC/DC **$35.00-40.00**

404, table, 1951, brown plastic, flared base, lower front slide rule dial, upper vertical grille bars, 2 knobs, BC, 6 tubes, AC/DC.. **$35.00-40.00**

405, table, 1951, ivory plastic, flared base, lower front slide rule dial, upper vertical grille bars, 2 knobs, BC, 6 tubes, AC/DC **$35.00-40.00**

408, table, 1950, mahogany plastic, center front raised half-round dial over horizontal bars, 2 thumbwheel knobs, BC, FM, 7 tubes, AC/DC **$35.00-45.00**

321, table, 1946, wood, center front slide rule dial, upper metal "woven" grille, 5 push-buttons, 2 knobs, BC, 6 tubes, AC/DC, $40.00-50.00.

410, table, 1951, wood, lower front slide rule dial, large upper grille, feet, 2 knobs, BC, 6 tubes, AC/DC **$35.00-40.00**

411, table, 1950, maroon plastic, large right front dial, left vertical grille bars, 2 knobs, BC, 5 tubes, AC/DC **$30.00-35.00**

412, table, 1952, black plastic, large right front dial, left vertical grille bars, 2 knobs, BC, 5 tubes, AC/DC **$30.00-35.00**

414, table, 1950, mahogany plastic, large right front dial, left horizontal grille bars, 2 knobs, BC, 5 tubes, AC/DC **$30.00-35.00**

415F, table, 1953, ivory plastic, large right front dial, left horizontal grille bars, 2 knobs, BC, 5 tubes, AC/DC **$30.00-35.00**

416, table, 1950, maroon plastic, large right front dial, left horizontal grille bars, 2 knobs, BC, 5 tubes, AC/DC **$30.00-35.00**

417, console-R/P, 1947, wood, inner right slide rule dial, 12 pushbuttons, left phono, fold-down front, lower grille area, 5 knobs, BC, SW, FM, FM1, 10 tubes, AC **$65.00-75.00**

417A, console-R/P, 1947, wood, inner right slide rule dial, 12 pushbuttons, left phono, fold-down front, lower grille area, 5 knobs, BC, SW, FM, FM1, 10 tubes, AC **$65.00-75.00**

419, table, 1954, plastic, right front round dial over large checkered grille area with horizontal & vertical bars, feet, 2 knobs, BC, 4 tubes, AC/DC **$20.00-25.00**

423, table, 1951, ivory plastic, lower front slide rule dial, upper recessed vertical grille bars, 2 knobs, BC, 6 tubes, AC/DC **$30.00-40.00**

424, table, 1954, mahogany plastic, recessed front with large center round dial knob and left grille with vertical louvers, step down sides, feet, 2 knobs, BC, 5 tubes, AC/DC............................... **$25.00-30.00**

425, table, 1954, ivory plastic, recessed front with large center round dial knob and left grille with vertical louvers, step down sides, feet, 2 knobs, BC, 5 tubes, AC/DC **$25.00-30.00**

428, table, 1955, plastic, raised center with half-round dial, vertical front bars, feet, 2 knobs, BC, 5 tubes, AC/DC **$35.00-40.00**

440, table, 1954, plastic, center front raised half-round dial over horizontal bars, 3 knobs, BC, FM, 7 tubes, AC/DC **$40.00-50.00**

442, table, 1955, plastic, lower front slide rule dial, upper recessed grille with vertical bars, 2 knobs, BC, 5 tubes, AC/DC **$35.00-45.00**

400, table, 1950, brown plastic, slanted right front dial, left vertical grille bars, 2 knobs, BC, 5 tubes, AC/DC, $35.00-40.00.

409, table, 1952, mahogany plastic, center front raised half-round dial over horizontal bars, 2 thumbwheel knobs, BC, FM, 7 tubes, AC/DC, $35.00-45.00.

450, table, C1955, plastic, large center front dial overlaps vertical grille bars, feet, 2 knobs, BC, 5 tubes, AC/DC **$25.00-30.00**

453, table, 1956, plastic, right front round dial over large checkered grille area with horizontal & vertical bars, feet, 2 knobs, BC, 4 tubes, AC/DC **$20.00-25.00**

470 "Musaphonic," table, 1956, mahogany plastic, left front lattice grille, right front round dial, 2 knobs, BC, 5 tubes, AC/DC **$15.00-20.00**

471 "Musaphonic," table, 1956, ivory plastic, left front lattice grille, right front round dial, 2 knobs, BC, 5 tubes, AC/DC **$15.00-20.00**

472 "Musaphonic," table, 1956, red plastic, left front lattice grille, right front round dial, 2 knobs, BC, 5 tubes, AC/DC **$20.00-25.00**

475 "Musaphonic," table, 1956, plastic, step-down top, left front lattice grille, right front round dial, feet, 2 knobs, BC, 5 tubes, AC/DC **$25.00-30.00**

500, table-C, 1950, mahogany plastic, upper front thumbwheel dial, left round clock, right horizontal grille bars, 4 knobs, BC, 5 tubes, AC **$40.00-50.00**

501, table-C, 1950, ivory plastic, upper front thumbwheel dial, left round clock, right horizontal grille bars, 4 knobs, BC, 5 tubes, AC **$40.00-50.00**

502, console-R/P, 1948, wood, inner right slide rule dial, 9 pushbuttons, door, left pull-out phono drawer, lower grille area, 5 knobs, BC, SW, FM, FM1, 14 tubes, AC **$75.00-85.00**

505, table-C, 1950, brown plastic, upper front thumbwheel dial, left alarm clock, right vertical grille bars, 5 knobs, BC, 5 tubes, AC ..**$40.00-50.00**

506, table-C, 1950, ivory plastic, upper front thumbwheel dial, left alarm clock, right vertical grille bars, 5 knobs, BC, 5 tubes, AC ..**$40.00-50.00**

507, table-C, 1950, maroon plastic, upper front thumbwheel dial, left alarm clock, right vertical grille bars, 5 knobs, BC, 5 tubes, AC **$40.00-50.00**

510, table-C, 1951, brown plastic, upper front thumbwheel dial, left alarm clock, right circular louvers, 4 knobs, BC, 5 tubes, AC ..**$40.00-50.00**

422, table, 1951, mahogany plastic, lower front slide rule dial, upper recessed vertical grille bars, 2 knobs, BC, 6 tubes, AC/DC, $35.00-40.00.

511, table-C, 1951, ivory plastic, upper front thumbwheel dial, left alarm clock, right circular louvers, 4 knobs, BC, 5 tubes, AC ..**$40.00-50.00**

514, table-C, 1953, mottled mahogany plastic, upper front thumbwheel dial, left round alarm clock, right horizontal grille bars, 4 knobs, BC, 5 tubes, AC **$40.00-50.00**

515, table-C, 1951, brown plastic, upper front thumbwheel dial, left round alarm clock, right vertical grille bars, 5 knobs, BC, 5 tubes, AC **$40.00-50.00**

516, table-C, 1951, ivory plastic, upper front thumbwheel dial, left round alarm clock, right vertical grille bars, 5 knobs, BC, 5 tubes, AC **$40.00-50.00**

516F, table-C, 1951, ivory plastic, upper front thumbwheel dial, left round alarm clock, right vertical grille bars, 5 knobs, BC, 5 tubes, AC **$40.00-50.00**

517F, table-C, 1951, maroon plastic, upper front thumbwheel dial, left round alarm clock, right vertical grille bars, 5 knobs, BC, 5 tubes, AC **$40.00-50.00**

518F, table-C, 1951, white plastic, upper front thumbwheel dial, left round alarm clock, right vertical grille bars, 5 knobs, BC, 5 tubes, AC **$40.00-50.00**

521, table-C, 1950, dark mahogany plastic, upper front thumbwheel dial, wrap-around panel with right horizontal grille bars & left round alarm clock, 5 knobs, BC, 5 tubes, AC **$40.00-50.00**

522, table-C, 1950, blonde mahogany plastic, upper front thumbwheel dial, wrap-around panel with right horizontal grille bars & left round alarm clock, 5 knobs, BC, 5 tubes, AC **$40.00-50.00**

430, table, 1952, mahogany, right front rectangular dial, left horizontal grille bars, 2 knobs, BC, 5 tubes, AC/DC, $35.00-45.00.

542, table-C, 1953, brown plastic, upper front thumbwheel dial, right vertical grille bars, left round alarm clock, 5 knobs, BC, 5 tubes, AC **$40.00-50.00**

543, table-C, 1953, ivory plastic, upper front thumbwheel dial, right vertical grille bars, left round alarm clock, 5 knobs, BC, 5 tubes, AC **$40.00-50.00**

548, table-C, 1953, plastic, lower front slide rule dial, right & left vertical grille bars, center clock, 5 knobs, BC, AC **$30.00-35.00**

549, table-C, 1953, plastic, lower front slide rule dial, right & left vertical grille bars, center clock, 5 knobs, BC, 5 tubes, AC **$30.00-35.00**

551, table-C, 1953, plastic, lower front slide rule dial, right & left vertical grille bars, center clock, 4 knobs, BC, 6 tubes, AC **$30.00-35.00**

555, table-C, 1954, ivory plastic, cross-hatch front, left front square clock face, right front dial knob, feet, 3 knobs, BC, 4 tubes, AC ..**$20.00-25.00**

555G, table-C, 1954, gray plastic, cross-hatch front, left front square clock face, right front dial knob, feet, 3 knobs, BC, 4 tubes, AC **$20.00-25.00**

556, table-C, 1954, red plastic, cross-hatch front, left front square clock face, right front dial knob, feet, 3 knobs, BC, 4 tubes, AC ..**$30.00-35.00**

560, table-C, 1954, brown plastic, "textured" front, center front round clock face, feet, 3 front knobs, 1 right side dial knob, BC, 5 tubes, AC **$20.00-25.00**

561, table-C, 1954, ivory plastic, "textured" front, center front round clock face, feet, 3 front knobs, 1 right side dial knob, BC, 5 tubes, AC **$20.00-25.00**

573, table-C, 1955, plastic, lower front slide rule dial, right & left vertical grille bars, center clock, 5 knobs, BC, 5 tubes, AC **$30.00-35.00**

515F, table-C, 1951, brown plastic, upper front thumb-wheel dial, left round alarm clock, right vertical grille bars, 5 knobs, BC, 5 tubes, AC, $40.00-50.00.

581 "**Musaphonic**," table-C, 1955, plastic, step-down top, front center lattice grille, left front square clock, right front square dial, feet, 5 knobs, BC, 5 tubes, AC $30.00-35.00

590, table-C, 1955, plastic, right front dial, left clock, raised center lattice grille, 5 knobs, BC, 6 tubes, AC.....................................$25.00-30.00

600, portable, 1950, plastic, lower front slide rule dial, upper recessed horizontal grille bars, handle, 2 thumbwheel knobs, BC, 4 tubes, battery $35.00-45.00

601, portable, 1950, maroon plastic, lower front slide rule dial, upper recessed horizontal grille bars, handle, 2 thumbwheel knobs, BC, 4 tubes, AC/DC/battery $35.00-45.00

603, portable, 1950, tan plastic, lower front slide rule dial, upper recessed horizontal grille bars, handle, 2 thumbwheel knobs, BC, 4 tubes, AC/DC/battery $35.00-45.00

604, portable, 1950, green plastic, lower front slide rule dial, upper recessed horizontal grille bars, handle, 2 thumbwheel knobs, BC, 4 tubes, AC/DC/battery $35.00-45.00

610, portable, 1951, maroon plastic, upper front half-round dial, lower vertical grille bars, handle, 2 knobs, BC, 5 tubes, AC/DC/battery $35.00-45.00

611, portable, 1951, green plastic, upper front half-round dial, lower vertical grille bars, handle, 2 knobs, BC, 5 tubes, AC/DC/battery ..$35.00-45.00

612, portable, 1953, black plastic, top round dial area, front vertical grille bars, double chrome handle, 2 knobs, BC, 4 tubes, AC/DC/battery $45.00-55.00

613, portable, 1953, red plastic, top round dial area, front vertical grille bars, double chrome handle, 2 knobs, BC, 4 tubes, AC/DC/battery $45.00-55.00

637, portable, 1955, plastic, large right front dial, left metal perforated grille, fold-down handle, 2 knobs, BC, 4 tubes, battery ..$35.00-40.00

648, portable, 1955, plastic, large right front dial with center crest over-laps perforated grille area, fold-down handle, 2 knobs, BC, 4 tubes, AC/DC/battery $45.00-55.00

650, portable, 1950, maroon plastic, upper front slide rule dial, lower horizontal grille bars, handle, 2 thumbwheel knobs, BC, 5 tubes, AC/DC/battery $35.00-45.00

741, console-R/P, 1952, wood, inner right dial, lower pull-out phono drawer, double doors, 3 knobs, BC, 6 tubes, AC $45.00-55.00

752, console-R/P, 1951, mahogany, inner right dial, lower pull-out phono drawer, double doors, 4 knobs, BC, FM, 8 tubes, AC....$50.00-65.00

753, console-R/P, 1951, blonde wood, inner right dial, lower pull-out phono drawer, double doors, 4 knobs, BC, FM, 8 tubes, AC........$50.00-65.00

755, console-R/P, 1951, mahogany, inner right dial, lower pull-out phono drawer, 2 knobs, BC, FM, 11 tubes, AC $50.00-65.00

535, table-C, 1951, mottled mahogany plastic, right front square dial, left square alarm clock, center vertical bars, 5 knobs, BC, 6 tubes, AC, $30.00-40.00.

546, table-C, 1953, plastic, lower front slide rule dial, right & left vertical grille bars, center clock, 5 knobs, BC, AC, $30.00-35.00.

860 "**Atomic**," table, 1957, mahogany plastic, sloping front edges with recessed lattice front, left front round dial with center "orbiting atom", left grille, 2 knobs, BC, 5 tubes, AC/DC $45.00-55.00

861 "**Atomic**," table, 1957, red plastic, sloping front edges with recessed lattice front, left front round dial with center "orbiting atom," left grille, 2 knobs, BC, 5 tubes, AC/DC $65.00-75.00

862 "**Atomic**," table, 1957, turquoise plastic, sloping front edges with recessed lattice front, left front round dial with center "orbiting atom," left grille, 2 knobs, BC, 5 tubes, AC/DC $55.00-65.00

870, table, 1956, plastic, right front round dial, raised left lattice grille area, 3 knobs, BC, 6 tubes, AC/DC $30.00-35.00

895, table-C, 1956, plastic, right front dial and left square clock over large checkered panel, feet, 3 knobs, BC, 4 tubes, AC $25.00-30.00

900, table-C, 1956, plastic, left front square clock with roman numerals, right front tuning dial, feet, 3 knobs, BC, 5 tubes, AC....$20.00-25.00

920 "**Musaphonic**," table-C, 1956, plastic, step-down top, front center lattice grille, left front square clock, right front square dial, feet, 5 knobs, BC, 5 tubes, AC $30.00-35.00

A-52, tombstone, 1936, wood, center front dial with oval escutcheon, upper cloth grille with cut-outs, 4 knobs, BC, SW, 5 tubes, AC $95.00-115.00

A-54, table, 1936, two-tone walnut, step-down top, upper right front window dial, left grille with cut-outs, 4 knobs, BC, SW, 5 tubes, AC/DC $65.00-75.00

A-55, console, 1936, wood, upper front dial with oval escutcheon, lower cloth grille with center vertical bars, 4 knobs, BC, SW, 5 tubes, AC...$110.00-130.00

A-63, tombstone, 1935, walnut veneer, Deco, center front window dial, upper cloth grille with vertical bars, 4 knobs, BC, SW, 6 tubes, AC $120.00-150.00

636, portable, 1955, plastic, large right front dial, left metal perforated grille, fold-down handle, 2 knobs, BC, 4 tubes, battery, $35.00-40.00.

General Electric

660 & 660A "Convertible," portable-C, 1956, plastic, combination clock (660A) and removable portable radio (660), radio has front metal perforated grille area and fold-down handle, 5 knobs, BC, 4 tubes, AC/battery, $50.00-65.00.

A-65, console, 1935, walnut-veneer, upper front window dial, lower cloth grille with vertical bars, 4 knobs, BC, SW, 6 tubes, AC ..**$95.00-115.00**

A-67, console, 1935, wood, upper front horizontal pointer dial, lower cloth grille with scrolled cut-outs, 4 knobs, BC, SW, 6 tubes, AC **$120.00-150.00**

A-70, tombstone, 1935, wood, center front horizontal pointer dial, upper & lower cloth grille areas with vertical bars, fluting, BC, SW, 7 tubes, AC **$95.00-115.00**

A-75, console, 1935, walnut-veneer, upper front horizontal pointer dial, lower cloth grille with 3 vertical bars, BC, SW, 7 tubes, AC......**$120.00-140.00**

A-82, tombstone, 1935, walnut, lower front horizontal pointer dial, upper cloth grille with cut-outs, 5 knobs, BC, SW, LW, 8 tubes, AC **$120.00-150.00**

A-83, tombstone, 1936, wood, center front horizontal pointer dial, upper & lower cloth grilles with vertical bars, 5 knobs, BC, SW, 8 tubes, AC **$120.00-150.00**

A-85, console, 1936, wood, upper front horizontal pointer dial, lower cloth grille with vertical bars, BC, SW, 8 tubes, AC....**$120.00-140.00**

A-87, console, 1935, wood, upper front horizontal pointer dial, lower vertical grille bars, feet, 4 band, 5 knobs, BC, SW, LW, 8 tubes, AC **$120.00-150.00**

A-125, console, 1935, wood, upper front horizontal pointer dial, lower grille with rectangular cut-outs, fluted sides, base, 5 band, 4 knobs, BC, SW, LW, 12 tubes, AC **$190.00-210.00**

BX, table, 1932, metal case with lacquer finish, right front dial, center round grille, 2 knobs, BC, 4 tubes, AC/DC **$75.00-85.00**

C403, table-C, antique white plastic, large right front dial over horizontal bars, left alarm clock, feet, 3 knobs, BC, 5 tubes, AC....**$15.00-20.00**

C404, table-C, Wedgwood blue plastic, large right front dial over horizontal bars, left alarm clock, feet, BC, 4 tubes, AC..............**$15.00-20.00**

A-53, tombstone, 1935, walnut finish, center front window dial, upper cloth grille with cut-outs, 3 knobs, BC, SW, 5 tubes, AC, $95.00-115.00.

C405, table-C, 1957, gray/white plastic, right front round dial over horizontal bars, off-center raised clock area, feet, BC, 4 tubes, AC ..**$15.00-20.00**

C405D, table-C, gray/white plastic, right front round dial over horizontal bars, off-center raised clock area, feet, BC, AC **$15.00-20.00**

C407, table-C, 1957, rose beige/white plastic, right front round dial over horizontal bars, off-center raised clock area, feet, BC, 4 tubes, AC...**$15.00-20.00**

C415, table-C, 1958, plastic, raised clock/dial panel, lower front slide rule dial, upper clock, right & left vertical bars, 4 knobs, BC, 5 tubes, AC **$30.00-35.00**

C433, table-C, 1960, antique white plastic, raised clock/dial panel, lower front slide rule dial, upper clock, right & left vertical bars, feet, 4 knobs, BC, 4 tubes **$20.00-25.00**

C434, table-C, 1960, rose beige plastic, raised clock/dial panel, lower front slide rule dial, upper clock, right & left vertical bars, feet, 4 knobs, BC, 4 tubes **$20.00-25.00**

C434C, table-C, 1960, plastic, raised clock/dial panel, lower front slide rule dial, upper clock, right & left vertical bars, feet, 4 knobs, BC.........**$20.00-25.00**

C436, table-C, 1964, antique white plastic, right front dial over checkered grille panel, left alarm clock, feet, 4 knobs, BC, 4 tubes, AC...**$15.00-20.00**

C437, table-C, 1964, pink plastic, right front dial over checkered grille panel, left alarm clock, feet, 4 knobs, BC, 4 tubes, AC ..**$15.00-20.00**

C437A, table-C, 1964, pink plastic, right front dial over checkered grille panel, left alarm clock, feet, 4 knobs, BC, AC **$15.00-20.00**

C438, table-C, 1964, mint green plastic, right front dial over checkered grille panel, left alarm clock, feet, 4 knobs, BC, 4 tubes, AC......**$15.00-20.00**

A-64, tombstone, 1935, wood, center front horizontal pointer dial, upper cloth grille with cut-outs, arched top, 4 knobs, BC, SW, 6 tubes, AC, $95.00-115.00.

C510, table-C, 1961, antique white plastic, right front vertical dial, left alarm clock, center textured grille area, 5 knobs, BC, FM, 7 tubes, AC **$15.00-20.00**

C510A, table-C, 1961, plastic, right front vertical dial, left alarm clock, center textured grille area, 5 knobs, BC, FM, AC **$15.00-20.00**

C-1479B, table-C, plastic, right front dial, left alarm clock face, center grille panel with vertical bars, 3 knobs, BC **$15.00-20.00**

E-50, table, 1937, wood, center front horizontal dial with surrounding 4-section cloth grille, 2 bands, 4 knobs, BC, SW, 5 tubes, AC ..**$65.00-75.00**

E-52, table, 1937, wood, center front horizontal dial with surrounding 4-section cloth grille, 4 knobs, BC, SW, 5 tubes, AC **$65.00-75.00**

E-61, tombstone, 1936, wood, rounded top, center front horizontal slide rule dial, upper cloth grille with cut-outs, 4 knobs, BC, SW, 6 tubes, AC **$120.00-140.00**

E-62, table, 1936, wood, left front slide rule dial, right grille area with cut-outs, 4 knobs, BC, SW, 6 tubes, AC **$50.00-65.00**

E-71, tombstone, 1936, two-tone wood, center front horizontal dial, large cloth grille with cut-outs, 4 knobs, BC, SW, 7 tubes, AC...........**$110.00-130.00**

E-72, table, 1936, wood, left front horizontal dial, right cloth grille with 3 vertical bars, 4 knobs, BC, SW, 7 tubes, AC **$40.00-50.00**

E-81, tombstone, 1936, wood, center front horizontal dial, upper grille with cut-outs, 4 knobs, BC, SW, 8 tubes, AC **$110.00-130.00**

E-155, console, 1936, wood, upper front center slide tuning dial with "colorama" tuning, large lower grille with three vertical bars, rounded shoulders, pedestal base, 5 knobs, BC, SW, LW, 15 tubes, AC...**$375.00-425.00**

F-51, table, 1937, plastic, Deco, right front vertical dial, rounded left side, horizontal wrap-around bars, 4 knobs, BC, 5 tubes, AC **$120.00-150.00**

F-53, table, 1937, wood, center front rectangular slide rule dial, upper & lower grilles with horizontal bars, 4 knobs, BC, SW, 5 tubes, AC................**$65.00-75.00**

F-65, console, 1937, wood, upper front rectangular dial, lower cloth grille with 3 vertical bars, 4 knobs, BC, SW, 6 tubes, AC ..**$110.00-130.00**

F-66, console, 1937, wood, upper front rectangular dial, lower cloth grille with 3 vertical bars, 4 knobs, BC, SW, 6 tubes, AC ..**$110.00-130.00**

F-74, table, 1938, wood, left front rectangular dial, tuning eye, right grille with 2 horizontal bars, 4 knobs, BC, SW, 7 tubes, AC ..**$85.00-95.00**

F-75, console, 1937, wood, upper front rectangular dial, lower cloth grille with vertical bars, 4 knobs, BC, SW, 7 tubes, AC **$110.00-130.00**

F-81, tombstone, 1937, wood, lower front rectangular dial, upper cloth grille with horizontal bars, 4 knobs, BC, SW, 8 tubes, AC **$120.00-150.00**

F-86, console, 1937, wood, upper front rectangular dial, lower cloth grille with 3 vertical bars, 4 knobs, BC, SW, 8 tubes, AC ..**$120.00-140.00**

F-96, console, 1937, wood, upper front rectangular dial, pushbuttons, lower cloth grille with 2 vertical bars, 5 knobs, BC, SW, 9 tubes, AC **$120.00-150.00**

F-107, console, 1937, wood, upper front rectangular dial, lower cloth grille with vertical bars, pushbuttons, 5 knobs, BC, SW, 10 tubes, AC **$120.00-150.00**

F-109, console-R/P, 1937, wood, upper front dial, lower cloth grille with vertical bars, inner phono, BC, SW, 10 tubes, AC.....**$120.00-150.00**

F-135, console, 1937, wood, upper front rectangular dial, lower cloth grille with vertical bars, pushbuttons, 5 knobs, BC, SW, 13 tubes, AC **$140.00-160.00**

C-415C, table-C, 1958, plastic, raised clock/dial panel, lower front slide rule dial, upper clock, right & left vertical grille bars, 4 knobs, BC, AC, $30.00-35.00.

F-665, chairside, 1937, walnut, top rectangular dial, front grille with vertical bars, step-down top, 4 knobs, BC, SW, 6 tubes, AC ..**$130.00-150.00**

FB-52, cathedral, 1937, wood, center front rectangular dial, cloth grille with vertical bars, 3 knobs, BC, 5 tubes, battery.........**$95.00-115.00**

FB-77, console, 1938, wood, upper front rectangular dial, lower cloth grille with 3 vertical bars, 4 knobs, BC, SW, 7 tubes, battery ..**$75.00-85.00**

FD-100, cathedral, C1940, wood, center front slide rule dial, upper cloth grille with vertical bars, 4 knobs, BC, SW, 10 tubes, AC/DC....**$150.00-180.00**

FE-112, table, 1940, wood, right front rectangular dial, left cloth grille with horizontal wrap-around bars, tuning eye, 4 knobs, BC, SW,LW, 11 tubes, AC **$95.00-115.00**

G-50, table, 1937, wood, right front round telephone dial, left cloth grille with vertical bars, 2 knobs, BC, 5 tubes, AC **$65.00-75.00**

G-55, console, 1938, wood, upper front round telephone dial, lower cloth grille with 2 vertical bars, BC, 5 tubes, AC **$120.00-140.00**

G-56, console, 1938, wood, 2 upper front dials, lower grille with vertical bars, pushbuttons, 4 knobs, BC, SW, 5 tubes, AC **$95.00-115.00**

G-61, table, 1938, wood, rounded right with 3 dials, left wrap-around grille with horizontal bars, pushbuttons, 4 knobs, BC, SW, 6 tubes, AC **$85.00-95.00**

G-64, table, 1939, wood, 2 right front slide rule dials, left wrap-around cloth grille with horizontal bars, pushbuttons, 4 knobs, BC, SW, 6 tubes, AC **$85.00-95.00**

G-68, console-R/P, 1938, wood, inner dial & phono, front grille with vertical bars, lift top, BC, SW, 6 tubes, AC.......................**$110.00-130.00**

G-75, console, 1938, wood, upper front center slide rule dial, tuning eye, lower grille with horizontal louvers, 4 knobs, BC, SW, 7 tubes, AC **$120.00-140.00**

G-76 "Radiogrande," console, 1938, wood, upper front dial, pushbuttons, tuning eye, large lower grille with cut-outs, 4 knobs, BC, SW, 7 tubes, AC **$200.00-230.00**

G-78, console, 1939, wood, upper front rectangular dial, lower cloth grille with horizontal bars, pushbuttons, 4 knobs, BC, SW, 7 tubes, AC **$120.00-150.00**

E-105, console, 1936, wood, upper front rotating tubular dial, lower cloth grille with 3 vertical bars, rounded shoulders, 5 knobs, BC, SW, 10 tubes, AC, $110.00-130.00.

G-85, console, 1938, wood, upper front dial, lower cloth grille with horizontal & vertical bars, tuning eye, 10 pushbuttons, 4 knobs, BC, SW, 8 tubes, AC **$120.00-140.00**

G-86, console, 1939, wood, two tone, extended and rounded front corners, upper front center slide rule dial, tuning eye, pushbuttons, lower grille with horizontal bars, 4 knobs, BC, SW, 8 tubes, AC...**$150.00-170.00**

G-87A, console, 1933, wood, lowboy, upper front window dial, lower cloth grille with cut-outs, 4 knobs, BC, 8 tubes, AC ..**$150.00-160.00**

G-97, console, 1938, wood, upper front dial, lower cloth grille with vertical bars, 7 pushbuttons, right top pop-up station timer, 4 knobs, BC, SW, 9 tubes, AC...**$190.00-210.00**

G-99, console, 1938, wood, upper front center slide rule dial, tuning eye, pushbuttons, large lower grille divided into 7 sections, 4 knobs, BC, SW, 9 tubes, AC...**$150.00-170.00**

G-105, console, 1938, wood, upper front dial, lower cloth grille with vertical bars, tuning eye, 14 pushbuttons, 4 knobs, BC, SW, 10 tubes, AC **$180.00-210.00**

GB-400, portable, 1948, luggage-style, center grille, handle, 2 thumbwheel knobs, BC, 4 tubes, battery................................**$30.00-35.00**

GD-41, table, 1938, two-tone wood, right front airplane dial, left cloth grille with 3 section cut-outs, 2 knobs, BC, 5 tubes, AC/DC .. **$50.00-65.00**

GD-50, table, 1938, wood, right front dial, left cloth grille with horizontal bars, 2 knobs, BC, 5 tubes, AC/DC **$40.00-50.00**

GD-51, table, 1938, wood, right front slide rule dial, left grille, 5 pushbuttons on right top front, 1 front and 1 side knob, BC, 5 tubes, AC/DC **$60.00-70.00**

GD-52, table, 1938, wood, slanted front, center grille, 6 pushbuttons, 2 thumbwheel knobs, BC, 6 tubes, AC..............................**$50.00-65.00**

GD-63, table, 1939, wood, slanted front with vertical wrap-over bars, pushbuttons, 2 thumbwheel knobs, BC, 6 tubes, AC/DC **$50.00-65.00**

F-63, table, 1937, walnut, left front gold dial, streamlined right side with Deco grille cut-outs, 4 knobs, BC, SW, 6 tubes, AC, $85.00-95.00.

F-70, table, 1937, wood, left front rectangular dial, right cloth grille with 4 horizontal bars, 4 knobs, BC, SW, 7 tubes, AC, $65.00-75.00.

GD-500, table, 1939, plastic, right front round "compass" dial, left grille with vertical wrap-over bars, 2 knobs, BC, 5 tubes, AC/DC **$65.00-75.00**

GD-520, table, 1939, plastic, Deco, small case, right front metal dial panel, left wrap-around horizontal bars, 2 knobs, BC, 5 tubes, AC/DC **$160.00-190.00**

GD-600, table, 1938, wood, right front rectangular dial, left cloth grille with vertical wrap-over bars, 2 knobs, BC, 6 tubes, AC/DC .. **$50.00-65.00**

H-32, console, 1931, walnut, lowboy, upper front window dial, lower grille with scrolled cut-outs, BC, 10 tubes, AC **$120.00-150.00**

H-73, table, 1939, wood, upper right front recessed and slanted slide rule dial, left wraparound grille with horizontal bars, pushbuttons, 4 knobs, BC, SW, 7 tubes, AC **$80.00-100.00**

H-77, console, 1939, wood, upper front recessed and slanted slide rule dial, lower grille with horizontal bars, pushbuttons, 4 knobs, BC, SW, 7 tubes, AC **$110.00-130.00**

H-78, console-R/P, 1939, wood, upper front slide rule dial, lower grille with three vertical bars, pushbuttons, lift-top with inner phono, 4 knobs, BC, SW, 7 tubes, AC **$90.00-110.00**

H-79, console-R/P, 1939, wood, large lower grille with three vertical bars, lift top with inner slide rule dial, pushbuttons, phono, 4 knobs, BC, SW, 7 tubes, AC..**$90.00-110.00**

H-87, console, 1939, wood, upper front slanted slide rule dial, pushbuttons, lower cloth grille with bars, 4 knobs, BC, SW, 8 tubes, AC **$120.00-140.00**

H-91 "Longfellow," grandfather clock, 1931, mahogany, Colonial design, inner dial & knobs, front door, upper clock face, 4 knobs, BC, 10 tubes, AC **$480.00-530.00**

H-400, table, 1939, plastic, right front round dial, left grille with wrap over top vertical lines, rounded corners and shoulders, 2 knobs, BC, 4 tubes, AC/DC **$90.00-110.00**

H-406U, table, 1939, plastic, right front round dial, left grille with wrap over top vertical lines, rounded corners and shoulders, 2 knobs, BC, 4 tubes, AC/DC **$120.00-140.00**

H-500, table, 1939, mottled brown plastic, Deco, step-down top, center front thumbwheel dial, left front lattice grille, 2 knobs, BC, 5 tubes, AC/DC **$140.00-150.00**

H-500W, table, 1939, ivory plastic, Deco, step-down top, center front thumbwheel dial, left front lattice grille, 2 knobs, BC, 5 tubes, AC/DC **$160.00-180.00**

G-53, table, 1938, wood, 2 right front slide rule dials, pushbuttons, left grille with vertical wrap-over bars, 4 knobs, BC, SW, 5 tubes, AC, $65.00-75.00.

H-500X, table, 1939, onyx "beetle" plastic, Deco, step-down top, center front thumbwheel dial, left front lattice grille, 2 knobs, BC, 5 tubes, AC/DC **$240.00-260.00**

H-501, table, 1939, mottled brown plastic, Deco, step-down top, center front thumbwheel dial, left front lattice grille, 2 knobs, BC, 5 tubes, AC/DC **$140.00-150.00**

H-501W, table, 1939, ivory plastic, Deco, step-down top, center front thumbwheel dial, left front lattice grille, 2 knobs, BC, 5 tubes, AC/DC **$160.00-180.00**

H-501X, table, 1939, onyx "beetle" plastic, Deco, step-down top, center front thumbwheel dial, left front lattice grille, 2 knobs, BC, 5 tubes, AC/DC **$240.00-260.00**

H-502, table, 1939, plastic, Deco, step-down top, center front thumbwheel dial, left lattice grille area, 2 knobs, BC, 5 tubes, AC/DC .. **$140.00-150.00**

H-503, table, 1939, wood, center front thumbwheel dial, left vertical grille wraps over top, 2 knobs, BC, 5 tubes, AC/DC **$75.00-85.00**

H-510, table, 1939, mottled brown plastic, Deco, step-down top, center front thumbwheel dial, left front lattice grille, 4 tuning "keys," 2 knobs, BC, 5 tubes, AC/DC **$140.00-150.00**

H-510W, table, 1939, ivory plastic, Deco, step-down top, center front thumbwheel dial, left front lattice grille, 4 tuning "keys," 2 knobs, BC, 5 tubes, AC/DC **$160.00-180.00**

H-510X, table, 1939, onyx "beetle" plastic, Deco, step-down top, center front thumbwheel dial, left front lattice grille, 4 tuning "keys," 2 knobs, BC, 5 tubes, AC/DC **$240.00-260.00**

GB-401, table, 1939, two-tone wood, slanted front with vertical wrap-over bars, 3 knobs, BC, 4 tubes, battery, $30.00-35.00.

H-511, table, 1939, mottled brown plastic, Deco, step-down top, center front thumbwheel dial, left front lattice grille, 4 tuning "keys," 2 knobs, BC, 5 tubes, AC/DC **$140.00-150.00**

H-511W, table, 1939, ivory plastic, Deco, step-down top, center front thumbwheel dial, left front lattice grille, 4 tuning "keys," 2 knobs, BC, 5 tubes, AC/DC **$160.00-180.00**

H-511X, table, 1939, onyx "beetle" plastic, Deco, step-down top, center front thumbwheel dial, left front lattice grille, 4 tuning "keys," 2 knobs, BC, 5 tubes, AC/DC **$240.00-260.00**

H-520, table, 1939, mottled brown plastic, Deco, step-down top, center front thumbwheel dial, left front lattice grille, 4 tuning "keys," 2 knobs, BC, 5 tubes, AC/DC **$140.00-150.00**

H-520W, table, 1939, ivory plastic, Deco, step-down top, center front thumbwheel dial, left front lattice grille, 4 tuning "keys," 2 knobs, BC, 5 tubes, AC/DC **$160.00-180.00**

H-520X, table, 1939, onyx "beetle" plastic, Deco, step-down top, center front thumbwheel dial, left front lattice grille, 4 tuning "keys," 2 knobs, BC, 5 tubes, AC/DC **$240.00-260.00**

H-521, table, 1939, mottled brown plastic, Deco, step-down top, center front thumbwheel dial, left front lattice grille, 4 tuning "keys," 2 knobs, BC, 5 tubes, AC/DC **$140.00-150.00**

H-521W, table, 1939, ivory plastic, Deco, step-down top, center front thumbwheel dial, left front lattice grille, 4 tuning "keys," 2 knobs, BC, 5 tubes, AC/DC **$160.00-180.00**

H-521X, table, 1939, onyx "beetle" plastic, Deco, step-down top, center front thumbwheel dial, left front lattice grille, 4 tuning "keys," 2 knobs, BC, 5 tubes, AC/DC **$240.00-260.00**

H-531, tombstone, 1939, wood, small case, lower right front dial, upper 2-section cloth grille, chassis mounted sideways, 2 knobs, BC, 5 tubes, AC/DC **$85.00-105.00**

H-600, table, 1939, mottled brown plastic, right front square dial, left lattice grille, horizontal case lines, 2 knobs, BC, 7 tubes, AC/DC **$95.00-115.00**

H-600W, table, 1939, ivory plastic, right front square dial, left lattice grille, horizontal case lines, 2 knobs, BC, 7 tubes, AC/DC .. **$120.00-140.00**

H-600X, table, 1939, onyx "beetle" plastic, right front square dial, left lattice grille, horizontal case lines, 2 knobs, BC, 7 tubes, AC/DC.. **$170.00-190.00**

H-601, table, 1939, mottled brown plastic, right front square dial, left lattice grille, horizontal case lines, 2 knobs, BC, 7 tubes, AC/DC **$95.00-115.00**

H-601W, table, 1939, ivory plastic, right front square dial, left lattice grille, horizontal case lines, 2 knobs, BC, 7 tubes, AC/DC .. **$120.00-140.00**

H-601X, table, 1939, onyx "beetle" plastic, right front square dial, left lattice grille, horizontal case lines, 2 knobs, BC, 7 tubes, AC/DC **$170.00-190.00**

H-610, table, 1939, mottled brown plastic, right front square dial, left lattice grille, horizontal case lines, 4 tuning "keys," 2 knobs, BC, 7 tubes, AC/DC **$95.00-115.00**

H-610W, table, 1939, ivory plastic, right front square dial, left lattice grille, horizontal case lines, 4 tuning "keys," 2 knobs, BC, 7 tubes, AC/DC.. **$120.00-140.00**

H-610X, table, 1939, onyx "beetle" plastic, right front square dial, left lattice grille, horizontal case lines, 4 tuning "keys," 2 knobs, BC, 7 tubes, AC/DC **$170.00-190.00**

H-611, table, 1939, mottled brown plastic, right front square dial, left lattice grille, horizontal case lines, 4 tuning "keys," 2 knobs, BC, 7 tubes, AC/DC **$95.00-115.00**

GD-60, table, 1938, wood, slanted front, center grille, 6 pushbuttons, 2 thumbwheel knobs, BC, 6 tubes, AC, $50.00-65.00.

H-611W, table, 1939, ivory plastic, right front square dial, left lattice grille, horizontal case lines, 4 tuning "keys," 2 knobs, BC, 7 tubes, AC/DC **$120.00-140.00**

H-611X, table, 1939, onyx "beetle" plastic, right front square dial, left lattice grille, horizontal case lines, 4 tuning "keys," 2 knobs, BC, 7 tubes, AC/DC **$170.00-190.00**

H-620, table, 1939, mottled brown plastic, right front square dial, left lattice grille, horizontal case lines, 4 tuning "keys," 3 knobs, BC, SW, 7 tubes, AC/DC **$95.00-115.00**

H-620W, table, 1939, ivory plastic, right front square dial, left lattice grille, horizontal case lines, 4 tuning "keys," 3 knobs, BC, SW, 7 tubes, AC/DC.. **$120.00-140.00**

H-620X, table, 1939, onyx "beetle" plastic, right front square dial, left lattice grille, horizontal case lines, 4 tuning "keys," 3 knobs, BC, SW, 7 tubes, AC/DC **$170.00-190.00**

H-621, table, 1939, mottled brown plastic, right front square dial, left lattice grille, horizontal case lines, 4 tuning "keys," 3 knobs, BC, SW, 7 tubes, AC/DC **$95.00-115.00**

H-116, console, 1939, wood, upper front slanted dial, 11 pushbuttons, lower grille with horizontal bars, tuning eye, 4 knobs, BC, SW, 11 tubes, AC, $220.00-240.00.

H-621W, table, 1939, ivory plastic, right front square dial, left lattice grille, horizontal case lines, 4 tuning "keys," 3 knobs, BC, SW, 7 tubes, AC/DC **$120.00-140.00**

H-621X, table, 1939, onyx "beetle" plastic, right front square dial, left lattice grille, horizontal case lines, 4 tuning "keys," 3 knobs, BC, SW, 7 tubes, AC/DC **$170.00-190.00**

H-622, table, 1939, wood, Deco rounded left side with wraparound grille, right rectangular dial and 4 tuning "keys," 3 knobs, BC, SW, 7 tubes, AC/DC.. **$85.00-105.00**

H-623, table, 1939, wood, Deco rounded left side with wraparound grille, right rectangular dial and 4 tuning "keys," 3 knobs, BC, SW, 7 tubes, AC/DC.. **$85.00-105.00**

H-630, table, 1939, wood, right front dial, 4 pushbuttons, left cloth wrap-over grille, 3 knobs, BC, SW, 7 tubes, AC/DC **$40.00-50.00**

H-632, table, 1939, wood, center front dial, pushbuttons, right & left side wrap-around grilles, 3 knobs, BC, SW, 5 tubes, AC **$50.00-65.00**

H-634, table, 1939, wood, right front slide rule dial, push buttons, left wrap-around grille, 4 knobs, BC, SW, 6 tubes, AC/DC .. **$55.00-65.00**

H-638, table-R/P, 1939, wood, right front slide rule dial, pushbuttons, left wraparound grille with horizontal bars, lift top with inner phono, 4 knobs, BC, SW, 6 tubes, AC **$40.00-50.00**

H-639, table-R/P, 1939, Deco, right front dial, pushbuttons, rounded left side with wrap-around horizontal grille louvers, lift top, inner phono, 2 knobs, BC, 6 tubes, AC **$40.00-50.00**

H-640, table, 1939, Deco, right front slide rule dial, pushbuttons, rounded left top grille, 4 knobs, BC, SW, 6 tubes, AC/DC **$200.00-240.00**

H-5100, table, 1939, plastic, Deco, step-down top, center front thumbwheel dial, left front lattice grille, 4 pushbuttons, 2 knobs, BC, battery **$140.00-150.00**

HB-402, portable, 1939, right front dial, left grille area, handle, 2 knobs, BC, 4 tubes **$30.00-35.00**

H-530, tombstone, 1939, wood, small case, lower right front dial, upper 2-section cloth grille, chassis mounted sideways, 2 knobs, BC, 5 tubes, AC/DC, $85.00-105.00.

HJ-1005, console, 1939, wood, upper front slanted dial, 9 pushbuttons, lower cloth grille with 3 vertical bars, rounded sides, tuning eye, 5 knobs, BC, SW, 10 tubes, AC, $190.00-210.00.

J-72, cathedral, 1932, wood, lower front window dial, upper cloth grille with cut-outs, 3 knobs, BC, 7 tubes, AC, $200.00-230.00.

HB-412, portable, 1939, leatherette, inner right front dial, left grille, fold-up front, handle, BC, 4 tubes, AC/DC/battery **$30.00-35.00**

HJ-514, table, C1939, wood, right front dial, left horizontal grille bars, 2 knobs, BC, 5 tubes, AC/DC **$35.00-45.00**

HJ-612, table, 1939, wood, right front square airplane dial, left grille with horizontal louvers, rounded front corners, 2 knobs, BC, SW, 6 tubes, AC/DC **$30.00-40.00**

HJ-624, table, 1939, wood, right front dial, pushbuttons, left wrap-around grille with horizontal bars, thumbwheel knobs, BC, 7 tubes, AC/DC **$85.00-95.00**

HJ-905, console, 1939, wood, recessed upper slanted front with slide rule dial, tuning eye, pushbuttons, lower grille with horizontal louvers, rounded front corners, 4 knobs, BC, SW, 9 tubes, AC ..**$190.00-210.00**

J-51, table, 1940, wood, upper front slide rule dial, lower horizontal louvers, 2 knobs, BC, 5 tubes, AC/DC **$40.00-50.00**

J-53, table, 1940, two-tone wood, upper front slide rule dial, lower horizontal louvers, 2 knobs, BC, 5 tubes, AC/DC................**$40.00-50.00**

J-54, table, 1940, mottled brown plastic, upper front slide rule dial, lower horizontal louvers, 2 knobs, BC, 5 tubes, AC/DC..........**$40.00-50.00**

J-62, table, 1941, mahogany, upper front slide rule dial, lower cloth grille with criss-cross cut-outs, side handles, decorative molding, 3 knobs, BC, 7 tubes, AC **$65.00-75.00**

J-63, table, 1941, two-tone wood, upper front slide rule dial, lower grille with horizontal bars, 4 knobs, BC, SW, 7 tubes, AC/DC **$40.00-50.00**

J-64, table, 1941, two-tone wood, large front slide rule dial, rounded left grille with horizontal bars, 5 pushbuttons, 4 knobs, BC, SW, 7 tubes, AC **$65.00-75.00**

J-71, table, 1941, wood, large center front slide rule dial, right & left wrap-around horizontal grille bars, 6 pushbuttons, 4 knobs, BC, SW, 7 tubes, AC **$85.00-95.00**

J-80, cathedral, 1932, wood, center front window dial, cloth grille with cut-outs, fluted columns, 3 knobs, BC, 8 tubes, AC.....**$300.00-320.00**

J-82, cathedral, 1932, wood, center front window dial, cloth grille with cut-outs, fluted columns, 3 knobs, BC, 8 tubes, AC ..**$300.00-320.00**

J-86, console, 1932, wood, lowboy, upper front window dial, lower grille with cut-outs, stretcher base, 3 knobs, BC, 8 tubes, AC........**$120.00-140.00**

J-88, console-R/P, 1932, wood, lower front window dial, upper grille with cut-outs, inner phono, 3 knobs, BC, 8 tubes, AC **$130.00-150.00**

J-501W, table, 1941, ivory plastic, upper front slide rule dial, lower horizontal louvers, 2 knobs, BC, 5 tubes, AC/DC...............**$35.00-45.00**

J-614, table, 1940, plastic, upper front slide rule dial, lower horizontal louvers, 2 knobs, BC, SW, 6 tubes, AC/DC **$35.00-45.00**

J-620, table, 1941, blond mahogany, upper front slide rule dial, lower cloth grille with criss-cross cut-outs, side handles, decorative molding, 3 knobs, BC, 7 tubes, AC **$65.00-75.00**

J-644, table, 1941, plastic, right front dial, left horizontal louvers, rounded top, 2 knobs, BC, 7 tubes, AC/DC **$35.00-45.00**

J-805, console, 1940, wood, upper front slide rule dial, lower cloth grille with bars, 6 pushbuttons, 4 knobs, BC, SW, 8 tubes, AC **$120.00-140.00**

J-809, console-R/P, 1940, mahogany, inner right front slide rule dial, door, left pull-out phono drawer, lower grille area, 4 knobs, BC, SW, 8 tubes, AC **$75.00-85.00**

JB-410, portable, 1940, leatherette/plastic, inner dial and horizontal grille bars, fold-open front, handle, BC, 4 tubes, battery........**$35.00-45.00**

J-54W, table, 1940, ivory plastic, upper front slide rule dial, lower horizontal louvers, 2 knobs, BC, 5 tubes, AC/DC, $40.00-50.00.

J-100, cathedral, 1932, wood, front window dial, upper cloth grille with cut-outs, 3 knobs, BC, 10 tubes, AC, $300.00-320.00.

JFM-90, table, C1941, wood, FM1 tuner, center front black dial, 6 pushbuttons, rounded front corners, 2 knobs, FM1, 9 tubes, AC, $30.00-35.00.

K-60-P, cathedral, 1933, wood, mantle-clock design, lower front window dial, upper round cloth grille with cut-outs, handle, 4 knobs, BC, 6 tubes, AC, $300.00-320.00.

JB-420, table, 1940, mahogany plastic, right front dial over horizontal wrap-around grille bars, 2 knobs, BC, 4 tubes, battery..**$35.00-45.00**

JCP-562, table, 1942, wood, right front dial, left cloth grille, 2 knobs, BC, 5 tubes, AC/DC **$35.00-45.00**

K-40-A, table, 1933, walnut, right front dial, center cloth grille with cut-outs, lower scalloped molding, 2 knobs, BC, 4 tubes, AC/DC **$85.00-95.00**

K-41, table, 1933, metal, right front dial, center round cloth grille, decorative case lines, 2 knobs, BC, AC **$85.00-95.00**

K-43-C, cathedral, 1933, wood, low case, center front dial surrounded by cloth grille with cut-outs, 4 knobs, BC, SW, 4 tubes, AC ..**$180.00-200.00**

K-50, cathedral, 1933, wood, lower right front window dial, upper cloth grille with cut-outs, 3 knobs, BC, 5 tubes, AC...........**$150.00-180.00**

K-50-P, cathedral, 1933, wood, lower right front window dial, upper cloth grille with cut-outs, 4 knobs, BC, 5 tubes, AC...........**$150.00-180.00**

K-51, table, 1932, wood, inner front window dial, cloth grille with cut-outs, double sliding carved doors, BC, 5 tubes, AC ..**$200.00-230.00**

K-51-P, table, 1932, wood, inner front window dial, cloth grille with cut-outs, double sliding carved doors, BC, 5 tubes, AC ..**$200.00-230.00**

K-52, cathedral, 1933, wood, lower right front window dial, upper cloth grille with cut-outs, 4 knobs, BC, SW, 5 tubes, AC **$240.00-270.00**

K-53-M, table, 1933, wood, right front window dial, left & right quarter-round grille cut-outs, 4 knobs, BC, SW, 5 tubes, AC ..**$85.00-115.00**

K-54 "Music Box," table-R/P, 1932, ornate case, right side controls, front grille with cut-outs, lift top, inner phono, BC, 5 tubes, AC **$85.00-115.00**

K-60, cathedral, 1933, wood, mantle-clock design, lower front window dial, upper round cloth grille with cut-outs, handle, 4 knobs, BC, 6 tubes, AC .... **$300.00-320.00**.

K-62, console, 1931, wood, lowboy, center front window dial, lower cloth grille with cut-outs, 6 legs, 3 knobs, BC, 9 tubes, AC ..**$150.00-180.00**

K-63, cathedral, 1933, wood, mantle-clock design, lower front window dial, upper cloth grille with cut-outs, 4 knobs, BC, SW, 6 tubes, AC **$240.00-270.00**

K-65, console, 1933, walnut, upper front window dial, lower cloth grille with cut-outs, 6 legs, stretcher base, 4 knobs, BC, 6 tubes, AC...**$120.00-150.00**

K-80, tombstone, 1933, wood, center front round dial, upper cloth grille with cut-outs, angled top, 4 knobs, BC, SW, 8 tubes, AC **$300.00-350.00**

K-82 "Georgian," grandfather clock, 1931, mahogany, Colonial design, inner dial & controls, front door, upper clock face, BC, 9 tubes, AC...**$480.00-530.00**

K-85, console, 1933, wood, upper front round dial, lower cloth grille with cut-outs, 6 legs, 4 knobs, BC, SW, 8 tubes, AC **$150.00-170.00**

K-106, console, 1933, wood, upper front window dial, lower grille with cut-outs, 6 legs, 5 knobs, BC, 10 tubes, AC **$150.00-180.00**

K-126, console, 1933, wood, upper front window dial, lower grille with cut-outs, 6 legs, 5 knobs, BC, SW, 12 tubes, AC **$180.00-200.00**

L-500, table, 1941, mahogany plastic, upper front slide rule dial, lower horizontal louvers, 2 knobs, BC, 5 tubes, AC/DC.......... **$35.00-45.00**

L-513, table, 1941, wood, upper center slanted slide rule dial, lower grille with horizontal louvers, feet, 2 knobs, BC, 5 tubes, AC/DC **$80.00-100.00**

K-43, cathedral, 1933, wood, low case, center front dial surrounded by cloth grille with cut-outs, 4 knobs, BC, SW, 4 tubes, AC, $180.00-200.00.

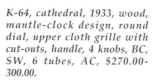

K-64, cathedral, 1933, wood, mantle-clock design, round dial, upper cloth grille with cut-outs, handle, 4 knobs, BC, SW, 6 tubes, AC, $270.00-300.00.

K-70, cathedral, wood, lower front window dial with escutcheon, upper 3-section cloth grille, 3 knobs, $160.00-190.00.

L-521, table, 1941, white plastic, upper center slanted slide rule dial, lower grille with horizontal louvers, top handle, 2 knobs, BC, 5 tubes, AC/DC **$40.00-50.00**

L-522, table, 1941, brown plastic, upper center slanted slide rule dial, lower grille with horizontal louvers, top handle, 2 knobs, BC, 5 tubes, AC/DC **$40.00-50.00**

L-550, table, 1941, ivory plastic, upper front slide rule dial, lower horizontal louvers, 2 knobs, BC, 5 tubes, AC/DC...................... **$35.00-45.00**

L-570, table, 1941, Catalin, upper front slide rule dial, lower horizontal louvers, handle, 2 ribbed knobs, BC, 5 tubes, AC/DC .... **$650.00+**

L-600, table, 1941, mahogany plastic, upper front slide rule dial, lower horizontal louvers, 2 knobs, BC, 6 tubes, AC/DC.......... **$35.00-45.00**

L-604, table, 1941, two-tone walnut, upper front slanted slide rule dial, lower horizontal louvers, 2 knobs, BC, AC **$35.00-45.00**

L-610, table, 1941, ivory plastic, upper front slanted slid rule dial, lower horizontal louvers, 2 knobs, BC, 6 tubes, AC **$35.00-45.00**

L-621, table, 1941, mahogany plastic, upper front slide rule dial, lower double grille with horizontal louvers, 2 knobs, BC, SW, 6 tubes, AC/DC **$40.00-50.00**

L-624, table, 1941, ivory plastic, upper front slanted slide rule dial, lower double grille with horizontal louvers, 2 knobs, BC, SW, 6 tubes, AC/DC... **$40.00-50.00**

L-630, table, 1940, two-tone wood, upper front slide rule dial, lower cloth grille with center horizontal bar, 4 knobs, BC, SW, 6 tubes, AC...**$40.00-50.00**

L-631, table, 1941, wood, upper front slanted slide rule dial, lower cloth grille with two vertical bars, 2 knobs, BC, SW, 6 tubes, AC/DC **$35.00-45.00**

K-105, console, 1933, wood, upper front window dial, lower grille with cut-outs, 6 legs, 5 knobs, BC, SW, 10 tubes, AC, $150.00-180.00.

L-632, table, 1941, wood, upper front slanted slide rule dial, lower horizontal louvers, 2 knobs, BC, SW, 6 tubes, AC/DC **$35.00-45.00**

L-633, table, 1941, walnut, upper front slanted slide rule dial, lower horizontal grille bars, rounded front sides, 2 knobs, BC, SW, 6 tubes, AC/DC **$50.00-65.00**

L-640, table, 1941, wood, upper front slide rule dial, lower grille area, 5 pushbuttons, 4 knobs, BC, SW, 6 tubes, AC **$50.00-65.00**

L-641, table, 1942, wood, upper front slide rule dial, lower grille with horizontal bars & center oval, 4 knobs, BC, SW, 6 tubes, AC..**$45.00-55.00**

L-660, table, 1941, wood, front slide rule dial with chrome escutcheon, 5 pushbuttons, 2 knobs, BC, 6 tubes, AC/DC **$45.00-55.00**

L-678, table-R/P, 1941, wood, center front dial, right & left wrap-around grilles, lift top, inner phono, BC, 6 tubes, AC **$30.00-35.00**

L-740, table, 1941, walnut, center front slide rule dial, 5 pushbuttons, top grille bars, 4 knobs, BC, SW, 7 tubes, AC **$65.00-75.00**

L-915, console, 1940, walnut, upper front slanted slide rule dial, pushbuttons, lower grille with vertical bars, BC, SW, 9 tubes, AC.........**$120.00-150.00**

L-916, console, 1941, wood, upper front slanted slide rule dial, pushbuttons, lower grille with vertical bars, BC, SW, 9 tubes, AC **$110.00-130.00**

LB-412, portable, 1941, two-tone case, inner dial and grille bars, fold-open front, handle, 2 knobs, BC, 4 tubes, battery.........**$40.00-50.00**

LB-502, portable, 1941, plastic, inner dial and horizontal grille bars, fold-open front, handle, 2 knobs, BC, 5 tubes, AC/DC/battery ..**$40.00-50.00**

LB-530, portable, 1940, leatherette, inner slide rule dial, fold-open top, front horizontal louvers, handle, 3 knobs, BC, 5 tubes, AC/battery **$30.00-35.00**

LB-530X, portable, 1940, leatherette, inner slide rule dial, fold-open top, front horizontal louvers, handle, 3 knobs, BC, 5 tubes, AC/battery **$30.00-35.00**

LB-603, portable, 1941, two-tone leatherette, inner right dial over horizontal grille bars, fold-up front, handle, 2 knobs, BC, 6 tubes, AC/DC/battery **$40.00-45.00**

L-50, table, 1932, ornate "carved" front & sides, right dial, center grille, handle, 2 knobs, BC, 5 tubes, AC/DC, $160.00-190.00.

LB-700, portable, 1940, cloth covered, upper front dial, lower horizontal grille bars, handle, 2 knobs, BC, 7 tubes, AC/DC/battery ..**$30.00-35.00**

LB-702, portable, 1941, cloth covered, inner top dial & knobs, lift-up lid, front horizontal grille bars, BC, 7 tubes, AC/DC/battery ..**$30.00-35.00**

LC-619, console-R/P, 1941, two-tone walnut, inner right front slide rule dial, left lift top, inner phono, BC, SW, 6 tubes, AC....**$110.00-130.00**

LC-638, table-R/P, 1941, walnut, front slide rule dial, horizontal louvers, lift top, inner phono, 4 knobs, BC, 6 tubes, AC **$40.00-45.00**

LC-648, console-R/P, 1941, two-tone walnut, inner right front slide rule dial, door, left lift top, inner phono, BC, 6 tubes, AC......**$85.00-95.00**

LC-658, table-R/P, 1941, mahogany veneer, outer front dial & grille, lift top, inner phono, 4 knobs, BC, 6 tubes, AC **$35.00-40.00**

LC-679, table-R/P, 1942, wood, center front dial, 6 pushbuttons, right & left side wrap-around cloth grilles with horizontal bars, lift top, inner phono, 2 knobs, BC, 7 tubes, AC **$45.00-50.00**

LF-115, console, 1940, walnut, upper front slanted slide rule dial, pushbuttons, lower grille with vertical bars, BC, SW, FM1, 11 tubes, AC...**$120.00-140.00**

LF-116, console, 1940, walnut, upper front slanted slide rule dial, pushbuttons, lower grille with vertical bars, BC, SW, FM1, 11 tubes, AC...**$110.00-130.00**

LFC-1118, console-R/P, 1940, walnut, inner right front slide rule dial, pushbuttons, door, left lift top, inner phono, BC, SW, FM1, 11 tubes, AC $120.00-140.00

LFC-1128, console-R/P, 1940, walnut, inner right front slide rule dial, pushbuttons, door, left pull-out phono drawer, BC, SW, FM1, 11 tubes, AC $110.00-140.00

M-42, tombstone, 1934, two-tone wood, lower front dial, 3-section cloth grille, 4 knobs, BC, 4 tubes, AC....................................$85.00-105.00

M-51A, tombstone, 1935, two-tone wood, rounded top, lower front square airplane dial, cloth grille with vertical bars, 4 knobs, BC, 5 tubes, AC $110.00-130.00

M-61, tombstone, 1934, wood, shouldered, center square airplane dial, upper grille with vertical bars, 5 knobs, BC, SW, 6 tubes, AC...$180.00-200.00

M-103, table, plastic, lower front curved slide rule dial, upper horizontal louvers, 2 knobs, BC $35.00-45.00

P-671, portable, 1958, black/white plastic, right side dial, horizontal front grille bars with GE logo, handle, 2 knobs, BC, 4 tubes, AC/DC/battery $20.00-25.00

P-673, portable, 1958, turquoise/white plastic, right side dial, horizontal front grille bars with GE logo, handle, 2 knobs, BC, 4 tubes, AC/DC/battery $20.00-25.00

P-700, portable, plastic, large right front dial, left grille with horizontal bars, fold-down handle, 2 knobs, BC $20.00-25.00

P-735A, portable, 1958, plastic, right side dial, large front grille area, handle, 2 knobs, BC, 4 tubes, AC/DC/battery.....................$20.00-25.00

S-22 "Junior," console, 1931, wood, lowboy, upper front window dial, lower cloth grille with cut-outs, 3 knobs, BC, 8 tubes ..$110.00-130.00

S-22 "Junior," tombstone, 1931, walnut, lower front window dial, upper floral cloth grille, top, brass handle, columns, 3 knobs, BC, 8 tubes, AC $200.00-230.00

L-613, table, 1941, two-tone wood, upper front slanted slide rule dial, lower horizontal louvers, 2 knobs, BC, SW, 6 tubes, AC/DC, $45.00-55.00.

S-22 "Junior," tombstone/stand, 1931, walnut, model S-22 with removable 4 legged stand, 3 knobs, BC, 8 tubes, AC.........$240.00-270.00

S-22A, tombstone, 1932, wood, lower front window dial, upper floral cloth grille, columns, 3 knobs, BC, 8 tubes, AC $190.00-210.00

S-22C, tombstone, 1934, wood, lower front window dial, upper floral cloth grille, columns, 3 knobs, BC, 8 tubes, AC $190.00-210.00

S-22X "Junior," tombstone-C, 1931, wood, lower front window dial, upper cloth grille with cut-outs & center clock, columns, top metal handle, 3 knobs, BC, 8 tubes, AC $270.00-300.00

S-42 "Junior," console, 1931, walnut, upper front window dial, lower cloth grille with cut-outs, 3 knobs, BC, 8 tubes, AC ..$120.00-140.00

S-42B, console, 1931, walnut, upper front window dial, lower cloth grille with vertical bars, 3 knobs, BC, 8 tubes, battery.........$85.00-105.00

T-12 "Midget," cathedral, 1931, wood, lower front window dial with escutcheon, upper cloth grille with cut-outs, 3 knobs, BC, 4 tubes, AC $180.00-200.00

T-101, table, slate gray plastic, large left front dial over horizontal grille bars, feet, 2 knobs, BC, 4 tubes $15.00-20.00

T-102, table, honey beige plastic, large left front dial over horizontal grille bars, feet, 2 knobs, BC, 4 tubes $15.00-20.00

T-103, table, mint green plastic, large left front dial over horizontal grille bars, feet, 2 knobs, BC, 4 tubes $15.00-20.00

T-115A, table, 1958, plastic, raised upper front slide rule dial, large lower lattice grille, 2 knobs, BC, 6 tubes, AC/DC $20.00-25.00

T-125A, table, 1959, pink plastic, right front dial, center lattice grille, 2 knobs, BC, 5 tubes, AC/DC $15.00-20.00

L-652, table, 1941, wood, large center front slide rule dial, 5 pushbuttons, top louvers, 2 knobs, BC, 6 tubes, AC/DC, $50.00-65.00.

T-125C, table, 1959, pink plastic, right front round dial, center lattice grille, feet, 2 knobs, BC, 5 tubes, AC/DC $15.00-20.00

T-126, table, 1959, beige plastic, right front dial, center lattice grille, 2 knobs, BC, 5 tubes, AC/DC $15.00-20.00

T-126A, table, 1959, beige plastic, right front dial, center lattice grille, 2 knobs, BC, 5 tubes, AC/DC $15.00-20.00

T-126C, table, 1959, beige plastic, right front round dial, center lattice grille, feet, 2 knobs, BC, 5 tubes, AC/DC $15.00-20.00

T-127, table, 1959, antique white plastic, right front dial, center lattice grille, 2 knobs, BC, 5 tubes, AC/DC $15.00-20.00

T-127A, table, 1959, white plastic, right front dial, center lattice grille, 2 knobs, BC, 5 tubes, AC/DC $15.00-20.00

T-127C, table, 1959, off-white plastic, right round dial, center lattice grille, feet, 2 knobs, BC, 5 tubes, AC/DC $15.00-20.00

T-128, table, 1959, yellow plastic, right round dial, center lattice grille, feet, 2 knobs, BC, 5 tubes, AC/DC $15.00-20.00

T-128C, table, 1959, yellow plastic, right front round dial, center lattice grille, feet, 2 knobs, BC, 5 tubes, AC/DC $15.00-20.00

T-129C, table, 1959, turquoise plastic, right round dial, center lattice grille, feet, 2 knobs, BC, AC/DC $15.00-20.00

T-140D, table, 1966, sage green plastic, large right front dial overlaps dual speaker lattice grille area, feet, 2 knobs, BC $15.00-20.00

T-141, table, 1966, rose beige plastic, large right front dial overlaps dual speaker lattice grille area, feet, 2 knobs, BC, 5 tubes $15.00-20.00

T-141D, table, 1966, rose beige plastic, large right front dial overlaps dual speaker lattice grille area, feet, 2 knobs, BC $15.00-20.00

T-142, table, 1966, antique white plastic, large right front dial overlaps dual speaker lattice grille area, feet, 2 knobs, BC, 5 tubes $15.00-20.00

M-81, tombstone, 1934, wood, center front square airplane dial, upper grille with vertical bars, 5 knobs, BC, SW, 8 tubes, AC, $120.00-150.00.

P-672, portable, 1958, terra cotta/white plastic, right side dial, horizontal front grille bars with GE logo, handle, 2 knobs, BC, 4 tubes, AC/DC/battery, $20.00-25.00.

T-142D, table, 1966, antique white plastic, large right front dial overlaps dual speaker lattice grille area, feet, 2 knobs, BC **$15.00-20.00**

T-143, table, 1966, walnut grain plastic, large right front dial overlaps dual speaker lattice grille area, feet, 2 knobs, BC, 5 tubes......**$15.00-20.00**

T-150 "Musaphonic," table, 1962, mahogany, lower front slide rule dial, large upper grille area, 4 knobs, BC, FM, 9 tubes **$15.00-20.00**

T-151 "Musaphonic," table, 1962, walnut, lower front slide rule dial, large upper grille area, 4 knobs, BC, FM **$15.00-20.00**

T-151B "Musaphonic," table, 1962, wood, lower front slide rule dial, large upper grille area, 4 knobs, BC, FM **$15.00-20.00**

T-165, table, 1961, Wedgwood blue/white plastic, lower right front dial panel over large textured grille area, 2 knobs, BC, 5 tubes, AC/DC **$20.00-25.00**

T-166, table, 1961, mocha/beige plastic, lower right front dial panel over large textured grille area, 2 knobs, BC, 5 tubes, AC/DC.. **$20.00-25.00**

T-170, table, 1961, cocoa/beige plastic, right front vertical dial, large left lattice grille area, 4 knobs, BC, FM, 8 tubes, AC...........**$20.00-25.00**

T-171, table, 1961, antique white plastic, right front vertical dial, large left lattice grille area, 4 knobs, BC, FM, 8 tubes, AC...........**$20.00-25.00**

T-180, table, 1961, antique white plastic, right front dial panel over large grille area with horizontal bars, feet, 2 knobs, FM, 6 tubes, AC/DC **$15.00-20.00**

T-185, table, 1961, Wedgwood blue/white plastic, lower right front dial panel over large textured grille area, FM only, 2 knobs, FM, 6 tubes, AC/DC **$15.00-20.00**

T-186, table, 1961, cocoa/beige plastic, lower right front dial panel over large textured grille area, FM only, 2 knobs, FM, 6 tubes, AC/DC **$15.00-20.00**

T-210 "Musaphonic," table, 1961, mocha/beige plastic, lower slanted slide rule dial, large upper cloth grille area, dual speakers, 4 knobs, BC, FM, 9 tubes, AC/DC.....................................**$20.00-25.00**

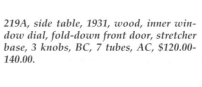

T-186A, table, 1961, cocoa/beige plastic, lower right front dial panel over large textured grille area, FM only, 2 knobs, FM, AC/DC, $15.00-20.00.

T-210B "Musaphonic," table, 1961, mocha/beige plastic, lower front slanted slide rule dial, large upper cloth grille area, dual speakers, 4 knobs, BC, FM, 9 tubes, AC/DC..................................**$20.00-25.00**

YRB-60-2, table, 1948, plastic, right front dial printed on flocked grille, horizontal wrap-around bands, 2 knobs, BC, 5 tubes, AC/DC **$40.00-50.00**

YRB 79-2, table, 1948, plastic, lower front slide rule dial, upper recessed horizontal louvers, 2 knobs, BC, 5 tubes, AC/DC.........**$35.00-45.00**

YRB 83-1, table, 1948, wood, lower front slide rule dial, upper horizontal louvers, 2 knobs, BC, 5 tubes, AC/DC **$35.00-45.00**

X-415, table, 1948, wood, center front multi-band dial, upper stepback top with horizontal louvers, 5 knobs, BC, SW, FM, 9 tubes, AC **$75.00-85.00**

GENERAL IMPLEMENT
General Implement Corp.
Terminal Tower, Cleveland, Ohio

9A5, table, 1948, plastic, right front square dial, left horizontal grille bars, handle, 2 knobs, BC, 5 tubes, AC/DC **$85.00-95.00**

GENERAL MOTORS

110MB "Little General," cathedral, C1932, wood, lower front window dial w/escutcheon, upper cloth grille with cut-outs, side switch, 3 knobs, BC, 6 tubes, AC, $300.00-320.00.

201 "Pioneer," console, 1931, wood, lowboy, inner dial, double doors, lower grille area, 4 knobs, BC, 7 tubes, battery............**$85.00-105.00**

250 "Little General," cathedral, 1931, walnut, lower front window dial, upper scalloped grille with cut-outs, 3 knobs, BC, 7 tubes, AC..**$300.00-320.00**

250A "Little General," cathedral, 1931, wood, lower front window dial, upper cloth grille with cut-outs, 3 knobs, BC, 7 tubes, AC **$300.00-320.00**

219A, side table, 1931, wood, inner window dial, fold-down front door, stretcher base, 3 knobs, BC, 7 tubes, AC, $120.00-140.00.

281, ashtray/remote control unit, metal, looks like an ashtray on floor stand, upper window dial, 2 knobs, BC, 2 tubes, AC, $180.00-210.00.

251 "Valere," console, 1931, wood, lowboy, upper front window dial, lower cloth grille with cut-outs, 3 knobs, BC, 8 tubes, AC **$120.00-140.00**

252 "Cosmopolitan," console, 1931, wood, inner front dial, small sliding door, lower vertical grille bars, 3 knobs, BC, 10 tubes, AC **$110.00-140.00**

GENERAL TELEVISION
General Radio & Television Corp.
Chicago, Illinois

4B5, table, 1947, plastic, right front square dial, left horizontal louvers, 2 knobs, BC, 5 tubes, AC/DC **$35.00-40.00**

6C5, table, 1948, plastic, right front square dial, left cloth grille with 3 vertical bars, 2 knobs, BC, 5 tubes, AC/DC **$45.00-55.00**

9B6, table, plastic, right front square dial, left horizontal grille bars, handle, 2 knobs, BC **$50.00-65.00**

9B6P, table, 1948, plastic, right front square dial over large metal wrap-around perforated grille, handle, 2 knobs, BC, 6 tubes, AC/DC **$35.00-45.00**

14A4F, table, 1946, plastic, right front square dial, left horizontal louvers, 2 knobs, BC, 4 tubes, battery **$30.00-35.00**

49, table, wood, right front square dial, left cloth grille, plastic grille bars/dial bezel/handle, 2 knobs, AC/DC, $65.00-75.00.

17A5, table, 1946, wood, right front square dial, left plastic horizontal grille louvers, zig-zag strip on base, 2 knobs, BC, 5 tubes, AC/DC **$40.00-50.00**

19A5, table, 1946, wood, right front square dial outlined in plastic, left plastic horizontal louvers, 2 knobs, BC, 5 tubes, AC/DC **$35.00-40.00**

21A4, portable, 1947, luggage-style, cloth with lower stripes, right front square dial, left grille, handle, 2 knobs, BC, 4 tubes, battery **$25.00-30.00**

22A5C, table-R/P, 1947, wood, right front square dial, left grille, lift top, inner phono, 2 knobs, BC, 5 tubes, AC **$30.00-35.00**

23A6, portable, 1947, luggage-style, cloth covered, right front square dial, left grille, handle, 2 knobs, BC, 4 tubes, AC/DC/battery ..**$30.00-35.00**

24B6, table, 1948, wood, right front square dial, left horizontal grille bars, handle, 2 knobs, BC, 6 tubes, AC/DC **$40.00-50.00**

25B5, portable, 1947, two-tone, right front square dial over large perforated grille, handle, 2 knobs, BC, 5 tubes, AC/DC/battery ..**$30.00-35.00**

26B5, portable, 1947, two-tone leatherette, right front dial panel over large grille area, handle, 2 knobs, BC, 5 tubes, AC/DC/battery **$25.00-30.00**

534 "Grand Piano," table-N, 1939, wood, looks like grand piano, inner right dial, left G-clef grille, lift top, 2 knobs, BC, 5 tubes, AC/DC, $320.00-350.00.

27C5, table, 1948, plastic, right front square dial, left cloth grille with 3 vertical bars, 2 knobs, BC, 5 tubes, AC/DC **$45.00-55.00**

526, table, 1940, wood, right front dial, left grille with horizontal bars, plastic dial bezel/handle, 2 knobs, BC, 5 tubes, AC/DC **$50.00-65.00**

591, table, 1940, Catalin with plastic trim, right front dial, left horizontal grille bars, handle, 2 knobs, BC, 5 tubes, AC/DC............... **$700.00+**

GENEVA
Cordonic Manufacturing Co.

36, cathedral, C1931, wood, right window dial with escutcheon, upper cloth grille with cut-outs, scalloped top, 3 knobs, BC, 7 tubes, AC, $300.00-320.00.

GILBERT
R.W. Gilbert
2357 W. Washington Blvd, Los Angeles, California

70, cathedral, 1931, wood, lower center window dial with escutcheon, upper grille with ornate cut-outs, 3 knobs, BC, 6 tubes, AC **$400.00-450.00**

GILFILLAN
Gilfillan Bros. Inc.
1815 Venice Boulevard, Los Angeles, California

The Gilfillan Company, originally formed as a smelting and refining outfit, began to manufacture and sell radio parts in 1922 and by 1924 they were advertising complete radios and soon grew to be one of the largest radio manufacturers on the west coast. The last radios made by Gilfillan were produced in 1948.

5, cathedral, 1932, wood, lower front window dial, upper cloth grille with cut-outs, scrolled top, 3 knobs, BC, 5 tubes, AC **$320.00-350.00**
5-F, table, 1941, plastic, right front dial, left horizontal louvers, 2 knobs, BC, 5 tubes **$45.00-55.00**
5-L, portable, 1941, striped, right front square dial over horizontal grille bars, handle, 2 knobs, BC, 5 tubes, AC/DC/battery **$40.00-45.00**
8-T, tombstone, 1934, wood, lower dual window dials, upper grille with ornate cut-outs, two-tone, 4 knobs, BC, SW, 8 tubes, AC **$300.00-350.00**
10, table, 1926, carved walnut, rectangular case, slanted front panel with center dial, BC, 5 tubes, battery **$150.00-180.00**

16H, table, wood, right front dial, left cloth grille with "X" cut-out, handle, 2 knobs, BC, AC/DC, $45.00-55.00.

20, console, 1926, mahogany, lowboy, upper slanted panel with center dial, lower built-in speaker, BC, 6 tubes, battery........**$200.00-230.00**
56B, table, 1946, wood, metal front panel with right square dial & left perforated grille, 2 knobs, BC, 5 tubes, AC/DC.................. **$45.00-55.00**
58M, table, 1948, plastic, Deco, rounded right with half-round dial, left horizontal wrap-around louvers, 2 knobs, BC, 5 tubes, AC/DC **$170.00-190.00**
58W, table, 1948, plastic, Deco, rounded right with half-round dial, left horizontal wrap-around louvers, 2 knobs, BC, 5 tubes, AC/DC **$170.00-190.00**
63X, tombstone, 1935, wood, center front round dial, upper grille with cut-outs, 3 band, 4 knobs, BC, SW, 6 tubes, AC **$120.00-150.00**
66AM, table, 1946, wood, upper front slanted slide rule dial, lower cloth grille, 2 knobs, BC, 6 tubes, AC....................................**$35.00-40.00**
66B "Overland," portable, 1946, leatherette, metal front panel with right dial & left perforated grille, double doors, handle, 2 knobs, BC, 6 tubes, AC/DC/battery **$40.00-50.00**
66PM "El Dorado," table-R/P, 1946, wood, inner right vertical dial, left phono, front grille, lift top, 4 knobs, BC, 6 tubes, AC **$25.00-30.00**
66S, table, 1939, wood, upper front dial, right & left side wrap-around grilles with horizontal bars, BC, 6 tubes, AC **$75.00-85.00**
68-48, console-R/P/Rec, 1949, wood, inner right slide rule dial, left pull-out phono/recorder drawer, doors, lower grille, 4 knobs, BC, 10 tubes, AC **$50.00-65.00**

56B-CB, table, 1946, wood, metal front panel with right square dial & left perforated grille, 2 knobs, BC, 5 tubes, AC/DC, $45.00-55.00.

68B-D, portable, 1948, alligator, metal front panel with right square dial & left perforated grille, handle, 2 knobs, BC, 6 tubes, AC/DC/battery **$35.00-40.00**
68F, table, 1948, wood, metal front panel with right square dial & left perforated grille, 3 knobs, BC, FM, 6 tubes, AC/DC **$40.00-45.00**
80, table, 1927, wood, low rectangular case, center front window dial, 3 knobs, BC, 6 tubes, AC **$150.00-180.00**
86U, tombstone, 1947, wood, center front slide rule dial, upper grille, 6 pushbuttons, 4 knobs, BC, SW, 8 tubes, AC **$75.00-85.00**
97, console, 1936, wood, upper front center round dial, lower large grille with center vertical bars plus left and right horizontal bars, two-tone, 5 knobs, BC, SW, 9 tubes, AC...................................**$300.00-340.00**
100, console, 1929, wood, lowboy, inner front dial, lower cloth grille with cut-outs, doors, 3 knobs, BC, 8 tubes, AC **$160.00-190.00**
105, console, 1929, wood, lowboy, upper front window dial, lower cloth grille, fluted columns, 3 knobs, BC, 9 tubes, AC........**$120.00-150.00**
108-48, console-R/P/Rec, 1949, wood, inner right front slide rule dial, left pull-out phono/recorder drawer, doors, 5 knobs, BC, FM, 15 tubes, AC **$65.00-75.00**
119, console, 1940, wood, lowboy, half-round Hepplewhite-style, upper front slide rule dial, BC, AC **$300.00-350.00**
GN-1 "Neutrodyne," table, 1924, wood, low rectangular case, inner panel, fold-down front, doors, BC, 5 tubes, battery ..**$160.00-190.00**
GN-2 "Neutrodyne," table, 1924, wood, low rectangular case, 3 dial front panel, BC, 5 tubes, battery **$120.00-150.00**
GN-3 "Neutrodyne," table, 1925, wood, high rectangular case, 2 dial slant front panel, BC, 4 exposed tubes, battery **$200.00-230.00**
GN-5 "Neutrodyne," table, 1925, mahogany, low rectangular case, 3 dial front panel, 5 knobs, BC, 5 tubes, battery..................**$140.00-160.00**
GN-6, table, 1925, mahogany, tall case, slanted front panel with 2 dials, BC, 4 exposed tubes, battery **$200.00-230.00**

GLOBAL

GR-7000, portable, plastic, right front dial, left grille with horizontal bars, made in Japan, 2 knobs, BC, 4 tubes, battery, $45.00-55.00.

GLOBE
Globe Electronics, Inc.
225 West 17th Street, New York, New York

5BP1, portable, 1947, luggage-style, inner left dial, right 2-section grille, fold-down front, handle, 3 knobs, BC, AC/DC/battery ..**$30.00-40.00**

6P1, table-R/P, 1947, wood, front slanted slide rule dial, lower grille, 3/4 lift top, inner phono, 2 knobs, BC, 6 tubes, AC **$40.00-45.00**

6U1, table, 1947, wood, upper front slanted slide rule dial, lower cloth grille, 2 knobs, BC, 6 tubes, AC/DC **$35.00-40.00**

7CP-1, console-R/P, 1947, wood, center front square dial, 4-section grille area, lower record storage, lift top, inner phono, 2 knobs, BC, 5 tubes, AC **$40.00-50.00**

51, table, 1947, swirled plastic, right front round dial, left horizontal wrap-around louvers, 2 knobs, BC, 5 tubes, AC/DC **$65.00-75.00**

62C, table-R/P, 1947, wood, upper front slanted slide rule dial, lower grille, 3/4 lift top, inner phono, 4 knobs, BC, SW, 6 tubes, AC ..**$35.00-40.00**

85, table-C, 1948, wood, large raised electric clock, right dial, 2 thumb-wheel knobs, BC, 5 tubes, AC **$50.00-65.00**

454, portable, 1948, plastic, inner dial, geometric grille, flip-open front, handle, 2 knobs, BC, 4 tubes, AC/DC/battery...............**$35.00-45.00**

456, portable, 1948, leatherette, lower front slide rule dial, upper grille, handle, 2 knobs, BC, battery **$25.00-30.00**

457, table, 1948, plastic, right front half-round dial, left horizontal wrap-around louvers, 2 knobs, BC, 4 tubes, AC/DC **$50.00-65.00**

500, portable, 1947, leatherette, inner top slide rule dial, fold-up lid, lower front horizontal louvers, 2 knobs, BC, 5 tubes, AC/DC .. **$35.00-40.00**

517, table-R/P, 1947, leatherette, left front dial, right perforated grille, open top phono, 2 knobs, BC, 5 tubes, AC/DC **$20.00-25.00**

552, table, 1947, plastic, streamline, right front dial over horizontal wrap-around louvers, 2 knobs, BC, 5 tubes, AC/DC **$110.00-130.00**

553, table, 1947, plastic, right front half-round dial, left horizontal wrap-around louvers, 2 knobs, BC, AC/DC **$50.00-65.00**

558, table-C, 1948, wood, large raised electric clock, right dial, 2 thumb-wheel knobs, BC, 5 tubes, AC **$50.00-65.00**

559, table-N, 1948, horse stands on wood base, horizontal grille slats, 2 thumbwheel knobs, BC, 5 tubes, AC/DC **$300.00-350.00**

GLOBE TROTTER
Globe Trotter Radio Co.

Globe Trotter, table-N, 1936, looks like a world globe on a stand, tunes by turning globe, 6-color maps, BC, 4 tubes, AC/DC **$530.00-580.00**

GLORITONE
United States Radio & Television Corporation
Chicago, Illinois

26P, cathedral, 1929, wood, center front window dial with escutcheon, upper cloth grille with cut-outs, 3 knobs, BC, 5 tubes, AC, $160.00-190.00.

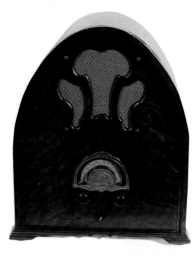

99, cathedral, 1931, wood, lower front half-round dial with escutcheon, upper 3-section cloth grille, 3 knobs, BC, $240.00-270.00.

5T10, table, plastic, lower front slide rule dial, upper 2-section grille area with horizontal bars, twin speakers, 2 knobs, BC **$30.00-35.00**

9B, console, 1932, wood, lowboy, upper front quarter-round dial, lower grille with cut-outs, 6 legs, BC, 9 tubes, AC **$140.00-160.00**

24, cathedral, 1933, wood, center front window dial, upper cloth grille with cut-outs, fluted columns, 2 knobs, BC, 4 tubes, AC ..**$270.00-300.00**

25A, table, 1932, wood, rectangular case, right front window dial, center cloth grille with cut-outs, BC, 5 tubes, AC.....................**$65.00-75.00**

26, cathedral, 1931, wood, center front window dial, upper grille with cut-outs, side columns, 3 knobs, BC, 5 tubes, AC **$150.00-180.00**

26B, console, 1931, wood, lowboy, upper front center window dial, lower grille with cut-outs, 4 legs, 3 knobs, BC, 5 tubes, AC ..**$110.00-130.00**

27, cathedral, 1930, wood, modern, 2 or more versions, lower right front thumbwheel dial, upper grille with cut-outs, 2 knobs, BC, 5 tubes, AC **$190.00-210.00**

27P, console-R/P, 1930, wood, center left front window dial, lower "clover-leaf" grille cut-outs, lift top with inner phono, 2 knobs, BC, 5 tubes, AC **$140.00-170.00**

27S "Spinet," console, 1930, wood, lowboy, upper left front window dial, lower "clover-leaf" grille cut-outs, rounded top, 2 knobs, BC, 5 tubes, AC **$200.00-230.00**

99A, cathedral, 1931, wood, lower front half-round dial with escutcheon, upper 3-section cloth grille, 3 knobs, BC **$240.00-270.00**

305, cathedral, two-tone wood, center front window dial, upper cloth grille with cut-outs, 2 knobs, BC **$240.00-270.00**

305-6, cathedral, two-tone wood, center front window dial, upper cloth grille with cut-outs, 2 knobs, BC, 5 tubes, AC...........**$240.00-270.00**

GOODYEAR
Goodyear Tire & Rubber Co.

015060, table, C1939, tali case, two-tone wood, center front dial with plastic escutcheon, tuning eye, 5 pushbuttons, 4 knobs, BC, SW, 7 tubes, AC/DC **$65.00-75.00**

GRANCO
Granco Products, Inc.
36-17 20th Avenue, Long Island, New York

601, table, 1959, plastic, upper right front window dial, lower lattice grille, FM only, 2 knobs, FM, 5 tubes, AC **$25.00-30.00**

610, table, 1955, plastic, center front horizontal dial over horizontal grille bars, 2 knobs, FM, 6 tubes, AC/DC **$20.00-25.00**

611, table, 1959, plastic, center front horizontal dial over large lattice grille, FM only, 2 knobs, FM, 6 tubes, AC/DC **$20.00-25.00**

704, table, 1962, plastic, lower left front 2-band dial panel over large lattice grille, feet, 2 knobs, BC, FM, 6 tubes, AC/DC **$25.00-30.00**

720, table, 1955, plastic, center front horizontal dial over horizontal grille bars, 2 knobs, BC, FM, 7 tubes, AC/DC...................... **$20.00-25.00**

750, table-R/P, 1956, wood, lower front slide rule dial, large upper grille area, 3/4 lift top, inner 3 speed phono, 4 knobs, BC, FM, 7 tubes, AC **$25.00-30.00**

770, table-C, 1957, plastic, left front dial over horizontal bars, right round alarm clock, 2 knobs, BC, FM, 7 tubes, AC...................**$25.00-30.00**

RP-1220, console-R/P, 1958, wood, inner right front dial, fold-down door, large lower grille area, left lift top, inner phono, hi-fi, 5 knobs, BC, FM, 12 tubes, AC **$65.00-75.00**

730A, table, 1955, plastic, lower front slide rule dial, upper horizontal grille bars, feet, 2 knobs, BC, FM, 7 tubes, AC/DC, $25.00-30.00.

GRANTLINE
W. T. Grant Co.
1441 Broadway, New York, New York

502 Series A, table, c1947, plastic, Deco, right front slide rule dial, left round grille with horizontal bars, 4 pushbuttons, 2 knobs, BC, 5 tubes, AC/DC, $120.00-140.00.

500, table, 1946, plastic, small right front dial, left horizontal grille bars, 2 knobs, BC, 5 tubes, AC/DC **$40.00-50.00**

501, table, 1946, plastic, small right front dial, left horizontal grille bars, 2 knobs, BC, 5 tubes, AC/DC **$40.00-50.00**

501A, table, 1946, plastic, small right front dial, left horizontal grille bars, 2 knobs, BC, 5 tubes, AC/DC **$40.00-50.00**

501-7, table, 1948, plastic, arched dial at top of semi-circular front grille design, 2 knobs, BC, 5 tubes, AC/DC **$50.00-65.00**

504-7, table, 1947, plastic, right front round dial over horizontal louvers, 2 knobs, BC, 5 tubes, AC/DC **$30.00-35.00**

508-7, portable, 1948, plastic & leatherette, arched dial at top of semi-circular front grille design, handle, 2 knobs, BC, 4 tubes, AC/DC/battery **$30.00-35.00**

510A, portable, 1947, cloth covered, upper front slide rule dial, lower metal grille, handle, 2 knobs, BC, 5 tubes, AC/DC/battery **$30.00-35.00**

605, table, 1946, plastic, streamline, right front half-round dial, left horizontal wrap-around grille bars, 6 pushbuttons, 2 knobs, BC, 6 tubes, AC/DC... **$160.00-190.00**

606, table, 1946, plastic, streamline, right front half-round dial, left horizontal wrap-around grille bars, 6 pushbuttons, 2 knobs, BC, 6 tubes, AC/DC... **$160.00-190.00**

651, table, 1947, plastic, upper front slanted slide rule dial, lower horizontal wrap-around louvers, 2 knobs, BC, 5 tubes, AC/DC **$45.00-55.00**

5610, end table, 1948, wood, front slide rule dial, grille cut-outs, raised top edge, 2 knobs, BC, 5 tubes, AC/DC..................... **$85.00-105.00**

6541, table-R/P, wood, upper front slanted slide rule dial, lower horizontal grille bars, lift top, inner phono, 3 knobs, BC, AC **$35.00-40.00**

6547, table-R/P, 1947, wood, upper front slanted slide rule dial, lower horizontal grille bars, lift top, inner phono, 4 knobs, BC, 5 tubes, AC **$35.00-40.00**

GRAYBAR
Graybar Electric Co.

GB-4, cathedral, 1931, wood, lower front window dial with escutcheon, upper 3-section cloth grille, 3 knobs, BC, 4 tubes, AC, $140.00-160.00.

310, table, 1928, wood, low rectangular case, center front dial, lift top, 1 switch, 3 knobs, BC, 7 tubes, AC $85.00-95.00

311, console, 1929, metal, Deco, rectangular case on high legs, center front window dial, 2 knobs, BC, 6 tubes, AC.............$110.00-130.00

330, table, 1929, wood, low rectangular case, center front window dial, lift top, 1 switch, 3 knobs, BC, 9 tubes, AC....................$85.00-95.00

GREBE
A. H. Grebe
10 Van Wyck Avenue, Richmond Hill, New York

A. H. Grebe began as a young man to produce crystal sets and by 1920 had formed A. H. Grebe & Company. The popular Grebe Synchrophase, introduced in the mid-twenties, was the highlight of the company's career. The ever-present Doctor Mu, the Oriental "sage of radio," and his advice on life were a regular feature of Grebe advertising. By 1932, the original Grebe Company was out of business.

CR-5, table, 1921, wood, low rectangular case, 2 dial black Bakelite front panel, 6 knobs, BC, SW, LW, 1 tube, battery, $690.00-740.00.

CR-18, table, 1926, wood, rectangular case, 2 front thumbwheel dials, top exposed meter coils, 5 knobs, SW, 2 tubes, battery, $2,000.00+.

60, cathedral, 1933, walnut, center front window dial with escutcheon, upper grille with cut-outs, 3 knobs, BC, 6 tubes, AC ..**$270.00-300.00**
80, tombstone, 1933, walnut, center front window dial with escutcheon, upper grille with cut-outs, 3 knobs, BC, 8 tubes, AC .**$160.00-190.00**
84, console, 1933, walnut, lowboy, inner front window dial, lower grille cut-outs, sliding doors, 6 legs, 3 knobs, BC, 8 tubes, AC ..**$190.00-210.00**
160, console, 1930, wood, lowboy, upper front window dial & carvings, lower cloth grille with cut-outs, 3 knobs, BC, AC **$190.00-210.00**
206-L, table, 1937, wood, step-down top, right front airplane dial, left cloth grille with 3 vertical bars, 4 knobs, BC, SW, 6 tubes, AC **$85.00-95.00**
270, console, 1929, wood, lowboy, upper front window dial, lower cloth grille with cut-outs, stretcher base, BC, AC **$160.00-190.00**
285, console, 1929, wood, upper front window dial, lower cloth grille with cut-outs, sliding doors, BC, AC **$180.00-200.00**
309-L, table, 1937, wood, step-down top, large right front telephone dial, left cloth grille with cut-outs, 5 knobs, BC, SW, 9 tubes, AC ..**$120.00-150.00**
370-C, table, 1936, wood, large center front dial, right & left cloth wrap-around grilles with horizontal bars, 4 knobs, BC, SW, 7 tubes, AC.................**$95.00-115.00**
450, console-R/P, 1929, wood, front window dial, lower cloth grille with cut-outs, stretcher base, inner phono, BC, AC **$150.00-180.00**
3016-4, console, 1937, walnut, upper front telephone dial, lower cloth grille with vertical bars, 5 knobs, BC, SW, 16 tubes, AC **$300.00-350.00**
AC-Six, table, 1928, wood, low rectangular case, front window dial with escutcheon, 2 knobs, BC, 7 tubes, AC **$180.00-200.00**
AHG-9, tombstone, 1935, wood, lower front round airplane dial, upper cloth grille with 3 vertical bars, 5 knobs, BC, SW, 9 tubes, AC.................**$150.00-170.00**
AHG-90, console, 1935, wood, upper front round airplane dial, lower grille with vertical bars, 5 knobs, BC, SW, 9 tubes, AC..**$200.00-240.00**
AHG-120, console, 1935, wood, upper front round airplane dial, lower cloth grille with cut-outs, 5 knobs, BC, SW, 12 tubes, AC.....**$240.00-280.00**
Challenger 5, table, 1938, plastic, center front square dial, right & left wrap-around grilles with horizontal bars, 2 knobs, 5 tubes, AC/DC **$65.00-75.00**
CR-3, table, 1920, wood, 2 styles, low rectangular case, 2 dial black front panel, lift top, 9 knobs, 1 tube, battery **$875.00-975.00**

MU-1 without chain "Synchrophase," table, 1925, wood, rectangular case, 3 diamond-shaped thumbwheel dials, without dial chain, 8 knobs, BC, 5 tubes, battery, $270.00-300.00.

CR-3A, table, 1920, wood, low rectangular case, 2 dial front panel, very rare, 4 knobs, 1 exposed tube, battery ....**$3,000.00+**
CR-8, table, 1921, wood, low rectangular case, 3 dial black Bakelite front panel, 9 knobs, BC, SW, LW, 1 tube, battery **$800.00-850.00**
CR-9, table, 1921, wood, low rectangular case, 2 dial black Bakelite panel, lift top, 8 knobs, BC, SW, LW, 3 tubes, battery **$690.00-740.00**
CR12, table, 1923, wood, low rectangular case, 2 dial black Bakelite front panel, 9 knobs, BC, 4 tubes, battery **$800.00-850.00**
CR-13, table, 1923, wood, low rectangular case, 3 dial black Bakelite front panel, lift top, 9 knobs, SW, 2 tubes, battery ..**$900.00-1,000.00**
CR-14, table, 1923, wood, low rectangular case, 2 dial black Bakelite panel, lift top, 7 knobs, BC, 3 tubes, battery **$740.00-800.00**
MU-1 with chain "Synchrophase," table, 1925, wood, rectangular case, 3 diamond-shaped thumbwheel dials, with dial chain, 8 knobs, BC, 5 tubes, battery **$270.00-300.00**
SK-4, console, 1930, wood, lowboy, large front dial escutcheon with thumbwheel tuning, lower round grille with cut-outs, 3 knobs, BC, 7 tubes, AC **$180.00-200.00**
Synchronette, table, 1933, wood with inlay, Deco, right front dial, center grille with cut-outs, stepped top, 2 knobs, BC, 5 tubes, AC **$95.00-115.00**

Synchrophase Seven, table, 1927, two-tone wood, low rectangular case, center thumbwheel dial, front pillars, 4 knobs, BC, 7 tubes, battery, $200.00-230.00.

GRUNOW
General Household Utilities Co.
Chicago, Illinois

7C, console, wood, upper front round airplane dial, lower shield-shaped grille with 2 vertical bars, 5 knobs **$120.00-150.00**
20, grandfather clock, 1932, wood, front window dial and knobs, upper clock face, scalloped top with finials, BC, AC **$480.00-530.00**
460, tombstone, 1934, wood, lower center front airplane dial, upper grille with decorative center vertical divider, rounded shoulders, 3 knobs, BC, 6 tubes, AC **$80.00-90.00**

450, tombstone, 1934, wood, small case, lower front dial, large grille with chrome cut-outs, 2 knobs, BC, SW, 4 tubes, AC, $200.00-230.00.

500, tombstone, 1933, wood, step-down top, center front window dial, upper cloth grille with chrome cut-outs, 2 knobs, BC, 5 tubes, AC, $270.00-300.00.

588, table, 1937, wood, right front Tele-dial, left wrap-around grille with center horizontal bar, 3 knobs, 5 tubes, $85.00-95.00.

470, tombstone, 1935, walnut, rounded shoulders, lower front dial, upper grille with cut-outs, 3 knobs, BC, 4 tubes, AC.............**$95.00-105.00**

490, tombstone, 1934, wood & chrome, lower right front dial, large upper cloth grille with chrome cut-outs, 2 knobs, BC, 6 tubes ..**$200.00-230.00**

501, table, 1933, two-tone wood, right front window dial, center grille with chrome cut-outs, 2 knobs, BC, 5 tubes, AC/DC **$160.00-190.00**

520, table, 1935, right & left front windows with escutcheons, center grille with vertical chrome bars, BC, 5 tubes, AC/DC **$130.00-160.00**

566, table, 1935, wood, right front round dial, left cloth grille with horizontal bars, 2 knobs, BC, SW, 5 tubes, AC.........................**$65.00-75.00**

580, tombstone, 1935, walnut, center front round dial, upper grille with cut-outs, 4 knobs, 5 tubes, AC **$120.00-150.00**

581, console, 1935, wood, upper front round dial, lower cloth grille with cut-outs, 4 knobs, BC, SW, 5 tubes, AC **$120.00-150.00**

589, console, 1937, wood, upper front Tele-dial, lower round cloth grille with 2 vertical bars, 4 knobs, BC, SW, 5 tubes, AC ..**$180.00-200.00**

594, table, 1937, ivory finish, "violin-shape," center front round chrome grille with center airplane dial, 2 knobs, BC, 5 tubes, AC/DC.. **$140.00-180.00**

640, tombstone, 1935, wood, center front round dial, upper cloth grille with cut-outs, 4 knobs, BC, SW, 6 tubes, AC **$110.00-130.00**

641, console, 1935, two-tone wood, upper front round dial, lower cloth grille with cut-outs, 4 knobs, BC, SW, 6 tubes, AC **$120.00-150.00**

653, console, 1937, walnut, upper front slanted Tele-dial, lower cloth grille with vertical bars, 4 knobs, BC, SW, 6 tubes, AC........**$200.00-230.00**

654, upright table, 1937, wood, upper front round airplane dial, lower horizontal grille bars, 4 knobs, BC, SW, 6 tubes, AC **$120.00-140.00**

670, tombstone, 1934, wood, center front round dial, upper cloth grille with cut-outs, 4 knobs, BC, SW, 6 tubes, AC **$120.00-150.00**

671, console, 1934, wood, upper front round dial, lower grille with cut-outs, 4 knobs, BC, SW, 6 tubes, AC **$120.00-140.00**

680, tombstone, 1935, wood, center front round dial, upper cloth grille with cut-outs, 4 knobs, BC, SW, 6 tubes, AC **$110.00-130.00**

681, console, 1935, wood, upper front round dial, lower cloth grille with vertical bars, 4 knobs, BC, SW, 6 tubes, AC **$120.00-140.00**

700, tombstone, 1933, wood, step-down top, center front window dial, upper cloth grille with chrome cut-outs, 5 knobs, BC, SW, 7 tubes, AC **$240.00-270.00**

750, tombstone, 1934, wood, step-down top, center front round dial, upper cloth grille with cut-outs, BC, SW, 7 tubes, AC **$120.00-140.00**

761, console, 1935, wood, upper front round dial, lower cloth grille with 2 vertical bars, 5 knobs, BC, SW, 7 tubes, AC **$120.00-150.00**

871, console, 1935, wood, upper front round dial, lower cloth grille with 2 vertical bars, 5 knobs, BC, SW, 8 tubes, AC **$220.00-260.00**

1081, console, 1937, two-tone walnut, upper front Tele-dial, lower grille with vertical bars, BC, SW, 10 tubes, AC **$240.00-280.00**

1161, console, 1935, wood, upper front round dial, lower grille with cut-outs, 3 knobs, BC, SW, 11 tubes, AC **$160.00-190.00**

1171, console, 1935, wood, upper front round dial, lower cloth grille with 2 vertical bars, 5 knobs, BC, SW, 11 tubes, AC **$160.00-190.00**

1183, console, 1937, wood, upper front Tele-dial, lower cloth grille with 6 vertical bars, 4 knobs, BC, SW, 11 tubes, AC **$300.00-350.00**

1191, console, 1936, wood, upper front round dial, tuning eye, lower cloth grille with horizontal bars, 3 knobs, BC, SW, 11 tubes, AC **$200.00-240.00**

1241, console, 1935, wood, upper front round dial, lower cloth grille with 2 vertical bars, BC, SW, 12 tubes, AC.......................**$170.00-200.00**

1291, console, 1936, wood, upper front Tele-dial, lower cloth grille with 5 vertical bars, 4 knobs, BC, SW, 12 tubes, AC **$270.00-300.00**

1541, console, 1936, wood, upper front Tele-dial, lower cloth grille with 7 vertical bars, 5 knobs, BC, SW, 15 tubes, AC **$320.00-350.00**

570, tombstone, 1935, two-tone wood, lower front round dial, upper cloth grille with cut-outs, 3 knobs, BC, SW, 5 tubes, AC, $120.00-140.00.

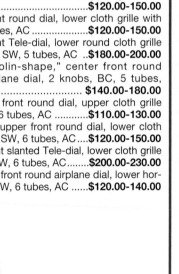

660, tombstone, 1934, wood, lower front round dial, upper cloth grille with cut-outs, fluting, 4 knobs, BC, SW, 6 tubes, AC, $150.00-160.00.

GUILD
Guild Radio & Television Co.
460 North Eucalyptus Avenue, Inglewood, California

380T *"Town Crier," table-N, 1956, wood, looks like an old lantern, inner vertical slide rule dial, front door, 4 knobs, BC, FM, 7 tubes, $150.00-180.00.*

556 "Country Belle," wall-N, 1956, wood, looks like an old wall telephone, side crank tunes stations, 2 side knobs, BC, 5 tubes, AC/DC **$65.00-75.00**
638B-A "Buccaneer Chest," table-N, 1965, wood, looks like an old treasure chest, inner panel with Old World map, slide rule dial, leather straps, 4 knobs, BC, FM, 7 tubes, AC **$120.00-150.00**
818 "Bonnet Box," console-R/P-N, 1959, wood, looks like an old dry sink, inner radio & phono, lift lid, 5 knobs, BC, FM, 18 tubes, AC **$150.00-180.00**
921ML "New Englander," console-R/P-N, wood, looks like a roll-top desk, top compartment with fold-back lid contains radio controls, phono is under roll-top, front grille, BC, FM **$320.00-350.00**
T/K 1577 "Teakettle," table-N, wood, china & brass, looks like an old tea kettle, top lifts for controls, bottom speaker **$120.00-150.00**

484 *"Spice Chest," table-N, 1956, wood, spice chest design, inner slide rule dial, double front shutter or panel doors, 2 drawers, 3 knobs, BC, 5 tubes, AC/DC, $120.00-140.00.*

785 *"Grafonola," table-R/P-N, 1959, wood, looks like an old crank phonograph complete with horn, top phono, side louvers, 5 knobs, BC, 7 tubes, AC, $150.00-180.00.*

GULBRANSEN
Gulbransen Co.
816 North Kedzie Avenue, Chicago, Illinois

130, cathedral, 1931, wood, center front window dial, upper cloth grille with lyre cut-out, fluted columns, 3 knobs, BC, 7 tubes, AC ..**$420.00-450.00**
135, console, 1931, wood, lowboy, upper front window dial, lower grille with cut-outs, stretcher base, BC, 6 tubes, AC **$120.00-150.00**
235, console, 1931, wood, upper front window dial, lower cloth grille with cut-outs, stretcher base, BC, AC...............................**$120.00-150.00**
9950, console, 1930, wood, highboy, upper front window dial, speaker grille underneath cabinet, 3 knobs, BC, 9 tubes, AC..**$150.00-180.00**

HALLDORSON
Halldorson Co.
1772 Wilson Ave., Chicago, Illinois

RD-400, table, 1925, wood, low rectangular case, 2 dial front panel, 4 knobs, BC, 4 tubes, battery **$110.00-130.00**
RF-500, table, 1925, wood, low rectangular case, 3 dial front panel, 5 knobs, BC, 5 tubes, battery **$110.00-130.00**

HALLICRAFTERS
The Hallicrafters Co.
5th & Kostner Avenues, Chicago, Illinois

The Hallicrafters Company was formed by Bill Halligan in 1933 for the manufacture of receivers and phonos for other companies. By 1935, Hallicrafters was producing its own ham radio equipment. During WW II, the company had many military contracts. Hallicrafters enjoyed a reputation for reasonable prices which they were able to offer due to their large volume of business.

5R10, *table, 1951, metal, large center front slide rule dial, top left perforated grille, 4 knobs, BC, SW, 5 tubes, AC/DC, $50.00-65.00.*

5R60, table, 1955, mahogany plastic, left front round dial, right checkered grille, feet, 2 center knobs, BC, 5 tubes, AC/DC, $30.00-35.00.

5R10A, table, 1952, metal, large center front slide rule dial, top left perforated grille, multi-band, 4 knobs, BC, SW, 5 tubes, AC/DC .. **$50.00-65.00**

5R11, table, 1951, plastic, center front round metal dial ring over perforated grille panel, 2 knobs, BC, 5 tubes, AC/DC **$40.00-50.00**

5R12, table, 1951, red plastic, center front round metal dial ring over perforated grille panel, 2 knobs, BC, 5 tubes, AC/DC **$40.00-50.00**

5R13, table, 1951, white plastic, center front round metal dial ring over perforated grille panel, 2 knobs, BC, 5 tubes, AC/DC .. **$40.00-50.00**

5R14, table, 1951, black plastic, center front round metal dial ring over perforated grille panel, 2 knobs, BC, 5 tubes, AC/DC .. **$40.00-50.00**

5R24, portable, 1952, leatherette, center front round dial over woven grille, handle, 2 knobs, BC, 4 tubes, AC/DC/battery **$30.00-35.00**

5R30A "Continental," table, 1952, plastic, right front slide rule dial, left checkered perforated grille, 3 knobs, BC, SW, 5 tubes, AC/DC **$40.00-50.00**

5R31A "Continental," table, 1952, beige plastic, right front slide rule dial, left checkered perforated grille, 3 knobs, BC, SW, 5 tubes, AC/DC **$40.00-50.00**

5R32A "Continental," table, 1952, plastic, right front slide rule dial, left checkered perforated grille, 3 knobs, BC, SW, 5 tubes, AC/DC **$40.00-50.00**

5R33A "Continental," table, 1952, plastic, right front slide rule dial, left checkered perforated grille, 3 knobs, BC, SW, 5 tubes, AC/DC **$40.00-50.00**

5R34A "Continental," table, 1952, blue plastic, right front slide rule dial, left checkered perforated grille, 3 knobs, BC, SW, 5 tubes, AC/DC **$40.00-50.00**

5R40 "Continental," portable, 1955, leatherette, right front dual band dial with worldwide cities, left perforated grille, top leather handle, 3 knobs, BC, SW, 4 tubes, AC/DC/battery......................**$35.00-45.00**

5R41 "Continental," portable, 1955, leatherette, right front dual band dial with worldwide cities, left perforated grille, top leather handle, 3 knobs, BC, SW, 4 tubes, AC/DC/battery......................**$35.00-45.00**

5R42 "Continental," portable, 1955, leatherette, right front dual band dial with worldwide cities, left perforated grille, top leather handle, 3 knobs, BC, SW, 4 tubes, AC/DC/battery......................**$35.00-45.00**

AT-CL-5, table-C, 1952, plastic, low center dial, left square clock, right grille, center "h" logo, 5 knobs, BC, 5 tubes, AC, $30.00-35.00.

5R50, table-C, 1952, blue plastic, right front slide rule dial, left square alarm clock, top checkered grille, 6 knobs, BC, SW, 5 tubes, AC **$40.00-50.00**

5R51, table-C, 1952, yellow plastic, right front slide rule dial, left square alarm clock, top checkered grille, 6 knobs, BC, SW, 5 tubes, AC.. **$40.00-50.00**

5R52, table-C, 1952, pink plastic, right front slide rule dial, left square alarm clock, top checkered grille, 6 knobs, BC, SW, 5 tubes, AC.. **$40.00-50.00**

5R61, table, 1955, ivory plastic, right front round dial, left checkered grille, feet, 2 center knobs, BC, 5 tubes, AC/DC **$30.00-35.00**

AT-CL-9, table-C, 1953, brown plastic, low center dial, left square clock, right grille, center "h" logo, 5 knobs, BC, 5 tubes, AC ..**$30.00-35.00**

AT-CL-10, table-C, 1953, green plastic, low center dial, left square clock, right grille, center "h" logo, 5 knobs, BC, 5 tubes, AC ..**$30.00-35.00**

AT-CL-11, table, 1953, white plastic, low center dial, left square clock, right grille, center "h" logo, 5 knobs, BC, 5 tubes, AC ..**$30.00-35.00**

EC-306, table-R/P, 1948, wood, center front dial, right & left grilles, lift top, inner phono, 4 knobs, BC, SW, 6 tubes, AC **$35.00-40.00**

EX-306, table-R/P, 1948, wood, center front dial, right & left grilles, lift top, inner phono, 4 knobs, BC, SW, 6 tubes, AC **$35.00-40.00**

S-55, table, 1949, metal, center front slide rule dial, top wrap-over perforated grille, 4 knobs, BC, FM, 11 tubes, AC/DC............ **$35.00-40.00**

S-58, table, 1949, metal, left rectangular front slide rule dial, right perforated grille with "h" logo, 4 knobs, BC, FM, 7 tubes, AC **$45.00-50.00**

S-80 "Defender," table, 1952, upper front slanted slide rule dial, lower perforated grille with "h" logo, 3 knobs, BC, SW, 4 tubes, battery **$45.00-55.00**

TW-25, portable, 1953, leatherette, large center front round metal dial ring over perforated grille panel, handle, 2 knobs, BC, 4 tubes, AC/DC/battery **$30.00-35.00**

TW100, portable, 1956, British tan leather, large center front metal dial ring overlaps lower grille cut-outs, handle, 2 knobs, BC, 4 tubes, AC/DC/battery, $30.00-35.00.

TW101, portable, 1956, Cordovan leather, large center front metal dial ring overlaps lower grille cut-outs, handle, 2 knobs, BC, 4 tubes, AC/DC/battery...**$30.00-35.00**

TW102, portable, 1956, champagne leather, large center front metal dial ring overlaps lower grille cut-outs, handle, 2 knobs, BC, 4 tubes, AC/DC/battery **$30.00-35.00**

TW103, portable, 1956, cherry red leather, large center front metal dial ring overlaps lower grille cut-outs, handle, 2 knobs, BC, 4 tubes, AC/DC/battery **$30.00-35.00**

TW104, portable, 1956, cloud blue leather, large center front metal dial ring overlaps lower grille cut-outs, handle, 2 knobs, BC, 4 tubes, AC/DC/battery **$30.00-35.00**

TW105, portable, 1956, bonanza yellow leather, large center front metal dial ring overlaps lower grille cut-outs, handle, 2 knobs, BC, 4 tubes, AC/DC/battery **$30.00-35.00**

TW200, portable, 1957, British tan leather, upper front right corner round tuning dial, lower center grille, top leather handle, 2 knobs, BC, 4 tubes, AC/DC/battery **$30.00-35.00**

TW201, portable, 1957, dove gray leather, upper front right corner round tuning dial, lower center grille, top leather handle, 2 knobs, BC, 4 tubes, AC/DC/battery $30.00-35.00

TW202, portable, 1957, forest green leather, upper front right corner round tuning dial, lower center grille, top leather handle, 2 knobs, BC, 4 tubes, AC/DC/battery $30.00-35.00

TW203, portable, 1957, cherry red leather, upper front right corner round tuning dial, lower center grille, top leather handle, 2 knobs, BC, 4 tubes, AC/DC/battery $30.00-35.00

TW-500, portable, 1954, green leatherette, inner multi-band slide rule dial, lattice grille, flip-up front with map, telescope antenna, handle, 2 knobs, BC, SW, LW, 5 tubes, AC/DC/battery.............$75.00-85.00

TW-600, portable, 1954, brown leatherette, inner multi-band slide rule dial, lattice grille, flip-up front with map, telescope antenna, handle, 2 knobs, BC, SW, LW, 5 tubes, AC/DC/battery.............$75.00-85.00

TW-2000 "World Wide," portable, 1955, leatherette, inner multi-band slide rule dial, flip-up front with map, telescope antenna, handle, 8 bands, 2 knobs, BC, SW, LW, 5 tubes, AC/DC/battery $120.00-150.00

TW-1000 "World Wide," portable, 1953, leatherette, inner multi-band slide rule dial, flip-up front with map, telescope antenna, handle, 8 bands, 2 knobs, BC, SW, LW, 5 tubes, AC/DC/battery, $120.00-150.00.

HALSON
Halson Radio Mfg. Co.
New York, New York

10, table, 1938, two-tone wood, rectangular dial, left cloth wrap-around grille with vertical bars, 3 knobs, BC, SW, 6 tubes, AC/DC $55.00-65.00

43B-A, table, 1933, walnut, step-down top, right front dial, center round grille with cut-outs, 2 knobs, BC, 4 tubes, AC/DC $85.00-95.00

50R, table, 1936, wood, center round airplane dial surrounded by octagonal grille, two tone wood, 3 knobs, BC, SW, 6 tubes, AC/DC.. $55.00-65.00

610, tombstone, 1934, wood, center front round dial, upper cloth grille with cut-outs, 3 knobs, BC, SW, 6 tubes, AC $120.00-150.00

CR53, table, wood with inlay, right front dial, center cloth grille with cut-outs, 2 knobs, BC $85.00-95.00

T10, table, 1937, wood, right front dial, left cloth grille with cut-outs, 2 knobs, BC, AC $40.00-50.00

A5, table, 1938, Catalin, small case, right front round dial, left cloth grille with horizontal wrap-around bars, 2 knobs, $800.00+.

HAMILTON-LLOYD
Plaza Music Co.

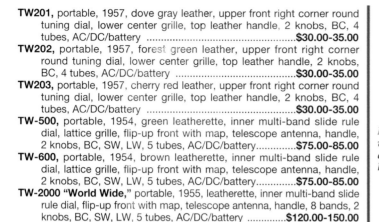

Model unknown, cathedral, c1931, wood, center front half round dial with escutcheon, upper grille with cut-outs, 3 knobs, BC, 5 tubes, AC, $260.00-290.00.

HANSEN
Hansen Storage Co.
120 Jefferson St., Milwaukee, Wisconsin

American Crest, table, 1925, wood, low rectangular case, 2 dial front panel, 3 knobs, BC, 6 tubes, battery $120.00-150.00

Bluebird, table, 1925, wood, step-down case, slanted two dial panel, 2 knobs, BC, 4 tubes, battery $150.00-170.00

Gold Finch, table, 1925, wood, low rectangular case, 2 dial front panel, 4 knobs, BC, 5 tubes, battery $120.00-140.00

HARMONY
Harmony Mfg. Co.
2812 Griffith Ave., Cincinnati, Ohio

5, table, 1925, wood, low rectangular case, front panel with left dial, 5 tubes, battery $120.00-140.00

HARPERS
Harpers International, Inc.
315 Fifth Avenue, New York, New York

GK-301, portable, 1962, plastic, right front dial overlaps wedge-shaped metal perforated grille area, fold-down handle, 2 knobs, BC, 4 tubes, battery, $45.00-55.00.

HARTMAN
Hartman Electrical Mfg. Co.
31 E. Fifth St., Mansfield, Ohio

12-A, console, 1925, wood, lowboy, inner left dial panel, right speaker grille with cut-outs, fold-down front, lower storage, BC, 5 tubes, battery $190.00-210.00

12-B, table, 1925, wood, low rectangular case, left dial panel, right speaker grille with cut-outs, BC, 5 tubes, battery $150.00-180.00

12-C, table, 1925, wood, low rectangular case, center 3 dial panel, BC, 5 tubes, battery $120.00-150.00

HERALD

P-156S, portable, plastic, right front dial, left lattice grille, fold-down handle, BC **$50.00-65.00**

HETEROPLEX
Heteroplex Mfg. Co.
423 Market St., Philadelphia, Pennsylvania

De Luxe, table, 1925, wood, low rectangular case, 2 dial front panel, top door, BC, 3 tubes, battery **$120.00-140.00**

HITACHI
Electronic Utilities Co.
Division of the Sampson Company
2244 South Western Avenue, Chicago, Illinois

H-501, table, plastic, right front dial panel, left lattice grille area, feet, switch, 2 knobs, BC, SW, 5 tubes **$30.00-35.00**

HOFFMAN
Hoffman Radio Corp.
3430 South Hill Street, Los Angeles, California

A-200, table, 1946, plastic, upper front slide rule dial, lower horizontal louvers, 2 knobs, BC, 5 tubes, AC/DC, $45.00-55.00.

A-300, table, 1946, wood, upper front slanted slide rule dial, lower horizontal louvers, 3 knobs, BC, 6 tubes, AC **$40.00-45.00**
A-301, table, wood, upper front slanted slide rule dial, pushbuttons, lower horizontal louvers, 3 knobs, BC **$40.00-50.00**
A-309, table, 1947, wood, upper front slide rule dial, lower cloth grille with metal cut-outs, 2 knobs, BC, 6 tubes, AC/DC **$45.00-55.00**
A-401, table-R/P, 1947, wood, upper front slide rule dial, lower grille, lift top, inner phono, 3 knobs, BC, 6 tubes, AC **$30.00-35.00**
A-500, console-R/P, 1946, wood, lowboy style, inner slide rule dial, 6 pushbuttons, lift top, 3 knobs, BC, 6 tubes, AC **$50.00-65.00**
A-501, console-R/P, 1946, wood, inner right slide rule dial, pushbuttons, door, lower front grille with horizontal bars, 5 knobs, BC, SW, 9 tubes, AC **$65.00-75.00**
A-700, portable, 1947, metal, upper front slide rule dial, lower lattice grille, handle, 2 knobs, BC, 5 tubes, AC/DC/battery **$40.00-45.00**
B-400, table-R/P, 1947, wood, upper front dial, lower, 3/4 lift top, inner phono, 2 knobs, BC, 5 tubes, AC **$30.00-35.00**
B-1000, console-R/P, 1947, wood, modern, tilt-out front, inner left dial, pushbuttons & right phono, 5 knobs, BC, SW, 10 tubes, AC **$65.00-75.00**
B-8002, console-R/P, 1958, wood, inner left dial, right phono, lift top, large front grille area, feet, 6 knobs, BC, FM, 14 tubes, AC **$50.00-65.00**
C-501, console-R/P, 1948, wood, modern, inner right slide rule dial, pushbuttons, door, left lift top, inner phono, 5 knobs, BC, SW, 11 tubes, AC **$65.00-75.00**

C-502, console-R/P, 1948, wood, modern, inner right slide rule dial, 6 pushbuttons, door, left lift top, inner phono, 5 knobs, BC, FM, 15 tubes, AC **$65.00-75.00**
C-503, console-R/P, 1948, wood, modern, inner right slide rule dial, 6 pushbuttons, door, left lift top, inner phono, 5 knobs, BC, SW, 14 tubes, AC **$65.00-75.00**
C-507, console-R/P, 1948, wood, inner right slide rule dial, left pull-out phono drawer, front doors fold open, 4 knobs, BC, FM, 10 tubes, AC **$50.00-65.00**
MP-402 "Nugget," portable, plastic, diagonally divided front with right dial area and left horizontal bars, right side dial, handle, BC ..**$120.00-180.00**

HORN
Herbert H. Horn Radio Manufacturing Co.
1201 South Olive Street, Los Angeles, California

Riviera PR, console-R/P, 1935, wood, Deco, round cabinet, inner front dial, double doors, lift top, inner phono, BC, SW, 6 tubes, AC ....**$550.00+**
Riviera R, console, 1935, wood, Deco, round cabinet, inner front dial, lower grille, double doors, BC, SW, 6 tubes, AC ....**$550.00+**

HOWARD
Howard Radio Company,
451-469 East Ohio Street, Chicago, Illinois

Howard began selling radio parts in 1922 and complete sets in 1924. By 1949, the company was out of business.

4BT, table, 1939, wood, upper front dial, lower cloth grille with cut-outs, 3 knobs, BC, 4 tubes, battery **$30.00-35.00**
20, cathedral, 1931, wood, center front window dial, upper grille with cut-outs, 3 knobs, BC, 7 tubes, AC **$270.00-300.00**
40, console, 1931, wood, lowboy, upper front window dial, lower grille with cut-outs, stretcher base, BC, 8 tubes, AC **$120.00-150.00**
60, console-R/P, 1931, wood, front window dial, lower grille cut-outs, lift top, inner phono, 3 knobs, BC, 9 tubes, AC **$150.00-180.00**
135-AC, console, 1927, wood, highboy, center front escutcheon with window dial, requires separate speaker, 4 legs, 3 knobs, BC, 7 tubes, AC **$100.00-120.00**
150, table, 1925, wood, low rectangular case, slanted 3 dial front panel, 6 knobs, BC, 5 tubes, battery **$95.00-105.00**
200, table, 1925, wood, low rectangular case, 3 dial front panel, 7 knobs, BC, 6 tubes, battery....................................**$110.00-130.00**
214, console, 1937, walnut, upper front oval dial, lower cloth grille with vertical bars, tuning eye, 5 knobs, BC, SW, 14 tubes, AC **$150.00-180.00**
218, console, 1937, walnut, upper front round dial, lower cloth grille with vertical bars, tuning eye, 4 knobs, BC, SW, 11 tubes, AC ..**$120.00-150.00**
225, table, 1937, wood, right front dial, left cloth grille with cut-outs, 4 knobs, BC, SW, 5 tubes, AC **$65.00-75.00**
250, console, 1925, wood, lowboy, inner 3 dial panel, fold-down front, built-in speaker, 6 knobs, BC, 5 tubes, battery **$180.00-200.00**
250, table, 1937, two-tone wood, right front dial, left vertical grille cut-outs, 4 knobs, BC, SW, 5 tubes, AC **$65.00-75.00**
256, table, 1937, walnut, right front round dial, left cloth grille with cut-outs, 3 knobs, BC, 5 tubes, AC **$40.00-50.00**
259-T, table, 1937, walnut with inlay, right front round dial, left cloth grille with vertical bars, BC, 7 tubes, AC/DC.........................**$45.00-55.00**
266-T, table, 1937, walnut, right front round dial, left cloth grille with cut-outs, 4 knobs, BC, 6 tubes, AC **$40.00-50.00**
303, console, 1939, walnut, upper front rectangular dial, 4 pushbuttons, lower grille with center vertical bar, BC, 6 tubes, AC ..**$120.00-140.00**
305, table, 1939, two-tone wood, lower front slide rule dial, pushbuttons, large upper grille, 4 knobs, BC, SW, 5 tubes, AC **$65.00-75.00**
307, table, 1940, two-tone wood, lower front slide rule dial, large upper grille, BC, SW, 5 tubes, AC **$55.00-65.00**
307-TP, table-R/P, 1941, wood, lower right front slide rule dial, left grille, lift top, inner phono, BC, SW, 5 tubes, AC **$30.00-35.00**
308-C, console, 1939, wood, upper front slide rule dial, pushbuttons, lower cloth grille with center vertical bar, BC, SW, 8 tubes, AC ..**$120.00-140.00**
308-TT, console, 1939, walnut, slanted top, pushbuttons, tuning eye, front horizontal grille bars, 4 knobs, BC, SW, 8 tubes, AC....**$150.00-170.00**

318-D, console, 1938, walnut, upper front slide rule dial, lower cloth grille with vertical bars, tuning eye, pushbuttons, 4 knobs, BC, SW, 7 tubes, AC **$110.00-130.00**

368, table, 1937, wood, right front dial, left wrap-over cloth grille with vertical bars, 4 knobs, BC, SW, 8 tubes, AC **$55.00-65.00**

375, table, 1938, wood, large right front slide rule dial, left wrap-around cloth grille with cut-outs, pushbuttons, 4 knobs, BC, SW, 7 tubes, AC **$85.00-95.00**

400, console, 1937, wood, upper front dial, lower cloth grille with horizontal bars, 4 knobs, BC, SW, 12 tubes, AC...................**$150.00-160.00**

418, console, 1938, wood, upper front slide rule dial, lower cloth grille with cut-outs, pushbuttons, 4 knobs, BC, SW, 11 tubes, AC ..**$120.00-150.00**

425, console, 1937, wood, upper front dial, lower cloth grille with horizontal bars, 4 knobs, BC, SW, 14 tubes, AC...................**$140.00-160.00**

468, table, 1938, wood, right front slide rule dial, left wrap-around cloth grille with cut-outs, pushbuttons, BC, SW, 8 tubes, AC ..**$65.00-75.00**

472AC, chairside-R/P, 1948, wood, top dial, upper front grille, lower pull-out phono drawer, storage, 4 knobs, BC, FM, 9 tubes, AC **$75.00-95.00**

472AF, console-R/P, 1948, wood, right front pull-out radio drawer, left pull-out phono drawer, lower criss-cross grille, 4 knobs, BC, FM, 9 tubes, AC **$65.00-75.00**

472C, chairside-R/P, 1948, wood, top dial, upper front grille, lower pull-out phono drawer, storage, 4 knobs, BC, FM, 9 tubes, AC **$75.00-95.00**

472F, console-R/P, 1948, wood, right front pull-out radio drawer, left pull-out phono drawer, lower criss-cross grille, 4 knobs, BC, FM, 9 tubes, AC **$55.00-65.00**

474, table, 1948, plastic, right front square dial over horizontal wrap-around bars, 3 knobs, BC, FM, 5 tubes, AC/DC **$40.00-50.00**

518-S, console, 1940, walnut, upper front rectangular dial, lower horizontal grille bars, tuning eye, 6 pushbuttons, 4 knobs, BC, SW, 12 tubes, AC **$200.00-240.00**

268, table, 1936, wood, step-down top, large right front round dial, left cloth grille with vertical bars, tuning eye, 4 knobs, BC, SW, 7 tubes, AC, $75.00-85.00.

575, table, 1939, two-tone walnut, center front slide rule dial, upper grille, 6 pushbuttons, 4 knobs, BC, SW, 6 tubes, AC **$65.00-75.00**

580, table, 1940, wood, center front slide rule dial, upper grille, 6 pushbuttons, tuning eye, 4 knobs, BC, SW, 8 tubes, AC **$65.00-75.00**

700, table, 1940, plastic, right front dial over horizontal wrap-around louvers, 2 knobs, BC, 5 tubes, AC **$40.00-50.00**

718-APC, console-R/P, 1940, walnut, inner right front slide rule dial, pushbuttons, tuning eye, inner left phono, doors, front grille with vertical bars, 4 knobs, BC, SW, 12 tubes, AC **$75.00-85.00**

718C, console, 1941, walnut, upper front rectangular dial, lower vertical grille bars, 6 pushbuttons, 4 knobs, BC, SW, 12 tubes, AC **$120.00-140.00**

718-FM, console, 1941, wood, upper front slide rule dial, lower cloth grille with vertical bars, pushbuttons, 4 knobs, BC, SW, 14 tubes, AC **$120.00-140.00**

780, table, 1941, two-tone wood, upper front slanted slide rule dial, lower criss-cross grille, 6 knobs, BC, SW, 11 tubes, AC **$50.00-65.00**

808CH, chairside-R/P, 1941, wood, top dial, front grille with cut-outs, lift top, inner phono, storage, BC, SW, 8 tubes, AC........**$110.00-130.00**

901A, table, 1946, two-tone wood, right front dial, left horizontal louvers, 2 knobs, BC, 5 tubes, AC/DC **$30.00-35.00**

901A-I, table, 1946, plastic, right front square dial, left horizontal louvers, horizontal wrap-around bars, 2 knobs, BC, 5 tubes, AC/DC **$45.00-55.00**

482, table, 1948, wood, fm tuner, cube shape, front slide rule dial, 3 knobs, FM, 7 tubes, AC, $55.00-65.00.

901AP, table-R/P, 1946, wood, right front square dial, left grille with horizontal bars, lift top, inner phono, 3 knobs, BC, 5 tubes, AC **$30.00-35.00**

906, table, 1947, wood, lower front slide rule dial, upper 2-section criss-cross grille, 4 knobs, BC, 6 tubes, AC **$40.00-45.00**

906C, chairside-R/P, 1947, wood, dial on top of case, upper front grille, lower pull-out phono drawer, record storage, 4 knobs, BC, 6 tubes, AC **$75.00-95.00**

906-S, table, 1948, wood, lower front slide rule dial, upper 2-section criss-cross grille, 4 knobs, BC, SW, 6 tubes, AC **$45.00-55.00**

906-SB, table, 1948, wood, lower front slide rule dial, upper 2-section criss-cross grille, 4 knobs, BC, SW, AC **$45.00-55.00**

909M, console-R/P, 1947, wood, right pull-out radio drawer, left pull-out phono drawer, lower criss-cross grille, 4 knobs, BC, SW, 9 tubes, AC **$65.00-75.00**

920, table, 1946, plastic, right front square dial, left horizontal louvers, horizontal wrap-around bars, 3 knobs, BC, 4 tubes, battery ..**$40.00-45.00**

A, table, 1925, wood, low rectangular case, 3 dial front panel, 8 knobs, BC, 5 tubes, battery...**$120.00-150.00**

B-13, table, 1934, wood, center "cathedral arch" grille, right side tuning knob, vertical side and horizontal top decorative lines, 2 knobs, BC, 5 tubes, AC/DC **$75.00-85.00**

F-17, console, 1934, wood, lowboy, upper front round dial, lower cloth grille with cut-outs, 6 legs, 4 knobs, BC, SW, 12 tubes, AC ..**$120.00-150.00**

Q, console, 1934, wood, lowboy, upper front dial, lower cloth grille with cut-outs, 6 legs, 3 knobs, BC, 8 tubes, AC **$160.00-190.00**

HUDSON
Wells-Gardner & Co.
2701 No. Kildare Avenue, Chicago, Illinois

Series OEL, console, 1936, wood, large upper front red dial, lower cloth grille with center vertical bars, tuning eye, 4 knobs, BC, SW, 11 tubes, AC **$120.00-150.00**

HUDSON-ROSS
Hudson-Ross Inc.
Chicago, Illinois

Three Little Pigs, cathedral, 1933, ivory or green wood, center front dial, upper grille with hand-painted 3 Little Pigs cut-out, side pig figures, 2 knobs, BC, 4 tubes, AC ....**$2,250.00+**

HYMAN
Henry Hyman & Co., Inc.
476 Broadway, New York, New York

V-60 "Bestone," table, 1925, wood, high rectangular case, 2 dial front panel, BC, 4 tubes, battery **$120.00-140.00**

JACKSON
Jackson Industries, Inc.
58E Cullerton Street, Chicago, Illinois

150, console-R/P, 1951, wood, inner front slide rule dial, lower pull-out phono drawer, double doors, 4 knobs, BC, 7 tubes, AC ..**$50.00-65.00**

254, console-R/P, 1952, wood, inner right front vertical slide rule dial, left pull-out phono drawer, double front doors, 4 knobs, BC, 7 tubes, AC **$50.00-65.00**

255, console-R/P, 1952, wood, inner right front vertical slide rule dial, left pull-out phono drawer, double doors, 4 knobs, BC, FM, 8 tubes, AC **$50.00-65.00**

350, console-R/P, 1951, wood, inner front slide rule dial, lower pull-out phono drawer, double doors, 4 knobs, BC, FM, 8 tubes, AC **$50.00-65.00**

DP-51, portable-R/P, 1952, luggage-style, inner right dial, lattice grille, left phono, lift top, handle, 3 knobs, BC, 5 tubes, AC **$20.00-25.00**

JP-50, portable-R/P, 1952, luggage-style, inner right dial, lattice grille, left phono, lift top, handle, 3 knobs, BC, 5 tubes, AC **$20.00-25.00**

JP-200, portable-R/P, 1952, leatherette, luggage-style, inner right half-round dial, left phono, lift top, handle, 3 knobs, BC, 5 tubes, AC **$20.00-25.00**

JACKSON-BELL
Jackson-Bell Company
Los Angeles, California

The Jackson-Bell Company began business in 1926 selling radios. The company is best known for its midget radios manufactured from 1930 to 1932 with which they grew to be one of the largest radio producers on the west coast. Jackson-Bell was out of business by 1935.

4, cathedral, 1932, wood, front window dial with escutcheon, upper cloth grille with cut-outs, 3 knobs, BC, 4 tubes, AC, $180.00-230.00.

4 "Peter Pan," cathedral, 1932, wood, front window dial, upper grille with Peter Pan cut-out, pointed top, 3 knobs, BC, 4 tubes, AC **$350.00-400.00**

6, table, 1930, wood, center front window dial, right & left scenic tapestry grilles, 3 knobs, BC, AC **$240.00-270.00**

25 "Peter Pan," tombstone, 1932, wood, shouldered, front window dial, upper cloth grille with Peter Pan cut-out, 3 knobs, BC, 5 tubes, AC **$350.00-400.00**

25AV "Pandora," table, 1932, wood, chest-style, carved case, lift top, inner window dial, storage, 3 knobs, BC, 5 tubes, AC..**$320.00-360.00**

26-SW, tombstone, 1932, wood, shouldered, lower front window dial, upper grille with cut-outs, 3 knobs, BC, SW, 6 tubes, AC.......**$150.00-180.00**

34, table, C1933, blue mirror glass case, center front round dial surrounded by grille cut-outs, 2 knobs, BC, 5 tubes, AC ....**$1,250.00+**

38, console, 1932, wood, lowboy, upper front window dial, lower cloth grille with cut-outs, 6 legs, BC, 8 tubes, AC **$150.00-160.00**

54 "Peter Pan," tombstone, 1935, wood, shouldered, lower front window dial, upper cloth grille with Peter Pan cut-out, 3 knobs, BC, 5 tubes, AC **$350.00-400.00**

59, cathedral, 1929, wood, right front thumbwheel dial, center Deco "sunburst" grille cut-outs, pointed top, BC, 7 tubes, AC ..**$180.00-200.00**

60, cathedral, 1929, wood, right front thumbwheel dial, center Deco "sunburst" grille cut-outs, pointed top, BC, 7 tubes, AC ..**$180.00-200.00**

62, cathedral, 1930, wood, lower front window dial, upper round "sunburst" grille, pointed top, 3 knobs, BC, 6 tubes, AC ..**$180.00-200.00**

62, cathedral, 1930, wood, lower front window dial, upper cloth grille with an cut-outs, 3 knobs, BC, 6 tubes, AC **$320.00-360.00**

68, cathedral, 1931, wood, center front window dial, upper cloth grille with tulip cut-outs, 3 knobs, BC, 8 tubes, AC **$300.00-320.00**

84, cathedral, 1931, wood, front window dial, upper cloth grille with Peter Pan cut-out, 3 knobs, BC, 4 tubes, AC **$350.00-400.00**

87, cathedral, 1931, wood, lower front half-round dial, upper cloth grille with tulip cut-outs, decorative spindles, 3 knobs, BC, 7 tubes, AC..**$300.00-320.00**

Peter Pan, cathedral or tombstone, various models, wood, front window dial, cloth grille with Peter Pan cut-out, 3 knobs, BC, AC.........**$350.00-400.00**

Swan, cathedral or tombstone, various models, wood, front window dial, cloth grille with a swan cut-out, 3 knobs, BC, AC **$320.00-360.00**

JEFFERSON-TRAVIS
Jefferson-Travis, Inc.
380 Second Avenue, New York, New York

MR-3, portable, 1947, leatherette, right front slide rule dial, left round grille with "JT" cut-out, handle, 3 knobs, BC, SW, 5 tubes, AC/DC/battery **$30.00-35.00**

JEWEL
Jewel Radio Corp.
583 Sixth Avenue, New York, New York

300, table, 1947, plastic, right front round dial, left horizontal wrap-around louvers, 2 knobs, BC, 4 tubes, AC/DC **$40.00-50.00**

304 "Pixie," portable, 1948, alligator, inner right dial, flip-open lid, outer perforated grille, strap, 2 knobs, BC, 4 tubes, battery ..**$40.00-50.00**

501, table, 1947, wood, upper front slanted slide rule dial, lower horizontal grille openings, 2 knobs, BC, 4 tubes, AC/DC......... **$35.00-40.00**

502, table, 1947, wood with inlay, upper front slanted slide rule dial, lower horizontal louvers, 2 knobs, BC, 4 tubes, AC/DC......... **$40.00-50.00**

504, table, 1947, wood, upper front slanted slide rule dial, lower grille with large block openings, 2 knobs, BC, 4 tubes, AC/DC...... **$45.00-55.00**

505 "Pin Up," wall-C, 1947, plastic, lower right front window dial, center clock over vertical wrap-over bars, 2 knobs, BC, 4 tubes, AC **$85.00-95.00**

801 "Trixie," portable, 1948, alligator, inner right dial, fold-open door, strap, 3 knobs, BC, 4 tubes, AC/DC/battery **$45.00-55.00**

814, portable, 1948, plastic, lower front recessed dial panel, top grille bars, strap, 2 knobs, BC, 4 tubes, battery......................**$40.00-50.00**

915, table-C, 1950, plastic, right front round dial, left clock, center perforated grille, 4 knobs, BC, 4 tubes, AC **$30.00-35.00**

935, table-C, 1949, plastic, right front round dial, left clock, center horizontal bars, 5 knobs, BC, 5 tubes, AC, $30.00-35.00.

281/521, table, 1921, mahogany, 2 units – receiver & 2 stage amp, 3 dial receiver panel, lift tops, 8 knobs, BC, SW, LW, 3 tubes, battery, $1,100.00-1,200.00.

311, portable, 1923, oak, inner left control panel, right storage, lift top, handle, BC, 1 exposed tubes, battery $850.00-950.00

366A, console, 1932, wood, lowboy, inner front quarter-round dial, lower grille with cut-outs, double front doors, 6 legs, 5 knobs, BC, SW, LW, 12 tubes, AC $200.00-230.00

525, table/amp, 1921, wood, tall rectangular case, 2 stage amp, 2 knobs, 2 tubes, battery $800.00-850.00

826B, console, 1930, wood, large console with two chassis-one for broadcast and one for shortwave-separate upper right & left front window dials, lower center grille with cut-outs, 2 front knobs, 2 right side knobs, BC, SW, 12 tubes, AC $580.00-690.00

III, portable, 1923, leatherette, inner black panel, lift-off cover with storage, handle, 4 knobs, BC, 3 exposed tubes, battery ..$850.00-950.00

VI, table, 1924, wood, tall rectangular case, 2 dial slant front panel, 4 knobs, BC, 4 exposed tubes, battery $650.00-700.00

X, table, 1923, mahogany, inner 2 dial slanted panel, fold-up top, lower speaker grille with cut-outs, 4 knobs, BC, 3 exposed tubes, battery $1,200.00-1,300.00

XI, table, 1924, mahogany, inner 2 dial slanted panel, fold-up top, lower speaker grille with cut-outs, 4 knobs, BC, 4 exposed tubes, battery $1,200.00-1,300.00

XV, table, 1924, wood, tall rectangular case, 2 dial slant front panel, 7 knobs, BC, 5 exposed tubes, battery $580.00-640.00

XXX, table, 1925, wood, rectangular case, slant front panel with 2 window dials, 5 knobs, BC, 5 tubes, battery....................$530.00-580.00

V, table, 1923, wood, high rectangular case, 2 dial slant front panel, 4 knobs, BC, 3 exposed tubes, battery, $530.00-580.00.

KENT

402A, table, 1939, metal, midget, right front dial over horizontal wrap-around bars, 2 knobs, BC, 3 tubes, AC/DC $85.00-95.00

422A, table, C1941, metal, midget, right front dial over horizontal wrap-around bars, handle, 2 knobs, BC, 4 tubes, AC/DC...... $85.00-95.00

422, table, 1940, metal, midget, right front dial over horizontal wrap-around bars, handle, 2 knobs, BC, 4 tubes, AC/DC, $85.00-95.00.

KING

King Quality Products, Inc., Buffalo, New York
King-Buffalo, Inc., Buffalo, New York
King-Hinners Radio Co., Inc., Buffalo, New York
King Manufacturing Corporation, Buffalo, New York

King Quality Products, Inc., began business in 1924. The company was owned by Sears, Roebuck and in the mid-twenties produced radios with both the Sears Silvertone as well as the King label. By the early 1930s, King was out of business.

10, table, 1926, wood, low rectangular case, 3 dial black front panel, 5 knobs, BC, 5 tubes, battery......................................$140.00-160.00

25, table, 1925, wood, low rectangular case, 3 dial front panel, meter, 5 knobs, BC, 5 tubes, battery......................................$120.00-150.00

25-C, console, 1925, wood, inner right 3 dial panel & left speaker grille with cut-outs, fold-down front, lower storage, meter, 5 knobs, BC, 5 tubes, battery..$200.00-230.00

30, table, 1925, wood, low rectangular case, slanted 3 dial front panel, 4 knobs, BC, 5 tubes, battery......................................$110.00-130.00

30-S, table, 1925, wood, low rectangular case, left front slanted 3 dial panel, right speaker grille with cut-outs, 4 knobs, BC, 5 tubes, battery $150.00-170.00

61, table, 1926, two-tone wood, low rectangular case, 3 dial front panel, 5 knobs, BC, 6 tubes, battery $110.00-130.00

61-H, console, 1926, wood, inner left 3 dial panel & right speaker grille with cut-outs, fold-down front, lower storage, 5 knobs, BC, 6 tubes, battery $200.00-230.00

62, table, 1926, two-tone wood, rectangular case, oval front panel with window dial, 3 knobs, BC, 6 tubes, battery.................$85.00-115.00

4, upright table, wood, small case, lower half-round dial, upper round grille with cut-outs, 2 knobs, $200.00-230.00.

80-H "Viking," console, 1927, wood, inner right 1 dial panel & right speaker grille with cut-outs, fold-down front, lower storage, 3 knobs, BC, 6 tubes, battery, $200.00-230.00.

63, console, 1926, wood, lowboy, inner window dial, doors, built in loud speaker, 4 legs with center stretcher, 3 knobs, BC, 6 tubes, battery $110.00-130.00
71 "Commander," table, 1926, wood, low rectangular case, center front window dial, loop antenna, feet, 2 knobs, BC, 6 tubes, battery $180.00-200.00
80 "Baronet," table, 1927, wood, low rectangular case, center front dial, fluted columns, 3 knobs, BC, 6 tubes, battery $110.00-130.00
81 "Crusader," table, 1927, two-tone wood, low rectangular case, oval front panel with 1 dial, 3 knobs, BC, 6 tubes, battery ..$95.00-115.00
81-H "Chevalier," console, 1927, walnut, highboy, inner 1 dial oval panel & upper round grille, double doors, 3 knobs, BC, 6 tubes, battery $180.00-200.00
97 "Royal," console, 1929, wood, upper center window dial with escutcheon, lower grille with decorative "spadelike" cut-outs, 4 legs with stretcher, 2 knobs, BC, 8 tubes, AC $120.00-140.00
98 "Imperial," console, 1929, wood, upper center window dial with escutcheon, lower grille with decorative "spadelike" cut-outs, 4 legs with stretcher, 2 knobs, BC, 9 tubes, AC $130.00-150.00
101 "Monarch," console, 1929, wood, upper center window dial with escutcheon, lower grille with decorative "spadelike" cut-outs, 4 legs with stretcher, 2 knobs, BC, 7 tubes, AC $110.00-130.00
FF, table, 1929, two-tone metal, low rectangular case, center front window dial, 3 knobs, BC, 6 tubes, AC................................$85.00-95.00

KINGSTON
Kingston Radio, Kokomo, Indiana

Founded in 1933, Kingston manufactured many farm battery radios which were sold under other labels, such as Airline and Truetone. The company was out of business by 1951.

55, table, 1934, wood, step-down sides, right front dial, center cloth grille with cut-outs, 2 knobs, BC, 5 tubes, AC/DC $75.00-95.00
600A, tombstone, 1934, wood, Deco, center front window dial, upper cloth grille with cut-outs, 3 knobs, BC, 6 tubes, AC ..$150.00-180.00
600B, console, 1934, wood, Deco, upper front dial, lower grille area, 3 knobs, BC, 6 tubes, AC $150.00-180.00

KITCHENAIRE
The Radio Craftsmen, Inc.
1341 South Michigan Avenue, Chicago, Illinois

No #, wall, 1946, metal, kitchen wall set with right & left side shelves, herringbone grille, top louvers, 2 knobs, BC, AC/DC $240.00-270.00

KNIGHT
Allied Radio Corporation
833 West Jackson Boulevard, Chicago, Illinois

4D-450, portable, 1948, leatherette & plastic, upper front slide rule dial, lower lattice grille, handle, 2 knobs, BC, 4 tubes, battery $30.00-35.00
4E-450, portable, 1948, leatherette & plastic, upper front slide rule dial, lower lattice grille, handle, 2 knobs, BC, 4 tubes, battery ..$30.00-35.00
4E-515, table, 1948, walnut plastic, upper right dial knob, left grille with horizontal bars, rounded corners and shoulders, 2 knobs, BC, 4 tubes, AC/DC $35.00-45.00
4E-516, table, 1948, ivory plastic, upper right dial knob, left grille with horizontal bars, rounded corners and shoulders, 2 knobs, BC, 4 tubes, AC/DC $35.00-45.00
4F-515, table, 1949, walnut plastic, upper right dial knob, left grille with horizontal bars, rounded corners and shoulders, 2 knobs, BC, 4 tubes, AC/DC $35.00-45.00
4F-516, table, 1949, ivory plastic, upper right dial knob, left grille with horizontal bars, rounded corners and shoulders, 2 knobs, BC, 4 tubes, AC/DC $35.00-45.00
4G-420, table-R/P, 1950, front slide rule dial, lift top, inner phono, 3 knobs, BC, 4 tubes, AC $30.00-35.00
5A-150, table, 1946, plastic, upper front slanted slide rule dial, lower horizontal louvers, 2 knobs, BC, 5 tubes, AC/DC.............$30.00-35.00
5A-152, table, 1947, plastic, upper front slanted slide rule dial, lower horizontal louvers, 2 knobs, BC, 5 tubes, AC/DC.............$30.00-35.00
5A-154, table, 1947, two-tone wood, upper front slanted slide rule dial, lower horizontal louvers, 2 knobs, BC, 5 tubes, AC/DC .. $45.00-55.00
5A-190, table, 1947, plastic, step-down top, right front dial, left horizontal grille bars, 2 knobs, BC, 9 tubes, AC/DC $50.00-65.00
5B-160, table-R/P, 1947, leatherette, slanted slide rule dial, front horizontal louvers, open top phono, 3 knobs, BC, 4 tubes, AC ..$25.00-30.00
5B-175, table, 1947, walnut plastic, right front square dial, left vertical wrap-over louvers, 2 knobs, BC, 5 tubes, AC/DC $45.00-55.00
5B-176, table, 1947, ivory plastic, right front square dial, left vertical wrap-over louvers, 2 knobs, BC, 5 tubes, AC/DC $45.00-55.00
5B-185, table-R/P, 1947, wood, upper front dial, lower criss-cross grille, lift top, inner phono, 2 knobs, BC, 4 tubes, AC $40.00-45.00
5C-185, table-R/P, 1947, wood, upper front dial, lower criss-cross grille, lift top, inner phono, 2 knobs, BC, 4 tubes, AC $40.00-45.00
5C-290, portable, 1947, leatherette, top dial, lower horizontal louvers, handle, 3 knobs, BC, 4 tubes, AC/DC/battery...............$20.00-25.00
5D-250, table, 1948, walnut plastic, raised top, upper front slanted slide rule dial, lower horizontal louvers, 2 knobs, BC, 5 tubes, AC/DC $40.00-50.00
5D-251, table, 1948, ivory plastic, raised top, upper front slanted slide rule dial, lower horizontal louvers, 2 knobs, BC, 5 tubes, AC/DC $40.00-50.00
5D-290, portable, 1948, leatherette, top dial, lower horizontal louvers, handle, 3 knobs, BC, 4 tubes, AC/DC/battery...............$20.00-25.00
5D-455, portable, 1948, leatherette/plastic, upper front slide rule dial, lower lattice grille, handle, 2 knobs, BC, 5 tubes, AC/DC/battery $30.00-35.00
5E-250, table, 1948, walnut plastic, raised top, upper front slanted slide rule dial, lower horizontal louvers, 2 knobs, BC, 5 tubes, AC/DC $40.00-50.00
5E-251, table, 1948, ivory plastic, raised top, upper front slanted slide rule dial, lower horizontal louvers, 2 knobs, BC, 5 tubes, AC/DC....... $40.00-50.00
5E-455, portable, 1948, leatherette/plastic, upper front slide rule dial, lower lattice grille, handle, 2 knobs, BC, 5 tubes, AC/DC/battery $30.00-35.00
5E-457, portable, 1949, plastic, lower front slide rule dial, upper grille with horizontal louvers, sloping sides and rounded shoulders, top leather handle, 2 knobs, BC, 5 tubes, AC/DC/battery....$50.00-60.00
5F-525, table, 1949, brown plastic, right front round dial, left checkerboard grille, ridged base, 2 knobs, BC, 5 tubes, AC/DC $35.00-45.00
5F-526, table, 1949, ivory plastic, right front round dial, left checkerboard grille, ridged base, 2 knobs, BC, 5 tubes, AC/DC $35.00-45.00
5F-565, portable, 1949, leatherette, right front square dial, horizontal louvers, handle, 3 knobs, BC, 5 tubes, AC/DC/battery $35.00-40.00
5F-600 "Lullaby," radio/bed lamp, 1949, walnut plastic, right front round dial, left vertical grille bars, built-in bed lamp, hooks for headboard mounting, 2 knobs, BC, 5 tubes, AC/DC $75.00-85.00

5F-601 "Lullaby," radio/bed lamp, 1949, ivory plastic, right front round dial, left vertical grille bars, built-in bed lamp, hooks for headboard mounting, 2 knobs, BC, 5 tubes, AC/DC **$75.00-85.00**

5H-570, table, 1951, plastic, diagonally divided front panel with right round dial, 2 knobs, BC, 5 tubes, AC/DC...................... **$25.00-30.00**

5H-605, table-C, 1951, plastic, lower right front dial over horizontal bars, upper square clock, 4 knobs, BC, 5 tubes, AC **$45.00-55.00**

5H-700, table-R/P, 1951, cloth-covered, right front square dial, left grille, switch, 3/4 lift top, inner phono, 3 knobs, BC, 5 tubes, AC..**$25.00-30.00**

5J-705, table, 1952, plastic, right front square dial, left vertical wrap-over grille bars, 2 knobs, BC, 5 tubes, AC............**$40.00-50.00**

5K-715, table-C, 1953, wood, right front square dial, left square alarm clock, raised center with vertical wrap-over grille bars, 5 knobs, BC, 5 tubes, AC **$30.00-35.00**

6A-122, table, 1946, wood, upper front slanted slide rule dial, lower cloth grille, 4 knobs, BC, SW, 6 tubes, AC/DC **$40.00-50.00**

6A-127, portable, 1946, leatherette, upper front slanted slide rule dial, lower criss-cross grille, handle, 3 knobs, BC, 6 tubes, AC/DC/battery **$30.00-35.00**

6A-195, table, 1947, plastic, right front square dial, left vertical wrap-over grille bars, 2 knobs, BC, 6 tubes, AC/DC **$40.00-50.00**

6B-122, table, 1947, wood, upper front slanted slide rule dial, lower rectangular grille, rounded front corners, 4 knobs, BC, SW, 6 tubes, AC/DC **$40.00-50.00**

6B-127, portable, 1947, leatherette, upper front slanted slide rule dial, lower criss-cross grille, top leather handle, 3 knobs, BC, 6 tubes, AC/DC/battery **$35.00-40.00**

6B-155, table, 1947, walnut plastic, upper front slanted slide rule dial, lower grille with horizontal bars, rounded corners, 2 top knobs, BC, 5 tubes, AC/DC **$50.00-60.00**

6B-156, table, 1947, ivory plastic, upper front slanted slide rule dial, lower grille with horizontal bars, rounded corners, 2 top knobs, BC, 5 tubes, AC/DC **$50.00-60.00**

6C-122, table, 1947, wood, upper front slanted slide rule dial, lower rectangular grille, rounded front corners, 4 knobs, BC, SW, 6 tubes, AC/DC **$40.00-50.00**

6C-127, portable, 1947, leatherette, upper front slanted slide rule dial, lower criss-cross grille, top leather handle, 3 knobs, BC, 6 tubes, AC/DC/battery **$35.00-40.00**

6C-225, table, 1947, walnut plastic, upper front slide rule dial, lower horizontal louvers, sloping sides and rounded shoulders, 3 knobs, BC, 6 tubes, AC/DC **$40.00-50.00**

6C-226, table, 1947, ivory plastic, upper front slide rule dial, lower horizontal louvers, sloping sides and rounded shoulders, 3 knobs, BC, 6 tubes, AC/DC **$40.00-50.00**

6D-225, table, 1948, walnut plastic, upper front slide rule dial, lower horizontal louvers, sloping sides and rounded shoulders, 3 knobs, BC, 6 tubes, AC/DC **$40.00-50.00**

6D-226, table, 1948, ivory plastic, upper front slide rule dial, lower horizontal louvers, sloping sides and rounded shoulders, 3 knobs, BC, 6 tubes, AC/DC **$40.00-50.00**

6D-235, table, 1948, wood, curved sides, right front dial, left vertical grille bars, 3 knobs, BC, AC/DC **$50.00-65.00**

6D-360, console-R/P, 1948, two-tone wood, upper front slide rule dial, center pull-out phono drawer, lower grille, 5 knobs, BC, SW, 6 tubes, AC **$75.00-85.00**

6F-235, table, 1949, wood, curved sides, right front dial, left vertical grille bars, 3 knobs, BC, AC/DC **$50.00-65.00**

6G-400 "Roamer," portable, 1950, leatherette, upper left front slide rule dial, lower grille with horizontal bars, top leather handle, 2 knobs, BC, 5 tubes, AC/DC/battery **$35.00-45.00**

6H-580, table, 1951, plastic, large front dial with horizontal decorative lines, 2 knobs, BC, 6 tubes, AC/DC **$30.00-35.00**

6K-718, portable, 1953, two-tone leatherette, center front round dial with inner perforated grille, handle, 2 knobs, BC, 5 tubes, AC/DC/battery **$40.00-50.00**

7B-220, table, 1947, wood, upper front slanted slide rule dial, lower criss-cross grille, 4 knobs, BC, FM, 6 tubes, AC/DC **$40.00-50.00**

7C-220, table, 1947, wood, upper front slanted slide rule dial, lower criss-cross grille, 4 knobs, BC, FM, 6 tubes, AC/DC **$40.00-50.00**

7D-405, table-R/P, 1948, wood, upper front slide rule dial, lower grille, lift top, inner phono, 4 knobs, BC, 6 tubes, AC **$30.00-35.00**

8B-210, table-R/P, 1947, wood, front dial, 3/4 lift top, inner phono, 4 knobs, BC, 8 tubes, AC **$30.00-35.00**

8G-200, table, 1950, mahogany plastic, right front airplane dial, left front grille, sloping sides, "pedestal" base, 4 knobs, BC, FM, 8 tubes, AC/DC **$55.00-65.00**

8G-201, table, 1950, ivory plastic, right front airplane dial, left front grille, sloping sides, "pedestal" base, 4 knobs, BC, FM, 8 tubes, AC/DC **$55.00-65.00**

11C-300, console-R/P, 1947, wood, inner right slide rule dial, fold-down door, left pull-out phono drawer, lower grille, 4 knobs, BC, FM, 11 tubes, AC **$65.00-75.00**

11D-302, console-R/P, 1949, wood, inner right slide rule dial, door, left fold-down phono, lower grille, 4 knobs, BC, FM, 11 tubes, AC **$65.00-75.00**

14F-490, console-R/P, 1949, wood, top lid with inner right slide rule dial and inner left phono, lower front grille behind double doors, tuning eye, 5 knobs, BC, FM, 14 tubes, AC **$80.00-90.00**

19F-492, console-R/P, 1949, wood, top lid with inner right slide rule dial and inner left phono, lower front grille behind double doors, tuning eye, two chassis, 5 knobs, BC, FM, 19 tubes, AC **$90.00-100.00**

49-J6, table, 1940, plastic, right front dial, left horizontal wrap-around bars, pushbuttons, 3 knobs, BC **$55.00-65.00**

68B-151K, table, wood, right front black oval dial, left cloth grille with cut-outs, tuning eye, 4 knobs, BC, 7 tubes, battery, $50.00-65.00.

94S-445, table-C, 1955, wood, right front square dial, left square alarm clock, center horizontal grille bars, 5 knobs, BC, 5 tubes, AC **$30.00-35.00**

96-326, table-R/P/Rec, 1951, leatherette, inner left dial, phono, recorder, lift top, handle, 4 knobs, BC, 6 tubes, AC **$25.00-30.00**

449, portable, 1950, leatherette, left front slide rule dial, lower horizontal grille bars, handle, 2 knobs, BC, 5 tubes, AC/DC/battery ..**$25.00-30.00**

2117, tombstone, wood, lower front large round dial with center sailing ship, upper cloth grille with cut-outs, 4 knobs, BC, SW.........**$120.00-140.00**

B17115, portable, 1941, leatherette, inner right front dial, left grille with horizontal bars, fold-in front, handle, 2 knobs, BC, 6 tubes, AC/DC/battery **$25.00-30.00**

KODEL
The Kodel Manufacturing Company
118 Third Street, West, Cincinnati, Ohio
The Kodel Radio Corporation
503 East Pearl Street, Cincinnati, Ohio

The Kodel Manufacturing Company was formed in 1924 by Clarence Ogden, an inventor of battery chargers. The company's radio business boomed along with their production of battery eliminators. The advent of AC radio, however, was the beginning of the end for Kodel and they were out of business by the 1930s.

Big Five "Logodyne," console, 1925, mahogany, desk-style, inner 3 dial panel, fold-down front, right built-in speaker, 7 knobs, BC, 5 tubes, battery **$180.00-200.00**

Big Five "Logodyne," table, 1925, mahogany, low rectangular case, slanted 3 dial front panel, 7 knobs, BC, 5 tubes, battery **$120.00-150.00**

C-11 "Gold Star," table, 1924, leatherette, tall rectangular case, 1 dial front panel, 2 knobs, BC, 1 tube, battery, $190.00-210.00.

C-12 "Gold Star," table, 1924, wood, rectangular case, center front dial, 3 knobs, BC, 2 tubes, battery $160.00-190.00

C-13 "Gold Star," table, 1924, wood, low rectangular case, 2 dial front panel, 5 knobs, BC, 3 tubes, battery $160.00-180.00

C-14, table, 1924, wood, low rectangular case, 2 dial front panel, 5 knobs, BC, 4 tubes, battery..$140.00-160.00

Standard Five "Logodyne," console, 1925, mahogany, slanted 3 dial center panel, right built-in speaker, door, 5 knobs, BC, 5 tubes, battery $180.00-200.00

Standard Five "Logodyne," table, 1925, mahogany, low rectangular case, 3 dial front panel, 5 knobs, BC, 5 tubes, battery $120.00-140.00

KOLSTER
Federal Telegraph Company
Woolworth Building, New York, New York
Federal-Brandes, Inc.
Newark, New Jersey

To avoid any confusion with the rival Federal Telephone & Telegraph Company, the Federal Telegraph Company used the Kolster name for its radio line which began in 1925. Plagued with internal problems from the beginning and after many reorganization attempts, Kolster was out of business by 1930.

6D, table, 1926, wood, rectangular case, center front dial with escutcheon, lift top, 3 knobs, BC, 6 tubes, battery, $75.00-85.00.

6E, console, 1926, wood, lowboy, upper front dial, center grille with fleur-de-lis cut-outs, lower storage, 3 knobs, BC, 6 tubes, battery $170.00-190.00

6G, console, 1926, wood, inner front dial, lower grille, double doors, storage, 3 knobs, BC, 6 tubes, battery $180.00-200.00

6H, console, 1926, wood, lowboy, inner front dial, lower grille, double doors, storage, 3 knobs, BC, 6 tubes, battery...........$180.00-200.00

6J, table, 1927, wood, low rectangular case, center front window dial with large escutcheon, 3 knobs, BC, 7 tubes, AC......$130.00-150.00

7A, table, 1926, two-tone wood, low rectangular case, center front dial, 3 knobs, BC, 7 tubes, battery.......................................$110.00-130.00

7B, table, 1926, two-tone wood, center front dial, upper built-in speaker, 3 knobs, BC, 7 tubes, battery $130.00-150.00

8A, table, 1926, wood, center front window dial with escutcheon, 3 knobs, BC, 8 tubes, battery $110.00-130.00

8B, console, 1926, wood, center front window dial, upper built-in speaker, left side loop antenna, 3 knobs, BC, 8 tubes, battery..$240.00-270.00

8C, console, 1926, wood, inner dial, fold-down front, upper speaker, built-in loop antenna, 3 knobs, BC, 8 tubes, battery..$270.00-300.00

K-20, table, 1928, wood & metal, rectangular case, center front window dial, carvings, paw feet, 3 knobs, BC, 7 tubes, AC $110.00-130.00

K-43, console, 1929, wood, inner dial with escutcheon, lower grille with cut-outs, double front doors, 3 knobs, BC, 8 tubes, AC $160.00-190.00

K-44, console, 1929, walnut, inner dial with escutcheon, lower grille with cut-outs, double front doors, stretcher base, 3 knobs, BC, 9 tubes, AC $150.00-180.00

K-45, console, 1928, wood, lowboy, right side window dial, large front floral grille cloth, remote control, BC, 11 tubes, AC ..$470.00-530.00

K-48, console, 1931, wood, lowboy, upper front window dial with escutcheon, lower grille with cut-outs, 3 knobs, BC, 7 tubes, AC $120.00-150.00

K-60, tombstone, 1931, wood, center front window dial, upper cloth grille with repwood cut-outs, 3 knobs, BC, 7 tubes, AC $130.00-160.00

K-70, console, 1931, wood, upper front window dial, lower cloth grille with cut-outs, 3 knobs, BC, 8 tubes, AC $130.00-150.00

K-80, console, 1931, wood, carved front panel with upper window dial, lower cloth grille with 2 vertical bars, 3 knobs, BC, 9 tubes, AC..$130.00-160.00

K-100, console, 1932, wood, upper front window dial, lower cloth grille with cut-outs, 3 knobs, BC, 7 tubes $140.00-160.00

K-110, tombstone, 1932, wood, shouldered, center front window dial, upper cloth grille with cut-outs, 3 knobs, BC, 8 tubes, AC..$130.00-150.00

K-114, tombstone, 1932, wood, shouldered, center front window dial, upper cloth grille with cut-outs, 3 knobs, BC, 9 tubes, battery..$85.00-105.00

K-120, console, 1932, wood, lowboy, upper front window dial, lower cloth grille with cut-outs, 3 knobs, BC, 8 tubes, AC ..$110.00-130.00

K-124, console, 1932, wood, upper front window dial, lower cloth grille with cut-outs, 3 knobs, BC, 9 tubes, battery...............$85.00-105.00

K-130, console, 1932, wood, lowboy, upper front window dial, lower cloth grille with cut-outs, 6 legs, BC, 9 tubes, AC......$130.00-150.00

K-140, console, 1932, wood, lowboy, upper front window dial, lower grille with cut-outs, doors, 6 legs, 3 knobs, BC, 10 tubes, AC $150.00-190.00

K-21, table, 1928, wood, rectangular case, center front window dial, front carvings, paw feet, 3 knobs, BC, 8 tubes, AC, $120.00-140.00.

K-90, console, 1931, wood, inner front window dial, lower cloth grille with 2 vertical bars, double sliding doors, 3 knobs, BC, 10 tubes, AC, $120.00-150.00.

KOYO

KR-4S1 "Parrot," portable, plastic, right front dial, left vertical grille bars, BC, battery..$85.00-115.00

KRAFT
Kraft Mfg. & Dist. Co.

Puppytune, table-lamp, 1949, radio/lamp shaped like puppy, right square dial, left grille, 2 knobs, BC, AC/DC $200.00-230.00

LAFAYETTE
Radio Wire Television, Inc.
Wholesale Radio Service Co., Inc.
100 Sixth Avenue, New York, New York

22, console, wood, upper front slide rule dial with center tuning eye, lower cloth grille with center vertical bars, 6 pushbuttons, 5 knobs, BC, SW $130.00-160.00

60, tombstone, 1935, wood, center front round dial, upper cloth grille with horizontal bars, 4 knobs, BC, SW $130.00-160.00

A-22, table, 1937, wood, left front rectangular dial, right front grille with cut-outs, 3 knobs, BC, SW, 6 tubes, AC/DC $35.00-45.00

A-23, table, 1937, wood, right front rectangular dial, left decorative grille with cut-outs, rounded top front edge, 4 knobs, BC, SW, LW, 7 tubes, AC/DC $50.00-60.00

B-14, table, 1938, two-tone wood, right front oval dial, left wrap-around grille with horizontal bars, tuning eye, 5 knobs, BC, SW, 8 tubes, AC $75.00-85.00

B-18, console, 1938, wood, upper front oval dial, lower cloth grille with 2 vertical bars, tuning eye, 5 knobs, BC, SW, 8 tubes, AC $120.00-150.00

B-20, console-R/P, 1938, wood, front oval dial, lower cloth grille with vertical bars, tuning eye, lift top, inner phono, 4 knobs, BC, SW, 8 tubes, AC $120.00-150.00

B-25, table, 1938, two-tone wood, right front round dial, left wrap-around cloth grille with horizontal bars, tuning eye, pushbuttons, 5 knobs, BC, SW, 8 tubes, AC $85.00-95.00

B-26, console, 1938, wood, upper front round dial, lower cloth grille with 2 vertical bars, tuning eye, pushbuttons, 5 knobs, BC, SW, 8 tubes, AC $150.00-190.00

B-34, console, 1938, wood, step-down top, upper front round dial, lower cloth grille with center vertical bar, tuning eye, pushbuttons, 5 knobs, BC, SW, 11 tubes, AC $150.00-190.00

B-38, console-R/P, 1938, walnut, front round dial, lower cloth grille with vertical bars, tuning eye, pushbuttons, lift top, inner phono, 5 knobs, BC, SW, 11 tubes, AC $150.00-180.00

B-44, console, 1938, wood, upper front round dial, lower cloth grille with center vertical bars, tuning eye, pushbuttons, 5 knobs, BC, SW, 13 tubes, AC $150.00-190.00

B-81, table, 1937, wood, right front oval dial with tuning eye above, left wrap-around grille with horizontal bars, 4 knobs, BC, SW, 8 tubes, AC $75.00-85.00

B-82, console, 1937, wood, upper front large oval dial with tuning eye above, lower grille with three vertical bars, 4 knobs, BC, SW, 8 tubes, AC $130.00-150.00

B-88, console, 1937, wood, upper front large oval dial with tuning eye above, lower grille with three vertical bars, rounded shoulders and front corners, 4 knobs, BC, SW, 11 tubes, AC $140.00-160.00

B-98, console, 1937, wood, upper front oval dial with tuning eye above, lower grille with three vertical bars, terraced shoulders, two speakers, 5 knobs, BC, SW, 13 tubes, AC $160.00-180.00

B-101, console, 1940, walnut, upper front slide rule dial, lower cloth grille with vertical bars, pushbuttons, 4 knobs, BC, SW, 9 tubes, AC $110.00-130.00

B-102, console-R/P, 1940, walnut, inner right dial, pushbuttons, inner left phono, lift top, front grille with horizontal bars, BC, SW, 9 tubes, AC $120.00-150.00

B-103, table, 1940, wood, right front slide rule dial, left horizontal grille bars, pushbuttons, 4 knobs, BC, SW, 9 tubes, AC $65.00-75.00

BA-1, chairside, 1938, wood, top round dial and, rounded front with lower horizontal grille bars, storage, 3 knobs, BC, SW, 7 tubes, AC/DC $160.00-180.00

BA-2, table, 1938, two-tone walnut, left front airplane dial, left wrap-around horizontal grille bars, tuning eye, 4 knobs, BC, SW, 8 tubes, AC/DC $75.00-85.00

BA-19, table, 1938, wood, right front round airplane dial, left cloth grille with horizontal bars, tuning eye, 3 knobs, BC, SW, 7 tubes, AC/DC $75.00-85.00

BB-27, table, 1939, wood, right front dial, curved left wrap-around grille, pushbuttons, tuning eye, 3 knobs, BC, SW, 6 tubes, AC/DC $65.00-75.00

BE-78, table, 1940, ivory plastic, small right side dial, round left grille with 2 horizontal bars, 6 pushbuttons, 2 knobs, BC, 5 tubes, AC/DC $120.00-150.00

BE-79, table, 1940, walnut plastic, small right side dial, round left grille with 2 horizontal bars, 6 pushbuttons, 2 knobs, BC, 5 tubes, AC/DC $120.00-150.00

C-3, table, 1938, ivory plastic, large center front airplane dial, right & left side wrap-around grilles with horizontal bars, 2 knobs, BC, 6 tubes, AC/DC $85.00-105.00

C-4, table, 1938, red plastic, large center front airplane dial, right & left side wrap-around grilles with horizontal bars, 2 knobs, BC, 6 tubes, AC/DC $110.00-130.00

C-5, table, 1938, black plastic, large center front airplane dial, right & left side wrap-around grilles with horizontal bars, 2 knobs, BC, 6 tubes, AC/DC $85.00-105.00

C-16, table, 1939, wood, right front slide rule dial, left grille with three horizontal bars, rounded corners, 3 knobs, BC, SW, 5 tubes, AC $40.00-50.00

C-19, table, 1939, wood, right front slide rule dial, left grille with three horizontal bars, rounded corners, tuning eye, 3 knobs, BC, SW, 6 tubes, AC $45.00-55.00

C-21, table, 1939, wood, right front large slide rule dial, left grille with vertical and horizontal bars, rounded top front, 4 knobs, BC, SW, 6 tubes, AC $50.00-60.00

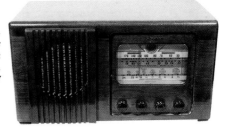

C-117, table, 1940, wood, right front slide rule dial, left grille with vertical bars, tuning eye, 4 knobs, BC, SW, 7 tubes, AC, $55.00-65.00.

145

C-119, table, 1941, wood, right front slide rule dial, left grille with horizontal louvers, 4 knobs, BC, SW, 10 tubes, AC/DC, $40.00-50.00.

C-47, table, 1937, wood, right front oval dial, left wrap-around grille with horizontal bars, tuning eye, 5 knobs, BC, SW, 9 tubes, AC/DC **$60.00-70.00**

C-48, table, 1937, wood, right front oval dial, left wrap-around grille with horizontal bars, tuning eye, 5 knobs, BC, SW, LW, 9 tubes, AC/DC **$60.00-70.00**

C-57, table, 1938, wood, right front dial, left cloth grille with horizontal bars, tuning eye, 5 knobs, BC, SW, 9 tubes, AC/DC **$65.00-75.00**

C-69 "Little Symphony," table-R/P, 1938, wood, left front dial, right cloth grille with 3 vertical bars, tuning eye, lift top, inner phono, 5 knobs, BC, SW, 9 tubes, AC/DC **$55.00-65.00**

C-77, table, 1938, wood, right front dial, left cloth grille with horizontal bars, tuning eye, 5 knobs, BC, SW, 12 tubes, AC/DC .. **$75.00-85.00**

C-81, table, 1938, wood, right front dial, left cloth grille with horizontal bars, tuning eye, 5 knobs, BC, SW, 12 tubes, AC **$75.00-85.00**

C-82, console, 1938, wood, upper front dial, lower cloth grille with center vertical bars, tuning eye, 5 knobs, BC, SW, 16 tubes, AC/DC **$160.00-190.00**

C-85, table, 1938, wood, right front dial, left cloth grille with horizontal bars, tuning eye, 5 knobs, BC, SW, 9 tubes, AC **$55.00-65.00**

C-86 "Little Symphony," table-R/P, 1938, wood, left front dial, right cloth grille with 3 vertical bars, tuning eye, lift top, inner phono, 5 knobs, BC, SW, 9 tubes, AC **$55.00-65.00**

C-87, table, 1939, wood, right front slide rule dial, left grille wraps over portion of top, rounded top front, 3 knobs, BC, SW, 6 tubes, AC/DC **$45.00-55.00**

C-88, table, 1939, wood, right front slide rule dial, left grille wraps over portion of top, rounded top front, tuning eye, 3 knobs, BC, SW, 7 tubes, AC/DC **$50.00-60.00**

C-89, console, 1938, wood, upper front dial, lower cloth grille with center vertical bars, tuning eye, 5 knobs, BC, SW, 16 tubes, AC **$160.00-190.00**

C-90, table, 1939, wood, right front slide rule dial with tuning eye, left wraparound grille with horizontal louvers, 4 knobs, BC, SW, 7 tubes, AC/DC **$50.00-60.00**

C-98, table, 1939, wood, large right front slide rule dial, left horizontal wrap-around louvers, 6 pushbuttons, tuning eye, 4 knobs, BC, SW **$55.00-65.00**

C-121, portable, 1940, brown & white leatherette, inner right front dial, left cloth grille, fold-in front, handle, 2 knobs, BC, 5 tubes, AC/DC/battery **$30.00-35.00**

C-121BL, portable, 1940, blue & white leatherette, inner right front dial, left cloth grille, fold-in front, handle, 2 knobs, BC, 5 tubes, AC/DC/battery **$30.00-35.00**

C-121BR, portable, 1940, brown leatherette, inner right front dial, left cloth grille, fold-in front, handle, 2 knobs, BC, 5 tubes, AC/DC/battery **$30.00-35.00**

C-125, portable, 1940, leatherette, inner right front dial, left cloth grille, fold-in front, handle, 3 knobs, BC, SW, 7 tubes, AC/DC/battery **$30.00-35.00**

C-127, table, 1940, walnut, right front dial, left grille with horizontal bars, 5 knobs, BC, SW, 13 tubes, AC/DC **$50.00-65.00**

CC-1, table, 1940, wood, large right front slide rule dial with tuning eye, left grille with horizontal and vertical bars, 4 knobs, BC, SW, 7 tubes, battery **$40.00-50.00**

CC-24, table, 1939, walnut plastic, slide rule dial on front center of top, front two section grille with vertical louvers, rounded corners, feet, 2 knobs, BC, 6 tubes, AC/DC **$45.00-55.00**

CC-25, table, 1939, ivory plastic, slide rule dial on front center of top, front two section grille with vertical louvers, rounded corners, feet, 2 knobs, BC, 6 tubes, AC/DC **$45.00-55.00**

CC-29, table, 1939, wood, right front slide rule dial with tuning eye, left wraparound grille with horizontal louvers, 4 knobs, BC, SW, 8 tubes, AC **$60.00-70.00**

CC-35, console-R/P, 1940, walnut, inner right dial panel, left phono, lift top, double front doors cover grille, BC, SW, 15 tubes, AC **$75.00-85.00**

CC-39, console-R/P, 1940, wheat finish, inner right dial panel, left phono, lift top, double front doors cover grille, BC, SW, 15 tubes, AC **$75.00-85.00**

CC-47, table, 1940, wood, right front slide rule dial, left grille with 3 vertical bars, 8 pushbuttons, 4 knobs, BC, SW, 12 tubes, AC/DC **$75.00-85.00**

CC-48, table, 1940, wood, right front slide rule dial, left grille with 3 vertical bars, 4 knobs, BC, SW, 12 tubes, AC/DC **$75.00-85.00**

CC-55, portable, 1939, striped cloth-covered, right front dial, left grille, handle, 2 knobs, BC, AC/DC/battery **$30.00-35.00**

CC-98, table, 1939, wood, right front slide rule dial with tuning eye, left wraparound grille with horizontal louvers, 4 knobs, BC, SW, 9 tubes, AC/DC **$55.00-65.00**

D-2, table, 1939, wood, upper right front slide rule dial, lower six pushbuttons, left wraparound grille with horizontal louvers, 3 knobs, BC, 6 tubes, AC **$40.00-50.00**

D-4, table, 1939, wood, upper right front slide rule dial with tuning eye, lower 6 pushbuttons, left wraparound grille with horizontal louvers, 4 knobs, BC, SW, 7 tubes, AC **$60.00-70.00**

D-5, table, 1939, wood, upper right front slide rule dial, lower 6 pushbuttons, left wraparound grille with horizontal louvers, 4 knobs, BC, SW, 7 tubes, AC/DC **$50.00-60.00**

D-10, table, 1937, wood, right front dial, left decorative grille with cut-outs, 2 knobs, BC, 4 tubes, AC **$30.00-40.00**

D-11, table, 1937, wood, right front airplane dial, left decorative grille, rounded top front edge, 3 knobs, BC, SW, 5 tubes, AC .. **$45.00-55.00**

D-13, table, 1937, wood, right front airplane dial, left grille, three decorative horizontal stripes, 3 knobs, BC, SW, 5 tubes, AC .. **$40.00-50.00**

D-14, tombstone, 1937, wood, lower center oval dial, upper grille with three horizontal bars, rounded corners, 3 knobs, BC, SW, 4 tubes, 6VDC **$50.00-60.00**

D-20, table, 1937, wood, right front oval dial, left decorative grille with cut-outs, rounded top front edge, 4 knobs, BC, SW, 6 tubes, AC **$55.00-65.00**

D-21, table, 1938, wood, right front airplane dial, left wrap-over cloth grille with center vertical divider, 3 knobs, BC, SW, 5 tubes, AC .. **$40.00-50.00**

D-22, table, 1938, wood, right front airplane dial, left wrap-over cloth grille with center vertical divider, tuning eye, 3 knobs, BC, 5 tubes, battery **$35.00-40.00**

D-23, table, 1938, wood, right front airplane dial, left cloth grille with horizontal bars, 3 knobs, BC, SW, 6 tubes, AC/DC **$40.00-45.00**

D-27, table, 1937, wood, right front airplane dial, left rectangular grille with three horizontal bars, 3 knobs, BC, SW, 5 tubes, battery **$30.00-40.00**

D-28, table, 1937, wood, right front oval dial, left grille with three horizontal bars, 4 knobs, BC, SW, 7 tubes, battery **$35.00-45.00**

D-30, console, 1937, wood, upper front large oval dial with tuning eye above, lower grille with three vertical bars, 4 knobs, BC, SW, 7 tubes, AC **$130.00-150.00**

D-31, table, 1937, wood, right front oval dial, left grille with cut-outs, upper front center tuning eye, 4 knobs, BC, SW, 7 tubes, AC **$75.00-85.00**

D-32, table, 1938, wood, right front dial, left wrap-around cloth grille with 2 horizontal bars, 5 knobs, BC, SW, 6 tubes, AC/6VDC .. **$50.00-65.00**

D-33, table, 1940, wood, right front slide rule dial with tuning eye, left front grille with vertical lines wraps over top, 4 knobs, BC, SW, 7 tubes, AC/DC **$50.00-60.00**

D-35, table, 1938, wood, right front airplane dial, left cloth grille with horizontal & vertical bars, tuning eye, 4 knobs, BC, SW, 6 tubes, AC **$50.00-65.00**

D-36, table, 1938, wood, right front airplane dial, left wrap-around cloth grille with horizontal bars, tuning eye, 4 knobs, BC, SW, 6 tubes, AC **$50.00-65.00**

D-38, table, 1937, wood, right front dial, left decorative grille with cut-outs, 2 knobs, BC, 5 tubes, AC **$40.00-50.00**

D-40, console, 1938, wood, upper front airplane dial, lower cloth grille with cut-outs, tuning eye, 4 knobs, BC, SW, 6 tubes, AC ..**$110.00-130.00**

D-41, table, 1938, wood, right front airplane dial, left wrap-over cloth grille with center vertical divider, 4 knobs, BC, SW, 6 tubes, battery **$35.00-40.00**

D-42, table, 1940, wood, right front slide rule dial with tuning eye, left front grille with vertical lines wraps over top, 4 knobs, BC, SW, 7 tubes, AC **$60.00-70.00**

D-48, table, 1938, wood, right front airplane dial, left wrap-over cloth grille with center vertical divider, tuning eye, 3 knobs, BC, SW, 7 tubes, AC/DC **$55.00-65.00**

D-49, table, 1938, wood, right front airplane dial, left cloth grille with cut-outs, tuning eye, 4 knobs, BC, SW, 7 tubes, AC **$65.00-75.00**

D-50, table, 1938, wood, right front airplane dial, left wrap-over cloth grille with vertical bars, tuning eye, 4 knobs, BC, SW, 8 tubes, AC **$65.00-75.00**

D-51, table, 1938, wood, right front telephone dial, left cloth grille with vertical bars, tuning eye, 4 knobs, BC, SW, 8 tubes, AC....**$85.00-105.00**

D-53, console, 1938, wood, upper front airplane dial, lower cloth grille with center vertical divider, tuning eye, 4 knobs, BC, SW, 8 tubes, AC **$95.00-115.00**

D-54, console, 1938, wood, upper front telephone dial, lower cloth grille with 3 center vertical bars, tuning eye, 4 knobs, BC, SW, 8 tubes, AC **$160.00-190.00**

D-55, console-R/P, 1938, wood, front airplane dial, lower cloth grille with center vertical bars, tuning eye, lift top, inner phono, 4 knobs, BC, SW, 8 tubes, AC.........**$95.00-115.00**

D-66, table, 1940, wood, right front airplane dial, left grille with horizontal bars, 2 knobs, BC, 6 tubes, AC/DC **$50.00-65.00**

D-68, table, 1938, wood, right front dial, left grille with horizontal bars, tuning eye, pushbuttons, 3 knobs, BC, 7 tubes, AC/DC......**$65.00-75.00**

D-69, table, 1940, wood, right side slide rule dial with tuning eye, left side grille with horizontal and vertical bars, rounded corners, feet, 3 knobs, BC, 8 tubes, AC **$45.00-55.00**

D-71, table, 1940, wood, right front slide rule dial with tuning eye, extended left side wraparound grille with horizontal louvers, 4 knobs, BC, SW, 8 tubes, AC **$60.00-70.00**

D-72, table, 1939, walnut plastic, streamline, right front dial, curved left with horizontal wrap-around louvers, 3 knobs, BC, 6 tubes, AC/DC **$110.00-130.00**

D-73, table, 1939, ivory plastic, streamline, right front dial, curved left with horizontal wrap-around louvers, 3 knobs, BC, 6 tubes, AC/DC **$110.00-130.00**

D-76, table, 1939, walnut plastic, streamline, right front dial, curved left with horizontal wrap-around louvers, 3 knobs, BC, 6 tubes, AC.........**$110.00-130.00**

D-77, table, 1939, ivory plastic, streamline, right front dial, curved left with horizontal wrap-around louvers, 3 knobs, BC, 6 tubes, AC **$110.00-130.00**

D-90, table, 1940, wood, right front airplane dial, left grille with horizontal bars, 2 knobs, BC, 6 tubes, AC **$45.00-55.00**

D-93 "Way-Fairer," portable, 1940, cloth-covered, right front inset dial, left inset grille, striped case, top leather handle, 3 knobs, BC, 5 tubes, AC/DC/battery **$30.00-40.00**

D-131, table, 1940, walnut plastic, right front dial, left vertical grille bars, 2 knobs, BC, 4 tubes, AC/DC.........**$35.00-45.00**

D-132, table, 1940, ivory plastic, right front dial, left vertical grille bars, 2 knobs, BC, 4 tubes, AC/DC **$35.00-45.00**

D-133 "Little Giant," table-R/P, 1940, brown leatherette, right front airplane dial, left grille area, lift top, inner phono, 2 knobs, BC, 4 tubes, AC.........**$30.00-35.00**

D-139, table, 1940, walnut plastic, streamline, right front airplane dial, curved left with horizontal wrap-around louvers, 2 knobs, BC, 5 tubes, AC/DC **$110.00-130.00**

D-140, table, 1940, ivory plastic, streamline, right front airplane dial, curved left with horizontal wrap-around louvers, 2 knobs, BC, 5 tubes, AC/DC **$110.00-130.00**

DA-11, table, 1937, wood, right front airplane dial, left decorative grille, rounded top front edge, 3 knobs, BC, SW, 5 tubes, AC..**$45.00-55.00**

DA-13, table, 1937, wood, right front airplane dial, left grille with three horizontal bars, rounded top front edge, 3 knobs, BC, SW, 5 tubes, AC **$40.00-50.00**

DA-20, table, 1937,wood, right front oval dial, left decorative grille with cut-outs, rounded top front edge, 4 knobs, BC, SW, 6 tubes, AC **$55.00-65.00**

M31-71, cathedral, 1935, wood, shouldered, center front half-round dial, upper 3-section cloth grille, 3 knobs, BC, 5 tubes, AC, $140.00-160.00.

DA-28, table, 1938, wood, right front dial, left cloth grille with horizontal & vertical bars, 4 knobs, BC, SW, 7 tubes, battery.........**$40.00-50.00**

DA-31, table, 1937, wood, right front oval dial, top front center tuning eye, left decorative grille with cut-outs, 4 knobs, BC, SW, 7 tubes, AC.........**$65.00-75.00**

E-60, table, 1940, wood, right front slide rule dial, left grille with horizontal bars, 4 knobs, BC, 5 tubes **$40.00-50.00**

E-62, table, 1940, onyx Catalin, step-down right top with pushbuttons, right front dial, left grille with horizontal wrap-around louvers, 2 knobs, BC, 5 tubes, AC/DC ....**$1,150.00+**

E-63, table, 1940, butterscotch Catalin, step-down right top with pushbuttons, right front dial, left grille with horizontal wrap-around louvers, 2 knobs, BC, 5 tubes, AC/DC ....**$1,150.00+**

E-64, table, 1940, walnut plastic, right front dial, left horizontal wrap-around louvers, 2 knobs, BC, 5 tubes, AC/DC **$35.00-45.00**

E-65, table, 1940, ivory plastic, right front dial, left horizontal wrap-around louvers, 2 knobs, BC, 5 tubes, AC/DC **$35.00-45.00**

E-74, table, 1939, walnut plastic, upper right front thumb dial knob, left wraparound grille with horizontal louvers, step-down top, 2 knobs, BC, 5 tubes, AC/DC **$25.00-35.00**

E-75, table, 1939, ivory plastic, upper right front thumb dial knob, left wraparound grille with horizontal louvers, step-down top, 2 knobs, BC, 5 tubes, AC/DC **$25.00-35.00**

E-76, table, 1939, walnut plastic, upper right front dial, left wraparound grille with horizontal louvers, rounded corners, 2 knobs, BC, 6 tubes, AC/DC.........**$30.00-40.00**

E-77, table, 1939, ivory plastic, upper right front dial, left wraparound grille with horizontal louvers, rounded corners, 2 knobs, BC, 6 tubes, AC/DC.........**$30.00-40.00**

E-186, table, 1940, walnut plastic, right front airplane dial, left horizontal wrap-around louvers, 3 knobs, BC, SW, 6 tubes, AC/DC..**$40.00-50.00**

E-187, table, 1940, ivory plastic, right front airplane dial, left horizontal wrap-around louvers, 3 knobs, BC, SW, 6 tubes, AC/DC **$40.00-50.00**

E-188, table, 1940, two-tone walnut, right front airplane dial, left grille with 3 vertical bars, 3 knobs, BC, SW, 6 tubes, AC/DC **$50.00-65.00**

E-189, table, 1940, two-tone walnut, right front slide rule dial, left horizontal grille bars, tuning eye, pushbuttons, 4 knobs, BC, SW, 9 tubes, AC **$75.00-95.00**

E-191 "Veri-Own," portable, 1940, leatherette, inner dial and vertical grille bars, fold-open door, handle, 2 knobs, BC, 4 tubes, battery.........**$30.00-40.00**

EB-8, table, 1937, wood, right front vertical oval dial, left grille with "rounded H" cut-out, rounded corners, pedestal base, two-tone, 3 knobs, BC, SW, 5 tubes, AC/DC **$45.00-55.00**

EB-52, table, 1938, wood, right front dial, left cloth grille with 2 vertical bars, 3 knobs, BC, 5 tubes, battery.........**$30.00-35.00**

EB-56, table, 1938, wood, right front telephone dial, left wrap-around cloth grille with 2 horizontal bars, 3 knobs, BC, 5 tubes, AC **$75.00-85.00**

EB-58, table, 1938, two-tone wood, right front telephone dial, left wrap-around cloth grille with 2 horizontal bars, 3 knobs, BC, 6 tubes, AC/DC.........**$75.00-85.00**

EB-65, chairside-R/P, 1938, wood, Deco, fold-back top, top telephone dial, front round cloth grille with vertical bars, inner phono, 4 knobs, BC, SW, 6 tubes, AC **$180.00-200.00**

EB-66, table, 1938, three-tone wood, right front telephone dial, left cloth grille, 4 knobs, BC, SW, 7 tubes, AC/DC **$75.00-85.00**

EB-67, table, 1938, wood, right front telephone dial, left cloth grille with Deco cut-outs, 4 knobs, BC, SW, 7 tubes, battery **$40.00-50.00**

EB-70, table, 1938, two-tone wood, right front telephone dial, left cloth grille area, 4 knobs, BC, SW, 6 tubes, AC **$75.00-85.00**

FA-10, table, 1938, ivory plastic, Deco case with step-down sides, front airplane dial, upper vertical grille bars, tuning eye, 4 knobs, BC, SW, 7 tubes, AC/DC .... **$700.00+**

FA-11, table, 1938, red plastic, Deco case with step-down sides, front airplane dial, upper vertical grille bars, tuning eye, 4 knobs, BC, SW, 7 tubes, AC/DC .... **$1,000.00+**

FA-12, table, 1938, ebony plastic, Deco case with step-down sides, front airplane dial, upper vertical grille bars, tuning eye, 4 knobs, BC, SW, 7 tubes, AC/DC .... **$500.00+**

FA-15W, table, 1947, walnut wood, small right front vertical slide rule dial, left horizontal louvers, 2 knobs, BC, 5 tubes, AC/DC **$35.00-45.00**

FA-15Y, table, 1947, ivory painted wood, small right front vertical slide rule dial, left horizontal louvers, 2 knobs, BC, 5 tubes, AC/DC **$35.00-45.00**

FE-5, table, 1940, walnut plastic, upper right front dial with 5 push-levers below, left wraparound grille with horizontal louvers, 1 front and 1 right side knob, BC, 6 tubes, AC/DC **$110.00-140.00**

FE-6, table, 1940, ivory plastic, upper right front dial with 5 push-levers below, left wraparound grille with horizontal louvers, 1 front and 1 right side knob, BC, 6 tubes, AC/DC **$110.00-140.00**

FE-35, table, 1940, wood, right front dial, left grille with horizontal bars, push-buttons, 1 front knob, 1 side knob, BC, 5 tubes, battery **$40.00-50.00**

FE-141, table, 1940, walnut plastic, Deco, step-down top, right front half-round dial, left horizontal bars, base, 6 pushbuttons, 1 front knob, 1 right side knob, BC, 6 tubes, AC/DC **$150.00-180.00**

FE-142, table, 1940, ivory plastic, Deco, step-down top, right front half-round dial, left horizontal bars, base, 6 pushbuttons, 1 front knob, 1 right side knob, BC, 6 tubes, AC/DC **$150.00-180.00**

FE-143, table, 1940, walnut plastic, Deco, step-down top, right front dial, left horizontal bars, 5 pushbuttons, 1 front knob, 1 right side knob, BC, 5 tubes, AC/DC **$150.00-180.00**

FE-144, table, 1940, ivory plastic, Deco, step-down top, right front dial, left horizontal bars, 5 pushbuttons, 1 front knob, 1 right side knob, BC, 5 tubes, AC/DC **$150.00-180.00**

FE-145, console-R/P, 1940, walnut veneer, inner right dial/left phono, lift top, double front grille doors, tuning eye, pushbuttons, 3 knobs, BC, SW, 11 tubes, AC **$120.00-150.00**

FE-146, console-R/P, 1940, wood, inner right dial/left phono, lift top, front grille area, tuning eye, pushbuttons, 3 knobs, BC, SW, 11 tubes, AC **$110.00-130.00**

FE-147, console-R/P, 1940, mahogany, inner right dial/left phono, lift top, double front doors, inner grille & storage, tuning eye, pushbuttons, 3 knobs, BC, SW, 11 tubes, AC **$110.00-130.00**

FE-147R, console-R/P, 1940, mahogany, inner right dial/left phono, lift top, double front doors, inner grille & storage, tuning eye, pushbuttons, 3 knobs, BC, SW, 11 tubes, AC **$110.00-130.00**

FE-149, console, 1940, walnut, upper front slanted slide rule dial, lower cloth grille with center vertical divider, tuning eye, 8 pushbuttons, 3 knobs, BC, SW, 11 tubes, AC **$120.00-150.00**

FE-151, console-R/P, 1940, mahogany, inner front dial & grille, double doors, lift top, inner phono, tuning eye, pushbuttons, 3 knobs, BC, SW, 11 tubes, AC..**$110.00-130.00**

FE-152, console-R/P, 1940, walnut, inner front dial & grille, double doors, lift top, inner phono, tuning eye, pushbuttons, 3 knobs, BC, SW, 11 tubes, AC..**$110.00-130.00**

FE-154, console-R/P, 1940, bleached mahogany, inner front dial & grille, double doors, lift top, inner phono, tuning eye, pushbuttons, 3 knobs, BC, SW, 11 tubes, AC **$110.00-130.00**

FE-155, console-R/P, 1940, wood, inner right dial/left phono, lift top, double front doors, inner grille & storage, tuning eye, pushbuttons, 3 knobs, BC, SW, 11 tubes, AC **$110.00-130.00**

FE-156, console-R/P, 1940, wood, inner right dial/left phono, lift top, double front grille doors, tuning eye, pushbuttons, 3 knobs, BC, SW, 11 tubes, AC **$120.00-150.00**

FS-16, table, 1938,wood, right front dial, left grille with 2 horizontal bars, 2 knobs, BC, 5 tubes, AC/DC **$35.00-40.00**

FS-29, table, 1938, walnut, right front airplane dial, left grille with cut-outs, 3 knobs, BC, SW, 10 tubes, AC/DC **$35.00-45.00**

FS-30, table, 1938, two-tone wood, right front airplane dial, left grille with cut-outs, tuning eye, 3 knobs, BC, SW, 11 tubes, AC/DC **$50.00-65.00**

FS-43, table, 1937, wood, right front dial, left wraparound grille with two horizontal bars, rounded front corners, 3 knobs, BC, SW, 6 tubes, AC/DC..**$40.00-50.00**

FS-47, console, 1938, wood, upper front dial, lower cloth grille with center vertical divider, tuning eye, 4 knobs, BC, SW, 11 tubes, AC/DC **$120.00-140.00**

FS-60, table-R/P, 1938, walnut, right front dial, left cloth grille with curved cut-outs, lift top, inner phono, 4 knobs, BC, 5 tubes, AC/DC **$35.00-40.00**

J-32, table, 1937, wood, right front dial, left grille with cut-outs, two tone, 2 knobs, BC, 4 tubes, AC/DC..**$30.00-40.00**

J-35, table, 1937, wood, right front dial, left grille with cut-outs, rounded shoulders and front corners, 2 knobs, BC, 5 tubes, AC/DC **$30.00-40.00**

J-43, table, 1937, wood, right front oval dial, left three section grille, rounded front corners, 3 knobs, BC, SW, 6 tubes, AC/DC **$35.00-45.00**

J50-M, table, 1947, marbleized plastic, upper right front dial knob, left grille with wraparound horizontal louvers, 2 knobs, BC, 5 tubes, AC/DC **$100.00-120.00**

J50-Y, table, 1947, ivory plastic, upper right front dial knob, left grille with wraparound horizontal louvers, 2 knobs, BC, 5 tubes, AC/DC **$50.00-60.00**

J-62C, table-R/P, 1947, wood, front slanted slide rule dial, lower grille, 3/4 lift top, inner phono, 4 knobs, BC, SW, 6 tubes, AC........**$35.00-40.00**

JA-35, table, 1937, wood, right front dial, left grille with cut-outs, rounded shoulders and front corners, 2 knobs, BC, 5 tubes, AC/DC **$30.00-40.00**

JA-84, table, 1940, ivory plastic, bowed front with upper slide rule dial and lower horizontal grille bars, 3 knobs, BC, 5 tubes, AC/DC **$40.00-50.00**

JA-87, table, 1940, walnut plastic, bowed front with upper slide rule dial and lower horizontal grille bars, 3 knobs, BC, 5 tubes, AC/DC **$40.00-50.00**

JA-89, table, 1940, walnut plastic, right front dial, left grille with horizontal louvers, 2 knobs, BC, 4 tubes, AC/DC **$40.00-50.00**

JA-93, table, 1940, ivory plastic, right front dial, left grille with horizontal louvers, 2 knobs, BC, 4 tubes, AC/DC **$40.00-50.00**

JS-129, console, 1940, walnut, upper front dial, lower grille with 2 vertical bars, tuning eye, 5 knobs, BC, SW, 8 tubes, AC........**$120.00-150.00**

JS-130, portable, 1940, brown/white leatherette, inner right dial, left grille, slide-in front, handle, 2 knobs, BC, 6 tubes, AC/DC/battery...........**$30.00-35.00**

JS-130BL, portable, 1940, blue/white leatherette, inner right dial, left grille, slide-in front, handle, 2 knobs, BC, 6 tubes, AC/DC/battery **$30.00-35.00**

JS-135, table, 1940, walnut, right front airplane dial, left grille area, 4 knobs, BC, SW, 6 tubes, AC **$45.00-55.00**

JS-168 "Symphonette," table-R/P, 1940, two-tone walnut, right front dial, left grille with center vertical bar, tuning eye, 5 knobs, BC, SW, 9 tubes, AC/DC **$40.00-45.00**

JS-173, table, 1940, two-tone walnut, right front dial, left grille with center vertical bar, tuning eye, 5 knobs, BC, SW, 8 tubes, AC ..**$65.00-75.00**

JS-175 "Symphonette," table-R/P, 1940, two-tone walnut, right front dial, left grille with center vertical bar, tuning eye, 5 knobs, BC, SW, 8 tubes, AC **$40.00-45.00**

JS-176, table-R/P/Rec, 1940, wood, right front dial, left grille with center vertical bar, tuning eye, lift top, inner phono/recorder, 5 knobs, BC, SW, 9 tubes, AC..**$40.00-45.00**

JS-177, table, 1940, walnut plastic, right front airplane dial, left grille with concentric squares, handle, 2 knobs, BC, 5 tubes, AC/DC **$45.00-55.00**

JS-178, table, 1940, ivory plastic, right front airplane dial, left grille with concentric squares, handle, 2 knobs, BC, 5 tubes, AC/DC **$45.00-55.00**

JS-179, table, 1940, walnut plastic, right front airplane dial, left cloth grille with cut-outs, handle, 3 knobs, BC, 5 tubes, AC/DC **$55.00-65.00**

JS-180, table, 1940, ivory plastic, right front airplane dial, left cloth grille with cut-outs, handle, 3 knobs, BC, 5 tubes, AC/DC **$55.00-65.00**

JS-181, table, 1940, walnut plastic, right front airplane dial, left cloth grille with cut-outs, handle, 4 knobs, BC, SW, 6 tubes, AC/DC ..**$55.00-65.00**

JS-182, table, 1940, ivory plastic, right front airplane dial, left cloth grille with cut-outs, handle, 4 knobs, BC, SW, 6 tubes, AC/DC **$55.00-65.00**

JS-183, table, 1940, two-tone walnut, right front dial, left horizontal grille bars, tuning eye, 4 knobs, BC, 8 tubes, AC..................**$65.00-75.00**

M-31, tombstone, 1937, wood, lower front round airplane dial, upper cloth grille with cut-outs, 4 knobs, BC, SW, 6 tubes, 32VDC ..**$50.00-65.00**

M-42, console, 1938, wood, large upper front round dial, lower cloth grille with 3 vertical bars, tuning eye, 4 knobs, BC, SW, 12 tubes, AC **$160.00-190.00**

MC-10B, table, 1947, black plastic, right front dial, left louvered grille, 2 knobs, BC, 5 tubes, AC/DC **$45.00-55.00**

MC-10Y, table, 1947, ivory plastic, right front dial, left louvered grille, 2 knobs, BC, 5 tubes, AC/DC **$45.00-55.00**

MC-11B, table, 1947, black plastic, rounded top, upper front slanted slide rule dial, lower grille, 3 knobs, BC, 6 tubes, AC/DC........ **$40.00-50.00**

MC-11Y, table, 1947, ivory plastic, rounded top, upper front slanted slide rule dial, lower grille, 3 knobs, BC, 6 tubes, AC/DC **$40.00-50.00**

MC-12B, table, 1947, black plastic, rounded top, upper front slanted slide rule dial, lower grille, 4 knobs, BC, SW, 6 tubes, AC/DC .. **$40.00-50.00**

MC-12Y, table, 1947, ivory plastic, rounded top, upper front slanted slide rule dial, lower grille, 4 knobs, BC, SW, 6 tubes, AC/DC .. **$40.00-50.00**

MC-13, table-R/P, 1947, wood, center front square dial, right/left cloth grilles, lift top, inner phono, 2 knobs, BC, 5 tubes, AC ..**$30.00-35.00**

MC-16, table, 1947, plastic, Deco, right front dial, left horizontal wrap-around louvers, 2 knobs, BC, 5 tubes, AC/DC **$75.00-85.00**

Novelette "Micro Super," portable, plastic, upper front round dial, can be used with either earphone or separate plug-in speaker, BC, 4 tubes, battery **$85.00-115.00**

S-49, table-R/P, 1940, wood, small right front dial, left cloth grille, lift top, inner phono, 2 knobs, BC, 5 tubes, AC **$30.00-35.00**

S-161 "Mini-Portable," portable, 1940, leatherette, top right dial, front grille, handle, 2 knobs, BC, 4 tubes, battery **$35.00-40.00**

S-165, table, 1940, walnut, upper front slide rule dial, lower grille area, 2 knobs, BC, 5 tubes, AC/DC **$40.00-50.00**

SB-7, table, 1938, walnut, right front dial, left cloth grille with horizontal bars, 2 knobs, BC, 5 tubes, AC **$40.00-50.00**

SB-8, table, 1938, walnut, right front dial, left cloth grille with horizontal bars, tuning eye, 2 knobs, BC, 6 tubes, AC....................**$40.00-50.00**

LAMCO
La Magna Mfg. Co., Inc.
51 Clinton Place, East Rutherford, New Jersey

1000, table, 1947, plastic, right front round dial, left horizontal wrap-around louvers, 2 knobs, BC, 5 tubes, AC/DC **$40.00-50.00**

3000, portable, 1948, two-tone leatherette, right front dial, left cloth grille, handle, 2 knobs, BC **$35.00-40.00**

LASALLE
LaSalle Radio Products Co.
140 Washington Street, New York, New York

LTUC "Trans-Universe," tombstone, 1935, wood, center front octagonal dial, upper cloth grille with cut-outs, 3 knobs, BC, SW, 7 tubes, AC **$120.00-150.00**

LEARADIO
Lear Incorporated
110 Ionia Avenue, N. W., Grand Rapids, Michigan

561, table, 1946, wood, upper front slide rule dial, lower cloth grille, 2 knobs, BC, 5 tubes, AC/DC **$30.00-35.00**

567, table, 1946, plastic, upper front slide rule dial, lower horizontal louvers with stylized "X," 2 knobs, BC, 5 tubes, AC/DC .. **$45.00-55.00**

1281-PC, console-R/P, 1948, wood, right front tilt-out slide rule dial, left pull-out phono drawer, 4 knobs, BC, FM, 12 tubes, AC..**$65.00-75.00**

6611PC, console-R/P, 1946, wood, right front pull-out drawer with dial, left pull-out phono drawer, 4 knobs, BC, SW, 6 tubes, AC **$65.00-75.00**

6615, table, 1946, wood, upper front slanted slide rule dial, lower cloth grille with horizontal bars, 3 knobs, BC, 6 tubes, AC/DC.. **$40.00-50.00**

6616, table, 1946, plastic, upper front slide rule dial, lower horizontal louvers, 3 knobs, BC, 6 tubes, AC/DC **$40.00-50.00**

566, table, 1946, plastic, upper front slide rule dial, lower horizontal louvers with stylized "X," 2 knobs, BC, 5 tubes, AC/DC, $45.00-55.00.

662/663/664/665, table, C1947, plastic, upper front slide rule dial, lower horizontal grille louvers, 3 knobs, BC, 5 tubes, AC/DC, $45.00-55.00.

6617PC, table-R/P, 1947, wood, chest-type, inner right slide rule dial, left phono, lift top, 3 knobs, BC, 6 tubes, AC **$30.00-35.00**

RM-402C "Learavian," portable, 1948, striped cloth, top slide rule dial, handle, side recessed grille, 3 knobs, BC, SW, LW, 7 tubes, AC/DC/battery **$25.00-30.00**

LEE
John Meck Industries
Plymouth, Indiana

400, table, 1948, flocked case, right front half-round dial/left on/off/volume markings printed on flocked grille, 2 knobs, BC, $150.00-180.00.

LEWOL
Lewol Manufacturing Co.

4L "Best," table, 1934, embossed leather, right front dial, center "leaf" cut-out, angled top, 2 knobs, BC, 4 tubes, AC/DC, $200.00-230.00.

LEWYT
Lewyt Corp.
60 Broadway, Brooklyn, New York

615A, table-R/P, 1947, wood, inner right slide rule dial, left phono, lift top, front grille, 4 knobs, BC, 6 tubes, AC $30.00-35.00
711, portable, 1948, plastic, lower front dial, upper grille with circular cut-outs, molded handle, 3 recessed knobs, BC, 4 tubes, AC/DC/battery $35.00-40.00

LEXINGTON
Bloomingdale Bros.
60th Street & Lexington Avenue, New York, New York

6545, table-R/P, 1947, wood, top slide rule dial, front criss-cross grille, open top phono, 3 knobs, BC, 5 tubes, AC....................$20.00-25.00

LIBERTY
American Communications Co.
306 Broadway, New York, New York

507A, table, 1947, plastic, right front square dial, left horizontal wrap-around louvers, 2 knobs, BC, 5 tubes, AC/DC $50.00-65.00
A6P, table, 1947, plastic, right front square dial, left horizontal wrap-around louvers, 2 knobs, BC, 6 tubes, AC/DC $50.00-65.00

LIBERTY TRANSFORMER
Liberty Transformer Co.
555 N. Parkside Avenue, Chicago, Illinois

Sealed Five, table, 1925, wood, low rectangular case, 3 dial front panel, BC, 5 tubes, battery..$120.00-150.00

LINCOLN
Allied Radio Corporation
833 West Jackson Boulevard, Chicago, Illinois

5A-110, table, 1946, wood, lower front slanted slide rule dial, large upper cloth grille, 2 knobs, BC, AC/DC $35.00-40.00
S13L-B, table, 1946, wood, upper front slanted slide rule dial, lower cloth grille with "X" cut-out, 2 knobs, BC, SW, 6 tubes, AC/DC $45.00-55.00

LOFTIN-WHITE
Electrad, Inc.

G, cathedral, wood, shouldered, lower front window dial, upper round grille with lyre cut-out, finials, 2 knobs, BC, 5 tubes, AC, $320.00-350.00.

LOG CABIN

Log Cabin, table-N, c1935, wood, looks like log cabin, speaker grille in door, knobs in windows, BC, 4 tubes, AC/DC $200.00-230.00

LYRIC
The Rauland Corporation
4245 Knox Avenue, Chicago, Illinois
All-American Mohawk Corporation
4201 Belmont Avenue, Chicago, Illinois

Wurlitzer Manufacturing Company was involved in building the Lyric line for All-American Mohawk. In 1934, Wurlitzer began producing and marketing its own radios under the "Lyric" name (see Wurlitzer Lyric).

J, cathedral, 1930, two-tone wood, scalloped top, lower front half-round dial, upper cloth grille with cut-outs, 3 knobs, BC, 6 tubes, AC, $320.00-350.00.

S-7, cathedral, 1931, wood, scalloped top, lower front half-round dial, upper cloth grille with cutouts, 3 knobs, BC, 7 tubes, AC, $320.00-350.00.

546T, table, 1946, plastic, right front square dial, left cloth grille with criss-cross center, 2 knobs, BC, 5 tubes, AC/DC **$45.00-55.00**

MAGIC-TONE
Radio Development & Research Corporation
233 West 54th Street
New York, New York

i504, table-N, 1947, liquor bottle shape, dial on bottle neck, cap is on/off/volume control, base, BC, 4 tubes, AC/DC, $380.00-410.00.

501, table, 1946, wood, upper front slide rule dial, lower grille with 4 horizontal bars, 2 knobs, BC, 5 tubes, AC/DC **$35.00-45.00**
510, portable, 1948, snakeskin, purse-type, dial on top of case, strap, 2 knobs, BC, 4 tubes, battery **$50.00-65.00**
900, table-N, 1948, keg lamp, keg front "spigot" is dial, keg top knob is volume control, base, BC, 4 tubes, AC/DC **$270.00-300.00**

MAGNAVOX
The Magnavox Company
Oakland, California

The Magnavox Company was formed in 1917 for the manufacture of microphones and loudspeakers and, during WW I, the company did much business with the US government. Magnavox soon began to produce radios but lost money throughout the 1920s due to many internal problems.

AM-20, table-C, plastic, large right side dial, left front square clock face over horizontal grille bars, 4 knobs, BC, AC, $30.00-35.00.

10, table, 1925, wood, low rectangular case, center front dial, 3 knobs, BC, 5 tubes, battery.....................................**$170.00-190.00**
25, table, 1925, wood, high rectangular case, lower 1 dial panel, upper built-in speaker grille, 3 knobs, BC, 5 tubes, battery..**$230.00-250.00**
28M, end table-R/P, 1941, wood, top dial, front grille with cut-outs, lift top, inner phono, BC, 7 tubes, AC..............................**$110.00-130.00**
75, console, 1925, mahogany, inner 1 dial panel, fold-down front, upper built-in speaker grille, 3 knobs, BC, 5 tubes, battery..**$300.00-320.00**
142B, console-R/P, wood, inner right dial, 8 push buttons, door, left pull-out phono drawer, 5 knobs, BC, SW, 7 tubes **$75.00-85.00**
154B, console-R/P, 1947, wood, inner right dial, 6 pushbuttons, door, left pull-out phono drawer, 5 knobs, BC, SW, 10 tubes, AC ..**$75.00-85.00**
155B "Regency Symphony," console-R/P, 1947, wood, inner right dial, 8 pushbuttons, door, left lift top, inner phono, 5 knobs, BC, SW, 13 tubes, AC **$65.00-75.00**
D, table, 1925, wood, high rectangular case, lower front pull-out chassis drawer, upper built-in speaker grille, BC, 5 tubes, battery **$200.00-230.00**
FM40, table, 1961, wood, lower front slide rule dial, large upper grille area with 2 speakers, 4 knobs, BC, FM, 7 tubes, AC/DC........**$20.00-25.00**
T, table, 1925, wood, inner right pull-out chassis drawer, left speaker, fold-down front, 3 knobs, BC, 5 tubes, AC **$150.00-170.00**
TRF-5, table, 1924, wood, low rectangular case, center front round dial, side cut-outs, feet, 3 knobs, BC, 5 tubes, battery......**$160.00-190.00**
TRF-50, table, 1924, wood, inner dial, built-in speaker, double doors with carvings, 3 knobs, BC, 5 tubes, battery **$280.00-300.00**

J "Junior," table, 1925, wood, square case, center front dial, lift top, 4 knobs, BC, 5 tubes, battery, $120.00-150.00.

MAGUIRE
Maguire Industries, Inc.
West Putnam, Greenwich, Connecticut

6L, table, C1946, plastic, step-back right with slide rule dial, left horizontal wrap-around louvers, 3 knobs, BC, SW, 6 tubes, AC/DC..**$40.00-50.00**

500BW, table, 1946, plastic, left front round dial, horizontal louvers, 2 knobs, BC, AC/DC **$40.00-45.00**

500DI, table, 1946, plastic, left front round dial, right horizontal grille bars and, 2 knobs, BC, AC/DC **$40.00-45.00**

561DW, table, 1946, plastic, left front round dial, horizontal grille bars, 2 knobs, BC, AC/DC **$40.00-50.00**

571, table, 1948, plastic, left front round dial, horizontal louvers, 2 knobs, BC, 5 tubes, AC/DC **$40.00-50.00**

661, table, 1947, plastic, left front round dial, horizontal wrap-around bars, handle, 2 knobs, BC, 5 tubes, AC/DC **$45.00-55.00**

700A, table-R/P, 1946, wood, lower front slide rule dial, upper horizontal louvers, 3/4 lift top, inner phono, 3 knobs, BC, 7 tubes, AC **$30.00-35.00**

700E, table-R/P, 1947, wood, lower front slide rule dial, upper criss-cross grille, 3/4 lift top, inner phono, 3 knobs, BC, 7 tubes, AC ..**$30.00-35.00**

MAJESTIC
Grigsby-Grunow Company
5801 Dickens Avenue, Chicago, Illinois
Majestic Radio & Television Corporation
St. Charles, Illinois

The Grigsby-Grunow Company was formed in 1928. The company's radio sales were extraordinary due to the superiority of their speakers over that of others on the market. However, the Depression soon caught up with Grigsby-Grunow, and by 1933 the company was bankrupt. The business was re-formed into the Majestic Radio & Television Corporation which made the Majestic line and General Household Utilities which made the Grunow line until 1937.

1 "Charlie McCarthy," table-N, 1938, plastic, small right front slide rule dial, rounded left with Charlie McCarthy figure, 2 knobs, BC, 6 tubes, AC, $1,000.00-1,170.00.

1A-50A, table, 1939, wood, upper right front slide rule dial, left grille with vertical louvers, rounded front corners, two-tone, 2 knobs, BC, 5 tubes, AC **$35.00-40.00**

1A-59, table, 1939, two-tone wood, right front slide rule dial, left horizontal wrap-around louvers, 2 knobs, BC, 5 tubes, AC **$50.00-65.00**

1BR50-B, portable, 1939, luggage-type, striped cloth, front dial, grille, handle, BC, 5 tubes, AC/DC/battery **$35.00-40.00**

2C60-P, console-R/P, 1939, wood, Deco, upper slide rule dial, pushbuttons, fold-down front, inner phono, 2 knobs, BC, SW, 6 tubes, AC **$120.00-150.00**

2D60, table, 1939, plastic, Deco, right front round airplane dial, left wrap-around grille, extended and rounded left side, 3 knobs, BC, SW, 6 tubes, AC/DC **$120.00-150.00**

3BC90-B, console, 1939, walnut, Deco, upper front slanted slide rule dial, lower vertical grille bars, pushbuttons, tuning eye, BC, SW, 9 tubes, AC **$180.00-200.00**

3C80, console, 1939, wood, upper front slide rule dial, lower grille & decorative horizontal bars, pushbuttons, tuning eye, BC, SW, 8 tubes, AC **$140.00-160.00**

4L1, portable, 1955, plastic, center front round dial with eagle, handle, 2 knobs, BC, 4 tubes, battery **$35.00-45.00**

5A430, table, 1946, wood, small upper front slide rule dial, lower cloth grille, 2 knobs, BC, 5 tubes, AC/DC **$35.00-45.00**

5A410, table, 1946, plastic, upper front raised slide rule dial, lower horizontal wrap-around louvers, 2 knobs, BC, 5 tubes, AC/DC, $75.00-95.00.

5A445, table-R/P, 1947, wood, right front dial, left criss-cross grille, lift top, inner phono, 3 knobs, BC, 5 tubes, AC **$35.00-40.00**

5A445R, table-R/P, 1947, wood, right front dial, left grille, lift top, inner phono, 3 knobs, BC, 5 tubes, AC **$35.00-40.00**

5AK711, table, 1947, plastic, low case, slide rule dial, top vertical grille bars, 2 knobs, BC, 5 tubes, AC/DC.............................**$85.00-115.00**

5AK780, end table-R/P, 1947, step down end table, top dial, phono in base with lift top, 3 knobs, BC, 5 tubes, AC **$75.00-85.00**

5C-2, table-C, 1952, plastic, upper front dial, center clock, right & left vertical bars, 5 knobs, BC, AC.......................................**$45.00-55.00**

5LA5, table, 1951, plastic, upper front raised slide rule dial, lower horizontal wrap-around louvers, 2 knobs, BC, 5 tubes, AC/DC ..**$75.00-95.00**

5LA7, table, 1951, plastic, raised top, upper front slanted slide rule dial, lower horizontal wrap-around louvers, 2 knobs, BC, 5 tubes, AC/DC **$55.00-65.00**

5M1, portable, 1955, plastic, center front round dial with eagle, fold-down handle, 2 knobs, BC, 4 tubes, AC/DC/battery **$35.00-45.00**

5T, table-C, 1939, plastic, Deco, center round dial surrounds clock face, rear grille, 2 knobs, BC, 5 tubes, AC/DC **$200.00-230.00**

6FM714, table, 1948, plastic, raised top, upper front slanted slide rule dial, lower right & left horizontal wrap-around louvers, 2 knobs, BC, FM, 6 tubes, AC/DC...**$55.00-65.00**

7P420, portable, 1947, leatherette, inner right dial, left grille with eagle, fold-down front, handle, telescope antenna, 3 knobs, BC, 7 tubes, AC/DC/battery, $45.00-55.00.

20, console, 1932, wood, lowboy, curved legs, center front window dial with escutcheon, lower grille with cut-outs, 3 knobs, BC, 8 tubes, AC, $120.00-150.00.

44B "Duo-Chief," table, C1934, wood, lower left front dial, upper cloth grille with aluminum cut-outs, 2 knobs, BC, SW, 4 tubes, AC, $180.00-200.00.

6FM773, console-R/P, 1949, wood, inner right dial, left phono, lift top, front criss-cross grille, 2 knobs, BC, FM, 6 tubes, AC ..**$50.00-65.00**

7C40, table-R/P, 1942, walnut, right front dial, left vertical grille bars, lift top, inner phono, 3 knobs, BC, 7 tubes, AC **$30.00-35.00**

7C432, table, 1947, wood, upper front slide rule dial, lower horizontal louvers, tubular feet, 4 knobs, BC, 7 tubes, AC **$40.00-50.00**

7C447, table-R/P, 1947, wood, inner right vertical dial, left phono, lift top, front criss-cross grille, 4 knobs, BC, 7 tubes, AC **$35.00-40.00**

7FM888, console-R/P, 1949, wood, inner right slide rule dial, left pull-out phono drawer, doors, 2 knobs, BC, FM, 7 tubes, AC/DC..**$65.00-75.00**

7JK777R, console-R/P, 1947, wood, inner right dial, left phono, lift top, front criss-cross grille, 4 knobs, BC, 7 tubes, AC **$50.00-65.00**

7JL866, end table-R/P, 1949, wood, step-down top, slide rule dial, front pull-out phono drawer, 4 knobs, BC, 7 tubes, AC.........**$65.00-75.00**

7K60, console, 1941, wood, upper front dial, lower grille with vertical bars, 3 knobs, BC, 7 tubes, AC/DC...........................**$120.00-150.00**

7T11, table, 1942, plastic, right front airplane dial, curved left with horizontal wrap-around bars, 3 knobs, BC, 7 tubes, AC/DC/battery **$150.00-180.00**

7YR752, table-R/P/Rec, 1947, wood, outer right front dial, left cloth grille, lift top, inner phono/recorder, 3 knobs, BC, 7 tubes, AC..**$35.00-40.00**

8FM744, table, 1947, wood, curved top, front slide rule dial over large cloth grille area, 2 knobs, BC, FM, 8 tubes, AC/DC **$40.00-50.00**

8FM775, console-R/P, 1947, wood, upper front slide rule dial, lower pull-out phono drawer, 3 knobs, BC, FM, 8 tubes, AC..........**$50.00-65.00**

8FM776, console-R/P, 1947, wood, inner right slide rule dial, left pull-out phono drawer, double doors, 3 knobs, BC, FM, 8 tubes, AC **$50.00-65.00**

8FM889, console-R/P, 1949, wood, inner right slide rule dial, left pull-out phono drawer, double doors, 3 knobs, BC, FM, 8 tubes, AC **$50.00-65.00**

8JL885, console-R/P, 1948, wood, upper front slide rule dial, center pull-out phono drawer, lower grille, 5 knobs, BC, SW, 8 tubes, AC..**$65.00-75.00**

8S452, table-R/P, 1946, wood, inner right dial, lift top, horizontal wrap-around louvers, 5 knobs, BC, SW, 8 tubes, AC..............**$40.00-45.00**

8S473, console-R/P, 1946, wood, inner right dial, left phono, lift-top, front criss-cross grille, 5 knobs, BC, SW, 8 tubes, AC **$55.00-65.00**

10FM891, console-R/P, 1949, wood, inner right slide rule dial, left pull-out phono, double doors, 4 knobs, BC, SW, FM, 10 tubes, AC...**$65.00-75.00**

12FM475, console-R/P, 1947, wood, inner right dial, left phono, lift top, front criss-cross grille, BC, SW, FM, 12 tubes, AC **$65.00-75.00**

12FM895, console-R/P, 1949, wood, inner right slide rule dial, left pull-out phono drawer, double doors, 4 knobs, BC, SW, FM, 12 tubes, AC **$65.00-75.00**

15, tombstone, 1932, wood, shouldered, center front window dial, upper cloth grille with cut-outs, 3 knobs, BC, 5 tubes, AC ..**$120.00-150.00**

31, cathedral, 1931, walnut, shouldered, right front window dial, upper cloth grille with cut-outs, small finials, 2 knobs, BC, 6 tubes, AC, $240.00-270.00.

50, cathedral/stand, 1931, wood with stand, shouldered, right front window dial, upper cloth grille with cut-outs, small finials, 2 knobs, BC, 8 tubes, AC, $240.00-270.00.

60, table, 1937, two-tone wood, Deco, right front oval dial, left cloth grille with cut-outs, 4 knobs, BC, SW, 6 tubes, AC, $85.00-105.00.

15A, tombstone, 1932, wood, shouldered, center front window dial, upper cloth grille with cut-outs, 3 knobs, BC, 5 tubes, AC **$120.00-150.00**

30, cathedral, 1930, wood, shouldered, right front window dial with escutcheon, upper cloth grille with cut-outs, small finials, 2 knobs, BC, 6 tubes, AC **$240.00-270.00**

44 "Duo-Chief," table, 1933, wood, lower left front dial, upper cloth grille with aluminum cut-outs, 2 knobs, BC, SW, 4 tubes, AC **$180.00-200.00**

49 "Duo-Modern," table, 1933, two-tone wood, lower left front dial, upper cloth grille with aluminum cut-outs, 2 knobs, BC, SW, 4 tubes, AC **$200.00-230.00**

50, cathedral, 1931, wood, shouldered, right front window dial, upper cloth grille with cut-outs, small finials, 2 knobs, BC, 8 tubes, AC **$180.00-200.00**

52, cathedral/stand, 1930, wood with stand, shouldered, right front window dial, upper cloth grille with cut-outs, top spires, 2 knobs, BC, 8 tubes, AC **$240.00-270.00**

52, table, 1938, plastic, upper right front dial, left grille with 2 horizontal bars, 2 knobs, BC, 5 tubes, AC/DC **$75.00-85.00**

55 "Duette," table, 1933, two-tone wood, left front dial, grille with aluminum lyre-shaped cut-out, 2 knobs, BC, SW, 5 tubes, AC **$200.00-230.00**

56 "Ardmore," cathedral, 1933, wood, peaked top, center front window dial, upper cloth grille with cut-outs, finials, 3 knobs, BC, 6 tubes, AC **$240.00-270.00**

90-B, console, 1929, wood, lowboy, upper front window dial, lower cloth grille, stretcher base, 3 knobs, BC, 8 tubes, AC, $140.00-160.00.

156 "Sherwood," grandfather clock, 1931, wood, front window dial, upper clock face, rounded top, finials, lower door with inner storage, 3 knobs, BC, 5 tubes, AC, $470.00-530.00.

57 "Berkshire," console, 1933, wood, lowboy, upper front window dial, lower cloth grille with cut-outs, 3 knobs, BC, 6 tubes, AC **$120.00-150.00**

59 "Studio," tombstone, 1933, two-tone wood, Deco, step-down top, lower front dial, upper grille with vertical aluminum bars, 2 knobs, BC, SW, 5 tubes, AC **$350.00-410.00**

65, tombstone, 1937, wood, lower front oval dial with escutcheon and tuning eye, upper grille with cut-outs, step-down top, 4 knobs, BC, SW, 6 tubes, AC...**$180.00-200.00**

66, table, 1937, wood, right front oval dial with escutcheon and tuning eye, left grille with center vertical bars, step-down corners, 4 knobs, BC, SW, 6 tubes, AC **$70.00-80.00**

67 "Barclay," console, 1933, wood, lowboy, upper front window dial, lower cloth grille with cut-outs, decorative fluting, 6 legs, BC, 6 tubes, AC **$120.00-150.00**

68 "Plaza," console, 1933, wood, upper front window dial, lower cloth grille with cut-outs, decorative fluting and carvings, 2 knobs, BC, 6 tubes, AC **$120.00-150.00**

69 "Savoy," console, 1933, wood, upper front window dial, lower cloth grille with scrolled cut-outs, 2 knobs, BC, 6 tubes, AC **$130.00-150.00**

71, console, 1928, walnut, upper front window dial, lower oval cloth grille w/cut-outs, 3 knobs, BC, 7 tubes, AC **$180.00-200.00**

161, tombstone, c1934, wood, step-down top, right front window dial, center cloth grille with chrome cut-outs, 3 knobs, BC, 6 tubes, AC, $240.00-270.00.

196 "Gothic," cathedral, 1933, wood, front window dial, upper cloth grille with cut-outs, fluted columns, 2 knobs, BC, 6 tubes, AC, $240.00-300.00.

310A, tombstone, 1933, wood, center front window dial with escutcheon, large cloth grille area with cut-outs, 3 knobs, BC, 7 tubes, AC, $110.00-130.00.

71B, console, 1929, wood, lowboy, upper front window dial with oval escutcheon, lower round cloth grille with cut-outs, 3 knobs, BC, 8 tubes, AC **$180.00-200.00**

75, tombstone, 1936, wood, lower front oval dial with escutcheon and tuning eye, upper front grille with cut-outs, rounded front corners, 4 knobs, BC,SW, 7 tubes, AC.......................................**$220.00-250.00**

76, table, 1936, wood, step-down top, front oval dial with escutcheon, left grille, tuning eye, 4 knobs, BC, SW, 7 tubes, AC ..**$85.00-105.00**

77 "Queen Anne," console, 1933, wood, upper front window dial, lower grille with cut-outs, Queen Anne legs, 3 knobs, BC, 7 tubes, AC **$150.00-180.00**

80FMP2, console-R/P, 1951, wood, inner right slide rule dial, door, left pull-out phono drawer, lower grille, 2 knobs, BC, FM, 8 tubes, AC **$65.00-75.00**

85, tombstone, 1936, wood, lower front oval dial with escutcheon and tuning eye, upper front and side front grilles, rounded front corners and shoulders, 4 knobs, BC, SW, 8 tubes, AC **$270.00-300.00**

86 "Hyde Park," console, 1931, walnut, upper front window dial, lower cloth grille with scrolled cut-outs, 3 knobs, BC, 8 tubes, AC ..**$140.00-150.00**

90, console, 1929, wood, lowboy, upper front window dial, lower cloth grille, stretcher base, 3 knobs, BC, 8 tubes, AC **$140.00-160.00**

91, console, 1929, walnut, lowboy, upper front window dial, lower cloth grille with cut-outs, stretcher base, 3 knobs, BC, 8 tubes, AC...**$120.00-150.00**

92, console, 1929, walnut, highboy, inner front window dial, oval cloth grille with cut-outs, double doors, 3 knobs, BC, 8 tubes, AC...**$130.00-150.00**

93, console, 1930, wood, lowboy, front window dial, lower cloth grille with cut-outs, stretcher base, 3 knobs, BC, 8 tubes, AC **$130.00-150.00**

102, console-R/P, 1930, wood, lowboy, front window dial, lower cloth grille with cut-outs, lift top, inner phono, storage, 3 knobs, BC, 8 tubes, AC **$110.00-130.00**

103, console-R/P, 1930, wood, lowboy, inner front window dial, lower cloth grille with cut-outs, double doors, lift top, inner phono, 3 knobs, BC, 8 tubes, AC **$110.00-130.00**

130, console, 1930, walnut, lowboy, upper front window dial, lower cloth grille with cut-outs, BC, 7 tubes, AC **$110.00-130.00**

130, portable, 1939, leatherette, small case, upper front round dial, angled top, handle, 3 knobs, BC, 3 tubes, battery **$75.00-95.00**

130U, portable, 1939, cloth-covered, upper front right dial, upper front left grille, leather handle, 3 knobs, BC, 3 tubes, battery **$30.00-40.00**

131, console, 1930, wood, lowboy, upper front window dial, lower cloth grille with cut-outs, BC, 7 tubes, AC **$120.00-140.00**

132, console, 1930, wood, highboy, inner front window dial, upper grille with cut-outs, double doors, stretcher base, BC, 7 tubes, AC...**$140.00-150.00**

151 "Havenwood," tombstone, 1931, wood, shouldered, center front window dial, upper cloth grille with cut-outs, 3 knobs, BC, 5 tubes, AC **$150.00-180.00**

153 "Ellswood," console, 1931, wood, lowboy, upper front window dial, lower cloth grille with cut-outs, 3 knobs, BC, 5 tubes, AC **$130.00-150.00**

200, console, 1932, wood, lowboy, upper front quarter-round dial, lower cloth grille with cut-outs, stretcher base, 3 knobs, BC, 8 tubes, AC, $120.00-140.00.

381 "Treasure Chest," table-N, 1933, wood with repwood trim, looks like treasure chest, inner dial, speaker in lid, 2 knobs, BC, 4 tubes, AC, $240.00-270.00.

463 "Century Six," table, 1933, walnut, right front window dial, left grille with Deco chrome cut-outs, 2 knobs, BC, 6 tubes, AC, $200.00-230.00.

155 "Castlewood," console-R/P, 1931, wood, lowboy, upper front window dial, lower cloth grille with cut-outs, lift top, inner phono, 3 knobs, BC, 5 tubes, AC $120.00-140.00

167, tombstone, 1939, wood, lower front large round dial, upper cloth grille with 5 vertical bars, BC, SW, 6 tubes, AC............$85.00-105.00

181, console-R/P, 1929, walnut, lowboy, inner front window dial, lower round grille with cut-outs, double doors, phono, 3 knobs, BC, 9 tubes, AC $140.00-150.00

194 "Gothic," cathedral, 1933, walnut finish, lower right front dial, upper cloth grille with cut-outs, 2 knobs, BC, SW, 4 tubes, AC...$200.00-230.00

195 "Gothic," cathedral, 1933, walnut finish, front window dial, upper cloth grille with cut-outs, 2 knobs, BC, SW, 5 tubes, AC $240.00-300.00

201 "Sheffield," tombstone, 1932, wood, Deco, lower front quarter-round dial, upper cloth grille with cut-outs, 3 knobs, BC, 8 tubes, AC $120.00-150.00

203 "Fairfax," console, 1932, wood, lowboy, Early English design, upper front quarter round dial, lower cloth grille with cut-outs, stretcher base, 3 knobs, BC, 8 tubes, AC..........................$120.00-150.00

211 "Whitehall," console, 1932, wood, highboy, Jobean design, lower front quarter-round dial, upper cloth grille with cut-outs, 3 knobs, BC, 10 tubes, AC $120.00-150.00

214 "Stratford," console, 1932, wood, lowboy, Art-Modern design, upper front quarter-round dial, lower cloth grille with cut-outs, 3 knobs, BC, 10 tubes, AC $120.00-150.00

215 "Croydon," console, 1932, wood, highboy, Early English design, front quarter-round dial, upper 2-section cloth grille with cut-outs, 3 knobs, BC, 10 tubes, AC $180.00-200.00

233, console-R/P, 1930, wood, lowboy, inner front window dial/grille, double doors, lift top, inner phono, BC, 7 tubes, AC..$150.00-180.00

250-MI "Zephyr," table, 1939, plastic, raised top, upper front slide rule dial, lower horizontal wrap-around louvers, top pushbuttons, 2 knobs, BC, 5 tubes, AC/DC...................$75.00-95.00

251 "Cheltenwood," tombstone/stand, 1931, wood, front quarter-round dial, upper cloth grille with cut-outs, stretcher base, 3 knobs, BC, 9 tubes, AC $150.00-180.00

253 "Brentwood," console, 1931, wood, lowboy, Jobean design, upper front quarter-round dial, lower cloth grille with cut-outs, stretcher base, 3 knobs, BC, 9 tubes, AC...............................$120.00-150.00

259-EB, table, 1939, walnut, front slide rule dial, curved left grille with cut-outs, pushbuttons, 2 knobs, BC, SW, 5 tubes, AC ..$75.00-95.00

291, tombstone, 1932, two-tone walnut, peaked top, Art Moderne design, lower front quarter-round dial, upper cloth grille with cut-outs, 3 knobs, BC, 9 tubes, AC $200.00-230.00

293, console, 1933, wood, lowboy, upper front quarter- round dial, lower cloth grille with cut-outs, 6 legs, 3 knobs, BC, 9 tubes, AC........$120.00-150.00

304, console, 1932, wood, inner front quarter-round dial, large lower cloth grille with cut-outs, double doors, 6 legs, stretcher base, 3 knobs, BC, 11 tubes, AC $140.00-150.00

311, tombstone, 1932, wood, center front window dial, large cloth grille area with cut-outs, 3 knobs, BC, 7 tubes, AC $110.00-130.00

314, console, 1932, wood, lowboy, upper front window dial, large cloth grille area with cut-outs, 6 legs, stretcher base, 3 knobs, BC, 7 tubes, AC $160.00-180.00

324, console, 1932, wood, lowboy, inner front quarter-round dial, lower 2-section cloth grille with cut-outs, double doors, 6 legs, stretcher base, 3 knobs, BC, 12 tubes, AC................$180.00-200.00

331, cathedral, 1933, wood, shouldered, center front window dial, upper grille with Gothic cut-outs, 3 knobs, BC, 7 tubes, AC ..$300.00-320.00

336, console, 1933, wood, lowboy, upper front window dial, lower cloth grille with cut-outs, 3 knobs, BC, 7 tubes, AC...........$120.00-140.00

344, console, 1933, wood, lowboy, inner window dial, doors, lower cloth grille with criss-cross cut-outs, twin speakers, 6 legs, 3 knobs, BC, 11 tubes, AC $120.00-150.00

351 "Collingwood," console, 1932, wood, lowboy, Tudor design, inner front quarter-round dial, lower cloth grille with cut-outs, double doors, BC, 10 tubes, AC $140.00-160.00

353 "Abbeywood," console-R/P, 1932, wood, ornate Charles II design, inner front dial, doors, right & left cloth grilles with cut-outs, lift top, inner phono, 4 knobs, BC, 10 tubes, AC $300.00-320.00

363, console, 1933, wood, lowboy, upper front quarter-round dial, pipe organ front panel with illuminated stained glass insert, lower grille with Gothic cut-outs, 6 legs, 3 knobs, BC, 11 tubes, AC $300.00-320.00

370, table, 1933, wood, rounded top, right front window dial, center cloth grille with cut-outs, 2 knobs, BC, 5 tubes, AC...........$110.00-130.00

371, table, 1933, wood, rounded top, right front window dial, center grille with Gothic cut-outs, 2 knobs, BC, 5 tubes, AC $110.00-130.00

373, table, 1933, wood, rounded top, right front window dial, upper grille with illuminated glass insert, 2 knobs, BC, 5 tubes, AC..$240.00-270.00

393, console, 1933, wood, lowboy, upper front window dial, lower cloth grille with "peacock" cut-out, 6 legs, 3 knobs, BC, 8 tubes, AC $150.00-190.00

400, table, 1941, plastic, raised top, upper front slide rule dial, lower horizontal wrap-around louvers, 2 knobs, BC, 5 tubes, AC/DC......$65.00-75.00

411 "DeLuxe," table, 1933, wood with inlay, Deco, front dial, center grille with aluminum cut-outs, 2 knobs, BC, 6 tubes, AC/DC..$180.00-200.00

448-2, table, 1940, wood, right front slide rule dial, left vertical wrap-over bars, battery.......................................$40.00-45.00

461 "Master Six," tombstone, 1933, wood, front window dial, upper chrome grille, vertical fluted front bar, top & side fluting, 3 knobs, BC, 6 tubes, AC $150.00-180.00

511, table, 1938, plastic, center front slide rule dial surrounded by circular grille area with horizontal louvers, 2 knobs, BC, 5 tubes, AC..$850.00+

560 "Chatham," console, 1933, birch & walnut, lowboy, upper front window dial, lower cloth grille with vertical bars, stretcher base, 2 knobs, BC, SW, 5 tubes, AC $110.00-130.00

566 "Tudor," console, 1933, oak, antique finish, upper front window dial, geometric grille cut-outs, stretcher base, 2 knobs, BC, SW, 5 tubes, AC $110.00-130.00

599 "Radiograph," table-R/P, 1931, walnut, left front dial, center cloth grille with cut-outs, lift top, inner phono, 2 knobs, BC, 5 tubes $75.00-95.00

666 "Ritz," console, 1933, two-tone wood, Deco, upper front window dial, "V" shaped grille with vertical cut-outs, 2 knobs, BC, SW, 6 tubes, AC $500.00-550.00

672, chairside/bar, 1937, wood, top dial, lift top, inner bar & glassware, front grille, storage, BC, SW, 6 tubes, AC $190.00-220.00

651, table, 1937, plastic, front round airplane dial, curved left with wrap-around horizontal bars, 3 knobs, BC, 5 tubes, AC/DC, $150.00-180.00.

750, console, 1937, wood, upper front oval dial with escutcheon and tuning eye, lower front grille with center vertical bars, rounded front corners and shoulders, 4 knobs, BC, SW, 7 tubes, AC ..**$240.00-270.00**

776 "Lido," console, 1933, five-tone wood, Deco, step-down top, upper front window dial, center vertical grille bars, 2 knobs, BC, SW, 6 tubes, AC **$500.00-550.00**

850, console,1937, wood, upper front oval dial with escutcheon and tuning eye, lower front center and corner grilles with vertical bars, 4 knobs, BC, SW, 8 tubes, AC **$300.00-350.00**

886 "Park Avenue," console, 1933, three-tone wood, modern, step-down top, right front window dial, left cloth grille, wrap-around horizontal bars, 2 knobs, BC, SW, 6 tubes, AC, $800.00-900.00.

906 "Riviera," console, 1933, four-tone wood, modern, upper front window dial, vertical grille bars, right shelves, 2 knobs, BC, SW, 6 tubes, AC **$530.00-580.00**

921 "Melody Cruiser," table-N, 1946, wood radio shaped like sailing ship, horizontal louvers, chrome sails, 2 knobs, BC, AC **$350.00-380.00**

1656, console, 1937, wood, large upper front rectangular escutcheon with dial, 12 pushbuttons and tuning eye, large "U" shaped grille below, step-down cabinet, feet, 5 knobs, BC, SW, 16 tubes, AC..**$1,200.00+**

P1A50, table-R/P, 1939, two-tone wood, right front slide rule dial, left horizontal louvers, lift top, inner phono, 3 knobs, BC, 5 tubes, AC ..**$35.00-45.00**

T081-A, table, 1940, wood, right front slide rule dial, left wrap-over vertical bars, 2 knobs, BC, 4 tubes, battery **$35.00-40.00**

T1019, table, 1940, walnut, right front dial, left grille with horizontal bars, 3 knobs, BC, SW **$45.00-55.00**

TP221-A, table-R/P, 1941, wood, right front dial, left horizontal louvers, lift top, inner phono, 3 knobs, BC, 6 tubes, AC **$35.00-40.00**

MANTOLA
The B. F. Goodrich Co.
500 South Main Street, Akron, Ohio

24B6, table, 1947, wood, right front square dial, left horizontal grille bars, handle, 2 knobs, BC, 6 tubes, AC/DC **$45.00-55.00**

92-521, table, 1949, plastic, right front round dial overlaps lower horizontal grille bars, 2 knobs, BC, 4 tubes, AC/DC **$30.00-35.00**

92-522, table, 1949, plastic, right front round dial overlaps lower horizontal grille bars, 2 knobs, BC, 4 tubes, AC/DC **$30.00-35.00**

92-529, table, 1951, wood, lower front slide rule dial, large upper cloth grille, 2 knobs, BC, FM, 8 tubes, AC **$30.00-35.00**

92-752, portable, 1949, front slide rule dial at top of recessed horizontal louvers, handle, 2 knobs, AC/DC/battery **$30.00-35.00**

477 5QL, table, plastic, Deco, right front dial, curved left, horizontal wrap-around louvers, step-down top with pushbuttons, 2 knobs, AC/DC **$120.00-150.00**

R-450A, table, plastic, Deco, right front dial, curved left, horizontal wrap-around louvers, 2 knobs **$75.00-95.00**

G45XJ45, table, plastic, right front dial, left grille with vertical bars, rounded top corners, 3 knobs, BC, SW, 5 tubes, AC/DC, 45.00-55.00.

R-643W, table, 1946, wood, upper front slanted slide rule dial, lower cloth grille with 4 horizontal bars, 2 knobs, BC, 4 tubes, battery **$35.00-40.00**

R-652, portable, 1946, luggage-style, inner right dial, left horizontal grille bars, fold-down front, handle, 2 knobs, BC, 5 tubes, AC/DC/battery...**$30.00-35.00**

R-654-PM, table, 1946, mahogany plastic, upper front slanted slide rule dial, lower horizontal louvers, 2 knobs, BC, 5 tubes, AC/DC......**$40.00-45.00**

R-654-PV, table, 1946, ivory plastic, upper front slide rule dial, lower horizontal louvers, 2 knobs, BC, 5 tubes, AC/DC **$40.00-45.00**

R-655-W, table-R/P, 1946, wood, upper front slide rule dial, lower grille with 2 horizontal bars, lift top, inner phono, 2 knobs, BC, 5 tubes, AC **$30.00-35.00**

R-662, portable, 1946, luggage-style, inner right dial, left horizontal grille bars, fold down front, handle, 2 knobs, BC, 6 tubes, AC/DC/battery...**$30.00-35.00**

R-664-PV, table, 1947, plastic, upper front slide rule dial, lower horizontal louvers, 2 knobs, BC, 6 tubes, AC/DC **$40.00-45.00**

R-7543, table, 1947, plastic, right front square dial, left horizontal louvers, handle, 2 knobs, BC, AC/DC **$50.00-65.00**

R-75143, table, 1948, wood, right front square dial, left horizontal plastic louvers, 2 knobs, BC, 5 tubes, AC/DC **$30.00-40.00**

R-75152, table-R/P, 1948, wood, lower front slide rule dial, upper criss-cross grille, lift top, inner phono, 4 knobs, BC, 5 tubes, AC.........**$30.00-35.00**

R-76162, console-R/P, 1948, wood, front tilt-out dial, center pull-out phono drawer, lower grille with 2 vertical bars, 4 knobs, BC, 6 tubes, AC **$65.00-75.00**

R-76262, chairside, 1948, wood, slide-out front radio unit, horizontal louvers, inner phono, 4 knobs, BC, 6 tubes, AC **$85.00-105.00**

R-78162, console-R/P, 1948, wood, inner right slide rule dial, fold-down door, left pull-out phono drawer, 4 knobs, BC, FM, 8 tubes, AC **$65.00-75.00**

MARLBORO

CDI, table/N, plastic with metal foil, looks like pack of Marlboro cigarettes, 13⅜" high, right side dial, front perforated grille area, made in Japan, BC, 5 tubes, $690.00-800.00.

MARSHALL

61590, table, three-tone wood, large front airplane dial, curved left grille with wrap-around horizontal bar, 4 knobs, BC, SW, 6 tubes, AC/DC, $85.00-115.00.

MARWOL
Marwol Radio Corporation

A-1, table, 1925, wood, low rectangular case, 3 dial front panel, 3 knobs, BC, 5 tubes, battery....................................$150.00-180.00
Baby Grand, table, 1925, low rectangular case, slanted 3 dial front panel, 5 knobs, BC, 5 exposed tubes, battery $270.00-300.00

MASON
Mason Radio Products Co.
Kingston, New York

45-1A, table, 1947, plastic, right front square dial, left horizontal louvers, 2 knobs, BC, AC/DC $45.00-55.00

MASTER
Master Radio Manufacturing Co.

70, cathedral, 1930, wood, right front window dial, upper cloth grille with cut-outs, decorative spindles, BC, 6 tubes, AC $190.00-210.00

MAYFAIR
Radiaphone Corporation
1142 South Wall Street, Los Angeles, California

355, table, black plastic, right front half-round dial, left grille with horizontal louvers, 2 knobs, BC...$40.00-50.00
393, table, white plastic, right front half-round dial, left grille with horizontal louvers, 2 knobs, BC...$40.00-50.00
510, table, 1947, plastic, right front dial, horizontal wrap-around grille bars, 2 knobs, BC, 5 tubes, AC/DC................................$40.00-50.00
520, table, 1947, plastic, upper front slide rule dial, lower horizontal wrap-around louvers, 3 knobs, BC, 5 tubes, AC/DC $40.00-50.00
530, table, 1947, two-tone wood, upper front slide rule dial, lower vertical grille bars, 2 knobs, BC, 5 tubes, AC/DC.....................$55.00-65.00
550, table-R/P, 1947, wood, upper front slanted slide rule dial, lower vertical grille bars, lift top, inner phono, 3 knobs, BC, 5 tubes, AC..$30.00-35.00

MAZDA
Mazda Radio Manufacturing Co.
3405 Perkins Ave., Cleveland, Ohio

Consomello Grand, table, 1925, wood, high rectangular case, lower 3 dial front panel, upper built-in speaker, 6 knobs, BC, 6 tubes, battery...$190.00-210.00
Consomello Jr., table, 1926, wood, small low rectangular case, 2 dial front panel, 3 knobs, BC, battery..............................$110.00-130.00

MECK
John Meck Industries
Liberty & Pennsylvania Avenues, Plymouth, Indiana

4C7, table, 1948, plastic, right front square dial, left & top horizontal louvers, 2 knobs, BC, 4 tubes, AC/DC $45.00-55.00
5A7-P11 "Trail Blazer," table, 1948, plastic, Deco, right front square dial, left horizontal wrap-around louvers, 2 knobs, BC, 5 tubes, AC/DC $65.00-75.00
5A7-PB11 "Trail Blazer," table, 1948, plastic, Deco, right front square dial, left horizontal wrap-around louvers, 2 knobs, BC, 5 tubes, AC/DC $65.00-75.00
5D7-WL18, portable, 1947, two-tone, left front round dial over horizontal louvers, handle, 2 knobs, BC, 4 tubes, AC/DC/battery ..$30.00-35.00
6A6-W4, table, 1947, two-tone wood, upper front slanted slide rule dial, large lower cloth grille, 2 knobs, BC, 6 tubes, AC/DC....$40.00-50.00
CD-500, table-R/P, 1948, wood, right front square dial, left horizontal grille bars, lift top, inner phono, 3 knobs, BC, 5 tubes, AC $30.00-35.00
CE-500, table, 1948, plastic, right front dial, left & top horizontal louvers, handle, 2 knobs, BC, 5 tubes, AC/DC $35.00-40.00
CM-500, portable, 1948, leatherette, left front round dial over horizontal louvers, handle, 2 knobs, BC, 4 tubes, AC/DC/battery ..$30.00-35.00
CR-500, table, 1948, wood, lower front slide rule dial, large upper slanted grille area, 4 knobs, BC, FM, 10 tubes, AC/DC $35.00-40.00
CW-500, table, 1948, plastic, right front dial, vertical wrap-over grille bars, 2 knobs, BC, 4 tubes, AC/DC $55.00-65.00
DA-601, table, 1950, plastic, right front dial, left vertical wrap-over grille bars, 2 knobs, BC, 4 tubes, AC/DC.............................$65.00-75.00
DB-602I, table, 1950, plastic, right front dial, left vertical wrap-over grille bars, 2 knobs, BC, 4 tubes, AC/DC.............................$65.00-75.00
EC-720, table, 1950, plastic, right front square dial, left horizontal wrap-around louvers, 2 knobs, BC, 5 tubes, AC/DC $65.00-75.00
EF-730, table, 1950, plastic, Deco, right front dial, rounded left with horizontal wrap-around louvers, 2 knobs, BC, 5 tubes, AC/DC $65.00-75.00
EV-760, portable, 1950, leatherette, left front dial over large perforated grille area, handle, 2 knobs, BC, 4 tubes, AC/DC/battery $20.00-25.00
PM-5C5-DW10 "Trail Blazer," table-R/P, 1946, wood, right front square dial, left wrap-around cloth grille with 2 horizontal bars, lift top, inner phono, 2 knobs, BC, 5 tubes, AC $30.00-35.00
PM-5C5-PW-10, table-R/P, 1947, wood, right front square dial, left cloth grille with horizontal bars, lift top, inner phono, 2 knobs, BC, 5 tubes, AC $30.00-35.00
RC-5C5-P "Trail Blazer," table, 1946, wood, right front dial, left wrap around grille with 2 horizontal bars, 2 knobs, BC, 5 tubes, AC/DC...$35.00-45.00

MEDCO
Telesonic Corp. of America
5 West 45th Street, New York, New York

1635, table, 1947, wood, right front square dial over horizontal louvers, 2 knobs, BC, 6 tubes, AC/DC..$30.00-40.00
1636, table, 1947, wood, upper front slide rule dial, large lower cloth grille, 3 knobs, BC, SW, 6 tubes, AC/DC......................$30.00-40.00
1642, table, 1947, plastic, upper front slide rule dial, lower horizontal louvers, 2 knobs, BC, 5 tubes, AC/DC $35.00-45.00
1643, table, 1947, plastic, upper front slide rule dial, lower horizontal louvers, feet, 3 knobs, BC, 5 tubes, AC/DC $35.00-45.00

MEISSNER
Meissner Mfg. Co.
Division of Maguire Industries, Inc.
Mt. Carmel, Illinois

9-1053, table, 1941, two-tone walnut, right front slide rule dial, left cloth grille with vertical bars, tuning eye, 4 knobs, BC, SW, FM, 17 tubes $65.00-75.00
9-1065, portable-R/P/Rec/PA, 1946, suitcase style, inner radio, phono, recorder, PA system, handle, BC, 7 tubes, AC $35.00-45.00

9-1085 "Tropicana," table, 1946, mirror glass & bamboo, mirrored front with right airplane dial, left etched design, bamboo sides, 3 knobs, BC, AC/DC ....**$1,150.00+**
16A, console-R/P, 1950, wood, inner right slide rule dial, left phono, hinged lift top, 5 knobs, BC, FM, 17 tubes, AC **$50.00-65.00**
2961, console-R/P, 1947, wood, inner right dial, left pull-out phono drawer, double doors, storage, tuning eye, 4 knobs, BC, SW, FM, 29 tubes, AC **$65.00-75.00**

MELODY BEER

Melody Beer Bottle, table-N, plastic, looks like large beer bottle, base, "The Beer with a Melody" slogan, BC, $350.00-410.00.

MELROSE

571 BX-20-94C, table, 1946, plastic, right front slide rule dial, left horizontal louvers, 2 knobs, BC, AC/DC, $45.00-55.00.

MERIDIAN
John Meck Industries
Liberty & Pennsylvania Avenues, Plymouth, Indiana

CA-500, table, 1946, two-tone wood, right front dial, left cloth grille area, 2 knobs, BC, 4 tubes, AC/DC, $35.00-45.00.

METEOR
Sears, Roebuck & Co.
925 South Homan, Chicago, Illinois

7125, table, wood, right front dial, left cloth grille with cutouts, 6 pushbuttons, 3 knobs, BC, $55.00-65.00.

7001, table, 1956, plastic, right front round dial, left geometric recessed grille, feet, BC, 4 tubes, AC/DC **$30.00-35.00**
7016A, table-C, 1958, plastic, right side dial, front oval clock, horizontal bars on three sides, 3 knobs, BC, 4 tubes, AC **$25.00-30.00**

METRODYNE
Metro Electric Company
2161-71 N. California Avenue, Chicago, Illinois

Super-Five, table, 1926, mahogany, low rectangular case, 3 dial black Bakelite front panel, 4 knobs, BC, 5 tubes, battery....**$110.00-130.00**
Super-Six, table, 1926, walnut, low rectangular case, front panel with 3 pointer dials, lift top, 4 knobs, BC, 6 tubes **$140.00-150.00**
Super-Seven, table, 1926, walnut, low rectangular case, 1 dial etched Bakelite front panel, 4 knobs, BC, 7 tubes, battery....**$200.00-230.00**
Super-Eight, console, 1928, two-tone wood, inner front dial, lower cloth grille with cut-outs, double doors, 4 knobs, BC, 8 tubes, AC **$240.00-300.00**

Super-Eight, table, 1928, two-tone walnut with carvings, low rectangular case, center front dial, 4 knobs, BC, 8 tubes, AC, $180.00-200.00.

MICHIGAN
Michigan Radio Corporation
32 Pearl Street, Grand Rapids, Michigan

Junior, table, 1923, wood, low rectangular case, 2 dial black front panel, right lift top, BC, 2 tubes, battery..............................**$150.00-180.00**
MRC-2, table, 1924, wood, high rectangular case, 2 dial slanted front panel, 4 levers, BC, 2 tubes, battery **$200.00-230.00**
MRC-3, table, 1923, wood with inlay, low rectangular case, 2 dial front panel, storage, 5 levers, BC, 3 tubes, battery **$270.00-300.00**

MRC-4, table, 1923, mahogany, low rectangular case, inner 2 dial panel, fold-down front, lift top, BC, 4 tubes, battery **$310.00-330.00**

MRC-7 Senior, table, 1922, mahogany, rectangular case, 2 dial black front panel, right lift top, 6 knobs, BC, 3 tubes, battery **$410.00-460.00**

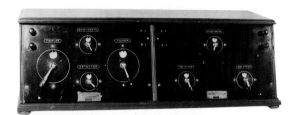

MRC-12, table, 1924, wood, detector/amplifier, low rectangular case, slant front black panel, 7 levers, BC, 3 tubes, battery, $350.00-410.00.

MICROPHONE RADIO

Novelty radios in the shape of microphones were produced for many different radio stations. Each radio features the station call letters and usually tunes in only that one station.

Various Styles, table-N, usually plastic, upper "microphone" with metal grille, lower base with louvers, 1 knob, BC, 5 tubes, AC **$120.00-150.00**

MIDLAND
Midland Mfg. Co.
Decorah, Iowa

M6A, table, 1946, wood, right front round dial, left grille with horizontal wrap-around bars, 2 knobs, BC, 5 tubes, AC/DC, $55.00-65.00.

M6B, table, 1946, wood, right front round dial, left grille with horizontal wrap-around bars, 2 knobs, BC, 5 tubes, AC/DC **$55.00-65.00**

MIDWEST
The Midwest Radio Company
808 Main Street, Cincinnati, Ohio
Midwest Radio Corporation
406-D East Eight Street, Cincinnati, Ohio

Midwest Radio Company was founded by A. G. Hoffman as a mail-order radio business. Many early sets were sold with the "Miraco" name – short for Midwest Radio Company.

16-37, console, 1937, wood, Deco case, upper front round dial, lower cloth grille with cut-outs, BC, SW, 16 tubes, AC........**$270.00-300.00**

422, table, 1940, metal, midget, right front dial, left horizontal grille bars, 2 knobs, BC, AC/DC, $75.00-95.00.

18-35, console, 1935, wood, Deco case, upper front round dial, lower cloth grille with vertical bars, BC, SW, 18 tubes, AC..**$300.00-320.00**

18-36, console, 1936, wood, Deco case, upper front round dial, lower cloth grille with cut-outs, 6 band, BC, SW, 18 tubes, AC **$410.00-460.00**

20-38, console, 1938, wood, large case, upper front round white dial, lower recessed grille with Deco cut-outs, 4 knobs, BC, SW, 20 tubes, AC **$530.00-580.00**

402, table, 1939, metal, midget, right front dial, left horizontal grille bars, 2 knobs, BC, AC/DC **$75.00-95.00**

M-32, tombstone, 1936, wood, step-down top, lower front round airplane dial, upper grille with "herringbone" cut-outs, 4 knobs ..**$150.00-180.00**

P-6, portable, 1947, luggage-style, upper front slanted slide rule dial, lower grille area, handle, 3 knobs, BC, 5 tubes, AC/DC/battery **$30.00-35.00**

PB-6, portable, 1947, luggage-style, upper front slanted slide rule dial, lower grille area, handle, 3 knobs, BC, 5 tubes, AC/DC/battery **$30.00-35.00**

RG-16, console-R/P, 1948, wood, inner right slide rule dial, pushbuttons, left pull-out phono, fold-down front, 6 knobs, BC, SW, FM, 16 tubes, AC **$120.00-150.00**

ST-16, console-R/P, 1947, wood, top slide rule dial, pushbuttons, front tilt-out phono, storage, 4 knobs, BC, SW, FM, 16 tubes, AC **$120.00-150.00**

TM-8, table, 1947, wood, large front slide rule dial, right grille with 2 vertical bars, 5 bands, tuning eye, 4 knobs, BC, SW, 8 tubes, AC..**$65.00-75.00**

Unitune 5, table, 1926, wood, low rectangular case, slanted front 1 dial Bakelite panel, BC, 5 tubes, battery **$120.00-140.00**

Unitune 8, table, 1928, wood, low rectangular case, center front window dial with escutcheon, BC, 8 tubes **$120.00-140.00**

816, console, 1947, wood, upper front slanted slide rule dial and controls with copper background, lower grille with 7 center vertical bars, rounded corners, tuning eye, 6 knobs, BC, SW, FM, 16 tubes, AC, $220.00-240.00.

MW "Miraco," table, 1923, mahogany, low rectangular case, 2 dial black front panel, lift top, 7 knobs, BC, 4 tubes, battery, $200.00-230.00.

Ultra 5 "Miraco," table, 1924, wood, low rectangular case, 3 dial front panel (several versions), lift top, 7 knobs, BC, 3 tubes, battery, $180.00-200.00.

MINERVA
Minerva Corp. of America
238 William Street, New York, New York

411, table, 1948, plastic, upper front slanted slide rule dial, lower lattice grille, 2 knobs, BC, 4 tubes, AC/DC $35.00-40.00
702H, table, 1947, plastic, upper front slanted slide rule dial, lower lattice grille, 3 knobs, BC, 6 tubes, AC/DC $35.00-40.00
729 "Portapal," portable, 1947, cloth-covered, right front slide rule dial over lattice grille area, handle, 3 knobs, BC, 5 tubes, AC/DC/battery $35.00-40.00
L-728, table, 1947, wood, rounded corners, upper front slanted slide rule dial, lower grille, 2 knobs, BC, 5 tubes, AC/DC $35.00-45.00
W-117-3, table, 1947, wood, right front dial over horizontal grille bars, 4 knobs, BC, SW, 8 tubes, AC/DC $35.00-45.00

W117 "Tropic Master," table, 1946, metal, inner right dial, left grille with "M" cut-out, fold down front, handle, 4 knobs, BC, SW, AC/DC, $45.00-55.00.

W-702, table, 1947, plastic, upper front slanted slide rule dial, lower grille with geometric pattern, 2 knobs, BC, 6 tubes, AC/DC ..$35.00-40.00
W-702B, table, 1947, plastic, upper front slanted slide rule dial, lower metal wrap-around grille, 2 knobs, BC, 6 tubes, AC/DC $40.00-50.00
W710A, table, 1946, wood, upper front slide rule dial, lower horizontal wooden louvers, 3 knobs, BC, AC/DC $30.00-35.00

MIRRORTONE
John Meck Industries
Liberty & Pennsylvania Avenues, Plymouth, Indiana

850 "Deluxe," table, plastic, Deco, small right front dial, left horizontal grille bars, decorative case lines, 2 knobs, BC, AC/DC $50.00-65.00
RC-6A7-P6, table, 1948, plastic, upper front slanted slide rule dial, large lower grille area, 3 knobs, BC, 6 tubes, AC/DC ..$35.00-40.00

MISSION BELL
Mission Bell Radio Mfg. & Distr. Co.
2117 West Pico, Los Angeles, California
Mission Bell began business in 1927.

386, table, 1938, wood, right front airplane dial, left wraparound grille, rounded corners and shoulders, 3 knobs, BC, SW, 6 tubes, AC $50.00-60.00
400, portable, 1939, cloth-covered, right front dial, left grille with 3 horizontal sections, handle, 2 knobs, BC, 4 tubes, battery ..$30.00-35.00
407, table, 1940, plastic, upper right front dial, left wraparound grille with horizontal louvers, pushbuttons on top right, 2 knobs, BC, 5 tubes, AC/DC $100.00-120.00
500, portable, 1939, right front slide rule dial, left grille with 3 horizontal sections, handle, 2 knobs, BC, 4 tubes, battery $30.00-35.00

MITCHELL
Mitchell Mfg. Co.
2525 North Clybourn Avenue, Chicago, Illinois

1268R, table-C, 1951, plastic, lower right front round dial over horizontal grille bars, upper clock, 4 knobs, BC, 5 tubes, AC, $35.00-40.00.

1250 "Lullaby," radio/bed lamp, 1949, plastic, front round dial, vertical grille bars, built-in bed lamp, 2 knobs, BC, 5 tubes, AC/DC $75.00-85.00
1251 "Lullaby," radio/bed lamp, 1949, plastic, front round dial, vertical grille bars, built-in bed lamp, 2 knobs, BC, 5 tubes, AC/DC $75.00-85.00
1252, table, 1952, plastic, right front round dial, large left grille area, 2 knobs, BC, 5 tubes, AC/DC $30.00-35.00
1254 "Madrigal," table, 1952, walnut plastic, round front dial ring with inner pointer overlaps large grille area, 2 knobs, BC, 6 tubes, AC/DC $30.00-35.00

1255 "Madrigal," table, 1952, ivory plastic, round front dial ring with inner pointer overlaps large grille area, 2 knobs, BC, 6 tubes, AC/DC **$30.00-35.00**

1256, portable, 1952, plastic, left side dial, front concentric rectangles, flex handle, 2 knobs, BC, 4 tubes, AC/DC/battery **$25.00-30.00**

1260 "Lumitone," table-lamp, 1940, plastic, lamp/radio, lower thumb-wheel dial, upper horizontal grille bars, 2 knobs, BC, 5 tubes, AC/DC **$150.00-180.00**

1267, table-C, 1952, plastic, lower right front round dial over horizontal grille bars, upper clock, 4 knobs, BC, 5 tubes, AC **$35.00-40.00**

1411 "Fiesta," table, mahogany plastic, right side dial, large front metal grille area, BC **$25.00-30.00**

1412 "Fiesta," table, gray plastic, right side dial, large front metal grille area, 2 knobs, BC **$25.00-30.00**

Cherokee, table, 1926, walnut, front window dial with large escutcheon, lift top, 3 knobs, BC, 6 tubes, battery **$110.00-130.00**

Chippewa, console, 1926, two-tone walnut, inner dial, fold-down front, lift top, 3 knobs, BC, 6 tubes, battery **$120.00-150.00**

Geneva, console, 1926, walnut, desk-style, inner dial, fold-down front, domed-top speaker grille, 3 knobs, BC, 6 tubes, battery ..**$200.00-230.00**

Iroquois, console, 1927, wood, inner window dial with escutcheon, fold-down front, upper grille area with cut-outs, 3 knobs, BC, 6 tubes, battery **$240.00-270.00**

Navajo, table, 1926, wood, front window dial with escutcheon, lift top, burl panels, 3 knobs, BC, 6 tubes, battery **$110.00-130.00**

Pocahontas, console, 1926, two-tone inlaid walnut, double front doors, inner dial, feet, 3 knobs, BC, 6 tubes, battery **$200.00-220.00**

Pontiac, console, 1926, walnut with burl front, inner dial, fold-down front door, upper grille, 3 knobs, BC, 6 tubes, battery........**$150.00-180.00**

Winona, table, 1926, walnut, low rectangular case, front window dial with escutcheon, lift top, 3 knobs, BC, 6 tubes, battery **$110.00-130.00**

1287 "Adventurer," portable, 1955, right front slide rule dial over horizontal grille bars, telescope antenna, handle, 4 knobs, BC, SW, 5 tubes, AC/DC/battery, $35.00-45.00.

A5, table, 1925, wood, high rectangular case, 1 dial slant front panel, 3 knobs, BC, 5 tubes, battery, $140.00-160.00.

MOHAWK
Mohawk Corporation of Illinois
2222 Diversey Parkway, Chicago, Illinois
All-American Mohawk Corporation
4201 Belmont Avenue, Chicago, Illinois

100, table, 1923, wood, high rectangular case, 1 dial slant front panel, 3 knobs, BC, 5 tubes, battery......................................**$120.00-140.00**

105, portable, 1925, leatherette, inner Bakelite panel with 2 dials, flip-up front with antenna, handle, 4 knobs, BC, 6 tubes, battery **$200.00-230.00**

110, table, 1925, wood, high domed-top case, 1 dial front panel, door, 3 knobs, BC, 5 tubes, battery......................................**$190.00-210.00**

115, console, 1925, wood, highboy, domed-top case, inner 1 dial front panel, door, 3 knobs, BC, 5 tubes, battery **$240.00-270.00**

MONARCH

Model unknown, tombstone, wood, lower center dial, upper grille with cut-outs, rounded top corners, 3 knobs, BC, SW, 7 tubes, AC/DC, $95.00-115.00.

44, table, 1927, wood, low rectangular case, center front dial with escutcheon, 2 knobs, BC, 6 tubes, battery, $110.00-130.00.

MONITOR
Monitor Equipment Co.
110 East 42nd Street, New York, New York

M-403, table-R/P, 1947, wood, right front dial, left grille with picture, open top phono, 3 knobs, BC, 4 tubes, AC...................**$25.00-30.00**

M-500, table, 1947, plastic, right front dial, left horizontal louvers, 2 knobs, BC, 5 tubes, AC/DC **$30.00-35.00**

M-510, portable, 1947, leatherette, right front dial over horizontal grille bars, handle, 2 knobs, BC, 4 tubes, AC/DC/battery **$25.00-30.00**

M-3070, console-R/P, 1947, wood, inner right slide rule dial, left pull-out phono drawer, doors, 4 knobs, BC, FM, 11 tubes, AC ..**$65.00-75.00**

RA-50, table-R/P, 1947, wood, upper front slide rule dial, lower horizontal grille bars, lift top, inner phono, 4 knobs, BC, 5 tubes, AC ..**$30.00-35.00**

TA56M, table, 1946, plastic, upper front slanted slide rule dial, lower horizontal louvers, 2 knobs, BC, 5 tubes, AC/DC **$40.00-50.00**

MOTOROLA
Galvin Mfg. Corporation
847 West Harrison Street, Chicago, Illinois

The Galvin Manufacturing Company was founded in 1928 by Paul Galvin in the business of producing radio power supplies. Soon branching out into the production of auto radios, the company grew to become one of the largest producers of radios and television under the Motorola brand name.

5A7A "Playmate Jr.," portable, 1948, metal, inner right dial, center horizontal louvers, set plays when flip-up lid opens, 2 knobs, BC, 5 tubes, AC/DC/battery, $40.00-50.00.

3A5 "Playboy," portable, 1941, maroon metal & chrome, inner right dial, left grille with cut-outs, set plays when flip-up lid opens, handle, 2 knobs, BC, 5 tubes, AC/DC/battery..............................**$40.00-50.00**

5A1, portable, 1946, maroon metal & chrome, inner right dial, left grille, set plays when flip-up lid opens, handle, 2 knobs, BC, 4 tubes, battery **$40.00-50.00**

5A5, portable, 1946, inner right dial, left grille, set plays when flip-up lid opens, handle, 2 knobs, BC, 5 tubes, AC/DC/battery **$40.00-50.00**

5A7, portable, 1947, metal, inner right dial, center horizontal louvers, set plays when flip-up lid opens, 2 knobs, BC, 5 tubes, AC/DC/battery **$40.00-50.00**

5A9M, portable, 1948, metal, inner right dial, center horizontal louvers, set plays when flip-up lid opens, flex handle, 2 knobs, BC, 5 tubes, AC/DC/battery **$40.00-50.00**

5C1 "Radio-Larm," table-C, 1950, plastic, right front round dial, center vertical grille bars with "M" logo, left alarm clock, 5 knobs, BC, 5 tubes, AC **$30.00-35.00**

5C11E, table-C, 1959, plastic, lower right front dial over vertical grille bars, left clock, feet, 3 knobs, BC, 5 tubes, AC.............**$20.00-25.00**

5C13B, table-C, 1959, blue plastic, off-center front dial over vertical grille bars, left clock, feet, 4 knobs, BC, 5 tubes, AC.............**$20.00-25.00**

5C13M, table-C, 1959, mahogany plastic, off-center front dial over vertical grille bars, left clock, feet, 4 knobs, BC, 5 tubes, AC **$20.00-25.00**

5C13P, table-C, 1959, pink plastic, off-center front dial over vertical grille bars, left alarm clock, feet, 4 knobs, BC, 5 tubes, AC....**$20.00-25.00**

5C13W, table-C, 1959, white plastic, off-center front dial over vertical grille bars, left clock, feet, 4 knobs, BC, 5 tubes, AC **$20.00-25.00**

5C22M, table-C, 1958, plastic, off-center front dial over vertical grille bars, left clock, feet, 4 knobs, BC, 5 tubes, AC.............**$20.00-25.00**

5H13U, table, 1950, green plastic, large center front round dial with stylized "M" logo over dotted grille, 2 knobs, BC, 5 tubes, AC/DC, $30.00-35.00.

5C23GW, table-C, 1958, plastic, left dial/clock panel over front horizontal grille bars, "M" logo, 4 knobs, BC, AC **$20.00-25.00**

5H11U, table, 1950, walnut plastic, large center front round dial with stylized "M" logo over dotted grille, 2 knobs, BC, 5 tubes, AC/DC..**$30.00-35.00**

5H12U, table, 1950, ivory plastic, large center front round dial with stylized "M" logo over dotted grille, 2 knobs, BC, 5 tubes, AC/DC..**$30.00-35.00**

5L1 "Music Box," portable, 1950, two-tone plastic, right front dial, center checkered grille, handle, 2 knobs, BC, 4 tubes, AC/DC/battery **$30.00-35.00**

5L1U, portable, 1950, two-tone plastic, right front dial, center checkered grille, handle, 2 knobs, BC, 5 tubes, AC/DC/battery **$30.00-35.00**

5M1 "Playmate Jr.," portable, 1950, metal, small case, inner right dial, flip-up front, handle, 2 knobs, BC, 4 tubes, AC/DC/battery......**$45.00-55.00**

5M1U, portable, 1950, metal, small case, inner right dial, flip-up front, handle, 2 knobs, BC, 4 tubes, AC/DC/battery...............**$45.00-55.00**

5P21N, portable, 1957, plastic, upper right front dial overlaps lower horizontal grille bars, stylized "M" logo, handle, 2 knobs, BC, 5 tubes, battery **$30.00-35.00**

5P22GW-1, portable, 1957, leatherette, right front round dial, lower horizontal bars, handle, 2 knobs, BC, 5 tubes, AC/DC/battery......**$30.00-35.00**

5P22RW-1, portable, 1957, leatherette, right front round dial, lower horizontal bars, handle, 2 knobs, BC, 5 tubes, AC/DC/battery......**$30.00-35.00**

5P22S-1, portable, 1957, leatherette, right front round dial, lower horizontal bars, handle, 2 knobs, BC, 5 tubes, AC/DC/battery..**$30.00-35.00**

5P23E-1, portable, 1957, leatherette & plastic, upper right front dial overlaps V-shaped grille area with vertical bars, handle, 2 knobs, BC, 5 tubes, AC/DC/battery **$40.00-50.00**

5P23PN-1, portable, 1957, leatherette & plastic, upper right front dial overlaps V-shaped grille area with vertical bars, handle, 2 knobs, BC, 5 tubes, AC/DC/battery **$40.00-50.00**

5P23WB-1, portable, 1957, leatherette & plastic, upper right front dial overlaps V-shaped grille area with vertical bars, handle, 2 knobs, BC, 5 tubes, AC/DC/battery **$40.00-50.00**

5J1 "Jewel Box," portable, 1950, plastic, inner right dial, center Oriental pattern grille, flip-up front, handle, 2 knobs, BC, 4 tubes, AC/DC/battery, $85.00-95.00.

5R11U, table, 1950, plastic, right front round dial, lower "hi-low" checkered panel, 2 knobs, BC, 5 tubes, AC/DC, $35.00-45.00.

5P31A, portable, 1957, gray leatherette & plastic, upper right front dial, lower lattice grille area, rotatable handle, 2 knobs, BC, 4 tubes, AC/DC **$35.00-40.00**

5P32C, portable, 1957, light blue leatherette & plastic, upper right front dial, lower perforated grille area with lower left "M" logo, handle, 2 knobs, BC, 4 tubes, AC/DC/battery...............................**$35.00-40.00**

5P32E, portable, 1957, navy blue leatherette & plastic, upper right front dial, lower perforated grille area with lower left "M" logo, handle, 2 knobs, BC, 4 tubes, AC/DC/battery...............................**$35.00-40.00**

5P32R, portable, 1957, red leatherette & plastic, upper right front dial, lower perforated grille area with lower left "M" logo, handle, 2 knobs, BC, 4 tubes, AC/DC/battery **$35.00-40.00**

5P32Y, portable, 1957, yellow leatherette & plastic, upper right front dial, lower perforated grille area with lower left "M" logo, handle, 2 knobs, BC, 4 tubes, AC/DC/battery **$35.00-40.00**

5R23G, table-R/P, 1958, front dial over large perforated grille, slanted lift top, inner phono, 3 knobs, BC, 5 tubes, AC **$30.00-35.00**

5T, tombstone, 1937, wood, lower front dial with escutcheon, upper grille with bars, 4 knobs, BC, SW, 5 tubes.........................**$110.00-130.00**

5T11G, table, 1959, green plastic, right front round dial, left lattice grille, 2 knobs, BC, 5 tubes, AC/DC.....................................**$35.00-40.00**

5T11M, table, 1959, mahogany plastic, right front round dial, left lattice grille, 2 knobs, BC, 5 tubes, AC/DC **$20.00-25.00**

5T11R, table, 1959, red plastic, right front round dial, left lattice grille, 2 knobs, BC, 5 tubes, AC/DC.....................................**$35.00-40.00**

5T11W, table, 1959, white plastic, right front round dial, left lattice grille, 2 knobs, BC, 5 tubes, AC/DC **$20.00-25.00**

5T13P, table, 1959, plastic, lower right front dial, upper & lower vertical bars, feet, 2 knobs, BC, 5 tubes, AC/DC.......................**$35.00-40.00**

5T21W, table, 1957, white plastic, recessed front grille with horizontal lines, lower right front dial, rounded shoulders, 2 knobs, BC, 5 tubes, AC/DC **$20.00-30.00**

5T22M, table, 1957, mahogany plastic, lower right front round raised dial area, horizontal grille bars, left foot, 2 knobs, BC, 5 tubes, AC/DC **$50.00-60.00**

5T22R, table, 1957, red plastic, lower right front round raised dial area, horizontal grille bars, left foot, 2 knobs, BC, 5 tubes, AC/DC ..**$65.00-75.00**

5T22W, table, 1957, white plastic, lower right front round raised dial area, horizontal grille bars, left foot, 2 knobs, BC, 5 tubes, AC/DC **$50.00-60.00**

5T22Y, table, 1957, yellow plastic, lower right front round raised dial area, horizontal grille bars, left foot, 2 knobs, BC, 5 tubes, AC/DC **$65.00-75.00**

5X11U, table, 1950, walnut plastic, center front round dial with inner perforated grille, metal stand, 2 knobs, BC, 5 tubes, AC/DC, $40.00-50.00.

5T23N, table, 1957, brown plastic, recessed front with lower right dial, left horizontal line grille with three vertical bars, feet, 2 knobs, BC, 5 tubes, AC/DC **$25.00-30.00**

5T23P, table, 1957, pink plastic, recessed front with lower right dial, left horizontal line grille with three vertical bars, feet, 2 knobs, BC, 5 tubes, AC/DC **$40.00-50.00**

5T23W, table, 1957, white plastic, recessed front with lower right dial, left horizontal line grille with three vertical bars, feet, 2 knobs, BC, 5 tubes, AC/DC **$25.00-30.00**

5T23Y, table, 1957, yellow plastic, recessed front with lower right dial, left horizontal line grille with three vertical bars, feet, 2 knobs, BC, 5 tubes, AC/DC **$40.00-50.00**

5X12U, table, 1950, ivory plastic, center front round dial with inner perforated grille, metal stand, 2 knobs, BC, 5 tubes, AC/DC ..**$40.00-50.00**

5X13U, table, 1950, black plastic, center front round dial with inner perforated grille, metal stand, 2 knobs, BC, 5 tubes, AC/DC ..**$40.00-50.00**

5X21U, table, 1951, plastic, center front round dial with inner perforated grille, metal stand, 2 knobs, BC, SW, 5 tubes, AC/DC ..**$40.00-50.00**

6F11, console-R/P, 1950, wood, upper front half-round dial, lower pull-out phono drawer, 4 knobs, BC, 6 tubes, AC **$50.00-65.00**

6L1 "Town & Country," portable, 1950, plastic, "U"-shaped dial with inner perforated grille, handle, 2 knobs, BC, 5 tubes, AC/DC/battery **$30.00-35.00**

6P25E, portable, 1958, navy, upper right front dial overlaps large lower grille area with lower left "M" logo, handle, 2 knobs, BC, 6 tubes, AC/DC/battery **$35.00-40.00**

6P25N, portable, 1958, brown, upper right front dial overlaps large lower grille area with lower left "M" logo, handle, 2 knobs, BC, 6 tubes, AC/DC/battery **$35.00-40.00**

6P25S, portable, 1958, tan, upper right front dial overlaps large lower grille area with lower left "M" logo, handle, 2 knobs, BC, 6 tubes, AC/DC/battery **$35.00-40.00**

6P34E "700 Ranger," portable, 1957, navy leatherette, upper right front dial, lower metal perforated grille with stylized "M" logo, handle, 2 knobs, BC, 5 tubes, AC/DC/battery, $35.00-40.00.

6P34S "700 Ranger," portable, 1957, suntan leatherette, upper right front dial, lower metal perforated grille with stylized "M" logo, handle, 2 knobs, BC, 5 tubes, AC/DC/battery.....................**$35.00-40.00**

6-T, table, 1937, wood, right front dial with large escutcheon, left cloth grille with 3 vertical bars, 4 knobs, BC, SW, 6 tubes, AC **$85.00-105.00**

6T15N "Custom 6," table, 1959, brown plastic, lower right front dial, upper vertical grille bars, slanted sides, 2 knobs, BC, 6 tubes, AC/DC **$35.00-40.00**

6T15S "Custom 6," table, 1959, tan plastic, lower right front dial, upper vertical grille bars, slanted sides, 2 knobs, BC, 6 tubes, AC/DC **$35.00-40.00**

6X11U, table, 1950, walnut plastic, center front round dial with inner perforated grille, 2 knobs, BC, 6 tubes, AC/DC **$40.00-50.00**

6X12U, table, 1950, ivory plastic, center front round dial with inner perforated grille, 2 knobs, BC, 6 tubes, AC/DC **$40.00-50.00**

7F11, console-R/P, 1950, wood, inner right half-round dial, left pull-out phono, double doors, 4 knobs, BC, 7 tubes, AC............**$50.00-65.00**

7XM21, table, 1950, plastic, large half-round dial, lower "hi-low" grille area with large pointer, 2 knobs, BC, FM, 6 tubes, AC/DC **$35.00-40.00**

8FM21, console-R/P, 1951, wood, upper half-round dial, lower pull-out phono drawer, 4 knobs, BC, FM, 8 tubes, AC...............**$45.00-55.00**

8S-515, portable, leatherette, upper right front dial, lower metal perforated grille with stylized "M" logo, rotatable handle, 2 knobs, BC, $40.00-50.00.

8S-534, portable, leatherette, right front half-round dial, vertical grille bars, rotatable handle, 2 knobs, BC **$40.00-45.00**

9A, chairside, 1937, two-tone wood, oval Deco case, top dial, tuning eye, front vertical grille bars, BC, SW, 9 tubes, AC...........**$180.00-200.00**

9FM21, console-R/P, 1950, wood, inner right half-round dial, left pull-out phono, doors, open storage, 4 knobs, BC, FM, 9 tubes, AC ..**$50.00-65.00**

10-Y-1, console, 1937, wood, upper front dial, lower cloth grille with vertical bars, tuning eye, 4 knobs, BC, SW, 10 tubes, AC..**$120.00-150.00**

12-Y-1, console, 1937, walnut, upper front dial, lower cloth grille with vertical bars, tuning eye, BC, SW, 12 tubes, AC **$150.00-180.00**

17-FM-41, console, 1941, wood, upper front slide rule dial, lower vertical grille bars, tuning eye, pushbuttons, BC, SW, FM1, 17 tubes, AC **$120.00-150.00**

40-60W, table, 1940, wood, right front square dial, left cloth grille, wooden handle, 3 knobs, BC, 6 tubes, AC/DC **$45.00-55.00**

40-65BP "Headliner," portable, 1940, cloth-covered, right front dial, left cloth grille, handle, 2 knobs, BC, 6 tubes, AC/DC/battery ..**$30.00-35.00**

40BK, console, 1940, wood, upper front dial, lower cloth grille with vertical bars, 3 knobs, BC, 4 tubes, battery **$110.00-130.00**

40BW, table, 1940, two-tone wood, right front square dial, raised left grille with cut-outs, 3 knobs, BC, 4 tubes, battery **$65.00-75.00**

41A, table, 1939, plastic, Deco, right front dial, raised left grille with graduated horizontal louvers, 3 knobs, BC, 4 tubes, battery **$50.00-65.00**

41B, table, 1939, plastic, right front dial, curved left grille with horizontal louvers, 3 knobs, BC, 4 tubes, battery **$35.00-45.00**

41D-1, portable, 1939, London tan leatherette, right front dial, left grille, handle, 2 knobs, BC, 4 tubes, battery **$30.00-35.00**

41D-2, portable, 1939, tan striped cloth, right front dial, left grille, handle, 2 knobs, BC, 4 tubes, battery **$30.00-35.00**

41E, table, 1939, two-tone wood, right front dial, left grille with cut-outs, 3 knobs, BC, 4 tubes, battery **$30.00-40.00**

41F, table, 1939, two-tone wood, right front dial, left grille with cut-outs, 3 knobs, BC, 4 tubes, battery **$30.00-40.00**

41H, portable, 1939, leatherette, right front dial, left cloth grille area, handle, 3 knobs, BC, 4 tubes, AC/DC/battery.....................**$25.00-30.00**

41S "Sporter," portable, 1939, leatherette, "camera-case" style, top dial, front grille, carrying strap, 2 knobs, BC, 4 tubes, battery ..**$45.00-55.00**

42B1, portable, 1953, two-tone, top right dial, front vertical grille bars, handle, 2 knobs, BC, battery **$30.00-35.00**

45B12, table, 1946, two-tone wood, right front dial, left cloth grille, 3 knobs, BC, 4 tubes, battery...**$30.00-35.00**

45P1 "Pixie," portable, 1956, plastic, right front metal dial plate, vertical grille bars, handle, 2 thumbwheel knobs, BC, 4 tubes, battery **$240.00-270.00**

45P2 "Pixie," portable, 1956, plastic, right front metal dial plate, vertical grille bars, handle, 2 thumbwheel knobs, BC, 4 tubes, battery **$240.00-270.00**

47B11, table, 1947, wood, right front half-round dial, left cloth grille with center "Motorola" logo, 3 knobs, BC, 4 tubes, battery ..**$35.00-40.00**

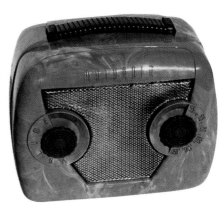

49L11Q, portable, 1949, plastic, right front dial over center metal grille, flex handle, 2 knobs, BC, 4 tubes, battery, $35.00-45.00.

48L11, portable, 1948, plastic, right front dial over center graduated horizontal louvers, handle, 2 knobs, BC, 4 tubes, battery **$35.00-45.00**

50X1, table, 1940, plastic, right front dial, left horizontal louvers, 2 knobs, BC, 5 tubes, AC/DC...**$35.00-45.00**

50XC "Circle Grill," table, 1940, Catalin, Deco, right front square dial, left round grille, handle, 2 hexagonal knobs, BC, 5 tubes, AC/DC ....**$2,000.00+**

50XC1 "Circle Grill," table, 1940, Catalin, Deco, right front square dial, left round grille, handle, 2 hexagonal knobs, BC, 5 tubes, AC/DC ....**$2,000.00+**

50XC2 "Circle Grill," table, 1940, Catalin, Deco, right front square dial, left round grille, handle, 2 hexagonal knobs, BC, 5 tubes, AC/DC ....**$2,000.00+**

50XC4 "Circle Grill," table, 1940, Catalin, Deco, right front square dial, left round grille, handle, 2 hexagonal knobs, BC, 5 tubes, AC/DC ....**$2,000.00+**

51A, table, 1939, plastic, Deco, right front dial, raised left grille with graduated horizontal louvers, 2 knobs, BC, 5 tubes, AC/DC....**$75.00-85.00**

51C, table, 1939, plastic, Deco, right front dial, raised left grille with graduated horizontal louvers, 2 knobs, BC, 5 tubes, AC/DC....**$75.00-85.00**

51D, portable, 1941, cloth-covered, inner right dial, left grille, fold-down front, handle, 3 knobs, BC, 5 tubes, AC/DC/battery **$30.00-35.00**

51X15 "S Grill," table, 1939, Catalin, right front square dial, left cloth grille with curved bars, tubular handle, 2 knobs, BC, 5 tubes, AC/DC ....**$3,000.00+**

51X16 "S Grill," table, 1939, Catalin, right front square dial, left cloth grille with curved bars, tubular handle, 2 knobs, BC, 5 tubes, AC/DC ....**$3,000.00+**

51X17, table, 1941, two-tone leatherette, right front square dial, left horizontal louvers, handle, 2 knobs, BC, 5 tubes, AC/DC....**$40.00-50.00**

51X18, table, 1941, ivory, upper front slanted slide rule dial, lower grille, 2 knobs, BC, 5 tubes, AC **$40.00-50.00**

51X19, table, 1942, wood, right front square dial, left horizontal plastic louvers, 2 knobs, BC, 5 tubes, AC/DC **$40.00-50.00**

52B1U, portable, 1953, plastic, top left dial, front vertical grille bars, handle, 2 knobs, BC, 4 tubes, AC/DC/battery.....................**$30.00-35.00**

52BW, table, 1940, walnut, right front slide rule dial, left horizontal louvers, 4 knobs, BC, SW, 5 tubes, battery **$35.00-40.00**

50XH1, table, 1940, plastic, right front dial, left horizontal louvers, 2 knobs, BC, 5 tubes, AC/DC, $40.00-50.00.

51X20, table, 1942, two-tone wood, upper front slanted slide rule dial, lower woven grille, 2 knobs, BC, 5 tubes, AC/DC, $45.00-55.00.

52C1, table-C, 1953, plastic, right front dial, left alarm clock, center vertical bars, 4 knobs, BC, 5 tubes, AC **$25.00-30.00**

52C4, table, 1939, Catalin, right front dial, left grille with 7 vertical louvers, 2 hexagonal knobs, BC, 5 tubes, AC/DC ....**$1,200.00+**

52C6, table-C, 1952, walnut plastic, right front dial, left alarm clock, center vertical grille bars, 5 knobs, BC, 5 tubes, AC............**$25.00-30.00**

52C7, table-C, 1952, ivory plastic, right front dial, left alarm clock, center vertical grille bars, 5 knobs, BC, 5 tubes, AC **$25.00-30.00**

52C8, table-C, 1952, green plastic, right front dial, left alarm clock, center vertical grille bars, 5 knobs, BC, 5 tubes, AC **$25.00-30.00**

52CW2, table/wall-C, 1953, white plastic, side dial, large upper front alarm clock, lower checkered panel with "M" logo, 5 knobs, BC, 5 tubes, AC **$30.00-35.00**

52CW3, table/wall-C, 1953, green plastic, side dial, large upper front alarm clock, lower checkered panel with "M" logo, 5 knobs, BC, 5 tubes, AC **$30.00-35.00**

52CW4, table/wall-C, 1953, red plastic, side dial, large upper front alarm clock, lower checkered panel with "M" logo, 5 knobs, BC, 5 tubes, AC **$30.00-35.00**

52H11U, table, 1952, walnut plastic, upper front dial with stick pointer, lower vertical bars, 1 knob, BC, 5 tubes, AC/DC **$30.00-35.00**

52H12U, table, 1952, ivory plastic, upper front dial with stick pointer, lower vertical bars, 1 knob, BC, 5 tubes, AC/DC **$30.00-35.00**

52H13U, table, 1952, green plastic, upper front dial with stick pointer, lower vertical bars, 1 knob, BC, 5 tubes, AC/DC **$30.00-35.00**

52H14U, table, 1952, gray plastic, upper front dial with stick pointer, lower vertical bars, 1 knob, BC, 5 tubes, AC/DC **$30.00-35.00**

52L1, portable, 1953, plastic, top right dial, front lattice grille & stylized "M," handle, 2 knobs, BC, 4 tubes, AC/DC/battery........**$30.00-35.00**

52CW1, table/wall-C, 1953, yellow plastic, side dial, large upper front alarm clock, lower checkered panel with "M" logo, 5 knobs, BC, 5 tubes, AC, $30.00-35.00.

52M1U, portable, 1952, small green case, inner right round dial, lower lattice grille, stylized "M" cut-out, flip-up front, 2 knobs, BC, 4 tubes, AC/DC/battery **$40.00-50.00**

52R12A, table, 1952, ivory plastic, right front round dial, left round grille disc with stylized "M," 2 knobs, BC, 5 tubes, AC/DC **$25.00-30.00**

52R11U, table, 1952, walnut plastic, right front round dial, left round grille disc with stylized "M," 2 knobs, BC, 5 tubes, AC/DC **$25.00-30.00**

52R12U, table, 1952, ivory plastic, right front round dial, left round grille disc with stylized "M," 2 knobs, BC, 5 tubes, AC/DC **$25.00-30.00**

52R13U, table, 1952, maroon plastic, right front round dial, left round grille disc with stylized "M," 2 knobs, BC, 5 tubes, AC/DC......**$25.00-30.00**

52R14U, table, 1952, gray plastic, right front round dial, left round grille disc with stylized "M," 2 knobs, BC, 5 tubes, AC/DC **$25.00-30.00**

52R15U, table, 1952, green plastic, right front round dial, left round grille disc with stylized "M," 2 knobs, BC, 5 tubes, AC/DC **$25.00-30.00**

52R16U, table, 1952, red plastic, right front round dial, left round grille disc with stylized "M," 2 knobs, BC, 5 tubes, AC/DC **$25.00-30.00**

53A, table, 1939, two-tone wood, right front dial, left horizontal wrap-around grille bars, 2 knobs, BC, 5 tubes, AC/DC **$65.00-75.00**

53C, table, 1939, plastic, Deco, right front dial, raised left grille with graduated horizontal louvers, 2 knobs, BC, 5 tubes, AC/DC....**$75.00-85.00**

53C1, table-C, 1954, walnut plastic, right front dial, left alarm clock, side horizontal bars, 3 knobs, BC, 5 tubes, AC.....................**$25.00-30.00**

53C2, table-C, 1954, ivory plastic, right front dial, left alarm clock, side horizontal bars, 3 knobs, BC, 5 tubes, AC.....................**$25.00-30.00**

53C3, table-C, 1954, green plastic, right front dial, left alarm clock, side horizontal bars, 3 knobs, BC, 5 tubes, AC.....................**$25.00-30.00**

53C4, table-C, 1954, red plastic, right front dial, left alarm clock, side horizontal bars, 3 knobs, BC, 5 tubes, AC.....................**$25.00-30.00**

52M2U, portable, 1952, small maroon case, inner right round dial, lower lattice grille, stylized "M" cut-out, flip-up front, 2 knobs, BC, 4 tubes, AC/DC/battery, $40.00-50.00.

53D1, table-C-N, 1954, clock/radio/desk set, center radio unit with round alarm clock, right & left pen holders, 5 knobs, BC, 5 tubes, AC **$50.00-65.00**

53F2, table-R/P, 1954, plastic, top round dial, vertical front grille bars, lift top, inner phono, 3 knobs, BC, 5 tubes, AC **$40.00-50.00**

53H1, table, 1954, ebony plastic, modern, lower front slide rule dial, large upper perforated grille area with center logo, 2 knobs, BC, 5 tubes, AC/DC **$75.00-85.00**

53H2, table, 1954, gray plastic, modern, lower front slide rule dial, large upper perforated grille area with center logo, 2 knobs, BC, 5 tubes, AC/DC **$75.00-85.00**

53H3, table, 1954, green plastic, modern, lower front slide rule dial, large upper perforated grille area with center logo, 2 knobs, BC, 5 tubes, AC/DC **$75.00-85.00**

53H4, table, 1954, red plastic, modern, lower front slide rule dial, large upper perforated grille area with center logo, 2 knobs, BC, 5 tubes, AC/DC **$75.00-85.00**

53LC1, portable-C, 1953, green plastic, upper right dial/left spring wound clock, large lower grille area with center logo, handle, 3 knobs, BC, 4 tubes, AC/DC/battery **$40.00-50.00**

53LC2, portable-C, 1953, maroon plastic, upper right dial/left spring wound clock, large lower grille area with center logo, handle, 3 knobs, BC, 4 tubes, AC/DC/battery...............................**$40.00-50.00**

53LC3, portable-C, 1953, gray plastic, upper right dial/left spring wound clock, large lower grille area with center logo, handle, 3 knobs, BC, 4 tubes, AC/DC/battery **$40.00-50.00**

53R1, table, 1954, walnut plastic, recessed vertical lattice front, upper right round dial, left grille, 2 knobs, BC, 5 tubes, AC/DC..........**$20.00-30.00**

53R2, table, 1954, ivory plastic, recessed vertical lattice front, upper right round dial, left grille, 2 knobs, BC, 5 tubes, AC/DC **$20.00-30.00**

53R3, table, 1954, yellow plastic, recessed vertical lattice front, upper right round dial, left grille, 2 knobs, BC, 5 tubes, AC/DC..........**$20.00-30.00**

53R4, table, 1954, gray plastic, recessed vertical lattice front, upper right round dial, left grille, 2 knobs, BC, 5 tubes, AC/DC **$20.00-30.00**

53R5, table, 1954, green plastic, recessed vertical lattice front, upper right round dial, left grille, 2 knobs, BC, 5 tubes, AC/DC **$20.00-30.00**

53R6, table, 1954, red plastic, recessed vertical lattice front, upper right round dial, left grille, 2 knobs, BC, 5 tubes, AC/DC **$20.00-30.00**

53X2, table, 1954, sand plastic, large half-round dial on case top, front horizontal grille bars with logo, 2 knobs, BC, 5 tubes, AC/DC..**$45.00-55.00**

53X3, table, 1954, green plastic, large half-round dial on case top, front horizontal grille bars with logo, 2 knobs, BC, 5 tubes, AC/DC..**$45.00-55.00**

53X4, table, 1954, rust plastic, large half-round dial on case top, front horizontal grille bars with logo, 2 knobs, BC, 5 tubes, AC/DC..**$45.00-55.00**

52X110, table, plastic, upper front raised slide rule dial, large lower perforated grille area, 2 knobs, BC, $30.00-35.00.

54L, portable, 1955, plastic, left side dial, large front metal perforated oval grille area with center crest, fold-down handle, 1 left side and 1 right side knob, BC, 4 tubes, AC/DC/battery **$30.00-35.00**

55B1, portable, 1955, leatherette, upper front dial, center lattice grille area, rotatable handle, 2 knobs, BC, 4 tubes, AC/DC/battery..**$35.00-40.00**

55B1U, portable, 1955, leatherette, upper front dial, center lattice grille area, rotatable handle, 2 knobs, BC, 5 tubes, AC/DC/battery..**$35.00-40.00**

55F11, table-R/P, 1946, wood, upper front slide rule dial, lower grille area, lift top, inner phono, 2 knobs, BC, 5 tubes, AC **$30.00-35.00**

55L2, portable, 1956, leatherette, right front round dial, "V" shaped checkered grille area, rotatable handle, 2 knobs, BC, 4 tubes, AC/DC/battery **$40.00-50.00**

55L3, portable, 1956, leatherette, right front round dial, "V" shaped checkered grille area, rotatable handle, 2 knobs, BC, 4 tubes, AC/DC/battery **$40.00-50.00**

55L3U, portable, 1956, leatherette, right front round dial, "V" shaped checkered grille area, rotatable handle, 2 knobs, BC, 4 tubes, AC/DC/battery **$40.00-50.00**

55L4, portable, 1956, leatherette, right front round dial, "V" shaped checkered grille area, rotatable handle, 2 knobs, BC, 4 tubes, AC/DC/battery **$40.00-50.00**

55M2, portable, 1956, leatherette, right front dial, plastic lattice grille area, rotatable handle, 2 knobs, BC, 4 tubes, AC/DC/battery..**$35.00-40.00**

55X11, table, 1946, brown plastic, upper front slide rule dial, lower horizontal louvers, 2 knobs, BC, 5 tubes, AC/DC **$30.00-35.00**

55X12, table, 1946, ivory plastic, upper front slide rule dial, lower horizontal louvers, 2 knobs, BC, 5 tubes, AC/DC **$30.00-35.00**

55X13, table, 1946, two-tone wood, upper front dial, lower cloth grille, 2 knobs, BC, 5 tubes, AC/DC..**$40.00-50.00**

53X1, table, 1954, walnut plastic, large half-round dial on case top, front horizontal grille bars with logo, 2 knobs, BC, 5 tubes, AC/DC, $45.00-55.00.

56CC, table-C, 1956, plastic, front center dial, left front grille with vertical louvers, right front clock, feet, 5 knobs, BC, 5 tubes, AC ..**$30.00-35.00**

56CD, table-C, 1956, plastic, front center dial, left front grille with vertical louvers, right front clock, feet, 5 knobs, BC, 5 tubes, AC ..**$30.00-35.00**

56CJ, table-C, 1956, plastic, left front dial, right alarm clock, center panel with "M" logo, 5 knobs, BC, 5 tubes, AC **$20.00-25.00**

56CS2A, table-C, 1956, plastic, lower right front dial over vertical grille bars, left alarm clock, feet, 2 knobs, BC, 5 tubes, AC....**$20.00-25.00**

56H, table, 1956, plastic, lower front conical dial over large textured grille area, feet, 2 knobs, BC, 5 tubes, AC/DC **$65.00-75.00**

56H1, table, 1956, plastic, lower front conical dial over large textured grille area, feet, 2 knobs, BC, 5 tubes, AC/DC **$65.00-75.00**

56H4, table, 1956, plastic, lower front conical dial over large textured grille area, feet, 2 knobs, BC, 5 tubes **$65.00-75.00**

56L1, portable, 1956, leatherette, right front half-round dial, vertical grille bars, rotatable handle, 2 knobs, BC, 4 tubes, AC/DC/battery **$35.00-40.00**

56L2, portable, 1956, leatherette, right front half-round dial, vertical grille bars, rotatable handle, 2 knobs, BC, 4 tubes, AC/DC/battery **$35.00-40.00**

56L2A, portable, 1956, leatherette, right front half-round dial, vertical grille bars, rotatable handle, 2 knobs, BC, 4 tubes, AC/DC/battery **$35.00-40.00**

56L4, portable, 1956, leatherette, right front half-round dial, vertical grille bars, rotatable handle, 2 knobs, BC, 4 tubes, AC/DC/battery **$35.00-40.00**

56M1, portable, 1956, leatherette, right front chrome dial plate, lattice grille area, rotatable handle, 2 knobs, BC, 4 tubes, AC/DC/battery **$40.00-50.00**

56M2, portable, 1956, leatherette, right front chrome dial plate, lattice grille area, rotatable handle, 2 knobs, BC, 4 tubes, AC/DC/battery **$40.00-50.00**

56R, table, 1956, plastic, recessed vertical lattice front, lower right dial, center grille, feet, 2 knobs, BC, 5 tubes, AC/DC **$25.00-30.00**

56X1, table, 1940, plastic, right front dial, left horizontal wrap-around louvers, 2 knobs, BC, 5 tubes, AC/DC **$45.00-55.00**

56X11, table, 1947, walnut plastic, right front square dial, left horizontal louvers, 2 knobs, BC, 5 tubes, AC/DC **$35.00-45.00**

56XA1, table, 1940, plastic, right front dial, left horizontal wrap-around louvers, 2 knobs, BC, 5 tubes, AC/DC **$50.00-65.00**

55L2U, portable, 1956, leatherette, right front round dial, "V" shaped checkered grille area, rotatable handle, 2 knobs, BC, 4 tubes, AC/DC/battery, $40.00-50.00.

56B1, portable, 1956, leatherette, right front dial, center plastic grille with "V" louvers, rotatable handle, 2 knobs, BC, 4 tubes, AC/DC/battery, $35.00-40.00.

56XAW, table, 1940, walnut, right front dial, left cloth grille with cut-out, 4 top right pushbuttons, 2 knobs, BC, 5 tubes, AC/DC **$50.00-65.00**

57A1, table, 1957, ebony plastic, lower right round dial over horizontal front bars, center "M" logo, 2 knobs, BC, 5 tubes, AC/DC **$30.00-35.00**

57A2, table, 1957, red plastic, lower right round dial over horizontal front bars, center "M" logo, 2 knobs, BC, 5 tubes, AC/DC **$30.00-35.00**

57A3, table, 1957, white plastic, lower right round dial over horizontal front bars, center "M" logo, 2 knobs, BC, 5 tubes, AC/DC **$30.00-35.00**

57CC2, table-C, 1957, plastic, center front dial, right alarm clock face, left vertical grille bars with upper left "M" logo, feet, 5 knobs, BC, 5 tubes, AC **$30.00-35.00**

57CE, table-C, 1957, plastic, lower right front dial over vertical grille bars, left alarm clock, feet, BC, 5 tubes, AC........................**$25.00-30.00**

57H1, table, 1957, black plastic, concave front with left slide rule dial and right grille, top on-off pushbutton, feet, 2 knobs, BC, 5 tubes, AC/DC **$30.00-35.00**

57H2, table, 1957, white plastic, concave front with left slide rule dial and right grille, top on-off pushbutton, feet, 2 knobs, BC, 5 tubes, AC/DC **$30.00-35.00**

57H3, table, 1957, green plastic, concave front with left slide rule dial and right grille, top on-off pushbutton, feet, 2 knobs, BC, 5 tubes, AC/DC **$40.00-50.00**

57H4, table, 1957, blue plastic, concave front with left slide rule dial and right grille, top on-off pushbutton, feet, 2 knobs, BC, 5 tubes, AC/DC **$40.00-50.00**

56M3, portable, 1956, leatherette, right front chrome dial plate, lattice grille area, rotatable handle, 2 knobs, BC, 4 tubes, AC/DC/battery, $40.00-50.00.

57R1, table, 1957, black plastic, lower right front dial over horizontal grille bars, feet, 2 "steering wheel" knobs, BC, 5 tubes, AC/DC..**$50.00-60.00**

57R2, table, 1957, white plastic, lower right front dial over horizontal grille bars, feet, 2 "steering wheel" knobs, BC, 5 tubes, AC/DC..**$50.00-60.00**

57R3, table, 1957, turquoise plastic, lower right front dial over horizontal grille bars, feet, 2 "steering wheel" knobs, BC, 5 tubes, AC/DC **$75.00-85.00**

57R4, table, 1957, pink plastic, lower right front dial over horizontal grille bars, feet, 2 "steering wheel" knobs, BC, 5 tubes, AC/DC, $75.00-85.00.

57X11, table, 1947, plastic, slanted sides, upper front slide rule dial, lower horizontal louvers, 2 knobs, BC, 5 tubes, AC/DC **$45.00-55.00**

58A11, table, 1948, plastic, right front square dial, left horizontal louvers, 2 knobs, BC, 5 tubes, AC/DC **$40.00-45.00**

58FRC, table-R/P, 1940, wood, right front slide rule dial, left cloth grille with cut-outs, lift top, inner phono, 3 knobs, BC, 5 tubes, AC ..**$40.00-45.00**

58G11, table, 1949, walnut plastic, right front square dial, left horizontal louvers, 2 bullet knobs, BC, 5 tubes, AC/DC..................**$30.00-35.00**

58G12, table, 1949, ivory plastic, right front square dial, left horizontal louvers, 2 bullet knobs, BC, 5 tubes, AC/DC..................**$30.00-35.00**

58L11, table, 1948, plastic, right front dial over graduated horizontal louvers, handle, 2 knobs, BC, 4 tubes, AC/DC/battery ..**$30.00-35.00**

58R11, table, 1948, plastic, raised center panel with right round dial & left lattice grille, 2 knobs, BC, 5 tubes, AC/DC **$30.00-35.00**

58R11A, table, 1949, plastic, raised center panel with right round dial & left lattice grille, 2 knobs, BC, 5 tubes, AC/DC **$30.00-35.00**

58X12, table, 1949, plastic, upper front slide rule dial, lower trapezoid cloth grille with 3 vertical bars, 2 knobs, BC, 5 tubes, AC/DC ..**$40.00-50.00**

59F11, portable-R/P, 1949, leatherette, inner dial, phono, record storage, lift top, handle, 3 knobs, BC, 5 tubes, AC **$25.00-30.00**

59H11U, table, 1950, brown plastic, dial numerals on horizontal grille bars, stick pointer, 2 knobs, BC, 5 tubes, AC/DC **$30.00-35.00**

59H12U, table, 1950, ivory plastic, dial numerals on horizontal grille bars, stick pointer, 2 knobs, BC, 5 tubes, AC/DC **$30.00-35.00**

59L12Q, portable, 1949, plastic, right dial over center wedged-shaped grille, flex handle, 2 knobs, BC, 4 tubes, AC/DC/battery..**$30.00-35.00**

59R11, table, 1949, plastic, right front round dial over checkered grille area, recessed base, 2 knobs, BC, 5 tubes, AC/DC **$30.00-35.00**

59T-4, table, 1938, wood, 4 pushbuttons, front cloth grille with cut-outs, 2 top thumbwheel, BC, 5 tubes, AC **$65.00-75.00**

59T-5, table, 1938, wood, right front slide rule dial, left grille with Deco cut-outs, pushbuttons, 4 knobs, BC, 5 tubes, AC............**$85.00-95.00**

59X12I, table, 1950, ivory plastic, large front half-round dial over horizontal grille bars, 2 knobs, BC, 5 tubes, AC/DC **$35.00-40.00**

59X21U, table, 1950, plastic, large front half-round dial over horizontal grille bars, 2 knobs, BC, SW, 5 tubes, AC/DC...............**$35.00-40.00**

60-X-1, table, 1940, plastic, right front dial, left horizontal wrap-around louvers, handle, 2 knobs, BC, 6 tubes, AC/DC **$40.00-50.00**

61A, table, 1939, plastic, right front dial, left horizontal wrap-around louvers, 5 pushbuttons, 2 knobs, BC, 5 tubes, AC/DC **$65.00-75.00**

61B, table, 1939, plastic, right front dial, left horizontal wrap-around louvers, 5 pushbuttons, 3 knobs, BC, SW, 5 tubes, AC/DC..**$65.00-75.00**

61C, table, 1939, wood, right front slide rule dial, left grille with horizontal bars, pushbuttons, 4 knobs, BC, SW, 6 tubes, AC **$65.00-75.00**

61-CA, table, 1940, wood, right front slide rule dial, left grille with horizontal bars, pushbuttons, 4 knobs, BC, SW, 6 tubes, AC **$65.00-75.00**

61D, console, 1939, wood, upper front slide rule dial, lower grille with 3 vertical bars, 6 pushbuttons, 4 knobs, BC, SW, 6 tubes, AC ..**$120.00-150.00**

61E, table, 1939, plastic, right front dial, left horizontal wrap-around louvers, 5 pushbuttons, 2 knobs, BC, 6 tubes, AC/DC **$65.00-75.00**

61F, table-R/P, 1939, wood, right front slide rule dial, left grille with cut-outs, lift top, inner phono, BC, 6 tubes, AC....................**$45.00-55.00**

61F23, console-R/P, 1941, wood, inner right dial, left phono, double lift top, front cloth grille with vertical bars, 4 knobs, BC, SW, 6 tubes, AC **$65.00-75.00**

61K23, console, 1942, wood, upper front slide rule dial, lower cloth grille with vertical bars, pushbuttons, 4 knobs, BC, SW, 6 tubes, AC...**$110.00-130.00**

61T22, table, 1941, wood, right front slide rule dial, left cloth grille with criss-cross cut-out, 5 pushbuttons, 4 knobs, BC, SW, 6 tubes, AC **$65.00-75.00**

62B, table, 1939, plastic, right front dial, left horizontal wrap-around louvers, 5 pushbuttons, 3 knobs, BC, SW, 6 tubes, AC/DC..**$65.00-75.00**

62C1, table-C, 1952, plastic, right front dial, center divider panel, left alarm clock, 5 knobs, BC, 6 tubes, AC **$20.00-25.00**

62C2, table-C, 1952, ivory plastic, right front dial, center divider panel, left alarm clock, 5 knobs, BC, 6 tubes, AC **$20.00-25.00**

62C3, table-C, 1952, green plastic, right front dial, center divider panel, left alarm clock, 5 knobs, BC, 6 tubes, AC **$20.00-25.00**

62E, table, 1939, plastic, right front dial, left horizontal wrap-around louvers, 5 pushbuttons, 2 knobs, BC, 6 tubes, AC/DC **$65.00-75.00**

62F1, console-R/P, 1940, wood, inner right slide rule dial, left phono, lift top, front cloth grille with 2 vertical bars, BC, SW, 6 tubes, AC..**$85.00-95.00**

57X12, table, 1947, ivory plastic, slanted sides, upper front slide rule dial, lower horizontal louvers, 2 knobs, BC, 5 tubes, AC/DC, $45.00-55.00.

62T1, table, 1940, walnut, right front slide rule dial, left cloth grille with horizontal bars, pushbuttons, 4 knobs, BC, SW, 6 tubes, AC..**$65.00-75.00**

62X21, table, 1954, plastic, upper front dial with stick pointer, lower vertical grille bars, stylized "M" logo, 2 knobs, BC, SW, 6 tubes, AC/DC **$35.00-40.00**

63C, table, 1955, plastic, large front oval clock face, right side dial, feet, 2 front and 2 side knobs, BC, 6 tubes, AC **$40.00-45.00**

63E, table, 1939, wood, right front dial, left grille with vertical bars, 5 pushbuttons, 2 knobs, BC, 6 tubes, AC **$65.00-75.00**

63L1, portable, 1953, plastic, upper front metal panel with slide rule dial, lower vertical grille bars with center logo, handle, 2 thumbwheel knobs, BC, 5 tubes, AC/DC/battery...............................**$35.00-40.00**

64X1, table, 1955, plastic, lower front slide rule dial, large upper grille area with 2 round speaker cut-outs under horizontal bars, 2 knobs, BC, 6 tubes, AC/DC..**$25.00-30.00**

65F11, table-R/P, 1946, wood, outer front dial & grille, lift top, inner phono, 2 knobs, BC, AC **$30.00-35.00**

65L11, portable, 1946, cloth-covered, inner right dial, left cloth grille, flip-up lid, 2 knobs, BC, 6 tubes, AC/DC/battery.................**$40.00-45.00**

65T21, table, 1946, wood, right front slide rule dial over large cloth grille, 4 knobs, BC, SW, 6 tubes, AC..**$50.00-55.00**

65X11, table, 1946, brown plastic, upper front slide rule dial, lower horizontal louvers, 2 knobs, BC, 6 tubes, AC/DC **$40.00-50.00**

65X12, table, 1946, ivory plastic, upper front slide rule dial, lower horizontal louvers, 2 knobs, BC, 6 tubes, AC/DC **$40.00-50.00**

58X11, table, 1949, brown plastic, upper front slide rule dial, lower trapezoid cloth grille with 3 vertical bars, 2 knobs, BC, 5 tubes, AC/DC, $40.00-50.00.

65X13, table, 1946, wood, upper front slide rule dial, lower grille with vertical bars, rounded front corners, 2 knobs, BC, 6 tubes, AC/DC **$40.00-50.00**

67F11, table-R/P, 1948, plastic, outer front vertical dial, right & left grille areas, pushbutton controls, lift top, inner phono, 2 knobs, BC, 6 tubes, AC...**$40.00-50.00**

67F12, table-R/P, 1948, walnut, outer front vertical dial, right & left grille areas, pushbutton controls, lift top, inner phono, 2 knobs, BC, 6 tubes, AC...**$35.00-40.00**

67F12B, table-R/P, 1948, blonde, outer front vertical dial, right & left grille areas, pushbutton controls, lift top, inner phono, 2 knobs, BC, 6 tubes, AC...**$35.00-40.00**

67F14, console-R/P, 1949, wood, step-down top, slide rule dial, center pull-out phono drawer, lower storage, 4 knobs, BC, 6 tubes, AC **$75.00-85.00**

67F61BN, table-R/P, 1948, wood, right front slide rule dial, left cloth grille, lift top, inner phono, 4 knobs, BC, SW, 6 tubes, AC........**$50.00-55.00**

67L11, portable, 1948, alligator, inner slide rule dial, center grille, lift-up front, 2 square knobs, BC, 5 tubes, AC/DC/battery **$40.00-45.00**

67X11, table, 1947, walnut plastic, upper front slide rule dial, lower horizontal wrap-around louvers, 2 knobs, BC, 6 tubes, AC/DC **$40.00-45.00**

67X12, table, 1947, ivory plastic, upper front slide rule dial, lower horizontal wrap-around louvers, 2 knobs, BC, 6 tubes, AC/DC ..**$40.00-45.00**

67X13, table, 1947, wood, upper front slide rule dial, lower cloth grille, 2 knobs, BC, 6 tubes, AC/DC **$40.00-45.00**

67XM21, table, 1948, plastic, upper front wrap-over slide rule dial, lower horizontal wrap-around louvers, 2 knobs, BC, FM, 5 tubes, AC/DC **$40.00-45.00**

68F11, table-R/P, 1949, plastic, outer vertical slide rule dial, right & left grille areas, lift top, inner phono, 2 knobs, BC, 6 tubes, AC **$50.00-55.00**

68F12, table-R/P, 1949, wood, outer front vertical slide rule dial, right & left grille areas, lift top, inner phono, 2 knobs, BC, 6 tubes, AC **$40.00-45.00**

68F14, console-R/P, 1949, wood, upper front vertical slide rule dial, criss-cross grille, lift top, inner phono, lower storage, 2 knobs, BC, 6 tubes, AC **$50.00-65.00**

68T11, table, 1949, plastic, upper front slanted slide rule dial, large lower cloth grille, 2 knobs, BC, 5 tubes, AC **$40.00-50.00**

68X11, table, 1949, two-tone plastic, upper front slanted slide rule dial, lower grille with geometric cut-outs, 2 knobs, BC, 6 tubes, AC/DC **$75.00-85.00**

59X11, table, 1950, mahogany plastic, large front half-round dial over horizontal grille bars, 2 knobs, BC, 5 tubes, AC/DC, $35.00-40.00.

62CW1, table-C, 1953, wood, lower front slide rule dial, large upper clock face, side grille, 2 knobs, BC, 6 tubes, AC, $35.00-40.00.

64X2, table, 1955, plastic, lower front slide rule dial, large upper grille area with 2 round speaker cut-outs under horizontal bars, 2 knobs, BC, 6 tubes, AC/DC, $25.00-30.00.

68X11Q, table, 1949, two-tone plastic, upper front slanted slide rule dial, lower grille with geometric cut-outs, 2 knobs, BC, 6 tubes, AC/DC **$75.00-85.00**

69L11, portable, 1949, plastic coated cloth with aluminum trim, suitcase-style, dial moves inside clear handle, 2 top thumbwheel knobs, BC, AC/DC/battery **$50.00-65.00**

71-A, table, 1940, walnut, right front slide rule dial, left wrap-around grille bars, pushbuttons, 4 knobs, BC, SW, 7 tubes, AC/DC ..**$65.00-75.00**

72XM21, table, 1952, plastic, large front half-round dial with inner checkered grille area, stylized "M" logo, 2 knobs, BC, FM, 6 tubes, AC/DC **$35.00-40.00**

75F21, console-R/P, 1947, wood, upper front slanted slide rule dial, center pull-out phono drawer, lower cloth grille, 4 knobs, BC, SW, 7 tubes, AC **$95.00-115.00**

75F31, console-R/P, 1947, wood, inner right slide rule dial, 6 pushbuttons, left phono, 2 lift tops, 4 knobs, BC, SW, FM, 7 tubes, AC..**$75.00-85.00**

76F31, console-R/P, 1948, wood, inner right slide rule dial, left pull-out phono, fold-down front, 4 knobs, BC, SW, FM, 7 tubes, AC **$75.00-85.00**

77FM21, console-R/P, 1948, wood, step-down top, wrap-over slide rule dial, center front pull-out phono drawer, lower storage, 4 knobs, BC, FM, 6 tubes, AC **$85.00-95.00**

77FM22, console-R/P, 1949, wood, right front vertical slide rule dial, left lift top, inner phono, lower storage, 4 knobs, BC, FM, 6 tubes, AC **$65.00-75.00**

77FM22M, console-R/P, 1948, wood, step-down top, wrap-over slide rule dial, center pull-out phono, lower storage, 4 knobs, BC, FM, 6 tubes, AC **$85.00-95.00**

77FM22WM, console-R/P, 1948, wood, step-down top, wrap-over slide rule dial, center pull-out phono, lower storage, 4 knobs, BC, FM, 6 tubes, AC **$85.00-95.00**

77FM23, console-R/P, 1948, wood, step-down top, wrap-over slide rule dial, center front pull-out phono, lower storage, 4 knobs, BC, FM, 6 tubes, AC **$85.00-95.00**

77XM21, table, 1948, walnut plastic, upper front slide rule dial, lower horizontal wrap-around louvers, 2 knobs, BC, FM, 6 tubes, AC/DC **$50.00-65.00**

77XM22B, table, 1948, blonde, top wrap-over slide rule dial, lower cloth wrap-around grille, 2 knobs, BC, FM, 6 tubes, AC/DC ..**$35.00-40.00**

78F11, console-R/P, 1949, wood, step-down top, upper front slide rule dial, center pull-out phono drawer, lower criss-cross grille, storage, 4 knobs, BC, 6 tubes, AC **$85.00-95.00**

78F12M, console-R/P, 1949, wood, right front vertical slide rule dial, lift top, inner phono, lower left storage, right criss-cross grille, 4 knobs, BC, 6 tubes, AC **$65.00-75.00**

78FM21, console-R/P, 1949, wood, step-down top, upper front slide rule dial, center pull-out phono drawer, lower storage, 4 knobs, BC, FM, 6 tubes, AC **$85.00-95.00**

78FM22, console-R/P, 1948, wood, right front vertical slide rule dial, left phono, lower grille & storage, 4 knobs, BC, FM, 6 tubes, AC.............**$75.00-85.00**

79FM21R, console-R/P, 1950, wood, upper front half-round dial, lower pull-out phono drawer, 4 knobs, BC, FM, 6 tubes, AC ..**$85.00-95.00**

79XM21, table, 1950, plastic, large front half-round dial with inner stick pointer & grille, 2 knobs, BC, FM, 6 tubes, AC/DC **$50.00-65.00**

81C, console, 1939, wood, slide rule dial, lower grille with vertical bars, 6 pushbuttons, BC, SW, 8 tubes, AC **$120.00-150.00**

81F21, console-R/P, 1941, wood, upper slide rule dial, 5 pushbuttons, pull-out phono drawer, 4 knobs, BC, SW, 8 tubes, AC........**$110.00-130.00**

81K31, console, 1941, wood, upper front slide rule dial, lower cloth grille with center vertical divider, pushbuttons, 4 knobs, BC, SW, 8 tubes, AC **$120.00-150.00**

82A, console, 1939, wood, slide rule dial, automatic tuning clock, vertical grille bars, 4 knobs, BC, SW, 8 tubes, AC **$150.00-180.00**

85F21, console-R/P, 1946, wood, slanted slide rule dial, 6 pushbuttons, pull-out phono, 4 knobs, BC, SW, 8 tubes, AC **$95.00-115.00**

63X, table, 1954, plastic, lower front slide rule dial, large upper grille area, 2 knobs, BC, 6 tubes, AC/DC, $25.00-30.00.

67T11, table, wood, upper front slide rule dial overlaps large criss-cross grille area, 2 knobs, BC, $40.00-45.00.

68L11, portable, 1948, plastic coated cloth with aluminum trim, suitcase-style, dial moves inside handle, 2 top thumbwheel knobs, BC, 5 tubes, AC/DC/battery, $50.00-65.00.

85K21, console, 1946, wood, slanted slide rule dial, cloth grille, contrasting veneer, 4 knobs, BC, SW, 8 tubes, AC **$95.00-115.00**

88FM21, console-R/P, 1949, wood, inner right slide rule dial, left pull-out phono drawer, 4 knobs, BC, FM, 8 tubes, AC...............**$65.00-75.00**

95F31, console-R/P, 1947, wood, right tilt-out slide rule dial, inner left phono, 4 knobs, BC, SW, FM, 9 tubes, AC **$75.00-85.00**

99FM21R, console-R/P, 1949, wood, inner right slide rule dial, left pull-out phono, storage, 4 knobs, BC, FM, 9 tubes, AC.......**$65.00-75.00**

101C31, console, 1941, wood, slanted upper front with round electric clock station presets and slide rule dial, lower grille with center vertical bar, rounded front corners, 4 knobs, BC, SW, 10 tubes, AC **$200.00-240.00**

107F31, console-R/P, 1948, wood, tilt-out dial, pushbuttons, pull-out phono drawer, 4 knobs, BC, SW, FM, 10 tubes, AC **$75.00-85.00**

107F31B, console-R/P, 1948, wood, tilt-out dial, pushbuttons, pull-out phono drawer, 4 knobs, BC, SW, FM, 10 tubes, AC **$75.00-85.00**

496BT-1, table, 1939, wood, right front dial, left grille with horizontal cut-outs, 3 knobs, BC, SW, 4 tubes, battery **$35.00-40.00**

A-1, portable, 1941, maroon metal & chrome, set turns on when lid is opened, handle, 2 knobs, BC, 4 tubes, battery **$50.00-65.00**

A1B, table, 1960, blue plastic, lower right front dial over horizontal grille bars, 2 knobs, BC, 5 tubes, AC/DC.................**$20.00-25.00**

A1N, table, 1960, brown plastic, lower right front dial over horizontal grille bars, 2 knobs, BC, 5 tubes, AC/DC.................**$20.00-25.00**

A1R, table, 1960, red plastic, lower right front dial over horizontal grille bars, 2 knobs, BC, 5 tubes, AC/DC.................**$20.00-25.00**

A1W, table, 1960, white plastic, lower right front dial over horizontal grille bars, 2 knobs, BC, 5 tubes, AC/DC.................**$20.00-25.00**

A4G15 "Custom 6," table, 1959, plastic, lower right front dial, large upper grille area with vertical bars, 2 knobs, BC, AC/DC **$25.00-30.00**

A15J3, table, 1960, plastic, lower right front dial over large grille area with horizontal bars, 2 knobs, BC, AC/DC **$20.00-25.00**

A18B3UL, table, plastic, large right front round dial over horizontal grille bars, feet, 2 knobs, BC, AC/DC.....................**$25.00-30.00**

69X11, table, 1950, plastic, large front half-round dial with stick pointer and inner woven grille area, 2 knobs, BC, 6 tubes, AC/DC, $45.00-50.00.

77XM22, table, 1948, walnut, top wrap-over slide rule dial, lower cloth wrap-around grille, 2 knobs, BC, FM, 6 tubes, AC/DC, $35.00-40.00.

A21N, table, 1963, beige plastic, large square off-center dial area over lattice front grille, feet, 2 knobs, BC, 5 tubes, AC/DC **$20.00-25.00**

A21W, table, 1963, white plastic, large square off-center dial area over lattice front grille, feet, 2 knobs, BC, 5 tubes, AC/DC **$20.00-25.00**

A22B, table, 1963, blue plastic, large square off-center dial area over lattice front grille, feet, 2 knobs, BC, 5 tubes, AC/DC **$20.00-25.00**

A22N, table, 1963, beige plastic, large square off-center dial area over lattice front grille, feet, 2 knobs, BC, 5 tubes, AC/DC **$20.00-25.00**

B-150, bike radio, 1940, mounts on bike handlebars, horizontal grille bars, separate battery pack, BC, 3 tubes, battery.........**$75.00-95.00**

C4B2, table-C, 1960, plastic, two-level case, center front dial, right round clock face, left vertical grille bars, feet, 4 tubes, BC, 5 tubes, AC **$30.00-35.00**

C5G, table-C, 1959, plastic, center round dial, pushbuttons, left alarm clock, right vertical bars, 7 knobs, BC **$20.00-25.00**

MURDOCK
Wm. J. Murdock Company
430 Washington Avenue, Chelsea, Massachusetts

The Wm. J. Murdock Company began business making radio parts and related items and the company produced its first complete radio in 1924. The Murdock Model 200, circa 1925, featured a very unusual loud speaker which screwed into the top of the set. By 1928, the company was out of the radio production business.

100, table, 1924, wood, low rectangular case, 3 dial front panel, top screw-in horn speaker, 5 knobs, BC, 5 tubes, battery **$180.00-200.00**

101, table, 1925, wood, low rectangular case, 3 dial front panel, 5 knobs, BC, 5 tubes, battery.....................................**$120.00-150.00**

200 "Neutrodyne," table, 1925, wood, low rectangular case, 3 dial panel, top screw-in horn speaker, 5 knobs, BC, 5 tubes, battery......**$180.00-200.00**

201, table, 1925, wood, low rectangular case, 3 dial front panel, 5 knobs, BC, 5 tubes, battery.....................................**$120.00-150.00**

203, table, 1925, wood, low rectangular case, 3 dial front panel, meter, 5 knobs, BC, 6 tubes, battery.....................................**$130.00-160.00**

204, console, 1925, wood, inner 2 dial panel, fold-down front, upper speaker grille, lower storage, 4 knobs, BC, 6 tubes, battery ..**$240.00-300.00**

CS-32, table, 1923, wood, low rectangular case, 3 dial black Bakelite front panel, 5 knobs, BC, 5 tubes, battery, $180.00-200.00.

MURPHY
G. C. Murphy Co.
531 5th Ave., McKeesport, Pennsylvania

113, table, 1946, wood, slant front, lower dial, upper horizontal louvers, 2 knobs, BC, 5 tubes, AC/DC $35.00-40.00

MUSIC MASTER
Music Master Corporation
Tenth and Cherry Streets, Philadelphia, Pennsylvania

The Music Master Corporation was formed in 1924 in the business of manufacturing horns for radios. The company began to produce radios in 1925 but, due to mismanagement and financial difficulties, was out of business by 1926.

175, table, 1925, mahogany, rectangular case, upper slanted 2 dial panel, lower speaker grille with cut-outs, 5 knobs, BC, 6 tubes, battery, $300.00-350.00.

60, table, 1925, mahogany, low rectangular case, 3 dial front panel, 3 knobs, BC, 5 tubes, battery $140.00-150.00
100, table, 1925, mahogany, low rectangular case, slanted 3 dial front panel, feet, 5 knobs, BC, 5 tubes, battery $140.00-160.00
140, table, 1925, wood, high rectangular case, center front dial over stylized "M" logo, lift top, 4 knobs, BC, 5 tubes, battery ..$410.00-460.00
215, console, 1925, mahogany, upper slanted 2 dial panel, lower speaker grille with cut-outs, spinet legs, 6 tubes, battery........$350.00-410.00
250, table, 1925, mahogany, low rectangular case, front window dial, self-contained antenna, 4 knobs, BC, 7 tubes, battery $200.00-230.00
460, console, 1925, mahogany, inner slanted 1 dial panel, fold-down front, bowed legs, 3 knobs, BC, 7 tubes, battery $270.00-300.00

MUSICAIRE

576-1-6A, table, 1946, wood, front plastic panel with upper slide rule dial, lower cloth grille with wooden vertical bars, 3 knobs, BC, 6 tubes, AC $65.00-75.00
ME6, portable, leatherette, upper front slanted slide rule dial, lower grille area, handle, 3 knobs, BC $30.00-35.00

576, table, 1946, wood, front plastic panel with upper slide rule dial, lower cloth grille with wooden vertical bars, 3 knobs, BC, 6 tubes, AC, $65.00-75.00.

NARRAGANSETT

Beer Barrel, table-N, wood, looks like beer barrel, lower front knobs and perforated grille area, center lighted oval Narragansett name & logo, top "ice" & two beer bottles, BC, $180.00-200.00.

NATIONAL UNION
National Union Radio Corp.
Newark, New Jersey

571, table, 1947, wood, upper right front slide rule dial overlaps large lattice grille, 2 knobs, BC, 5 tubes, AC/DC $25.00-30.00
G-613 "Commuter," portable, 1947, leatherette, upper front slide rule dial, lower cloth grille, handle, 1 switch, 2 knobs, BC, 6 tubes, AC/DC/battery $30.00-35.00
G-619 "Presentation," table, 1947, wood, upper front slanted slide rule dial, lower cloth grille, 2 knobs, BC, 6 tubes, AC/DC $30.00-35.00

NAYLOR
Sterling Manufacturing Company

Sterling Five, table, wood, low rectangular case, 2 dial black Bakelite front panel, 4 knobs, BC, 5 tubes, battery, $120.00-150.00.

NEUTROWOUND
Neutrowound Radio Mfg. Co.
Divison of Advance Automobile Accessories Corp.
Homewood, Illinois

1926, table, 1926, metal, very low rectangular case with 3 top raised dial areas, 6 knobs, BC, 6 tubes w/top caps, battery ....$550.00+

1927, table, 1927, metal, very low rectangular case with 3 top raised dial areas, 7 knobs, BC, 6 tubes w/top caps, battery, $550.00+.

Super Allectric, table, 1927, wood, low rectangular case, upper slanted panel with off-center thumbwheel dial, lower knobs & meter, 4 knobs, BC, 6 tubes, AC $240.00-300.00

NEW YORKER

5C1, table-C, plastic, step-down top, right front dial overlaps lattice grille area, left alarm clock, feet, 4 knobs, BC, AC, $30.00-35.00.

OLD LAGER

Radio Keg, table-N, 1933, wood, looks like keg with metal hoops, front dial, rear grille with vertical bars, BC, AC/DC $350.00-410.00

OLYMPIC
Olympic Radio & TV/Hamilton Radio
510 Avenue of the Americas, New York, New York

6-606-A, portable, 1947, leatherette, luggage style, front plastic panel with slide rule dial & horizontal grille bars, handle, 2 knobs, BC, 6 tubes, AC/DC/battery, $35.00-40.00.

6-501V, table, 1946, ivory plastic, right front round slanted dial, left horizontal wrap-around louvers, 2 knobs, BC, 5 tubes, AC/DC $75.00-85.00
6-501W, table, 1946, walnut plastic, right front round slanted dial, left horizontal wrap-around louvers, 2 knobs, BC, 5 tubes, AC/DC $75.00-85.00
6-502, table, 1946, wood, right front slanted panel with round dial, horizontal wrap-around grille bars, 2 knobs, BC, 5 tubes, AC/DC $50.00-65.00
6-502P, table, 1946, wood, right front slanted panel with round dial, left vertical grille bars, 2 knobs, BC, 5 tubes, AC/DC $50.00-65.00

6-617, table-R/P, 1946, wood, front slanted slide rule dial, horizontal louvers, lift top, inner phono, 4 knobs, BC, 6 tubes, AC, $30.00-35.00.

6-504L, table-R/P, 1946, top right round dial, left flip-up top covers phono only, 3 knobs, BC, 5 tubes, AC $25.00-30.00
6-601V, table, 1946, ivory plastic, upper front slanted slide rule dial, lower horizontal grille bars, 4 knobs, BC, SW, 6 tubes, AC $40.00-50.00
6-601W, table, 1946, walnut plastic, upper front slanted slide rule dial, lower horizontal grille bars, 4 knobs, BC, SW, 6 tubes, AC $40.00-50.00
6-604V, table, 1947, ivory plastic, upper front slanted slide rule dial, lower horizontal wrap-around louvers, 4 knobs, BC, SW, 6 tubes, AC/DC $40.00-50.00
6-604W, table, 1947, walnut plastic, upper front slanted slide rule dial, lower horizontal wrap-around louvers, 4 knobs, BC, SW, 6 tubes, AC/DC $40.00-50.00
6-606, portable, 1946, leatherette, luggage style, front plastic panel with slide rule dial & horizontal grille bars, handle, 2 knobs, BC, 6 tubes, AC/DC/battery $35.00-40.00
6-606-U, portable, 1947, luggage style, front plastic panel with slide rule dial & horizontal grille bars, handle, 2 knobs, BC, 6 tubes, AC/DC/battery $35.00-40.00
7-421V, table, 1949, ivory plastic, right front round slanted dial, left horizontal wrap-around louvers, 2 knobs, BC, 5 tubes, AC/DC $75.00-85.00
7-421W, table, 1949, walnut plastic, right front round slanted dial, left horizontal wrap-around louvers, 2 knobs, BC, 5 tubes, AC/DC $75.00-85.00
7-435V, table, 1948, ivory plastic, right front round slanted dial, left horizontal wrap-around louvers, 3 knobs, BC, SW, 5 tubes, AC/DC $75.00-85.00
7-435W, table, 1948, walnut plastic, right front round slanted dial, left horizontal wrap-around louvers, 3 knobs, BC, SW, 5 tubes, AC/DC $75.00-85.00
7-526, portable, 1947, leatherette, front plastic panel with slide rule dial & horizontal grille bars, handle, 2 knobs, BC, 5 tubes, AC/DC/battery $35.00-40.00

402, table-C, 1955, plastic, right side dial over horizontal bars, center front alarm clock, feet, 5 knobs, BC, 5 tubes, AC, $30.00-35.00.

501, table-R/P, two-tone wood, right front square dial, left cloth grille, lift top, inner phono, 3 knobs, BC, AC, $35.00-40.00.

LP-163, table, plastic, right front round slanted dial, left horizontal wrap-around louvers, 2 knobs, $75.00-85.00.

7-532V, table, 1948, ivory plastic, upper front slide rule dial, lower horizontal wrap-around louvers, 4 knobs, BC, FM, 6 tubes, AC/DC $40.00-50.00

7-532W, table, 1948, walnut plastic, upper front slide rule dial, lower horizontal wrap-around louvers, 4 knobs, BC, FM, 6 tubes, AC/DC $40.00-50.00

7-537, table, 1948, plastic, right front round slanted dial, left horizontal wrap-around louvers, 3 knobs, BC, FM, 6 tubes, AC/DC ..$75.00-85.00

7-622, table-R/P, 1948, wood, upper front slide rule dial, lower horizontal grille bars, lift top, inner phono, 4 knobs, BC, 6 tubes, AC ..$35.00-40.00

7-638, console-R/P, 1948, wood, upper front slide rule dial, cloth grille with cut-outs, lift top, inner phono, lower storage, 4 knobs, BC, 6 tubes, AC $50.00-65.00

7-724, console-R/P, 1947, wood, inner right slide rule dial, storage, door, left lift top, inner phono, 4 knobs, BC, SW, 8 tubes, AC..$65.00-75.00

7-925, console-R/P, 1948, wood, inner right slide rule dial, door, left pull-out left phono drawer, 4 knobs, BC, FM, 10 tubes, AC..$65.00-75.00

8-451, portable, 1948, plastic, inner right slide rule dial, left lattice grille, flip-up top, handle, 2 knobs, BC, 4 tubes, battery.........$40.00-50.00

8-533V, table, 1949, plastic, upper front slanted slide rule dial, lower horizontal wrap-around louvers, 4 knobs, BC, FM, 6 tubes, AC/DC $40.00-50.00

8-533W, table, 1949, plastic, upper front slanted slide rule dial, lower horizontal wrap-around louvers, 4 knobs, BC, FM, 6 tubes, AC/DC $40.00-50.00

8-618, table-R/P, 1948, wood, upper front slanted slide rule dial, lower horizontal grille bars, lift top, inner phono, 4 knobs, BC, SW, 6 tubes, AC $35.00-40.00

8-934, console-R/P, 1948, wood, inner right slide rule dial, lower storage, door, left lift top, inner phono, 4 knobs, BC, FM, 10 tubes, AC $65.00-75.00

412, table-R/P, 1959, two-tone, center front dial, 3/4 lift top, inner phono, high-fidelity, 3 knobs, BC, 5 tubes, AC/DC $25.00-30.00

FM-15, table, 1960, plastic, trapezoid case, upper front slide rule dial over large checkered grille, 3 knobs, BC, FM, $25.00-30.00.

445, portable, 1954, plastic, top dial, large front checkered grille area, handle, 2 knobs, BC, 4 tubes, AC/DC/battery...............$30.00-35.00

450, portable, 1957, plastic, right front round dial overlaps horizontal grille bars, fold-down handle, 2 knobs, BC, 4 tubes, battery ..$25.00-30.00

450-V, portable, 1957, plastic, right front round dial overlaps horizontal grille bars, fold-down handle, 2 knobs, BC, 4 tubes, battery.....$25.00-30.00

461, portable, 1959, plastic, large round front dial overlaps lower perforated grille area, fold-down handle, telescope antenna, 2 knobs, BC, 4 tubes, AC/DC/battery $40.00-45.00

465, table-C, 1959, plastic, right front dial panel, left alarm clock, center lattice grille, feet, 3 knobs, BC, 4 tubes, AC $25.00-30.00

489, portable, 1951, plastic, inner slide rule dial, left lattice grille, set plays when flip-up front opens, 2 knobs, BC, 4 tubes, battery ..$40.00-50.00

552, table, 1960, plastic, raised top with slide rule dial, lower checkered grille area, 2 knobs, BC, 5 tubes, AC/DC $25.00-30.00

555, table-C, 1959, plastic, lower front slide rule dial, upper checkered grille with center alarm clock, feet, 4 knobs, BC, 5 tubes, AC....$25.00-30.00

PT-51, portable, 1941, leatherette, inner right dial, left cloth grille, slide-in door, handle, 2 knobs, BC, 5 tubes, AC/DC/battery $30.00-35.00

PQ-61, portable, 1941, leatherette, inner right dial, left grille, fold-down front, handle, 2 knobs, BC, 6 tubes, AC/DC/battery $30.00-35.00

LP-3244, table, plastic, large center front dial overlaps textured grille area, lower "Olympic" logo, feet, 2 knobs, BC, $40.00-50.00.

OPERADIO
The Operadio Corporation
8 South Dearborn Street, Chicago, Illinois

628-B, table, plastic, lower front slide rule dial, upper grille area with horizontal bars, 5 pushbuttons, 2 knobs, BC, SW...............$45.00-55.00

1925, portable, 1925, leatherette, inner 2 dial panel, lower grille with "sun-burst" cut-out, removable cover contains antenna, meter, 4 knobs, BC, 6 tubes, battery, $240.00-300.00.

OZARKA
Ozarka, Inc.
804 Washington Boulevard, Chicago, Illinois

Ozarka, Incorporated began manufacturing radios in 1922. Despite the stock market crash, Ozarka's business remained strong. However, the company was out of business by 1932.

95, cathedral, 1932, wood, fancy scrolled cabinet, center front window dial, upper cloth grille with cut-outs, feet, 3 knobs, BC, 8 tubes, $530.00-580.00.

78 "Armada," table, 1928, wood, looks like treasure chest, center front window dial, side handles, 3 knobs, BC, 7 tubes AC or 6 tubes battery, AC or battery versions $350.00-410.00

89, table, 1928, metal, low rectangular case, center front window dial with thumbwheel tuning, 2 thumbwheel knobs, BC, 9 tubes, AC $120.00-150.00

Corona, table, 1927, wood, low case with curved sides & carvings, center front dial, 3 knobs, BC, 6 tubes, battery................$300.00-320.00

J-1 "Junior," table, 1925, wood, slanted top, lower built-in speaker grille with cut-outs, 5 knobs, BC, 5 exposed tubes, battery ..$350.00-410.00

Minuet, console, wood, upper front dial, large lower speaker grille with cut-outs, 3 knobs, BC, 6 tubes, battery.....................$240.00-300.00

S-1 "Senior," table, 1925, wood, high rectangular case, 3 dial slanted front panel, 5 knobs, BC, 5 tubes, battery.................$240.00-270.00

S-5 "Senior," table, 1925, wood, high rectangular case, slanted 3 dial panel, lift top, 5 knobs, BC, 5 tubes, battery $240.00-300.00

S-7 "Senior," table, 1926, wood, high rectangular case, slanted 3 dial panel, lift top, 5 knobs, BC, 7 tubes, battery $270.00-320.00

V-16, console, 1932, wood, large Gothic cabinet with carvings, upper front window dial, lower cloth grille with cut-outs, 2 speakers, 4 knobs, BC, 16 tubes, AC, $580.00-700.00.

PACKARD-BELL
Packard-Bell Company
1115 South Hope Street, Los Angeles, California

Packard-Bell began business in 1933, during the Depression and always enjoyed a reputation for good quality radios. Packard-Bell had many government contracts during WW II for electrical equipment. The company was sold in 1971.

5D8, table, 1948, plastic, right front airplane dial, left horizontal louvers, handle, 2 knobs, BC, 5 tubes, AC/DC $45.00-55.00

5DA, table, 1947, plastic, right front airplane dial, left horizontal louvers, handle, 2 knobs, BC, 5 tubes, AC/DC $45.00-55.00

5FP, table, 1946, plastic, right front airplane dial, left horizontal louvers, 2 knobs, BC, 5 tubes, AC $40.00-50.00

5R1, table, 1957, plastic, dial numerals over large front checkered grille area, 2 knobs, BC, 5 tubes, AC/DC $35.00-40.00

6RC1, table-C, 1958, plastic, lower front slide rule dial, upper horizontal louvers with center alarm clock, BC, 6 tubes, AC $25.00-30.00

47, table, 1935, wood, center front round airplane dial, right & left horizontal wrap-around louvers, 5 knobs, BC, SW, 7 tubes, AC..$85.00-95.00

65A, table, 1940, wood, right front square dial, left cloth grille with horizontal bars, handle, 3 knobs, BC, 6 tubes, AC $50.00-65.00

100, table, 1949, plastic, right front dial, left grille with horizontal bars, decorative case lines, handle, 2 knobs, BC, 5 tubes, AC/DC $45.00-55.00

100A, table, 1949, plastic, right front dial, left grille with horizontal bars, decorative case lines, handle, 2 knobs, BC, 5 tubes, AC/DC ..$45.00-55.00

471, portable, 1947, luggage-style, leatherette, right front dial, left grille, handle, 3 knobs, BC, 4 tubes, AC/DC/battery...............$30.00-35.00

501, table, C1949, plastic, large right front dial, left horizontal louvers, handle, 2 knobs, BC, 5 tubes, AC/DC $45.00-55.00

531, table, 1954, plastic, large center front dial over perforated grille, 2 knobs, BC, 5 tubes, AC/DC...$25.00-30.00

551, table, 1946, plastic, upper front curved slide rule dial, lower vertical grille bars, handle, 2 knobs under handle, BC, 5 tubes, AC.........$50.00-65.00

561, table-R/P, 1946, leatherette, inner left front dial, right grille, fold-up lid, inner phono, 3 knobs, BC, 5 tubes, AC $30.00-35.00

568, portable-R/P, 1947, leatherette, inner right front dial, left grille, fold-up lid, inner phono, 3 knobs, BC, 5 tubes, AC $30.00-35.00

572, table, 1947, two-tone wood, upper front curved dial, lower horizontal louvers, handle, 2 knobs under handle, BC, 5 tubes, AC/DC $65.00-75.00

602, table, C1949, wood, large center front dial with two slide rule dial scales, one marked Southwest/one marked Northwest, top vertical grille bars, 2 knobs, BC, 6 tubes, AC/DC $40.00-50.00

621, table-C, 1952, plastic, right front square dial, left alarm clock, top grille bars, 5 knobs, BC, 6 tubes, AC...............................$30.00-35.00

5R5, table, 1959, plastic, dial numerals over front horizontal bars, large dial pointer, feet, 2 knobs, BC, 5 tubes, AC/DC, $20.00-25.00.

631, table, 1954, plastic, large front perforated metal grille with raised dial numerals, 3 knobs, BC, 6 tubes, AC/DC **$30.00-35.00**

651, table, 1946, wood, upper front curved slide rule dial, lower horizontal louvers, handle, 2 knobs under handle, BC, SW, 6 tubes, AC ..**$65.00-75.00**

661, table-R/P, 1946, wood, upper front dial, lower grille, 3/4 lift top, inner phono, 4 knobs, BC, 6 tubes, AC **$30.00-35.00**

662, console-R/P, 1947, wood, desk-style, inner slide rule dial, phono, fold-up top, 4 knobs, BC, 6 tubes, AC **$85.00-95.00**

682, table, 1949, right front square dial, left criss-cross grille, handle, 3 knobs, BC, 6 tubes, AC/DC..**$45.00-55.00**

771, table, 1948, wood, upper front slanted slide rule dial, lower criss-cross grille, 4 knobs, BC, SW, 7 tubes, AC **$35.00-40.00**

861 "Phonocord," console-R/P/Rec/PA, 1947, wood, inner slide rule dial, phono/recorder/PA, lift top, front criss-cross grille, 4 knobs, BC, 8 tubes, AC **$75.00-85.00**

880, console-R/P, 1948, wood, inner right slanted slide rule dial, left phono, fold-up front, 4 knobs, BC, 8 tubes, AC **$75.00-85.00**

880-A, chairside-R/P, 1948, wood, top slide rule dial, slide-in lid, inner phono, lower storage area, 4 knobs, BC, 8 tubes, AC ..**$75.00-85.00**

881-A, console-R/P/Rec, 1948, wood, inner right slanted slide rule dial, left phono/recorder, fold-up front, 4 knobs, BC, 8 tubes, AC..**$75.00-85.00**

881-B, chairside-R/P/Rec, 1948, wood, top slide rule dial, slide-in lid, inner phono/recorder, lower storage area, 4 knobs, BC, 8 tubes, AC **$75.00-85.00**

884, table-R/P, 1949, wood, upper front slide rule dial, lower criss-cross grille, lift top, inner phono, 4 knobs, BC, FM, 8 tubes, AC ..**$30.00-35.00**

892, console-R/P, 1949, wood, upper front slide rule dial, center pull-out phono, lower criss-cross grille, 4 knobs, BC, FM, 8 tubes, AC..**$50.00-65.00**

1052A, table-R/P/Rec/PA, 1946, wood, inner left front dial, right grille, phono/recorder/PA, fold-up top, 4 knobs, BC, SW, 10 tubes, AC **$30.00-35.00**

1054-B, console-R/P/Rec/PA, 1947, wood, top slanted slide rule dial, center front pull-out phono/recorder/PA drawer, 6 knobs, BC, SW, 10 tubes, AC **$65.00-75.00**

1063, console-R/P/Rec/PA, 1947, wood, inner right dial, 6 pushbuttons, left phono/recorder/PA, lift top, drop front, 4 knobs, BC, SW, 10 tubes, AC **$75.00-85.00**

464, table, wood, two right front dial scales, left 2-section cloth grille, 6 pushbuttons, 3 knobs, BC, SW, AC, $75.00-85.00.

1181, console-R/P/Rec, 1949, wood, inner right slanted slide rule dial, left phono/recorder, fold-back top, 5 knobs, BC, FM, 12 tubes, AC **$75.00-85.00**

1273, console-R/P, 1948, wood, center front pull-out drawer with slide rule dial, phono, 5 knobs, BC, FM, 13 tubes, AC **$75.00-85.00**

PAN AMERICAN
Pan American Electric Co.
132 Front Street, New York, New York

"Clock," table-N, 1946, wood, arched case looks like mantle clock, round plastic dial, 2 knobs, BC, 5 tubes, AC/DC **$75.00-85.00**

PARAGON
Adams-Morgan Co.
16 Alvin Place, Upper Montclair, New Jersey
The Paragon Electric Corporation
Upper Montclair, New Jersey

The Adams-Morgan Company began business in 1910 selling wireless parts. By 1916 their first Paragon radio was marketed. After much internal trouble between the company executives leading to the demise of the Adams-Morgan Company and the creation of the Paragon Electric Corporation in 1926, the company finally went out of business completely in 1928.

RB-2, table, 1923, mahogany, low rectangular case, 3 dial black front panel, lift top, 10 knobs, BC, 3 tubes, battery, $725.00-825.00.

DA-2, table, 1921, oak, detector/2-stage amplifier, black front panel, 5 knobs, 3 tubes, battery **$1,150.00-1,250.00**

RA-10, table, 1921, oak, low rectangular case, 2 dial black front panel, 9 knobs, tuner only-no tubes....................................**$900.00-1,000.00**

RA10/DA2, table, 1921, two rectangular case units, RA 10-receiver & DA 2-two stage amplifier, 14 knobs, 3 tubes, battery ..**$1,900.00-2,100.00**

RD-5, table, 1922, wood, low rectangular case, 7 knobs, battery **$900.00-1,000.00**

Two, table, 1924, mahogany finish, low rectangular case, 1 center front dial, 3 knobs, BC, 2 tubes, battery **$350.00-400.00**

IIIA, table, 1924, wood, inner black Bakelite panel, double front doors, lift top, 8 knobs, BC, 3 tubes, battery **$900.00-1,000.00**

RD-5/A-2, table, 1922, two rectangular case units, RD5-receiver & A2-two stage amplifier, 10 knobs, BC, battery, $1,450.00-1,550.00.

PARSON'S
Parson's Laboratories, Inc.
1471 Selby Ave., St. Paul, Minnesota

66A, table, 1932, wood, right front half-round dial with escutcheon, left scalloped cloth grille, BC, 6 tubes, battery $65.00-75.00

PASTIME

No #, miniature console, wood, 8" high, inner thumbwheel dial and cloth grille with cut-outs, double front doors, BC, 2 tubes..$350.00-410.00

PATHE
Pathe Phonograph & Radio Corp.
20 Grand Ave., Brooklyn, New York

B-5, table, 1925, wood, low rectangular case, slanted 3 dial front panel, BC, 5 tubes, battery...................................$120.00-150.00
Minute Man, table, 1925, wood, low rectangular case, 3 dial front panel, BC, 5 tubes, battery...................................$120.00-150.00

PEER

35SW, table, wood, right front dial, center cloth grille with cut-outs, 2 knobs, BC, AC/DC...$85.00-95.00

PEERLESS

LP400, portable, plastic, right front dial, left lattice grille area, fold-down handle, BC, battery, $40.00-45.00.

PENNCREST
J.C. Penney

621-5121, table, 1963, plastic, large right front round dial overlaps horizontal grille bars, 2 knobs, BC, 5 tubes, AC/DC $15.00-20.00
626-5844, table, 1962, wood, right front round dial, left grille with logo, 3 knobs, BC, FM, 6 tubes, AC/DC $15.00-20.00
626-5845, table, 1962, wood, right front round dial, left grille with logo, 3 knobs, BC, FM, 6 tubes, AC/DC $15.00-20.00
3123, table-C, 1964, plastic, lower right front dial overlaps upper lattice grille area, left clock, BC, 5 tubes $15.00-20.00
3129, table-C, 1964, plastic, top right dial, front off-center clock over horizontal grille bars, feet, 3 knobs, BC, 5 tubes, AC $15.00-20.00
3622, table-C, 1962, plastic, right front dial overlaps horizontal wrap-around grille bars, left clock, feet, BC, 5 tubes, AC........$20.00-25.00
3625, table-C, 1964, plastic, top right dial, front off-center clock, feet, BC, 5 tubes, AC $20.00-25.00
3845, table-C, 1962, plastic, right front dial, center clock, left grille area with logo, 5 knobs, BC, FM, 6 tubes, AC $20.00-25.00
3934, table-C, 1965, walnut finish, right front dial panel, left clock, center lattice grille area, feet, 6 knobs, BC, FM, 5 tubes, AC....$20.00-25.00
5335, table, 1965, plastic, right front dial panel, large left criss-cross grille area, feet, 4 knobs, BC, FM, 6 tubes, AC/DC $15.00-20.00

5340, table, 1962, plastic, lower right front dial panel overlaps large textured grille area, feet, BC, FM, 6 tubes, AC/DC.............$15.00-20.00
5343, table, 1962, plastic, lower right front dial panel overlaps large textured grille area, feet, BC, FM, 7 tubes, AC/DC.............$15.00-20.00
5836, table, 1963, wood, lower left front slide rule dial panel overlaps large grille area, upper left logo, 2 speakers, 4 knobs, BC, FM, 5 tubes, AC/DC...$15.00-20.00
5837, table, 1963, wood, lower left front slide rule dial panel overlaps large grille area, upper left logo, 2 speakers, 4 knobs, BC, FM, 5 tubes, AC/DC...$15.00-20.00

PEPSI
The Pepsi-Cola Company

Pepsi Bottle, table-N, plastic, looks like large Pepsi bottle, base, BC, AC, $600.00-650.00.

PCR-5 "Cooler," table-N, plastic, looks like Pepsi-Cola cooler, right side dial looks like bottle cap, lower front horizontal grille bars, upper Pepsi logo, BC $600.00-650.00

PERRY

3856, cathedral, 1932, wood, center front quarter-round dial with escutcheon, upper cloth grille with cut-outs, 3 knobs, BC, AC, $300.00-350.00.

PERWAL
Perwal Radio & Television Co.
140 North Dearborn Street, Chicago, Illinois

51, table, 1937, wood, right front 3 color dial, left cloth grille with Deco cut-outs, BC, 4 tubes, AC/DC $55.00-65.00
52, table, 1937, two-tone wood, center front airplane dial, top grille with cut-outs, 3 knobs, BC, 5 tubes, AC/DC......................$75.00-85.00

581, table, 1937, center front round airplane dial, top grille with cut-outs, 2 knobs, BC, 5 tubes, AC/DC **$75.00-85.00**

741, table, 1937, wood, right front round dial, tuning eye, left grille with vertical bars, 3 knobs, BC, SW, 7 tubes, AC/DC............**$75.00-85.00**

PFANSTIEHL
Pfanstiehl Radio Co.
11 South La Salle Street, Chicago, Illinois
Fansteel Products Company, Inc.
North Chicago, Illinois

The Pfanstiehl Radio Company was formed in 1924 and in that same year marketed its first radio. During the late 1920s business gradually declined and by 1930, the company was out of the radio business.

18, table, 1926, wood, low rectangular case, front panel with half-round double-pointer dial, 3 knobs, BC, 5 tubes, battery, $120.00-140.00.

7 "Overtone," table, 1924, wood, low rectangular case, 3 dial front panel, 8 knobs, BC, 5 tubes, battery **$120.00-140.00**

8, table, 1924, wood, low rectangular case, slanted 2 dial front panel, BC, 5 tubes, battery **$110.00-130.00**

10 "Overtone," table, 1924, wood, low rectangular case, 1 dial front panel, BC, 6 tubes, battery **$110.00-130.00**

10-C, console, 1924, wood, highboy, inner 1 dial panel, fold-down front, upper speaker, BC, 6 tubes, battery **$200.00-230.00**

10-S "Overtone," console, 1924, wood, 1 dial front panel & left built-in speaker on detachable stand, BC, 6 tubes, battery ..**$150.00-160.00**

20, table, 1926, wood, rectangular case, 1 dial front panel, BC, 6 tubes, battery **$85.00-105.00**

50, table, 1927, wood, low rectangular case, center window dial with escutcheon, BC, 7 tubes, AC **$85.00-115.00**

181, console, 1926, wood, inner dial panel with half-round pointer dial, fold-down front, storage, 3 knobs, BC, 5 tubes, battery **$150.00-180.00**

PHILCO
Philadelphia Storage Battery Company
Ontario & C Streets, Philadelphia, Pennsylvania
Philco Corporation
Tioga & C Streets, Philadelphia, Pennsylvania

Philco began business in 1906 as the Philadelphia Storage Battery Company, a maker of batteries and power supplies. In 1927 the company produced its first radio and grew to be one of the most prolific of all radio manufacturers.

14LZX "Lazy X," chairside/remote speaker, 1933, wood, Queen Anne-style chairside unit with inner top dial connects to remote speaker unit with 25 ft. cable, 4 knobs, BC, SW, 9 tubes, AC ..**$320.00-350.00**

14X, console, 1933, walnut, upper front dial, lower inclined grille with 3 vertical bars, fluted columns, 4 knobs, BC, SW, 9 tubes, AC **$140.00-160.00**

15DX, console, 1932, wood, inner front dial & controls, bowed tambour doors, lower inclined grille, shadow tuning meter, 4 knobs, BC, 11 tubes, AC **$240.00-270.00**

15X, console, 1932, walnut, upper front window dial, lower inclined grille with vertical columns, 4 knobs, BC, 11 tubes, AC **$200.00-230.00**

4, table/console top, 1931, wood, short-wave converter, rectangular enclosure, upper center window dial, 3 knobs, SW, 3 tubes, AC, $110.00-135.00.

14 or 14B, cathedral, 1933, wood, center front window dial, upper cloth grille with cut-outs, some versions with BC only, 4 knobs, BC, SW, 9 tubes, AC, $300.00-350.00.

16B, cathedral, 1933, two-tone wood, center front window dial, upper cloth grille with cut-outs, shadow tuning meter, 4 knobs, BC, SW, 11 tubes, AC **$240.00-300.00**

16B, tombstone, 1933, two-tone wood, Deco look, center front window dial, upper cloth grille with 3 vertical decorative bars, tapered top, shadow tuning meter, 4 knobs, BC, SW, 11 tubes, AC **$240.00-270.00**

16L, console, 1933, wood, lowboy, upper front window dial, lower cloth grille with cut-outs, shadow tuning meter, 4 knobs, BC, SW, 11 tubes, AC **$150.00-170.00**

16RX, chairside/remote speaker, 1933, wood, chairside unit with top dial, remote speaker with inclined grille, 4 knobs, BC, SW, 11 tubes, AC **$320.00-350.00**

16X, console, 1933, wood, upper front window dial, lower cloth grille with vertical bars, shadow tuning meter, 4 knobs, BC, SW, 11 tubes, AC **$120.00-150.00**

17B, cathedral, 1933, wood, center front window dial, upper cloth grille with cut-outs, shadow tuning meter, 4 knobs, BC, SW, 11 tubes, AC, $240.00-300.00.

18H, console, 1933, wood, lowboy, upper front window dial, lower cloth grille with cut-outs, 6 legs, shadow tuning meter, 4 knobs, BC, SW, 8 tubes, AC, $150.00-180.00.

21B, cathedral, 1930, wood, center front window dial, upper cloth grille with cut-outs, fluted columns, 3 knobs, BC, 7 tubes, AC, $320.00-350.00.

18X, console, 1933, wood, upper front dial, lower inclined grille with 3 vertical bars, fluted columns, 4 knobs, BC, SW, 8 tubes, AC **$120.00-150.00**

19H, console, 1933, wood, lowboy, upper front window dial, lower cloth grille with cut-outs, 6 legs, shadow tuning meter, 4 knobs, BC, SW, 6 tubes, AC **$120.00-150.00**

20, cathedral, 1930, wood, center front window dial, upper cloth grille with scrolled cut-outs, 3 knobs, BC, 7 tubes, AC **$240.00-300.00**

20, console, 1930, wood, small case, lowboy, upper front window dial, lower cloth grille, 3 knobs, BC, 7 tubes, AC **$120.00-150.00**

20 Deluxe, cathedral, 1930, two-tone wood, center front window dial, upper cloth grille with scrolled cut-outs, 3 knobs, BC, 7 tubes, AC..**$240.00-300.00**

20B, cathedral, 1930, wood, center front window dial, upper cloth grille with scrolled cut-outs, 3 knobs, BC, 7 tubes, AC **$270.00-300.00**

22L, console-R/P, 1932, wood, lowboy, front window dial, lower cloth grille with cut-outs, lift top, inner phono, 6 legs, 4 knobs, BC, 7 tubes, AC **$120.00-150.00**

28C, table, 1934, wood, front window dial, right & left "butterfly wing" grilles, 4 knobs, BC, SW, 6 tubes, AC/DC.................**$130.00-160.00**

28L, console, 1934, wood, lowboy, upper front window dial, lower cloth grille with cut-outs, 4 knobs, BC, SW, 6 tubes, AC/DC **$150.00-170.00**

29TX, table/remote speaker, 1934, wood, table set with front window dial, shadow tuning meter, remote speaker cabinet with grille cut-outs, 4 knobs, BC, SW, 6 tubes, AC **$200.00-230.00**

29X, console, 1934, wood, upper front window dial, lower inclined grille with 3 vertical columns, 4 knobs, BC, SW, 6 tubes, AC **$150.00-180.00**

32L, console, 1934, wood, lowboy, upper front window dial, lower cloth grille with cut-outs, DC, 4 knobs, BC, SW, 6 tubes, DC ..**$85.00-115.00**

34B, tombstone, 1935, wood, shouldered, center front dial, upper cloth grille with cut-outs, 4 knobs, BC, SW, 7 tubes, battery..**$75.00-85.00**

17D, console, 1933, wood, highboy, inner front dial & controls, double doors, 6 legs, 4 knobs, BC, SW, 11 tubes, AC **$150.00-170.00**

17L, console, 1933, wood, lowboy, upper center window dial, lower grille with decorative cut-outs, 4 legs, stretcher base, shadow tuning meter, 4 knobs, BC, SW, 11 tubes, AC **$130.00-150.00**

17RX, chairside/remote speaker, 1934, wood, chairside unit with top dial, remote speaker with inclined grille, 4 knobs, BC, SW, 11 tubes, AC **$320.00-350.00**

17X, console, 1933, wood, upper front dial, lower inclined open grille, shadow tuning meter, 4 knobs, BC, SW, 11 tubes, AC **$120.00-150.00**

18B, cathedral, 1933, two-tone wood, center front window dial, 3-section cloth grille, 4 knobs, BC, 8 tubes, AC **$300.00-320.00**

18D, console, 1933, wood, lowboy, inner front window dial and controls, lower cloth grille with cut-outs, double doors, 6 legs, 4 knobs, BC, SW, 8 tubes, AC...**$170.00-190.00**

18L, console, 1933, wood, lowboy, upper front window dial, lower cloth grille with cut-outs, stretcher base, shadow tuning meter, 4 knobs, BC, SW, 8 tubes, AC **$130.00-150.00**

18MX, console, 1934, mahogany with black trim, upper front window dial, lower cloth grille with 2 vertical bars, 4 knobs, BC, SW, 8 tubes, AC **$120.00-150.00**

18RX, chairside/remote speaker, 1933, wood, chairside unit with top dial, remote speaker with inclined grille, 4 knobs, BC, SW, 8 tubes, AC **$320.00-350.00**

19, cathedral, 1932, wood, recessed front panel with center window dial, upper cloth grille with cut-outs, shadow tuning meter, 4 knobs, BC, SW, 6 tubes, AC, $270.00-300.00.

34, cathedral, 1935, wood, center front window dial, upper 3-section cloth grille, 4 knobs, BC, SW, 7 tubes, battery, $240.00-260.00.

37-38B, tombstone, 1937, wood, shouldered, center front round dial, upper cloth grille with cut-outs, 4 knobs, BC, SW, 6 tubes, battery, $75.00-85.00.

37-602C, table, 1937, wood, finished front & back, right front round dial, left cloth grille with Deco cut-outs, top cut-outs, 2 knobs, BC, 5 tubes, AC/DC, $85.00-95.00.

34L, console, 1934, wood, lowboy, upper front window dial, lower cloth grille with cut-outs, 4 knobs, BC, SW, 7 tubes, battery ..**$85.00-115.00**

37-9X, console, 1937, two-tone wood, upper front round automatic tuning dial, lower cloth grille with 3 vertical bars, 6 knobs, BC, SW, 9 tubes, AC **$150.00-180.00**

37-10X, console, 1937, two-tone wood, upper front round automatic tuning dial, lower cloth grille with 3 vertical bars, 6 knobs, BC, SW, 9 tubes, AC **$150.00-180.00**

37-11X, console, 1937, two-tone wood, upper front round automatic tuning dial, lower cloth grille with 4 vertical bars, 6 knobs, BC, SW, 10 tubes, AC **$150.00-180.00**

37-33B, cathedral, 1937, two-tone wood, lower round dial, upper grille with vertical cut-outs, 2 knobs, BC, 5 tubes, battery ..**$85.00-115.00**

37-33F, console, 1937, wood, upper front round dial, lower cloth grille with cut-outs, 2 knobs, BC, 5 tubes, battery................**$85.00-105.00**

37-34B, cathedral, 1937, two-tone wood, lower round dial, upper grille with vertical cut-outs, 3 knobs, BC, 5 tubes, 6VDC **$85.00-115.00**

37-34F, console, 1937, wood, upper front round dial, lower cloth grille with cut-outs, 3 knobs, BC, 5 tubes, 6VDC.................**$85.00-105.00**

37-38F, console, 1937, wood, upper front round dial, lower cloth grille with 3 vertical bars, 4 knobs, BC, SW, 6 tubes, battery **$85.00-105.00**

37-38J, console, 1937, wood, upper front round dial, lower cloth grille with 3 vertical bars, 4 knobs, BC, SW, 6 tubes, battery........**$85.00-105.00**

37-60B, cathedral, 1937, wood, center front round dial, upper cloth grille with 6 cut-outs, 4 knobs, BC, SW, 5 tubes, AC.........**$150.00-170.00**

37-60B, tombstone, 1937, wood, center front round dial, upper cloth grille with 2 large and 4 small cut-outs, 4 knobs, BC, SW, 5 tubes, AC **$120.00-140.00**

37-60F, console, 1937, wood, upper front round dial, lower cloth grille with 4 cut-outs, 4 knobs, BC, SW, 5 tubes, AC.........**$120.00-150.00**

37-61B, cathedral, 1937, wood, center front round dial, upper cloth grille with cut-outs, 4 knobs, BC, SW, 5 tubes, AC **$140.00-160.00**

37-61F, console, 1937, wood, upper front round dial, lower cloth grille with cut-outs, 4 knobs, BC, SW, 5 tubes, AC **$120.00-140.00**

37-62C, table, 1937, two-tone wood, right front round dial, left cloth grille with Deco cut-outs, 3 knobs, BC, SW, 5 tubes, AC **$85.00-95.00**

37-89B, cathedral, 1937, wood, center front round dial, upper cloth grille with 6 cut-outs, 4 knobs, BC, SW, 6 tubes, AC.........**$130.00-160.00**

37-89F, console, 1937, wood, upper front round dial, lower cloth grille with 4 cut-outs, 4 knobs, BC, SW, 6 tubes, AC.........**$120.00-140.00**

37-93B, cathedral, 1937, wood, lower round dial, upper cloth grille with vertical bars, 2 knobs, BC, 5 tubes, AC **$110.00-130.00**

37-116X, console, 1937, wood, upper front automatic tuning dial, lower cloth grille with 5 vertical bars, lower right & left front cut-outs, 7 knobs, BC, SW, 15 tubes, AC **$200.00-230.00**

37-600C, table, 1937, wood, finished front & back, right front round dial, left cloth grille with Deco cut-outs, top cut-outs, 2 knobs, BC, 4 tubes, AC **$85.00-95.00**

37-604C, table, 1937, wood, dial on top of case, front round cloth grille with horizontal bars, 3 knobs, BC, SW, 5 tubes, AC/DC **$110.00-130.00**

37-610B, tombstone, 1937, wood, center front round dial, upper cloth grille with cut-outs, 4 knobs, BC, SW, 5 tubes, AC....**$110.00-130.00**

37-610J, console, 1937, wood, upper front round dial, lower cloth grille with 3 vertical bars, 4 knobs, BC, SW, 5 tubes, AC ..**$110.00-130.00**

37-611B, tombstone, 1937, wood, shouldered, center front round dial, upper cloth grille with cut-outs, 4 knobs, BC, SW, 5 tubes, AC/DC **$110.00-130.00**

37-611F, console, 1937, wood, upper front round dial, lower cloth grille with four cut-outs, 4 knobs, BC, SW, 5 tubes, AC/DC **$110.00-130.00**

37-611J, console, 1937, wood, upper front round dial, lower cloth grille with three vertical bars, 4 knobs, BC, SW, 5 tubes, AC/DC ..**$110.00-130.00**

37-611T, table, 1937, wood, Deco, off-center round dial, rounded left, cloth grille with horizontal bars, 4 knobs, BC, SW, 5 tubes, AC/DC **$120.00-150.00**

37-84B, cathedral, 1937, wood, lower front round dial, upper cloth grille with vertical bars, 2 knobs, BC, 4 tubes, AC, $110.00-130.00.

37-610T, table, 1937, wood, Deco, off-center round dial, rounded left, cloth grille with horizontal bars, 4 knobs, BC, SW, 5 tubes, AC, $120.00-150.00.

37-620B, tombstone, 1937, two-tone wood, center front dial, cloth grille with cut-outs, 4 knobs, BC, SW, 6 tubes, AC, $110.00-130.00.

38-4XX, console, 1938, wood, upper front slanted automatic tuning dial, lower cloth grille with 4 vertical bars, 4 knobs, BC, SW, 8 tubes, AC, $120.00-150.00.

37-620J, console, 1937, wood, upper front round dial, lower cloth grille, 4 knobs, BC, SW, 6 tubes, AC **$110.00-130.00**

37-623B, tombstone, 1937, two-tone wood, rounded shoulders, round dial, 6 grille cut-outs, 4 knobs, BC, SW, 6 tubes, battery **$75.00-85.00**

37-623J, console, 1937, wood, upper front round dial, lower cloth grille with 3 vertical bars, 4 knobs, BC, SW, 6 tubes, battery ..**$75.00-85.00**

37-624B, tombstone, 1937, two-tone wood, rounded shoulders, round dial, 6 grille cut-outs, 4 knobs, BC, SW, 6 tubes, 6VDC ..**$75.00-85.00**

37-624J, console, 1937, wood, upper front round dial, lower cloth grille with 3 vertical bars, 4 knobs, BC, SW, 6 tubes, 6VDC ..**$75.00-85.00**

37-630T, table, 1937, wood, Deco, right front round dial, left cloth grille with Deco cut-outs, shadow tuning meter, 4 knobs, BC, SW, 6 tubes, AC **$95.00-105.00**

37-630X, console, 1937, wood, recessed front, upper round dial, lower cloth grille with 3 vertical bars, shadow tuning meter, 4 knobs, BC, SW, 6 tubes, AC...**$120.00-150.00**

37-640B, tombstone, 1937, wood, rounded shoulders, center front round dial, upper cloth grille with vertical cut-outs, shadow tuning meter, 4 knobs, BC, SW, 7 tubes, AC **$120.00-140.00**

37-640MX, console, 1937, wood, upper front round dial, lower cloth grille with four vertical cut-outs, shadow tuning meter, 4 knobs, BC, SW, 7 tubes, AC **$120.00-150.00**

37-640X, console, 1937, wood, rounded shoulders, upper front round dial, lower cloth grille with three vertical bars, shadow tuning meter, 4 knobs, BC, SW, 7 tubes, AC...................................**$120.00-150.00**

37-641B, tombstone, 1937, wood, rounded shoulders, center front round dial, upper cloth grille with vertical cut-outs, shadow tuning meter, 4 knobs, BC, SW, 7 tubes, AC/DC **$110.00-130.00**

37-641MX, console, 1937, wood, upper front round dial, lower cloth grille with four vertical cut-outs, shadow tuning meter, 4 knobs, BC, SW, 7 tubes, AC/DC **$110.00-130.00**

37-641X, console, 1937, wood, upper front round dial, lower cloth grille with three vertical bars, shadow tuning meter, 4 knobs, BC, SW, 7 tubes, AC/DC **$110.00-130.00**

37-643B, tombstone, 1937, wood, rounded shoulders, center front round dial, upper cloth grille with cut-outs, shadow tuning meter, 4 knobs, BC, SW, 7 tubes, battery **$85.00-95.00**

37-643X, console, 1937, wood, upper front round dial, lower cloth grille with cut-outs, shadow tuning meter, 6 feet, 4 knobs, BC, SW, 7 tubes, battery **$75.00-85.00**

37-650B, tombstone, 1937, wood, center front dial, upper cloth grille with cut-outs, shadow tuning meter, 4 knobs, BC, SW, 8 tubes, AC **$120.00-150.00**

37-650X, console, 1937, wood, upper front round dial, lower cloth grille with 3 vertical bars, shadow tuning meter, 4 knobs, BC, SW, 8 tubes, AC **$120.00-150.00**

37-660B, tombstone, 1937, wood, rounded shoulders, center front round dial, upper cloth grille with cut-outs, shadow tuning meter, 4 knobs, BC, SW, 9 tubes, AC **$120.00-150.00**

37-660X, console, 1937, wood, upper front round dial, lower cloth grille with cut-outs, shadow tuning meter, 6 feet, 4 knobs, BC, SW, 9 tubes, AC **$120.00-150.00**

37-665B, tombstone, 1937, wood, rounded shoulders, center front round dial, upper cloth grille with cut-outs, 4 knobs, BC, SW, 9 tubes, AC **$120.00-150.00**

38, cathedral, 1930, two-tone wood, center front window dial, upper cloth grille with cut-outs, 4 knobs, BC, SW, 5 tubes, battery, $130.00-150.00.

38-15T, table, 1938, wood & Bakelite versions, right front dial, left wrap-around cloth grille with cut-outs, 3 knobs, BC, SW, 5 tubes, AC, $55.00-65.00.

38-35B, tombstone, 1938, two-tone wood, lower front dial, upper cloth grille with cut-outs, 2 knobs, BC, 5 tubes, AC/6VDC, $75.00-85.00.

38-93B, tombstone, 1938, two-tone wood, rounded shoulders, lower front round dial, cloth grille with cut-outs, 2 knobs, BC, 5 tubes, AC, $110.00-130.00.

37-665X, console, 1937, wood, upper front round dial, lower cloth grille with cut-outs, shadow tuning meter, 6 feet, 4 knobs, BC, SW, 9 tubes, AC **$120.00-150.00**

37-670B, tombstone, 1937, wood, center front round dial, upper cloth grille with vertical bars, shadow tuning meter, 4 knobs, BC, SW, 11 tubes, AC **$140.00-160.00**

37-670X, console, 1937, wood, upper front round dial, lower cloth grille with 4 vertical bars, shadow tuning meter, 4 knobs, BC, SW, 11 tubes, AC **$150.00-180.00**

37-675X, console, 1937, wood, upper front round automatic tuning dial, lower cloth grille with cut-outs, 6 feet, 7 knobs, BC, SW, 12 tubes, AC **$180.00-200.00**

37-690X, console, 1937, wood, inner automatic tuning dial, grille cut-outs, double doors, 3 speakers, 7 knobs, BC, SW, 20 tubes, AC **$580.00-700.00**

37-2620B, console, 1937, two-tone wood, center front dial, cloth grille with cut-outs, 4 knobs, BC, SW, LW, 6 tubes, AC **$110.00-130.00**

37-2620J, console, 1937, wood, upper front round dial, lower cloth grille with 3 vertical bars, 4 knobs, BC, SW, LW, 6 tubes, AC **$110.00-130.00**

37-2650B, tombstone, 1937, wood, rounded shoulders, center front round dial, upper cloth grille with cut-outs, shadow tuning meter, 4 knobs, BC, SW, LW, 8 tubes, AC **$120.00-150.00**

37-2650X, console, 1937, wood, upper front round dial, lower cloth grille with 3 vertical bars, shadow tuning meter, 4 knobs, BC, SW, LW, 8 tubes, AC **$110.00-130.00**

37-2670B, tombstone, 1937, wood, center front round dial, upper cloth grille with vertical bars, shadow tuning meter, 4 knobs, BC, SW, LW, 11 tubes, AC **$140.00-160.00**

37-2670X, console, 1937, wood, upper front round dial, lower cloth grille with 4 vertical bars, shadow tuning meter, 4 knobs, BC, SW, LW, 11 tubes, AC **$140.00-160.00**

38-1XX, console, 1938, wood, upper front slanted automatic tuning dial, lower cloth grille with 5 vertical bars, 6 knobs, BC, SW, 12 tubes, AC **$160.00-190.00**

38-2XX, console, 1938, wood, upper front slanted automatic tuning dial, lower cloth grille with cut-outs, 6 knobs, BC, SW, 11 tubes, AC **$160.00-190.00**

38-3XX, console, 1938, wood, upper front slanted automatic tuning dial, lower cloth grille with 4 vertical bars, 6 knobs, BC, SW, 9 tubes, AC **$120.00-150.00**

38-5X, console, 1938, wood, upper front round dial, lower cloth grille with 3 vertical bars, 4 knobs, BC, SW, 8 tubes, AC **$110.00-130.00**

38-5, tombstone, 1938, two-tone wood, rounded shoulders, center front round dial, upper cloth grille with cut-outs, 4 knobs, BC, SW, 8 tubes, AC **$110.00-130.00**

38-7CS, chairside, 1938, wood, Deco, top dial, lower round cloth grille with horizontal bars, center storage, 4 knobs, BC, SW, 6 tubes, AC **$150.00-180.00**

38-7T, table, 1938, wood, right front round dial, rounded left side, cloth grille with Deco cut-outs, 4 knobs, BC, SW, 6 tubes, AC ..**$85.00-95.00**

38-62F, console, 1938, wood, upper front round dial, lower cloth grille with 3 vertical bars, 3 knobs, BC, SW, 5 tubes, AC, $110.00-130.00.

39-70F, console, 1939, wood, upper center square dial, lower grille with 3 vertical bars, 2 knobs, BC, 4 tubes, battery, $85.00-105.00.

39-71T, portable, 1939, striped cloth covered, right front dial, left grille area, leather handle, 2 knobs, BC, 4 tubes, battery, $30.00-35.00.

40-120C, table, 1940, wood, right front square dial, left horizontal louvers, handle, tubular feet, 3 knobs, BC, SW, 6 tubes, AC/DC, $55.00-65.00.

38-7XX, console, 1938, wood, upper front slanted automatic tuning dial, lower cloth grille with vertical bars, 4 knobs, BC, SW, 6 tubes, AC **$110.00-130.00**

38-8X, console, 1938, wood, upper front round dial, lower cloth grille with 3 vertical bars, shadow tuning meter, 4 knobs, BC, SW, 6 tubes, AC **$110.00-130.00**

38-9K, console, 1938, two-tone wood, upper front round dial, lower cloth grille with three vertical bars and left & right cut-outs, 4 knobs, BC, SW, 6 tubes, AC.......................................**$120.00-150.00**

38-9T, table, 1938, wood, right front round dial, rounded left side, cloth grille with Deco cut-outs, 4 knobs, BC, SW, 6 tubes, AC ..**$85.00-95.00**

38-10F, console, 1938, wood, upper front round dial, lower cloth grille with 2 vertical bars, 4 knobs, BC, SW, 5 tubes, AC ..**$110.00-130.00**

38-10T, table, 1938, wood, right front round dial, rounded left side, cloth grille with Deco cut-outs, 4 knobs, BC, SW, 5 tubes, AC...........**$95.00-115.00**

38-12C, table, 1938, wood & Bakelite versions, right front dial, left cloth grille with bars or cut-outs, 2 knobs, BC, 5 tubes, AC ..**$50.00-65.00**

38-12T, table, 1938, wood, right front dial, left wrap-around cloth grille with cut-outs, 3 knobs, BC, 5 tubes, AC **$50.00-65.00**

39-116RX, console, 1939, walnut, inner slide rule dial, fold-up lid, lower cloth grille with vertical bars, automatic remote control, 4 thumbwheel knobs, BC, SW, 14 tubes, AC, $240.00-270.00.

38-14T, table, 1938, wood & Bakelite versions, right front dial, left wrap-around cloth grille with cut-outs, 3 knobs, BC, SW, 5 tubes, AC/DC **$50.00-65.00**

38-22CS, chairside, 1938, wood, Deco, top dial, lower front round grille with horizontal bars, center storage, 4 knobs, BC, SW, 6 tubes, AC/DC **$150.00-180.00**

38-22T, table, 1938, wood, right front round dial, left cloth grille with Deco cut-outs, 4 knobs, BC, SW, 6 tubes, AC/DC **$85.00-95.00**

38-22XX, console, 1938, wood, upper front slanted automatic tuning dial, lower cloth grille with vertical bars, 4 knobs, BC, SW, 6 tubes, AC/DC **$110.00-130.00**

38-23K, console, 1938, two-tone wood, upper front round dial, lower cloth grille with three vertical bars and left & right cut-outs, 4 knobs, BC, SW, 6 tubes, AC/DC **$120.00-140.00**

38-23T, table, 1938, wood, right front round dial, rounded left side, Deco grille cut-outs, 4 knobs, BC, SW, 6 tubes, AC/DC **$95.00-115.00**

38-23X, console, 1938, wood, upper front round dial, lower grille area, 4 knobs, BC, SW, 6 tubes, AC/DC **$120.00-140.00**

38-33B, tombstone, 1938, wood, lower front rectangular dial, upper cloth grille with cut-outs, 2 knobs, BC, 5 tubes, battery **$75.00-85.00**

38-33F, console, 1938, wood, upper front dial, lower cloth grille with 2 vertical bars, 2 knobs, BC, 5 tubes, battery **$75.00-85.00**

38-34B, tombstone, 1938, wood, center front round dial, cloth grille with cut-outs, 2 knobs, BC, 5 tubes, 6VDC **$75.00-85.00**

38-34F, console, 1938, wood, upper front dial, lower cloth grille with 2 vertical bars, 2 knobs, BC, 5 tubes, 6VDC **$75.00-85.00**

38-35F, console, 1938, wood, upper front dial, lower cloth grille with 2 vertical bars, 2 knobs, BC, 5 tubes, AC/6VDC **$75.00-85.00**

38-38K, console, 1938, two-tone wood, upper front round dial, lower cloth grille with three vertical bars and left & right cut-outs, 4 knobs, BC, SW, 6 tubes, battery **$85.00-95.00**

38-38T, table, 1938, wood, right front round dial, rounded left with Deco grille cut-outs, 4 knobs, BC, SW, 6 tubes, battery **$65.00-75.00**

38-38X, console, 1938, wood, upper front round dial, lower cloth grille with three center vertical bars, 4 knobs, BC, SW, 6 tubes, battery **$75.00-85.00**

40-125C, table, 1940, wood, right front dial, left vertical grille bars, 6 push-buttons, handle, 3 knobs, BC, SW, 6 tubes, AC/DC, $65.00-75.00.

40-140T, table, 1940, wood, upper front slide rule dial, lower cloth grille with Deco cut-outs, 4 knobs, BC, SW, 6 tubes, AC, $50.00-65.00.

41-221C, table, 1941, wood, front walnut plastic dial panel with right dial & left horizontal louvers, handle, feet, 3 knobs, BC, SW, 6 tubes, AC/DC, $45.00-55.00.

38-39K, console, 1938, two-tone wood, upper front round dial, lower cloth grille with three vertical bars and left & right cut-outs, 4 knobs, BC, SW, 6 tubes, 6VDC **$85.00-95.00**

38-39T, table, 1938, wood, right front round dial, rounded left with Deco grille cut-outs, 4 knobs, BC, SW, 6 tubes, 6VDC **$50.00-65.00**

38-39X, console, 1938, wood, upper front round dial, lower cloth grille with three center vertical bars, 4 knobs, BC, SW, 6 tubes, 6VDC **$75.00-85.00**

38-40K, console, 1938, two-tone wood, upper front round dial, lower cloth grille with three vertical bars and left & right cut-outs, 4 knobs, BC, SW, 6 tubes, AC/6VDC....................................**$85.00-95.00**

38-40T, table, 1938, wood, Deco, right front round dial, left cloth grille with cut-outs, 4 knobs, BC, SW, 6 tubes, AC/6VDC **$55.00-65.00**

38-40X, console, 1938, wood, upper front round dial, lower cloth grille with three center vertical bars, 4 knobs, BC, SW, 6 tubes, AC/6VDC..**$75.00-85.00**

38-60F, console, 1938, wood, center front round dial, lower grille with two vertical bars, rounded corners with vertical trim, 4 knobs, BC, SW, 5 tubes, AC...**$95.00-105.00**

38-60B, tombstone, 1938, two-tone wood, center front round dial, upper 2-section grille, 4 knobs, BC, SW, 5 tubes, AC **$110.00-130.00**

38-62T, table, 1938, two-tone wood, right front round dial, left cloth grille with Deco cut-outs, 3 knobs, BC, SW, 5 tubes, AC **$55.00-65.00**

38-89K, console, 1938, two-tone wood, upper front round dial, lower cloth grille with cut-outs, 4 knobs, BC, SW, 6 tubes, AC **$110.00-130.00**

38-89B, tombstone, 1938, two-tone wood, center front round dial, cloth grille with cut-outs, 4 knobs, BC, SW, 6 tubes, AC....**$110.00-130.00**

38-116XX, console, 1938, wood, upper front slanted automatic tuning dial, lower cloth grille with vertical bars, lower right & left front cut-outs, 7 knobs, BC, SW, 15 tubes, AC **$200.00-230.00**

38-610J, console, 1938, wood, upper center round dial, lower grille w/3 vertical bars, rounded shoulders, 4 knobs, BC, SW, 5 tubes, AC **$120.00-140.00**

38-610B, tombstone, 1938, wood, center front round dial, upper grille w/8 cut-outs, 4 knobs, BC, SW, 5 tubes, AC **$110.00-130.00**

38-620T, table, 1938, wood, Deco, right front round dial, rounded left with Deco grille cut-outs, 4 knobs, BC, SW, 6 tubes, AC **$90.00-115.00**

38-623K, console, 1938, wood, upper front round dial, lower cloth grille with cut-outs, 4 knobs, BC, SW, 6 tubes, battery **$85.00-95.00**

38-623T, table, 1938, wood, Deco, right front round dial, rounded left with Deco grille cut-outs, 4 knobs, BC, SW, 6 tubes, battery ..**$75.00-85.00**

38-624K, console, 1938, wood, upper front round dial, lower cloth grille with cut-outs, 4 knobs, BC, SW, 6 tubes, 6VDC **$85.00-95.00**

38-624T, table, 1938, wood, Deco, right front round dial, rounded left with Deco grille cut-outs, 4 knobs, BC, SW, 6 tubes, 6VDC ..**$75.00-85.00**

38-630K, console, 1938, wood, upper front round dial, lower cloth grille with cut-outs, shadow tuning meter, 4 knobs, BC, SW, 6 tubes, AC **$120.00-140.00**

38-643B, tombstone, 1938, wood, rounded shoulders, center front round dial, upper cloth grille with cut-outs, shadow tuning meter, 4 knobs, BC, SW, 7 tubes, battery **$95.00-115.00**

38-643X, console, 1938, wood, upper front round dial, lower cloth grille with 3 vertical bars, shadow tuning meter, 4 knobs, BC, SW, 7 tubes, battery...**$85.00-95.00**

38-665X, console, 1938, wood, upper front round dial, lower cloth grille with 3 vertical bars, shadow tuning meter, 4 knobs, BC, SW, 9 tubes, AC **$140.00-160.00**

38-665B, tombstone, 1938, wood, rounded shoulders, center front round dial, upper cloth grille with cut-outs, shadow tuning meter, 4 knobs, BC, SW, 9 tubes, AC **$120.00-140.00**

38-690XX, console, 1938, wood, upper front slanted automatic tuning dial, lower cloth grille with cut-outs, right & left front vertical bars, 3 speakers, 7 knobs, BC, SW, 20 tubes, AC **$480.00-580.00**

38-2620, table, 1938, wood, Deco, right front round dial, rounded left with Deco grille cut-outs, 4 knobs, BC, SW, LW, 6 tubes, AC..**$90.00-115.00**

40-501P, table-R/P, 1940, two-tone wood, right front dial, left cloth grille with cut-outs, open top phono, 3 knobs, BC, 5 tubes, AC, $30.00-35.00.

41-226C, table, 1941, wood, Deco, front plastic dial panel with right dial & left horizontal grille bars, fluted left side, 6 upper pushbuttons, 3 knobs, BC, SW, 6 tubes, AC/DC, $110.00-130.00.

41-235T, table, 1941, wood, upper front slanted slide rule dial, lower cloth grille, plastic trim, 4 knobs, BC, SW, 7 tubes, AC, $45.00-55.00.

41-250T, table, 1941, wood, Deco, slanted front, inset plastic panel with slide rule dial/8 pushbuttons left horizontal grille bars, 4 knobs, BC, SW, 8 tubes, AC, $85.00-115.00.

38-2630, console, 1938, wood, upper front round dial, lower cloth grille with cut-outs, shadow tuning meter, 4 knobs, BC, SW, LW, 6 tubes, AC **$120.00-140.00**

38-2650X, console, 1938, wood, upper front round dial, lower cloth grille with 3 vertical bars, shadow tuning meter, 4 knobs, BC, SW, LW, 8 tubes, AC **$140.00-160.00**

38-2650B, tombstone, 1938, wood, rounded shoulders, center front round dial, upper cloth grille with cut-outs, shadow tuning meter, 4 knobs, BC, SW, LW, 8 tubes, AC **$120.00-140.00**

38-2670X, console, 1938, wood, upper center round dial, lower grille w/4 vertical bars, 4 knobs, BC, SW, LW, 11 tubes, AC **$150.00-180.00**

38-2670B, tombstone, 1938, wood, center round dial, upper grille with 6 cut-outs, shadow tuning meter, 4 knobs, BC, SW, LW, 11 tubes, AC **$130.00-180.00**

38A, cathedral, 1933, wood, center front window dial, upper cloth grille with cut-outs, 4 knobs, BC, SW, 5 tubes, battery **$150.00-180.00**

38L, console, 1933, wood, lowboy, upper front window dial, lower cloth grille with cut-outs, 4 knobs, BC, SW, 5 tubes, battery **$120.00-150.00**

39-6C, table, 1939, walnut with inlay, right front airplane dial, left cloth grille with Deco cut-outs, 2 knobs, BC, 5 tubes, AC **$55.00-65.00**

39-6CI, table, 1939, ivory paint, right front airplane dial, left cloth grille with Deco cut-outs, 2 knobs, BC, 5 tubes, AC **$55.00-65.00**

39-7C, table, 1939, walnut, right front dial with pushbuttons above, left cloth grille with cut-outs, 2 knobs, BC, 5 tubes, AC **$55.00-65.00**

39-7T, table, 1939, walnut, right front dial with pushbuttons above, left cloth grille with 3 horizontal bars, 2 knobs, BC, 5 tubes, AC **$55.00-65.00**

39-8T, table, 1939, wood, right front airplane dial, left cloth grille w/horizontal bars, 2 knobs, BC, 5 tubes, AC/DC **$55.00-65.00**

39-12CB, table, 1939, walnut plastic, right front airplane dial, left cloth grille with two horizontal bars wraps around corner, 2 knobs, BC, 5 tubes, AC/DC **$55.00-65.00**

39-12CBI, table, 1939, ivory plastic, right front airplane dial, left cloth grille with two horizontal bars wraps around corner, 2 knobs, BC, 5 tubes, AC/DC...**$55.00-65.00**

39-12T, table, 1939, wood, right front airplane dial, left cloth grille wraps around corner, 2 knobs, BC, 5 tubes, AC/DC **$55.00-65.00**

39-14CB, table, 1939, walnut plastic, right front airplane dial, left cloth grille with two horizontal bars wraps around corner, 2 knobs, BC, 5 tubes, AC/DC...**$55.00-65.00**

39-14CBI, table, 1939, ivory plastic, right front airplane dial, left cloth grille with two horizontal bars wraps around corner, 2 knobs, BC, 5 tubes, AC/DC...**$55.00-65.00**

39-14T, table, 1939, wood, right front airplane dial, left cloth grille wraps around corner, 2 knobs, BC, 5 tubes, AC/DC **$55.00-65.00**

39-15CB, table, 1939, walnut plastic, right front airplane dial, left cloth grille with two horizontal bars wraps around corner, 2 knobs, BC, 5 tubes, AC/DC...**$55.00-65.00**

39-15CBI, table, 1939, ivory plastic, right front airplane dial, left cloth grille with two horizontal bars wraps around corner, 2 knobs, BC, 5 tubes, AC/DC...**$55.00-65.00**

39-15T, table, 1939, wood, right front airplane dial, left cloth grille wraps around corner, 2 knobs, BC, 5 tubes, AC/DC **$55.00-65.00**

39-17F, console, 1939, wood, upper front slide rule dial, large lower cloth grille with 3 vertical bars, 6 top pushbuttons, 2 side knobs, BC, 5 tubes, AC **$120.00-150.00**

41-245T, table, 1941, wood, upper front slanted slide rule dial, lower cloth grille with horizontal bars, 6 pushbuttons, 4 knobs, BC, SW, 7 tubes, AC, $65.00-75.00.

41-280X, console, 1941, wood, upper front slanted slide rule dial, lower grille with vertical bars, 8 pushbuttons, 4 knobs, BC, SW, 8 tubes, AC, $110.00-130.00.

41-290X, console, 1941, wood, upper front slanted slide rule dial, lower grille with wrap-over vertical bars, 8 pushbuttons, 4 knobs, BC, SW, 10 tubes, AC, $120.00-140.00.

42-340T, table, 1942, two-tone wood, upper front slanted slide rule dial, lower rectangular cloth grille, 4 knobs, BC, SW, 7 tubes, AC, $50.00-65.00.

39-17T, table, 1939, wood, upper front slide rule dial, large lower cloth grille with 3 vertical bars, 6 pushbuttons, 2 side knobs, BC, 5 tubes, AC **$65.00-75.00**

39-18F, console, 1939, wood, upper front slide rule dial, large lower cloth grille with 3 vertical bars, 6 pushbuttons, 2 side knobs, BC, 5 tubes, AC/DC **$120.00-150.00**

39-19F, console, 1939, wood, upper front slide rule dial, large lower cloth grille with 3 vertical bars, 6 pushbuttons, 3 side knobs, BC, SW, 5 tubes, AC **$120.00-150.00**

39-19T, table, 1939, wood, upper front slide rule dial, lower cloth grille with zig-zag cut-outs, top pushbuttons, 3 side knobs, BC, SW, 5 tubes, AC **$65.00-75.00**

39-25T, table, 1939, wood, slant front, right slide rule dial, left cloth grille with Deco cut-outs, 8 pushbuttons, 4 knobs, BC, 5 tubes, AC **$75.00-85.00**

39-25XF, console, 1939, wood, upper front slanted slide rule dial, lower cloth grille with vertical bars, 8 pushbuttons, 4 knobs, BC, SW, 5 tubes, AC **$120.00-150.00**

39-30T, table, 1939, wood, slant front, right slide rule dial, left cloth grille with Deco cut-outs, 8 pushbuttons, 4 knobs, BC, SW, 6 tubes, AC **$75.00-85.00**

39-31XF, console, 1939, walnut, 2 styles, upper front slanted slide rule dial, lower cloth grille with vertical bars, 8 pushbuttons, 4 knobs, BC, SW, 6 tubes, AC.......................................**$120.00-150.00**

39-35XX, console, 1939, wood, upper front slanted slide rule dial, lower cloth grille with 4 vertical bars, pushbuttons, 4 knobs, BC, SW, 6 tubes, AC **$110.00-130.00**

39-36XX, console, 1939, walnut, upper front slanted slide rule dial, lower cloth grille with 4 vertical bars, 8 pushbuttons, 4 thumbwheel knobs, BC, SW, 6 tubes, AC **$110.00-130.00**

39-40XX, console, 1939, walnut, upper front slanted slide rule dial, lower cloth grille with vertical bars, pushbuttons, 4 thumbwheel knobs, BC, SW, 8 tubes, AC **$120.00-140.00**

39-45XX, console, 1939, walnut, inner dial, pushbuttons, fold-up lid, lower cloth grille with vertical bars, 4 thumbwheel knobs, BC, SW, 9 tubes, AC **$120.00-150.00**

39-55RX, console, 1939, wood, inner slide rule dial, fold-up lid, lower cloth grille with vertical bars, wireless "Mystery" remote control, 4 thumbwheel knobs, BC, 11 tubes, AC......................**$150.00-180.00**

39-70B, tombstone, 1939, wood, rounded shoulders, lower front square dial, upper cloth grille with cut-outs, 2 knobs, BC, 4 tubes, battery **$75.00-85.00**

39-80B, table, 1939, wood, lower front dial surrounded by large cloth grille area with cut-outs, 2 knobs, BC, 4 tubes, battery **$85.00-95.00**

39-80XF, console, 1939, wood, upper front dial on slanted face, lower grille with 3 vertical bars, 2 knobs, BC, 4 tubes, battery **$85.00-105.00**

39-85B, table, 1939, wood, lower front dial surrounded by large cloth grille area with cut-outs, pushbuttons, 3 knobs, BC, SW, 4 tubes, battery **$85.00-95.00**

39-85XF, console, 1939, wood, upper front dial on slanted face, lower grille with 3 vertical bars, pushbuttons, 3 knobs, BC, SW, 4 tubes, battery **$85.00-105.00**

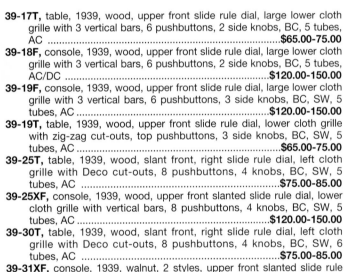

42-321T, table, 1942, wood, upper front slanted slide rule dial, lower rectangular cloth grille, feet, 2 knobs, BC, 6 tubes, AC/DC, $40.00-50.00.

42-350T, table, 1942, wood, upper front slide rule dial, lower horizontal wrap-around grille bars, 6 pushbuttons, 4 knobs, BC, SW, FM1, 7 tubes, AC, $85.00-95.00.

42-842T, portable, 1942, leatherette, upper front plastic panel with right airplane dial & left horizontal grille bars, handle, 2 knobs, BC, 7 tubes, AC/DC/battery, $35.00-40.00.

42-KR3, table, 1942, wood, rounded case, recessed front panel with right dial & left horizontal louvers, base, 2 knobs, BC, 5 tubes, AC/DC, $40.00-50.00.

39-117F, console, 1939, wood, upper front slide rule dial, lower cloth grille with 3 vertical bars, 6 top pushbuttons, 2 side knobs, BC, 5 tubes, AC **$110.00-130.00**

39-117T, table, 1939, two-tone wood, upper front slide rule dial, lower cloth grille with Deco cut-outs, 6 top pushbuttons, 2 side knobs, BC, 5 tubes, AC **$65.00-75.00**

39-118F, console, 1939, wood, upper front slide rule dial, lower cloth grille with 3 vertical bars, 6 top pushbuttons, 2 side knobs, BC, 5 tubes, AC/DC **$110.00-130.00**

39-119F, console, 1939, wood, upper front slide rule dial, lower cloth grille with 3 vertical bars, 6 pushbuttons, 3 side knobs, BC, SW, 5 tubes, AC **$110.00-130.00**

40-74T, portable, 1940, striped cloth covered, right front dial, left grille area, handle, 2 knobs, BC, 4 tubes, battery **$30.00-35.00**

40-81T, portable, 1940, striped cloth covered, right front square dial, left grille area, handle, 2 knobs, BC, 4 tubes, battery **$30.00-35.00**

40-82T, portable, 1940, striped cloth covered, inner right dial, left grille area, fold-down front, handle, 2 knobs, BC, 4 tubes, battery **$30.00-35.00**

40-88T, portable, 1940, striped cloth covered, right front dial, left grille area, handle, 3 knobs, BC, SW, 5 tubes, battery...........**$30.00-35.00**

40-90CB, table, 1940, plastic, right front dial, left cloth grille with 2 horizontal bars, 2 knobs, BC, 4 tubes, battery **$35.00-40.00**

40-95F, console, 1940, wood, upper center slide rule dial, lower grille with 4 vertical bars, 2 knobs, BC, 4 tubes, battery **$120.00-140.00**

40-95T, table, 1940, wood, upper front slide rule dial, lower cloth grille with cut-outs, 2 knobs, BC, 4 tubes, battery..................**$40.00-50.00**

40-115C, table, 1940, wood, right front dial, left cloth grille with 2 "wavy" horizontal bars, 3 knobs, BC, SW, 6 tubes, AC **$45.00-55.00**

40-120CI, table, 1940, ivory paint, right front square dial, left horizontal louvers, handle, tubular feet, 3 knobs, BC, SW, 6 tubes, AC/DC **$55.00-65.00**

40-124C, table, 1940, wood, right front dial, left cloth grille with Deco cut-outs, 6 pushbuttons, 3 knobs, BC, SW, 6 tubes, AC **$65.00-75.00**

40-130T, table, 1940, wood, upper front slide rule dial, lower cloth grille with diagonal cut-outs, 4 knobs, BC, SW, 6 tubes, AC..**$50.00-65.00**

40-135T, table, 1940, wood, upper front slide rule dial, lower cloth grille with diagonal cut-outs, 6 pushbuttons, 4 knobs, BC, SW, 6 tubes, AC **$65.00-75.00**

40-145T, table, 1940, wood, upper front slide rule dial, lower cloth grille with Deco cut-outs, 6 pushbuttons, 4 knobs, BC, SW, 6 tubes, AC..**$65.00-75.00**

40-150T, table, 1940, wood, slant front, right slide rule dial, left cloth grille with Deco cut-outs, 8 pushbuttons, 4 knobs, BC, SW, 7 tubes, AC **$85.00-105.00**

40-155T, table, 1940, wood, slant front, right slide rule dial, left cloth grille with Deco cut-outs, 8 pushbuttons, 4 knobs, BC, SW, 8 tubes, AC **$85.00-105.00**

40-158F, console, 1940, wood, upper front dial, lower cloth grille with vertical bars, 6 pushbuttons, 4 knobs, BC, SW, 6 tubes, AC........**$110.00-130.00**

40-160F, console, 1940, wood, upper front dial, lower cloth grille with vertical bars, 6 pushbuttons, 4 knobs, BC, SW, 6 tubes, AC........**$110.00-130.00**

40-165F, console, 1940, wood, upper front dial, lower cloth grille with vertical bars, 6 pushbuttons, 4 knobs, BC, SW, 6 tubes, AC........**$120.00-150.00**

40-170CS, chairside, 1940, wood, all sides finished, top dial, 6 pushbuttons, cloth grille with horizontal bars, 4 knobs, BC, SW, 6 tubes, AC **$160.00-180.00**

40-180XF, console, 1940, wood, upper front slanted slide rule dial, lower vertical grille bars, 8 pushbuttons, 4 knobs, BC, SW, 7 tubes, AC **$120.00-150.00**

40-185XX, console, 1940, wood, upper front slanted slide rule dial, lower cloth grille with 4 vertical bars, 8 pushbuttons, 4 knobs, BC, SW, 8 tubes, AC **$120.00-150.00**

42-1002, table-R/P, 1942, wood, front slanted slide rule dial, lower horizontal grille bars, lift top, inner phono, 2 knobs, BC, 6 tubes, AC, $30.00-35.00.

42-PT91, table, 1942, brown plastic, right front dial, right & left horizontal wrap-around louvers, left grille, 2 knobs, BC, 5 tubes, AC/DC, $45.00-50.00.

42-PT95, table, 1942, wood, front plastic panel with right dial & left horizontal grille bars, handle, feet, 2 knobs, BC, 5 tubes, AC/DC, $45.00-55.00.

40-190XF, console, 1940, wood, upper front slanted slide rule dial, lower cloth grille with 6 vertical bars, 8 pushbuttons, 4 knobs, BC, SW, 8 tubes, AC $120.00-150.00

40-195XX, console, 1940, wood, upper front slanted slide rule dial, lower cloth grille with vertical bars, 8 pushbuttons, 4 thumbwheel knobs, BC, SW, 10 tubes, AC $130.00-160.00

40-200XX, console, 1940, wood, inner slide rule dial, 8 pushbuttons, fold-up lid, large lower cloth grille with vertical bars, 4 thumbwheel knobs, BC, SW, 11 tubes, AC $140.00-160.00

40-201XX, console, 1940, wood, inner slide rule dial, pushbuttons, fold-up lid, lower cloth grille with vertical bars, right & left front cut-outs, 4 thumbwheel knobs, BC, SW, 10 tubes, AC $150.00-190.00

40-205RX, console, 1940, walnut, inner dial, fold-up lid, lower cloth grille with vertical bars, wireless automatic remote control, 4 thumbwheel knobs, BC, 11 radio tubes/1 remote tube, AC $160.00-190.00

40-215RX, console, 1940, walnut, inner dial, fold-up lid, lower cloth grille with vertical bars, wireless automatic remote control, 4 thumbwheel knobs, BC, SW, 11 radio tubes/1 remote tube, AC....$160.00-190.00

40-216RX, console, 1940, walnut, inner dial, fold-up lid, lower cloth grille with vertical bars, wireless automatic remote control, 4 thumbwheel knobs, BC, SW, 13 radio tubes/1 remote tube, AC....$180.00-200.00

40-300X, console, 1940, wood, inner slide rule dial, 7 pushbuttons, fold-up lid, large lower vertical grille louvers, BC, SW, 12 tubes, AC $150.00-190.00

40-504P, portable-R/P, 1940, cloth covered, left front dial, right grille area, handle, lift top, inner crank phono, 3 knobs, BC, 4 tubes, battery $35.00-45.00

40-525P, console-R/P, 1940, wood, front dial, pushbuttons lower cloth grille with 3 vertical bars, lift top, inner phono, 4 knobs, BC, SW, 6 tubes, AC $95.00-115.00

45, table, 1934, wood, Deco, center front window dial, right & left "butterfly wing" grilles, top louvers, 4 knobs, BC, SW, 6 tubes, AC, $130.00-160.00.

46-350, portable, 1946, wood & leatherette, upper front slide rule dial, lower horizontal grille bars, tambour cover, handle, 2 knobs, BC, 6 tubes, AC/DC/battery, $40.00-50.00.

41-22CL, table-C, 1941, wood, right front square airplane dial, center grille with horizontal bars, left front clock, 3 knobs, BC, 6 tubes, AC $75.00-95.00

41-81T, portable, 1941, cloth covered, front plastic dial panel with right dial & left horizontal grille bars, handle, 2 knobs, BC, 4 tubes, battery $30.00-35.00

41-95T, table, 1941, two-tone wood, upper front slanted slide rule dial, lower vertical grille bars, 2 knobs, BC, 5 tubes, battery ..$40.00-45.00

41-100T, table, 1941, wood, upper front slide rule dial, lower 3 section grille, 6 pushbuttons, 2 knobs, BC, 5 tubes, battery $45.00-55.00

41-220C, table, 1941, wood, right front dial, left cloth grille, handle, feet, 3 knobs, BC, SW, 6 tubes, AC/DC $45.00-55.00

41-221CI, table, 1941, wood, front ivory plastic dial panel with right dial & left horizontal louvers, handle, feet, 3 knobs, BC, SW, 6 tubes, AC/DC $45.00-55.00

41-225C, table, 1941, two-tone wood, right front square dial, left cloth grille, 6 pushbuttons, 3 knobs, BC, SW, 6 tubes, AC/DC $55.00-65.00

41-230T, table, 1941, brown plastic, upper front slanted slide rule dial, lower cloth grille, 4 knobs, BC, SW, 7 tubes, AC $50.00-65.00

41-231T, table, 1941, wood, Deco, right front dial, left horizontal louvers, rounded left side, 6 pushbuttons, 3 knobs, BC, SW, 6 tubes, AC/DC $85.00-105.00

41-240T, table, 1941, wood, upper front slanted slide rule dial, lower cloth grille with horizontal bars, 4 knobs, BC, SW, 7 tubes, AC $50.00-65.00

46-1201, table-R/P, 1946, wood, curved front, top slide rule dial, center cloth grille, lower slide-in record slot, 2 knobs, BC, 5 tubes, AC, $75.00-85.00.

46-1226, console-R/P, 1946, wood, upper front slanted slide rule dial, lower tilt-out phono, 4 knobs, BC, SW, 8 tubes, AC, $95.00-115.00.

48-200, table, 1948, walnut plastic, right front dial, right & left horizontal wrap-around louvers, 2 knobs, BC, 5 tubes, AC/DC, $40.00-50.00.

41-246T, table, 1941, wood, upper front slanted slide rule dial, lower cloth grille with horizontal bars, 6 pushbuttons, 4 knobs, BC, SW, 7 tubes, AC **$65.00-75.00**

41-255T, table, 1941, wood, Deco, slanted front, inset plastic panel with slide rule dial/8 pushbuttons left horizontal grille bars, 4 knobs, BC, SW, 9 tubes, AC...**$85.00-115.00**

41-256T, table, 1941, wood, Deco, slanted front, inset plastic panel with slide rule dial/8 pushbuttons left horizontal grille bars, 4 knobs, BC, SW, 9 tubes, AC...**$85.00-115.00**

41-258F, console, 1941, wood, upper front dial, lower cloth grille with 4 vertical bars, 3 knobs, BC, SW, 6 tubes, AC **$95.00-115.00**

41-260F, console, 1941, wood, upper front slide rule dial, lower cloth grille with vertical bars, pushbuttons, 4 knobs, BC, SW, 7 tubes, AC **$110.00-130.00**

41-265K, console, 1941, wood, upper front slide rule dial, lower grille with vertical bars, 6 pushbuttons, 4 knobs, BC, SW, 7 tubes, AC **$110.00-130.00**

41-285X, console, 1941, wood, upper front slanted slide rule dial, lower grille with vertical bars, 8 pushbuttons, 4 knobs, BC, SW, 9 tubes, AC **$110.00-130.00**

41-287X, console, 1941, wood, inner slide rule dial, pushbuttons, fold-up lid, large lower cloth grille with cut-outs, 4 knobs, BC, SW, 9 tubes, AC **$110.00-130.00**

41-295X, console, 1941, walnut, upper front slanted slide rule dial, lower grille with vertical bars, 8 pushbuttons, 4 thumbwheel knobs, BC, SW, 11 tubes, AC..**$120.00-150.00**

41-296X, console, 1941, walnut, upper front slanted slide rule dial, lower grille with vertical bars, 8 pushbuttons, 4 thumbwheel knobs, BC, SW, 9 tubes, AC...**$120.00-150.00**

41-300X, console, 1941, walnut, inner slide rule dial, 8 pushbuttons, fold-up lid, vertical front panels, 4 thumbwheel knobs, BC, SW, 12 tubes, AC **$150.00-180.00**

41-315X, console, 1941, walnut, inner slide rule dial, 8 pushbuttons, fold-up lid, lower cloth grille with vertical bars, 4 thumbwheel knobs, BC, SW, 12 tubes, AC...**$150.00-180.00**

41-316RX, console, 1941, wood, inner slide rule dial, 8 pushbuttons, fold-up lid, lower cloth grille with vertical bars, wireless remote control, 4 thumbwheel knobs, BC, SW, 14 radio tubes/1 remote tube, AC **$200.00-230.00**

41-601P, table-R/P, 1941, wood, upper front slide rule dial, lower horizontal louvers, lift top, inner phono, 2 knobs, BC, 5 tubes, AC **$35.00-40.00**

41-603P, table-R/P, 1941, wood, center front square dial, right & left horizontal grille bars, lift top, inner phono, 3 knobs, BC, SW, 6 tubes, AC **$35.00-40.00**

41-608P, console-R/P/Rec, 1941, wood, upper front slide rule dial, tilt-out front, inner phono/recorder, 6 pushbuttons, 4 knobs, BC, SW, 9 tubes, AC **$110.00-130.00**

41-625P, console-R/P, 1941, wood, upper front rectangular dial, tilt-out front with vertical bars, inner phono, 3 knobs, BC, SW, 7 tubes, AC...**$120.00-140.00**

41-842T, portable, 1941, leatherette, front plastic panel with right dial & left horizontal grille bars, handle, 2 knobs, BC, 7 tubes, AC/DC/battery **$30.00-35.00**

41-843T, portable, 1941, leatherette, inner plastic panel with right dial & left horizontal grille bars, fold-down front, handle, 2 knobs, BC, 7 tubes, AC/DC/battery **$35.00-40.00**

47-204, table, 1947, leatherette, center front plastic panel with right dial & left horizontal grille bars, 2 knobs, BC, 5 tubes, AC/DC, $35.00-40.00.

48-206, table, 1948, leatherette, front plastic panel with right dial & left horizontal grille bars, rounded corners, 2 knobs, BC, 5 tubes, AC/DC, $40.00-45.00.

48-225, table, 1948, plastic, right front square dial, left perforated grille, rounded top, 2 knobs, BC, 5 tubes, AC/DC, $35.00-45.00.

48-461, table, 1948, wood, upper front slanted slide rule dial, lower recessed cloth grille, 2 knobs, BC, 6 tubes, AC/DC, $35.00-40.00.

41-844T, portable, 1941, wood, inner plastic panel with right dial & left horizontal grille bars, tambour door, handle, 2 knobs, BC, 7 tubes, AC/DC/battery **$40.00-45.00**

41-851T, portable, 1941, leatherette, front plastic panel with right dial & left horizontal grille bars, 3 knobs, BC, SW, 5 tubes, AC/DC/battery **$30.00-35.00**

41-KR, table/refrigerator-C, 1941, wood, this set was marketed as a kitchen radio and has an arched base to fit the top of a refrigerator of the era, right front dial, left clock, center vertical grille bars, 2 knobs, BC, 5 tubes, AC **$50.00-65.00**

42-1-T-96, table, 1942, wood, right front dial with red pointer, left square cloth grille, 2 knobs, BC......................................**$45.00-55.00**

42-22CL, table-C, 1942, wood, right front square airplane dial, center grille with horizontal bars, left front clock, 3 knobs, BC, SW, 6 tubes, AC **$75.00-95.00**

42-122T, table, 1942, wood, upper center slanted slide rule dial with plastic bezel, lower grille with 3 cut-outs, 2 knobs, BC, 5 tubes, battery **$50.00-65.00**

42-123F, console, 1942, wood, upper center slanted slide rule dial with plastic bezel, lower grille with vertical bars, 2 knobs, BC, 5 tubes, battery **$65.00-85.00**

42-322T, table, 1942, wood, upper front slanted slide rule dial, lower horizontal louvers, 3 knobs, BC, SW, 6 tubes, AC/DC **$50.00-65.00**

42-327T, table, 1942, two-tone wood, upper front slide rule dial, lower cloth grille with 2 horizontal bars, 6 pushbuttons, 3 knobs, BC, SW, 6 tubes, AC/DC **$50.00-65.00**

42-345T, table, 1942, wood, upper front slide rule dial, lower cloth grille, 6 pushbuttons, 4 knobs, BC, SW, 7 tubes, AC **$50.00-65.00**

42-355T, table, 1942, walnut, right front slide rule dial, left cloth grille with horizontal bars, 9 pushbuttons, 4 knobs, BC, SW, FM1, 8 tubes, AC **$75.00-85.00**

48-460, table, 1948, plastic, step-down top, curved dial on top of case, lower horizontal wrap-around louvers, 2 top knobs, BC, 6 tubes, AC/DC, $45.00-55.00.

42-358F, console, 1942, wood, upper center slanted slide rule dial with plastic bezel, lower grille with vertical bars, 2 knobs, BC, 6 tubes, AC/DC **$95.00-115.00**

42-360F, console, 1942, wood, upper center slanted slide rule dial with plastic bezel, lower grille with vertical bars, 4 knobs, BC, SW, 7 tubes, AC **$110.00-130.00**

42-365K, console, 1942, wood, upper center slanted slide rule dial with plastic bezel, lower grille with vertical bars, 6 pushbuttons, 4 knobs, BC, SW, 7 tubes, AC **$110.00-130.00**

42-380X, console, 1942, walnut, upper front slanted slide rule dial, lower vertical bars, 9 pushbuttons, 4 knobs, BC, SW, 8 tubes, AC ..**$120.00-140.00**

42-390X, console, 1942, wood, upper front slanted slide rule dial with plastic escutcheon, lower vertical grille bars, pushbuttons, 4 knobs, BC, SW, FM1, 8 tubes, AC **$120.00-140.00**

42-395X, console, 1942, wood, upper front slanted slide rule dial with plastic escutcheon, lower inset grille with 9 vertical bars, 10 pushbuttons, 4 knobs, BC, SW, FM1, 9 tubes, AC **$120.00-140.00**

42-400X, console, 1942, wood, inner slanted slide rule dial, slide-down lid, lower vertical grille bars, pushbuttons, thumbwheel tuning, 4 knobs, BC, SW, FM1, 11 tubes, AC **$120.00-150.00**

42-1001, table-R/P, 1942, wood, front inset slide rule dial, lower horizontal grille bars, lift top, inner phono, 2 knobs, BC, 5 tubes, AC ..**$30.00-35.00**

42-1003, table-R/P, 1942, wood, front slide rule dial, right & left horizontal wrap-around louvers, lift top, inner phono, 3 knobs, BC, SW, 7 tubes, AC **$30.00-35.00**

42-1004, console-R/P, 1942, wood, upper front slide rule dial, lower tilt-out front with vertical bars & inner phono, 2 knobs, BC, 6 tubes, AC **$110.00-130.00**

42-1005, console-R/P, 1942, wood, upper front slide rule dial, lower tilt-out front with vertical bars & inner phono, 3 knobs, BC, SW, 7 tubes, AC **$110.00-130.00**

42-1006, console-R/P, 1942, wood, upper slanted slide rule dial, lower tilt-out front with vertical bars & inner phono, 3 knobs, BC, 7 tubes, AC **$110.00-130.00**

42-1008, console-R/P, 1942, wood, upper slanted slide rule dial, lower tilt-out front with vertical bars & inner phono, 6 pushbuttons, 4 knobs, BC, SW, 9 tubes, AC **$110.00-130.00**

48-482, table, 1948, wood, lower front slanted slide rule dial, upper cloth grille, 10 pushbuttons, 4 knobs, BC, SW, FM, 9 tubes, AC, $55.00-65.00.

48-1262, console-R/P, 1948, two-tone wood, upper front slanted slide rule dial, lower tilt-out phono, 4 knobs, BC, 6 tubes, AC, $85.00-105.00.

42-1009, console-R/P, 1942, wood, ornate cabinet, upper slanted slide rule dial, lower center grille, 6 pushbuttons, 4 knobs, BC, SW, 9 tubes, AC **$160.00-190.00**

42-1010, console-R/P, 1942, wood, upper slanted slide rule dial, lower grille with vertical bars, ten pushbuttons, 4 knobs, BC, SW, 10 tubes, AC **$150.00-180.00**

42-1011, console-R/P, 1942, wood, ornate cabinet, inner slanted slide rule dial with fold up cover, lower center grille with cathedral arches, 10 pushbuttons, 4 knobs, BC, SW, 10 tubes, AC **$160.00-190.00**

42-1012, console-R/P, 1942, walnut, inner dial, 10 pushbuttons, fold-up cover, tilt-out front with inner phono, 4 knobs, BC, SW, FM1, 10 tubes, AC **$150.00-180.00**

42-1013, console-R/P, 1942, walnut, inner dial, 10 pushbuttons, fold-up cover, lower criss-cross grille, tilt-out front with inner phono, 4 knobs, BC, SW, FM1, 10 tubes, AC **$150.00-180.00**

42-1015, console-R/P, 1942, wood, inner slide rule dial, 12 pushbuttons, fold-up lid, double front doors, tilt-out phono, 4 knobs, BC, SW, FM1, 12 tubes, AC **$150.00-180.00**

42-KR5, table/refrigerator-C, 1942, wood, this set was marketed as a kitchen radio and has an arched base to fit the top of a refrigerator of the era, rounded sides, recessed front panel with right dial, left clock & center horizontal grille bars, 2 knobs, BC, 5 tubes, AC..**$50.00-65.00**

42-PT-2, table, 1942, brown plastic, upper front slide rule dial, lower horizontal wrap-around louvers, 2 knobs, BC, 5 tubes, AC/DC **$40.00-45.00**

42-PT4, table, 1942, ivory plastic, upper front slide rule dial, lower horizontal wrap-around louvers, 2 knobs, BC, 5 tubes, AC/DC ..**$40.00-45.00**

42-PT7, table, 1942, wood, upper front slide rule dial, lower horizontal grille, rounded shoulders, feet, 2 knobs, BC, 5 tubes, AC/DC **$45.00-50.00**

49-503, table, 1949, plastic, modernistic dial & grille, rounded top, slanted sides, 2 knobs, BC, 5 tubes, AC/DC, $85.00-115.00.

42-PT10, table, 1942, brown plastic, upper front slide rule dial, lower horizontal wrap-around louvers, 2 knobs, BC, 6 tubes, AC/DC **$40.00-45.00**

42-PT87, portable, 1942, leatherette, front plastic panel with right airplane dial & left horizontal grille bars, handle, 2 knobs, BC, 5 tubes, AC/DC/battery **$35.00-40.00**

42-PT92, table, 1942, ivory plastic, right front dial, right & left horizontal wrap-around louvers, left grille, 2 knobs, BC, 5 tubes, AC/DC..**$45.00-50.00**

42-PT93, table, 1942, wood, right front dial, left cloth grille, center vertical divider, handle, feet, 2 knobs, BC, 5 tubes, AC/DC **$45.00-55.00**

42-PT94, table, 1942, wood, front plastic panel with right dial & left horizontal grille bars, handle, feet, 2 knobs, BC, 5 tubes, AC/DC ..**$45.00-55.00**

43B, cathedral, 1932, wood, center front window dial, upper cloth grille with cut-outs, 4 knobs, BC, SW, 8 tubes, AC **$270.00-300.00**

43H, console, 1932, wood, lowboy, upper front window dial, lower cloth grille with cut-outs, 6 legs, 4 knobs, BC, SW, 8 tubes, AC **$120.00-140.00**

43X, console, 1932, wood, upper front window dial with escutcheon, lower inclined grille area, 4 knobs, BC, SW, 8 tubes, AC **$120.00-140.00**

44B, cathedral, 1933, wood, center front window dial, upper cloth grille with cut-outs, 4 knobs, BC, SW, 6 tubes, AC **$240.00-270.00**

44H, console, 1933, wood, lowboy, upper front window dial, lower cloth grille with cut-outs, 6 legs, 4 knobs, BC, SW, 6 tubes, AC **$120.00-140.00**

45C, table, 1934, wood, Deco, center front window dial, right & left "butterfly wing" grilles, top louvers, 4 knobs, BC, SW, 6 tubes, AC..**$130.00-160.00**

45L, console, 1934, wood, lowboy, upper front window dial, lower cloth grille with cut-outs, 4 knobs, BC, SW, 6 tubes, AC **$120.00-150.00**

46, cathedral, 1931, wood, center front window dial, upper cloth grille with cut-outs, DC, 3 knobs, BC, 7 tubes, DC **$350.00-410.00**

46-131, table, 1946, plastic, upper front slide rule dial, lower horizontal louvers, 2 knobs, BC, 4 tubes, battery **$35.00-40.00**

46-132, table, 1946, wood, upper front slide rule dial, lower cloth grille with center horizontal bar, 2 knobs, BC, 5 tubes, battery **$30.00-35.00**

49-500, table, 1949, walnut plastic, right front dial, right & left horizontal wrap-around louvers, 2 knobs, BC, 5 tubes, AC/DC, $40.00-50.00.

49-601, portable, 1949, plastic, lower front slide rule dial, upper horizontal grille bars, handle, 2 knobs, BC, 4 tubes, battery, $40.00-45.00.

49-909, table, 1949, wood, center front slide rule dial, large upper woven grille, 4 knobs, BC, FM, 9 tubes, AC, $40.00-45.00.

46-142, table, 1946, plastic, upper front slanted slide rule dial, lower horizontal louvers, 2 knobs, BC, 5 tubes, battery **$35.00-40.00**

46-200, table, 1946, walnut plastic, right front dial, right & left horizontal wrap-around louvers, 2 knobs, BC, 5 tubes, AC/DC......**$45.00-50.00**

46-200-I, table, 1946, ivory plastic, right front dial, right & left horizontal wrap-around louvers, 2 knobs, BC, 5 tubes, AC/DC......**$45.00-50.00**

46-250, table, 1946, walnut plastic, upper front slide rule dial, lower horizontal louvers, 2 knobs, BC, 5 tubes, AC/DC **$40.00-50.00**

46-250-I, table, 1946, ivory plastic, upper front slide rule dial, lower horizontal louvers, 2 knobs, BC, 5 tubes, AC/DC **$40.00-50.00**

46-251, table, 1946, walnut plastic, upper front slide rule dial, lower recessed grille, 2 knobs, BC, 5 tubes, AC/DC...............**$40.00-50.00**

46-420, table, 1946, plastic, step-down top, curved dial on top of case, lower horizontal wrap-around louvers, 2 knobs, BC, 6 tubes, AC/DC **$45.00-55.00**

46-420-I, table, 1946, plastic, step-down top, curved dial on top of case, lower horizontal wrap-around louvers, 2 knobs, BC, 6 tubes, AC/DC **$45.00-55.00**

46-421, table, 1946, walnut, upper front slide rule dial, lower oblong cloth grille, 2 knobs, BC, 6 tubes, AC/DC **$50.00-65.00**

46-421-I, table, 1946, ivory, upper front slide rule dial, lower oblong cloth grille, 2 knobs, BC, 6 tubes, AC/DC **$50.00-65.00**

46-427, table, 1946, wood, upper front slide rule dial, lower horizontal louvers, 3 knobs, BC, SW, 6 tubes, AC/DC....................**$50.00-55.00**

46-480, console, 1946, wood, upper front slanted slide rule dial, lower cloth grille with vertical bars, 4 knobs, BC, SW, FM, 7 tubes, AC **$110.00-130.00**

46-1203, table-R/P, 1946, wood, right front vertical dial, left horizontal louvers, lift top, inner phono, 3 knobs, BC, AC **$35.00-40.00**

50, cathedral, 1931, wood, center front window dial, upper cloth grille with cut-outs, 3 knobs, BC, 5 tubes, AC, $170.00-200.00.

50-520, table, 1950, brown plastic, lower front slide rule dial, upper horizontal louvers, feet, 2 knobs, BC, 5 tubes, AC/DC, $35.00-40.00.

46-1209, console-R/P, 1946, wood, 2 upper front slide rule dials, lower tilt-out phono, pushbuttons, 4 knobs, BC, SW, 8 tubes, AC........**$110.00-130.00**

46-1213, console-R/P, 1946, wood, inner right slide rule dial, 10 pushbuttons, doors, left fold-out phono, 4 knobs, BC, SW, FM, 11 tubes, AC **$85.00-95.00**

46-1217, console-R/P, 1946, wood, inner left dial, fold-up lid, right pullout phono, lower grille with cut-outs, AC **$85.00-105.00**

47-205, table, 1947, leatherette & plastic, right front dial, left horizontal louvers, 2 knobs, BC, 5 tubes, AC/DC **$35.00-40.00**

47-1227, console-R/P, 1947, wood, upper front slanted slide rule dial, lower tilt-out phono, 4 knobs, BC, FM, 9 tubes, AC ..**$110.00-130.00**

47-1230, console-R/P, 1947, wood, upper front slide rule dial, lower tilt-out phono, pushbuttons, 4 knobs, BC, SW, FM, 9 tubes, AC..**$110.00-130.00**

48-141, table, 1948, walnut plastic, upper front slide rule dial, lower horizontal louvers, 2 knobs, BC, 4 tubes, battery **$40.00-45.00**

48-145, table, 1948, ivory plastic, upper front slide rule dial, lower horizontal louvers, 2 knobs, BC, 4 tubes, battery **$40.00-45.00**

48-150, table, 1948, wood, upper front slanted slide rule dial, lower perforated metal grille, 2 knobs, BC, 5 tubes, battery **$40.00-45.00**

48-200-I, table, 1948, ivory plastic, right front dial, right & left horizontal wrap-around louvers, 2 knobs, BC, 5 tubes, AC/DC......**$40.00-50.00**

48-214, table, 1948, wood, right front dial, left lattice grille, 2 knobs, BC, 5 tubes, AC/DC **$40.00-45.00**

48-230, table, 1948, plastic, modernistic dial & grille, rounded top, slanted sides, 2 knobs, BC, 5 tubes, AC/DC **$85.00-105.00**

48-250, table, 1948, walnut plastic, upper front slide rule dial, lower horizontal wrap-around louvers, 2 knobs, BC, 5 tubes, AC/DC **$40.00-50.00**

48-250-I, table, 1948, ivory plastic, upper front slide rule dial, lower horizontal wrap-around louvers, 2 thumbwheel knobs, BC, 5 tubes, AC/DC **$40.00-50.00**

48-300, portable, 1948, leatherette, upper front slide rule dial, lower horizontal louvers, handle, 2 knobs, BC, 5 tubes, AC/DC/battery ..**$35.00-40.00**

48-360, portable, 1948, alligator, inner slide rule dial, lower horizontal wood louvers, tambour lid, handle, 2 thumbwheel knobs, BC, 6 tubes, AC/DC/battery **$45.00-50.00**

48-460-I, table, 1948, ivory plastic, step-down top, curved dial on top of case, lower horizontal wrap-around louvers, 2 top knobs, BC, 6 tubes, AC/DC..**$45.00-55.00**

51-538, table-C, 1951, plastic, top left thumbwheel dial, left front alarm clock panel overlaps horizontal wrap-around grille bars, 5 knobs, BC, 5 tubes, AC, $45.00-50.00.

51-631, portable, 1951, plastic, upper front slide rule dial, wrap-over vertical bars, metal handle, 2 side knobs, BC, 4 tubes, AC/DC/battery, $40.00-45.00.

52-544-I, table-C, 1952, plastic, raised left top with thumbwheel dial, lower left front clock panel overlaps horizontal wrap-around grille bars, 5 knobs, BC, 5 tubes, AC, $45.00-50.00.

48-464, table, 1948, brown plastic, upper front slanted slide rule dial, lower horizontal louvers, 4 knobs, BC, SW, 6 tubes, AC/DC **$50.00-55.00**

48-472, table, 1948, walnut plastic, upper front slanted slide rule dial, lower horizontal louvers, 4 knobs, BC, FM, 8 tubes, AC/DC......**$40.00-50.00**

48-472-I, table, 1948, ivory plastic, upper front slanted slide rule dial, lower horizontal louvers, 4 knobs, BC, FM, 8 tubes, AC/DC......**$40.00-50.00**

48-475, table, 1948, wood, raised top, upper front slanted slide rule dial, lower cloth grille area, 6 pushbuttons, 4 knobs, BC, FM, 8 tubes, AC **$65.00-75.00**

48-485, console, 1948, mahogany, upper front slanted slide rule dial, front tilt-out phono, 4 knobs, BC, 6 tubes, AC **$65.00-75.00**

48-703, table, 1948, plastic, modernistic dial & grille, rounded top, slanted sides, 2 knobs, BC, AC/DC **$85.00-105.00**

48-1201, table-R/P, 1948, wood, curved front, top slide rule dial, center cloth grille, lower slide-in record slot, 2 knobs, BC, 5 tubes, AC **$75.00-85.00**

48-1253, table-R/P, 1948, walnut, front slide rule dial, lower horizontal louvers, 3/4 lift top, inner phono, 2 knobs, BC, 5 tubes, AC..**$40.00-45.00**

48-1256, table-R/P, 1948, wood, right front vertical slide rule dial, horizontal grille bars, lift top, inner phono, 3 knobs, BC, 6 tubes, AC..**$35.00-40.00**

48-1260, console-R/P, 1948, wood, inner right slide rule dial, inner left slide-in record slot, large lower grille, 2 knobs, BC, 5 tubes, AC..**$50.00-65.00**

48-1263, console-R/P, 1948, walnut, upper front slanted slide rule dial, lower tilt-out phono, 4 knobs, BC, SW, 8 tubes, AC **$85.00-105.00**

48-1264, console-R/P, 1948, walnut, upper front slide rule dial, center pull-out phono, lower criss-cross grille, 4 knobs, BC, FM, 9 tubes, AC **$75.00-85.00**

48-1266, console-R/P, 1948, wood, inner dial, 6 pushbuttons, double doors, center pull-out phono, lower criss-cross grille, 4 knobs, BC, SW, FM, 9 tubes, AC **$75.00-85.00**

48-1270, console-R/P, 1948, wood, inner right slide rule dial, pushbuttons, door, left pull-out phono, 4 knobs, BC, SW, FM, 13 tubes, AC **$75.00-85.00**

48-1274 "Hepplewhite," console-R/P, 1948, mahogany, inner dial, fold-up lid, front tilt-out front phono, 4 knobs, BC, SW, FM, 16 tubes, AC **$75.00-85.00**

48-1276 "Sheraton," console-R/P, 1948, wood, inner slide rule dial, pushbuttons, fold-up lid, front tilt-out phono, 4 knobs, BC, SW, FM, 16 tubes, AC **$75.00-85.00**

48-1284, console-R/P, 1948, wood, inner right slide rule dial, door, left pull-out phono, lower grille & storage, 4 knobs, BC, SW, 7 tubes, AC **$65.00-75.00**

48-1286, console-R/P, 1948, wood, inner slide rule dial, lift-up lid, front tilt-out phono, storage, 4 knobs, BC, FM, 11 tubes, AC..**$75.00-85.00**

48-1290, console-R/P, 1948, wood, inner right vertical dial, pushbuttons, door, left pull-out phono, 4 knobs, BC, SW, FM, 13 tubes, AC **$85.00-95.00**

48-1401, table-R/P, 1948, wood & plastic, modern, top right slide rule dial, left arched grille, front slide-in phono, AC **$120.00-150.00**

49-100, table, 1949, brown plastic, upper front slide rule dial, lower horizontal louvers, 2 knobs, BC, 4 tubes, battery **$40.00-45.00**

49-101, table, 1949, plastic, lower front slide rule dial, upper vertical wrap-over grille bars, 2 knobs, BC, 4 tubes, battery......**$40.00-45.00**

49-472, table, 1949, plastic, upper front slanted slide rule dial, lower horizontal louvers, 4 knobs, BC, FM **$50.00-55.00**

49-500-I, table, 1949, ivory plastic, right front dial, right & left horizontal wrap-around louvers, 2 knobs, BC, 5 tubes, AC/DC......**$40.00-50.00**

49-501, table, 1949, brown plastic, modern, right front round dial, left arched perforated grille, 2 knobs, BC, 5 tubes, AC/DC **$300.00-320.00**

49-501-I, table, 1949, ivory plastic, modern, right front round dial, left arched perforated grille, 2 knobs, BC, 5 tubes, AC/DC **$300.00-320.00**

49-504, table, 1949, walnut plastic, upper front slide rule dial, lower horizontal louvers, 2 knobs, BC, 5 tubes, AC/DC **$40.00-50.00**

52-643, portable, 1952, plastic, lower front slide rule dial, upper lattice grille, flex handle, 2 knobs, BC, 5 tubes, AC/DC/battery, $35.00-40.00.

52-540, table, 1952, plastic, lower front slide rule dial, upper horizontal grille bars, 2 knobs, BC, 5 tubes, AC/DC, $35.00-40.00.

53-563, table, 1953, plastic, modern, right front slide rule dial, raised left checkered grille, 2 knobs, BC, SW, 5 tubes, AC/DC, $55.00-65.00.

49-504-I, table, 1949, ivory plastic, upper front slide rule dial, lower horizontal louvers, 2 knobs, BC, 5 tubes, AC/DC **$40.00-50.00**

49-505, table, 1949, plastic, center slide rule dial, curved-in checkerboard front, 2 knobs, BC, 5 tubes, AC/DC **$55.00-65.00**

49-506, table, 1949, wood, right dial/center decorative "wedge" over plastic checkered grille, 2 knobs, BC, 5 tubes, AC/DC ..**$50.00-65.00**

49-602, portable, 1949, plastic, lower front slide rule dial, upper horizontal louvers, handle, 2 knobs, BC, 4 tubes, AC/DC/battery ..**$40.00-45.00**

49-603, table/easel style, 1949, leather & plastic, folds open, tiny window dial, horizontal grille bars, 2 thumbwheel knobs, BC, 5 tubes, AC/DC **$55.00-65.00**

49-605, portable, 1949, plastic, upper front slide rule dial, large lower grille area, handle, 2 thumbwheel knobs, BC, 6 tubes, AC/DC/battery **$50.00-65.00**

49-607, portable, 1949, alligator & wood, upper front slide rule dial, lower horizontal wooden grille bars, handle, 2 knobs, BC, 6 tubes, AC/DC/battery **$55.00-65.00**

49-900-E, table, 1949, ebony plastic, step-down top, curved dial on top of case, lower horizontal wrap-around louvers, 2 knobs, BC, 6 tubes, AC/DC **$50.00-65.00**

49-900-I, table, 1949, ivory plastic, step-down top, curved dial on top of case, lower horizontal wrap-around louvers, 2 knobs, BC, 6 tubes, AC/DC **$50.00-65.00**

49-901, table, 1949, plastic, modern, large right station selector, left raised grille with circular cut-outs, BC, 5 tubes, AC/DC **$95.00-105.00**

49-902, table, 1949, plastic, right front dial, right & left horizontal grille bars, 2 knobs, BC, 6 tubes, AC/DC **$40.00-50.00**

49-904, table, 1949, plastic, large right slide rule dial on see-through plastic, left grille, 4 knobs, BC, SW, 6 tubes, AC/DC **$40.00-50.00**

49-905, table, 1949, plastic, angled front design, right dial, left horizontal louvers, 3 knobs, BC, FM, 6 tubes, AC/DC **$40.00-45.00**

49-906, table, 1949, plastic, upper front slide rule dial, lower horizontal grille bars, 4 knobs, BC, FM, 8 tubes, AC/DC **$40.00-45.00**

49-1100, console, 1949, mahogany, upper center slide rule dial, large lower grille with 3 vertical bars, 4 knobs, BC, 6 tubes, AC **$65.00-75.00**

49-1101, console, 1949, mahogany, upper front dial, large lower cloth grille with 3 vertical bars, 4 knobs, BC, FM, 9 tubes, AC **$65.00-75.00**

53-702, table-C, 1953, plastic, step-down top, right front round dial overlaps horizontal grille bars, left square clock, 5 knobs, BC, SW, 5 tubes, AC, $30.00-35.00.

60MB, tombstone, 1934, wood, center front round window dial, upper cloth grille with Deco cutouts, 4 knobs, BC, SW, 5 tubes, AC, $110.00-130.00.

49-1401, table-R/P, 1949, wood & plastic, modern, top right slide rule dial, left arched grille, front slide-in phono, 3 knobs, BC, 5 tubes, AC **$120.00-150.00**

49-1405, table-R/P, 1949, wood, right front square dial, left horizontal louvers, lift top, inner phono, 3 knobs, BC, 5 tubes, AC **$40.00-45.00**

49-1600, console-R/P, 1949, wood, upper front slide rule dial, center fold-out phono, lower criss-cross grille, 4 knobs, BC, 5 tubes, AC..**$65.00-75.00**

49-1602, console-R/P, 1949, wood, upper front slanted slide rule dial, front tilt-out phono, 4 knobs, BC, 6 tubes, AC....**$65.00-75.00**

49-1603, console-R/P, 1949, wood, upper front slanted slide rule dial, front tilt-out phono, 4 knobs, BC, 6 tubes, AC **$65.00-75.00**

49-1604, console-R/P, 1949, wood, upper front slide rule dial, center pull-out phono, lower grille area, record storage, 4 knobs, BC, 6 tubes, AC/DC..**$65.00-75.00**

49-1605, console-R/P, 1949, wood, upper front slanted slide rule dial, front tilt-out phono, 4 knobs, BC, 6 tubes, AC **$65.00-75.00**

49-1606, console-R/P, 1949, wood, upper front slide rule dial, center fold-out phono, lower grille, storage, 4 knobs, BC, FM, 7 tubes, AC **$75.00-85.00**

49-1613, console-R/P, 1949, wood, inner right slide rule dial, lower storage, door, left fold-out phono, 4 knobs, BC, FM, 11 tubes, AC..**$65.00-75.00**

49-1615, console-R/P, 1949, wood, inner left slide rule dial, pushbuttons, door, right fold-out phono, lower grille, 5 knobs, BC, FM, 11 tubes, AC..**$75.00-85.00**

49B, cathedral, 1934, two-tone wood, center front window dial, 3 section cloth grille, DC, 4 knobs, BC, SW, 7 tubes, DC.........**$200.00-230.00**

49H, console, 1934, wood, lowboy, upper front window dial, lower cloth grille with cut-outs, DC, 4 knobs, BC, SW, 7 tubes, DC..**$120.00-150.00**

66B, tombstone, 1935, wood, center front round window dial, upper cloth grille with Deco cutouts, 4 knobs, BC, SW, 5 tubes, AC, $120.00-140.00.

53-706, lamp/radio/clock, 1953, wood, tall rectangular case, lower front dial, center grille, upper alarm clock, upper lamp, 5 knobs, BC, SW, 5 tubes, AC **$85.00-105.00**

53-707, table-C, 1953, wood, tall rectangular case, lower front grille, upper alarm clock, 5 knobs, BC, SW, 5 tubes, AC..**$65.00-75.00**

53-804, table-C, 1953, plastic, right front round dial, left alarm clock, center checkered grille, 2 band, 5 knobs, BC, SW, 6 tubes, AC ..**$30.00-35.00**

53-950, table, 1953, plastic, right front dial, left lattice grille with stylized "P," brown/ivory, 2 knobs, BC, SW, 5 tubes, AC/DC **$40.00-45.00**

53-952, table, 1953, plastic, lower slanted slide rule dial, upper slanted lattice grille, 2 knobs, BC, SW, 5 tubes, AC/DC **$40.00-45.00**

53-954, table, 1953, wood, lower center slide rule dial, upper recessed lattice grille, mahogany/blond, 2 knobs, BC, SW, 5 tubes, AC/DC **$40.00-45.00**

53-956, table, 1953, plastic, right front square dial, left lattice grille, 3 knobs, BC, FM, 6 tubes, AC/DC **$35.00-40.00**

91 or 91B, cathedral, 1932, two-tone wood, center front window dial, upper cloth grille with cut-outs, some versions with BC only, 4 knobs, BC, SW, 9 tubes, $300.00-350.00.

53-958, table, 1953, wood, right & left front vertical dials, center cloth grille, 3 knobs, BC, FM, AC/DC **$35.00-40.00**

53-960, table, 1953, wood, right front recessed 9-band vertical slide rule dial, left grille area, 5 knobs, BC, SW, 8 tubes, AC **$50.00-65.00**

53-1350, table-R/P, 1953, plastic, lower front slide rule dial, upper grille, lift top, inner phono, 2 knobs, BC, SW, 5 tubes, AC **$30.00-35.00**

53-1750, end table-R/P, 1953, wood, drop-leaf, top dial, lower pull-out phono drawer, 2 front knobs, BC, SW, 5 tubes, AC **$85.00-105.00**

53-1754, console-R/P, 1953, wood, inner front slide rule dial, lower phono, storage, double doors, 4 knobs, BC, SW, 6 tubes, AC **$50.00-65.00**

54C, table, 1933, walnut with inlay, right front dial, center cloth grille with cut-outs, top louvers, 2 knobs, BC, SW, 5 tubes, AC/DC..**$85.00-95.00**

54S, table, 1934, two-tone wood, "owl-eye" front design, right front dial, center cloth grille with cut-outs, top louvers, 2 knobs, BC, SW, 5 tubes, AC/DC **$85.00-95.00**

57C, table, 1933, wood, right front dial, center cloth grille with cut-outs, top louvers, 2 knobs, BC, 4 tubes, AC **$85.00-95.00**

59C, table, 1935, walnut with inlay, right front dial, center cloth grille with cut-outs, top louvers, 2 knobs, BC, 4 tubes, AC...........**$85.00-95.00**

59S, table, 1935, two-tone wood, "owl-eye" front design, right front dial, center cloth grille with cut-outs, top louvers, 2 knobs, BC, 4 tubes, AC...**$85.00-95.00**

60B, cathedral/various styles, 1934, wood, center front window dial, upper cloth grille with cut-outs, 4 knobs, BC, SW, 5 tubes, AC...**$140.00-160.00**

60F, console, C1935, wood, upper front window dial with escutcheon, lower cloth grille with cut-outs, 4 knobs, BC, SW, 5 tubes, AC **$110.00-130.00**

60L, console, 1933, wood, lowboy, upper front window dial, lower cloth grille with cut-outs, 4 knobs, BC, SW, 5 tubes, AC **$110.00-130.00**

65, console, 1929, wood, lowboy, upper front window dial, lower cloth grille with "oyster-shell" cut-out, 4 knobs, BC, 6 tubes, AC ..**$110.00-130.00**

65, console, 1929, wood, highboy, inner front window dial w/escutcheon, tapestry grille, folding doors, side fleur-de-lis cut-outs, stretcher base, 4 knobs, BC, 6 tubes, AC.................................**$120.00-140.00**

96, console, 1930, wood, low-boy, upper front window dial with escutcheon, lower cloth grille with vertical bars, 4 knobs, BC, 9 tubes, AC, $120.00-150.00.

65, console, 1929, wood, "deluxe" highboy, inner front window dial w/escutcheon, tapestry grille, sliding doors, side fleur-de-lis cut-outs, stretcher base, 4 knobs, BC, 6 tubes, AC **$140.00-160.00**

65, table, 1929, metal, low rectangular case, center front window dial with escutcheon, lift-off lid, 4 knobs, BC, 6 tubes, AC........**$120.00-150.00**

66B, cathedral, 1935, wood, center front window dial, upper cloth grille with cut-outs, 4 knobs, BC, SW, 5 tubes, AC **$200.00-230.00**

66L, console, 1935, wood, lowboy, upper front window dial, lower cloth grille with cut-outs, 4 knobs, BC, SW, 5 tubes, AC....**$120.00-140.00**

66S, tombstone, 1935, two-tone wood, center front window dial, shield-shaped cloth grille with center vertical bars, 4 knobs, BC, SW, 5 tubes, AC **$95.00-115.00**

70 or 370 "Lazyboy," chairside, 1931, cabinet designed by Norman Bel Geddes, top recessed controls, front grille area, 2 knobs, BC, 7 tubes, AC **$160.00-190.00**

70 or 270, console-R/P, 1931, walnut, lowboy, upper front window dial, lower cloth grille with cut-outs, lift top, inner phono, 4 knobs, BC, 7 tubes, AC **$150.00-180.00**

70 or 570, grandfather clock, 1932, wood, Colonial-style, front window dial, lower cloth grille with cut-outs, upper clock face, 4 knobs, BC, 7 tubes, AC **$430.00-500.00**

118B, tombstone, 1935, two-tone wood, shouldered, center front dial, upper cloth grille with cut-outs, shadow tuning meter, 4 knobs, BC, SW, 8 tubes, AC, $120.00-140.00.

511, table, 1928, two-tone Spanish brown metal, rectangular case, center front window dial, 3 knobs, BC, 7 tubes, AC, $85.00-105.00.

70B, cathedral, 1931, wood, center front window dial, upper cloth grille with cut-outs, fluted columns, 4 knobs, BC, 7 tubes, AC **$350.00-380.00**

70L, console, 1931, wood, lowboy, upper front window dial, lower cloth grille with shield-shaped cut-out, 4 knobs, BC, 7 tubes, AC ..**$120.00-140.00**

71 "Lazyboy," chairside, 1932, cabinet designed by Norman Bel Geddes, top controls, front grille area, 2 knobs, BC, 7 tubes, AC **$150.00-180.00**

71H, console, 1932, wood, lowboy, upper front window dial, lower cloth grille with cut-outs, 6 legs, 4 knobs, BC, 7 tubes, AC ..**$120.00-140.00**

71L, console, 1932, wood, lowboy, upper front window dial, lower cloth grille with shield-shaped cut-out, 4 knobs, BC, 7 tubes, AC ..**$120.00-140.00**

76, console, 1929, wood, lowboy, upper front window dial, lower cloth grille with "oyster-shell" cut-out, 4 knobs, BC, 7 tubes, AC ..**$110.00-130.00**

76, console, 1929, wood, highboy, inner front window dial w/escutcheon, tapestry grille, folding doors, side fleur-de-lis cut-outs, stretcher base, 4 knobs, BC, 7 tubes, AC..................................**$130.00-150.00**

76, console, 1929, wood, "deluxe" highboy, inner front window dial w/escutcheon, tapestry grille, sliding doors, side fleur-de-lis cut-outs, stretcher base, 4 knobs, BC, 7 tubes, AC **$140.00-160.00**

77, console, 1930, wood, lowboy, upper front window dial, lower cloth grille with vertical bars, 4 knobs, BC, 7 tubes, AC **$120.00-140.00**

81B "Junior," cathedral, 1933, two-tone wood, center front window dial, upper cloth grille with cut-outs, 3 knobs, BC, SW, 4 tubes, AC **$140.00-170.00**

86, console, 1929, wood, highboy, inner window dial with escutcheon, upper round cloth grille with cut-outs, small right & left doors, large double front doors, drawer, 3 knobs, BC, 8 tubes, AC ..**$120.00-150.00**

86, console, 1929, wood, upper front window dial with escutcheon, lower round cloth grille with cut-outs, lift top, 3 knobs, BC, 8 tubes, AC **$140.00-160.00**

87, console, 1929, wood, lowboy, upper front window dial, lower scalloped grille with cut-outs, 4 knobs, BC, 8 tubes, AC..**$140.00-160.00**

87, console, 1929, wood, highboy, inner front window dial w/escutcheon, tapestry grille, folding doors, side fleur-de-lis cut-outs, stretcher base, 4 knobs, BC, 8 tubes, AC..................................**$130.00-150.00**

87, console, 1929, wood, "deluxe" highboy, inner front window dial w/escutcheon, tapestry grille, sliding doors, side fleur-de-lis cut-outs, stretcher base, 4 knobs, BC, 8 tubes, AC **$140.00-160.00**

551, table-N, 1932, wood, Colonial mantle clock-style, upper clock face, top finials, 3 knobs, BC, 5 tubes, AC, $320.00-345.00.

89, Queen Anne console, C1933, wood, looks like small Queen Anne chest of drawers, inner window dial and, fold down front door, 4 knobs, BC, SW, 6 tubes, AC **$270.00-320.00**

89B, cathedral/various styles, 1932-1936, two-tone wood, center front dial, upper cloth grille with cut-outs, some version with BC only, 3 or 4 knobs, BC, SW, 6 tubes, AC..................................**$200.00-230.00**

89F, console, 1935, wood, upper front window dial, lower cloth grille with cut-outs, 4 knobs, BC, SW, 6 tubes, AC **$110.00-130.00**

90H, console, 1931, wood, lowboy, inner front window dial, cloth grille with cut-outs, double front doors, 4 knobs, BC, 9 tubes, AC ..**$150.00-180.00**

90L, console, 1931, walnut, lowboy, upper front window dial, cloth grille with cut-outs, 4 legs, 4 knobs, BC, 9 tubes, AC **$150.00-180.00**

90X, console, 1932, wood, upper front window dial, lower inclined grille area, 4 knobs, BC, 9 tubes, AC **$160.00-190.00**

91L, console, 1932, wood, lowboy, upper front window dial, lower cloth grille with cut-outs, 4 knobs, BC, SW, 9 tubes, AC **$160.00-180.00**

620, tombstone, 1936, wood, shouldered, center front oval dial, upper cloth grille with cut-outs, 4 knobs, BC, SW, 6 tubes, AC, $110.00-130.00.

91X, console, 1933, wood, upper front window dial with escutcheon, lower inclined grille area, 4 knobs, BC, SW, 9 tubes, AC **$160.00-185.00**

95, console, 1929, wood, lowboy, upper front window dial, lower cloth grille with "oyster-shell" cut-out, 4 knobs, BC, 9 tubes, AC ..**$140.00-160.00**

95, console, 1929, wood, highboy, inner front window dial w/escutcheon, tapestry grille, folding doors, side fleur-de-lis cut-outs, stretcher base, 4 knobs, BC, 9 tubes, AC..................................**$150.00-170.00**

95, console, 1929, wood, "deluxe" highboy, inner front window dial w/escutcheon, tapestry grille, sliding doors, side fleur-de-lis cut-outs, stretcher base, 4 knobs, BC, 9 tubes, AC **$185.00-210.00**

96H, console, 1930, wood, upper front window dial, lower cloth grille with cut-outs, stretcher base, 4 knobs, BC, 9 tubes, AC ..**$120.00-150.00**

112, console, 1931, wood, lowboy, designed by Norman Bel Geddes, recessed front panel with upper window dial & lower cloth grille with cut-outs, 4 knobs, BC, 11 tubes, AC......................**$180.00-200.00**

112X, console, 1933, wood, upper front window dial with escutcheon, lower inclined grille area, 4 knobs, BC, 11 tubes, AC..**$180.00-200.00**

116B, tombstone/two styles, 1936, wood, center front oval dial, upper cloth grille with cut-outs, shadow tuning meter, one style with shouldered cabinet, 4 knobs, BC, SW, LW, 11 tubes, AC ..**$110.00-130.00**

116PX, console-R/P, 1936, wood, front oval dial, lower cloth grille with cut-outs, right & left cut-outs, lift top, inner phono, 4 knobs, BC, LW, 11 tubes, AC..**$160.00-190.00**

116X, console, 1936, walnut, upper front oval dial, lower cloth grille with vertical bars, right & left cut-outs, 4 knobs, BC, SW, LW, 11 tubes, AC **$160.00-190.00**

118B, cathedral, 1935, two-tone wood, center front window dial, upper 3-section cloth grille, shadow tuning meter, 4 knobs, BC, SW, 8 tubes, AC **$300.00-350.00**

118H, console, 1935, wood, upper front window dial, lower cloth grille with cut-outs, shadow tuning meter, 4 knobs, BC, SW, 8 tubes, AC **$140.00-160.00**

118MX, console, 1935, wood, upper front window dial, lower cloth grille with 2 vertical bars, shadow tuning meter, 4 knobs, BC, SW, 8 tubes, AC **$120.00-150.00**

118RX, chairside/remote speaker, 1935, wood, chairside unit with top dial, separate speaker with Deco grille cut-outs, shadow tuning meter, 4 knobs, BC, SW, 8 tubes, AC **$200.00-230.00**

118X, console, 1935, wood, upper front window dial, lower cloth grille with 3 vertical bars, shadow tuning meter, 4 knobs, BC, SW, 8 tubes, AC **$120.00-150.00**

144B, cathedral, 1935, wood, center front window dial, 3-section cloth grille, shadow tuning meter, 4 knobs, BC, SW, 6 tubes, AC **$240.00-270.00**

144H, console, 1935, wood, upper front window dial, lower cloth grille with cut-outs, shadow tuning meter, 4 knobs, BC, SW, 6 tubes, AC **$120.00-140.00**

144X, console, 1935, wood, upper front window dial, lower cloth grille with 3 vertical bars, shadow tuning meter, 4 knobs, BC, SW, 6 tubes, AC **$120.00-140.00**

200X, console, 1934, wood, upper front window dial, lower cloth grille with center bars, right & left cut-outs, shadow tuning meter, 4 knobs, BC, 10 tubes, AC **$130.00-150.00**

201X, console, 1934, wood, upper front window dial, lower grille cloth with center bars, shadow tuning meter, 4 knobs, BC, SW, 10 tubes, AC **$130.00-150.00**

212, console-R/P, 1931, wood, lowboy, designed by Norman Bel Geddes, front window dial, lower cloth grille with cut-outs, lift top, inner phono, 4 knobs, BC, 11 tubes, AC **$150.00-180.00**

296, console-R/P, 1930, wood, lowboy, front window dial, lower cloth grille with vertical bars, lift top, inner phono, 4 knobs, BC, 9 tubes, AC **$140.00-160.00**

470, console, 1932, wood, lowboy, upper combination BC receiver and SW converter with separate window dials, lower grille cloth, 4 legs, 7 knobs, BC, SW, 9 tubes, AC **$160.00-180.00**

630B, tombstone, 1936, wood, shouldered, center front oval dial, upper cloth grille with cut-outs, shadow tuning meter, 4 knobs, BC, SW, 6 tubes, AC, $110.00-130.00.

490, console, 1932, wood, lowboy, upper combination BC receiver and SW converter with separate window dials, lower grille cloth, 4 legs, 7 knobs, BC, SW, 11 tubes, AC **$160.00-180.00**

500X, console-R/P, 1935, wood, front window dial, lower inclined grille with 2 vertical bars, lift top, inner phono, shadow tuning meter, 4 knobs, BC, SW, 11 tubes, AC **$160.00-190.00**

501X, console-R/P, 1935, wood, front window dial, lower inclined grille with 2 vertical bars, lift top, inner phono, shadow tuning meter, 4 knobs, BC, SW, 11 tubes, AC **$160.00-190.00**

505L, console-R/P, 1935, wood, lowboy, upper front window dial, lower cloth grille with cut-outs, lift top, inner phono, 6 legs, 4 knobs, BC, SW, 5 tubes, AC...**$110.00-130.00**

512, table, 1928, two-tone Mandarin red metal, rectangular case, center front window dial, hand-painted flowers, 3 knobs, BC, 7 tubes, AC **$120.00-140.00**

513, table, 1928, two-tone Labrador gray metal, rectangular case, center front window dial, hand-painted flowers, 3 knobs, BC, 7 tubes, AC **$120.00-140.00**

514, table, 1928, two-tone Nile green metal, rectangular case, center front window dial, hand-painted flowers, 3 knobs, BC, 7 tubes, AC..**$120.00-140.00**

515 "Impressionistic," table, 1928, gold metal, rectangular case, center front window dial, hand-painted green, red & blue leaves, 3 knobs, BC, 7 tubes, AC **$120.00-140.00**

650X, console, 1936, two-tone wood, upper front oval dial, lower cloth grille with 3 vertical bars, shadow tuning meter, 4 knobs, BC, SW, LW, 8 tubes, AC, $120.00-140.00.

531, console, 1928, wood, lowboy, upper fold down front, lower center grille, 4 legs, 3 knobs, BC, 7 tubes, AC **$120.00-140.00**

610, console, 1936, wood, upper front oval dial, lower cloth grille with cut-outs, fluting, 4 knobs, BC, SW, 5 tubes, AC **$110.00-130.00**

610, table, 1936, wood, right front oval dial, rounded left, left cloth grille with Deco cut-outs, 4 knobs, BC, SW, 5 tubes, AC **$85.00-115.00**

610, tombstone, 1936, wood, shouldered, center front oval dial, upper cloth grille with cut-outs, 4 knobs, BC, SW, 5 tubes, AC........**$120.00-140.00**

620F, console, 1936, wood, upper front oval dial, lower cloth grille with cut-outs, 4 knobs, BC, SW, 6 tubes, AC **$110.00-130.00**

623, tombstone, 1935, wood, shouldered, center front oval dial, upper grille with cut-outs, 4 knobs, BC, SW, 6 tubes, battery......**$65.00-75.00**

623F, console, 1935, wood, upper front oval dial, lower cloth grille with cut-outs, 4 knobs, BC, SW, 6 tubes, battery..................**$75.00-95.00**

624, console, 1935, wood, upper front oval dial, lower cloth grille with cut-outs, 4 knobs, BC, SW, 6 tubes, battery..................**$75.00-95.00**

624, tombstone, 1935, wood, shouldered, center front oval dial, upper grille with cut-outs, 4 knobs, BC, SW, 6 tubes, battery......**$65.00-75.00**

625J, console, 1936, wood, upper front oval dial, lower cloth grille with cut-outs, 4 knobs, BC, SW, 6 tubes, AC **$95.00-115.00**

630CSX, chairside, 1936, two-tone wood, top recessed controls and oval dial, front cloth grille with 3 vertical bars, shadow tuning meter, 4 top knobs, BC, SW, 6 tubes, AC **$150.00-180.00**

630X, console, 1936, wood, upper front oval dial, lower cloth grille with decorative vertical bars, shadow tuning meter, 4 knobs, BC, SW, 6 tubes, AC **$110.00-130.00**

655B, tombstone, 1936, wood, rounded shoulders, center front oval, upper cloth grille with cut-outs, shadow tuning meter, 4 knobs, BC, SW, 8 tubes, AC, $130.00-150.00.

A52CK-1, table-C, C1941, wood, lower right airplane dial, lower left grille with cut-outs, upper center clock, 2 knobs, BC, SW, 5 tubes, AC, $75.00-95.00.

635B, tombstone, 1936, wood, shouldered, center front oval dial, upper cloth grille with cut-outs, shadow tuning meter, 4 knobs, BC, SW, 6 tubes, AC **$110.00-130.00**

635PF, console-R/P, 1936, wood, upper front oval dial, lower cloth grille with cut-outs, lift top, inner phono, shadow tuning meter, 4 knobs, BC, SW, 6 tubes, AC **$110.00-130.00**

635X, console, 1936, wood, upper front oval dial, lower cloth grille with 3 vertical bars, shadow tuning meter, 4 knobs, BC, SW, 6 tubes, AC **$110.00-130.00**

640B, tombstone, 1936, wood, shouldered, center front oval dial, upper cloth grille with cut-outs, shadow tuning meter, 4 knobs, BC, SW, LW, 7 tubes, AC **$120.00-140.00**

640X, console, 1936, wood, upper front oval dial, lower cloth grille with cut-outs, shadow tuning meter, 4 knobs, BC, SW, LW, 7 tubes, AC **$120.00-150.00**

641B, tombstone, 1936, wood, shouldered, center front oval dial, upper cloth grille with cut-outs, shadow tuning meter, 4 knobs, BC, SW, 7 tubes, DC **$85.00-105.00**

641X, console, 1936, wood, upper front oval dial, lower cloth grille with 3 vertical bars, shadow tuning meter, 4 knobs, BC, SW, 7 tubes, DC **$85.00-105.00**

642B, tombstone, 1936, wood, shouldered, center front oval dial, upper cloth grille with cut-outs, 4 knobs, BC, SW, 7 tubes, DC(32V) **$85.00-105.00**

642F, console, 1936, wood, upper front oval dial, lower decorative grille with 5 cut-outs, 4 knobs, BC, SW, 7 tubes, DC(32V) ..**$85.00-105.00**

643B, tombstone, 1936, wood, shouldered, center front oval dial, upper cloth grille with cut-outs, 4 knobs, BC, SW, LW, 7 tubes, battery **$85.00-105.00**

A-361, console, 1941, wood, upper slanted slide rule dial, lower grille with 7 vertical bars, 2 knobs, BC, 6 tubes, AC, $95.00-115.00.

643X, console, 1936, wood, upper front oval dial, lower cloth grille with 3 vertical bars, 4 knobs, BC, SW, LW, 7 tubes, battery ..**$85.00-105.00**

645B, tombstone, 1936, wood, shouldered, center front oval dial, upper cloth grille with cut-outs, shadow tuning meter, 4 knobs, BC, SW, 7 tubes, AC **$120.00-140.00**

645X, console, 1936, wood, upper front oval dial, lower cloth grille with cut-outs, shadow tuning meter, 4 knobs, BC, SW, 7 tubes, AC...**$110.00-130.00**

650B, tombstone, 1936, wood, shouldered, center front oval dial, upper cloth grille with cut-outs, shadow tuning meter, 4 knobs, BC, SW, LW, 8 tubes, AC...**$130.00-150.00**

650H, console, 1936, wood, lowboy, inner top dial & controls, pop-up lid, front oval grille with lyre cut-out, shadow tuning meter, 4 knobs, BC, SW, LW, 8 tubes, AC **$120.00-140.00**

650MX, console, 1936, wood, inner top dial & controls, lift lid, front cloth grille with 4 vertical bars, shadow tuning meter, 4 knobs, BC, SW, LW, 8 tubes, AC...**$120.00-150.00**

650PX, console-R/P, 1936, two-tone wood, upper front oval dial, lower cloth grille with vertical bars, lift top, inner phono, shadow tuning meter, 4 knobs, BC, SW, LW, 8 tubes, AC **$120.00-150.00**

650RX, chairside/remote speaker, 1936, wood, chairside table with top dial, separate speaker unit with vertical grille bars, shadow tuning meter, 4 knobs, BC, SW, LW, 8 tubes, AC **$200.00-230.00**

655H, console, 1936, wood, lowboy, inner top dial & controls, pop-up lid, front oval grille with lyre cut-out, shadow tuning meter, 4 knobs, BC, SW, 8 tubes, AC...**$150.00-170.00**

655MX, console, 1936, wood, inner top dial & controls, lift lid, front cloth grille with 4 vertical bars, shadow tuning meter, 4 knobs, BC, SW, 8 tubes, AC **$120.00-150.00**

B-570, table, 1953, plastic, right front round dial over horizontal grille bars, arched base, sand/red, 2 knobs, BC, 5 tubes, AC/DC, $30.00-35.00.

655PX, console-R/P, 1936, wood, upper front oval dial, lower cloth grille with vertical bars, lift top, inner phono, shadow tuning meter, 4 knobs, BC, SW, 8 tubes, AC **$140.00-150.00**

655X, console, 1936, wood, upper front oval dial, lower cloth grille with 3 vertical bars, shadow tuning meter, 4 knobs, BC, SW, 8 tubes, AC **$120.00-150.00**

660X, console, 1936, two-tone wood, upper front oval dial, lower cloth grille with 3 vertical bars, shadow tuning meter, 4 knobs, BC, SW, LW, 10 tubes, AC..**$120.00-140.00**

665X, console, 1936, wood, upper front oval dial, lower cloth grille with 3 vertical bars, shadow tuning meter, 4 knobs, BC, SW, LW, 10 tubes, AC **$120.00-140.00**

680X, console, 1935, wood, inner top dial & controls, lift lid, front cloth grille with vertical bars, right & left front cut-outs, shadow tuning meter, 6 knobs, BC, SW, LW, 15 tubes, AC **$150.00-180.00**

777, table-C, 1962, blue & ivory plastic, lower right front dial overlaps horizontal bars, large upper alarm clock face, feet, BC, 5 tubes, AC **$25.00-30.00**

780, table-C, 1962, ivory or mocha plastic, right front lattice grille area, left alarm clock face with lower dial, feet, BC, 5 tubes, AC ..**$25.00-30.00**

782, table-C, 1962, beige/ivory or ivory/aqua plastic, wedge-shaped case, lower right front dial, upper alarm clock face, left horizontal grille bars, BC, 5 tubes, AC **$20.00-25.00**

783, table-C, 1962, white/pink or white/beige plastic, wedge-shaped case, lower front horizontal dial, upper right alarm clock face, upper left grille area, BC, 5 tubes, AC **$20.00-25.00**

784, table-C, 1962, white/aqua or beige/ivory plastic, wedge-shaped case, lower left slide rule dial, large upper lattice grille area, right alarm clock face, pushbuttons, BC, AC........................**$20.00-25.00**

785, table-C, 1962, ivory or black plastic, lower front slide rule dial, 2 upper modules right speaker grille/left alarm clock face, pushbuttons, BC, 5 tubes, AC **$30.00-35.00**

851, table, 1962, ivory plastic, lower right front dial panel overlaps large textured grille area, feet, 2 knobs, BC, 5 tubes, AC/DC ..**$15.00-20.00**

852, table, 1962, ivory/mocha or ivory/pink plastic, wedge-shaped case, lower right front dial overlaps large upper grille area with horizontal bars, BC, 5 tubes, AC/DC **$15.00-20.00**

853, table, 1962, aqua/white or beige/white plastic, wedge-shaped case, right front dial panel, left grille with horizontal bars, BC, 5 tubes, AC/DC **$15.00-20.00**

855, table, 1962, white/mocha or white/aqua plastic, wedge-shaped case, lower front slide rule dial, large upper 2-section grille area, handle, 2 knobs, BC, 5 tubes, AC/DC **$15.00-20.00**

856, table, 1962, mocha/ivory, charcoal/ivory or aqua/ivory plastic, wedge-shaped case, lower right front slide rule dial, large upper lattice grille area, 2 knobs, BC, 5 tubes, AC/DC **$25.00-30.00**

858, table, 1962, black or ivory plastic, lower front slide rule dial, two upper speaker modules, 2 knobs, BC, 5 tubes, AC/DC **$25.00-30.00**

910, table, 1962, ivory/black plastic, right front slide rule dial, left lattice grille area, 2 knobs, FM, 6 tubes, AC.............................**$15.00-20.00**

914, table, 1962, aqua/ivory or black/ivory plastic, wedge-shaped case, lower front round dial, upper grille area with vertical bars, 2 speakers, 2 knobs, BC, FM, AC **$20.00-25.00**

A-801, chairside, 1941, wood, Deco, top vertical slide rule dial, lower open storage, pushbuttons, 3 knobs, BC, 8 tubes, AC **$120.00-140.00**

B-569, table, 1954, plastic, right front half-round dial, left horizontal grille bars, 2 knobs, BC, 5 tubes, AC/DC..................................**$25.00-30.00**

B-572, table, 1953, plastic, large right front dial, left horizontal grille bars, feet, sand/green/maroon, 2 knobs, BC, 5 tubes, AC/DC..**$35.00-40.00**

B-574 "Multiwave," table, 1953, plastic, right front dial, left horizontal grille bars, feet, green/black/red, 2 knobs, BC, SW, 5 tubes, AC/DC **$35.00-40.00**

B-578 "Transitone-Multiwave," table, 1953, plastic, right front dial with center "P" logo, left horizontal grille bars, feet, green/mahogany, 2 knobs, BC, SW, 5 tubes, AC/DC, $35.00-40.00.

B-650, portable, 1953, plastic, center front grille with circular cut-outs, foldback handle, thumbwheel knobs, BC, 4 tubes, battery **$35.00-40.00**

B-651, portable, 1953, plastic, upper center slide rule dial, lower vertical grille, fold-down handle, sand/driftwood/green, 2 knobs (1 each side), BC, 4 tubes, AC/DC/battery....................................**$40.00-45.00**

B-652, portable, 1953, plastic, upper front center half-round dial, lower lattice with "PHILCO," top plastic handle, green/cherry/gray, 2 knobs (1 each side), BC, 4 tubes, AC/DC/battery **$40.00-45.00**

B-656, portable, 1953, plastic, lower center slide rule dial, upper lattice grille, leather fold down handle, beige/green/gray, 2 front knobs, 1 side knob, BC, SW, 5 tubes, AC/DC/battery **$40.00-45.00**

B-710, table-C, 1953, plastic, right front dial, left alarm clock, center lattice grille, 5 knobs, BC, 5 tubes, AC **$30.00-35.00**

B-711, table-C, 1953, plastic, right front dial, left alarm clock, center lattice grille, 5 knobs, BC, 5 tubes, AC **$30.00-35.00**

B-712, table-C, 1953, plastic, right front dial, left alarm clock, center lattice grille, 5 knobs, BC, SW, 5 tubes, AC **$30.00-35.00**

B-714X "Transitone," table-C, 1954, plastic, step-down top, right front round dial over horizontal bars, left alarm clock, 5 knobs, BC, SW, 5 tubes, AC **$30.00-35.00**

C580, table, 1955, plastic, right front round dial, lower metal "houndstooth" perforated grille, 2 knobs, BC, 4 tubes, AC/DC, $30.00-35.00.

B-804, table-C, 1953, plastic, right front dial, left alarm clock, center lattice grille, 5 knobs, BC, SW, 6 tubes, AC **$30.00-35.00**

B-956, table, 1953, plastic, off-center dial with stylized "P" logo overlaps front lattice grille, feet, 3 knobs, BC, FM, 6 tubes, AC/DC ..**$40.00-45.00**

B-962, table, 1953, plastic, right front dial, left lattice grille with stylized "P," 2 knobs, BC, SW, 6 tubes, AC/DC **$40.00-45.00**

B-964, table, 1953, plastic, lower slanted slide rule dial, upper slanted lattice grille, 2 knobs, BC, SW, 6 tubes, AC/DC **$40.00-45.00**

B-1349, table-R/P, 1954, plastic, lower front slide rule dial, upper lattice grille, lift top, inner phono, 2 knobs, BC, 5 tubes, AC **$40.00-45.00**

B-1350, table-R/P, 1953, plastic, lower front slide rule dial, upper grille, lift top, inner phono, 2 knobs, BC, SW, 5 tubes, AC **$30.00-35.00**

B-1352, table-R/P, 1953, wood, lower front slide rule dial, upper grille, lift top, inner phono, 2 knobs, BC, SW, 5 tubes, AC **$30.00-35.00**

B-1750, end table-R/P, 1953, wood, drop-leaf, top dial, lower pull-out phono drawer, 2 front knobs, BC, SW, 5 tubes, AC **$85.00-105.00**

B-1754, console-R/P, 1953, wood, double doors, inside upper slide rule dial, pull-out phono, lower grille below doors, 4 knobs, BC, SW, 6 tubes, AC **$55.00-65.00**

C-660, portable, 1955, plastic, center front grille panel with circular cut-outs, handle, 2 top thumbwheel knobs, BC, 4 tubes, battery **$30.00-35.00**

C-663, portable, 1955, plastic, top right dial, front vertical grille bars with center stylized "P" logo, handle, BC, 4 tubes, AC/DC/battery ..**$30.00-35.00**

C-666, portable/flashlight, 1955, plastic, lower front slide rule dial, upper lattice grille, top flashlight switch, handle, 3 knobs, BC, 5 tubes, AC/DC/battery **$50.00-65.00**

C-667, portable/flashlight, 1955, plastic, 2 lower front slide rule dials, upper lattice grille, top flashlight switch, handle, 3 knobs, BC, SW, 5 tubes, AC/DC/battery **$50.00-65.00**

C-720, table-C, 1955, plastic, lower right front dial, large upper clock face, side grille bars, 4 knobs, BC, 5 tubes, AC **$45.00-55.00**

D-597, table, 1956, plastic, right front dial, left horizontal bars with center stylized "P" logo, feet, BC, 5 tubes **$25.00-30.00**

D-665, portable, 1956, vanity-case style, inner controls, lift-up mirrored lid, front grille with center stylized "P" logo, 2 knobs, BC, 4 tubes, AC/DC/battery **$65.00-75.00**

D-1345, table-R/P-C, 1957, inner right dial, outer left front clock overlaps perforated grille, lift top, inner phono, handle, 3 knobs, BC, 5 tubes, AC **$40.00-50.00**

E-810, table, 1957, plastic, right front dial over checkered panel, left metal perforated grille, feet, 2 knobs, BC, 5 tubes, AC/DC, $25.00-30.00.

F-673, portable, 1957, leather case, right front half-round dial, metal perforated grille with wedge-shaped cut-outs, handle, BC, $30.00-35.00.

E-672, portable, 1957, leather, right front half-round dial, large grille area with checkered cut-outs, handle, 2 knobs, BC, 4 tubes, AC/DC/battery **$30.00-35.00**

E-675, portable, 1957, leather, right front half-round dial overlaps metal perforated grille, handle, 2 knobs, BC, 4 tubes, AC/DC/battery **$30.00-35.00**

E-812, table, 1957, plastic, large right round dial overlaps perforated panel & lower horizontal grille bars, 2 knobs, BC, 5 tubes, AC/DC..**$25.00-30.00**

E-818, table, 1958, wood & plastic, center front slide rule dial, twin speakers, lower right "P" logo, 2 knobs, BC, 6 tubes, AC/DC..**$25.00-30.00**

E-1370, table-R/P, 1957, right side dial, large front perforated grille with logo, lift top, inner phono, handle, 2 knobs, BC, 5 tubes, AC **$25.00-30.00**

F-238, table-C, plastic, lower right front dial, upper alarm clock, left horizontal grille bars, feet, BC, AC..**$20.00-25.00**

F-675, portable, 1957, leather case, right front dial overlaps large center perforated grille, handle, AC/DC/battery **$30.00-35.00**

F-809, table, 1958, plastic, center front round dial overlaps horizontal wrap-around grille bars, feet, 2 knobs, BC, 5 tubes, AC ..**$20.00-25.00**

F-974, table, 1959, plastic, large center front round dial overlaps lattice grille, 2 knobs, BC, FM, 7 tubes, AC/DC **$25.00-30.00**

G-681, portable, 1959, plastic, left front dial, right checkered grille, "Scantenna" handle, 2 knobs, BC, 4 tubes, AC/DC/battery........**$30.00-35.00**

G-822 "Deluxe," table, 1959, plastic, lower front off-center dial overlaps vertical grille bars, 2 knobs, BC, 5 tubes, AC/DC **$20.00-25.00**

H-691, portable, plastic, left front leatherette panel with lower dial, right checkered grille area, rotatable handle, BC, AC/DC/battery...........**$25.00-30.00**

F-752, table-C, 1958, plastic, lower right front dial, upper alarm clock, left lattice grille, feet, 2 knobs, BC, 5 tubes, AC, $25.00-30.00.

H-765, table-C, plastic, modern, step-down base contains lower vertical grille bars, top clock module with 4 pushbuttons, 2 knobs, BC, AC **$65.00-85.00**

H-836, table, plastic, modern, vertically divided front, lower right dial overlaps lattice grille area, twin speakers, feet, BC........**$20.00-25.00**

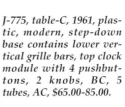

J-775, table-C, 1961, plastic, modern, step-down base contains lower vertical grille bars, top clock module with 4 pushbuttons, 2 knobs, BC, 5 tubes, AC, $65.00-85.00.

L-799, table-C, 1963, plastic, lower right slide rule dial & upper alarm clock face overlap textured front panel, 4 knobs, BC, FM, 6 tubes, AC **$25.00-30.00**

PT-2, table, 1941, brown plastic, upper front slide rule dial, lower horizontal wrap-around louvers, 2 knobs, BC, 5 tubes, AC/DC ..**$40.00-45.00**

PT-4, table, 1941, ivory plastic, upper front slide rule dial, lower horizontal wrap-around louvers, 2 knobs, BC, 5 tubes, AC/DC **$40.00-45.00**

PT-6, table, 1941, two-tone wood, upper front slide rule dial, lower cloth grille with 3 horizontal bars, 2 knobs, BC, 5 tubes, AC/DC **$45.00-50.00**

PT-25, table, 1940, brown plastic, right front square dial overlaps horizontal louvers, 2 knobs, BC, 5 tubes, AC/DC **$45.00-50.00**

PT-26, table, 1940, brown plastic, right front square dial overlaps horizontal louvers, 2 knobs, BC, 5 tubes, AC/DC **$45.00-50.00**

PT-27, table, 1940, ivory plastic, right front square dial overlaps horizontal louvers, 2 knobs, BC, 5 tubes, AC/DC **$45.00-50.00**

PT-28, table, 1940, ivory plastic, right front square dial overlaps horizontal louvers, 2 knobs, BC, 5 tubes, AC/DC **$45.00-50.00**

PT-29, table, 1940, brown plastic, right front square dial overlaps horizontal louvers, 2 knobs, BC, SW, 5 tubes, AC/DC **$45.00-50.00**

PT-30, table, 1941, brown plastic, right front dial, left wraparound grille with horizontal bars, rounded shoulders, 2 knobs, BC, 5 tubes, AC/DC **$45.00-50.00**

PT-31, table, 1940, ivory plastic, right front square dial overlaps horizontal louvers, 2 knobs, BC, SW, 5 tubes, AC/DC **$45.00-50.00**

PT-33, table, 1940, plastic, right front dial overlaps horizontal bars, handle, 2 knobs, BC, 5 tubes, AC/DC **$45.00-50.00**

PT-35, table, 1940, plastic, two color modern case, right side dial and knobs and left wraparound grille in cream, balance in ebony, 2 knobs, BC, SW, 5 tubes, AC/DC **$130.00-160.00**

PT-36, table, 1940, plastic, two color modern case, right side dial and knobs and left wraparound grille in cream, balance in ebony, 2 knobs, BC, 5 tubes, AC/DC **$130.00-160.00**

PT-37, table, 1940, brown plastic, right front square dial overlaps horizontal louvers, 2 knobs, BC, SW, 5 tubes, AC/DC **$45.00-50.00**

PT-38, table, 1940, walnut, right front dial, left cloth grille with Deco cut-outs, 2 knobs, BC, SW, 5 tubes, AC/DC **$50.00-55.00**

PT-39, table, 1940, walnut, right front square airplane dial, left grille with Deco cut-outs, 2 knobs, BC, 5 tubes, AC/DC **$50.00-55.00**

PT-41, table, 1940, walnut, right front square airplane dial, left cloth grille with Deco cut-outs, 2 knobs, BC, 5 tubes, AC/DC **$50.00-55.00**

PT-43, table, 1940, wood & plastic, right front dial, left horizontal wrap-around grille bars, handle, 2 knobs, BC, SW, 5 tubes, AC/DC **$65.00-75.00**

PT-44, table, 1941, wood, case has curved sides and top, right front dial, left vertical grille bars, 2 knobs, BC, 5 tubes, AC/DC **$75.00-85.00**

PT-45, table, 1940, brown plastic, right front dial and knobs, left grille with horizontal bars, upper center front 6 pushbuttons, 2 knobs, BC, 5 tubes, AC/DC **$50.00-55.00**

PT-47, table, 1940, ivory plastic, right front dial, left mitered louvers, 6 pushbuttons, 2 knobs, BC, 5 tubes, AC/DC **$55.00-65.00**

PT-48, table, 1940, ivory plastic, right front dial, left mitered louvers, 6 pushbuttons, 2 knobs, BC, 5 tubes, AC/DC **$55.00-65.00**

PT-49, table, 1941, wood, right front dial and knobs, left grille with three vertical bars, two front "feet," inlaid veneer, 2 knobs, BC, 5 tubes, AC/DC **$55.00-65.00**

PT-50, table, 1940, maple, right front dial, left cloth grille with 3 horizontal bars, 2 knobs, BC, 5 tubes, AC/DC................................**$50.00-55.00**

PT-51, table, 1940, ivory plastic, right front dial, left mitered louvers, 6 pushbuttons, 2 knobs, BC, 5 tubes, AC/DC **$55.00-65.00**

PT-55, table, 1940, plastic, two color case, right side dial and knobs and left wraparound grille in cream, balance in ebony, handle, 2 knobs, BC, SW, 5 tubes, AC/DC **$130.00-160.00**

PT-57, table, 1940, brown plastic, right front dial and knobs, left grille with horizontal bars, upper center front 6 pushbuttons, handle, 2 knobs, BC, 5 tubes, AC/DC..**$55.00-65.00**

PT-59, table, 1940, plastic, two color modern case, right side dial and knobs and left wraparound grille in amber, balance in brown, 2 knobs, BC, SW, 5 tubes, AC/DC **$130.00-160.00**

PT-61, table, 1940, two-tone wood, Deco, step-down top, right front dial, left horizontal louvers, curved base, 2 knobs, BC, 5 tubes, AC/DC **$130.00-160.00**

PT-63, portable, 1940, cloth covered, "airplane cloth," right front square dial, left cloth grille, handle, 2 knobs, BC, 5 tubes, battery **$30.00-35.00**

PT-65, table, 1940, wood, right front dial and knobs, left grille with horizontal louvers, upper center front 6 pushbuttons, handle, rounded shoulders, 2 knobs, BC, 5 tubes, AC/DC **$55.00-65.00**

PT-12, table, 1941, two-tone wood, upper front slanted slide rule dial, lower horizontal louvers, 2 knobs, BC, 5 tubes, AC/DC, $40.00-45.00.

PT-66, table, 1940, wood & plastic, right front dial, left grille, base, handle, 6 pushbuttons, 2 knobs, BC, 5 tubes, AC/DC **$55.00-65.00**

PT-67, table, 1940, plastic, two color modern case, right side dial and knobs and left wraparound grille in amber, balance in brown, 6 pushbuttons, handle, 2 knobs, BC, SW, 5 tubes, AC/DC....**$130.00-160.00**

PT-69, table-C, 1940, wood, trapezoid-shaped, lower right front dial, left cloth grille with horizontal bars, upper clock, 2 knobs, BC, 5 tubes, AC **$85.00-105.00**

PT-87, portable, 1941, leather & plastic, front plastic dial panel with right dial & left horizontal grille bars, handle, 2 knobs, BC, 5 tubes, AC/DC/battery **$30.00-35.00**

PT-88, portable, 1941, leather & plastic, inner plastic dial panel with right dial & left horizontal grille bars, fold-down front, handle, 2 knobs, BC, 5 tubes, AC/DC/battery **$30.00-35.00**

PT-89C, portable, 1941, plastic, "camera" look with shoulder strap, two tone, top knobs, front center grille with horizontal louvers, 2 knobs, BC, 4 tubes, battery.....................................**$85.00-105.00**

TH-1, table, 1939, wood, right front gold dial, left cloth grille with horizontal bars, 2 knobs, BC, 5 tubes, AC/DC **$45.00-55.00**

TH-3, table, 1939, plastic, right front dial, left wraparound grille with horizontal bars, rounded shoulders, 2 knobs, BC, 5 tubes, AC **$45.00-50.00**

PT-42, table, 1941, two-tone wood, right front square dial, left cloth grille, tapered sides, 2 knobs, BC, 5 tubes, AC/DC, $50.00-55.00.

TH-4, table, 1939, plastic, right front dial, left grille with horizontal bars, brown/ivory, 2 knobs, BC, 5 tubes, AC/DC **$45.00-50.00**

TH-5, table, 1939, plastic, right front dial, left grille with horizontal bars, upper front center 6 pushbuttons, brown/ivory, 2 knobs, BC, 5 tubes, AC/DC...**$45.00-50.00**

TH-14, table, 1940, wood, right front dial and knobs, left grille with horizontal cut-outs, handle, 2 knobs, BC, 5 tubes, AC/DC ..**$55.00-65.00**

TH-15, table, 1940, wood, right front dial, left grille with horizontal louvers, 6 upper front center pushbuttons, handle, rounded shoulders, 2 knobs, BC, 5 tubes, AC/DC **$55.00-65.00**

TH-16, table, 1940, plastic, right front dial and knobs, left grille with horizontal louvers, handle, 2 knobs, BC, 5 tubes, AC/DC....**$45.00-50.00**

TH-17, table, 1940, brown plastic, right front dial and knobs, left grille with horizontal bars, upper center front 6 pushbuttons, handle, 2 knobs, BC, 5 tubes, AC/DC...**$45.00-50.00**

TH-18, table, 1940, plastic, right front dial, left grille with horizontal bars, brown/ivory, 2 knobs, BC, SW, 5 tubes, AC/DC **$45.00-50.00**

TP-4, table, 1939, plastic, right front dial, left grille with horizontal bars, brown/ivory, 2 knobs, BC, SW, 5 tubes, AC/DC **$45.00-50.00**

TP-5, table, 1939, plastic, right front dial, left grille with horizontal bars, upper front center 6 pushbuttons, brown/ivory, 2 knobs, BC, SW, 5 tubes, AC/DC...**$45.00-50.00**

TP-10, table, 1939, plastic, two color modern case, right side dial and knobs and left wraparound grille in ivory, balance in brown, 2 knobs, BC, SW, 5 tubes, AC/DC **$130.00-160.00**

TP-11, table, 1939, plastic, two color modern case, right side dial and knobs and left wraparound grille in ivory, balance in brown, upper front center 6 pushbuttons, 2 knobs, BC, SW, 5 tubes, AC/DC...**$130.00-160.00**

TP-12, table, 1939, wood, right side dial and knobs, left grille, horizontal wraparound trim, rounded shoulders, 2 knobs, BC,SW, 5 tubes, AC/DC..**$50.00-55.00**

TP-20, table, 1940, plastic, two color modern case, right side dial and knobs and left wraparound grille in cream, balance in ebony, handle, 2 knobs, BC, SW, 5 tubes, AC/DC **$130.00-160.00**

PT-46, table, 1940, brown plastic, right front dial, left mitered louvers, 6 pushbuttons, 2 knobs, BC, 5 tubes, AC/DC, $55.00-65.00.

TP-21, table, 1940, plastic, two color modern case, right side dial and knobs and left wraparound grille in amber, balance in brown, 6 pushbuttons, handle, 2 knobs, BC, 5 tubes, AC/DC ..**$130.00-160.00**

PHILHARMONIC
Espey Mfg. Co., Inc.
528 East 72nd Street, New York, New York

100C, console-R/P, 1948, wood, inner right slide rule dial, phono, lift top, front criss-cross grille, 4 knobs, BC, 7 tubes, AC **$50.00-65.00**
100T "Minuet," table-R/P, 1948, wood, upper front slide rule dial, lower horizontal grille bars, lift top, inner phono, 4 knobs, BC, 5 tubes, AC **$30.00-35.00**
149-C, console-R/P, 1949, wood, inner right dial, left phono, lift top, front criss-cross grille, 4 knobs, BC, 7 tubes, AC **$55.00-65.00**
249-C, console-R/P, 1949, wood, inner right dial, lift top, left pull-out phono drawer, lower criss-cross grille, 4 knobs, BC, 7 tubes, AC **$65.00-75.00**
349-C, console-R/P, 1949, wood, inner right slide rule dial, door, left pull-out phono drawer, lower front criss-cross grille, 5 knobs, BC, FM, 7 tubes, AC **$65.00-75.00**
8712, console-R/P, 1947, wood, inner right slide rule dial, record storage, door, left lift top, inner phono, 2, 4 knobs, BC, SW, AC ..**$65.00-75.00**

PHILLIPS 66
Phillips Petroleum Co.
Bartlesville, Oklahoma

3-12A, portable, 1948, upper front slanted slide rule dial, lower horizontal louvers, handle, 2 knobs, battery....................................**$35.00-40.00**
3-20A, table-R/P, 1948, wood, upper front slanted slide rule dial, lower horizontal louvers, 3/4 lift top, inner phono, BC, AC **$30.00-35.00**
3-81A, console-R/P, 1948, wood, inner right slide rule dial, door, left pull-out phono drawer, 4 knobs, BC, SW, FM, 14 tubes, AC ..**$75.00-85.00**

PILOT
Pilot Electrical Manufacturing Company
323 Berry Street, Brooklyn, New York
Pilot Radio & Television Corporation
Pilot Radio and Tube Corporation
Lawrence, Massachusetts
Pilot Radio Corporation
37-06 36th Street, Long Island, New York

The Pilot Electrical Manufacturing Company began business in 1922 making batteries and parts and eventually expanded into the production of radios.

53, tombstone, 1934, wood, center front round dial, upper cloth grille with cut-outs, 4 knobs, BC, SW, 5 tubes, AC **$160.00-180.00**

L-8, cathedral, 1933, wood, center front half-round dial with escutcheon, upper cloth grille with cut-outs, 4 knobs, BC, SW, 8 tubes, AC, $300.00-320.00.

T-601 "Pilotuner," table/console top, 1947, wood, FM tuner, compact, center airplane dial, rounded top shoulders, 2 knobs, FM, AC, $45.00-65.00.

63, tombstone, 1934, wood, center front round dial, upper cloth grille with cut-outs, BC, SW, 6 tubes, AC **$150.00-160.00**
93, table, 1934, walnut with inlay, center front cloth grille with cut-outs, BC, SW, 5 tubes, AC/DC **$75.00-85.00**
114, tombstone, 1934, wood, center front round dial, upper cloth grille, BC, SW, 11 tubes, AC **$140.00-150.00**
133, table, 1940, wood, right front dial, tuning eye, left horizontal wrap-around louvers, 4 knobs, BC, SW, battery **$65.00-75.00**
193, table, 1936, wood, right front large round dial, left cloth grille with horizontal bars, 4 knobs, BC, SW, LW, 5 tubes, AC **$65.00-75.00**
293, tombstone, 1936, wood, lower front large round dial, upper cloth grille with vertical bars and center tuning eye, 4 knobs, BC, SW, 7 tubes, AC **$160.00-190.00**
298, tombstone, 1936, wood, lower front large round dial, upper cloth grille with vertical bars and center tuning eye, DC, 4 knobs, BC, SW, 7 tubes, DC **$110.00-130.00**
423, table, 1937, wood, rounded top, lower front large round dial, upper cloth grille with cut-outs, 4 knobs, BC, SW, 7 tubes, AC/DC **$85.00-105.00**
B-2, table, 1934, walnut, Deco, right front window dial, center grille cut-outs, 2 knobs, BC, 4 tubes, AC/DC **$85.00-105.00**
B-3, table, 1946, plastic, upper front slide rule dial, lower grille with horizontal bars, 3 knobs, BC, SW, 6 tubes, AC/DC.............**$40.00-50.00**
B1151 "Lone Ranger," table, 1939, plastic, right front dial with Lone Ranger & Silver, left horizontal louvers, handle, 2 knobs, BC, 5 tubes, AC/DC **$85.00-95.00**
C-63, console, 1934, wood, upper front round dial, lower cloth grille, feet, 4 knobs, BC, SW, 6 tubes, AC....................................**$120.00-150.00**
C-193, console, 1937, wood, upper front large round dial, lower cloth grille with vertical bars, tuning eye, 4 knobs, BC, SW, 6 tubes, AC...**$120.00-150.00**
C-293, console, 1936, wood, upper front large round dial, lower cloth grille with center vertical divider, tuning eye, 4 knobs, BC, SW, 7 tubes, AC **$120.00-150.00**
CG-184, console, 1936, wood, upper front large round dial, lower cloth grille with center vertical divider, tuning eye, 4 knobs, BC, SW, 7 tubes, AC/DC **$120.00-150.00**
CX-304, console, 1937, walnut, upper front large round dial, lower cloth grille with center vertical divider & horizontal bars, tuning eye, 4 knobs, BC, SW, 11 tubes, AC/DC **$150.00-160.00**
E-20, table, 1934, burl walnut, Deco, step-down top, right front window dial, center grille cut-outs, 3 knobs, BC, 6 tubes, AC/DC........**$85.00-115.00**
G-852, table, 1936, two-tone wood, right front large round dial, left cloth wrap-around grille, 3 knobs, BC, SW, 5 tubes, AC **$65.00-75.00**
PG-184, console-R/P, 1938, wood, upper front large round dial, lower cloth grille with center vertical divider, tuning eye, lift top, inner phono, 4 knobs, BC, SW, 8 tubes, AC/DC **$120.00-150.00**
PG-674, console-R/P, 1938, wood, upper front large round dial, lower cloth grille with center vertical divider, tuning eye, lift top, inner phono, 4 knobs, BC, SW, 7 tubes, AC **$120.00-150.00**
RG-184, console-R/P, 1937, wood, inner right round dial, left phono, lift top, lower front grille area, BC, SW, 7 tubes, AC/DC ..**$85.00-115.00**
RG-584, console-R/P, 1937, wood, inner right round dial, left phono, lift top, lower front grille area, BC, SW, AC **$85.00-115.00**
RG-674, console-R/P, 1937, wood, inner right round dial, left phono, lift top, lower front grille area, BC, SW, AC **$85.00-115.00**
T-3, table, 1946, wood, upper front slide rule dial, lower horizontal louvers, 3 knobs, BC, SW, 6 tubes, AC/DC **$50.00-65.00**

T-301, table, 1941, walnut, upper front slanted slide rule dial, lower cloth grille with 2 horizontal bars, BC, FM, 8 tubes, AC..........**$50.00-65.00**

T-341, table, 1941, walnut, right front slide rule dial, left vertical grille bars, pushbuttons, 8 bands, BC, SW, 10 tubes, AC/DC........**$85.00-105.00**

T-411-U, table, 1947, wood, center front vertical slide rule dial, right & left grille areas, 4 knobs, BC, SW, 6 tubes, AC **$40.00-45.00**

T-500U, table, 1947, plastic, large center front dial, right & left horizontal wrap-around grille bars, 3 knobs, BC, SW, 5 tubes, AC/DC **$85.00-95.00**

T-511, table, 1946, wood, center front vertical slide rule dial, right & left grille areas, 4 knobs, BC, SW, 6 tubes, AC/DC.............**$40.00-45.00**

T-521, table, 1947, wood, lower front slide rule dial, large upper grille area, 4 knobs, BC, FM, 8 tubes, AC/DC **$35.00-40.00**

T-531AB, table, 1947, wood, lower front slide rule dial, upper horizontal louvers, 4 knobs, BC, SW, FM, 8 tubes, AC/DC **$40.00-45.00**

T-741, table, 1948, wood, lower front slide rule dial, upper horizontal louvers, 4 knobs, BC, SW, 7 tubes, AC/DC **$40.00-45.00**

T-1252, table, 1939, wood, right front dial, left horizontal wrap-around louvers, handle, 3 knobs, BC, SW, 6 tubes, AC/DC **$45.00-55.00**

T-1451, portable, 1939, cloth covered, inner right square dial, left grille area, fold-in cover, 2 knobs, BC, 6 tubes, AC/DC/battery **$30.00-35.00**

TG-56, tombstone, 1937, wood, lower front large round dial, upper cloth grille with vertical bars, 4 knobs, BC, SW, battery **$75.00-85.00**

TG-162, table, 1937, wood, right front large round dial, left wrap-around cloth grille with horizontal bars, 3 knobs, BC, SW, 5 tubes, AC/DC **$50.00-65.00**

TG-184, table, 1937, wood, right front large round dial, left cloth grille with horizontal bars, tuning eye, 4 knobs, BC, SW, 8 tubes, AC/DC **$75.00-85.00**

TG-528 "Dragon IV," tombstone, 1937, wood, lower front large 5-band slide rule dial, upper cloth grille with vertical bars, tuning eye, 6 knobs, BC, SW, 12 tubes, AC **$180.00-190.00**

TG-584, table, 1937, wood, right front round dial, left wrap-over cloth grille with vertical bars, tuning eye, 4 knobs, BC, SW, 8 tubes, AC **$75.00-85.00**

TG-674, table, 1938, wood, right front round dial, left cloth grille with horizontal bars, tuning eye, 4 knobs, BC, SW, 5 tubes, AC ..**$75.00-85.00**

TG-752, table, 1937, wood, right front large round dial, left wrap-around cloth grille with horizontal bars, 3 knobs, BC, SW, 5 tubes, AC....**$50.00-65.00**

TG-5206, tombstone, 1937, wood, lower front large round dial, upper cloth grille with vertical bars, 4 knobs, BC, SW, battery ..**$75.00-85.00**

TP-32, table-R/P, 1941, walnut, right front slide rule dial, left horizontal wrap-around louvers, lift top, inner phono, 4 knobs, BC, SW, 6 tubes, AC **$35.00-40.00**

TP-423, table-R/P, 1937, wood, lower front round dial, upper cloth grille with center horizontal bar, lift top, inner phono, 4 knobs, BC, SW, 7 tubes, AC/DC...**$40.00-50.00**

Super Wasp - DC, table, 1928, kit, receiver, metal front panel with two window dials, plug-in coils, DC, 4 knobs, BC, SW, 4 tubes, battery, $430.00-470.00.

WX-201, tombstone, 1937, walnut plastic, lower front round dial, upper cloth grille with vertical bars, 3 knobs, BC, 5 tubes, AC/DC **$180.00-200.00**

X3, table, 1946, wood, upper front slanted slide rule dial, lower horizontal louvers, 3 knobs, BC, SW, 6 tubes, AC/DC..................**$40.00-45.00**

X-304 "Challenger," tombstone, 1938, wood, lower front round dial, upper cloth grille with cut-outs & center tuning eye, 4 knobs, BC, SW, 11 tubes, AC/DC **$150.00-180.00**

Super Wasp - AC, table, 1928, kit, receiver, metal front panel with two window dials, plug-in coils, 3 knobs, BC, SW, 4 tubes, AC..**$430.00-470.00**

Wasp, table, 1928, kit, receiver, metal front panel with left window dial, plug-in coils, 4 knobs, BC, SW, 3 tubes, battery........**$320.00-350.00**

PIONEER

578, tombstone, wood with inlay, lower front round dial, upper cloth grille with cut-outs, "Pioneer" name plate, 3 knobs...........**$110.00-120.00**

PLA-PAL

No #, table-N, two-tone wood, Deco, sides and top open for bar & storage, right front dial, center cloth grille with chrome cut-outs, 2 knobs, BC, AC/DC..**$350.00-410.00**

PORT-O-MATIC
The Port-O-Matic Corp.
50 E. 77th St., New York, New York

25-A, portable, 1938, cloth covered, fold down front lid, inner right front airplane dial, left octagonal grille, tuning eye, top handle, 4 knobs, BC, SW, LW, 8 tubes, AC/DC **$40.00-50.00**

61-A, portable-R/P, 1941, cloth covered, inner right dial, left round grille area, fold-down front, handle, lift top, inner phono, 6 tubes, AC **$30.00-35.00**

PORTO BARADIO
Porto Products
412 North Orleans Street, Chicago, Illinois

PB-520, table-N, 1948, plastic bar/radio, lower front slide rule dial, upper horizontal louvers, side handles, open top bar, 2 knobs, BC, 5 tubes, AC/DC, $240.00-270.00 w/glassware.

TP-1062, table-R/P, 1941, wood, recessed right front dial, left horizontal wrap-around louvers, lift top, inner phono, 3 knobs, BC, SW, 6 tubes, AC/DC, $35.00-40.00.

TX-42, table-R/P, 1941, wood, right front slide rule dial, left criss-cross grille, lift top, inner phono, 4 knobs, BC, SW, 6 tubes, AC...........**$35.00-40.00**

UG-184, tombstone, 1938, wood, lower front large round dial, upper cloth grille with cut-outs and center tuning eye, 4 knobs, BC, SW, 8 tubes, AC/DC **$160.00-180.00**

VG-352, table, 1937, ivory plastic, right front round dial overlaps criss-cross grille area with center horizontal bar, 3 knobs, BC, SW, 5 tubes, AC/DC...**$65.00-75.00**

VX-201, tombstone, 1937, ivory plastic, lower front round dial, upper cloth grille with vertical bars, 3 knobs, BC, 5 tubes, AC/DC..**$180.00-200.00**

WG-352, table, 1937, walnut plastic, right front round dial overlaps criss-cross grille area with center horizontal bar, 3 knobs, BC, SW, 5 tubes, AC/DC...**$65.00-75.00**

PA-510, table-N, 1949, plastic bar/radio, lower front slide rule dial, upper horizontal louvers, side handles, open top bar, 2 knobs, BC, 5 tubes, AC/DC ....**$240.00-270.00 w/glassware**

PRECEL
Precel Radio Mfg. Co.
227 Erie St., Toledo, Ohio

Superfive, table, 1925, wood, tall rectangular case, slanted 3 dial panel, lower storage, BC, 5 tubes, battery **$150.00-180.00**

PREMIER
Premier Crystal Laboratories, Inc.
63 Park Row, New York, New York

15LW, table, 1946, wood, rounded corners, upper front slide rule dial, lower cloth grille, 2 knobs, BC, AC/DC **$40.00-45.00**

PRIESS
Priess Radio Corporation
693 Broadway, New York, New York

The Priess Radio Corporation began business in 1924. Beset by financial difficulties, the company was bankrupt by 1927.

PR4 "Straight 8," table, 1925, wood, low rectangular case, center front dial, top loop antenna, 4 knobs, BC, 8 tubes, battery, $240.00-270.00.

PR3, table, 1925, mahogany, low rectangular case, 2 dial front panel, top loop antenna, 4 knobs, BC, 5 tubes, battery **$200.00-220.00**
Straight Eight, console, 1925, two-tone walnut, inner dial panel and speaker grille with cut-outs, double front doors, 4 knobs, BC, 8 tubes, battery..**$300.00-320.00**
Straight Eight, table, 1925, two-tone mahogany with inlay, low rectangular case, top loop antenna, storage, 3 knobs, BC, 8 tubes, battery **$240.00-270.00**
Straight Nine, table, 1926, mahogany, low rectangular case, center front dial, top loop antenna, 4 knobs, BC, 9 tubes, battery ..**$270.00-310.00**

PRIVAT-EAR
Electronics Systems Corp.
Kansas City, Missouri

Pocket Radio, portable, 1951, plastic, upper front dial, no speaker-earphone only, telescoping antenna, subminiature tubes, BC, battery **$530.00-580.00**

PROMENETTE
The Promenette Radio & Television Corp.
1721 Elmwood Ave., Buffalo, New York

501, table, right front dial, left grille with horizontal bars, 2 knobs, BC, 5 tubes, AC/DC..**$30.00-35.00**

601, table, right front dial, left cloth grille with center horizontal bar, 2 knobs, BC **$30.00-35.00**

PURITAN
Pure Oil Co.
35 Wacker Drive, Chicago, Illinois

501, table, 1946, walnut plastic, upper front slide rule dial, lower criss-cross grille, 2 knobs, BC, 5 tubes, AC/DC....................**$40.00-45.00**
502, table, 1946, ivory plastic, upper front slide rule dial, lower criss-cross grille, 2 knobs, BC, 5 tubes, AC/DC....................**$40.00-45.00**
503, table-R/P, 1946, wood, top vertical dial, front cloth grille, lift top, inner phono, 3 knobs, BC, 5 tubes, AC **$30.00-35.00**
504, table, 1946, wood, upper front slanted slide rule dial, lower criss-cross grille, 4 knobs, BC, SW, AC **$40.00-45.00**
506, table, 1946, ivory plastic, step-down top, upper front slide rule dial, lower horizontal wrap-around louvers, 3 knobs, BC, 6 tubes, AC/DC **$65.00-75.00**
507, table, 1946, mahogany, step-down top, upper front slide rule dial, lower horizontal wrap-around louvers, 3 knobs, BC, 6 tubes, AC/DC **$65.00-75.00**
508, table, 1946, wood, upper front slanted slide rule dial, lower cloth grille, 4 knobs, BC, SW, 7 tubes, AC **$40.00-50.00**
509, portable, 1947, upper front slanted slide rule dial, lower horizontal grille bars, handle, 2 knobs, BC, 6 tubes, AC/DC/battery **$30.00-35.00**
515, table, 1947, wood, upper front slanted slide rule dial, lower two-tone cloth grille, 2 knobs, BC, 5 tubes, AC/DC **$40.00-45.00**

PUROTONE
PuroTone Radio Corporation

4516, table, two-tone wood, upper front slanted slide rule dial, lower grille area with horizontal and vertical bars, 3 knobs, BC, 6 tubes, AC/DC **$40.00-50.00**

R. K. RADIO LABORATORIES
Chicago, Illinois

S-4233 "Radio Keg," table-N, 1933, looks like keg with copper hoops, front window dial & knobs, rear grille, 2 knobs, BC, 5 tubes, AC/DC, $350.00-410.00.

RADIO LAMP
Radio Lamp Company of America
Chicago, Illinois

Radio Lamp, table-N, several styles, metal lamp base with lower built-in radio chassis and speaker, BC, AC/DC....................**$240.00-300.00**

RADIO VISION

414, tombstone, wood, lower right front dial, left cloth grille with shield-shaped cut-out, upper panel with battleships, planes, Statue of Liberty and water that "moves" when radio plays, $320.00-350.00.

RADIOBAR
Radiobar Co. of America
296 Broadway, New York, New York

200-RBP, console-R/P/bar, 1940, wood, inner left dial, door, right pull-out phono drawer, upper lighted bar unit with double doors & lift top, BC, SW, 8 tubes, AC ....**$650.00-750.00 w/glassware**
508, console/bar, 1933, wood, lower front dial & grille, upper bar unit with double doors & lift top, BC, SW, 8 tubes, AC ....**$650.00-750.00 w/glassware**
510, console/bar, 1933, walnut, inner front dial & grille, doors, upper bar unit with double doors & lift top, BC, SW, 10 tubes, AC ....**$750.00-850.00 w/glassware**
528, console/bar, 1933, wood, Deco, inner front dial & grille, upper bar unit with double doors & lift top, BC, SW, 8 tubes, AC ....**$850.00-950.00 w/glassware**
No #/Philco chassis, console/bar, 1936, wood, lower front dial, cloth grille with cut-outs, upper bar unit with double doors and lift top, 4 knobs..**$550.00-650.00 w/glassware**

RADIOETTE
Alamo Electronics Corp.
San Antonio, Texas

PR-2, portable, 1948, trapezoid shape, front dial, left concentric circular grille bars, handle, 3 knobs, BC, 4 tubes, AC/DC/battery ..**$30.00-35.00**

RADIOLA
Radio Corp. of America
Home Instrument Division
Camden, New Jersey

61-8, table, 1947, walnut plastic, upper front slanted slide rule dial, lower horizontal wrap-around grille bars, 2 knobs, BC, 5 tubes, AC/DC, $40.00-50.00.

76ZX11, table, 1948, plastic, upper front slanted slide rule dial, lower horizontal wrap-around grille bars, 2 knobs, BC, 6 tubes, AC/DC, $40.00-50.00.

61-1, table, 1947, plastic, upper front slanted slide rule dial, lower horizontal wrap-around louvers, 3 knobs, BC, AC/DC **$45.00-55.00**
61-3, table, 1947, wood, upper front slanted slide rule dial, lower horizontal louvers, 3 knobs, BC, AC/DC **$40.00-45.00**
61-5, table, 1947, upper front slanted slide rule dial with stars, lower horizontal louvers, 3 knobs, BC, SW, 6 tubes, AC/DC **$45.00-50.00**
61-9, table, 1947, ivory plastic, upper front slanted slide rule dial, lower horizontal wrap-around grille bars, 2 knobs, BC, 5 tubes, AC/DC **$40.00-50.00**
61-10 "Postone," table, 1947, plastic, upper front slanted slide rule dial, lower horizontal grille bars, 3 knobs, BC, SW, 6 tubes, AC/DC **$40.00-50.00**
75ZU, table-R/P, 1948, wood, upper front dial, lower horizontal grille bars, lift top, inner phono, 2 knobs, BC, 5 tubes, AC **$30.00-35.00**
76ZX12, table, 1948, plastic, upper front slanted slide rule dial, lower horizontal wrap-around grille bars, 2 knobs, BC, 6 tubes, AC/DC **$40.00-50.00**
501, table, 1941, ivory plastic, midget, right front dial, left horizontal wrap-around louvers, 2 knobs, BC, 5 tubes, AC/DC......**$75.00-85.00**
510, table, 1940, mahogany plastic, right front dial, left vertical grille bars, 2 knobs, BC, 5 tubes, AC/DC **$40.00-50.00**
511, table, 1940, ivory plastic, right front dial, left vertical grille bars, 2 knobs, BC, 5 tubes, AC/DC **$40.00-50.00**
512, table, 1941, wood, right front dial, left cloth grille, flared base, 2 knobs, BC, 5 tubes, AC/DC **$65.00-75.00**
513, table, wood, right front dial, left grille with diagonal bars, 2 knobs, BC, 5 tubes, AC/DC..**$45.00-55.00**
515, table, 1941, wood, upper front slanted slide rule dial, lower horizontal louvers, 3 knobs, BC, SW, 6 tubes, AC/DC **$40.00-50.00**
516, table, 1942, plastic, upper front slanted slide rule dial, lower vertical grille bars, handle, 2 knobs, BC, 5 tubes, AC/DC **$40.00-50.00**
520, table, 1942, wood, right front dial, left horizontal grille bars, 2 knobs, BC, 5 tubes, AC/DC..**$40.00-45.00**

500, table, 1941, walnut plastic, midget, right front dial, left horizontal wrap-around louvers, 2 knobs, BC, 5 tubes, AC/DC, $75.00-85.00.

517, table, 1942, two-tone wood, upper front slanted slide rule dial, lower horizontal louvers, 2 knobs, BC, 5 tubes, AC/DC, $40.00-50.00.

522, table, 1942, wood, upper front slanted slide rule dial, lower horizontal louvers, 2 knobs, BC, 5 tubes, AC/DC $40.00-45.00
526, table, 1942, plastic, upper front slanted slide rule dial, lower vertical grille bars, handle, 2 knobs, BC, SW, 5 tubes, AC/DC ..$40.00-50.00
527, table, 1942, wood, upper front slanted slide rule dial, lower vertical grille bars, 2 knobs, BC, SW, 5 tubes, AC/DC...............$40.00-50.00
B-50, table, 1940, wood, right front dial, left horizontal grille bars, 2 knobs, BC, 4 tubes, battery $35.00-40.00
B-52, table, 1940, wood, right front slide rule dial, left horizontal grille bars, 3 knobs, BC, 5 tubes, battery $35.00-40.00
P-5, portable, 1940, right front dial, left horizontal grille bars, 3 knobs, BC, AC/DC/battery $30.00-35.00
R560P, table-R/P, 1942, wood, right front dial, left grille area, lift top, inner phono, 3 knobs, BC, 5 tubes, AC $30.00-35.00

RAMWAY

R-17, table, wood, low rectangular case, front panel with 3 pointer dials & metal escutcheons, ram's head logo, $200.00-230.00.

RAYENERGY
RayEnergy Radio & Television Corp.
32 West 22nd Street, New York, New York

AD, table, 1946, wood, right front dial, left cloth grille with cut-outs, 2 knobs, BC, 5 tubes, AC/DC $40.00-50.00
AD4, table, 1946, wood, right front dial, left contrasting horizontal louvers, 2 knobs, BC, 5 tubes, AC/DC $40.00-50.00
SRB-1X, table, 1947, plastic, upper front slide rule dial, lower horizontal louvers, 2 knobs, BC, 5 tubes, AC/DC $40.00-50.00

RAYTHEON
Raytheon Manufacturing Co.
TV & Radio Division
5921 Dickens Avenue, Chicago, Illinois

R-51, table, C1952, mahogany plastic, right front triangular dial area, left horizontal wrap-around grille bars, 2 knobs, BC, 5 tubes, AC/DC $40.00-45.00

R-52, table, C1952, white plastic, right front triangular dial area, left horizontal wrap-around grille bars, 2 knobs, BC, 5 tubes, AC/DC ..$40.00-45.00

RCA
Radio Corporation of America
233 Broadway, New York, New York

RCA was formed in 1919 and soon became one of the largest distributors of radios. The company was one of the pioneers of early radio and broadcasting and began the National Broadcasting Company (NBC) in 1926. As well as being one of the most prolific of radio manufacturers, RCA also made vacuum tubes, Victrolas, marine apparatus, transmitters, and other broadcasting equipment. Their mascot, "Nipper," was featured in many company logos listening at the horn for "his master's voice."

1-BX-62, portable, 1958, plastic, upper front curved dial, large lower grille area with horizontal bars, Nipper logo, rotatable antenna, handle, 2 knobs, BC, 4 tubes, AC/DC/battery.....................$30.00-35.00
1-BX-64, portable, 1958, plastic, upper front curved dial, large lower grille area with horizontal bars, Nipper logo, rotatable antenna, handle, 2 knobs, BC, 4 tubes, AC/DC/battery.....................$30.00-35.00
1-BX-78, portable, 1958, plastic, upper front dial, lower lattice grille area, Nipper logo, rotatable antenna, handle, 2 knobs, BC, 4 tubes, AC/DC/battery $30.00-35.00
1-F-2E, table, plastic, center front round dial over large lattice grille area, feet, 2 knobs, FM, AC $25.00-30.00
1R81 "Livingston," table, 1952, plastic, center front large round dial overlaps horizontal bars, 4 side knobs, BC, FM, 8 tubes, AC ..$30.00-35.00
1-RA-11 "Accent," table, 1962, gray plastic, right front round dial overlaps horizontal bars, Nipper logo, feet, 2 knobs, BC, 5 tubes, AC $20.00-25.00
1-RA-20 "Hardy," table, 1962, white plastic, right front round dial overlaps horizontal bars, Nipper logo, feet, 2 knobs, BC, 5 tubes, AC $20.00-25.00
1-RA-23 "Hardy," table, 1962, pink plastic, right front round dial overlaps horizontal bars, Nipper logo, feet, 2 knobs, BC, 5 tubes, AC $20.00-25.00
1-RA-25 "Hardy," table, 1962, turquoise plastic, right front round dial overlaps horizontal bars, Nipper logo, feet, 2 knobs, BC, 5 tubes, AC $20.00-25.00
1-RA-26 "Hardy," table, 1962, beige plastic, right front round dial overlaps horizontal bars, Nipper logo, feet, 2 knobs, BC, 5 tubes, AC $20.00-25.00
1-RA-45, table, 1962, plastic, wedge-shaped, large right front dial over horizontal grille bars, Nipper logo, feet, 2 knobs, BC, 5 tubes, AC $20.00-25.00
1-RA-64, table, 1962, plastic, wedge-shaped case, lower front raised panel with oval dial overlaps horizontal bars, 2 knobs, BC, 5 tubes, AC $30.00-35.00
1-RC-30, table-C, 1962, white plastic, wedge-shaped case, lower front slide rule dial, upper right alarm clock, upper left lattice grille, top pushbuttons, feet, 2 knobs, BC, FM, 6 tubes, AC.........$25.00-30.00
1-RC-31, table-C, 1962, white/charcoal plastic, wedge-shaped case, lower front slide rule dial, upper right alarm clock, upper left lattice grille, top pushbuttons, feet, 2 knobs, BC, FM, 6 tubes, AC $25.00-30.00
1-RC-34, table-C, 1962, espresso/white plastic, wedge-shaped case, lower front slide rule dial, upper right alarm clock, upper left lattice grille, top pushbuttons, feet, 2 knobs, BC, FM, 6 tubes, AC.............$25.00-30.00

1-C-5JE, table-C, plastic, wedge-shaped case, left front slide rule dial & alarm clock overlap horizontal bars, rear handhold, feet, top drowse alarm button, BC, AC, $25.00-30.00.

1-RD-56, table-C, plastic, wedge-shaped, lower right front dial, upper alarm clock with drowse button, feet, BC, AC...............**$25.00-30.00**

1X, table, 1941, plastic, right front dial, left vertical grille bars, decorative case lines, 2 knobs, BC, 5 tubes, AC/DC, $50.00-65.00.

1X2, table, 1941, plastic, right front dial, left vertical grille bars, decorative case lines, 2 knobs, BC, 5 tubes, AC/DC **$50.00-65.00**

1-X-4EJ, table, 1961, plastic, wedge-shaped, lower front oval dial area, upper grille area with horizontal bars, Nipper logo, 2 knobs, BC **$30.00-35.00**

1X51, table, 1952, maroon plastic, upper front half-round dial, lower horizontal grille bars, 2 knobs, BC, 5 tubes, AC/DC **$35.00-40.00**

1X52, table, 1952, ivory plastic, upper front half-round dial, lower horizontal grille bars, 2 knobs, BC, 5 tubes, AC/DC **$35.00-40.00**

1X53, table, 1952, green plastic, upper front half-round dial, lower horizontal grille bars, 2 knobs, BC, 5 tubes, AC/DC **$35.00-40.00**

1X54, table, 1952, tan plastic, upper front half-round dial, lower horizontal grille bars, 2 knobs, BC, 5 tubes, AC/DC **$35.00-40.00**

1X55, table, 1952, blue plastic, upper front half-round dial, lower horizontal grille bars, 2 knobs, BC, 5 tubes, AC/DC **$35.00-40.00**

1X57, table, 1952, white plastic, upper front half-round dial, lower horizontal grille bars, 2 knobs, BC, 5 tubes, AC/DC **$35.00-40.00**

1X591, table, 1952, maroon plastic, lower front thin slide rule dial, upper pleated gold grille, 2 side knobs, BC, 5 tubes, AC/DC **$45.00-50.00**

1X592, table, 1952, ivory plastic, lower front thin slide rule dial, upper pleated gold grille, 2 side knobs, BC, 5 tubes, AC/DC ..**$45.00-50.00**

2B400, portable, 1952, gray plastic, center front round dial, lower metal perforated grille, fold-down handle, 2 knobs, BC, 4 tubes, battery **$35.00-40.00**

2B402, portable, 1952, ivory plastic, center front round dial, lower metal perforated grille, fold-down handle, 2 knobs, BC, 4 tubes, battery **$35.00-40.00**

2B403, portable, 1952, green plastic, center front round dial, lower metal perforated grille, fold-down handle, 2 knobs, BC, 4 tubes, battery **$35.00-40.00**

2B404, portable, 1952, tan plastic, center front round dial, lower metal perforated grille, fold-down handle, 2 knobs, BC, 4 tubes, battery **$35.00-40.00**

2B405, portable, 1952, red plastic, center front round dial, lower metal perforated grille, fold-down handle, 2 knobs, BC, 4 tubes, battery **$35.00-40.00**

2BX63, portable, 1953, plastic, upper front slide rule dial, lower horizontal bars, handle, 2 side knobs, BC, 5 tubes, AC/DC/battery ..**$30.00-35.00**

2-C-511, table-C, 1953, black & gray plastic, right side dial, center front round alarm clock face, top switch, 4 knobs, BC, 4 tubes, AC **$45.00-55.00**

2-C-512, table-C, 1953, ivory plastic, right side dial, center front round alarm clock face, top switch, 4 knobs, BC, 4 tubes, AC..**$45.00-55.00**

2-C-513, table-C, 1953, red plastic, right side dial, center front round alarm clock face, top switch, 4 knobs, BC, 4 tubes, AC..**$45.00-55.00**

2-C-514, table-C, 1953, two-tone gray plastic, right side dial, center front round alarm clock face, top switch, 4 knobs, BC, 4 tubes, AC **$45.00-55.00**

2-C-522, table-C, 1953, ivory plastic, right front round dial, left alarm clock, center horizontal bars, 5 knobs, BC, 5 tubes, AC **$25.00-30.00**

2-C-527, table-C, 1953, white plastic, right front round dial, left alarm clock, center horizontal bars, 5 knobs, BC, 5 tubes, AC ..**$25.00-30.00**

1X56, table, 1952, red plastic, upper front half-round dial, lower horizontal grille bars, 2 knobs, BC, 5 tubes, AC/DC, $35.00-40.00.

2-S-7, console-R/P, 1953, wood, inner right slide rule dial, lower pull-out phono, left storage, double doors, lower front grille, 2 knobs, BC, 6 tubes, AC **$50.00-65.00**

2-S-10, console-R/P, 1953, wood, inner right dial, upper phono, lower grille, left storage, double doors, 5 knobs, BC, FM, 10 tubes, AC **$65.00-75.00**

2-X-52, table, 1952, plastic, dial on top of case, center front horizontal louvers, 2 knobs, BC, AC/DC **$40.00-50.00**

2-X-62, table, 1953, ivory plastic, dial on top of case, center front horizontal louvers, 2 knobs, BC, 6 tubes, AC/DC **$40.00-50.00**

2-XF-91 "Forbes," table, 1953, maroon plastic, right front FM dial, left front BC dial, center horizontal bars, 4 knobs, BC, FM, 8 tubes, AC/DC **$35.00-40.00**

2-XF-931 "Townley," table, 1953, maroon plastic, right front FM dial, left front BC dial, center horizontal bars, 4 knobs, BC, FM, 8 tubes, AC **$35.00-40.00**

2-XF-932 "Townley," table, 1953, ivory plastic, right front FM dial, left front BC dial, center horizontal bars, 4 knobs, BC, FM, 8 tubes, AC **$35.00-40.00**

2-XF-933 "Townley," table, 1953, green plastic, right front FM dial, left front BC dial, center horizontal bars, 4 knobs, BC, FM, 8 tubes, AC **$35.00-40.00**

2-XF-934 "Townley," table, 1953, red plastic, right front FM dial, left front BC dial, center horizontal bars, 4 knobs, BC, FM, 8 tubes, AC **$35.00-40.00**

2-XF-935 "Townley," table, 1953, beige plastic, right front FM dial, left front BC dial, center horizontal bars, 4 knobs, BC, FM, 8 tubes, AC **$35.00-40.00**

3-BX-51, portable, 1954, brown plastic, large front checkered grille area, fold-down handle, 1 left & 1 right side knob, BC, 4 tubes, AC/DC/battery **$35.00-40.00**

3-BX-52, portable, 1954, tan plastic, large front checkered grille area, fold-down handle, 1 left & 1 right side knob, BC, 4 tubes, AC/DC/battery **$35.00-40.00**

3-BX-53, portable, 1954, green plastic, large front checkered grille area, fold-down handle, 1 left & 1 right side knob, BC, 4 tubes, AC/DC/battery **$35.00-40.00**

2B401, portable, 1952, black plastic, center front round dial, lower metal perforated grille, fold-down handle, 2 knobs, BC, 4 tubes, battery, $35.00-40.00.

2-C-521, table-C, 1953, maroon plastic, right front round dial, left alarm clock, center horizontal bars, 5 knobs, BC, 5 tubes, AC, $25.00-30.00.

3-BX-54, portable, 1954, red plastic, large front checkered grille area, fold-down handle, 1 left & 1 right side knob, BC, 4 tubes, AC/DC/battery **$35.00-40.00**

3-BX-671 "Strato-World," portable, 1954, leather, inner front slide rule dial, flip-up front with map, telescope antenna, 7 bands, 5 knobs, BC, SW, 5 tubes, AC/DC/battery.................................**$85.00-115.00**

3-RA-30 "Luster," table, 1963, antique white plastic, wedge-shaped case, right front dial, left checkered grille area, feet, 2 knobs, BC, 5 tubes, AC **$20.00-25.00**

3-RA-31 "Luster," table, 1963, charcoal/antique white plastic, wedge-shaped case, right front dial, left checkered grille area, feet, 2 knobs, BC, 5 tubes, AC **$20.00-25.00**

3-RA-32 "Luster," table, 1963, aqua/antique white plastic, wedge-shaped case, right front dial, left checkered grille area, feet, 2 knobs, BC, 5 tubes, AC **$20.00-25.00**

3-RA-34 "Luster," table, 1963, espresso/autumn smoke plastic, wedge-shaped case, right front dial, left checkered grille area, feet, 2 knobs, BC, 5 tubes, AC **$20.00-25.00**

3-RA-50 "Radiant," table, 1963, iceberg white plastic, wedge-shaped case, lower front raised dial panel overlaps horizontal bars, 2 knobs, BC, 5 tubes, AC **$20.00-25.00**

3-RA-51 "Radiant," table, 1963, iceberg white/black pearl plastic, wedge-shaped case, lower front raised dial panel overlaps horizontal bars, 2 knobs, BC, 5 tubes, AC **$20.00-25.00**

3-RA-52 "Radiant," table, 1963, dark blue/iceberg white plastic, wedge-shaped case, lower front raised dial panel overlaps horizontal bars, 2 knobs, BC, 5 tubes, AC **$20.00-25.00**

3-RA-54 "Radiant," table, 1963, autumn smoke/espresso plastic, wedge-shaped case, lower front raised dial panel overlaps horizontal bars, 2 knobs, BC, 5 tubes, AC **$20.00-25.00**

3-RA-60 "Splendor," table, 1963, mist brown/iceberg white plastic, wedge-shaped case, lower front raised dial panel overlaps horizontal bars, 2 knobs, BC, 5 tubes, AC **$20.00-25.00**

2US7, table-R/P, 1952, wood, upper front slide rule dial, lower grille, 3/4 lift top, inner phono, 2 knobs, BC, 6 tubes, AC, $30.00-35.00.

3-RA-63 "Splendor," table, 1963, iceberg white/shrimp plastic, wedge-shaped case, lower front raised dial panel overlaps horizontal bars, 2 knobs, BC, 5 tubes, AC **$20.00-25.00**

3-RA-65 "Splendor," table, 1963, dark green/iceberg white plastic, wedge-shaped case, lower front raised dial panel overlaps horizontal bars, 2 knobs, BC, 5 tubes, AC **$20.00-25.00**

3-RB-16 "Squire," table, 1963, Sahara plastic, left front vertical slide rule dial, right checkered grille area, 2 knobs, FM, 5 tubes, AC/DC **$15.00-20.00**

3-RB-31, table, 1963, black/iceberg white plastic, left front vertical slide rule dial, right checkered grille area, switch, 2 knobs, FM, 5 tubes, AC/DC **$15.00-20.00**

3-RB-32, table, 1963, academy blue/iceberg white plastic, left front vertical slide rule dial, right checkered grille area, switch, 2 knobs, FM, 5 tubes, AC/DC...................................**$15.00-20.00**

3-RB-34, table, 1963, espresso/iceberg white plastic, left front vertical slide rule dial, right checkered grille area, switch, 2 knobs, FM, 5 tubes, AC/DC...**$15.00-20.00**

3-RC-11 "Bulletin," table, 1964, black plastic, left front vertical slide rule dial, right checkered grille area, switch, 2 knobs, BC, FM, 6 tubes, AC **$15.00-20.00**

3-RC-14 "Bulletin," table, 1964, espresso plastic, left front vertical slide rule dial, right checkered grille area, switch, 2 knobs, BC, FM, 6 tubes, AC **$15.00-20.00**

3-RD-40 "Daybreak," table-C, 1963, iceberg white plastic, wedge-shaped case, lower front dial panel & upper alarm clock overlap horizontal bars, feet, 4 knobs, BC, 5 tubes, AC **$15.00-20.00**

3-RD-41 "Daybreak," table-C, 1963, iceberg white/black pearl plastic, wedge-shaped case, lower front dial panel & upper alarm clock overlap horizontal bars, feet, 4 knobs, BC, 5 tubes, AC **$15.00-20.00**

3-RD-43 "Daybreak," table-C, 1963, Sahara/shrimp plastic, wedge-shaped case, lower front dial panel & upper alarm clock overlap horizontal bars, feet, 4 knobs, BC, 5 tubes, AC **$15.00-20.00**

2-X-61, table, 1953, maroon plastic, dial on top of case, center front horizontal louvers, 2 knobs, BC, 6 tubes, AC/DC, $40.00-50.00.

3-RD-45 "Daybreak," table-C, 1963, dark green/iceberg white plastic, wedge-shaped case, lower front dial panel & upper alarm clock overlap horizontal bars, feet, 4 knobs, BC, 5 tubes, AC **$15.00-20.00**

3-RD-50 "Dawnette," table-C, 1963, black pearl/iceberg white plastic, wedge-shaped case, lower front dial panel & upper alarm clock overlap horizontal bars, drowse button, feet, 4 knobs, BC, 5 tubes, AC **$15.00-20.00**

3-RD-52 "Dawnette," table-C, 1963, iceberg white/starlight blue plastic, wedge-shaped case, lower front dial panel & upper alarm clock overlap horizontal bars, drowse button, feet, 4 knobs, BC, 5 tubes, AC **$15.00-20.00**

3-RD-54 "Dawnette," table-C, 1963, autumn smoke/espresso plastic, wedge-shaped case, lower front dial panel & upper alarm clock overlap horizontal bars, drowse button, feet, 4 knobs, BC, 5 tubes, AC **$15.00-20.00**

3-RD-57 "Dawnette," table-C, 1963, iceberg white/maple sugar plastic, wedge-shaped case, lower front dial panel & upper alarm clock overlap horizontal bars, drowse button, feet, 4 knobs, BC, 5 tubes, AC **$15.00-20.00**

3-RD-61 "Gloaming," table-C, 1963, black pearl/iceberg white plastic, wedge-shaped case, lower front dial panel & upper alarm clock overlap horizontal bars, drowse button, feet, 4 knobs, BC, 5 tubes, AC **$15.00-20.00**

3-RD-65 "Gloaming," table-C, 1963, dark green/iceberg white plastic, wedge-shaped case, lower front dial panel & upper alarm clock overlap horizontal bars, drowse button, feet, 4 knobs, BC, 5 tubes, AC **$15.00-20.00**

3-RD-67 "Gloaming," table-C, 1963, maple sugar/iceberg white plastic, wedge-shaped case, lower front dial panel & upper alarm clock overlap horizontal bars, drowse button, feet, 4 knobs, BC, 5 tubes, AC **$15.00-20.00**

3-RD-69 "Gloaming," table-C, 1963, mist brown/iceberg white plastic, wedge-shaped case, lower front dial panel & upper alarm clock overlap horizontal bars, drowse button, feet, 4 knobs, BC, 5 tubes, AC **$15.00-20.00**

3-X-521, table, 1954, brown plastic, right front dial, left checkered grille area, 2 knobs, BC, 5 tubes, AC/DC **$20.00-25.00**

3-X-532, table, 1954, ivory plastic, right front dial, left checkered grille area, 2 knobs, BC, 5 tubes, AC/DC **$20.00-25.00**

3-X-533, table, 1954, green plastic, right front dial, left checkered grille area, 2 knobs, BC, 5 tubes, AC/DC **$20.00-25.00**

3-X-536, table, 1954, white plastic, right front dial, left checkered grille area, 2 knobs, BC, 5 tubes, AC/DC **$20.00-25.00**

4C533, table-C, 1955, plastic, right front round dial, left round clock face, center grille area, 3 knobs, BC, 5 tubes, AC **$35.00-40.00**

3-RA-61 "Splendor," table, 1963, iceberg white/black pearl plastic, wedge-shaped case, lower front raised dial panel overlaps horizontal bars, 2 knobs, BC, 5 tubes, AC, $20.00-25.00.

4C541, table-C, 1955, plastic, right front round dial, left round clock face, center checkered grille area, feet, 4 knobs, BC, 5 tubes, AC **$35.00-40.00**

4C544, table-C, 1955, plastic, right front round dial, left round clock face, center checkered grille area, feet, 4 knobs, BC, 5 tubes, AC **$35.00-40.00**

4QB, table, 1940, plastic, lower front slanted dial, upper grille area, 2 knobs, BC, SW, 4 tubes, battery **$35.00-40.00**

4QB4, table, 1940, plastic, lower front slanted dial, upper grille area, 2 knobs, BC, SW, LW, 4 tubes, battery **$35.00-40.00**

4X, tombstone, 1936, two-tone wood, lower right front dial, upper cloth grille with 3 center bars, 2 knobs, BC, 4 tubes, AC/DC..**$75.00-85.00**

4X3, tombstone, 1936, mahogany finish, lower right front dial, upper cloth grille, base, 2 knobs, BC, 4 tubes, AC/DC **$75.00-85.00**

4X4, tombstone, 1936, white finish with contrasting knobs, lower right front dial, upper cloth grille, 2 knobs, BC, 4 tubes, AC/DC **$75.00-85.00**

4-X-551, table, 1955, plastic, top right thumbwheel dial, left front horizontal grille bars, 2 knobs, BC, 5 tubes, AC/DC **$50.00-55.00**

4-X-641, table, 1954, plastic, lower front horizontal slide rule dial, large upper checkered grille area, 2 knobs, BC, 6 tubes, AC/DC **$35.00-40.00**

4-X-648, table, 1956, plastic, lower front horizontal slide rule dial, large upper checkered grille area, 2 knobs, BC, 6 tubes, AC/DC **$35.00-40.00**

4-Y-511, table-R/P, 1954, plastic, right front round dial overlaps large grille, lift top, inner 45 phono, 3 knobs, BC, 5 tubes, AC............**$40.00-45.00**

5BT, tombstone, 1936, wood, center front dial, cloth grille with vertical bars, 2 knobs, BC, 5 tubes, battery **$120.00-150.00**

3-RF-91 "Woodland," table, 1952, maroon plastic, center front large round dial over horizontal decorative lines, 2 knobs each side, BC, FM, 9 tubes, AC, $45.00-55.00.

5-BX-41, portable, 1955, plastic, upper front flip-up dial, lower horizontal grille bars, 1 left & 1 right side knob, BC, 4 tubes, AC/DC/battery **$40.00-45.00**

5-C-581, table-C, 1955, plastic, lower base with slide rule dial, large upper clock area with round alarm clock face, 4 knobs, BC, 5 tubes, AC **$50.00-65.00**

5-C-591, table-C, 1955, plastic, lower base with slide rule dial, large upper clock area with round alarm clock face, 4 knobs, BC, 5 tubes, AC **$50.00-65.00**

5-C-592, table-C, 1955, plastic, lower base with slide rule dial, large upper clock area with round alarm clock face, 4 knobs, BC, 5 tubes, AC **$50.00-65.00**

5Q1, tombstone, 1940, wood, center front slide rule dial, upper cloth grille with 2 horizontal bars, 3 knobs, BC, SW, 5 tubes, AC ...**$75.00-85.00**

5Q2, tombstone, 1940, wood, lower front slide rule dial, upper patterned cloth grille, 3 knobs, BC, SW, 5 tubes, AC **$75.00-85.00**

5Q2X, tombstone, 1940, wood, lower front slide rule dial, upper patterned cloth grille, 3 knobs, BC, SW, 6 tubes including ballast, AC/DC **$75.00-85.00**

5Q4, table, 1940, wood, right front slide rule dial, left cloth grille with 2 horizontal bars, 3 knobs, BC, SW, 5 tubes, AC **$50.00-65.00**

5Q5, table, 1940, plastic, lower front slanted slide rule dial, upper metal grille, 3 knobs, BC, SW, 5 tubes, AC **$45.00-55.00**

5Q6, table, 1940, plastic, lower front slanted slide rule dial, upper grille area, 3 knobs, BC, SW, 6 tubes including ballast, AC/DC **$45.00-55.00**

5Q8E, table, 1940, brown plastic, lower front slanted slide rule dial, upper grille area, 3 knobs, BC, SW, LW, 6 tubes including ballast, AC/DC **$45.00-55.00**

5Q8F, table, 1940, black plastic, lower front slanted slide rule dial, upper grille area, 3 knobs, BC, SW, LW, 6 tubes including ballast, AC/DC **$45.00-55.00**

5Q8G, table, 1940, ivory plastic, lower front slanted slide rule dial, upper grille area, 3 knobs, BC, SW, LW, 6 tubes including ballast, AC/DC **$45.00-55.00**

3-X-535, table, 1954, red plastic, right front dial, left checkered grille area, 2 knobs, BC, 5 tubes, AC/DC, $20.00-25.00.

4T, cathedral, 1935, wood, center front window dial, cloth grille with cut-outs, 2 knobs, BC, 5 tubes, AC, $140.00-150.00.

5Q8H, table, 1940, maroon plastic, lower front slanted slide rule dial, upper grille area, 3 knobs, BC, SW, LW, 6 tubes including ballast, AC/DC **$45.00-55.00**

5Q12, table, 1940, plastic, lower front slanted slide rule dial, upper grille area, 3 knobs, BC, SW, 5 tubes, AC **$45.00-55.00**

5T4, table, 1936, wood, right front dial, left cloth grille with horizontal wrap-around bars, 4 knobs, BC, SW, 5 tubes, AC **$75.00-85.00**

5T5, tombstone, 1936, wood, lower front dial, upper cloth grille with vertical bars, 4 knobs, BC, SW, 5 tubes, AC **$85.00-115.00**

5T6, table, 1936, wood, right front dial, rounded left corner, left cloth grille with horizontal wrap-around and vertical bars, 4 knobs, BC, SW, 5 tubes, AC...**$75.00-85.00**

5T7, table, 1936, wood, right front dial, rounded left corner, left cloth grille with horizontal wrap-around and vertical bars, 4 knobs, BC, SW, 5 tubes, AC...**$75.00-85.00**

5T8, table, 1936, wood, right front dial, left cloth grille with vertical bars, rounded top, decorative base edging, 4 knobs, BC, SW, 5 tubes, AC **$75.00-85.00**

5U, tombstone-R/P, 1936, wood, lower front dial, upper cloth grille with vertical bars, lift top, inner phono, 4 knobs, BC, SW, 5 tubes, AC **$85.00-115.00**

5X2, tombstone, 1936, wood, lower center airplane dial, upper round grille with two horizontal bars, 3 knobs, BC, SW, 5 tubes, AC/DC **$85.00-95.00**

5X3, table, 1936, wood, center front airplane dial, top louvers, base, round shoulders, 3 knobs, BC, SW, 5 tubes, AC/DC **$85.00-95.00**

5X4, table, 1936, white lacquer/black base/contrasting knobs, center front airplane dial, round shoulders, feet, 3 knobs, BC, SW, 5 tubes, AC/DC **$65.00-75.00**

4-X-552, table, 1955, plastic, top right thumbwheel dial, left front horizontal grille bars, 2 knobs, BC, 5 tubes, AC/DC, $50.00-55.00.

5X5I, table, 1939, ivory finish, right raised dial panel, left horizontal grille bars, 2 knobs, BC, 5 tubes, AC/DC **$45.00-55.00**

5X5W, table, 1939, walnut finish, right raised dial panel, left horizontal grille bars, 2 knobs, BC, 5 tubes, AC/DC **$45.00-55.00**

5X564, table, 1955, plastic, front see-through dial panel over large checkered grille area, 3 knobs, BC, 5 tubes, AC/DC **$30.00-35.00**

6B4A, portable, 1956, plastic, large upper front dial overlaps wedge-shaped lattice grille area, fold-down handle, 2 knobs, BC, 4 tubes, battery **$30.00-35.00**

6B4B, portable, 1956, plastic, large upper front dial overlaps wedge-shaped lattice grille area, fold-down handle, 2 knobs, BC, 4 tubes, battery **$30.00-35.00**

6BK, console, 1936, wood, upper front center dial, lower grille with center vertical bar, rounded shoulders, fluted front corners, 4 knobs, BC, SW, 6 tubes, battery **$110.00-130.00**

6BK6, console, 1936, wood, upper front center dial, lower grille with center vertical bar, rounded shoulders, fluted front corners, 4 knobs, BC, SW, 6 tubes, 6VDC **$110.00-130.00**

6BT, tombstone, 1936, wood, center rectangular black dial, upper "rounded X" grille with cut-outs, fluted front corners, 4 knobs, BC, SW, 6 tubes, battery **$85.00-95.00**

6BT6, tombstone, 1936, wood, center rectangular black dial, upper "rounded X" grille with cut-outs, fluted front corners, 4 knobs, BC, SW, 6 tubes, 6VDC **$85.00-95.00**

6-BX-6A, portable, 1955, plastic, side dial, large front grille area with horizontal bars, Nipper logo, handle, 1 left & 1 right side knob, BC, 4 tubes, AC/DC/battery **$35.00-40.00**

6-BX-8A, portable, plastic, front checkered grille area with Nipper logo, fold-down handle, 2 knobs, BC, 4 tubes, AC/DC/battery ..**$35.00-40.00**

6-BX-8B, portable, plastic, front checkered grille area with Nipper logo, fold-down handle, 2 knobs, BC, 4 tubes, AC/DC/battery ..**$35.00-40.00**

5Q55, table, 1939, brown plastic, lower front slanted slide rule dial, upper cloth grille, 2 knobs, BC, SW, 5 tubes, AC, $45.00-55.00.

6-BX-63, portable, 1952, plastic, upper front slide rule dial, lower horizontal grille bars, 1 left & 1 right side knob, BC, 5 tubes, AC/DC/battery **$30.00-35.00**

6K, console, 1936, wood, upper front dial, lower cloth grille with 2 vertical bars, 4 knobs, BC, SW, 6 tubes, AC **$110.00-130.00**

6K1, console, 1936, wood, upper front dial, lower cloth grille with 2 vertical bars, 4 knobs, BC, SW, 6 tubes, AC **$110.00-130.00**

6K2, console, 1936, wood, upper front dial, lower cloth grille with vertical bars, 4 knobs, BC, SW, 6 tubes, AC **$110.00-130.00**

6Q1, table, 1940, plastic, lower front slanted slide rule dial, upper grille area, 2 knobs, BC, SW, 6 tubes, AC **$45.00-55.00**

6Q4, table, 1940, plastic, lower front slanted slide rule dial, upper grille area, 2 knobs, BC, SW, LW, 6 tubes, AC **$45.00-55.00**

6Q4X, table, 1940, plastic, lower front slanted slide rule dial, upper grille area, 2 knobs, BC, SW, LW, 7 tubes including ballast, AC/DC **$45.00-55.00**

6Q7, table, 1940, striped walnut, lower front slide rule dial, upper grille area, 3 knobs, BC, SW, 6 tubes, AC **$50.00-65.00**

6Q8, table, 1940, wood, step-down top, lower front slide rule dial, upper grille area, tuning eye, 2 knobs, BC, SW, LW, 6 tubes, AC **$50.00-65.00**

6-RF-9, table, 1956, mahogany, center front large round dial, right & left side knobs, BC, FM, 9 tubes **$35.00-40.00**

6T, tombstone, 1936, wood, center airplane dial, upper "rounded X" grille with cut-outs, fluted front corners, 4 knobs, BC, SW, 6 tubes, AC **$120.00-150.00**

6T2, tombstone, 1936, wood, center front black dial, upper cloth grille with cut-outs, 4 knobs, BC, SW, 6 tubes, AC **$120.00-150.00**

6T10, tombstone, 1936, black lacquer/chrome frame, center front dial, upper round cloth grille with center vertical chrome bar, chrome stand, 4 knobs, BC, SW, 6 tubes, AC **$530.00-580.00**

6X2, table, 1942, plastic, right front dial, left vertical grille bars, 2 knobs, BC, 5 tubes, AC/DC...**$40.00-50.00**

6X5, table, plastic, right front dial overlaps large lattice grille, left Nipper logo, feet, BC, 5 tubes, AC/DC **$15.00-20.00**

6-X-5A, table, 1956, plastic, right front dial overlaps large lattice grille, left Nipper logo, feet, BC, 5 tubes, AC/DC **$15.00-20.00**

6-X-5B, table, 1956, plastic, right front dial overlaps large lattice grille, left Nipper logo, feet, BC, 5 tubes, AC/DC **$15.00-20.00**

6-X-7B, table, 1956, plastic, right front dial over checkered grille area, upper left Nipper logo, feet, BC, AC/DC **$15.00-20.00**

6-X-7C, table, 1956, plastic, right front dial over checkered grille area, upper left Nipper logo, feet, BC, AC/DC **$15.00-20.00**

6-XD-5A, table, 1956, plastic, lower front dial, large upper lattice grille with center Nipper logo, 2 knobs, BC, 5 tubes, AC/DC **$30.00-35.00**

6-XD-5B, table, 1956, plastic, lower front dial, large upper lattice grille with center Nipper logo, 2 knobs, BC, 5 tubes, AC/DC ..**$30.00-35.00**

6-XD-5C, table, 1956, plastic, lower front dial, large upper lattice grille with center Nipper logo, 2 knobs, BC, 5 tubes, AC/DC ..**$30.00-35.00**

7-BX-5F, portable, 1955, plastic, front lattice grille area with Nipper logo, fold-down handle, right & left side knobs, BC, AC/DC/battery **$30.00-35.00**

7-BX-5H, portable, 1955, plastic, front lattice grille area with Nipper logo, fold-down handle, right & left side knobs, BC, AC/DC/battery **$30.00-35.00**

5T, tombstone, 1936, wood, center front dial, upper cloth grille with cut-outs, 4 knobs, BC, SW, 5 tubes, AC, $120.00-150.00.

7-BX-5JJ, portable, 1955, plastic, front lattice grille area with Nipper logo, fold-down handle, right & left side knobs, BC, AC/DC/battery **$30.00-35.00**

7-BX-6E, portable, 1956, plastic, right front dial overlaps lattice grille area with Nipper logo, top rotatable antenna bar, handle, 2 knobs, BC, 4 tubes, AC/DC/battery **$30.00-35.00**

7-BX-6J, portable, 1956, plastic, right front dial overlaps lattice grille area with Nipper logo, top rotatable antenna bar, handle, 2 knobs, BC, 4 tubes, AC/DC/battery **$30.00-35.00**

7-BX-6L, portable, 1956, plastic, right front dial overlaps lattice grille area with Nipper logo, top rotatable antenna bar, handle, 2 knobs, BC, 4 tubes, AC/DC/battery **$30.00-35.00**

7-BX-7J, portable, 1957, plastic, right front dial overlaps metal lattice grille area, top rotatable antenna bar, handle, 2 knobs, BC, 4 tubes, AC/DC/battery **$30.00-35.00**

7-BX-8L "Globe Trotter," portable, 1957, plastic, upper front slide rule dial, lower horizontal grille bars, handle, top rotatable antenna bar, 2 knobs, BC, 5 tubes, AC/DC/battery..............................**$30.00-35.00**

7-BX-9H "Yachtsman," portable, 1957, plastic, upper front slide rule dial, lower horizontal grille bars, handle, top rotatable antenna bar, 2 knobs, BC, SW, 5 tubes, AC/DC/battery.......................**$30.00-35.00**

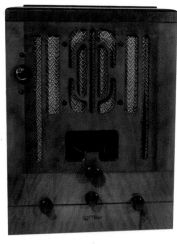

5T1, tombstone, 1936, wood, center front dial, upper cloth grille with cut-outs, tuning eye, 4 knobs, BC, SW, 5 tubes, AC, $120.00-150.00.

7-C-6F "Deluxe," table-C, 1956, plastic, right front half-round dial over lattice grille area, large left alarm clock face, 4 knobs, BC, 5 tubes, AC **$20.00-25.00**

7-HFR-1, console-R/P/Rec, 1957, wood, upper left front dial, lower pull-out phono, inner top right reel-to-reel recorder, 5 receiver knobs, BC, FM, 18 tubes, AC **$65.00-75.00**

7K, console, 1936, wood, upper front dial, lower cloth grille with 3 vertical bars, 4 knobs, BC, SW, 7 tubes, AC **$110.00-130.00**

7K1, console, 1937, wood, upper front dial, lower cloth grille with 3 vertical bars, tuning eye, 4 knobs, BC, SW, 7 tubes, AC ..**$120.00-150.00**

7Q4, table, 1940, wood, upper front slanted slide rule dial, large lower grille area, tuning eye, 3 knobs, BC, SW, LW, 7 tubes, AC **$45.00-55.00**

7Q4X, table, 1940, wood, upper front slanted slide rule dial, large lower grille area, tuning eye, 3 knobs, BC, SW, LW, 7 tubes, AC.........**$40.00-50.00**

7QB, table, 1941, wood, right front slide rule dial, left grille with 2 horizontal wrap-around bars, 4 knobs, BC, SW, 8 tubes AC/7 tubes DC, AC & DC versions **$50.00-65.00**

7QBK, console, 1941, wood, upper front slide rule dial, lower cloth grille with center vertical bars, 4 knobs, BC, SW, 8 tubes AC/7 tubes DC, AC & DC versions **$110.00-130.00**

7T, tombstone, 1936, wood, center front rectangular dial, upper cloth grille with cut-outs, 4 knobs, BC, SW, 7 tubes, AC....**$110.00-130.00**

7U, console-R/P, 1936, wood, front rectangular dial, lower cloth grille with cut-outs, tuning eye, lift top, inner phono, 4 knobs, BC, SW, 7 tubes, AC **$120.00-150.00**

7U2, console-R/P, 1936, wood, front rectangular dial, lower cloth grille with center vertical bar, tuning eye, lift top, inner phono, 4 knobs, BC, SW, 7 tubes, AC **$120.00-150.00**

7X, tombstone, 1936, wood, center front rectangular dial, upper cloth grille with cut-outs, decorative base edging, 4 knobs, BC, SW, 7 tubes, AC/DC...**$130.00-150.00**

5X, table, 1936, wood, rounded sides, finished front & back, center front dial, top louvers, 3 knobs, BC, SW, 5 tubes, AC/DC, $85.00-115.00.

6-BX-6B, portable, 1955, plastic, side dial, large front grille area with horizontal bars, Nipper logo, handle, 1 left & 1 right side knob, BC, 4 tubes, AC/DC/battery, $35.00-40.00.

7X1, tombstone, 1936, wood, center front rectangular dial, upper cloth grille with cut-outs, decorative base edging, 4 knobs, BC, SW, 7 tubes, AC/DC **$130.00-150.00**

8B41 "Jewel Box," portable, 1949, black plastic, inner round dial, grille bars, flip-open lid, handle, 2 knobs, BC, 4 tubes, battery ..**$40.00-45.00**

8B42 "Jewel Box," portable, 1949, brown plastic, inner round dial, grille bars, flip-open lid, handle, 2 knobs, BC, 4 tubes, battery ..**$40.00-45.00**

8B43 "Jewel Box," portable, 1949, red plastic, inner round dial, grille bars, flip-open lid, handle, 2 knobs, BC, 4 tubes, battery..........**$40.00-45.00**

8B46 "Jewel Box," portable, 1949, ivory plastic, inner round dial, grille bars, flip-open lid, handle, 2 knobs, BC, 4 tubes, battery **$40.00-45.00**

8BK, console, 1936, wood, upper front center dial, lower grille with center vertical bars and cut-outs, rounded shoulders, 4 knobs, BC, SW, 8 tubes, battery **$120.00-140.00**

8BK6, console, 1936, wood, upper front center dial, lower grille with center vertical bars and cut-outs, rounded shoulders, 4 knobs, BC, SW, 8 tubes, 6VDC **$120.00-140.00**

8BT, tombstone, 1936, wood, center rectangular black dial, upper ornate cut-out grille, decorative base edging, 4 knobs, BC, SW, 8 tubes, battery **$95.00-115.00**

8BT6, tombstone, 1936, wood, center rectangular black dial, upper ornate cut-out grille, decorative base edging, 4 knobs, BC, SW, 8 tubes, 6VDC **$95.00-115.00**

8BX5, portable, 1948, "snakeskin" & plastic, front round dial overlaps horizontal bars, handle, 2 knobs, BC, 5 tubes, AC/DC/battery...**$40.00-50.00**

8BX5F, portable, 1948, plastic, front lattice grille area with Nipper logo, fold-down handle, 2 knobs, BC, 5 tubes, AC/DC/battery..........**$25.00-30.00**

6-X-7, table, 1956, plastic, right front dial over checkered grille area, upper left Nipper logo, feet, 2 knobs, BC, 5 tubes, AC/DC, $15.00-20.00.

8BX6E, portable, 1956, plastic, right front dial overlaps horizontal grille bars, top rotatable antenna bar, handle, BC, AC/DC/battery......**$30.00-35.00**

8BX6L, portable, 1956, plastic, right front dial overlaps horizontal grille bars, top rotatable antenna bar, handle, BC, AC/DC/battery......**$30.00-35.00**

8BX54, portable, 1948, plastic, front round dial overlaps horizontal grille bars, handle, 2 knobs, BC, 5 tubes, AC/DC/battery **$30.00-35.00**

8BX55, portable, 1948, wood grain plastic, front round dial overlaps horizontal grille bars, handle, 2 knobs, BC, 5 tubes, AC/DC/battery **$35.00-40.00**

8C5L, table-C, plastic, step-down top, lower right front window dial over horizontal bars, left alarm clock, BC, AC **$25.00-30.00**

8F43, table, 1950, wood, upper front slanted slide rule dial, lower horizontal louvers, 2 knobs, BC, 4 tubes, battery **$30.00-35.00**

8K, console, 1936, wood, upper front rectangular dial, lower cloth grille with cut-outs, tuning eye, 4 knobs, BC, SW, 8 tubes, AC **$120.00-150.00**

8Q1, tombstone, 1940, wood, lower front slide rule dial, upper cloth grille, tuning eye, 4 knobs, BC, SW, 8 tubes, AC/DC **$75.00-85.00**

8Q2, table, 1940, wood, lower front slide rule dial, upper cloth grille, tuning eye, 2 knobs, BC, SW, 8 tubes, AC **$75.00-85.00**

8Q4, table, 1940, wood, center front slide rule dial, curved right & left cloth grilles with horizontal wrap-around bars, 4 knobs, BC, SW, 8 tubes, AC/DC..**$85.00-105.00**

8QB, tombstone, 1940, wood, upper front slide rule dial, lower cloth grille with center horizontal divider, 4 knobs, BC, SW, 8 tubes, AC/DC **$65.00-75.00**

8QBK, console, 1940, wood, upper front slide rule dial, lower cloth grille with 3 vertical bars, 4 knobs, BC, SW, 8 tubes, AC/DC.........**$120.00-150.00**

8QU5C, table-R/P, 1940, wood, lower front slide rule dial, upper cloth grille area, tuning eye, lift top, inner phono, 2 knobs, BC, SW, 8 tubes, AC **$35.00-45.00**

6-XF-9, table, 1956, plastic, center front dial panel, right & left checkered grilles, feet, 4 knobs, BC, FM, 8 tubes, AC, $40.00-45.00.

8QU5M, table-R/P, 1940, wood, lower front slide rule dial, upper cloth grille area, tuning eye, lift top, inner phono, 2 knobs, BC, SW, 8 tubes, AC **$35.00-45.00**

8R72, table, 1949, ivory plastic, recessed dial on top of case, large front cloth grille area, 4 knobs, BC, FM, 7 tubes, AC.............**$40.00-50.00**

8R74, table, 1949, mahogany plastic, recessed dial on top of case, large front cloth grille area, 4 knobs, BC, FM, 7 tubes, AC **$40.00-50.00**

8R75, table, 1949, walnut plastic, recessed dial on top of case, large front cloth grille area, 4 knobs, BC, FM, 7 tubes, AC **$40.00-50.00**

8R76, table, 1949, blonde plastic, recessed dial on top of case, large front cloth grille area, 4 knobs, BC, FM, 7 tubes, AC **$40.00-50.00**

8-RF-13, console on legs, 1958, wood, front slide rule dial overlaps cloth grille with horizontal bars, long legs, BC, FM, 13 tubes, AC.........**$35.00-40.00**

8T, tombstone, 1936, wood, lower front rectangular dial, upper cloth grille with cut-outs, tuning eye, 4 knobs, BC, SW, 8 tubes, AC **$170.00-190.00**

8T10, tombstone, 1936, black lacquer/chrome frame, center front dial, upper cloth grille with two vertical bars, chrome stand, 4 knobs, BC, SW, 8 tubes, AC...**$530.00-580.00**

8U, console-R/P, 1936, wood, upper front rectangular dial, lower cloth grille with 3 vertical bars, tuning eye, lift top, inner phono, 4 knobs, BC, SW, 8 tubes, AC **$120.00-150.00**

8V7, console-R/P, 1949, wood, inner right dial, left phono, 2 lift tops, lower front horizontal grille bars, 3 knobs, BC, 7 tubes, AC......**$65.00-75.00**

8V90, console-R/P, 1949, wood, inner right vertical slide rule dial, left phono, double doors, lower criss-cross grille, 4 knobs, BC, FM, 9 tubes, AC **$65.00-75.00**

8V111, console-R/P, 1949, wood, right tilt-out slide rule dial, left fold-down phono, 4 knobs, BC, FM, 11 tubes, AC **$65.00-75.00**

8V151, console-R/P, 1949, wood, right tilt-out dial, 8 push buttons, left fold-down phono, 6 knobs, BC, SW, FM, 15 tubes, AC ..**$65.00-75.00**

8X5D, table, 1957, black plastic, large right front round dial overlaps lattice grille area with upper left Nipper logo, feet, 2 knobs, BC, 5 tubes, AC/DC **$20.00-25.00**

8X5E, table, 1957, white plastic, large right front round dial overlaps lattice grille area with upper left Nipper logo, feet, 2 knobs, BC, 5 tubes, AC/DC **$20.00-25.00**

8X5F, table, 1957, pink plastic, large right front round dial overlaps lattice grille area with upper left Nipper logo, feet, 2 knobs, BC, 5 tubes, AC/DC **$20.00-25.00**

8X5H, table, 1957, green plastic, large right front round dial overlaps lattice grille area with upper left Nipper logo, feet, 2 knobs, BC, 5 tubes, AC/DC **$20.00-25.00**

8X6E, table, 1957, white plastic, large right front round dial overlaps lattice grille area with upper left Nipper logo, feet, 2 knobs, BC, 5 tubes, AC/DC **$20.00-25.00**

8X6F, table, 1957, pink plastic, large right front round dial overlaps lattice grille area with upper left Nipper logo, feet, 2 knobs, BC, 5 tubes, AC/DC **$20.00-25.00**

7-BX-8J "Globe Trotter," portable, 1957, plastic, upper front slide rule dial, lower horizontal grille bars, handle, top rotatable antenna bar, 2 knobs, BC, 5 tubes, AC/DC/battery, $30.00-35.00.

8X6J, table, 1957, gray plastic, large right front round dial overlaps grille area with upper left Nipper logo, feet, 2 knobs, BC, 5 tubes, AC/DC **$20.00-25.00**

8X6M, table, 1957, yellow plastic, large right front round dial overlaps lattice grille area with upper left Nipper logo, feet, 2 knobs, BC, 5 tubes, AC/DC **$20.00-25.00**

8X8N, table, plastic, lower front slide rule dial, upper 2- section lattice grille with twin speakers, feet, 2 knobs, BC...................**$20.00-25.00**

8X9J, table, 1954, plastic, lower front slide rule dial, large upper lattice grille area, 2 knobs, BC, AC/DC **$25.00-30.00**

8X51, table, 1957, maroon plastic, large right front round dial overlaps lattice grille area with upper left Nipper logo, feet, 2 knobs, BC, 5 tubes, AC/DC..**$20.00-25.00**

8X53, table, 1948, wood, upper front slanted slide rule dial, lower horizontal grille openings, 2 knobs, BC, 5 tubes, AC/DC **$40.00-50.00**

8X71, table, 1949, maroon plastic, upper front dotted slide rule dial overlaps horizontal grille bars, 3 knobs, BC, FM, 7 tubes, AC/DC ..**$40.00-45.00**

8X72, table, 1949, ivory plastic, upper front dotted slide rule dial overlaps horizontal grille bars, 3 knobs, BC, FM, 7 tubes, AC/DC..**$40.00-45.00**

8X522, table, 1948, ivory plastic, round dial on case top, front horizontal louvers, 2 knobs, BC, 5 tubes, AC/DC **$45.00-55.00**

7-BX-10 "Stra-toworld," portable, 1954, leather case, inner slide rule dial, flip-up front with map, telescoping antenna, 5 knobs, BC, SW, 5 tubes, AC/DC/battery, $85.00-115.00.

8-X-541, table, 1949, maroon plastic, center front round dial overlaps horizontal grille bars, decorative brass pointer/top strip, 2 knobs, BC, 5 tubes, AC/DC..**$35.00-45.00**

8-X-542, table, 1949, ivory plastic, center front round dial overlaps horizontal grille bars, decorative brass pointer/top strip, 2 knobs, BC, 5 tubes, AC/DC..**$35.00-45.00**

8-X-545, table, 1949, plastic, center front round dial overlaps horizontal grille bars, decorative brass pointer/top strip, 2 knobs, BC, 5 tubes, AC/DC **$45.00-50.00**

8-X-547, table, 1949, white plastic, center front round dial overlaps horizontal grille bars, decorative brass pointer/top strip, 2 knobs, BC, 5 tubes, AC/DC..**$35.00-45.00**

8X682, table, 1949, ivory plastic, center front large round dial with inner grille, 4 thumbwheel knobs, BC, SW, 6 tubes, AC/DC ..**$50.00-65.00**

9BX5, portable, 1948, leatherette & plastic, center front round dial overlaps perforated grille area, handle, 2 knobs, BC, 5 tubes, AC/DC/battery **$35.00-45.00**

9BX56, portable, 1949, plastic, upper front dial, lower textured panel, wire stand, 1 left & 1 right side knob, BC, 4 tubes, AC/DC/battery **$40.00-50.00**

9C7FE, table-C, plastic, lower front slide rule dial, large upper right alarm clock over horizontal grille bars, feet, BC, AC **$25.00-30.00**

9K2, console, 1936, wood, upper front dial, lower cloth grille with horizontal & vertical bars, tuning eye, 5 knobs, BC, SW, 9 tubes, AC **$120.00-150.00**

9Q1, table, 1940, wood, top recessed slide rule dial, front grille area, 3 knobs, BC, SW, 9 tubes, AC **$40.00-50.00**

9Q4, table, 1940, wood, top recessed slide rule dial, front grille area, 3 knobs, BC, SW, 9 tubes, AC **$40.00-50.00**

7T1, tombstone, 1936, wood, center front rectangular dial, upper cloth grille with vertical bars, tuning eye, 4 knobs, BC, SW, 7 tubes, AC, $150.00-160.00.

8BX6 "Globe Trotter," portable, 1948, aluminum & plastic, upper front slide rule dial, lower horizontal grille bars, handle, 2 thumbwheel knobs, BC, 6 tubes, AC/DC/battery, $40.00-50.00.

9QK, console, 1940, wood, top recessed slide rule dial, front cloth grille with 2 vertical bars, 3 knobs, BC, SW, 9 tubes, AC ..**$110.00-130.00**

9SX1 "Little Nipper," table, 1939, walnut plastic, Deco, right front round dial, left horizontal louvers, 2 ivory knobs, BC, SW, 5 tubes, AC/DC **$160.00-190.00**

9SX2 "Little Nipper," table, 1939, walnut/ivory plastic, Deco, right front round dial, left horizontal louvers, 2 walnut knobs, BC, SW, 5 tubes, AC/DC **$200.00-230.00**

9SX3 "Little Nipper," table, 1939, ivory plastic, Deco, right front round dial, left horizontal louvers, 2 red knobs, BC, SW, 5 tubes, AC/DC **$200.00-230.00**

9SX4 "Little Nipper," table, 1939, red/ivory plastic, Deco, right front round dial, left horizontal louvers, 2 red knobs, BC, SW, 5 tubes, AC/DC **$350.00-380.00**

9SX5 "Little Nipper," table, 1939, black/marble plastic, Deco, right front round dial, left horizontal louvers, 2 jet knobs, BC, SW, 5 tubes, AC/DC **$380.00-410.00**

9SX6 "Little Nipper," table, 1939, blue/onyx plastic, Deco, right front round dial, left horizontal louvers, 2 blue knobs, BC, SW, 5 tubes, AC/DC **$410.00-430.00**

9SX7 "Little Nipper," table, 1939, onyx plastic, Deco, right front round dial, left horizontal louvers, 2 maroon knobs, BC, SW, 5 tubes, AC/DC **$380.00-410.00**

8K1, console, 1936, wood, upper front rectangular dial, lower cloth grille with vertical bars, tuning eye, 4 knobs, BC, SW, 8 tubes, AC, $120.00-150.00.

9T, tombstone, 1935, wood, lower front dial, upper cloth grille with vertical bars, tuning eye, 5 knobs, BC, SW, 9 tubes, AC ..**$170.00-190.00**

9TX1, table, 1938, walnut plastic, right front dial (knob), left horizontal wrap-around louvers, 2 knobs, BC, 5 tubes, AC/DC......**$45.00-55.00**

9TX2, table, 1938, ivory plastic, right front dial (knob), left horizontal wrap-around louvers, 2 knobs, BC, 5 tubes, AC/DC......**$45.00-55.00**

9TX3, table, 1938, two-tone wood, right front dial (knob), left horizontal wrap-around louvers, 2 knobs, BC, 5 tubes, AC/DC......**$45.00-55.00**

9TX4, table, 1938, Catalin, right front dial (knob), left horizontal wrap-around louvers, 2 knobs, BC, 5 tubes, AC/DC ....**$850.00+**

9TX21, table, 1939, walnut plastic, right front dial, left horizontal grille bars, 2 tan knobs, BC, 5 tubes, AC/DC........................**$45.00-55.00**

9TX22, table, 1939, ivory plastic, right front dial, left horizontal grille bars, 2 knobs, BC, 5 tubes, AC/DC **$45.00-55.00**

9TX23 "Little Nipper," table, 1939, wood, Deco, right front dial with thermometer-type tuning, left grille area, 2 knobs, BC, 5 tubes, AC/DC **$75.00-95.00**

9TX31 "Little Nipper," table, 1939, walnut plastic, right front dial, left horizontal wrap-around grille bars, 2 tan knobs, BC, 5 tubes, AC/DC **$65.00-75.00**

9TX32 "Little Nipper," table, 1939, ivory plastic, right front dial, left horizontal wrap-around grille bars, 2 knobs, BC, 5 tubes, AC/DC..**$65.00-75.00**

9TX33 "Little Nipper," table, 1939, wood, Deco, right front vertical "V" dial, left grille area, 2 knobs, BC, 5 tubes, AC/DC..........**$75.00-85.00**

9TX50, table, 1939, wood, off center front dial panel with thermometer-type tuning overlaps horizontal grille bars, handle, 2 knobs, BC, 5 tubes, AC/DC **$55.00-65.00**

9U, console-R/P, 1936, wood, center front dial, lower cloth grille with horizontal & vertical bars, tuning eye, lift top, inner phono, 5 knobs, BC, SW, LW, 9 tubes, AC **$140.00-160.00**

8R71, table, 1949, maroon plastic, recessed dial on top of case, large front cloth grille area, 4 knobs, BC, FM, 7 tubes, AC, $40.00-50.00.

9W101, console-R/P, 1949, wood, inner right slide rule dial, inner left pull-out phono drawer, storage, doors, lower grille, 4 knobs, BC, FM, 10 tubes, AC **$65.00-75.00**

9W103, console-R/P, 1949, wood, inner right slide rule dial, inner left pull-out phono drawer, storage, doors, lower grille, 4 knobs, BC, FM, 10 tubes, AC **$65.00-75.00**

9W106, console-R/P, 1950, wood, inner right slide rule dial, left pull-out phono drawer, lower grille & storage, doors, 3 knobs, BC, FM, 10 tubes, AC **$65.00-75.00**

9X6, table, 1938, wood, right front dial, left cloth grille with horizontal cut-outs, 2 right side knobs, BC, 4 tubes, AC/DC...............**$35.00-45.00**

9-X-10FE, table, 1958, pink plastic, lower front slide rule dial, large upper lattice grille area with Nipper logo, wire swivel base, twin speakers, 2 knobs, BC, 5 tubes, AC/DC..**$30.00-35.00**

9-X-10JE, table, 1958, gray plastic, lower front slide rule dial, large upper lattice grille area with Nipper logo, wire swivel base, twin speakers, 2 knobs, BC, 5 tubes, AC/DC..**$30.00-35.00**

9-X-10ME, table, 1958, maple sugar plastic, lower front slide rule dial, large upper lattice grille area with Nipper logo, wire swivel base, twin speakers, 2 knobs, BC, 5 tubes, AC/DC **$30.00-35.00**

9X11, table, 1938, Catalin-green, right front dial, left cloth grille with "W" cut-out, 2 right side knobs, BC, 4 tubes, AC/DC ....**$1,000.00+**

9X12, table, 1938, Catalin-black, right front dial, left cloth grille with "W" cut-out, 2 right side knobs, BC, 4 tubes, AC/DC ....**$1,000.00+**

9X13, table, 1938, Catalin-ivory, right front dial, left cloth grille with "W" cut-out, 2 right side knobs, BC, 4 tubes, AC/DC ....**$1,000.00+**

9X14, table, 1938, Catalin-brown, right front dial, left cloth grille with "W" cut-out, 2 right side knobs, BC, 4 tubes, AC/DC ....**$1,000.00+**

9X562, table, 1950, ivory plastic, lower front narrow slide rule dial, upper concentric circular grille bars, 1 left & 1 right side knob, BC, 5 tubes, AC/DC **$40.00-50.00**

9X571, table, 1950, maroon plastic, lower front narrow slide rule dial, upper "bull-horn" louvers, 1 right & 2 left side knobs, BC, 5 tubes, AC/DC **$55.00-65.00**

9X572, table, 1949, ivory plastic, lower front narrow slide rule dial, upper "bull-horn" louvers, 1 right & 2 left side knobs, BC, 5 tubes, AC/DC **$55.00-65.00**

9X641, table, 1950, maroon plastic, upper front slanted slide rule dial, lower horizontal grille bars, 2 knobs, BC, 6 tubes, AC/DC **$40.00-50.00**

9X642, table, 1950, ivory plastic, upper front slanted slide rule dial, lower horizontal grille bars, 2 knobs, BC, 6 tubes, AC/DC **$40.00-50.00**

9X651, table, 1950, brown plastic, upper front slanted slide rule dial, lower horizontal louvers, 3 knobs, BC, SW, 6 tubes, AC/DC **$40.00-50.00**

9X652, table, 1950, ivory plastic, upper front slanted slide rule dial, lower horizontal louvers, 3 knobs, BC, SW, 6 tubes, AC/DC ..**$40.00-50.00**

9Y51, table-R/P, 1950, plastic, upper front slide rule dial, lower horizontal grille bars, 3/4 lift top, inner 45 RPM phono, 2 side knobs, BC, 5 tubes, AC **$40.00-50.00**

8X8J, table, plastic, lower front slide rule dial, upper 2- section lattice grille with twin speakers, feet, 2 knobs, BC, $20.00-25.00.

9Y510, table-R/P, 1951, plastic, upper front slide rule dial, lower horizontal grille bars, 3/4 lift top, inner 45 RPM phono, 2 knobs, BC, 5 tubes, AC **$40.00-50.00**

10K, console, 1936, wood, upper front dial, lower cloth grille with cutouts, tuning eye, 5 knobs, BC, SW, 10 tubes, AC **$140.00-150.00**

10Q1, tombstone, 1940, wood, lower front slide rule dial, upper cloth grille with vertical wrap-over bars, tuning eye, 4 knobs, BC, SW, 10 tubes, AC **$85.00-115.00**

10T, tombstone, 1936, wood, center front dial, upper cloth grille with 2 vertical bars, tuning eye, 5 knobs, BC, SW, 10 tubes, AC **$150.00-180.00**

10T11, tombstone, 1937, black lacquer with chrome supports, center front dial, upper cloth grille with 2 vertical bars, tuning eye, chrome stand, 5 knobs, BC, SW, LW, 10 tubes, AC **$550.00-610.00**

10X "Little Nipper," table, 1940, plastic, upper front slide rule dial, lower horizontal grille bars, 2 knobs, BC, 5 tubes, AC/DC **$40.00-50.00**

11Q4, tombstone, 1938, wood, upper front curved slide rule dial, lower rectangular grille with horizontal bars, tuning eye, motorized pushbutton tuning, 4 knobs, BC, SW, 11 tubes, AC **$220.00-260.00**

11QK, console, 1938, wood, upper front curved slide rule dial, lower cloth "shield-like" grille with vertical bars, tuning eye, motorized pushbutton tuning, 4 knobs, BC, SW, 11 tubes, AC ..**$150.00-170.00**

11QU, console-R/P, 1938, wood, ornate grain, enclosed slide rule dial and knobs, lower cloth grille with vertical bars, tuning eye, motorized pushbutton tuning, 4 knobs, BC, SW, 11 tubes, AC ..**$220.00-260.00**

11X1, table, 1940, plastic, upper front slide rule dial, lower horizontal grille bars, 2 knobs, BC, 5 tubes, AC/DC **$40.00-50.00**

8X521, table, 1948, maroon plastic, round dial on case top, front horizontal louvers, 2 knobs, BC, 5 tubes, AC/DC, $45.00-55.00.

12Q4, tombstone, 1938, wood, ornate grain, upper front curved slide rule dial, lower cloth grille with center vertical bars, tuning eye, two chassis, 5 knobs, BC, SW, 12 tubes, AC & DC versions ..**$220.00-260.00**

12QK, console, 1938, wood, upper front curved slide rule dial, lower cloth grille with center vertical bars, tuning eye, two chassis, 5 knobs, BC, SW, 12 tubes, AC & DC versions **$150.00-170.00**

12QU, console-R/P, 1938, wood, ornate grain, enclosed slide rule dial and knobs, lower cloth grille with vertical bars, tuning eye, two chassis, 5 knobs, BC, SW, 12 tubes, AC **$220.00-260.00**

12X, table, 1942, brown plastic, upper front slide rule dial, lower horizontal grille bars, 2 knobs, BC, 5 tubes, AC/DC **$40.00-50.00**

12X2, table, 1942, antique ivory plastic, upper front slide rule dial, lower horizontal grille bars, 2 knobs, BC, 5 tubes, AC/DC **$40.00-50.00**

13K, console, 1936, wood, upper front dial, lower cloth grille with center vertical bars, tuning eye, 5 knobs, BC, SW, LW, 13 tubes, AC **$180.00-200.00**

14AX, table, 1941, walnut plastic, upper front slide rule dial, lower horizontal grille bars, 2 knobs, BC, SW, 5 tubes, AC/DC **$40.00-50.00**

14AX2, table, 1941, ivory plastic, upper front slide rule dial, lower horizontal grille bars, 2 knobs, BC, SW, 5 tubes, AC/DC **$40.00-50.00**

14BK, console, 1940, wood, upper front dial, lower cloth grille with 3 vertical bars, 3 knobs, BC, 4 tubes, battery **$65.00-75.00**

14BT1, table, 1940, plastic, right front dial, left vertical grille bars, 3 knobs, BC, 4 tubes, battery...**$35.00-40.00**

14BT2, table, 1940, wood, right front dial, left horizontal louvers, 3 knobs, BC, 4 tubes, battery **$35.00-40.00**

14X, table, 1941, walnut plastic, upper front slanted slide rule dial, lower horizontal louvers, 2 knobs, BC, SW, 5 tubes, AC/DC ..**$40.00-50.00**

14X2, table, 1941, ivory plastic, upper front slanted slide rule dial, lower horizontal louvers, 2 knobs, BC, SW, 5 tubes, AC/DC ..**$40.00-50.00**

15BP-1 "Pick-Me-Up," portable, 1940, walnut plastic, right front dial, left vertical grille bars, optional carrying case, 3 knobs, BC, 5 tubes, AC/DC/battery **$40.00-50.00**

8X681, table, 1949, maroon plastic, center front large round dial with inner grille, 4 thumbwheel knobs, BC, SW, 6 tubes, AC/DC, $50.00-65.00.

9K, console, 1936, wood, upper front dial, lower cloth grille with horizontal & vertical bars, tuning eye, 5 knobs, BC, SW, LW, 9 tubes, AC, $110.00-130.00.

15BP-2 "Pick-Me-Up," portable, 1940, brown cloth covered, right front dial, left grille area, handle, 3 knobs, BC, 5 tubes, AC/DC/battery $30.00-35.00

15BP-3, portable, 1940, gray cloth covered, right front dial, left grille area, handle, 3 knobs, BC, 5 tubes, AC/DC/battery $30.00-35.00

15BP-4, portable, 1940, brown leatherette, right front dial, left grille area, handle, 3 knobs, BC, 5 tubes, AC/DC/battery...............$30.00-35.00

15BP-5, portable, 1940, blue leatherette, right front dial, left grille area, handle, 3 knobs, BC, 5 tubes, AC/DC/battery...............$30.00-35.00

15BP-6, portable, 1940, wood, right front dial, left horizontal grille bars, handle, optional carrying case, 3 knobs, BC, 5 tubes, AC/DC/battery $40.00-45.00

15BT, table, 1940, wood, right front slide rule dial overlaps horizontal bars, 4 knobs, BC, SW, 5 tubes, battery $35.00-40.00

16K, console, 1940, wood, upper front slide rule dial, lower cloth grille with 3 vertical bars, pushbuttons, 4 knobs, BC, SW, 6 tubes, AC $110.00-130.00

16T2, table, 1940, wood, right front slide rule dial over horizontal bars, 4 knobs, BC, SW, 6 tubes, AC $50.00-65.00

9K1, console, 1936, wood, upper front dial, lower cloth grille with vertical bars, tuning eye, 4 knobs, BC, SW, 9 tubes, AC, $120.00-150.00.

16T3, table, 1940, wood, right front slide rule dial panel overlaps horizontal bars, 5 pushbuttons, 4 knobs, BC, SW, 6 tubes, AC..**$55.00-65.00**

16X1, table, 1941, mahogany plastic, upper front slanted dial, lower horizontal grille bars, 3 knobs, BC, 6 tubes, AC/DC **$40.00-50.00**

16X2, table, 1941, ivory plastic, upper front slanted dial, lower horizontal grille bars, 3 knobs, BC, 6 tubes, AC/DC **$40.00-50.00**

16X3, table, 1941, wood, upper front slanted dial, lower horizontal louvers, 3 knobs, BC, 6 tubes, AC/DC **$40.00-50.00**

16X4, table, 1941, two-tone wood, upper front dial, lower grille area, pushbuttons, 3 knobs, BC, 6 tubes, AC/DC **$40.00-50.00**

16X11, table, 1940, plastic, upper front slanted slide rule dial, lower horizontal grille bars, 3 knobs, BC, SW, 6 tubes, AC/DC **$40.00-45.00**

16X13, table, 1940, wood, upper front slanted slide rule dial, lower horizontal louvers, 3 knobs, BC, SW, 6 tubes, AC/DC **$45.00-55.00**

16X14, table, 1940, wood, upper front slanted slide rule dial, lower horizontal grille bars, pushbuttons, 3 knobs, BC, 6 tubes, AC/DC **$50.00-65.00**

19K, console, 1940, walnut, upper front oblong slide rule dial, lower vertical grille bars, 6 pushbuttons, 4 knobs, BC, SW, 9 tubes, AC **$110.00-130.00**

24BT-1, table, 1940, plastic, right front dial, left vertical grille bars, 2 knobs, BC, 4 tubes, battery..**$35.00-40.00**

24BT-2, table, 1940, wood, right front dial overlaps horizontal bars, 2 knobs, BC, 4 tubes, battery..**$35.00-40.00**

25BK, console, 1940, wood, upper front slide rule dial, lower cloth grille with vertical bars, 4 knobs, BC, SW, 5 tubes, battery **$65.00-75.00**

25BP "Pick-Me-Up," portable, 1941, two-tone leatherette, right front dial, left horizontal louvers, handle, 3 knobs, BC, 5 tubes, AC/DC/battery **$30.00-35.00**

9K3, console, 1936, wood, upper front dial, lower cloth grille with center divider, tuning eye, 5 knobs, BC, SW, 9 tubes, AC, $110.00-130.00.

25BT-2, table, 1942, wood, right front slide rule dial, left horizontal grille bars, 3 knobs, BC, 5 tubes, battery................................**$35.00-40.00**

25BT-3, table, 1940, wood, right front slide rule dial, left vertical grille bars, 4 knobs, BC, SW, 5 tubes, battery **$40.00-45.00**

25X, table, 1942, wood, right front dial overlaps horizontal bars, 2 knobs, BC, 5 tubes, AC/DC..**$40.00-50.00**

26X-1, table, 1941, plastic, upper front slanted slide rule dial, lower horizontal louvers, 3 knobs, BC, SW, 6 tubes, AC/DC **$40.00-50.00**

26X-3, table, 1941, upper front slanted slide rule dial, lower horizontal louvers, 3 knobs, BC, SW, 6 tubes, AC/DC...................**$40.00-50.00**

26X4, table, 1941, wood, upper front slanted slide rule dial, lower horizontal louvers, pushbuttons, 3 knobs, BC, SW, 6 tubes, AC/DC..**$50.00-65.00**

27K, console, 1942, wood, upper front slide rule dial, lower cloth grille with center vertical bar, pushbuttons, 4 knobs, BC, SW, 7 tubes, AC **$110.00-130.00**

28X5, table, 1941, wood, upper front slanted slide rule dial, lower horizontal louvers, 5 pushbuttons, 4 knobs, BC, SW, 8 tubes, AC/DC..**$50.00-65.00**

29K, console, 1941, wood, upper front slanted slide rule dial, lower vertical grille bars, pushbuttons, 4 knobs, BC, SW, 9 tubes, AC ..**$110.00-130.00**

29K2, console, 1941, wood, raised top, upper front slanted slide rule dial, lower vertical grille bars, pushbuttons, 4 knobs, BC, SW, 9 tubes, AC **$120.00-150.00**

34X, table, 1942, wood, upper front slanted slide rule dial, lower horizontal grille bars, 2 knobs, BC, SW, 5 tubes, AC/DC **$40.00-50.00**

36X, table, 1941, wood, upper front slanted slide rule dial, lower horizontal wrap-around louvers, 3 knobs, BC, 6 tubes, AC/DC **$40.00-50.00**

40X30 "Little Nipper," table, 1939, walnut plastic, right front dial, left horizontal wrap-around louvers, 2 knobs, BC, 5 tubes, AC/DC **$50.00-65.00**

40X31 "Little Nipper," table, 1939, ivory plastic, right front dial, left horizontal wrap-around louvers, 2 knobs, BC, 5 tubes, AC/DC **$50.00-65.00**

40X50 "Modern Blonde," table, 1939, wood, right front dial, left 3-section cloth grille, handle, feet, 2 knobs, BC, 5 tubes, AC/DC ..**$45.00-55.00**

40X52, table, 1939, ivory finish, right front dial, left horizontal louvers, handle, 2 knobs, BC, 5 tubes, AC/DC.....................**$45.00-55.00**

40X54 "Treasure Chest," table, 1939, wood, nautical-type, right front dial, left "ship's wheel" grille, side rope handles, 2 knobs, BC, 5 tubes, AC/DC.................................**$180.00-200.00**

40X55, table, 1939, wood, right front dial, left grille with horizontal bars, handle, 2 knobs, BC, 5 tubes, AC/DC **$45.00-55.00**

9SX8 "Little Nipper," table, 1939, marble plastic, Deco, right front round dial, left horizontal louvers, 2 jet knobs, BC, SW, 5 tubes, AC/DC, $410.00-460.00.

40X57 "San Francisco Expo," table, 1939, Repwood, Golden Gate Bridge pressed into front, right dial, left grille, handle, 2 knobs, BC, 5 tubes, AC/DC **$900.00-1,000.00**

45-E, side table/bookcase, 1940, maple finish wood, upper front vertical slide rule dial, right & left horizontal bars, lower 2-shelf book case, 2 knobs, BC, 5 tubes, AC/DC.............................**$55.00-65.00**

45-EM, side table/bookcase, 1940, mahogany finish wood, upper front vertical slide rule dial, right & left horizontal bars, lower 2-shelf book case, 2 knobs, BC, 5 tubes, AC/DC **$55.00-65.00**

45-EW, side table/bookcase, 1940, walnut finish wood, upper front vertical slide rule dial, right & left horizontal bars, lower 2-shelf book case, 2 knobs, BC, 5 tubes, AC/DC **$55.00-65.00**

45-W-10, console-R/P, 1951, wood, inner right pull-out drawer with slide rule dial & phono, left storage, 5 knobs, BC, FM, 10 tubes, AC **$50.00-65.00**

45X1, table, 1940, brown plastic, right front dial, left horizontal wrap-around louvers, 2 knobs, BC, 5 tubes, AC/DC **$55.00-65.00**

45X3, table, 1940, wood, right front dial, left grille area, 2 knobs, BC, 5 tubes, AC/DC..**$40.00-50.00**

45X4, table, 1940, wood, right front dial, left horizontal grille bars, 2 knobs, BC, 5 tubes, AC/DC...**$45.00-55.00**

45X5, table, 1940, walnut plastic, right front dial, left horizontal wrap-around grille bars, 2 knobs, BC, 5 tubes, AC/DC **$50.00-65.00**

45X6, table, 1940, ivory plastic, right front dial, left horizontal wrap-around grille bars, 2 knobs, BC, 5 tubes, AC/DC **$50.00-65.00**

45X11, table, 1940, brown plastic, right front dial, left vertical grille bars, 2 knobs, BC, 5 tubes, AC/DC...**$50.00-65.00**

45X12, table, 1940, ivory plastic, right front dial, left vertical grille bars, 2 knobs, BC, 5 tubes, AC/DC...**$50.00-65.00**

45X13, table, 1940, two-tone wood, right front dial, left horizontal louvers, 2 knobs, BC, 5 tubes, AC/DC **$45.00-55.00**

45X17, table, 1940, wood, right front dial, left vertical grille bars, 2 knobs, BC, 5 tubes, AC/DC..**$45.00-55.00**

9X561, table, 1950, maroon plastic, lower front narrow slide rule dial, upper concentric circular grille bars, 1 left & 1 right side knob, BC, 5 tubes, AC/DC, $40.00-50.00.

45X111, table, 1940, mahogany plastic, right front dial, left vertical grille bars, 2 knobs, BC, 5 tubes, AC/DC **$50.00-65.00**

45X112, table, 1940, ivory plastic, right front dial, left vertical grille bars, 2 knobs, BC, 5 tubes, AC/DC...................................**$50.00-65.00**

45X113, table, 1940, wood, right front dial, left horizontal louvers, 2 knobs, BC, 5 tubes, AC/DC....................................**$45.00-55.00**

46X1, table, 1940, mahogany plastic, right front dial, left vertical grille bars, 2 knobs, BC, 6 tubes including ballast, AC/DC **$50.00-65.00**

46X2, table, 1940, ivory plastic, right front dial, left vertical grille bars, 2 knobs, BC, 6 tubes including ballast, AC/DC **$50.00-65.00**

46X3, table, 1939, two-tone wood, right front dial, left horizontal louvers, 2 knobs, BC, 6 tubes including ballast, AC/DC **$45.00-55.00**

46X11, table, 1940, mahogany plastic, right front dial, left vertical grille bars, 3 knobs, BC, SW, 5 tubes, AC/DC **$50.00-65.00**

46X12, table, 1939, ivory plastic, right front dial, left vertical grille bars, 3 knobs, BC, SW, 5 tubes, AC/DC **$50.00-65.00**

46X13, table, 1940, wood, right front dial, left square grille area, 3 knobs, BC, SW, 5 tubes, AC/DC **$45.00-55.00**

46X21, table, 1940, walnut plastic, right front dial, left vertical grille bars, 3 knobs, BC, 5 tubes, AC/DC **$45.00-55.00**

46X24, table, 1940, walnut, right front dial, left grille area, pushbuttons, 3 knobs, BC, SW, 6 tubes including ballast, AC/DC **$55.00-65.00**

54B1, portable, 1946, inner round dial, perforated grille, thumbwheel knob, flip open lid, handle, BC, 4 tubes, battery **$40.00-50.00**

54B2, portable, 1946, inner round dial, perforated chrome grille, thumbwheel knob, flip open lid, handle, BC, 4 tubes, battery ..**$40.00-50.00**

54B3, portable, 1946, inner round dial, perforated chrome grille, thumbwheel knob, flip open lid, handle, BC, 4 tubes, battery ..**$40.00-50.00**

54B5, portable, 1947, plastic, left front round dial, right horizontal wrap-around louvers, handle, 2 knobs, BC, 4 tubes, battery ..**$40.00-50.00**

55F, table, 1946, wood, right front slide rule dial, left horizontal louvers, 3 knobs, BC, 5 tubes, battery **$35.00-40.00**

55U, table-R/P, 1946, wood, upper front slide rule dial, lower horizontal louvers, lift top, inner phono, 2 knobs, BC, 5 tubes, AC..**$35.00-40.00**

56X, table, 1946, walnut plastic, upper front dial with red dot pointer, lower horizontal louvers, 3 knobs, BC, 6 tubes, AC/DC ..**$40.00-50.00**

56X2, table, 1946, ivory plastic, upper front dial with red dot pointer, lower horizontal louvers, 3 knobs, BC, 6 tubes, AC/DC **$40.00-50.00**

9Y7, table-R/P, 1949, wood, upper front slide rule dial, lower horizontal grille bars, 3/4 lift top, inner 45 RPM phono, 2 knobs, BC, 6 tubes, AC, $35.00-40.00.

15K, console, 1936, wood, upper front dial, lower cloth grille with center vertical divider, tuning eye, 5 knobs, BC, SW, LW, 15 tubes, AC, $180.00-200.00.

56X3, table, 1946, two-tone wood, upper front slanted slide rule dial, lower horizontal louvers, 3 knobs, BC, 6 tubes, AC/DC ..**$40.00-50.00**

56X10, table, 1946, plastic, upper front slanted slide rule dial, lower horizontal louvers, 3 knobs, BC, SW, 6 tubes, AC/DC **$40.00-50.00**

56X11, table, 1946, plastic, upper front slanted slide rule dial, lower horizontal louvers, 3 knobs, BC, SW, 6 tubes, AC/DC **$40.00-50.00**

58AV, console-R/P, 1946, wood, inner right slide rule dial, 6 pushbuttons, left phono, lift top, 4 knobs, BC, SW, 8 tubes, AC **$50.00-65.00**

59AV1, console-R/P, 1946, wood, inner right slide rule dial, 6 pushbuttons, door, left pull-out phono, 6 knobs, BC, SW, 9 tubes, AC **$65.00-75.00**

61-8, table, 1948, brown plastic, upper front slanted slide rule dial, lower horizontal wrap-around louvers, 2 knobs, BC, 5 tubes, AC/DC **$45.00-55.00**

61-9, table, 1948, ivory plastic, upper front slanted slide rule dial, lower horizontal wrap-around louvers, 2 knobs, BC, 5 tubes, AC/DC **$45.00-55.00**

64F3, table, 1946, wood, burl graining, upper front slanted slide rule dial, lower horizontal louvers, 2 knobs, BC, 4 tubes, battery ..**$35.00-45.00**

65AU, table-R/P, 1947, wood, upper front slide rule dial, lower horizontal louvers, lift top, inner phono, 2 knobs, BC, 5 tubes, AC..**$35.00-40.00**

15X, table, 1940, mahogany plastic, upper front slanted dial with red dot pointer, lower horizontal louvers, 3 knobs, BC, 6 tubes, AC/DC, $40.00-50.00.

65BR9, portable, 1947, leatherette, center front round dial, lower horizontal grille bars, handle, built-in battery charger, 2 knobs, BC, 5 tubes, AC/battery **$40.00-50.00**

65F, table, 1948, wood, right front slide rule dial, left horizontal louvers, 3 knobs, BC, 5 tubes, battery **$35.00-40.00**

65U, table-R/P, 1947, wood, upper front slide rule dial, lower horizontal louvers, lift top, inner phono, 2 knobs, BC, 5 tubes, AC..**$35.00-40.00**

65X2, table, 1946, plastic, upper front slanted slide rule dial, lower horizontal louvers, 2 knobs, BC, 5 tubes, AC/DC **$40.00-45.00**

66BX "Globe Trotter," portable, 1946, aluminum/plastic, upper front flip-up dial lid, lower horizontal grille bars, handle, 2 knobs, BC, 6 tubes, AC/DC/battery **$40.00-50.00**

66X1, table, 1946, brown plastic, upper front curved slide rule dial, lower cloth grille, rear hand-hold, 3 knobs, BC, SW, 6 tubes, AC/DC...**$45.00-55.00**

66X3, table, 1946, two-tone wood, upper front curved slide rule dial, lower "zebra" cloth grille, 3 knobs, BC, SW, 6 tubes, AC/DC ..**$50.00-65.00**

66X4, table, 1946, wood, upper front curved slide rule dial, lower horizontal grille bars, 3 knobs, BC, SW, 6 tubes, AC/DC **$50.00-65.00**

66X7, table, 1946, dark blue Catalin, upper front curved slide rule dial, lower horizontal grille bars, 3 knobs, BC, SW, 6 tubes, AC/DC...**$550.00+**

66X9, table, 1946, green swirl Catalin, upper front curved slide rule dial, lower horizontal grille bars, 3 knobs, BC, SW, 6 tubes, AC/DC ....**$550.00+**

66X11, table, 1947, brown plastic, upper front slanted slide rule dial, lower concentric rectangular grille cut-outs, 3 knobs, BC, 6 tubes, AC/DC **$45.00-55.00**

66X12, table, 1947, ivory plastic, upper front slanted slide rule dial, lower concentric rectangular grille cut-outs, 3 knobs, BC, 6 tubes, AC/DC **$45.00-55.00**

16T4, table, 1940, wood, right front slide rule dial, left curved grille with horizontal bars, 5 pushbuttons, 4 knobs, BC, SW, 6 tubes, AC, $75.00-85.00.

66X14, table, 1948, blonde wood, upper front slanted slide rule dial, lower horizontal louvers, brass trim, 3 knobs, BC, 6 tubes, AC/DC..**$40.00-50.00**

66X15, table, 1948, mahogany wood, upper front slanted slide rule dial, lower horizontal louvers, brass trim, 3 knobs, BC, 6 tubes, AC/DC **$40.00-50.00**

67AV1, console-R/P, 1946, wood, dial & in right tilt-out drawer, left lift top, inner phono, 4 knobs, BC, SW, 7 tubes, AC **$75.00-85.00**

68R1, table, 1947, brown plastic, lower front slide rule dial, upper vertical grille bars, 4 knobs, BC, FM, 8 tubes, AC **$40.00-50.00**

68R2, table, 1947, ivory plastic, lower front slide rule dial, upper vertical grille bars, 4 knobs, BC, FM, 8 tubes, AC **$40.00-50.00**

68R3, table, 1946, wood, lower front slide rule dial, large upper grille area, 4 knobs, BC, FM, 8 tubes, AC **$40.00-45.00**

68R4, table, 1946, wood, lower front slide rule dial, upper vertical grille bars, 4 knobs, BC, FM, 8 tubes, AC **$40.00-50.00**

75X11, table, 1948, maroon plastic & brass, right front dial, left cloth grille with vertical bars, 2 knobs, BC, 5 tubes, AC/DC...........**$65.00-85.00**

75X12, table, 1948, ivory plastic & brass, right front dial, left cloth grille with vertical bars, 2 knobs, BC, 5 tubes, AC/DC...........**$65.00-85.00**

75X14, table, 1948, mahogany plastic & brass, right front dial, left cloth grille with vertical bars, 2 knobs, BC, 5 tubes, AC/DC ..**$65.00-85.00**

75X15, table, 1948, walnut plastic & brass, right front dial, left cloth grille with vertical bars, 2 knobs, BC, 5 tubes, AC/DC...........**$65.00-85.00**

75X16, table, 1948, blonde plastic & brass, right front dial, left cloth grille with vertical bars, 2 knobs, BC, 5 tubes, AC/DC............**$65.00-85.00**

75X17, table, 1948, lacquered cabinet with oriental designs, right front dial, left vertical grille bars, brass trim, 2 knobs, BC, 5 tubes, AC/DC **$150.00-180.00**

75ZU, table-R/P, 1949, upper front dial, lower horizontal grille bars, lift top, inner phono, 2 knobs, BC, 5 tubes, AC **$30.00-35.00**

76ZX11, table, 1948, walnut plastic, upper front slanted slide rule dial, lower horizontal wrap-around bars, 2 knobs, BC, 6 tubes, AC/DC **$45.00-55.00**

76ZX12, table, 1948, ivory plastic, upper front slanted slide rule dial, lower horizontal wrap-around bars, 2 knobs, BC, 6 tubes, AC/DC **$45.00-55.00**

77U, table-R/P, 1948, wood, upper front slide rule dial, lower horizontal louvers, lift top, inner phono, 2 knobs, BC, 6 tubes, AC..**$35.00-40.00**

77V1, console-R/P, 1948, wood, inner right slide rule dial, left phono, lift top, 3 knobs, BC, 7 tubes, AC **$50.00-65.00**

77V2, console-R/P, 1948, wood, right front tilt-out slide rule dial, left lift top, inner phono, 4 knobs, BC, SW, 7 tubes, AC **$50.00-65.00**

79-10, tombstone, wood, lower front round dial, upper cloth grille with vertical bars, tuning eye, 5 knobs **$150.00-170.00**

84BT, tombstone, 1937, wood, rounded top, lower front dial, cloth grille with cut-outs, 2 knobs, BC, 4 tubes, battery.................**$75.00-95.00**

84BT6, tombstone, 1937, wood, rounded top, lower front dial, cloth grille with cut-outs, 2 knobs, BC, 4 tubes, 6VDC...................**$75.00-95.00**

85BK, console, 1937, wood, upper square pointer dial, lower ornate grille cloth with center vertical bar, 3 knobs, BC, SW, 5 tubes, battery **$95.00-115.00**

17K, console, 1940, wood, upper front oblong slide rule dial, lower cloth grille with vertical bars, pushbuttons, 4 knobs, BC, SW, 7 tubes, AC, $85.00-115.00.

85BT, tombstone, 1937, wood, lower square pointer dial, upper grille area with cut-outs, 3 knobs, BC, SW, 5 tubes, battery..........**$85.00-105.00**

85BT6, table, 1937, wood, right front dial, left grille with center horizontal cut-outs, horizontal trim, 3 knobs, BC, SW, 5 tubes, 6VDC ..**$45.00-55.00**

85E, chairside, 1937, walnut finish, Deco, top square dial, front grille with horizontal bars, storage, 3 knobs, BC, SW, 5 tubes, AC **$150.00-180.00**

85K, console, 1937, wood, upper center dial, lower grille with center vertical bar, tiered upper front corners, 3 knobs, BC, SW, 5 tubes, AC **$85.00-105.00**

85T, table, 1936, wood, right front square dial, left cloth grille with 2 horizontal bars, 3 knobs, BC, 5 tubes, AC..........................**$45.00-55.00**

85T5, tombstone, 1937, wood, lower rectangular dial, upper grille with two horizontal bars, 3 knobs, BC, SW, 5 tubes, AC **$85.00-105.00**

85T8, tombstone, 1937, wood, lower slide rule dial, upper "U-shaped" grille, 3 knobs, BC, SW, 5 tubes, AC **$85.00-105.00**

86E, chairside, 1937, wood, rounded right side, front grille with horizontal bars, lift up top, 3 knobs, BC, SW, 7 tubes, AC **$295.00-320.00**

86K, console, 1937, wood, upper square dial, lower grille with center vertical bar, 3 knobs, BC, SW, 7 tubes, AC **$120.00-150.00**

18T, table, 1940, wood, upper front slanted slide rule dial, lower cloth grille, 6 pushbuttons, 4 knobs, BC, SW, 8 tubes, AC, $50.00-65.00.

86K7, console, 1937, wood, upper square dial, lower grille with two vertical bars, 3 knobs, BC, SW, 7 tubes, AC **$120.00-150.00**

86T, table, 1937, wood, Deco, right front dial, rounded left side, left cloth grille with center horizontal bar, 3 knobs, BC, SW, 6 tubes, AC **$65.00-75.00**

86T1, table, 1937, wood, right front dial, left cloth grille with horizontal bars, 3 knobs, BC, SW, 6 tubes, AC **$50.00-65.00**

86T3, tombstone, 1937, wood, center front slide rule dial with plastic escutcheon, upper cloth grille with vertical bars, 3 knobs, BC, SW, 6 tubes, AC **$95.00-115.00**

86T6, table, 1938, wood, right front slide rule dial, rounded left side, left cloth grille with curved cut-out, pushbuttons, 3 knobs, BC, SW, 6 tubes, AC **$85.00-95.00**

87K, console, 1937, wood, upper square dial, lower grille with three center vertical bars, 3 knobs, BC, SW, 7 tubes, AC **$120.00-150.00**

87K1, console, 1937, wood, upper front slanted slide rule dial, lower cloth grille with vertical bars, pushbuttons, tuning eye, 2 knobs, BC, SW, 7 tubes, AC...**$120.00-150.00**

87K2, console, 1937, wood, upper front slide rule dial, lower cloth grille with vertical bars, pushbuttons, tuning eye, 2 knobs, BC, SW, 7 tubes, AC **$120.00-150.00**

87T, table, 1937, wood, right front dial, left wrap-around cloth grille with center horizontal bars, 3 knobs, BC, SW, 7 tubes, AC ..**$65.00-75.00**

87T1, table, 1937, wood, right front slide rule dial, left wrap-around cloth grille with cut-outs, tuning eye, 3 knobs, BC, SW, 7 tubes, AC **$85.00-95.00**

87T2, table, 1937, wood, lower front slide rule dial, upper cloth grille, tuning eye, 6 pushbuttons, 2 knobs, BC, SW, 7 tubes, AC ..**$85.00-95.00**

91B, portable/table, 1933, metal, center grille with cut-outs, blue top and sides, silver front and back, 2 knobs, BC, 3 tubes, battery ..**$85.00-95.00**

94BK, console, 1938, wood, upper front dial, lower cloth grille with center vertical bar, 2 knobs, BC, 4 tubes, battery **$85.00-95.00**

28T, table, 1941, wood, upper front slanted slide rule dial, lower cloth grille, 6 pushbuttons, 4 knobs, BC, SW, 8 tubes, AC, $50.00-65.00.

28X, table, 1941, wood, upper front slanted slide rule dial, lower horizontal louvers, 4 knobs, BC, SW, 8 tubes, AC/DC, $50.00-65.00.

94BK1, console, 1938, wood, upper front dial, lower cloth grille with center vertical bar, 2 knobs, BC, 4 tubes, battery $85.00-95.00

94BK2, console, 1938, wood, upper front slide rule dial, lower cloth grille with center vertical bar, pushbuttons, 2 knobs, BC, SW, 4 tubes, battery $85.00-95.00

94BP1, portable, 1939, cloth, right front square dial, left grille area, handle, 2 knobs, BC, 4 tubes, battery $35.00-40.00

94BP4-B, portable, 1939, "buffalo" covering, right front dial, left grille area, handle, 2 knobs, BC, 4 tubes, battery $35.00-40.00

94BP4-C, portable, 1939, "cowhide" covering, right front dial, left grille area, handle, 2 knobs, BC, 4 tubes, battery $35.00-40.00

94BP4-R, portable, 1939, "rawhide" covering, right front dial, left grille area, handle, 2 knobs, BC, 4 tubes, battery $35.00-40.00

94BP61, portable, 1940, dark brown, small right front dial, left grille area, handle, 2 knobs, BC, 4 tubes, battery $30.00-35.00

94BP62, portable, 1940, tan, small right front dial, left grille area, handle, 2 knobs, BC, 4 tubes, battery $30.00-35.00

94BP64, portable, 1940, light brown, small right front dial, left grille area, handle, 2 knobs, BC, 4 tubes, battery $30.00-35.00

94BP66, portable, 1940, gray, small right front dial, left grille area, handle, 2 knobs, BC, 4 tubes, battery $30.00-35.00

94BP80, portable, 1940, brown leather, small right front dial, left grille area, handle, 2 knobs, BC, 4 tubes, battery $30.00-35.00

94BP81, portable, 1940, black leather, small right front dial, left grille area, handle, 2 knobs, BC, 4 tubes, battery $30.00-35.00

94BT, tombstone, 1938, wood, lower front airplane dial, upper cloth grille with center horizontal divider, 2 knobs, BC, 4 tubes, battery $55.00-65.00

94BT2, table, 1939, two-tone wood, right front slide rule dial, left cloth grille with cut-outs, pushbuttons, 2 knobs, BC, SW, 4 tubes, battery $40.00-45.00

35X, table, 1942, wood, upper front slanted slide rule dial, lower horizontal grille bars, 2 knobs, BC, 5 tubes, AC/DC, $40.00-50.00.

94BT6, tombstone, 1938, wood, lower front airplane dial, upper cloth grille with center horizontal divider, 2 knobs, BC, 4 tubes, battery $55.00-65.00

94BT61, tombstone, 1938, wood, lower front airplane dial, upper cloth grille with 2 splayed bars, 2 knobs, BC, 4 tubes, battery..$50.00-65.00

94X, table, 1938, wood, lower front round dial, upper cloth grille with horizontal bars, 2 knobs, BC, 4 tubes, AC/DC $65.00-75.00

94X-1, table, 1938, wood, 6 top pushbuttons provide electric tuning of six pre-selected stations, top on/off/volume knob, front cloth grille area, BC, 4 tubes, AC/DC $85.00-105.00

94X-2, table, 1938, wood, 6 top pushbuttons provide electric tuning of six pre-selected stations, top on/off/volume knob, front cloth grille area, BC, 4 tubes, AC/DC $85.00-105.00

95T, table, 1938, wood, large center front dial, right & left grilles with horizontal wrap-around bars, 2 knobs, BC, 5 tubes, AC......$65.00-75.00

95T5LW, table, 1938, wood, lower front slide rule dial, upper cloth grille with vertical bars, 6 pushbuttons, 2 knobs, BC, 5 tubes, AC $65.00-75.00

95X, table, 1938, wood, lower front dial, upper cloth grille with vertical bars, 2 knobs, BC, 5 tubes, AC/DC...............................$65.00-75.00

95X1, table, 1938, wood, lower front dial, upper cloth grille with center horizontal bars, top pushbuttons, 2 knobs, BC, 5 tubes, AC/DC $75.00-85.00

95X6, table, 1938, wood, lower front dial, upper cloth grille with vertical bars, 2 knobs, BC, 5 tubes, AC/DC..............................$65.00-75.00

95X11, table, 1938, wood, lower front dial, upper cloth grille with center horizontal bars, top pushbuttons, 2 knobs, BC, 5 tubes, AC/DC $75.00-85.00

95X, table, 1938, wood, lower front dial, upper cloth grille with vertical bars, rounded front corners, 2 knobs, BC, 5 tubes, AC/DC $65.00-75.00

40X53 "La Siesta," table, 1939, wood, painted with Mexican scene, right front dial, left cloth grille, handle, 2 knobs, BC, 5 tubes, AC/DC, $640.00-690.00.

95XL, table, 1938, wood, lower front dial, upper cloth grille, ornate cabinet, base moulding, 2 knobs, BC, 5 tubes, AC/DC........$75.00-95.00

95XLW, table, 1938, wood, lower front dial, upper cloth grille with vertical bars, 2 knobs, BC, LW, 5 tubes, AC/DC $65.00-75.00

96BK6, console, 1939, wood, upper front slide rule dial, lower cloth grille with center vertical divider, pushbuttons, 2 knobs, BC, SW, 6 tubes, battery $75.00-85.00

96BT6, table, 1939, two-tone wood, right front slide rule dial, left cloth grille with cut-outs, pushbuttons, 2 knobs, BC, SW, 6 tubes, battery $50.00-55.00

96E, chairside, 1938, wood, Deco, top dial & pushbuttons, front grille with vertical center bar, 2 knobs, BC, 6 tubes, AC $140.00-160.00

96E2, chairside, 1939, two-tone wood, half-round, top dial/knobs/pushbuttons, front grille with vertical bars, 2 knobs, BC, SW, 6 tubes, AC $200.00-230.00

96K, console, 1938, wood, upper front slide rule dial, lower grille with center vertical bar, 6 pushbuttons, 2 knobs, BC, SW, 6 tubes, AC..$110.00-130.00

96K2, console, 1938, wood, upper front slide rule dial, lower grille with center vertical bar, pushbuttons, 2 knobs, BC, SW, 6 tubes, AC..$110.00-130.00

96K5, console, 1939, wood, upper front slide rule dial, lower cloth grille with center vertical divider, pushbuttons, 2 knobs, BC, SW, 6 tubes, AC **$110.00-130.00**

96K6, console, 1939, wood, upper front slide rule dial, lower cloth grille with center vertical bar, 6 pushbuttons, 2 knobs, BC, SW, 6 tubes, AC **$110.00-130.00**

96T, table, 1938, wood, lower front slide rule dial, upper cloth grille with vertical bars, pushbuttons, 2 knobs, BC, 6 tubes, AC....**$75.00-85.00**

96T1, table, 1938, two-tone wood, lower front slide rule dial, upper vertical grille bars, pushbuttons, 2 knobs, BC, 6 tubes, AC..**$75.00-85.00**

96T2, table, 1938, wood, lower front slide rule dial, upper cloth grille with vertical bars, 6 pushbuttons, 2 knobs, BC, SW, 6 tubes, AC **$65.00-75.00**

96T3, table, 1938, wood, lower front slide rule dial, upper cloth grille with horizontal bars, 6 pushbuttons, 2 knobs, BC, SW, 6 tubes, AC **$65.00-75.00**

96T4, table, 1939, wood, lower front slide rule dial, upper cloth grille with 2 horizontal chrome bars, 5 pushbuttons, 2 knobs, BC, SW, 6 tubes, AC/DC **$85.00-95.00**

96T5, table, 1939, wood, lower front slide rule dial, upper cloth grille with 2 horizontal bars, 5 pushbuttons, 2 knobs, BC, SW, 6 tubes, AC/DC **$75.00-85.00**

96T6, table, 1939, wood, lower front slide rule dial, large upper grille area, 5 pushbuttons, 2 knobs, BC, SW, 6 tubes, AC/DC **$50.00-65.00**

40X56 "1939 World's Fair," table, 1939, Repwood, Trylon & Perisphere pressed into front, right dial, left cloth grille, handle, 2 knobs, BC, 5 tubes, AC/DC, $900.00-1,000.00.

96T7, table, 1939, wood, lower front slide rule dial, upper cloth grille with 2 horizontal bars, pushbuttons, 2 knobs, BC, SW, 6 tubes, AC **$75.00-85.00**

96X2, table, 1939, black plastic, Deco, step-down top, right front dial, curved left with horizontal wrap-around louvers, 3 knobs, BC, SW, 6 tubes, AC/DC...**$150.00-180.00**

96X3, table, 1939, walnut/ivory plastic, Deco, step-down top, right front dial, curved left with horizontal wrap-around louvers, 3 knobs, BC, SW, 6 tubes, AC/DC **$150.00-180.00**

96X4, table, 1939, ivory plastic, Deco, step-down top, right front dial, curved left with horizontal wrap-around louvers, 3 knobs, BC, SW, 6 tubes, AC/DC...**$150.00-180.00**

96X11, table, 1939, walnut plastic, Deco, step-down top, right front dial, curved left with horizontal wrap-around louvers, pushbuttons, 3 knobs, BC, SW, 6 tubes, AC/DC **$150.00-180.00**

96X12, table, 1939, black plastic, Deco, step-down top, right front dial, curved left with horizontal wrap-around louvers, pushbuttons, 3 knobs, BC, SW, 6 tubes, AC/DC **$150.00-180.00**

96X13, table, 1939, walnut/ivory plastic, Deco, step-down top, right front dial, curved left with horizontal wrap-around louvers, pushbuttons, 3 knobs, BC, SW, 6 tubes, AC/DC **$150.00-180.00**

96X14, table, 1939, ivory plastic, Deco, step-down top, right front dial, curved left with horizontal wrap-around louvers, pushbuttons, 3 knobs, BC, SW, 6 tubes, AC/DC **$150.00-180.00**

97E, chairside, 1938, wood, top dial/pushbuttons/tuning eye, front grille with horizontal bars, 2 knobs, BC, SW, 7 tubes, AC ..**$110.00-130.00**

45X2, table, 1940, ivory plastic, right front dial, left horizontal wrap-around louvers, 2 knobs, BC, 5 tubes, AC/DC, $55.00-65.00.

97K, console, 1939, wood, upper front slide rule dial, lower cloth grille with vertical bars, tuning eye, pushbuttons, 2 knobs, BC, SW, 7 tubes, AC **$120.00-150.00**

97K2, console, 1939, wood, upper front slide rule dial, lower cloth grille with vertical bars, pushbuttons, 2 knobs, BC, SW, 7 tubes, AC **$120.00-150.00**

97KG, console, 1938, wood, upper front slanted slide rule dial, lower cloth grille with vertical bars, tuning eye, pushbuttons, 2 knobs, BC, SW, 7 tubes, AC..**$120.00-150.00**

97T, table, 1938, wood, lower front slide rule dial, upper cloth grille with wrap-over vertical bars, tuning eye, pushbuttons, 2 knobs, BC, SW, 7 tubes, AC **$75.00-85.00**

97T2, table, 1939, wood, lower front slide rule dial, large upper grille area, pushbuttons, 2 knobs, BC, SW, 7 tubes, AC **$75.00-85.00**

97X, table, 1938, wood, lower front slide rule dial, upper cloth grille with vertical bars, pushbuttons, 2 knobs, BC, 7 tubes, AC/DC......**$65.00-75.00**

97Y, console, 1938, wood, upper front slide rule dial, lower cloth grille with center vertical divider, pushbuttons, 2 knobs, BC, SW, 7 tubes, AC/DC **$110.00-130.00**

98EY, chairside, 1938, wood, top dial & pushbuttons, front cloth grille with horizontal bars, 2 knobs, BC, SW, 8 tubes, AC/DC **$110.00-130.00**

98K, console, 1938, wood, upper front dial, lower cloth grille with center vertical bar, tuning eye, 8 pushbuttons, 4 knobs, BC, SW, 8 tubes, AC **$120.00-140.00**

98K2, console, 1939, wood, upper front slide rule dial, lower cloth grille with vertical bars, tuning eye, pushbuttons, 2 knobs, BC, SW, 8 tubes, AC **$120.00-140.00**

98T, table, 1939, wood, lower front slide rule dial, upper cloth grille with horizontal bars, pushbuttons, 2 knobs, BC, SW, 8 tubes, AC ..**$65.00-75.00**

98T2, table, 1938, wood, lower front slide rule dial, upper cloth grille with horizontal bars, tuning eye, pushbuttons, 2 knobs, BC, SW, 8 tubes, AC/DC **$65.00-75.00**

98YG, console, 1938, wood, upper front slanted slide rule dial, lower cloth grille with vertical bars, tuning eye, pushbuttons, 2 knobs, BC, SW, 8 tubes, AC/DC **$120.00-140.00**

99K, console, 1938, wood, upper front curved dial, lower cloth grille with vertical bars, 8 pushbuttons, 4 knobs, BC, SW, 9 tubes, AC ..**$120.00-140.00**

99T, table, 1938, wood, lower front slide rule dial, upper cloth grille with vertical bars, tuning eye, 8 pushbuttons, 4 knobs, BC, SW, 9 tubes, AC **$75.00-85.00**

45X16, table, 1940, two-tone wood, right front dial, left horizontal louvers, 2 knobs, BC, 5 tubes, AC/DC, $45.00-55.00.

46X23, table, 1940, wood, right front airplane dial, left horizontal louvers, 3 knobs, BC, SW, 6 tubes including ballast, AC/DC, $45.00-55.00.

100, cathedral, 1933, wood, center front dial, cloth grille with cut-outs, side moldings, 4 knobs, BC, SW, 4 tubes, AC **$180.00-200.00**

101, tombstone, 1933, wood, center front dial, upper cloth grille with horizontal bars, two-tone wood, 4 knobs, BC, SW, 4 tubes, AC ..**$180.00-200.00**

102, table, 1934, metal, right front dial, center cloth grille with Deco cut-outs, 2 knobs, BC, 4 tubes, AC/DC **$85.00-95.00**

110, cathedral, 1933, wood, front window dial, upper cloth grille with cut-outs, side moldings, 4 knobs, BC, 5 tubes, AC **$270.00-300.00**

110K2, console, 1941, wood, upper front oblong slide rule dial, lower vertical grille bars, pushbuttons, 4 knobs, BC, SW, 10 tubes, AC **$120.00-150.00**

111, table, 1934, inlaid walnut, right front window dial, center cloth grille with scalloped cut-outs, 4 knobs, BC, SW, 5 tubes, AC..**$95.00-115.00**

111K, console, 1941, wood, upper front oblong slide rule dial, lower grille with vertical bars, pushbuttons, 4 knobs, BC, SW, 11 tubes, AC **$120.00-150.00**

114, table, 1934, two-tone wood, right front dial, center 3-section cloth grille, 2 knobs, BC, SW, 5 tubes, AC/DC.......................**$85.00-95.00**

115, table, 1933, wood, right front window dial, center cloth grille with vertical cut-outs, tiered top, base moulding, 4 knobs, BC, SW, 5 tubes, AC **$110.00-140.00**

117, tombstone, 1934, wood, rounded shoulders, lower front round dial, upper cloth grille with vertical bars, 4 knobs, BC, SW, 5 tubes, AC..**$85.00-115.00**

118, tombstone, 1934, wood, center front round airplane dial, upper cloth grille with vertical bars, 4 knobs, BC, SW, 5 tubes, AC..**$120.00-150.00**

119, tombstone, 1935, wood, arched top, lower front round dial, cloth grille with vertical bars, 4 knobs, BC, SW, 5 tubes, AC **$110.00-130.00**

121, cathedral, 1933, wood, lower front round airplane dial, upper cloth grille with cut-outs, side & top moldings, 4 knobs, BC, SW, 6 tubes, AC **$270.00-300.00**

55X, table, 1942, wood, center front dial, right & left grilles with horizontal louvers, 2 knobs, BC, 5 tubes, AC/DC, $45.00-55.00.

56X5 "The 12000 Miler," table, 1946, wood, upper front slanted slide rule dial, lower horizontal louvers, 3 knobs, BC, SW, 6 tubes, AC/DC, $50.00-65.00.

122, tombstone, 1933, wood, lower front round airplane dial, upper cloth grille with vertical bars, rounded top, "pedestal" look base, 4 knobs, BC, SW, 6 tubes, AC **$190.00-230.00**

124, tombstone, 1934, wood, right front window dial, upper ornate flowery grille, "pedestal" look base, 4 knobs, BC, SW, 6 tubes, AC..**$270.00-300.00**

125, tombstone, 1934, wood, arched top, front round airplane dial, upper 4-section cloth grille, fluting, 4 knobs, BC, SW, 6 tubes, AC ..**$85.00-115.00**

127, tombstone, 1934, wood, lower front round airplane dial, upper cloth grille with vertical bars, rounded top, "pedestal" look base, 4 knobs, BC, SW, 6 tubes, 220VDC **$150.00-170.00**

140, tombstone, 1934, wood, scalloped shoulders, lower front round airplane dial, upper cloth grille with cut-outs, 4 knobs, BC, SW, 8 tubes, AC **$300.00-350.00**

141, tombstone, 1934, wood, rounded shoulders, lower front round airplane dial, upper cloth grille with cut-outs, 4 knobs, BC, SW, 8 tubes, AC **$240.00-260.00**

141-E, tombstone, 1934, wood, rounded shoulders, lower front airplane dial, upper cloth grille with cut-outs, 4 knobs, BC, SW, LW, 8 tubes, AC **$240.00-260.00**

142-B, cathedral, 1933, wood, front window dial, upper cloth grille with cut-outs, side & top moldings, 4 knobs, BC, 8 tubes, battery..**$150.00-180.00**

143, tombstone, 1933, wood, shouldered, rounded top, round airplane dial, upper cloth grille with vertical bars, 5 knobs, BC, SW, 8 tubes, AC **$320.00-370.00**

211, console, 1934, wood, lowboy, upper front round dial, lower cloth grille with cut-outs, 4 knobs, BC, SW, 5 tubes, AC....**$120.00-150.00**

211K, console, 1941, wood, upper front slanted slide rule dial, lower vertical grille bars, pushbuttons, 2 speakers, 4 knobs, BC, SW, 11 tubes, AC **$150.00-180.00**

214, console, 1935, wood, upper front round dial, lower cloth grille with cut-outs, 4 knobs, 5 tubes, AC **$110.00-130.00**

220, console, 1933, wood, lowboy, upper front round airplane dial, lower cloth grille with cut-outs, 6 legs, 4 knobs, BC, 6 tubes, AC........**$120.00-140.00**

224, console, 1934, wood, lowboy, upper front round dial, lower cloth grille with cut-outs, 6 legs, 5 knobs, BC, SW, 6 tubes, AC **$120.00-140.00**

225, console, 1935, wood, upper front round airplane dial, lower cloth grille with cut-outs, 4 knobs, BC, SW, 6 tubes, AC....**$120.00-140.00**

226, console, 1934, wood, upper front round dial, lower cloth grille with vertical cut-outs, 5 knobs, BC, SW, 6 tubes, AC........**$120.00-140.00**

65X1, table, 1948, plastic, upper front slanted slide rule dial, lower horizontal louvers, 2 knobs, BC, 5 tubes, AC/DC, $40.00-45.00.

66X2, table, 1946, ivory plastic, upper front curved slide rule dial, lower cloth grille, rear hand-hold, 3 knobs, BC, SW, 6 tubes, AC/DC, $45.00-55.00.

66X13, table, 1948, walnut wood, upper front slanted slide rule dial, lower horizontal louvers, brass trim, 3 knobs, BC, 6 tubes, AC/DC, $40.00-50.00.

240 "All-Wave," console, 1933, wood, lowboy, upper front round dial, lower cloth grille with cut-outs, 6 legs, 4 knobs, BC, SW, 8 tubes, AC **$120.00-150.00**

240E "All-Wave," console, 1933, wood, lowboy, upper front round dial, lower cloth grille with cut-outs, 6 legs, 4 knobs, BC, SW, LW, 8 tubes, AC **$130.00-160.00**

242, console, 1934, wood, lowboy, upper front round airplane dial, lower cloth grille with cut-outs, 6 legs, 5 knobs, BC, SW, LW, 8 tubes, AC **$120.00-150.00**

260, console, 1933, wood, lowboy, upper front window dial, lower cloth grille with cut-outs, 6 legs, 5 knobs, BC, 10 tubes, AC..**$120.00-150.00**

262, console, 1934, wood, lowboy, upper front round dial, lower grille with cut-outs, 6 legs, BC, SW, LW, 10 tubes, AC **$120.00-150.00**

280, console, 1933, wood, lowboy, upper front window dial, lower cloth grille with cut-outs, 6 legs, 5 knobs, BC, SW, 12 tubes, AC....**$140.00-160.00**

281, console, 1934, wood, lowboy, inner round dial, lower cloth grille with cut-outs, double doors, 6 legs, BC, SW, LW, 12 tubes, AC....**$180.00-200.00**

300 "Duo," table-R/P, 1933, wood, front dial and cloth grille with cut-outs, lift top, inner phono, 3 knobs, BC, 4 tubes, AC ..**$85.00-115.00**

310 "Duo," console-R/P, 1933, wood, highboy, front window dial, cloth grille with cut-outs, stretcher base, BC, SW, 5 tubes, AC **$110.00-130.00**

320, console-R/P, 1934, wood, highboy, lower front round airplane dial, upper cloth grille with cut-outs, stretcher base, lift-top, 4 knobs, BC, SW, 6 tubes, AC..**$110.00-130.00**

321, console-R/P, 1934, wood, lowboy, upper front round airplane dial, lower cloth grille with vertical cut-outs, lift-top, 4 knobs, BC, SW, 6 tubes, AC **$110.00-130.00**

322, console-R/P, 1934, wood, lowboy, upper front round airplane dial, lower cloth grille with cut-outs, lift-top, 5 knobs, BC, SW, 6 tubes, AC **$120.00-140.00**

327, console-R/P, 1934, wood, lowboy, upper front round airplane dial, lower cloth grille with vertical cut-outs, lift-top, 4 knobs, BC, SW, 6 tubes, 220VDC...**$95.00-115.00**

340 "All Wave Duo," console-R/P, 1934, wood, lowboy, center front round dial, lower cloth grille with cut-outs, 6 legs, 4 knobs, BC, SW, 8 tubes, AC **$120.00-150.00**

340E "All Wave Duo," console-R/P, 1934, wood, lowboy, center front round dial, lower cloth grille with cut-outs, 6 legs, 4 knobs, BC, SW, LW, 8 tubes, AC...**$130.00-160.00**

341, console-R/P, 1934, wood, lowboy, center front round dial, lower cloth grille with lyre cut-out, lift top, inner phono, BC, SW, LW, 8 tubes, AC **$120.00-140.00**

381, console-R/P/Rec, 1934, wood, lowboy, inner front round dial, doors, right & left side storage, lift top, inner phono, BC, SW, LW, 12 tubes, AC **$180.00-200.00**

610V2, console-R/P, 1948, wood, inner right slide rule dial, 6 pushbuttons, door, left pull-down phono, lower grille, 4 knobs, BC, FM, 10 tubes, AC **$65.00-75.00**

612V3, console-R/P, 1947, wood, pull-down front door with inner slide rule dial/8 pushbuttons/top phono, 6 knobs, BC, SW, FM, 12 tubes, AC **$75.00-85.00**

710V2, console-R/P, 1948, wood, right tilt-out slide rule dial left pull-out phono drawer, lower grille, 4 knobs, BC, FM, 10 tubes, AC.............**$65.00-75.00**

711V2, console-R/P, 1947, wood, right tilt-out dial/6 pushbuttons, left fold-out phono, lower grille, 2 knobs, BC, SW, FM, 11 tubes, AC **$65.00-75.00**

711V3, console-R/P, 1947, wood, right tilt-out dial/6 pushbuttons, left fold-out phono, lower grille, 2 knobs, BC, SW, FM, 11 tubes, AC **$75.00-85.00**

810K1, console, 1937, wood, upper front square dial, lower cloth grille with 3 vertical bars, tuning eye, 3 knobs, BC, SW, 9 tubes, AC..**$140.00-160.00**

66X8, table, 1946, maroon Catalin, upper front curved slide rule dial, lower horizontal grille bars, 3 knobs, BC, SW, 6 tubes, AC/DC, $650.00+.

75X18, table, 1948, lacquered cabinet with Oriental designs, right front dial, left vertical grille bars, brass trim, 2 knobs, BC, 5 tubes, AC/DC, $150.00-180.00.

85T1, table, 1936, wood, right front dial, left wrap-around cloth grille with 2 horizontal bars, 3 knobs, BC, SW, 5 tubes, AC, $45.00-55.00.

811K, console, 1937, wood, upper front slide rule dial, lower cloth grille with 3 vertical bars, tuning eye, pushbuttons, 6 knobs, BC, SW, 11 tubes, AC $120.00-150.00

811T, tombstone, 1937, wood, lower front slide rule dial, upper cloth grille with 3 horizontal bars, tuning eye, pushbuttons, tiered sides, 6 knobs, BC, SW, 11 tubes, AC $110.00-130.00

812K, console, 1937, wood, upper front slide rule dial, lower cloth grille with horizontal bars, tuning eye, pushbuttons, 6 knobs, BC, SW, 12 tubes, AC $180.00-200.00

812X, tombstone, 1937, wood, lower square dial, upper rectangular grille area, tuning eye, 4 knobs, BC, SW, LW, 12 tubes, AC/DC $110.00-130.00

813K, console, 1937, wood, upper front curved dial, lower horizontal grille bars, pushbuttons, tuning eye, 6 knobs, BC, SW, 13 tubes, AC $180.00-200.00

910KG, console, 1938, wood, upper front curved dial, lower cloth grille with 2 vertical bars, tuning eye, pushbuttons, 4 knobs, BC, SW, 10 tubes, AC $150.00-180.00

911K, console, 1938, wood, upper front curved dial, lower vertical grille bars, tuning eye, pushbuttons, 4 knobs, BC, SW, 11 tubes, AC $170.00-190.00

A55, console-R/P, 1950, wood, upper front slide rule dial, lower right pull-out phono drawer, 4 knobs, BC, 5 tubes, AC $50.00-65.00

B-411, portable, 1951, plastic, center front round dial, lower grille area, handle, 2 knobs, BC, 4 tubes, battery $40.00-45.00

BC7-9, console, 1935, wood, upper front dial, lower cloth grille with cut-outs, 4 knobs, BC, SW, 7 tubes, battery $75.00-85.00

BK-41, console, 1939, wood, upper front dial, lower cloth grille with vertical bars, 2 knobs, BC, 4 tubes, battery $75.00-75.00

BK-42, console, 1939, wood, upper front slide rule dial, lower cloth grille with vertical bars, BC, 4 tubes, battery $85.00-85.00

BT6-3, table, 1935, wood, lower front half-round dial, upper cloth grille with cut-outs, 4 knobs, BC, SW, 6 tubes, battery $50.00-65.00

94BT1, tombstone, 1938, wood, lower front airplane dial, upper cloth grille with 2 splayed bars, 2 knobs, BC, 4 tubes, battery, $55.00-65.00.

BT6-5, tombstone, 1935, wood, lower front round airplane dial, upper cloth grille with cut-outs, 5 knobs, BC, SW, 6 tubes, battery $65.00-75.00

BT7-8, tombstone, 1935, wood, rounded shoulders, lower front round dial, cloth grille with cut-outs, 4 knobs, BC, SW, battery $65.00-75.00

BT40, table, 1939, two-tone wood, right front dial, left 3-section cloth grille, 2 knobs, BC, 4 tubes, battery $30.00-35.00

BT41, table, 1939, two-tone wood, right front dial, left cloth grille with horizontal bars, 2 knobs, BC, 4 tubes, battery $30.00-35.00

BT42, table, 1940, two-tone wood, right front slide rule dial, left square grille area, 2 knobs, BC, 4 tubes, battery $50.00-65.00

BX55, portable, 1950, plastic with "alligator" panels, upper front dial, lower horizontal louvers, handle, 1 left & 1 right side knob, BC, 4 tubes, AC/DC/battery $45.00-55.00

BX57, portable, 1950, plastic with "alligator" panels, upper front dial, lower horizontal louvers, handle, 1 left & 1 right side knob, BC, 4 tubes, AC/DC/battery $45.00-55.00

C1E, table-C, 1959, plastic, lower right front dial overlaps vertical grille bars, left alarm clock, 3 knobs, BC, 5 tubes, AC...........$25.00-30.00

C-3HE, table-C, 1959, plastic, lower right front window dial, large left front alarm clock face, lattice grille area, feet, 3 knobs, BC, 5 tubes, AC $30.00-35.00

C7-6, console, 1935, wood, upper front dial, lower cloth grille with cut-outs, rounded front corners, 4 knobs, BC, SW, 7 tubes, AC ..$110.00-130.00

C8-19, console, 1936, wood, upper front dial, lower cloth grille with cut-outs, tuning eye, 4 knobs, BC, SW, 8 tubes, AC $120.00-150.00

C8-20, console, 1936, wood, upper front dial, lower cloth grille with cut-outs, tuning eye, six feet, 4 knobs, BC, SW, 8 tubes, AC $130.00-160.00

C9-4, console, 1935, wood, upper front round dial, lower cloth grille with cut-outs, tuning eye, 5 knobs, BC, SW, 9 tubes, AC..$120.00-150.00

C11-1, console, 1935, wood, upper front dial, lower cloth grille with horizontal & vertical bars, tuning eye, 5 knobs, BC, SW, 11 tubes, AC $120.00-150.00

86T2, table, 1937, two-tone wood, Deco, right front slide rule dial, rounded left side, left cloth grille with curved cut-out, 3 knobs, BC, SW, 6 tubes, AC, $75.00-85.00.

95T5, table, 1938, wood, lower front slide rule dial, upper cloth grille with vertical bars, 6 pushbuttons, 2 knobs, BC, 5 tubes, AC, $65.00-75.00.

96X1, table, 1939, walnut plastic, Deco, step-down top, right front dial, curved left with horizontal wrap-around louvers, 3 knobs, BC, SW, 6 tubes, AC/DC, $150.00-180.00.

C13-2, console, 1935, wood, inner front dial & tuning eye, double doors, lower cloth grille with criss-cross cut-outs, 5 knobs, BC, SW, LW, 13 tubes, AC **$220.00-260.00**

C13-3, console, 1935, wood, inner front dial & tuning eye, double doors, lower cloth grille with vertical bars, 5 knobs, BC, SW, LW, 13 tubes, AC **$220.00-260.00**

C15-3, console, 1935, wood, inner front dial & tuning eye, lower grille with criss-cross cut-outs behind double doors, 5 knobs, BC, SW, LW, 15 tubes, AC...**$280.00-320.00**

C15-4, console, 1935, wood, inner front dial & tuning eye, lower grille with cut-outs, 5 knobs, BC, SW, LW, 15 tubes, AC ..**$280.00-320.00**

D7-7, console-R/P, 1935, wood, upper front dial, lower cloth grille with cut-outs, lift-top, 4 knobs, BC, SW, 7 tubes, AC........**$110.00-130.00**

D8-28, console-R/P, 1936, wood, upper front dial, lower cloth grille with cut-outs, tuning eye, lift-top, 4 legs, 4 knobs, BC, SW, 8 tubes, AC..**$120.00-150.00**

D9-19, console-R/P, 1935, wood, upper front round dial, lower cloth grille with vertical bars, tuning eye, lift top, inner phono, 5 knobs, BC, SW, 9 tubes, AC **$120.00-150.00**

D11-2, console-R/P, 1935, wood, front dial, lower cloth grille with horizontal & vertical bars, tuning eye, lift top, inner phono, 5 knobs, BC, SW, 11 tubes, AC...**$120.00-150.00**

D-22, console-R/P/Rec, 1935, wood, inner front dial & tuning eye, double doors, lower grille with criss-cross cut-outs, lift top, inner phono, 5 knobs, BC, SW, 22 tubes, AC ....**$650.00+**

HF-2, console, 1938, wood, upper front curved dial, lower cloth grille with vertical bars, pushbuttons, 4 knobs, BC, SW, 12 tubes, AC ..**$180.00-200.00**

98X, table, 1938, wood, lower front slide rule dial, upper cloth grille with wrap-over vertical bars, tuning eye, pushbuttons, 2 knobs, BC, SW, 8 tubes, AC/DC, $75.00-85.00.

103, tombstone, 1934, wood, lower front round dial, upper cloth grille with vertical cut-outs, decorative fluting, 4 knobs, BC, SW, 4 tubes, AC, $85.00-95.00.

HF-4, console, 1938, wood, 18th Century-style, half-round, inner dial & knobs, double doors, 4 knobs, BC, SW, 12 tubes, AC ..**$180.00-200.00**

HF-6, console, 1938, wood, upper front curved dial, lower cloth grille with vertical bars, pushbuttons, 7 bands, 5 knobs, BC, SW, 14 tubes, AC **$180.00-200.00**

HF-8, console, 1938, wood, inner dial & tuning eye, lower grille, double doors, 5 knobs, BC, SW, 16 tubes, AC **$190.00-210.00**

K-50, console, 1939, wood, upper front slide rule dial, lower cloth grille with center vertical divider, pushbuttons, BC, 5 tubes, AC ..**$110.00-130.00**

K-61, console, 1940, wood, upper front slide rule dial, lower cloth grille with 2 vertical bars, pushbuttons, 4 knobs, BC, SW, 6 tubes, AC **$110.00-130.00**

K-62, console, 1940, wood, upper front slide rule dial, lower cloth grille with center vertical divider, pushbuttons, 4 knobs, BC, SW, 6 tubes, AC **$110.00-130.00**

K-81, console, 1939, wood, upper front slide rule dial, lower 3-section cloth grille, pushbuttons, 5 knobs, BC, SW, 8 tubes, AC........**$120.00-150.00**

K-82, console, 1940, wood, upper front slide rule dial, lower vertical grille bars, pushbuttons, 4 knobs, BC, SW, 8 tubes, AC **$110.00-130.00**

K-105, console, 1940, wood, upper front slide rule dial, lower vertical grille bars, pushbuttons, BC, SW, 10 tubes, AC **$120.00-140.00**

K130, console, 1939, wood, inner slide rule dial, pushbuttons, double doors, lower vertical grille bars, BC, SW, 13 tubes, AC..............**$150.00-180.00**

110K "Presidential," console, 1940, wood, upper front oblong slide rule dial, lower vertical grille bars, 6 pushbuttons, 4 knobs, BC, SW, 10 tubes, AC, $150.00-180.00.

120, cathedral, 1933, wood, right front window dial, upper cloth grille with cut-outs, side & top moldings, 4 knobs, BC, SW, 6 tubes, AC, $270.00-300.00.

221, console, 1934, wood, lowboy, upper front round airplane dial, lower cloth grille with cut-outs, 4 knobs, BC, SW, 6 tubes, AC, $110.00-130.00.

P31, portable, 1932, leatherette, inner wood panel with window dial, right & left 3-section grilles, snap-off front, handle, BC, 8 tubes, battery **$180.00-200.00**

PX600, portable, 1952, plastic, upper front slide rule dial, lower perforated grille with circular cut-outs, handle, 2 side knobs, BC, 5 tubes, AC/DC/battery **$40.00-45.00**

Q11, table, 1942, wood, upper front slanted slide rule dial, lower horizontal wrap-around louvers, 3 knobs, BC, SW, 5 tubes, AC/DC..**$40.00-50.00**

Q12, table, 1942, plastic, upper front slanted slide rule dial, lower horizontal louvers, 3 knobs, BC, SW, 5 tubes, AC/DC **$40.00-50.00**

Q14, table, 1942, wood, upper front slanted slide rule dial, lower cloth grille area, 3 knobs, BC, SW, 5 tubes, AC **$40.00-50.00**

Q14E, table, 1942, wood, upper front slanted slide rule dial, lower cloth grille area, 3 knobs, BC, SW, 5 tubes, AC **$40.00-50.00**

Q15, table, 1942, wood, upper front slanted slide rule dial, lower cloth grille area, 3 knobs, BC, SW, 5 tubes, AC **$40.00-50.00**

Q15E, table, 1942, wood, upper front slanted slide rule dial, lower cloth grille area, 3 knobs, BC, SW, 5 tubes, AC **$40.00-50.00**

Q16, table, 1942, wood, lower front slide rule dial, upper grille area, 3 knobs, BC, SW, 5 tubes, AC **$50.00-65.00**

Q16E, table, 1942, wood, lower front slide rule dial, upper grille area, 3 knobs, BC, SW, 5 tubes, AC **$50.00-65.00**

Q17, table, 1942, wood, lower front slide rule dial, upper grille area, 3 knobs, BC, SW, 5 tubes, AC **$50.00-65.00**

Q18, table, 1942, wood, lower front slanted slide rule dial, upper cloth grille area, BC, SW, 6 tubes, AC **$40.00-50.00**

Q20, table, 1940, plastic, right front dial, left vertical grille bars, 3 knobs, BC, SW, 5 tubes, AC **$45.00-55.00**

Q21, table, 1940, wood, right front dial, left cloth grille, 3 knobs, BC, SW, 5 tubes, AC **$40.00-45.00**

Q23, table, 1942, wood, lower front slide rule dial, upper vertical grille bars, 3 knobs, BC, SW, 6 tubes, AC **$50.00-65.00**

Q25, table, 1941, wood, upper front slide rule dial, lower grille area, 3 knobs, BC, SW, 6 tubes, AC **$50.00-65.00**

Q27, table, 1942, wood, upper front slanted slide rule dial, lower grille area, 3 knobs, BC, SW, 6 tubes, AC **$50.00-65.00**

Q30, table, 1942, wood, lower front slide rule dial, upper grille area, BC, SW, 6 tubes, AC..**$55.00-65.00**

Q31, table, 1942, wood, lower front slide rule dial, upper grille area, BC, SW, 6 tubes, AC..**$55.00-65.00**

QB9, table, 1941, wood, upper front slanted slide rule dial, lower horizontal louvers, BC, SW, 5 tubes, battery............................**$40.00-45.00**

QB55X, table, 1948, plastic, upper front slanted slide rule dial, lower horizontal louvers, 3 knobs, BC, SW, LW, 4 tubes, battery..**$40.00-45.00**

QU51C, console-R/P, 1942, wood, inner left vertical dial/knobs/tuning eye, door, right lift top, inner phono, lower front grille, BC, SW, 8 tubes, AC **$75.00-85.00**

128, tombstone, 1934, wood, shouldered, rounded top, center front round dial, upper cloth grille with cut-outs, 5 knobs, BC, SW, 6 tubes, AC, $270.00-300.00.

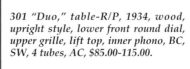

301 "Duo," table-R/P, 1934, wood, upright style, lower front round dial, upper grille, lift top, inner phono, BC, SW, 4 tubes, AC, $85.00-115.00.

816K, console, 1937, wood, upper front curved dial, lower cloth grille with horizontal bars, pushbuttons, tuning eye, 6 knobs, BC, SW, 16 tubes, AC, $270.00-300.00.

BX6 "Globe Trotter," portable, 1950, leatherette & aluminum, inner slide rule dial, slide-down cover, lower horizontal grille bars, 2 thumbwheel knobs, BC, 5 tubes, AC/DC/battery, $40.00-50.00.

QU51M, console-R/P, 1942, wood, inner left vertical dial/knobs/tuning eye, door, right lift top, inner phono, lower front grille, BC, SW, 8 tubes, AC **$75.00-85.00**

R-4 "Superette," cathedral, 1932, wood, front window dial with escutcheon, upper 3-section cloth grille, fluted columns, 3 knobs, BC, 7 tubes, AC **$320.00-350.00**

R-5 "Radiolette," cathedral, 1931, wood, lower front window dial, upper 3-section cloth grille, 3 knobs, BC, 4 tubes, AC **$170.00-190.00**

R-6, console, 1932, wood, lowboy, upper front window dial, lower cloth grille with cut-outs, 3 knobs, BC, 7 tubes, AC...........**$120.00-150.00**

R-7A "Superette," tombstone, 1931, wood, shouldered, lower front window dial, upper 3-section cloth grille, 3 knobs, BC, 8 tubes, AC **$120.00-150.00**

R-10, console, 1931, wood, lowboy, upper front window dial, lower cloth grille with cut-outs, 3 knobs, BC, 8 tubes, AC...........**$120.00-140.00**

R-22W, table, 1933, wood, front dial, center cloth grille with cut-outs, sloped sides, BC, 5 tubes, AC/DC...............................**$85.00-115.00**

R-27, table, 1933, wood, right front dial, center cloth grille with cut-outs, sloped sides, BC, 4 tubes, AC/DC...............................**$75.00-95.00**

R-28, cathedral, 1933, wood, lower front window dial, upper cloth grille with cut-outs, 4 knobs, BC, 5 tubes, AC **$160.00-190.00**

R-28A "Carryette," table, 1933, walnut, lower right front window dial, cloth grille with cut-outs, 4 knobs, BC, 5 tubes, AC **$75.00-85.00**

R-28B "Carryette," table, 1933, wood, lower right front window dial, cloth grille with cut-outs, 4 knobs, BC, 5 tubes, AC **$75.00-85.00**

R-28C "Carryette," table, 1933, wood, chest-type, lower right front window dial, 3-section cloth grille, side handles, 3 knobs, BC, 5 tubes, AC **$85.00-115.00**

R-28D "Carryette," table, 1933, wood, rounded front with tambour doors, inner window dial, cloth grille with cut-outs, 3 knobs, BC, 5 tubes, AC **$140.00-160.00**

R-28E "Carryette," table, 1933, wood, inner right front window dial, cloth grille with cut-outs, doors, 3 knobs, BC, 5 tubes, AC ..**$85.00-115.00**

R-28P, tombstone, 1933, wood, lower front round dial, upper cloth grille with vertical bars, 4 knobs, BC, SW, 5 tubes **$110.00-130.00**

R-32 "Victor," console, 1929, wood, lowboy, upper front sliding dial with wood escutcheon, large lower cloth grille, BC, 10 tubes, AC **$110.00-130.00**

R-34 "Victor," console, 1929, wood, lowboy, upper front sliding dial with wood escutcheon, lower grille with 2 vertical bars, stretcher base, 3 knobs, BC, 8 tubes, AC **$110.00-130.00**

R37P, cathedral, 1933, wood, lower front window dial, upper cloth grille with cut-outs, side & top moldings, 4 knobs, BC, SW, 6 tubes, AC...**$300.00-350.00**

R38, console, 1933, wood, lowboy, upper front window dial, lower cloth grille with cut-outs, 6 legs, stretcher base, 3 knobs, BC, 6 tubes, AC **$120.00-150.00**

R-43, console, 1931, wood, center front window dial, lower cloth grille with cut-outs, 3 knobs, BC, 8 tubes, battery.................**$85.00-95.00**

BP-10, portable, 1941, leatherette & plastic, inner dial, flip-open front, handle, 2 thumbwheel knobs, BC, 4 tubes, battery, $65.00-75.00.

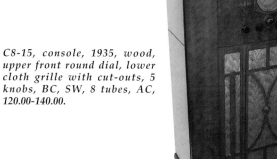

C8-15, console, 1935, wood, upper front round dial, lower cloth grille with cut-outs, 5 knobs, BC, SW, 8 tubes, AC, 120.00-140.00.

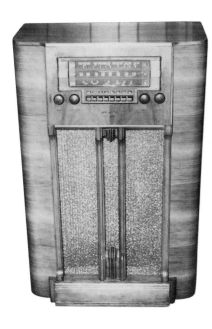

K-60, console, 1939, wood, upper front slide rule dial, lower cloth grille with 2 vertical bars, 8 pushbuttons, 4 knobs, BC, SW, 6 tubes, AC, $110.00-130.00.

Q36, table, 1947, wood, center front vertical multi-band slide rule dial, right & left cloth grilles, tuning eye, 5 knobs, BC, SW, 11 tubes, AC, $50.00-65.00.

R-50, console, 1931, wood, upper front window dial, lower cloth grille with cut-outs, 3 knobs, BC, 10 tubes, AC ....**$110.00-130.00.**

R-71, tombstone, 1932, wood, front window dial with escutcheon, cloth grille with cut-outs, 3 knobs, BC, 8 tubes, AC...........**$150.00-180.00.**

R-72, console, 1932, wood, upper front window dial, lower cloth grille with cut-outs, 3 knobs, BC, 8 tubes, AC ....**$120.00-140.00.**

R-73, tombstone, 1933, wood, shouldered, lower front window dial, cloth grille with cut-outs, right side switch, 3 knobs, BC, 8 tubes, AC ....**$150.00-180.00.**

R-74, tombstone, 1932, wood, shouldered, lower front window dial, cloth grille with cut-outs, 3 knobs, BC, 10 tubes, AC..........**$150.00-180.00.**

R-75, console, 1932, wood, upper front window dial, lower cloth grille with cut-outs, 6 legs, 3 knobs, BC, 8 tubes, AC ....**$110.00-130.00.**

R-76, console, 1932, wood, upper front window dial, lower cloth grille with cut-outs, 3 knobs, BC, 10 tubes, AC ....**$120.00-140.00.**

R-78, console, 1933, wood, lowboy, inner front dial & grille, double doors, 6 legs, stretcher base, 3 knobs, BC, 12 tubes, AC .....**$150.00-180.00.**

R110, tombstone, 1933, wood, shouldered, lower front window dial, cloth grille with cut-outs, 3 knobs....................................**$130.00-150.00.**

Radiola III, table, 1924, wood, square case, top black Bakelite 1 dial panel, 2 knobs & 1 lever, BC, 2 exposed tubes, battery..........**$120.00-150.00.**

Radiola IV, table, 1923, mahogany, rectangular case, inner left dial panel, inner right speaker, double doors, lift top, 3 knobs, BC, 3 tubes, battery ....**$580.00-640.00.**

Radiola V, table, 1923, metal with mahogany finish, rectangular case, wood base & top, 2 dials, 6 knobs, BC, 3 tubes, battery ....**$480.00-530.00.**

Radiola VI, table, 1923, metal with mahogany finish, rectangular case, wood base & top, 2 dials, 8 knobs, BC, 6 tubes, battery ......**$900.00-1,000.00.**

Radiola VII, table, 1923, wood, rectangular case, 2 dial black Bakelite front panel, 7 knobs, BC, 5 tubes, battery ....**$4,000.00+**

Radiola VIIB, table, 1924, wood, inner panel, lift top, front oval cloth grille with cut-outs, 7 knobs, BC, 5 exposed tubes, battery ......**$3,000.00+**

Radiola VIII "Super-VIII," console, 1924, wood, lowboy, inner 2 dial panel, fold-down front, upper built-in speaker, lower storage, BC, 6 tubes, battery ....**$580.00-640.00.**

Radiola 16, table, 1927, wood, low rectangular case, right front oval dial, lift top, 2 knobs, BC, 6 tubes, battery ....**$85.00-105.00.**

Radiola 17, table, 1927, wood, low rectangular case, center front dial with escutcheon, lift top, 2 knobs, BC, 7 tubes, AC ......**$85.00-95.00.**

Radiola 18, table, 1927, wood, low rectangular case, center front dial with escutcheon, lift top, 2 knobs, BC, 7 tubes, AC ......**$85.00-95.00.**

Radiola 20 "Floor Model," console, 1925, two-tone wood, table model 20 on wooden base, slanted front panel with 2 thumbwheel dials, lift top, 4 knobs, BC, 5 tubes, battery..............................**$180.00-210.00.**

Radiola 20, table, 1925, two-tone wood, slanted front panel with 2 thumbwheel dials, lift top, 4 knobs, BC, 5 tubes, battery ......**$160.00-180.00.**

Radiola 24, portable, 1925, leatherette, 2 inner dials, upper cloth grille with vertical bars, removable front cover stores loop antenna, handle, BC, 6 tubes, battery ....**$350.00-380.00.**

K-80, console, 1938, wood, upper front slide rule dial, lower cloth grille with 3 vertical bars, pushbuttons, 4 knobs, BC, SW, 8 tubes, AC, $120.00-150.00.

R-7 "Superette," tombstone, 1931, wood, shouldered, lower front window dial, upper 3-section cloth grille, 3 knobs, BC, 8 tubes, AC, $120.00-150.00.

R-8 "Superette," tombstone, 1931, wood, lower front window dial, upper cloth grille with Gothic cut-outs, 3 knobs, BC, 8 tubes, AC, $140.00-170.00.

R-12, console, 1931, wood, lowboy, upper front window dial, lower cloth grille with cut-outs, 3 knobs, BC, 8 tubes, AC, $110.00-130.00.

Radiola 28, console, 1925, wood, highboy, slanted front panel, 2 thumbwheel dials, top, loop antenna, 4 knobs, BC, 8 tubes, battery **$240.00-270.00**

Radiola 30, console, 1926, wood, lower front fold-out dial panel, upper round cloth grille with cut-outs, fluted legs, 4 knobs, BC, 8 tubes, battery **$240.00-300.00**

Radiola 30A, console, 1927, wood, lowboy, inner panel with 2 thumb-wheel dials, double front doors, stretcher base, 4 knobs, BC, 8 tubes, AC **$200.00-230.00**

Radiola 33, console, 1929, metal, Deco, rectangular case on high legs, center front diamond-shaped dial, 3 knobs, BC, 7 tubes, AC...**$110.00-130.00**

Radiola 33, table, 1929, metal, Deco, rectangular case, center front diamond-shaped dial, 3 knobs, BC, 7 tubes, AC **$75.00-95.00**

Radiola 43, table, two-tone wood, lower rectangular case, center front window dial with pressed wood escutcheon, lift top, switch..**$85.00-105.00**

Radiola 44, table, 1929, wood, low rectangular case, center front window dial with escutcheon, 1 knob, BC, 5 tubes, AC **$150.00-180.00**

Radiola 48, console, 1930, wood, lowboy, ornate case, upper front window dial, lower cloth grille with cut-outs, 2 knobs, BC, 7 tubes, AC **$150.00-180.00**

Radiola 60, console/desk, 1928, wood, highboy, inner panel with window dial & left speaker grille with cut-outs, drop-front, 2 knobs, BC, 9 tubes, AC **$270.00-300.00**

Radiola 60, table, 1928, two-tone walnut, low rectangular case, center front window dial, feet, 2 knobs, BC, 9 tubes, AC......**$120.00-150.00**

Radiola 60 w/matching speaker table, 1928, wood, Radiola 60 table model on a four-legged speaker table, stretcher base, 2 knobs, BC, 9 tubes, AC **$240.00-270.00**

Radiola 62, console, 1928, walnut with maple inlay, highboy, inner front dial, double doors, stretcher base, 2 knobs, BC, 9 tubes, AC...**$240.00-270.00**

Radiola 64, console, 1928, wood, lowboy, inner right dial, upper snap-out cloth grille with cut-outs, large double doors, BC, 11 tubes, AC **$320.00-350.00**

Radiola 66, console, 1929, wood, lowboy, center front tapestry panel with right window dial, 2 knobs, BC, 8 tubes, AC **$180.00-200.00**

Radiola 80, console, 1930, wood, lowboy, upper front window dial, lower grille with cut-outs, 3 knobs, BC, 9 tubes, AC...........**$180.00-200.00**

Radiola 86, console-R/P/Rec, 1930, wood, inner front dial, lower cloth grille with cut-outs, double doors, lift top, inner phono & recorder, 3 knobs, BC, 9 tubes, AC **$410.00-460.00**

Radiola AR-812, portable, 1924, wood, low rectangular case, 2 dial front panel, handle, storage, 4 knobs, BC, 6 tubes, battery..**$180.00-200.00**

Radiola Grand, table, 1922, wood, chest-style, inner 1 dial panel, lift top, front cloth grille with cut-outs, BC, 4 exposed tubes, battery..**$760.00-880.00**

Radiola Nine-Eighteen, console-R/P, 1928, wood, Radiola 64 chassis and record player in large console cabinet, inner radio and record player, record storage, double doors, BC, 11 tubes, AC..........**$480.00-530.00**

R-11, console, 1931, wood, upper front window dial, lower 3-section cloth grille, 3 knobs, BC, 9 tubes, AC, $120.00-140.00.

R-22S, table, 1933, ornate pressed wood case, right front dial, center cloth grille with cut-outs, metal handle, 2 knobs, BC, 5 tubes, AC/DC, $120.00-150.00.

R37, cathedral, 1933, wood, lower front window dial, upper cloth grille with cut-outs, side & top moldings, 3 knobs, BC, 6 tubes, AC, $300.00-350.00.

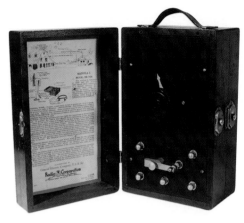

Radiola I, table, 1923, wood, model ER-753A, box-type, crystal set, fold-open front, storage, handle, 1 knob, BC, $850.00-1,000.00.

Radiola RS, table, 1923, wood, square case, lift top, inner 1 dial black panel, 2 knobs & 1 lever, BC, 2 exposed tubes, battery **$420.00-480.00**

Radiola Senior, table, 1923, wood, square case, inner black 1 dial panel, hinged top, BC, 1 exposed tubes, battery.................**$240.00-300.00**

Radiola Senior/Radiola AC, table, 1923, wood, 2 boxes, receiver /amplifier, BC, 1 exposed tubes, battery **$580.00-640.00**

RAE-26, console-R/P, 1931, wood, lower front window dial, upper 3-section cloth grille, inner phono, BC, 9 tubes, AC **$150.00-180.00**

RAE-45, console-R/P, 1931, wood, lowboy, inner sliding dial with wood escutcheon, double front doors, lift top, inner phono, AC ..**$190.00-210.00**

RAE-59, console R/P/Rec, 1931, wood, inner dial, double doors, lower cloth grille with cut-outs, lift top, inner phono & recorder, 3 knobs, BC, 10 tubes, AC **$240.00-270.00**

RAE-84, console R/P/Rec, 1933, wood, lowboy, inner front dial, lower grille, double doors, 6 legs, stretcher base, 3 knobs, BC, 12 tubes, AC **$220.00-260.00**

RE-19, console-R/P, 1932, wood, lowboy, lower front window dial, upper cloth grille with cut-outs, inner phono, 3 knobs, BC, 8 tubes, AC **$180.00-200.00**

RE-45 "Victor," console-R/P, 1929, wood, lowboy, inner sliding dial with wood escutcheon, lower grille, double doors, lift top, inner phono, BC, 10 tubes, AC **$120.00-150.00**

RE-73, console-R/P, 1931, wood, lowboy, center front sliding dial, lower cloth grille with cut-outs, lift top, inner phono, 4 knobs, BC, 8 tubes, AC **$120.00-150.00**

RE-80, console-R/P, 1932, wood, lowboy, center front window dial, lower cloth grille with cut-outs, lift top, inner phono, 3 knobs, BC, 8 tubes, AC **$130.00-150.00**

RFA11V, table, 1965, white plastic, right front dial over vertical grille bars, feet, 3 knobs, BC, 5 tubes, AC/DC **$15.00-20.00**

RGA12A, table, 1966, blue plastic, right front dial overlaps textured grille area, lower left on/off/volume knob, feet, BC, 5 tubes ..**$15.00-20.00**

RGA12G, table, 1966, green plastic, right front dial overlaps textured grille area, lower left on/off/volume knob, feet, BC, 5 tubes **$15.00-20.00**

RGA12Y, table, 1966, white plastic, right front dial overlaps textured grille area, lower left on/off/volume knob, feet, BC, 5 tubes ..**$15.00-20.00**

RHD17A, table-C, 1967, blue/slate plastic, off-center front panel with lower right front window dial, large round alarm clock face, 5 knobs, BC, 5 tubes, AC **$20.00-25.00**

RHD17J, table-C, 1967, alabaster/green plastic, off-center front panel with lower right front window dial, large round alarm clock face, 5 knobs, BC, 5 tubes, AC **$20.00-25.00**

RHD17Y, table-C, 1967, white/gray plastic, off-center front panel with lower right front window dial, large round alarm clock face, 5 knobs, BC, 5 tubes, AC **$20.00-25.00**

RV151, console-R/P, 1949, wood, right front tilt-out dial, left pull-out phono unit, storage, BC, FM, AC..................**$65.00-75.00**

SHF-1, console/R/P/Rec, 1958, wood, inner left slide rule dial, lower pull-out phono & tape recorder drawers, feet, two separate speakers, tuning eye, 5 receiver knobs, BC, FM, 33 tubes, AC..**$150.00-180.00**

SHF-2, console-R/P, 1958, wood, inner left slide rule dial, lower pull-out phono drawer, right grille, doors, tuning eye, 5 receiver knobs, BC, FM, 17 tubes, AC **$50.00-65.00**

T4-8, cathedral, 1934, wood, lower front round dial, 3-section cloth grille, 2 knobs, BC, 4 tubes, AC **$150.00-180.00**

R-70, cathedral, 1933, wood, lower front window dial with escutcheon, upper cloth grille with cut-outs, 3 knobs, BC, 7 tubes, AC, $240.00-270.00.

Radiola II, portable, 1923, mahogany, 2 dial inner panel, removable fold-open front, handle, 4 knobs, BC, 2 tubes, battery, $420.00-480.00.

Radiola III-A, table, 1924, wood, low rectangular case, top 1 dial black panel, 3 knobs & 1 lever, BC, 4 exposed tubes, battery, $180.00-200.00.

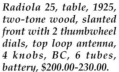

Radiola 25, table, 1925, two-tone wood, slanted front with 2 thumbwheel dials, top loop antenna, 4 knobs, BC, 6 tubes, battery, $200.00-230.00.

T4-9, table, 1935, two-tone wood, right front dial, left cloth grille with cut-outs, 2 knobs, BC, 4 tubes, AC **$55.00-65.00**
T4-10, table, 1935, two-tone wood, front round dial, center 3-section cloth grille, 2 knobs, BC, 4 tubes, AC/DC **$65.00-75.00**
T5-2, tombstone, 1935, wood, small case, center front dial, upper cloth grille with cut-outs, 4 knobs, BC, SW, 5 tubes, AC **$95.00-115.00**
T8-18, tombstone, 1936, wood, lower front dial, cloth grille with vertical bars, tuning eye, 4 knobs, BC, SW, 8 tubes, AC.......**$120.00-140.00**
T10-1, tombstone, 1936, wood, lower front round airplane dial, cloth grille with cut-outs, 5 knobs, BC, SW, 10 tubes, AC..**$150.00-180.00**
T-55, table, 1940, wood, available in wood finish with metal escutcheon and silver painted finish with chrome escutcheon, right front slide rule dial, left cloth grille, 6 pushbuttons, 2 knobs, BC, 5 tubes, AC......................**$65.00-75.00**
T-56, table, 1940, wood, right front slide rule dial, left cloth grille, 6 pushbuttons, 2 knobs, BC, 5 tubes, AC **$65.00-75.00**
T-62, table, 1940, wood, right front slide rule dial, left cloth grille, 6 pushbuttons, 4 knobs, BC, SW, 6 tubes, AC **$65.00-75.00**
T-63, table, 1940, wood, right front slide rule dial, left cloth grille, 6 pushbuttons, 4 knobs, BC, SW, 6 tubes, AC **$65.00-75.00**
T-64, table, 1940, two-tone wood, lower front slide rule dial, upper cloth grille, pushbuttons, 2 knobs, BC, SW, 6 tubes, AC.......**$65.00-75.00**
T-65, table, 1940, two-tone wood, lower front slide rule dial, upper cloth grille, pushbuttons, 2 knobs, BC, SW, 6 tubes, AC........**$65.00-75.00**
T-80, table, 1939, two-tone wood, lower front slide rule dial, upper cloth grille, tuning eye, 6 pushbuttons, BC, SW, 8 tubes, AC ..**$85.00-95.00**
U-8M, table-R/P, 1939, blonde mahogany finish, right front dial with thermometer-type tuning, left horizontal grille bars, open top phono, BC, 5 tubes, AC **$25.00-30.00**

U-8W, table-R/P, 1939, walnut finish, right front dial with thermometer-type tuning, left horizontal grille bars, open top phono, BC, 5 tubes, AC **$25.00-30.00**
U-9, table-R/P, 1940, wood, right front slide rule dial, left cloth grille with cut-outs, lift top, inner phono, 2 knobs, BC, 5 tubes, AC ..**$35.00-40.00**
U-10, table-R/P, 1940, wood, right front slide rule dial, left cloth grille, pushbuttons, lift top, inner phono, 3 knobs, BC, 5 tubes, AC....**$35.00-40.00**
U-12, table-R/P, 1939, wood, right front slide rule dial, left cloth grille with curved cut-out, pushbuttons, lift top, inner phono, 4 knobs, BC, SW, 7 tubes, AC **$40.00-45.00**
U-20, console-R/P, 1939, wood, upper front slide rule dial, lower cloth grille with crossed bars, pushbuttons, lift top, inner phono, 4 knobs, BC, SW, 7 tubes, AC **$110.00-130.00**
U-26, console-R/P, 1939, wood, inner top right slide rule dial, pushbuttons, left phono, lift top, front grille area, BC, SW, 8 tubes, AC.................................**$95.00-115.00**
U-30, console-R/P, 1939, wood, inner slide rule dial and knobs, motorized pushbutton tuning, large front cross hatch grille, tuning eye, 4 knobs, BC, SW, 10 tubes, AC **$170.00-190.00**
U-40, console-R/P, 1939, wood, inner dial/pushbuttons/knobs/phono, double doors, lower cloth grille with vertical bars, 4 knobs, BC, SW, 7 tubes, AC **$110.00-130.00**
U-42, console-R/P, 1939, walnut, inner dial/pushbuttons/knobs/phono, double doors, lower cloth grille with vertical bars, tuning eye, separate power chassis, 4 knobs, BC, SW, 8 tubes, AC ..**$120.00-150.00**
U-44, console-R/P, 1939, wood, inner top right slide rule dial & pushbuttons, left phono, lift top, lower front grille area, tuning eye, 2 knobs, BC, SW, 10 tubes, AC **$120.00-150.00**
U-46, console-R/P, 1940, wood, inner right slide rule dial, pushbuttons, left phono, double doors, lower grille area with doors, tuning eye, BC, SW, 13 tubes, AC **$120.00-150.00**

Radiola X, table, 1924, wood, tall case, lower front 2 dial panel, upper speaker grille with cut-outs, 5 knobs, BC, 4 tubes, battery, $530.00-580.00.

Radiola 26, portable, 1925, walnut, inner 2 dial panel, lower cloth grille with cut-outs, fold-open front with rotatable antenna, handle, 4 knobs, BC, 6 tubes, battery, $350.00-410.00.

Radiola Regenoflex, table, 1924, wood, low rectangular case, 2 dial front panel, side compartments, 5 knobs, BC, 4 tubes, battery, $410.00-440.00.

T7-5, tombstone, 1935, wood, lower front dial, upper cloth grille with cut-outs, fluting, 4 knobs, BC, SW, 7 tubes, AC, $110.00-130.00.

U-50, portable-R/P, 1939, cloth covered, inner slide rule dial, front grille area with RCA logo, lift top, handle, BC, SW, 5 tubes, AC **$30.00-35.00**

U-104, table-R/P, 1939, wood, lower front dial, upper cloth grille with cut-outs, open top phono, BC, 5 tubes, AC **$30.00-35.00**

U-105, console-R/P, 1937, wood, lift-top with inner dial/knobs/tuning eye and phono, large front grille area with vertical bars, 3 knobs, BC, SW, 10 tubes, AC.......**$120.00-150.00**

U-106, console,1938, wood, lift-top with inner dial/knobs/tuning eye and phono, large front grille area with vertical bars, 2 knobs, BC, SW, 9 tubes, AC **$120.00-150.00**

U-107, console-R/P, 1937, wood, double front doors with inner square dial/knobs/tuning eye, lower grille with horizontal bars, lift-top for phono, electric pushbutton tuning, 3 knobs, BC, SW, 10 tubes, AC **$140.00-180.00**

U-108, console-R/P, 1937, wood, double front doors with inner slide rule dial/knobs/tuning eye and lower grille, lift-top for phono, six feet, electric pushbutton tuning, 6 knobs, BC, SW, 16 tubes, AC **$220.00-260.00**

U-109, console-R/P, 1937, wood, double front doors with inner slide rule dial/knobs/tuning eye, lower grille with vertical bars, lift-top for phono, electric pushbutton tuning, 6 knobs, BC, SW, 16 tubes, AC **$220.00-260.00**

U-111, table-R/P, 1939, wood, left front dial, right cloth grille with horizontal bars, lift top, inner phono, BC, 5 tubes, AC **$30.00-35.00**

U-112, table-R/P, 1939, wood, left front dial, right cloth grille with cut-outs, lift top, inner phono, BC, 5 tubes, AC.......**$30.00-35.00**

U-115, table-R/P, 1939, wood, lower front slide rule dial, upper vertical grille bars, pushbuttons, lift top, inner phono, 2 knobs, BC, 6 tubes, AC **$40.00-45.00**

U-119, table-R/P, 1939, wood, lower front slide rule dial, upper cloth grille with vertical bars, pushbuttons, lift top, inner phono, BC, SW, 6 tubes, AC **$40.00-45.00**

U-121, console-R/P, 1939, wood, lift-top with dial/pushbuttons/knobs and phono, large front grille with vertical bars, electric pushbutton tuning, 3 knobs, BC, 6 tubes, AC **$150.00-180.00**

U-122E, chairside-R/P, 1938, wood, top dial/pushbuttons/knobs, lift top, inner phono, front cloth grille with horizontal bars, lower storage, BC, SW, 6 tubes, AC **$95.00-115.00**

U-123, console-R/P, 1939, wood, lift-top with dial/pushbuttons/knobs and phono, large front grille with vertical bars, electric pushbutton tuning, 3 knobs, BC, 6 tubes, AC **$150.00-180.00**

U-124, console-R/P, 1939, wood, inner top right vertical dial & pushbuttons, left phono, lift top, front cloth grille with 2 vertical bars, BC, SW, 6 tubes, AC.......**$95.00-115.00**

U-125, console-R/P, 1939, wood, inner top right dial/knobs/pushbuttons, left phono, lift top, front cloth grille with horizontal & vertical bars, BC, SW, 8 tubes, AC **$95.00-115.00**

U-126, console-R/P, 1938, wood, inner slide rule dial and knobs, motorized pushbutton tuning, large front grille with center vertical bar, tuning eye, 4 knobs, BC, SW, 10 tubes, AC **$150.00-180.00**

U-127E, chairside-R/P, 1939, wood, top dial/pushbuttons/knobs, lift top, inner phono, front horizontal grille bars, lower storage, 3 knobs, BC, 6 tubes, AC **$150.00-180.00**

U-128, console-R/P, 1938, wood, inner slide rule dial and knobs, motorized pushbutton tuning, large front grille with center vertical bar, tuning eye, 4 knobs, BC, SW, 10 tubes, AC **$150.00-180.00**

U-129, console-R/P, 1939, wood, inner slide rule dial and knobs, motorized pushbutton tuning, large front grille horizontal bars, tuning eye, 4 knobs, BC, SW, 10 tubes, AC.......**$170.00-190.00**

U-130, console-R/P, 1938, wood, inner slide rule dial and knobs, motorized pushbutton tuning, large front cross hatch grille, tuning eye, 4 knobs, BC, SW, 12 tubes, AC **$180.00-200.00**

U-132, console-R/P, 1938, wood, lift-top with inner dial/knobs/tuning eye and phono, large front grille area with dual "X" pattern, electric pushbutton tuning, 5 knobs, BC, SW, 14 tubes, AC.......**$220.00-260.00**

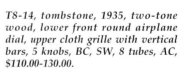

Radiola Special, table, 1923, tall rectangular case, inner black panel with controls, cover, 4 knobs, BC, 1 tube, battery, $740.00-800.00.

T8-14, tombstone, 1935, two-tone wood, lower front round airplane dial, upper cloth grille with vertical bars, 5 knobs, BC, SW, 8 tubes, AC, $110.00-130.00.

T-60, table, 1940, two-tone wood, right front slide rule dial, left cloth grille with horizontal bars, 6 pushbuttons, 4 knobs, BC, SW, 6 tubes, AC, $65.00-75.00.

U-134, console-R/P, 1938, wood, lift-top with inner dial/knobs/tuning eye and phono, front grille area behind double doors, electric pushbutton tuning, 5 knobs, BC, SW, 16 tubes, AC $240.00-280.00

UY-122E, chairside-R/P, 1938, wood, top dial/push buttons/knobs, lift top, inner phono, front cloth grille with horizontal bars, lower storage, 2 knobs, BC, SW, 7 tubes, AC/DC $150.00-180.00

UY-124, console-R/P, 1939, wood, inner top right vertical dial & pushbuttons, left phono, lift top, front cloth grille with 2 vertical bars, 2 knobs, BC, SW, 7 tubes, AC/DC $95.00-115.00

V-101, table-R/P, 1940, wood, right front slide rule dial, left grille area, lift top, inner phono, 3 knobs, BC, 7 tubes including ballast, AC......$40.00-45.00

V-102, table-R/P, 1941, wood, right front slide rule dial, left vertical grille bars, pushbuttons, lift top, inner phono, 3 knobs, BC, 7 tubes, AC $40.00-45.00

V-105, table-R/P, 1942, wood, right front dial, left grille area, lift top, inner phono, 3 knobs, BC, 5 tubes, AC $35.00-40.00

V-170, console-R/P, 1940, wood, lift-top with inner dial/knobs and phono, front grille area with three vertical bars, pushbutton tuning, 4 knobs, BC, SW, 6 tubes, AC $120.00-150.00

V-200, console-R/P, 1940, wood, lift-top with inner dial/knobs/pushbuttons and phono, front grille area with cross hatch, 4 knobs, BC, SW, 7 tubes, AC $120.00-150.00

V-201, console-R/P, 1940, wood, center front slide rule dial, pushbuttons, lower grille with center vertical bars, lift-top for phono, 4 knobs, BC, SW, 7 tubes, AC $120.00-150.00

V-205, console-R/P, 1940, wood, inner right slide rule dial & pushbuttons, door, left lift top, inner phono, lower cloth grille with center divider, 5 knobs, BC, SW, 9 tubes, AC $120.00-150.00

V-209, console-R/P, 1942, wood, lift-top with inner dial/knobs and phono, front recessed grille area with vertical bars, 4 knobs, BC, SW, 8 tubes, AC...$120.00-150.00

V-210, console-R/P, 1942, wood, double front doors with inner dial/knobs/pushbuttons and phono, front recessed grille area with vertical bars, 4 knobs, BC, SW, 8 tubes, AC $120.00-150.00

V-215, console-R/P, 1942, wood, inner right slide rule dial & pushbuttons, door, left fold-out phono, lower grille with vertical bars, 6 knobs, BC, SW, 9 tubes, AC $120.00-150.00

V-225, console-R/P, 1941, wood, inner right slide rule dial & pushbuttons, door, left pull-out phono, lower cloth grille with cut-outs, 6 knobs, BC, SW, 9 tubes, AC $120.00-150.00

V-135, table-R/P, 1941, wood, right front dial, left grille with horizontal bars, lift top, inner phono, 3 knobs, BC, 5 tubes, AC, $30.00-35.00.

X-2HE, table, plastic, large right front round dial over vertical grille bars, lower left on/off/volume knob, feet, BC, AC/DC $20.00-25.00

X-2JE, table, plastic, large right front round dial over vertical grille bars, lower left on/off/volume knob, feet, BC, AC/DC $20.00-25.00

X-4EF "Filteramic," table, 1960, plastic, center dial area over lattice front panel, dual speakers, feet, 2 knobs, BC, 5 tubes, AC $25.00-30.00

X5HE, table, plastic, lower front slide rule dial, large upper lattice grille, 2 knobs, BC, AC $20.00-25.00

X-55, table, 1942, two-tone wood, right front slide rule dial, left cloth grille, 6 pushbuttons, 2 knobs, BC, 5 tubes, AC/DC $50.00-65.00

X-551, table, 1951, maroon plastic, semi-circular grille bars around center front dial, top strip, 2 knobs, BC, 5 tubes, AC/DC, $40.00-50.00.

X-60, table, 1942, wood, right front slide rule dial, left cloth grille with horizontal bars, pushbuttons, 4 knobs, BC, SW, 6 tubes, AC/DC....$50.00-65.00

X-552, table, 1951, ivory plastic, semi-circular grille bars around center front dial, top strip, 2 knobs, BC, 5 tubes, AC/DC $40.00-50.00

V-100, table-R/P, 1939, two-tone wood, right front dial, left horizontal grille bars, lift top, inner phono, 3 knobs, BC, 5 tubes, AC, $35.00-40.00.

X-711, table, 1951, plastic, upper dotted slide rule dial over large grille area, 3 knobs, BC, FM, 7 tubes, AC/DC, $25.00-30.00.

RECORDIO
Wilcox-Gay Corporation
604 Seminary Street, Charlotte, Michigan

1J10, table-R/P/Rec, 1951, suitcase-style, inner left dial, right disc recorder, lift top, handle, 3 knobs, BC, 5 tubes, AC **$25.00-30.00**

6B10, table-R/P/Rec/PA, 1946, leatherette, inner front dial/controls/oval grille area, fold-down front, lift top, inner phono, pushbuttons, tuning eye, 4 knobs, BC, 8 tubes, AC.....................................**$30.00-35.00**

6B30M, table-R/P/Rec/PA, 1946, wood, right front dial & controls, left oval grille, lift top, inner phono, pushbuttons, tuning eye, 4 knobs, BC, 8 tubes, AC **$35.00-40.00**

7D44, console-R/P/Rec, 1948, wood, left front tilt-out dial, pushbuttons, right pull-out phono drawer, 4 knobs, BC, FM, 15 tubes, AC **$65.00-75.00**

7E40, console-R/P/Rec, 1948, wood, inner right slide rule dial, left pull-out phono drawer, 4 knobs, BC, FM, 12 tubes, AC..............**$65.00-75.00**

7E44, console-R/P/Rec, 1948, wood, inner slide rule dial, double doors, lower phono/recorder, cloth grille with vertical bars, 4 knobs, BC, FM, 12 tubes, AC **$65.00-75.00**

8J10, table-R/P/Rec, 1949, leatherette, inner left dial, grille, right phono, lift top, handle, 3 knobs, BC, 5 tubes, AC **$25.00-30.00**

9G10, table-R/P/Rec, 1950, leatherette, inner slide rule dial, phono, lift top, handle, 5 knobs, BC, FM, 7 tubes, AC **$25.00-30.00**

9G40M, console-R/P/Rec, 1950, wood, inner right vertical slide rule dial, left phono, fold-down door, lower front grille area, 5 knobs, BC, FM, 7 tubes, AC **$50.00-65.00**

9H40B, console-R/P, 1950, wood, inner right vertical slide rule dial, inner left phono, fold-down door, lower front grille & storage, 5 knobs, BC, FM, 7 tubes, AC **$50.00-65.00**

REGAL
Regal Electronics Corporation
20 West 20th Street, New York, New York

205, table, 1947, plastic, upper front slanted slide rule dial, lower horizontal louvers, 2 knobs, BC, 5 tubes, AC/DC **$40.00-50.00**

271, table, 1953, plastic, large front half-round dial over horizontal louvers, 2 knobs, BC, 5 tubes, AC/DC **$25.00-30.00**

472, table, 1953, plastic, lower front half-round dial overlaps upper checkered panel, top louvers, 2 knobs, BC, 5 tubes, AC/DC ..**$30.00-35.00**

575, table, 1953, plastic, upper front slide rule dial, lower horizontal louvers wrap-around right side, 2 knobs, BC, 5 tubes, AC/DC **$40.00-50.00**

747, portable, 1947, metal & plastic, inner slide rule dial, upper horizontal louvers, flip-up front, 2 knobs, BC, 4 tubes, AC/DC/battery **$35.00-40.00**

777, portable, 1949, metal & plastic, inner slide rule dial, flip-up front, 2 knobs, BC, 4 tubes, AC/DC/battery...............................**$35.00-40.00**

1049, table, 1947, plastic, upper front slide rule dial, lower horizontal wrap-around louvers, 3 knobs, BC, SW, 6 tubes, AC/DC..........**$40.00-50.00**

1107, table, 1948, plastic, upper front slanted slide rule dial, 3 rows of decorative grille circles, 2 knobs, BC, 4 tubes, AC/DC ..**$40.00-50.00**

1500, table, 1948, plastic, upper front slanted slide rule dial, lower horizontal wrap-around louvers, 3 knobs, BC, SW, 4 tubes, battery **$25.00-30.00**

1749, table, 1947, plastic, upper front slanted slide rule dial, lower horizontal wrap-around louvers, 3 knobs, BC, SW, 6 tubes, AC/DC..**$40.00-50.00**

1877, portable, 1952, plastic, lower front dial, upper checkered grille, handle, 2 knobs, BC, 4 tubes, AC/DC/battery...............**$40.00-50.00**

7152, table, 1949, plastic, upper front slanted slide rule dial, lower horizontal louvers, 3 knobs, BC, SW, 5 tubes, AC/DC **$35.00-40.00**

7162, table, 1949, plastic, upper front slanted slide rule dial, lower raised lattice grille, 3 knobs, BC, SW, 6 tubes, AC/DC **$40.00-50.00**

7163, table, 1949, plastic, upper front slanted slide rule dial, lower raised lattice grille, 3 knobs, BC, SW, 6 tubes, AC/DC **$40.00-50.00**

7251, table, 1948, plastic, slant-down top, lower front slide rule dial, upper lattice grille, 2 knobs, BC, 5 tubes, AC/DC **$40.00-50.00**

BP48, portable, 1948, inner slide rule dial, horizontal grille bars, flip-open top, handle, 2 knobs, BC, 4 tubes, battery **$35.00-45.00**

C-527, table-C, 1952, plastic, lower front dial, upper alarm clock face, decorative case lines, 5 knobs, BC, 5 tubes, AC............**$30.00-35.00**

FM78, table, 1949, plastic, upper front slanted slide rule dial, lower raised lattice grille, 3 knobs, BC, FM, 8 tubes, AC/DC.............**$40.00-50.00**

L-76, table, 1946, wood, upper front slanted slide rule dial, lower cloth grille with center horizontal bar, 2 knobs, BC, 6 tubes, AC/DC..**$30.00-35.00**

P-175, portable, 1952, alligator, inner right airplane dial, left grille, fold-down lid, handle, 3 knobs, BC, SW, 6 tubes, AC/DC/battery **$30.00-35.00**

W800, table, 1947, plastic, upper front slanted slide rule dial, lower horizontal louvers, 2 knobs, BC, 6 tubes, AC/DC **$40.00-45.00**

W801, table, 1947, plastic, upper front slide rule dial, lower horizontal louvers, 2 knobs, BC, 6 tubes, AC/DC **$40.00-45.00**

W901, table, 1947, plastic, upper front slide rule dial, lower horizontal wrap-around louvers, 3 knobs, BC, SW, 6 tubes, AC/DC **$40.00-45.00**

REMLER
Remler Co., Ltd.
2101 Bryant Street, San Francisco, California

21-3, cathedral, 1932, wood, flat top, lower front curved dial, upper cloth grille with cut-outs, 3 knobs, BC, 4 tubes, AC, $200.00-230.00.

10, cathedral, 1932, wood, flat top, lower front dial, upper cloth grille with cut-outs, fluted columns, 3 knobs, BC, 6 tubes, AC ..**$270.00-320.00**

15, cathedral, 1932, wood, flat top, lower front dial, upper cloth grille with cut-outs, fluted columns, 3 knobs, BC, 7 tubes, AC ..**$270.00-320.00**

15-C, console, 1932, wood, lowboy, upper front dial, lower cloth grille with cut-outs, 3 knobs, BC, 7 tubes, AC **$120.00-150.00**

19, console, 1932, wood, lowboy, upper front dial, lower cloth grille with cut-outs, BC, SW, 10 tubes, AC **$120.00-150.00**

40 "Scottie," table, 1936, plastic, right front dial, center cloth grille with Deco cut-outs & Scottie logo, 2 knobs, BC, 4 tubes, AC **$240.00-300.00**

41 "Scottie," table, 1936, plastic, center front grille with Deco cut-outs & Scottie logo, 2 knobs, BC, SW, 5 tubes, AC **$240.00-300.00**

43 "Esquire," table, 1936, wood, center front black dial surrounded by grille cut-outs, 4 knobs, BC, SW, 7 tubes, AC...............**$75.00-85.00**

51 "Skipper," table, 1936, plastic, center front dial surrounded by grille cut-outs, 2 knobs, BC, 4 tubes, AC **$75.00-85.00**

53, tombstone, wood, lower front dial, upper cloth grille with cut-outs, decorative fluting, 2 knobs, BC, 5 tubes, AC.............**$110.00-130.00**

54, table, 1938, plastic, right front dial, left "Venetian blind" louvered grille, 2 knobs, 5 tubes, AC **$55.00-65.00**

61, table, 1938, wood, upper front slide rule dial, lower horizontal wrap-around louvers, pushbuttons, 3 knobs, BC, 6 tubes, AC..**$55.00-65.00**

62 "Grenadier," table, 1936, wood, center front black dial surrounded by grille cut-outs, 4 knobs, BC, SW, 5 tubes, AC...............**$75.00-85.00**

88, tombstone, 1936, wood, shouldered, lower front dial, upper cloth grille with cut-outs, 2 speakers, BC, SW, 10 tubes, AC **$160.00-190.00**

471, table-R/P/Rec, 1940, wood, left front slide rule dial, right grille with horizontal bars, lift top, inner phono, BC, 7 tubes, AC ..**$30.00-35.00**

5300BI "Scottie," table-R/P, 1947, two-tone plastic, upper front slide rule dial, lower horizontal louvers, Scottie logo, lift top, inner phono, 2 knobs, BC, 5 tubes, AC **$180.00-200.00**

5310BL, table-R/P, 1948, blonde, inner right dial, phono, lift top, front grille doors, 4 knobs, BC, 6 tubes, AC **$35.00-40.00**

5310M, table-R/P, 1948, mahogany, inner right dial, phono, lift top, front grille doors, 4 knobs, BC, 6 tubes, AC **$35.00-40.00**

5400 "Scottie," portable, 1948, leatherette/walnut plastic, upper front slide rule dial, upper horizontal grille bars with center Scottie logo, handle, 2 knobs, BC, 5 tubes, AC/DC/battery............**$95.00-115.00**

5410 "Scottie," portable, 1948, leatherette/white plastic, lower front slide dial, upper horizontal grille bars with center Scottie logo, handle, 2 knobs, BC, 5 tubes, AC/DC/battery $120.00-150.00

5500 "Scottie Pup," table, 1948, walnut plastic, "upholstered"-style, lower front slide rule dial, upper vertical grille bars with Scottie logo, 2 knobs, BC, 5 tubes, AC/DC $180.00-200.00

5505 "Scottie Pup," table, 1948, ebony/white plastic, lower front slide rule dial, upper horizontal grille bars with center Scottie logo, handle, 2 knobs, BC, 5 tubes, AC/DC $200.00-230.00

5510 "Scottie Pup," table, 1948, white plastic, lower front slide rule dial, upper horizontal grille bars with center Scottie logo, handle, 2 knobs, BC, 5 tubes, AC/DC......................................$180.00-200.00

5515 "Scottie Pup," table, 1948, red/white plastic, lower front slide rule dial, upper horizontal grille bars with center Scottie logo, handle, 2 knobs, BC, 5 tubes, AC/DC..$240.00-270.00

5520 "Scottie Junior," table, 1947, walnut plastic, "upholstered"-style, lower front slide rule dial, upper vertical grille bars with Scottie logo, 2 knobs, BC, 5 tubes, AC/DC $180.00-200.00

5530 "Scottie Junior," table, 1947, white plastic, "upholstered"-style, lower front slide rule dial, upper vertical grille bars with Scottie logo, 2 knobs, BC, 5 tubes, AC/DC $180.00-200.00

5535 "Scottie Pup," table, 1948, red/white plastic, lower front slide rule dial, upper horizontal grille bars with center Scottie logo, handle, 2 knobs, BC, 5 tubes, AC/DC..$240.00-270.00

6000 "Scottie," table, 1949, plastic, top wrap-over dial, lower horizontal grille bars, Scottie logo, 2 knobs, BC, 6 tubes, AC/DC..$120.00-150.00

MP5-5-3 "Scottie," table, 1946, plastic, top wrap-over dial, lower horizontal louvers, handle, Scottie logo, 2 knobs, BC, 5 tubes, AC $160.00-180.00

RESAS
Resas, Inc.
112 Chambers St., New York, New York

5T "Tone-A-Dyne," table, 1925, wood, low rectangular case, 3 dial front panel, 5 tubes, battery $160.00-180.00

REVERE
Revere Camera Company
320 East 21st Street, Chicago, Illinois

Patrician, table, 1931, wood, front window dial with escutcheon, upper built-in speaker with arched top & grille cut-outs, BC, 5 tubes, AC, $200.00-230.00.

Jr., cathedral, wood, center front window dial with escutcheon, upper cloth grille with cut-outs..$300.00-350.00

Minuette, cathedral, 1932, wood, small case with flat top, lower dial, upper grille with cut-outs, 3 knobs, 4 tubes $160.00-180.00

400, portable, 1955, leather, purse-style, inner aluminum panel with left dial & right perforated grille, lift-up lid, strap, BC, 4 tubes, AC/DC/battery, $120.00-150.00.

ROBERT-LAWRENCE
Robert-Lawrence Electronics Corporation

02-L-6T, portable, 1948, alligator, left front airplane dial, right grille area, handle, 3 knobs, BC, SW, 6 tubes, AC/DC $30.00-35.00

ROLAND
Roland Radio Corporation
12-30 Anderson Avenue, Mt. Vernon, New York

5P2, portable, 1954, plastic, upper right front round dial, center lattice grille, handle, 2 knobs, BC, 4 tubes, AC/DC/battery, $25.00-30.00.

C2, table-C, 1957, plastic, right side dial, left front alarm clock, right lattice grille, BC, 5 tubes, AC...$25.00-30.00

4P2 "Riviera," portable, plastic, upper right front dial, large left lattice grille area, handle, BC, battery $25.00-30.00

4T1, table, 1953, plastic, right front round dial overlaps horizontal wrap-around grille bars, 2 knobs, BC, 4 tubes, AC/DC $40.00-50.00

5C1, table-C, 1953, plastic, right side dial, center front round clock over horizontal louvers, 5 knobs, BC, 5 tubes, AC $30.00-35.00

5C2, table-C, 1953, plastic, right front dial, left alarm clock, center vertical bars, 6 knobs, BC, 5 tubes, AC $30.00-35.00

5C5, table-C, 1956, plastic, right side dial, left front alarm clock, right lattice grille, 5 knobs, BC, 5 tubes, AC $25.00-30.00

5P5, portable, 1956, plastic, right front round dial, vertical grille bars, handle, 2 knobs, BC, 4 tubes, AC/DC/battery...............$25.00-30.00

5T1E, table, 1953, plastic, right front round dial over large recessed grille, feet, 2 knobs, BC, 5 tubes, AC/DC $35.00-40.00

5T1V, table, 1953, plastic, right front round dial over large recessed grille, feet, 2 knobs, BC, 5 tubes, AC/DC $35.00-40.00

5T2M, table, 1953, plastic, center front round dial over large recessed grille, feet, 2 knobs, BC, 5 tubes, AC/DC $35.00-40.00

5T3, table, 1954, plastic, center front round dial over horizontal louvers, 2 knobs, BC, 5 tubes, AC/DC....................................$20.00-25.00

5T5, table, 1954, plastic, right front diagonal half-round dial over recessed lattice grille, 2 knobs, BC, 5 tubes, AC/DC $30.00-35.00

5T6, table, 1956, plastic, right front diagonal half-round dial over recessed lattice grille, feet, 2 knobs, BC, 5 tubes, AC/DC **$30.00-35.00**

5X6U, table-R/P, 1956, wood, right front vertical slide rule dial over large grille area, lift top, inner phono, 3 right side knobs, BC, 5 tubes, AC **$30.00-35.00**

6P2, portable, 1954, plastic, upper front slide rule dial, lower lattice grille, handle, 2 knobs, BC, 5 tubes, AC/DC/battery................**$25.00-30.00**

6T1M, table, 1953, plastic, lower front slide rule dial, upper woven grille, 2 knobs, BC, 6 tubes, AC/DC **$30.00-35.00**

8FT1M, table, 1953, plastic, lower front slide rule dial, upper woven grille, 2 knobs, BC, FM, 7 tubes, AC/DC **$30.00-35.00**

8XF1, table-R/P, 1953, upper front slide rule dial, lower grille, lift top, inner phono, 3 knobs, BC, FM, 7 tubes, AC **$30.00-35.00**

10TF1, table, 1954, wood, lower front slide rule dial, upper grille, 4 knobs, BC, FM, 10 tubes, AC **$30.00-35.00**

10XF1, console-R/P, 1955, wood, right front slide rule dial, left pull-out phono drawer, lower grille area, 5 knobs, BC, FM, 10 tubes, AC **$50.00-65.00**

54B, table, plastic, center front round dial over large horizontal louvers, 1 lower knob, BC, $25.00-30.00.

ROSKO

TP-6, portable, plastic, large front lattice grille area, fold-down handle, right & left side knobs, BC, 4 tubes, battery **$35.00-45.00**

ROYAL
Royal Radio Co.
10 West 33rd Street, New York, New York

AN150, portable, 1952, leatherette, inner right dial, left grille, fold-in front, handle, 3 knobs, BC, SW, 6 tubes, AC/DC/battery **$35.00-40.00**

SCOTCH COOLER

No #, portable-N, metal, looks like a plaid picnic cooler, top controls, handle, BC, battery **$150.00-180.00**

SCOTT
E.H. Scott Radio Laboratories, Inc.
4450 Ravenswood Avenue, Chicago, Illinois

E.H. Scott was a native of New Zealand who emigrated to the United States at the end of World War I. After an initial interest in automobiles, he became fascinated with radio, writing many articles on the best performing radio circuitry of the day. In the second half of the 1920s, Scott began manufacturing radio transformers and offered a variety of high performance radio kits. In the 1930s, Scott began custom manufacturing expensive, state-of-the-art radios, "The Stradivarius of Radio Receivers," typically featuring high tube counts, chrome plated chassis, and high fidelity audio. His motto was "the fine things are aways made by hand." During World War II, Scott manufactured many radio receivers for the armed forces. E.H. Scott sold his interest in his company during the latter part of World War II and terminated any association with the company in 1945. Scott Radio Laboratories continued in business into the 1950s.

Scott radios are some of the most highly sought collector radios. The radios were purchased separately from the cabinets, resulting in a wide variety of possible radio and cabinet combinations. The listings below indicate values of the basic radio models themselves and then the additional value of the particular cabinet illustrated in the photos is also noted. The value of any given Scott radio in a cabinet is the total of the radio value and the cabinet value. A key value criteria is the completeness of the radio (i.e. includes all chassis and speaker as indicated) and the condition of any chrome-plated chassis, with significant rust and/or pitting resulting in a serious reduction in the listed values.

800BT, console, 1948, wood, 800B on left side in Chippendale cabinet with right side projection TV, 7 radio knobs, 5 TV knobs, BC, SW, FM, TV, 13 main receiver tubes, 11 power supply/amplifier/FM subsytem tubes, 31 TV tubes, AC, $2000.00-2400.00.

800B, console, 1946, wood, chrome-plated receiver chassis, chrome-plated power supply/amplifier/FM subsystem, speaker, pushbutton electric tuning, slide rule dial, two tuning eyes, optional phono and remote, 7 knobs, BC, SW, FM, 13 main receiver tubes, 11 power supply/amplifier/FM subsytem tubes, AC **$500.00-650.00**

A.C. 10, table/console, 1929, wood, many cabinet styles/no cabinet, kit/factory build, several variations, front center escutcheon w/single vertical dial, separate power pack/amp chassis, 3 knobs, BC, optional SW converter, 8 receiver tubes, 3-4 power supply/amplifier tubes, AC, $900.00-1,050.00.

Allwave (2 Volt), console/table, 1933, wood, many cabinet styles/no cabinet, several radio design variations, basic 2 piece design consists of chrome-plated receiver chassis and speaker, receiver has escutcheon with one center vertical window dial (photo shown with "Orleans" cabinet), 3 knobs & 1 bandswitch lever, BC, SW, 11 or 12 tubes, battery, $1,750.00-2,000.00, "Orleans" cabinet $750.00.

Allwave 12 Two-Dial, console/table, 1931, wood, many cabinet styles/no cabinet, several radio design variations, basic 3 piece design consists of chrome-plated receiver chassis/power supply/amplifier chassis and speaker, receiver has escutcheon with two center vertical window dials, plug-in coils select BC or SW bands (photo shown with "Lancaster" cabinet), 4 knobs, BC, SW, 9 receiver tubes, 3 power supply/amplifier tubes, AC, $750.00-900.00, "Lancaster" cabinet $500.00.

Allwave 15, console/table, 1934, wood, many cabinet styles/no cabinet, several radio design variations, basic 3 piece design consists of chrome-plated receiver chassis/chrome-plated power supply/amplifier chassis and speaker, receiver has escutcheon with one center vertical window dial, BC, SW, 12 receiver tubes, 3 power supply/amplifier tubes, AC.....................................**$1,100.00-1,250.00**

Philharmonic (pointer dial), console, 1937, wood, many cabinet styles/no cabinet, chrome-plated receiver chassis, chrome-plated power supply/amplifier, speaker with built-in crossover for additional speakers, receiver has large airplane dial with pointer indicator, two tuning eyes, optional remote control, 7 knobs, BC, SW, LW, 24 receiver tubes, 6 power supply/amplifier tubes, AC **$2,000.00-2,400.00**

Shield Grid 9, table, 1928, wood/no case, kit, front panel w/center panel meter & two vertical dials, separate AC power supply/amp (photo shown with "Nelson" cabinet), 5 knobs, BC, optional SW, 8 receiver tubes, 3 power supply/amplifier tubes, AC or battery without power supply ....**$1,100.00-1,300.00 w/supply, "Nelson" cabinet $200**

Super XII, console, 1938, wood, many cabinet styles/no cabinet, chrome-plated receiver chassis with on-board power supply, speaker, receiver has large airplane dial, 5 knobs, BC, SW, 12 tubes, AC **$750.00-900.00**

Super XII, console, 1939, wood, many cabinet styles/no cabinet, chrome-plated receiver chassis, chrome-plated power supply, speaker, receiver has large airplane dial, 5 or 7 knobs, BC, SW, 11 receiver tubes, 1 power supply tube, AC....................**$750.00-900.00**

World's Record Super 10, table, 1926, wood/no case, kit, wood component base, Bakelite front panel w/two left front window dials, typically two right front panel meters, 5 knobs, BC, 10 tubes, battery **$1,500.00-1,700.00**

Allwave 12 Deluxe, console/table, 1932, wood, many cabinet styles/no cabinet, several radio design variations, basic 3 piece design consists of chrome-plated receiver chassis/chrome-plated power supply/amplifier chassis and speaker, receiver has escutcheon with one center vertical window dial (photo shown with "Lido" cabinet), 3 knobs & 1 bandswitch lever, BC, SW, 9 receiver tubes, 3 power supply/amplifier tubes, AC, $800.00-950.00, "Lido" cabinet $1,600.00.

Allwave 23 (5 knob), console, 1935, wood, many cabinet styles/no cabinet, chrome-plated receiver chassis, chrome-plated power supply/amplifier, typically 3 speakers, receiver has escutcheon with one center vertical window dial (photo shown with "Tasman" cabinet), 5 knobs & 1 bandswitch lever, BC, SW, 17 receiver tubes, 6 power supply/amplifier tubes, AC, $1,350.00-1,550.00, "Tasman" cabinet $1,250.00.

Allwave 23 (7 knob), console, 1936, wood, many cabinet styles/no cabinet, chrome-plated receiver chassis, chrome-plated power supply/amplifier, typically 3 speakers, receiver has escutcheon with one center vertical window dial (photo shown with "Laureate Grande" cabinet), 7 knobs & 1 bandswitch lever, BC, SW, 17 receiver tubes, 6 power supply/amplifier tubes, AC, $1,400.00-1,600.00, "Laureate Grande" cabinet $2,500.00.

Masterpiece, console, 1939, wood, many cabinet styles/no cabinet, chrome-plated receiver chassis, chrome-plated power supply/amplifier, speaker, receiver has large airplane dial (photo shown with "Louis XV" cabinet), 7 knobs, BC, SW, 11 receiver tubes, 3 power supply/amplifier tubes, AC, $950.00-1,150.00, "Louis XV" cabinet $3,000.00.

Laureate, console, 1941, wood, many cabinet styles/no cabinet, chrome-plated receiver chassis, chrome-plated power supply, speaker, slide rule dial, tuning eye (photo shown with "Regent" cabinet), BC, SW, FM1, optional FM w/converter, 16 receiver tubes, 2 power supply tubes, AC, $1,000.00-1,200.00, "Regent" cabinet $1,250.00.

Phantom, console, 1938, wood, many cabinet styles/no cabinet, chrome-plated receiver chassis, chrome-plated power supply/amplifier, speaker, slide rule tuning dial, tuning eye, optional remote control (photo shown with "Westwood" cabinet), 7 knobs, BC, SW, 13 receiver tubes, 6 power supply/amplifier tubes, AC, $1,150.00-1,350.00, "Westwood" cabinet $1,300.00.

Philharmonic ("beam-of-light"), console, 1939, wood, many cabinet styles/no cabinet, chrome-plated receiver chassis, chrome-plated power supply/amplifier, speaker with built-in crossover for additional speakers, receiver uses "beam-of-light" as dial indicator, several dial variations, two tuning eyes, optional remote control (photo shown with "Waverly Grande" cabinet), 7 or 9 knobs, BC, SW, LW, 24 receiver tubes, 6 power supply/amplifier tubes, AC, $2,000.00-2,400.00, "Waverly Grande" cabinet $2,250.00.

Phantom (FM), console, 1940, wood, many cabinet styles/no cabinet, chrome-plated receiver chassis, chrome-plated power supply/amplifier, speaker, slide rule tuning dial, tuning eye, optional remote control (photo shown with "Acousticraft" cabinet), 8 knobs, BC, SW, FM1, optional FM w/converter, 22 receiver tubes, 6 power supply/amplifier tubes, AC, $1,250.00-1,450.00, "Acousticraft" cabinet $1,500.00.

Philharmonic (FM), console, 1940, wood, many cabinet styles/no cabinet, chrome-plated receiver chassis, chrome-plated power supply/amplifier, several speaker variations, receiver uses "beam-of-light" as dial indicator, two tuning eyes, optional remote control (photo shown with "Gothic Grande" cabinet), BC, SW, LW, FM1, optional FM w/converter, 27 receiver tubes, 6 power supply/amplifier tubes, AC, $2,100.00-2,500.00, "Gothic Grande" cabinet $2,500.00.

Phantom Deluxe, console, 1939, wood, many cabinet styles/no cabinet, chrome-plated receiver chassis, chrome-plated power supply/amplifier, speaker, slide rule tuning dial, tuning eye, optional remote control (photo shown with "Braemar" cabinet), 8 knobs, BC, SW, 14 receiver tubes, 6 power supply/amplifier tubes, AC, $1,150.00-1,350.00, "Braemar" cabinet $750.00.

Shield Grid 9, table, 1928, wood/no case, kit, front panel w/center panel meter & two vertical dials, 5 knobs, BC, 9 tubes, battery, $900.00-1,050.00.

Shield Grid 9B, table, 1928, wood/no case, kit, front panel w/center panel meter & two vertical dials (photo shown with "Nelson" table cabinet), 5 knobs, BC, optional SW, 9 tubes, battery, $900.00-1,050.00, "Nelson" cabinet $200.00.

Symphony, table/console, 1929, wood/no case, large front center escutcheon, single vertical dial, built-in AC supply, 3 knobs, BC, 5 tubes, AC, $2,100.00-2,300.00.

Sixteen, console/chairside, 1937, wood, many cabinet styles/no cabinet, chrome-plated receiver chassis, chrome-plated power supply/amplifier, speaker, receiver has large metal airplane dial, tuning eye (photo shown with "Braeside" cabinet), 5 knobs & 1 push-pull switch, BC, SW, 12 receiver tubes, 4 power supply/amplifier tubes, AC, $800.00-950.00, "Braeside" cabinet $2,500.00.

World's Record Super 8, table, 1926, wood/no case, kit, several radio design variations, wood component base, Bakelite front panel, two window dials, 4 or 5 knobs, BC, 8 tubes, battery, $1,000.00-1,200.00.

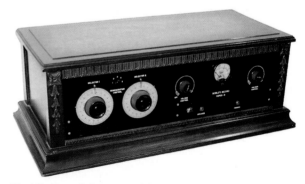

World's Record Super 9, table, 1925, wood/suitcase style/no case, kit, several radio design variations, wood component base, front panel w/two dials, may have panel meter, typically 6 knobs, BC, optional SW, 9 tubes, battery, $1,100.00-1,300.00.

World's Record Super 9 Deluxe, table, 1926, wood/no case, kit, wood component base, Bakelite front panel w/two left front dials, typically two right front panel meters, 8 knobs, BC, optional SW, 9 tubes, battery, $1,200.00-1,400.00.

World's Record Super 10, table, 1927, wood/no case, kit, wood component base, Bakelite front panel w/center panel meter & two vertical dials, 5 knobs, BC, 10 tubes, battery, $1,500.00-1,700.00.

SENTINEL
Sentinel Radio Corp.
2020 Ridge Avenue, Evanston, Illinois

1U-345, portable, 1952, plastic, right front round dial, diagonal grille with vertical bars, handle, 2 knobs, BC, 4 tubes, AC/DC/battery, $40.00-45.00.

1U-312PW, portable, 1950, plastic, upper front slanted slide rule dial, lower 2-section grille with center stylized "S," flex handle, 2 top thumbwheel knobs, BC, 5 tubes, AC/DC/battery **$40.00-45.00**
1U-339K, table-R/P, 1950, wood, center front dial, right & left grilles, lift top, inner phono, 4 knobs, BC, 5 tubes, AC **$35.00-40.00**
1U-340C, console-R/P, 1951, wood, upper right front dial, left pull-out phono drawer, lower grille, 4 knobs, BC, 5 tubes, AC....**$65.00-75.00**

195ULTWD, table, 1940, walnut, right front dial, left wrap-around cloth grille with 2 horizontal bars, top right pushbuttons, handle, 2 knobs, BC, 5 tubes, AC/DC, $75.00-85.00.

1U-355P, portable, 1956, plastic, right side round dial, front horizontal bars with center logo, handle, 2 knobs, BC, 4 tubes, AC/DC/battery **$30.00-35.00**
1U-360, table, 1956, plastic, right side dial, right & left side horizontal bars, front grille area, 2 knobs, BC, 4 tubes, AC/DC......**$25.00-30.00**
1U-363, table, 1956, plastic, right side dial, front recessed horizontal grille bars with center logo, 2 side knobs, BC, 5 tubes, AC/DC...**$25.00-30.00**
8, console, 1930, two-tone walnut, highboy, upper front window dial, lower cloth grille with "oyster shell" cut-out, 3 knobs, BC, 8 tubes, AC **$120.00-140.00**
11, console, 1930, walnut, lowboy, Deco, upper front window dial, lower octagonal cloth grille with cut-outs, 2 knobs, BC, 7 tubes, AC **$130.00-150.00**
76AC, console, 1937, wood, upper front round dial, lower cloth grille with center vertical bars, 5 knobs, BC, SW, 11 tubes, AC ..**$120.00-140.00**
108A, cathedral, 1931, wood, center front window dial, upper cloth grille with cut-outs, 3 knobs, BC, 7 tubes, AC **$300.00-320.00**
108A, console, 1931, wood, lowboy, upper front window dial, lower cloth grille with scrolled cut-outs, 3 knobs, BC, 7 tubes, AC..**$120.00-150.00**
109, console, 1931, wood, upper front window dial, lower cloth grille with cut-outs, BC, 9 tubes, AC **$120.00-150.00**
111, cathedral, 1931, wood, center front dial, upper cloth grille with cut-outs, BC, 4 tubes, AC **$240.00-300.00**
125AC-CB, console-R/P, 1939, wood, upper front slide rule dial, pushbuttons, lower grille with vertical bars, lift top, inner phono, BC, SW, 6 tubes, AC **$130.00-150.00**

220T460, table, 1940, wood, right front slide rule dial with plastic escutcheon, left cloth grille with 4 horizontal bars, 4 knobs, BC, SW, 7 tubes, AC, $45.00-55.00.

248G, table-R/P, 1941, two-tone wood, right front dial, left cloth grille with center vertical divider, lift top, inner phono, 2 knobs, BC, 5 tubes, AC, $35.00-40.00.

137UT, table, 1939, plastic, upper right front streamlined thumbwheel dial, horizontal grille bars, decorative case lines, 2 knobs, BC, 5 tubes including ballast, AC/DC $75.00-85.00

168BC, console, 1939, wood, upper front slanted slide rule dial, lower cloth grille with vertical bars, 4 knobs, BC, SW, 5 tubes, battery $75.00-85.00

168BT, table, 1939, walnut, right front slide rule dial, left cloth grille with vertical bars, 4 knobs, BC, SW, 5 tubes, battery............$45.00-50.00

170BL, portable, 1939, brown leatherette, right front dial, left grille, handle, 2 knobs, BC, 3 tubes, battery $30.00-35.00

175BCT, console, 1939, walnut, upper front slanted dial, lower cloth grille with center vertical bars, front fluting, 2 knobs, BC, 4 tubes, battery $75.00-85.00

175BT, table, 1939, walnut plastic, right front dial, left horizontal wrap-around louvers, 2 knobs, BC, 4 tubes, battery $35.00-40.00

175BTW, table, 1940, walnut, right front square dial, left horizontal louvers, feet, 2 knobs, BC, 4 tubes, battery $35.00-40.00

176BT, table, 1939, walnut, right front dial, left horizontal grille bars, fluted top & base, pushbuttons, BC, SW, 6 tubes, battery..$35.00-40.00

177UT, table, 1939, plastic, upper right front streamlined thumbwheel dial, horizontal grille bars, decorative case lines, 2 knobs, BC, 5 tubes, AC/DC $75.00-85.00

178BL, portable, 1939, striped cloth covered, right front dial, left grille, handle, 2 knobs, BC, 4 tubes, battery $30.00-35.00

180XL, portable, 1939, cloth covered, inner right dial, left grille, fold-down front, handle, 4 knobs, BC, 5 tubes, AC/DC/battery........$30.00-35.00

284NI, table, 1946, Catalin, upper front slanted slide rule dial, lower inset curved horizontal grille bars, 2 knobs, BC, 5 tubes, AC/DC, $850.00+.

181BL-CB, portable-R/P, 1940, cloth covered, inner right dial, left grille, fold-down front, lift top, inner crank phono, 2 knobs, BC, 4 tubes, battery $40.00-45.00

194UTI, table, 1940, ivory plastic, right front dial, left horizontal wrap-around louvers, 2 knobs, BC, 5 tubes, AC/DC $50.00-65.00

194UTR, table, 1940, red plastic, right front dial, left horizontal wrap-around louvers, 2 knobs, BC, 5 tubes, AC/DC $65.00-75.00

194UTW, table, 1940, walnut plastic, right front dial, left horizontal wrap-around louvers, 2 knobs, BC, 5 tubes, AC/DC $50.00-65.00

195ULT, table, 1939, Catalin, right front dial, left horizontal wrap-around louvers, step-down top right with pushbuttons, 2 knobs, BC, 5 tubes, AC/DC ....$1,150.00+

195ULTO, table, 1940, plastic, right front dial, left horizontal wrap-around louvers, step-down top right with pushbuttons, 2 knobs, BC, 5 tubes, AC/DC..$85.00-95.00

198ALCE, console, 1940, walnut with inlay, upper front dial, lower cloth grille with vertical bars, pushbuttons, 4 knobs, BC, SW, 8 tubes, AC $120.00-150.00

198ALT, table, 1940, wood, right front dial, left cloth grille with vertical center bar, pushbuttons, 4 knobs, BC, SW, 7 tubes, AC $65.00-75.00

199ACE, console, 1939, wood, upper front slanted slide rule dial, lower cloth grille with 3 vertical bars, 4 knobs, BC, SW, 11 tubes, AC..$140.00-160.00

203ULT, table, 1940, wood, right front dial, left cloth grille with 2 horizontal bars, step-down top right with pushbuttons, 4 knobs, BC, SW, 6 tubes, AC/DC..$75.00-85.00

204AT, table, 1940, two-tone walnut, raised right top, right front dial, left wrap-around cloth grille, BC, 5 tubes, AC.....................$50.00-65.00

205BL, portable, 1940, striped cloth covered, lower front slide rule dial, upper grille, handle, 2 knobs, BC, 4 tubes, battery $30.00-35.00

314W, table, 1948, walnut plastic, upper front slide rule dial, lower horizontal wrap-around louvers, 2 knobs, BC, 5 tubes, AC/DC, $45.00-50.00.

238-V, table-N, 1941, looks like stack of books, maroon leatherette, inner right dial, left grille, lift top, 2 knobs, BC, 5 tubes, AC ..$170.00-190.00

242, table, 1940, wood, right front slide rule dial, left cloth grille with center vertical bar, 3 knobs, BC, 5 tubes, battery................$45.00-55.00

243T, table, 1940, wood, right front slide rule dial, left cloth grille with center vertical bar, 5 knobs, BC, SW, 5 tubes, battery ..$40.00-50.00

247P, portable, 1942, inner dial & horizontal grill bars, fold-open front, handle, BC, 5 tubes, AC/DC/battery $40.00-45.00

248K, table-R/P, 1942, wood, center front dial, right & left grilles with horizontal bars, lift top, inner phono, 2 knobs, BC, 5 tubes, AC $35.00-40.00

248NI, table, 1941, Catalin, right front dial, left horizontal wrap-around louvers, 2 knobs, BC, 5 tubes, AC/DC ....$1,150.00+

249I, table, 1941, ivory plastic, right front dial, left horizontal wrap-around louvers, 2 knobs, BC, 6 tubes, AC..................................$50.00-65.00

263I, table, 1941, plastic, upper front slide rule dial, lower horizontal wrap-around louvers, 2 knobs, BC, 6 tubes, AC/DC......$40.00-50.00

264I, table, 1942, plastic, upper front slide rule dial, lower horizontal wrap-around louvers, 4 knobs, BC, SW, 6 tubes, AC/DC $40.00-50.00

265T, table, 1942, wood, right front dial, left cloth grille with center vertical divider, 2 knobs, BC, 4 tubes, battery $30.00-35.00

268T, table, 1942, two-tone wood, right front slide rule dial, left cloth grille with center vertical bars, 4 knobs, BC, SW, 7 tubes, AC..$55.00-65.00

269C, console, 1942, wood, upper front slanted slide rule dial, lower cloth grille with vertical bars, pushbuttons, 4 knobs, BC, SW, 9 tubes, AC $120.00-140.00

284GA, table-R/P, 1947, wood, lower front slide rule dial, upper grille, lift-top, inner phono, 2 knobs, BC, 5 tubes, AC **$40.00-45.00**

284I, table, 1946, plastic, upper front slide rule dial, lower horizontal wrap-around louvers, 2 knobs, BC, 5 tubes, AC/DC.....**$55.00-65.00**

284NB, table, 1946, Catalin, upper front slanted slide rule dial, large lower cloth grille, 2 knobs, BC, 5 tubes, AC/DC ....**$800.00+**

284NR, table, 1946, Catalin, upper front slanted slide rule dial, lower inset curved horizontal grille bars, 2 knobs, BC, 5 tubes, AC/DC ..**$850.00+**

285P, portable, 1946, leatherette, luggage-style, upper front slide rule dial, lower grille area, handle, 3 knobs, BC, 6 tubes, AC/DC/battery **$35.00-40.00**

286P, portable, 1947, plastic, inner right dial, center metal perforated grille, flip-up lid, 2 thumbwheel knobs, BC, 5 tubes, AC/DC/battery **$40.00-50.00**

286PR, portable, 1947, plastic, inner right thumbwheel dial, center metal perforated grille, flip-up lid, 2 thumbwheel knobs, BC, 5 tubes, AC/DC/battery **$45.00-55.00**

289T, table, 1946, wood, upper front slide rule dial, large lower cloth grille, 2 knobs, BC, 4 tubes, battery **$35.00-40.00**

292K, table-R/P, 1947, wood, upper front slide rule dial, lower grille area, lift top, inner phono, 3 knobs, BC, 6 tubes, AC **$35.00-40.00**

293CT, console-R/P, 1947, wood, front slanted slide rule dial, grille area, lift top, inner phono, 3 knobs, BC, 6 tubes, AC **$50.00-65.00**

293I, table, 1946, plastic, upper front slanted slide rule dial, lower horizontal louvers, 3 knobs, BC, 6 tubes, AC/DC **$50.00-65.00**

293W, table, 1946, plastic, upper front slanted slide rule dial, lower horizontal louvers, 3 knobs, BC, 6 tubes, AC/DC **$50.00-65.00**

294I, table, 1946, plastic, upper front slanted slide rule dial, lower vertical grille bars, 4 knobs, BC, SW, 6 tubes, AC/DC...............**$50.00-65.00**

294T, table, 1946, wood, upper front slanted slide rule dial with plastic trim, lower grille, 4 knobs, BC, SW, 6 tubes, AC/DC......**$40.00-45.00**

295T, table, 1947, two-tone wood, lower front slide rule dial, upper grille area, 4 knobs, BC, SW, 6 tubes, AC/battery **$75.00-85.00**

296M, console-R/P, 1948, wood, inner right slide rule dial/pushbuttons, left pull-out phono, fold-down front, lower grille, 2 knobs, BC, FM, 10 tubes, AC **$65.00-75.00**

302, table, 1948, wood, upper front slanted slide rule dial, lower cloth grille area, 4 knobs, BC, FM, 6 tubes, AC/DC **$40.00-50.00**

302I, table, 1948, ivory plastic, upper front slanted slide rule dial, lower vertical grille bars, 4 knobs, BC, FM, 6 tubes, AC/DC....**$50.00-65.00**

302W, table, 1948, walnut plastic, upper front slanted slide rule dial, lower vertical grille bars, 4 knobs, BC, FM, 6 tubes, AC/DC **$50.00-65.00**

305I, table, 1948, ivory plastic, upper front slanted slide rule dial, lower vertical grille bars, 4 knobs, BC, SW, 6 tubes, AC/DC ..**$50.00-65.00**

305W, table, 1948, walnut plastic, upper front slanted slide rule dial, lower vertical grille bars, 4 knobs, BC, SW, 6 tubes, AC/DC **$50.00-65.00**

309I, table, 1947, ivory plastic, right front dial over horizontal wrap-around grille bars, 2 knobs, BC, 5 tubes, AC/DC **$45.00-50.00**

309R, table, 1947, red plastic, right front dial over horizontal wrap-around grille bars, 2 knobs, BC, 5 tubes, AC/DC **$55.00-65.00**

309W, table, 1947, walnut plastic, right front dial over horizontal wrap-around grille bars, 2 knobs, BC, 5 tubes, AC/DC **$45.00-50.00**

313I, table, 1948, ivory plastic, upper front slanted slide rule dial, lower horizontal wrap-around louvers, 3 knobs, BC, 6 tubes, AC/DC **$45.00-50.00**

313W, table, 1948, walnut plastic, upper front slanted slide rule dial, lower horizontal wrap-around louvers, 3 knobs, BC, 6 tubes, AC/DC **$45.00-50.00**

314E, table, 1948, black plastic, upper front slide rule dial, lower horizontal wrap-around louvers, 2 knobs, BC, 5 tubes, AC/DC **$45.00-50.00**

314I, table, 1948, ivory plastic, upper front slide rule dial, lower horizontal wrap-around louvers, 2 knobs, BC, 5 tubes, AC/DC.....**$45.00-50.00**

315I, table, 1948, ivory plastic, upper front slanted slide rule dial, lower horizontal wrap-around louvers, 3 knobs, BC, FM, 6 tubes, AC/DC **$45.00-50.00**

315W, table, 1948, walnut plastic, upper front slanted slide rule dial, lower horizontal wrap-around louvers, 3 knobs, BC, FM, 6 tubes, AC/DC **$45.00-50.00**

316P, portable, 1948, plastic, lower front slide rule dial, upper vertical grille bars, handle, 2 knobs, BC, 4 tubes, AC/DC/battery **$30.00-35.00**

316PM, portable, 1948, plastic, lower front slide rule dial, upper vertical grille bars, handle, 2 knobs, BC, 4 tubes, AC/DC/battery ..**$30.00-35.00**

329I, table, 1948, ivory plastic, right front airplane dial over horizontal wraparound grille bars, 2 knobs, BC, 5 tubes, AC/DC..**$40.00-50.00**

329R, table, 1948, red plastic, right front airplane dial over horizontal wraparound grille bars, 2 knobs, BC, 5 tubes, AC/DC ..**$50.00-60.00**

335PI, portable, 1950, ivory plastic, lower front slide rule dial, upper grille area, flex handle, 2 knobs, BC, 4 tubes, AC/DC/battery, $35.00-40.00

329W, table, 1948, walnut plastic, right front airplane dial over horizontal wraparound grille bars, 2 knobs, BC, 5 tubes, AC/DC ..**$40.00-50.00**

331I, table, 1949, ivory plastic, right front half-round dial, large left cloth grille area, rounded sides, 2 knobs, BC, 5 tubes, AC/DC ..**$45.00-50.00**

331R, table, 1949, red plastic, right front half-round dial, large left cloth grille area, rounded sides, 2 knobs, BC, 5 tubes, AC/DC **$50.00-60.00**

331W, table, 1949, walnut plastic, right front half-round dial, large left cloth grille area, rounded sides, 2 knobs, BC, 5 tubes, AC/DC ..**$45.00-50.00**

332I, table, 1949, ivory plastic, upper front slide rule dial with large numerals, lower cloth grille, 3 knobs, BC, 6 tubes, AC/DC........**$40.00-45.00**

332W, table, 1949, walnut plastic, upper front slide rule dial with large numerals, lower cloth grille, 3 knobs, BC, 6 tubes, AC/DC **$40.00-45.00**

335PG, portable, 1950, green plastic, lower front slide rule dial, upper grille area, flex handle, 2 knobs, BC, 4 tubes, AC/DC/battery.**$45.00-50.00**.

335PM, portable, 1950, maroon plastic, lower front slide rule dial, upper grille area, flex handle, 2 knobs, BC, 4 tubes, AC/DC/battery **$45.00-50.00**

335PW, portable, 1950, walnut plastic, lower front slide rule dial, upper grille area, flex handle, 2 knobs, BC, 4 tubes, AC/DC/battery **$35.00-40.00**

338I, table, 1951, ivory plastic, right front dial, left checkered grille, feet, 2 knobs, BC, 5 tubes, AC/DC......................................**$35.00-40.00**

338R, table, 1951, red plastic, right front dial, left checkered grille, feet, 2 knobs, BC, 5 tubes, AC/DC......................................**$45.00-50.00**

338W, table, 1951, walnut plastic, right front dial, left checkered grille, feet, 2 knobs, BC, 5 tubes, AC/DC **$35.00-40.00**

344, table, 1953, plastic, large center front half-round dial with inner louvers, 3 knobs, BC, AC/DC **$40.00-45.00**

623, table, 1933, wood, upper right front window dial, center grille with decorative cut-outs, wavy sides with flared base, 4 knobs, BC, SW, 6 tubes, AC **$100.00-120.00**

5721, tombstone, 1934, two-tone wood, lower front dial, upper cloth grille with Deco cut-outs, BC, SW, AC **$120.00-140.00**

IU-355P, portable, 1956, plastic, front grille area with horizontal bars and center logo, handle, right side knobs, BC, 4 tubes **$30.00-35.00**

Duotrola, chairside-R/P-2 piece, 1930, wood, chairside case contains tuning controls, speaker case contains phono, AC **$240.00-270.00**

Portrola, chairside, 1930, wood, top dial & controls, front cloth grille with cut-outs, case finished on all sides, 8 tubes.............. **$240.00-270.00**

SETCHELL-CARLSON
Setchell Carlson, Inc.
2233 University Avenue, St. Paul, Minnesota

23, tombstone, 1939, wood, center front dial, upper cloth grille with 3 horizontal bars, 4 knobs, BC, SW, 4 tubes, battery........**$65.00-75.00**

63, tombstone, 1939, wood, center front dial, upper cloth grille with 3 horizontal bars, 4 knobs, BC, SW, 5 tubes, battery........**$65.00-75.00**

408, table, 1948, plastic, top raised slide rule dial, lower horizontal louvers, 2 thumbwheel knobs, BC, 5 tubes, AC/DC...........**$65.00-75.00**

427, table, 1947, plastic, top raised slide rule dial, lower horizontal louvers, 2 thumbwheel knobs, BC, 6 tubes, AC/DC, $70.00-90.00.

413, table, 1941, wood, right front slide rule dial, left horizontal louvers, intercom, 5 knobs, BC, SW, 6 tubes, AC.........................**$65.00-75.00**

415, table, 1948, plastic, top raised slide rule dial, lower horizontal wrap-around louvers, 2 thumbwheel knobs, BC **$65.00-75.00**

416, table, 1946, plastic, top raised slide rule dial, lower horizontal wrap-around louvers, 2 thumbwheel knobs, BC, 5 tubes, AC/DC..**$70.00-90.00**

437, table, 1948, plastic, top raised slide rule dial, lower horizontal louvers, 2 thumbwheel knobs, BC, 7 tubes, 32VDC **$65.00-75.00**

447, portable, 1948, leatherette, upper front step-back slide rule dial, lower vertical plastic grille bars, handle, 2 thumbwheel knobs, BC, 5 tubes, AC/DC/battery **$50.00-65.00**

449, portable, 1949, leatherette, upper front left slide rule dial, lower horizontal grille bars, handle, 2 knobs, BC, 5 tubes, battery ..**$35.00-40.00**

458-RD, table, 1950, plastic, upper front slide rule dial, lower rounded grille area with vertical bars, 4 top pushbuttons, can be used with matching speaker as an intercom unit, 2 knobs, BC, 4 tubes, AC/DC **$85.00-105.00**

469, table, 1950, plastic, top raised slide rule dial, lower horizontal louvers, 2 top thumbwheel knobs, FM, 7 tubes, AC/DC **$65.00-75.00**

570, table, 1950, cylindrical shape, upper front slide rule dial, handle, removable speaker, 2 knobs, BC, 5 tubes, AC/DC **$85.00-95.00**

588, table, 1939, two-tone wood, right front dial, left wrap-around cloth grille with center horizontal bar, 3 knobs, BC, 5 tubes, AC.........**$45.00-55.00**

4130, table, 1940, wood, lower front slide rule dial, large upper cloth grille, 3 knobs..**$40.00-50.00**

WT16 "Whisper-Tone," radio/bed lamp, painted wood, cylindrical shape, front slide rule dial, horizontal grille bars, light, 2 knobs **$50.00-65.00**

SHAMROCK

Model unknown, table, wood, rectangular case, center escutcheon with window dial, lift top, 1 knob, BC, battery, $90.00-100.00.

SHOWERS

20 "Consola," table, wood, low rectangular case, gold decorated metal front panel with two pointer dials, BC, 5 tubes, battery **$180.00-200.00**

SIGNAL
Signal Electronics, Inc.
114 East 16th Street, New York, New York

141, portable, 1948, plastic, inner metal grille with horizontal grille bars, flip-open front, handle, 2 thumbwheel knobs, BC, 4 tubes, battery **$40.00-50.00**

241 "Concerto," table, 1948, wood with metal front panel, lower front slide rule dial, upper "sunburst" grille, 2 knobs, BC, 5 tubes, AC/DC **$65.00-75.00**

341-A, portable, 1948, snakeskin, upper front slide rule dial, large lower perforated grille, handle, 2 knobs, BC, 4 tubes, AC/DC/battery **$35.00-40.00**

341T, portable, 1947, snakeskin, lower front slide rule dial, upper perforated grille, handle, 2 knobs, BC, 4 tubes, AC/DC/battery ..**$30.00-35.00**

AF252, table, 1948, plastic with metal front panel, upper front slide rule dial, lower raised vertical grille bars, 3 knobs, BC, FM, 6 tubes, AC/DC **$65.00-75.00**

SILVERTONE
Sears, Roebuck & Co.
925 South Homan Street, Chicago, Illinois

1, table, 1950, metal, right front round dial, cloth grille with horizontal bars, 2 knobs, BC, 4 tubes, AC/DC, $65.00-75.00.

2, table, 1950, metal, right front round dial, cloth grille with horizontal bars, 2 knobs, BC, 4 tubes, AC/DC **$65.00-75.00**

4-233, table-N, 1951, plastic, right front round dial with either gun or hat pointer, left cowboy & horse over horizontal grille bars, BC, AC.......**$350.00-400.00**

10, table-C, 1951, brown plastic, 2-section front panel with right front round dial & left round alarm clock face, 6 knobs, BC, 5 tubes, AC **$30.00-35.00**

11, table-C, 1951, ivory plastic, 2-section front panel with right front round dial & left round alarm clock face, 6 knobs, BC, 5 tubes, AC **$30.00-35.00**

16, table, 1951, plastic, right front dial, left diagonal grille bars, stylized "S" logo, 3 knobs, BC, 6 tubes, AC/DC.........................**$35.00-40.00**

18, table, 1951, plastic, right front dial, left diagonal grille bars, stylized "S" logo, 3 knobs, BC, FM, 8 tubes, AC **$35.00-40.00**

24, table, 1929, metal, low rectangular case, front off-center window dial, switch, 2 knobs, battery.................................**$65.00-75.00**

25, console, 1929, wood, lowboy, inner front window dial, fold-down front, lower cloth grille with cut-outs, lift top, battery ..**$85.00-105.00**

26, console, 1929, wood, lowboy, inner front dial, upper speaker grille with cut-outs, double doors, lower storage, battery **$85.00-105.00**

33, table-R/P, 1950, leatherette, inner right dial, phono, lift top, handle, 3 knobs, BC, 5 tubes, AC **$20.00-25.00**

58, console-R/P, 1930, walnut, lowboy, inner front window dial, lower cloth grille with cut-outs, double doors, lift top, inner phono, 8 tubes, AC **$120.00-140.00**

15, table, 1951, plastic, right front dial, left diagonal grille bars, stylized "S" logo, 3 knobs, BC, 6 tubes, AC/DC, $35.00-40.00.

1250, cathedral, 1931, wood, lower center window dial, upper grille, decorative columns on front sides, 3 knobs, BC, 5 tubes, AC, $260.00-290.00.

60, console-R/P, 1930, wood, lowboy, inner front window dial, lower cloth grille with cut-outs, double doors, lift top, inner phono, 9 tubes, AC **$120.00-150.00**

64, console-R/P, 1950, wood, right front tilt-out slide rule dial, inner left phono, lower storage, doors, BC, FM, AC.....................**$65.00-75.00**

72, table-R/Rec, 1951, suitcase-style, inner left dial, right disc recorder, lift top, handle, 3 knobs, BC, 5 tubes, AC **$25.00-30.00**

117, console, wood, upper front window dial with escutcheon, lower cloth grille with cut-outs, stretcher base **$120.00-140.00**

210, portable, 1950, plastic, right side dial, front vertical wrap-over grille bars, handle, 2 knobs, BC, 4 tubes, battery **$35.00-40.00**

215, portable, 1950, plastic, right front dial over horizontal grille bars, flex handle, 2 knobs, BC, 4 tubes, AC/DC/battery...............**$35.00-40.00**

220, portable, 1950, plastic, upper front dial, lower checkered grille area, flex handle, 2 knobs, BC, 4 tubes, AC/DC/battery **$35.00-40.00**

222X, tombstone, 1932, wood, lower front dial, upper cloth grille with cut-outs, 5 knobs, BC **$95.00-115.00**

225, portable, 1950, alligator, upper front slide rule dial, lower grille area, handle, 2 knobs, BC, 5 tubes, AC/DC/battery...............**$30.00-35.00**

1017, table, 1952, mahogany wood, center front half-round dial with inner pointer overlaps large cloth grille, feet, 4 knobs, BC, 5 tubes, AC/DC **$30.00-35.00**

1018, table, 1952, blonde wood, center front half-round dial with inner pointer overlaps large cloth grille, feet, 4 knobs, BC, 5 tubes, AC/DC **$30.00-35.00**

1032, table-R/P, 1952, plastic, right front round dial, left vertical grille bars, open top phono, 3 knobs, BC, 5 tubes, AC **$35.00-40.00**

1053, console-R/P, 1952, wood, upper front dial, center pull-out phono drawer, lower grille, 3 knobs, BC, 6 tubes, AC **$40.00-50.00**

1055, console-R/P, 1952, wood, upper front dial, center pull-out phono drawer, lower grille, 3 knobs, BC, FM, 8 tubes, AC........**$40.00-50.00**

1260, console-R/P, 1931, walnut, lowboy, center front window dial, lower cloth grille with cut-outs, lift top, inner phono, BC, 6 tubes, AC **$110.00-130.00**

1290, cathedral, 1931, wood, lower front window dial, upper cloth grille with cut-outs, fluted columns, 4 knobs, BC, 6 tubes, battery **$120.00-150.00**

1292, console, 1931, walnut, lowboy, upper front window dial, lower cloth grille with cut-outs, stretcher base, BC, 6 tubes, battery..**$85.00-95.00**

1330, console-R/P, 1931, walnut, lowboy, center front window dial, lower cloth grille with cut-outs, lift top, inner phono, BC, 7 tubes, AC **$95.00-115.00**

1561, table, 1940, wood, right front slide rule dial, left cloth grille with cut-outs, pushbuttons, 4 knobs, BC, 6 tubes, AC **$50.00-65.00**

1580, console, 1932, wood, lowboy, upper front quarter-round dial, lower cloth grille with cut-outs, 5 knobs, BC, SW, 7 tubes, AC...........**$120.00-140.00**

1589, cathedral, 1932, burl walnut, lower front quarter-round dial, upper cloth grille with cut-outs, 5 knobs, BC, 7 tubes **$270.00-300.00**

1631, console, 1931, wood, lowboy, upper front quarter-round dial, lower cloth grille with cut-outs, 6 legs, 5 knobs, BC, 9 tubes, AC........**$120.00-140.00**

1641, console, 1932, walnut, upper front quarter round dial, large lower grille with cut-outs, 2 speakers, 5 knobs, BC, SW, 12 tubes, AC **$140.00-160.00**

1650, console, 1935, wood, lowboy, upper front quarter-round dial, lower cloth grille with cut-outs, 6 legs, BC, SW, 10 tubes, AC ..**$120.00-140.00**

1660, cathedral, 1935, wood, lower front window dial with escutcheon, upper cloth grille with cut-outs, 3 knobs, BC, 5 tubes, AC **$190.00-210.00**

1670, console, 1933, wood, lowboy, upper front quarter-round dial, lower cloth grille with cut-outs, 6 legs, BC, 11 tubes, AC....**$120.00-140.00**

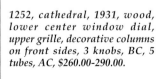

640, table, plastic, small upper front dial, large lower horizontal louvers, 2 thumbwheel knobs, BC, $75.00-85.00.

1252, cathedral, 1931, wood, lower center window dial, upper grille, decorative columns on front sides, 3 knobs, BC, 5 tubes, AC, $260.00-290.00.

1403, cathedral, 1931, wood, lower front window dial, upper cloth grille with cut-outs, fluted columns, 3 knobs, BC, 6 tubes, AC, $270.00-300.00.

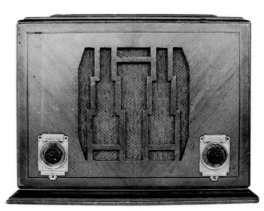

1705, table, 1933, wood, Deco, lower right front dial, center cloth grille with cut-outs (2 front, 2 rear), 4 knobs, BC, SW, 6 tubes, AC, $85.00-95.00.

1720, console, 1933, wood, lowboy, upper front window dial with escutcheon, lower cloth grille with cut-outs, 3 knobs, BC, 10 tubes, AC **$110.00-130.00**

1745, tombstone, 1933, wood, double step-down top, center front round dial, upper cloth grille with cut-outs, 5 knobs, 6 tubes.. **$180.00-230.00**

1800, cathedral, 1934, two-tone wood, center front window dial, upper cloth grille with cut-outs, 2 knobs, BC, SW, 4 tubes, AC.......**$150.00-180.00**

1806, console, 1934, wood, upper front dial, lower cloth grille with cut-outs, 5 knobs, BC, SW, 7 tubes, AC **$120.00-150.00**

1822, console, 1935, wood, Deco, upper front dial, lower cloth grille with curled cut-outs, 5 knobs, BC, SW, 14 tubes, AC **$140.00-170.00**

1835, console, 1935, wood, upper front round dial, lower cloth grille with cut-outs, 5 knobs, BC, SW, 9 tubes, AC **$120.00-140.00**

1850, tombstone, 1935, wood, Deco, double step-down top, center front round dial, upper cloth grille with cut-outs, 4 knobs, BC, SW, 6 tubes, battery...**$120.00-140.00**

1851, console, 1935, wood, upper front round dial, lower cloth grille with cut-outs, 4 knobs, BC, SW, 6 tubes including ballast, battery..**$95.00-105.00**

1852, tombstone, 1935, walnut, Deco, curved shoulders, center front dial, upper cloth grille with cut-outs, 4 knobs, BC, SW, 6 tubes including ballast, battery **$75.00-95.00**

1905, tombstone, 1936, wood, lower front round dial with escutcheon, upper cloth grille with cut-outs, 5 knobs, BC, SW, 9 tubes, AC **$95.00-115.00**

1906, tombstone, 1936, wood, lower front round dial, upper cloth grille with cut-outs, 4 knobs, BC, SW, 6 tubes, AC **$120.00-140.00**

1911, console, 1936, wood, upper front round dial, lower cloth grille with vertical bars, BC, SW, 6 tubes, AC **$110.00-130.00**

1921, tombstone, 1936, wood, shouldered, center front round dial, upper cloth grille with bars, 4 knobs, 6 tubes, battery..........**$120.00-150.00**

1938, tombstone, 1936, wood, lower front round dial, upper cloth grille with cut-outs, 4 knobs, BC, SW, 6 tubes, AC **$110.00-130.00**

1945, console, 1936, walnut, upper front round dial, lower cloth grille with cut-outs, tuning eye, BC, SW, 9 tubes, AC **$120.00-140.00**

1954, tombstone, 1936, wood, lower front round dial, upper cloth grille with cut-outs, 4 knobs, BC, SW, 6 tubes, AC **$95.00-115.00**

1972, console, 1936, wood, upper front round dial, lower cloth grille with 3 splayed bars, BC, SW, 8 tubes, AC **$120.00-140.00**

1993, console, 1936, wood, upper front round dial, lower cloth grille with 3 splayed bars, 5 knobs, BC, SW, 7 tubes including ballast, battery **$85.00-95.00**

2001, table, 1950, brown metal, right front round dial overlaps criss-cross grille, lower left knob, BC, AC/DC **$75.00-85.00**

2002, table, 1950, ivory metal, right front round dial overlaps criss-cross grille, lower left knob, BC, AC/DC **$75.00-85.00**

2003, table, 1953, brown plastic, upper front slide rule dial, lower checkered grille, feet, 2 knobs, BC, 5 tubes, AC/DC **$20.00-25.00**

2004, table, 1953, ivory plastic, upper front slide rule dial, lower checkered grille, feet, 2 knobs, BC, 5 tubes, AC/DC **$20.00-25.00**

2006, table, 1953, green plastic, upper front slide rule dial, lower checkered grille, feet, 2 knobs, BC, 5 tubes, AC/DC **$20.00-25.00**

2007, table-C, 1953, plastic, center front round dial, right checkered grille, left alarm clock, 5 knobs, BC, 4 tubes, AC **$30.00-35.00**

2016, table, 1956, ivory plastic, right rectangular dial, left criss-cross grille, 3 knobs, BC, 6 tubes, AC/DC **$35.00-45.00**

2021, table, 1962, plastic, right front round dial, large left grille area with vertical bars, 3 knobs, BC, FM, 7 tubes, AC/DC **$20.00-25.00**

1582, cathedral, 1932, two-tone wood, lower front quarter-round dial, upper cloth grille with cut-outs, 5 knobs, BC, SW, 7 tubes, AC, $270.00-300.00.

1743, tombstone, 1933, two-tone wood, lower front round dial, upper cloth grille with cut-outs, 3 knobs, BC, SW, 5 tubes, AC, $85.00-115.00.

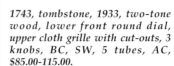

1955, tombstone, 1936, wood, step-down top, lower front round dial, upper cloth grille with 3 vertical bars, 5 knobs, BC, SW, 9 tubes, AC, $140.00-160.00.

2014, table, 1956, green plastic, right rectangular dial, left criss-cross grille, 3 knobs, BC, 6 tubes, AC/DC, $35.00-45.00.

2022, table, 1953, plastic, right front dial, left diagonal grille bars, stylized "S" logo, 3 knobs, BC, SW, AC/DC **$35.00-40.00**

2028, table, 1953, wood, front half-round metal dial over large grille area, 2 knobs, BC, 4 tubes, battery **$25.00-30.00**

2041, table-R/P, 1953, leatherette, right front round dial, 3/4 lift top inner phono, handle, 3 knobs, BC, 5 tubes, AC **$30.00-35.00**

2056, console-R/P, 1953, wood, upper front slide rule dial, center pull-out phono drawer, lower grille, storage, 2 knobs, BC, 6 tubes, AC **$50.00-65.00**

2061, console-R/P, 1953, wood, inner right front slide rule dial, pull-out phono, left storage, double doors, lower grille, 2 knobs, BC, 8 tubes, AC **$50.00-65.00**

2225, portable, 1953, alligator, right front half-round dial overlaps lattice grille, handle, 2 knobs, BC, 5 tubes, AC/DC/battery **$30.00-35.00**

2411, table, 1939, wood, right front rectangular dial, left cloth grille with fluted vertical bars, 4 knobs, BC, SW, 5 tubes, battery..**$45.00-55.00**

2761, table, 1939, wood, lower front slide rule dial, upper cloth grille with 3 vertical bars, 5 pushbuttons, 5 knobs, BC, SW, 6 tubes, battery **$75.00-85.00**

3002, table, 1954, ivory plastic, upper front thumbwheel dial, "V" shaped grille with cloth & checkered panels, BC, 4 tubes, AC ..**$40.00-45.00**

3004, table, 1954, plastic, right front dial, left horizontal grille bars, feet, 2 knobs, BC, 5 tubes, AC/DC **$25.00-30.00**

3032, table-R/P, 1953, plastic, right front round dial, left vertical grille bars, open top phono, 3 knobs, BC, AC **$40.00-45.00**

3040, table-R/P, 1953, plastic, front half-round dial with inner louvers, 3/4 lift top, inner phono, 2 knobs, BC, 5 tubes, AC **$40.00-45.00**

3040A, table-R/P, 1955, plastic, front half-round dial with inner louvers, 3/4 lift top, inner phono, 2 knobs, BC, 5 tubes, AC........**$40.00-45.00**

3045, table-R/P, 1953, wood, large front metal half-round dial over cloth grille, lift top, inner phono, 2 knobs, BC, 5 tubes, AC **$30.00-35.00**

3068, console-R/P, 1955, wood, right front tilt-out slide rule dial, left pull-down phono door, lower grille, 3 knobs, BC, FM, 8 tubes, AC..**$50.00-65.00**

3145, table-R/P, wood, large front metal half-round dial over cloth grille, lift top, inner phono, 2 knobs, BC, AC **$30.00-35.00**

3210, portable, 1953, plastic, center front round dial overlaps lower horizontal wrap-around bars, fold-down handle, 2 knobs, BC, 4 tubes, battery **$30.00-35.00**

3215, portable, 1954, maroon plastic, center front round dial overlaps upper horizontal grille bars, fold-down handle, 2 knobs, BC, 4 tubes, AC/DC/battery **$30.00-35.00**

3216, portable, 1954, green plastic, center front round dial overlaps upper horizontal grille bars, fold-down handle, 2 knobs, BC, 4 tubes, AC/DC/battery **$30.00-35.00**

3217, portable, 1954, gray plastic, center front round dial overlaps upper horizontal grille bars, fold-down handle, 2 knobs, BC, 4 tubes, AC/DC/battery **$30.00-35.00**

3451, table, 1940, plastic, Deco, left front "candy cane" dial, wrap-over vertical grille bars, 4 pushbuttons, 2 knobs, BC, 5 tubes, AC/DC **$85.00-95.00**

3561, table, 1941, plastic, Deco, left front "candy cane" dial, wrap-over vertical grille bars, 4 pushbuttons, 2 knobs, BC, 5 tubes, AC/DC **$85.00-95.00**

4032, table-R/P, 1955, plastic, center front half-round dial, open top phono, 3 knobs, BC, 6 tubes, AC/DC **$35.00-40.00**

4035, table-C, 1954, blue plastic, right front vertical slide rule dial, round alarm clock face, left grille with horizontal bars, feet, BC, 5 tubes, AC **$15.00-20.00**

4036, table-C, ivory plastic, right front vertical slide rule dial, round alarm clock face, left grille with horizontal bars, feet, BC, 5 tubes, AC **$15.00-20.00**

4037, table-C, beige plastic, right front vertical slide rule dial, round alarm clock face, left grille with horizontal bars, feet, BC, 5 tubes, AC **$15.00-20.00**

4038, table-C, pink plastic, right front vertical slide rule dial, round alarm clock face, left grille with horizontal bars, feet, BC, 5 tubes, AC **$15.00-20.00**

4068A, console-R/P, 1955, wood, inner right slide rule dial, left fold-down phono door, lower grille, 3 knobs, BC, FM, 10 tubes, AC..**$65.00-75.00**

2005, table, 1953, red plastic, upper front slide rule dial, lower checkered grille, feet, 2 knobs, BC, 5 tubes, AC/DC, $20.00-25.00.

3001, table, 1954, brown plastic, upper front thumbwheel dial, "V" shaped grille with cloth & checkered panels, 2 knobs, BC, 4 tubes, AC, $40.00-45.00.

3011, table, plastic, upper left rectangular airplane dial, right grille, decorative lines, 2 knobs, BC, 5 tubes, AC/DC, $65.00-75.00.

4200, table, 1955, plastic, right front trapezoid dial, left horizontal grille bars, feet, 3 knobs, BC, FM, 8 tubes, AC **$25.00-30.00**

4204, table, 1954, maroon plastic, recessed front with right dial and left cloth grille, 3 knobs, BC, FM, 8 tubes, AC......................**$35.00-40.00**

4210, portable, 1955, plastic, center front round dial overlaps lower horizontal wrap-around grille bars, top thumbwheel knob, handle, BC, 4 tubes, battery **$30.00-35.00**

4212, portable, 1955, right front round dial knob, left lattice grille with Silvertone logo, BC, 4 tubes, battery **$35.00-40.00**

4225, portable, 1955, cloth covered, lower front dial, upper grille area, handle, BC, 5 tubes, AC/DC/battery **$30.00-35.00**

4418, table, 1937, wood, center front round dial, top speaker grille, 3 knobs, BC, SW, 4 tubes, battery **$40.00-50.00**

4464, tombstone, 1936, two-tone wood, lower front round dial, upper cloth grille with cut-outs, 4 knobs, BC, SW, 6 tubes, AC **$120.00-140.00**

4485, console, 1937, wood, upper front round dial, lower cloth grille with vertical bars, tuning eye, 5 knobs, BC, SW, 8 tubes, AC **$110.00-130.00**

4486, console, 1937, wood, upper front round dial, lower cloth grille with vertical bars, tuning eye, 5 knobs, BC, SW, 10 tubes, AC ..**$110.00-130.00**

4487, console, 1937, wood, upper front round self-tuning dial, lower cloth grille with cut-outs, 5 knobs, BC, SW, 11 tubes, AC..**$120.00-150.00**

4500 "Election," table, 1936, plastic, right front round dial, left cloth grille with vertical wrap-over bars, BC, 5 tubes, AC.............**$95.00-115.00**

4500A, table, 1936, plastic, right front round dial, left cloth grille with vertical wrap-over bars, BC, 5 tubes, AC **$95.00-115.00**

4563, table, 1936, wood, rounded left, right front round dial, left cloth grille with Deco cut-outs, 4 knobs, BC, SW, 6 tubes, AC **$65.00-75.00**

4565, table, 1936, wood, off-center round dial with tuning eye, right & left cloth grilles with cut-outs, 5 knobs, BC, SW, 8 tubes, AC ..**$65.00-75.00**

3461, table, 1940, plastic, Deco, left front "candy cane" dial, wrap-over vertical grille bars, 4 pushbuttons, 2 knobs, BC, 6 tubes, AC/DC, $85.00-95.00.

4585, console, 1936, wood, upper front round dial, lower cloth grille with vertical bars, tuning eye, 5 knobs, BC, SW, 8 tubes, AC **$120.00-150.00**

4612, table, 1937, wood, right front dial, left cloth grille with 2 vertical bars, 4 knobs, BC, SW, 6 tubes, 32VDC **$35.00-40.00**

4619, tombstone, 1937, walnut with maple inlays, center front dial, upper cloth grille with bars, 4 knobs, BC, SW, 6 tubes, 32VDC ..**$85.00-95.00**

4652, console, 1938, wood, upper front dial, lower cloth grille with 3 vertical bars, fluted columns, 4 knobs, BC, SW, 6 tubes, battery..**$95.00-105.00**

4660, table, 1937, two-tone wood, left front dial, right grille with cut-outs, tuning eye, 3 knobs, BC, SW, 6 tubes, AC **$65.00-75.00**

4663, upright table, 1938, wood, center front dial, curved top with vertical grille bars, tuning eye, 4 knobs, BC, SW, 6 tubes, AC ..**$95.00-115.00**

4664, table, 1937, wood, right front dial, left cloth grille with Deco cut-outs, tuning eye, 4 knobs, BC, SW, 7 tubes, AC...........**$65.00-75.00**

4665, tombstone, 1938, wood, center front slanted slide rule dial, upper cloth grille with 3 vertical bars, tuning eye, 4 knobs, BC, SW, 8 tubes, AC **$95.00-115.00**

4666, table, 1938, wood, upper front rolling slide rule dial, center automatic tuning, side grille bars, BC, SW, 10 tubes, AC **$120.00-150.00**

4668, table-R/P, 1938, wood, right front dial, left cloth grille with vertical bars, fluted columns, lift top, inner phono, 4 knobs, BC, SW, 6 tubes, AC..**$40.00-45.00**

4685, console, 1938, wood, upper front slide rule dial, lower cloth grille with vertical bars, tuning eye, 4 knobs, BC, SW, 8 tubes, AC..**$110.00-130.00**

4686, console, 1938, wood, upper front slide rule dial, automatic tuning, lower cloth grille with vertical bars, 4 knobs, BC, SW, 10 tubes, AC **$120.00-140.00**

4688, console, 1938, wood, upper front slide rule dial, lower cloth grille with vertical bars, pushbuttons, tuning eye, motorized tuning, 5 knobs, BC, SW, 14 tubes, AC **$200.00-240.00**

4763, table, 1938, wood, off-center dial with tuning eye above, left wraparound cloth grille with cut-outs, 4 knobs, BC, SW, 6 tubes, AC **$75.00-85.00**

4765, table, 1938, wood, left front slide rule dial with tuning eye left, grille with vertical bars wraps over top, 4 knobs, BC, SW, 8 tubes, AC **$120.00-140.00**

3351 "Commentator," table, 1940, plastic, Deco, left front "candy cane" dial, wrap-over vertical grille bars, 4 pushbuttons, 2 knobs, BC, 5 tubes, AC/DC, $85.00-95.00.

4206, table, 1954, ivory plastic, recessed front with right dial and left cloth grille, 3 knobs, BC, FM, 8 tubes, AC, $35.00-40.00.

4414, table, 1936, plastic, right front round dial, left cloth grille with wrap-over vertical bars, 2 knobs, BC, 5 tubes, AC, $95.00-115.00.

4564, tombstone, 1936, wood, lower front round airplane dial with globe, upper cloth grille with cut-outs, 4 knobs, BC, SW, 6 tubes, AC, $95.00-115.00.

4766, table, 1938, wood, top front edge slide rule dial with tuning eye, lower rotary pushbuttons, step-down top, right and left side wrap-around grilles, 4 knobs, BC, SW, 10 tubes, AC.........**$200.00-240.00**
4769, table, 1938, wood, upper right front slide rule dial and tuning eye, lower right rotary pushbuttons, left wraparound grille, rounded left side, 3 knobs, BC, SW, 8 tubes, AC **$140.00-160.00**
4784, console, 1938, wood, upper front center dial with tuning eye, lower cloth grille with three vertical bars, 4 knobs, BC, SW, 7 tubes, AC **$120.00-140.00**
4786, console, 1938, wood, top front edge slide rule dial with tuning eye, lower rotary pushbuttons, step-down top, lower grille with three vertical bars, rounded front corners, 4 knobs, BC, SW, 10 tubes, AC **$160.00-180.00**
4787, console, 1938, wood, upper front center slide rule dial and tuning eye, rotary pushbuttons, lower cloth grille with center vertical bars, step-down top, 4 knobs, BC, SW, 12 tubes, AC........**$200.00-240.00**
4788, console, 1938, wood, recessed front with upper front slide rule dial, large lower cloth grille with vertical and horizontal bars, pushbuttons, tuning eye, step-down top, motorized tuning, 5 knobs, BC, SW, 14 tubes, AC...**$240.00-280.00**
4789, console, 1938, wood, upper front center slide rule dial and tuning eye, rotary pushbuttons, lower recessed cloth grille with three vertical bars, step-down top, 3 knobs, BC, SW, 8 tubes, AC ..**$140.00-160.00**
4790, console, 1938, wood, top front edge slide rule dial with tuning eye, lower cloth grille, step-down top, wood inlay, 5 tubes, BC, SW, 10 tubes, AC **$170.00-190.00**
4799, console, 1938, wood, wide cabinet, upper front center slide rule dial, large lower cloth grille with two vertical bars, pushbuttons, tuning eye, step-down top and rounded corners, motorized tuning, 5 knobs, BC, SW, 14 tubes, AC **$280.00-320.00**
5016, table, 1956, mahogany, right front plastic half-round dial, left cloth grille, 3 knobs, BC, 6 tubes, AC/DC **$20.00-25.00**
5017, table, 1956, blonde oak, right front plastic half-round dial, left cloth grille, 3 knobs, BC, 6 tubes, AC/DC **$20.00-25.00**

4522, tombstone, 1936, wood, lower front round dial with globe, upper cloth grille with cut-outs, 3 knobs, BC, 6 tubes, battery, $85.00-105.00.

5032, table-R/P, 1955, plastic, front center half round dial over horizontal louver grille, exposed top phono, 3 knobs, BC, 4 tubes, AC **$30.00-35.00**
5227, portable, 1955, leatherette, inner slide rule dial, flip-up front with map, telescope antenna, BC, SW, 5 tubes, AC/DC/battery........**$55.00-65.00**
6000, table, 1966, plastic, lower right front dial overlaps upper horizontal grille bars, 2 knobs, BC, 4 tubes, AC/DC **$15.00-20.00**
6002, table, 1946, metal, midget, small upper right front dial, horizontal louvers, 2 knobs, BC, 4 tubes, AC/DC **$65.00-75.00**
6010, table, plastic, right front round dial, left cloth grille with vertical wrap-over bars, BC, 4 tubes, battery **$50.00-65.00**
6012, table, 1947, plastic, lower front slide rule dial, upper vertical grille bars, pushbuttons, handle, 2 knobs, BC, 5 tubes, AC/DC **$45.00-55.00**
6016, table, 1947, plastic, right front square dial on front/side/top, handle, 3 knobs, BC, 6 tubes, AC/DC **$45.00-55.00**
6018, table-C, 1956, plastic, step-down top, right front round dial, left alarm clock, side louvers, 5 knobs, BC, 4 tubes, AC.....**$30.00-35.00**
6021, table-C, 1956, ivory plastic, trapezoid shape, lower front slide rule dial, large upper clock face, 5 knobs, BC, 5 tubes, AC..**$30.00-35.00**
6022, table, 1938, wood, right front slide rule dial with inner tuning eye, left grille with cut-outs, 6 pushbuttons, 4 knobs, BC, SW, 7 tubes, AC **$75.00-85.00**
6042, table, 1939, two-tone wood, right front dial, left oval grille with center decorative bar, 2 knobs, battery.............................**$35.00-40.00**
6051, table, 1947, two-tone wood, lower right front dial, left & upper cloth grille areas with cut-outs, 2 knobs, battery **$35.00-40.00**
6052, tombstone, 1939, walnut with inlay, shouldered, lower front dial, upper cloth grille with cut-outs, pushbuttons, 2 knobs, BC, 6 tubes, battery **$65.00-75.00**

6020, table-C, 1956, brown plastic, trapezoid shape, lower front slide rule dial, large upper clock face, 5 knobs, BC, 5 tubes, AC, $30.00-35.00.

6050, table, 1947, wood, right front round dial, left cloth grille with 3 horizontal bars, 3 knobs, BC, AC/DC, $50.00-65.00.

6057A, console-R/P, 1956, wood, upper front slide rule dial, center pull-out phono drawer, storage, 2 knobs, BC, 6 tubes, AC ..$75.00-85.00
6064, console, 1939, wood, upper front slanted dial, lower cloth grille with 3 vertical bars, 4 knobs, BC, 6 tubes, battery $85.00-95.00
6068, console, 1939, walnut, upper front slanted slide rule dial, lower cloth grille with 2 vertical bars, BC, SW, 7 tubes, battery $85.00-95.00
6071, table-R/P, 1947, wood, right front round dial, left cloth grille with 3 horizontal bars, lift top, inner phono, 3 knobs, BC, 6 tubes, AC $35.00-40.00
6072, table-R/P, 1947, wood, lower front slide rule dial, upper oblong cloth grille with 3 horizontal bars, lift top, inner phono, 2 knobs, BC, 5 tubes, AC $35.00-40.00
6093, console, 1946, wood, upper front slide rule dial, lower cloth grille with bars, pushbuttons, 4 knobs, BC, SW, 8 tubes, AC $85.00-105.00
6100, console-R/P, 1946, wood, upper front slanted dial, center pull-out phono drawer, lower cloth grille, 4 knobs, BC, 5 tubes, AC.............$85.00-105.00
6105, console-R/P, 1946, wood, upper front slanted slide rule dial, center pull-out phono drawer, lower grille, pushbuttons, 4 knobs, BC, SW, 8 tubes, AC $85.00-105.00
6111, console-R/P, 1946, wood, inner right slide rule dial, pushbuttons, fold-down door, left pull-out phono drawer, lower grille, 4 knobs, BC, SW, 8 tubes, AC $75.00-85.00
6111A, console-R/P, 1947, wood, inner right slide rule dial, 8 pushbuttons, fold-down door, left pull-out phono drawer, lower grille, 4 knobs, BC, SW, 8 tubes, AC $75.00-85.00
6122, table, two-tone wood, right front slide rule dial, left cloth grille with cut-outs, tuning eye, 6 pushbuttons, 4 knobs, BC, SW, 7 tubes, AC $75.00-85.00
6138, console,1939, wood, upper front slanted slide rule dial, lower cloth grille with center vertical divider, 8 pushbuttons, tuning eye, 4 knobs, BC, SW, 13 tubes, AC $120.00-150.00

6129, table, wood, upper right front slide rule dial, left cloth grille with 3 vertical bars, 8 pushbuttons, tuning eye, 4 knobs, BC, SW, 8 tubes, AC, $75.00-85.00.

6217, portable, 1956, maroon plastic, upper left front dial area, right horizontal wrap-around bars, handle, 2 knobs, BC, 4 tubes, AC/DC/battery, $25.00-30.00.

6156, console, wood, upper slanted slide rule dial with inner tuning eye, lower grille with 2 vertical bars, 8 pushbuttons, 4 knobs, BC, SW, 11 tubes, AC $120.00-150.00
6177-A, table, 1939, plastic, Deco, right front round dial, rounded left with horizontal wrap-around louvers, BC, 5 tubes, AC/DC ..$140.00-180.00
6178-A, table, 1939, plastic, Deco, right front round dial, rounded left with horizontal wrap-around louvers, BC, 5 tubes, AC/DC ..$140.00-180.00
6192, console, wood, upper front slanted slide rule dial, lower cloth grille with 3 vertical bars, tuning eye, 8 pushbuttons, 4 knobs, BC, SW, 11 tubes, AC $120.00-140.00
6200A, table, 1946, plastic, lower front slide rule dial, large upper cloth grille, 2 knobs, BC, 4 tubes, battery $30.00-35.00
6216A, portable, 1956, gray plastic, upper left front dial area, right horizontal wrap-around bars, handle, 2 knobs, BC, 4 tubes, AC/DC/battery $25.00-30.00
6218, portable, 1956, green plastic, upper left front dial area, right horizontal wrap-around bars, handle, 2 knobs, BC, 4 tubes, AC/DC/battery $25.00-30.00

6231, console, 1939, wood, upper center slanted face with airplane dial, lower grille with 2 vertical bars, 5 pushbuttons, tuning eye, 4 knobs, BC, SW, 7 tubes, AC, $120.00-150.00.

6251, table, 1939, wood, upper right front airplane dial, left grille with cut-outs, 5 pushbuttons, tuning eye, 4 knobs, BC, SW, 7 tubes, AC, $80.00-90.00.

6541, portable, 1940, cloth covered, right front rectangular airplane dial, left grille with horizontal bars, handle, 2 knobs, BC, 4 tubes, battery, $25.00-30.00.

6220A, table, 1946, wood, lower front slide rule dial, upper cloth grille with cut-outs, 2 knobs, BC, 5 tubes, battery.................**$30.00-35.00**

6230A, table, 1947, wood, lower front slide rule dial, upper cloth grille with scrolled sides, 2 knobs, BC, SW, 5 tubes, battery..**$45.00-55.00**

6327, table, 1939, wood, upper front slanted slide rule dial, lower cloth grille with crossed cut-outs, 5 pushbuttons, 2 knobs, BC, 6 tubes, AC/DC **$75.00-85.00**

6372, table, 1940, wood, right front vertical slide rule dial, left cloth grille, handle, 2 knobs, BC, 4 tubes, battery **$35.00-40.00**

6425, table, 1939, wood, lower front slide rule dial, upper horizontal louvers, pushbuttons, tuning eye, BC, SW, 8 tubes, AC **$65.00-75.00**

6437, console, 1940, wood, upper front slanted slide rule dial, lower cloth grille with crossed cut-outs, pushbuttons, BC, SW, 12 tubes, AC **$120.00-140.00**

6491-A, end table, 1940, wood, round end table on 4 legged base, inner dial &, double front doors, 4 knobs, BC, 6 tubes, AC ..**$200.00-230.00**

7006, table, 1967, brown plastic, step-down top, front off-center dial, left cloth grille area, 2 knobs, BC, AC/DC **$25.00-30.00**

7007, table, 1967, ivory plastic, step-down top, front off-center dial, left cloth grille area, 2 knobs, BC, AC/DC **$25.00-30.00**

7014, table, 1957, plastic, lower front slide rule dial, large upper lattice grille area with center "V" logo, 2 speakers, 2 knobs, BC, 6 tubes, AC/DC **$25.00-30.00**

7020, table, 1941, Deco, left front "candy cane" dial, wrap-over vertical grille bars, 2 knobs, BC, 5 tubes, AC/DC **$85.00-95.00**

7021, table, 1947, plastic, lower front slide rule dial, large upper grille, 4 pushbuttons, 4 knobs, BC, 6 tubes, AC/DC **$40.00-45.00**

7022, table, 1946, Deco, left front "candy cane" dial, wrap-over vertical grille bars, 2 knobs, BC, 5 tubes, AC/DC **$85.00-95.00**

7024, table, 1941, Deco, left front "candy cane" dial, wrap-over vertical grille bars, 2 knobs, BC, 5 tubes, AC/DC **$85.00-95.00**

7025, table, 1947, plastic, Deco, left front "candy cane" dial, wrap-over vertical grille bars, 2 knobs, BC, 5 tubes, AC/DC **$85.00-95.00**

7036A, table, 1941, wood, upper front slanted slide rule dial, lower cloth grille with horizontal bars, 5 pushbuttons, 3 knobs, BC, SW, 6 tubes, AC **$65.00-75.00**

7038, table, 1941, wood, lower front slide rule dial, upper cloth grille with horizontal bars, 6 pushbuttons, 4 knobs, BC, SW, 8 tubes, AC **$50.00-65.00**

7039, table, 1941, wood, Deco, lower front slide rule dial, upper cloth grille with horizontal bars, 8 pushbuttons, 2 knobs, BC, SW, 9 tubes, AC **$85.00-95.00**

7054, table, 1947, wood, lower front slide rule dial, upper grille area, 4 pushbuttons, 4 knobs, BC, 6 tubes, AC/DC **$35.00-40.00**

7070, table-R/P, 1947, plastic, right front dial, left vertical louvers, curved left side, open top phono, 2 knobs, BC, 5 tubes, AC **$30.00-35.00**

7085, table-R/P/Rec, 1947, wood, inner right vertical slide rule dial, phono/wire recorder, lift top, front horizontal grille bars, 4 knobs, BC, 8 tubes, AC **$30.00-35.00**

7086, table-R/P/Rec, 1947, wood, inner right vertical slide rule dial, phono/wire recorder, lift top, front horizontal grille bars, 4 knobs, BC, 7 tubes, AC **$30.00-35.00**

7090, console, 1947, wood, upper front slanted dial, lower cloth grille with 2 vertical bars, 4 pushbuttons, 4 knobs, BC, SW, 6 tubes, AC/DC **$85.00-95.00**

7100, console-R/P, 1947, wood, inner right slide rule dial, left phono, lift top, front cloth grille with cut-outs, 4 knobs, BC, 6 tubes, AC ..**$85.00-95.00**

7102, console-R/P/Rec, 1947, wood, inner right slide rule dial, left phono/wire recorder, lift top, front criss-cross grille, 4 knobs, BC, 8 tubes, AC **$65.00-75.00**

7103, console-R/P/Rec, 1947, wood, inner right slide rule dial, left phono/wire recorder, lift top, front criss-cross grille, 4 knobs, BC, 7 tubes, AC **$65.00-75.00**

7108, table, 1941, wood, upper front slide rule dial, lower horizontal grille bars, 4 knobs, BC, SW, 5 tubes, battery **$35.00-40.00**

7111, console-R/P, 1947, wood, inner right slide rule dial/lower storage, door, left lift top, inner phono, 4 knobs, BC, SW, 8 tubes, AC **$65.00-75.00**

6402, table, 1940, plastic, midget, small right front dial over horizontal wrap-around louvers, 2 knobs, BC, 4 tubes, AC/DC, $75.00-85.00.

6821, portable, cloth covered, right front dial, left metal perforated grille, handle, 2 knobs, BC, 6 tubes, AC/DC/battery, $30.00-35.00.

7031A, table, 1942, two-tone wood, upper front slanted slide rule dial, lower cloth grille with 2 horizontal bars, 4 knobs, BC, SW, 6 tubes, AC, $50.00-65.00.

7115, console-R/P, 1947, wood, upper front slanted slide rule dial, center pull-out phono drawer, lower grille, 4 knobs, BC, FM, AC ..**$85.00-95.00**

7116, console-R/P, 1947, wood, right tilt-out slide rule dial, inner phono, lower front grille, BC, FM, AC **$65.00-75.00**

7166, portable, 1946, inner right dial, upper horizontal grille bars, flip-up lid, handle, BC, 4 tubes, AC/DC/battery **$40.00-45.00**

7206, table, 1957, ivory plastic, 2 front right slide rule dials, left cloth grille, 3 knobs, BC, FM, 8 tubes, AC **$25.00-30.00**

7210, table-R/P, 1948, wood, lower front slide rule dial, upper cloth grille with crossed bars, lift top, inner phono, side phono crank, 2 knobs, BC, 4 tubes, battery...**$40.00-45.00**

7222, portable, 1957, upper front slide rule dial, large lower grille area, handle, BC, 5 tubes, AC/DC/battery **$25.00-30.00**

7226, table, 1948, wood, lower front slanted slide rule dial, upper cloth grille, 2 knobs, BC, 6 tubes, AC/DC/battery **$45.00-55.00**

7244, table-R/P, 1939, wood, right front dial, left cloth grille with 2 horizontal bars, lift top, inner phono, BC, 6 tubes, AC **$40.00-45.00**

8000, table, 1948, upper right front dial, lower perforated wrap-under grille, flared base, 2 knobs, BC, 4 tubes, AC/DC...........**$65.00-75.00**

8004, table, 1949, ivory metal, midget, small upper right front dial, horizontal louvers, 2 knobs, BC, 4 tubes, AC/DC **$75.00-85.00**

8005, table, 1948, plastic, upper front slide rule dial, lower aluminum grille, 2 knobs, BC, 5 tubes, AC/DC **$40.00-50.00**

8020, table, 1948, plastic, upper front slide rule dial, lower perforated metal grille, 4 knobs, BC, FM, AC/DC **$40.00-50.00**

7050, console, 1941, wood, upper center slanted face with slide rule dial, lower grille with 4 vertical bars, 8 push-buttons, 5 knobs, BC, SW, 10 tubes, AC, $120.00-140.00.

7104, table, 1941, wood, upper front slanted slide rule dial, lower cloth grille with 2 vertical bars, 3 knobs, BC, 5 tubes, battery, $35.00-40.00.

8021, table, 1949, plastic, upper front slide rule dial, lower perforated metal grille, 4 knobs, BC, FM, 7 tubes, AC/DC **$40.00-50.00**

8024, table, 1949, plastic, lower front slide rule dial, upper vertical grille bars, 2 knobs, BC, FM, 8 tubes, AC **$35.00-40.00**

8036, table-C, autumn gold plastic, modern wedge-shaped case, side controls, large front alarm clock face, BC, AC **$25.00-30.00**

8037, table-C, light beige plastic, modern wedge-shaped case, side controls, large front alarm clock face, BC, AC **$25.00-30.00**

8038, table-C, light blue plastic, modern wedge-shaped case, side controls, large front alarm clock face, BC, AC **$25.00-30.00**

8041, table-R/P, 1958, top raised slide rule dial, wrap-over front grille, lift top, inner phono, handle, 3 knobs, BC, 5 tubes, AC.....**$35.00-40.00**

8050, table, 1948, two-tone wood, lower front slide rule dial, upper cloth grille with cut-outs, 2 knobs, BC, 5 tubes, AC/DC **$35.00-40.00**

8051, table, 1948, two-tone wood, lower front slide rule dial, upper cloth grille with cut-out, 2 knobs, BC, 5 tubes, AC/DC **$35.00-40.00**

8052, table, 1949, wood, lower front slide rule dial, upper cloth grille, raised pushbuttons, 4 knobs, BC, AC/DC.....................**$40.00-45.00**

8055B, console-R/P, 1959, wood, left dial &, right lift top, inner phono, large front grille area, legs, 5 knobs, BC, FM, 10 tubes, AC **$40.00-50.00**

8057, console-R/P, 1958, wood, inner left dial/right 4 speed phono, lift top, large front grille area, legs, 3 knobs, BC, 6 tubes, AC **$40.00-50.00**

8073, table-R/P, 1950, plastic, right front round dial, left vertical grille bars, open top phono, BC, 5 tubes, AC **$40.00-45.00**

8080, table-R/P, 1948, plastic, upper front slide rule dial, lower grille area, lift top, inner phono, 4 knobs, BC, 5 tubes, AC.............**$40.00-45.00**

8086A, table-R/P/Rec, 1949, wood, inner vertical slide rule dial/phono/wire recorder, lift top, front horizontal grille bars, 4 knobs, BC, 8 tubes, AC **$30.00-35.00**

8090, console, 1948, wood, upper front slanted slide rule dial, lower cloth grille with 2 vertical bars, 4 knobs, BC, 5 tubes, AC/DC..**$65.00-75.00**

8100, console-R/P, 1948, wood, inner right slide rule dial/left phono, lift top, front cloth grille, 4 knobs, BC, 5 tubes, AC **$50.00-65.00**

7204, table, 1957, brown plastic, 2 right front slide rule dials, left cloth grille, 3 knobs, BC, FM, 8 tubes, AC, $25.00-30.00.

8003, table, 1949, blue metal, midget, small upper right front dial, horizontal louvers, 2 knobs, BC, 4 tubes, AC/DC, $75.00-85.00.

9001, table, 1949, plastic, diagonally divided front with right dial & graduated vertical wrap-over grille bars, 2 knobs, BC, AC/DC, $50.00-65.00.

8101C, console-R/P, 1949, wood, inner right vertical slide rule dial/left phono, lift top, front criss-cross grille, 4 knobs, BC, 5 tubes, AC **$50.00-65.00**

8103, console-R/Rec, 1949, wood, inner right vertical slide rule dial/left recorder, lift top, front criss-cross grille, 4 knobs, BC, 7 tubes, AC **$50.00-65.00**

8105A, console-R/P, 1948, wood, inner right vertical dial/pushbuttons/left phono, lift top, front cloth grille, 4 knobs, BC, SW, 6 tubes, AC..**$50.00-65.00**

8108A, console-R/P, 1949, wood, right front tilt-out slide rule dial, left pull-out phono drawer, lower criss-cross grille, 4 knobs, BC, FM, AC **$65.00-75.00**

8115B, console-R/P, 1949, wood, right front tilt-out slide rule dial, pushbuttons, left pull-out phono drawer, lower grille area, 4 knobs, BC, FM, 9 tubes, AC...**$65.00-75.00**

8200, table, 1949, plastic, upper front slide rule dial, lower metal perforated grille, 2 knobs, BC, 4 tubes, battery **$30.00-35.00**

8210, table-R/P, 1949, wood, inner left vertical dial, phono, lift top, front cloth grille with cut-outs, crank phono, 2 knobs, BC, 4 tubes, battery **$35.00-40.00**

8217, portable, 1957, tan plastic, vertical grille bars, top antenna knob, swing handle, right & left side knobs, BC **$40.00-45.00**

8218, portable, 1957, aqua plastic, vertical grille bars, top antenna knob, swing handle, right & left side knobs, BC **$40.00-45.00**

8219, portable, 1957, coral plastic, vertical grille bars, top antenna knob, swing handle, right & left side knobs, BC **$40.00-45.00**

8230, table, 1949, wood, lower front slide rule dial, upper criss-cross grille, 2 knobs, BC, SW, 6 tubes, AC/DC/battery **$40.00-50.00**

8270A, portable, 1949, plastic & metal, inner slide rule dial, flip-up top, lower front grille area, 2 thumbwheel knobs, BC, 6 tubes, AC/DC/battery **$35.00-40.00**

9000, table, 1949, plastic, diagonally divided front with right dial & graduated vertical wrap-over grille bars, 2 knobs, BC, 5 tubes, AC/DC **$50.00-65.00**

9002, table, 1959, brown plastic, modern, lower right front dial overlaps upper recessed horizontal bars, feet, 2 knobs, BC, 5 tubes, AC/DC **$40.00-45.00**

9003, table, 1959, ivory plastic, modern, lower right front dial overlaps upper recessed horizontal bars, feet, 2 knobs, BC, 5 tubes, AC/DC **$40.00-45.00**

9006, table, 1949, white plastic, upper front V-shaped slide rule dial, lower vertical grille bars, 2 knobs, BC, 5 tubes, AC/DC **$35.00-40.00**

9012, table, 1959, plastic, right front vertical slide rule dial, large center grille area, 4 knobs, BC, 6 tubes, AC/DC **$25.00-30.00**

9022, table, 1949, plastic, right front square dial, wrap-around vertical grille bars, 3 knobs, BC, FM, 8 tubes, AC **$45.00-50.00**

9028, table-C, 1959, plastic, lower front dial, upper alarm clock, right & left grille areas, feet, BC, 6 tubes, AC **$25.00-30.00**

9049, console-R/P, 1959, wood, inner dial & 4 speed phono, lift top, large front grille area, legs, BC, FM, 12 tubes, AC **$40.00-50.00**

9054, table, 1949, wood, right front vertical slide rule dial over criss-cross grille, 4 knobs, BC, SW, 6 tubes, AC **$40.00-45.00**

9061, console-R/P, 1959, wood, controls under top "piano-lid" cover, lower right front pull-out phono, legs, BC, FM, 15 tubes, AC **$40.00-50.00**

9073B, table-R/P, 1950, plastic, right front round dial, left vertical grille bars, open top phono, BC, 5 tubes, AC **$40.00-50.00**

9082, table-R/P, 1950, wood, center front dial over large grille area, lift top, inner phono, 4 knobs, BC, 5 tubes, AC **$30.00-35.00**

9105, console-R/P, 1950, wood, upper front dial with right & left cut-outs, center pull-out phono drawer, lower grille area, 3 knobs, BC, FM, 8 tubes, AC **$50.00-65.00**

9201, table, 1959, plastic, wedge-shaped case, right vertical dial, left vertical dial, large center cloth grille, 2 speakers, 4 knobs, BC, FM, 6 tubes, AC **$30.00-35.00**

8010, table-C, 1948, plastic, slide rule dial lights through lower front grille, upper clock face, 5 knobs, BC, 5 tubes, AC, $65.00-75.00.

9005, table, 1949, mahogany plastic, upper front V-shaped slide rule dial, lower vertical grille bars, 2 knobs, BC, 5 tubes, AC/DC, $35.00-40.00.

R71, console, 1940, wood, upper center slanted face with slide rule dial, lower grille with 4 vertical bars, 6 pushbuttons, 2 knobs, BC, SW, 7 tubes, AC, $120.00-150.00.

9260, portable, 1948, plastic, lower right front dial, upper vertical metal wrap-over grille bars, fold-down handle, 2 knobs, BC, 5 tubes, AC/DC/battery **$40.00-45.00**

9270, portable, 1950, leatherette, upper front slide rule dial, lower grille area, handle, 2 knobs, BC, 5 tubes, AC/DC/battery **$25.00-30.00**

9280, portable, 1950, alligator, luggage-style, upper front slide rule dial, lower grille area, handle, 2 knobs, BC, 5 tubes, AC/DC/battery **$25.00-30.00**

Neutrodyne, table, 1924, wood, low rectangular case, 3 dial black front panel, lift top, 5 tubes, battery **$120.00-150.00**

R1261, table, 1940, two-tone wood, front off-center slide rule dial, right & left cloth grille areas with bars, 5 pushbuttons, 4 knobs, BC, SW, 6 tubes, AC **$65.00-75.00**

R1181, table, 1940, wood, lower front slide rule dial, upper 3-section cloth grille, 6 pushbuttons, 2 knobs, BC, SW, 8 tubes, AC, $65.00-75.00.

SIMPLEX
Simplex Radio Co.
Sandusky, Ohio

H, cathedral, 1930, wood, center front window dial, upper round cloth grille with cut-outs, 2 knobs, BC, 5 tubes, AC...........**$160.00-190.00**

N, cathedral, 1932, two-tone wood, center front window dial, upper cloth grille with cut-outs, 3 knobs, BC, 5 tubes, AC...........**$160.00-190.00**

NT, console, 1936, wood, upper front oval black dial, lower cloth grille with 3 vertical bars, tuning eye, 4 knobs, BC, SW, 10 tubes, AC **$120.00-140.00**

P, tombstone, 1932, two-tone wood, lower front window dial, upper cloth grille with lyre cut-out, 3 knobs, BC, SW, 5 tubes, AC ..**$180.00-200.00**

Q, cathedral, 1932, two-tone wood, center front window dial, upper cloth grille with cut-outs, 3 knobs, BC, 5 tubes, AC...........**$200.00-230.00**

RF, table, 1925, wood, low rectangular case, 2 dial front panel, 4 tubes, battery **$140.00-150.00**

RS5, table, 1925, mahogany, low rectangular case, 3 dial front panel, 5 tubes, battery...**$110.00-130.00**

RX, table, 1925, wood, square case, 2 dial front panel, 4 tubes, battery **$110.00-130.00**

SR8, table, 1925, mahogany, low rectangular case, slanted 3 dial front panel, 5 tubes, battery **$110.00-120.00**

NT, tombstone, 1936, wood, center front oval dial, upper cloth grille with horizontal bars, tuning eye, 4 knobs, BC, SW, 10 tubes, AC, $110.00-130.00.

SIMPLON
Industrial Electronic Corp.
505 Court Street, Brooklyn, New York

CA-5, table-R/P, 1947, cloth covered, upper front slanted dial, lower grille, handle, 3/4 lift-top, inner phono, 2 knobs, BC, 5 tubes, AC **$20.00-25.00**

WVV2, table, 1947, wood, upper front slanted slide rule dial, lower cloth grille with 4 horizontal bars, rounded right shoulder, rounded left side, 2 knobs, BC, 5 tubes, AC/DC **$40.00-45.00**

SKY CHIEF

Model unknown, portable, alligator, upper right front airplane dial, left cloth grille, handle, 2 knobs, BC, 5 tubes, AC/DC/battery, $40.00-50.00.

SKY KNIGHT
Butler Bros.
Randolph & Canal Streets, Chicago, Illinois

CB-500-P, table, 1947, wood, right front square dial, left 3-section cloth grille, 2 knobs, BC, 5 tubes, battery **$25.00-30.00**

SKYROVER
Butler Bros.
Randolph & Canal Streets, Chicago, Illinois

9022-N, table, 1946, plastic, upper front slanted slide rule dial, lower horizontal louvers with 3 vertical bars, 3 knobs, BC, 6 tubes, AC, $40.00-45.00.

22B5, console, wood, upper front round airplane dial, lower cloth grille with cut-outs, 4 knobs, BC, SW, 12 tubes, AC **$120.00-140.00**
C-10, cathedral, wood, lower front window dial with escutcheon, upper cloth grille with cut-outs, 3 knobs **$200.00-230.00**
N5-RD-250, table, 1946, plastic, upper front slanted slide rule dial, lower horizontal louvers with 3 vertical bars, 3 knobs, BC, 6 tubes, AC/DC **$40.00-45.00**
N5-RD295, table, 1947, plastic, right front square dial, left vertical grille bars, decorative case lines, 2 knobs, BC, 5 tubes, AC/DC **$50.00-65.00**
P-71, cathedral, wood, scalloped top, center front quarter-round dial, upper cloth grille with cut-outs, 3 knobs **$240.00-300.00**

SMOKERETTE
Porto Products, Inc.

SR-600W "Smokerette," table-N, 1947, plastic, combination radio/pipe rack/humidors/ashtray, left front slide rule dial, lower cloth grille with plastic cut-outs, 2 knobs, BC, AC, $200.00-230.00.

SONGBIRD

Model unknown, table, wood, rectangular case with inlaid decorative lines, right dial, center grille with brass "Songbird" nameplate, 2 knobs, BC, 6 tubes, AC/DC, $130.00-150.00.

SONIC
Sonic Industries, Inc.
19 Wilbur Street, Lynbrook, New York

415, table-R/P, 1958, plastic, inner right front dial, 3 speed record player, lift top, handle, 2 knobs, BC, 5 tubes, AC **$15.00-20.00**
465, table-R/P, 1958, center front dial overlaps horizontal grille bars, 3/4 lift top, inner phono, handle, BC, 5 tubes, AC **$20.00-25.00**

SONORA
Sonora Radio & Television Corp.
325 North Hoyne Avenue, Chicago, Illinois

100, table, 1948, plastic, upper front curved slide rule dial, lower horizontal louvers, 2 knobs, BC, 5 tubes, AC/DC **$40.00-45.00**
101, portable, 1948, plastic, lower front slide rule dial, upper curved horizontal louvers, handle, 2 knobs, BC, battery **$30.00-35.00**
102, portable, 1949, plastic, lower front slide rule dial, upper curved horizontal louvers, handle, 2 knobs, BC, 5 tubes, AC/DC/battery ..**$30.00-35.00**
170-6B, table, 1949, wood, right front dial, left grille with cut-outs, 4 knobs, BC, SW, 6 tubes, battery **$35.00-40.00**
171, table, 1950, plastic, lower front slide rule dial, upper horizontal grille bars, 2 knobs, BC, 5 tubes, AC/DC.........................**$45.00-50.00**
183, table, 1942, wood, right front square dial, left six section grille, rounded front corners, 2 knobs, BC, 4 tubes, battery **$30.00-40.00**
306, table-R/P, 1950, wood, center front dial, right & left criss-cross grille areas, lift top, inner phono, 4 knobs, BC, 5 tubes, AC ..**$30.00-35.00**
379, table, 1954, plastic, large front dial with decorative lines, 2 knobs, BC, 6 tubes, AC/DC..**$25.00-30.00**
389, table, 1954, plastic, recessed front with large center half round dial, left front perforated grille, feet, 2 knobs, BC, 5 tubes, AC/DC ..**$30.00-35.00**
390, table, 1954, plastic, recessed front with large center half round dial, left front perforated grille, feet, 2 knobs, BC, 5 tubes, AC/DC ..**$30.00-35.00**
401, console-R/P, 1948, wood, small cabinet, upper front square dial, lower storage, lift top, inner phono, 4 knobs, BC, 5 tubes, AC **$50.00-65.00**
538, portable, 1957, plastic, large lower perforated grille with "V," handle, 2 upper front thumbwheel knobs, BC, 4 tubes, AC/DC/battery **$30.00-35.00**
568, table, 1957, wood, lower front slide rule dial, large upper cloth grille, 2 knobs, BC, 6 tubes, AC/DC **$30.00-35.00**
652, table, plastic, right front dial, left grille panel with decorative lines & circular cut-outs, 2 knobs, BC, AC/DC **$25.00-30.00**
A-11, table, 1938, plastic, right front slide rule dial, left horizontal grille bars, horizontal wrap-around case lines, 2 knobs, BC, 5 tubes, AC/DC **$50.00-65.00**
C-22, table, 1938, plastic, right front slide rule dial over horizontal bars, left lattice grille, 2 knobs, BC, 6 tubes, AC **$50.00-65.00**
C-221, table, 1939, two-tone wood, right front dial, left horizontal grille bars, 2 knobs, BC, 6 tubes, AC **$45.00-55.00**

D-800, table, 1926, wood, low rectangular case, two front window dials with thumbwheel tuning, lift top, 4 knobs, BC, battery, $150.00-180.00.

D-12, table, 1938, wood, right front slide rule dial, rounded left with horizontal louvers, 4 knobs, BC, SW, 6 tubes, AC/DC **$75.00-85.00**

DD-14, table, 1939, wood, right front slide rule dial, left horizontal louvers, 3 knobs, BC, SW, 6 tubes, AC/DC **$40.00-45.00**

DDA-14, table, 1938, wood, right front slide rule dial, left horizontal grille bars, 4 pushbuttons, 3 knobs, 6 tubes, AC/DC............**$45.00-55.00**

EA-33, table, 1938, wood, upper right front slide rule dial, left horizontal wrap-around grille bars, 6 pushbuttons, 4 knobs, BC, SW, 6 tubes, AC/DC **$65.00-75.00**

FA-55, table, 1938, wood, right front slide rule dial, left horizontal wrap-around louvers, pushbuttons, 4 knobs, BC, SW, 7 tubes, AC............**$65.00-75.00**

GA-66, table, 1938, wood, center front slide rule dial, right & left horizontal wrap-around louvers, pushbuttons, 4 knobs, BC, SW, 9 tubes, AC **$65.00-75.00**

GA-88, console, 1938, wood, upper front slide rule dial, lower cloth grille with 2 vertical bars, pushbuttons, 4 knobs, BC, SW, 9 tubes, AC **$110.00-130.00**

KBU-168, portable, 1941, cloth covered, inner right round dial, left grille area, fold-down front, handle, 3 knobs, BC, 5 tubes, AC/DC/battery **$30.00-35.00**

KF, table, 1941, two-tone plastic, small case, top right dial, front vertical grille bars, 2 knobs, BC, 4 tubes, AC/DC **$75.00-85.00**

KG-80 "Candid Portable," portable, 1940, plastic, right front round grille area, handle, 2 top knobs, BC, 4 tubes, battery **$45.00-55.00**

KG-132 "Brownie," portable, 1941, brown plastic, front round grille, handle, left side knobs, BC, 4 tubes, battery........................**$45.00-55.00**

E-865, console, 1927, wood, lowboy with double doors, upper center window dial, middle grille with cut-outs, lower battery storage, 4 legs, stretcher base, 3 knobs, BC, 6 tubes, battery, $140.00-160.00.

KL-185, console-R/P/Rec, 1942, wood, inner right slide rule dial/pushbuttons/knobs, left phono/recorder, lift top, front grille, BC, SW, 9 tubes, AC **$85.00-95.00**

KM "Coronet," table, 1941, Catalin, right front square dial, left horizontal grille bars, handle, 2 knobs, BC, 5 tubes, AC/DC ....**$900.00+**

KM-450, table, 1941, wood, right front square dial, left angled grille with horizontal bars, 2 knobs, BC, 5 tubes, AC/DC **$50.00-65.00**

KNF-99, table-R/P, 1940, walnut, right front square dial, left cloth grille with horizontal & vertical bars, lift top, inner phono, 3 knobs, BC, 5 tubes, AC **$35.00-40.00**

KNF-148, table-R/P, 1941, walnut, right front square dial, left lattice grille, lift top, inner phono, 3 knobs, BC, 5 tubes, AC.............**$35.00-40.00**

KT "Cameo," table, 1941, plastic, right front airplane dial, left horizontal louvers, 2 knobs, BC, 5 tubes, AC/DC **$40.00-50.00**

KT-87 "Cameo," table, 1941, tan/brown plastic, right front dial, left horizontal louvers, 2 knobs, BC, 5 tubes, AC/DC **$40.00-45.00**

KT-89 "Cameo," table, 1941, ivory plastic, right front dial, left horizontal louvers, 2 knobs, BC, 5 tubes, AC/DC **$40.00-45.00**

KXF-95, console-R/P, 1940, wood, inner right slide rule dial, left phono, front grille with horizontal and vertical bars, 5 knobs, BC, SW, 6 tubes, AC/DC..**$110.00-130.00**

KY-94, console, 1940, walnut, upper front slanted slide rule dial, lower cloth grille with horizontal & vertical bars, pushbuttons, 5 knobs, BC, SW, 7 tubes, AC..**$110.00-130.00**

KZ-111, table, 1940, wood, right front dial, left cloth grille with vertical bars, 2 knobs, 4 tubes, battery **$35.00-40.00**

LD-93, table, 1941, walnut, right front square dial, left horizontal louvers, 3 knobs, BC, SW, 5 tubes, AC/DC **$40.00-50.00**

RBU-176, table, 1946, plastic, upper front slanted slide rule dial, lower horizontal louvers, 2 knobs, BC, 5 tubes, AC/DC, $40.00-45.00.

LKS-180, table, 1942, walnut, right front airplane dial, raised left grille area with horizontal cut-outs, 3 knobs, BC, 6 tubes, AC/DC ..**$50.00-65.00**

LLS-179, table, 1942, walnut, right front dial, left cloth grille with horizontal & vertical bars, 2 knobs, BC, 6 tubes, AC/DC **$50.00-65.00**

LM "Stratoliner," table, 1942, plastic, upper front slanted slide rule dial, lower horizontal grille bars, 2 knobs, BC, 5 tubes, AC/DC..**$40.00-45.00**

LQ "Clipper," table, 1942, plastic, lower front slide rule dial, upper horizontal grille bars, 2 knobs, BC, 5 tubes, AC/DC **$40.00-45.00**

LR-147 "Triple Play," portable, 1941, leatherette, lower front slide rule dial, upper horizontal grille bars, handle, 3 knobs, BC, 5 tubes, AC/DC/battery **$30.00-35.00**

LTF-465, table-R/P, 1942, walnut, right front square dial, left horizontal louvers, lift top, inner phono, 3 knobs, BC, 5 tubes, AC..**$30.00-35.00**

LV-186, console-R/P, 1942, wood, upper front slanted dial, center pull-out phono, lower grille area, 4 knobs, BC, SW, 7 tubes, AC..**$95.00-115.00**

M-22, table, 1949, plastic, right front slide rule dial over horizontal bars, left lattice grille, 2 knobs, BC, 6 tubes, battery **$40.00-45.00**

Navigator, table-N, 1940, looks like world globe, radio tunes by rotating the globe on its axis, switch and volume control in base, BC, 5 tubes, AC/DC **$240.00-350.00**

P-99 "Teeny-Weeny," table, 1938, wood, midget, right front dial, left grille with 2 horizontal bars, 2 knobs, BC, 4 tubes, AC/DC......**$65.00-75.00**

P-100 "Teeny-Weeny," table, 1938, plastic, midget, right front dial, left grille with 2 horizontal bars, 2 knobs, BC, 4 tubes, AC/DC **$75.00-85.00**

P-101 "Jubilee," table, 1938, plastic, midget, right front dial, left grille with 2 horizontal bars, 2 knobs, BC, 4 tubes, AC/DC **$75.00-85.00**

P-106 "Metro," table, 1939, plastic, midget, right front dial, left grille with vertical bars, 2 knobs, BC, 4 tubes, AC/DC **$75.00-85.00**

PL-29 "Playboy," portable, 1939, striped cloth covered square case, front dial & grille, handle, BC, 4 tubes, battery **$40.00-45.00**

PS-102, table, 1938, plastic, midget, right front dial, left vertical grille bars, BC, 5 tubes, AC/DC **$75.00-85.00**

QA-33, table, 1949, wood, upper right front slide rule dial, left grille with horizontal wrap-around bars, 6 pushbuttons, 4 knobs, BC, SW, 6 tubes, battery **$45.00-50.00**

RBMU-176, table, 1947, plastic, upper front slanted slide rule dial, lower horizontal louvers, 2 knobs, BC, 5 tubes, AC/DC **$40.00-45.00**

RBU-175, table, 1946, plastic, upper front slanted slide rule dial, lower horizontal louvers, 2 knobs, BC, 5 tubes, AC/DC **$40.00-45.00**

RBU-177, table, 1946, plastic, upper front slanted slide rule dial, lower horizontal louvers, 2 knobs, BC, 5 tubes, AC/DC **$40.00-45.00**

RCU-208, table, 1946, wood, right front square dial, curved left side with vertical louvers, 3 knobs, BC, 6 tubes, AC/DC **$65.00-75.00**

RDU-209, table, 1946, two-tone wood, upper front slide rule dial, lower horizontal louvers, 3 knobs, BC, 6 tubes, AC/DC **$50.00-65.00**

RET-210, table, 1947, wood, right front square dial, left cloth grille, 4 knobs, BC, SW, 7 tubes, AC **$45.00-50.00**

RGMF-230, table-R/P, 1947, wood, right front dial, left horizontal grille bars, lift top, inner phono, 2 knobs, BC, 5 tubes, AC **$30.00-35.00**

RKRU-215, table-R/P, 1946, wood, upper front dial, lower grille, lift top, inner phono, 2 knobs, BC, 6 tubes, AC **$30.00-35.00**

RMR-219, console-R/P, 1947, wood, inner right dial/pushbuttons, left phono, lift top, front grille with vertical bars, 4 knobs, BC, SW, 8 tubes, AC **$65.00-75.00**

RQU-222, table, 1946, plastic, upper front curved slide rule dial, lower 2-section grille with horizontal louvers, 3 knobs, BC, 6 tubes, AC/DC **$50.00-65.00**

RX-223, table, 1947, wood, right front square dial with plastic escutcheon, left cloth grille with bars, 2 knobs, BC, 4 tubes, battery **$40.00-45.00**

TH-46, table, 1940, wood, right front vertical slide rule dial, left cloth grille, BC, 4 tubes, battery **$30.00-35.00**

TJ-62, table, 1939, plastic, right front airplane dial, left horizontal grille bars, 2 knobs, BC, 5 tubes, AC/DC **$40.00-45.00**

TJ-63, table, 1939, wood, right front airplane dial, left vertical grille bars, 2 knobs, BC, 5 tubes, AC/DC **$45.00-50.00**

TK-44, table, 1939, walnut with gold band overlay, right front dial, left horizontal grille bars, 2 knobs, BC, 4 tubes, AC/DC **$45.00-50.00**

TN-45, table, 1939, wood, right dial panel over large wrap-around front grille, 2 knobs, BC, 5 tubes, AC/DC **$50.00-65.00**

TNE-60, table-R/P, 1939, wood, lower front square dial, right & left wrap-over cloth grilles, lift top, inner phono, 2 knobs, BC, LW, 5 tubes, AC **$35.00-40.00**

TP-108 "Teeny-Weeny," table, 1939, plastic, midget, right front dial, left grille area, BC, 4 tubes, AC/DC **$75.00-85.00**

TSA-105 "Cosmo," table, 1939, plastic, right front half-round dial, left horizontal louvers, "Air Magnet" antenna, 2 knobs, BC, 5 tubes, AC/DC **$50.00-65.00**

TT-52, table, 1939, walnut, center front slide rule dial, upper wrap-over cloth grille, pushbuttons, 2 knobs, BC, 5 tubes, AC **$65.00-75.00**

RBU-207, table, 1946, wood, upper front slanted slide rule dial, lower horizontal grille bars, 2 knobs, BC, 5 tubes, AC/DC, $40.00-45.00.

WAU-243, table, 1939, plastic, Deco, large round dial on right top of case, left horizontal wrap-around grille bars, right front pushbuttons, 2 knobs, BC, 5 tubes, AC/DC, $150.00-180.00.

TT-128, table, 1940, wood, right front slide rule dial, rounded left with horizontal wrap-around grille bars, pushbuttons, 2 knobs, BC, 5 tubes, AC **$65.00-75.00**

TV-48, table, 1939, plastic, center front round dial, right & left vertical grille bars, BC, 4 tubes, AC/DC **$75.00-85.00**

TW-49, table, 1939, plastic, Deco, large round dial on right top of case, left horizontal wrap-around grille bars, right front pushbuttons, 2 knobs, BC, 5 tubes, AC/DC **$150.00-180.00**

TX-53, table, 1941, wood, right front slide rule dial, left wrap-around grille area, pushbuttons, 4 knobs, BC, SW, 6 tubes, AC **$65.00-75.00**

TY-54, table, 1939, wood, center front slide rule dial, right and left wrap-around grille areas, pushbuttons, 4 knobs, BC, SW, 7 tubes, AC **$65.00-75.00**

TZ-56, console, 1939, wood, upper front slanted slide rule dial, lower cloth grille with vertical bars, pushbuttons, 4 knobs, BC, SW, 12 tubes, AC **$110.00-130.00**

WBRU-239, table-R/P, 1948, wood, right front dial, left grille, lift top, inner phono, 4 knobs, BC, 5 tubes, AC **$35.00-40.00**

WCU-246, radio/lamp, 1948, plastic, controls right & left sides of case, top grille bars, front lamp switch, 2 knobs, BC, 5 tubes, AC/DC **$65.00-75.00**

WDU-233, portable, 1947, two-tone, upper front slide rule dial, lower perforated grille, handle, 2 knobs, BC, 4 tubes, AC/DC/battery ..**$35.00-40.00**

WDU-249, portable, 1948, mottled case with plastic accents, upper front slide rule dial, lower perforated grille, handle, 2 top thumbwheel knobs, BC, 4 tubes, AC/DC/battery **$40.00-45.00**

WEU-262, table, 1948, plastic, right front dial, left cloth grille, decorative case lines, 4 knobs, BC, FM, 8 tubes, AC/DC **$65.00-75.00**

WGFU-241, table-R/P, 1947, plastic, right front round dial, left vertical grille bars, open top phono, 3 knobs, BC, 5 tubes, AC ..**$40.00-50.00**

WGFU-242, table-R/P, 1947, plastic, right front round dial, left vertical grille bars, open top phono, 3 knobs, BC, 5 tubes, AC ..**$40.00-50.00**

WJU-252, table, 1948, plastic, midget, top right dial, front/back/top grille bars, 2 knobs, BC, 4 tubes, AC/DC **$95.00-115.00**

WKRU-254A, console-R/P, 1948, wood, inner right dial, left phono, lift top, front grille, 4 knobs, BC, FM, 8 tubes, AC **$50.00-65.00**

WLRU-219A, console-R/P, 1948, wood, inner right half-round dial, left phono, lift top, front grille with vertical columns, 4 knobs, BC, FM, 9 tubes, AC **$65.00-75.00**

YB-299, table, 1950, plastic, right front half-round dial, left horizontal louvers, 2 knobs, BC, 5 tubes, AC/DC **$40.00-45.00**

SOUND, INC.
Sound, Inc.
221 East Cullerton Street, Chicago, Illinois

5R2, table, 1947, two-tone, upper right front dial, center horizontal grille bars, 2 pointer knobs, BC, 4 tubes, AC/DC..................**$30.00-35.00**

SPARTON
Sparks-Withington Company
Jackson, Michigan

The Sparks-Withington Company began to manufacture radios in 1926. In the 1930s, their introduction of Deco-styled mirrored radios, along with other Deco cabinet designs by Walter Dorwin Teague, helped make the Sparton line one of the most sought after by collectors of Deco radios. The company produced one of the most expensive-to-own radios in today's collecting world — the 1936 Nocturne, a Deco, 46" round mirrored console which currently sells for over, $25,000.

6CL66, table, 1948, leatherette, right front rectangular dial, left cloth grille, 3 knobs, $30.00-35.00.

5AW16, table, 1947, walnut plastic, raised top, upper front slanted slide rule dial, lower vertical grille bars, 2 knobs, BC, 5 tubes, AC/DC **$50.00-55.00**
6-66A, table, 1948, leatherette, right front rectangular dial, left cloth grille, 3 knobs, BC, SW, 6 tubes, AC/DC **$30.00-35.00**
6A66, table, 1948, metal, right front rectangular dial, left round grille area, 3 knobs **$50.00-65.00**
6AM06, portable, 1948, leatherette, inner right dial, left grille area, fold-down front, handle, 2 knobs, BC, 6 tubes, AC/DC/battery **$35.00-40.00**
6AW26PA, table-R/P, 1947, wood, inner right slide rule dial, left phono, lift top, front grille area, 4 knobs, BC, SW, 6 tubes, AC.......**$35.00-40.00**
16984, console-R/P, 1946, wood, upper front slide rule dial, lower cloth grille with 2 vertical bars, tilt-out phono, 4 knobs, AC..**$95.00-115.00**
7AM46, console, 1946, wood, upper front slide rule dial, lower cloth grille with 2 vertical bars, 4 knobs, BC, SW, 7 tubes, AC **$95.00-115.00**
9, console, 1931, wood, lowboy, front window dial, lower cloth grille with cut-outs, 2 knobs, BC, 5 tubes, AC..........................**$120.00-150.00**
10AM76-PA, console-R/P, 1947, wood, inner right slide rule dial, door, left pull-out phono, lower horizontal louvers, tuning eye, 4 knobs, BC, SW, FM, 10 tubes, AC **$95.00-105.00**
10BW76PA, console-R/P, 1947, wood, inner right slide rule dial, door, left pull-out phono drawer, lower cloth grille with vertical bars, tuning eye, 4 knobs, BC, SW, FM, 10 tubes, AC **$85.00-95.00**
14, console, 1932, wood, lowboy, front half-round dial, lower cloth grille with cut-outs, 6 legs, 3 knobs, BC, 8 tubes, AC **$110.00-130.00**
15, console, 1931, wood, lowboy, front half-round dial, lower cloth grille with cut-outs, decorative front carvings, 3 knobs, BC, 8 tubes, AC...**$120.00-150.00**
18, console, 1932, wood, lowboy, upper front half-round dial, lower cloth grille with vertical bars, 4 knobs, BC, 10 tubes, AC ..**$120.00-150.00**
20, console-R/P, 1932, wood, lowboy, center front half-round dial, lower cloth grille with cut-outs, lift top, inner phono, AC **$150.00-170.00**
25, console, 1931, wood, upper front half-round dial, lower cloth grille with cut-outs, 3 knobs, BC, 10 tubes, AC **$140.00-160.00**

5-15, table, 1925, wood, rectangular cabinet, 3 window dials, lift top, upper center Sparton "S," 4 knobs, BC, 5 tubes, battery, $110.00-130.00.

4AW17, table, 1948, plastic, raised top, upper front slanted slide rule dial, lower vertical grille bars, 2 knobs, BC, 4 tubes, battery ..**$35.00-40.00**
5, cathedral, 1931, wood, lower front window dial, upper round cloth grille with cut-outs, 2 knobs, BC, 5 tubes, AC............**$240.00-270.00**
5AI16, table, 1947, ivory plastic, raised top, upper front slanted slide rule dial, lower vertical grille bars, 2 knobs, BC, 5 tubes, AC/DC........**$50.00-55.00**
5AM26-PS, table-R/P, 1946, wood, upper front slide rule dial, lower grille area, lift top, inner phono, 2 knobs, BC, AC **$35.00-40.00**
5AW06, table, 1946, plastic, upper front slide rule dial, lower horizontal wrap-around louvers, 2 knobs, BC, 5 tubes, AC/DC......**$50.00-55.00**

5-26, table, 1925, wood, rectangular cabinet, 3 window dials, lift top, upper center Sparton nameplate, fold down front, 6 knobs, BC, 5 tubes, battery, $110.00-130.00.

10, tombstone, 1931, wood, shouldered, lower front half-round dial, upper cloth grille with cut-outs, 3 knobs, BC, 7 tubes, AC, $110.00-130.00.

27, console, 1932, wood, inner half-round dial, lower cloth grille with cut-outs, double front doors, BC, 13 tubes, AC $130.00-150.00

28 "Triolian," console, 1932, wood, inner dial, double front doors, front & side cut-outs, BC, 13 tubes, AC $180.00-200.00

53, table, 1934, wood, front round dial, center grille with cut-outs, 2 knobs, BC, SW, 5 tubes, AC/DC $75.00-85.00

57, table, 1934, walnut with inlay, front round dial, center grille with cut-outs, 2 knobs, BC, SW, 5 tubes, AC/DC $75.00-85.00

61/62, table, 1933, wood with inlay, right front dial, center cloth grille with cut-outs and center Sparton logo, BC, SW, 5 tubes, AC/DC......$75.00-85.00

62, table, 1926, wood, low rectangular case, center front window dial with escutcheon, 3 knobs, BC, 7 tubes, AC $140.00-150.00

65, tombstone, 1934, wood, lower front round airplane dial, upper cloth grille with cut-outs, 5 knobs, BC, SW, 6 tubes, AC $140.00-150.00

67, tombstone, 1934, two-tone wood, center front round airplane dial, upper cloth grille with cut-outs, 4 knobs, BC, SW, 6 tubes, AC $140.00-150.00

68, console, 1934, wood, lowboy, upper front round airplane dial, lower cloth grille with cut-outs, 4 knobs, BC, SW, 6 tubes, AC $110.00-130.00

69, table, 1928, two-tone wood, low rectangular case, center front window dial with escutcheon, lift top, 3 knobs, BC, 7 tubes, AC ..$95.00-115.00

71, tombstone, 1933, wood, center front window dial, upper cloth grille with cut-outs, 4 knobs, BC, SW, 6 tubes, AC $120.00-150.00

72, console, 1933, wood, lowboy, upper front half-round dial, lower cloth grille with cut-outs, 6 legs, BC, SW, 7 tubes, AC $120.00-140.00

74, console, 1933, wood, upper front half-round dial, lower cloth grille with cut-outs, 4 knobs, BC, SW, 9 tubes, AC $120.00-140.00

75A, tombstone, 1933, wood, lower front half-round dial, upper cloth grille with cut-outs, 5 knobs, BC, SW, 8 tubes, AC $120.00-140.00

80, console, 1934, wood, upper front round dial, lower cloth grille with cut-outs, 4 knobs, BC, SW, 8 tubes, AC $110.00-130.00

132, table, 1950, plastic, oblong case, right front half-round dial, metal perforated grille, 2 knobs, BC, 5 tubes, AC/DC, $75.00-95.00.

83, console, 1934, wood with inlay, upper front round airplane dial, lower cloth grille with cut-outs, feet, BC, SW, 8 tubes, AC..$110.00-130.00

89-A, console, 1928, wood, inner window dial, lower cloth grille with cut-outs, double doors, 3 knobs, BC, 9 tubes, AC $180.00-200.00

100, table, 1948, plastic, upper front slide rule dial, lower horizontal wrap-around louvers, 2 knobs, BC, 5 tubes, AC/DC $45.00-55.00

104, console, 1934, wood, upper front round airplane dial, lower cloth grille with cut-outs, 4 knobs, BC, SW, 10 tubes, AC..$120.00-150.00

134 "Triolian," console, 1934, walnut, lowboy, inner front dial, lower cloth grille with cut-outs, double doors, 5 knobs, BC, SW, 13 tubes, AC $180.00-200.00

139, table, 1950, plastic, oblong case, right front half-round dial, metal perforated grille, 2 knobs, BC, 5 tubes, AC/DC.............$75.00-95.00

141A, table, 1950, wood, lower front slanted slide rule dial, large upper grille area, 4 knobs, BC, FM, 8 tubes, AC................$35.00-40.00

152, portable, 1950, plastic, inner dial, lower checkered grille, flip-up front, handle, 2 thumbwheel knobs, BC, 4 tubes, AC/DC/battery $40.00-45.00

230, table, 1953, black plastic, oblong case, right front half-round dial, center woven grille area, 2 knobs, BC, 5 tubes, AC/DC..$75.00-95.00

232, table, 1953, maroon plastic, oblong case, right front half-round dial, center woven grille area, 2 knobs, BC, 5 tubes, AC/DC ..$75.00-95.00

141XX, table, 1951, wood, lower front plastic panel with slide rule dial, large upper grille area, 4 knobs, BC, FM, 8 tubes, AC, $50.00-65.00.

239, table, 1953, ivory plastic, oblong case, right front half-round dial, center woven grille area, 2 knobs, BC, 5 tubes, AC/DC..$75.00-95.00

301 "Equasonne," console, 1929, carved wood, highboy, inner dial, double front doors, lower back panel, 3 knobs, BC, 10 tubes, AC $690.00-740.00

301, portable, 1953, brown plastic covered, left front dial, center lattice grille, handle, 2 knobs, BC, 4 tubes, AC/DC/battery $40.00-45.00

305, portable, 1953, green plastic covered, left front dial, center lattice grille, handle, 2 knobs, BC, 4 tubes, AC/DC/battery $40.00-45.00

309, portable, 1953, ivory plastic covered, left front dial, center lattice grille, handle, 2 knobs, BC, 4 tubes, AC/DC/battery $40.00-45.00

345, table, 1953, plastic, left front round dial, center concentric circular louvers over perforated grille, 2 knobs, BC, 5 tubes, AC/DC..$35.00-40.00

409-GL, table, 1938, blue mirror glass, 7 sided Deco case, right front dial, left round grille, 2 black feet, 2 knobs, BC, 5 tubes including ballast, AC/DC ....$2,150.00+

410 "Junior," upright table, 1930, wood, arched top, lower front window dial, upper round cloth grille with cut-outs, finials, feet, 2 knobs, BC, 6 tubes, AC $250.00-300.00

500-C "Cloisonne," table, 1939, Catalin, enamel & chrome, Deco, right front slide rule dial, left round cloth grille with horizontal bars, 2 knobs, BC, 5 tubes, AC/DC ....$2,200.00+

500-DG, table, 1939, wood with inlay, step-down sides, right front dial, left vertical grille bars, 2 knobs, BC, 5 tubes, AC/DC $45.00-55.00

506, table, 1935, wood, center front round airplane dial over cloth grille with cut-outs, BC, SW, 5 tubes, AC $85.00-115.00

510-DG, table, 1939, wood, right front airplane dial, left grille with vertical bars, center front wood accent inlay, rounded top front, 2 knobs, BC, 5 tubes, AC/DC...$50.00-60.00

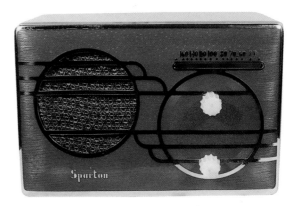

500 "Cloisonne," table, 1939, Catalin, enamel & chrome, Deco, right front slide rule dial, left round cloth grille with horizontal bars, 2 knobs, BC, 5 tubes, AC/DC, $2,200.00+.

506 "Bluebird," table, 1936, round blue or peach mirror glass with chrome cents, Deco, round front dial, feet, 3 knobs, BC, SW, 5 tubes, AC, $3,500.00+.

557, table, 1936, blue or peach mirror glass, Deco, front square dial, horizontal chrome fins wrap-around right side, black or brown base, 3 knobs, BC, SW, 5 tubes, AC/DC, $2,000.00+.

510-DR, table, 1939, wood, right front airplane dial, left grille with vertical bars, dual horizontal wood accent inlays, rounded front corners, 2 knobs, BC, 5 tubes, AC/DC **$50.00-60.00**

510-W, table, 1939, wood, upper right front dial, left wraparound grille, rounded corners and shoulders, 2 knobs, BC, 5 tubes, AC/DC **$50.00-60.00**

516, tombstone, 1935, wood, shouldered, center front round dial, upper cloth grille with vertical bars, 4 knobs, BC, SW, 5 tubes, AC **$110.00-130.00**

537, upright table, 1936, wood, large center front round dial, top grille, 4 knobs, BC, SW, 5 tubes, AC **$85.00-95.00**

558, table, 1937, blue or peach mirror glass, Deco, front square dial, horizontal chrome fins wrap-around right side, black or brown base, 4 knobs, BC, SW, 5 tubes, AC/DC..**$2,000.00+**

567, console, 1936, wood, upper front round dial, lower grille with cut-outs, 3 knobs, BC, SW, 5 tubes, AC **$110.00-130.00**

570-M, table, 1936, wood, right front slide rule dial, raised left grille with vertical bars, 4 pushbuttons, 3 knobs, BC, SW, 5 tubes, AC/DC **$85.00-95.00**

577, console, 1936, wood, upper front round dial, lower cloth grille with center vertical bars, 4 knobs, BC, SW, 5 tubes, AC ..**$110.00-130.00**

589, console, 1930, wood, carved cabinet with side lion‚s head decorations, inner dial, double front doors, upper grille area with ornate cut-outs & pillars, 3 knobs, BC, 10 tubes, AC **$1,000.00-1,100.00**

616, tombstone, 1935, wood, Deco, lower front airplane dial, upper cloth grille with cut-outs, 4 knobs, BC, SW, 6 tubes, AC....**$150.00-180.00**

617, tombstone, 1936, wood, center front round dial, upper cloth grille with horizontal bars, 4 knobs, BC, SW, 6 tubes, AC ..**$150.00-180.00**

637, tombstone, 1937, wood, lower front round dial, upper cloth grille with 4 horizontal bars, 4 knobs, BC, SW, 6 tubes, battery..**$150.00-180.00**

666, console, 1935, wood, upper front dial, lower cloth grille with vertical bars, 4 knobs, BC, SW, 6 tubes, AC **$110.00-130.00**

667, console, 1936, wood, upper front round dial, lower 3-section cloth grille, 4 knobs, BC, SW, 6 tubes, AC **$120.00-150.00**

678, console, 1937, wood, upper front dial, lower cloth grille with vertical bars & circular cut-outs, pushbuttons, tuning eye, 4 knobs, BC, SW, 6 tubes, AC **$180.00-200.00**

716, tombstone, 1935, wood, lower front round airplane dial, upper cloth grille with cut-outs, 4 knobs, BC, SW, 7 tubes, AC....**$120.00-150.00**

766, console, 1935, wood, upper front round dial, lower cloth grille with cut-outs, tuning eye, 4 knobs, BC, SW, 7 tubes, AC..**$150.00-180.00**

768, console, 1937, wood, upper front dial, lower cloth grille with horizontal & vertical bars, tuning eye, 5 knobs, BC, SW, 7 tubes, AC **$150.00-180.00**

867, console, 1936, wood, upper front round dial, lower cloth grille with vertical center bars, BC, SW, 8 tubes, AC.................**$180.00-200.00**

931, console, 1929, wood, inner dial, lower cloth grille with cut-outs, double front doors, stretcher base, 3 knobs, BC, 9 tubes AC, 8 tubes DC, AC and DC versions **$110.00-130.00**

536, tombstone, 1935, wood, shouldered, center brass escutcheon with multicolor airplane dial, upper grille with cut-outs, 4 knobs, BC, SW, 5 tubes, AC, $120.00-140.00.

930 "Equasonne," console, 1929, wood, inner dial, lower cloth grille with cut-outs, double front doors, stretcher base, 3 knobs, BC, 9 tubes, AC, $120.00-150.00.

36987, tombstone, wood, lower front round airplane dial, upper cloth grille with cut-outs, 5 knobs, BC, SW, $140.00-150.00.

966, console, 1935, wood, upper front round dial, lower cloth grille with cut-outs, tuning eye, 4 knobs, BC, SW, 9 tubes, AC..**$120.00-150.00**

987, console, 1936, wood, upper front round dial, lower cloth grille with splayed bars, tuning eye, 6 knobs, BC, SW, 9 tubes, AC..**$200.00-220.00**

997, tombstone, 1937, wood, center front round dial, upper cloth grille with 4 horizontal bars, tuning eye, 5 knobs, BC, SW, 9 tubes, AC **$150.00-180.00**

1003, console-R/P, 1949, wood, "chest of drawers," inner right half-round dial/pushbuttons, left pull-out phono drawer, 4 knobs, BC, SW, FM, 13 tubes, AC **$150.00-180.00**

1006, console-R/P, 1947, wood, inner right slide rule dial, door, left pull-out phono drawer, lower criss-cross grille, 2 knobs, BC, FM, 8 tubes, AC **$75.00-85.00**

1010, console-R/P, 1948, wood, inner right dial, left phono, lift top, lower front criss-cross grille, 4 knobs, BC, 7 tubes, AC **$65.00-75.00**

1030, console-R/P, 1948, wood, fold-down front with inner slide rule dial/phono, lower grille area, 4 knobs, BC, 6 tubes, AC ..**$65.00-75.00**

1040, console-R/P, 1949, wood, right tilt-out slide rule dial, left pull-out phono drawer, 2 knobs, BC, FM, 9 tubes, AC...............**$65.00-75.00**

1051, console-R/P, 1949, wood, upper left slide rule dial, lower tilt-out phono, right grille & storage, 4 knobs, BC, SW, 6 tubes, AC **$65.00-75.00**

1059, console-R/P, 1949, wood, upper left slide rule dial, lower tilt-out phono, right grille & storage, 4 knobs, BC, FM, 8 tubes, AC **$65.00-75.00**

1068, console, 1937, wood, upper front dial, lower cloth grille with 4 vertical bars, 2 tuning eyes, pushbuttons, 5 knobs, BC, SW, 10 tubes, AC **$180.00-200.00**

1160, console, 1939, wood, upper front slide rule dial, lower horizontal grille bars, pushbuttons, 5 knobs, BC, SW, 11 tubes, AC **$180.00-200.00**

1166, console, 1935, wood, upper front round dial, lower cloth grille with vertical bars, tuning eye, 5 knobs, BC, SW, 11 tubes, AC ..**$150.00-190.00**

1167, console, 1936, wood, upper front round dial, lower cloth grille with vertical bars, BC, SW, 11 tubes, AC **$160.00-190.00**

1186 "Nocturne," console, 1936, blue or rose mirror glass & chrome, designed by Walter Dorwin Teague, 46" round Deco design, upper front round dial, lower cloth grille with horizontal bars, tuning eye, 5 knobs, BC, SW, 11 tubes, AC ....**$25,000.00+**

1288-P, console-R/P, 1937, wood, front dial, lower cloth grille with vertical bars, tuning eye, pushbuttons, side storage, lift top, inner phono, BC, SW, 12 tubes, AC **$200.00-230.00**

1466 "Triolian," console, 1935, wood, upper front round dial, lower cloth grille with cut-outs, lower right & left side cut-outs, tuning eye, BC, SW, 14 tubes, AC...**$200.00-230.00**

1567, console, 1936, wood, upper front round dial, lower cloth grille with vertical bars, tuning eye, BC, SW, 15 tubes, AC **$240.00-270.00**

1867 "Triolian," console, 1936, leather & walnut, Deco, upper front round dial, lower cloth grille with cut-outs, tuning eye, 3 speakers, 5 knobs, BC, SW, 18 tubes, AC **$470.00-580.00**

8618, console, 1938, wood, upper front slanted slide rule dial, lower cloth grille with 3 vertical bars, pushbuttons, 5 knobs, BC, SW, 8 tubes, AC **$150.00-180.00**

SPLITDORF
Splitdorf Radio Corporation
Newark, New Jersey

R-500, table, 1924, wood, low rectangular case, metal 3 dial front panel, lift top, 5 knobs, BC, 5 tubes, battery, $120.00-150.00.

Abbey, table, 1927, wood, 6-sided case, upper front window dial with escutcheon, lift top, 2 knobs, BC, 6 tubes, battery **$150.00-180.00**

R-100, table, 1925, wood, low rectangular case, 3 dial front panel, 5 knobs, BC, 5 tubes, battery **$140.00-160.00**

R-V-695, table, 1926, two-tone wood, rectangular case, metal 2 dial slanted front panel, 4 knobs, BC, 6 tubes, battery, $120.00-150.00.

ST. REGIS
International Radio Corporation
Ann Arbor, Michigan

676X, table, 1937, wood, black dial, upper grille with horizontal bars and rectangular cut-out, 2 knobs, BC, 6 tubes including ballast, AC/DC, $65.00-75.00.

STANDARD
Standard Radio Corp.
Worcester, Massachusetts
Standard Polyrad Corp.
521 Broadway, Cincinnati, Ohio

B5 "Standardyne," table, 1925, wood, low rectangular case, 3 dial black front panel, lift top, 5 tubes, battery.............................$120.00-140.00

BH "Standardyne," console, 1925, wood, inner 3 dial black panel, fold-down lid, upper speaker grille with cut-outs, lower storage, battery $160.00-190.00

STANTEX

PC-200, portable, plastic, upper right front thumbwheel dial, lower right side on/off knob, no speaker, earphone only, made in Japan, BC, battery $40.00-45.00

STARK
Stark Sound Engineering
2131 Fairfield Avenue, Fort Wayne, Indiana

1010, table, 1950, plastic, raised top, right front dial, left cloth grille with horizontal bars, 2 knobs, BC, 4 tubes, AC/DC $40.00-50.00

1020, table, 1950, plastic, raised top, upper front slanted slide rule dial, lower horizontal wrap-around louvers, 2 knobs, BC, 5 tubes, AC/DC $50.00-65.00

STARR
Starr Equipment Corp.
366 Hamilton Ave., Brooklyn, New York

D "Starr-Harmonic," table, 1925, wood, low rectangular case, 3 dial front panel, feet, 5 tubes, battery...............................$140.00-160.00

STEELMAN
Steelman Radio & Phonograph Co., Inc.
12-30 Anderson Avenue, Mt. Vernon, New York

3A16U, table-R/P, 1956, cloth covered, right front vertical slide rule dial overlaps large grille, lift top, inner phono, handle, 3 right side knobs, BC, 5 tubes, AC $25.00-30.00

3AR1, table-R/P, 1953, cloth covered, right front round dial, left square grille, lift top, inner phono, handle, 4 knobs, BC, 5 tubes, AC $30.00-35.00

3AR4, table-R/P, 1956, cloth covered, right front round dial, left grille, lift top, inner phono, handle, 4 knobs, BC, 5 tubes, AC $25.00-30.00

3AR5U, table-R/P, 1956, cloth covered, right side dial, large front grille, lift top, inner phono, handle, 3 knobs, BC, 5 tubes, AC $25.00-30.00

3RP1, table-R/P, 1953, cloth covered, center front round dial over grille, lift top, inner phono, 3 knobs, BC, 5 tubes, AC.............$25.00-30.00

3RP4, table-R/P, 1956, cloth covered, inner right dial, 3 speed record player, lift top, handle, 3 knobs, BC, 5 tubes, AC $25.00-30.00

3RP8, table-R/P, 1959, cloth covered, inner front dial, phono, lattice grille, lift top, handle, 2 knobs, BC, 4 tubes, AC $20.00-25.00

4AR12, console-R/P, 1959, wood, inner dial & 4 speed phono, lift top, large front grille area, legs, 2 knobs, BC, 5 tubes, AC....$40.00-50.00

4RP7, table-R/P, 1958, inner front half-round dial, 4 speed record player, lift top, handle, BC, 4 tubes, AC $20.00-25.00

450, table-C, 1952, plastic, right front round dial, left round alarm clock, center vertical grille bars, 5 knobs, BC, 5 tubes, AC......$30.00-35.00

517, table-R/P, 1952, suitcase-style, inner right dial, phono, lift top, handle, 4 knobs, BC, 5 tubes, AC $20.00-25.00

595, table-R/P, 1952, leatherette, right side dial/ round grille with Steelman logo, lift top, inner phono, 4 knobs, BC, 5 tubes, AC $25.00-30.00

597, table-R/P, 1952, leatherette, right front half-round dial, left grille, lift top, inner phono, 4 knobs, BC, 5 tubes, AC $25.00-30.00

601, portable, 1952, center front round dial overlaps perforated grille, handle, 2 knobs, BC, 4 tubes, battery $20.00-25.00

602, portable, 1952, leatherette, upper front dial, lower perforated grille, handle, 2 knobs, BC, 4 tubes, AC/DC/battery...............$25.00-30.00

5101, table, 1952, wood, off-center dial over large front grille area, 3 knobs, BC, 5 tubes, AC/DC $25.00-30.00

6000, portable, 1952, leatherette & wood, inner center front round dial, fold-in front, handle, 2 knobs, BC, 5 tubes, AC/DC/battery $25.00-30.00

AF1100, table, 1952, plastic, lower front slide rule dial, large upper grille area, 4 knobs, BC, FM, 10 tubes, AC $25.00-30.00

STEINITE
Steinite Labs
Atchinson, Kansas

991, table, 1927, wood, two front window dials with large escutcheons, center voltmeter, 4 knobs, BC, 7 tubes, AC, $150.00-180.00.

40, console, 1929, wood, highboy, recessed center panel with upper window dial with escutcheon, lower decorative grille with cut-outs, 4 legs with stretcher base, 3 knobs and 1 thumbwheel dial, BC, 8 tubes, AC...$120.00-140.00

45, console, 1929, wood, highboy, center panel with lower window dial with escutcheon, upper decorative grille with cut-outs, 4 legs with stretcher base, 3 knobs and 1 thumbwheel dial, BC, 8 tubes, AC..$120.00-140.00

102, console-R/P, 1929, walnut, lowboy, ornate cabinet, inner front window dial, lower cloth grille with cut-outs, double front doors, 3 knobs, BC, 9 tubes, AC $240.00-270.00

261, table, 1928, wood, rectangular box, center window dial with escutcheon, lift up top lid, 1 front volume knob, 1 front thumbwheel dial, BC, 7 tubes, AC $100.00-120.00

263, console, 1928, wood, lowboy, upper front center window dial with escutcheon, lower large grille, 4 legs, 1 front volume knob, 1 front thumbwheel dial, BC, 7 tubes, AC............................$130.00-150.00

265, console, 1928, wood, lowboy desk style, drop down upper door with inside front center window dial with escutcheon, lower double doors with inner grille, 1 front volume knob, 1 front thumbwheel dial, BC, 7 tubes, AC $150.00-170.00

266, console, 1928, wood, lowboy, upper double doors with inner front center window dial with escutcheon and upper grille, 4 legs with stretcher base, 1 front volume knob, 1 front thumbwheel dial, BC, 7 tubes, AC $150.00-170.00

605, table-R/P, 1931, wood, upright table with peaked top, center front window dial, upper grille area, lower pull-out phono drawer, BC, 8 tubes, AC $240.00-300.00

700, cathedral, 1931, wood, center front window dial, upper cloth grille with cut-outs, 3 knobs, BC, 5 tubes, AC $270.00-310.00

712, console, 1931, wood, lowboy, upper front window dial, lower cloth grille with cut-outs, BC, 8 tubes $120.00-150.00

990, table, 1927, wood, two front window dials with large escutcheons, center voltmeter, rounded front corners, 4 knobs, BC, 7 tubes, AC ..$150.00-180.00

993, console, 1927, wood, lowboy, two upper front window dials with large escutcheons and center voltmeter, lower grille with vertical cut-outs, 4 legs, 4 knobs, BC, 7 tubes, AC $170.00-190.00

STELLAR

Roger Maris/Mickey Mantle, table-N, 1959, wood, right front round dial with diamond-shaped pointer, left perforated grille with baseball batter, "autographed" by Roger Maris & Mickey Mantle, BC..$580.00-690.00

STERLING
The Sterling Manufacturing Co.
Cleveland, Ohio

LS-4, portable, plastic, diagonally divided front, right round dial overlaps lower perforated chrome grille, fold-down handle, BC, 4 tubes, battery, $45.00-55.00.

5 "Concertone," tombstone, 1931, wood, small case, shouldered, lower right front dial, upper 3-section cloth grille, 5 tubes .. **$150.00-180.00**

7 "Concertone," tombstone, 1931, wood, shouldered, center front quarter-round dial, upper 3-section cloth grille, 3 knobs ..**$150.00-180.00**

8 "Concertone," console, 1931, wood, lowboy, upper front quarter-round dial, lower cloth grille with cut-outs, 3 knobs, 8 tubes **$160.00-190.00**

A-2-60 "Troubador," console, 1929, walnut, highboy, inner window dial, lower round cloth grille with cut-outs, double doors, 8 tubes, AC **$190.00-210.00**

A-3-60 "Serenader," console, 1929, walnut, lowboy, upper front window dial, lower cloth grille with cut-outs, AC **$120.00-150.00**

B-2-60 "Imperial," console, 1929, walnut, upper front window dial with escutcheon, lower square cloth grille with cut-outs, AC ..**$120.00-150.00**

STEWART-WARNER
Stewart-Warner Corp.
1826 Diversey Parkway, Chicago, Illinois

07-51H, table, 1940, plastic, streamlined, right front dial, rounded left with horizontal wraparound louvers, 2 knobs, BC, 5 tubes, AC/DC, $85.00-95.00.

01-5D9, table-R/P, 1939, wood, right front dial, left cloth grille with horizontal bars, lift top, inner phono, 2 knobs, AC **$40.00-45.00**

01-5H7, console, 1939, walnut, upper front slide rule dial, lower cloth grille with 2 vertical bars, pushbuttons, BC, SW, 4 tubes, AC **$120.00-150.00**

01-6A7, console, 1939, wood, upper front slanted slide rule dial, lower cloth grille with 3 vertical bars, pushbuttons, 4 knobs, BC, SW, AC...**$140.00-150.00**

01-6B9, console-R/P, 1939, walnut, upper front slide rule dial, lower vertical grille bars, pushbuttons, 4 knobs, BC, SW, 8 tubes, AC...**$120.00-150.00**

3, console, 1932, wood, lowboy, rounded shoulders, combination BC receiver and SW converter, 2 window dials, lower grill with cut-outs, 6 knobs, BC, SW, 11 tubes, AC, $220.00-260.00.

01-6C9, console-R/P, 1939, wood, upper front left and right sets of pushbuttons and knobs, larger lower grille with five vertical bars, lift top with inner phono and slide rule dial, 4 knobs, BC, SW, 8 tubes, AC **$150.00-180.00**

01-8A7, console, 1939, wood, upper front slide rule dial, lower cloth grille with vertical bars, pushbuttons, 4 knobs, BC, SW, 8 tubes, AC **$140.00-160.00**

01-8B7, console, 1940, wood, upper front slide rule dial, lower cloth grille with vertical bars, 8 pushbuttons, 4 knobs, BC, SW, 8 tubes, AC **$140.00-160.00**

01-611, table, 1939, wood, right front dial, raised left horizontal louvers, pushbuttons, 4 knobs, BC, SW, 6 tubes, AC **$50.00-65.00**

01-817, console, 1939, wood, upper front slide rule dial, lower cloth grille with 2 vertical bars, pushbuttons, 2 band, 3 knobs, BC, SW, 8 tubes, AC **$140.00-160.00**

02-411, portable, 1939, striped cloth covered, right front dial, left grille, handle, 2 knobs, BC, 4 tubes, battery **$30.00-35.00**

03-5C1, table, 1939, two-tone wood, right front dial, left horizontal louvers, 2 knobs, BC, 5 tubes, AC/DC **$40.00-50.00**

03-5E1, upright table, 1939, plastic, center front airplane dial, upper horizontal louvers, 7 pushbuttons, 2 knobs, BC, 5 tubes, AC/DC **$120.00-150.00**

13-5U, table, 1939, two-tone wood, right front dial, rounded left grille with cut-outs, 2 knobs, BC, 5 tubes, AC/DC, $50.00-65.00.

51T136, table, 1947, wood, upper front slanted slide rule dial, large lower cloth grille, 2 knobs, BC, 5 tubes, AC/DC, $35.00-40.00.

03-5K3 "The Magician," table, 1939, plastic, streamlined, right front dial, rounded left with horizontal wrap-around louvers, BC, 5 tubes, AC/DC..**$85.00-95.00**

07-5B "Senior Varsity," table, 1939, plastic, Deco, right front dial, left round grille with "wavy" cut-outs, 2 knobs, BC, 5 tubes, AC/DC...**$240.00-300.00**

07-5B3Q "Dionne Quints," table-N, 1939, plastic, Deco, decals of quints, right front dial, left round grille with "wavy" cut-outs, 2 knobs, BC, 5 tubes, AC/DC ....**$1,100.00+**

07-5R3, table, 1940, ivory plastic, streamlined, right front slide rule dial, rounded left with horizontal wrap-around louvers, 2 knobs, BC, SW, 5 tubes, AC/DC **$85.00-95.00**

07-55BK, bed, 1939, wood, bed made by Jiranek, waterfall headboard with built-in radio, large dial, grille cut-outs, 2 knobs, BC, 5 tubes, AC/DC **$300.00-350.00**

07-512 "Campus," table, 1939, plastic, streamlined, right front dial, rounded left with horizontal wrap-around louvers, optional school letters or initials, 2 knobs, BC, 5 tubes, AC/DC.............**$85.00-95.00**

07-513 "Gulliver's Travels," table-N, 1939, plastic, streamlined, decals of Gulliver's Travels, right front dial, rounded left with horizontal wrap-around louvers, 2 knobs, BC, 5 tubes, AC/DC...........**$700.00+**

07-513H, table, 1939, plastic, streamlined, right front dial, rounded left with horizontal wrap-around louvers, 2 knobs, BC, 5 tubes, AC/DC **$85.00-95.00**

07-513Q "Dionne Quints," table-N, 1938, plastic, streamlined, decal of quints, right front dial, rounded left with horizontal wrap-around louvers, 2 knobs, BC, 5 tubes, AC/DC...................................**$1,000.00+**

07-514, table, 1939, two-tone wood, Deco, right front dial, left horizontal wrap-around louvers, 2 knobs, BC, 5 tubes, AC/DC......**$65.00-75.00**

07-516 "Fireside," chairside, 1939, wood, slanted front dial, horizontal louvers, lower magazine shelf, 4 legs, 2 knobs, BC, 5 tubes, AC/DC **$120.00-150.00**

4B4, table, 1940, two-tone wood, center front slide rule dial, right & left grilles with horizontal bars, 2 knobs, BC, 4 tubes, battery ..**$50.00-65.00**

4C1, table, 1940, wood, right front dial, left cloth grille with cut-outs, 2 knobs, BC, 4 tubes, battery **$40.00-45.00**

4D1, table, 1940, two-tone wood, right front dial, left cloth grille with cut-outs & vertical bars, 2 knobs, BC, 4 tubes, battery **$50.00-55.00**

91-513 "Spade," table, 1938, wood, triangular case, front slide rule dial, 4 pushbuttons, cloth grilles with cut-outs on all four sides, 2 knobs, BC, 5 tubes, AC, $400.00-450.00.

5R7, table, 1940, walnut, center front slide rule dial, right & left grilles with vertical bars, 2 knobs, BC, SW, 5 tubes, AC/DC............**$65.00-75.00**

5V9, table-R/P, 1941, wood, right front dial, left cloth grille with horizontal bars, lift top, inner phono, 3 knobs, BC, 5 tubes, AC **$35.00-40.00**

6T8, table-R/P, 1940, inner right dial, left grille, fold-down front, lift top, inner phono, handle, 4 knobs, BC, SW, 6 tubes, AC.....**$35.00-40.00**

6U2GA, portable, 1942, upper front slanted slide rule dial, lower grille area, handle, 3 knobs, 6 tubes, AC/DC/battery..............**$35.00-40.00**

9B7, console, 1940, wood, upper front slide rule dial, lower cloth grille with vertical center divider & bars, pushbuttons, 4 knobs, BC, SW, 9 tubes, AC **$110.00-130.00**

50, console, 1932, wood, lowboy, upper front dial, lower cloth grille with cut-outs, 6 legs, BC, SW, 11 tubes, AC **$140.00-160.00**

51, console, 1932, wood, lowboy, inner dial, double doors, lower cloth grille with cut-outs, 5 legs, BC, SW, 11 tubes, AC **$150.00-180.00**

51T56, table, 1948, wood, upper front slanted slide rule dial, large lower grille area, 2 knobs, BC, 5 tubes, AC/DC **$35.00-40.00**

61T16, table, 1946, mahogany plastic, upper front slanted slide rule dial, lower cloth grille, 3 knobs, BC, 6 tubes, AC/DC **$35.00-40.00**

61T26, table, 1946, ivory plastic, upper front slide rule dial, lower horizontal louvers, 3 knobs, BC, 6 tubes, AC/DC **$40.00-45.00**

62T16, table, 1946, wood, right front slide rule dial, left cloth grille with 2 horizontal bars, 6 pushbuttons, 4 knobs, BC, SW, 6 tubes, AC **$55.00-65.00**

62T36, table, 1946, Catalin, upper front slanted slide rule dial, lower inset horizontal louvers, 3 knobs, BC, SW, 6 tubes, AC **$480.00-580.00**

62TC16, table, 1946, wood, right front slide rule dial, left wrap-around cloth grille with horizontal bars, 6 pushbuttons, 4 knobs, BC, SW, 6 tubes, AC **$65.00-75.00**

72CR26, console-R/P, 1947, wood, inner right slide rule dial/6 pushbuttons, door, left pull-out phono drawer, 4 knobs, BC, SW, 7 tubes, AC **$65.00-75.00**

91-511, table, 1938, walnut, right front slide rule dial, left horizontal louvers, pushbuttons, 2 knobs, BC, 5 tubes, AC **$65.00-75.00**

62TC18, table, 1946, wood, right front slide rule dial, left cloth wrap-around grille with horizontal bars, pushbuttons, 4 knobs, BC, SW, $65.00-75.00.

300, table, 1925, wood, low rectangular case, front panel with 3 half-round dials, 5 knobs, BC, 5 tubes, battery, $85.00-105.00.

91-512, table, 1938, wood, right front slide rule dial, left wrap-around horizontal louvers, 4 pushbuttons, 2 knobs, BC, 5 tubes, AC..**$65.00-75.00**

91-514, table, 1938, black & ivory, Deco, right front slide rule dial, left vertical grille bars, pushbuttons, 2 knobs, BC, 5 tubes, AC..**$150.00-170.00**

91-531, upright table, 1938, walnut, center front dial, upper cloth grille with vertical bars, pushbuttons, BC, SW, 5 tubes, AC ..**$85.00-95.00**

91-536, chairside, 1938, wood, half-round, top dial/pushbuttons, front grille with horizontal bars, BC, SW, 5 tubes, AC **$200.00-230.00**

91-537, console, 1938, wood, upper front dial, lower cloth grille with center vertical bar, pushbuttons, 2 knobs, BC, SW, 5 tubes, AC........**$120.00-150.00**

91-617, console, 1938, wood, upper front dial, lower cloth grille with center divider, pushbuttons, 4 knobs, BC, SW, 6 tubes, AC ..**$110.00-130.00**

91-621, table, 1938, wood, right front dial, left horizontal wrap-around louvers, tuning eye, pushbuttons, 2 knobs, BC, SW, 6 tubes, AC **$85.00-95.00**

91-627, console, 1938, wood, upper front dial, lower cloth grille with horizontal bars, tuning eye, pushbuttons, 2 knobs, BC, SW, 6 tubes, AC **$120.00-140.00**

91-817, console, 1938, wood, upper front horizontal dial, lower cloth grille with center vertical divider, base, tuning eye, pushbuttons, 3 knobs, BC, SW, 8 tubes, AC **$140.00-160.00**

91-1117, console, 1938, wood, upper front dial, lower horizontal grille bars, tuning eye, pushbuttons, 4 knobs, BC, SW, 11 tubes, AC **$140.00-160.00**

95-514, table, two-tone wood, Deco, upper right front slide rule dial, left cloth grille with vertical bars, 4 pushbuttons, 2 knobs..**$180.00-200.00**

97-521, table, 1938, walnut, right front slide rule dial, left horizontal louvers, pushbuttons, 2 knobs, BC, 6 including ballast, AC/DC **$65.00-75.00**

97-524, table, 1938, black & ivory, Deco, right front slide rule dial, left vertical grille bars, pushbuttons, 2 knobs, BC, 6 including ballast, AC/DC **$150.00-170.00**

97-562, table, 1939, plastic, Deco, right front dial, left round grille with "wavy" cut-outs, BC, 5 tubes including ballast, AC/DC ..**$240.00-300.00**

303, table, wood, rectangular case, slanted black 3 dial front panel, lift top, 5 knobs, BC, 5 tubes, battery, $120.00-150.00.

305 "Aeromaster," table, 1925, wood, rectangular case, slanted 3 dial front panel, 6 knobs, BC, 5 tubes, battery..................**$120.00-150.00**

310, console, 1925, wood, inner panel with 3 half-round dials, fold-down front, upper cloth grille with cut-outs, lower storage, 5 knobs, BC, 5 tubes, battery..**$200.00-230.00**

325, table, 1925, wood, low rectangular case, metal front panel with 3 half-round pointer dials, lift top, 5 knobs, BC, 5 tubes, battery **$110.00-130.00**

350, table, 1926, wood, high rectangular case, center front dial with escutcheon, lower cloth grille with cut-outs, 3 knobs, BC, 6 tubes, battery **$150.00-180.00**

355, console, 1926, wood, upper front dial with escutcheon, center cloth grille with cut-outs, lower storage, 3 knobs, BC, 6 tubes, battery **$180.00-200.00**

360, console, 1926, wood, inner dial with escutcheon, fold-down front, upper left cloth grille with cut-outs, storage, 3 knobs, BC, 6 tubes, battery **$160.00-190.00**

385, table, 1927, wood, low rectangular case, center front dial, 3 knobs, BC, 6 tubes, battery..**$85.00-105.00**

520, console, 1927, wood, lowboy, upper front window dial, lower round metal grille with dancing girl cut-outs, 3 knobs, BC, 6 tubes, battery **$350.00-410.00**

801, table, 1928, metal, low rectangular case, center front dial, switch, 2 knobs, BC, 6 tubes, AC **$85.00-95.00**

802, table, 1928, metal, low rectangular case with top built-in speaker, center front dial, switch, 2 knobs, BC, 6 tubes, AC....**$110.00-130.00**

900, table w/speaker stand, metal & wood, 900AC on wooden speaker stand painted to match, center grille, 4 legs, 3 knobs, BC, 8 tubes, AC, $200.00-220.00.

900, console, 1929, walnut, lowboy, upper front window dial with escutcheon, lower round cloth grille with cut-outs, 3 knobs, BC, 8 tubes, AC **$110.00-130.00**

900AC, table, 1929, metal, low rectangular case, center front window dial, lift-off top, 3 knobs, BC, 8 tubes, AC.....................**$85.00-95.00**

1101, table, 1933, wood, rounded top, center front window dial, right & left cloth grilles with cut-outs, 3 knobs, 10 tubes, AC ..**$85.00-115.00**

1102, console, 1933, wood, lowboy, upper front window dial, lower cloth grille with cut-outs, 3 knobs, 10 tubes **$110.00-130.00**

1104, side table, 1933, wood, Duncan Phyfe-style, inner window dial, right & left cloth grilles with cut-outs, fold-down front, 10 tubes, AC **$120.00-150.00**

1105, console, 1933, wood, small French commode-style case, inner window dial, fold-down front, 2 lower drawers, 10 tubes, AC **$120.00-150.00**

1106, console/bookcase, 1933, wood, shouldered top, inner window dial, double doors, upper & lower bookshelves, 10 tubes, AC........**$240.00-270.00**

1111, table, 1933, walnut, front dial, center grille with figural cut-out, fluted metal wrap-over bands, 2 knobs, BC, SW, 6 tubes, AC ..**$240.00-300.00**

1116, table-N, 1933, red leatherette, looks like stack of 3 books, inner dial and "S/W" cut-out, fold-open front, 2 knobs, BC, SW, 6 tubes, AC **$240.00-300.00**

9001-D, console, 1946, wood, decorative lowboy cabinet with 4 legs, pull-down three false drawer front, pushbuttons, slide rule dial, 4 knobs, BC, SW, 6 tubes, AC, $240.00-270.00.

9002-B, table, 1948, plastic, upper front slanted slide rule dial, lower horizontal louvers, 3 knobs, BC, 6 tubes, AC/DC, $40.00-50.00.

1117, table-N, 1933, green leatherette, looks like stack of 3 books, inner dial and "S/W" cut-out, fold-open front, 2 knobs, BC, SW, 6 tubes, AC **$240.00-300.00**

1118, table-N, 1933, brown leather, looks like stack of 3 books, inner dial and "S/W" cut-out, fold-open front, 2 knobs, BC, SW, 6 tubes, AC **$240.00-300.00**

1119, table, 1933, jade green enamel, front dial, center grille with figural cut-out, fluted silver metal wrap-over bands, 2 knobs, BC, SW, 6 tubes, AC **$240.00-300.00**

1152, side table, 1933, wood, Duncan Phyfe-style, inner dial & cloth grille with cut-outs, fold-down front, BC, SW, 6 tubes, AC..**$120.00-150.00**

1153, side table, 1933, wood, Duncan Phyfe-style, inner window dial, right & left cloth grilles with cut-outs, fold-down front, BC, SW, 6 tubes, AC **$120.00-150.00**

1154, console, 1933, wood, small French commode-style case, inner window dial, fold-down front, 2 lower drawers, BC, SW, 6 tubes, AC **$120.00-150.00**

1155, table, 1933, wood, front dial, center cloth grille with cut-outs, fluted side panels, BC, SW, 6 tubes, AC **$75.00-85.00**

1262 "Stuart," tombstone, 1934, wood, lower front quarter-round dial, upper cloth grille with cut-outs, 4 knobs, BC, SW, 7 tubes, AC...**$180.00-200.00**

1264, console, 1934, wood, lowboy, upper front quarter-round dial, lower cloth grille, 4 knobs, BC, SW, 7 tubes, AC......**$140.00-160.00**

1265, console, 1934, wood, lowboy, upper front quarter-round dial, lower cloth grille with cut-outs, 6 legs, BC, SW, 7 tubes, AC ..**$140.00-160.00**

1401, tombstone, 1935, two-tone wood, 2 lower front windows with escutcheon, upper cloth grille with cut-outs, 2 knobs, BC, SW, 5 tubes, AC **$140.00-160.00**

1421, table, 1936, two-tone wood, center front round dial, upper right cloth grille with cut-outs, 2 knobs, BC, 5 tubes, AC **$75.00-85.00**

9151-A, table, 1950, plastic, right front raised see-through dial overlaps checkered grille, 2 knobs, BC, FM, 7 tubes, AC/DC, $40.00-45.00.

1461, table, 1936, wood, large right front round airplane dial, left step-down top with front and side grille sections, rounded shoulders and corners, 4 knobs, BC, SW, 7 tubes, AC.....................**$100.00-120.00**

1691, table, 1936, wood, large front center airplane dial, top grille with cut-outs, rounded top front edge, 4 knobs, BC, SW, 5 tubes, AC **$80.00-100.00**

1711, table, 1936, wood, right front airplane dial, left grille with vertical cut-outs, rounded front corners, 3 knobs, BC, SW, 5 tubes, AC/DC **$45.00-55.00**

1721, table, 1936, wood, upper right front large round airplane dial and tuning eye, left front and side grille with vertical cut-outs, rounded shoulders, 4 knobs, BC, SW, 6 tubes, AC.................**$110.00-130.00**

1731, tombstone, 1936, wood, lower front center large round airplane dial and tuning eye, upper grille with cut-outs, step-down shoulders, 4 knobs, BC, SW, 7 tubes, AC **$120.00-140.00**

1735, console, 1936, wood, upper front center large round airplane dial and tuning eye, lower recessed grille with three bars, 4 knobs, BC, SW, 7 tubes, AC..**$130.00-160.00**

1883, chairside, 1937, walnut, half-round case, top dial under glass, front cloth grille w 3/horizontal bars, BC, SW, 6 tubes including ballast, AC/DC **$200.00-230.00**

3041, table, 1937, rectangular case lays down or stands up, slide rule dial, wrap-around grille with cut-outs, BC, 5 tubes, AC **$85.00-95.00**

9000-B, table, 1947, wood, upper front slanted slide rule dial, lower horizontal louvers, 3 knobs, BC, SW, 6 tubes, AC/DC **$50.00-65.00**

9001-E, end table, 1946, wood, drop leaf-style, inner slide rule dial, pushbuttons, fold-down front, 4 knobs, BC, SW, 6 tubes, AC **$120.00-150.00**

9180-H, table, 1954, black plastic, right front raised round dial, left recessed lattice grille, 2 knobs, BC, 4 tubes, AC/DC, $35.00-40.00.

9001-F, end table, 1946, wood, inner slide rule dial, pushbuttons, fold-down front, lower 4-legged base, 4 knobs, BC, SW, 6 tubes, AC..**$130.00-160.00**

9002-A, table, 1948, plastic, upper front curved slide rule dial, large lower grille area, 3 knobs, BC, 6 tubes, AC/DC **$40.00-50.00**

9007-F, portable, 1946, luggage-style, inner right dial, left grille, fold down front, handle, 3 knobs, BC, 6 tubes, AC/DC/battery........**$30.00-35.00**

9150-D, console-R/P, 1950, wood, right front tilt-out dial, left pull-down phono door, lower storage & grille, 3 knobs, BC, FM, 8 tubes, AC **$75.00-85.00**

9152-A, table, 1950, plastic, right round dial over vertical front grille bars, feet, 2 knobs, BC, 5 tubes, AC/DC **$35.00-40.00**

9152-B, table, 1950, plastic, right round dial over vertical front grille bars, feet, 2 knobs, BC, 5 tubes, AC/DC **$35.00-40.00**

9153-A, table, 1950, plastic, lower right front dial, large upper perforated metal grille, 2 knobs, BC, 4 tubes, AC/DC/battery **$30.00-35.00**

9154-C, console-R/P, 1951, wood, upper front dial, center pull-out phono drawer, lower grille, 3 knobs, BC, 6 tubes, AC **$50.00-65.00**

9160-AU, table, 1952, mahogany plastic, right front round dial, left lattice grille, 2 knobs, BC, 5 tubes, AC/DC **$35.00-40.00**

9160-BU, table, 1952, yellow plastic, right front round dial, left lattice grille, 2 knobs, BC, 5 tubes, AC/DC **$35.00-40.00**

9160-CU, table, 1952, blue plastic, right front round dial, left lattice grille, 2 knobs, BC, 5 tubes, AC/DC **$35.00-40.00**

A6-1Q "Dionne Quints," table-N, 1938, plastic, decals of Dionne quints, wrap-over vertical bars, 2 top thumbwheel knobs, BC, 3 tubes, AC/DC, $1,000.00+.

R-172-A, table, 1936, wood, right front round black dial, left front & side cloth grilles with vertical bars, 4 knobs, BC, SW, 6 tubes, AC, $55.00-65.00.

9160-DU, table, 1952, rust plastic, right front round dial, left lattice grille, 2 knobs, BC, 5 tubes, AC/DC **$35.00-40.00**

9160-EU, table, 1952, tan plastic, right front round dial, left lattice grille, 2 knobs, BC, 5 tubes, AC/DC **$35.00-40.00**

9162, table-C, 1952, plastic, left front half-round dial over alarm clock, upper horizontal bars, lower right circular cut-outs, feet, 6 knobs, BC, 5 tubes, AC **$35.00-40.00**

9162E, table-C, 1952, plastic, left front half-round dial over alarm clock, upper horizontal bars, lower right circular cut-outs, feet, 6 knobs, BC, 5 tubes, AC **$35.00-40.00**

9165-A, table, 1953, black & yellow plastic, right front half-round dial over dotted grille area, feet, 2 knobs, BC, 6 tubes, AC/DC....**$25.00-30.00**

9165-B, table, 1953, rust & tan plastic, right front half-round dial over dotted grille area, feet, 2 knobs, BC, 6 tubes, AC/DC....**$25.00-30.00**

9170-B "Gadabout," portable, 1954, green plastic, top dial, 2-section front lattice grille, fold-down handle, 2 top thumbwheel knobs, BC, 4 tubes, AC/DC/battery **$25.00-30.00**

9170-C "Gadabout," portable, 1954, gray plastic, top dial, 2-section front lattice grille, fold-down handle, 2 top thumbwheel knobs, BC, 4 tubes, AC/DC/battery **$25.00-30.00**

9170-D "Gadabout," portable, 1954, maroon plastic, top dial, 2-section front lattice grille, fold-down handle, 2 top thumbwheel knobs, BC, 4 tubes, AC/DC/battery **$25.00-30.00**

9178-C, table-R/P, 1955, wood, right side dial, large front grille area, lift top, inner phono, 3 side knobs, BC, 6 tubes, AC **$30.00-35.00**

9180-B, table, 1954, green plastic, right front raised round dial, left recessed lattice grille, 2 knobs, BC, 4 tubes, AC/DC **$35.00-40.00**

9181-A, table, 1954, mahogany plastic, recessed front with right front large round dial with civil defense marks, left front grille, bandswitch on back, 2 knobs, BC, SW, 5 tubes, AC/DC **$40.00-45.00**

9181-C, table, 1954, gray plastic, recessed front with right front large round dial with civil defense marks, left front grille, bandswitch on back, 2 knobs, BC, SW, 5 tubes, AC/DC **$40.00-45.00**

9181-D, table, 1954, maroon plastic, recessed front with right front large round dial with civil defense marks, left front grille, bandswitch on back, 2 knobs, BC, SW, 5 tubes, AC/DC **$50.00-55.00**

9181-E, table, 1954, yellow plastic, recessed front with right front large round dial with civil defense marks, left front grille, bandswitch on back, 2 knobs, BC, SW, 5 tubes, AC/DC **$50.00-55.00**

9181-F, table, 1954, blue plastic, recessed front with right front large round dial with civil defense marks, left front grille, bandswitch on back, 2 knobs, BC, SW, 5 tubes, AC/DC **$50.00-55.00**

A-6S "Air Pal," table, 1938, plastic, front & back vertical wrap-over grille bars, 2 top thumbwheel knobs, BC, 3 tubes, AC/DC ..**$120.00-150.00**

A51T3 "Air Pal," table, 1947, plastic, upper front slide rule dial, lower vertical grille bars, 2 large top knobs, BC, 5 tubes, AC/DC ..**$120.00-150.00**

A51T4 "Air Pal," table, 1947, plastic, upper front slide rule dial, lower vertical grille bars, 2 large top knobs, BC, 5 tubes, AC/DC ..**$120.00-150.00**

A61CR3, console, 1948, wood, upper front recessed slanted dial, center pull-out phono drawer, lower grille, 3 knobs, BC, 6 tubes, AC **$50.00-65.00**

A61P1, portable, 1948, leatherette, inner right dial, left vertical grille bars, fold-down front, handle, 3 knobs, BC, 6 tubes, AC/DC/battery **$35.00-40.00**

R-110-A, tombstone, 1933, two-tone wood, center front window dial with escutcheon, upper cloth grille with cut-outs, 4 knobs, BC, SW, 10 tubes, AC, $180.00-200.00.

R-1301-A, tombstone, 1935, wood, rounded/step-down top, lower front round dial, upper cloth grille with cut-outs, 4 knobs, BC, SW, 5 tubes, AC, $180.00-200.00.

R-1495, console, 1936, wood, large center front round black airplane dial, lower cloth grille with 4 vertical bars, 5 knobs, BC, SW, LW, 12 tubes, AC, $140.00-160.00.

A72T3, table, 1948, wood, upper front slanted slide rule dial, lower criss-cross grille, 3 knobs, BC, FM, 7 tubes, AC/DC $40.00-45.00

A92CR6, console-R/P, 1947, wood, inner right slide rule dial/6 pushbuttons, door, left pull-out phono drawer, lower criss-cross grille, 4 knobs, BC, FM, 9 tubes, AC $65.00-75.00

B51T2 "Air Pal," table, 1949, plastic, upper front slanted slide rule dial, lower grille area with "X," 2 top knobs, BC, 5 tubes, AC/DC......$120.00-150.00

B61T1, table, 1949, ivory plastic, upper front slide rule dial, left wrap-around horizontal louvers, 3 knobs, BC, 6 tubes, AC/DC $40.00-45.00

B61T2, table, 1949, mahogany plastic, upper front slide rule dial, left wrap-around horizontal louvers, 3 knobs, BC, 6 tubes, AC/DC $40.00-45.00

B72CR1, console-R/P, 1948, wood, upper front wrap-over slide rule dial, center front pull-out phono drawer, lower grille area, 4 knobs, BC, FM, 7 tubes, AC...$65.00-75.00

B92CR1, console-R/P, 1949, wood, inner right recessed dial, door, left lift top, inner phono, lower front criss-cross grille, 3 knobs, BC, FM, 9 tubes, AC...$55.00-65.00

C51T1, table, 1948, ivory plastic, right front half-round dial, left horizontal wrap-around louvers, 2 knobs, BC, 5 tubes, AC/DC......$40.00-50.00

C51T2, table, 1948, mahogany plastic, right front half-round dial, left horizontal wrap-around louvers, 2 knobs, BC, 5 tubes, AC/DC $40.00-50.00

R-104, chairside, 1932, wood, front half-round dial, lower right & left side cloth grilles with cut-outs, right & left side handle, BC, 6 tubes, AC $200.00-230.00

R-108, table, 1934, metal, low front center dial over vertically slotted grille, left and right sloping top, rounded shoulders, 4 round feet, 2 knobs, BC, 4 tubes, AC/DC.....................................$100.00-120.00

R-109-A, cathedral, 1932, wood, center front window dial, upper cloth grille with cut-outs, fluted columns, 3 knobs, BC, 6 tubes, AC...$240.00-270.00

R-110-AT, table, 1933, wood, center front window dial with escutcheon, right & left cloth grilles with cut-outs, 2 speakers, 4 knobs, BC, SW, 10 tubes, AC $120.00-150.00

R-116-AH, table, 1933, wood, right front dial & volume windows, left cloth grille with horizontal bars, 2 knobs, BC, 5 tubes, AC $75.00-85.00

R-192 "Good Companion," table, 1937, Deco, round case design with base, upper front half round dial, center circular grille area, 3 knobs, BC, SW, 6 tubes, battery ....$600.00+

R-1235A, tombstone, 1935, wood, lower front dial, upper cloth grille with aluminum cut-outs, top fluting, BC, 4 tubes, AC.......$240.00-270.00

R-1262A, tombstone, 1934, two-tone wood, step-down sides, lower front quarter-round dial, upper cloth grille with cut-outs, 4 knobs, BC, SW, 7 tubes, AC...$270.00-300.00

R-1361-A, tombstone, 1934, two-tone wood, center front round airplane dial, upper cloth grille with cut-outs, 4 knobs, BC, SW, 7 tubes, AC $180.00-200.00

R-1725-A, console, 1936, wood, upper front round black dial, lower cloth grille with 3 bars, 4 knobs, BC, SW, 6 tubes, AC $120.00-150.00

R-3042-A, table, 1937, wood, right front slide rule dial, left wrap-around cloth grille with cut-outs, 2 knobs, BC, 5 tubes, AC $50.00-65.00

R-3043-A, table, 1937, wood, rectangular case lays down or stands up, slide rule dial, cloth grille with bars, 2 knobs, BC, 5 tubes, AC..$75.00-95.00

STRATOVOX
Grossman Music Co.
210 Prospect Street, Cleveland, Ohio

579-1-58A, table, 1946, wood, upper front slanted slide rule dial, lower cloth grille with 2 horizontal bars, 2 knobs, BC, AC/DC ..$40.00-50.00

STROMBERG-CARLSON
Stromberg-Carlson Company
100 Carlson Road, Rochester, New York

Stromberg-Carlson was formed in 1894 for the production of telephone equipment. The company began to make radio parts and by 1923 was producing complete radios. Stromberg-Carlson was well known for its commitment to quality and their products are often called the "Rolls Royce" of radios.

1-A, table, 1924, wood, low rectangular case, 3 dial black Bakelite front panel, BC, 5 tubes, battery, $180.00-200.00.

1-B, table, 1924, wood, low rectangular case, 3 dial black Bakelite front panel, lift top, 5 knobs, BC, 5 tubes, battery $180.00-200.00

2, console, 1924, wood, inner three dial panel, fold-down front, lower storage, 5 knobs, BC, 5 tubes, battery $240.00-300.00

19, console, 1931, wood, lowboy, upper front window dial, lower cloth grille with cut-outs, BC, 9 tubes, AC $140.00-170.00

20, console, 1931, wood, highboy, upper front window dial, lower cloth grille with cut-outs, stretcher base, BC, 9 tubes, AC ..$160.00-190.00

22, console, 1931, walnut, lowboy, inner window dial, lower cloth grille with cut-outs, double doors, carved legs, 4 knobs, BC, 10 tubes, AC $160.00-190.00

24, console-R/P, 1932, wood, lowboy, inner window dial, lower cloth grille with cut-outs, double doors, lift top, inner phono, 6 legs, 4 knobs, BC, 10 tubes, AC $160.00-190.00

25, console, 1931, wood, lowboy, upper front window dial, lower cloth grille with cut-outs, stretcher base, BC, 8 tubes, AC ..$120.00-140.00

27, console, 1931, walnut, highboy, inner window dial, lower cloth grille with vertical bars, double doors, 6 legs, tuning meter, 4 knobs, BC, 10 tubes, AC $190.00-210.00

37, console, 1932, walnut finish, lowboy, upper front window dial, lower cloth grille with cut-outs, tuning meter, 3 knobs, BC, 9 tubes, AC...$120.00-150.00

38, console, 1932, wood, lowboy, upper front window dial, lower cloth grille with cut-outs, bowed legs, tuning meter, 3 knobs, BC, 9 or 10 tube versions, AC...$140.00-160.00

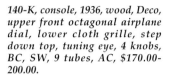

49, console, 1933, wood, lowboy, inner window dial, lower cloth grille with circular cut-outs, double doors, tuning meter, 4 knobs, BC, 11 tubes, AC, $180.00-200.00.

140-K, console, 1936, wood, Deco, upper front octagonal airplane dial, lower cloth grille, step down top, tuning eye, 4 knobs, BC, SW, 9 tubes, AC, $170.00-200.00.

39, console, 1932, wood, lowboy, inner window dial, lower cloth grille with circular cut-outs, double doors, stretcher base, tuning meter, 3 knobs, BC, 9 or 10 tube versions, AC **$160.00-190.00**

40, console, 1932, walnut, inner window dial, lower cloth grille with cut-outs, double doors, tuning meter, 3 knobs, BC, 9 or 10 tube versions, AC **$140.00-160.00**

41, console-R/P, 1932, wood, lowboy, inner window dial, lower cloth grille with cut-outs, double doors, lift top, inner phono, 6 legs, tuning meter, 3 knobs, BC, 9 or 10 tube versions, AC **$180.00-200.00**

51, console-R/P, 1933, wood, lowboy, inner window dial, lower cloth grille with cut-outs, double doors, lift top, inner phono, 6 legs, tuning meter, 4 knobs, BC, 11 tubes, AC **$180.00-200.00**

52, console, 1933, wood, lowboy, inner window dial, lower cloth grille with cut-outs, double doors, carved legs, 4 knobs, BC, 12 tubes, AC **$180.00-200.00**

54, console-R/P, 1933, wood, lowboy, inner window dial, lower cloth grille with cut-outs, double doors, lift top, inner phono, 6 legs, BC, 12 tubes, AC **$180.00-200.00**

55 "Te-lek-tor-et," console w/remote, 1933, wood, speaker & amplifier cabinet, chest-type wired remote control with inner dial, 2 knobs on remote, BC, 6 amplifier tubes, 2 remote tubes, AC....**$270.00-320.00**

56, console, 1933, wood, Deco, hinged front door hides knobs & dial, lower cloth grille with Deco cut-outs, BC, 8 tubes, AC **$240.00-270.00**

56-R, console, 1933, wood, Deco, removable tuning mechanism for remote control, hinged front door hides knobs & dial, lower cloth grille with Deco cut-outs, BC, 8 tubes, AC **$240.00-270.00**

58-L, console, 1935, wood, upper front octagonal airplane dial, lower cloth grille with cut-outs, 3 knobs, BC, SW, 6 tubes, AC **$110.00-130.00**

58-T, tombstone, 1935, wood, lower front octagonal dial, upper cloth grille with vertical bars, 3 knobs, BC, SW, 6 tubes, AC........**$150.00-180.00**

58-W, console, 1935, wood, upper front octagonal airplane dial, lower cloth grille with cut-outs, 3 knobs, BC, SW, 6 tubes, AC........**$110.00-130.00**

60-H "Treasure," console, 1934, walnut finish, highboy, inner window dial, lower cloth grille with vertical bars, double sliding doors, 6 legs, 4 knobs, BC, SW, 7 tubes, AC....................................**$140.00-160.00**

60-L "Treasure," console, 1934, walnut, upper front window dial, lower cloth grille with vertical bars, 4 knobs, BC, SW, 7 tubes, AC **$120.00-140.00**

60-M, console, 1935, wood, lowboy, upper front dial, lower cloth grille with cut-outs, 6 legs, 4 knobs, BC, SW, 7 tubes, AC ..**$120.00-140.00**

60-PR "Treasure," console-R/P, 1935, walnut, inner front window dial & phono, double doors, lower cloth grille with vertical bars, 4 knobs, BC, SW, 7 tubes, AC **$120.00-150.00**

60-T "Treasure," tombstone, 1934, two-tone wood, center front window dial, upper cloth grille with 2 horizontal bars and cut-outs, 4 knobs, BC, SW, 7 tubes, AC **$120.00-150.00**

61-L, console, 1936, wood, upper front octagonal airplane dial, lower cloth grille with cut-outs, 3 knobs, BC, SW, 7 tubes, AC **$120.00-150.00**

61-N, console, 1936, wood, upper front octagonal dial, lower cloth grille with cut-outs, feet, BC, SW, 7 tubes, AC **$130.00-150.00**

61-T, tombstone, 1935, wood, lower front octagonal dial, upper cloth grille with vertical bars, 3 knobs, BC, SW, 7 tubes, AC........**$120.00-150.00**

61-U, tombstone, 1935, wood, step-down top, lower front octagonal airplane dial, upper 5-section cloth grille, 3 knobs, BC, SW, 7 tubes, AC **$140.00-160.00**

61-H, table, 1935, wood, Deco, front off-center octagonal dial, right & left cloth grills with cut-outs, 3 knobs, BC, SW, 7 tubes, AC, $85.00-95.00.

225-H, table, 1937, wood, right front octagonal dial, left cloth grille with floral cut-outs, 4 knobs, BC, SW, 6 tubes including ballast, AC, $95.00-115.00.

235-H, table, 1938, wood, right front dial, left cloth grille with cut-outs, tuning eye, 6 pushbuttons, 4 knobs, BC, SW, 8 tubes, AC, $85.00-105.00.

61-W, console, 1935, wood, upper front octagonal airplane dial, lower cloth grille with cut-outs, 3 knobs, BC, SW, 7 tubes, AC........**$120.00-140.00**

61-Y, table, 1936, wood, off center octagonal airplane dial, right & left cloth grille areas with bars, 3 knobs, BC, SW, 7 tubes, AC/DC..**$75.00-85.00**

61-Z, console, 1936, wood, upper front octagonal airplane dial, lower cloth grille with cut-outs, 3 knobs, BC, SW, 7 tubes, AC/DC ..**$120.00-140.00**

62, console, 1935, walnut, upper front octagonal dial, lower cloth grille with cut-outs, 5 knobs, BC, SW, 8 tubes, AC **$120.00-150.00**

63, console, 1935, wood, upper front octagonal dial, lower cloth grille with cut-outs, feet, 5 knobs, BC, SW, 8 tubes, AC **$140.00-150.00**

64, console, 1934, wood, Deco, upper front dial, lower cloth grille with cut-outs, feet, 5 knobs, BC, SW, 8 tubes, AC...........**$150.00-190.00**

65 "Te-lek-tor-et," console w/remote, 1935, wood, speaker & amplifier cabinet, chest-type wired remote control with inner dial, 2 knobs on remote, BC, 6 amplifier tubes, 2 remote tubes, AC....**$270.00-320.00**

68, console, 1934, wood, Deco, upper front octagonal airplane dial, lower cloth grille with cut-outs, tuning eye, 4 knobs, BC, SW, 10 tubes, AC **$190.00-210.00**

68R, console, 1935, wood, lowboy, inner dial, double front doors, 6 legs, stretcher base, 4 knobs, BC, SW, 10 tubes, AC **$120.00-150.00**

69, console/table top, 1934, wood, short-wave converter only, large center octagonal dial, rounded shoulders and front corners, 3 knobs, SW, 4 tubes, AC..**$110.00-130.00**

70, console, 1935, wood, lowboy, inner dial, double front doors, lower cloth grille with cut-outs, 2 speakers, 6 legs, 5 knobs, BC, SW, 13 tubes, AC **$240.00-300.00**

345-F, console, 1939, mahogany, upper front square dial, lower cloth grille with center cut-outs, tuning eye, pushbuttons, BC, SW, 10 tubes, AC, $150.00-180.00.

72, console-R/P, 1935, wood, inner dial & phono, double front doors, lower vertical grille bars, 2 speakers, 6 feet, 5 knobs, BC, SW, 13 tubes, AC **$240.00-270.00**

74, console-R/P, 1935, wood, inner dial & phono, double front doors, lower vertical grille bars, 2 speakers, 6 feet, 5 knobs, BC, SW, 16 tubes, AC **$300.00-350.00**

80, console, 1936, wood, upper front octagonal airplane dial, lower cloth grille with vertical bars, 6 feet, tuning meter, 5 knobs, BC, SW, 9 tubes, AC **$150.00-160.00**

82, console, 1935, walnut, upper front octagonal airplane dial, lower cloth grille with cut-outs, tuning meter, 4 knobs, BC, SW, 10 tubes, AC **$150.00-160.00**

83, console, 1935, walnut, upper front octagonal airplane dial, lower cloth grille with cut-outs, tuning meter, 4 knobs, BC, SW, 11 tubes, AC **$150.00-160.00**

84, console, 1935, wood, upper front octagonal airplane dial, lower cloth grille with cut-outs, tuning meter, 6 feet, 5 knobs, BC, SW, 12 tubes, AC **$190.00-210.00**

115, console, 1936, wood, upper front octagonal dial, lower cloth grille with cut-outs, 3 knobs, BC, SW, 7 tubes, 6VDC **$95.00-115.00**

125-H, table, 1936, two-tone wood, right front octagonal dial, left cloth grille with vertical bars, 4 knobs, BC, SW, 5 tubes, AC/DC........**$65.00-75.00**

127-H, table, 1936, wood, slightly right of center octagonal dial with tuning eye above, left grille with horizontal bars, rounded front corners, 4 knobs, BC, SW, 9 tubes, AC/DC **$65.00-75.00**

340-V, console, 1939, maple, corner-style, upper front square dial, lower cloth grille with vertical bars, tuning eye, pushbuttons, 4 knobs, BC, SW, 9 tubes, AC, $140.00-160.00.

501, table, 1926, wood, low rectangular case, front panel with 2 pointer dials, center meter, lift top, 4 knobs, BC, 5 tubes, battery, $150.00-180.00.

130-H, table, 1936, wood, front off-center octagonal dial, left cloth grille with crossed bars, 4 knobs, BC, SW, 7 tubes, AC **$65.00-75.00**

130-J "Treasure Chest," table, 1937, wood, Deco, step-down top, right front octagonal dial, left vertical grille bars, 4 knobs, BC, SW, 7 tubes, AC **$120.00-150.00**

130-L, console, 1936, wood, upper front octagonal dial, lower cloth grille with 2 vertical bars, 4 knobs, BC, SW, 7 tubes, AC ..**$110.00-130.00**

130-M, console, 1936, wood, upper front octagonal dial, lower cloth grille with vertical bars, tuning eye, 4 knobs, BC, SW, 8 tubes, AC...**$110.00-130.00**

130-R, table, 1936, two-tone wood, Deco, front off-center octagonal dial, left grille, tuning eye, 4 knobs, BC, SW, 8 tubes, AC ..**$95.00-115.00**

130-U, tombstone, 1936, wood, lower front octagonal dial, upper cloth grille with horizontal bars, 4 knobs, BC, SW, 7 tubes, AC **$130.00-160.00**

140-H, table, 1936, wood, rectangular case, front octagonal dial, left horizontal louvers, tuning eye, 4 knobs, BC, SW, 9 tubes, AC **$85.00-105.00**

140-L, console, 1936, wood, upper front octagonal dial, lower cloth grille with vertical bars, tuning eye, 4 knobs, BC, SW, 9 tubes, AC...**$160.00-190.00**

140-M, console, 1937, wood, upper front octagonal dial, center cloth grille with horizontal bars, tuning eye, feet, 4 knobs, BC, SW, 9 tubes, AC **$160.00-190.00**

635/635-B "Treasure Chest," table, 1928, two-tone walnut, low rectangular case, front window dial with escutcheon, 3 knobs, BC, 7 tubes, AC, $120.00-150.00.

140-P, console-R/P, 1936, wood, front octagonal dial, lower cloth grille with vertical bars, tuning eye, feet, 5 knobs, BC, SW, 9 tubes, AC **$180.00-200.00**

145-L, console, 1936, wood, upper front dial, lower cloth grille with cut-outs, feet, tuning eye, 5 knobs, BC, SW, LW, 10 tubes, AC **$190.00-210.00**

145-SP, console-R/P, 1937, wood, front dial with escutcheon, lower cloth grille with center vertical bars, tuning eye, inner phono, 5 knobs, BC, SW, LW, 10 tubes, AC **$160.00-190.00**

150-L, console, 1936, wood, upper front dial, lower cloth grille, feet, 5 knobs, BC, SW, LW, 12 tubes, AC **$200.00-230.00**

160-L, console, 1936, wood, upper front dial, lower "U"-shaped cloth grille, feet, tuning eye, 5 knobs, BC, SW, LW, 14 tubes, AC ..**$200.00-230.00**

160-P, console, 1936, wood, ornate cabinet, double front doors, flared feet, tuning eye, 5 knobs, BC, SW, LW, 14 tubes, AC ..**$230.00-250.00**

180-L, console, 1936, wood, upper double doors enclose dial and knobs, lower recessed grille with lower horizontal bars, tuning eye, 5 knobs, BC, SW, LW, 17 tubes, AC **$320.00-360.00**

228-H, table, 1937, wood, right front octagonal dial, left cloth grille with vertical bars, tuning eye, 4 knobs, BC, SW, 6 tubes, AC..**$75.00-85.00**

228-L, console, 1937, wood, upper front octagonal dial, lower cloth grille with vertical bars, 4 knobs, BC, SW, 6 tubes, AC...**$110.00-130.00**

229-P, console-R/P, 1937, wood, front octagonal dial, lower cloth grille with horizontal bars, tuning eye, 5 knobs, BC, SW, 8 tubes, AC...**$150.00-180.00**

230-H, table, 1937, wood, rectangular case, right front dial, left horizontal grille bars, tuning eye, 4 knobs, BC, SW, 7 tubes, AC ..**$85.00-95.00**

230-L, console, 1937, wood, upper front dial, lower cloth grille with center vertical bars, 4 knobs, BC, SW, 7 tubes, AC..**$110.00-130.00**

642/642-A, console, 1929, wood, high-boy, decorative carving, upper window dial, lower cloth grille with cut-outs, 3 knobs, BC, 7 tubes, AC, $150.00-180.00.

231-F, chairside, 1937, wood, Deco, mirrored top with center dial, horizontal side louvers, tuning eye, 4 knobs, BC, SW, 7 tubes, AC...**$350.00-410.00**

231-P, console-R/P, 1937, wood, broad face cabinet, lower center recessed grille, lift-top, rounded front corners, six feet, 4 knobs, BC, SW, 7 tubes, AC...**$200.00-230.00**

231-R, chairside, 1937, wood, Deco, half-round, mirrored top with dial, front horizontal wrap-around louvers, tuning eye, 4 knobs, BC, SW, 7 tubes, AC **$410.00-460.00**

240-H, table, 1937, wood, front dial, rounded left side with horizontal wrap-around louvers, tuning eye, 5 knobs, BC, SW, 11 tubes, AC...**$95.00-115.00**

240-L, console, 1937, wood, upper front dial, center grille with horizontal bars & cut-outs, 5 knobs, BC, SW, 11 tubes, AC **$180.00-200.00**

240-M, console, 1937, wood, upper front dial, lower cloth grille with bars, tuning eye, 5 knobs, BC, SW, 11 tubes, AC **$180.00-200.00**

240-R, console, 1937, wood, half-round case, inner dial/pushbuttons, double doors, lower front horizontal wrap-around louvers, 5 knobs, BC, SW, 11 tubes, AC **$530.00-580.00**

240-S, console, 1937, wood, ornate cabinet, upper decorative double doors, beveled front corners, 4 feet, 5 knobs, BC, SW, 11 tubes, AC **$200.00-230.00**

240-W, console/desk, 1937, wood, looks like Governor Winthrop desk, inner dial & controls, 5 knobs, BC, SW, 11 tubes, AC ..**$580.00-700.00**

250-L, console, 1937, wood, upper front dial, lower cloth grille with curved horizontal bars, feet, tuning eye, 6 knobs, BC, SW, 13 tubes, AC **$200.00-230.00**

1000-H, table, 1941, plastic, arched top, right front square dial, left cloth grille with vertical bars, 3 knobs, BC, 6 tubes, AC/DC, $50.00-65.00.

1101, table, 1946, plastic, raised top, upper front slanted slide rule dial, lower horizontal wrap-around louvers, rear hand-hold, 2 knobs, BC, 6 tubes, AC/DC, $50.00-65.00.

255-L, console, 1937, wood, upper front dial, lower cloth grille with curved horizontal bars, tuning eye, feet, 6 knobs, BC, SW, 13 tubes, AC **$200.00-230.00**

260-L, console, 1937, wood, upper front dial, center cloth grille with horizontal bars, tuning eye, 6 knobs, BC, SW, 16 tubes, AC **$240.00-270.00**

310-H, table, 1938, wood, center front dial, left cloth grille with cut-out, 3 knobs **$55.00-65.00**

320-H, table, 1938, two-tone wood, right front dial, left cloth grille with cut-outs, 3 knobs, BC, SW, 5 tubes, AC **$55.00-65.00**

320-T, side table, 1938, mahogany, drop leaf Duncan Phyfe design, inner dial, 3 knobs, BC, SW, 5 tubes, AC **$110.00-130.00**

325-H, table, 1938, wood, center front dial, left cloth grille with cut-outs, 6 right pushbuttons, 3 knobs, BC, SW, 5 tubes, AC **$75.00-85.00**

325-J, table, 1938, walnut, center front dial, left cloth grille with "horseshoe" cut-out, 6 right pushbuttons, 3 knobs, BC, SW, 5 tubes, AC...**$65.00-75.00**

325-N, side table, 1938, mahogany, Chippendale design, inner dial, 3 knobs, BC, SW, 5 tubes, AC **$130.00-160.00**

325-S, side table, 1938, maple, drop leaf Early American design, inner dial, 3 knobs, BC, SW, 5 tubes, AC **$130.00-160.00**

335-H, table, 1939, wood, rectangular case, right front dial, left cloth grille with center cut-out, pushbuttons, tuning eye, 4 knobs, BC, SW, 7 tubes, AC...**$85.00-95.00**

335-L, console, 1939, walnut, upper front dial, lower cloth grille with horizontal & vertical bars, tuning eye, pushbuttons, 4 knobs, BC, SW, 7 tubes, AC **$120.00-150.00**

336-P, chairside, 1939, walnut, top dial/6 pushbuttons/tuning eye, front cloth grille with vertical bars, storage, 5 knobs, BC, SW, 7 tubes, AC **$150.00-180.00**

337-H, table, 1939, walnut, right front dial, left cloth grille with 3 vertical bars, tuning eye, 6 pushbuttons, 4 knobs, BC, SW, 7 tubes, AC **$85.00-95.00**

1101-HW, table, 1946, wood, small upper front slide rule dial, lower horizontal louvers, 2 knobs, BC, 6 tubes, AC/DC, $40.00-45.00.

337-L, console, 1939, walnut, upper front dial, lower grille bars, tuning eye, 6 pushbuttons, 4 knobs, BC, SW, 7 tubes, AC ..**$150.00-180.00**

340-F, console, 1939, maple, front square dial, lower cloth grille with vertical bars, tuning eye, pushbuttons, 4 knobs, BC, SW, 9 tubes, AC **$150.00-180.00**

340-H, table, 1939, rosewood, right front dial, left cloth grille with horizontal bars, tuning eye, pushbuttons, 4 knobs, BC, SW, 9 tubes, AC **$85.00-105.00**

340-M, console, 1939, walnut, upper front square dial, lower cloth grille with vertical bars, tuning eye, pushbuttons, 4 knobs, BC, SW, 9 tubes, AC **$140.00-160.00**

340-P, console-R/P, 1939, walnut, upper front square dial, lower cloth grille with horizontal bars, inner phono, tuning eye, pushbuttons, 4 knobs, BC, SW, 9 tubes, AC **$150.00-180.00**

340-W, console, 1938, walnut, corner-style, upper front square dial, lower cloth grille with vertical bars, tuning eye, pushbuttons, 4 knobs, BC, SW, 9 tubes, AC **$150.00-180.00**

340-Y, console, 1938, walnut, corner-style, upper front square dial, lower cloth grille with vertical bars, tuning eye, pushbuttons, 4 knobs, BC, SW, 9 tubes, AC...**$150.00-180.00**

341-P, console-R/P, 1939, wood, broad face cabinet, large lower center recessed grille with center vertical bars, lift-top, six feet, 4 knobs, BC, SW, 9 tubes, AC **$150.00-180.00**

341-R, chairside, 1938, walnut, half-round, top dial/8 pushbuttons/tuning eye, lower front horizontal grille bars, 4 knobs, BC, SW, 9 tubes, AC **$240.00-300.00**

345-M, console, 1939, walnut, upper front square dial, lower cloth grille with cut-outs, tuning eye, pushbuttons, BC, SW, 10 tubes, AC **$150.00-180.00**

1105, portable, 1947, cloth covered, right front window dial, Deco grille design, handle, 2 knobs, BC, 6 tubes, AC/DC/battery, $40.00-45.00.

345-X, console, 1939, wood, upper front dial, lower cloth grille with 3 vertical cut-outs, pushbuttons, BC, SW, 10 tubes, AC ..**$170.00-200.00**

350-M, console, 1938, walnut, upper front dial, center horizontal grille bars, tuning eye, 8 pushbuttons, 5 knobs, BC, SW, 11 tubes, AC **$180.00-200.00**

350-R, console, 1938, wood, half-round case, inner dial/pushbuttons, double doors, lower front horizontal wrap-around louvers, 5 knobs, BC, SW, 11 tubes, AC **$530.00-580.00**

350-S, console, 1938, wood, upper front center dial with pushbuttons above, lower grille with two horizontal bars, rounded front corners, 5 knobs, BC, SW, 11 tubes, AC **$180.00-200.00**

350-V, console, 1939, walnut, corner-style, upper front dial, lower cloth grille with vertical bars, tuning eye, pushbuttons, 5 knobs, BC, SW, 11 tubes, AC **$200.00-220.00**

360-M, console, 1939, walnut, upper front dial, lower cloth grille with cut-outs, tuning eye, pushbuttons, motorized remote tuning, 5 knobs, BC, SW, 12 tubes, AC **$180.00-200.00**

370-M, console, 1939, walnut, inner dial, double doors, center cloth grille with vertical bars, motorized remote tuning, BC, SW, 14 tubes, AC **$190.00-220.00**

400-H, table, 1939, wood, right rectangular dial with knobs below, left grille with cut-outs, rounded front corners, 3 knobs, BC, 5 tubes, AC **$55.00-65.00**

400-N, side table, 1939, mahogany, Chippendale design, inner dial, 3 knobs, BC, 5 tubes, AC **$110.00-130.00**

400-S, side table, 1939, wood, double front doors, solid side legs with connecting stretcher, 3 knobs, BC, 5 tubes, AC **$110.00-130.00**

402-H, portable, 1939, cloth covered, right front dial and knobs, left grille, decorative lower trim, handle, 2 knobs, BC, 4 tubes, battery **$45.00-55.00**

405-H, table, 1939, wood, six vertical pushbuttons right side, rectangular dial with knobs below, left grille with cut-outs, rounded top front edge, 4 knobs, BC, 5 tubes, AC/DC **$55.00-65.00**

410-H, table, 1939, wood, right slide rule dial with knobs below, left grille with two vertical bars, decorative front corners, 3 knobs, BC, SW, 5 tubes, AC **$55.00-65.00**

410-J, table, 1939, wood, right slide rule dial with knobs below, left grille with two "bed-post" vertical bars, decorative base moulding, 3 knobs, BC, SW, 5 tubes, AC **$65.00-75.00**

410-T, side table, 1939, wood, front center "drawer-like" door, rounded sides, single center support leg flares into four feet, 3 knobs, BC, SW, 5 tubes, AC..**$120.00-140.00**

411-PT, table-R/P, 1939, walnut, right front slide rule dial, left cloth grille with cut-outs, lift top, inner phono, 4 knobs, BC, SW, 4 tubes, AC **$55.00-65.00**

411-PF, side table-R/P, 1939, wood, front center "drawer-like" door, four legs with lower shelf, 4 knobs, BC, SW, 4 tubes, AC ..**$110.00-130.00**

420-H, table, 1939, wood, right slide rule dial with background tuning eye, pushbuttons below dial, left grille with cut-outs, round front corners, 4 knobs, BC, SW, 7 tubes, AC **$75.00-85.00**

420-F, console, 1939, wood, top center slide rule dial with background tuning eye, pushbuttons below dial, lower grille with vertical bars, 4 knobs, BC, SW, 7 tubes, AC **$150.00-180.00**

420-L, console, 1939, wood, top center slide rule dial with background tuning eye, pushbuttons below dial, lower grille with vertical bars, corner fluted columns, 4 knobs, BC, SW, 7 tubes, AC **$150.00-180.00**

420-PL, console-R/P, 1939, wood, broad face cabinet, large lower center recessed grille with center vertical bars, lift-top, 4 knobs, BC, SW, 7 tubes, AC **$150.00-180.00**

420-PR, chairside-R/P, 1939, wood, face up slide rule dial and knobs, lift-top, front grille with decorative vertical bars, 4 knobs, BC, SW, 7 tubes, AC **$220.00-260.00**

430-H, table, 1939, wood, right front slide rule dial with background tuning eye, pushbuttons below dial, left grille with cut-outs, lower front decorative trim, 4 knobs, BC, SW, 9 tubes, AC.............**$75.00-85.00**

430-L, console, 1939, wood, top center slide rule dial with background tuning eye, pushbuttons below dial, lower recessed grille with center vertical bars, 4 knobs, BC, SW, 9 tubes, AC **$150.00-180.00**

430-M, console, 1939, wood, top center slide rule dial with background tuning eye, pushbuttons below dial, lower grille with vertical and horizontal bars, 4 knobs, BC, SW, 9 tubes, AC..........**$150.00-180.00**

430-PF, console-R/P, 1939, wood, "chest-of-drawers look" cabinet, inside slide rule dial with background tuning eye, pushbuttons, 4 knobs, BC, SW, 9 tubes, AC **$150.00-180.00**

430-PL, console-R/P, 1939, wood, broad face cabinet with large lower grille area with three vertical bars, inside slide rule dial with background tuning eye, pushbuttons, 4 knobs, BC, SW, 9 tubes, AC..**$150.00-180.00**

1500-HR "Dynatomic," table, 1951, maroon plastic, raised top, upper front curved slide rule dial, lower horizontal wrap-around louvers, 2 knobs, BC, 5 tubes, AC, $50.00-65.00.

440-M, console, 1939, wood, upper center front slide rule dial with background tuning eye, pushbuttons and knobs below dial, lower grille with three decorative horizontal bars, 4 feet, optional remote, 5 knobs, BC, SW, 10 tubes, AC **$240.00-270.00**

450-M, console, 1939, wood, upper center front slide rule dial with background tuning eye, pushbuttons and knobs below dial, lower grille with four vertical bars, 6 feet, optional remote, 5 knobs, BC, SW, 11 tubes, AC...**$260.00-290.00**

480-M, console, 1940, wood, inner dial & pushbuttons, double doors, lower cloth grille with cut-outs, tuning eye, motorized remote tuning, 6 knobs, BC, SW, FM1, 20 tubes, AC **$360.00-410.00**

500-H, table, 1940, plastic, right front dial, left cloth grille with horizontal bars, decorative case lines, 3 knobs, BC, 6 tubes, AC/DC...........**$50.00-65.00**

500-U, table, 1940, two-tone wood, right front airplane dial, left grille with horizontal bars, 3 knobs, BC, 6 tubes, AC/DC **$55.00-65.00**

500-S, table, 1940, walnut, right front airplane dial, left grille with horizontal bars, curved side scrolls, 3 knobs, BC, 6 tubes, AC/DC ..**$120.00-150.00**

505-H, table, 1940, wood, right front dial, left vertical grille bars, 3 knobs, FM1, 9 tubes, AC **$75.00-85.00**

515-M, console, 1940, wood, upper front dial, lower cloth grille with horizontal & vertical bars, pushbuttons, 2 chassis, tuning eye, 4 knobs, BC, SW, FM1, 17 tubes, AC **$300.00-350.00**

520-L, console, 1940, wood, upper front center slide rule dial with background tuning eye, pushbuttons below dial, lower recessed grille with two vertical bars, 4 knobs, BC, SW, 7 tubes, AC **$150.00-180.00**

523, table, 1927, mahogany, low rectangular case, front panel with 2 pointer dials, center meter, 4 knobs, BC, 8 tubes, AC.........**$150.00-180.00**

524, console, 1927, walnut, highboy, inner panel with 2 pointer dials, center meter, fold-down front, 4 knobs, BC, 8 tubes, AC ..**$180.00-200.00**

535-M, console, 1940, wood, inner dial & pushbuttons, double front doors, lower cloth grille with four vertical bars, 5 knobs, BC, SW, FM1, 15 tubes, AC **$290.00-320.00**

585-M, console, 1941, wood, upper double doors with inside slide rule dial, tuning eye, pushbuttons, lower grille with decorative latticework, motorized tuning, remote control, 5 knobs, BC, SW, FM1, 19 tubes, AC **$360.00-410.00**

600-H, table, 1941, plastic, right front dial, rounded left side with horizontal bars, 3 knobs, BC, AC/DC **$50.00-65.00**

636-A, console, 1928, wood, inner window dial, fold-down front, stretcher base, 3 knobs, BC, 7 tubes, AC **$150.00-180.00**

638, console, 1929, wood, highboy, center window dial, upper cloth grille with vertical bars, 3 knobs, BC, 8 tubes, AC **$150.00-180.00**

641-A "Treasure Chest," table, 1929, walnut finish, low rectangular case, upper front window dial, lift top, 3 knobs, BC, 7 tubes, AC **$95.00-115.00**

900-H, table, 1941, two-tone plastic, right front dial, left vertical grille bars, 3 knobs, BC, 6 tubes, AC/DC **$45.00-50.00**

920-L, console, 1941, wood, upper front slide rule dial, large lower criss-cross grille, pushbuttons, 4 knobs, BC, SW, 7 tubes, AC **$120.00-150.00**

1210-H "Courier," table, 1948, two-tone wood, 3 right front dials, left cloth criss-cross grille, 4 knobs, BC, FM, 11 tubes, AC, $40.00-45.00.

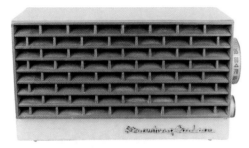

T-4, table, 1955, plastic, right side dial & volume knobs, front brick-like grille panel, BC, 5 tubes, AC/DC, $25.00-30.00.

920-PG, console-R/P, 1941, wood, double upper front doors for receiver and phono, inner slide rule dial and pushbuttons, lower double grille, four feet, 4 knobs, BC, SW, 7 tubes, AC **$120.00-150.00**

925-PF, console-R/P, 1941, wood, double upper front doors for receiver and phono, inner slide rule dial and pushbuttons, tuning eye, lower double grille, four feet, 5 knobs, BC, SW, FM1, 14 tubes, AC **$130.00-160.00**

935PL, console-R/P, 1941, walnut, Hepplewhite cabinet, four front doors, inner slide rule dial, pushbuttons, tuning eye, 5 knobs, BC, SW, FM1, 16 tubes, AC **$130.00-160.00**

935-PR, console-R/P, 1941, wood, English Regency cabinet, two large front doors, inner slide rule dial, pushbuttons, tuning eye, 5 knobs, BC, SW, FM1, 16 tubes, AC **$130.00-160.00**

955-PF "Georgian," console-R/P, 1941, wood, inner slide rule dial, pushbuttons, phono, scalloped base, BC, SW, FM1, 16 tubes main receiver, 4 tube amplifier, AC.....................................**$180.00-200.00**

1000-J, table, 1941, wood, right front square dial, left grille with vertical bars, rounded shoulders and sides, feet, 3 knobs, BC, 6 tubes, AC/DC **$120.00-140.00**

1035-PLW "Wilfred Pelletier," console-R/P, 1942, wood, inner right slide rule dial/pushbuttons/knobs, inner left pull-out phono, lower grille, doors, BC, SW, AC...**$65.00-75.00**

1100-H, table, 1947, wood, right front square dial, left cloth grille, 3 knobs, BC, 6 tubes, AC/DC ....**$35.00-40.00.**

1101-HPW, table-R/P, 1948, wood, right front curved dial, horizontal wrap-around grille bars, lift top, inner phono, 3 knobs, BC, 6 tubes, AC **$40.00-45.00**

1110-HW, table, 1947, wood, center front vertical slide rule dial, right & left horizontal wrap-around louvers, 6 pushbuttons, 4 knobs, BC, SW, 6 tubes, AC..**$65.00-75.00**

1110 "Series 10," table, 1947, wood, center front vertical slide rule dial, right & left horizontal wrap-around louvers, 6 pushbuttons, 4 knobs, BC, SW, 6 tubes, AC **$65.00-75.00**

1121LW, console, 1946, wood, upper front slide rule dial, lower criss-cross grille, pushbuttons, 4 knobs, BC, SW, 11 tubes, AC **$95.00-115.00**

1135PLW, console-R/P, 1947, wood, inner right slide rule dial/pushbuttons, door, left pull-out phono drawer, 2 knobs, BC, SW, FM, 16 tubes, AC **$120.00-140.00**

1202, table-R/P, 1949, wood, right front curved dial, horizontal wrap-around grille bars, lift top, inner phono, 3 knobs, BC, 5 tubes, AC...**$40.00-45.00**

1204, table, 1948, plastic, lower front slide rule dial, upper grille area, 4 knobs, BC, FM, 7 tubes, AC/DC **$50.00-65.00**

1204-HM, table, 1948, wood & leatherette, lower front slide rule dial, large upper cloth grille area, 4 knobs, BC, FM, 7 tubes, AC/DC **$40.00-45.00**

1210PLM, console-R/P, 1948, wood, 3 inner right dials, door, left pull-out phono drawer, lower criss-cross grille, 4 knobs, BC, FM, 11 tubes, AC **$75.00-85.00**

1220-PL, console-R/P, 1948, wood, inner right slide rule dial, left phono, lift top, lower front criss-cross grille, 4 knobs, BC, SW, 7 tubes, AC **$65.00-75.00**

1235-PLM, console-R/P, 1948, wood, inner right slide rule dial, pushbuttons, door, left pull-out phono drawer, tone switches, 2 knobs, BC, SW, FM, 16 tubes, AC **$85.00-95.00**

1400, table, 1949, plastic, raised top, upper front slide rule dial, lower horizontal wrap-around louvers, 2 knobs, BC, 5 tubes, AC/DC **$50.00-65.00**

1400-H, table, 1949, plastic, raised top, upper front slide rule dial, lower horizontal wrap-around louvers, 2 knobs, BC, 5 tubes, AC/DC **$50.00-65.00**

1407PFM, console-R/P, 1949, wood, inner right slide rule dial, left pull-out phono drawer, lower storage & grille, double front doors, 4 knobs, BC, FM, 10 tubes, AC **$65.00-75.00**

1409PGM, console-R/P, 1949, wood, inner right slide rule dial, door, left pull-out phono drawer, 4 knobs, BC, FM, 14 tubes, AC ..**$75.00-85.00**

1500, table, 1951, plastic, raised top, upper front slide rule dial, lower horizontal wrap-around louvers, 2 knobs, BC, 5 tubes, AC/DC **$50.00-65.00**

1507, console-R/P, 1951, wood, inner right slide rule dial, door, left pull-out phono drawer, lower criss-cross grille, 4 knobs, BC, FM, 10 tubes, AC **$65.00-75.00**

1608, console-R/P, 1951, wood, inner right slide rule dial, left phono, lower storage & grille, double doors, 5 knobs, BC, 8 tubes, AC **$65.00-75.00**

AWP-8, portable, 1956, leatherette, inner slide rule dial, fold-up front with world map, handle, 8 band, 4 knobs, BC, SW, LW, 6 tubes, AC/DC/battery **$110.00-130.00**

C-1, table-C, 1951, plastic, right front dial, left alarm clock, center checkered panel, 5 knobs, BC, 5 tubes, AC **$40.00-45.00**

C-3, table-C, 1955, plastic, right side dial, left front clock, right circular louvers, BC, 5 tubes, AC **$30.00-35.00**

C-5 Deluxe, table-C, 1955, plastic, right side dial, left front alarm clock, right perforated grille area, 5 knobs, BC, 5 tubes, AC....**$30.00-35.00**

EP-2, portable, 1955, top dial and on/off/volume knobs, front grille with decorative "V," rounded sides, handle, BC, 4 tubes, AC/DC/battery **$45.00-55.00**

FR-506 "Jupiter," console-R/P, 1957, wood, inner dial/knobs/phono, lower front grille panels, feet, BC, FM, AC.....................**$50.00-65.00**

FR-711M, console-R/P, 1958, wood, inner right dial, left phono, lift top, large front grille, legs, BC, FM, 11 tubes, AC **$40.00-50.00**

SR-407, table, 1957, center front slide rule dial, 4 pushbuttons, high fidelity, 4 knobs, BC, FM, 12 tubes, AC.........................**$30.00-35.00**

SUPREME (LIPAN)
Aim Industries
41 Union Square, New York, New York

750, table-R/P, 1949, leatherette, inner right dial, phono, lift top, 4 knobs, BC, 5 tubes, AC **$20.00-25.00**

SYLVANIA
Sylvania Electric Products (Colonial Radio & TV)
254 Rand Street, Buffalo, New York

5T13, table, 1961, plastic, wedge-shaped case, center front round dial overlaps vertical bars, left grille area, 2 knobs, BC **$25.00-30.00**

430L, portable, 1952, leatherette, center front panel with round dial overlaps cloth grille, handle, 2 knobs, BC, 4 tubes, AC/DC/battery **$25.00-30.00**

433B, portable, 1955, black plastic, top dial, large front checkered grille area, handle, 2 top knobs, BC, 4 tubes, AC/DC/battery**$25.00-30.00**

433GR, portable, 1955, green plastic, top dial, large front checkered grille area, handle, 2 top knobs, BC, 4 tubes, AC/DC/battery..**$25.00-30.00**

433H, portable, 1955, ivory plastic, top dial, large front checkered grille area, handle, 2 top knobs, BC, 4 tubes, AC/DC/battery..**$25.00-30.00**

433RE, portable, 1955, red plastic, top dial, large front checkered grille area, handle, 2 top knobs, BC, 4 tubes, AC/DC/battery..**$25.00-30.00**

433YE, portable, 1955, yellow plastic, top dial, large front checkered grille area, handle, 2 top knobs, BC, 4 tubes, AC/DC/battery..**$25.00-30.00**

454BR "Sky Lark," portable, 1954, brown plastic, large center front round dial overlaps right metal perforated grille area, fold-down handle, 2 knobs, BC, 4 tubes, battery **$30.00-35.00**

454GR "Sky Lark," portable, 1954, green plastic, large center front round dial overlaps right metal perforated grille area, fold-down handle, 2 knobs, BC, 4 tubes, battery **$30.00-35.00**

454H "Sky Lark," portable, 1954, ivory plastic, large center front round dial overlaps right metal perforated grille area, fold-down handle, 2 knobs, BC, 4 tubes, battery **$30.00-35.00**

454RE "Sky Lark," portable, 1954, red plastic, large center front round dial overlaps right metal perforated grille area, fold-down handle, 2 knobs, BC, 4 tubes, battery **$30.00-35.00**

510B, table, 1950, black plastic, raised top area, right front round dial overlaps horizontal louvers, 2 knobs, BC, 5 tubes, AC/DC **$30.00-35.00**

510H, table, 1950, ivory plastic, raised top area, right front round dial overlaps horizontal louvers, 2 knobs, BC, 5 tubes, AC/DC **$30.00-35.00**

510W, table, 1950, walnut plastic, raised top area, right front round dial overlaps horizontal louvers, 2 knobs, BC, 5 tubes, AC/DC........**$30.00-35.00**

511B, table, 1952, black plastic, right front round dial, bowed front panel with checkered grille, 2 knobs, BC, 5 tubes, AC/DC......**$25.00-30.00**

511H, table, 1952, ivory plastic, right front round dial, bowed front panel with checkered grille, 2 knobs, BC, 5 tubes, AC/DC......**$25.00-30.00**

511M, table, 1952, mahogany plastic, right front round dial, bowed front panel with checkered grille, 2 knobs, BC, 5 tubes, AC/DC ..**$25.00-30.00**

513B, table, 1953, black plastic, recessed concave front with center rectangular panel, right front dial, left two section grille with square perforations, 2 knobs, BC, 5 tubes, AC/DC **$25.00-30.00**

513CH, table, 1953, chartreuse plastic, recessed concave front with center rectangular panel, right front dial, left two section grille with square perforations, 2 knobs, BC, 5 tubes, AC/DC........**$35.00-40.00**

513GR, table, 1953, green plastic, recessed concave front with center rectangular panel, right front dial, left two section grille with square perforations, 2 knobs, BC, 5 tubes, AC/DC....................**$35.00-40.00**

1102RE, table, 1957, red plastic, right side dial, front lattice grille, auxiliary intercom unit, 2 side knobs, BC, 5 tubes, AC/DC, $20.00-25.00.

513H, table, 1953, ivory plastic, recessed concave front with center rectangular panel, right front dial, left two section grille with square perforations, 2 knobs, BC, 5 tubes, AC/DC **$25.00-30.00**

513M, table, 1953, mahogany plastic, recessed concave front with center rectangular panel, right front dial, left two section grille with square perforations, 2 knobs, BC, 5 tubes, AC/DC....................**$25.00-30.00**

513RE, table, 1953, red plastic, recessed concave front with center rectangular panel, right front dial, left two section grille with square perforations, 2 knobs, BC, 5 tubes, AC/DC **$35.00-40.00**

513YE, table, 1953, yellow plastic, recessed concave front with center rectangular panel, right front dial, left two section grille with square perforations, 2 knobs, BC, 5 tubes, AC/DC....................**$35.00-40.00**

519, table, 1956, plastic, right side dial, front horizontal grille bars, 2 side knobs, BC, 5 tubes, AC/DC **$20.00-25.00**

540MA "Tune-Riser," table-C, 1951, plastic, upper right front slide rule dial, right & left horizontal grille bars, center alarm clock, 4 knobs, BC, 5 tubes, AC **$30.00-35.00**

542BR, table-C, 1952, brown plastic, lower front slide rule dial, large upper alarm clock face, side horizontal bars, 3 knobs, BC, 5 tubes, AC **$30.00-35.00**

542CH, table-C, 1952, chartreuse plastic, lower front slide rule dial, large upper alarm clock face, side horizontal bars, 3 knobs, BC, 5 tubes, AC **$30.00-35.00**

542GR, table-C, 1952, green plastic, lower front slide rule dial, large upper alarm clock face, side horizontal bars, 3 knobs, BC, 5 tubes, AC **$30.00-35.00**

Z5T17, table, plastic, center front dial panel overlaps checkered grille area with upper right logo, feet, 2 knobs, BC, $30.00-35.00.

542RE, table-C, 1952, red plastic, lower front slide rule dial, large upper alarm clock face, side horizontal bars, 3 knobs, BC, 5 tubes, AC **$30.00-35.00**

542YE, table-C, 1952, yellow plastic, lower front slide rule dial, large upper alarm clock face, side horizontal bars, 3 knobs, BC, 5 tubes, AC **$30.00-35.00**

1102GR, table, 1957, green plastic, right side dial, front lattice grille, auxiliary intercom unit, 2 side knobs, BC, 5 tubes, AC/DC..**$20.00-25.00**

1102H, table, 1957, ivory plastic, right side dial, front lattice grille, auxiliary intercom unit, 2 side knobs, BC, 5 tubes, AC/DC..**$20.00-25.00**

1202, table, 1957, plastic, aluminum front panel with large center round dial, feet, 2 knobs, BC, 5 tubes, AC/DC **$25.00-30.00**

2108, table-C, 1959, plastic, right side round dial, left front alarm clock, right horizontal bars, 3 knobs, BC, 4 tubes, AC **$20.00-25.00**

2109TU, table-C, 1959, plastic, lower right front round dial overlaps horizontal wrap-around louvers, left alarm clock, 4 knobs, BC, 5 tubes, AC **$25.00-30.00**

2302H, table-C, 1957, plastic, lower center front slide rule dial, upper alarm clock with day-date, 5 knobs, BC, 5 tubes, AC........**$25.00-30.00**

3303TA, portable, 1957, leather, center front round compass over grille, strap, 2 side knobs, BC, 4 tubes, AC/DC/battery **$40.00-45.00**

4501, table-R/P, 1958, two-tone, top dial, wrap-over front grille, lift top, inner phono, handle, 3 knobs, BC, 6 tubes, AC **$20.00-25.00**

AK17, table-C, 1963, plastic, right front see-through panel with inner vertical slide rule dial & alarm clock, left lattice grille area, 4 knobs, BC, 5 tubes, AC **$25.00-30.00**

SYMPHONY
Symphony Radio & Television Corporation

401, cathedral, two-tone wood, lower front round airplane dial, upper cloth grille with cut-outs, 3 knobs, $270.00-300.00.

200, table/lamp/planter, 1948, lamp radio with trapezoid-shaped case, right front dial, left trapezoid-shaped grille, 2 top plant pots, BC, 5 tubes, AC $120.00-180.00

200L-R, table/lamp/planter, 1948, lamp radio with trapezoid-shaped case, right front dial, left trapezoid-shaped grille, 2 top plant pots, BC, 5 tubes, AC/DC.....................................$120.00-180.00

250, portable, 1949, upper right front dial, lower round grille with vertical bars, handle, 2 knobs, BC, 4 tubes, battery $35.00-45.00

260 "Hollywood," table-N, 1948, striped grasscloth with painted palm trees, left front dial panel, handle, 2 knobs, BC, 4 tubes, battery.....................................$150.00-180.00

348, portable, 1948, leatherette, inner right half-round dial, left round grille with horizontal bars, flip-up front, 2 knobs, BC, 5 tubes, AC/DC/battery $35.00-45.00

TECH-MASTER

538, table, two-tone wood, upper front slanted slide rule dial, lower horizontal wrap-around grille bars, 3 knobs, BC $40.00-50.00

TELE KING
Tele King Corp.
601 West 26th Street, New York, New York

RK41, table, 1953, plastic, right front round dial overlaps raised checkered grille panel, 2 knobs, BC, 4 tubes, AC/DC $30.00-35.00

RK51A, table, 1953, plastic, right front round dial overlaps raised checkered grille panel, 2 knobs, BC, 5 tubes, AC/DC $30.00-35.00

RKP-53-A, portable, 1954, plastic, right side dial, large front checkered grille area, handle, 2 right side knobs, BC, 4 tubes, AC/DC/battery $30.00-35.00

TELE-TONE
Tele-tone Radio Corp.
609 West 51st Street, New York, New York

117, table, 1946, wood, slanted front with lower slide rule dial, upper grille with circular cut-outs, 2 knobs, BC, 6 tubes, AC/DC, $40.00-45.00.

100, table, 1946, wood, lower front slide rule dial, upper horizontal grille bars, 2 knobs, BC, 5 tubes $35.00-40.00

109, table, 1946, plastic, lower front slide rule dial, upper grille with circular cut-outs, 2 knobs, BC, 5 tubes, AC/DC $45.00-55.00

111, table, 1948, wood, slanted lower front with slide rule dial, upper patterned grille, 2 knobs, BC, 5 tubes, AC/DC $40.00-45.00

117A, table, 1946, wood, slanted front with lower slide rule dial, upper grille with circular cut-outs, 2 knobs, BC, 6 tubes, AC/DC.......$40.00-45.00

133, table-R/P, 1947, wood, lower front dial, upper grille, lift top, inner phono, 4 knobs, BC, 8 tubes, AC $25.00-30.00

134, table-R/P, 1947, inner front slanted slide rule dial, fold-up front, handle, lift top, inner phono, 4 knobs, BC, 8 tubes, AC $35.00-40.00

135, table, 1947, plastic, upper front slide rule dial, lower lattice grille, 2 knobs, BC, 5 tubes, AC/DC $40.00-50.00

138, table, 1947, two-tone plastic, lower front slide rule dial, upper lattice grille, 2 knobs, BC, SW, 5 tubes, AC/DC.........................$40.00-50.00

145, portable, 1947, leatherette, upper front slide rule dial, lower horizontal grille bars, handle, 2 knobs, BC, 4 tubes, AC/DC/battery ..$35.00-40.00

148, table, 1947, plastic, upper front slide rule dial, lower lattice grille, 2 knobs, BC, 5 tubes, AC/DC $40.00-45.00

150, table, 1948, plastic, upper front slide rule dial, lower lattice grille, 2 knobs, BC, 4 tubes, AC/DC $35.00-40.00

152, portable, 1948, plastic, inner slide rule dial, lower horizontal grille bars, fold-down front, handle, 2 knobs, BC.........................$35.00-40.00

156, portable, 1948, plastic, upper front slide rule dial, recessed horizontal louvers, handle, 2 knobs, BC, 4 tubes, battery.........$35.00-40.00

157, table, 1948, plastic, upper front slide rule dial, lower horizontal wrap-around louvers, 2 knobs, BC, 5 tubes, AC/DC $45.00-50.00

159, table, 1948, plastic, lower front slide rule dial, upper vertical grille bars, 2 knobs, BC, 5 tubes, AC/DC.........................$45.00-50.00

160, table, 1948, two-tone plastic, lower front raised dial overlaps recessed checkered grille area, 2 knobs, BC, 5 tubes, AC/DC........$45.00-50.00

165, table, 1948, plastic, right front round dial overlaps lower horizontal grille bars, 2 knobs, BC, 4 tubes, AC/DC $30.00-35.00

166, table, 1948, plastic, upper front slide rule dial, lower horizontal wrap-around louvers, handle, 2 knobs, BC, 5 tubes, AC/DC ..$40.00-45.00

185, portable, 1948, plastic, inner slide rule dial, lattice grille, fold-down front, handle, 2 knobs, BC, 5 tubes, AC/DC/battery ...$30.00-35.00

190, portable, 1949, plastic, lower front slide rule dial, upper lattice grille, handle, 2 knobs, BC, 5 tubes, AC/DC/battery...............$30.00-35.00

195, table, 1949, plastic, right front round dial overlaps lower horizontal grille bars, 2 knobs, BC, 4 tubes, AC/DC $30.00-35.00

198, table, 1949, wood, lower front slanted slide rule dial, upper slanted grille area, 2 knobs, BC, FM, 8 tubes, AC $35.00-40.00

201, table, 1949, plastic, lower front raised dial overlaps recessed checkered grille area, 2 knobs, BC, 6 tubes, AC/DC $45.00-50.00

205, table, 1949, plastic, large right front round dial overlaps lower horizontal grille bars, 2 knobs, BC, 5 tubes, AC/DC $30.00-35.00

206, table, 1951, plastic, lower front slide rule dial, upper vertical grille bars, 2 knobs, BC, FM, 8 tubes, AC $30.00-35.00

228, portable, 1951, plastic, lower front half-round dial/louvers, flex handle, 2 knobs, BC, 5 tubes, AC/DC/battery $45.00-50.00

235, console-R/P, 1951, wood, upper front slide rule dial, center pull-out phono drawer, lower grille area, 2 knobs, BC, FM, 8 tubes, AC $50.00-55.00

TELECHRON
Telechron, Inc.
Ashland, Massachusetts

8H67 "Musalarm," table-C, 1948, plastic, step-down top, left square alarm clock, right horizontal wrap-around grille bars, 4 knobs, BC, 5 tubes, AC, $35.00-40.00.

8H59 "Musalarm," table-C, 1950, plastic, trapezoid shape, lower right front dial, upper circular grille cut-outs, left round alarm clock, BC, AC $45.00-55.00

TELEVOX
Televox, Inc.
451 South 5th Avenue, Mt. Vernon, New York

RP, table-R/P, 1947, wood, inner right vertical slide rule dial, left phono, lift top, 4 knobs, BC, 5 tubes, AC $25.00-30.00

TEMPLE
Templetone Radio Mfg. Corp.
New London, Connecticut

E-511, table-R/P, 1947, wood, upper front slanted slide rule dial, lower horizontal louvers, lift top, inner phono, 2 knobs, BC, 5 tubes, AC, $40.00-45.00.

E-514, table, 1946, wood, upper front slanted slide rule dial, lower cloth grille, 2 knobs, BC, 5 tubes, AC/DC $35.00-40.00
F-611, portable, 1946, luggage-style, upper front slanted slide rule dial, lower grille area, handle, 2 knobs, BC, 6 tubes, AC/DC/battery $30.00-35.00
F-616, table, 1946, wood, upper front slanted slide rule dial, lower cloth warp-around grille, 2 knobs, BC, AC/DC....................$40.00-45.00
G-410, portable, 1947, leatherette, upper front slide rule dial, lower grille area, handle, 2 knobs, BC, 4 tubes, AC/DC/battery $30.00-35.00
G-415, portable, 1948, inner dial, upper vertical grille bars, flip-open door, handle, power changeover switch, 2 knobs, BC, 4 tubes, AC/DC/battery $35.00-40.00
G-418, table, 1947, metal, right front dial, left graduated horizontal louvers, 2 knobs, BC, 4 tubes, AC/DC $75.00-85.00
G-419, table, 1947, metal, right front dial, left graduated horizontal louvers, 2 knobs, BC, 4 tubes, AC/DC $75.00-85.00
G-513, table, 1947, plastic, upper front slide rule dial, lower horizontal louvers, 2 knobs, BC, 5 tubes, AC/DC $40.00-45.00
G-515, table, 1947, wood, upper front slanted slide rule dial, large lower cloth grille, 2 knobs, BC, 5 tubes, AC/DC $40.00-45.00
G-516, table-R/P, 1947, wood, upper front slanted slide rule dial, lower criss-cross grille, lift top, inner phono, 4 knobs, BC, 5 tubes, AC $35.00-40.00
G-518, table-R/P, 1947, wood, upper front slanted slide rule dial, lower grille area, lift top, inner phono, 4 knobs, BC, 5 tubes, AC $35.00-40.00
G-521, portable, 1947, upper front slide rule dial, lower lattice grille, telescoping antenna, strap, 3 knobs, BC, SW, 5 tubes, AC/DC/battery $35.00-40.00
G-522, table, 1947, wood, upper front slanted slide rule dial, large lower grille area, 4 knobs, BC, SW, 5 tubes, AC/DC...............$35.00-40.00
G-619, table, 1947, wood, upper front slanted slide rule dial, large lower cloth grille area, 2 knobs, BC, 6 tubes, AC/DC $35.00-40.00
G-722, console-R/P, 1947, wood, right front slide rule dial, 6 pushbuttons, left pull-out phono drawer, lower grille, 4 knobs, BC, SW, 7 tubes, AC $75.00-85.00
G-724, table, 1948, wood, upper front slanted slide rule dial, lower criss-cross grille, 4 knobs, BC, FM, 7 tubes, AC/DC $35.00-40.00
G-725, console-R/P, 1948, wood, inner right slide rule dial, door, left pull-out phono drawer, lower grille area, 4 knobs, BC, FM, 7 tubes, AC $75.00-85.00
G-1430, console-R/P, 1948, wood, inner right slide rule dial, door, left pull-out phono drawer, lower grille, 4 knobs, BC, SW, FM, 14 tubes, AC $75.00-85.00

F-617, table-R/P, 1947, wood, upper front slanted slide rule dial, lower horizontal louvers, lift top, inner phono, 4 knobs, BC, 6 tubes, AC, $40.00-45.00.

G-4108, table, 1947, metal, right front dial, left graduated horizontal louvers, 2 knobs, BC, AC/DC $75.00-85.00
H-411 "Playmate," portable, 1948, oblong front panel with right round dial & left horizontal louvers, handle, 2 knobs, BC, 4 tubes, battery **$50.00-65.00**
H-622, console-R/P, 1948, wood, inner right slide rule dial, door, left pull-out phono drawer, lower criss-cross grille, 4 knobs, BC, SW, 6 tubes, AC **$65.00-75.00**

TEMPOTONE
Barker Bros. Co.
7th & Figueroa Street, Los Angeles, California

500E, table, 1946, plastic, left front panel with round dial overlaps horizontal louvers, 2 knobs, BC, 5 tubes, AC/DC $25.00-30.00

THERMIODYNE
Thermiodyne Radio Corp.
Plattsburg, New York

TF6, table, 1925, wood, rectangular case, front panel with center dial, lift top, 7 knobs, BC, 6 tubes, battery...........................$120.00-150.00

THOMPSON
R. E. Thompson Mfg. Co.
30 Church St., New York, New York

S-70 "Concert Grand," table, 1925, wood, rectangular case, slanted 3 dial front panel, 5 knobs, BC, 6 tubes, battery $130.00-160.00
V-50 "Grandette," table, 1925, wood, rectangular case, 3 dial front panel, 5 knobs, BC, 5 tubes, battery $120.00-140.00

S-60 "Parlor Grand," table, 1925, wood, rectangular case, slanted 3 dial front panel, 5 knobs, BC, 5 tubes, battery, $120.00-150.00.

THOROLA
Reichmann Company
1725-39 West 74th Street, Chicago, Illinois

57, table, 1926, wood, rectangular case, black front panel with 2 pointer dials and gold trim, 4 knobs, BC, 5 tubes, battery, $140.00-160.00.

50 "Islodyne," table, 1925, leatherette with metal corner accents, low rectangular case, 3 dial black front panel, 5 knobs, BC, 5 tubes, battery $150.00-180.00

TIFFANY TONE
Herbert H. Horn Radio Manufacturing Co.
1201 South Olive Street, Los Angeles, California

60, cathedral, C1931, wood, right thumbwheel dial, upper decorative grille, 3 knobs, BC, 7 tubes, AC, $270.00-300.00.

67, table, wood, right front dial, right side horizontal wrap-around louvers, left grille area with decorative bars, tuning eye, 4 knobs..$45.00-55.00
156A, wood, 1934, wood, left and right front window dials, center grille with cut-outs, step-down top, decorative side molding, 4 feet, 4 knobs, BC, SW, 5 tubes, AC $180.00-200.00

TRAV-LER
Trav-Ler Karenola Radio & Television Corp.
571 West Jackson Boulevard, Chicago, Illinois

41, table, 1936, wood, small case, center front dial, finished on both front & back, 2 knobs, BC, 4 tubes, AC/DC............................$65.00-75.00
53, tombstone, 1935, wood, lower front dial, upper cloth grille with cut-outs, BC, SW, 5 tubes, AC..$120.00-150.00

55-37, table, 1955, plastic, right front dial, left checkered grille, 2 knobs, BC, 5 tubes, AC/DC......................................$40.00-45.00
55-38, table, 1955, plastic, center front half-round dial over patterned grille, 2 knobs, BC, 5 tubes, AC/DC $30.00-35.00
55C42, table-C, 1955, plastic, right side dial, center front alarm clock, left checkered grille, BC, 5 tubes, AC $30.00-35.00
125, console, 1937, walnut, upper front round airplane dial, lower cloth grille with 3 splayed bars, BC, SW, 5 tubes, battery $50.00-65.00
131, console, 1937, walnut, upper front oval dial, lower cloth grille with center vertical bars, tuning eye, 5 knobs, BC, SW, 11 tubes, AC..$120.00-140.00
135, console, 1937, wood, upper front round dial, lower cloth grille with cut-outs, 4 knobs, BC, SW, 7 tubes, AC $110.00-130.00
135-M, console, 1937, wood, upper front round dial, lower cloth grille with cut-outs, tuning eye, 4 knobs, BC, SW, 7 tubes, AC ..$110.00-130.00
149, console, 1937, wood, upper front round dial, lower cloth grille with 3 splayed bars, 3 knobs, BC, SW, 6 tubes, AC $110.00-130.00
149-M, console, 1937, wood, upper front round dial, lower cloth grille with 3 splayed bars, tuning eye, 3 knobs, BC, SW, 6 tubes, AC $120.00-140.00
173, console, 1937, wood, upper front round dial, lower cloth grille with cut-outs, 4 knobs, BC, SW, 7 tubes, battery..................$65.00-75.00
315, table, 1939, two-tone wood, right front horizontal wrap-around dial, left round grille with horizontal bars, 2 knobs, BC, SW, 6 tubes, AC/DC $150.00-170.00
325, table-C, 1939, walnut & leatherette, center front slide rule dial, right clock, left grille, 2 knobs, BC, 5 tubes, AC $50.00-65.00
431, table, 1937, two-tone wood, right front dial, left 3-section cloth grille, 2 knobs, BC, 4 tubes, AC/DC............................$45.00-55.00
431-SW, table, 1937, two-tone wood, right front dial, left 3-section cloth grille, 2 knobs, BC, SW, 4 tubes, AC/DC......................$50.00-65.00
442, table, 1936, walnut, small oval case, center front dial surrounding by cut-out grille, feet, 2 knobs, BC, 5 tubes, AC/DC $200.00-240.00
502, table, 1937, wood, rectangular front panel with center dial, side grills with horizontal bars, 2 knobs, BC, 5 tubes, AC/DC........$65.00-75.00
512, table, 1936, wood, oblong case, center front dial over cloth grille with horizontal bars, 2 knobs, BC, 5 tubes, AC/DC.....$95.00-115.00
522, table, 1937, wood, right front oval dial, left oval grille with "H" cut-out, 3 knobs, BC, SW, 5 tubes, AC/DC $65.00-75.00
525, tombstone, 1937, wood, lower front round dial, upper cloth grille with curved cut-outs, 3 knobs, BC, 5 tubes, battery..........$85.00-95.00
527, table, 1937, walnut, right front automatic tuning dial, left grille area, 3 knobs, 5 tubes $65.00-75.00
539-M, table, 1939, wood, front slide rule dial, upper wrap-over grille, tuning eye, pushbuttons, 4 knobs, BC, SW, LW, 9 tubes, AC $65.00-75.00
549, table, 1937, wood, right front round dial, left cloth grille with Deco cut-outs, 3 knobs, BC, SW, 5 tubes, AC $65.00-75.00
550, table, 1937, wood, right front round dial, left cloth grille with Deco cut-outs, 3 knobs, BC, SW, 6 tubes, AC/DC.................$65.00-75.00
635, table, 1937, wood, right front round dial, left cloth grille with horizontal bars, 4 knobs, BC, SW, 7 tubes, AC.........................$65.00-75.00
635-M, table, 1937, wood, right front round dial, left cloth grille with horizontal bars, tuning eye, 4 knobs, BC, SW, 7 tubes, AC ..$65.00-75.00

5002, table, plastic, right front dial with red pointer, left vertical wrap-over grille bars, 2 knobs, BC, 6 tubes, AC/DC, $40.00-50.00.

701, table, 1937, wood, center front panel with half-round dial, side grills with horizontal bars, tuning eye, 3 knobs, BC, SW, 7 tubes, AC/DC **$75.00-85.00**

733, tombstone, 1937, wood, lower front round dial, upper cloth grille with cut-outs, 4 knobs, BC, SW, 7 tubes, battery **$85.00-95.00**

802, table, 1940, wood, right front slide rule dial, left cloth grille with horizontal bars, pushbuttons, 3 knobs, 7 tubes, AC **$65.00-75.00**

5000I, table, 1947, plastic, step-down top, right front dial, left cloth grille with horizontal bars, 2 knobs, BC, 5 tubes, AC/DC........**$40.00-50.00**

5008, table, 1946, two-tone wood, upper front slanted slide rule dial, lower cloth grille, 3 knobs, BC, 6 tubes, AC/DC **$35.00-40.00**

5009, table, 1946, wood, upper front slanted slide rule dial, lower cloth grille, 3 knobs, BC, 6 tubes, AC/DC **$35.00-40.00**

5010, table, 1946, wood, upper front slanted slide rule dial, lower cloth grille with "X" cut-out, 4 knobs, BC, SW, 6 tubes, AC/DC.........**$35.00-40.00**

5015, table, 1948, plastic, raised top, upper front slanted slide rule dial, lower horizontal louvers, 2 knobs, BC, 5 tubes, AC/DC ..**$40.00-45.00**

5019, portable, 1947, leatherette, right front dial, left cloth grille, handle, 2 knobs, BC, 4 tubes, battery...**$25.00-30.00**

5020, portable, 1947, luggage-style, right front square dial, left cloth grille, handle, 3 knobs, BC, 4 tubes, AC/DC/battery **$25.00-30.00**

5021, table, 1948, plastic, right front square dial, left vertical wrap-over louvers, 2 knobs, BC, 4 tubes, battery **$35.00-40.00**

5022, portable, 1950, alligator & plastic, right front dial overlaps horizontal grille bars, handle, 3 knobs, BC, 4 tubes, AC/DC/battery..**$40.00-50.00**

5027, portable, 1948, leatherette, upper front dial, lower horizontal louvers, handle, 3 knobs, BC, 4 tubes, AC/DC/battery **$35.00-40.00**

5028-A, portable, 1947, snakeskin, right front dial, left plastic horizontal grille bars, handle, 3 knobs, BC, 5 tubes, AC/DC/battery, $40.00-50.00.

5028, portable, 1948, leatherette, right front dial, left horizontal grille bars, handle, 3 knobs, BC, 5 tubes, AC/DC/battery...............**$40.00-45.00**

5029, portable, 1948, leatherette, right front dial, left horizontal grille bars, handle, 2 knobs, BC, 4 tubes, battery **$35.00-40.00**

5036, table-R/P, 1949, right front slide rule dial, left cloth grille, lift top, inner phono, 3 knobs, BC, AC **$30.00-35.00**

5049, portable, 1948, alligator, right front dial, left horizontal louvers, handle, 2 knobs, BC, 4 tubes, battery **$35.00-40.00**

5051, table, 1948, plastic, right front square dial, left vertical wrap-over grille bars, 2 knobs, BC, 5 tubes, AC/DC **$45.00-50.00**

5056-A, table, 1950, plastic, right front round dial, left checkered grille, BC, AC/DC..**$30.00-35.00**

5060, table, 1950, plastic, upper front slanted slide rule dial, lower horizontal grille bars, 2 top knobs, BC, 5 tubes, AC/DC **$55.00-65.00**

5061, table, 1950, plastic, upper front slanted slide rule dial, lower horizontal wrap-around grille bars, 2 top knobs, BC, 5 tubes, AC/DC **$55.00-65.00**

5066, table, 1948, plastic, upper front slanted slide rule dial, lower lattice grille, 2 knobs, BC, 6 tubes, AC/DC **$40.00-45.00**

5170, table-C, 1952, wood, right front square dial with inner perforated grille, left square alarm clock, 5 knobs, BC, 5 tubes, AC..**$30.00-35.00**

5220, portable, plastic, right side dial, left side on/off/volume knob, large front perforated grille area, handle, BC, AC/DC/battery ..**$25.00-30.00**

5300, portable, 1953, plastic, left dial, lower grille area, fold-down handle, 2 thumbwheel knobs, BC, 4 tubes, battery **$30.00-35.00**

5054, table, 1948, midget, upper right front dial, left horizontal grille bars, 2 knobs, BC, 4 tubes, AC/DC, $75.00-85.00.

5301, portable, 1953, alligator & plastic, right front dial over horizontal bars, left grille, handle, 3 knobs, BC, 4 tubes, AC/DC/battery ..**$30.00-35.00**

5310, table-R/P, 1953, wood, upper front slanted slide rule dial, lower grille, lift top, inner phono, 4 knobs, BC, 5 tubes, AC **$30.00-35.00**

5356, table, plastic, right front dial, left checkered grille area, BC, AC **$40.00-45.00**

5372, portable-R/P, 1954, leatherette, inner right square dial, left phono, lift top, handle, 3 knobs, BC, 5 tubes, AC **$30.00-35.00**

5510, table-R/P, 1956, wood, front half-round dial over grille, lift top, inner phono, 4 knobs, BC, 5 tubes, AC **$35.00-40.00**

6040, table-R/P, 1948, wood, upper front slide rule dial, lower grille, lift top, inner phono, 4 knobs, BC, 6 tubes, AC **$30.00-35.00**

6050, table-R/P, 1949, wood, upper front slanted slide rule dial, lower grille, lift top, inner phono, 4 knobs, BC, 5 tubes, AC **$30.00-35.00**

6300, portable, 1957, plastic, left dial, lower grille area, fold-down handle, 2 thumbwheel knobs, BC, 4 tubes, battery **$25.00-30.00**

6528, console-R/P, 1959, wood, inner dial, 4 speed phono, lift top, large front grille area, legs, 5 knobs, BC, 6 tubes, AC **$40.00-50.00**

T-200, table, 1959, plastic, off-center "steering wheel" dial over recessed horizontal bars, 2 knobs, BC, 5 tubes, AC/DC **$50.00-65.00**

T-201, table, 1959, plastic, off-center "steering wheel" dial over recessed horizontal bars, 2 knobs, BC, 5 tubes, AC/DC **$50.00-65.00**

M, cathedral, two-tone wood, center front window dial, upper cloth grille with cut-outs, scalloped top, 3 knobs, BC, $200.00-230.00.

TROPHY

Bowling Ball, table-N, 1941, plastic, shaped like a bowling ball, lower front vertical bars, lower rear speaker, base, right & left side knobs, BC, 5 tubes, AC/DC...**$470.00-580.00**

Baseball, table-N, 1941, molded cardboard, shaped like a baseball, top and lower front screens, base, right & left side knobs, BC, 5 tubes, AC/DC, $690.00-800.00.

TROY
Troy Radio & Television Co.
1142-1144 South Olive Street, Los Angeles, California

The Troy Radio Manufacturing Company began in 1933; the company was named for the USC Trojans. Troy made radios for many other companies besides their own. As a result of strict quality control standards, Troy was one of the few West Coast radio manufacturers to receive the Underwriters approval. With the beginning of WW II, Troy ceased radio production.

45-M, table, 1938, peach, silver, blue or green etched mirror glass, right front dial, left grille, 2 knobs, BC, 5 tubes, AC ....**$2100.00+**
75PC, table-R/P, 1936, wood, center front dial, right & left horizontal grille bars, lift top, inner phono, 3 knobs, BC, 5 tubes, AC **$35.00-40.00**
100, table, 1937, wood, rounded right, right front telephone dial, left cloth grille with horizontal bars, 3 knobs, BC, 5 tubes, AC **$75.00-85.00**
113-AW, table, 1938, two-tone wood, right front dial, left horizontal wrap-around louvers, tuning eye, 4 knobs, BC, SW, 11 tubes, AC ..**$65.00-75.00**
825, table, 1938, wood, front off-center dial, left wrap-around cloth grille with cut-outs, 6 pushbuttons, 3 knobs, BC, 5 tubes, AC ..**$65.00-75.00**
C-170-PC, console-R/P, 1938, wood, inner right dial & knobs, left phono, lift top, front cloth grille with vertical bars, AC **$110.00-130.00**

TRUETONE
Western Auto Supply Co.
2107 Grand Avenue, Kansas City, Missouri

636, table, 1938, plastic, Deco, right front dial, left horizontal wrap-around bars, 5 pushbuttons, 1 front & 1 side knob, BC, SW, $75.00-85.00.

585, tombstone, wood, lower front round airplane dial, upper cloth grille with cut-outs, 3 knobs, BC, SW **$110.00-130.00**
D-725, table, 1936, wood, large right front round airplane dial, left cloth grille with vertical bars, 4 knobs, BC, SW, 5 tubes, AC..**$50.00-65.00**
D-727, table, 1937, wood, right front dial, left cloth grille with horizontal bars, tuning eye, pushbuttons, 4 knobs, BC, SW, 9 tubes, AC..**$75.00-85.00**
D-910-B, table, 1939, wood, center front slide rule dial, upper recessed vertical grille bars, 6 pushbuttons, 4 knobs, BC, SW, 6 tubes, AC..**$65.00-75.00**
D-941, table, 1939, plastic, Deco, right front vertical wrap-over dial, left horizontal wrap-around louvers, 4 pushbuttons, 2 knobs, BC, 6 tubes, AC/DC..**$110.00-140.00**
D-1002, table, 1939, wood, right front airplane dial, left cloth grille with cut-outs, 4 knobs, BC, SW, 7 tubes, AC **$50.00-65.00**
D-1011, table, 1939, plastic, upper right front slide rule dial, left vertical grille bars, center vertical divider, 6 pushbuttons, base, 2 knobs, BC, 6 tubes, AC/DC **$75.00-85.00**
D-1046A, console-R/P, 1950, wood, upper front slide rule dial, lower pull-out phono drawer, 4 knobs, BC, FM, AC....................**$65.00-75.00**
D-1117, table, 1940, wood, upper front slide rule dial, lower cloth grille with cut-outs, decorative molding, side handles, 3 knobs, BC, SW, 7 tubes, AC/DC..**$65.00-75.00**
D-1210, console, 1942, wood, upper front slanted slide rule dial, lower cloth grille with 2 vertical bars, tuning eye, 6 pushbuttons, 6 knobs, BC, SW, 8 tubes, AC **$120.00-150.00**
D-1240A, console-R/P, 1952, wood, inner right slide rule dial, lower pull-out phono drawer, left storage, double doors, lower front grille, 4 knobs, BC, FM, 8 tubes, AC **$65.00-75.00**

D-723, table, 1939, wood, large right front round airplane dial, left cloth grille with cut-outs, 4 knobs, BC, SW, 7 tubes, AC, $65.00-75.00.

D-1612, end table, 1947, wood, front tilt-out radio with slide rule dial & top pie-crust edge, 3 knobs, BC, 6 tubes, AC............**$110.00-130.00**
D-1644, console-R/P, 1947, wood, upper front slide rule dial, lower grille, open storage, lift top, inner phono, 4 knobs, BC, 6 tubes, AC.......**$40.00-50.00**
D-1645, console-R/P, 1946, wood, upper front slanted slide rule dial, lower cloth grille with cut-out, 4 knobs, BC, SW, 6 tubes, AC **$110.00-130.00**
D-1752, console-R/P, 1948, wood, upper front slanted slide rule dial, horizontal grille bars, inner pull-out phono & record storage, double doors, 4 knobs, BC, FM, 8 tubes, AC **$85.00-105.00**
D-1835, console, 1948, wood, upper front slanted slide rule dial, lower cloth grille, 4 knobs, BC, SW, 6 tubes, AC **$85.00-105.00**
D-1836A, console-R/P, 1948, wood, upper front slide rule dial, lower cloth grille, tilt-out phono, 4 knobs, BC, FM, 7 tubes, AC **$85.00-105.00**
D-1840, console-R/P, 1948, wood, right front dial, left lift top, inner phono, lower grille & storage, 5 knobs, BC, 6 tubes, AC **$65.00-75.00**
D-1845, console-R/P, 1948, wood, upper front slanted slide rule dial, lower pull-out phono drawer, 4 knobs, BC, SW, 6 tubes, AC **$85.00-95.00**
D-1846A, console-R/P, 1948, two-tone wood, upper front slanted slide rule dial, lower pull-out phono drawer, 4 knobs, BC, FM, 7 tubes, AC **$95.00-105.00**
D-1850, console-R/P, 1948, wood, inner right slide rule dial, door, left pull-out phono drawer, lower grille, 4 knobs, BC, FM, 10 tubes, AC **$75.00-85.00**
D-1949, console-R/P, 1949, wood, inner right "sun burst" dial, door, left pull-out phono drawer, lower grille, 3 knobs, BC, FM, 8 tubes, AC **$75.00-85.00**
D-2017, table, 1950, walnut plastic, modern, right black half-round dial, left arched cloth grille, 2 knobs, BC, 6 tubes, AC/DC..**$180.00-200.00**

D-2018, table, 1950, ivory plastic, modern, right black half-round dial, left arched cloth grille, 2 knobs, BC, 6 tubes, AC/DC **$180.00-200.00**

D-2020, table, 1950, plastic, lower front slide rule dial, upper horizontal grille bars with vertical wrap-over center strip, 2 knobs, BC, FM, AC/DC **$45.00-50.00**

D-2025A, table, 1950, wood, right front square dial overlaps large grille area, 4 knobs, BC, FM, 7 tubes, AC **$30.00-35.00**

D-2027A, table, 1950, wood, right front square dial overlaps large grille area, 4 knobs, BC, FM, 8 tubes, AC **$35.00-40.00**

D-2121, table w/antenna, wood, upper front slanted slide rule dial, large lower cloth grille area, top antenna, 3 knobs, BC, 5 tubes, battery **$85.00-95.00**

D-2145, table-R/P, 1953, wood, right front square dial, left grille, 2/3 lift top, inner phono, 2 knobs, BC, 5 tubes, AC **$35.00-40.00**

D-2205, table-C, 1953, plastic, right front half-round dial, left alarm clock, center perforated grille area, 5 knobs, BC, 4 tubes, AC ..**$30.00-35.00**

D-2210, table, 1941, metal with wood finish, right front dial, left wrap-around cloth grille with horizontal bars, chrome trim, 2 knobs, BC, 5 tubes, AC/DC...**$130.00-160.00**

D-2214A, table, 1953, plastic, large front dial with inner horizontal grille bars, 2 knobs, BC, 5 tubes, AC/DC................................**$25.00-30.00**

D-2226, table, 1953, plastic, center front half-round dial overlaps large perforated grille area, 2 knobs, BC, FM, 9 tubes, AC **$30.00-35.00**

D-2237A, table, 1952, plastic, slanted sides, center front dial, large cloth grille, feet, 2 knobs, BC, 6 tubes, AC/DC **$30.00-35.00**

D-2255, table-R/P, 1953, wood, center front dial, right & left grills, lift top, inner phono, 2 knobs, BC, 5 tubes, AC **$35.00-40.00**

D-2263, table, 1953, wood, lower front slide rule dial, large upper grille area, 2 knobs, BC, 4 tubes, battery................................**$25.00-30.00**

D-2270, table-R/P, 1953, leatherette, inner left dial, phono, lift top, front grille, handle, 3 knobs, BC, 5 tubes, AC **$20.00-25.00**

D-2325-A, table, 1953, plastic, lower front half-round dial with crest overlaps large grille area, 2 knobs, BC, 6 tubes, AC **$30.00-35.00**

D-1014, table, 1940, wood, right front dial, left horizontal wrap-around louvers, pushbuttons, 3 knobs, BC, SW, 7 tubes, AC/DC, $55.00-65.00.

D-2383, table, 1953, plastic, upper front slanted slide rule dial, lower horizontal louvers, 3 knobs, BC, SW, 5 tubes, AC/DC **$40.00-45.00**

D-2389, table-C, 1954, plastic, right side round dial, front alarm clock over checkered grille, 5 knobs, BC, 4 tubes, AC............**$30.00-35.00**

D-2418, table-C, 1954, black plastic, right front round dial, left front round clock, center grille, 4 knobs, BC, 4 tubes, AC......**$45.00-50.00**

D-2419, table-C, 1954, red plastic, right front round dial, left front round clock, center grille, 4 knobs, BC, 4 tubes, AC **$50.00-60.00**

D-2420, table-C, 1954, white plastic, right front round dial, left front round clock, center grille, 4 knobs, BC, 4 tubes, AC......**$40.00-45.00**

D-2483, table, 1954, plastic, lower front slide rule dial, upper grille area, 3 knobs, BC, SW, 6 tubes, AC/DC **$30.00-35.00**

D-2556A, table-R/P, 1955, wood, right side dial, large front grille area, lift top, inner phono, 3 right side knobs, BC, 6 tubes, AC ..**$25.00-30.00**

D-2560A, table-R/P, 1955, two-tone leatherette, center front round dial, lift top, inner phono, handle, 2 knobs, BC, 5 tubes, AC **$30.00-35.00**

D-2582A, table, 1955, plastic, right front half-round dial, horizontal grille bars, feet, 2 knobs, BC, 4 tubes, AC/DC........................**$25.00-30.00**

D-2610, table, 1946, plastic, large center front square dial, right & left side horizontal louvers, 2 knobs, BC, 5 tubes, AC/DC ..**$75.00-85.00**

D-1126, console, 1942, wood, upper front slanted slide rule dial, lower cloth grille with 2 vertical bars and "x" center, tuning eye, 6 pushbuttons, 4 knobs, BC, SW, 11 tubes, AC, $130.00-160.00.

D-2613, table, 1947, plastic, upper front slanted slide rule dial, lower criss-cross grille with crossed bars, 3 knobs, BC, SW, 6 tubes, AC/DC **$40.00-45.00**

D-2615 "Stratoscope," table, 1946, plastic, upper right front slide rule dial, left vertical grille bars, center vertical divider, 6 pushbuttons, base, 2 knobs, BC, 6 tubes, AC/DC **$85.00-95.00**

D-2616, table, 1946, plastic, upper front slanted slide rule dial, lower curved louvers, 6 pushbuttons, 2 knobs, BC, 6 tubes, AC/DC **$40.00-50.00**

D-2616B, table, 1948, plastic, upper front slanted slide rule dial, lower curved louvers, 6 pushbuttons, 2 knobs, BC, 6 tubes, AC/DC **$40.00-50.00**

D-2619, table, 1947, wood, lower front slanted slide rule dial, large upper grille area, 2 knobs, BC, 6 tubes, AC/DC **$40.00-45.00**

D-2620, table, 1946, two-tone wood, upper front slanted slide rule dial, lower cloth grille with 2 horizontal bars, 2 knobs, BC, 5 tubes, AC/DC **$40.00-50.00**

D-2621, table, 1946, two-tone wood, upper front slanted slide rule dial, lower cloth grille with cutouts, 2 knobs, BC, 4 tubes, battery **$30.00-40.00**

D-2622, table, 1947, wood, rounded corners, upper front slanted slide rule dial, large lower cloth grille, 2 knobs, BC, 5 tubes, AC/DC...**$45.00-55.00**

D-2623, table, 1947, wood, upper front slide rule dial over large cloth grille area, 4 knobs, BC, 6 tubes, AC.............................**$40.00-45.00**

D-2624, table, 1946, wood, upper front slanted slide rule dial, lower metal criss-cross grille, 3 knobs, BC, SW, 7 tubes, AC/DC **$40.00-45.00**

D-2626, table, 1948, wood, upper front slanted slide rule dial, lower criss-cross grille, 4 knobs, BC, SW, 6 tubes, AC **$40.00-45.00**

D-2015, table, C1939, plastic, upper right front slide rule dial, left vertical grille bars, center vertical divider, 6 pushbuttons, base, 2 knobs, BC, 6 tubes, AC/DC, $95.00-115.00.

D-2026, table, plastic, lower front black dial over checkered panel, upper cloth grille, 2 knobs, BC, FM, $40.00-45.00.

D-2630, table, 1946, plastic, upper front slanted slide rule dial, lower cloth grille, 3 knobs, BC, SW, 7 tubes, AC/DC **$40.00-45.00**

D-2637A, table, 1956, plastic, center front recessed round dial over horizontal bars, 2 knobs, BC, 6 tubes, AC/DC **$30.00-35.00**

D-2640, table-R/P, 1948, wood, lower front slanted slide rule dial, upper criss-cross grille, lift top, inner phono, 2 knobs, BC, 5 tubes, AC **$30.00-35.00**

D-2642, table-R/P, 1947, wood, upper front slide rule dial, lower grille with 3 vertical bars, lift top, inner phono, 2 knobs, BC, 5 tubes, AC **$30.00-35.00**

D-2644, table, 1947, wood, upper front slanted slide rule dial, lower criss-cross grille, 2 knobs, BC, 4 tubes, battery.....................**$30.00-35.00**

D-2645, table-R/P, 1946, wood, top right vertical slide rule dial, front cloth grille, lift top, inner phono, 4 knobs, BC, SW, 6 tubes, AC **$30.00-35.00**

D-2661, table, 1946, plastic, large center front square dial, right & left side horizontal louvers, 2 knobs, BC, 4 tubes, battery ..**$75.00-85.00**

D-2663, table, 1947, wood, upper front slanted slide rule dial, lower cloth grille with center horizontal bar, 2 knobs, BC, 4 tubes, battery **$35.00-40.00**

D-2665, table, 1947, metal, center front dial, right & left cloth grills, chrome accents, rounded shoulders, 2 knobs, BC, 4 tubes, battery **$50.00-65.00**

D-2692, table, 1948, wood, upper front slanted slide rule dial, lower horizontal grille bars, 2 knobs, BC, 6 tubes, AC/DC **$35.00-40.00**

D-2709, table, 1947, plastic, right front dial, left lattice grille, base, 2 knobs, BC, 4 tubes, AC/DC..**$45.00-55.00**

D-2710, table, 1947, plastic, upper front slanted slide rule dial, large lower grille area, 2 knobs, BC, 5 tubes, AC/DC.............**$40.00-50.00**

D-2718, table, 1947, plastic, upper front slide rule dial, lower horizontal wrap-around louvers, 3 knobs, BC, SW, 7 tubes, AC/DC..**$50.00-65.00**

D-2718B, table, 1947, plastic, upper front slide rule dial, lower horizontal wrap-around louvers, 3 knobs, BC, SW, 7 tubes, AC/DC..**$50.00-65.00**

D-2743, table-R/P, 1947, wood, right front dial, left horizontal louvers, open top phono, 3 knobs, BC, 4 tubes, AC...................**$20.00-25.00**

D-2748, table-R/P, 1947, wood, lower front slide rule dial, upper horizontal louvers, lift top, inner phono, 4 knobs, BC, 5 tubes, AC..**$30.00-35.00**

D-2612, table, 1946, plastic, upper front slanted slide rule dial, lower criss-cross metal grille with crossed bars, 3 knobs, BC, 6 tubes, AC/DC, $40.00-45.00.

D-2806, table, 1948, plastic, right front round dial overlaps lower horizontal louvers, 2 knobs, BC, 4 tubes, AC/DC **$35.00-40.00**

D-2807, table, 1948, plastic, right front round dial overlaps lower horizontal louvers, 2 knobs, BC, 4 tubes, AC/DC **$35.00-40.00**

D-2815, table, 1948, plastic, upper front slanted slide rule dial, lower curved louvers, pushbuttons, 2 knobs, BC, 6 tubes, AC/DC **$50.00-65.00**

D-2819, table, 1948, plastic, upper front slide rule dial, lower horizontal wrap-around louvers, 4 knobs, BC, FM, 7 tubes, AC **$50.00-65.00**

D-2836A, table, 1958, plastic, upper right front BC dial/upper left front FM dial over large grille area with center horizontal bar, 4 knobs, BC, FM, 8 tubes, AC **$25.00-30.00**

D-2851, table-R/P, 1948, wood, upper front slanted slide rule dial, lower grille, lift top, inner phono, 4 knobs, BC, 5 tubes, AC **$35.00-40.00**

D-2857A, table, 1958, plastic, right side dial, horizontal front louvers with center vertical divider & crest, feet, BC, 5 tubes, AC/DC..**$25.00-30.00**

D-2907, table, 1949, plastic, right front round dial overlaps raised center lattice grille area, 2 knobs, BC, 4 tubes, AC/DC **$35.00-40.00**

D-2910, table, 1949, plastic, upper front slanted slide rule dial, large lower grille area, 2 knobs, BC, AC/DC........................**$40.00-45.00**

D-2919, table, 1949, plastic, lower front slide rule dial, upper lattice grille, horizontal decorative bands, 4 knobs, BC, FM, 6 tubes, AC/DC **$35.00-40.00**

D-2923, table, wood, upper front slide rule dial overlaps large grille area, 4 knobs, BC, SW, 6 tubes, AC......................................**$40.00-45.00**

D-2963, table, 1949, plastic, upper front slanted slide rule dial, large lower grille area, 2 knobs, BC, 4 tubes, battery............**$30.00-35.00**

D-3120A, portable, 1953, plastic, upper front slide rule dial, left front horizontal bars, handle, 2 side knobs, BC, 4 tubes, AC/DC/battery **$30.00-35.00**

D-3210A, portable, 1953, plastic, right side dial, front & rear horizontal bars, handle, 2 side knobs, BC, 4 tubes, AC/DC/battery **$30.00-35.00**

D-2634, table, 1947, wood, lower front see-through slide rule dial over large cloth grille area, 3 knobs, BC, 6 tubes, AC, $35.00-40.00.

D-3265A, portable, 1952, leatherette & plastic, upper front round dial, handle, 2 knobs, BC, 5 tubes, AC/DC/battery................**$30.00-35.00**

D-3300, portable, 1953, plastic, large center front round dial over horizontal bars, fold-down handle, 2 knobs, BC, 4 tubes, battery......**$30.00-35.00**

D-3490, portable, 1955, plastic, large center front round dial over lower horizontal grille bars, fold-down handle, 2 knobs, BC, 4 tubes, battery **$30.00-35.00**

D-3600A, portable, 1957, plastic, left dial, lower front grille, fold-down handle, 2 thumbwheel knobs, BC, 4 tubes, battery **$30.00-35.00**

D-3615, portable, 1947, leatherette, upper right front half-round dial, center lattice grille area, handle, BC, AC/DC/battery **$25.00-30.00**

D-3619, portable, 1946, luggage-style, upper front slide rule dial, lower grille area, handle, 2 top knobs, BC, AC/DC/battery......**$25.00-30.00**

D-3630, portable, 1947, luggage-style, inner right dial overlaps horizontal louvers, fold-down front, handle, 2 knobs, BC, 5 tubes, AC/DC/battery **$30.00-35.00**

D-3720, portable, 1947, leatherette, small lower right front round dial overlaps woven grille area, handle, 2 knobs, BC, 4 tubes, AC/DC/battery **$30.00-35.00**

D-3721, portable, 1948, leatherette, lower front slide rule dial, plastic grille with horizontal bars, handle, 2 knobs, BC, 4 tubes, AC/DC/battery **$30.00-35.00**

D-3722, portable, 1948, leatherette, plastic front panel, right dial overlaps horizontal louvers, handle, 2 knobs, BC, 4 tubes, AC/DC/battery **$30.00-35.00**

D-2810, table, 1948, plastic, upper front slanted slide rule dial, lower cloth grille, 2 knobs, BC, 5 tubes, AC/DC, $40.00-45.00.

D-3780A, portable, 1957, leather, upper right round dial, front grille cut-outs, handle, 2 knobs, BC, 4 tubes, battery $25.00-30.00

D-3784A, portable, 1957, leather, upper right round dial, front grille cut-outs, handle, 2 knobs, BC, 4 tubes, AC/DC/battery $25.00-30.00

D-3789A, portable, 1957, leather, right side dial, front grille cut-outs, handle, 2 knobs, BC, 5 tubes, AC/DC/battery....................$25.00-30.00

D-3809, portable, 1948, plastic, small upper front slide rule dial, lower recessed horizontal louvers, handle, 2 knobs, BC, 4 tubes, battery $30.00-35.00

D-3810, portable, 1948, plastic, small upper front slide rule dial, lower recessed horizontal louvers, handle, 2 knobs, BC, 5 tubes, AC/DC/battery $30.00-35.00

D-3811, portable, 1948, plastic, inner right dial, upper grille bars, radio plays when flip-up lid opens, power changeover switch, 2 knobs, BC, 4 tubes, AC/DC/battery $40.00-45.00

D-3840, portable, 1948, leatherette, inner right dial, left vertical grille bars, fold-down front, handle, 3 knobs, BC, 6 tubes, AC/DC/battery $30.00-35.00

D-3910, portable, 1949, plastic, lower right front dial, upper horizontal grille bars, handle, 2 knobs, BC, 4 tubes, AC/DC/battery $30.00-35.00

DC2154, table, plastic, upper right front dial panel, large lattice grille area with logo, feet, BC $15.00-20.00

DC2980A, table, 1959, plastic, right front round dial, left lattice grille, 2 knobs, BC, 4 tubes, AC/DC $15.00-20.00

DC2989A, table-C, 1959, plastic, wedge-shaped, upper right front dial, left alarm clock, center horizontal bars, feet, BC, 6 tubes, AC...$20.00-25.00

DC3800, portable, 1959, plastic, front perforated grille, collapsible handle, 2 side knobs, BC, 4 tubes, AC/DC/battery $20.00-25.00

DC5987A, table-R/P, 1959, right front dial, upper random-patterned perforated grille, handle, lift top, inner phono, 4 knobs, BC, 6 tubes, AC..$35.00-40.00

Junior, table, plastic, small right front dial, left and lower horizontal louvers, 2 knobs, BC...$75.00-85.00

D-2819E, table, 1948, plastic, upper front slide rule dial, lower horizontal wrap-around louvers, 4 knobs, BC, FM, 7 tubes, AC, $50.00-65.00.

TUSKA
The C.D. Tuska Co.
Hartford, Connecticut

222, table, 1922, wood, low rectangular case, 2 dial black front panel, 6 knobs, BC, 1 tube, battery, $800.00-900.00.

224, table, 1922, wood, low rectangular case, 2 dial black front panel, 4 knobs, BC, 1 tube, battery...$480.00-580.00

225 Double Panel, table, 1923, mahogany, low rectangular case, 2 dial black Bakelite double panel, 6 knobs, BC, 3 tubes, battery $690.00-740.00

228 "Superdyne," table, 1924, wood, low rectangular case, 2 dial black front panel, 6 knobs, BC, 4 tubes, battery.................$250.00-300.00

300, table, 1924, wood, low rectangular case, 2 dial black front panel, lift top, 6 knobs, BC, 4 tubes, battery.............................$480.00-530.00

301 "Junior," table, 1925, wood, low rectangular case, 3 dial front panel, 5 knobs, BC, 3 tubes, battery $240.00-300.00

305 "Superdyne," table, 1925, wood, low rectangular case, black front panel with 2 window dials, 6 knobs, BC, 4 tubes, battery..........$200.00-230.00

225 Single Panel, table, 1923, mahogany, low rectangular case, 2 dial black Bakelite single panel, 6 knobs, BC, 3 tubes, battery, $480.00-530.00.

401, table, 1925, wood, low rectangular case, black front panel with 3 gold half-round pointer dials, 4 knobs, BC, battery, $300.00-320.00.

20TH CENTURY
Electronic Devices Corp.
601 West 26th Street, New York, New York

100X, table, wood, right front square black dial, left cloth grille with vertical bars, 3 knobs, BC, SW, AC/DC $40.00-45.00

101, table, 1947, wood, right front square black dial, left criss-cross grille, 3 knobs, BC, SW, AC/DC **$40.00-50.00**

TYRMAN
Tyrman Electric Corporation
Tyrman Radio Company

50, portable, leatherette, inner wooden panel with window dial, upper grille area, fold-open front with built-in antenna, handle, 3 knobs, BC, battery..**$260.00-300.00**

U. S. RADIO
U.S. Radio & Televison Corporation
Chicago, Illinois

9-A, tombstone, 1932, wood, center front quarter-round dial, upper cloth grille with cut-outs, 4 knobs, BC, 9 tubes, AC, $160.00-190.00.

3040, console, 1933, wood, lowboy, upper front window dial, lower cloth grille with cut-outs, 6 legs, BC, 5 tubes, AC **$120.00-150.00**
3074, console, 1933, wood, lowboy, upper front dial, lower cloth grille with cut-outs, 6 legs, 7 tubes **$120.00-150.00**
3084, cathedral, 1933, wood, center front window dial, upper cloth grille with cut-outs, 3 knobs, 5 tubes **$120.00-150.00**
3086, cathedral, 1933, wood, lower front window dial, upper cloth grille with cut-outs, 3 knobs, 5 tubes **$120.00-150.00**
3092, table, 1933, wood with inlay, front dial, center cloth grille with cut-outs, BC, 5 tubes, AC/DC **$75.00-85.00**

USL RADIO
U-S-L Radio, Inc.
Niagara Falls, New York
USL Battery Corporation
Oakland, California

DC-6, table, C1928, wood, center front window dial, lift top, 2 knobs, BC, 6 tubes, battery, $75.00-95.00.

ULTRADYNE
Regal Electronics Corp.
20 West 20th Street, New York, New York

L-43, table, 1946, wood, right front black dial, left cloth grille with "V" cut-out, 2 knobs, 4 tubes, AC/DC, $40.00-50.00.

L-46, table, 1946, wood, right front half-round dial, left cloth grille with curved bars, 2 knobs, BC, 6 tubes, AC/DC **$40.00-45.00**

ULTRATONE
Audio Industries
Michigan City, Indiana

355, table-R/P, 1956, right side dial, large front grille area, handle, lift top, inner phono, 3 right side knobs, BC, 5 tubes, AC **$20.00-25.00**

UNITED AIR CLEANER
United Air Cleaner Company

Model unknown, cathedral, C1931, wood, center brass escutcheon with window dial, upper decorative grille, scalloped top, 3 knobs, BC, 7 tubes, AC, $320.00-350.00.

UNITED UTILITIES

1021TB, table, plastic, upper front slanted slide rule dial, lower woven grille area, 3 knobs, BC, $40.00-50.00.

UNITONE
Union Electronics Corp.
38-01 Queens Boulevard, Long Island, New York

88, table, 1946, wood, upper front slanted slide rule dial, lower cloth grille with 2 horizontal bars, 2 knobs, BC, SW, AC/DC **$40.00-45.00**

UNIVERSAL
Universal Battery Company
Universal Radio & Television Corporation

72A6, tombstone, 1935, wood, lower front round dial, upper cloth grille with cut-outs, BC, SW, battery **$65.00-75.00**
73A6, console, 1935, wood, upper front round dial, lower cloth grille with cut-outs, BC, SW, battery **$65.00-75.00**
7222, console, 1935, wood, upper front round dial, lower cloth grille with cut-outs, battery **$65.00-75.00**
7232, tombstone, 1935, wood, lower front round dial, upper cloth grille with cut-outs, battery.....................................**$65.00-75.00**
DS-85, table, plastic, small case, right front half-round dial, left checkered grille area, feet, BC **$25.00-30.00**

VAL-KEEN

572, table, 1946, wood, upper right front slide rule dial, lower & left cloth grille areas with horizontal bars, 3 knobs, AC, $40.00-45.00.

VAN CAMP
Van Camp Hardware & Iron Co.
401 West Maryland Street, Indianapolis, Indiana

576-1-6A, table, 1946, wood, upper front slide rule dial, lower cloth grille with vertical bars, 3 knobs, BC, 6 tubes, AC/DC............**$55.00-65.00**

VICTOREEN

345, console, 1930, wood, inner window dial and knobs, double doors, Queen Anne style cabinet with double stretcher base, 2 chassis, 11 tubes **$300.00-350.00**

VIKING
Viking Radio Laboratories/Ozarka Radio
433 N. LaSalle St., Chicago, Illinois

5-A, table, 1926, wood, low rectangular case, 3 dial front panel, 5 knobs, BC, 5 tubes, battery.....................................**$120.00-140.00**
5-A, console, 1926, wood, inner three dial panel, fold-down front, upper speaker grille, lower storage, 5 knobs, BC, 5 tubes, battery **$180.00-200.00**

599, table, 1926, two-tone cardboard & leatherette, large center front dial, lift back, 3 knobs, BC, 5 tubes, battery, $180.00-200.00.

VIZ
Molded Insulation Co.
335 East Price Street, Philadelphia, Pennsylvania

RS-1, table, 1947, plastic, right front round dial, left horizontal wrap-around louvers, BC, 5 tubes, AC/DC, $40.00-50.00.

VOGUE
Sheridan Electronics Corp.
2850 South Michigan Avenue, Chicago, Illinois

2554R, table, 1946, plastic, right front half-round dial, left horizontal wrap-around louvers, handle, 2 knobs, BC, 5 tubes, AC/DC **$45.00-55.00**

WAGNER

72AE-184, table, two-tone wood, right front dial, left cloth grille with horizontal bars, tuning eye, 4 knobs, 5 tubes, AC, $65.00-75.00.

WARE
Ware Radio Corporation
529-549 West 42nd Street, New York, New York

B1 "Bantam," cathedral, 1931, two-tone wood, right front dial, upper cloth grille with cut-outs, fluted columns, finials, BC, 7 tubes, AC, $320.00-370.00.

L, table, 1925, wood, low rectangular case, 3 dial black front panel, lift top, 4 knobs, BC, 5 tubes, battery.............................$120.00-140.00
TU, console, 1926, wood, inner panel, lift top, inner front speaker grille, double doors, 3 knobs, BC, 3 exposed tubes, battery $350.00-380.00
W, table, 1924, walnut, low rectangular case, 3 dial front panel, meter, 4 knobs, BC, 5 tubes, battery......................................$120.00-150.00
WU, console, 1925, wood, inner slanted 3 dial panel, upper speaker grille, double doors, 4 knobs, BC, 5 tubes, battery $180.00-200.00
X, table, 1925, walnut, low rectangular case, 3 dial front panel, meter, 4 knobs, BC, 5 tubes, battery......................................$120.00-140.00

T, table, 1924, mahogany, high rectangular case, slanted 2 dial panel, 3 knobs, BC, 3 exposed tubes, battery, $300.00-320.00.

WATTERSON
Watterson Radio Mfg. Co.
2700 Swiss Avenue, Dallas, Texas

4581, table, 1946, wood, right front square dial overlaps horizontal grille bars, 2 knobs, BC, 5 tubes, AC/DC...............................$40.00-45.00
4582, table, 1946, wood, right front square dial, left cloth grille with horizontal bars, 2 knobs, BC $30.00-35.00
4782, table, 1947, two-tone wood, right front dial, left cloth grille with cut-outs, 2 knobs, BC, 4 tubes, battery $40.00-45.00

4790, table, 1947, two-tone wood, right front dial, left cloth grille with horizontal bars, 3 knobs, BC, 6 tubes, AC/DC $40.00-45.00
4800, table, 1948, wood, front oblong slide rule dial over large grille area, 4 knobs, BC, FM, 6 tubes, AC/DC.............................$30.00-35.00
ARC-4591A, table-R/P, 1947, wood, top right vertical slide rule dial, front horizontal louvers, lift top, inner phono, 4 knobs, BC, 6 tubes, AC $30.00-35.00
RC-4581, table-R/P, 1947, wood, right front square dial, left horizontal grille bars, lift top, inner phono, 3 knobs, BC, 5 tubes, AC $30.00-35.00

WELLS
Wells Mfg. Co.
Fond du Lac, Wisconsin

24, table, 1925, wood, low rectangular case, black front panel with center dial, BC, 4 tubes, battery $130.00-150.00

WESTERN AIR PATROL

5E, tombstone, wood, center front half-round dial, upper cloth grille with cut-outs, 3 knobs...$120.00-140.00
268, table, wood, center front vertical slide rule dial, right and left cloth grille areas, 6 pushbuttons, 3 knobs $75.00-85.00

WESTERN ELECTRIC

Western Electric began business in 1872 making Bell Telephone equipment. In the early 1920s, the company began radio production — at first only for commercial interests.

4B, table, 1923, wood, low rectangular case, 2 dial black front panel, battery $740.00-850.00
4C, table, c1924, wood, low rectangular case, 2 dial front panel, battery $800.00-900.00
4D, table, c1924, wood, low rectangular case, 2 dial front panel, battery $580.00-700.00

7A, table/amp, wood, amplifier, black Bakelite front panel, $530.00-580.00.

WESTINGHOUSE
Westinghouse Electric Corp., Home Radio Division
Sunbury, Pennsylvania

The Westinghouse company sold its line of radios through RCA until 1930. The company is well known for its slogan: "You Can Be Sure If It's Westinghouse."

Aeriola Jr., table, 1922, wood, crystal set, square case, lift top, inner control panel, storage, lever dial, BC.......................$360.00-410.00
H-103, table, 1946, wood, curved top, recessed front, lower slide rule dial, upper horizontal louvers, 4 knobs, BC, SW $55.00-65.00

Aeriola Sr., table, 1922, wood, square case, inner 1 dial panel, lift top, 2 knobs, 1 lever, BC, 1 tube, battery, $180.00-230.00.

H-130, table, 1946, wood, top recessed slide rule dial, lower front cloth grille, 4 knobs, AC/DC, $45.00-55.00.

H-104, table, 1946, wood, curved top, recessed front, lower slide rule dial, upper horizontal louvers, 6 pushbuttons, 4 knobs, BC, SW, 7 tubes, AC **$55.00-65.00**

H-117, console-R/P, 1947, wood, upper slide rule dial, 6 pushbuttons, inner pull-out phono, double doors, 4 knobs, BC, SW, FM, 14 tubes, AC **$85.00-95.00**

H-119, console-R/P, 1947, wood, inner left slide rule dial/6 pushbuttons, door, left pull-out phono drawer, 4 knobs, BC, SW, FM, 14 tubes, AC **$85.00-95.00**

H-124 "Little Jewel"/"Refrigerator," portable, 1945, dark green plastic with metal center panel, upper front dial, lower cloth grille with vertical bars, fold-down handle, 2 knobs, BC, 6 tubes, AC/DC..**$85.00-105.00**

H-125 "Little Jewel"/"Refrigerator," portable, 1945, light green plastic with metal center panel, upper front dial, lower cloth grille with vertical bars, fold-down handle, 2 knobs, BC, 6 tubes, AC/DC..**$85.00-105.00**

H-126 "Little Jewel"/"Refrigerator," portable, 1945, ivory plastic with metal center panel, upper front dial, lower cloth grille with vertical bars, fold-down handle, 2 knobs, BC, 6 tubes, AC/DC ..**$85.00-105.00**

H-127 "Little Jewel"/"Refrigerator," portable, 1945, burgundy plastic with metal center panel, upper front dial, lower cloth grille with vertical bars, fold-down handle, 2 knobs, BC, 6 tubes, AC/DC ..**$85.00-105.00**

H-133, table, 1947, two-tone wood, upper front slanted slide rule dial, lower cloth grille, 3 knobs, BC **$40.00-45.00**

H-142, table, 1948, wood, upper front slanted slide rule dial, lower grille area, top fluting, 5 knobs, BC, SW, 9 tubes, AC **$75.00-85.00**

H-147, table, 1948, plastic, right front dial panel overlaps large cloth grille area, 2 knobs, BC, 5 tubes, AC/DC................................**$40.00-50.00**

H-148, portable, 1947, leatherette, small upper right front dial over large criss-cross grille area, handle, 2 knobs, BC, 4 tubes, AC/DC/battery **$30.00-35.00**

H-157, table, 1948, wood, lower front slide rule dial, large upper recessed cloth grille, 2 knobs, BC, 6 tubes, AC/DC **$35.00-40.00**

H-161, table, 1948, wood, right front curved dial over large cloth grille, 4 knobs, BC, FM, 8 tubes, AC **$40.00-45.00**

H-165, portable, 1948, inner dial, upper horizontal grille bars, fold-down front, handle, 4 knobs, BC, 5 tubes, AC/DC/battery **$30.00-35.00**

H-166, console-R/P, 1948, wood, inner left slide rule dial, door, right pull-out phono drawer, lower grille, 4 knobs, BC, FM, 12 tubes, AC **$65.00-75.00**

H-168, console-R/P, 1948, wood, inner right curved dial, left phono, lift top, front grille cut-outs, 4 knobs, BC, FM, 8 tubes, AC..**$65.00-75.00**

H-168A, console-R/P, 1948, wood, inner right curved dial, left phono, lift top, front grille cut-outs, 4 knobs, BC, FM, 8 tubes, AC..**$65.00-75.00**

H-169, console-R/P, 1948, wood, inner left slide rule dial, door, right pull-out phono drawer, 4 knobs, BC, SW, FM, 14 tubes, AC ..**$85.00-95.00**

H-171, console-R/P, 1948, wood & plastic, front plastic radio unit detaches from wood console cabinet, radio case has top slide rule dial/lower horizontal louvers, console cabinet has lift top/inner phono, 4 knobs, BC, 6 tubes, AC **$110.00-130.00**

H-178, table, 1948, two-tone wood, upper front slanted slide rule dial, lower cloth grille, 3 knobs, BC, 5 tubes, battery **$35.00-40.00**

H-182, table, 1949, plastic, upper front slanted slide rule dial, lower cloth grille, decorative case lines, 3 knobs, BC, FM, 6 tubes, AC/DC **$40.00-45.00**

H-138, console-R/P, 1946, wood, front slide rule dial with upper horizontal louvers, lower cloth grille with 2 vertical bars, 6 pushbuttons, 4 knobs, BC, SW, AC, $75.00-85.00.

H-122, table-R/P, 1946, front plastic radio unit detaches from wood phono case, radio case has top dial/lower horizontal louvers, 4 knobs, BC, AC/DC, $50.00-65.00.

H-188, table, 1948, plastic, Oriental design, right front dial, left cloth grille with cutouts, 2 knobs, BC, 5 tubes, AC/DC, $75.00-85.00.

H-183A, console-R/P, 1948, wood, inner right dial, door, left pull-out phono drawer, lower grille & storage, 4 knobs, BC, 6 tubes, AC **$65.00-75.00**

H-185, portable, 1949, plastic, upper front slide rule dial, lower horizontal grille bars, handle, 2 knobs, BC, 4 tubes, AC/DC/battery ..**$35.00-40.00**

H-186, console-R/P, 1949, wood, inner right slide rule dial/pushbuttons, door, left pull-out phono drawer, lower front grille, 4 knobs, BC, FM, 12 tubes, AC **$75.00-85.00**

H-190, console-R/P, 1949, wood, upper front slide rule dial, center pull-out phono drawer, lower grille, 4 knobs, BC, FM, 8 tubes, AC..**$65.00-75.00**

H-191, console-R/P, 1949, wood, inner right slide rule dial, left pull-out phono drawer, double doors, 4 knobs, BC, FM, 8 tubes, AC **$65.00-75.00**

H-191A, console-R/P, 1949, wood, inner right slide rule dial, left pull-out phono drawer, double doors, 4 knobs, BC, FM, 8 tubes, AC **$65.00-75.00**

H-195, portable, 1949, leatherette, upper front slide rule dial, lower cloth grille, handle, 2 knobs, BC, 4 tubes, AC/DC/battery **$35.00-40.00**

H-198, table, 1949, wood, lower front slide rule dial, large upper cloth grille, 2 knobs, BC, FM, 8 tubes, AC **$30.00-35.00**

H-202, table, 1948, plastic, upper front slanted slide rule dial, large lower grille area, decorative case lines, 3 knobs, BC, FM........**$40.00-50.00**

H-203, console-R/P, 1949, wood, inner right slide rule dial, door, left pull-out phono drawer, lower grille & open storage, 2 knobs, BC, FM, 8 tubes, AC **$65.00-75.00**

H-204A, table, 1948, plastic, upper front slanted slide rule dial, lower cloth grille with Oriental cut-outs, decorative case lines, 3 knobs, BC, FM, 6 tubes, AC/DC **$45.00-55.00**

H-210, portable, 1949, plastic, right front vertical slide rule dial, wrap-around horizontal louvers, handle, 2 knobs, BC, 5 tubes, AC/DC **$40.00-45.00**

H-211, portable, 1949, plastic, right front vertical slide rule dial, wrap-around horizontal louvers, handle, 2 knobs, BC, 5 tubes, AC/DC **$40.00-45.00**

H-214A, console-R/P, 1949, wood, upper front slide rule dial, center pull-out phono drawer, lower grille, right & left storage, 2 knobs, BC, 6 tubes, AC **$65.00-75.00**

H-204, table, 1948, plastic, upper front slanted slide rule dial, lower cloth grille with Oriental cut-outs, decorative case lines, 3 knobs, BC, FM, 6 tubes, AC/DC, $45.00-55.00.

H301T5, table, 1950, plastic, lower front slide rule dial, large upper grille area, 2 knobs, BC, 5 tubes, AC/DC **$35.00-40.00**

H-302P5, portable, 1950, leatherette, luggage-style, upper front slide rule dial, lower grille, handle, 2 knobs, BC, 5 tubes, AC/DC/battery **$35.00-40.00**

H303P4, portable, 1950, plastic, upper front slide rule dial, lower horizontal louvers, handle, 2 knobs, BC, 4 tubes, AC/DC/battery **$40.00-45.00**

H-307T7, table, 1950, brown plastic, lower front slide rule dial, upper horizontal louvers, 2 knobs, BC, FM, 7 tubes, AC/DC **$35.00-40.00**

H-308T7, table, 1950, ivory plastic, lower front slide rule dial, upper horizontal louvers, 2 knobs, BC, FM, 7 tubes, AC/DC..........**$35.00-40.00**

H-309P5, portable, 1950, plastic, upper front slide rule dial, lower horizontal louvers, handle, 2 knobs, BC, 5 tubes, AC/DC/battery **$35.00-40.00**

H-311T5, table, 1950, plastic, lower front slide rule dial, upper vertical wrap-over grille bars, 2 knobs, BC, 5 tubes, AC/DC **$35.00-40.00**

H-312P4, portable, 1950, plastic, upper front slide rule dial, lower contrasting grille, handle, 2 knobs, BC, 4 tubes, AC/DC/battery ..**$40.00-45.00**

H-315P4, portable, 1950, red plastic, upper front center slide rule dial, lower grille, leather handle, 2 knobs, BC, 4 tubes, AC/DC/battery, $45.00-50.00.

H-316C7, console-R/P, 1950, wood, inner left slide rule dial over large grille area, right pull-out phono drawer, double doors, 2 knobs, BC, FM, 7 tubes, AC **$50.00-65.00**

H318T5, table, 1950, plastic, slanted front design, right round dial over perforated grille, 2 knobs, BC, 5 tubes, AC/DC.............**$30.00-35.00**

H-321T5, table, 1950, plastic, lower front slide rule dial, upper cloth grille with geometric plastic cut-outs, 2 knobs, BC, 5 tubes, AC/DC **$40.00-50.00**

H-324T7U, table, 1950, plastic, lower front slide rule dial, upper horizontal louvers, 2 knobs, BC, FM, 7 tubes, AC/DC **$40.00-45.00**

H-331P4U, portable, 1952, green plastic, upper front slide rule dial, lower lattice grille, handle, 2 top thumbwheel knobs, BC, 4 tubes, AC/DC/battery **$40.00-45.00**

H-333P4U, portable, 1952, brown plastic, upper front slide rule dial, lower lattice grille, handle, 2 top thumbwheel knobs, BC, 4 tubes, AC/DC/battery **$40.00-45.00**

H-334T7UR, table, 1951, plastic, large center front curved dial overlaps grille area, 2 knobs, BC, 7 tubes, AC/DC **$40.00-45.00**

H-336T5U, table, 1951, plastic, slanted front design, right round dial over perforated grille, 2 knobs, BC, 5 tubes, AC/DC.............**$35.00-40.00**

H-338T5U, table, 1951, plastic, large right front round dial with inner pointer over woven grille, 2 knobs, BC, 5 tubes, AC/DC **$40.00-45.00**

H-341T5U, table, 1951, plastic, large right front round dial with inner pointer over woven grille, 2 knobs, BC, 5 tubes, AC/DC **$40.00-45.00**

H-343P5U, portable, 1951, plastic, large center front round dial with inner perforated grille, fold-back handle, 2 thumbwheel knobs, BC, 5 tubes, AC/DC/battery **$45.00-50.00**

H-350T7, table, 1951, brown plastic, large center front curved dial overlaps grille area, 2 knobs, BC, FM, 7 tubes, AC/DC **$40.00-45.00**

H-351T7, table, 1951, ivory plastic, large center front curved dial overlaps grille area, 2 knobs, BC, FM, 7 tubes, AC/DC **$40.00-45.00**

H-354C7, console-R/P, 1952, wood, upper front curved dial overlaps grille area, lower pull-out phono, right & left storage, 2 knobs, BC, FM, 7 tubes, AC **$75.00-85.00**

H-355T5, table-C, 1952, maroon plastic, right front thumbwheel dial, left alarm clock, center grille with horizontal divider, 6 knobs, BC, 5 tubes, AC **$40.00-45.00**

H-357C10, console-R/P, 1952, wood, inner left curved dial/lower grille, right pull-out phono, storage, double front doors, 3 knobs, BC, FM, 10 tubes, AC **$75.00-85.00**

H-357T5, table-C, 1952, brown plastic, right front thumbwheel dial, left alarm clock, center grille with horizontal divider, BC, AC **$40.00-45.00**

H-359T5, table, 1953, brown plastic, large center front half-round dial with inner textured grille, 2 knobs, BC, 5 tubes, AC/DC..........**$30.00-35.00**

H-360T5, table, 1953, ivory plastic, large center front half-round dial with inner textured grille, 2 knobs, BC, 5 tubes, AC/DC **$30.00-35.00**

H-361T6, table, 1952, plastic, large right front round dial with inner pointer over cloth grille, 2 knobs, BC, 6 tubes, AC/DC **$30.00-35.00**

H-365T5, table, 1952, brown plastic, right front round dial, left recessed "tic/tac/toe" grille, 2 knobs, BC, 5 tubes, AC/DC **$30.00-35.00**

H-366T5, table, 1952, ivory plastic, right front round dial, left recessed "tic/tac/toe" grille, 2 knobs, BC, 5 tubes, AC/DC **$30.00-35.00**

H-371T7, table, 1953, brown plastic, large center front round dial with inner pointer, 2 knobs, BC, FM, 7 tubes, AC/DC............**$30.00-35.00**

H-374T5, table-C, 1952, plastic, right front thumbwheel dial, left alarm clock, center lattice grille, 5 knobs, BC, 5 tubes, AC **$30.00-35.00**

H-378T5, table, 1953, plastic, large right front round dial overlaps lower horizontal bars, feet, 2 knobs, BC, 5 tubes, AC/DC **$20.00-25.00**

H-379T5, table, 1953, plastic, large right front round dial overlaps lower horizontal bars, feet, 2 knobs, BC, 5 tubes, AC/DC **$20.00-25.00**

H-380T5, table, 1953, plastic, large right front round dial overlaps lower horizontal bars, feet, 2 knobs, BC, 5 tubes, AC/DC **$20.00-25.00**

H-381T5, table, 1953, plastic, large right front round dial overlaps lower horizontal bars, feet, 2 knobs, BC, 5 tubes, AC/DC **$20.00-25.00**

H-382T5, table, 1953, brown plastic, right front half-round dial over horizontal bars, 2 knobs, BC, 5 tubes, AC/DC **$20.00-25.00**

H-345T5, table, 1951, plastic, large right front round dial with inner pointer over woven grille, slanted sides, 2 knobs, BC, 5 tubes, AC/DC, $40.00-45.00.

H-388T5, table-C, 1953, plastic, right front dial, left alarm clock, center "woven" panel, 4 knobs, BC, 5 tubes, AC **$30.00-35.00**

H-393T6, table, 1953, plastic, large center front half-round dial with inner textured grille, 2 knobs, BC, 6 tubes, AC/DC **$40.00-45.00**

H-397T5, table-C, 1954, maroon plastic, small tombstone style, center front slide rule dial, upper alarm clock, lower grille, 5 knobs, BC, 5 tubes, AC **$40.00-50.00**

H-398T5, table-C, 1954, ivory plastic, small tombstone-style, center front slide rule dial, upper alarm clock, lower grille, 5 knobs, BC, 5 tubes, AC **$40.00-50.00**

H-409P4, portable, 1954, plastic, upper front dial, large lower lattice grille with "W" logo, handle, optional AC supply, 2 knobs, BC, 4 tubes, battery **$40.00-45.00**

H-410P4, portable, 1954, plastic, upper front dial, large lower lattice grille with "W" logo, handle, optional AC supply, 2 knobs, BC, 4 tubes, battery **$40.00-45.00**

H-411P4, portable, 1954, plastic, upper front dial, large lower lattice grille with "W" logo, handle, optional AC supply, 2 knobs, BC, 4 tubes, battery **$40.00-45.00**

H-417T5, table, 1954, maroon plastic, center front round dial over large lattice grille, wire stand, 2 knobs, BC, 5 tubes, AC/DC ..**$40.00-45.00**

H-418T5, table, 1954, ivory plastic, center front round dial over large lattice grille, wire stand, 2 knobs, BC, 5 tubes, AC/DC **$40.00-45.00**

H-420T5, table-C, 1955, brown plastic, right front square dial, center grille with diamond perforations, left square clock, 3 knobs, BC, 5 tubes, AC **$40.00-45.00**

H-356T5, table-C, 1952, ivory plastic, right front thumbwheel dial, left alarm clock, center grille with horizontal divider, 6 knobs, BC, 5 tubes, AC, $40.00-45.00.

H-421T5, table-C, 1955, ivory plastic, right front square dial, center grille with diamond perforations, left square clock, 3 knobs, BC, 5 tubes, AC **$40.00-45.00**

H-422P4, portable, 1954, maroon plastic, upper front center slide rule dial, lower grille with horizontal louvers, fold-down plastic top handle, 2 thumbwheel knobs, BC, 4 tubes, AC/DC/battery **$40.00-45.00**

H-423P4, portable, 1954, coral plastic, upper front center slide rule dial, lower grille with horizontal louvers, fold-down plastic top handle, 2 thumbwheel knobs, BC, 4 tubes, AC/DC/battery **$40.00-45.00**

H-424P4, portable, 1954, beige plastic, upper front center slide rule dial, lower grille with horizontal louvers, fold-down plastic top handle, 2 thumbwheel knobs, BC, 4 tubes, AC/DC/battery **$35.00-40.00**

H-425P4, portable, 1954, black plastic, upper front center slide rule dial, lower grille with horizontal louvers, fold-down plastic top handle, 2 thumbwheel knobs, BC, 4 tubes, AC/DC/battery **$35.00-40.00**

H-434T5, table, 1955, black plastic, lower front raised slide rule dial, upper horizontal bars with center divider, twin speakers, 2 knobs, BC, 5 tubes, AC/DC..**$30.00-35.00**

H-435T5, table, 1955, ivory plastic, lower front raised slide rule dial, upper horizontal bars with center divider, twin speakers, 2 knobs, BC, 5 tubes, AC/DC..**$30.00-35.00**

H-436T5, table, 1955, maroon plastic, lower front raised slide rule dial, upper horizontal bars with center divider, 2 knobs, BC, 5 tubes, AC/DC **$45.00-50.00**

H-437T5, table, 1955, tan plastic, lower front raised slide rule dial, upper horizontal bars with center divider, 2 knobs, BC, 5 tubes, AC/DC **$30.00-35.00**

H-437T5A, table, 1955, tan plastic, lower front raised slide rule dial, upper horizontal bars with center divider, 2 knobs, BC, 5 tubes, AC/DC **$30.00-35.00**

H-438T5, table, 1955, green plastic, lower front raised slide rule dial, upper horizontal bars with center divider, 2 knobs, BC, 5 tubes, AC/DC **$45.00-50.00**

H-438T5A, table, 1955, green plastic, lower front raised slide rule dial, upper horizontal bars with center divider, 2 knobs, BC, 5 tubes, AC/DC **$30.00-35.00**

H-370T7, table, 1953, black plastic, large center front round dial with inner pointer, 2 knobs, BC, FM, 7 tubes, AC/DC, $30.00-35.00.

H-383T5, table, 1953, ivory plastic, right front half-round dial over horizontal bars, 2 knobs, BC, 5 tubes, AC/DC, $20.00-25.00.

H-440T5, table, 1955, gray plastic, lower front raised slide rule dial, upper horizontal bars with center divider, 2 knobs, BC, AC/DC ..**$30.00-35.00**

H-447T4, table, 1955, brown plastic, right front dial, lower horizontal grille bars, feet, 2 knobs, BC, 4 tubes, AC/DC.........................**$20.00-25.00**

H-448T4, table, 1955, gray plastic, right front dial, lower horizontal grille bars, feet, 2 knobs, BC, 4 tubes, AC/DC........................**$20.00-25.00**

H-449T4, table, 1955, aqua plastic, right front dial, lower horizontal grille bars, feet, 2 knobs, BC, 4 tubes, AC/DC........................**$20.00-25.00**

H-471T5, table-C, 1955, gray plastic, step-down top, right front dial over checkered grille area, left alarm clock, 4 knobs, BC, 5 tubes, AC **$35.00-40.00**

H-472T5, table-C, 1955, ivory plastic, step-down top, right front dial over checkered grille area, left alarm clock, 4 knobs, BC, 5 tubes, AC **$35.00-40.00**

H-473T5, table-C, 1955, rose plastic, step-down top, right front dial over checkered grille area, left alarm clock, 4 knobs, BC, 5 tubes, AC **$35.00-40.00**

H-482PR5, table-R/P, 1955, lower front slide rule dial, large upper grille with "W" logo, right side knob, handle, lift top, inner phono, BC, 5 tubes, AC **$30.00-35.00**

H-486T5, table-C, 1955, ivory plastic, lower front slide rule dial, large upper alarm clock face, metal bezel, 5 metal knobs, BC, 5 tubes, AC **$30.00-35.00**

H-487T5, table-C, 1955, maroon plastic, lower front slide rule dial, large upper alarm clock face, metal bezel, 5 metal knobs, BC, 5 tubes, AC **$40.00-45.00**

H-488T5, table-C, 1955, black plastic, lower front slide rule dial, large upper alarm clock face, metal bezel, 5 metal knobs, BC, 5 tubes, AC **$30.00-35.00**

H-435T5A, table, 1955, ivory plastic, lower front raised slide rule dial, upper horizontal bars with center divider, 2 knobs, BC, 5 tubes, AC/DC, $30.00-35.00.

H-489T5, table-C, 1955, gray plastic, lower front slide rule dial, large upper alarm clock face, metal bezel, 5 metal knobs, BC, 5 tubes, AC **$30.00-35.00**

H-499T5A, table, 1955, black plastic, right front dial over perforated grille, 2 knobs, BC, 5 tubes, AC/DC **$30.00-35.00**

H-500T5A, table, 1955, red plastic, right front dial over perforated grille, 2 knobs, BC, 5 tubes, AC/DC..**$40.00-45.00**

H-501T5A, table, 1955, brown plastic, right front dial over perforated grille, 2 knobs, BC, 5 tubes, AC/DC **$30.00-35.00**

H-502T5A, table, 1955, green plastic, right front dial over perforated grille, 2 knobs, BC, 5 tubes, AC/DC **$40.00-45.00**

H-536T6, table, 1956, plastic, lower front slide rule dial, upper horizontal grille bars, 2 knobs, BC, 6 tubes, AC/DC **$25.00-30.00**

H-537P4, portable, 1957, gray plastic, top dial, front metal perforated grille, handle, feet, BC, AC/DC/battery **$30.00-35.00**

H-538T4, table-C, 1955, black plastic, right front round dial over perforated grille, extended left front square clock, feet, 3 knobs, BC, 4 tubes, AC **$50.00-60.00**

H-539T4, table-C, 1955, ivory plastic, right front round dial over perforated grille, extended left front square clock, feet, 3 knobs, BC, 4 tubes, AC **$50.00-60.00**

H-540T4, table-C, 1955, red plastic, right front round dial over perforated grille, extended left front square clock, feet, 3 knobs, BC, 4 tubes, AC **$80.00-90.00**

H-558P4, portable, 1957, white & sand plastic, top dial, front metal grille, handle, feet, 2 thumbwheel knobs, BC, 4 tubes, AC/DC/battery **$30.00-35.00**

H-559P4, portable, 1957, gray & black plastic, top dial, front metal grille, handle, feet, 2 thumbwheel knobs, BC, 4 tubes, AC/DC/battery **$30.00-35.00**

H-474T5, table-C, 1955, light green plastic, step-down top, right front dial over checkered grille area, left alarm clock, 4 knobs, BC, 5 tubes, AC, $35.00-40.00.

H-562P4, portable, 1957, plastic, upper right front dial, lower perforated grille, side strap, 2 top thumbwheel knobs, BC, 4 tubes, battery **$20.00-25.00**

H-563P4A, portable, 1957, plastic, upper right front dial, lower perforated grille, side strap, 2 top thumbwheel knobs, BC, 4 tubes, battery **$25.00-30.00**

H-570T4, table-C, 1956, mocha plastic, right front dial, large left front clock face, feet, 4 knobs, BC, 4 tubes, AC **$25.00-30.00**

H-571T4, table-C, 1956, ivory plastic, right front dial, large left front clock face, feet, 4 knobs, BC, 4 tubes, AC **$25.00-30.00**

H-572T4, table-C, 1956, pink plastic, right front dial, large left front clock face, feet, 4 knobs, BC, 4 tubes, AC **$40.00-45.00**

H-574T4, table, 1956, black plastic, raised right front panel with round dial, left criss-cross grille, feet, 2 knobs, BC, 4 tubes, AC/DC ..**$25.00-30.00**

H-575T4, table, 1956, ivory plastic, raised right front panel with round dial, left criss-cross grille, feet, 2 knobs, BC, 4 tubes, AC/DC ..**$25.00-30.00**

H-576T4, table, 1956, pink plastic, raised right front panel with round dial, left criss-cross grille, feet, 2 knobs, BC, 4 tubes, AC/DC ..**$25.00-30.00**

H-577T4, table, 1956, red plastic, raised right front panel with round dial, left criss-cross grille, feet, 2 knobs, BC, 4 tubes, AC/DC ..**$25.00-30.00**

H-627, table, plastic, right front round dial over large grille area, BC **$20.00-25.00**

H-627T6U, table, 1951, plastic, lower front slide rule dial, upper cloth grille with geometric plastic cut-outs, 2 knobs, BC, AC/DC **$35.00-40.00**

H-632T5A, table, plastic, lower front slide rule dial, large upper grille area with horizontal & vertical bars, 2 knobs, BC, AC/DC......**$20.00-25.00**

H-636T6, table, 1958, ivory/white plastic, lower front slide rule dial, large upper grille area with horizontal & vertical bars, feet, 5 knobs, BC, 6 tubes, AC/DC..**$20.00-25.00**

H-638T6, table, 1958, charcoal/white plastic, lower front slide rule dial, large upper grille area with horizontal & vertical bars, feet, 5 knobs, BC, 6 tubes, AC/DC...**$20.00-25.00**

H-666P5, portable, 1959, upper right front round dial, lower lattice grille, telescope antenna, handle, BC, 5 tubes, AC/DC/battery..**$25.00-30.00**

H-677T4, table-C, 1959, champagne plastic, right side round dial, large front alarm clock, feet, 3 knobs, BC, 4 tubes, AC **$20.00-25.00**

H-678T4, table-C, 1959, coral plastic, right side round dial, large front alarm clock, feet, 3 knobs, BC, 4 tubes, AC **$20.00-25.00**

H-679T4, table-C, 1959, aqua plastic, right side round dial, large front alarm clock, feet, 3 knobs, BC, 4 tubes, AC **$20.00-25.00**

H-681T5, table, 1959, coral/white plastic, wedge-shaped case, lower right front round dial, horizontal bars, 2 knobs, BC, 5 tubes, AC/DC **$20.00-25.00**

H-682T5, table, 1959, aqua/white plastic, wedge-shaped case, lower right front round dial, horizontal bars, 2 knobs, BC, 5 tubes, AC/DC **$20.00-25.00**

H-683T5, table, 1959, charcoal/white plastic, wedge-shaped case, lower right front round dial, horizontal bars, 2 knobs, BC, 5 tubes, AC/DC **$20.00-25.00**

H-475T5, table-C, 1955, ivory plastic, lower front slide rule dial, upper alarm clock, metal bezel, 5 metal knobs, BC, 5 tubes, AC, $30.00-35.00.

H-704T5, table, 1960, chestnut brown/white plastic, wedge-shaped case, right front round dial, large left grille area with horizontal bars, twin speakers, 2 knobs, BC, 5 tubes, AC/DC **$20.00-25.00**

H-705T5, table, 1960, turquoise/white plastic, wedge-shaped case, right front round dial, large left grille area with horizontal bars, twin speakers, 2 knobs, BC, 5 tubes, AC/DC.................................**$20.00-25.00**

H-706T5, table, 1960, ivory/white plastic, wedge-shaped case, right front round dial, large left grille area with horizontal bars, twin speakers, 2 knobs, BC, 5 tubes, AC/DC...**$20.00-25.00**

H-743TA, table, 1956, shadow white plastic, raised right front panel with round dial, left criss-cross grille, feet, BC, 4 tubes, AC..**$30.00-35.00**

H-744TA, table, 1956, carnation pink plastic, raised right front panel with round dial, left criss-cross grille, feet, BC, 4 tubes, AC..**$30.00-35.00**

H-816L5, table-C, 1962, white plastic, right front dial, large left alarm clock area with oversize numerals, feet, 4 knobs, BC, 5 tubes, AC..**$20.00-25.00**

HR102BN, console-R/P, 1958, wood, inner right round dial, left phono, lift top, large front grille, 6 knobs, BC, FM, 11 tubes, AC **$40.00-50.00**

WR-5, console, 1930, walnut, upper front window dial, lower cloth grille with cut-outs, 3 knobs, BC, 9 tubes, AC **$120.00-140.00**

WR-7, console-R/P, 1930, walnut, lowboy, inner front window dial, lower cloth grille with cut-outs, double front doors, lift top, inner phono, 4 knobs, BC, 9 tubes, AC **$120.00-150.00**

WR-8 "Columaire," grandfather clock, 1931, wood, Deco, right side dial/knobs/switch, upper front clock face, top speaker, BC, 9 tubes, AC **$360.00-410.00**

WR-8-R "Columaire," grandfather clock, 1931, wood, Deco, right side dial/knobs/switch, upper front clock face, top speaker, remote control, BC, 9 tubes, AC **$420.00-480.00**

H-503T5A, table, 1955, light gray plastic, right front dial over plaid metal perforated grille, 2 knobs, BC, 5 tubes, AC/DC, $30.00-35.00.

WR-10A "Columette," tombstone, 1931, two-tone walnut, lower front window dial, upper 3-section cloth grille, 3 knobs, BC, 8 tubes, AC **$85.00-115.00**

WR-10-AH, console, 1931, wood, inner window dial, lower cloth grille with cut-outs, sliding doors, 3 knobs, BC, 8 tubes, AC **$120.00-150.00**

WR-10-AL, console, 1931, walnut, lower front window dial, upper 3-section cloth grille, 3 knobs, BC, 8 tubes, AC.................**$110.00-130.00**

WR-12 "Columaire Jr.," console, wood, grandfather clock-shaped cabinet without the clock face, Deco, center front window dial, top speaker, 3 knobs, BC, 8 tubes, AC **$260.00-300.00**

WR-12C "Columaire Jr.," grandfather clock, 1931, wood, Deco, center front window dial, upper clock face, top speaker, 3 knobs, BC, 8 tubes, AC **$360.00-410.00**

WR-12X3, table, 1941, wood, upper front slanted slide rule dial, lower horizontal louvers, 2 knobs, BC, 5 tubes, AC/DC **$35.00-40.00**

WR-12X4, table, 1941, wood, upper right front dial, left horizontal louvers, 5 pushbuttons, 2 knobs, BC, 5 tubes, AC/DC **$40.00-50.00**

WR-12X8, table, 1942, plastic, upper front slanted slide rule dial, lower horizontal grille bars, 2 knobs, BC, SW, 5 tubes, AC/DC **$40.00-45.00**

WR-12X10, table, 1942, plastic, upper front slanted slide rule dial, lower horizontal grille bars, 3 knobs, BC, 6 tubes, AC/DC **$40.00-45.00**

WR-12X12, table, 1942, plastic, upper front slanted slide rule dial, lower horizontal grille bars, 3 knobs, BC, SW, 6 tubes, AC/DC ..**$40.00-45.00**

WR-12X14, table, 1942, wood, upper front slanted slide rule dial, lower horizontal louvers, 6 pushbuttons, 3 knobs, BC, 6 tubes, AC/DC **$50.00-55.00**

WR-12X15, table, 1942, wood, right front slide rule dial, left horizontal louvers, 5 pushbuttons, 3 knobs, BC, SW, 6 tubes, AC/DC..**$50.00-55.00**

WR-12X16, table, 1941, wood, upper front slanted slide rule dial, lower horizontal louvers, 5 pushbuttons, 4 knobs, BC, SW, 8 tubes, AC/DC **$50.00-65.00**

WR-13, console-R/P, 1931, wood, lower front window dial, upper 3-section cloth grille, lift top, inner phono, 3 knobs, BC, 8 tubes, AC **$110.00-130.00**

H-557P4, portable, 1957, two-tone green plastic, top dial, front metal grille, feet, handle, 2 thumbwheel knobs, BC, 4 tubes, AC/DC/battery, $30.00-35.00.

Westinghouse

H-637T6, table, 1958, coral/white plastic, lower front slide rule dial, large upper grille area with horizontal & vertical bars, feet, 5 knobs, BC, 6 tubes, AC/DC, $20.00-25.00.

WR-14, cathedral, 1931, two-tone wood, lower front window dial, upper 3-section cloth grille, 3 knobs, BC, 4 tubes **$120.00-150.00**

WR-15, grandfather clock, 1931, wood, Deco, center front window dial, upper gold clock face, top speaker, 3 knobs, BC, 9 tubes, AC...**$360.00-410.00**

WR-20, table, 1934, wood, front dial, center cloth grille with cut-outs, decorative case lines, 2 knobs, BC, 4 tubes, AC/DC **$65.00-75.00**

WR-21, table, 1934, wood, front dial, center cloth grille with horizontal bars, 2 knobs, BC, SW, 5 tubes, AC **$65.00-75.00**

WR-22, tombstone, 1934, wood, center front window dial, upper cloth grille with Deco cut-outs, 3 knobs, BC, SW, 5 tubes, AC **$110.00-130.00**

WR-23, tombstone, 1934, wood, lower front quarter-round dial, upper vertical grille bars, 4 knobs, BC, SW, 7 tubes, AC **$140.00-160.00**

WR-24, console, 1934, wood, upper front quarter-round dial, lower cloth grille with 3 vertical bars, 4 knobs, BC, SW, 7 tubes, AC..........**$110.00-130.00**

WR-27, table, 1934, wood, front dial, center cloth grille with cut-outs, 2 knobs, BC, 4 tubes, AC **$75.00-85.00**

WR-28, tombstone, 1934, wood, center front round dial, upper cloth grille with cut-outs, 4 knobs, BC, SW, 6 tubes, AC **$120.00-150.00**

WR-29, console, 1934, wood, upper front round dial, lower cloth grille with cut-outs, 4 knobs, BC, SW, 6 tubes, AC **$110.00-130.00**

WR-30, console, 1934, wood, upper front quarter-round dial, lower cloth grille with cut-outs, decorative medallions, 4 knobs, BC, SW, 10 tubes, AC **$140.00-160.00**

WR-42X1, table-R/P, 1941, wood, right front dial, left grille area, lift top, inner phono, 3 knobs, BC, 5 tubes, AC **$30.00-35.00**

WR-42X7, console-R/P, 1942, walnut, upper front slanted dial, center pull-out phono drawer, lower grille, 4 knobs, BC, SW, 7 tubes including ballast, AC **$85.00-95.00**

WR-62K1 "Carryette," portable, 1941, striped cloth covered, right front dial, left grille, handle, 3 knobs, BC, 6 tubes, AC/DC/battery **$30.00-35.00**

H-715T5, table, 1960, ivory/white plastic, FM only, wedge-shaped case, right front round dial, large left grille area with horizontal bars, twin speakers, 1 front & 1 side knob, FM, 5 tubes, AC, $20.00-25.00.

WR-62K2 "Carryette," portable, 1941, leatherette, inner right dial, left grille, fold-down front, handle, 3 knobs, BC, 6 tubes, AC/DC/battery **$30.00-35.00**

WR-100, tombstone, 1935, wood, lower front round dial, upper cloth grille with cut-outs, 2 knobs, BC, 5 tubes, AC...........**$120.00-150.00**

WR-101, table, 1935, wood, lower front dial, upper cloth grille with cut-outs, 4 knobs, BC, SW, 6 tubes, AC/DC **$75.00-85.00**

WR-102, table, 1936, wood, right front dial, left cloth grille, 3 knobs, BC, 5 tubes, AC/DC **$45.00-50.00**

WR-103, table, 1936, wood, right front oval dial, left 3-section cloth grille, 3 knobs, BC, 6 tubes, AC/DC **$50.00-65.00**

WR-120, table, 1937, plastic, right front dial, left grille area, 3 knobs, BC, SW, 6 tubes, AC/DC **$50.00-55.00**

WR-152, table, 1939, wood, right front dial, left cloth grille with center horizontal bars, 2 knobs, BC, 6 tubes, AC/DC **$50.00-55.00**

WR-154, table, 1939, wood, right front dial, left wrap-around cloth grille with horizontal bars, BC, 6 tubes including ballast, AC/DC **$50.00-65.00**

WR-162, table, 1939, wood, right front slide rule dial, left wrap-around cloth grille with horizontal bars, tuning eye, 4 knobs, BC, SW, 8 tubes, AC/DC...**$65.00-75.00**

WR-165M, table, 1939, wood, right front round dial, left horizontal wrap-around louvers, BC, 5 tubes, AC **$45.00-55.00**

WR-166A, table, 1939, plastic, right front round dial, left & right horizontal wrap-around bars, 2 knobs, BC, 5 tubes, AC/DC **$45.00-55.00**

H-742TA, table, 1956, aqua plastic, raised right front panel with round dial, left criss-cross grille, feet, BC, 4 tubes, AC $30.00-35.00.

WR-168, table, 1939, wood, right front slide rule dial, left cloth grille with 2 horizontal bars, 2 knobs, BC, 5 tubes, AC/DC **$50.00-65.00**

WR-169, table, 1939, wood, right front slide rule dial, left cloth grille with vertical bars, 5 pushbuttons, 2 knobs, BC, 5 tubes, AC/DC **$65.00-75.00**

WR-170, table, 1939, two-tone walnut, right front slide rule dial, left wrap-around cloth grille with horizontal bars, 6 pushbuttons, 2 knobs, BC, SW, 5 tubes, AC/DC **$75.00-85.00**

WR-172, table, 1939, wood, right front slide rule dial, left wrap-around cloth grille with horizontal metal bars, pushbuttons, 4 knobs, BC, SW, 6 tubes, AC/DC **$75.00-85.00**

WR-182, table, 1940, two-tone walnut, right front dial, left grille area, 3 knobs, BC, SW, 5 tubes, AC/DC **$50.00-65.00**

WR-186, table, 1941, two-tone wood, right front slide rule dial, left vertical grille bars, 6 pushbuttons, 4 knobs, BC, SW, 5 tubes, AC/DC **$75.00-85.00**

WR-201, tombstone, 1935, wood, lower front round dial, upper cloth grille with cut-outs, BC, SW, 5 tubes, AC **$85.00-105.00**

WR-203, tombstone, 1935, wood, lower front round dial, upper cloth grille with cut-outs, 4 knobs, BC, SW, 6 tubes, AC....**$120.00-150.00**

WR-204, tombstone, 1935, wood, lower front round dial, upper cloth grille with cut-outs, 4 knobs, BC, SW, 7 tubes, AC....**$120.00-150.00**

WR-205, tombstone, 1935, wood, lower front round dial, upper cloth grille with cut-outs, 4 knobs, BC, SW, 8 tubes, AC....**$120.00-150.00**

WR-207 "Trumpter," table, 1935, wood, front off-center round black & white dial, left grille area, 4 knobs, BC, SW, 5 tubes, AC ..**$40.00-50.00**

WR-208 "Jubileer," table, 1935, wood, front off-center round black & white dial, left grille area, 4 knobs, BC, SW, 5 tubes, AC **$45.00-55.00**

WR-210, table, 1936, wood, right front oval dial, left cloth grille with center horizontal bar, 3 knobs, BC, SW, 5 tubes, AC **$50.00-65.00**

WR-211, table, 1936, wood, right front oval dial, left cloth horseshoe-shaped grille with center horizontal bar, 4 knobs, BC, SW, 6 tubes, AC **$55.00-65.00**

WR-212, table, 1936, wood, right front round dial, left cloth grille with vertical bars, tuning eye, 4 knobs, BC, SW, 8 tubes, AC......**$75.00-85.00**

WR-214, tombstone, 1936, wood, lower front oval dial, upper cloth grille with cut-outs and center tuning eye, 4 knobs, BC, SW, 10 tubes, AC **$150.00-180.00**

WR-217, table, 1937, wood, right front oval dial, left cloth horseshoe-shaped grille with cut-outs, BC, SW, 5 tubes, AC..........**$55.00-65.00**

WR-222, table, 1937, wood, large right front dial, left cloth grille with cut-outs, 4 knobs, BC, SW, 5 tubes, AC **$40.00-50.00**

WR-224, table, 1937, wood, large right front dial, left cloth grille with horizontal bars, 4 knobs, BC, SW, 5 tubes, AC....................**$40.00-50.00**

WR-228, table, 1937, walnut, right front dial, left wrap-around grille with vertical bars, tuning eye, 4 knobs, BC, SW, 8 tubes, AC..**$50.00-65.00**

WR-256, table, 1939, wood, right front dial, left wrap-around cloth grille with horizontal bars, 2 knobs, BC, 5 tubes, AC.............**$45.00-55.00**

WR-262, table, 1939, wood, right front slide rule dial, left wrap-around cloth grille with horizontal bars, tuning eye, pushbuttons, 4 knobs, BC, SW, 6 tubes, AC **$65.00-75.00**

WR-264, table, 1939, wood, lower front slide rule dial, upper cloth grille with vertical bars, tuning eye, pushbuttons, BC, SW, 7 tubes, AC **$65.00-75.00**

H-875LN6, table-C, wood/charcoal plastic, right vertical dial, left alarm clock, center grille with horizontal bars, feet, band switch, 4 knobs, BC, FM, 6 tubes, AC, $30.00-35.00.

WR-270, table, 1939, wood, right front slide rule dial, left wrap-around cloth grille with horizontal bars, 6 pushbuttons, 2 knobs, BC, 5 tubes, AC **$65.00-75.00**

WR-274, table, 1939, wood, right front slide rule dial, left wrap-around horizontal grille bars, tuning eye, pushbuttons, 4 knobs, BC, SW, 7 tubes, AC **$75.00-85.00**

WR-288, table, 1940, wood, right front slide rule dial, left horizontal grille bars, 5 pushbuttons, 4 knobs, BC, SW, 6 tubes, AC **$65.00-75.00**

WR-290, table, 1941, wood, upper front slanted slide rule dial, lower grille area, 6 pushbuttons, 4 knobs, BC, SW, 8 tubes, AC **$50.00-65.00**

WR-303, console, 1935, wood, upper front round dial, lower cloth grille with cut-outs, 4 knobs, BC, SW, 6 tubes, AC **$110.00-130.00**

WR-304, console, 1935, wood, upper front round dial, lower cloth grille with cut-outs, 4 knobs, BC, SW, 7 tubes, AC **$110.00-130.00**

WR-305, console, 1935, wood, upper front round dial, lower cloth grille with cut-outs, 4 knobs, BC, SW, 8 tubes, AC **$120.00-140.00**

WR-306, console, 1935, wood, upper front round dial, lower cloth grille with cut-outs, 4 knobs, BC, SW, 10 tubes, AC **$120.00-140.00**

WR-311, console, 1936, wood, upper front round dial, lower cloth grille with center vertical bars, 4 knobs, BC, SW, 6 tubes, AC **$110.00-130.00**

WR-312, console, 1936, wood, upper front round dial, lower cloth grille with vertical bars & cut-outs, tuning eye, 4 knobs, BC, SW, 8 tubes, AC **$120.00-140.00**

WR-314, console, 1936, wood, upper front oval dial, lower cloth grille with 2 vertical bars, tuning eye, 4 knobs, BC, SW, 10 tubes, AC **$120.00-140.00**

RC (RA/DA), table, 1922, wood, 2 boxes-receiver & amp, black front panels, 1 dial, lift top, 5 knobs, BC, 3 tubes, battery, $300.00-350.00.

WR-315, console, 1936, wood, upper front oval dial, lower cloth grille with center vertical divider, tuning eye, 5 knobs, BC, SW, 12 tubes, AC **$140.00-170.00**

WR-316, console, 1936, wood, upper front round dial, lower cloth grille with vertical bars & cut-outs, BC, SW, LW, 7 tubes including ballast, AC/DC...**$110.00-130.00**

WR-326, console, 1937, walnut, upper front dial, lower cloth grille with center vertical bar, tuning eye, 4 knobs, BC, SW, 7 tubes, AC...**$120.00-140.00**

WR-328, console, 1937, wood, upper front dial, lower cloth grille with 2 vertical bars, tuning eye, 4 knobs, BC, SW, 8 tubes, AC **$120.00-140.00**

WR-334, console, 1937, wood, upper front half-round dial, lower cloth grille with center vertical bar, 5 knobs, BC, SW, 12 tubes, AC...**$140.00-160.00**

WR-336, console, 1937, wood, upper front half-round dial with automatic tuning, lower cloth grille with center vertical bar, 5 knobs, BC, SW, 12 tubes, AC **$140.00-160.00**

WR-338, chairside, 1939, wood, slanted front dial, lower grille area, tuning eye, 4 knobs, BC, SW, 7 tubes, AC **$140.00-170.00**

WR-342, console, 1939, wood, upper front half-round dial with automatic tuning, lower cloth grille with center vertical bars, tuning eye, 5 knobs, BC, SW, 8 tubes, AC **$130.00-150.00**

WR-6, console, 1930, wood, lowboy, inner front window dial w/repwood escutcheon, lower repwood grille, double front doors, 3 knobs, BC, 9 tubes, AC, $120.00-150.00.

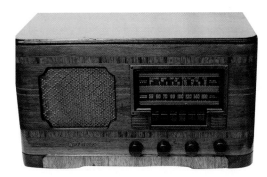

WR-12X7, table, 1941, wood, right front slide rule dial, left cloth grille, 6 pushbuttons, 4 knobs, BC, SW, 5 tubes, AC/DC, $50.00-65.00.

WR-366, console, 1939, wood, upper front slide rule dial, lower cloth grille with vertical bars, tuning eye, pushbuttons, 4 knobs, BC, SW, 8 tubes, AC **$120.00-140.00**

WR-370, console, 1939, wood, upper front slide rule dial, lower cloth grille with splayed bars, tuning eye, pushbuttons, 4 knobs, BC, SW, 12 tubes, AC **$120.00-150.00**

WR-372, console, 1939, wood, upper front slide rule dial, lower cloth grille with vertical bars, 6 pushbuttons, 4 knobs, BC, SW, 6 tubes, AC **$110.00-130.00**

WR-373, console, 1939, wood, upper front slide rule dial, lower cloth grille with center vertical bars, tuning eye, pushbuttons, 4 knobs, BC, SW, 7 tubes, AC **$110.00-130.00**

WR-373-Y, console, 1939, wood, upper front slide rule dial, lower cloth grille with center vertical bars, tuning eye, pushbuttons, 4 knobs, BC, SW, 7 tubes, AC/DC **$110.00-130.00**

WR-374, console, 1939, wood, upper front slide rule dial, lower cloth grille with center vertical bars, pushbuttons, 4 knobs, BC, SW, 8 tubes, AC **$120.00-140.00**

WR-388, console, 1940, wood, upper front slide rule dial, lower cloth grille with bars, 6 pushbuttons, 4 knobs, BC, SW, 9 tubes, AC **$110.00-130.00**

WR-468, table-R/P, 1939, two-tone wood, right front dial, left cloth grille with horizontal bars, lift top, inner phono, 2 knobs, BC, 5 tubes, AC **$35.00-40.00**

WR-470, table-R/P, 1939, wood, right front slide rule dial, left wrap-around cloth grille with horizontal bars, pushbuttons, lift top, inner phono, 3 knobs, BC, 5 tubes, AC **$40.00-45.00**

WR-472, table-R/P, 1939, wood, left front dial, right cloth grille with horizontal bars, lift top, inner phono, 3 knobs, BC, 5 tubes, AC **$40.00-45.00**

WR-473, console-R/P, 1939, wood, inner right dial, left phono, lift top, front cloth grille with center vertical bars, 4 knobs, BC, SW, 7 tubes, AC **$65.00-75.00**

WR-258, table, 1938, wood, lower front slide rule dial, upper cloth grille with horizontal bars, 6 pushbuttons, 2 knobs, BC, 5 tubes, AC, $50.00-65.00.

WR-474, console-R/P, 1939, wood, inner right dial, left phono, lift top, front cloth grille with 4 vertical bars, 4 knobs, BC, SW, 8 tubes, AC **$65.00-75.00**

WR-478, table-R/P, 1948, two-tone wood, right front dial, left grille, lift top, inner phono, 3 knobs, BC, 5 tubes, AC **$35.00-40.00**

WR-480, table-R/P, 1940, wood, right front slide rule dial, left cloth grille with center horizontal bars, pushbuttons, lift top, inner phono, 3 knobs, BC, 5 tubes, AC **$40.00-45.00**

WR-602, tombstone, 1935, wood, center front round dial, upper cloth grille with cut-outs, BC, SW **$85.00-95.00**

WR-603, tombstone, 1936, wood, lower front round dial, upper 3-section cloth grille, 4 knobs, BC, 4 tubes, battery **$85.00-95.00**

WR-605, tombstone, 1936, wood, center front round dial, upper 3-section cloth grille, 4 knobs, BC, SW, 6 tubes, battery.......**$85.00-95.00**

WR-606, console, 1936, wood, upper front round dial, lower cloth grille with center vertical bars, 4 knobs, BC, SW, 4 tubes, battery **$65.00-75.00**

WR-608, console, 1936, wood, upper front round dial, lower cloth grille with center vertical bars, 4 knobs, BC, SW, 6 tubes, battery **$65.00-75.00**

WR-675 "Carryette," portable, 1939, cloth covered, right front slide rule dial, left grille area, handle, 2 knobs, BC, 4 tubes, battery **$35.00-40.00**

WR-675A "Carryette," portable, 1939, cloth covered, right front slide rule dial, left grille area, handle, 2 knobs, BC, 4 tubes, battery..**$35.00-40.00**

WR-678 "Carryette," portable, 1940, brown & white cloth covered, upper front dial, lower grille area, handle, 2 knobs, BC, 5 tubes, AC/DC/battery **$35.00-40.00**

WR-679 "Carryette," portable, 1940, two-tone leatherette, upper front dial, lower grille area, handle, 2 knobs, BC, 5 tubes, AC/DC/battery **$35.00-40.00**

WR-209, table, 1936, wood, right front oval dial, left cloth grille with horizontal bars, 3 knobs, BC, SW, 5 tubes, AC, $50.00-65.00.

WR-272, table, 1939, wood, right front slide rule dial, left wrap-around cloth grille with horizontal metal bars, pushbuttons, 4 knobs, BC, SW, 6 tubes, AC, $75.00-85.00.

WR-682, portable, 1941, inner horizontal chrome bars, right window dial, left cloth grille, flip-open front, BC, 4 tubes, battery **$55.00-65.00**

WR-368, console, 1938, wood, upper front slide rule dial, lower cloth grille with vertical bars, tuning eye, pushbuttons, 4 knobs, BC, SW, 10 tubes, AC, $120.00-150.00.

WILCOX-GAY
Wilcox-Gay Corp.
Charlotte, Michigan

5A6-75, tombstone, 1935, wood, center front round airplane dial, upper cloth grille with cut-outs, 4 knobs, BC, 6 tubes, battery..**$85.00-95.00**
A-17, table, 1936, circular case with ebony finish, Deco, center front dial, decorative vertical bars, feet, 4 knobs, BC, SW, AC/DC .....**$550.00+**
A-32, table, 1937, two-tone wood, upper front slide rule dial, center automatic tuning, right & left grille areas, AC **$65.00-75.00**
A-37, console, 1937, wood, upper front slide rule dial & telephone dial, lower cloth grille, 5 knobs, BC, SW, 6 tubes, AC **$150.00-170.00**
A-50, table, 1938, wood, sloping front panel, center dial, upper grille with horizontal louvers, 3 knobs, BC, 5 tubes, AC/DC **$50.00-60.00**
A-51, table, 1938, plastic, right front dial, left round cloth grille with wrap-around horizontal bars, 2 knobs, BC, 4 tubes, AC/DC ..**$55.00-65.00**
A-52, table, 1938, walnut, right front slide rule dial, left cloth grille with Deco cut-outs, 3 knobs, BC, 5 tubes, AC **$55.00-65.00**
A-53 "Thin Man," table, 1939, plastic, thin case can stand, lie or hang, front dial, cloth grille with bars, decorative case lines, 2 knobs, BC, 5 tubes, AC/DC **$65.00-75.00**
A-54, table, 1939, walnut, right front slide rule dial, left wrap-around louvers, pushbuttons, 5 knobs, BC, SW, 7 tubes, AC **$65.00-75.00**
A-55, console, 1939, walnut, upper front slide rule dial, lower horizontal grille bars, pushbuttons, 5 knobs, BC, SW, 7 tubes, AC **$110.00-130.00**
A-58, table, 1940, wood, right front slide rule dial, left cloth grille with cut-outs, 4 tubes **$50.00-65.00**
A-69, console-R/P, 1939, walnut, inner dial/phono, lift top, front grille, lower record storage, BC, 5 tubes, AC **$150.00-180.00**
A-111, console-R/P, 1941, wood, inner left slide rule dial, lower storage, right grille with horizontal bars, lift top, inner phono, BC, FM, 9 tubes, AC **$120.00-150.00**
TXF-67, console-R/P, 1940, wood, inner right dial, left phono, lift top, lower front grille area, BC, SW, AC **$130.00-160.00**

WILMAK
Wilmak Corp.
RR 3, Benton Harbor, Michigan

W-446 "Denchum," table, 1947, wood, top plastic handle with built-in thumbwheel dials, side louvers, BC, AC/DC **$75.00-85.00**

540, table, two-tone wood, right front dial, center cloth grille with slanted cut-outs, base, 2 knobs, BC, AC/DC, $75.00-85.00.

01006, table, 1938, wood, large right front dial, left cloth grille with Deco cut-outs, 6 pushbuttons, 3 knobs, BC, SW, 5 tubes, AC/DC..**$75.00-85.00**
Cigarette Pack, table-N, looks like a pack of Wings cigarettes, 16" high, dial and knobs are located either on the front or the right side **$580.00-690.00**

WOOLAROC
Phillips Petroleum Co.
Bartlesville, Oklahoma

3-2A, table, 1946, plastic, streamline, upper front slanted slide rule dial, lower horizontal louvers wrap around left side, 3 knobs, BC, 6 tubes, AC/DC **$50.00-65.00**
3-3A, table, 1946, wood, upper front slanted slide rule dial, lower cloth grille, 4 knobs, BC, SW, 7 tubes, AC **$40.00-50.00**
3-5A, table, 1947, two-tone plastic, right front square dial, left horizontal grille bars, handle, 2 knobs, BC, 5 tubes, AC/DC **$65.00-75.00**
3-6A/5, table, 1947, wood, upper front slanted slide rule dial, large lower cloth grille, 2 knobs, BC, 5 tubes, AC/DC **$40.00-45.00**
3-9A, table, 1946, ivory plastic, upper front slide rule dial, lower criss-cross grille, feet, 2 knobs, BC, 5 tubes, AC/DC.............**$50.00-55.00**
3-10A, table, 1946, plastic, upper front slide rule dial, lower criss-cross grille, feet, 2 knobs, BC, 5 tubes, AC/DC **$45.00-50.00**
3-11A, table, 1946, wood, upper front slanted slide rule dial, lower criss-cross grille, 4 knobs, BC, SW, 6 tubes, AC **$40.00-45.00**
3-12A/3, portable, 1947, leatherette, upper front slanted slide rule dial, lower metal grille, handle, 2 knobs, BC, 6 tubes, AC/DC/battery **$30.00-35.00**
3-15A, table, 1948, metal, right front dial, left graduated horizontal louvers, 2 knobs, BC, 4 tubes, AC/DC **$65.00-75.00**
3-17A, table, 1948, plastic, upper front slide rule dial, lower horizontal louvers, 2 knobs, BC, 5 tubes, AC/DC **$45.00-50.00**

3-1A, table, 1946, plastic, streamline, upper front slanted slide rule dial, lower horizontal louvers wrap around left side, 3 knobs, BC, 6 tubes, AC/DC, $50.00-65.00.

3-20A, table-R/P, 1947, wood, upper front slanted slide rule dial, lower horizontal louvers, lift top, inner phono, 4 knobs, BC, 5 tubes, AC **$40.00-45.00**
3-29A, table-R/P, 1946, wood, top right vertical slide rule dial, right front grille, left lift top, inner phono, 3 knobs, BC, 5 tubes, AC ..**$30.00-35.00**
3-70A, console-R/P, 1948, wood, inner right slide rule dial, door, left pull out phono drawer, lower front grille, 4 knobs, BC, SW, 7 tubes, AC **$65.00-75.00**
3-71A, console-R/P, 1948, wood, inner right slide rule dial, door, left pull-out phono drawer, lower front grille, 4 knobs, BC, FM, 7 tubes, AC **$65.00-75.00**

WORKRITE
The Workrite Manufacturing Co.
1806 East 30th Street, Cleveland, Ohio

17, table, 1927, two-tone wood, low rectangular case, slanted front panel with center window dial, 2 knobs, BC, 6 tubes, battery..**$85.00-105.00**
18, table, 1928, two-tone wood, low rectangular case, slanted front panel with center window dial, 2 knobs, BC, 7 tubes, AC ..**$110.00-130.00**
38, table, 1928, wood, rectangular case, center front window dial with escutcheon, 2 knobs, 9 tubes, AC.............................**$120.00-150.00**
Air Master, table, 1924, wood, high rectangular case, slanted 3 dial front panel, 5 knobs, BC, 5 tubes, battery **$120.00-150.00**
Aristocrat, console, 1924, mahogany, inner slanted 3 dial panel, fold-down front, inner left speaker, inner right storage, 5 knobs, BC, 5 tubes, battery...**$240.00-280.00**
Chum, table, 1924, wood, high rectangular case, slanted 2 dial front panel, 3 knobs, BC, 3 exposed tubes, battery **$240.00-280.00**
Radio King, table, 1924, mahogany, tall case, lower front slanted 3 dial panel, upper enclosed speaker with grille cut-outs, 5 knobs, BC, 5 tubes, battery...**$240.00-270.00**

WURLITZER LYRIC
Rudolph Wurlitzer Mfg. Co.
North Tonawanda, New York

408, console, 1935, two-tone wood, upper front window dial, lower cloth grille with cut-outs, feet, BC, SW................................**$110.00-130.00**
470-B, tombstone, 1935, wood, center front round dial, upper cloth grille with cut-outs, vertical fluting, 4 knobs, BC, SW, 7 tubes, AC **$120.00-150.00**
470-W, console, 1935, wood, upper front round dial, lower cloth grille with cut-outs, vertical fluting, 4 knobs, BC, SW, 7 tubes, AC **$110.00-130.00**
C-4-LI, table, 1934, wood, right front dial, center grille with horizontal louvers, 2 band, 2 knobs, BC, 4 tubes, AC/DC **$55.00-65.00**
M-4-L, table, 1934, wood, right front dial, left horizontal wrap-around louvers, 2 band, 2 knobs, BC, 4 tubes, AC/DC **$55.00-65.00**
M-4-LI, table, 1934, two-tone wood, right front dial, left horizontal wrap-around louvers, 2 band, 2 knobs, BC, 4 tubes, AC/DC **$65.00-75.00**
SA-5-L, tombstone, 1934, wood, shouldered, center front window dial, upper cloth grille with cut-outs, 3 knobs, BC, 5 tubes, AC **$120.00-150.00**
SA-46, console, 1934, wood, lowboy, upper front window dial, lower cloth grille with cut-outs, BC, 4 tubes **$110.00-130.00**
SA-99, console, 1934, wood, lowboy, upper front window dial, lower cloth grille with cut-outs, 6 legs, 4 knobs, BC, 9 tubes, AC ..**$120.00-150.00**
SA-120, console, 1934, wood, lowboy, upper front half-round dial, lower cloth grille with cut-outs, 6 legs, 4 knobs, BC, 12 tubes, AC **$140.00-170.00**
SA-133, console, 1934, wood, upper front quarter-round dial, lower cloth grille with cut-outs, 3 knobs, BC, 13 tubes, AC..........**$160.00-190.00**
SU-5 "Duncan Phyfe," side table, 1934, wood, Duncan Phyfe style, inner dial, fold-down front, 2 knobs, BC, SW, 5 tubes, AC/DC **$120.00-150.00**
SU-5 "Queen Ann," side table, 1934, wood, Queen Ann style, inner dial, fold-down front, 2 knobs, BC, SW, 5 tubes, AC/DC ..**$120.00-150.00**
SW-88, tombstone, 1934, two-tone wood, step-down top, center front window dial, upper horizontal grille bars, 4 knobs, BC, SW, 8 tubes, AC **$120.00-150.00**
SW-89, console, 1934, wood, upper front window dial, lower cloth grille with cut-outs, 6 legs, 4 knobs, BC, SW, 8 tubes, AC ..**$120.00-140.00**

ZANEY-GILL
Zaney-Gill Corp.
Los Angeles, California

Clarion, cathedral, 1930, mahogany, lower front dial with ornate bronze-finished escutcheon, upper round grille, BC, AC........**$240.00-300.00**
Legionair, cathedral, 1930, mahogany, peaked top, Deco, center front dial, upper grille with "sun-burst" cut-outs, BC, AC ..**$300.00-320.00**

2445 "Music Box," cathedral, 1930, wood, center front window dial, upper cloth grille with cut-outs, small fluted columns, 2 knobs, BC, 6 tubes, AC, $240.00-300.00.

ZENITH
Zenith Radio Corporation
Chicago, Illinois

The Zenith company began as Chicago Radio Labs in 1918 and the name "Zenith" came from the station call letters of its founders — 9ZN. Commander Eugene McDonald built Zenith into one of the most successful and prolific of radio manufacturers. Some of the most sought after Zenith sets today are the black dial sets of the 1930s. The Zenith "Stratospheres" are some of the highest value collector sets. Zenith model numbers were often stamped on sets and tended to fade. Because of this fact, chassis numbers of some models are also included as an aid in determining the specific model.

4-B-131, tombstone, 1936, walnut, lower front round dial, upper cloth grille with cut-outs, decorative fluting, 3 knobs, BC, 4 tubes, 6VDC, $120.00-150.00.

3-R, table, 1923, wood, low rectangular case with slanted front panel, large center tuning dial with multiple other adjustment dials, 9 knobs, BC, 4 tubes, battery **$580.00-690.00**

4-B-132, table, 1936, wood, cube-shaped, step-down sides, front round dial, top grille, 3 knobs, BC, 4 tubes, 6VDC **$85.00-115.00**

4-B-231, table, 1937, wood, lower front black dial, upper cloth grille with vertical bars, 2 knobs, BC, 4 tubes, 6VDC **$55.00-65.00**

4-B-313, table, 1939, plastic, right front dial, rounded left with horizontal wrap-around grille bars, 2 knobs, BC, 4 tubes, 6VDC....**$65.00-85.00**

4-B-314, table, 1939, plastic, right front dial, rounded left with horizontal wrap-around grille bars, 5 pushbuttons, 2 knobs, BC, 4 tubes, 6VDC **$65.00-85.00**

4-B-317, table, 1939, wood, right front dial, rounded left wrap-around grille with vertical glass bars, pushbuttons, 2 knobs, BC, 4 tubes, 6VDC **$140.00-160.00**

4-B-355, console, 1939, wood, upper front slanted dial, lower cloth grille with vertical bars, 2 knobs, BC, 4 tubes, 6VDC..............**$85.00-95.00**

4-B-422, table, 1940, plastic, right front dial, rounded left with horizontal wrap-around grille bars, 2 knobs, BC, 4 tubes, 6VDC....**$65.00-85.00**

4-B-437, table, 1940, walnut, right front dial, left wrap-around grille with horizontal bars, 2 knobs, BC, 4 tubes, 6VDC **$40.00-50.00**

4-B-466, console, 1940, wood, upper front dial, lower cloth grille with vertical bars, 2 knobs, BC, 4 tubes, 6VDC **$75.00-85.00**

4-J-40, portable, plastic, top dial & on/off/volume knobs, front round perforated grille area with center crest, handle, BC, AC/battery, $40.00-45.00.

4-B-515, table, 1941, plastic, right front dial, rounded/raised left with horizontal wrap-around louvers, 2 knobs, BC, 4 tubes, 6VDC **$110.00-130.00**

4-B-535, table, 1941, walnut, right front dial, left wrap- around grille with horizontal bars, 2 knobs, BC, 4 tubes, 6VDC **$40.00-50.00**

4-B-536, table, 1941, wood, right front dial, left cloth grille with cut-outs, 2 knobs, BC, 4 tubes, 6VDC **$45.00-55.00**

4-B-639, table, 1942, wood, right front black dial, left cloth grille with crossed bars, 2 knobs, BC, 4 tubes, 6VDC **$45.00-50.00**

4-F-227, table, 1937, wood, lower front black dial, upper cloth grille with vertical bars, 2 knobs, BC, 4 tubes, battery **$55.00-65.00**

4-G-800, portable, 1948, plastic, inner left dial, large lattice grille area, flip-up front, handle, 2 recessed knobs, BC, 4 tubes, AC/DC/battery **$40.00-45.00**

4-G-800Z, portable, 1948, plastic, inner left dial, large lattice grille area, flip-up front, handle, 2 recessed knobs, BC, 4 tubes, AC/DC/battery **$40.00-45.00**

4-G-903, portable, 1949, plastic, flip-over dial, inner checkered grille area, handle, 2 knobs, BC, 4 tubes, AC/DC/battery **$30.00-35.00**

4-G-903Y, portable, 1949, plastic, flip-over dial, inner checkered grille area, handle, 2 knobs, BC, 4 tubes, AC/DC/battery **$30.00-35.00**

4-K-016, table, 1946, plastic, front inverted V-shaped dial & louvers, handle, 2 knobs, BC, 4 tubes, battery **$45.00-50.00**

4-K-035, table, 1946, walnut veneer, right front black dial, left cloth grille with horizontal bars, 2 knobs, BC, 4 tubes, battery........**$50.00-55.00**

4-K-035G, table, 1946, limed walnut, right front black dial, left cloth grille with horizontal bars, 2 knobs, BC, 4 tubes, battery........**$50.00-55.00**

4-K-331, table, 1939, wood, right front dial, left wrap-around cloth grille with horizontal bars, 2 knobs, BC, 4 tubes, battery........**$50.00-55.00**

4-R, table, 1923, wood, low rectangular case, 1 dial brown or black front panel, 6 knobs, BC, 4 tubes, battery, $580.00-690.00.

4-K-402D, portable, 1940, cloth-covered, inner right dial, left grille, fold-down front, handle, BC, 4 tubes, battery........................**$40.00-45.00**

4-K-402L, portable, 1940, leather, inner right dial, left grille, fold-down front, handle, BC, 4 tubes, battery.................................**$40.00-45.00**

4-K-402M, portable, 1940, cloth-covered, inner right dial, left grille, fold-down front, handle, BC, 4 tubes, battery........................**$40.00-45.00**

4-K-402Y, portable, 1940, cloth-covered, inner right dial, left grille, fold-down front, handle, BC, 4 tubes, battery........................**$40.00-45.00**

4-K-422, table, 1940, plastic, right front dial, rounded left with horizontal wrap-around bars, 2 knobs, BC, 4 tubes, battery **$75.00-85.00**

4-K-435, table, 1940, wood, right front dial, left wrap-around cloth grille with horizontal bars, 2 knobs, BC, 4 tubes, battery.......**$45.00-55.00**

4-K-465, console, 1940, wood, upper front dial, lower cloth grille with 2 vertical bars, 2 knobs, BC, 4 tubes, battery **$85.00-95.00**

4-K-515, table, 1941, plastic, right front dial, rounded/raised left with horizontal wrap-around louvers, 2 knobs, BC, 4 tubes, battery ..**$110.00-130.00**

4-K-570, console, 1941, wood, large upper front dial, lower cloth grille with vertical bars, 2 knobs, BC, 4 tubes, battery...........**$85.00-95.00**

4-K-600 "Poketradio," portable, 1942, black plastic & leatherette, inner right dial, center round grille with curved louvers & "Z" logo, plays when cover opens, handle, 2 knobs, BC, 4 tubes, battery **$75.00-85.00**

4-K-600G "Poketradio," portable, 1942, two-tone green plastic & leatherette, inner right dial, center round grille with curved louvers & "Z" logo, plays when cover opens, handle, 2 knobs, BC, 4 tubes, battery **$85.00-95.00**

4-K-600P "Poketradio," portable, 1942, red/white/blue plastic & leatherette, inner right dial, center round grille with curved louvers & "Z" logo, plays when cover opens, handle, 2 knobs, BC, 4 tubes, battery **$85.00-95.00**

4-K-600R "Poketradio," portable, 1942, red plastic & leatherette, inner right dial, center round grille with curved louvers & "Z" logo, plays when cover opens, handle, 2 knobs, BC, 4 tubes, battery **$85.00-95.00**

4-K-600W "Poketradio," portable, 1942, ivory plastic & leatherette, inner right dial, center round grille with curved louvers & "Z" logo, plays when cover opens, handle, 2 knobs, BC, 4 tubes, battery **$75.00-85.00**

5-D-611, table, 1942, brown plastic, right front black airplane dial over large horizontal louvers, 2 knobs, BC, 5 tubes, AC/DC, $45.00-50.00.

Zenith

5-G-2617, table, 1942, wood, front black "boomerang" dial, lower cloth grille with vertical bars, 4 pushbuttons, 2 knobs, BC, 5 tubes, AC/DC/battery, $65.00-75.00.

4-K-616, table, 1942, plastic, upper front black "boomerang" dial with inner concentric circular louvers, 2 knobs, BC, 4 tubes, battery **$45.00-55.00**

4-K-635, table, 1942, wood, right front black "boomerang" dial, left cloth grille with 2 vertical bars, 2 knobs, BC, 4 tubes, battery..**$40.00-50.00**

4-K-640, table, 1942, wood, right front black "boomerang" dial, left cloth grille with diagonal bars, 4 pushbuttons, 3 knobs, BC, SW, 4 tubes, battery **$45.00-55.00**

4-K-658, console, 1942, wood, upper front black "boomerang" dial, lower cloth grille with vertical bars, 2 knobs, BC, 4 tubes, battery..**$95.00-115.00**

4-T-26, tombstone, 1935, wood, lower front black dial, upper cloth grille with Deco cut-outs, 3 knobs, BC, SW, 4 tubes, AC ..**$110.00-130.00**

4-T-51, console, 1935, wood, upper front black dial, lower cloth grille with cut-outs, 3 knobs, BC, SW, 4 tubes, AC **$120.00-140.00**

4-V-31, tombstone, 1935, wood, lower front round black dial, upper cloth grille with cut-outs, 3 knobs, BC, 4 tubes, battery **$120.00-140.00**

4-V-59, console, 1935, wood, upper front round black dial, lower cloth grille with cut-outs, 3 knobs, BC, 4 tubes, battery **$85.00-95.00**

5-D-011 "Consoltone," table, 1946, swirl plastic, right front black dial, left cloth grille, off/on bull's eye, 1 knob, BC, 5 tubes, AC/DC..**$50.00-55.00**

5-D-011W "Consoltone," table, 1946, white plastic, right front black dial, left cloth grille, off/on bull's eye, 1 knob, BC, 5 tubes, AC/DC ..**$50.00-55.00**

5-D-011Y "Consoltone," table, 1946, black plastic, right front black dial, left cloth grille, off/on bull's eye, 1 knob, BC, 5 tubes, AC/DC..**$50.00-55.00**

5-R-216, table, 1937, wood, off-center round black dial, left front grille cut-outs, feet, 2 knobs, BC, 5 tubes, AC, $120.00-140.00.

5-D-011Z "Consoltone," table, 1946, plastic, right front black dial, left cloth grille, off/on bull's eye, 1 knob, BC, 5 tubes, AC/DC **$50.00-55.00**

5-D-011ZW "Consoltone," table, 1946, plastic, right front black dial, left cloth grille, off/on bull's eye, 1 knob, BC, 5 tubes, AC/DC..**$50.00-55.00**

5-D-027 "Consoltone," table, 1946, two-tone wood, right front black dial, left cloth grille, fluted sides, 1 knob, BC, 5 tubes, AC/DC **$50.00-55.00**

5-D-610, table, 1941, brown plastic, right front black dial over horizontal wrap-around louvers, 2 knobs, BC, 5 tubes, AC/DC......**$50.00-55.00**

5-D-610W, table, 1941, ivory plastic, right front black dial over horizontal wrap-around louvers, 2 knobs, BC, 5 tubes, AC/DC......**$50.00-55.00**

5-D-611W, table, 1942, ivory plastic, right front black airplane dial over large horizontal louvers, 2 knobs, BC, 5 tubes, AC/DC..**$45.00-50.00**

5-D-627, table, 1942, wood, right front black dial, left cloth grille with cut-outs, 2 knobs, BC, 5 tubes, AC/DC **$55.00-65.00**

5-D-810, table, 1949, plastic, right front round dial over recessed metal grille, feet, 2 knobs, BC, AC/DC **$40.00-45.00**

5-F-134, tombstone, 1941, wood, lower front round black dial, upper cloth grille with horizontal bars, 4 knobs, BC, SW, 5 tubes, battery **$120.00-150.00**

5-R-312, table, 1938, plastic, right front dial, rounded/raised left with horizontal wrap-around louvers, pushbuttons, 2 knobs, BC, 5 tubes, AC, $120.00-150.00.

5-F-233, table, 1937, wood, front off-center round black dial, left grille cut-outs, feet, 3 knobs, BC, SW, 5 tubes, battery..........**$85.00-95.00**

5-F-251, console, 1937, wood, upper front round black dial, lower cloth grille with vertical bars, 3 knobs, BC, SW, 5 tubes, battery **$120.00-140.00**

5-G-003, portable, 1947, plastic, concentric semi-circular front grille bars with left dial, flex handle, 1 knob, BC, 4 tubes, AC/DC/battery **$35.00-40.00**

5-G-003ZZ, portable, 1947, plastic, concentric semi-circular front grille bars with left dial, flex handle, 1 knob, BC, 4 tubes, AC/DC/battery **$35.00-40.00**

5-G-036, table, 1947, wood, right front black dial, left cloth grille with horizontal bars, tone switches, 2 knobs, BC, 5 tubes, AC/DC/battery **$40.00-45.00**

5-G-401D, portable, 1940, cloth covered, inner right dial, left grille, fold-down front, handle, 2 knobs, BC, 5 tubes, AC/DC/battery **$35.00-40.00**

5-G-401L, portable, 1940, leather, inner right dial, left grille, fold-down front, handle, 2 knobs, BC, 5 tubes, AC/DC/battery **$35.00-40.00**

5-G-401M, portable, 1940, cloth covered, inner right dial, left grille, fold-down front, handle, 2 knobs, BC, 5 tubes, AC/DC/battery **$35.00-40.00**

5-G-401Y, portable, 1940, cloth covered, inner right dial, left grille, fold-down front, handle, 2 knobs, BC, 5 tubes, AC/DC/battery..**$35.00-40.00**

5-G-403, portable, 1940, two-tone wood, upper right front dial, left grille area with horizontal bars, handle, 2 knobs, BC, AC/DC/battery **$85.00-95.00**

5-G-441, table, 1940, wood, right front slide rule dial, left wrap-around cloth grille with horizontal bars, pushbuttons, 2 knobs, BC, SW, 5 tubes, AC/DC/battery **$65.00-75.00**

5-G-442, table, 1940, wood, lower front slide rule dial, upper cloth grille with vertical bars, pushbuttons, 2 knobs, BC, SW, 5 tubes, AC/DC/battery **$75.00-85.00**

5-G-484M, portable-R/P, 1940, cloth covered, right front dial, left grille, lift top, inner phono, BC, 5 tubes, AC/DC/battery **$35.00-40.00**

5-G-500, portable, 1941, cloth covered, inner right black dial, left grille, fold-down front, handle, 2 "Z" knobs, BC, 5 tubes, AC/DC/battery **$30.00-35.00**

5-G-500L, portable, 1941, leather, inner right dial, left grille, fold-down front, handle, 2 knobs, BC, 5 tubes, AC/DC/battery **$30.00-35.00**

5-G-500M, portable, 1941, cloth covered, inner right dial, left grille, fold-down front, handle, 2 knobs, BC, 5 tubes, AC/DC/battery **$30.00-35.00**

5-G-572, console, 1941, wood, upper front black dial, lower horizontal grille bars, 2 knobs, BC, SW, 5 tubes, AC/DC/battery..**$130.00-150.00**

5-G-603M, portable, 1942, striped cloth covered, right front black dial, left grille with sailboat design, handle, 2 knobs, 5 tubes, AC/DC/battery **$35.00-40.00**

5-G-617, table, 1942, plastic, front "boomerang" dial with inner curved grille bars, 4 pushbuttons, 2 knobs, BC, 5 tubes, AC/DC/battery **$55.00-65.00**

5-G-636, table, 1942, wood, right front "boomerang" dial, left cloth grille with Deco cut-outs, 4 pushbuttons, 2 knobs, BC, 5 tubes, AC/DC/battery **$65.00-75.00**

5-J-217, table, 1937, wood, cube-shaped, center front round black dial, top grille cut-outs, 3 knobs, BC, SW, 5 tubes, AC/6VDC **$150.00-180.00**

5-J-247, chairside, 1937, wood, step-down top with round black dial, lower storage, 3 knobs, BC, SW, 5 tubes, AC/6VDC..**$140.00-160.00**

5-J-255, console, 1937, wood, upper front round black dial, lower cloth grille with vertical bars, 3 knobs, BC, SW, 5 tubes, AC/6VDC ..**$95.00-115.00**

5-K-637, table, 1942, wood, right front "boomerang" dial, left cloth grille with Deco cut-outs, 4 pushbuttons, 2 knobs, BC, 5 tubes, battery **$50.00-55.00**

5-S-29, tombstone, 1935, wood, lower front round black dial, upper cloth grille with cut-outs, 4 knobs, BC, SW, 5 tubes, AC, $160.00-190.00.

5-R-086, table-R/P, 1946, wood, right front black dial, left cloth grille with cut-outs, lift top, inner phono, 1 knob, BC, 5 tubes, AC..**$35.00-40.00**

5-R-135, tombstone, 1937, wood, lower front black dial, upper cloth grille with 3 center vertical bars, 3 knobs, BC, 5 tubes, AC ..**$120.00-150.00**

5-R-216W, table, 1937, bone white, off-center round black dial, left front grille cut-outs, feet, 2 knobs, BC, 5 tubes, AC **$120.00-140.00**

5-R-226, table, 1937, wood, miniature child's console, upper front round black dial, lower 2-section cloth grille, 2 knobs, BC, 5 tubes, AC **$200.00-230.00**

5-R-236, chairside, 1937, wood, top round dial, vertical grille bars, lower & side storage, feet, 2 knobs, BC, 5 tubes, AC **$130.00-150.00**

5-R-236W, chairside, 1937, bone white, top round dial, vertical grille bars, lower & side storage, feet, 2 knobs, BC, 5 tubes, AC..**$130.00-150.00**

5-R-316, table, 1938, wood, right front dial, left cloth grille with horizontal bars, pushbuttons, 2 knobs, BC, 5 tubes, AC **$65.00-75.00**

5-R-317, table, 1937, wood, right front dial, rounded left wrap-around grille with vertical glass bars, 5 pushbuttons, 2 knobs, BC, 5 tubes, AC **$240.00-300.00**

5-R-337, chairside, 1938, wood, top dial & pushbuttons, front grille, lower open storage, 2 knobs, BC, 5 tubes, AC **$110.00-130.00**

5-R-680, table-R/P, 1942, wood, right front black dial, left cloth grille with cut-outs, lift top, inner phono, 3 knobs, BC, 5 tubes, AC ..**$40.00-45.00**

5-R-686, table-R/P, 1942, wood, right front black dial, left cloth grille with vertical bars, lift top, inner phono, 3 knobs, BC, 5 tubes, AC **$40.00-45.00**

6-D-015 "Consoltone," table, 1946, walnut plastic, right front quarter-round dial, right & left concentric quarter-round louvers, metal center strip, handle, 1 knob, BC, 6 tubes, AC/DC, $55.00-65.00.

5-S-56, console, 1936, wood, upper front round black dial, lower vertical grille bars, 4 knobs, BC, SW, 5 tubes, AC **$140.00-160.00**

5-S-119, table, 1936, wood, right front round black dial, left cloth grille with cut-outs, 4 knobs, BC, SW, 5 tubes, AC **$95.00-115.00**

5-S-126, table, 1936, wood, cube-shaped, center front round black dial, top grille cut-outs, 4 knobs, BC, SW, 5 tubes, AC **$150.00-180.00**

5-S-127, tombstone, 1936, wood, lower front round black dial, upper cloth grille with horizontal bars, 4 knobs, BC, SW, 5 tubes, AC **$180.00-200.00**

5-S-128, table, 1937, wood, cube-shaped, center front round black dial, top grille cut-outs, 4 knobs, BC, SW, 5 tubes, AC **$150.00-180.00**

5-S-150, console, 1937, wood, upper front round black dial, lower cloth grille with vertical bars, 4 knobs, BC, SW, 5 tubes, AC..**$150.00-180.00**

5-S-151, console, 1936, wood, upper front round black dial, lower cloth grille with vertical bar, 4 knobs, BC, SW, 5 tubes, AC ..**$180.00-200.00**

5-S-161, console, 1937, wood, upper front round black dial, lower cloth grille with vertical bars, 4 knobs, BC, SW, 5 tubes, AC..**$150.00-180.00**

5-S-218, table, 1937, wood, front off-center round black dial, left grille cut-outs, feet, 3 knobs, BC, SW, 5 tubes, AC **$140.00-160.00**

5-S-220, table, 1937, wood, large center front round black dial, feet, 3 knobs, BC, SW, 5 tubes, AC **$150.00-180.00**

5-S-220Y, table, 1937, ebony finish, large center round black dial, feet, 3 knobs, BC, SW, 5 tubes, AC **$180.00-200.00**

5-S-228, tombstone, 1937, wood, lower front round black dial, upper cloth grille with cut-outs, feet, 3 knobs, BC, SW, 5 tubes, AC **$150.00-180.00**

5-S-228W, tombstone, 1937, bone white, lower front round black dial, upper cloth grille with cut-outs, feet, 3 knobs, BC, SW, 5 tubes, AC **$150.00-180.00**

6-D-030, table, 1946, walnut, right front quarter-round black dial, right & left cloth grille areas, metal center strip, 1 knob, BC, 6 tubes, AC/DC, $45.00-55.00.

6-D-117, table, 1936, wood, right front round black dial, left cloth grille with horizontal bars, 3 knobs, BC, SW, 6 tubes, AC/DC, $75.00-85.00.

5-S-237, chairside, 1938, wood, Deco, step-down top with round dial, front vertical grille bars, lower shelf, 3 knobs, BC, SW, 5 tubes, AC $150.00-180.00

5-S-237W, chairside, 1938, bone white, Deco, step-down top with round dial, front vertical grille bars, lower shelf, 3 knobs, BC, SW, 5 tubes, AC $150.00-180.00

5-S-237Y, chairside, 1938, ebony, Deco, step-down top with round dial, front vertical grille bars, lower shelf, 3 knobs, BC, SW, 5 tubes, AC $150.00-180.00

5-S-250, console, 1937, wood, upper front round black dial, lower cloth grille with vertical bars, 3 knobs, BC, SW, 5 tubes, AC..$120.00-150.00

5-S-252, console, 1937, wood, upper front round black dial, lower cloth grille with vertical bars, 3 knobs, BC, SW, 5 tubes, AC..$120.00-150.00

5-S-319, table, 1937, wood, front oblong gold dial, left wrap-around cloth grille with horizontal bars, 5 pushbuttons, 4 knobs, BC, SW, 5 tubes, AC $85.00-115.00

5-S-320, table, 1939, wood, front oblong gold dial, left horizontal wrap-around grille bars, 5 pushbuttons, 4 knobs, BC, SW, 5 tubes, AC...$85.00-115.00

5-S-327, tombstone, 1938, wood, lower front oblong gold dial, upper cloth grille with horizontal bars, pushbuttons, 4 knobs, BC, SW, 5 tubes, AC $180.00-200.00

5-S-338, chairside, 1939, wood, top dial & push buttons, front grille, lower open storage, 4 knobs, BC, SW, 5 tubes, AC ..$150.00-180.00

5-S-339M, chairside, 1939, wood, top dial & pushbuttons, front grille, lower open storage, 4 knobs, BC, SW, 5 tubes, AC ..$160.00-190.00

5-X-230, tombstone, 1939, wood, lower front round black dial, upper cloth grille with cut-outs, 4 knobs, BC, SW, 5 tubes, 32VDC $120.00-140.00

5-X-248, chairside, 1939, wood, half-round, top round black dial, front grille, 4 knobs, BC, SW, 5 tubes, 32VDC.................$110.00-130.00

5-X-274, console, 1939, wood, upper front round black dial, lower cloth grille with vertical bars, 4 knobs, BC, SW, 5 tubes, 32VDC $110.00-130.00

6-B-129, tombstone, 1936, wood, lower front black dial, upper cloth grille with cut-outs and scalloped top edge, 5 knobs, BC, SW, 6 tubes, battery $150.00-180.00

6-B-164, console, 1937, wood, upper front black dial, lower cloth grille with vertical bars, 5 knobs, BC, SW, 6 tubes, battery $150.00-170.00

6-B-321, table, 1939, wood, front round dial, left wrap-around grille, pushbuttons, 4 knobs, BC, SW, 6 tubes, battery $75.00-85.00

6-D-317, table, 1938, wood, right front dial, rounded left wrap-around grille with vertical glass bars, pushbuttons, 2 knobs, BC, 6 tubes including ballast, AC/DC, $250.00-300.00.

6-D-014, table, 1946, swirl plastic, front inverted V-shaped dial & louvers, handle, 2 knobs, BC, 6 tubes, AC/DC $50.00-65.00

6-D-014W, table, 1946, white plastic, front inverted V-shaped dial & louvers, handle, 2 knobs, BC, 6 tubes, AC/DC $50.00-65.00

6-D-014Y, table, 1946, black plastic, front inverted V-shaped dial & louvers, handle, 2 knobs, BC, 6 tubes, AC/DC $50.00-65.00

6-D-015W "Consoltone," table, 1946, ivory plastic, right front quarter-round dial, right & left concentric quarter-round louvers, metal center strip, handle, 1 knob, BC, 6 tubes, AC/DC $55.00-65.00

6-D-015Y "Consoltone," table, 1946, black plastic, right front quarter-round dial, right & left concentric quarter-round louvers, metal center strip, handle, 1 knob, BC, 6 tubes, AC/DC $55.00-65.00

6-D-029, table, 1946, walnut, front inverted V-shaped black dial, lower cloth grille, 2 knobs, BC, 6 tubes, AC/DC $50.00-55.00

6-D-029G, table, 1946, lime walnut, front inverted V-shaped black dial, lower cloth grille, 2 knobs, BC, 6 tubes, AC/DC $50.00-55.00

6-D-030E, table, 1946, mahogany, right front quarter-round black dial, right & left cloth grille areas, metal center strip, 1 knob, BC, 6 tubes, AC/DC $45.00-55.00

6-D-116, table, 1936, wood, right front round black dial, left cloth grille with horizontal bars, 3 knobs, BC, SW, 6 tubes, AC/DC $75.00-85.00

6-D-118, table, 1936, wood, right front round black dial, left cloth grille with vertical bars, 3 knobs, BC, SW, 6 tubes, AC/DC $65.00-75.00

6-D-510, table, 1941, brown plastic, right front black dial over horizontal wrap-around grille bars, handle, 2 knobs, BC, 6 tubes, AC/DC, $50.00-65.00.

6-D-219, table, 1937, wood, rounded right top, right front round dial, left cloth grille with horizontal bars, 3 knobs, BC, SW, 6 tubes, AC/DC $75.00-85.00

6-D-219W, table, 1937, bone white, rounded right top, right front round dial, left cloth grille with horizontal bars, 3 knobs, BC, SW, 6 tubes, AC/DC $75.00-85.00

6-D-219Y, table, 1937, ebony, rounded right top, right front round dial, left cloth grille with horizontal bars, 3 knobs, BC, SW, 6 tubes, AC/DC $75.00-85.00

6-D-221, table, 1937, wood, right front round black dial, left cloth grille with cut-outs, feet, 3 knobs, BC, SW, 6 tubes, AC/DC ..$65.00-75.00

6-D-311, table, 1938, plastic, Deco, right front half-round dial, left horizontal wrap-around louvers, 1 "Z" knob, BC, 6 tubes including ballast, AC/DC $180.00-200.00

6-D-312, table, 1938, plastic, right front dial, rounded/raised left with horizontal wrap-around louvers, pushbuttons, 2 knobs, BC, 6 tubes including ballast, AC/DC $150.00-180.00

6-D-315, table, 1938, plastic, Deco, right front half-round dial, left horizontal wrap-around louvers, handle, "Z" knob, BC, 6 tubes including ballast, AC/DC $180.00-200.00

6-D-316, table, 1938, wood, right front dial, left cloth grille with horizontal bars, pushbuttons, 2 knobs, BC, 6 tubes including ballast, AC/DC $65.00-75.00

6-D-326, table, 1938, wood, miniature child's console, upper front half-round dial, lower cloth grille with center vertical bar, 1 "Z" knob, BC, 6 tubes including ballast, AC/DC..............................$200.00-230.00

6-D-336, chairside, 1938, wood, top dial, slanted grille with horizontal bars, legs, 1 knob, BC, 6 tubes including ballast, AC/DC $120.00-150.00

6-D-337, chairside, 1938, wood, top dial & pushbuttons, front grille, lower open storage, 2 knobs, BC, 6 tubes including ballast, AC/DC **$120.00-150.00**

6-D-410, table, 1939, brown plastic, right front dial, left vertical wrap-over grille bars, 1 tuning & 1 thumbwheel knob, BC, 6 tubes including ballast, AC/DC **$75.00-85.00**

6-D-411, table, 1939, plastic, right front dial, left vertical wrap-over grille bars, 1 tuning & 1 thumbwheel knob, BC, 6 tubes including ballast, AC/DC **$75.00-85.00**

6-D-413, table, 1939, brown plastic, front off-center dial, left vertical wrap-over grille bars, 5 pushbuttons, 1 tuning & 1 thumbwheel knob, BC, 6 tubes including ballast, AC/DC **$95.00-115.00**

6-D-414, table, 1939, plastic, front off-center dial, left vertical wrap-over grille bars, 5 pushbuttons, 1 tuning & 1 thumbwheel knob, BC, 6 tubes including ballast, AC/DC **$95.00-115.00**

6-D-425, table, 1939, wood, right front dial, left cloth grille with vertical bars, 1 tuning & 1 thumbwheel knob, BC, 6 tubes including ballast, AC/DC **$50.00-65.00**

6-D-426, table, 1939, wood, right front dial, left cloth grille with vertical spiral bars, pushbuttons, 1 tuning & 1 thumbwheel knob, BC, 6 tubes including ballast, AC/DC **$75.00-85.00**

6-D-427, table, 1939, wood, right front dial, left cloth grille with horizontal bars, pushbuttons, 1 tuning & 1 thumbwheel knob, BC, 6 tubes including ballast, AC/DC **$65.00-75.00**

6-D-446, chairside, 1940, wood, top dial & pushbuttons, front grille, right & left storage, 1 tuning & 1 thumbwheel knob, BC, 6 tubes including ballast, AC/DC **$120.00-150.00**

6-D-455, bookcase, 1940, wood, inner dial & grille, fold-down front, 2 lower shelves, 1 tuning & 1 thumbwheel knob, BC, 6 tubes, AC/DC **$200.00-230.00**

6-D-510W, table, 1941, ivory plastic, right front black dial over horizontal wrap-around grille bars, handle, 2 knobs, BC, 6 tubes, AC/DC **$50.00-65.00**

6-D-516, table, 1940, plastic, right front black dial over horizontal wrap-around grille bars, handle, 2 knobs, BC, 6 tubes, AC/DC, $50.00-65.00.

6-D-520, table, 1941, two-tone walnut plastic, right front black dial over wrap-around lattice grille, handle, 2 knobs, BC, 6 tubes, AC/DC **$50.00-65.00**

6-D-520W, table, 1941, plastic, right front black dial over wrap-around lattice grille, handle, 2 knobs, BC, 6 tubes, AC/DC **$50.00-65.00**

6-D-526, table, 1941, walnut, "waterfall" front, right dial, left vertical grille bars, 2 knobs, BC, 6 tubes, AC/DC **$65.00-75.00**

6-D-538, table, 1941, wood, right front black dial, left horizontal & vertical grille cut-outs, decorative case lines, 2 knobs, BC, 6 tubes, AC/DC **$65.00-75.00**

6-D-614 "Consoltone," table, 1942, plastic, front black "boomerang" dial with inner concentric circular louvers, handle, 2 knobs, BC, 6 tubes, AC/DC **$50.00-65.00**

6-D-614W "Consoltone," table, 1942, black & white plastic, front black "boomerang" dial with inner concentric circular louvers, 2 knobs, BC, 6 tubes, AC/DC **$50.00-65.00**

6-D-615 "Consoltone," table, 1942, plastic, front "boomerang" dial with inner curved grille bars, 4 pushbuttons, handle, 2 knobs, BC, 6 tubes, AC/DC **$50.00-65.00**

6-D-525, table, 1941, walnut, right front black dial, left raised horizontal grille bars, 2 "Z" knobs, BC, 6 tubes, AC/DC, $75.00-85.00.

6-D-615W "Consoltone," table, 1942, white plastic, front "boomerang" dial with inner curved grille bars, 4 pushbuttons, handle, 2 knobs, BC, 6 tubes, AC/DC **$50.00-65.00**

6-D-620, table, 1942, plastic, front black "boomerang" dial with inner concentric circular louvers, handle, 2 knobs, BC, SW, 6 tubes, AC/DC **$50.00-65.00**

6-D-620W, table, 1942, black & white plastic, front black "boomerang" dial with inner concentric circular louvers, handle, 2 knobs, BC, SW, 6 tubes, AC/DC **$50.00-65.00**

6-D-629, table, 1942, wood, front black "boomerang" dial, lower cloth grille with cut-outs, 2 knobs, BC, 6 tubes, AC/DC **$50.00-65.00**

6-D-630, table, 1942, wood, front black "boomerang" dial, center round cloth grille with cut-outs, 4 pushbuttons, 2 knobs, BC, 6 tubes, AC/DC **$55.00-65.00**

6-D-644, table, 1942, wood, front black "boomerang" dial, center cloth grille with cut-outs, 2 knobs, BC, SW, 6 tubes, AC/DC..**$55.00-65.00**

6-D-815Y, table, 1949, plastic, front round dial with numbers on clear plastic over large metal grille area, flex handle, 2 knobs, BC, 6 tubes, AC/DC **$35.00-40.00**

6-D-2615, table, 1942, wood, arched top, front black "boomerang" dial, lower cloth grille with vertical bars, 4 pushbuttons, 2 knobs, BC, 6 tubes, AC/DC **$55.00-65.00**

6-G-001Y "Universal," portable, 1946, black leatherette, inner right quarter-round dial, right & left concentric quarter-round louvers, metal center strip, flip up lid, handle, 2 knobs, BC, 6 tubes, AC/DC/battery **$50.00-60.00**

6-G-038, table, 1948, wood, right front black dial, left criss-cross grille, pushbuttons, telescoping antenna, 2 knobs, BC, SW, 6 tubes, AC/DC/battery **$45.00-50.00**

6-G-560, console, 1941, wood, upper front black dial, lower cloth grille with center vertical bar, 2 knobs, BC, 6 tubes, AC/DC/battery **$120.00-150.00**

6-D-612, table, 1942, brown plastic, right front recessed black dial, horizontal wrap-around grille bars, handle, 2 knobs, BC, 6 tubes, AC/DC, $50.00-65.00.

6-D-612W, table, 1942, white plastic, right front recessed black dial, horizontal wrap-around grille bars, handle, 2 knobs, BC, 6 tubes, AC/DC, $50.00-65.00.

6-G-601D, portable, 1942, blue/gray cloth covered, inner right black dial, left grille with sailboat, fold-down front, handle, 2 knobs, BC, 6 tubes, AC/DC/battery **$55.00-65.00**

6-G-601M, portable, 1941, brown cloth covered, inner right black dial, left grille with sailboat, fold-down front, handle, 2 knobs, BC, 6 tubes, AC/DC/battery **$55.00-65.00**

6-G-601MH, portable, 1941, brown/ivory cloth covered, inner right black dial, left grille with sailboat, fold-down front, handle, 2 knobs, BC, 6 tubes, AC/DC/battery **$55.00-65.00**

6-G-601ML, portable, 1942, brown "alligator," inner right black dial, left grille with sailboat, fold-down front, handle, 2 knobs, BC, 6 tubes, AC/DC/battery **$55.00-65.00**

6-G-601Y, portable, 1948, leatherette, inner right quarter- round dial, right & left concentric quarter-round louvers, metal center strip, flip up lid, handle, 2 knobs, BC, 6 tubes, AC/DC/battery **$45.00-50.00**

6-G-638, table, 1942, wood, right front black dial, left cloth grille with cut-outs, pushbuttons, 2 knobs, BC, SW, 6 tubes, AC/DC/battery **$65.00-75.00**

6-G-660, console, 1942, wood, upper front slanted black dial, lower cloth grille with vertical bars, pushbuttons, 2 knobs, BC, SW, 6 tubes, AC/DC/battery **$120.00-150.00**

6-G-801, portable, 1949, plastic, inner dial & grille, fold-open front doors, flex handle, pull-up antenna, 2 knobs, BC, 6 tubes, AC/DC/battery **$40.00-50.00**

6-J-230, tombstone, 1937, wood, lower front round black dial, upper cloth grille with cut-outs, 4 knobs, BC, SW, 6 tubes, AC/6VDC **$150.00-170.00**

6-J-257, console, 1937, wood, upper front round black dial, lower cloth grille with center vertical divider, 4 knobs, BC, SW, 6 tubes, AC/6VDC **$160.00-190.00**

6-D-628, table, 1942, wood, right front black dial, left cloth grille with cut-outs, 2 knobs, BC, 6 tubes, AC/DC, $50.00-65.00.

6-J-322, table, 1939, wood, step-down top, right front dial, rounded left grille with horizontal bars, pushbuttons, 4 knobs, BC, SW, 6 tubes, AC/6VDC **$85.00-95.00**

6-J-357, console, 1939, wood, front round black dial, lower cloth grille with vertical bars, pushbuttons, 4 knobs, BC, SW, 6 tubes, AC/6VDC **$190.00-220.00**

6-J-436, tombstone, 1940, wood, lower front round black dial, upper wrap-over grille with vertical bars, pushbuttons, BC, SW, 6 tubes, AC/6VDC **$120.00-150.00**

6-J-463, console, 1940, wood, upper front round black dial, lower cloth grille with vertical bars, pushbuttons, BC, SW, 6 tubes, AC/6VDC **$275.00-325.00**

6-P-416, table, 1940, brown plastic, right front dial, left vertical wrap-over grille bars, 1 tuning & 1 thumbwheel knob, BC, 6 tubes including ballast, AC **$65.00-75.00**

6-P-417, table, 1940, plastic, right front dial, left vertical wrap-over grille bars, BC, 6 tubes, AC **$65.00-75.00**

6-P-418, table, 1940, brown plastic, right front dial, left horizontal wrap-around louvers, pushbuttons, handle, BC, 6 tubes, AC ..**$50.00-65.00**

6-P-419, table, 1940, plastic, right front dial, left horizontal wrap-around louvers, pushbuttons, handle, 1 tuning & 1 thumbwheel knob, BC, 6 tubes including ballast, AC **$50.00-65.00**

6-P-429, table, 1940, wood, right front dial, left wrap-around cloth grille with horizontal bars, pushbuttons, 1 tuning & 1 thumbwheel knob, BC, 6 tubes including ballast, AC **$65.00-75.00**

6-D-815, table, 1949, plastic, front round dial with numbers on clear plastic over large metal grille area, flex handle, 2 knobs, BC, 6 tubes, AC/DC, $35.00-40.00.

6-P-430, table, 1940, step-down top, right front dial, rounded left with horizontal wrap-around louvers, pushbuttons, BC, 6 tubes, AC....................................**$85.00-115.00**

6-R-060, console, 1946, walnut, upper front slanted black dial, large lower cloth grille with 3 vertical bars, BC, 6 tubes, AC..........**$110.00-130.00**

6-R-084, table-R/P, 1947, wood, front black "boomerang" dial, cloth grille, lift top, inner phono, feet, 2 knobs, BC, 6 tubes, AC....................................**$40.00-45.00**

6-R-087, console-R/P, 1946, walnut, upper front black dial, center pull-out phono, lower cloth grille, 2 knobs, BC, 6 tubes, AC **$85.00-95.00**

6-R-480, table-R/P, 1940, wood, right front dial, left cloth grille with cut-outs, feet, open top phono, BC, 6 tubes, AC **$40.00-45.00**

6-R-481, table-R/P, 1940, wood, right front dial, rounded left with grille cut-outs, lift top, inner phono, 2 knobs, BC, 6 tubes including ballast, AC....................................**$120.00-150.00**

6-R-583, table-R/P, 1941, walnut, right front black dial, left grille, lift top, inner phono, 3 knobs, BC, 6 tubes, AC **$40.00-45.00**

6-R-683, table-R/P, 1942, wood, right front black dial, left cloth grille with 2 vertical bars, lift top, inner phono, 4 knobs, BC, 6 tubes, AC **$40.00-45.00**

6-R-684, table-R/P, 1942, wood, right front black dial, left cloth grille with vertical bars, lift top, inner phono, 4 knobs, BC, 6 tubes, AC **$40.00-45.00**

6-R-687, console-R/P, 1942, walnut, inner right black dial/left phono, lift top, front cloth grille with lyre cut-out, 4 knobs, BC, 6 tubes, AC **$150.00-180.00**

6-G-001YX "Universal," portable, 1946, black leatherette, inner right quarter-round dial, right & left concentric quarter-round louvers, metal center strip, flip up lid, handle, 2 knobs, BC, 6 tubes, AC/DC/battery, $50.00-60.00.

6-G-601L, portable, 1942, leather, inner wood panel with right black dial & left grille with sailboat, fold-down front, handle, 2 knobs, BC, 6 tubes, AC/DC/battery, $55.00-65.00.

6-R-687R, console-R/P, 1942, mahogany, inner right black dial/left phono, lift top, front cloth grille with lyre cut-out, 4 knobs, BC, 6 tubes, AC **$150.00-180.00**

6-R-688 "Modern," console-R/P, 1942, blonde, inner right black dial/left phono, lift top, front cloth grille with cut-outs, feet, 4 knobs, BC, 6 tubes, AC **$110.00-130.00**

6-R-886, table-R/P, 1948, wood, front round dial/louvers, fold-back cover, inner phono, 2 knobs, BC, 6 tubes, AC **$40.00-45.00**

6-S-27, tombstone, 1935, wood, lower front round black dial, upper grille with cut-outs & scalloped top edge, 4 knobs, BC, SW, 6 tubes, AC **$270.00-300.00**

6-S-52, console, 1935, wood, upper front round black dial, lower cloth grille with cut-outs, 4 knobs, BC, SW, 6 tubes, AC **$270.00-300.00**

6-S-137 "Zephyr," tombstone, 1936, wood, lower front black dial, upper cloth grille with horizontal wrap-around louvers, 5 knobs, BC, SW, 6 tubes, AC **$270.00-300.00**

6-S-147 "Zephyr," chairside, 1936, wood, Deco, top dial, lower horizontal wrap-around louvers, 5 knobs, BC, SW, 6 tubes, AC..**$200.00-230.00**

6-S-157 "Zephyr," console, 1936, wood, upper front black dial, lower horizontal wrap-around louvers, 5 knobs, BC, SW, 6 tubes, AC **$350.00-400.00**

6-S-203 (5638 chassis), chairside-R/P, 1937, wood, top round dial, lift top, inner phono, lower record storage, BC, SW, 6 tubes, AC **$150.00-180.00**

6-S-203W (5638 chassis), chairside-R/P, 1937, bone white, top round dial, lift top, inner phono, lower record storage, BC, SW, 6 tubes, AC **$150.00-180.00**

6-S-222 (5638 chassis), table, 1937, wood, cube-shaped, center front round black dial, top grille with cut-outs, 4 knobs, BC, SW, 6 tubes, AC **$150.00-180.00**

6-S-223 (5638 chassis), table, 1937, wood, right front round black dial, left cloth grille with cut-outs, feet, 4 knobs, BC, SW, 6 tubes, AC **$150.00-180.00**

6-S-238, chairside, 1938, wood, half-round, top dial, front grille with vertical bars, BC, SW, 6 tubes, AC....................**$240.00-270.00**

6-S-239 (5638 chassis), chairside, 1937, wood, step-down top with round black dial, lower open storage, 4 knobs, BC, SW, 6 tubes, AC **$180.00-200.00**

6-S-241 (5638 chassis), chairside/bar, 1937, wood, top round dial & front cloth grille with vertical bars, storage & bar area, 4 knobs, BC, SW, 6 tubes, AC....................**$200.00-230.00**

6-S-241W (5638 chassis), chairside/bar, 1937, bone white, top round dial &, front cloth grille with vertical bars, storage & bar area, 4 knobs, BC, SW, 6 tubes, AC **$200.00-230.00**

6-S-249, chairside, 1938, wood, half-round, top dial, lower front horizontal wrap-around louvers, BC, SW, 6 tubes, AC **$240.00-270.00**

6-S-254H (5644 chassis), console, 1937, wood, upper front black triangular dial, lower cloth grille with vertical bars, 4 knobs, BC, SW, 6 tubes, AC **$240.00-270.00**

6-S-254W (5644 chassis), console, 1937, bone white, upper front black triangular dial, lower cloth grille with vertical bars, 4 knobs, BC, SW, 6 tubes, AC **$240.00-270.00**

6-S-254Y (5644 chassis), console, 1937, ebony, upper front black triangular dial, lower cloth grille with vertical bars, 4 knobs, BC, SW, 6 tubes, AC **$240.00-270.00**

6-S-256 (5644 chassis), console, 1937, wood, upper front black triangular dial, lower recessed cloth grille with center vertical divider, 4 knobs, BC, SW, 6 tubes, AC **$250.00-280.00**

6-S-275, console, 1938, wood, upper front round black dial, lower cloth grille with vertical bars, 4 knobs, BC, SW, 6 tubes, AC..**$240.00-270.00**

6-G-004Y "Universal," portable, 1947, black leatherette, inner right quarter-round dial, right & left concentric quarter-round louvers, metal center strip, flip up lid, handle, 2 knobs, BC, SW, 6 tubes, AC/DC/battery, $75.00-85.00.

6-R-631, table, 1941, wood, front black "boomerang" dial, lower cloth grille with cut-outs, pushbuttons, 2 knobs, BC, 6 tubes, AC, $75.00-85.00.

6-S-128, tombstone, 1936, wood, lower front black dial, upper cloth grille with horizontal bars, 5 knobs, BC, SW, 6 tubes, AC, $270.00-300.00.

6-S-229 (5638 chassis), tombstone, 1937, wood, lower front round black dial, upper cloth grille with cut-outs, 4 knobs, BC, SW, 6 tubes, AC, $180.00-200.00.

6-S-301 (5651 chassis), chairside-R/P, 1939, wood, top dial, lift top, inner phono, rounded front with horizontal wrap-around louvers, 4 knobs, BC, SW, 6 tubes, AC **$240.00-270.00**

6-S-305 (5651 chassis), console-R/P, 1938, wood, inner left dial/push-buttons, right phono, lift top, front cloth grille with center vertical bar, 4 knobs, BC, SW, 6 tubes, AC **$160.00-190.00**

6-S-322 (5651 chassis), table, 1939, wood, step-down top, right front dial, left wrap-around cloth grille with horizontal bars, pushbuttons, 4 knobs, BC, SW, 6 tubes, AC.....................................**$85.00-105.00**

6-S-330 (5648 chassis), tombstone, 1938, wood, lower front round black dial, upper cloth grille with cut-outs, pushbuttons, 4 knobs, BC, SW, 6 tubes, AC...**$180.00-200.00**

6-S-340 (5651 chassis), chairside, 1939, wood, half-round, top dial & pushbuttons, wrap-around vertical grille bars, 4 knobs, BC, SW, 6 tubes, AC **$240.00-270.00**

6-S-341 (5649 chassis), chairside, 1938, wood, Deco, half-round, top dial, lower front horizontal wrap-around louvers, 4 knobs, BC, SW, 6 tubes, AC **$240.00-270.00**

6-S-361 (5648 chassis), console, 1939, wood, upper front round black dial, lower cloth grille with vertical bars, pushbuttons, 4 knobs, BC, SW, 6 tubes, AC..**$200.00-230.00**

6-S-362 (5649 chassis), console, 1939, wood, upper front round black dial, lower cloth grille with vertical bars, pushbuttons, 4 knobs, BC, SW, 6 tubes, AC..**$200.00-230.00**

6-S-439 (5678 chassis), table, 1940, wood, front black slide rule dial, left wrap-around cloth grille with horizontal bars, pushbuttons, 2 knobs, BC, SW, 6 tubes, AC **$85.00-115.00**

6-S-469 (5678 chassis), console, 1940, wood, upper front slide rule dial, lower cloth grille with vertical bars, pushbuttons, 2 knobs, BC, SW, 6 tubes, AC **$120.00-150.00**

6-S-511 (6A13 chassis), table, 1941, brown plastic, right front dial, left horizontal wrap-around grille bars, pushbuttons, handle, 2 knobs, BC, SW, 6 tubes, AC **$55.00-65.00**

6-S-511W (6A13 chassis), table, 1941, ivory plastic, right front dial, left horizontal wrap-around grille bars, pushbuttons, handle, 2 knobs, BC, SW, 6 tubes, AC **$55.00-65.00**

6-S-528 (6A02 chassis), table, 1941, wood, right front black dial, left cloth grille with vertical bars, pushbuttons, 3 knobs, BC, SW, 6 tubes, AC **$75.00-85.00**

6-S-532, table, 1941, wood, large front black dial, wrap-around grille, pushbuttons, 2 knobs, BC, SW, 6 tubes, AC **$75.00-85.00**

6-S-546 (6A05 chassis), chairside, 1941, wood, top black dial & pushbuttons, front cloth grille, casters, 2 knobs, BC, SW, 6 tubes, AC...**$110.00-130.00**

6-S-556 (6A05 chassis), console, 1941, wood, upper front black dial, lower cloth grille with vertical bars, pushbuttons, 2 knobs, BC, SW, 6 tubes, AC **$150.00-180.00**

6-S-580 (6A04 chassis), table-R/P, 1941, wood, right front black dial, left vertical grille bars, pushbuttons, lift top, inner phono, BC, SW, 6 tubes, AC **$45.00-50.00**

6-S-632 (6B08 chassis), table, 1942, wood, front black dial, left wrap-around cloth grille with horizontal bars, pushbuttons, 2 knobs, BC, SW, 6 tubes, AC...**$55.00-65.00**

6-S-646 (6B08 chassis), chairside, 1942, walnut, top black dial & push-buttons, front cloth grille with cut-outs, 2 knobs, BC, SW, 6 tubes, AC **$130.00-150.00**

6-S-152, console, 1936, wood, upper front black dial, lower cloth grille with 3 vertical bars, 5 knobs, BC, SW, 6 tubes, AC, $240.00-270.00.

6-S-254 (5644 chassis), console, 1937, wood, upper front black triangular dial, lower cloth grille with vertical bars, 4 knobs, BC, SW, 6 tubes, AC, $240.00-270.00.

6-S-321 (5651 chassis), table, 1937, wood, right front dial, left wrap-around cloth grille with center horizontal bars, pushbuttons, 4 knobs, BC, SW, 6 tubes, AC, $75.00-85.00.

6-S-892, table, wood, front black dial, left wrap-around cloth grille with 2 horizontal bars, pushbuttons, 2 knobs, BC, SW, 6 tubes, $75.00-85.00.

6-S-646R (6B08 chassis), chairside, 1942, mahogany, top black dial & pushbuttons, front cloth grille with cut-outs, 2 knobs, BC, SW, 6 tubes, AC **$130.00-150.00**

6-S-656 (6B08 chassis), console, 1942, wood, upper front black dial, lower cloth grille with vertical bars, pushbuttons, 2 knobs, BC, SW, 6 tubes, AC **$120.00-140.00**

6-V-27, tombstone, 1935, wood, lower front round black dial, upper cloth grille with cut-outs & scalloped top edge, 4 knobs, BC, SW, 6 tubes, battery **$150.00-180.00**

6-V-62, console, 1936, wood, upper front round black dial, lower cloth grille with cut-outs, 4 knobs, BC, SW, 6 tubes, battery **$150.00-180.00**

7-D-126, table, 1936, wood, cube-shaped, center front round black dial, top grille cut-outs, 4 knobs, BC, SW, 7 tubes including ballast, AC/DC **$150.00-180.00**

7-D-127, tombstone, 1937, wood, lower front round black dial, upper cloth grille with horizontal bars, 4 knobs, BC, SW, 7 tubes including ballast, AC/DC **$160.00-190.00**

7-D-138 "Zephyr," tombstone, 1936, wood, lower front round black dial, upper cloth grille with horizontal wrap-around louvers, 4 knobs, BC, SW, 7 tubes, AC/DC **$200.00-230.00**

7-D-148 "Zephyr," chairside, 1936, wood, top dial, sliding glass cover, front horizontal wrap-around louvers, 4 knobs, BC, SW, 7 tubes, AC **$180.00-200.00**

7-D-168 "Zephyr," console, 1936, wood, upper front round black dial, lower horizontal wrap-around louvers, 4 knobs, BC, SW, 7 tubes, AC/DC **$340.00-380.00**

7-D-203, chairside-R/P, 1937, wood, top round black dial, lift top, inner phono, lower grille & record storage, 4 knobs, BC, SW, 7 tubes including ballast, AC/DC **$150.00-180.00**

7-D-203W, chairside-R/P, 1938, bone white, top round dial, lift top, inner phono, lower grille & record storage, 4 knobs, BC, SW, 7 tubes including ballast, AC/DC **$150.00-180.00**

7-D-222, table, 1937, wood, cube-shaped, center front round black dial, top grille cut-outs, 4 knobs, BC, SW, 7 tubes including ballast, AC/DC **$150.00-180.00**

7-D-223, table, 1937, wood, right front round black dial, left cloth grille with cut-outs, feet, 4 knobs, BC, SW, 7 tubes including ballast, AC/DC **$150.00-180.00**

7-D-229, tombstone, 1937, wood, lower front round black dial, upper cloth grille with cut-outs, 4 knobs, BC, SW, 7 tubes including ballast, AC/DC **$180.00-200.00**

7-D-239, chairside, 1937, wood, step-down top with round black dial, lower open storage, 4 knobs, BC, SW, 7 tubes including ballast, AC/DC **$150.00-180.00**

6-S-527 (6A02 chassis), table, 1941, wood, right front dial, left horizontal grille bars, pushbuttons, 3 knobs, BC, SW, 6 tubes, AC, $65.00-75.00.

7-D-241, chairside/bar, 1937, wood, top round dial, front cloth grille with vertical bars, storage & bar area, 4 knobs, BC, SW, 7 tubes including ballast, AC/DC **$160.00-190.00**

7-D-241W, chairside/bar, 1937, bone white, top round dial, front cloth grille with vertical bars, storage & bar area, 4 knobs, BC, SW, 7 tubes including ballast, AC/DC **$160.00-190.00**

7-D-243, chairside, 1937, wood, Deco, step-down top with dial, large front horizontal wrap-around louvers, 4 knobs, BC, SW, 7 tubes including ballast, AC/DC **$200.00-230.00**

7-D-253, console, 1937, wood, upper front round black dial, lower cloth grille with vertical bars, 4 knobs, BC, SW, 7 tubes including ballast, AC/DC **$200.00-230.00**

7-H-820, table, 1948, plastic, center front round concentric circular louvers and dial, 3 knobs, BC, FM, FM1, 7 tubes, AC/DC ..**$45.00-55.00**

7-H-820Z, table, 1948, plastic, center front round concentric circular louvers and dial, 3 knobs, BC, FM, FM1, 7 tubes, AC/DC ..**$45.00-55.00**

7-H-822, table, 1949, plastic, diagonally divided front with left black dial & right perforated grille area with crest, 3 knobs, BC, FM, AC/DC **$35.00-40.00**

7-H-920, table, 1949, plastic, center front round concentric circular louvers and dial, 3 knobs, BC, FM, AC/DC **$45.00-55.00**

7-H-921, table, 1949, plastic, diagonally divided front with left black dial & right perforated grille area with crest, 3 knobs, BC, FM, 7 tubes, AC/DC **$35.00-40.00**

7-H-921Z, table, 1949, plastic, diagonally divided front with left black dial & right perforated grille area with crest, 3 knobs, BC, FM, 7 tubes, AC/DC **$35.00-40.00**

7-H-922, table, 1950, plastic, diagonally divided front with left black dial & right perforated grille area with crest, flex handle, 3 knobs, BC, FM, AC/DC **$35.00-40.00**

7-J-259, console, 1937, wood, upper front black "robot" dial, lower cloth grille with center vertical bars, 4 knobs, BC, SW, 7 tubes, AC/6VDC **$240.00-300.00**

7-J-328, table, 1939, wood, front black "robot" dial, left wrap-around cloth grille with horizontal bars, pushbuttons, BC, SW, 7 tubes, AC/6VDC **$85.00-115.00**

7-J-368, console, 1939, wood, upper front black "robot" dial, large lower horizontal wrap-around louvers, pushbuttons, 1 knob, BC, SW, 7 tubes, AC/6VDC **$350.00-400.00**

7-K-01, table, plastic, center front round dial with inner metal perforated grille area, handle, 2 knobs, BC, FM, AC/DC **$50.00-55.00**

7-G-605 "Trans-Oceanic Clipper," portable, 1941, simulated alligator, inner black dial, left grille with airplane or sailboat, fold-down front, handle, 6 pushbutton band selectors, collapsible antenna, 4 "radioorgan" tone switches, 2 knobs, BC, SW, 7 tubes, AC/DC/battery, $245.00-295.00.

7-H-918, table, 1949, plastic, center front round dial with inner perforated grille, 2 knobs, FM, AC/DC, $40.00-45.00.

7-M-918, table, plastic, center front round dial with inner perforated grille area, 2 knobs, FM **$40.00-45.00**

7-R-070, table-R/P, 1948, leatherette & plastic, front plastic "automobile" grille, lift top, inner phono, 2 knobs, BC, 7 tubes, AC **$50.00-65.00**

7-R-887, console-R/P, 1949, wood, upper front slanted black dial, pushbuttons, center fold-down phono door, lower grille, BC, 7 tubes, AC **$110.00-130.00**

7-S-28, tombstone, 1936, wood, lower front round black dial, upper cloth grille with cut-outs, 4 knobs, BC, SW, 7 tubes, AC....**$240.00-270.00**

7-S-53, console, 1936, wood, upper front round black dial, lower cloth grille with vertical bars, 4 knobs, BC, SW, 7 tubes, AC **$240.00-270.00**

7-S-232 "Walton's" (5709 chassis), tombstone, 1937, wood, large case, lower front black "robot" dial, upper 2-section cloth grille, 4 knobs, BC, SW, 7 tubes, AC **$800.00-900.00**

7-S-240 (5709 chassis), chairside, 1938, wood, Deco, top black "robot" dial, front cloth grille with vertical bars, storage, 4 knobs, BC, SW, 7 tubes, AC **$270.00-320.00**

7-S-240W (5709 chassis), chairside, 1937, bone white, Deco, top black "robot" dial, front cloth grille with vertical bars, storage, 4 knobs, BC, SW, 7 tubes, AC **$270.00-320.00**

7-S-242 (5709 chassis), chairside, 1937, wood, Deco, top "robot" dial, large horizontal wrap-around louvers, 4 knobs, BC, SW, 7 tubes, AC **$300.00-350.00**

7-S-242W (5709 chassis), chairside, 1937, ebony finish, Deco, top "robot" dial, large horizontal wrap-around louvers, 4 knobs, BC, SW, 7 tubes, AC **$300.00-350.00**

7-S-258W (5709 chassis), console, 1937, bone white, upper front black "robot" dial, lower cloth grille with vertical bars, tuning eye, 4 knobs, BC, SW, 7 tubes, AC **$300.00-320.00**

7-S-260 (5709 chassis), console, 1937, wood, upper front black "robot" dial, lower cloth grille with vertical bars, 4 knobs, BC, SW, 7 tubes, AC **$300.00-320.00**

7-S-260Y (5709 chassis), console, 1937, ebony finish, upper front black "robot" dial, lower cloth grille with vertical bars, 4 knobs, BC, SW, 7 tubes, AC **$300.00-320.00**

7-S-261 (5709 chassis), console/bookcase, 1937, wood, upper front black "robot" dial, lower cloth grille with cut-outs, right & left side book shelves, 4 knobs, BC, SW, 7 tubes, AC **$600.00-700.00**

7-J-232 "Walton's," tombstone, 1937, wood, large case, lower front black "robot" dial, upper 2-section cloth grille, 4 knobs, BC, SW, 7 tubes, AC/6VDC, $690.00-800.00.

7-S-258 (5709 chassis), console, 1937, wood, upper front black "robot" dial, lower cloth grille with vertical bars, tuning eye, 4 knobs, BC, SW, 7 tubes, AC, $300.00-320.00.

7-S-323 (5714 chassis), table, 1939, wood, front round black dial, left wrap-around cloth grille with horizontal bars, pushbuttons, tuning eye, 1 knob, BC, SW, 7 tubes, AC................................**$85.00-115.00**

7-S-342 (5714 chassis), chairside, 1939, wood, top black dial & pushbuttons, front grille with vertical bars, right & left side shelves, tuning eye, 1 knob, BC, SW, 7 tubes, AC..............................**$150.00-180.00**

7-S-343 (5714 chassis), chairside, 1939, wood, top black dial & pushbuttons, front scalloped cloth grille with cut-outs, feet, tuning eye, 1 knob, BC, SW, 7 tubes, AC **$150.00-180.00**

7-S-364 (5714 chassis), console, 1939, wood, upper front slanted round black dial, lower cloth grille with vertical bars, pushbuttons, tuning eye, 1 knob, BC, SW, 7 tubes, AC..............................**$200.00-230.00**

7-S-366 (5714 chassis), console, 1939, wood, ornate cabinet with carvings, upper front round black dial, lower grille area, pushbuttons, tuning eye, 1 knob, BC, SW, 7 tubes, AC **$300.00-350.00**

7-S-432 (5724 chassis), table, 1939, wood, right front dial, rounded left with horizontal wrap-around bars, pushbuttons, 2 knobs, BC, SW, 7 tubes, AC **$85.00-95.00**

7-S-433 (5724 chassis), table, 1939, wood, lower front slide rule dial, upper cloth grille with horizontal bars, pushbuttons, 2 knobs, BC, SW, 7 tubes, AC..**$85.00-105.00**

7-S-434 (5724 chassis), table, 1939, wood, lower front slide rule dial, upper half-round cloth grille with cut-outs, pushbuttons, columns, 2 knobs, BC, SW, 7 tubes, AC **$120.00-150.00**

7-S-449 (5724 chassis), chairside, 1939, wood, top dial & push buttons, front grille with curved vertical bars, 2 knobs, BC, SW, 7 tubes, AC **$150.00-180.00**

7-S-363 (5714 chassis), console, 1939, wood, upper front round black dial, lower cloth grille with vertical bars, pushbuttons, tuning eye, 1 knob, BC, SW, 7 tubes, AC, $240.00-270.00.

7-S-529 (7A02 chassis), table, 1941, wood, front black dial, left wrap-around cloth grille with horizontal bars, pushbuttons, 2 knobs, BC, SW, 7 tubes, AC, $85.00-105.00.

8-D-510, table, plastic, right front black dial with white pointer over horizontal wrap-around grille bars, handle, 2 knobs, $45.00-55.00.

7-S-453, table, 1939, wood, front round black dial, left wrap-around cloth grille with horizontal bars, pushbuttons, BC, SW, 7 tubes **$150.00-180.00**

7-S-458 (5724 chassis), console, 1939, wood, upper front slide rule dial, lower cloth grille with vertical bars, pushbuttons, 2 knobs, BC, SW, 7 tubes, AC **$130.00-150.00**

7-S-461 (5724 chassis), console, 1939, wood, upper front slide rule dial, lower cloth grille with vertical bars, pushbuttons, 2 knobs, BC, SW, 7 tubes, AC **$140.00-170.00**

7-S-462 (5724 chassis), console/bookcase, 1939, wood, upper front slide rule dial, lower vertical grille bars, pushbuttons, 2 drawers, right & left shelves, BC, SW, 7 tubes, AC **$250.00-300.00**

7-S-530 (7A02 chassis), table, 1941, wood, right front black dial, left grille with vertical bars, pushbuttons, 2 knobs, BC, SW, 7 tubes, AC...**$85.00-105.00**

7-S-547 (7A02 chassis), chairside, 1941, wood, top black dial & pushbuttons, front grille area, casters, 2 knobs, BC, SW, 7 tubes, AC...**$150.00-180.00**

7-S-557 (7A02 chassis), console, 1941, wood, upper front black dial, lower cloth grille with vertical bars, pushbuttons, 2 knobs, BC, SW, 7 tubes, AC **$150.00-180.00**

7-S-558 (7A02 chassis), console, 1941, wood, upper front black dial, lower cloth grille with vertical bars, pushbuttons, 2 knobs, BC, SW, 7 tubes, AC **$150.00-180.00**

7-S-581, chairside-R/P, 1941, wood, top dial & pushbuttons, lift top, inner phono, front horizontal grille bars, BC, SW, 7 tubes, AC **$160.00-190.00**

7-S-582, console-R/P, 1941, wood, upper front black dial, center phono, lower vertical grille bars, pushbuttons, BC, SW, 7 tubes, AC......**$150.00-180.00**

7-S-585 (7A01 chassis), console-R/P, 1941, wood, step-down top, upper front black dial, center phono, lower vertical grille bars, push-buttons, 2 knobs, BC, SW, 7 tubes, AC **$150.00-180.00**

7-S-598, console-R/P, 1941, wood, inner right dial & pushbuttons, inner left phono, double doors, lower front grille, 2 knobs, BC, SW, 7 tubes, AC **$120.00-150.00**

7-S-633 (7B01 chassis), table, 1942, wood, front black dial, left wrap-around cloth grille with horizontal bars, pushbuttons, 2 knobs, BC, SW, 7 tubes, AC..**$85.00-95.00**

7-S-634 (7B01 chassis), table, 1942, wood, right front black dial, left cloth grille with vertical spiral bars, pushbuttons, 2 knobs, BC, SW, 7 tubes, AC **$85.00-95.00**

7-S-635, table, 1942, wood, front black dial, left wrap-around cloth grille with horizontal bars, pushbuttons, 2 knobs, BC, SW, 7 tubes, AC **$85.00-95.00**

7-S-657 (7B01 chassis), console, 1942, wood, upper front slanted black dial, lower cloth grille with vertical bars, pushbuttons, 2 knobs, BC, SW, 7 tubes, AC.....................................**$120.00-140.00**

7-S-681 "Westchester" (7B02 chassis), chairside-R/P, 1941, wood, top black dial & pushbuttons, front pull-out phono unit, 2 knobs, BC, SW, 7 tubes, AC.....................................**$110.00-130.00**

7-S-682 "Beverly" (7B02 chassis), console-R/P, 1942, wood, upper front black dial, center pull-out phono, lower cloth grille with vertical bars, pushbuttons, 2 knobs, BC, SW, 7 tubes, AC **$110.00-130.00**

7-S-685 "Carleton" (7B02 chassis), console-R/P, 1942, wood, inner right black dial & pushbuttons, door, left lift top, inner phono, front vertical grille bars, 2 knobs, BC, SW, 7 tubes, AC **$110.00-130.00**

7-X-075, console-R/P, 1946, wood, upper front black dial, center pull-out phono, lower cloth grille, BC, 7 tubes, battery **$75.00-85.00**

8-D-363, console, 1939, wood, upper front round black dial, lower cloth grille with vertical bars, pushbuttons, tuning eye, BC, SW, 8 tubes, AC/DC **$250.00-300.00**

8-G-005YTZ1 "Transoceanic," portable, 1948, black leatherette, inner dial & grille, fold-up front, telescoping antenna, handle, 6 pushbutton band selectors, 4 tone switches, 2 knobs, BC, SW, 8 tubes, AC/DC/battery **$95.00-125.00**

8-G-005YTZ2 "Transoceanic," portable, 1949, black leatherette, inner dial & grille, fold-up front, telescoping antenna, handle, 6 pushbutton band selectors, 4 tone switches, 2 knobs, BC, SW, 8 tubes, AC/DC/battery **$95.00-125.00**

8-H-023, table, 1946, plastic, large front half-round dial with inner concentric semi-circular louvers, 2 knobs, BC, FM, FM1, 8 tubes, AC/DC **$40.00-50.00**

8-H-061, console, 1946, wood, upper front slanted black dial, lower cloth grille with vertical bars, pushbuttons, 2 knobs, BC, FM, FM1, 8 tubes, AC **$110.00-130.00**

8-H-832, table, 1948, wood, lower front black dial with brass & plastic escutcheon, upper cloth grille, tone switches, 3 knobs, BC, FM, FM1, 8 tubes, AC...**$40.00-50.00**

8-S-129 (5801 chassis), tombstone, 1936, wood, lower front black dial, upper cloth grille with vertical bars, 5 knobs, BC, SW, 8 tubes, AC..**$240.00-270.00**

7-S-634R (7B01R chassis), table, 1942, wood, right front black dial, left cloth grille with vertical spiral bars, pushbuttons, 2 knobs, BC, SW, 7 tubes, AC, $85.00-95.00.

8-G-005Y "Transoceanic" (8C40 chassis), portable, 1946, black leatherette, inner dial & grille, fold-up front, telescoping antenna, handle, 6 pushbutton band selectors, 4 tone switches, 2 knobs, BC, SW, 8 tubes, AC/DC/battery, $95.00-125.00.

8-H-034, table, 1946, wood, front curved black dial, lower cloth grille area, feet, 2 knobs, BC, FM, FM1, 8 tubes, AC/DC, $45.00-55.00.

8-S-154 (5801 chassis), console, 1936, wood, step-down top, upper front black dial, lower cloth grille with vertical bars, 5 knobs, BC, SW, 8 tubes, AC..**$295.00-345.00**

8-S-443 (5808 chassis), table, 1940, wood, step-down top, right front round black dial, left vertical wrap-over bars, pushbuttons, 1 knob, BC, SW, 8 tubes, AC **$120.00-150.00**

8-S-451 (5808 chassis), chairside, 1940, wood, top round black dial & pushbuttons, front grille with cut-outs, 1 knob, BC, SW, 8 tubes, AC **$185.00-235.00**

8-S-531 (8A02 chassis), table, 1941, wood, step-down top, right front round black dial, left vertical grille bars, pushbuttons, 1 knob, BC, SW, 8 tubes, AC.....................................**$150.00-180.00**

8-S-548 (8A02 chassis), chairside, 1941, wood, top round black dial & pushbuttons, front cloth grille with cut-outs, 1 knob, BC, SW, 8 tubes, AC **$185.00-235.00**

8-S-563X, console, 1942, wood, upper front round black dial, lower cloth grille with vertical bars, pushbuttons, 1 knob, BC, SW, 8 tubes, AC **$250.00-300.00**

8-S-647, chairside, 1942, wood, top black dial & pushbuttons, front cloth grille with center vertical divider, 1 knob, BC, SW, 8 tubes, AC **$180.00-200.00**

9-H-079, console-R/P, 1946, wood, large black dial on top of case, center pull-down phono door, lower grille, 2 knobs, BC, FM, FM1, 9 tubes, AC **$95.00-115.00**

9-H-081, console-R/P, 1946, wood, large black dial on top of case, center pull-down phono door, lower grille, 2 knobs, BC, FM, FM1, 9 tubes, AC **$95.00-115.00**

9-H-088R, console-R/P, 1946, wood, right front tilt-out black dial, left pull-out phono, lower criss-cross grille, 2 knobs, BC, FM, FM1, 9 tubes, AC **$95.00-115.00**

9-H-881, console-R/P, 1948, wood, dial on top of case, center pull-out phono, lower criss-cross grille, 3 knobs, BC, FM, FM1, 9 tubes, AC **$85.00-95.00**

8-S-563 (8A02 chassis), console, 1941, wood, upper front round black dial, lower cloth grille with horizontal bars, pushbuttons, 1 knob, BC, SW, 8 tubes, AC, $250.00-300.00.

9-H-984LP, console-R/P, 1949, wood, dial on top of case, center fold-down phono door, lower criss-cross grille, BC, FM, AC..**$75.00-85.00**

9-H-995, console-R/P, 1949, wood, right front tilt-out black dial, left fold-down phono door, tone switches, 3 knobs, BC, FM, 9 tubes, AC **$75.00-85.00**

9-S-30, tombstone, 1936, wood, lower front round black dial, upper cloth grille with cut-outs, 4 knobs, BC, SW, 9 tubes, AC....**$240.00-270.00**

9-S-54, console, 1936, wood, upper front round black dial, lower cloth grille with cut-outs, 4 knobs, BC, SW, 9 tubes, AC....**$350.00-400.00**

9-S-55, console, 1936, wood, shouldered, upper front round black dial, lower cloth grille with cut-outs, 4 knobs, BC, SW, 9 tubes, AC..**$350.00-400.00**

9-S-204, console-R/P, 1937, wood, upper front black "robot" dial, lower cloth grille with center vertical bars, inner phono, BC, SW, 9 tubes, AC **$300.00-320.00**

9-S-232 "Walton's" (5905 chassis), tombstone, 1937, wood, large case, lower front black "robot" dial, upper 2-section cloth grille, tuning eye, 4 knobs, BC, SW, 9 tubes, AC **$1,000.00-1,100.00**

9-S-242 (5905 chassis), chairside, 1937, wood, step-down top with "robot" dial, large horizontal wrap-around louvers, tuning eye, 4 knobs, BC, SW, 9 tubes, AC **$320.00-370.00**

9-S-242Y (5905 chassis), chairside, 1937, ebony finish, step-down top with "robot" dial, large horizontal wrap-around louvers, tuning eye, 4 knobs, BC, SW, 9 tubes, AC **$320.00-370.00**

8-S-463 (5808 chassis), console, 1939, wood, upper front round black dial, lower cloth grille with vertical bars, pushbuttons, 1 knob, BC, SW, 8 tubes, AC, $325.00-375.00.

8-S-661, console, 1942, wood, upper front black dial, lower cloth grille with center vertical bar, pushbuttons, 1 knob, BC, SW, 8 tubes, AC, $180.00-200.00.

8-T-01C "Universal," portable, black leatherette, inner right quarter-round dial, right & left concentric quarter-round louvers, metal center strip, flip up lid, handle, 2 knobs, BC, 8 tubes, AC/DC/battery, $40.00-50.00.

11-E, table, 1927, wood, rectangular case, slanted front panel with center thumbwheel dial, 2 knobs, BC, 7 tubes, AC, $150.00-180.00.

9-S-244 (5905 chassis), chairside, 1937, wood, top "robot" dial, front cloth grille with vertical bars, tuning eye, 4 knobs, BC, SW, 9 tubes, AC $320.00-370.00

9-S-262 (5905 chassis), console, 1937, wood, upper front black "robot" dial, lower cloth grille with 2 vertical bars, tuning eye, 4 knobs, BC, SW, 9 tubes, AC....................$320.00-370.00

9-S-263 (5905 chassis), console, 1937, wood, upper front black "robot" dial, lower cloth grille with vertical bars, tuning eye, 4 knobs, BC, SW, 9 tubes, AC.......................$320.00-370.00

9-S-264 (5905 chassis), console, 1937, wood, low cabinet, upper front black "robot" dial, lower cloth grille with vertical bars, tuning eye, 4 knobs, BC, SW, 9 tubes, AC $550.00-650.00

9-S-319, table, 1938, wood, front oblong gold dial, left wrap-around cloth grille with horizontal bars, pushbuttons, 4 knobs, BC, SW, 9 tubes $85.00-115.00

9-S-324 (5907 chassis), table, 1939, wood, front black "robot" dial, left wrap-around cloth grille with horizontal bars, pushbuttons, tuning eye, 1 knob, BC, SW, 9 tubes, AC.............................$200.00-230.00

9-S-344 (5907 chassis), chairside, 1939, wood, top "robot" dial & pushbuttons, lower horizontal wrap-around louvers, tuning eye, 1 knob, BC, SW, 9 tubes, AC $300.00-320.00

9-S-365 (5906 chassis), console, 1939, wood, upper front black "robot" dial, lower cloth grille with vertical bars, pushbuttons, tuning eye, 4 knobs, BC, SW, 9 tubes, AC $300.00-350.00

9-S-369 (5907 chassis), console, 1939, wood, step-down top, upper front black "robot" dial, lower cloth grille with vertical bars, pushbuttons, tuning eye, 1 knob, BC, SW, 9 tubes, AC..........$400.00-450.00

10, console, 1931, wood, lowboy, upper front dial, lower cloth grille with cut-outs, 3 knobs, BC, 8 tubes, AC............................$160.00-190.00

10-H-551, chairside, 1941, wood, top round black dial & pushbuttons, front grille with vertical bars, BC, SW, FM1, 10 tubes, AC $300.00-350.00

10-H-562, console, 1941, wood, spinet piano-style, upper front slanted round black dial, lower cloth grille with "lyre" cut-out, pushbuttons, spindles, BC, SW, 10 tubes, AC $395.00-445.00

10-H-571, console, 1941, wood, spinet piano-style, upper front slanted round black dial, lower cloth grille with "lyre" cut-out, pushbuttons, spindles, BC, SW, FM1, 10 tubes, AC.....................$395.00-445.00

10-H-573, console, 1941, wood, upper front slanted round black dial, lower cloth grille with cut-outs, pushbuttons, BC, SW, FM, 10 tubes, AC $270.00-320.00

10-S-130 (1004 chassis), tombstone, 1936, wood, lower front black dial, upper cloth grille with cut-outs, 5 knobs, BC, SW, 10 tubes, AC $350.00-400.00

10-S-147 "Zephyr" (1004 chassis), chairside, 1936, wood, top black dial, large lower horizontal wrap-around louvers, 5 knobs, BC, SW, 10 tubes, AC $270.00-300.00

10-S-153 (1004 chassis), console, 1936, wood, upper front black dial, lower cloth grille with splayed bars, 5 knobs, BC, SW, 10 tubes, AC $425.00-475.00

10-S-155 (1004 chassis), console, 1936, wood, upper front black dial, lower cloth grille with vertical bars, 5 knobs, BC, SW, 10 tubes, AC $300.00-350.00

10-S-156 (1004 chassis), console, 1936, wood, upper front black dial, lower cloth grille with vertical bars, 5 knobs, BC, SW, 10 tubes, AC $300.00-350.00

10-S-157 "Zephyr" (1004 chassis), console, 1936, wood, upper front black dial, large lower horizontal wrap-around grille bars, tuning eye, 5 knobs, BC, SW, 10 tubes, AC..........................$500.00-550.00

10-S-160 (1004 chassis), console, 1936, wood, upper front black dial, lower cloth grille with center vertical bar, 5 knobs, BC, SW, 10 tubes, AC $350.00-400.00

10-S-443 (1005 chassis), table, 1940, wood, step-down top, right front round black dial, left vertical wrap-over grille bars, pushbuttons, 1 knob, BC, SW, 10 tubes, AC $150.00-180.00

9-S-367 (5907 chassis), console, 1938, wood, upper front round black "robot" dial, lower horizontal wrap-around louvers, pushbuttons, tuning eye, 1 knob, BC, SW, 9 tubes, AC, $400.00-450.00.

11-S-474 (1103 chassis), console, 1940, wood, upper front round black dial, lower cloth grille with vertical bars, pushbuttons, 1 knob, BC, SW, 11 tubes, AC, $375.00-425.00.

12-S-232 "Walton's" (1204 chassis), tombstone, 1937, wood, large case, lower front black "robot" dial, upper 2-section cloth grille, tuning eye, 4 knobs, BC, SW, 12 tubes, AC, $1,200.00-1,300.00.

288, tombstone, 1934, two-tone wood, Deco, center front window dial, upper cloth grille with cut-outs, 6 knobs, BC, SW, 8 tubes, AC, $200.00-260.00.

10-S-452 (1005 chassis), chairside, 1940, wood, half-round, top black dial & pushbuttons, lower horizontal wrap-around grille bars, 1 knob, BC, SW, 10 tubes, AC **$300.00-350.00**

10-S-464 (1005 chassis), console, 1940, wood, upper front round black dial, lower cloth grille with horizontal bars, pushbuttons, 1 knob, BC, SW, 10 tubes, AC..**$320.00-370.00**

10-S-470 (1005 chassis), console, 1940, wood, upper front round black dial, lower concave grille area, pushbuttons, 1 knob, BC, SW, 10 tubes, AC **$500.00-550.00**

10-S-491, console-R/P, 1940, wood, upper front black dial, center pull-out phono, lower horizontal wrap-around louvers, pushbuttons, 1 knob, BC, SW, 10 tubes, AC **$400.00-450.00**

10-S-531 (10A1 chassis), table, 1941, wood, step-down top, right front round black dial, left vertical grille bars, pushbuttons, 1 knob, BC, SW, 10 tubes, AC..**$140.00-160.00**

10-S-549 (10A1 chassis), chairside, 1940, walnut, top round black dial & pushbuttons, front cloth grille with cut-outs, storage, 1 knob, BC, SW, 10 tubes, AC...**$270.00-300.00**

10-S-566 (10A1 chassis), console, 1941, wood, upper front round black dial, lower cloth grille with vertical bars, pushbuttons, 1 knob, BC, SW, 10 tubes, AC...**$295.00-345.00**

10-S-567, console, 1941, wood, upper front round black dial, lower vertical grille bars, pushbuttons, BC, SW, 10 tubes, AC ..**$295.00-345.00**

10-S-568, console, 1941, wood, upper front round black dial, lower vertical grille bars, pushbuttons, BC, SW, 10 tubes, AC ..**$270.00-320.00**

10-S-589 (10A2 chassis), console-R/P, 1941, wood, upper front round black dial, center pull-out phono, lower horizontal wrap-around louvers, pushbuttons, 1 knob, BC, SW, 10 tubes, AC **$345.00-395.00**

10-S-599, console-R/P, 1941, wood, inner right black dial, inner left phono, double doors, lower vertical grille bars, BC, SW, 10 tubes, AC **$180.00-200.00**

10-S-669 (10B1 chassis), console, 1939, wood, upper front black dial, lower cloth grille with vertical bars, pushbuttons, 1 knob, BC, SW, 10 tubes, AC **$160.00-185.00**

10-S-690 "Wilshire" (10B2 chassis), console-R/P, 1942, wood, inner right black dial, door, left pull-out phono, lower vertical grille bars, BC, SW, 10 tubes, AC **$120.00-150.00**

11, console, 1931, wood, lowboy, upper front window dial, lower cloth grille with cut-outs, stretcher base, 3 knobs, BC, 8 tubes, AC..**$150.00-180.00**

11, table, 1927, walnut, rectangular case, slanted front panel with center thumbwheel dial, 2 knobs, BC, 6 tubes, battery **$150.00-180.00**

12, console, 1931, wood, highboy, inner front dial, double doors, arched stretcher base, 3 knobs, BC, 8 tubes, AC **$150.00-180.00**

12, table, 1927, mahogany, rectangular case, slanted front panel with off-center dial, 2 knobs, BC, 6 tubes, battery **$120.00-150.00**

12-A-57, console, 1936, wood, upper front round black dial, lower cloth grille with cut-outs, 4 knobs, BC, SW, 12 tubes, AC..**$500.00-550.00**

12-A-58, console, 1936, wood, upper front round black dial, lower cloth grille with "torch" cut-out, 2 speakers, 4 knobs, BC, SW, 12 tubes, AC **$500.00-550.00**

12-H-090, console-R/P, 1946, wood, right front tilt-out dial/pushbuttons, left fold-down phono door, lower cloth grille with cut-outs, 3 knobs, BC, SW, FM, FM1, 12 tubes, AC **$110.00-130.00**

12-H-092R, console-R/P, 1946, mahogany, right front tilt-out black dial/pushbuttons, left fold-down phono door, lower cloth grille with cut-outs, 3 knobs, BC, SW, FM, FM1, 12 tubes, AC..**$110.00-130.00**

12-H-093R, chairside-R/P, 1946, wood, top dial/pushbuttons, front pull-out phono, side cloth grille with cut-outs, 3 knobs, BC, SW, FM, FM1, 12 tubes, AC **$120.00-150.00**

12-H-094E, console-R/P, 1946, bleached mahogany, right front tilt-out dial/pushbuttons, left pull-out phono, lower criss-cross grille, 3 knobs, BC, SW, FM, FM1, 12 tubes, AC **$110.00-130.00**

12-H-650 "Lenox," chairside, 1942, wood, top black dial/pushbuttons, front cloth grille with vertical bars, BC, SW, FM1, 12 tubes, AC..**$120.00-150.00**

15-U-269, console, 1937, wood, upper front black "robot" dial, lower cloth grille with horizontal & vertical bars, tuning eye, 4 knobs, BC, SW, 15 tubes, AC, $800.00-900.00.

705, table, 1933, wood, flared base, right front window dial, center cloth grille with cut-outs, side fluting, 2 knobs, BC, 6 tubes, AC, $120.00-150.00.

715, tombstone, 1933, wood, shouldered, center front window dial, upper cloth grille with cut-outs, 4 knobs, BC, 8 tubes, AC, $270.00-320.00.

805, cathedral, 1934, two-tone wood, center front window dial, upper cloth grille with cut-outs, 4 knobs, BC, SW, 5 tubes, AC, $200.00-230.00.

12-H-670 "Newport," console, 1941, wood, upper front slanted black dial, lower cloth grille with vertical bars, pushbuttons, BC, SW, FM, 12 tubes, AC **$150.00-180.00**

12-H-679, console-R/P, 1941, wood, inner dial/phono, double front doors, lower cloth grille, BC, SW, FM1, 12 tubes, AC **$120.00-150.00**

12-H-689 "Kenwood," console-R/P, 1942, wood, upper front black dial, center pull-out phono drawer, lower cloth grille with vertical bars, pushbuttons, storage, 1 knob, BC, SW, 12 tubes, AC..**$120.00-150.00**

12-H-691 "Chatham," chairside, 1942, wood, top dial/pushbuttons, front pull-out phono drawer, side criss-cross grille, BC, SW, FM1, 12 tubes, AC **$120.00-150.00**

12-H-695 "Williamsburg," console-R/P, 1942, wood, inner right black dial, door, left lift top, inner phono, lower front cloth grille, storage, 1 knob, BC, SW, FM1, 12 tubes, AC **$120.00-150.00**

12-H-696 "Georgetown," console-R/P, 1942, wood, inner right black dial, door, left lift top, inner phono, lower front cloth grille, storage, BC, SW, 12 tubes, AC **$120.00-150.00**

12-S-205 (1204 chassis), console-R/P, 1937, wood, inner "robot" dial & phono, lift top, front cloth grille with horizontal & vertical bars, storage, tuning eye, 4 knobs, BC, SW, 12 tubes, AC **$500.00-550.00**

12-S-245 (1204 chassis), chairside, 1937, wood, recessed center top with black "robot" dial, side cloth grille with horizontal bars, tuning eye, 4 knobs, BC, SW, 12 tubes, AC **$330.00-380.00**

12-S-265 (1204 chassis), console, 1937, wood, upper front black "robot" dial, lower cloth grille with center vertical bar, tuning eye, 4 knobs, BC, SW, 12 tubes, AC **$425.00-475.00**

770B, console, 1933, wood, upper front dial with elaborate 4 section escutcheon, lower cloth grille with scrolled cut-outs, 6 feet, 4 knobs, BC, 12 tubes, AC, $345.00-395.00.

12-S-266 (1204 chassis), console, 1937, wood, upper front black "robot" dial, lower arched cloth grille with cut-outs, tuning eye, 4 knobs, BC, SW, 12 tubes, AC......................................**$450.00-500.00**

12-S-267 (1204 chassis), console, 1937, wood, upper front black "robot" dial, lower cloth grille with vertical bars, tuning eye, 4 knobs, BC, SW, 12 tubes, AC...**$425.00-475.00**

12-S-268 (1204 chassis), console, 1937, wood, wide cabinet, upper front black "robot" dial, lower cloth grille with horizontal & vertical bars, tuning eye, 4 knobs, BC, SW, 12 tubes, AC **$600.00-700.00**

12-S-345 (1206 chassis), chairside, 1939, wood, top black "robot" dial & pushbuttons, front circular cloth grille with horizontal bars, tuning eye, 1 knob, BC, SW, 12 tubes, AC............................**$370.00-420.00**

12-S-370 (1206 chassis), console, 1939, wood, upper front black "robot" dial, lower grille with horizontal bars, pushbuttons, tuning eye, 1 knob, BC, SW, 12 tubes, AC **$600.00-700.00**

12-S-371 (1206 chassis), console, 1939, wood, half-round, upper front black "robot" dial, lower cloth grille with vertical bars, pushbuttons, tuning eye, 1 knob, BC, SW, 12 tubes, AC **$525.00-600.00**

12-S-445 (1207 chassis), table, 1940, wood, step-down top, right front "robot" dial, left vertical wrap-over grille bars, pushbuttons, 1 knob, BC, SW, 12 tubes, AC **$240.00-270.00**

12-S-453 (1207 chassis), chairside, 1945, wood, top "robot" dial/push-buttons, bowed front grille, storage, feet, 1 knob, BC, SW, 12 tubes, AC **$240.00-300.00**

12-S-471 (1207 chassis), console, 1940, wood, upper front black "robot" dial, lower grille with center vertical panel with cut-outs, pushbuttons, 1 knob, BC, SW, 12 tubes, AC **$800.00-1,000.00**

12-S-550 (12A3 chassis), chairside, 1941, wood, top "robot" dial/push-buttons, front cloth grille with center vertical divider, feet, 1 knob, BC, SW, 12 tubes, AC **$260.00-300.00**

12-S-568 (12A3 chassis), console, 1940, wood, step-down top, upper front "robot" dial, lower cloth grille with vertical bars, pushbuttons, 1 knob, BC, SW, 12 tubes, AC **$370.00-420.00**

12-S-569 (12A3 chassis), console, 1940, wood, upper front slanted "robot" dial, lower vertical grille bars, pushbuttons, 1 knob, BC, SW, 12 tubes, AC **$410.00-460.00**

827, table, 1934, wood, right front window dial, center cloth grille with vertical chrome bars, 4 knobs, BC, SW, 7 tubes, AC, $180.00-200.00.

A-508B, table, plastic, lower right front dial over large lattice grille area with center crest, feet, BC, $30.00-35.00.

B-600 "Trans-Oceanic" (6A40 chassis), portable, 1959, leatherette, inner slide rule dial & left side speaker grille, fold-up front, telescoping antenna, handle, 7 pushbutton band selectors, 4 tone switches, 2 knobs, BC, SW, 6 tubes, AC/DC/battery, $95.00-125.00.

12-U-158 (1203 chassis), console, 1936, wood, upper front round black dial, lower cloth grille with vertical bars, 5 knobs, BC, SW, 12 tubes, AC $450.00-500.00

12-U-159 (1203 chassis), console, 1936, wood, upper front round black dial, lower cloth grille with center vertical panel with cut-outs, 5 knobs, BC, SW, 12 tubes, AC $475.00-525.00

14-H-789, console-R/P, 1948, wood, right front tilt-out dial/pushbuttons, left fold-down phono door, lower grille, 3 knobs, BC, SW, FM, FM1, 14 tubes, AC $85.00-95.00

15-S-372 (1502 chassis), console, 1939, wood, upper front black "robot" dial, lower cloth grille with center vertical bars, pushbuttons, tuning eye, 1 knob, BC, SW, 15 tubes, AC............................$725.00-825.00

15-S-373 (1502 chassis), console, 1939, wood, upper front black "robot" dial, lower horizontal wrap-around louvers, pushbuttons, tuning eye, 1 knob, BC, SW, 15 tubes, AC $800.00-900.00

15-U-246, chairside, 1938, wood, recessed center top with black "robot" dial, side cloth grille with horizontal bars, tuning eye, 4 knobs, BC, SW, 15 tubes, AC...$530.00-640.00

16-A-61 "Stratosphere," console, 1936, wood, upper front round black dial, lower concave grille area, 2 speakers, 5 knobs, BC, SW, LW, 16 tubes, AC...$6,000.00+

16-A-63 "Stratosphere," console, 1936, wood, ornate cabinet, inner black dial, double front doors, lower concave grille area, 2 speakers, 5 knobs, BC, SW, LW, 16 tubes, AC................................$8,000.00+

17E, console, 1927, wood, looks like spinet piano, slanted front with dial & escutcheon, meter, 3 knobs, BC, 7 tubes, AC $180.00-200.00

27, table, 1927, wood, rectangular case, slanted panel with 2 pointer dials, right/left eliminator storage, AC $240.00-270.00

33-X, table, 1928, wood, rectangular case, slanted thumbwheel dial with escutcheon, decorative rosettes, 3 knobs, BC, 7 tubes, AC..$180.00-200.00

35-PX, console, 1928, wood, highboy, inner thumbwheel dial, upper cloth grille with cut-outs, double doors, 3 knobs, BC, 9 tubes, AC...$180.00-200.00

40-A, console-R/P, 1929, wood, massive ornate carved cabinet, upper front dial, lower grille cut-outs, "automatic tuning" pushbuttons, 3 knobs, BC, 10 tubes, AC...$1,000.00+

52, console, 1929, wood, lowboy, upper front thumbwheel dial with escutcheon, lower cloth grille with cut-outs, pushbuttons, 3 knobs, BC, 9 tubes, AC $320.00-370.00

54, console, 1929, wood, lowboy, upper front thumbwheel dial with escutcheon, lower cloth grille with cut-outs, pushbuttons, 3 knobs, BC, 9 tubes, AC $360.00-410.00

55, console, 1929, wood, lowboy, ornate case, upper front thumbwheel dial with escutcheon, lower cloth grille with cut-outs, pushbuttons, remote control, 3 knobs, BC, 9 tubes, AC.................$360.00-410.00

61, console, 1930, wood, lowboy, upper front dial, lower cloth grille with cut-outs, 3 knobs, BC, 9 tubes, AC...........................$300.00-350.00

64, console, 1930, wood, lowboy, upper front dial, lower cloth grille with cut-outs, inner pushbuttons, 3 knobs, BC, 9 tubes, AC $360.00-410.00

67, console, 1930, wood, massive ornate lowboy, upper front dial, lower cloth grille with cut-outs, inner pushbuttons, 3 knobs, BC, 9 tubes, AC $410.00-460.00

210 "Zenette," cathedral, 1932, wood, lower front window dial, upper scalloped cloth grille with cut-outs, 3 knobs, BC, 7 tubes, AC...$300.00-350.00

210-5 "Zenette," cathedral, 1932, wood, lower front window dial, upper scalloped cloth grille with cut-outs, 4 knobs, BC, LW, 7 tubes, AC...$300.00-350.00

215 "Zenette," cathedral, 1932, wood, center front window dial, upper scalloped cloth grille with cut-outs, fluted columns, 4 knobs, BC, 7 tubes, AC $300.00-350.00

220, console, 1932, wood, lowboy, upper front window dial, lower cloth grille with cut-outs, 3 knobs, BC, 7 tubes, AC...........$120.00-150.00

230 "Zenette," tombstone, 1930, wood, peaked top, center front window dial, upper cloth grille with cut-outs, 4 knobs, BC, 8 tubes, AC $270.00-300.00

240, console, 1932, wood, lowboy, upper front window dial, lower cloth grille with cut-outs, 6 legs, 4 knobs, BC, 8 tubes, AC ..$140.00-160.00

A-600L "Trans-Oceanic" (6A41 chassis), portable, 1957, brown leather, inner slide rule dial & left side speaker grille, fold-up front, telescoping antenna, handle, 7 pushbutton band selectors, 4 tone switches, BC, SW, 6 tubes, AC/DC/battery, $160.00-210.00.

G-500 "Trans-Oceanic" (5G40 chassis), portable, 1950, leatherette, inner airplane dial & grille, fold-up front, telescoping antenna, handle, 6 pushbutton band selectors, 4 tone switches, 2 knobs, BC, SW, 5 tubes, AC/DC/battery, $95.00-125.00.

G-510Y, table, 1950, plastic, right front round dial over large metal criss-cross grille, feet, 2 knobs, BC, 5 tubes, AC/DC, $35.00-40.00.

G-730, table, wood, lower front slide rule dial, large upper grille area, 2 knobs, BC, FM, AC, $30.00-35.00.

245, console, 1932, wood, lowboy, upper front window dial, lower cloth grille with cut-outs, inner pushbuttons, 6 legs, 4 knobs, BC, 8 tubes, AC **$240.00-270.00**

250, cathedral, 1932, wood, center front window dial, upper scalloped cloth grille with cut-outs, 5 knobs, BC, SW, 9 tubes, AC.......**$350.00-380.00**

260, console, 1932, wood, upper front window dial, lower cloth grille with cut-outs, 6 legs, 5 knobs, BC, SW, 9 tubes, AC **$180.00-200.00**

270, console-R/P, 1932, wood, lowboy, front window dial, lower cloth grille with cut-outs, lift top, inner phono, 3 knobs, BC, 7 tubes, AC...**$140.00-160.00**

293, console, 1933, wood, lowboy, upper front window dial, lower cloth grille with cut-outs, 6 legs, 6 knobs, BC, SW, 8 tubes, AC **$140.00-160.00**

672, console, 1930, wood, massive ornate lowboy, upper front dial, lower cloth grille with cut-outs, inner pushbuttons, 3 knobs, BC, 9 tubes, AC **$480.00-580.00**

701, table, 1933, wood with inlay, right front dial, center cloth grille with cut-outs, side fluting, 2 knobs, BC, 5 tubes, AC/DC ..**$120.00-150.00**

705-2, table, 1933, wood, flared base, right front window dial, center cloth grille with cut-outs, side fluting, 2 knobs, BC, 6 tubes, AC **$120.00-150.00**

706, table, 1933, wood, right front window dial, center cloth grille with horizontal bars, 2 knobs, BC, 6 tubes, AC..................**$85.00-115.00**

707, table, 1933, wood with inlay, right front window dial, center cloth grille with cut-outs, 2 knobs, BC, 6 tubes, AC...........**$120.00-150.00**

711, table, 1933, wood, flared base, right front window dial, center cloth grille with cut-outs, 2 knobs, BC, 6 tubes, AC...........**$120.00-150.00**

755, console, 1933, wood, lowboy, upper front window dial, lower cloth grille with cut-outs, 6 legs, 4 knobs, BC, 8 tubes, AC ..**$180.00-200.00**

760, console, 1933, wood, upper front dial with elaborate 4 section escutcheon, lower cloth grille with scrolled cut-outs, 6 feet, 4 knobs, BC, 9 tubes, AC **$200.00-230.00**

765, console, 1933, wood, inner dial with elaborate 4 section escutcheon, lower cloth grille with scrolled cut-outs, double sliding doors, 6 legs, 4 knobs, BC, 9 tubes, AC **$270.00-300.00**

801, table, 1934, wood, step-down top, right front dial, center cloth grille with cut-outs, 2 knobs, BC, 5 tubes, AC/DC.............**$120.00-150.00**

807, tombstone, 1933, wood, lower front round dial, upper cloth grille with cut-outs, 4 knobs, BC, SW, 5 tubes, AC **$180.00-200.00**

808, tombstone, 1934, wood, lower front round dial, upper cloth grille with vertical bars, 4 knobs, BC, SW, 6 tubes, AC **$180.00-200.00**

809, tombstone, 1934, wood, front round dial, upper cloth grille with Deco chrome cut-outs, 4 knobs, BC, SW, 6 tubes, AC **$300.00-320.00**

829, tombstone, 1934, wood, lower front round dial, upper cloth grille with chrome cut-outs, 4 knobs, BC, SW, 7 tubes, AC **$345.00-395.00**

845, console, 1934, wood, upper front window dial, lower cloth grille with cut-outs, 4 knobs, BC, SW, 5 tubes, AC **$150.00-180.00**

847, console, 1934, wood, upper front window dial, lower cloth grille with cut-outs, 4 knobs, BC, SW, 5 tubes, AC **$150.00-180.00**

850, console, 1934, wood, upper front round dial, lower cloth grille with cut-outs, 4 knobs, BC, SW, 5 tubes, AC **$150.00-180.00**

860, console, 1934, wood, upper front round airplane dial, lower cloth grille with cut-outs, 6 legs, 4 knobs, BC, SW, 6 tubes, AC ..**$150.00-180.00**

861, console, 1934, wood, upper front round dial, lower cloth grille with cut-outs, 4 knobs, BC, SW, 6 tubes, AC **$150.00-180.00**

970, console, 1934, wood, upper front round dial, lower cloth grille with scrolled cut-outs, 6 legs, 4 knobs, BC, SW, 9 tubes, AC ..**$300.00-350.00**

975, console, 1934, wood, upper front round dial, lower cloth grille with cut-outs, sliding doors, 6 legs, 4 knobs, BC, SW, 9 tubes, AC...**$300.00-350.00**

1000-Z "Stratosphere," console, 1934, multi-tone wood, upper front round black dial covered by sliding doors, step-down top, ornate decorative trim, lower concave grille with multiple vertical openings, 3 speakers, 6 knobs, BC, SW, 25 tubes, AC ....**$30,000.00+**

1117, tombstone, 1935, wood, lower front round dial, upper cloth grille with cut-outs, 4 knobs, BC, SW, 6 tubes, AC **$150.00-180.00**

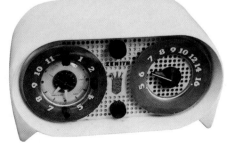

G-516W, table-C, 1950, plastic, right front round metal dial/left round alarm clock over perforated grille with center crest, 5 knobs, BC, 5 tubes, AC, $45.00-50.00.

H-511 "Consoltone," table, 1951, plastic, oblong case, right front half-round dial, center horizontal metal strip, feet, 2 knobs, BC, 5 tubes, AC/DC, $45.00-50.00.

H-664, table-R/P, 1951, plastic, front raised round metal dial with inner perforated grille, lift top, inner phono, 3 knobs, BC, 6 tubes, AC, $65.00-85.00.

A-400 "Holiday," portable, 1957, plastic, large front wrap-over grille with crest, handle, 2 side knobs, BC, 4 tubes, AC/DC/battery ..$40.00-45.00

A-402 "Sea Shore," portable, 1957, plastic, upper front dial, lower checkered grille area with crest, handle, 3 knobs, BC, 4 tubes, AC/DC/battery **$30.00-35.00**

A-404L "Carousel," portable, 1957, leather, front grille area with crest, handle, 2 side knobs, BC, 4 tubes, AC/DC/battery **$35.00-40.00**

A-504 "Sun Valley," portable, 1958, plastic, upper front dial, lower checkered grille area with crest, handle, 3 knobs, BC, 5 tubes, AC/DC/battery **$30.00-35.00**

A-513G, table, 1958, plastic, large front oval checkered grille area with center crest, 2 side knobs, BC, 5 tubes, AC/DC **$30.00-35.00**

A-513R, table, 1958, plastic, large front oval checkered grille area with center crest, 2 side knobs, BC, 5 tubes, AC/DC **$30.00-35.00**

A-515Y, table-C, 1957, plastic, step-down top, right front dial/left alarm clock overlap center horizontal bars with crest, 3 knobs, BC, 5 tubes, AC **$30.00-35.00**

A-519Y, table-C, 1958, plastic, center front dial/right clock face over large checkered grille with crest, feet, 4 knobs, BC, 5 tubes, AC **$25.00-30.00**

A-600 "Trans-Oceanic" (6A40 chassis), portable, 1957, black leatherette, inner slide rule dial & left side speaker grille, fold-up front, telescoping antenna, handle, 7 pushbutton band selectors, 4 tone switches, 2 knobs, BC, SW, 6 tubes, AC/DC/battery **$95.00-125.00**

A-615F, table, plastic, center black oval dial overlaps horizontal front bars, crest logo, feet, 2 knobs, BC, AC/DC....................**$25.00-30.00**

B-400L, portable, plastic, large front metal perforated wrap-over grille with crest, handle, BC **$30.00-35.00**

B-513V, table, 1959, plastic, lower right front dial, large front oval grille with vertical bars & center crest, BC, AC/DC **$25.00-30.00**

B-514F, table-C, 1959, plastic, right front oval dial/left oval clock over large checkered grille area with center crest, 3 knobs, BC, 5 tubes, AC **$25.00-30.00**

B-615F, table, 1959, plastic, lower right dial, large front oval grille with vertical bars & center logo, left side knob, feet, 2 front knobs & 1 side knob, BC, 6 tubes, AC/DC **$20.00-25.00**

B-728C, table-C, 1959, plastic, lower front slide rule dial, upper center clock face, right & left grille areas, 4 knobs, BC, FM, 7 tubes, AC/DC **$25.00-30.00**

C-730, table, 1955, wood, lower front slide rule dial, large upper plastic woven grille area, 2 knobs, BC, FM, 7 tubes, AC/DC **$30.00-35.00**

F-508B, table, 1961, blue plastic, upper right front dial overlaps lower vertical bars, feet, BC, AC/DC **$15.00-20.00**

J-615, table, 1952, walnut plastic, center front half-round dial with inner circular grille louvers & crest, feet, flex handle, 2 knobs, BC, 6 tubes, AC/DC, $40.00-45.00.

F-508L, table, 1961, beige plastic, upper right front dial overlaps lower vertical bars, feet, BC, AC/DC **$15.00-20.00**

F-508V, table, 1961, pink plastic, upper right front dial overlaps lower vertical bars, feet, BC, AC/DC **$15.00-20.00**

F-508W, table, 1961, white plastic, upper right front dial overlaps lower vertical bars, feet, BC, AC/DC **$15.00-20.00**

G-503 "Universal," portable, 1950, leatherette, flip-over dial with crest, inner metal grille, handle, 2 knobs, BC, 5 tubes, AC/DC/battery **$45.00-55.00**

G-503Y "Universal," portable, 1950, leatherette, flip-over dial with crest, inner metal grille, handle, 2 knobs, BC, 5 tubes, AC/DC/battery **$45.00-55.00**

G-511, table, 1950, plastic, right front round dial over large metal criss-cross grille, flex handle, 2 knobs, BC, 5 tubes, AC **$40.00-45.00**

G-516, table-C, 1950, plastic, right front round metal dial/left round alarm clock over perforated grille with center crest, 5 knobs, BC, 5 tubes, AC **$45.00-50.00**

G-615, table, 1950, plastic, center front round metal dial over metal criss-cross grille, flex handle, 2 knobs, BC, 6 tubes, AC/DC ..**$40.00-45.00**

G-660, table-R/P, 1950, plastic, front square dial with inner perforated grille, lift top, inner phono, 4 knobs, BC, 6 tubes, AC **$40.00-45.00**

G-723, table, 1950, plastic, diagonally divided front with left dial & right perforated grille area with crest, 3 knobs, BC, FM, 7 tubes, AC/DC **$35.00-40.00**

G-724, table, 1950, plastic, diagonally divided front with left dial & right perforated grille area with crest, flex handle, 3 front knobs & 1 side knob, BC, FM, 7 tubes, AC/DC **$35.00-40.00**

G-725, table, 1950, plastic, center front round dial with crest, flex handle, 3 knobs, BC, FM, 7 tubes, AC/DC.................................**$45.00-50.00**

G-882, console-R/P, 1950, wood, inner right dial, lower storage, doors, left pull-out phono, lower grille, 3 knobs, BC, FM, 8 tubes, AC **$75.00-85.00**

H-401, portable, 1952, plastic, center front round dial with inner perforations, handle, 2 knobs, BC, 4 tubes, AC/DC/battery......**$40.00-45.00**

H-500 "Trans-Oceanic" (5H40 chassis), portable, 1951, black leatherette, inner airplane dial & left side speaker grille, fold-up front, telescoping antenna, handle, 7 pushbutton band selectors, 4 tone switches, 2 knobs, BC, SW, 5 tubes, AC/DC/battery ..**$85.00-115.00**

K-412Y, portable, 1953, plastic, center concentric circular louvers with crest, handle, 2 "owl-eye" knobs, BC, 4 tubes, AC/DC, $65.00-75.00.

H-725, table, 1951, plastic, center front round dial with inner perforated grille, flex handle, 3 knobs, BC, FM, 7 tubes, AC/DC, $40.00-45.00.

K-526, table, 1953, plastic, center front round dial with inner lattice grille & crest, flex handle, 3 knobs, BC, 5 tubes, AC/DC, $40.00-45.00.

K-725, table, 1953, plastic, large center front round metal dial with inner perforated grille & crest, flex handle, 3 knobs, BC, FM, 7 tubes, AC/DC, $45.00-50.00.

H-503, portable, 1951, leatherette, inner round dial with crest & inner grille area, fold-back front, handle, 2 knobs, BC, 5 tubes, AC/DC/battery **$50.00-55.00**

H-511W "Consoltone," table, 1951, plastic, oblong case, right front half-round dial, center horizontal metal strip, feet, 2 knobs, BC, 5 tubes, AC/DC **$45.00-50.00**

H-615, table, 1951, plastic, center front square dial with inner metal criss-cross grille, flex handle, 2 knobs, BC, 6 tubes, AC/DC ..**$40.00-45.00**

H-615W, table, 1951, plastic, center front square dial with inner metal criss-cross grille, flex handle, 2 knobs, BC, 6 tubes, AC/DC **$40.00-45.00**

H-615Z, table, 1952, plastic, center front square dial with inner metal criss-cross grille, feet, 2 knobs, BC, 6 tubes, AC/DC **$40.00-45.00**

H-615Z1, table, 1952, plastic, center front square dial with inner metal criss-cross grille, flex handle, 2 knobs, BC, 6 tubes, AC/DC **$40.00-45.00**

H-661R, table-R/P, 1951, leatherette, center front round dial overlaps large grille area, lift top, inner phono, 4 knobs, BC, 6 tubes, AC **$30.00-35.00**

H-723, table, 1951, plastic, off-center round dial, criss-cross grille with crest, feet, 3 knobs, BC, FM, 7 tubes, AC/DC...............**$35.00-40.00**

H-723Z, table, 1951, plastic, off-center round dial, criss-cross grille with crest, feet, 3 knobs, BC, FM, 7 tubes, AC/DC...............**$35.00-40.00**

H-724, table, 1951, plastic, off-center round dial, criss-cross grille with crest, flex handle, feet, 3 front knobs & 1 side knob, BC, FM, 7 tubes, AC/DC..**$35.00-40.00**

H-724Z, table, 1951, plastic, off-center round dial, criss-cross grille with crest, flex handle, feet, 3 front knobs & 1 side knob, BC, FM, 7 tubes, AC/DC..**$35.00-40.00**

H-724Z1, table, 1952, plastic, off-center round dial, cloth grille with crest, flex handle, feet, 3 front knobs & 1 side knob, BC, FM, 7 tubes, AC/DC **$35.00-40.00**

H-724Z2, table, 1952, plastic, off-center round dial, cloth grille with crest, flex handle, right side knob, 3 front knobs & 1 side knob, BC, FM, 7 tubes, AC/DC...**$35.00-40.00**

H-845 "Super Interlude," table, 1964, wood, left front vertical slide rule dial, large grille area with vertical bars and center crest, 3 knobs, BC, FM, 8 tubes, AC **$20.00-25.00**

H-880R, console-R/P, 1951, wood, inner right dial with crest, door, left pull-out phono, lower grille area, 3 knobs, BC, FM, 8 tubes, AC **$65.00-75.00**

H-880RZ, console-R/P, 1950, wood, inner right dial with crest, lower storage, doors, left pull-out phono, lower grille, 3 knobs, BC, FM, 8 tubes, AC **$65.00-75.00**

HF-660F, table-R/P, 1959, left front dial, large grille area, lift top, inner phono, handle, 3 knobs, BC, 6 tubes, AC **$20.00-25.00**

HF-772R, console-R/P, 1957, wood, inner right slide rule dial, left phono, lift top, large front grille area, 4 knobs, BC, 7 tubes, AC..**$45.00-50.00**

HF-1286RD, console-R/P, 1958, wood, inner left slide rule dial/pull-out phono, door, right criss-cross grille, 5 knobs, BC, FM, 11 tubes, AC **$50.00-65.00**

J-402, portable, 1952, plastic, top left dial, top right on/off/volume knob, front circular perforated grille with center crest, handle, 2 knobs, BC, 4 tubes, AC/DC/battery **$40.00-45.00**

J-420T, table, 1952, plastic, oblong case, right front half-round dial, center horizontal metal strip, feet, 2 knobs, BC, SW, 4 tubes, battery **$35.00-40.00**

J-506 "Pacemaker," table, 1964, plastic, upper right front dial overlaps lower vertical bars, feet, 2 knobs, BC, 5 tubes, AC/DC..**$15.00-20.00**

J-508B, table, 1963, plastic, upper right front dial overlaps lower vertical bars, feet, 2 knobs, BC, 5 tubes, AC/DC.......................**$15.00-20.00**

J-512W "Executive," table, 1964, plastic, left front dial, large right metal perforated grille area with metal oval & center crest, feet, 2 knobs, BC, 5 tubes, AC/DC...**$15.00-20.00**

J-514, table-C, 1952, plastic, oblong case, right front dial, left alarm clock, center horizontal bars, 5 knobs, BC, 5 tubes, AC...........**$40.00-45.00**

J-615F, table, 1952, green plastic, center front half-round dial with inner circular grille louvers & crest, feet, flex handle, 2 knobs, BC, 6 tubes, AC/DC **$40.00-45.00**

J-615G, table, 1952, gray plastic, center front half-round dial with inner circular grille louvers & crest, feet, flex handle, 2 knobs, BC, 6 tubes, AC/DC **$40.00-45.00**

J-615W, table, 1952, white plastic, center front half-round dial with inner circular grille louvers & crest, feet, flex handle, 2 knobs, BC, 6 tubes, AC/DC **$40.00-45.00**

J-615Y, table, 1952, black plastic, center front half-round dial with inner circular grille louvers & crest, feet, flex handle, 2 knobs, BC, 6 tubes, AC/DC **$40.00-45.00**

K-622, table-C, 1953, plastic, step-down top, right front dial/left alarm clock overlap center horizontal bars with crest, 5 knobs, BC, 6 tubes, AC, $40.00-45.00.

K-731, table, 1963, wood & plastic, center slide rule dial, upper "wicker" grille, 4 feet, 3 knobs, BC, FM, 7 tubes, AC/DC, $40.00-50.00.

L, cathedral, 1931, two-tone wood, lower front window dial, upper cloth grille with cut-outs, 3 knobs, BC, 5 tubes, AC, $200.00-230.00.

J-616, table-C, 1952, plastic, oblong case, right front dial, left alarm clock, center horizontal bars with crest, 5 knobs, BC, 6 tubes, AC..**$40.00-45.00**

J-733, table-C, 1952, walnut plastic, left front square dial & right square clock face overlap textured grille with center crest, feet, 6 knobs, BC, 7 tubes, AC **$30.00-35.00**

J-733G, table-C, 1952, green plastic, left front square dial & right square clock face overlap textured grille with center crest, feet, 6 knobs, BC, 7 tubes, AC **$30.00-35.00**

J-733R, table-C, 1952, mahogany plastic, left front square dial & right square clock face overlap textured grille with center crest, feet, 6 knobs, BC, 7 tubes, AC **$30.00-35.00**

J-733Y, table-C, 1952, ebony plastic, left front square dial & right square clock face overlap textured grille with center crest, feet, 6 knobs, BC, 7 tubes, AC **$30.00-35.00**

K-412R, portable, 1953, plastic, center concentric circular louvers with crest, handle, 2 "owl-eye" knobs, BC, 4 tubes, AC/DC ..**$65.00-75.00**

K-412W, portable, 1953, plastic, center concentric circular louvers with crest, handle, 2 "owl-eye" knobs, BC, 4 tubes, AC/DC ..**$65.00-75.00**

K-508 "Emblem," table, 1964, plastic, large right front dial, left textured grille area, feet, 2 knobs, BC, 5 tubes, AC/DC **$15.00-20.00**

K-510W, table, 1952, plastic, center front round dial with inner perforations, 2 knobs, BC, 5 tubes, AC/DC **$40.00-45.00**

K-518, table-C, 1952, plastic, oblong case, right front dial, left alarm clock, center horizontal bars with crest, feet, BC, AC **$40.00-45.00**

K-615B, table, 1963, plastic, wedge-shaped case, lower front slanted slide rule dial, large upper grille area with vertical bars & center crest, 2 knobs, BC, 5 tubes, AC/DC **$25.00-30.00**

K-615C, table, 1963, plastic, wedge-shaped case, lower front slanted slide rule dial, large upper grille area with vertical bars & center crest, 2 knobs, BC, 5 tubes, AC/DC **$25.00-30.00**

K-666R, table-R/P, 1953, plastic, step-down front with lower half-round metal dial, lift top, inner phono, 3 knobs, BC, 6 tubes, AC..**$40.00-50.00**

K-777R, console-R/P, 1953, wood, inner right vertical slide rule dial, left pull-out phono, fold-down front, lower grille area, 3 knobs, BC, 7 tubes, AC **$50.00-65.00**

L-515W, table, 1954, plastic, oblong case, right front dial, left alarm clock, center horizontal grille bars, feet, 5 knobs, BC, 5 tubes, AC, $40.00-45.00.

L-622, table-C, 1953, plastic, step-down top, right front dial & left alarm clock overlap horizontal grille bars with center crest, feet, 5 knobs, BC, 6 tubes, AC, $30.00-35.00.

L-403F, portable, 1953, green plastic, center grille with horizontal louvers, fold down plastic handle, right and left front recessed thumbwheel knobs, BC, 4 tubes, AC/DC/battery..............................**$45.00-50.00**

L-403G, portable, 1953, gray plastic, center grille with horizontal louvers, fold down plastic handle, right and left front recessed thumbwheel knobs, BC, 4 tubes, AC/DC/battery..............................**$35.00-40.00**

L-403R, portable, 1953, maroon plastic, center grille with horizontal louvers, fold down plastic handle, right and left front recessed thumbwheel knobs, BC, 4 tubes, AC/DC/battery **$35.00-40.00**

L-403Y, portable, 1953, black plastic, center grille with horizontal louvers, fold down plastic handle, right and left front recessed thumbwheel knobs, BC, 4 tubes, AC/DC/battery..............................**$45.00-50.00**

L-406, portable, 1953, plastic, top dial & on/off/volume knobs, front round perforated grille with center crest, handle, BC, SW, AC/DC/battery **$35.00-40.00**

L-406R, portable, 1953, plastic, top dial, front round perforated grille with center crest, handle, 3 knobs, BC, SW, 4 tubes, AC/DC/battery **$35.00-40.00**

L-505, portable, 1953, plastic, center top dial, front perforated metal wrap-over grille panel with center crest, handle, 2 knobs, BC, 5 tubes, AC/DC/battery **$35.00-40.00**

L-507, portable, 1954, leatherette, inner dial, flip up front with world map, handle, 2 knobs, BC, SW, 5 tubes, AC/DC/battery **$50.00-65.00**

L-509 "Sovereign," table, 1964, plastic, left front dial overlaps large textured grille area, BC, AC/DC **$15.00-20.00**

L-513 "Reminder," table-C, 1964, plastic, left front dial, right & left horizontal bars, center alarm clock, 4 knobs, BC, 5 tubes, AC......**$15.00-20.00**

L-515, table, 1954, plastic, oblong case, right front dial, left alarm clock, center horizontal grille bars, feet, 5 knobs, BC, 5 tubes, AC **$40.00-45.00**

L-516B "Sandman," table-C, 1964, plastic, right front dial, left alarm clock, center grille area with crest, BC, AC **$25.00-30.00**

L-518, table-C, 1953, plastic, oblong case, right front dial, left alarm clock, center horizontal louvers with crest, 5 knobs, BC, 5 tubes, AC **$40.00-45.00**

L-520R, table-C, 1954, plastic, step-down top, right front dial & left alarm clock overlap horizontal grille bars with center crest, feet, 5 knobs, BC, 5 tubes, AC **$30.00-35.00**

L-566, table-R/P, 1954, plastic, step-down front with lower half-round metal dial, lift top, inner phono, 2 knobs, BC, 5 tubes, AC **$45.00-50.00**

LH "Zenette," cathedral, 1931, two-tone wood, lower front window dial, upper scalloped cloth grille with cut-outs, 3 knobs, BC, 7 tubes, AC, $300.00-350.00.

M-510R, table, 1955, plastic, oblong case, right front round dial overlaps large checkered grille area, fold-down handle, 2 knobs, BC, 5 tubes, AC/DC, $45.00-50.00.

L-600 "Trans-Oceanic" (6L40 chassis), portable, 1954, black leatherette, inner slide rule dial & left side speaker grille, fold-up front, telescoping antenna, handle, 7 pushbutton band selectors, 4 tone switches, 2 knobs, BC, SW, 6 tubes, AC/DC/battery **$110.00-140.00**

L-721, table, 1954, plastic, diagonally divided front with left black dial & right perforated grille area with crest, 3 knobs, BC, FM, 7 tubes, AC/DC **$35.00-40.00**

L-727 "Empress," table-C, 1964, plastic, right front round dial over checkered grille area, left alarm clock face, 4 knobs, BC, FM, 7 tubes, AC **$20.00-25.00**

L-846, chairside-R/P, 1954, wood, top dial, front louvered pull-out phono drawer, legs, BC, FM, AC **$50.00-65.00**

L-880, console-R/P, 1954, wood, inner right dial, lower storage, doors, left pull-out phono, lower grille, 3 knobs, BC, FM, 8 tubes, AC **$65.00-75.00**

LP "Zenette," cathedral, 1931, two-tone wood, lower front window dial, upper cloth grille with cut-outs, 3 knobs, BC, 5 tubes, AC **$200.00-230.00**

M-505, portable, 1953, plastic, top round dial, front gold metal grille with center logo, handle, right & left side knobs, AC/DC/battery **$40.00-45.00**

R-509V, table, 1955, plastic, right side dial, left side volume knob, large front lattice grille area with center crest, feet, 2 side knobs, BC, 5 tubes, AC/DC..**$25.00-30.00**

R-510G, table, 1955, plastic, oblong case, right front round dial overlaps large checkered grille area, fold-down handle, 2 knobs, BC, 5 tubes, AC/DC **$45.00-50.00**

R-510R, table, 1955, plastic, oblong case, right front round dial overlaps large checkered grille area, fold-down handle, 2 knobs, BC, 5 tubes, AC/DC **$45.00-50.00**

R-510Y, table, 1955, plastic, oblong case, right front round dial overlaps large checkered grille area, fold-down handle, 2 knobs, BC, 5 tubes, AC/DC **$45.00-50.00**

R-510Z1, table, 1955, plastic, oblong case, right front round dial overlaps large checkered grille area, fold-down handle, 2 knobs, BC, 5 tubes, AC/DC **$45.00-50.00**

S-829, tombstone, 1934, wood, raised top, lower front round dial over Deco chrome grille cut-outs, 4 knobs, BC, SW, 7 tubes, AC, $350.00-380.00.

R-511R, table, 1955, plastic, right front half-round dial, center checkered grille with crest, fold-down handle, feet, 2 knobs, BC, 5 tubes, AC/DC **$40.00-45.00**

R-511V, table, 1955, plastic, right front half-round dial, center checkered grille with crest, fold-down handle, feet, 2 knobs, BC, 5 tubes, AC/DC **$40.00-45.00**

R-600 "Transoceanic" (6R40 chassis), portable, 1954, black leatherette, inner slide rule dial & left side speaker grille, fold-up front, telescoping antenna, handle, 7 pushbutton band selectors, 4 tone switches, 2 knobs, BC, SW, 6 tubes, AC/DC/battery **$110.00-140.00**

R-615F, table, plastic, upper front half-round dial, inner circular louvers with center crest, handle, feet, 2 knobs, BC **$40.00-45.00**

R-615G, table, plastic, upper front half-round dial, inner circular louvers with center crest, handle, feet, 2 knobs, BC **$40.00-45.00**

SF-177E, console-R/P, 1959, wood, modern, inner left dial, lower pull-out phono, door, right grille area, stretcher base, 6 knobs, BC, 7 tubes, AC **$50.00-65.00**

Super-Zenith VII, table, 1924, mahogany, low and long rectangular case, front panel with 2 pointer dials, right & left storage compartments, 5 knobs, BC, 6 tubes, battery......................................**$200.00-230.00**

Super-Zenith VIII, console, 1924, mahogany, model "Super-Zenith VII" on legs, right & left storage compartments, 5 knobs, BC, 6 tubes, battery **$240.00-300.00**

Super-Zenith IX, console, 1924, model "Super-Zenith VII" on legs with built-in speaker & battery storage, 5 knobs, BC, 6 tubes, battery **$300.00-320.00**

Super-Zenith X, console, 1924, wood, front panel with 2 pointer dials, upper built-in speaker with grille, lower battery storage, 5 knobs, BC, 6 tubes, battery..**$300.00-320.00**

T-402, portable, 1955, plastic, right front dial, center horizontal grille bars, fold-back handle, rear crest, 2 thumbwheel knobs, BC, 4 tubes, battery **$50.00-55.00**

T-521R, table-C, 1956, plastic, right front dial, left alarm clock, center lattice grille with inner perforations, feet, 6 knobs, BC, 5 tubes, AC **$30.00-35.00**

R-511F, table, 1955, plastic, right front half-round dial, center checkered grille with crest, fold-down handle, feet, 2 knobs, BC, 5 tubes, AC/DC, $40.00-45.00.

T-521G, table-C, 1956, plastic, right front dial, left alarm clock, center lattice grille with inner perforations, feet, 6 knobs, BC, 5 tubes, AC, $30.00-35.00.

T-825, table, 1955, plastic, large center front round metal dial with inner perforations, handle, 2 knobs, BC, FM, 8 tubes, AC/DC, $40.00-45.00.

T-524R, table-C, 1955, plastic, step-down top, right front dial, left alarm clock face, center grille with horizontal bars, feet, 5 knobs, BC, 5 tubes, AC **$35.00-40.00**

T-545, table-R/P, 1955, plastic, large front square dial with inner perforations, lift top, inner phono, 4 knobs, BC, 5 tubes, AC **$45.00-50.00**

T-600 "Trans-Oceanic" (6T40 chassis), portable, 1955, black leatherette, inner slide rule dial & left side speaker grille, fold-up front, telescoping antenna, handle, 7 pushbutton band selectors, 4 tone switches, 2 knobs, BC, SW, 6 tubes, AC/DC/battery **$95.00-125.00**

U-723, table, plastic, off-center round dial over checkered grille with crest, feet, 3 knobs, BC, FM **$30.00-35.00**

WH, console, 1931, wood, lowboy, upper front window dial, lower cloth grille with cut-outs, stretcher base, 3 knobs, BC, 7 tubes, AC **$120.00-150.00**

X-306, table, plastic, right front round dial overlaps large textured grille area, switch, feet, 2 knobs, FM, AC..............................**$15.00-20.00**

X-509R, table, plastic, right side dial, left side volume knob, large front lattice grille area with center crest, feet, BC **$25.00-30.00**

Y-506L, portable, 1957, leather, front lattice grill & crest, handle, 2 side knobs, BC, 5 tubes, AC/DC/battery...............................**$30.00-35.00**

Y-513, table, 1956, plastic, large front oval checkered grille area with center crest, fold-down handle, 2 side knobs, BC, 5 tubes, AC/DC **$30.00-35.00**

Y-600 "Trans-Oceanic" (6T40Z chassis), portable, 1956, black leatherette, inner slide rule dial & left side speaker grille, fold-up front, telescoping antenna, handle, 7 pushbutton band selectors, 4 tone switches, 2 knobs, BC, SW, 6 tubes, AC/DC/battery **$95.00-125.00**

Y-723, table, 1956, plastic, off-center round dial over checkered grille with crest, handle, side knob, 3 knobs, BC, FM, 7 tubes, AC/DC **$30.00-35.00**

Y-825, table, 1956, plastic, large center front round dial with inner metal perforated grille, handle, 2 knobs, BC, FM, AC/DC........**$40.00-45.00**

Y-832, table, 1956, wood, large center front round metal dial ring over perforated grille area, 3 knobs, BC, FM, 8 tubes, AC/DC **$35.00-40.00**

Y-724, table, 1956, plastic, off-center round dial over checkered grille with crest, handle, side knob, 3 front knobs & 1 side knob, BC, FM, 7 tubes, AC/DC, $30.00-35.00.

Z-316W, table, plastic, right front dial overlaps large textured grille area, feet, BC, FM...**$20.00-25.00**

Z-508V, table, 1957, plastic, lower right front dial over large checkered grille area with center crest, feet, 2 knobs, BC, 5 tubes, AC/DC **$25.00-30.00**

Z-550G, table-R/P, 1957, left side dial, large front grille with crest, lift top, inner phono, handle, 2 knobs, BC, 5 tubes, AC **$25.00-30.00**

Z-615F, table, 1957, plastic, center front oval dial overlaps horizontal grille bars, feet, 2 front knobs & 1 side knob, BC, 6 tubes, AC/DC **$25.00-30.00**

Z-733, table-C, 1956, plastic, step-down top, left front dial/right alarm clock over large textured grille with center crest, 6 knobs, BC, FM, 7 tubes, AC **$30.00-35.00**

ZEPHYR
Zephyr Radio Co.
13139 Hamilton Avenue, Detroit, Michigan

1, table, plastic, right front dial over horizontal grille bars, 2 knobs, BC, 4 tubes **$15.00-20.00**

35Y12, console, 1937, walnut, upper front large round dial, lower cloth grille with vertical bars, tuning eye, 4 knobs, BC, SW, 12 tubes, AC...**$200.00-230.00**

41X6, table, 1937, walnut with inlay, right front dial, left grille, base, 3 knobs, BC, 6 tubes including ballast **$65.00-75.00**